JOHN MAYNARD KEYNES

The Economist as Saviour 1920–1937

Robert Skidelsky is Professor of Political Economy at the University of Warwick. His books include *Politicians and the Slump* and *Oswald Mosley*, as well as the bestselling *John Maynard Keynes: Hopes Betrayed* and *The Economist as Saviour*.

JOHN MAYNARD
KEYNES

VOLUME TWO

THE ECONOMIST AS SAVIOUR

1920–1937

a biography by

Robert Skidelsky

PAPERMAC

TO

EDWARD

WHO HAS HELPED ME
MORE THAN HE KNOWS

First published 1992 by Macmillan London

This edition published 1994 by Papermac
an imprint of Macmillan Publishers Limited
25 Eccleston Place, London SW1W 9NF
Basingstoke and Oxford
Associated companies throughout the world
www.macmillan.co.uk

ISBN 0 333 58499 6

3 5 7 9 8 6 4 2

A CIP catalogue record for this book is available from
the British Library.

Phototypeset by Intype, London
Printed and bound in Great Britain by
Mackays of Chatham plc, Chatham, Kent

Contents

BRITISH RETAIL PRICE INDEX   viii

LIST OF ILLUSTRATIONS   ix

PICTURE ACKNOWLEDGEMENTS   x

ACKNOWLEDGEMENTS   xi

INTRODUCTION   xv

PROLOGUE: *What Is One to Do with One's Brains?*   xxxi

PART ONE: THE ECONOMIC CONSEQUENCES OF THE WAR

1. THE LIVES OF KEYNES   3
    I. Cambridge   II. Bloomsbury   III. Official Circles
    IV. Money-Making

2. THE TRANSITION TO PEACE   31
    I. Europe's Unfinished Civil War   II. Enter Miss
    Bentwich   III. Unendurable Facts   IV. Rubbish about
    Milliards   v. All in the Mind?   VI. The Mad Woman

3. KEYNES'S PHILOSOPHY OF PRACTICE   56
    I. Unfinished Business   II. The Principles of Conduct
    III. The Science of Government   IV. The Value of
    Tragedy   v. The Reception of the *Treatise*   APPENDIX 1.
    Philosophic Background to the *Treatise*   APPENDIX 2.
    Probability   APPENDIX 3. Scholarship Old and New

4. RUSSIAN AND GERMAN AFFAIRS   90
    I. Charleston and Cambridge.   II. Lydia Lopokova
    III. The Reconstruction of Europe   IV. The Genoa
    Conference   v. The Proprieties   VI. The Unlucky
    Experts   VII. Keynes-Melchior

5. MONETARY REFORM   130
    I. The British Disease?   II. A Greater Nation   III. Second
    Thoughts Are Best   IV. The Three Devils: Deflation,
    Population, Protection   v. 'In The Long Run We Are All
    Dead'   VI. Reactions   APPENDIX 1. Boom, Slump and

'Unemployment Equilibrium', 1919–1925: Graphical
Summary APPENDIX 2. Note on Monetary Reform

PART TWO: THE CROSS OF GOLD

6. GOLD AND MARRIAGE   173
   I. New Beginnings   II. Marriage Prospects   III. Does
   Unemployment Need a Drastic Remedy?   IV. Why
   Gold?   V. Efforts at Persuasion   VI. *The Economic
   Consequences of Mr. Churchill*   VII. Was Keynes
   Right?   VIII. Mr and Mrs J.M. Keynes

7. KEYNES'S MIDDLE WAY   219
   I. Victorian Presuppositions   II. The Liberal Context
   III. The End of *Laissez-Faire*   IV. The Political Economy
   of Stabilisation   V. The Politics of the Middle Way
   VI. The Love of Money   VII. The Jews   VIII. Conclusion
   APPENDIX

8. LIBERALISM AND INDUSTRY   242
   I. Run-up to the General Strike   II. The Break with
   Asquith   III. The Liberal Industrial Inquiry
   IV. Conclusion

9. THE CASE OF THE MISSING SAVINGS   272
   I. Hatching Dennis's Egg   II. Writing the *Treatise*
   III. Aspects of Keynes   IV. The Economics of
   Inertia   APPENDIX 1. Robertson's Economics   APPENDIX 2.
   The Transfer Problem   APPENDIX 3. Labordère

10. SUMMING UP THE 1920s: *A TREATISE ON MONEY*   314
    I. Introduction   II. Definitions   III. Excess Bearishness and
    Excess Saving   IV. The *Modus Operandi* of the Bank
    Rate   V. Wages   VI. The Uses of History   VII. Central
    Banks to the Rescue

11. THE SLUMP   338
    I. Did He Foresee It?   II. The Macmillan Committee
    III. The Committee of Economists   IV. Maynard's
    Cheerfulness   V. American Interlude   VI.
    Dégringolade   VII. The End to Champagne   APPENDIX

PART THREE: THE ECONOMIST TO THE RESCUE

12. PORTRAIT OF AN UNUSUAL ECONOMIST   405
    I. The *Zeitgeist*   II. The Personality of an Economist
    III. 'It's All in Marshall'   IV. The Master-Economist?
    APPENDIX

13. THE PRACTICAL VISIONARY   431
    I. Patterns of Persuasion   II. Influences   III. Half-Forged
    Weapons   IV. The Means to Prosperity   V. Let Goods
    be Homespun   VI. Farewell to the Conference

14. NEW DEALS   483
    I. Social Experiments   II. An Open Letter to the
    President   III. Sharpening the Tools   IV. An American
    Journey   V. Still Working   VI. Keynes versus Marx   VII.
    'Modest Preparations for the Good Life'   VIII. Final
    Touches

15. FIRING AT THE MOON   537
    I. The Vision   II. The *General Theory*

16. WHOSE GENERAL THEORY?   572
    I. Reactions   II. Keynes and the Classics   III. Vision into
    Algebra   APPENDIX 1 Retail Price Index   APPENDIX 2
    Hicks's 'little apparatus'

17. 'MY BREATHING MUSCLES WERE SO WONKY . . .'   624

    BIBLIOGRAPHY AND SOURCES   636

    REFERENCES   652

    DRAMATIS PERSONAE   685

    INDEX   709

British Retail Price Index

Year	Index	Factor
1913	100.0	37.8
1915	125.0	30.3
1920	250.0	15.1
1925	175.0	21.6
1930	158.3	23.9
1935	144.4	26.2
1940	183.3	20.6
1945	202.8	18.7
1950	233.3	16.2
1955	302.8	12.5
1960	347.2	10.9
1965	411.1	9.2
1970	513.9	7.4
1975	950.0	4.0
1980	1855.6	2.0
1985	2627.8	1.4
1990	3502.8	1.1
1992	3783.3	1.0

List of Illustrations

Maynard Keynes and Lydia Lopokova, *c.* 1922
Lydia Lopokova as Mariuccia, 1918
Maynard Keynes with Virginia Woolf, 1923
Lydia Lopokova, John Sheppard and Cecil Taylor, 1923
Peter Lucas, Dadie Rylands and Sebastian Sprott, 1922
Dennis Robertson, Ted Spencer, Roger Mynors, Austin Robinson and
Fred Burgess, 1925
Lydia and Maynard Keynes
Famous Economist Weds Ballerina
Maynard Keynes in Russia, 1925
Maynard Keynes at the Russian Academy of Sciences, Petrograd, 1925
Samuel Courtauld
Vera Bowen
Maynard Keynes and Lydia in Berlin, 1928
Piero Sraffa, Maynard Keynes and Dennis Robertson at Tilton, 1927
From Hubert Henderson's copy of the Liberal *Yellow Book*
Robert Brand
Maynard Keynes and Lloyd George, Liberal Summer School, 1927.
Cartoon by Vanessa Bell, 1927
'An Extra One', the resignation of Sir Oswald Mosley, 1930
Punch, February 1931
Hubert Henderson
Richard Kahn and Lydia at Tilton *c.* 1931
F. Hayek, 1931
Oswald Falk
Lydia and G. Edwards in *A Doll's House*
Lydia and Dadie Rylands in *Comus*
Arts Theatre Logo
Maynard Keynes and Bertil Ohlin, 1935
Maynard Keynes and General Jan Smuts, 1933
Maynard Keynes, Beatrice and Sydney Webb, *c.* 1928
George Bernard Shaw and Maynard Keynes, 1936
Maynard Keynes's letter of condolence to Reginald Macaulay on the death
of his brother
Low caricature of Maynard Keynes

PICTURE ACKNOWLEDGEMENTS

The author and publisher wish to thank Dr Milo Keynes, who kindly provided, from his collection, the majority of the illustrations. Grateful thanks also to the following individuals and collections for their kind permission to reproduce other documents and illustrations: Mrs Roland Falk; Mr James Fox; Angelica Garnett; Mrs Clarissa Heald; Sir Nicholas Henderson; Hulton Picture Company; Professor Richard Keynes; the Provost and Scholars of King's College, Cambridge, King's College Library; the Estate of David Low; Dr George Rylands; Solo Syndication.

Acknowledgements

The number of debts I have acquired in researching and writing this book beggars my ability to repay them adequately. Many scholars have sent me articles or papers, relating to some aspect of Keynes's work as an economist, philosopher and political thinker; others have generously answered my queries on points of theory or interpretation. I have talked to many people who knew Keynes; others have written to me about him. Colleagues and friends have read parts of the manuscript, and I have directly benefited from their comments. And it seems to me I must have bored all my friends, as well as my family, to distraction by talking obsessively about Keynes over many years. When my eldest son Edward was three years old, he got a postcard from my mother-in-law. It was of Gwen Raverat's famous watercolour of Keynes as a young man. 'This is a gentleman who you and Mummy and Daddy will soon grow to hate v. enormously I suspect. He looks a bit furtive to me.' Edward is now nineteen. My wife and children have been heroic in putting up with me and Keynes for so long. Augusta finally said she could stand it no longer and forced me to finish this book. But there is still volume 3 . . .

There are some deep sorrows. My mother died before I was able to complete the second volume, but not before we had talked a lot about Lydia Lopokova and the Russian temperament. And I miss my conversations with Nicky Kaldor. All I can do here is to thank those whose ideas and observations seem to me to have had a direct effect on what I have written.

I would like to thank especially Joseph Altham, Quentin Bell, Meghnad Desai, Jean Floud, Milton Friedman, Geoffrey Harcourt, Dorothea Hauser, Michael Holroyd, Vijay Joshi, Milo Keynes, Deepak Lal, Harry and Margaret Lintott, Ian Little, Roderick O'Donnell, Don Patinkin, John Presley, Dr George 'Dadie' Rylands, Larry Siedentop and Edward Skidelsky, who have read and pronounced on individual chapters or groups of chapters. Don Patinkin has reproached me with having adopted a 'post-Keynesian' interpretation of Keynes's economics. If I am guilty of this fallacy, I can say only that this is how Keynes's economics appeared to me, being the person I am. I have had an equally interesting discussion with Roderick O'Donnell concerning the respective merits of a formal and a biographical treatment of Keynes's thought. O'Donnell finds much more consistency than I do between Keynes's epistemology, ethics, economics and politics, seeing that consistency to lie in his 'general theory' of rationality. I would argue that this consistency is formal, or can be made formal, but that a biographer's task is to pay attention to the points of tension, and the distribution of sympathy and passion, in a thinker's ideas.

I would also like to acknowledge the help and/or stimulus I received from Noel Annan, the late Dennis Arundell, the late Frederick Ashton, Mark Blaug, Richard Brain, the late Richard Braithwaite, Katherine Burk, David Calleo, Anna Carabelli, the late Ruth Cohen, Paul Davidson, Stanley Dennison, Margaret Drabble, Mrs M. P. G. Draper, James Fox, Donald Gillies, Andrew Graham, Frank Hahn, Liam Halligan, Frederic Harmer, Suzanne Helburn, Nico Henderson, Martin Hollis, the late David Hubback, Terence Hutchison, the late Richard Kahn, Clarissa Kaldor, Hermione Lee, Bruce Littleboy, Deirdre McMahon, James Meade, Robin Medley, Alan Megill, Marcus Miller, Gary Mongiovi, Basil Moore, Nigel Nicolson, Wayne Parsons, George Peden, Austin Robinson, the late Joan Robinson, S. P. Rosenbaum, the late Victor Rothschild, Steven Runciman, Stephen Schuker, Raymond Seitz, the late George Shackle, Hans Singer, Mark Skousen, Frances Spalding, Ferdinando Targetti, Federico Varese, Andrew Weller, Philip Williamson and Richard Wright.

The chief unpublished manuscript sources used in this volume are deposited in the Library of King's College, Cambridge. I would like to thank the Librarian, Peter Jones, the Modern Archivist, Michael Halls, and his successor, Jacqueline Cox, for putting up with my presence and questions over long periods. I have consulted other manuscript collections in Britain and the United States, which are listed on pp. 635–8. I would like to extend a general thanks to the Keepers and Archivists of these papers for facilitating my use of them. I have a happy memory of a visit to Jersey to look at Oswald Falk's papers, in the possession of his daughter-in-law, Mrs Roland Falk, and of a weekend spent near Dieppe, with Henrietta Garnett, going through Vanessa Bell's letters to her grandfather, Duncan Grant. My chief failure in research has been to locate Keynes's letters to the French 'amateur' economist, Marcel Labordère, if indeed they survive. Labordère was a poet of money, exactly the kind of person Keynes worshipped (as Labordère worshipped Keynes). This is certainly one of the most intriguing correspondences in his life. In the Keynes Papers at King's, filed under PP/45, there are sixty letters from Labordère to Keynes; only five from Keynes to Labordère dating from the last years of his life, sometimes addressed to 'My dear Alchemist'. Judging from the Labordère letters, the correspondence was particularly rich and fruitful in the 1920s, when the two men are discussing the psychology of investment. Perhaps a more determined historical detective than I am will succeed in tracking down the fifty-five missing letters.

I would like to thank the following for permission to quote from manuscript and other material: King's College, Cambridge, for Keynes family letters, personal and economic; the Strachey Trust, and the Society of Authors for letters by Lytton and James Strachey; Mrs Angelica Garnett for letters by Vanessa Bell; Professor Quentin Bell for letters by Clive Bell; Mrs Henrietta Garnett for letters by Duncan Grant; Mrs Clarissa Heald for Harold Bowen's unpublished diary; Mrs Roland Falk for Oswald Falk's letters in her possession; the Hon. Lady Ford for the Robert Brand letters to his wife; the Bank of England; the Bodleian Library for letters by C. P. Scott; the British Library for letters by Samuel Courtauld; Churchill College, Cambridge, for papers by Ralph Hawtrey; Harvard University Library for letters by Thomas Lamont and J. A. Schumpeter; House of Lords Library for letters by Lloyd George; Library of Congress for letters by Felix Frankfurter and Emmanuel Goldenweiser; Nuffield College, Oxford, for letters by Hubert Henderson; Public Record Office; Yale University for letters by Russell C. Leffingwell, Walter Lippmann; the Secretary for permission to quote from the papers of the Tuesday Club; Professor Stanley Dennison for Dennis Robertson's letters; King's College, Cambridge, for Roy Harrod's letters.

Part of the research for this book was made possible by a Personal Research Award from the ESRC. I am grateful to the Australian National University for giving me a Visiting Fellowship in 1983; and for King's College, Cambridge, for High Table rights in the academic year, 1986–7. Finally, I would like to thank Roland Philipps, my publisher at Macmillan, for his constant encouragement. In Peter James, I had an editor whose eye missed nothing.

The author and publishers would like to express their gratitude to the following who have very kindly given their permission for the use of copyright materials: Neville Brown for permission to quote from *Dissenting Forbears*. Cambridge University Press for permission to quote from *Essays on John Maynard Keynes*, edited by Milo Keynes; and from *Principia Ethica* by G. E. Moore. Jonathan Cape Ltd for permission to quote from *The Political Diary of Hugh Dalton*, edited by Ben Pimlott. Chatto & Windus Ltd for permission to quote from *The Letters of Roger Fry*, edited by Denys Sutton. Hamish Hamilton Ltd for permission to quote from *Come Dance with Me* by Ninette de Valois. William Heinemann Ltd for permission to quote from *Books Do Furnish a Room* by Anthony Powell. Hodder & Stoughton Ltd for permission to quote from *An Ambassador of Peace* by Lord D'Abernon. Houghton Mifflin Co. for permission to quote from *The Coming of the New Deal* by Arthur Schlesinger. The Institute of Economic Affairs for permission to quote from *Keynes's General Theory: Fifty Years On*, edited by John Burton. The Macmillan Press Ltd for permission to quote from *Autobiography of an Economist* by Lionel Robbins; and from 'Keynes as an Economic Adviser' by N. Kaldor in *Keynes as a Policy Adviser*, edited by A. P. Thirlwall. John

Murray (Publishers) Ltd for permission to quote from *Dancing for Diaghilev* by Lydia Sokolova. Penguin Books for permission to quote from *The Age of Keynes: A Biographical Study* by Robert Lekachman. Virago Press Ltd for permission to quote from *The Diary of Beatrice Webb*, edited by Norman and Jean MacKenzie. Every effort has been made to trace all copyright holders, but if any have inadvertently been overlooked, the author and publishers will be pleased to make the necessary arrangements at the first opportunity.

Introduction

I

'My purpose is to tell of bodies which have been transformed into shapes of a different kind.' This second volume of biography tells the story of Keynes's metamorphosis from aesthete, philosopher and administrator into world saviour. It is a reshaping of life-purpose which gives his middle and later years a melancholy afterglow, despite their extraordinary achievement.

After the First World War, Keynes set out to save a capitalist system he did not admire. He found himself in a world emptied by war of its old faiths and certainties; one in which monsters prowled, ready to devour what remained of Europe's civilisation. The collapse of the American economy in 1929 closed, so it seemed, the circle of despair. In 1939, the European war, suspended in 1918, broke out again. 'We can regard what is now happening,' Keynes wrote in June 1940, 'as the final destruction of the optimistic liberalism which Locke inaugurated. . . . For the first time for more than two centuries Hobbes has more message for us than Locke. . . .'

The contrast with the cloistered, but hopeful, world of prewar Cambridge in which he grew up could not have been starker. He was the child of a late-flowering Edwardian Enlightenment which believed – against much evidence, to be sure – that a new age of reason had dawned. The brutality of the closure applied in 1914 helps explain Keynes's reading of the interwar years, and the nature of his mature efforts. This book is about his attempt to restore the expectation of stability and progress in a world cut adrift from its nineteenth-century moorings. He brought in the State to redress the failings of society, not because he loved it, but because he saw it as the last resource. His genius was to have developed an analysis of economic disorder which justified forms of state intervention compatible with traditional liberal values. He was the last of the great English Liberals.

It is worth recalling the main features of his early story. Professor John Vincent, in reviewing the first volume of my biography in the *Sunday Times* of 6 November 1983, wrote, 'Had Keynes died in 1925, he would be remembered as a minor don, an economic technician of obsolete views, a powerful wartime civil servant, a fringe figure in Bloomsbury, and a good College bursar; in other words, not remembered at all.' This is wrong: he would have been remembered for *The Economic Consequences of the Peace*, his outburst against the Treaty of Versailles. But, apart from this, Vincent is right. In 1920, Keynes was thirty-seven, and had given no hint of greatness in the sphere in which he would excel – economics. But for the war, it is not clear that he would have stuck to economics, or the life of a Cambridge don.

Keynes was born and bred for success. He was the product of two Nonconformist stocks, distinguished by brains, religious and didactic vocation and practical ability. A strong sense that one's duty to oneself entailed duty to others ran through both sides of the family, though with Maynard Keynes's father, Neville Keynes, this was a cheerless credo, his passions being much more clearly of a private nature. Those who see the imaginative flair coming from the Brown–Ford side of the family, and the administrative ability as the Keynes legacy, ignore the large role which aesthetic enjoyments – particularly those of the theatre and music – played in Neville Keynes's life. Maynard Keynes was very much his father's son, minus the anxiety which made intellectual work a misery to Neville Keynes. His tendency to preach to mankind, and legislate for its welfare, he got from his mother.

Keynes's was a precocious, pampered, but above all *successful* childhood. There was no 'unhappy' upbringing to overcome. This was partly due to the supportive nature of his home background and the enlightened regime of College at Eton. But Keynes also realised from an early age that his cleverness gave him a pathway to success in dealing with adults. Cleverness was the alternative to submission or rebellion: or, to put it another way, through cleverness one can manipulate any situation to one's advantage. But to what end? At school, Keynes excelled in both classics and mathematics; a notable gift for friendship coexisted with a facility for administration. He was cut off from normal 'boyhood' by his exceptional intelligence and lack of physical grace; at the same time he quickly learnt how to manipulate that 'normal' world, and at Eton was both an intellectual leader and a social success. His cleverness, his breadth of interests and the contrast between his private allegiances and the public nature of his abilities already mark him out as exceptionally interesting.

As a Cambridge undergraduate and postgraduate, a clerk in the India Office and Fellow of King's College, Cambridge, Keynes, before the war, played out the dichotomies of his childhood on a larger stage. The main contrast in this period is between the esoteric nature of his ideals and friendships, centred on the philosophy of G. E. Moore, the Apostles, Bloomsbury and the cult of homosexuality, and the growing range of his public activities as a civil servant, College administrator, economist, occasional politician and member of a Royal Commission. Between 1906 and 1914 nothing seemed so important to Keynes as the pursuit of knowledge and love. His *Treatise on Probability* was finished in 1914; the passionate phase of his love affair with the painter Duncan Grant came to an end in

March 1909, when Duncan Grant told him that he was no longer in love with him, while retaining an affection that was 'exceedingly strong'.

> His feelings towards people [Duncan Grant wrote to James Strachey on 22 April 1909], their strength and fullness, their purity of substance, even his lack of moods make him to me a most lovable character. But I cannot any longer believe myself to be *in* love with a person who sometimes bores me, sometimes irritates me, & from whom I can live apart without being unhappy, however much I like to be with him.

Although Keynes was to have other boyfriends, the period 1908–11 is the high point of his absorption in the abstract passions of the mind, and the secret affairs of the heart, though the pattern of mental work in the context of a loving relationship was to be reproduced when he married the ballerina Lydia Lopokova in 1925.

In the First World War, Keynes's 'divided nature' came out in his simultaneous opposition to the official war aim of a fight to the finish with Germany and his work, at the Treasury, for 'a government I despise for ends I think criminal'. As he put it to Duncan Grant in 1917, 'I pray for the most absolute financial crash (and yet I strive to prevent it – so all I do is a contradiction to all I feel).' The tug within him between the rational, pacifist values of Bloomsbury – 'I had become I suppose in a sense unpatriotic, as I suppose most artists must do,' Duncan Grant wrote to his father – and the calculations of Whitehall is seen at its sharpest in this period. It was not in Keynes's nature to give up *either* – an attitude he tried to rationalise by using his official position to protect his friends from conscription, and deploying financial arguments to minimise Britain's involvement in military fighting on the Western Front. This was Keynes's version of the Faustian bargain: intelligence could play a part in mitigating barbarism. The alternative interpretation of his conduct was put by his friend David Garnett: 'Who are you? Only an intelligence they need in their extremity. . . . A genie taken incautiously out of King's . . . by savages to serve them faithfully for their savage ends, and then – back you go in to the bottle.' The tension of this double loyalty drove Keynes to breaking point. In 1916 he declared himself a conscientious objector to conscription, although he had already been exempted by the Treasury; and he did finally break down at the Paris Peace Conference in 1919, returning, shattered, to England, to denounce Lloyd George's peace policy with a vehemence made more savage by pent-up hostility to his war policy. *The Economic Consequences of the Peace* (1919) made Keynes a world figure. Thus one could say that, in the end, he got the better of the bargain, since his Treasury experience, and the uses to which he put it in his book, gave him the position of intellectual leadership which he needed to remould economic theory and policy in the inter-war years.

II

It is hard even now to get Keynes's personality and achievement into focus. My own treatment has been greatly influenced by Alasdair Macintyre's fine book, *After Virtue*, published in 1981: a discussion of what happens to a culture when the attempt to justify ethics by religion or tradition comes to be seen as offensive to 'reason'. In such a culture, Macintyre suggests, moral discussion becomes interminable, since unaided reason provides no basis for agreement. Values are privatised or personalised, habitual virtues undermined; public discourse shifts to means, to technique – the one area in which rational agreement might still be sought and achieved. Such a culture produces two kinds of representative character: the Aesthete and the Manager. The aesthete pursues sensual enjoyment without limit; the manager manipulates social relations in the interests of stability. The twentieth-century 'characters' thus embody the impasse which moral discourse has reached. They are the inheritors of the collapsed Christian world-view. On occasion, Macintyre writes, the two characters may be found 'in one and the same person who partitions his life between them'.

Keynes is a leading, possibly the leading, twentieth-century example of this type of 'partitioned' character, the finest flower of an autumnal civilisation. The main cleavage running through his life is precisely that between the worlds of Bloomsbury and Whitehall. Someone who avowed his lifelong commitment to G. E. Moore's ideal of friendship and beauty was also the conscious stabiliser of social systems. But what is the connection here between private and public duty, one's duty to oneself and one's duty to the world?

Moore evaded the dilemma. He held ethical ends – conceived as states of mind – to be self-evidently good or bad. Apart from this, there was an inherited world of rules and duties. Moore argued that it was only for the sake of good states of mind – 'in order that as much of them as possible may at some time exist . . . that any one can be justified in performing any public or private duty'. But there was no obvious connection between the ethical programme he advanced and the inherited morality to which he subscribed. Keynes tried to improve on Moore by detaching the question of what we ought to do from conventional morality, and linking it instead to individual judgement of probabilities attaching to different courses of action. Thus he tried to close the circle of reason. The theme of his *Treatise on Probability*, at which he worked for eight years prior to 1914, is that probability can be, and should be, the 'guide of life'. But Keynes's judgements of probability, no less than Moore's ethical judgements, rest on intuition. This attempt to ground moral reasoning in the judgements of rational individuals breaks down when it becomes apparent that people's intuitions of goodness and right conduct differ, and there is no appeal outside individual intuition by reference to which those differences might be resolved. The result is moral disorder.

Looking back, it seems clear that the Moore–Keynes programme of secularising moral philosophy rested, as Keynes later admitted in 'My Early Beliefs', on the tacit assumption that human beings in England, or more narrowly Cambridge, in 1900 or thereabouts were already so constituted by their history as to be 'reliable, rational, decent people, influenced by truth and objective standards, who can be safely released from the outward restraints of convention and traditional standards and inflexible rules of conduct, and left, from now onwards, to their own sensible devices, pure motives and reliable intuitions of the good'. It presupposed, that is, that, left free to choose, individuals would choose what was good and right; and that these choices would add up to what was good and right for the whole community. Eventually Keynes came to understand that the search for truth could take place fruitfully only within a shared cultural framework. In economics one could not have good conversations unless there had been a prior meeting of minds on the intuitive level. But as a young man his faith in the ability of unanchored rational argument to discover the truth was complete.

Everyone agrees that Keynes was the most intuitive of men. But if we abandon his own early view of intuition as a culture-free insight into logical relations or, more generally, the nature of 'truth', there are interesting questions to be asked about the sources of his own intuitions. He used to say that his best ideas came to him from 'messing about with figures and *seeing* what they must mean' (italics added). From his earliest years Keynes was fascinated by numbers, which were perhaps more 'real' to him than people or situations. Yet he was famously sceptical about econometrics – the application of mathematical and statistical methods to the analysis of economic data, chiefly for the purpose of explanation and forecasting. The truth seems to be that numbers were for him simply clues, triggers of the imagination, rather like anecdotes are for the non-mathematically minded. People often talked about the 'magical' quality of his mind. His imagination was filled with the legends, fairy tales, myths, secular and Christian, of his childhood, which he freely drew on, much like Freud, to make patterns of the behaviour of his own times. The legend of King Midas, for example, is a recurring motif in his work, the clue to the riddle of economic stagnation. What made Keynes more (and in the opinion of some less) than an economist was that his understanding of what was happening was influenced much more by the drama and poetry of the West, which remained lifelong companions, than by the theorems of classical economics, many of which never got 'under his skin'. Economics was a game he could play, a language he could use, a powerful tool of thought; but the sources of his understanding of economic life lay outside, or beneath, its own characteristic ways of reasoning.

Keynes became more thoughtful as he grew older, without losing the sharp edge of his mind. For the young Keynes and his friends, casting off Christian 'hocus pocus' was pure gain. It liberated morality from its dependence on superstition. Keynes habitually referred to Victorian moral discourse as 'medieval' or 'barbarous', echoing the eighteenth century's contempt for the Christian world-view of the Middle Ages revived in Victorian England. The result of shedding superstition was confidently expected to be an improvement in morals, but even more importantly an improvement in the language of moral justification. The age of reason had dawned for a second time after the Victorian night. Later in life, Keynes was not so sure. 'Our generation – yours & mine . . . owed a great deal to our fathers' religion,' he told Virginia Woolf in 1934. 'And the young . . . who are brought up without it, will never get so much out of life. They're trivial: like dogs in their lusts. We had the best of both worlds. We destroyed Xty yet had its benefits.' In practice, Keynes's own life was shaped by the Cambridge tradition in which he grew up. This embedded the quest for individual excellence in a setting of public duty. For it was to their ancient universities that Victorian England looked for its 'clerisy' – its spiritual and intellectual leaders. But this tradition, too, had become a fragment of a vanishing whole, and was kept going by habit rather than by reflection. Indeed, when Keynes actually reflected on the problem of reconciling one's 'duty to oneself' with one's 'duty to the world' – notably in his essay on 'Egoism' in 1906, but intermittently throughout his life – he reached the familiar modern conclusion that these duties were in fact irreconcilable. Thus the lack of any close connection between private and public virtue, or rather the lack of a language in which such a connection could be conclusively demonstrated, first emerges as a problem in Keynes's moral philosophy, though he continued to live his own life as though such a connection existed.

The difficulty of getting Keynes's 'character' right arises to an unusual extent from the weakening of the Nonconformist culture which had previously 'formed' character and held unruly propensities in check. The strong, well-defined 'characters' of Victorian biographies were not just the fictions of conventional biographical language; rather the kind of language being used about them had itself helped form their characters. The biographer of a 'modern' subject like Keynes has a more difficult task. The notion of character has been replaced by the concept of 'personality' or 'nature'. Implicit in such formulations is an absence of coherence: one's 'nature' is a bundle of possibilities, a myriad of sensations, spilling out in different directions, more like a stream than a compact building. Heredity, family, school, class all play their part in Keynes's formation. But the way he developed also reflected the dissolution of the Puritan character-type. What Daniel Bell, in his book *The Cultural Contradictions of Capitalism*, calls the 'disjuncture' between the moral and material orders finds in Keynes its representative expression. Keynes's 'character' was a set of stratagems, a matter of checks and balances which allowed his life's work to unfold. His sense of duty triumphed in the end because the world needed to be saved from its folly.

Such a nature is difficult to grasp for the uncomplicated, and it eluded his contemporaries. Discerning associates were well aware that Keynes was 'not of a piece', and were puzzled to know what, if anything, the pieces added up to. Oswald Falk, who perhaps knew him best of all in the years covered by this book, saw him as a succession of 'masks', and wondered whether he could have 'any identity in solitude'. The masks were physical as well as mental. The playful eyes and sensual mouth were covered up by the conventional disguises – the military moustache, the dark suits and homburgs which he wore even on picnics – of the man of affairs.

Kingsley Martin did a profile of him for the *New Statesman* of 28 October 1933 (to go with Low's famous cartoon, reproduced on the last page of the plates section), which emphasised his liquidity of mind and temperament, so 'terrifying and bewildering to the cautious and the solidly rooted'. But the point is that the solidly rooted found the world crumbling beneath them and needed to be rescued by a liquid mind able 'to run round and over an obstacle rather than to dispose of it'.

> Since he is troubled with sympathies and prejudices rather than with principles [the *New Statesman* assessment continues], the best policy is to find him a new premise; in a few minutes he may be successfully discovering for you all the arguments in support of your own conclusion.

This comment is representative of many. Keynes used to say, 'Every morning I wake up like a new born babe.' Quentin Bell recalls his immense persuasiveness in arguing any theory which at the time he believed, or perhaps just interested him, or amused him. Partly this was a sheer delight in showing off his cleverness. But people wondered: where was the core of him? His intellectual playfulness led Beatrice Webb into a spectacular but understandable misjudgement: 'Keynes is not serious about economic problems; he plays chess with them. The only serious cult with him is aesthetics: the Chinese conception of the art of a pleasurable or happy man with a secured and sufficient livelihood. . . .' This was written in her diary on 19 June 1936, four months after the publication of the *General Theory*! Dennis Robertson likened his mind to a powerful searchlight, moving from object to object, ignoring the interconnections of the whole. But suppose there were no interconnections left, only fragments? The rapidity with which he took up and discarded plans was equally startling. He was the first to realise when a cause was lost, and adapt himself to the new situation with equal elan, while the more solid were still trying to catch with his project of the day before yesterday. Yet looking at his ideas and plans over his lifetime there is a remarkable consistency in his *understanding* of his age.

Keynes is so affectionate, loyal and warm blooded [the *New Statesman* goes on] that until one meets him in opposition one may not understand where he gets his reputation for arrogance. He has an unavoidable consciousness that he is intellectually superior to the great ruck of mortals. He does not suffer fools. He minds about culture and personal freedom, but not at all about equality; he hates waste more than he hates suffering, and he is quite capable of being ruthless when he wants his own way. He is the most benevolent, impish, dangerous and persuasive promoter of ideas, and his eyes, arresting, commanding and challenging at times, are at others as soft and lively as bees' bottoms in blue flowers.

We must turn to Oswald Falk for the most penetrating analysis of Keynes's 'mental fabric':

... I wonder [he wrote to Keynes on 2 February 1936] ... whether analysis is your fundamental mental process, whether it doesn't follow, with a somewhat grudging struggle at rational justification, rather than precede synthetic ideas, which are your real delight, and with which from time to time you startle and shock the majority. Didn't Newton once say that his ideas reached him by some mysterious route which he could not explain? And isn't there something in the view that a new idea ... may ... be the product of the ... moral feeling of an age, floating around us, and ready for apprehension by the most *sensitive* minds by other than reasoning processes? And isn't it the artist rather than the scientist who apprehends these ideas? Is your mind really so typically western as superficially it appears to be? I believe not. Brilliant as your analysis may be, I believe it is a veneer rather than the substance of your mental fabric. And that explains perhaps in part the hostility which you arouse amongst the more truly western minds of some of your fellow economists, scientists in the narrower sense, bogged in the muddles of their analysis ... and either unwilling to admit or unable to realise that an idea, which is attainable, is something very different from a truth, which is not, and that the attainable idea is essential for the conduct of our lives.

Keynes's economics, at their most general, can be seen as the reflection of the 'moral feeling' of the age, intuited by an extraordinarily *sensitive* mind; but a mind also habituated to responsibility and duty. The decay of Victorian values freed Keynes to experiment with new ways of living and also alerted him to the need for new forms of social control. We have here a clue to the paradox of how the speculator in morals, ideas and money could win over the solid men in City suits to revolutionary concepts of economic management. He was not, after all, improbably cast as the 'saviour of capitalism'. Social systems are never saved by true believers, the virtues appropriate to going down with the ship rarely being suitable for the arts of navigation. The manipulation of economies by governments was but an extension of the management of external relations which Keynes had long practised to protect his private life. The projects conjured up by his nimble mind fitted a world no longer solidly rooted in Victorian certainties.

For Keynes's teacher Alfred Marshall, the connections between economics and culture, wealth and welfare, were still relatively unproblematic. Material prosperity, Marshall believed, was the necessary condition of moral growth: a 'gentleman' needed £500 a year. And business life was, for Marshall, itself a form of moral and moralising activity: sacrificing present enjoyment to make things which people needed to make them good. By the twentieth century this reciprocal connection between commerce, culture and morals, too readily assumed by the Victorians, could not be taken for granted, decreasingly so as the century unfolded. Today the main object of business activity is to make a quick profit, the quicker the better. The main object of contemporary statecraft is to make societies ever richer. To what end, and with what effect on individual and social virtue, we no longer ask, and scarcely dare think about. Keynes was the last great economist to hold economics in some sort of relation with the 'good life'. But already the language available to him to talk about the relationship sounded threadbare. What, in fact, was the connection between being rich and being good? Keynes was troubled by such questions but could make little progress in answering them. It became sufficient to keep the existing system of wealth-creation going, because its collapse would be more horrible than its success.

Keynes started devising his projects of economic management at a moment when the Victorian certainties had broken down – irretrievably shattered by the First World War – and Victorian motives to virtuous behaviour and self-improvement had weakened. The breakdown of the self-regulating market was the most spectacular example of the weakening of the civil society inherited from the Victorians. The chief symptom of this breakdown was persisting mass unemployment, though it was some time before Keynes identified it as the problem which it was to be his life's work to solve. He was a monetary economist and he always approached economic disorder from the side of money. The disturbing influence of money on the real economy – on the production of goods and services – is a constant factor in his thinking from his earliest pre-war economic writings to his *General Theory*. But the role of money in his theory of economic disorder shifted over time, though how much this was due to a change of terminology rather than a change in his understanding of the world is unclear.

He starts with the theme that the specific virtues associated with economic self-regulation – he singles out self-restraint and long-run thinking – presuppose, or depend on, stability of the price level. The earliest symptom of post-war economic disorder was the collapse of the stable measuring rod – money – in terms of which economic activities were valued and proportioned to each other. However, it was not the fact of inflation or deflation which caused economic activity to oscillate, but the uncertainty about the future course of prices on the minds of economic decision-makers. The effect of uncertainty on economic behaviour – on decisions to save, invest and provide employment – emerges as a major theme of Keynes's earliest theoretical book, *A Tract on Monetary Reform* (1923). In these circumstances, the duty of the monetary authority is to secure a supply of money consistent with establishing a firm expectation of zero inflation. It is deeply ironic that a theory which started off by proclaiming the necessity of stable prices for stable production should have degenerated into the dogma that 'inflation doesn't matter'.

Two paths led on from this early statement to Keynes's mature theory. First, he came to see money not so much as a cause of uncertainty as a way of dealing with uncertainty. The function of money as generalised purchasing power offered the possibility of withholding it from production and consumption, and Keynes almost implies it was invented for this purpose. Depressions arise, Keynes wrote in his *Treatise on Money* (1931), when money is shifted from the 'industrial circulation' into the 'financial circulation'. The emphasis Keynes placed on the function of money as a store of wealth, as an escape from commitment, as a measure, not of purchasing power, but of mistrust of the future, was one of his original contributions to economics. That wealth-holders should want to keep their assets liquid in an unsettled world was not perhaps a surprising revelation to this most liquid of men.

Keynes's second contribution, in the *General Theory of Employment, Interest, and Money* (1936), was to show that an economy had no natural tendency to full employment; that it could be naturally adjusted to a low level of inactivity, like an invalid to ill-health; and that, in these circumstances, an external intervention was required to restore it to vigour. This challenged head-on the inherited economic doctrine that no equilibrium position short of full employment was possible. Thus the withdrawal from investment, which the existence of money made possible, could set up a train of repercussions which left the economy in stable equilibrium short of full employment.

These are simple expressions of technical ideas in economics. But in his more philosophical writings Keynes links the power of money to disturb economic self-regulation to the tendency for money itself to become an object of desire, rather than a means to satisfy desires. His most profound and poetical pages on economics have to do with the encroachment of money values on use values, the triumph of making money over making things. For Keynes, as for the classical economists, Depressions are the wages of sin, only the sin is not spending too much, but spending too little on the things which make for a 'good life'. From this standpoint the Keynesian Revolution may be seen as an attempt to remoralise the capitalist economy – in Ruskin's words, to produce 'wealth' rather than 'illth'. This was undoubtedly part of its attraction to many on the left. These are the moral resonances in Keynes's technical arguments which can be heard by those willing to listen. They are not part of the logic of the arguments themselves. Economics was already too far removed from being a moral science for it to carry moral arguments. It was another fragment of a vanishing whole, soon to disappear into the black hole of mathematics.

Keynes did the best he could with the intellectual and cultural means at his disposal. It is impossible to think of anyone who could have done better. It is unfair to accuse him of trying to treat a moral crisis with a technical fix. The most palpable failure of individualism at the time was economic. He saw the state as a yet unexploited resource, our 'iron rations'. Moderate collectivism, applied in time, could avert the more extreme varieties then on offer. The risk seemed small compared to the risk of doing nothing. Who is to say that he was wrong? We have since learnt something about the pathology of governments, and of the economic and welfare systems managed and regulated by governments. The chief question for our own time is whether measures to stabilise economies can be combined with effective checks on governments, bureaucracies and producer groups. It is not a question we can put to Keynes.

III

I have divided this volume into three parts. The first, which I have called 'The Economic Consequences of the War', locates the post-war economic problem in the failure to overcome the economic and political havoc which the First World War had wrought to the internal balances and external relations of the belligerents. Of particular importance was the overhang of undetermined debt left by the Treaty of Versailles and the collapse of Tsarist Russia. The four-year impasse on wartime debts and reparations (1919–23) not only absorbed the energies of statesmen better directed to other goals, but stymied international efforts to stabilise currencies and reconstruct the shattered economies of Central Europe.

Keynes's position, spelt out in his *Economic Consequences of the Peace*, did not waver. He called for a cancellation of all inter-Ally war debts and the immediate fixing of a modest annual payment by Germany, which would go largely to France. Keynes did not play a leading part in sorting out the mess left by the peacemakers, but his role was far from negligible. Specifically, he made a direct contribution to the British Treasury Plan for settling the reparation problem at the end of 1922, and, through his friendship with Carl Melchior, acted almost as unofficial adviser to the German government in 1922–3, a curiously under-researched role. His maximum point of influence came during the brief premiership of Bonar Law, his second wartime

Treasury chief; but there is little evidence, for the period as a whole, that *The Economic Consequences of the Peace* had cut Keynes off from 'official circles', though he remained *persona non grata* to Lloyd George.

The historical thought prompted by Keynes's plans and activities is that he wanted, if possible, to keep America out of Europe. The point of reducing the mountain of war obligations to a modest annual transfer from Germany to France was precisely to avoid what in fact happened: the use of the debt as an engine of American lending, foisting the yoke of New York bankers on Europe. Like most Englishmen of his generation, Keynes was distressed by the passing of financial power from London to New York, and sought to build up Germany as a fit partner to Britain in resisting the Americanisation of the world – a role which Germany consistently refused to play. His realisation that a return by Britain to the gold standard at the prewar sterling–dollar parity entailed, under the new conditions, London's dependence on New York for the maintenance of the standard, was an important motive for his opposition to the policy adopted by Churchill in 1925.

By the end of this period, Keynes's attention had shifted to the effects of the war on Britain's economic position. Although he was perfectly aware of the severe problems of structural adjustment facing the British economy, his fire was concentrated on the deflationary policy adopted by the Treasury and the Bank of England in order to put the pound back on to gold, attributing the bulk of the heavy unemployment which emerged in the years 1921–2 to this mistaken policy. He fired the first shot in what was to become the Keynesian Revolution in December 1922, when he told the Institute of Bankers that the policy of forcing down wages to the deflated level of prices was 'almost hopeless', and that the only way to secure increased employment was by 'an increase in the level of prices'. His *Tract on Monetary Reform* was written in 1923 to argue that high and stable employment in Britain required keeping the British price level under the control of the British monetary authority, and not subject to the caprice of the Federal Reserve Board.

The second section, 'The Cross of Gold', which takes the story from 1925 to 1931, might just as well have been entitled 'The Economic Consequences of the Gold Standard'. Four central themes may be noticed. The first is Keynes's campaign against the return to the gold standard, his coruscating attack on the return in his *Economic Consequences of Mr. Churchill* (1925), and his efforts, between 1928 and 1931, to develop an employment policy within the constraints of the gold-standard system.

The second is his writing, mainly between 1925 and 1928, of *A Treatise on Money*, conceived initially as an attempt to analyse the emergence of a disequilibrium between saving and investment in a 'quantity theory of money' framework, with particular reference to an economy like Britain's with downwardly rigid money wages and interest rates determined by membership of a fixed-exchange-rate system. His exposition of the theory of the *Treatise* to the Macmillan Committee in 1930 marks the birth of Keynesian economics and the start of the Keynesian revolution in policy-making. In his excellent book, *The Keynesian Revolution in the Making* (1988), Peter Clarke has shown how the *Treatise* was 'derailed' in 1928–9 as a result of Keynes's need to meet the Treasury's objection to his own, and Lloyd George's, advocacy, in the run-up to the general election of 1929, of public works to cure unemployment. The theoretical reshaping of the *Treatise* held up its publication till 1931, and led to a lack of harmony in its parts, which was the immediate spur to Keynes's decision to start writing what became the *General Theory*.

The third theme is Keynes's rapprochement with his old *bête noire* Lloyd George in 1926, and his part in shaping the policy of the Lloyd George Liberal Party over the next three years. Lloyd George looked to Keynes to provide the economic programme which would win the Liberals at least a share of power; Keynes saw Lloyd George as the most promising instrument for getting his economic plans taken up by government. Keynes's reconciliation with Lloyd George involved a personal breach with the Asquiths which gave him great pain. In return, Keynes 'sold' Lloyd George his 'cure' for unemployment which the former Prime Minister expounded with all the fervour of a Welsh revivalist preacher on the hustings in the 1929 general election. These three years, in which Keynes served on the Liberal Industrial Inquiry, mark the high point of his involvement in politics. Its product was his political philosophy of the Middle Way, first outlined in 'The End of *Laissez-Faire*' (1924). The Lloyd George campaign failed, and the world economy collapsed into depression in 1929. After vainly trying his arts of persuasion on the Labour government of 1929–31, Keynes retreated into his ivory tower at King's to engage, at the age of forty-eight, in a supreme intellectual effort to save Western civilisation from the engulfing tide of barbarism which economic collapse was bringing on.

Finally, in a turnabout which amazed his friends, Keynes emerged from his homosexual cocoon to marry the Russian ballerina Lydia Lopokova in 1925. He had first met her in 1918, and started wooing her at the end of 1921 when she returned to London to star in Diaghilev's ill-fated ballet, *The Sleeping Princess*. It was a real love affair, not a marriage of convenience, the heterosexual expression of Keynes's lifelong reverence for the artist. From the early 1920s Lydia became the centre of his life, providing the indispensable emotional security for his work, while he took on the management of her career. Their love for each other was lifelong. There is some evidence that they tried to have a child in 1927. His marriage caused a breach with Bloomsbury, but not with Bloomsbury values. Keynes lavished his growing wealth and power on the arts, changing from Bloomsbury's friend into its Maecenas.

A sub-plot which runs through the 1920s is Keynes's increasing involvement in money-making. The wartime Treasury for him, as for others, was a jumping-off point into the City. In the 1920s, he lost and made small fortunes in speculation, and got to understand, in a way few economists do, the volatile character of unregulated capitalism and the deep social resistances to a system which made livelihoods and employment 'the by-product of the activities of a casino'. The line to the *General Theory* runs as clearly from his association with Oswald Falk in the City as it does from Cambridge monetary theory, Kahn's multiplier, and his debates with his fellow economists.

Part Three, 'The Economist to the Rescue', deals with Keynes's theoretical and practical response to the great depression in a period (1931–7) when he was further away from the centres of power and influence in Britain than at any time since the start of the First World War. His retreat to the cloister in the 1930s was an affirmation of his conviction that, politics having failed, the world could be saved only by thought. The fruit of this thought was his *General Theory of Employment, Interest, and Money* (1936), a profound exploration of the logic of economic behaviour under uncertainty, with curious subterranean links to all his other reflections on the problems of behaviour in a world bereft of moral guidance. A central argument is that, knowledge of the future being unattainable, we fall back on conventions which are too flimsy to provide steadiness of purpose. But is not this picture of an economic universe driven by *fashion* also a comment on the world of value relativism? True enough, from a philosophical point of view, the future was no more uncertain in 1930 than in 1870. The difference was that conventions and expectations were much more robust in 1870. And this must have had something to do with the fact that behaviour still took place in a moral framework which encouraged people to do their duty, 'come what may', a framework which made economic self-regulation work.

The simple message of Keynes's economics seems to be that, when a society's self-governing mechanisms break down, it needs more governing from the centre. This is the 'managerial' response to the breakdown of values. The aesthetic response is to substitute personal for public ends. Keynes combined the two by saying that good states of mind could not be enjoyed in collapsing societies. Moreover, his economic theory, which justified putting idle resources to work by means of public expenditure, could be invoked in support of his aesthetic ideals. 'If I had the power today,' he wrote in 1933, 'I would surely set out to endow our capital cities with all the appurtenances of art and civilisation on the highest standards . . . convinced that what I could create I could afford – and believing that money thus spent would not only be better than any dole, but would make unnecessary any dole. For with what we have spent on the dole in England since the war we could have made our cities the greatest works of man in the world.'

Keynes was as good as his word. Even as he was putting the finishing touches to his *magnum opus* in 1935, he was financing and supervising the building of the Cambridge Arts theatre – his personal contribution to the

ideal of the civilised society. The strain of doubling his artistic and managerial roles proved too much for a constitution already enfeebled by pleurisy
in 1931. He collapsed with a coronary thrombosis in May 1937. He never
fully recovered his health. But apart from two relatively idle years (1937–9),
he did not abate his activities, and the Second World War would provide
the heroic climax to his life.

What Is One to Do with One's Brains?

The date is 21 June 1921; the place, the Ivy Restaurant, London. John Maynard Keynes is about to make an after-dinner speech. He is the author of the best-selling *Economic Consequences of the Peace* and has just sent off the proofs of his long-delayed *Treatise on Probability* to the printer. Having served in the Treasury during the war, he is now back in his old job as Fellow of King's College, Cambridge. Yet it is not as author or administrator, economist or philosopher that he speaks tonight, but as this year's President of the Apostles, the exclusive Cambridge Conversazione Society, whose annual dinner has just been eaten. He is only thirty-eight, tall, with a slight stoop, and still slim, though balding. His most remarkable feature is his eyes – 'riotous eyes', Frank Harris called them, which 'mirror every thought of the "leaping mind"'. He starts a little hesitantly, and reads what he says, because, although his voice is precise and cultivated, he is no orator. His subject is the Society, its past and present.

About thirty-five have eaten dinner. One or two of them – Keynes mentions the jurist Sir Frederick Pollock and the banker Walter Leaf – date back from the Society's antiquity. But the majority are his contemporaries or near contemporaries; it is a middle-aged gathering. Keynes mentions the absent brethren. Some have no truck with the Post Office and so have not bothered to reply to his invitations; some are too old or too infirm to come. Others are abroad. Bertrand Russell – he reads out his letter – is in Peking, lecturing to the Chinese on Einstein, behaviourism and Bolshevism. He strongly urges Keynes to join him at a huge salary. James Strachey is in Vienna being psychoanalysed by Freud. E. M. Forster is at Chhatarpur writing a novel on India in the intervals of trying to repair the cars of the Maharaja of Dewas. Lytton Strachey is rumoured to be present, disguised in a beard.

Turning to the active brethren – the undergraduate Apostles who meet every Saturday evening in Cambridge – Keynes remarks that after a 'slight flicker towards phenomenal events' (Apostles' slang for the affairs of the world), the Society has 'withdrawn itself into a monastic seclusion, and, except that they talk too much about the herd instinct, are much more like the Society always was than the outside world is what it used to be'. That world is seen by the young men, perhaps by everyone, as a 'sort of Juggernaut, an independent Juggernaut, one which it would be absurd to suppose one could affect or influence in any way. The Juggernaut is a feared and hated monster, which one does not mention often and from which one averts one's eyes'. The point would be well understood by his audience. In late Victorian and Edwardian times the young men of the Society had turned their gaze inwards because the outside world seemed to be progressing so satisfactorily; now they did so because it seemed too awful to contemplate, too out of control to influence. Keynes had some sympathy with this view.

Now he turns to the brothers who had died since the last dinner. Arthur Sidgwick and J. E. Symes are soon disposed of, but J. F. Moulton is a more interesting case, and it is around Moulton that the rest of Keynes's address revolves. Moulton had been elected an Apostle in 1867. He was a brilliant mathematician, Senior Wrangler in fact, and a Fellow of Christ's College, Cambridge. But he had forsaken scholarship for the Bar and, unusually for an Apostle, had gone in for money-making, although his intellectual capacities, Keynes remarked in a typical sally, 'were much in excess of those usually associated with the love of money'. Keynes had last met him at the Paris Peace Conference in 1919 when Moulton, who was then associated with British Dyestuffs, had sought him out at the Hotel Majestic to promote a scheme by which German dyes could be secured and held off the market, to the advantage of British dye interests but at the expense of the British taxpayer. 'The old man, then in his seventy-fifth year, a Lord of Appeal, with his great career behind him and substantial wealth at his command, a little palsied and his slightly heavy features a little quivering, but with his intellect apparently undimmed, was not ashamed to employ that intellect once again . . . to impose a sophistry on the junior Treasury official in front of him.'

A discreditable story, indeed: had the brethren been wrong, perhaps, to make Moulton one of their number in 1867? Not necessarily, Keynes thought, and quoted some lines from Ben Jonson's *Volpone*, one of his favourite plays, in which Volpone says, 'Yet I glory / More in the *cunning purchase* of my wealth / Than in the glad possession . . .' (Keynes's italics). Moulton's act in 1919, Keynes says, might be considered one of 'artistry, not of avarice'. Generalising his theme he asks his audience to imagine a man of great intellectual power and objectivity of mind. In youth he has feasted on art, science and philosophy. But suppose that, while his intellect and vitality are great, his powers of creation are feeble; that he has 'the egotism of the artist but not his powers of achievement'. Such a man generally goes one of three ways: 'He may become a pedant; he may play games; or he may follow, in some shape or form, in some degree or other, the career of Moulton. Would you have preferred Moulton a pedant? Would you have had him spend his declining years at the bridge table? In the stir and bustle of the world, pitting his wits, at a price, against all comers, an honourable servant of those who employed him, exercising a variety of conjoined gifts in the quarters of phenomenal existence . . . Moulton may have come, as near as he was capable . . . to the satisfactions of the artist.'[1]

Keynes has offered a subtle defence of worldliness in terms which alone might satisfy an audience which prized itself on its unworldliness. Moulton's motives were at heart *aesthetic*. He was an artist of action. But Moulton, one feels, is of no importance, either to Keynes or to his hearers. He is the peg on which Keynes hangs the question which really interests him: what is a person to do with his life who has the temperament or longing of the artist without the capacity to create works of art? A life devoted to art or pure thought, Keynes seems to be saying, is all very well for those who have genuine creative power, but not for those who, while hearing 'clear echoes of the voice divine', cannot find 'fit music for their visions'.[2]

Keynes himself is at a transition in his life. While he seems to be talking about Moulton it is easy to imagine that he is talking about himself – discussing, perhaps justifying, his life choices before the jury of his peers. He too had spent much of his early adulthood in the cloister, scribbling away on his theory of probability. As his father noted at the time, he had returned to Cambridge in 1908 to resume a 'student's life'. But as he worked on probability he came to realise that the achievements of a Moore or a Russell were beyond him. His inclinations and capacities were activist, not reclusive.

Even before 1914, economics had won out decisively over philosophy. Economics appealed to the two sides of Keynes's mind – imagining things and counting things. It connected the ivory tower to the world of action. By the accident of having spent two years at the India Office, Keynes found himself in demand as an expert on Indian currency matters. Without the war, the 'active middle period' to which his friend Archie Rose urged him might well have started in Delhi rather than in Whitehall; for was not the empire a well-recognised outlet for aesthete–administrators, and had not two of Keynes's best friends, Bernard Swithinbank and Gordon Luce, gone east? By 1914, too, Keynes was starting to apply economics to money-making – for himself and for his friends.

His emotional world was changing too. Even before 1914, London life had started to break down the homosexuality of the pre-war Cambridge Apostles. These Edwardian rebels may not have been growing up into what is called maturity. But they were growing older and more worldly. They had lives to build beyond the confines of Cambridge colleges. Even without the war, Bloomsbury might have turned towards domesticity. Keynes's love affair with Duncan Grant had come to an end in 1911. He never found a replacement. His own first experiments in heterosexuality date from the war years. Here was another transition.

There was no 'single' Keynes, no identity in solitude. People remember him by his masks, by the magic with which he invested his parts. He was a playful person. One talks naturally about the play of his eyes, his words, his ideas. Yet his playfulness, or artistry, was in the service of serious things. Keynes's answer to the Moulton problem seemed to be this: it is a person's state of mind, not the end which he pursues, or the rules which he follows, which is important in judging the worth of his life. To be morally valuable, even great humanitarian benefactions had to be 'cunningly purchased'. And did Keynes not also understand, by 1921, that what was needed was a new kind of history, to be made by a new kind of 'man of action', one for whom action was a kind of playfulness rather than a matter of life or death? Was this not the message, and point, of the quotation from Ben Jonson?

However, the precise sphere of Keynes's artistry was not fixed by 1921, because the consequences of the war had not worked themselves out. His stint at the Treasury had distanced him from pure scholarship while greatly enlarging the opportunities and attractions of influencing policy and making money. He would not have been happy as a career civil servant, but he enjoyed the role of the 'inside-outsider', a kind of naughty son of the Establishment. *The Economic Consequences of the Peace* had identified him as an expert on reparations and a leader of the younger generation in its revolt against the old men of politics. Yet, though the book gave Keynes technical and moral authority, its tone was not idealistic but ironic. Woodrow Wilson was a fake Colossus who could easily have taken his place in Lytton Strachey's gallery of *Eminent Victorians*. The world was to be saved by intelligence, not by morals. The book set Keynes's course for the 1920s. As long as financial diplomacy dominated international relations, he would be in demand for comment, plans, counsel and consultancies. It also made him a power in the Asquithian section of the Liberal Party.

On the other side, the shift from Whitehall to the City has always been easy, and indeed natural, in England, the two worlds forming an institutional nexus from which industry was traditionally excluded. Once Keynes became 'available', offers of lucrative business were not slow to come from bankers and financiers he had got to know in the war. But he was reluctant, as he put it in response to one money-making proposition, 'to make it, for some time at least, more or less my life's work'. Ideally, he wanted to be at the meeting point of his several worlds – intellect, public life, money-making and the arts.

Yet the war was, in the end, to drive him back to creative thought in a way he could not have anticipated in 1921. The question of what would have become of Keynes but for the war is inseparable from the question of what would have happened to Britain, and indeed the world, but for the war. What would the really big problems have been in a world which had not experienced that catastrophe? There was a functioning world order in 1914, based on a cosmopolitan ruling class and a set of conventions, norms and rules of the game governing both political and economic relations. By 1918 essential props of this bourgeois order had disappeared, and what was stitched together again looked alarmingly threadbare. If it was doomed in any case, its passing, but for the war, would surely have been much slower, the shocks more muted and spaced out. Britain's own place in that order would no doubt have continued to decline, but at a more leisurely rate. Money would have remained 'sound'. Unemployment would not have developed on such a scale or persisted for so long. The Liberal Party would still have been a challenger for power. Would Keynes or anyone else have felt that such a world – a world which had not been mortally wounded between 1914 and 1918 – required a new economic theory to explain, a new style to set right? Would he have striven so mightily?

Keynes would surely have made a mark on affairs in any case. The rhythm of his development pointed him, like Moulton, in that direction. But the nature of his involvement was set by events. It was events which gave direction to capacities and efforts which, as he himself half recognised, might easily have dissipated themselves in transient activities.

PART ONE

THE ECONOMIC CONSEQUENCES OF THE WAR

MOSES: It is not the business of a Ruler to be truthful, but to be politick; he must fly even from Virtue herself, if she sit in a different Quarter from Expediency. It is his Duty to *sacrifice* the Best, which is impossible, to a *little Good*, which is close at hand.

MR LOKE: . . . If Men were told the Truth, might not they believe it? If the Opportunity of Virtue and Wisdom is never to be offer'd 'em, how can we be sure that they would not be willing to take it? Let Rulers be *bold* and *honest*, and it is possible that the Folly of their Peoples will disappear.

(From 'A Dialogue' 'apparently in the writing of Voltaire' published 'for the first time' in Lytton Strachey's *Books and Characters* (1922), dedicated to 'John Maynard Keynes')

CHAPTER ONE

The Lives of Keynes

I

It was *The Economic Consequences of the Peace* that established Keynes's claim to attention. Until then he had been known only to small groups. In 1919 his qualities were broadcast to the world. A book written in a moment of passion and despair set its author on his life-long course. He had spoken like an angel with the knowledge of an expert. This mastery of science *and* words was to be the basis of all his achievement. But there was something else. Keynes asserted not only his own claim to attention but the claim of economic science to shape the future. The princes of the old world had left a dreadful mess; it was the task of the scientist to clean it up. This was a message with a powerful appeal to the rising generation. And it immediately raised the question with which Keynes was to wrestle for the next sixteen years of his life: was the inherited economics of the nineteenth century adequate to its new task? Or was that, too, part of the old world which had been swept away in the war? His eventual answer was given in *The General Theory of Employment, Interest, and Money*.

A few intimates apart, it was Cambridge undergraduates who first heard Keynes's denunciations of the Treaty of Versailles. Having quit the Treasury, he returned to King's College, Cambridge in October 1919 and gave his autumn lectures, 'The Economic Aspects of the Peace Treaty', from the proofs of his forthcoming book. They made a powerful impression on those who heard them. The idea that the world was being ruined by stupidity rather than by wickedness was a doctrine with obvious appeal to the clever.[1] This was to be the attraction of the Keynesian Revolution itself. Like his new American friend, Walter Lippmann, Keynes was moved to wrath not so much by a 'fiery passion for justice and equality', as by 'an impatience with how badly society was managed'.[2] This was the new liberal mood. The twentieth-century claim to rule would be based on competence not ideals. Ideals were too costly.

But the effect of Keynes's utterance was paradoxical. *The Economic Consequences of the Peace* made him a hero of the left, to which, as Kingsley Martin remarked, 'he never belonged'. Henceforth the intelligentsia of the left always listened with one ear to what Keynes was saying. The Labour Party emerged from the war as the Conservative Party's main challenger for power. Keynes's ability to speak to both sides of the political divide from a position in the centre was to be crucial to the making of the Keynesian Revolution.

Kingsley Martin, the son of a Nonconformist clergyman, had just come up to Magdalene College. 'It was wonderful for us', he later wrote, 'to have a high authority saying with inside knowledge of the Treaty what we felt emotionally.'[3] This was a minority view. Cambridge celebrated victory in suitable patriotic style. On Armistice Day, medical students smashed up the bookshop and art gallery of C. K. Ogden, editor of the anti-war *Cambridge Magazine*, flinging canvas after canvas by Vanessa Bell, Duncan Grant and Roger Fry through the shattered plate-glass window.[4] The rowdiness had still not subsided when Keynes returned.

Keynes sought out the small group of pacifist undergraduates who were having a hard time. Richard Braithwaite, who had started to read mathematics at King's in October 1919, remembered the great man coming up to him at a freshmen's party. They talked for an hour about Freud, after which Keynes remarked, 'Thank God, there's an intelligent man in College.' Braithwaite was a Quaker who, like Kingsley Martin, had served in the Friends' Ambulance Unit during the war. But Keynes never told Braithwaite about his own conscientious objection to conscription.[5] This remained unknown outside old Bloomsbury. By his silence on this, and by turning the argument from the iniquities of the war to those of the peace, Keynes limited his breach with the Establishment. He wanted to appeal to the young without losing the ear of the old.

Keynes's return to King's College established a pattern for the next eighteen years of his life. Generally, he was in Cambridge in term time from Thursday evening till Tuesday afternoon. Mid-week would be spent in London. Vacations were divided between London, foreign travel and Sussex. Keynes did not much like Cambridge out of full term, needing 'the pulse and movement of the College working in all its arteries to keep him happy'.[6] There were no sabbaticals in those days, and Keynes took only one term off teaching between 1919 and 1937. His writing as well as his other activities had to be fitted into the normal framework of the academic year.

What did he do in his long 'weekends'? His teaching responsibilities were much reduced from before the war, his livelihood no longer depending on 'selling economics by the hour'. Having given up his Girdler's lectureship, he confined himself to just eight lectures a year, compared to the hundred he had given in 1910–11. These took place in the autumn or summer terms, usually on Friday or Monday mornings. They were generally early drafts of books he was writing. After 1922 he lectured on 'The Theory of Money' for ten years, before changing to 'The Monetary Theory of Production' in 1932. His first two sets of lectures in 1919 and 1920 attracted audiences of hundreds. Many were not studying economics at all. They came simply to hear Keynes tell how to set the world to rights.

Keynes was responsible for the economics teaching at King's. He conducted his tutorials or supervisions, generally in groups of three or four, on Friday or Saturday evenings before dinner. At first there were not that many economics undergraduates at King's – no more than half a dozen a year. Keynes took no first-year students; he farmed out most of his college teaching to Gerald Shove, a pupil and friend from before the war, who initially held no College or University appointment. Shove was the carthorse of inter-war Cambridge economics, a role dictated by financial need as well as by an aversion to publication. He taught prodigiously, influenced many, but wrote almost nothing himself.

The Political Economy Club – or Keynes Club, as it was known – which Keynes had founded in 1909 continued to meet most Monday evenings in his drawing room overlooking Webb's Court – 'the pleasantest sitting room I have ever been in', Virginia Woolf wrote after a visit in 1923. By then Vanessa Bell and Duncan Grant had covered up Grant's pre-war murals of semi-nude dancers and grape-pickers with eight panels of allegorical figures representing the Muses. Membership of the Keynes Club was by invitation. It consisted of Keynes's closest colleagues in the Economics Faculty, graduate students and the best of the second- and third-year undergraduates. The proceedings were modelled on those of the Apostles. Someone – it might be Keynes himself or a distinguished visitor – would read a paper, then lots were drawn giving the order in which members had to make comments on it. 'If they had none to make they had still got to get up, go over to the fireplace and say so.'[7] The senior members in 1923 were Professor Pigou and Gerald Shove (King's – though Pigou rarely came), Dennis Robertson and Frank Ramsey (Trinity), Austin Robinson (Corpus), Frederick Lavington (Emmanuel), Philip Sargant-Florence (Caius) and Maurice Dobb (Clare). The brightest economics student of the early post-war period, Joan Maurice (later Robinson), who came up to Girton in 1922, was excluded from this all-male gathering.

Cambridge economics was in the doldrums after the war. Two of the Faculty's cleverest pre-war members, Walter Layton and Hubert Henderson, left Cambridge. There was a 'missing generation' – those who had fought, in many cases died, between 1914 and 1918 instead of going to university. The quality of the post-war economics undergraduates was not high. The post-war students turned at first to history and psychology, no doubt the better to understand the war. Only two of the early post-war candidates for the economics tripos – Austin Robinson and Maurice Dobb – got College teaching jobs in the 1920s. So the post-war faculty had a distinctly pre-war look till at least the mid–1920s. The renaissance of Cambridge economics – what Shackle calls the 'years of high theory' – only starts in 1926 with the publication of Dennis Robertson's *Banking Policy and the Price Level* and the arrival of Piero Sraffa from Italy.

Again there is something of a paradox here. As a result of his *Economic Consequences of the Peace* Keynes had gained a reputation as the most radical of the younger economists. But partly because of the way his life was arranged – and especially because of his incessant involvement in public controversy – he made no important theoretical contribution to his discipline till the appearance of his *Treatise on Money* in 1930. His polemics of the 1920s were directed against the mistakes of the policymakers, not against the theories they held. It was not till Britain's return to the gold standard in 1925 that Keynes started to think that mistaken policy was the result of mistaken theory. After that his policy critique took on an increasingly theoretical turn. But till the early 1930s his policy proposals leapt ahead of his theory, which remained relatively conservative.

At King's Keynes spent the first few years after the war teaching a succession of second-class men who went off into the family business. There were only two King's firsts in the economics tripos in the five years after the war – Rupert Trouton, a mature student who had been with Keynes in the Treasury, and J. V. Joshi, who later became deputy governor of the Reserve Bank of India. The situation improved only with the arrival of Frederick Harmer and Richard Kahn in 1924.

The oldest fixed point in Keynes's Cambridge life was the Saturday after-dinner meetings of the Apostles. The Society was another of the war's casualties. Discontinued between 1914 and 1918, it was revived by F. L. ('Peter') Lucas, the last of the pre-war 'births'. Lucas had returned to Cambridge in 1919 after a harrowing war, in which he had been wounded and gassed (Keynes eventually got him a job in Intelligence). In 1920 King's appointed him a Fellow in classics before he had even graduated from Trinity. Like Wilfred Owen and Siegfried Sassoon, Lucas had hated the madness of war, while responding passionately to the 'comradeship of the trenches'. The unresolved conflict between rationalism and romanticism stamped his character. 'Good prim priggish bright-eyed Peter', as Virginia Woolf called him, soon became a Fellow in English, slicing up English literature 'very prettily, with a pocket knife'.[8] But he was really a Georgian survivor, who hated the post-war world, loathed the Leavisite revolution in English studies and, as King's Librarian, would refuse to stock T. S. Eliot.

In setting out to revive the Apostles, Lucas had the support not only of Keynes, but of Keynes's oldest College intimate, John Sheppard, Fellow in classics at King's, by now a somewhat wizened cherub. Sheppard's contribution to the revival was James Hamilton Doggart, a pretty surgeon probationer, who preferred rugby to philosophy. Intellectual ballast was provided by two King's men, Alexander Penrose and 'Scanes' Spicer: all three were 'born' in November 1919. The two 'births' in 1920–1 were Jack (known as Sebastian) Sprott of Clare College, and Penrose's younger brother

Lionel from St John's, later an eminent geneticist. Frank Ramsey, George ('Dadie') Rylands and Richard Braithwaite were added the following year. This was the immediate post-war circle of Maynard Keynes's 'young men'. The new generation of Apostles was less homoerotic than the pre-war one, and showed a distressing tendency to early matrimony, Lucas setting the trend by marrying the novelist 'Topsy' Jones in 1921.

In his first two years back at Cambridge, Keynes went to the Saturday evening meetings fairly regularly ; he was an intermittent attender throughout the inter-war years. The problem for the young, as indeed for Keynes himself, was how to come to terms with the war. Perhaps the explanation lay with Freud and the 'death instinct'. There was also Rupert Brooke's disturbing wartime remark to ponder: 'I've never been quite so happy in my life' – a sentiment echoed by another pre-war Apostle, Ferenc Békássy, on his way to his death in the Bukovina. Békássy's friend Lucas had felt the same way. Keynes never ceased to be troubled by the paradox of progress – the tendency of technical advance to liquidate the conditions which give rise to terror and pity, tragedy and heroism.

Cambridge for Keynes also meant family – lots of it. His parents Neville and Florence Keynes remained solid presences at his birthplace, 6 Harvey Road, and most Sundays in term time Keynes would walk up there from King's, for lunch or tea and a gossip about the great world. Neville Keynes was sixty-six when the war ended, though he remained University Registrary till 1925. As his duties contracted, so did his anxieties, and he moved into tranquil old age with a new hobby: collecting and listening to gramophone records. His wife Florence, eight years his junior, was in no mood to retire. As Neville's life gratefully subsided, hers rose to a peak of activity. She became a town councillor and magistrate, helped establish the Papworth Village colony for tubercular patients, and spent much of her time working for the National Council of Women. Both parents took immense pleasure in their son's growing fame, a pleasure unclouded by jealousy or criticism, though attended by spasms of worry. Both continued to exert moral authority over him, Florence, in particular, reminding him that he came from a line of preachers and benefactors.

Childless himself, Maynard was embedded in an extended family of Browns and Keyneses. Although he was the only one touched by genius, the overall standard of achievement, though not of charm, was impressively high – a tribute to both heredity and family tradition. His younger brother Geoffrey, who had married Margaret Darwin in 1917, was a junior at St Bartholomew's Hospital, London, and starting to build an international reputation as a surgeon and bibliographer. Geoffrey and Margaret gave Maynard four nephews: Richard (1919), Quentin (1921), Milo (1924) and Stephen (1927). Maynard's sister Margaret was married to physiologist and Nobel prizewinner A. V. Hill. When they moved to Highgate in 1923, Margaret followed her mother's lead and became a borough councillor in

Hornsey, much concerned with the housing problems of the poor and elderly. They had four children: Polly (1914), David (1915), Janet (1918) and Maurice (1919). Maynard's grandparents, Dr John Brown, the 'Baptist bishop', and his wife Ada Haydon Brown were still living in Hampstead when the war ended. He died in 1922, she in 1929, both aged ninety-two.

The Sunday luncheon parties at 6 Harvey Road were proper family affairs, increasingly attended as time went on by Browns who settled in Cambridge – brothers and sisters of Florence, heavy in mind and body – and children from both sides of the family studying in Cambridge. Neville Brown, son of Harold Brown, read economics at Sidney Sussex College in the early 1920s, becoming secretary of the Keynes Club.

> Like other undergraduate members of the family, I was often invited to what, in those days, was a jolly family party. . . . Food would rumble up from the kitchen below in a hoist which would then disappear into the floor. My uncle Neville would circulate excellent claret: conversation was always easy and, if Maynard was present, sure to be very amusing.[9]

If Keynes was oppressed by the weight of these family connections, he did not show it. He was always generous with advice and practical help, particularly to the younger generation.

King's College remained his spiritual home, increasingly so as the years went on. 'That King's men are a religious order and their home a monastery is self-evident,' commented his friend Marcel Labordère in 1937. Keynes was never a University politician – his stint on the Council of Senate in the mid–1920s was agony for him. But he was a product of Eton and King's; and the idea of a fellowship of learning, linking up his childhood to his adult life, and a 500-year past to the present and the future, made a strong appeal to his imagination and feelings. This was Keynes's Burkean side. When he talked of protecting civilisation from its wreckers and destroyers, he thought first of the College in its setting. By civilisation he meant an endowed aristocracy of learning and the arts, with a strong sense of duty. He was never an egalitarian. Even his orthodox belief in equality of opportunity was tempered by the thought that 'certain small [family] "connections" have produced eminent characters out of all proportion to their size'.[10] Keynes rarely used the word, but he thought of himself as part of the 'clerisy' – a secular priesthood, setting standards of value and behaviour, practising the arts of leadership and mutual accommodation.

Keynes took a full part in the College's corporate life. He was, of course, a member of the College Council, or governing body, which met weekly on Saturdays (and sometimes on Mondays too), often for four or five hours, interrupted by lunch. But his influence was chiefly felt on three committees: Estates, Building and Fellowship. The first he totally dominated, even before he became first bursar in 1924. In the early 1920s he started a revolutionary policy of switching the College's investments from land into securities. By November 1920 he had sold off almost a third of the College estates. As he explained to his former Treasury colleague Basil Blackett, 'few non-resident landlords can hope at the present time to secure a net rental much above 3% of the selling value of agricultural estates'. Investing the proceeds of sales yielded 6 per cent. By 1925 he calculated that his policy had made the college £235,000 richer.[11] Changing economic circumstances, and perhaps values, brought a switch back to land in the later 1920s, and Keynes took personal charge of an experiment in direct farming by the College of 3000 acres in north Lincolnshire. He also dominated the Buildings Committee, planning and supervising a grandiose rebuilding programme which stuttered its way into the 1930s. Building appealed to his imagination for the reason it has appealed to all master-builders: he wanted to leave his footprint on earth. His monument is the Arts Theatre he had built in Cambridge in 1935.

As a Fellowship Elector his influence was less overwhelming, but it was rare that a candidate who had Keynes's backing failed to secure an appointment at King's. Friends and protégés who became Fellows included Peter Lucas (1920), Richard Braithwaite and Frank Ramsey (1924), Gerald Shove (1926), Dadie Rylands (1927) and Richard Kahn (1930). All except Kahn were Apostles. Here, as in other areas of College life, much of Keynes's influence rested on his friendship with Sheppard, who became vice-provost in 1929.

Keynes was a busy man, and increasingly looked it. To many undergraduates 'he can only have been a figure in their time, a tall man with an odd face and a restless eye, walking fast with a slight stoop up the aisle in Hall and holding on to the selvedge of his gown with both hands in front of him; pacing the Back Lawn with a companion in the summer; or hurrying across the Court with his black brief-case on the way to London'.[12] However, Keynes's work habits were so efficient that, though busy, he rarely seemed rushed; and he was able to carve himself out a surprising amount of free time. In the early 1920s he took up riding again, on Saturday afternoons, with Sebastian Sprott; Fridays would often see him pottering to David's the bookseller, 'Glyphoon's' the antique dealer, or Bodgers, his tailor, from whom he ordered not just suits, but silk shirts, collars, underwear and socks. Sunday was writing time – a paper, a lecture or an article to be started or polished off in the morning; a family lunch; perhaps a small dinner party for undergraduates, with a glass of claret as a reward; and then a concert in Chapel or a visit to one of Sheppard's At Homes for an hour of irreverent gossip. And after any dinner in Hall there might be a game of bridge or patience in the Combination Room.

This was a not unusual busy don's life. However, Cambridge was only one of Keynes's worlds – and for much of the 1920s not his most important one.

II

During the war Keynes had worked in Whitehall and relaxed in Bloomsbury. Bloomsbury was both where he lived and the collective name of the group of friends with whom he lived. Bloomsbury in this second sense was Keynes's conscience, the guardian of the unworldly ideal he had accepted as a young man. The tension between Whitehall and Bloomsbury shaped his life.

By taking over the lease of 46 Gordon Square in 1918, Keynes had possessed himself of what Clive Bell had called Bloomsbury's chief *monument historique*. He continued to share it, until his marriage in 1925, with Clive and his wife Vanessa, who themselves led partly separate lives. The Gordon Square houses, like those of neighbouring Tavistock Square, were spacious five-storey Georgian structures framing shared gardens of ample proportions, unlike the miniaturised houses and squares of Islington further to the east. They were not grand, and they were no longer fashionable, but they had been built to be occupied by people of means. Number 46 had its basement of kitchen, pantry and servants' sitting room. On the ground floor was the communal dining room, which Keynes, in Duncan Grant's view, contrived to make look like a company boardroom. On the first floor was a large L-shaped drawing room, decorated with murals by Vanessa Bell and Duncan Grant. Here Bloomsbury would often assemble for evening entertainment and gossip. On the floor above were Keynes's bedroom and study – the latter a book-lined room containing a bust of Julius Caesar. The two floors above that were initially occupied by the Bells and their children when they were in London. Servants' bedrooms were in the attic. The house's front door was painted in vermilion, to advertise the iconoclasm of its inhabitants.

With the end of the war, returning Bloomsbury grouped itself round Number 46 in such numbers that Lytton Strachey foresaw that Gordon Square would become 'a sort of College . . . the *rencontres* in the garden I shudder to think of'.[13] His mother, the still vigorous Lady Strachey, and assorted daughters were installed at Number 51, where Lytton also had a *pied-à-terre*. His brother James and Alix Sargant-Florence, married in 1920, lived at Number 41, when they were not being psychoanalysed by Freud in Vienna. Portions of this house were sub-let to a succession of younger Bloomsberries. Virginia Woolf's brother Adrian Stephen and his wife Karen – daughter of Keynes's old friend Mary Berenson – set up as practising psychoanalysts at Number 50. To Virginia Woolf, who still lived in far-off Richmond, Gordon Square seemed like a 'lion's house at the Zoo. One goes from cage to cage. All the animals are dangerous, rather suspicious of each other and full of fascination and mystery.'[14] The Bloomsbury animals spread to outer cages in Tavistock and Brunswick Squares, Great Ormond, Bernard and Fitzroy Streets. Walter Sickert, still living in Whistler's old studio in Fitzroy Street, kept alive the atmosphere of the 1890s. Lady Ottoline Morrell, wrinkled and powdered, came back to Bedford Square, Garsington at last emptied of its troublesome wartime house-guests. One of the last of these had gone off with 113 of Philip Morrell's favourite hens. 'Such a difficult thing to do,' Violet Bonham-Carter remarked to Keynes.

As before the war members of Bloomsbury enjoyed living cheek by jowl, seeing the same people for dinner as they had for lunch – often in Keynes's dining room. Other favourite meeting places were the 1917 Club in Gerrard Street, and the bookshop opened by 'Bunny' Garnett and Frankie Birrell in Taviton Street. Garnett married Ray Marshall in 1921 to a 'universal howl of execration from Bloomsbury'.[15] Her livelier sister Frances tried to restore financial order to the bookshop, where Birrell's slovenly dress, eccentric greetings and habit of covering 'stock' with fingerprints and cigarette ash rapidly reduced the clientele to the Bloomsbury hard-core. The older and younger generations also came together for inventive parties, marked by passionate dancing and witty, bawdy entertainments, sometimes written by Virginia Woolf or Lytton Strachey. One of the characters in Anthony Powell's *Books Do Furnish a Room* tried to imagine Gordon Square in the 1920s: 'Every house stuffed with Moderns from cellar to garret. High-pitched voices adumbrating absolute values, rational states of mind, intellectual integrity, civilized personal relationships, significant form. . . . The Fitzroy Street Barbera is uncorked. *Le Sacre du Printemps* turned on, a hand slides up a leg. . . . All are at one now, values and lovers.'[16]

Although Bloomsbury houses had their standard quota of servants, they were quite unlike well-regulated middle-class houses in which there was a place for everything, and everyone knew his place. It was never quite clear who was occupying what bedroom or with whom. Clive Bell came back to Number 46 one day to find 'Bunny' Garnett sleeping in his spare room, the WCs out of order, mutiny in the kitchen and the prospect of being 'nose to nose' with Alix Sargant-Florence for a whole month.[17] Soon afterwards Duncan Grant recorded a 'riot' at Number 41 – 'Alix went away without leaving an address or money or directions for a fortnight. The servants thought they had been marooned. . . .'[18] The masters and mistresses of Bloomsbury did not look or sound like other domestic employers, their studied shabbiness of dress being accompanied by exaggerations of speech which reminded Wyndham Lewis of 'the sounds associated with the spasms of a rough Channel passage'. Under these circumstances many of the servants went to pieces. Some actually went mad, like Vanessa's housemaid Mary Wilson. Others took to drink, steamed open their employers' letters and tried to emulate their feats of cohabitation. Keynes returned to Gordon Square from Charleston one evening in 1920 to find his cook Blanche in loving embrace with a Mr Bam in the basement, and Clive Bell and Mary Hutchinson similarly occupied above him. More alarmingly, Mr Bam took to painting. Soon they both left, to be replaced by Mr and Mrs Harland, he smelling strongly of whisky, who stayed till 1931. Keynes recorded all these goings-on with amused irony. Yet, in a strange throw-back to the morals of 6 Harvey Road, he at first refused to invite James Strachey to his end-of-ballet-season party in July 1919 on the ground that he had 'ruined two young ladies'. He relented only when Duncan Grant attacked him for moral hypocrisy.[19]

The Bloomsbury properties were rented or leased, mainly from the Bedford Estate, which owned most of that part of London. Keynes never owned a house in his life. This was quite normal for the time. Only 10 per cent of domestic property was owner-occupied in 1914, and the proportion did not change much till the 1930s. Bloomsbury's savings were invested in bonds, not houses. The Marxist writer Prince Mirsky was to describe them as 'theoreticians of the passive, dividend-drawing ... section of the bourgeoisie ... extremely intrigued by their own minutest inner experiences'.[20] Keynes had a complicated response to this *rentier* inheritance which, as we shall see, influenced his economic theories.

The pattern of communal London living, disrupted by the war, gradually dissolved as the Bloomsberries grew older and formed their own separate households, in the country or even abroad. They visited, of course, corresponded relentlessly and retained London bases. But the close-knit character of the pre-war group was gone, as Vanessa Bell later acknowledged. Two attempts to institutionalise themselves testify to the breakdown of the spontaneous sense of community. On 5 February 1920 Keynes gave a luncheon party at the Café Royal to which Duncan Grant's 'oldest friends' were asked to celebrate his first one-man show at the Paterson and Carfax Gallery. What a pity, Lytton Strachey said, they couldn't have such a party once a week. A month later, and perhaps as a direct result of this reunion, the Memoir Club came into existence, with Molly MacCarthy as its convenor. Ostensibly formed to help her husband Desmond write his long-awaited literary masterpiece, it met regularly during the inter-war years, chiefly to listen to Old Bloomsberries talking about themselves. Keynes read it *Dr Melchior* in 1921 and *My Early Beliefs* in 1938. In 1924 David Garnett and Francis Birrell founded the Cranium Club, whose members dined at the Verdi Restaurant in Wardour Street on the first Thursday of every month. Cranium's membership gives the best snapshot of the world of Bloomsbury men in the 1920s. Sixteen had been in or around Bloomsbury before the First World War; eleven were wartime or post-war additions – chiefly relations, friends and lovers of the older generation. Curiously, Keynes was not asked to join till 1929. Someone must have blackballed him.*

Keynes's place in this family of friends remained as complicated after the war as it had been before it. They loved him for his brilliant and restless mind; they were amused by his roving eye; but they continually criticised him for being worldly, domineering, manipulative, acerbic, wilful – flaws of character which, in their view, were not redeemed by aesthetic sensibility. Of all the Bloomsberries, with the exception of Clive Bell, his character was the most contested. By contrast, Keynes was almost pathetically loyal to his friends. They were not just his friends but his ideal. Lytton Strachey, it is said, was asked in the war why he was not fighting for civilisation. 'Madam,' he replied, 'I *am* the civilisation for which they are fighting.' Lytton's joke was Maynard's belief; his life was spent fighting for the civilisation which his Bloomsbury friends at least partially represented. His friends' criticisms of his character were often acute; but he was also being judged by rarefied standards. Bloomsbury's ideal was that of the enchanted adolescent, from which point of view all the compromises involved in growing up look like treachery. But Maynard understood better that the enchanted garden would become a wilderness unless it was defended from outside. As he mellowed, and the Bloomsberries entered middle age, their appreciation of him grew; in the end, they became, as Clive Bell called them, 'old friends'. But there was much passionate argument on the way.

Bloomsbury had not approved of Keynes's part in the war. However, with his resignation from the Treasury and his attack on the peace treaty, 'everything was transformed'[21] For a short time he enjoyed his friends' restrained approval. Chief among them were his Charleston 'family'. Charleston was the Sussex farmhouse near Lewes, which Vanessa Bell had

---

*The Cranium Club's members at that time were: Francis Birrell, Lowes Dickinson, David Garnett, George Kennedy (Keynes's favourite architect), Tom Marshall (the sociologist and brother of Ray Garnett and Frances Partridge), Bertrand Russell, Oliver Strachey (a brother of Lytton), Garrow Tomlin (brother of the sculptor Stephen Tomlin), Arthur Waley (the translator of Chinese poetry, previously Arthur Schloss), Gerald Brenan, Roger Fry, Duncan Grant, Raymond Mortimer, Alexander Penrose, Sebastian Sprott, Charles Sanger (a pre-war Apostle), Stephen Tomlin (lover of Duncan Grant), Eddy Sackville-West, Leonard Woolf, Frank Dobson (the sculptor), E. M. Forster, Gerald Heard (the scientific writer), Leo Myers (the novelist), C. H. C. Prentice (publisher), Lytton Strachey, Adrian Stephen, Saxon Sydney-Turner (Bloomsbury's silent man) and Ralph Wright (a partner in the Birrell–Garnett bookshop). Compare Frances Partridge, *Memories* (1981): 'The original "members" [of Bloomsbury] were still far from old, and around them a host of quite young fringe-Bloomsburies had collected – some from Oxford like Raymond Mortimer, Eddy Sackville-West, Bob and Eddie Gathorne-Hardy; some from Cambridge like the Davidson brothers and Dadie Rylands; musicians like Constant Lambert; Arthur Waley; the sculptor Stephen Tomlin (always known as Tommy), young Bells, young Stracheys, young MacCarthys, Slade students and many, many more' (p. 90). Quentin Bell commented on the Cranium Club list: 'more than half seem to me to have nothing to do with Bloomsbury'. It is a hopeless business trying to use the word in a way that satisfies everyone!

taken in 1916 to provide a home for Duncan Grant and Bunny Garnett, two of Bloomsbury's conscientious objectors assigned to agricultural labour. It was Keynes's weekend retreat during the war and he wrote *The Economic Consequences of the Peace* there in the summer of 1919. He spent the following two summers at Charleston as well, working on the proofs of his *Treatise on Probability* in 1920, and writing *A Revision of the Treaty* in 1921. He contributed £60 a year to its upkeep, a third of the cost.

Keynes's affair with Duncan Grant had ended in 1911, Bunny Garnett's affair with Duncan in 1919. Duncan decided to make his home with Vanessa, as Lytton Strachey had done with Dora Carrington. He still fell in love with young men, and needed fairly frequent interludes from domesticity. But he understood that only Vanessa could provide him with the stable background he needed to paint, which is what he cared about most. Their relationship was never again so threatened as it had been during the Bunny interlude, though he continued to cause Vanessa great suffering. Their daughter Angelica was born on Christmas Day 1918, Maynard agreeing to be god-father. 'Oh Lord, how guilty I shall feel if it's not a boy,' Vanessa had joked. When Angelica was born, Keynes sent a present of £200 (£4000 in today's values) from the Paris Peace Conference. One of Angelica's first memories is of having a bath at 46 Gordon Square, in a bathroom lined with jars of bath salts, and of Maynard 'in his elegant City suit, standing over me and showering me with these as I sat in the water'.[22] Maynard's favourite Bloomsbury child was Quentin, the younger of Vanessa's two boys by Clive Bell. He took both Julian and Quentin to the ballet soon after the war, noting that while Julian (aged ten) enjoyed the juggling best, Quentin (eight) seemed 'fascinated by the ballet itself'.[23] Quentin remembers him as completely a part of 'the enclosed little world in which we lived'.[24] What tied Maynard to Charleston was his love for Duncan, which never faded. He supported Duncan right through the inter-war years, and in 1937 settled a substantial income on him. Keynes was the rich, generous, worldly, slightly wicked uncle to the Charleston family, which is why his marriage to someone completely outside it came as such a shock to them.

On 8 November 1919 Lytton Strachey was telling his brother James 'I do not like [Pozzo]' – his special name for Maynard, invented in 1908 and intended to suggest a sewer. But he seems to have been won round by *The Economic Consequences of the Peace*, which he praised lavishly. The success of Lytton's own *Eminent Victorians* (1918) had mellowed him. He still aimed to 'deal little words that poison vast monsters of falsehood'.[25] But his manner, his friends noticed, had become uniformly amiable and affectionate.[26] By the time his *Queen Victoria* was published in 1921, it was clear that his satire had lost its sting, the jokes were for their own sake. 'I ought to do something particularly outrageous for my next book in order to retrieve my reputation,' he wrote to his brother James on 10 April 1921. 'It's alarming to be welcomed with open arms by Gosse, Jack Squire and *The Times* – though I suppose it's paying too.'* In fact, Maynard himself had taken energetic charge of the negotiations for the sale of the American rights of *Queen Victoria*, landing Strachey a contract with his own publisher, Harcourt, Brace & Co., which, according to Strachey's biographer, 'over the years deprived Strachey and his literary executor of many thousands of pounds'.[27†]

Lytton became notably less critical of Maynard in the last decade of his life, though no less amusing about him. He found the atmosphere 'sympathetic' when he stayed at King's in May 1920, despite the presence of Lord Chalmers, formerly of the Treasury, who made pompous, long-winded speeches. 'How Pozzo can take such obvious absurdities at all seriously quite beats me,' Strachey complained to Carrington.[28] He reported to his brother on another visit in 1921: 'a typical incident walking back with Pozzo' over a field after they had taken tea with Sebastian Sprott. 'He suddenly said he wanted to pump [urinate], and did so, walking along all the time in the most extraordinary way with legs apart, though there were people all about. "Oh, it's alright, it's alright, one can't be seen, as long as one keeps walking." He looked like a monstrosity of a gardener with an inefficient watering-pot. . . .'[29]

Virginia Woolf remained unreconciled. On 13 February 1920 she noted in her diary that it was to the credit of Cambridge that Keynes was unmoved by his success and had become more, rather than less, modest. But she could not resist a slighting reference to his book – 'a book which influences the world without being in the least a work of art'.[30] Visiting Charleston on 22 September 1920 she 'had a vivid sight of Maynard by lamplight – like a gorged seal, double chin, ledge of red lip, little eyes, sensual, brutal, unimaginative. One of those visions that come from a chance attitude, lost so soon as he turned his head. I suppose though it illustrates something I feel about him. Then he's read neither of my books.'[31‡]

If Virginia Woolf's diary often gives the impression that she disliked Keynes, so do Leonard Woolf's letters. The feelings of both go back to the 1900s, when Keynes had 'stolen' Arthur Hobhouse and later Duncan Grant from Lytton Strachey, who responded by blackening his character to Leonard, then in Ceylon, and to Virginia in London. What particularly depressed Virginia in 1920 was that both Lytton and Maynard were famous while she was not. Nor could Maynard have endeared himself to her by telling her to stick to non-fiction.[32] Not till *Jacob's Room* was published in 1921 did the

---

*Edmund Gosse and John Collings Squire were pillars of the literary establishment and favourite butts of Bloomsbury.
†The negotiations can be followed in the Keynes-Strachey correspondence at King's College, Cambridge. Keynes got Strachey $10,000, or just over £2000 for the American rights. To earn that he had to sell 15,000 copies in hardback. Of course *Queen Victoria* sold many more. This is not to say that Strachey did not need the money at the time.
‡*The Voyage Out* (1915) and *Night and Day* (1919).

1921 did the critics realise a genius had flowered, and did Virginia Woolf start to feel more secure.

That Bloomsbury found it hard to come to terms with the post-war world is shown by Clive Bell's book, *Civilisation*, published in 1928. Its mood is Edwardian, somewhat elegiac. It looks back to the eighteenth century, the last and, in Clive Bell's view, the greatest epoch of civilisation. Civilisation, he says, has nothing to do with morals, democracy, patriotism, technology, social justice or the 'life of action'. Action is the disease of those 'incapable of passionate love, profound aesthetic emotions, subtle thought, charming conversation, or attractive vices'; it is the disease of those 'inapt for civilised pleasures'. A civilised society is one which contains an 'optimate' of highly civilised men and women, living off the labour of others, and capable of leavening the mass. England was far from meeting these requirements. English life was so Philistine that it forced the gifted into mere individualism and eccentricity – in fact, made outlaws of them. Virginia Woolf commented ironically, 'he has great fun in the opening chapters but in the end it turns out that civilisation is a lunch party at 50 Gordon Square'.[33]

Bell's book captures something of the passivity and escapism often associated with Bloomsbury – its longing to retreat into its enchanted garden. Bell foresaw the rise of military despotism, but argued that this posed no long-run threat to culture, as military rulers always like to restore culture as quickly as possible. Few Bloomsberries could accept such a doctrine in its full rigour. Leonard Woolf's answer to Bell's hetairac conception came in a short essay, 'The Civilised Man', describing an ideal epitomised by Erasmus, with his hatred of cruelty and unreason. Quentin Bell gives a more balanced summary than his father managed. Bloomsbury, he wrote, was willing to 'sacrifice the heroic virtues in order to avoid the heroic vices'. Bloomsbury could not be heroic in the way in which Rupert Brooke or Békássy or later Julian Bell were heroic, that is happiest under fire. But it could happily *contemplate* the spectacle of heroism in Michelangelo, Coriolanus or in the character of Perceval which Virgina Woolf created in her novel *The Waves* – perhaps an evocation of her brother Thoby, the 'Goth' who had died of typhoid in 1906.

Still less does Clive Bell's book help us locate Keynes. Keynes was never an intellectual of the salon but a member of the British clerisy. Bell's ideal of the civilised life did justice neither to Keynes's interests nor to his capacities, and ignored both his patriotism and his sense of duty. His talk to Bloomsbury's Memoir Club in 1938 may be read as his gentle rebuke to the Clive Bell ideal. Retracing the 'early beliefs' of his Cambridge circle, of which Bell had formed a part, he criticised them for 'classifying as aesthetic experience what is really human experience and somehow sterilising it by this mis-classification'; of ignoring 'certain powerful and valuable springs of feeling . . . concerned with the order and pattern of life amongst communities'; of forgetting that 'civilisation was a thin and precarious crust erected by the personality and the will of a very few, and only maintained by rules and conventions skilfully put across and guilefully preserved'. By 1938 such reassessments were needed.[34]

Bloomsbury's position between the wars is paradoxical. It seemed to wield immense cultural power; at the same time the world's springs of action were increasingly remote from its own. In a sense it triumphed. Its writers, painters and publicists all rose to the height of their success and influence in the 1920s. They became arbiters of taste, the conduit through which writers like Dostoievsky, Proust and Chekhov, painters like Cézanne, Matisse and Picasso and thinkers like Freud entered British consciousness. Apart from its translations, the Hogarth Press, started by Leonard and Virginia Woolf, specialised in publishing experimental writing and experimental thought. Together with the Sitwells, Bloomsbury championed the cause of the ballet; the products of the Omega Workshops influenced furniture design. Bloomsbury morals, too, seem to have spread everywhere.

But Vanessa Bell was right to say Bloomsbury died in 1914, and not just as a closely knit group. Its rootedness in the Edwardian era distanced it alike from the post-war avant-garde and the new Victorianism. The truth is that many of the post-war experiments in life, letters and art were fed not by hope but by despair, a despair which also lay at the heart of the puritan revival in public life. These were all complicated reactions to the war: and Old Bloomsbury had no imaginative contact with the war. Its rationalism rebelled against a heroic view of life; its individualism shuddered at the thought of collective renewals. Even its espousal of Freud – there were four practising Bloomsbury psychoanalysts – seemed a superficial concession to the existence of unreason, rather than a coming to terms with tragic events: 'when reason dies, monsters are born'. Members of Bloomsbury were Voltairean survivors, by now subversive by habit, but anxious to retain their dividends and beautiful Georgian houses.

Lytton Strachey's irony caught a temporary mood; but the real irony was that it was his civilisation rather than that of his *Eminent Victorians* which had gone down to defeat – something which he recognised when he wrote *Queen Victoria*. The authentic voices of the 1920s were Evelyn Waugh and T. S. Eliot. Waugh's novels were littered with vile bodies; Eliot's poetry evoked a world of fragments, 'shored against my ruins'. In painting the iconoclasm of post-impressionism gave way to the horrors of surrealism, reminiscent of Bosch, Brueghel and Goya. Bloomsbury had grown up in the sunlight of Asquithian Liberalism, its natural habitat. Its project – if one can call it that – was to permeate the governing class with civilised values, just as the Fabians had tried to permeate it with collectivist ones. From its immaculate London squares it now looked out with irony and detachment as feeble Reaction shaped up to the onslaught of revolutionary conditions. Baldwin and MacDonald, George V and Queen Mary, were not Edwardian uncles but Victorian grandparents. So was Sir William Joynson Hicks,

Baldwin's censorious Home Secretary, who presided over the prosecution, for obscenity, of D. H. Lawrence's *Lady Chatterley's Lover* and Radclyffe Hall's *The Well of Loneliness*. The trade union leaders were another lot of Victorian dinosaurs raised to prominence by the war. What did Bloomsbury have to do with this world, or indeed the far madder world of the 1930s which followed it? What indeed is a Voltaire to do when the *ancien régime* has been abolished?

Keynes, a man of Bloomsbury, was also a man of Whitehall. *His* project was to bring a new machinery of progress to the aid of Edwardian liberalism. As he memorably expressed it at the end of his life, the important thing was to keep alive 'the possibility of civilisation'.

III

OFFICIAL CIRCLES

By the end of the war, Keynes was the dominating influence in the Treasury on all matters to do with external finance. According to Roy Harrod he threw all this away by publishing *The Economic Consequences of the Peace*. 'He incurred great odium in official circles,' Harrod writes, 'and was for many years in the wilderness.'[35] In a contemporary letter, Oswald Falk, who served with Keynes in 'A' Division, took a similar line: 'It has already done Keynes a great deal of harm, even amongst those who agree with him, and this is itself a pity. But one of the results is that people are unwilling to employ Keynes or work with him and so his cause is damaged, because he is undoubtedly one of the ablest if not the ablest economist living [sic].'[36] However, the easy inference that Keynes lacked influence between the wars because he had 'spilled the beans' or 'told the truth' in *The Economic Consequences* is wrong. In fact Keynes had much more influence than he himself was willing to acknowledge. When his suggestions were not heeded, it was usually because policymakers disagreed with them. And as Elizabeth Johnson has remarked, he never lost his 'habit of responsibility'.

The question of Keynes's relationship with the 'official mind' of the interwar years is highly complex. There *was* a 'Bloomsbury problem' about Keynes. Russell Leffingwell, an American Treasury official at the Paris Peace Conference, wrote in 1931:

> Keynes is always perverse, Puckish. He attacks anything sound or established or generally accepted, partly for the fun of it, partly for the purpose of stimulating debate. In doing so he is utterly irresponsible. He doesn't care how much harm he does. . . . He is just a bright boy, shocking his admiring elders by questioning the existence of God, and the Ten Commandments.[37]

However, Leffingwell never made the mistake of thinking that Keynes was uninfluential. In a letter to Walter Lippmann dated 30 December 1931, he refers to 'Keynes and all his school, which means all the Treasury civil servants who to a greater or less extent follow him . . . Strakosch, Blackett, Salter, Hawtrey, etc.', in his ' "inflation theory".'[38] We need to question how this could have seemed to be the case, when Keynes himself had described his writings, in the very same year, as the 'croakings of a Cassandra who could never influence the course of events in time'.[39]

The answer is complicated. Keynes's influence waxed and waned between the wars; his views and personality excited a large range of responses. Also, Keynes's theories and policies changed, and those who supported his views on 'managed money' in the 1920s by no means supported the theory of 'unbalanced budgets' in the 1930s. It is important to remember, though, that at no time was he the only actor on the stage. Keynes's scenes were always full of Top People from the interlocking worlds of banking, politics, administration, economics, journalism, not just in Britain, but in America and in Europe. Most of them no doubt were fascinated by the very qualities they mistrusted. Sound men like the American banker Bernard Baruch thought his facility with words was his undoing. But he was never booted off stage. And his voice always gave a distinct flavour to the conversation.

Keynes was certainly not cut off as a policy-adviser from the moment his *Economic Consequences of the Peace* appeared. Within a couple of months of its publication in December 1919, Austen Chamberlain, the first post-war Chancellor of the Exchequer, was consulting him on monetary policy as though he had never left the Treasury. His Treasury friend and admirer Basil Blackett occupied the new key position of controller of finance at the Treasury. On reparations, as we shall see, he was (uniquely) consulted by both the British and the German governments. If Keynes received a snub at this point, it was not from 'official circles', but from the academic profession, when in July 1920 the annual general meeting of the British Academy rejected his nomination for a fellowship in the Economic Section. This most unusual step was taken at the behest of 'archaeologists and literary men' who disapproved of Keynes's book. Keynes was so incensed by this, and also by Pigou's exclusion the previous year because he had been a pacifist in the war, that he instructed his sponsor, Professor W. R. Scott of the University of Glasgow, not to put his name forward again. After Pigou was elected in 1927, he relented and was himself elected in 1929.[40]

Keynes's loss of influence at the Treasury was gradual and can be explained in two ways. In 1922 power in his old department passed from Basil Blackett to Otto Niemeyer, who succeeded him as controller of finance when Blackett took up an appointment as finance member of the Viceroy's Council in Delhi. Niemeyer was the new Puritan broom at the Treasury. Keynes's influence was at its lowest during his ascendancy, which lasted till he left for the Bank of England in 1928.

More fundamentally, as Henry Roseveare has pointed out, the Treasury's finance division had become 'thoroughly cosmopolitan' in its outlook as the result of the development of 'A' Division during the war and the Treasury's subsequent involvement in the Paris Peace Conference, the reparations issue and efforts at European reconstruction.[41] Treasury officials like Bradbury, McFadyean and Leith-Ross served on the Reparation Commission in Paris during the first years of the peace, while Ralph Hawtrey, director of financial enquiries since 1919, was the main author of the resolution at Genoa in 1922 calling for a general resumption of the gold standard. The common position of these internationalists was that recovery from the war required putting the pre-war structure of the international economy back into place, whereas Keynes increasingly took the view that each country must first balance its own economy with the least social cost to itself. He became steadily more insular in outlook, whereas the previously insular Treasury became steadily more international: a conflict he dramatised in his *Tract on Monetary Reform* (1923). Keynes's falling out with the Bank of England, and particularly its governor Montagu Norman, in 1922 has to do with the same issue. Norman championed the debt settlement with the United States; Keynes attacked it. For all his peculiarities (he was declared insane by Jung!), Montagu Norman was a visionary banker, trying to build up a government of central bankers to replace the old 'automatic' gold standard. Keynes was not against the idea; but he sensed (rightly) that countries had to solve their own problems first. International finance would prosper once domestic adjustment had been secured; it could not be the means to force it. This perception was really the start of the Keynesian Revolution.

Of course, the Treasury and Bank of England were directly involved in the financial diplomacy of the 1920s and Keynes was not. In that sense his book did cut him off from official circles. More importantly, it made him *persona non grata* with the French, whose prime minister and policy he had so mauled, and with much liberal opinion in the United States: Bernard Baruch, for example, never forgave him for his ridicule of Woodrow Wilson.[42] That Keynes contributed importantly to American isolationism or French intransigence is far-fetched. What has not been sufficiently appreciated is the extent to which Keynes was anti-American in the 1920s – partly as a result of his disillusionment with the quality of American statesmanship, partly because he resented American money-power. This feeling affected his attitude both to reparations and to the question of Britain's return to the gold standard. For much of the 1920s he wanted to keep America out of Europe; early on he hankered after an Anglo-German understanding as the foundation of European reconstruction. He never visited the United States in the 1920s, despite repeated invitations: a striking case of reverse isolationism.

In publishing *Economic Consequences of the Peace*, Keynes took a calculated gamble that he could do more good trying to persuade the public of the iniquity of the Treaty than working from the inside to try to improve it. In any case, he had committed himself to a line of argument which made attendance by him at conferences of 'experts' superfluous. This was that nothing good could come out of reconstruction efforts till the economic clauses of the Versailles Treaty were scrapped and inter-Ally war debts forgiven. Since this was not practical politics, he had nothing to contribute except 'violent and ruthless truth-telling', which would work 'even if slowly'.[43]

By 1929, Keynes thought he was becoming 'more fashionable again'.[44] By this time an influential body of opinion had come to agree with him that the return to the gold standard in 1925 had been a mistake. The Labour government made him a member of the Royal Commission on Finance and Industry and of the Economic Advisory Council, and he dominated both. In the 1930s, he forged a wary relationship with a new generation of Treasury knights like Richard Hopkins and Frederick Phillips. However, the 1930s were very different from the 1920s; on balance, Keynes was more isolated – further from the corridors of power – in the second than in the first decade of peace. The main reason for this was the collapse of the Liberal Party and of the intellectual nexus, which would have called itself Liberal, through which he had tried to exert influence in the 1920s.

He could have had a political career in the Liberal Party had he wanted one. He was on excellent terms with Asquith and McKenna, leaders of the 'old' Liberalism, and continued to spend weekends at the Wharf. Few believed that the Liberal Party was finished. In 1920 Margot Asquith sent him a characteristic note from Paisley, where her husband was fighting a (successful) by-election to get back into Parliament, warning him against 'the snob movement towards Labour . . . like the snob movement towards Ugliness in Art, Discord in Music & Sexlessness in Women. But there is nothing eternal in chic.'

Keynes had no intention of joining Labour, but he would not come to the rescue of the sinking Asquithian ship. He turned down three offers in 1920 to stand for Parliament, including one from Cambridge which tempted him most; and he continued to resist further offers throughout the inter-war years. His personal involvement in the making of Liberal policy started only when Lloyd George took over the leadership from Asquith in 1926. He hoped for a serious Liberal revival and a power-sharing government with Labour, and invested a great deal of intellectual energy in providing such a combination with a programme of action.

The disintegration of these hopes, together with the collapse of the Liberal Party itself in 1931, left Keynes politically homeless. He was not sympathetic to the redivision of politics along lines of class and ideology, and in the 1930s, while remaining a semi-detached Liberal, refused to commit himself to either the Conservative or the Labour cause. Nevertheless, his notion of a 'managed capitalism' found support among the younger generation in both parties.

Until 1931, the intellectual and academic Establishment was overwhelmingly Liberal, and Keynes was part of a network of well-connected Liberal mandarins. Indeed, the powerful stream of Middle Way opinion generated by this group helps explain the moderation of politics in the Baldwin Age, though their influence has scarcely been recognised.

Who were these people? In his biography of Walter Layton, David Hubback talks about a 'tightly knit group' of 'Liberal radicals', members of which:

> met each other constantly in Whitehall, in the Westminster lobbies, in clubs, in Fleet Street, the City, and at the ancient universities. Layton, Keynes, Hubert Henderson and Dennis Robertson, all Cambridge economists, were at the centre of this network whose members included such remarkable ex-civil servants as William Beveridge, Josiah Stamp and Arthur Salter, businessmen with a strong social conscience such as Ernest Simon and Seebohm Rowntree, bankers such as R. H. Brand of Lazards, political thinkers such as Gilbert Murray, Graham Wallas and Ramsay Muir and idealistic politicians such as Philip Noel-Baker, Charles Masterman and Philip Kerr.[45]

As for public persuasion, Keynes, Layton and Henderson, together with Ernest Simon, came to edit, control or sit on the boards of three important weeklies: the *Nation, New Statesman* and *The Economist.*

Keynes was much closer to some of these men than to others. He had little real contact with those whom Hubback calls the 'political thinkers' and the 'idealistic politicians'. There are also some notable omissions from the names given above: Reginald McKenna, Keynes's wartime Treasury boss, chairman of the Midland Bank since 1919, should certainly be included in any mandarin circuit: one wonders what would have happened to Keynes had he become Chancellor again, as he almost did in 1922.

Economists were exposed to Keynes's views at monthly meetings in London of the Political Economy Club, founded in 1822. But the main 'inside' institution through which Keynes tried out his ideas was the Tuesday Club, an economic dining club started by Oswald Falk in 1917, also meeting once a month. Its core members were Falk himself and the four Cambridge economists. The City was represented by Charles Addis, Bob Brand, Reginald McKenna and Henry Strakosch, the Treasury by Basil Blackett and Otto Niemeyer, public service by John Anderson and Josiah Stamp; and financial journalism by A. W. Kiddy and Hartley Withers. Keynes addressed the Club on fifteen occasions and chaired many other meetings; guests who heard him included Montagu Norman.

Falk has described some of those 'whose talk was decisive in shaping the character of our discussions': the banker Charles Addis, with 'a charming smile and the gracious manners of an earlier generation', but possessed of 'great elasticity of mind'; Josiah Stamp, formerly of the Inland Revenue, 'a great gun loaded with documents'; Reginald McKenna, 'friendly, gentle, and even childish in his country home', but highly competitive in argument, particularly against Keynes, with whom he almost always agreed. Robert Brand of Lazards, formidably clever on paper, but lacking in self-confidence, was another leading figure. Henry Strakosch, a banker with South African interests, was a friend of both Keynes and Montagu Norman. But Keynes was the dominant force, as Falk recalled:

> We were in a changing world, and new ideas about it had to be tentative – none more so than those of Keynes, who, in our company, could indulge his delight in playing with them and be thoroughly reckless and irresponsible. In this manner, in spite of false scents, he caught up with the march of events more rapidly than others did . . . In our early years we had enjoyed Keynes's passion for dramatising events, and we were amused when, less consciously, he dramatised himself. He loved the footlights and was impatient if he was off stage for a minute, almost more impatient if he was not the central figure on it. He described Newton as Copernicus and Faustus in one, and doubtless he thought he resembled them both. His repertoire was unlimited. Can those who are always in the public eye and always dramatic have any identity in solitude? Or must they, like Lord Mellifont in the Henry James story, vanish and become nothing the moment they leave the stage? To the man behind the masks of Keynes there is no clue.[46]

Keynes, as Falk suggests, was an uncomfortable colleague even in this like-minded company. Few could keep up with him, as his ideas changed so quickly. Yet, when they were in his mind, he defended them passionately and ruthlessly, with a cutting-edge so sharp, and a command of language (as well as insult) so effortless, that even formidable intelligences were made to feel foolish in opposing them. At the same time, he was, like most of them, an intellectual administrator. He had a civil-service mind; in this kind of circle he stood out by the speed, fertility and energy with which he applied abstract ideas to the practical problems of the hour.

The Keynesian Revolution has been so exclusively presented as a revolution in economic theory that it is easy to forget that it was part of a continuing revolution in government, a return to the medieval practice of involving the clergy in the affairs of state. As a result of the increasing absorption of academics into government service, political and intellectual authority started to merge. The growing use of experts in government was a response both to the 'fear of the masses' and to the greater complexity of governing an urban, industrial society. But it also reflected the demand of bright university men for new careers to replace the reduced attraction of the priestly and imperial calling. The recruitment of the higher civil service by competitive examination after 1870 was the key step in professionalising public administration. But it was the First World War which opened up government to university academics. They got to know their way around Whitehall running shipping or rationing schemes; some of them stayed; others never ceased to see themselves as an extended arm of the state. The First World War experience led to a marked change in intellectual climate. There was more of a disposition to look to government to solve problems, less to look to the market or private enterprise: indeed contempt for the businessman's capacity became a fixed point with the new clerisy. From this perspective the Keynesian Revolution in economics is a key episode in the takeover of the governing function, as well as of the agenda of government, by the universities.

Not just Keynes's role, but the history of government and politics in the inter-war years thus calls for a more nuanced approach. There was no 'wilderness'. Till 1931 consensus politics and Middle Way economics marched hand in hand – much as they did in the 1950s and 1960s. Disputes over doctrine and policy (which were often fierce) belie the fact that policy was rarely intransigently applied. After 1931 there was a change. Business Conservatism was in the ascendant – much as in the 1980s – until it was discredited by appeasement. Yet the reality of much of the inter-war years is not of a right-wing orthodoxy, deeply entrenched, but of a political Middle Way looking for an economic doctrine to fit its socially appeasing inclinations. This Keynes eventually supplied.

IV

MONEY-MAKING

Keynes's average annual income from 1919–20 to 1928–9 inclusive was £5068 (gross). Of this, 'academic income' was £2372 a year, or a little under half. However, 'academic income' included income from 'lectures, Fellowship, examining, the Royal Economic Society, books and articles and his position as Bursar of King's College, Cambridge'.[47] Keynes's teaching and RES income did not exceed £700 a year in the 1920s, or about 14 per cent of the total. Income from 'books and articles' thus came to about one-third of total income over the period. This shows the importance of Keynes's writing in sustaining his life-style. This source of income was at its peak in the years 1920–3 when it provided almost 80 per cent of the total. But even in the late 1920s about 20 per cent of Keynes's income still derived from his writing. The share of investment, directorship and consultancy income in total income rose from 21 per cent between 1919–20 and 1922–3 to over 70 per cent between 1923–4 and 1928–9.

His income went up sharply in the last ten years of his life. Except for one year – 1938–9 – it never fell below £10,000 a year from 1936–7 till his death, though the cost of living was somewhat lower than in the 1920s. This was practically all investment income and reflects his huge gains on the Stock Exchange in the recovery from depression. Only in the 1930s did he become rich. Not that Keynes was by any means poor in the 1920s. An annual income of £5000 in the mid–1920s would have been worth something like £110,000 in 1992 prices – roughly what a top British company director would be getting, and about three to four times as much as a top academic salary.

Keynes's chief business collaborator was Oswald Toynbee ('Foxy') Falk. Keynes brought Foxy into the Treasury in 1917 and Foxy brought Keynes into the City after the war. Their friendship was often explosive, for they both had brilliant minds, powerful personalities and the utmost confidence in their own ideas. It lasted till Keynes's death, though it cooled in the 1930s, after a series of business clashes on the boards of companies they both controlled.

Falk, a partner in the stockbroking firm of Buckmaster and Moore, was a very tall man, with a fine head, aquiline features and the broad shoulders of a golfer, a sport at which he excelled. He loved pictures and adored the ballet – he had an affair with Pavlova. Prodigiously gifted intellectually, his faults were hauteur and impetuosity: he was much better at making fortunes (for himself as well as his clients) than keeping them. His hatred of socialism, which proved permanent, dated from the First World War, when the government acquired his Picassos, which he had sent to America for safekeeping, for what he considered a grossly inadequate amount of dollars. But he was just as intolerant as was Keynes of stupidity in high places: he never spoke to his friend Montagu Norman again after the return to the gold standard. Keynes learnt about financial markets under Falk's tutelage. Nicholas Davenport, who knew both men well, wrote that Falk 'would play the gilt-edged market as a virtuoso would his violin'; Thomas Balogh claims that Keynes's theory of liquidity preference originated in the way they both played this market in the 1920s.[48] To Falk, as well as to Marcel Labordère, Keynes owes his superb understanding of the unruly financial mechanisms of capitalism – something which distinguishes his work from that of all other economists of the age.

It was Falk and Geoffrey Marks who arranged for Keynes's appointment to the Board of the National Mutual Life Assurance Company in 1919; he became its chairman in 1921. As always he knew immediately how the business should be run. 'A Life Office', he declared on the day of his appointment, 'ought to have only one investment and it should be changed every day.' Seconded by Falk, and encouraged by Marks, Keynes initiated what was called an 'Active Investment Policy', which combined investing in real assets – at that time considered revolutionary – with constant switching between short-dated and long-dated securities, based on predictions of changes in the interest rate. From the start Keynes was a commanding influence, but the investment policy of the National Mutual was not quite as active as he wanted: indeed he would say later that by the time he could persuade the Board to buy a stock it was time to sell it. And he was far from revolutionary in all things, on one occasion defending from the platform at the annual general meeting the old custom whereby directors' fees were paid free of tax, as enormously beneficial to life assurance.

There was always a strong reciprocal connection between Keynes's money-making and his economic theory. 'Speculation', wrote Nicholas Davenport, 'improved his economics and economics improved his speculation.'[49] Gambling on currencies and commodities in the early 1920s produced an expert account of the theory of forward exchanges, which he included in his *Tract on Monetary Reform* in 1923. He followed the 'credit cycle investment' theory, just mentioned, which involved buying and selling market leaders in accord with predicted movements of the business cycle right through the 1920s, with very moderate results. This experience may have convinced him that investment was more than a risky, it was a radically uncertain, business. At any rate, after he was virtually wiped out in 1928–9, he came to believe that, correct anticipation of major turning points being impossible, a rational investment policy should be based on a 'steadfast holding' of a few fairly large units of balanced stock, 'through thick and thin'.[50] He was both fascinated and disgusted by the psychology of capitalism as revealed by the love and pursuit of money, and concerned about the social and ethical implications of a system which, as he was to put it in 1930, exalted and rewarded 'some of the most distasteful human qualities'.[51]

Unlike most of his Bloomsbury friends, Keynes had no inherited capital, so he badly needed to make money to support his expanded life-style. His money-making immediately after the war took two main forms: currency speculation and journalism. He and Falk had spent such spare time as they had at the Paris Peace Conference talking about how they might make money out of the uncertain future of currencies.[52] Keynes started gambling on currencies in the intervals of writing his *Economic Consequences of the Peace* at Charleston in 1919, finding it both amusing and challenging: the injustices and stupidities of the Peace Treaty could be made into a double source of profit. 'I feel absolutely confident that the right thing to do is to bull dollars and bear marks,' he wrote on 1 September to Falk, who replied, 'I came away . . . feeling more than ever that it is right to be a bear of sterling, francs, and lire.'[53] The story of Keynes's disastrous currency speculations of 1920 is told in chapter 2, where it is interwoven with the collapse of the great post-war boom and the advice he was giving the government on monetary policy at a critical moment in his own personal fortunes. His own financial collapse was fortunately not permanent. Like the British economy, he recovered, though only to a moderate prosperity.

His 'specs' as Keynes called them were only one way of getting him the

income he wanted. There were directorships and consultancies. Apart from
chairmanship of the National Mutual Life Assurance Company, which
brought him £1000 a year, he and Falk became financial consultants to the
chairman of Debenhams, at £500 each a year.[54] Other City directorships
followed, usually in companies started or controlled by Falk. Keynes's mid-
weeks in London were largely spent on this City business.

Keynes's other main way of making money was through journalism. He
wanted to address the public in any case, and he proved an eloquent
populariser of abstract ideas. But between 1920 and 1923 he was much
more of a writer for hire than he would ever be again. This was partly
because he needed the money. He wrote only four newspaper articles in
1920. There were fourteen in 1921, twenty-five in 1922 and fifty-one in 1923,
his peak year, which coincided with his becoming proprietor of the *Nation
and Athenaeum*. If we take worldwide syndication and special journalistic
assignments into account, we are talking of income supplements of about
£1500 in 1921 and over £4000 (say £90,000 today) in 1922. Keynes's failure
to produce a major work of theory till 1930 was the direct result of the way
he spent the first few years after the war.

The basis of his journalistic career was *The Economic Consequences of the
Peace*. It started with a long article on reparations and Woodrow Wilson
which he wrote for the American magazine *Everybody's* in May 1920, and
for which he was paid '£220 for three days' work'. More opportunities
opened up in 1921 and 1922 when financial diplomacy was at its height.
Keynes got most of his journalistic income in 1921–2 not through the dribs
and drabs of individual articles, but in three carefully planned operations,
one for the *Sunday Times*, two for the *Manchester Guardian*. In August–September 1921 he wrote a series of five, well-paid (£50 each) articles for the *Sunday
Times* on economic problems, planning for which he started in May. He
said he attached little importance to them, but evidently enough to arrange
worldwide syndication, which brought his total receipts for the series to
over £1000. Encouraged by this success, he organised and edited the twelve
issues of the *Manchester Guardian Commercial*'s Reconstruction Supplements
in 1922 for £2400, plus additional payments for his own articles; and he
was its special correspondent at the Genoa Conference in April 1922, receiving £300 for 10,000 words. (Worldwide, the articles brought him £1250.)
Notable by its absence was any work for *The Times*. He was not asked to
write anything – a single book review excepted – till 1933; the editor Geoffrey
Dawson turned down his offer of two articles on the return to the gold
standard in 1925. (Beaverbrook snapped them up for the *Evening Standard*;
they were turned into his most famous pamphlet *The Economic Consequences
of Mr. Churchill*.) *The Times*'s hostility to Keynes's ideas is the best indication
of his distance from the 'official' mind of the 1920s.

In the United States, Keynes's main journalistic outlet was the highbrow
weekly *New Republic* – a connection which started when it serialised three

extracts from *The Economic Consequences of the Peace* in December 1919–January 1920. It was edited by Herbert Croly, and Walter Lippmann worked on it till 1922. Ronald Steel has written that 'Without being radical, the magazine was just far enough to the left of the liberal consensus to be stimulating with its elitist emphasis on intellect and leadership.'[55] It took a large proportion of Keynes's English journalism in the 1920s. It was financed by Dorothy Straight, whose son Michael he would teach at Cambridge in the 1930s.

Keynes had no similarly secure French and German outlets. Paul Franck, the French translator of *The Economic Consequences*, managed to get some of his articles placed in financial journals like *L'Information* or *Le Cablegramme*. But the excoriator of Clemenceau did not appear in the most influential French newspapers. In Germany, the problem was not lack of eagerness to publish him, but lack of foreign currency to pay him. German newspapers resorted to printing large extracts from his English articles without, of course, paying him for them. Outside the United States, France and Germany, which Keynes intermittently tried to deal with himself, he left syndication to well-known agencies like the London General Press.

Although he wrote mainly to influence people, it was not in Keynes's nature to disregard the financial and business sides of his literary arrangements. In his personal papers there are long runs of letters dealing with minor discrepancies in payments. In these matters he acted as though he believed that 'if you look after the pennies, the pounds will look after themselves'. However, he was never a journalistic hack. He rejected some lucrative assignments outright; in other cases he used price carefully to ration calls on his time. He was also alive to the public repercussions of what he wrote, turning down £50 from the *Financial Times* early in 1921 on the ground that it was not 'in the public interest' that he should comment on the war-debt question just then.[56] He had other sticking points. He had a horror of personal interviews and declared that 'he had made a general principle of not making any communications with the Press whatever in this particular form'.[57] He rarely allowed his speeches to be published as articles, and nearly always refused to sign circulars or write prefaces to other people's books. The Keynes Papers reveal his enviable facility as a journalist. Many of his articles are preserved there hand-written, often in pencil. They seem to be both first and final drafts, with a minimum of crossing out. Although Keynes no longer matched his Eton performances in speed writing,[58] it looks as if a typical article of 1200 words took him no more than a couple of hours to be ready for the typist, and then dispatch to the printer.

Keynes always insisted that wealth should not be hoarded but spent on civilised living. Practising what he preached, he earmarked some of his first profits from currency speculation to buying pictures. Although he was not much moved by visual art, he tried to live his life by aesthetic standards, and having pictures was part of being civilised. He invariably bought on the advice of Duncan Grant and Vanessa Bell, but the timing of his purchases depended on the state of his balance with Buckmaster and Moore. He acquired some of his best paintings between the autumn of 1919 and the spring of 1920 when his currency speculations prospered. In November 1919 he bought Seurat's *Promenades* for £320 from the Chelsea Book Club, London agents of the Vildrac Galleries in Paris: one of twenty-eight oil studies for his masterpiece *La Grande Jatte*. Works by Picasso, Signac, Matisse and Derain were added over the next few months. This phase of picture-buying ended with his purchase of Renoir's *Head of a Boy* in Paris in May 1920, at a cost of £300. Except for a Cézanne acquired in 1924 on his own initiative ('the worst picture Cézanne ever painted', his friends remarked cattily), Keynes bought no more works of important French painters till 1935, when he was again making large profits on the stock market, though he bought many English pictures in the interval, chiefly the work of his friends, and supported their activities in other ways.[59]

The main areas of Keynes's life were already mapped out in 1920. No one would have predicted that his principal contribution would be to economic theory. Rather, the war had revealed him as a very unusual type of public servant, exceptional in his ability to apply economic theory incisively to the financial problems of government. Then came *The Economic Consequences of the Peace*, which showed his unique power as a persuader. In this book he put forward the revolutionary claim that economics should control the peace, not that the peace required a revolution in economics. Yet there are hints that economics would need to be revolutionised too, which only Dennis Robertson spotted. For in chapter 2 Keynes attributed the prosperity of the nineteenth century to the 'organisation and psychology of society'. The war had shattered the delicate social machinery of wealth-creation – the rules, conventions and domestic and international relations which tacitly underpinned the optimistic vision of what Keynes would call classical economics. The message of chapter 2 is that post-war capitalism would be radically unstable. The ground of economic discussion, as Robertson noted, is shifted to 'issues of psychology, and not of figures', to 'what people feel and think'. The 'business of forming a rational judgement becomes much more elusive and precarious'.[60] Keynes's own speculations in currencies and commodities, starting with Falk while he was writing his book, point to the form capitalist activities would typically take in a world too uncertain to plan for a secure future. Keynes's intuitions of doom and experience of financial markets were thus already starting to open up paths of thought which would lead in time to *The General Theory of Employment, Interest, and Money*. Though he did not yet know the precise turn his life's work would take, his instinct had already told him it would lie in the sorting out of the problems created by the war and the peace.

If we aim deliberately at the impoverishment of Central Europe, vengeance, I dare predict, will not limp. Nothing can then delay for very long that final civil war between the forces of Reaction and the despairing convulsions of Revolution, before which the horrors of the late German war will fade into nothing, and which will destroy, whoever is victor, the civilisation and the progress of our generation . . . In one way only can we influence these hidden currents – by setting in motion those forces of instruction and imagination which change *opinion*. The assertion of truth, the unveiling of illusion, the dissipation of hate, the enlargement and instruction of men's hearts and minds, must be the means.[61]

This was the mood in which Keynes confronted the 1920s.

CHAPTER TWO

The Transition to Peace

I

EUROPE'S UNFINISHED CIVIL WAR

The lives of Keynes and his generation were blighted by the failure to overcome the consequences of the First World War. That failure meant there could be no sustained economic and political recovery from the effects of the war. The shakily restored international system collapsed into world depression in 1929, and into world war in 1939. Totalitarianism gained a deadly grip over a large part of the world's population. Keynes lived to see a Soviet empire arise in Eastern Europe on the ruins of the Nazi empire. Not for nearly half a century was that final consequence of the war cancelled.

Any chance the world had of regaining political, economic and moral equilibrium was fatally undermined by the inability of American and European statesmen to liquidate the twin and connected problems of inter-Allied war debts and German reparations. The dominance of these questions unsettled everything for the first five post-war years. They absorbed the best energies of the world leaders; they produced an atmosphere of continual crisis which choked off attempts to normalise economic relations. They detached the United States from Europe, broke up the Anglo-French *entente* and almost destroyed the fledgling Weimar Republic. This last aspect was especially important. The contribution of the reparations issue to the rise of Hitler is well known. More significantly in the long run, the collapse of Germany's economic role in Eastern Europe was crucial in consolidating the Stalinist tyranny under the slogan 'Socialism in One Country'. When the clouds partly lifted in the mid–1920s, it was too late to undo the damage. The expectational environment had become hopelessly soured.

Keynes had declared his own position in *The Economic Consequences of the Peace*. Germany could not possibly pay what the British and French had committed themselves to demand. Keynes reckoned that Germany *could* pay a total of £1500m. (or 30b. gold marks) in thirty annual instalments of £50m., or 1000m. marks. Beyond this, he had argued that until the whole problem of German reparations and inter-Allied war debts was liquidated – by a reasonable settlement of the first and cancellation of the second – the economic life of the West would remain fundamentally disturbed. Nothing could be done to cure the monetary and currency disorders of Europe, the necessary outflow of American reconstruction money, reanchor expectations to normality, enable Russia to be rebuilt 'through the agency of German enterprise and organisation'. Keynes was agnostic about the permanence of Communism, 'but we may surely predict with some certainty that . . . the revival of trade, of the comforts of life and of ordinary economic motive are not likely to promote the extreme forms of those doctrines of violence and tyranny which are the children of war and despair'.[1]

The more time passes, the more redoubtable does Keynes's analysis seem, the more trifling the attacks of his critics. He was widely accused at the time of being anti-French, pro-German, and this label has stuck. There is some truth in it. The war had not caused him to renounce the view, common to his generation, that an economically dynamic Germany was an asset, not a liability to Europe – a view which if anything had been strengthened by the Bolshevik Revolution. Thus Keynes pooh-poohed the French alternative of trying to cut Germany down to France's size, politically and economically, in order to restore a pre–1870 balance of power between the two countries. 'You cannot restore Central Europe to 1870', he wrote, 'without setting up such strains in the European structure and letting loose such human and spiritual forces as, pushing beyond frontiers and races, will overwhelm not only you and your "guarantees", but your institutions, and the existing order of your society.'[2] Keynes also attacked the greed of the French representatives in bidding up their financial claims.[3]

On the other hand, it was Lloyd George more than the French whom he blamed for the reparations chapter of the Treaty.[4] The essence of Clemenceau's policy, as he saw it, was to 'weaken and destroy Germany in every way possible', not to extract a huge indemnity from it, which implied a 'vast commercial activity in Germany'.[5] America was also to blame for offering 'no constructive proposals' to alleviate France's financial problems.[6] Keynes's own suggestions were designed to secure France a larger share of a smaller (and he thought payable) reparations total. Britain should 'waive altogether' its own cash claims on Germany. In addition the French debt to Britain and the United States was to be cancelled; and France was to be the main beneficiary of a reconstruction loan.[7]

Recent scholarship, based on the opening of the French Foreign Office archives in 1972, has provided a fresh stream of criticism of Keynes's book. Keynes depicted the French aim of dismembering Germany as an act of economic barbarism. The American scholar Walter McDougall has pointed out that it was precisely the division of Germany after 1945 which made possible (West) European economic integration. From this point of view, France's attempt to separate the Rhineland from Germany can be seen as a forward-looking effort to achieve Franco-German economic co-operation within a political framework which guaranteed French security. It was Wilsonian nationalism, not Clemenceau's balance-of-power calculations, which was old-fashioned.[8] Keynes shared the general Anglo-Saxon myopia in not recognising that a balance between France and Germany was the precondition of European stability – and that this was prevented by the policy of preserving Bismarck's Reich.

Today this argument seems less convincing than it may have done in the 1970s. Keynes's alternative to both Wilsonian nationalism and a return to 1870 was to give Germany an eastern outlet for its organising and wealth-creating energy.[9] This was never tried. The German problem was 'solved' after 1945, not by restoring a Franco-German balance on the Rhine, but by the division of Europe (including Germany) into American and Soviet protectorates, which made French fears and German hopes alike irrelevant. But this was just as artificial an arrangement as what the French were proposing in 1919. Sooner or later the natural balance of Europe had to be restored, with Eastern Europe gravitating towards Germany rather than the Soviets. What Keynes saw far more clairvoyantly than the Quai d'Orsay, or its new apologists, was that a gamble on Germany had to be taken – as it does once more today. As he put it in a talk to Shrewsbury schoolboys in July 1920, there were two alternative hypotheses. Either the Germans had learnt their lesson, or they were irretrievably wicked. If the second were true, 'Europe is finished and the mantle of civilisation will once more sweep onto other shoulders.'[10] The trouble was that Keynes's alternative to the 'Carthaginian peace' was not practical politics, so the gamble on Germany was made too ungenerously to work.

Marc Trachtenberg comes to France's defence on another front. Keynes claimed that Germany *could* not transfer a sum of the order of £3000–£4000m. to the European Allies. Trachtenberg says it is much more a case of *would* not. Keynes muddied the waters by talking about capacity, when he should have been talking about willingness. The 'whole point of the notion of capacity', Trachtenberg argues, 'is to abstract from the notion of will: it makes no sense to say that the Germans could not pay because they did not want to pay'. The debate about 'capacity' has generated much technical literature. But the basic issue is simple. Both sides agreed that Germany's capacity to pay reparations was determined by the size of its export surplus. But, whereas Keynes claimed that this balance was fixed, the French in particular argued that it was largely a function of the Germans' willingness to reduce their own living standards in order to make room for increased exports. The reparations problem, in other words, was a budgetary, not a transfer problem. Trachtenberg endorses Jacob Viner's retrospective view that Keynes's argument was technically defective, but that economists refrained from pointing this out because they accepted his political con-clusions. It follows that demands for reparations of the order of £3000m.–£4000m. were not self-evidently absurd; in particular, there is no need to see in the French claim a 'pretext for dismembering Germany by force', as Keynes tended to.[11]

Trachtenberg's point is sound – as far as it goes. But Keynes's argument is not much damaged. His estimates of Germany's capacity were made 'having regard to the political, social, and human factors as well as the economic'.[12] In other words, Keynes's argument, correctly interpreted, is not about what Germany could have paid under a Ceaucescu, but what its people could be made to pay under a government similar to those which existed in Britain and France. And here he was surely more nearly right than those who talked of really large payments. Germany was not willing to pay the kind of tribute envisaged by the Allies, and there was no way of making it do so except by confiscating its production, as Russia was able to do in East Germany after the Second World War. Where Keynes may have been wrong was in thinking that the Germans were willing to pay anything.

If the new historiography establishes anything beyond doubt it is that French policy was in a frightful muddle – more so than Keynes realised. McDougall and Trachtenberg find justifications for different strands of French thinking – breaking up Germany on the one hand, exacting large reparations on the other – which were incompatible in theory and never resolved in practice. Keynes's alternative project retains its intellectual lustre. The worse that can be said about it was that it was ahead of its time. The 'cunning of reason' decreed much more tyranny, convulsion and slaughter before Europe could start to come together again. But then Keynes was never a Hegelian.

II

ENTER MISS BENTWICH

Keynes's private life was played out against the background of impending catastrophe. Its character was quite different from that of pre-war, not just because he was older, more famous and more in demand, but because no one with his capacity and sense of duty could ignore public affairs in the way that his generation had been able to do before 1914, when the politics of militarism were simply the amusements of the daily newspaper. Public events between the wars were too clamant to make possible good states of mind. As Keynes often said, they created in him a state of nervous excitement, whose relief demanded his active involvement in them.

But 1920 was an interlude; and Charleston in 1920 provided a last precise reminiscence of those extended pre-war summer house-parties when Bloomsberries and their friends assembled for their annual festivals of intellect, art and sexual intrigue, undisturbed by the political projects which were to play serpent to their paradise. As before, the familiar cast of characters came and went through August to October, each in his or her familiar part. Maynard worked on the proofs of his book on probability, Duncan Grant and Vanessa Bell painted in a new makeshift studio beyond the walled garden, Lytton Strachey read them his *Queen Victoria*, and Mary Hutchinson stopped Clive Bell from working at all. Bunny Garnett 'turned up in a motor', followed by Peter Lucas, 'perfectly charming as ever' and having a calming effect on the manic mathematician, Harry Norton. Virginia Woolf, breaking off from *Jacob's Room*, would drop in from neighbouring Rodmell for argument and gossip over lunch or supper. Maynard insisted that life be ordered on 'Charleston time' – one hour ahead of summer time – which led to inconveniently early teas, revolts in the kitchen and dark mutterings from Clive Bell. 'How mad they all are,' Lytton wrote to Carrington. 'The result is extremely Tchekhovesque. But luckily the atmosphere is entirely comic. . . . Everyone laughs and screams and passed on.'[13]

Maynard had hoped to have the Cambridge undergraduate Sebastian Sprott for the last part of his stay. 'We – that is Clive Bell, Duncan Grant, Norton, Lucas and I – are desolated that you can't come,' he wrote to him on 3 October. 'But families are families I know.' Instead, Maynard went up to London on 6 October and brought back Gabriel Atkin, a young painter and musician of moderate talent, who served as an occasional boyfriend to him as well as to Siegfried Sassoon. On this occasion, though, Atkin was distinctly *hors de combat*, having an abscess on the cheek and being forced to spend, as Duncan reported with some glee to Vanessa, his time 'in bed . . . alone'.[14]

Unattached since the break-up of his affair with Duncan Grant in 1911, Maynard no longer hankered after a grand passion – or so he told his friends. 'The shallow waters are the attraction. Up to the middle, not head over ears at my age,' he ambiguously informed Lytton.[15] Sebastian Sprott fitted the bill perfectly, and from October 1920 Keynes was considered by Bloomsbury to be 'married' to Sprott. The product of a dominating mother and a tough boarding school (Felsted), Sprott had come up to Cambridge in 1919 to read moral sciences, in which he got a double first. He became the intimate of stars like Keynes, Strachey and Morgan Forster, but was never a star himself, despite a stagey presence modelled on Ronald Firbank. He fitted in: unambitious, presentable, clever, sympathetic – an ideal house-guest or holiday companion. Strachey once sent him a letter in an envelope addressed: 'Kind Cambridge postman, please do not / Forget, through loitering, love or talk, / To leave this letter with the Sprott / Who lives at 7 Brunswick Walk'. Strachey specialised in addresses of this kind. The letters arrived punctually.

Sprott made no secret of his tastes. After reading Hirschfeld, he wrote to Maynard in 1921, 'I suspect I am tainted with Transvestitismus, Autonomosexualität, and Hermaphroditismus . . . to say nothing of Homosexualität and Onanie. . . . My love, yours ever Sebastian.' Maynard's approach was more subtle. Signing himself 'Ever yours affectionately, JMK', he wrote to

Sebastian on 4 January 1921: 'You say my parties are Greek. But have you applied the Method of Difference? Do you know what they are like when you are not there?'[16] In fact, few of Sprott's letters to Maynard have survived. Either Maynard or, more likely, his brother Geoffrey destroyed most of them, and the most indiscreet of those from Gabriel Atkin.

Sprott was the type of aesthetic middle-class homosexual mainly attracted to working-class youths. He blazed the trail to the Berlin night clubs later followed by Christopher Isherwood and W. H. Auden. In the 1930s he and his friend Joe Ackerley would roam the pubs in Portsmouth and Dover looking for low-life adventure with which to titillate the prim Morgan Forster. When he went to Nottingham University in 1925 as a lecturer in psychology, he dropped the Bloomsbury 'Sebastian' for the more proletarian 'Jack', and used discharged prisoners as domestic helpers in his grim Victorian terraced house. Quentin Bell remembers a paper he read to the Memoir Club in the 1950s, describing his friendship with the public hangman. Keynes never shared his taste for the low life. He refused to idealise the working class, British or German. He worshipped artists, not toughs. His ideal universe never included working-class 'mates' – something which distanced him from those who approached their socialism by this route.

In any event, Keynes's own sexuality was in a state of transition. He could contemplate at least the possibility of a love affair with someone of the opposite sex. There had been his flirtation with Barbara Hiles in 1917. Apparently this had continued after she became Barbara Bagenal: there is a strange letter from Duncan Grant to Vanessa Bell in 1920, written with characteristic disregard for the existence of Mr Bagenal, in which he wonders whether 'Barbara would be a good mother for Maynard's children'.[17] In Charleston mythology, Barbara Bagenal is the wife Keynes should have had.[18] Even more elusive was his relationship with his new secretary, Naomi Bentwich.

It was Naomi Bentwich herself who suggested, in August 1920, that she become Keynes's secretary on a part-time basis. She was then earning a precarious living on the register of Miss Pate's Cambridge secretarial agency. In that capacity she had typed chapters of Keynes's *Economic Consequences of the Peace* with growing excitement and enthusiasm, and conceived the plan of working for him. On 23 August Keynes wrote to her offering her a half-time job, at £300 p.a., combining work for him (taking his dictation, typing his articles), with compiling the decennial index of the *Economic Journal*, which he edited. 'Is this the kind of work you had in mind?' he wrote. It was; and she took her first dictation when Keynes returned to King's in the middle of October 1920. She remained his secretary for seven months. During that time (and for several years afterwards) she experienced the most turbulent feelings towards him, and about him, which she recorded in her diary. She later used these records, together with letters she and

Keynes exchanged, as the basis of an unpublished autobiography, 'Lucifer by Starlight: A Human Document'.

Naomi Bentwich came to Keynes with an unusual background for a secretary. She was a dark-haired, attractive, intelligent, idealistic young woman of twenty-nine, born into a prominent Anglo-Jewish family. After taking a secretarial course, she read moral sciences at Newnham College until 1917. She had been active in the No-Conscription Fellowship, visiting Garsington with Bertrand Russell. W. E. Johnson had been her tutor. Thinking it a shame that Johnson had never written a book, and that it was important for his logical thought to endure, she offered to take down his thoughts in short-hand, without charge. This was evidently the incentive he needed, and she spent much of her free time from 1915 to 1920 writing down Johnson's dictation, typing it out and contributing, by her comment and criticism, to the fashioning of what became the three volumes of his *Logic*, published in 1921, 1922 and 1924. It is generally agreed that without Naomi's help Johnson could never have produced these books.[19]

But this was not all. Johnson, a fifty-seven-year-old widower in 1915, fell in love with her. Naomi Bentwich, who found the sexual emotion 'disturbing', resisted his advances, telling him that her love for him must always be that of a 'daughter to a very dear father', but offering a consolation prize of a kiss 'twice a day'. Johnson capitulated. 'You are too far above me,' he wrote to her, 'to let me feel anything but a very distantly admiring love.' This response made Naomi Bentwich 'completely happy'. But soon there were signs that Johnson's feelings were not quite as distant as he had led her to believe. Naomi told him they must fight the 'animal passion' together for the sake of his work. Eventually, in 1920, they decided to marry. But the plan was abandoned in face of ferocious resistance from Johnson's sister and housekeeper Fanny, who said she would go mad, and from Naomi's own father, who could not bear the thought of his daughter marrying a Gentile. It was thus on the rebound from the passionate Johnson that she first confronted the subtle, almost invisible, sexuality of Keynes.

> I wasn't prepared [she wrote in her memoir] for that big room of his over the Queen's Lane entrance to King's College with its startling wall paintings by Duncan Grant . . . where a nude negress . . . alongside a cardinal in scarlet . . . proclaimed the free individualism which Keynes's literary style had led me to expect . . . All the same I was happier in the little inner room with its crimson curtains, his study, in which I was almost always alone with him. I usually sat there in a big armchair in front of the fireplace, and he sat at his desk by the window with his back to me. I can't remember that we shook hands at that first meeting; certainly there was no tea; his manner was abrupt.

Miss Bentwich would go to Keynes two or three times a week, sometimes of an evening, usually by previous appointment, but occasionally summoned by the King's College porter. Keynes would dictate his correspondence to her, and dismiss her. Their relationship was purely formal. One afternoon in November 1920 she came to him just after he had finished lunch with W. E. Johnson. He told her that he remembered Johnson talking logic with his father when he was 'so high' – and stretched out his hand about three foot from the ground. Why did Naomi think that Johnson's work was so important? Because he had deflected logical thought out of the groove into which Russell had led it, she replied. 'At that he sat back in his desk chair and looked over his shoulder at me. I seemed to sink into deep pools of sympathy, and by the lovely look in his eyes and his smile . . . knew that he understood as no one else understood.'

Naomi Bentwich later wrote that she had 'never known a man whose expression made such a difference to his whole person. Keynes, with his large restless eyes which lighted quickly, could be a graceful, Pan-like, mischievous boy; or a haughty overseer; or a scowling antagonist; or a graceful, soulful companion . . . I observed in him (like Diana of the Crossways of Dacier)"a singular conflicting of a buoyant animal nature with a curb of studiousness, as if the fardels of age were piling up on his shoulders before youth had quitted its pastures . . .".'

III

UNENDURABLE FACTS

When Keynes returned to Cambridge in October 1920, the hectic post-war boom had collapsed, prices had started to tumble and Britain was moving into the deepest depression of modern times. Keynes himself had experienced traumatic changes of fortune in his speculations on foreign currencies. On 18 December Harold Laski wrote in one of his regular political reports to Felix Frankfurter, 'And yet I think Ireland is less important than the industrial situation. We now have more than a million unemployed, and perhaps three times that number on short time. The government has no policy whatever. . . .'[20] The unemployment problem had arrived. Keynes could not foresee that it would dominate the rest of his life, and establish his enduring claim to fame.

His advice, indeed, had helped to create the depression. As an ex-Treasury man he was consulted in February 1920 on what course monetary policy should take. He said bank rate should be put up to 10 per cent if necessary and held there as long as needed to break the boom.[21] Keynes later claimed (1942) that 'with all methods of control . . . excluded, I feel myself that I should give today exactly the same advice as I gave then, namely, a swift and severe dose of dear money, sufficient to break the market. . . .'.[22]

Keynes's remedy was taken, but too timidly and too late. Bank rate was put up to 7 per cent on 15 April and held there for a year. In the same month the government imposed new taxes designed to increase its already substantial budget surplus. Austen Chamberlain had reported Keynes as saying that he did not believe that a 'dear money' policy 'would lead to unemployment'. As in the early 1980s, the government believed it could deflate the economy without causing a depression. And Keynes's opinion was one which Chamberlain especially respected.

The First World War had been followed by an inflationary boom. Wages had risen faster than prices in the last two years of the war, but rationing had prevented people from spending their increased money incomes on consumption goods. With the removal of controls the public went on a spending spree, prices rising by 50 per cent between April 1919 and April 1920. 'The prime cause of the rise in prices during the boom', wrote E. V. Morgan, 'was the impossibility of increasing output sufficiently to meet the violent rise in private expenditure, first on consumption goods and then on capital goods.'[23] Money wages now lagged behind the rise in prices, producing what Keynes would later call a 'profit inflation'.

Once the boom got going, prices were pushed higher and higher by gambling in commodities, shares, property, while interest rates were held down. Who would not borrow at 4 per cent a year, with prices going up 4 per cent a *month*? Old companies were bought and sold, and new ones floated, as an almost daily occurrence. Keynes's friend Robert Brand, a director of Lloyds Bank as well as Lazards, recalled that at the bank's Board meetings at the time 'we ladled out money; we did it because everybody said they were making and were going to make high profits; and while you had an uneasy feeling yet you thought that while they were making large profits there could be nothing said about ladling out the money'.[24] Keynes added his memory. 'Practically every country,' he wrote in 1929, 'was off the gold standard, and money was the one commodity to the rapid manufacture of which there was no serious impediment.'[25] Britain itself had formally abandoned the gold standard in March 1919 because of fear of social unrest if demobilisation led straight to the dole queue. The Cabinet interpreted a general strike on the Clyde in April 1919 as a revolutionary uprising. So banking and political logic combined to keep money amazingly cheap long after the boom showed signs of getting out hand. As in the war, the government was using inflation to solve its problems, because it could think of nothing else.

Keynes was fiercely opposed to the inflationary policy, especially as he detected behind it the evil genius of his old enemy Lloyd George. To him it was a rerun of his wartime battles against the profligate Welsh Wizard. The Prime Minister certainly saw the danger. 'We are spending more, we are earning less; we are consuming more, we are producing less. These are the facts of the situation and it cannot last,' he told the House of Commons on 18 August 1919. But, worried by the perceived revolutionary threat, he hesitated to take action. He wanted cheap money to finance his 'homes for heroes'. Montagu Norman noted on 4 February 1920 that 'PM & Bonar L[aw] & Bankers are pressing the C of E to *reduce* rates to allow issue of Housing Bonds' (italics added).[26] Being a primitive Keynesian long before Keynes became a sophisticated one, Lloyd George instinctively mistrusted the advice of Treasury officials. He brushed aside the Treasury's warnings that 'capital was not unlimited' with the remark that 'his wartime experiences refuted the Treasury view'.[27] His Chancellor, Austen Chamberlain, also resisted Bank of England pressure to put up the Treasury Bill rate (or cost of government borrowing), without which a higher bank rate could not be made effective.

As Susan Howson tells it, the emergence of the 'dear money' policy in the winter of 1919–20 is really the story of how the Bank of England, aided and abetted by Sir John Bradbury of the Treasury, regained control of financial policy from the politicians who had usurped it during the war. The copper-bottom argument put by the officials was that inflation had to be rapidly liquidated, and indeed reversed, if sterling was ever to return to the gold standard at its pre-war parity with the dollar. This objective, proclaimed by the Cunliffe Report in August 1918, had been accepted by all the political parties. Implementation of the objective required balanced budgets, the active use of interest-rate policy to stop credit expansion, and legal limitation of the note issue.[28] Lloyd George, Bonar Law and Austen Chamberlain accepted the end but shrank from the means. Yet, because they accepted the end, they ran out of arguments for opposing the means, especially once inflation had got out of control. And they might have had less depression later on had they acted sooner to curb the boom.

Keynes himself never regarded the return to the pre-war gold standard as the overriding aim of policy. But he hated inflation, for reasons he gave in *The Economic Consequences of Peace*, where he quoted a remark, attributed to Lenin, that 'the best way to destroy the capitalist system was to debauch the currency'.[29] Thus he found himself on the side of the Treasury and the Bank against the politicians. He supported Chamberlain's decision on 28 December 1919 to limit the issue of currency notes to a fixed amount.[30] His pencilled notes for a talk to the Tuesday Club on 8 January 1920 acknowledged that Treasury and Bank policy would delay post-war reconstruction and cause unemployment, but 'boom and good employment need capital. If we haven't got capital, is it any good *pretending* that we have it?'[31] At the Tuesday Club on 8 July he attacked the Coalition for its fiscal extravagance. He now wanted bank rate to rise to 8 per cent, and demanded heavy cuts in public spending, even though they risked depression, because he put so high 'the danger of going on with our present [inflationary] diseases'. His call for an 8 per cent bank rate was echoed by the Governor of the Bank, Montagu Norman, who attended that meeting, but was vetoed by Chamberlain.[32]

In fact the combination of a fiscal and monetary squeeze and falling real wages had already brought the boom to an end; no one, least of all Keynes, expected the severity of the collapse which followed. In September 1920 Norman thought the best that could be hoped for was 'a very slight reduction in our total inflation . . . during the current financial year'.[33] Consumer spending fell first, followed by investment spending. Prices started to tumble in October; unemployment rose sharply in November. Output fell by 15 per cent over the next twelve months; unemployment rose to 22 per cent. In an unprecedented, and final, display of price and wage flexibility, wholesale prices were almost halved, money wages fell by one-third in the same period. Later Sir Josiah Stamp shrewdly observed that the collapse was started by 'the refusal to mature of an anticipated inflation. . . . it is just the feeling you have when you go upstairs in the dark and tread on a top step which is not there'.[34]

Keynes, too, had taken part in the gambling mania, and like the others felt he was gambling on a certainty. As we have seen he had started speculating on currencies with Foxy Falk in the autumn of 1919. He believed that, as British prices rose faster than American ones, sterling would go down against the dollar; whereas, with the inflation rate in France, Germany and Italy higher than in Britain, sterling could be expected to appreciate against their currencies. For a time this assumption proved correct. From March 1919, when the sterling–dollar exchange was uncoupled, till February 1920, sterling fell from $4.70 to $3.40, and by the end of 1919 Keynes's realised profits were over £6000. Encouraged by these results he decided to form a syndicate with Falk, who was also his broker at Buckmaster and Moore. It started operations in January 1920 with a paid-up capital of £30,000, half provided by Falk, the other half by Keynes, who invested £8000 of his own money (mainly lent by his father and his brother-in-law A. V. Hill), £4500 of Duncan Grant's and Vanessa Bell's and £2500 of his brother's. Keynes had sole control of his half of the operation. The sleeping partners handed over their money to Keynes with the most sublime confidence in his wakeful ability to multiply it for them, a confidence Keynes appeared to have shared. As he explained to his father on 11 December 1919, 'The affair is, of course, risky. But Falk and I, seeing that our reputations depend on it, intend to exercise a good deal of caution.' Given Neville Keynes's obsessive anxiety, his decision to finance his son's gambling to the tune of £5000 was almost heroic.*

At first all went well. The Keynes group bought rupees and sold francs

---

*Donald Moggridge writes: '[Keynes's] strategy was straightforward: to sell short in the forward market the currencies of France, Italy, Holland and, after March 1920, Germany, and to go long in U.S. dollars, Norwegian and Danish krone and Indian rupees.' (CW, xii, 7.) The forward market in exchange was adapted to the new situation of floating currencies and was chiefly designed to insure traders against losses. A speculator would make contracts to buy and sell currencies for delivery and payment at some future date, hoping that when the transaction was completed he would have made a profit from a change in the currency's value. No cash had to change hands till the maturity of the contract, though the speculator was required to deposit a 10 per cent 'cover' with his broker. The total speculation could thus be a very large multiple of the speculator's assets. This feature greatly increased the risks and rewards of the game.

and lire, and by the week ending 27 February 1920 realised profits stood at
£8643 and book profits at £18,525 on a total investment of £200,000. 'My
debt of gratitude to you increases (like my capital) by geometrical pro-
gression,' wrote Geoffrey Keynes to his brother. Early in March the Syndicate took the fateful decision to go long in dollars, buying £150,000 worth
at 3.68 dollars to the pound. But sterling refused to fall. 'Dollars are certainly
puzzling,' wrote Falk to Keynes on 30 March, as the pound rose to $3.89.
It is plain that he and Keynes were gambling that action on the bank rate
would be postponed till May.[35] In fact it was put up on 15 April, and had
already been anticipated.

For the time being losses on dollars were more than compensated by
profits on francs, and in mid-March Keynes swept Vanessa Bell and Duncan
Grant off for a six-week Easter holiday in Italy, starting at the Hotel de
Russie in Rome. The visitors were less impressed by the grim industrial and
political situation than by the stunning fall in the value of the lire: 25 to the
pound in 1914, it was 35 in March 1919, 81 on 3 April 1920 and almost
100 by 16 April. Keynes informed his companions that spending was more
than a pleasure, it was a duty. They went on a shopping spree, buying over
£300 worth of furniture and fabric. Keynes's purchases including seventeen
pairs of gloves as presents. 'Win or lose, this high stake gambling amuses
me,' he wrote to his father from Rome. Neville Keynes's reaction can be
imagined.

The holiday ended at the end of April with a few days at I Tatti,
where Keynes had stayed before the war. Bernard Berenson had mobilised
Florentine society to meet the world-famous economist. Feeling perhaps left
out, Vanessa Bell wrote to Roger Fry in her most lordly Bloomsbury style:
'If only he [B.B.] could be honestly a stockbroker one would be quite at
one's ease. I'm sure he has no more notion of what's important in a painting
than a flea has.'[36] The climax of the stay was a grand dinner party given in
Keynes's honour by the American collector Charles Loeser, at which
Duncan Grant, mistaken for Keynes, was closely questioned about the
reparation problem, while Keynes, posing as 'il pittore Grant', gave his
expert opinion on his host's Cézannes. No one seems to have been amused
when the prank was discovered. Keynes never went to I Tatti again.*

A few weeks after returning to England Keynes was ruined. Francs, lire
and marks had all started to appreciate against sterling. The movement did
not last long, but long enough to clean Keynes out. Falk, he told Vanessa
on 22 May, was being 'a brick all through', and he was still holding on.

---

*The story has often been told, with many variations. The fullest version is contained in an
account Duncan Grant wrote out for the Memoir Club in the 1940s, original in possession of
Mr Richard Shone. Keynes supplied one variant in 1927: 'It was at his [Loeser's] party that
Duncan was introduced as the famous Mr. Keynes and accepted the description without
complaint because he found that it was accompanied by port and strawberries and cream. . . .'
(J.M.K. to Lydia Keynes, 21 February 1927.)

But finally on 27 May Keynes was forced to liquidate his positions. He lost all his group's capital, and owed his broker nearly £5000. His debts, that is – including his 'moral debts' to his family and friends – came to just under £20,000.

Keynes somehow made his remaining capital add up to £21,500, thus claiming that he was still solvent. Fortunately, most of the debts were to family and friends. His father immediately wrote off £2000 of his own loan, and made it clear that all his resources were at his son's disposal. ('All we can do we will do,' he cabled on 27 May). Florence took Maynard's reverses stoically. 'It was perhaps necessary to throw something overboard to propitiate the Gods – and if they are content with money, we will not grudge it to them,' she wrote in her birthday letter of 3 June. From Bloomsbury Keynes never received a word of reproach. Critical as his friends were of his aesthetic and political judgements, they never lost faith in his financial genius. None of them seemed to doubt for a moment that they would get their money back.

Nor were they wrong. Keynes paid off his immediate debt to Falk with a £5000 loan from the financier and philanthropist Sir Ernest Cassel, a supporter of the Papworth Community for tubercular patients, which Florence Keynes had helped establish in 1919. With £1500 on account from his publisher Daniel Macmillan, and £500 from Basil Blackett,[37] Keynes was in again almost immediately, convinced, as he told Cassel on 26 May, that it must be right to 'sell marks, francs, and lire forward' if one could stand the racket for a couple of months.[38] He formed a new syndicate with his former pupil Sidney Russell Cooke, a stockbroker with Capel, Cure and Terry. This time he was right. 'My finances have been prospering pretty well lately,' he told his father on 13 September. By the end of 1920 he had repaid Cassel and Blackett and had a small profit. In 1921 he formed another syndicate with Reginald McKenna. The 'moral debts' to Duncan and the others were cleared off in 1922, by the end of which Keynes had 'something between £25,000 and £30,000' left over for himself.[39*]

Keynes's gains and losses were short-term. Many economists at the time believed that economies reacted to shocks like alert individuals: rapid losses followed by quick recoveries, with agents switching into new lines of business just as Keynes switched into new currencies and commodities. The great lesson of the first post-war depression was that economies are much more sluggish than individuals. Once prices started to fall after July 1920 the expectation that they would go on falling caused everyone to act in ways which ensured that they did go on falling. Dealers unloaded their stocks;

*Stephen Schuker has claimed that Keynes 'used his privileged access to financial information to speculate on the forward exchanges. If he ever wondered whether he was involved in a conflict of interests, he gave no sign of it.' (Stephen A. Schuker, 'The Collected Writings of John Maynard Keynes' (volumes 17 and 18), *Journal of Economic Literature*, xviii, March 1980, 124–6.) It is hard to see what privileged information was available about currency movements.

owners sold their property and businesses as the banks called in mortgages; manufacturers stopped hiring labour; workers resisted employers' attempt to cut their wages, so real wages went up as profits fell, which added to bankruptcies, and so on. The cumulative effects of all their actions was to push economic activity down, not up. The economy, evidently, was not like a central-heating system, producing a thermostatically controlled temperature. When the temperature dropped, economists looked for the automatic adjustment and discovered there was none – or that it was much feebler than they had imagined.

Keynes's autumn lectures on 'The Present Disorders of the World's Monetary System' – 300 students turned up to the first one at twelve o'clock on Monday, 18 October – reflected his own as well as his nation's experience. His style was not dramatic; it was his ability to relate economics to dramatic events which drew students to him. His theme was how monetary disorders could have serious consequences for production and employment. Keynes started by observing that 'a change in prices and wages as measured by money is capable of transferring wealth from one class to another, and redistributing fortune in a way which baffles anticipation and upsets design. It is for that reason that we have to concentrate on what is nothing more than an intermediary and not an object of consumption.' Monetary instability, he went on to say, undermines the *virtue* of the capitalist system, and 'the nature of the defence' which can be made by the businessman for his existence. The prevalence of monetary disorders after the war constituted 'an essential change in the social structure'.

By monetary disorder Keynes meant inflation. Deflation, although its immediate evils are greater, was a derived phenomenon, brought about by the inevitable collapse of the inflationary boom. That is why Keynes, like all the monetary reformers of the 1920s, attached supreme importance to price stability: stable money is necessary for stable capitalism. Inflation, he said, was a device to enable a community, for a time, to consume its capital unawares. Both wage-earners and businessmen can make windfall gains at the expense of investors (savers). However, as the cost of borrowing capital rises, the windfall profits disappear, and the struggle between wages and profits starts. If trade unions resist wage reductions, unemployment results. But this can be postponed. Businessmen for some time will accept lower than normal profits rather than close their businesses; and even when that moment comes, 'the trade union could then claim government subsidies'. This is a stylised account of what was actually happening in the autumn of 1920.

This new interaction of government, business and unions to keep an inflationary boom going beyond the point when it would 'naturally' collapse, constituted in Keynes's view another fundamental change from the pre-war position. In his fourth lecture on public finance Keynes noted that 'under pressure of war governments learn a new mode of covert taxation by manufacturing money' – a discussion which foreshadows his section on the 'inflation tax' in the *Tract on Monetary Reform*. He said that governments and municipalities should learn to stop borrowing, though he recognised that balancing the budget can become politically impossible if the system of subsidy has become too widespread. He advocated a central bank entirely independent of governments: it should not be required to 'print notes to meet the requirements of the Treasury'. More interestingly, he agreed with the proposal to restore currencies to the 'old gold standard'. 'There is a great deal to be said against gold, but nearly all the more significant and scientific arrangements depend on confidence in governments. The advantage of the gold standard is the convention behind it that it is . . . disgraceful to tamper with gold.'

In his seventh lecture, entitled 'Do We Want Prices to Fall?', Keynes revealed the nub of his disagreement with the actual policy being pursued by the Treasury and the Bank of England. Inflation must be liquidated, and he was prepared to accept the unemployment cost of doing so. But he insisted that it should not be carried so far as to bring about a severe *actual* fall in price level. 'Having reached a level here and now – whatever that level may be – we should fix ourselves there, and not aim at getting back to what, after all, was a perfectly arbitrary pre-war level.' Devaluation should be preferred to further deflation – that is, 'we should accept a permanently diminished value for the standard coin measured in gold'.

Here Keynes felt he was restating orthodox doctrine in face of revolutionary innovations by the monetary authority. As Morgan remarks, the maintenance of a high bank rate during the long period of collapsing prices and activity was 'diametrically opposed to the established practice of reducing the rate as soon as the peak of the boom had been passed'.[40] In retrospect, Keynes felt that 'most of the troubles' which followed might have been averted had steps been taken to stabilise the situation towards the end of 1920 when the rate of inflation reached zero. (Though whether monetary policy alone could have done this is very doubtful.) As Pigou subsequently noted, the aim of the monetary authorities 'was not simply to arrest an inflation . . . [but] to restore our currency to pre-war gold parity in the near future'.[41] And this meant forcing down the British price level in line with the American price level. Since the British inflation had been greater than America's, its deflation had to be greater too.

However, Keynes rejected a purely monetary explanation of 'monetary disorders'. Monetary disorder 'is the way in which people may postpone and cover up what may be almost unendurable facts. . . . People struggle to maintain their previous standards by living off their capital; and the whole apparatus of monetary unsoundness allows the country . . . to put off the worst day without recognising what it is doing.' The 'unendurable fact' was that Europe's standard of living had to come down, not just because of the wartime destruction, but because – as he had already observed in

The Economic Consequences of the Peace – of the tendency of the real cost of
Europe's cereal imports from the United States to rise. 'A great deal of
monetary disorder is in essence a blind reaction against those natural forces
which are inevitably tending to lower the standard of life.' Europe was
overpopulated: 'The period during which the law of diminishing returns
was suspended is at an end, there must now be a tendency for the level of
life to fall just as inevitably as the tendency was for the level of life to rise
in the nineteenth century.' The problem is: 'are we going to reduce our
population or are we going to return to the lower standards of life which
have existed during the greater part of Europe's history?' On this gloomily
prophetic note Keynes left his 300 students, among whom were C. R. Fay,
Austin Robinson, Rupert Trouton, Maurice Dobb, R. W. Procter, F. W.
Paish and Arcadius Skidelsky.[42]

Regrettably these lectures have not been included in Keynes's *Collected
Writings*. They reveal what he was thinking about Europe's post-war economic problems at a time when other evidence is scanty. In essence they
show Keynes applying pre-war theory to the new situation caused by the
unfinished war. Some of the lectures, themselves based on much earlier
lecture material, are first drafts of chapters which would appear in the *Tract
on Monetary Reform* in 1923. A more innovative feature is the way Keynes
connects monetary disorder to the psychology and institutions of society.
Inflations are devices for enabling workers, businessmen and governments
to prosper temporarily by consuming or confiscating the 'real wealth' of
savers. Great inflations are driven by social and political pathology; this
makes their control and reversal without severe economic collapse exceptionally difficult. A third strand is Keynes's neo-Malthusianism. Europe's standard of living will have to come down if its population is to be properly fed.
And here there is a gap in the analysis. How is the policy of stabilising
prices to be combined with one of reducing real wages? A fuller discussion
of this conundrum must wait till later.

IV

RUBBISH ABOUT MILLIARDS*

Throughout 1920 Keynes had watched in fascinated horror the experts and
statesmen tramp round the holiday resorts of Europe talking what he called
'rubbish about milliards' in their efforts to determine Germany's reparation
bill. Officially this was the job of the Reparation Commission in Paris,
which was supposed to report in May 1921. However, the British and

---

*What they then called milliards, we now call billions – thousands of millions. All reparation
calculations were made in pre-war gold values, when the pound was worth twenty marks.

French recognised the inconvenience of leaving the German liability undetermined for so long, and started direct negotiations among themselves and
with the Germans. The French, in particular, were keen to get their hands
on German resources as quickly as possible to reconstruct their devastated
regions.

The prime mover in all this activity was Lloyd George, who now emerged
as Europe's great hope. He took credit for postponing the fixing of a definite
sum until the 'hot passions' of 1919 had had time to cool – forgetting his
part in inflaming them.[43] Free of the encumbrance of the Heavenly Twins,*
he now wanted to keep Germany's annual payments as small as possible,
wavering between Keynes's view that Germany could not pay large annual
sums, and alarm at the effects on British trade if it did. However, his bid
for moderation was weakened by the stony isolation of the United States,
especially by its refusal to scale down the debts it was owed by the Allies.
This left him à deux with the French, whose position became steadily more
intransigent. Deprived of the prospect of American assistance, they now
relied on Germany to pay the whole cost of restoring their invaded provinces.
However, they were much more interested in payments in kind than in
cash, which they hoped to achieve through direct negotiations with the
Germans, backed by threats to seize German mines and forests. Nor, without
American backing, could Lloyd George offer them the security guarantee
for which they might have traded large reparations. Instead they pursued
plans for setting up an independent Rhineland, which conflicted with their
aim of securing an economic agreement with Germany. The Germans played
a waiting game. They evaded the Allied proposals at Spa. They turned
down the French Seydoux Plan.† They defaulted on their interim coal
deliveries.

These were the balls Lloyd George had to juggle with. His policy was to
get Germany to accept the appearance of a large debt and France to accept
the reality of a small one. His unrivalled repertoire of blandishments and
threats was directed now at his Ally, now at his erstwhile enemy. With
much expert adjustment of the figures the prize seemed within his grasp,
but always just eluded him. Finally, his patience, though not his stamina,
ran out. At the end of 1920 he told the French that they must determine a
joint position forthwith. Briand, the new French Prime Minister, agreed. A
conference was summoned to meet in Paris in January 1921.

*Lords Cunliffe and Sumner, members of the British delegation to the Paris Peace Conference,
who wanted Germany to pay the 'whole cost' of the war.
†Under the Seydoux Plan, devised in the autumn of 1920, France attempted to secure deliveries
in kind for five years, to be paid for by German deposits of marks into a fund, which could be
drawn on by French importers to pay German businessmen supplying their orders. This would
have avoided the transfer problem, making Germany's capacity a matter of its willingness to
tax itself. The Germans showed little willingness, first saying that their overall liability must
be fixed in advance, then linking acceptance to a satisfactory outcome on Upper Silesia. (M.
Trachtenberg, *Reparations in World Politics*, 161f.)

Keynes's summary of Lloyd George's performances reflected the fascination with which he watched them. The Prime Minister, he conceded, had devoted his energies to 'protecting Europe from as many of the evil consequences of his own Treaty, as it lay within his power to prevent, with a craft few could have bettered, preserving the peace, though not the prosperity of Europe, seldom expressing the truth, yet often acting under its influence. He could claim, therefore, that by devious paths, a faithful servant of the possible, he was serving man.'[44] Not that Lloyd George's bravura lifted his own deep pessimism: 'It seems to me as certain as anything can be', he wrote to the American Alonzo Taylor on 27 November 1920, 'that the standard of life in Europe is bound to decline seriously below its pre-war level, until the influences of emigration, birth-rate and disease have brought about a new equilibrium.'[45]

At Paris in January 1921, Lloyd George had to endure a long exposition from the French President, Paul Doumer, demanding German payments of £600m. (or 12 billion gold marks) a year for forty-two years. Keynes's influence is apparent in his quick rejoinder: 'The question I would like to ask M. Doumer is, where are the 12 milliard gold marks to come from? I have been on the look-out for them for a couple of years . . . they are certainly not in Germany's exports.'[46] The juggling with milliards produced the usual magical formula. Germany was to pay two series of forty-two annuities, the first fixed, the second variable. The fixed amounts would rise from £100m. to £250m. a year over the first eleven years, and thereafter remain at £300m. The second series would amount to 12 per cent of Germany's exports. The capitalised amount was estimated at 226 billion gold marks, or £11 billion.

Keynes had accepted an invitation from C. P. Scott of the *Manchester Guardian* to comment on the Paris conference. His articles, which appeared on 31 January and 1 February 1921, marked the start of his highly profitable association with that newspaper. Keynes estimated that Germany would be required to pay £400m. a year over the whole period – 'double the highest figure that . . . any competent person here or in the United States has ever attempted to justify'. The only conclusion to be drawn was that the proposals could not be meant seriously.

> They are simply another move in the game, by which the players at any rate are no longer taken in. Mr. Lloyd George feels that he is making progress (perhaps he is) when he succeeds in persuading M. Briand to agree with him that 2 plus 2 does not make 12 but only 8; M. Briand hopes that, being eloquent, he may after all be able in the French Chamber to make a good enough song about 8 to defeat M. Poincaré as to how much better it would be for France if 2 plus 2 made 12.

They would never escape from the coils of war by such tricks. The truth had to be proclaimed loud and clear. 'The thought of the two Prime Ministers in Paris muddling over silly formulas, with M. Loucheur buzzing about between them . . . is, for anyone who realises what it is like, a thought of gibbering nightmare.'[47]

To the French economist, Henry de Peyser, who objected to this image, Keynes wrote with passion, 'I will be no party to a continuation of a European blood feud, however great the past guilt. In Cambridge here, this term we are performing the Aeschylean trilogy . . . I want to see the Furies turned into Eumenides, clothed in red robes, and pacifically housed in the Acropolis.' In a letter to a British correspondent, Neil Malcolm, Keynes expressed the hope that the Germans would reply to these preposterous proposals, sensibly and with dignity, and not put forward 'semi-sensible and semi-sophistical counter-proposals'.[48]

But the German counter-moves at the London Conference of 1 March 1921 gave an impression of 'evasiveness and insincerity'.[49] Dr Simons, the German Foreign Minister, fiddled with the Paris annuities in an effort to show that their current value amounted to only £50m. a year, which Germany would consider paying for five years, at the end of which the rate of repayment would be reconsidered; this was in any case contingent on German retention of Upper Silesia and the removal of all restrictions on German trade. General von Seeckt appeared in London with uniform, sword and monocle, a caricature of the Prussian warlord. Lloyd George dismissed the German offer with contempt; he and Briand, alleging German default in delivering war criminals for trials and making interim payments, announced a package of penalties. Allied troops marched into Duisburg and Düsseldorf on 8 March.

At Cambridge, the *Oresteia* had its first performance on 3 March, the day Lloyd George denounced the German proposals. Playing Elektra (opposite Donald Beves's Orestes) was a pink-faced, blue-eyed, yellow-haired King's freshman, George ('Dadie') Rylands, plucked by Sheppard from College at Eton, who was to become one of Maynard's closest College intimates. The next day, Keynes's secretary Miss Bentwich received a summons from Keynes. Her diary takes up the story:

> He was sitting at his dinner-table in the big room with a girl and two other men when I arrived, and he rose at once and walked through to his study. There he threw me half-a-dozen letters to deal with, said he had scarcely anything for me, and dictated two short notes. The people in the next room, he remarked, had come to see the Greek play, and he was going to see it himself that evening: had I seen it? 'Yes.' 'What was it like?' 'Magnificent. But please had he attended the Conference when he was in London?' 'What conference?' he shot out. 'Reparations.' 'Oh, I saw Bradbury for an hour yesterday. All they are doing at the Conference is trying to see how the Treaty can

be interpreted so as to enable us to put soldiers into Germany before May 1st.' 'Can't you do anything?' 'What's the good.'

However, the next day Keynes's valet appeared with a message that she was wanted at 2.15 p.m. 'I've written an article, quite short, Miss Bentwich,' he told her. 'It has to be cabled to the *Manchester Guardian*. I want you to find out the time, rates, forms for cabling, and bring it back here at 4.30. Mr. Asquith is coming to look at it before it goes.' (Keynes had invited Asquith to Cambridge for the Greek play.) She returned at 5.15 p.m. to find his room full of people, but no Asquith. 'Greek play,' he exclaimed with a flourish. 'You liked it. What did you think of the grand manner?' Eventually, at 6.40 p.m., when Asquith still hadn't come, Keynes sent her off to the post office in a taxi.

By next morning, Keynes had prepared a condensed version of the article for cabling to the United States, which Miss Bentwich took down in his study. At 12.15 p.m., 'when I was on the last page, he came in with someone he called Gabriel [Atkin] – a sickly yellow haired youth with white spats'.

> To-day at 1 o'clock [her diary continues] I went to lunch with Dr. [G. E.] Moore . . . Trevelyan (the translator of the *Oresteia*) was there, and he and I argued all the time about 'the grand style' and psychological drama. At 6pm. I was at Keynes again – Bursary letters at a tremendous pace about the transfer of King's property – land into shares – and one letter with a string of names of Impressionist artists – Cézanne, Degas, Matisse, Renoir, Sisley. As I was going he announced: 'The article you copied yesterday will be all over America to-morrow morning.' 'To whom did you send it?' 'The United Press Syndicate.' 'It wasn't as good as the other I thought.' 'Probably because it was for American consumption.'

Unknown to Keynes, his *Manchester Guardian* article, which appeared on 5 March, had already been extensively quoted in the United States, so his condensed version found only one outlet. While criticising the German proposals as 'ill-judged', Keynes mainly condemned Allied sanctions against Germany as illegal. 'The penalties,' he wrote,

> can hardly . . . be intended to raise money, and are rather designed to frighten Germany into putting her name to what she cannot and does not intend to perform by threatening a serious step in the direction of the French policy of permanently detaching the Rhine provinces from the German Commonwealth. The grave feature in the Allies' communication lies partly in our lending ourselves to a furtherance of this policy, and partly in contempt for the due form and processes of law. . . . The same attitude of mind and the same morality are responsible for the latest pronouncement, as for reprisals in Ireland. And if it is persisted in, it will lead to equal disaster.'[50]

V

ALL IN THE MIND?

By this time, Naomi Bentwich had fallen passionately in love with Keynes, a love which she was convinced he had deliberately kindled in her. As she took his dictation that Lent term she became aware of 'personal moments'. Once their hands met as she passed him a paper and she blushed deeply. Another time he slipped some *Economic Journal* writing paper into her hands 'in such a way that his lovely long fingers fluttered gently over the backs of my hands with an electric touch'. Once he asked her to turn round so that he could look at her – she felt – in profile. On 13 March he began dictating a letter and halted suddenly, gazing intently at her for what seemed an age:

> My heart was throbbing, but, with the image of Johnson before me, I kept my eyes down. I was confronted with the love of a man I adored, and yet blindly I fought. Suddenly I was aware of tugging against him with all my might. My whole being was concentrated in resistance; and the silence endured for so long that I felt as if my will would snap. Then, to my profound relief, he stuttered, and I dared to look up imploringly at him. His chin was resting in his hand and his brow was puckered up; he blinked rapidly, and I felt his pride making a determined stand for mastery. After what seemed 5 minutes, but may have been one, he stumbled in a quizzical embarrassed voice: 'Who can you suggest as finance minister for Albania?'

She noted in her diary, 'He is too confident; there is no *Weltschmerz* in him at all. But how attractive he is. I have never seen any man so beautiful as he looked on Friday and again to-day: his long, exquisitely graceful lines, his face pale and nervous, his eye-lashes long and black, half obscuring his liquid, lustrous eyes.'

Naomi Bentwich was now daily expecting some explicit indication of Keynes's love, or at least desire, for her. He had dictated a letter to her in which he said that he would be inaccessible to correspondence for three weeks, and she imagined that he might be about to sweep her off on a holiday. But, on going to take dictation at 46 Gordon Square for the first time on 17 March 1921, she noticed 'two passports on a small table in front of us. I choked down my disappointment as well as I could.' Two days later she came back for more dictation. Keynes was in an angry mood, told her the indexing of the *Economic Journal* was going too slowly, but then remarked amiably that he was going to Algiers for a lazy sixteen days in the desert. He left on 20 March, with Sebastian Sprott as 'companion secretary'. In the desert they went through the proofs of his book on probability, Sprott compiling the index. It was on this holiday that Keynes apparently refused to increase a tip he had given to a shoe-shine boy, remarking, 'I will not be be party to debasing the currency.' They were back in London on 12 April.

At home for the vacation, Naomi Bentwich analysed her feelings for Keynes. If only he had confessed his love, 'I should not have hesitated to become his wife at a day's notice. . . .' But he wasn't a good man: he reminded her of Sir Willoughby Patterne in Meredith's *The Egoist*. Her task was to make him a better man. 'It is a more difficult task than getting Johnson to write the Logic, and it needs absolutely different talents – subtlety, humour, tact, brilliance – all sorts of qualities I haven't got. . . . But I shall never despair of myself so long as I can see clearly what ought to be done. . . .'

Miss Bentwich returned to her secretarial duties at Cambridge with Meredith's line in her head: 'The pristine male, if resisted in his suing, concludes that he is scorned, and is infuriated.' Everything Keynes now did seemed to confirm her suspicion that he was angry because scorned. His notes were curt; he was evil and sentimental by turns. 'If only he would have dropped the pretence of officialdom, but he would not.' She wrote in her diary for Thursday, 28 April, 'To-day I expected him to drop the veil, and was strung right up to refuse him. But he had himself well under control, tried his best to make me talk politics in a friendly way; he told me he was writing another article over the weekend, and when I asked him if it would have to be cabled he blinked.' Next day he was in a fury. He dictated his article fast. 'I can always remember how furiously he hissed: "I didn't" when I queried what seemed like a contradiction.'

This was the last dictation Miss Bentwich took from Keynes. Confident that she had a sexual hold over him, she determined to take the offensive, without waiting for the signs of amorousness which Johnson had shown.

My most dear Keynes [she wrote him that same day]

I do understand you – I'm sure I do. You see, I must not be broken by your passion, because it would only mean misery to us both later on, for I am simply not the kind of person you thought I was when you tried to win me that way. But neither am I the intriguing thing you thought me this evening. I have been playing your game simply for your sake; because I have for you the kind of love that sees the loved one's faults and wants to cure them. There is a strength in goodness that there is in nothing else in the Universe; and with that strength added to the power for good that you have in you, you would be the veritable King of Kings I love to think you.

Your great fault is your egoism. It makes you unwilling to take any risks, and that is a great practical weakness. It has put you in my power twice, for instance, in this silly game of intrigue that we've been playing together. But worse than that, it makes you terribly cruel sometimes: to protect yourself, or to get what you want, you allow yourself to do ignoble things which I know you condemn in an hour of cool judgment.

It seems to me, if I can make you love me in a self-forgetful way, it would be a way of giving you the strength you need. That is all I am trying to do.

Keynes's reply came a few hours later. Incredulously Miss Bentwich read:

Your letter just received has filled me with more surprise than I can say. The whole thing is a disastrous misunderstanding on your part. I have no feelings of any kind such as you imagine, and never have had any. I can't even remember most of the incidents on which your imagination seems to have built meanings. I thought your manner a little odd sometimes and a little abrupt – and I stupidly put it down to overwork.

I am immensely sorry to have been the unintentional cause of so much unhappiness. Clearly you can't go on being my secretary and we must bring the arrangement to an end. But I hope you will go on with the *Economic Journal* Index. If you would like to see me, I shall be here at 6 o'clock this evening. But do not come, if you think better not.

Don't think this letter unkind, but I want it to be absolutely clear.

She turned up at 6 p.m. on 30 April. Keynes had no inkling that she was on the verge of hysteria. He flung himself in his chair, stretched out to his full length with his hands in his pocket, and with a mischievous gleam in his eye said, 'Oh Miss Bentwich, that letter, how could you!' He denied he had ever tried to arouse emotions in her. If Miss Pate or others heard of these incidents they would think them figments of her imagination. 'I've been extraordinarily stupid,' he said, flinging his head back and starting to stride round the room.

Miss Bentwich tried to recover from her mistake. 'Well, if I'm mistaken I'm very glad, and let's go on as before.' But Keynes would not have it.

'Oh, no, impossible – quite impossible' and he went on striding about. I told him I was unconvinced and stood up to go. He opened the door, and I was slowly going down the stairs, puzzled, disappointed, half-defiant, when suddenly he darted to the top of the staircase, and resting his forehead on his raised forearm, he looked down at me with the sweetest expression on his face, and the most wonderful look in his eyes – a look which penetrated my soul. A celestial rapture seized me – a beauty overpowering all analysis; then it was that there passed between us that mysterious exchange of looks, full of meaning, in which all was true. . . . I saw God in his eyes – the God in us that loves. . . . I never looked on Keynes again.

VI

'THE MAD WOMAN'

The last article Keynes dictated to Naomi Bentwich appeared in the *Manchester Guardian* on 6 May. It was a comment on the decision of the Reparation Commission, published on 27 April, to fix a total German debt of 132 billion gold marks, or £6.6 b. This turned out to be the lowest figure that was politically possible. Yet when the conjurors had done their work, it became clear that this, too, had been whittled down to no more than 50 billion marks – 'the sum', Lloyd George wrote, 'suggested by the German negotiators at Versailles'.[51] The trick was done by requiring Germany to issue three sets of bonds, but to pay interest and sinking-fund payments only on the first two – which came to 50 billion marks. As a Belgian official, Gaston Furst, put it, 'the Schedule of Payments elegantly resolved the difficulty on which all previous negotiations had foundered: the German debt was reduced in fact to a reasonable amount but this reduction was sufficiently carefully disguised to keep public opinion free from perceiving it and becoming aroused'.[52]

In his article, Keynes praised the Reparation Commission's verdict as 'a signal triumph for the spirit of justice which the German people themselves will not fail to recognise'. He urged the German government to accept the schedule of payments, though he did not believe it could be fulfilled. The Germans did accept, though only after the usual political crisis leading to the formation of a 'government of fulfilment' headed by Joseph Wirth and Walter Rathenau. Keynes 'claimed some credit for having urged the Germans to accept the Ultimatum and said that he had taken particular pains to have the article advising acceptance telegraphed in full to the German press'.[53]

Keynes has been criticised for not recognising that the so-called 'C' bonds were a fiction – that he had won. But Keynes's point was that Germany could not pay even the reduced annuity of £150m. Hence the crisis of default had only been postponed. In this he was proved right. He can be criticised, though, for not emphasising the fictional nature of the 'C' bonds. The existence of the fictional debt undermined any political will to pay off the real debt.

Naomi Bentwich felt she knew exactly what Keynes meant. Her Keynes had always been a partly fictional character, and as time went on she found it easier to create a dream world in which his denials could be interpreted as 'denying not me, but his own thwarted desire', and his writings on reparations as a secret code by which he conducted a subterranean affair with her. In November 1921 she wrote him thirty-two pages setting out her ethical beliefs. 'Here most beautiful Maynard Keynes is my soul.' He sent them back with a short note: 'Thanks for letting me see the enclosed.' On 16 November she wrote, 'Come here and carry me off.'

Keynes now contacted members of the Bentwich family: Naomi should not be left alone. But the passionate, accusing letters continued; occasionally Keynes wrote brief, perfunctory replies. In his circle she was known as the Mad Woman. Had Keynes stopped writing articles, or had she confined her newspaper reading to the religious column of *The Times*, as she vowed to, she might have come to terms with the fact of his indifference. But every public word by him, or mention of him, revived her feelings. Keynes's answers sounded like a stuck gramophone record: 'I don't reply to your letters', he wrote on 27 April 1924, 'because I fear that whatever I may say your imagination will twist it to some illusion. . . . The articles in the *Manchester Guardian* to which you refer are not written by me and I have nothing to do with them.'

Had Keynes, after all, played a subtle game with her? His sexuality was changing. Had he put his toe in the water, only to draw back in alarm when she fell in head over heels? We will never know. In 'My Early Beliefs', Keynes wrote that 'I still suffer incurably from attributing an unreal rationality to other people's beliefs and behaviour. . . .' He was singularly ill-equipped to deal with a severe attack of hysteria. In September 1926, Naomi Bentwich had a complete breakdown and was sent to Switzerland for a cure. Gradually she picked up the pieces of her life. In April 1928 she married Jonas Birnberg, a vegetarian schoolmaster of stern morals who had waited for her for ten years with the patience of Job. 'For us our union would make no heroic demands,' Miss Bentwich wrote.

Naomi Bentwich is the only tragic figure in Keynes's story. In a better world, she would have married W. E. Johnson and lived happily ever, or for many years, afterwards. By the time she came to Keynes she was already emotionally distraught. If, indeed, Keynes played a mild flirtation game with her – and there is only her unreliable intuition to suggest that he did – it was quite the wrong game to play with someone in her state of mind. In the end she recovered her balance and settled for something well short of her dreams and capacities. She survived into her nineties, a tiny woman in Blackheath, convinced that something had happened, after all, those many years ago.

CHAPTER THREE

Keynes's Philosophy of Practice

I

UNFINISHED BUSINESS

On 22 July 1920, Keynes wrote a letter to his mother: 'I've found my Probability MS. (Did I tell you I had lost it?)' *A Treatise on Probability* had been set up in proof in 1913, but its publication was held up by the war. Now, as Keynes told his publisher Daniel Macmillan, he found he had to make an 'enormous number of corrections on his proof' as his 'style of exposition' had greatly improved in the intervening seven years.[1] By 13 September 1920 he had sent off 200 pages to Macmillan for a second proof. He worked at it through the winter of 1920–1. By May 1921 the corrections were finished. 'I feel a little sentimental', Keynes wrote to Macmillan on 22 May, 'at writing the last words of what has occupied me for fifteen years and, apart from the five years interlude of war, has been a pretty constant companion. I shall never attempt anything again on so large a scale.'[2] *A Treatise on Probability* was published in August 1921. Keynes paid £767 11*s* out of his own pocket for 2500 bound volumes.

Despite the corrections, the *Treatise* was a pre-war book, reflecting the way pre-war Cambridge did its philosophy. Its distinctive philosophical ingredients are Rationalism – the appeal to reason rather than observation as the source of knowledge – and Platonism or Realism – the doctrine that ideas are independent objects, Platonic Forms, capable of being perceived by the mind. Thus probability is for Keynes a 'real objective' relation we 'cognise', just as, for G. E. Moore, 'good' was a non-material property of things, whose presence we 'intuit'. This way of doing philosophy was old-fashioned by the 1920s. Wittgenstein asked, '*Where in* the world is a meta-physical subject to be noted?' The question exposes the theological root of Keynes's enterprise. Pre-war Cambridge wanted a metaphysics without God. Platonism was its alternative to Christianity.

Keynes's theory goes all the way back to a paper he read to the Apostles in 1904 when, still an undergraduate, he had attacked G. E. Moore's theory of how people ought to behave in the face of uncertainty.[3] His endeavour was inspired by his determination to enlarge the scope of individual judgement and narrow that of custom as the 'guide of life'. This, in his view, required linking the concept of probability to beliefs rather than to empirical regularities. From this seed grew a massive scholarly tome which, as Dr O'Donnell was the first to point out, became a general theory of rationality, within which the problem of probability is situated.[4] Its published form in 1921 still carries the trace of the quest by Keynes's generation of Apostles for a liberating science of morals to complement G. E. Moore's liberation of ethics from the utilitarian straitjacket of the Victorians.

Substantial as it is, the *Treatise on Probability* is a mere fragment of a larger design for a philosophy of practice which Keynes sketched out half playfully in the summer of 1905. In some notes he called 'Miscellanea Ethica', he had proposed a 'complete ethical treatise' divided into the two divisions of 'Speculative and Practical Ethics'. The first (to be written by Moore) would explore the notion of what was 'good in itself' and erect on it a 'Catalogue Raisonné' of good feelings and fit objects. The second would investigate, or formulate, maxims of conduct, considered as means of attaining these goods, based on the 'curious connexion between "probable" and "ought",' and embracing a science of politics as well as of education.[5] By the time he wrote these notes, Keynes had already mapped out two areas of the 'second division': his paper to the Apostles of 23 January 1904 on 'Ethics in Relation to Conduct' just mentioned, and his essay of November 1904 on 'The Political Doctrines of Edmund Burke', which won the University Members Prize for English Essay. *A Treatise on Probability* is the development of the first paper; the essay on Burke may be seen as prolegomena to the treatise on government he never wrote, but which would have been a fitting, and much needed, complement to his theory of economics. The fact that he chose to work on practical ethics – the second division of his 'complete ethical treatise' – indicates his orientation towards the world rather than the cloister. But Keynes never lost his sense of the conflict between the two – that, as he put it, 'doing good' might interfere with 'being good'. The complete treatise sketched in 'Miscellanea Ethica' would consider the 'nature of beauty and tragedy and love' as well as the 'nature and value of virtue'. On these matters, too, Keynes produced fragments in his early years and throughout his life which influenced his philosophy of practice; in particular, it may be argued, his perception of the ethical value of certain states of mind connected with tragic events limited his enthusiasm for social reform.

II

The origins of Keynes's theory of probability lie in his perception of 'the curious connexion between "probable" and "ought" '. We ought, according to Moore, to act in such a way as to bring about the greatest possible amount of goodness in the universe. But our knowledge of the effects of our actions is bound to be, at best, probabilistic. The best we can hope to have is an expectation or belief that action A will be followed by result B. But what is it that makes such an expectation rational? It was what he considered Moore's failure to answer this question satisfactorily which set Keynes on his intellectual journey.

In the chapter of *Principia Ethica* entitled 'Ethics in Relation to Conduct' Moore had argued that it was impossible to know the probable effects of actions stretching into a remote future. In the absence of such knowledge, the best we could do, in most cases, was to follow moral rules which were generally useful and generally practised, as Hume had suggested. This conclusion stuck in the young Keynes's gullet. 'Before heaven,' he recalled in 1938, 'we claimed to be our own judge in our own case.' He cited the 'unsurpassable individualism of our philosophy", as well as his desire to escape from Victorian morality and Christian 'hocus-pocus'.[6] Moore, he said in 1904, was working with the wrong theory of probability. He was confusing knowledge of probabilities with knowledge of relative frequencies of occurrence, and claiming that if we do not have such knowledge – and particularly if we do not know for certain that any good we can achieve in the near future will not be outweighed by harm in the far future – we have no rational basis for individual judgement. Keynes said this was wrong. All we had to have was *no reason to believe* that any immediate good we achieved would be overturned by distant consequences.[7] Ignorance was not a barrier to individual judgement, but a way of neutralising the unknown. More generally, probabilistic knowledge was a kind of logical knowledge, concerning the 'bearing of evidence' on conclusions.[8] It was to do with beliefs, not with what actually happened. The *Treatise on Probability*, published seventeen years later, was a working out of this audacious insight.

It was conceived as an answer to the question: what are the principles of rational choice and action when the future is unknown or uncertain? It was concerned, that is, with the rationality of means, rather than of ends, though the young Keynes believed that the rightness of actions had to be judged by reference to both. Keynes claimed that the mind could often 'reduce' uncertainty to probability, intuiting that some outcomes are more or less likely than others, or, as he put it, 'perceiving' a probability relation between the evidence a person has (the premiss) and the conclusion of an argument. This perception sanctions a 'degree of belief' in the conclusion. The logic he proposes, that is, is one of partial entailment. The conclusion is any outcome of interest to us: 'It will rain tomorrow,' 'Interest rates will come down in the next six months,' 'There will be an election within the next two years,' 'If I do this, that.'

Probability, it will be seen, has two sides. It is subjective, in the sense of being relative to our knowledge and reasoning power. But, given these, the probability relation is 'unique and objective': everyone similarly equipped in these respects would perceive the same probability, would draw the same conclusion and should act on the same hypothesis. Keynes thought of his theory of probability as the general theory of logical or rational thought, with the deductive logic of certainty as a 'special case'.

Keynes's view of probability as logical *insight* was conceived as an attack on the dominant theory of his day – the frequency theory – which said that probability was a *fact of nature*, which is to say that if one in ten smokers dies of cancer the probability of smokers dying of cancer is 10 per cent. The identification of probability with frequency, Keynes writes, 'is a very grave departure from the established use of words; for it clearly excludes a great number of judgements which are generally believed to deal with probability'.[9] Moreover, the frequency theory assumed the 'inductive hypothesis' and other direct judgements (such as judgements of relevance) which could not themselves be derived from frequencies, but presupposed criteria. Relative frequency of occurrence could be part of the data which enable us to judge a probability; it could not be a probability itself.

The important implication of this is that we can and do have probabilities without numbers. We can have good grounds for preferring one conclusion to another, without having any basis for saying 'This is three times as probable as that.' In fact, most probabilities in Keynes's *Treatise* are non-numerical; they permit approximate rather than exact comparison – 'more or less likely' – with the possibility of being able to assign numbers to probabilities limited to certain restricted states of knowledge. Sometimes, though, probabilities are unknown; sometimes we know them but cannot rank (compare) them. Keynes gives the following example of the difficulty of comparing probabilities based on different arguments:

> Is our expectation of rain, when we start out for a walk, always *more* likely than not, or *less* likely than not, or *as* likely as not? I am prepared to argue that on some occasions *none* of these alternatives hold, and that it will be an arbitrary matter to decide for or against the umbrella. If the barometer is high, but the clouds are black, it is not always rational that one should prevail over another in our minds, or even that we should balance them – though it will be rational to allow caprice to determine us and to waste no time on the debate.[10]

Rational judgement, in other words, might be determined by caprice, non-numerical probabilities or by frequencies, when available.

The domain of rational judgement was thus much more extensive than Hume or Moore had allowed. We can have probabilities when we don't have frequencies; and, even when we have frequencies, all we know for certain is that there is a probability of the conclusion being right: probability begins and ends with probability. Thus Keynes's theory is both optimistic about the power of human reason and pessimistic about its ability to penetrate the secrets of the universe. We have only limited insight into the 'nature of reality'. He quoted Locke to the effect that 'in the greatest part of our concernment, God has afforded only the Twilight, as I may so say, of Probability, suitable, I presume, to the state of Mediocrity and Probationership He has been pleased to place us in here'.[11]

However, we are still some way from a complete statement of Keynes's theory of rational *behaviour* under uncertainty. The requirements of action can be distinguished from the requirements of judgement. In deciding how we ought to act, we need to take into account two further considerations independent of probability which Keynes called 'the weight of argument' and 'moral risk'. By the first Keynes means roughly the *amount* of evidence supporting the probability judgement. This does not necessarily alter the probability, but can alter the amount of confidence we have in our judgement of the probability. For example, in estimating the likely result of a general election one is justified in having more confidence in a large number of opinion polls than in a small number, though both might indicate the same result. The principle of 'moral risk' suggests that it is more rational to aim for a smaller good which seems more probable of attainment than to aim for a larger one which seems less, when the two courses of action have equal probable goodness. Other things being equal, therefore, 'a high weight and the absence of risk increase *pro tanto* the desirability of the action to which they refer'.[12]

One important conclusion for action is that, in most cases, it is more rational to aim for an immediate good than to aim for a remote one, since the first is more likely to have behind it both a greater weight of argument and a higher probability of attainment. Considerations of this kind certainly influenced Keynes's ideas about what it is rational for a reformer to aim at. In particular, they help explain his hostility to revolutionary socialism, which prefers a greater good with a lower probability of attainment to a smaller one with a higher probability of attainment.

In preparing his thesis on probability for publication before the First World War, Keynes added extra sections on induction and statistical inference. Two points only may be mentioned. A thoroughgoing empiricist, he wrote, cannot make use of induction without inconsistency, for the use of the inductive method requires that a prior probability be assigned to its validity.[13] The 100-odd pages on statistical inference are remarkable chiefly for Keynes's attempt to reduce the domain of its validity to those sets of cases for which *stable* as opposed to *average* frequencies are available.[14] He does not tell us, in the *Treatise*, how stable he thought social, as opposed to natural, structures were. It is characteristic of Keynes that he always wanted his data in a raw, not 'cooked' form, and much preferred tables to graphs, so that 'vigilant observation' of changing reality was not hampered by concoctions and manipulations which *assumed* that reality was unchanging. This is the root of his objection to the misuse of econometrics in social science, which goes back to his debate with Karl Pearson in 1910. These additions to the *Treatise* reinforce its central message, which is that the perception of probability, 'weight' and 'risk' are all highly dependent on judgement. Whether or not there is a map in heaven, there is none on earth. Reason, at all times, controls probability, choosing and shaping the data presented to our senses to yield arguments in which one can have greater or lesser degrees of justified belief. That is why Keynes thought of his theory as a branch of logic, to distinguish it from mere belief on one side and statistics on the other.

Students of Keynes have only recently rescued his *Treatise of Probability* from its long neglect. There is now a thriving scholarship, marked by the usual noisy discussion, concerning its intellectual origins, the nature of its epistemology and the question of its links with his economic theory. Interested readers can investigate these matters, as well as a more formal account of the theory itself, in the three appendices to this chapter. The most important point to grasp is that Keynes's concern with the rationality of judgement and behaviour under conditions of uncertainty was lifelong; it gives a distinctive flavour, or style, to his utterances; it is the intellectual motif of his life.

III

THE SCIENCE OF GOVERNMENT

Keynes never produced a treatise on politics, though he clearly felt the need for one.[15] All he left was a 100-page undergraduate essay on the political doctrines of Edmund Burke, the founder of British conservatism.[16] The science of government, Keynes makes clear, is not a direct, but an indirect, means to the attainment of Moore's ethical ends. Its aim is not to bring about states of affairs 'good intrinsically and in isolation', but to facilitate the pursuit of such goods by members of the community.[17] The presumption is that the more prosperous and contented a community is, and the juster its social arrangements, the better will be the states of mind of its inhabitants. The implications of these ideas for economic policy will become clearer later.

Ignoring the claims of Hume, Keynes commended Burke as the first utilitarian political philosopher – the first to espouse consistently the 'greatest happiness' principle. But he emphasises that Burke regarded this as a political, not an ethical, principle, and that he agrees with Burke on this point.[18] The purpose of government is to secure the contentment of the people as constrained by the principle of equity. Keynes accepts equity in the Burkean (or Hayekian) sense of the absence in law or policy of 'artificial discrimination in regard to individuals or to classes'.[19] It is primarily in this sense that Keynes deploys the term 'social justice' in his mature writings. Keynes's main argument for price stability is that its absence produces inequity, which leads to social discontent. Equity, as defined here, can be defended on utilitarian grounds. Keynes never showed himself much interested in the distribution issue raised by an appeal to justice.

The object of politics is social contentment. Keynes emphasises such goods as 'physical calm' and 'material comfort'.[20] The first is especially interesting. Throughout his life Keynes was personally affected by what he calls 'bad states of nerves' produced by disturbing public events. He then assumes, without further argument, that 'the government that sets the happiness of the governed before it will serve a good purpose, whatever the ethical theory from which it draws its inspiration'.[21]

Turning to the methods of politics, Keynes endorses the Moore–Burke criterion of 'moral risk', which, as we have seen, he was to incorporate in his *Treatise on Probability*:

> Burke ever held, and held rightly, that it can seldom be right . . . to sacrifice a present benefit for a doubtful advantage in the future. . . . It is not wise to look too far ahead; our powers of prediction are slight, our command over results infinitesimal. It is therefore the happiness of our own contemporaries that is our main concern; we should be very chary of sacrificing large numbers of people for the sake of a contingent end, however advantageous that may appear. . . . We can never know enough to make the chance worth taking. There is this further consideration that is often in need of emphasis: it is not sufficient that the state of affairs which we seek to promote should be better than the state of affairs which preceded it; it must be sufficiently better to make up for the evils of the transition.[22]

As Keynes was to put it in his *Tract on Monetary Reform* (1923): 'But this *long run* is a misleading guide to current affairs. *In the long run* we are all dead.'[23]

The undergraduate Keynes criticised Burke, as he did Moore, not for his 'method', which he regarded as correct, but for his assumption that the best results on the whole are to be got by sticking to 'rules', even if these are based on irrational prejudices. In short, Burke put the claims of peace and expediency over those of truth and rationality. The nearest he came to forsaking his own maxim was when he decided to speak out against the French Revolution. 'For, on this occasion,' Keynes wrote, 'he maintained that the best possible course for a rational man was to expound the truth and take his chance on the event.' But remarks like this cannot be construed as advocacy of truth-telling 'regardless of consequences', for what Keynes was arguing against Burke (and in the spirit of Mill) was that 'whatever the immediate consequences of a new truth may be, there is a high probability that truth will in the long run lead to better results than falsehood'.[24] The politics of lying, as Keynes would later say of Lloyd George, was self-defeating even in its own terms. Truth-telling was thus an important element in Keynes's philosophy of practice. His commitment to it is the most important example of rule-consequentialism and long-run perspectives in his thinking.

Keynes explained Burke's mistrust for truth in two ways: he felt the masses would be more contented and the state as well as morals more secure if customs were left undisturbed, and he 'suspected the current grounds of right action were, in many cases, baseless . . .'.[25] The second argument is the same he attributed to Moore; the *Treatise on Probability* can thus be seen as his answer to both Moore and Burke. Keynes went to some lengths to argue that rationality is compatible with democracy because, in practice, the scope of democracy is severely limited, and because over time its exercise might improve the rationality of citizens.[26] However, the second was never an important strand in his thinking. He looked to an 'educated bourgeoisie' to set political standards for the community, just as he looked to groups like Bloomsbury to set aesthetic standards. His efforts to separate the technical from the political aspects of ruling are consistent with the views he expressed in his Burke essay.

If Burke's mistrust of reason pushed Keynes away from political conservatism, another set of arguments in Burke, concerning property rights, pushed him away from socialism. Burke defended existing property rights on two grounds. Redistribution of wealth would make no real difference to the poor, since they greatly outnumbered the rich. But, in addition, it would 'considerably reduce in numbers those who could enjoy the undoubted benefits of wealth and who would confer on the state the advantages which the presence of wealthy citizens always brings'. Keynes felt that this double argument 'undoubtedly carried very great weight: in certain types of communities it is overwhelming, and it must always be one of the most powerful rejoinders to any scheme which has equalisation as its ultimate aim'. However, Burke carried his defence of existing property rights to extremes which conflicted with his own principle of expediency. He was so concerned to defend the 'outworks' of the property system that he did not see that this might endanger the 'central system' itself.[27] There could be no absolute sacredness of contract. It was the 'absolutists of contract', Keynes wrote in his *Tract on Monetary Reform*, 'who are the parents of Revolution'[28] – a good Burkean attitude, but one that Burke himself sometimes ignored.

In his political philosophy, Keynes married two key elements of Burkean conservatism – contentment as the purpose of government, together with avoidance of risk – to two key elements in reforming liberalism – a commitment to truth-telling and belief in the possibility of rational individual judgement. He rejected those elements in Burke which may be called 'unthinking conservatism' and those elements in socialism which aimed at ideal states and used means which infringe the principle of 'least risk'. This was very much the political temper of the Middle Way which Keynes espoused in the inter-war years.

IV

THE VALUE OF TRAGEDY

Neither Keynes's politics nor his economics was logically or morally entailed by Moore's *Principia Ethica*. Keynes did, in fact, usually make the judgement that the more contented, more prosperous people were, the better, ethically, the world would be. But he thought of this, not as a necessary conclusion, but as one which always rested on a balance of probabilities. It is his scepticism concerning the self-evident connection between ethical goodness and social reform which distances him most strikingly from the general run of social reformers of his day. Understanding the intellectual sources of this scepticism explains, therefore, much that is otherwise puzzling in Keynes's philosophy of practice.

In his ethical beliefs, Keynes remained an unreconstructed follower of G. E. Moore. 'I see no reason to shift from the fundamental intuitions of *Principia Ethica*. . . . It is still my religion under the surface,' he declared in 1938, thirty-five years after the appearance of Moore's 'New Testament'. 'By far the most valuable things which we know or can imagine', wrote Moore in his final chapter on 'The Ideal', 'are certain states of consciousness, which may be roughly described as the pleasures of human intercourse and the enjoyment of beautiful objects.' He added that it is 'only for the sake of these things – in order that as much as possible of them may at some time exist – that anyone can be justified in performing any public or private duty; that they are the *raison d'être* of virtue; that it is they . . . that form the rational ultimate end of human action and the sole criterion of social progress: these appear to be truths which have been generally overlooked.'[29]

This criterion poses an obvious problem for the social reformer. (We leave to one side the insuperable problem that we have no direct knowledge of any states of mind other than our own.) The increase in prosperity, contentment, justice, GDP or whatever it is we use to measure progress is clearly not the same thing as an increase in ethical goodness as Moore conceived it. Any social reformer who accepts Moore's ethics (or for that matter those Christian ethics which emphasise holiness or sainthood as the human ideal) is obliged to make a judgement about the consequences of material progress on the states of mind of those experiencing it.

Moore offers one way forward. Good states of mind, he says, are 'highly complex *organic unities*' which contain both an experiencing subject and an appropriate object of experience. Such objects need have no ethical value of their own. But, if they do not exist, the value of the experience will be less good than if they did. The social reformer can then claim that by improving the quality of the objects of experience he is increasing the ethical goodness of the universe, even though his policies do not improve at all good states of mind in isolation. This is a cogent argument, and Keynes undoubtedly acted on it as philanthropist, as builder and by accepting the chairmanship of the Arts Council at the end of his life. A follower of Moore might also interest himself in raising standards of education and of comfort insofar as these improved the intelligence, sensibility and comeliness of the population.

The snag comes with Moore's class of 'mixed goods', in which good states of mind *depend* on the existence of evil states of affairs. Moore gave as an example the dependence of pity on suffering.[30] Keynes was acutely aware of the 'mixed goods' problem. Feelings of compassion, courage, justice, which have positive ethical value, could be said to depend on the existence of suffering, danger, injustice: the First World War was a prime example of the 'mixed goods' dilemma. To the extent that social reform rids the world of bad states of affairs, it may be decreasing the total of ethical goodness. Keynes's hesitating line of argument in face of his dilemma is illustrated by a passage in a paper he first read to the Apostles in 1910, and which he read again in 1921. Keynes is discussing tragedy:

> I am not certain that all tragic states of affairs are bad on the whole, when everything has been taken into account, or that the goodness of the states of mind, if it is very great, may not outweigh the badness of states of affairs. . . . [But] it is possible, I think, to imagine two states of affairs, one of which is tragic or unjust, and the other not, such that the states of mind in each are of exactly equal value, and to believe that the tragic state of affairs is less desirable than the other.

But how is this to be arranged? Keynes gave an ingenious, if unconvincing, answer in a letter he wrote to Peter Lucas, whose book on tragedy had just been published, in 1928:

> In actual life many of the feelings which we deem noblest and most worth having are apt to be associated with troubles, misfortunes, and disasters. In itself we generally judge the state of mind of the hero going into battle as good – but it is such a pity that he should be killed. Similarly, feelings of sympathy are good in themselves. In fact,

the worst of real life is that feelings good in themselves are too often stimulated or occasioned or provoked by evil happenings. If, on the other hand, it were possible to sympathise with, enjoy at second hand, or admire, the noble feelings *without* the evil happenings which generally accompany them in real life, we would get the best of both worlds. Now, as it seems to me, the object of Tragedy is precisely to secure for us a conjuncture in which this comes about. . . . We come into contact with noble feelings and escape the bad practical consequences. . . .

All of this is connected with my favourite dilemma – the difficulty or impossibility of both being good and doing good. In Tragedy we can witness the spectacle of people being good in a realm which is completely divorced from all consequences, so that we do not have to weigh up against the excellence of being good the appalling nature of the consequences of such behaviour and the events associated with it.[31]

The cost of heroism, or pity, in other words, can be reduced to the price of a theatre ticket: a good bargain for the social reformer, but hardly likely to convince the sceptic that the states of mind of the spectator hero and the real hero are of equal value.

Moore's *Principia Ethica*, to whose fundamental intuitions Keynes remained faithful to the end, thus offers no philosophically based justification for extensive social reform. The doctrine of organic unities may be interpreted to provide a limited criterion for social reform, and Keynes did so interpret it. But it is extremely hard to know, by reference to it, whether ethical progress is taking place. This is because many of Moore's goods are 'mixed goods'. Moore's 'ideal' utilitarianism is clearly inferior as a criterion for social action to Bentham's hedonistic utilitarianism, which proportions goodness straightforwardly to pleasurable feelings, and thus gives strong support to the judgement that an improvement in material welfare adds to the sum of goodness. Keynes does generally make the straightforward Benthamite judgement that an increase in happiness will increase the sum of goodness. But when he tries to reconcile hedonistic with ideal utilitarianism he exhibits considerable intellectual discomfort. And his recognition of the ethical gap between the two concepts, as well as his commitment to, and understanding of, Moore's ethics did serve to limit his *passion* for social reform.

V

THE RECEPTION OF THE *TREATISE*

Keynes's early speculations on ethics and politics remained in the private domain. His *Treatise on Probability* was, however, published. The earliest reviews were appreciative. C. D. Broad, a follower of Moore and Russell, and four years younger than Keynes, expressed himself in 'substantial agreement' with him. In his review in *Mind* he gave a homely illustration of the 'essential relativity of probability':

> Thus, if the only fact that you know about a man is that he has recently swallowed arsenic, it is highly probable that he will be dead in the next half hour. If you afterwards get the additional piece of information that he has taken an emetic, the probability that he will die in the next half hour, on the combined data, is much smaller. Neither probability is in any way more 'correct' than the other.[32]

Bertrand Russell considered 'the mathematical calculus' to be 'astonishingly powerful' and 'the book as a whole one which it is impossible to praise too highly'. But he refused to accept the twin theses that probability was indefinable and that many probabilities are not numerically measurable. Russell hankered after a 'modified form' of the frequency theory.[33]

The old Apostle and statistician Charles Sanger was pleased that Keynes 'does not prefer algebra to earth', and quoted approvingly a sentence from the *Treatise* to the effect that 'sensible investigators only employ the correlation coefficient to test or confirm conclusions at which they have arrived on other grounds'. The *Spectator*'s 'S' found that 'Professor Keynes's equations demand a mental activity which does not accord well with reading.'[34]

Young Cambridge was unconvinced. Keynes wrote to Broad on 31 January 1922,

> I find that Ramsey and the other young men . . . are quite obdurate, and still believe that *either* Probability is a definitely measurable entity, probably connected with frequency, *or* it is of merely psychological importance and is definitely non-logical. I recognise that they can raise some very damaging criticisms against me on these lines. But all the same I feel great confidence that they are wrong.[35]

Frank Ramsey had come up to Trinity from Winchester in 1920, aged seventeen. Keynes thought him 'by far and away the most brilliant undergraduate who has appeared for many years on the borderline between Philosophy and Mathematics'.[36] A theorem he wrote as a schoolboy was up to fellowship-dissertation standard, in the opinion of his father, the President of Magdalene College; his brother became Archbishop of Canterbury. Ramsey was a huge, shambling bear of a man, worshipped for his intellect and loved for his sweetness of character. He became an Apostle in 1921 and was elected a Fellow of King's in 1924. As a member of the Society he struck a new note. After yet another endless discussion of the value of different states of mind, Ramsey told the brethren that such discussion 'although a pleasant way of passing the time, is not discussing *anything whatever*, but simply comparing notes' (italics added).[37] This was the authentic philosophical voice of the post-war generation, soon to be turned on Keynes's pre-war edifice.

To appreciate the damage that Ramsey was able to inflict on the *Treatise*, one must understand that Keynes's enterprise was a product of the pre-war Cambridge way of doing philosophy. At the time Moore, Russell and Keynes were all philosophic realists: they insisted on the *reality* of the intuitive knowledge which was the foundation of all knowledge. They believed that to *perceive* qualities or logical relations was to perceive *something*; that the indefinable objects of thought had a 'real' existence, and that this reality was in some way necessary to guarantee the truth of the intuition. To Moore 'good' and 'bad' were non-natural properties which *existed* by virtue of their being objects of thought. Russell confessed that when he wrote *The Principles of Mathematics* he shared with Frege a belief in the Platonic reality of numbers, which people a timeless realm 'of Being'.[38] Keynes, too, wrote that probability is a 'real objective relation' which we 'cognise'.[39] All three, that is, believed in the existence of a Platonic world of adjectives and fractions. If this now seems a curious aberration, it has to be set in the context of the quest for a new scientific metaphysics to assuage post-theological *Angst* and hold at bay the 'cosmos of chaos' which had so alarmed Henry Sidgwick. Russell wanted 'absolutely impersonal certain knowledge' in the 'kind of way in which people want religious faith'.[40] Keynes, too, hoped that 'When we allow that probable knowledge is, nevertheless, "real", a new method of argument can be introduced into metaphysical discussions.'[41] His metaphysical longings are expressed somewhat more ecstatically in a letter to Strachey on 7 February 1906: 'Only when after a thousand existences and a thousand loves we have become purified from Not-Being and are a perfect harmony, may we fly on wings of love into the heaven of Pythagoras and Plato and McTaggart. . . . I am sure it must all be true. We are mystic numbers and the sum is not yet solved.'

This way of doing philosophy was to be uprooted by Wittgenstein and Ramsey. In 1920, Ramsey was collaborating with C. K. Ogden in translating a mysterious manuscript Wittgenstein had sent to Cambridge from Italy. Little was known in Keynes's circle of Wittgenstein's fate, or work, when the war ended. He had left Cambridge in 1914, enlisted in the Austrian army, fought, survived and been taken prisoner by the Italians a few days after the armistice. In the war, he had written a book which, he now claimed in a letter to Russell, 'had solved our problems finally'. He expressed himself in similar terms to Keynes, in a postcard dated 12 June 1919: 'Have you done any more work on probability? My MS contains a few lines about it which, I believe, solve the essential question' – not the most tactful of remarks.[42] But then Wittgenstein did not know what tact was. That was the secret of his genius.

Wittgenstein was the major figure in the downfall of Keynes's theory, though he never referred to it. It was not the few paragraphs which he devoted to probability in the *Tractatus Logico-Philosophicus* (1922) which proved fatal but his denial of the existence of the self-evident truths on which the constructions of Moore, Russell and Keynes were based. Logic – or philosophy – could not penetrate to reality. Its 'necessary truths' were all 'empty tautologies' which tell us nothing about matters of fact.[43] There were no such things as metaphysical facts.

Wittgenstein carried to a heroic conclusion Russell's austere view of language. The essential business of language, thought Russell, was to assert or deny facts. A logical proposition, Wittgenstein argued, is a picture, true or false, of a fact, and has in common with this fact a certain structure. 'In the picture and the pictured there must be something identical in order that one can be a picture of the other at all.'[44] But what is in common between the structure of the sentence and the structure of the fact cannot be 'said' if sentences were simply pictures of facts. Practically the whole of philosophy had been an enquiry into what connects what we say with what exists. Almost the whole of philosophy was, therefore, a grammatical mistake. In his wartime notebooks Wittgenstein wrote, 'The correct method in philosophy would really be to say nothing except what can be said, i.e. what belong to natural science . . . and then whenever someone else tried to say something metaphysical to show him that he had not given any reference to certain signs in his sentence.'[45] Or as he put it aphoristically in the *Tractatus*, 'What can be said at all must be said clearly, and whereof one cannot speak thereof one must be silent.' Keynes's theory of probability was, strictly speaking, meaningless.

Wittgenstein's pronunciamentos constitute the most important philosophical manifesto of this century. They redefined the business of philosophy. Its job was not to sift the true from the false (this is left to science), but to determine the frontier between sense and nonsense, between real questions and pseudo-questions. Obviously, once it had done this, it would become redundant. One fruit of the *Tractatus* was the doctrine of logical positivism, which identified knowledge with mathematics and science, and declared all the rest of language to be meaningless utterance. This was true to the letter, but not to the spirit, of Wittgenstein. Wittgenstein did not think non-sense was nonsense in the dismissive sense of the term. Contained in non-sense were the profoundest questions of life. But they were beyond the reach of language. The contrast Bruce Duffy draws between Russell and Wittgenstein applies here to Keynes and Wittgenstein too: 'whereas Russell was the Enlightenment man who felt that everything could be rationally discussed and attained through diligent effort, Wittgenstein, that most impatient of men, was the desert mystic, subsisting on bread, rainwater, and silence'.[46] In fact, all three were great talkers, but whereas Russell and Keynes were excellent conversationalists, Wittgenstein was a tortured monologist, who gave the impression of trying to expel words from his system.

Wittgenstein's co-translator, Frank Ramsey, had two bites at Keynes's theory. In the *Cambridge Magazine* of October 1921, he accused Keynes of muddling up the perception with the existence of probability relations, pointing out the lack of necessary correspondence between the two. His fundamental attack was launched in the paper called 'Truth and Logic' read to the Cambridge Moral Science Club in 1925. After an hour or so of beautiful demolition work little of the baroque edifice of the *Treatise* was left standing.

Probability, Ramsey said, had both an objective and a subjective side. Both statistical and epistemological interpretations of the concept had a basis in ordinary language. Probability often meant proportion. If we say the probability of recovery from smallpox is three-quarters, we mean that is the proportion of smallpox cases which recover. Probability is thus a property of nature. But we also have the authority of language for thinking of it as 'partial belief'. When someone says that three-quarters of smallpox victims will recover, we may reply, 'That is probably true.' How do we justify the second statement? Keynes says, 'We perceive it.' We proceed in other words from full belief in the evidence to partial belief in the conclusion that recovery is three-quarters likely in any particular case or set of cases.

Ramsey's criticism was direct. He denied that there were:

> any such things as the probability relations he [Keynes] describes. He supposes that, at any rate in certain cases, they can be perceived; but speaking for myself I feel confident that this is not true. I do not perceive them, and if I am to be persuaded that they exist it must be by argument; moreover I shrewdly suspect that others do not perceive them either, because they are able to come to so very little agreement as to which of them relates any two given propositions.[47]

Ramsey's statement, once made, seemed obvious. The Emperor had no clothes. All Keynes had established was that we make judgements of probability, not that there were objective probability relations corresponding to them.

Keynes's mistake, Ramsey felt, lay in mixing up factual and logical arguments. We may infer a factual conclusion from a factual premiss, but we cannot say the conclusion is logically necessary. The main requirement in logic is that arguments should be non-contradictory. But with Keynes's probability arguments 'we could accept the premises and utterly reject the conclusions without any sort of inconsistency or contradiction'.[48] Inductive arguments are not weaker versions of deductive ones. They are to do with the acquisition of beliefs, deductive arguments with the laws of thought. Keynes's theory of probability mixed up the logic of discovery with the logic of implication.

Ramsey tackled the problem of what made beliefs rational along different lines. Agents are conceived of as adopting strategies for getting what they want, that is they are assumed to be equipped with consistent preferences. The rationality of such strategies is to be judged by their success. People start by attaching probabilities to different possible outcomes. These probabilities are subjective – they have no necessary sanction in logic or nature. Ramsey next construes these subjective degrees of belief as betting rates: all probabilities can be reduced to numbers. The first rationality requirement is that the odds agents are willing to offer on different propositions must not be such that a clever gambler can make a 'Dutch book' or profit against them whatever happens.[49] The second requirement is that strategies should be consistent with the facts. Personal or subjective probabilities are brought closer to objective probabilities through a learning process. Full rationality is reached when, in the words of Martin Hollis, 'starting price odds reflect the merits of the horses'.[50] Ramsey gives the following example: from the observation that a toadstool is yellow, a person proceeds to infer that it is unwholesome. The degree of belief which it would be best for him to have in this idea is clearly that which equalled the fraction of toadstools which were in fact unwholesome. The learning process is inductive. Unlike Keynes, Ramsey takes a pragmatic view of induction. It is a 'mental habit'. The only way of judging mental habits is to ask whether they 'work'. Whatever its status in epistemology, induction is a useful mental habit.[51]

Ramsey's critique won the day. By the early 1930s, Ramsey's friend Richard Braithwaite was calling Keynes's theory of probability 'very puzzling indeed'. 'Does Keynes really perceive his logical relations of probability holding between two propositions? If he does not, what reason is there to suppose they exist? For they are quite unlike other logical relations.' Moore's ethical theory too was in retreat, Cambridge philosophers – Broad excepted – analysing ethical propositions in terms of subjective statements of approval and disapproval. Modern philosophy had arrived. A Chinese philosopher visiting Cambridge to learn about the nature of truth discovered he had learnt a great deal about the correct use of the English language.[52]

Although it is often said that Ramsey merely 'developed' Keynes's theory in a constructive way, the two approaches come out of different mental universes. In Keynes's world, notions of objective goodness and probability form the foundation stones of ethical and practical reason. Without such foundations thought is 'adrift'. Ramsey's world is made up of preferences and bets. It is a world in which the subjective and pragmatic character of thought is accepted. We use techniques which work. Keynes's people are thinkers, and he equips them with the tools of thought: logic. Ramsey's people are actors, and he equips them with the tools of action: calculating power.

The contrast between the two men is generational. Whereas Keynes's generation saw in metaphysics a salvation from doubt, Ramsey's generation threw it out because they felt it responsible for the First World War. Show that some statement is nonsense, they seemed to be saying, and perhaps people will stop arguing about it, and concentrate their energies on problems which can be solved. Channel reason into science, not metaphysics, and you will get a peaceful, prosperous world. Thus one illusion replaced another: the metaphysical illusion giving way to the positivist illusion that fanaticism is a kind of error rather than a need, that evil is solely due to defective thinking and that 'human behaviour is completely determined by the state of knowledge'.[53]

Keynes appreciated the contrast between the pre-war and post-war worlds, but he was loath to surrender the truths hard won by Moore, himself and the pre-war Apostles, or perhaps merely salvaged from the wreck of religion. He also had sufficient historical culture to feel disquiet at the suggestion that mankind's past philosophical efforts were all mistakes which should be jettisoned in the interests of mental hygiene. He sets his one published comment on the *Tractatus* in the context of the post-war mood.

> Progress is a soiled creed [he wrote in 1923] black with coal dust and gunpowder; but we have not discarded it. We believe and disbelieve, and mingle faith with doubt. . . .
>
> We today are the most creedless of men. Every one of our religious and political constructions is moth-eaten. Our official religions have about as much practical influence on us as the monarchy of the Lord Mayor's coach. But we no longer substitute for them the militant scepticism of Voltaire and Hume, or the humanitarian optimism of Bentham and Comte and Mill, or the far-fetched abstractions of Hegel. Our newest Spinoza [Wittgenstein] gives us frozen comfort: 'We feel that even if all *possible* questions of knowledge be answered, our problems of life are still not touched at all. But in that event there is obviously no question left; and just this is the answer.'[54]

How far Keynes was shaken out of his pre-war beliefs by Wittgenstein and Ramsey is hard to tell. (See Appendix 3 at the end of this chapter for further discussion.) Keynes spent many hours talking and arguing with Wittgenstein on the latter's return to Cambridge in 1929 and it must be supposed that they talked philosophy. But no trace of these conversations has survived. It was characteristic of Keynes to admire the brilliance of Ramsey's performance and love him for it. Following Ramsey's death at the age of twenty-six in 1930, Richard Braithwaite edited a collection of his published and unpublished writings. Keynes must have had in mind Ramsey's critique of his *Treatise* when he wrote, in a review of the Braithwaite collection, that the essays were a 'remarkable example of how the young can take up the story at the point to which the previous generation had brought it a little out of breath, and then proceed forward without taking more than about a week thoroughly to digest everything which had been done up to date . . .'.

In his review, Keynes declared that the published version of Ramsey's criticism of his own theory of probability was very interesting 'both in itself and as showing in some detail how far his mind was departing . . . from the formal and objective treatment of his immediate predecessors.' He acknowledged his own debt to Russell, whose early work had suggested that the field of logic could be 'enormously extended'. But the 'gradual perfection of the formal treatment' at the hands of Russell, Wittgenstein and Ramsey himself had been to 'empty it of content and to reduce it more and more to dry bones, until finally it [logic] seemed to exclude not only all experience, but most of the principles, usually reckoned logical, of reasonable thought'. Ramsey had been led to a concept of 'human logic' as distinct from 'formal logic'. He had argued:

> against the view which I had put forward, that probability is concerned not with objective relations between propositions but (in some sense) with degrees of belief . . . Thus the calculus of probabilities belongs to formal logic. But the basis of our degrees of belief – or the *a priori* probabilities, as they used to be called – is part of our human outfit . . . So far I yield to Ramsey – I think he is right. But in attempting to distinguish 'rational' degrees of belief from belief in general he was not yet, I think, quite successful. It is not getting to the bottom of induction merely to say that it is a useful mental habit. Yet in attempting to distinguish a 'human' logic from formal logic on the one hand and descriptive psychology on the other, Ramsey may have been pointing the way to the next field of study when formal logic has been put into good order and its highly limited scope properly defined.[35]

This was Keynes's only published comment on reactions to his book. By the time it came out his attention had switched once more to the reparations issue. Naturally there was some correspondence – with Broad, with the young French logician Jean Nicod, with Professor Bachelier of Dijon University. In 1927 there was discussion of a German edition. But Keynes no longer thought about probability, though probability permeated his thought.

APPENDIX I

Philosophic Background to the Treatise

Keynes worked on his thesis on probability in 1906 'under the joint influence of Moore's *Principia Ethica* and Russell's *Principia Mathematica*'.[56] What he got equally from Moore and Russell (but perhaps also from his father) was the idea that logic was the foundation of philosophy, and that the foundational truths of ethics, mathematics and science were self-evident logical propositions, incapable of proof or disproof. A crucial debt was to Russell's extension of logic from its traditional subject–predicate form, exemplified by the syllogism, to include 'real' or 'external' relations, asymmetrical and transitive, like greater and less, similar and different. Russell calls a relation such as 'A is greater than B' or 'A is redder than B' 'a fundamental notion, which is not capable of definition'.[57] The recognition of such relations was fundamental to any principle of ordering, or ranking. Equally important was Russell's distinction between magnitude and quantity. A magnitude is 'anything which is greater or less than something else'; but magnitudes differ from quantities in the sense of being indivisible, and therefore not expressible as fractions of each other.[58] It makes sense to call A happier than B, not to say he is 50 per cent more happy. Russell's emphasis on the relational aspect of logic was fundamental to Keynes's theory of probability, though Keynes extended the scope of logical relations to include non-demonstrative inference.

This revival of Cambridge Platonism has to be set in the context of the revolt against philosophic Idealism or Hegelianism, which, by denying the reality of external relations, seemed to make impossible a 'science' of ethics or mathematics or practical conduct.

Idealism is the doctrine that reality is mental. Idealism is contrasted with Realism, the belief that reality exists independently of our perception of it. To Realists, beliefs do not construct reality, but picture it.

Empiricism and Rationalism are two contrasted methods of knowing. Empiricists hold that all our knowledge of the world rests on experience, given through the senses. Rationalism holds that reason is a prior source of knowledge, giving us the concepts needed to 'make sense' of experience. The two ways of knowing are compatible with either Idealism or Realism, but historically the usual pairings are Idealism/Empiricism and Realism/ Rationalism.

Idealism arises from the familiar paradox of empiricism. From the chain of propositions that we know the world only through experience, that we experience only appearances or sense data, not things in themselves, and that these appearances depend on us experiencing them, we are led to the hasty conclusion that all things that exist – all objects of knowledge – must be in our minds: 'esse est percipi'. A theory of knowledge which claims to tell us about the world tells us only about ourselves.

Idealism has its own answer to radical scepticism: the world is independent of our minds after all because it is in God's mind. Reality is what God knows, and we have privileged access to the contents of the divine mind. God's existence is the guarantee of an objective reality outside ourselves; it validates our science and ethics. This was Bishop Berkeley's famous argument for deism.

Abolish God, and we are back in the hole. Kant tried to get us out of it by saying that the facts of experience are grasped by means of transcendental truths. But, since these truths are supplied by us, reality is still trapped in the circle of our thought. As Russell pointed out, to say that logic is contributed by our nature does not guarantee the truth of logic, because our nature may change.[59]

After Kant came Hegel and the refloating of Idealism in the form in which Moore and Russell attacked it. The problem was familiar, the tools were partly new. Given the identity of reality and experience, how can we escape from subjectivity? Experience tells us, Hegel said, that history is the unfolding of Spirit or Reason, the 'cunning of reason' being its utilisation of men's passionate conflicts to further its self-realisation. The rational is fully realised when men's actions conform to its laws. Thus Spirit or Idea is the objective principle in the universe which grows with thought itself.[60]

Hegelianism came to Cambridge via the Oxford-trained philosopher Francis Herbert Bradley, whose monumental *Appearance and Reality*, published in 1893, started, by the reaction it provoked, the whole modern movement in Anglo-Saxon philosophy. Assuming that 'to be real is to be indissolubly one thing with sentience', Bradley proceeded to prove, by an amazing dialectical display, that the only reality that exists is Absolute Reality. Only of the Absolute can we say it is true or good or beautiful or anything else without contradiction.

The centrepiece of the demonstration is Bradley's doctrine of internal relations. Any relation, he said, must penetrate the *being* of both its terms, so they would both be something else if they were parts of a different relation. The same man cannot be both father and son, 'because he is modified in one way by the relationship of fatherhood and in another by the relation of sonship'. This meant, as Russell pointed out, that there can never be two facts concerning the same thing.[61] We cannot know any single thing apart from all its possible relations, which is a way of saying that nothing *really* exists or *is* or has logical stability except some entity which contains all the possible relations in the universe, which Bradley called the Absolute, and Russell called a pot of treacle.*

*Technically, only the Absolute can be the subject of predicates. Stated this way Idealism is certainly a 'system for extremists'. (G. J. Warnock, *English Philosophy since 1900*, 53.)

That Hegel came to Cambridge via Bradley was bad for his reputation, but fatal for Bradley's. Whether Bradley believed that only the Absolute is real is doubtful. He saw the Absolute as the Spirit within the world of appearance trying to 'real-ise' itself. It is this quality of striving for wholeness which makes the parts of the universe more than appearances. All this was true to Hegel's spirit. It was the fanaticism of Bradley's attempt to reduce Hegel's vision to formal logic which proved his undoing. For it then enabled Hegelianism to be attacked as bad grammar, which is really the form which the revolt against Idealism took.

Moore and Russell felt themselves to be drowning in Bradley's pot of treacle. They wanted to know that science and ethics were true and not part of the contradictory world of appearances. At the end of the 1890s, they both abandoned Hegelianism. In place of the striving Spirit they postulated a reality – a conceptual order – independent of, and above, experience, thus reinstating the Platonic dichotomy between experience and reason, appearance and reality, which Hegel had tried to overcome. Their aim was not to bury metaphysics, but to rescue it from the Idealists.

Moore and Russell disagreed with the Idealists not about ultimate values but about how to do philosophy. Moore did not attack the beliefs of Bradley and McTaggart but what he saw as their bad arguments. Typically, he would take some Idealist proposition – for example, that Reality is Spiritual – and then try to *isolate* the crucial argument which purported to establish the conclusion (a method which Idealist philosophers would have rejected). He would then show that the argument as stated was ambiguous, restate it in a form which seemed to him intelligible and proceed to show that, in this form, it was false. Not surprisingly, Idealists found that, after their arguments had been remoulded by Moore, they seemed much less convincing than the originals. Bosanquet complained that Moore's method never allowed the 'central reasonings' of great thinkers to emerge; and the same could be said of Russell. But their aim, in all this, was reconstruction. That, largely as a result of their demolition work, all metaphysical statements came to be regarded as nonsense was no part of their intention.

The Platonist tradition goes back to the Cambridge Platonists of the seventeenth century. It accepts that reality is spiritual or conceptual, while denying that it is mental; hence the postulate of a non-natural order. As against the empiricists it claims that what the mind 'receives' are not just sense data but messages from the Platonic world of Ideas or Forms, 'suprasensible . . . more real than the common world of sense, the unchangeable world of ideas, which alone gives to the world of sense whatever pale reflection of reality may belong to it.'[62] These ideas, which Russell calls universals, are the foundational truths of ethics, logic, science and mathematics. Reason is the source of knowledge.

The attempt to retrieve a true metaphysics started at Cambridge just before Keynes got interested in probability. Moore's classical article, 'The Refutation of Idealism' (*Mind*, 1903) accused the Idealists of confusing the existence of the object with the awareness of it. Russell's main attack from 1901 onwards was on Bradley's doctrine of organic or internal relations: the view that the terms of any relation so modify each other that nothing has a stable existence, or can be known, except Absolute Reality. The tendency and aim of these attacks was to establish the independence of the object known from the act of knowing, and more especially to argue that our knowledge of the world presupposes the existence of a class of self-evident truths independent of experience. By 1913 Idealism was generally regarded as overthrown, at least in Cambridge. McTaggart alone of the established philosophers upheld the older doctrine.

Keynes's *Treatise on Probability* bears the impress of this way of doing philosophy. Reason, not experience, is the source of our knowledge of probabilities. Probability is not an appearance, but a 'real objective relation'. Our perception of this relationship is the foundation for all our common-sense and scientific reasonings; in particular, it underlies all inductive arguments.

APPENDIX 2

Probability

The history of probability, as Ian Hacking notes, is both epistemological and statistical.[63] It is about what it is reasonable to believe and what is likely to happen, and about the relationship between the two. Someone looking to probability to 'guide conduct' was bound to approach the subject from the side of belief, since if knowledge of probabilities is confined to statistical regularities, probability is not much of a 'guide of life'.

In approaching it from this angle, Keynes was reviving a semi-dormant tradition. It was Leibniz who first argued cogently that 'probability is in proportion to what we know'. But, by the time Keynes took up the subject, probability had come to mean a ratio of favourable to total events, a matter of natural arrangements in the universe.

In chapter 7 of the *Treatise* Keynes provides a sparkling historical account. The oldest doctrine was Aristotle's: the probable is what 'usually happens'. We know that an event will probably happen if some other event to which it has been joined in the past happens. All empirical theories of probability stem from arguments of this kind. The main early issue was about what kinds of evidence or experience were relevant to our knowledge of probabilities: 'testimony of persons' or 'testimony of things'.[64]

This was roughly the doctrine when the French mathematicians got hold of it in the seventeenth and eighteenth centuries. They pointed out correctly that many judgements of probability do not depend on experience. When we toss a coin, heads and tails are judged equally likely without our necessarily knowing that they had occurred in that ratio on past trials. How do we *know* that the probability of heads turning up is ½? This, according to Jacques Bernoulli, was an *a priori* probability given by the mathematical principle of non-sufficient reason which asserts that all alternatives are equally probable on the data unless there is a known reason for believing the contrary. According to Bernoulli's law of large numbers, frequencies of occurrence would tend to approximate to *a priori* probabilities if the number of trials was sufficiently large.

Laplace inverted this by saying that *a priori* probabilities could be inferred from frequency of occurrence. He used the principle of non-sufficient reason to establish his 'rule of succession', which held that if an event has occurred m times out of $m + n$, the probability that it will occur at the $m + n + 1th$ trial is $(m + 1)$ $(m + 1 + 2)$. This led to the absurd result that 'the influence of any experience, *however limited*, could be numerically measured, and . . . [Laplace] purported to prove that, if B has been seen to accompany A twice, it is two to one that B will again accompany A on A's next appearance. It seemed to follow that the less information we had the more precise our knowledge of probabilities, the primary qualification for one who would be well informed being 'an equally balanced ignorance'.[65]*

Keynes accepted the important claim of the mathematical theory that all probabilities were known *a priori*. However, as it stood, the theory failed to tell us anything about the real world; the 'obvious reaction' from it was back 'into the arms of empiricism'. In his *Logic of Chance* (1866), the Cambridge philosopher John Venn denied that the measurement of probabilities depends on the application of Bernoulli's theorem. Probability statements are a class of statements about the real world. 'He holds that the probability of an event's having a certain attribute is simply the fraction expressing the proportion of cases in which, as a matter of fact, the attribute is present.'[66] This is the basis of the frequency theory. Probability is a number measuring the ratio of variable to constant attributes over repeated observation of a class of things.

The success of Venn's theory was due to the fact that a large number of natural and artificial arrangements do in fact exhibit stable long-run frequencies, which is useful for a variety of practical purposes – like insuring against loss. This is important in business life, since it enables uncertainty to be reduced to calculable risk. In such cases it seems plausible to identify

*The assumption which underpinned the formula was that if p (the *a priori* probability) is unknown, then Bernoulli's equiprobability theorem $(1 + n)$ can be applied to any pair of events so that the probability of m/n is ½. Keynes pointed out the fallacy of this in the *Treatise on Probability*. (*CW*, viii, 407–8.)

probability with frequency.* Venn held that the *a priori* probabilities of the mathematicians were simply 'abridgements' of experience: they could be established by frequent trials, though it would be tedious to do so. He did not deny that people make probability judgements which were not based on frequency; but he thought that these, being 'vague knowledge', were of no scientific interest.

Keynes's objection to Venn's identification of probability with frequency was twofold. First, it is 'a very grave departure from the established use of words; for it clearly excludes a great number of judgements which are generally believed to deal with probability'. If therefore the meaning of probability is confined to situations which exhibit stable frequencies 'we must allow that probability is *not* the guide of life, and that in following it we are not acting according to reason'.[67] But, secondly, the frequency theory assumed the 'inductive hypothesis' and other direct judgements (such as judgements of relevance) which could not themselves be derived from frequencies, and so was circular.

Venn's empirical theory in turn stimulated a reformulation of the mathematical theory by the German von Kries. But we have said enough to show in what direction Keynes's solution to these dilemmas was likely to go. Probability, said Keynes, is a logical not an empirical fact, known *a priori*. Thus far he sides with the mathematicians against the statisticians. However, probability is not necessarily a number, it may be only a magnitude. You get the mathematicians' numbers only when you empty probability of experience; and experience plays a vital part in the formation of Keynes's probabilities. But experience by itself does not give us a probability. It only provides information to be used in forming probabilities.

Keynes's crucial innovation was thus not to make probability a branch of logic, for the mathematical theory was already that, but to make it a general theory of logic, of which the deductive or syllogistic logic was a special case.[68] In Russell's summary:

> Logic is accustomed to considering the relation between premiss and conclusion which enables us to infer the latter with certainty from the former, but this Mr. Keynes regards as only the extreme degree of probability-relation which subsists whenever one proposition has any bearing, favourable or unfavourable, upon the truth of another.[69]

Or in Keynes's own summary: 'Inasmuch as it is always assumed that we can sometimes judge directly that a conclusion *follows from* a premiss, it is no great extension of this assumption to suppose that we can sometimes recognise that conclusion *partly follows from*, or stands in a relation of probability to, a premiss.'[70] Keynes holds that it is rational to believe in a

---

*Though, as Keynes pointed out, many of the frequencies used by insurers were bogus – more like odds called by bookmakers. (*CW*, viii, 24.)

conclusion to the extent that the premiss entails it. 'Degree of rational belief' thus corresponds to 'degree of logical entailment'. Keynes wrote, 'We believe that there is some real objective relation between Darwin's evidence and his conclusions, which is independent of the mere fact of our belief, and which is just as real and objective, though of a different degree, as that which would exist if the argument were as demonstrative as a syllogism.'[71]

Keynes's fundamental symbol for probability is a/h where h is the premiss or evidence and a the conclusion of the argument. In cases of certainty the value of a/h is 1; in cases of impossibility, zero. Probability falls between certainty and impossibility; alternatively, certainty can be considered a case of maximum probability.[72]

Probability is always objective and unique. Given the evidence there is only one probability of the conclusion being true. Keynes is particularly insistent that probability is not mere belief. 'When once the facts are given which determine our knowledge, what is probable and improbable in these circumstances had been fixed objectively, and is independent of our opinion.'[73] 'Degree of justified belief' thus corresponds to 'real objective' probability.

Degrees of rational belief arise from knowledge of secondary propositions which predicate a characteristic of primary propositions. If the primary proposition p is that 'It will rain', then the secondary proposition q describes a peculiar property of it, namely its probable relation to the evidence h. (Keynes got this distinction between primary and secondary propositions – between knowledge about a proposition and knowledge of it – from W. E. Johnson.) We know q by intuition: it is perceived as self-evidently true. This knowledge gives us our justified belief in p. However, we may also have knowledge of, and not merely knowledge about, the primary proposition: either directly (as in direct acquaintance) or indirectly if our knowledge of q justifies a belief in p amounting to certainty.[74]

To assert that one conclusion is more probable than another is to assert that there is more evidence in its favour. One compares the probabilities of different arguments by using the principle of indifference. 'According to this principle we must rely upon direct judgement for discriminating between the relevant and irrelevant parts of the evidence. We can only discard those parts of the evidence which are irrelevant by *seeing* that they have no logical bearing on the conclusion.'[75] We can then come to one of three judgements. Conclusions may be equally probable; others we can rank into 'more or less probable'. And the probabilities of others may be non-comparable.

It is only in the first case that we can give probabilities numbers. However, Keynes limits the application of Bernoulli's principle by rechristening the principle of non-sufficient reason the principle of indifference. We must have positive reasons for thinking the alternatives are symmetrical between a number of exclusive and exhaustive probabilities, and not just no reasons for thinking they are not. This provides a much smaller class than the mathematicians' equiprobabilities, and one basically confined to games of chance. Keynes's principle of indifference is much more strongly dependent on judgements of relevance than is the principle of non-sufficient reason.[76]

It is the second class which chiefly interested Keynes in the *Treatise*; in fact he wrote the book to show it existed. He argues that we can rank or compare probabilities without being able to measure them, and this is what we normally do when we speak of an event being more or less probable.[77] Ordinal comparison normally measures some degrees of closeness or likeness to a standard object, as in 'degrees of blueness'. By analogy 'we can say that one argument is more probable than another (i.e. nearer to certainty) in the same kind of way as we can describe one object as more like than another to a standard object of comparison'.[78] But it may make as little sense to say one argument is twice as probable as another as it does to say that some shade of colour is twice as blue as another. The analogy presupposes that we are acquainted with a standard example of certainty by reference to which we can recognise the degree to which it is present in other cases; we know what conditions must exist for us to be certain the conclusion is correct, and we can recognise the extent to which these conditions are present or absent.

Here is an example of ordinal comparison. Suppose the conclusion which interests us is whether it will rain in the next half-hour. We can rank each state of nature in terms of its likely association with rain. With a clear blue sky the probability of rain may be judged to be zero, with thick black clouds overhead it may be judged one; intermediate states are ranked from one to zero. But of any pair of such probabilities it might make no sense to say that one is twice as probable as the other.

However, some probabilities are non-comparable. 'If we are given two distinct arguments,' Keynes writes, 'there is no general presumption that their two probabilities and certainty can be placed in an order.'[79] The problem arises from the fact that, though we know the probabilities of the different arguments, we cannot decide which bits of evidence are relevant to the conclusion of interest. In the case of the probability of rain, the barometer might be high, but the clouds black. Each gives an opposite probability. The case of non-comparable probabilities must be distinguished from the case of unknown probabilities. Here it is a question of our knowledge being too scanty for our logical intuition to perceive the probability. It exists, but it may be unknown. However, the power of logical insight varies, so probabilities may be known to some which, on the same evidence, would escape others.[80] But given the premisses 'which our subjective powers and circumstances supply to us . . . the conclusions, which it is rational for us to draw, stand to those premisses in an objective and wholly logical relation.'[81] When a person cannot perceive a probability, or compare the probabilities of two arguments, he may, using a terminology drawn from recent discussion, be said to be in a state of radical, or complete, uncertainty.

How much uncertainty Keynes thought was cognitively justifiable, or whether it applied to some classes of events more than others, is difficult to say. But the *Treatise* was conceived in an optimistic frame of mind. It is at any rate improbable that Keynes would have championed probability as a 'guide of life' had he thought that probabilities were generally inaccessible; because then his position would, in practice, have been the same as Moore's, and the whole labour in vain.

A word may be said in conclusion about induction. The use of inductive methods requires an 'inductive hypothesis', namely that the structure of the universe exhibits 'limited independent variety', its atoms cohering together 'in groups of invariable connection' finite in number.[82] To the question of why one should accept the inductive hypothesis, Keynes could find no 'conclusive or perfectly satisfactory answer'.[83] It presents itself as 'neither a self-evident logical axiom nor an object of direct acquaintance'; rather as a 'valid principle darkly present in our minds, even though it still eludes the peering eyes of philosophy'.[84] Nor can it be 'self-evidently applicable to every kind of object and to all possible experiences.'[85] It was more like a working principle, which science and experience tend to confirm. Keynes concluded optimistically that science might, after all, establish *a posteriori* what the mathematical 'professors of probability' had always assumed *a priori*: that nature was like an urn 'containing white and black balls in fixed proportions.'[86]

APPENDIX 3

Scholarship Old and New

Until recently students of Keynes almost completely ignored his *Treatise on Probability*. Biographical studies hardly mentioned it.[87] Studies of Keynes's economics either ignored it or referred to it in passing.[88] Even economists like Shackle, who emphasised the role of uncertainty in Keynes's *General Theory*, considered attempts to link Keynes's probability theory with his economic theory 'pointless', since investment behaviour in the *General Theory* is 'irrational'.[89]

Recently, attempts have been made to track down Keynesian uncertainty to its roots in his theory of probability. The new scholarship is part of a more general revival of interest in the 'early Keynes'. It studies Keynes's philosophy in order to get a better understanding of his economics, and perhaps to make his economics seem more attractive. It thus reflects both the feeling that new insights into 'what Keynes meant' can be won only indirectly, and a disenchantment with the 'hydraulic' Keynesianism of the 1950s and 1960s which came to grief in the 1970s. The 'philosophic' Keynesians include Bradley Bateman, Anna Carabelli, John Davis, Roderick O'Donnell, Athol Fitzgibbons, Suzanne Helburn, Tony Lawson, Bruce Littleboy and Ted Winslow. The most substantial works in this genre have, so far, been by Carabelli and O'Donnell.[90] O'Donnell's dissertation, 'Keynes: Philosophy and Economics', submitted for a D.Phil. at Cambridge in 1982, inaugurated the new wave. Volume 1 of my biography of Keynes, dating from 1983, was the first published account which made use of Keynes's early unpublished philosophical and political writings and, indeed, alerted the world of Keynes scholarship to their existence.

The result of all this has been what Bradley Bateman calls a 'noisy dining hall of conversations' about what the early Keynes 'really meant'.[91] There are a number of such conversations, and new discussants are always being added. One important divide is between the 'ethical' Keynesians and the 'probability' Keynesians, who conduct noisy conversations among themselves as well as with each other – the first concentrating on Keynes's ethical beliefs (what I have called division one of his 'complete ethical treatise' sketched in 'Miscellanea Ethica'), the second on division two – his philosophy of practice, in which considerations of probability are central. Recently P. V. Mini has attempted to relate Keynes's economics to the culture of Bloomsbury.[92]

A full account of these conversations will not be attempted here. The crucial contention of the new scholarship is that the epistemic roots of Keynes's treatment of expectations in the *General Theory* are to be found in his early writings, notably the *Treatise on Probability*. What follows will concentrate on three issues connected with the *Treatise on Probability* which seem relevant to such a claim. What is the philosophic character of Keynes's theory of probability? What continuity is there, if any, between the epistemology in the *Treatise* and in the *General Theory*? Finally, did Keynes have a theory of rational behaviour under conditions of radical or *irreducible* uncertainty, and, if so, what was it?

Under the first head, the two main (and linked) topics of discussion are about the connection between reason and truth in Keynes's theory, and about whether Keynes thought of the universe as atomic or organic. The crucial issue here is whether Keynes considered his theory of rationality as a 'logic based on truth' or a 'logic of opinion'.

There is a long-standing connection in epistemology between knowledge and existence. It is often said that we cannot know something unless it exists. What exists, in turn, is often referred to as 'real' or 'objective' or 'a matter of fact' to distinguish it from products of our imagination or 'matters of opinion'. Knowledge is connected with truth: it is sometimes called 'true belief' or 'justified true belief'. One cannot believe truly that grass is blue, or that mice are taller than men, or that Edinburgh is south of London. True beliefs, it can then be said, are beliefs in things which exist independently of the beliefs.

To Keynes, rational and true are not synonyms. A rational belief, whether probable or certain, is not the same as a true belief. A belief that it will rain tomorrow is true if it does in fact rain tomorrow. But one can have a rational belief that it will rain tomorrow even if it does not; conversely, one can have a true belief that it will rain tomorrow which need not be rational. However, Keynes insisted that rational beliefs, or rational degrees of belief, are connected to knowledge or true beliefs; and knowledge must be knowledge of something. It is in this sense that Keynes, like Moore and Russell, was a Realist, or Platonist. This is roughly O'Donnell's interpretation, and it is certainly the most acceptable reading of the theory of the *Treatise*.

In the light of this it is surprising to find Anna Carabelli characterise Keynes's theory of probability as a 'logic of opinion, rather than . . . of truth', akin to religious belief, coming out of a tradition of 'rhetorical argument', with 'reasonableness' rather than 'reason' as its benchmark.[93] She thinks that a logic of 'non-demonstrative inference' must mean a logic of opinion, and hence of subjective argument. In making a radical separation between language and truth, Keynes anticipated the breakdown of 'neo-positivism' in the 1960s. He also anticipated the later Wittgenstein's notion of rationality as an 'expectation . . . embedded in a situation, which is rooted in human customs and ordinary language'.[94]

Carabelli's argument is internally consistent, granted the premiss that Keynes rejected both Empiricist and Rationalist theories of knowledge. If probability is disconnected from knowledge and truth, then it is bound to be a matter of 'opinion' only.

The only trouble with this argument is that it ignores Keynes's own insistence that probability is a 'real objective relation', and that all rational beliefs have reference to true propositions, though they are not identical with them. Carabelli maintains her interpretation by the simple expedient of denying that Keynes said these things, or, more subtly, by leaving out or reinterpreting those passages in which he did say them.

Consider his claim that all probabilities are based on true propositions. A rational degree of belief in hypothesis a derives from knowledge of a secondary proposition q asserting a probability relation a/h; and 'we cannot', Keynes writes, 'know a proposition unless it is in fact true'. But, whereas Keynes calls the secondary proposition q both 'true and certain', Carabelli calls it only 'certain'. She accepts that Keynes's probable beliefs are based on certain beliefs. But Keynes says they are based on *true* beliefs.[95]

Keynes's probabilities are also connected to truth through a knowledge of causal truths which are included in the data, h, of the argument, knowledge of h authorising a rational degree of belief in a. Carabelli, as well as Fitzgibbons, makes a great deal of Keynes's distinction (in a footnote on p. 306 of the *Treatise*) between the medieval terms *causa essendi* and *causa cognoscendi* – between the cause of an event and the cause of our knowledge of it. According to Carabelli, Keynes claimed we can never know the true causes of things, but only the causes according to our theories.[96] But Keynes insisted that our theories tell us something about the world.

In one of McTaggart's lectures which Keynes attended as an undergraduate, McTaggart gave the following example: 'Rain in the night may be the *causa essendi* of wet roads in the morning; while wet roads in the morning may at the same time be the *causa cognoscendi* of rain in the night.'[97] Here rain is the cause of the roads being wet; the wetness of the roads is the cause of us knowing it 'probably' rained in the night. Or, to put it more exactly, the wetness of the roads in the morning, together with our knowledge of causal relationships, provides the premiss of an argument justifying a rational degree of belief in the conclusion 'it rained in the night'.

It is true that rational beliefs are always relative to 'the actual relational and cognitive conditions' in which the beliefs are asserted. Keynes says it would be absurd to say that something had not been 'really' probable, relative to some knowledge, because new knowledge had altered the probability. Citing Frazer's *Golden Bough* he argues that even primitive beliefs dismissed as irrational by later times may have been 'justified', relative to magical belief-systems of an earlier day. But this does not make his logic a 'logic of opinion'. By a logic related to truth Keynes means a method of reasoning which is always the same. 'Opinion' refers to the data h which are variable. In a scientific age, a mistake in judgement is involved in constructing an argument from a magical premiss, except for purely hypothetical purposes.[98]

Carabelli's argument, as we can see, has some affinity with Ramsey's identification of probability with subjective belief, such belief being related to the 'human outfit'. The strongest argument for calling Keynes's theory of probability subjective is that at various points in the *Treatise* he calls probability 'relative in a sense to the principles of human reason', or relative to the 'knowledge of the individual'. He even talks of logical principles as 'relative to the constitution of the human mind'. Such passages, as O'Donnell notes, 'apparently subjectivise Keynes's theory to the point of self-contradiction';[99] and this was certainly the view of Ramsey and Braithwaite. O'Donnell has argued that Keynes was not throwing over the notion of objective logical relations, but emphasising our 'limited logical insight' into these relations. 'It is not the relations of logic which are relative to the individual, but the knowledge of these relations.'[100] This defence is conclusive against the charge that Keynes's probability relations were necessarily subjective; but not against Carabelli's contention that the grounds of personal beliefs are cultural.

The question of the ability of 'opinion' to penetrate 'reality' is bound up with the question of the nature of the universe. We may say there are two sources of uncertainty: randomness in nature and ignorance. O'Donnell holds that Keynes was a determinist as regards the natural world, but that his position on causality in social science was much more complex.

As against this, Fitzgibbons argues that Keynes believed the universe to be chaotic. He interprets Keynes to believe in the randomness of nature. He argues that Keynes independently discovered the Greek notion of the 'errant or wandering cause'. The universe is an 'atomic buzz', a 'Heraclitean flux', into which it is 'bad faith' to pretend that we have any insight.[101] If the universe is chaotic, the primary quality of action becomes not so much logical intuition as creativity or virtue.

Carabelli's interpretation is philosophically more explicit. Central to her interpretation of Keynes's probability as 'opinion' is that he held the ontology of the universe to consist of structures *too complex* to be penetrated by reason. By this she seems to mean that he held reality to be 'organic' rather than 'atomic'.[102] Moreover, he held 'markedly organicist views on probability'. Probability can approach reality only by means of analogy; there is no truth outside the constructs of our own mind. Carabelli notes that Keynes's belief in the 'organic and complex character of the material under investigation and in the adoption of the methodological approach based on ordinary language, intuition and non-demonstrative arguments . . . is now defended in its applicability with [sic] natural sciences themselves'. If reality is 'organic' there are no 'external relations' of the kind Russell postulated in his *Principles of Mathematics* and we are back to Bradley's 'jar of treacle'. It is *prima facie* highly unlikely that Keynes developed a theory of probability under the joint influence of Moore's *Principia Ethica* and Russell's *Principles of Mathematics* in order to reinstate Idealism.

The idea that Keynes held reality to be organic *in general* cannot be sustained, since his theory of probability rests, as we have seen, on the hypothesis of 'atomism and limited variety'. However, Keynes accepted, with Moore, that ethical and aesthetic structures are organic, in the sense that an addition of a part affects the value not just of the whole, but of the other parts. So judgement in this area may be defeated by the existence of non-comparable arguments – that is, a situation of radical uncertainty. There is no doubt that Keynes came to think of 'closed' economic structures as organic in this way. In the *Treatise* he did not distinguish between natural structures and social structures; his examples are all drawn from games of chance, insurance, lotteries and so on. The thought that social structures might be impermeable to probability did not occur explicitly, and, if it had, he would probably have rejected it.

Keynes was not the most systematic of thinkers, and it is not surprising that such conflicts of interpretation should arise. I agree with Carabelli that Keynes thought of knowledge of probabilities as a kind of social knowledge; at the same time it seems indisputable that he thought of social knowledge as improving over time in its ability to 'penetrate' a reality which existed outside it.

The second question concerns the continuity between the *Treatise* and the way Keynes theorised about economies after the war. A formal continuity is not difficult to establish. The 'unknown' probabilities of the *Treatise* become the 'irreducible' uncertainty of the *General Theory* and after. The concept of the 'weight of argument' is roughly translatable into the 'state of confidence'. The epistemological claim that uncertainty can be irreducible, which Keynes in the *General Theory* applies to long-term expectations, is, therefore, foreshadowed in the *Treatise on Probability*. The question to be answered is why irreducible uncertainty appears to be the general case in the *General Theory*, whereas, like certainty, it is very much a special case in the *Treatise on Probability*. Or to put the question as Fitzgibbons does: why has the 'twilight of probability' turned, by 1936, into the 'dark night' of uncertainty?

It may be that nothing much needs to be said about this beyond the fact that Keynes's attention had shifted. Before the war Keynes was chiefly interested in asserting the claims of individual judgement against a social system of rules and conventions of 'correct behaviour'. In the 1930s his attention was directed to the performance of economic systems. Nevertheless, there is a distinct change of mood between the two periods. First, by the inter-war years Keynes had acquired a much sharper sense than he had had before the war of the distinction between the social and natural sciences. Knowledge of a world in which agents' expectations influenced what happened was much harder to come by than one where (for example) the apple's intentions did not have to be considered as complications to the law of gravity. In other words, he did come to believe that social structures were more organic than atomistic. But the basic cause of the change of mood was the First World War, and its destruction of pre-war 'norms' of behaviour and belief in the rationality of behaviour. The less predictable human behaviour is, the less probabilistic the world seems for those who try to behave rationally, because human behaviour is part of the world whose probable outcomes have to be 'intuited'. From this point of view it was the shift from stable to unstable social structures – or more generally the increase in historical turbulence – which caused Keynes to theorise the economic problem in terms of irreducible uncertainty. If this interpretation is true, uncertainty itself is a historical variable, its scope, like that of probability, depending on time and place.

The final question is whether the economic behaviour Keynes depicts in his mature economics is properly called rational or irrational. Four interpretative positions may be identified.

In Fitzgibbons's view Keynes believed that the only rational behaviour under conditions of radical, or irreducible, uncertainty such as obtained in the world of the *General Theory* was to do one's duty, without giving a thought to the consequences. Keynes's logic of practical reason is a logic of duty, an 'ethics of motives rather than consequences'.[103] Doing one's duty in economics means going on investing 'as a way of life', and not selling shares just because everyone else is. Thus the essential rational principle when uncertainty is complete is 'faithfulness' or 'steadfastness'. Keynes says economies collapse because of agents' 'bad faith'. The epitome of bad faith is pretence to knowledge. Businessmen and investors resort to conventions of calculability which pretend to a greater knowledge of consequences than is available. This is irrational. In the *General Theory* Keynes treats actual behaviour as irrational; irrational behaviour is what causes the trouble. In arguing thus, Fitzgibbons blurs Keynes's distinction between behaviour which is individually rational but socially irrational.

Fitzgibbons thus confirms G. L. S. Shackle's well-known view that Keynes, in the *General Theory*, assumed agent behaviour to be *in fact* irrational. But for Shackle, though not for Fitzgibbons, this is necessarily so, given the existence of radical uncertainty. His epitome of irrationality is 'animal spirits', which Fitzgibbons interprets as a form of 'faithfulness'. Since the world of the *General Theory* is not one of probability, Shackle thinks it 'pointless' to try to 'link Keynes's probability theory with his economic theory'.[104]

Winslow agrees that the patterns of behaviour described in the *General Theory* are irrational, but argues that the source of irrationality is as much psychological as epistemological – what he calls 'a personal incapacity for rationality'. One starting point for this line of argument is Keynes's repudiation in his 1938 paper 'My Early Beliefs' of his 'early belief' that human nature is reasonable; this shift, according to Winslow, 'had an important effect on Keynes's economics'. Winslow argues that Freudian ideas were increasingly important to Keynes after the First World War. Specifically, a psychological propensity which Keynes identifies as 'the hoarding instinct', or 'love of money' lies at the heart of the malfunctioning of the capitalist system. Winslow's argument is that this trait (typical, incidentally, of many economists!) closely corresponds to Freud's notion of the anal-sadistic character, and that Keynes was perfectly aware of this, though veiling his knowledge in order not to overstep the limits of economics. Thus unconscious impulses shape and distort so-called rational purposive behaviour. Mini agrees with Winslow when he writes, 'It is not simply, or even mainly, that calculation is impossible because of the omnipresence of uncertainty. It is that *a calculated expectation of positive returns has never been the main source of action.*'[105]

These views stand in sharp contrast to those of O'Donnell, Carabelli and Lawson, who interpret Keynes to defend conventional behaviour patterns – including those which cause economies to collapse – as rational strategies, ways of 'getting by' in face of the unknown. O'Donnell, unlike Carabelli, identifies a shift of emphasis, within the conceptual terrain mapped out by the *Treatise on Probability*, from strong to weak rationality as Keynes's attention shifts from the pre-war to the post-war world. Various investment 'conventions' described by Keynes in the *General Theory* are identified by O'Donnell as forms of weak rationality.[106] Carabelli agrees: Keynes considered 'perfectly reasonable the behaviour grounded on conventions in a situation in which the lack of knowledge does not supply better reasons for acting. In this case the label irrationalism seems misplaced.'[107] Lawson believes that Keynes treated conventions as an important repository of relevant social knowledge.[108] On this view, convention, viewed by O'Donnell as a weak form of rationality, is the buckle which links the *Treatise on Probability* and the *General Theory*. It seems an odd conclusion to a life's work which started out as a defiant proclamation of the individual's rational right to freedom from conventions!

Whether or not Keynes changed his view of human nature between the *Treatise on Probability* and the *General Theory* may be thought irrelevant to the question of the epistemological continuity between the two books. That is to say, Keynes may have concluded that human beings were less rational than he supposed, without changing his view of what constituted rational behaviour. Yet the issue is not quite so easily disposed of, for in his economic writings he may have been trying to rationalise – give a rational account of – behaviour which he believed to be irrational. This, I believe, is a crucial point of tension which a biographer needs to notice, which emerges in the gap between the language Keynes uses and the thoughts he thinks. As he was to write, we know more than we can say precisely.

CHAPTER FOUR

Russian and German Affairs

I

Keynes spent his third post-war summer holiday at Charleston writing his third post-war book – *A Revision of the Treaty* – which he describes as a 'sequel' to *The Economic Consequences of the Peace* and which was partly a history, partly a defence against critics of the earlier book, and very much a scissors-and-paste job. His mother helped him once more with newspaper cuttings. By 1921, Georges Clemenceau, the French Prime Minister, 'dry in soul and empty of hope', had left the scene for his family home in the Vendée. 'The great thing about this wood,' said Clemenceau about his pine forest, 'is that, here, there is not the slightest chance of meeting Lloyd George or President Wilson. Nothing, here, but squirrels.' In his introduction, Keynes commented wryly, 'I wish that I could claim the same advantages for this book.' But it was 'this Faustus of ours', Lloyd George, who continued to excite his theological imagination: 'The deeper and the fouler the bogs into which Mr. Lloyd George leads us, the more credit is his for getting us out. He leads us in to satisfy our desires; he leads us out to save our souls. . . . Who, ever before, enjoyed the best of heaven and hell as we do?'

A Revision of the Treaty was not the only thing Keynes wrote that summer. In August and September, five articles by him on 'Europe's Economic Outlook' appeared in the *Sunday Times*. They covered much of the ground of his lectures the previous autumn. The first, published on 21 August, made the greatest impact. Keynes predicted that 'some time between February and August 1922 Germany will succumb to an inevitable default'. The Paris correspondent of the *Sunday Times* wrote, 'Rarely – probably never in the history of international politics – has a single and opinionative article had such far-reaching effects.'[1] One can see what he meant. The mark plummeted, the great German inflation started and Germany obliged by applying for a moratorium, slightly ahead of schedule, at the end of 1921. Maynard's father thought he had been 'wise' to close his mark account at Buckmaster and Moore before his article appeared.[2] This was an ethical, not an economic, judgement. Keynes was in an odd position. He was perfectly entitled to bet on his predictions; but such was his authority that his predictions, when published, were also a cause, though no doubt a minor one, of their coming true. By October he was busily selling marks again, and with increasing profit.

Two other themes are worth noting. Keynes proclaimed the duty of the banking system to offset the 'miscalculations of merchants' by raising interest rates 'at once' when a boom is in progress and lowering them equally promptly when 'merchants are depressed by falling prices'.[3] Here was a sharp criticism of the actual conduct of British monetary policy since 1919, with bank rate not put up till April 1920, and then held at 7 per cent for a year, while the economy moved into even deeper depression. Secondly, the strong strain of neo-Malthusianism persists. Real wages will have to come down, not just in Europe, but in England too. 'The losses of American speculators have been a useful means of feeding Europe for two years past; but it would be imprudent to rely on this source of income as a permanency.'[4] It was a typical thought of this time, typically expressed.

Keynes spent the summer of 1921 at Charleston with Vanessa Bell and Duncan Grant, visited by Cambridge friends like Sebastian Sprott, Peter Lucas and Douglas Davidson – the last having just joined his brother Angus at Magdalene College. When, in October, Vanessa, Duncan and the children left to spend the winter in St Tropez, Keynes sent them books, tinned food, advice on currency movements, and the Cambridge gossip they loved to hear.

> Last night [he reported to Vanessa on 19 October] I had to give the Princess [Elizabeth Bibesco, Asquith's daughter] her long promised dinner, theatre and tête-à-tête. She groped me in the stalls without the least concealment from the company and when the lights went up it turned out that her neighbour on the other side was my friend Mr. Cockerell of the Fitzwilliam Museum – which ought to be very good for my reputation.

Jack Sheppard was trying for the Greek professorship and Keynes spent ten exhausting hours as an Elector, attending the lectures of the ten candidates. On the great day, 15 November, when each candidate had to deliver an oration, Sheppard ruined his chances, Keynes reported to his absent friends, by a histrionic address 'in the style of the Baptist Ministry'. Though Maynard's Eton friend 'Dilly' Knox, another candidate, made a 'superb effort of great intellectual merit', the chair went to a sixty-year-old classicist, Alfred Chilton Pearson, who occupied it with no great distinction till 1928.[5]

Keynes saddled himself with two large extra-University commitments. He accepted an invitation from his old friend Edwin Montagu, Secretary of State for India, to go out to India early in 1922 as vice-chairman of a Royal Commission to advise on Indian fiscal policy – 'a last effort, almost certainly doomed to futility, to save India for modified Free Trade'.[6] After a visit to Manchester on 24 October he accepted an invitation from C. P. Scott, editor of the *Manchester Guardian*, to edit twelve supplements for that paper's *Commercial*. He boasted to Vanessa that his income for 1922 would be £8000.[7]

All this he took in his stride, but 'what tends to break me down (and spoil my handwriting)', he wrote to Vanessa Bell on 12 December, 'is not work, but too many parties, hospitality and drink. I've entertained enormously at Cambridge this term.' His engagement diary shows that much of his hospitality was directed at Sebastian Sprott, Douglas Davidson and Dadie Rylands. Maynard's circle of young men in the early 1920s included not just the four Penrose brothers (Alec, Lionel, Roland and Bernard – the first two, Apostles) but the Davidson brothers, Angus and Douglas, who were taken up by Bloomsbury. Douglas, an aspiring painter, gentle, modest, with a slight stammer, became a lifelong friend of his contemporary Dadie Rylands; Angus became secretary of the London Artists' Association which Maynard started in 1928. Dadie was the outstanding undergraduate actor of his time, excelling in female parts. He and Maynard became close friends, drawn to each other by a mutual love of the theatre and English literature. In 1921, Dadie was a pretty, naughty, high-spirited youth, who took to the intimacy and eccentricity of King's like a duck to water; he is still in residence in 1992, a perfectly preserved period piece. Lytton Strachey, who had revisited his old haunts to support Sheppard on Greek professorship election day, wrote to his brother James on 26 November:

> [Keynes's] activities seemed terrific – particularly the social ones, and he confessed he was terrifically exhausted keeping it up. I don't know whether there are other reasons for his exhaustion, but on the whole I should think so. Sebastian is his prime favourite, and they are coming here for Christmas. . . . I saw Sheppard, who was in a regular stew over the Greek Professorship, even Dadie, even the Freshmen, in abeyance. . . . His salon was deserted, which perhaps partly accounted for his gloom, Pozzo having become the fashion on Sunday night. . . . Whether the result of the Professorship has shattered him I don't know, but I rather gather he has consoled himself with a freshman of extraordinary promise and unequalled fascination, unfortunately athletic, but still. . . .

'The old rogue,' Maynard informed Vanessa on 12 December, 'does no stroke of work and lolls in the arms of his two attendants [Carrington and her lover Ralph Partridge] sipping old claret and fingering old books.' Having got out of his American publisher a promise of thousands of dollars for his next book, Lytton proposed to fob him off with a volume of reviews he had written for the *Spectator* fifteen years before. Strachey's *Books and Characters* was published in 1922. It was dedicated to Maynard Keynes, with whom, fifteen years earlier, he had fought for the love of Duncan Grant.

II

LYDIA LOPOKOVA

Although Maynard and Sebastian spent a 'quiet and very happy Christmas with Lytton' at Tidmarsh, Maynard's personal life was about to take a turn which would astound his personal friends. The first hint of impending rearrangements came in a letter he wrote to Vanessa at St Tropez on 22 December 1921: 'Loppy came to lunch last Sunday, and I again fell very much in love with her. She seems to me perfect in every way. One of her new charms is the most knowing and judicious use of English words. I am going to the ballet to-morrow, and am asking her to supper with me at the Savoy.' His engagement diary for Sunday, 18 December records a day enigmatically poised: '1.30 Loppy . . . 8.00 Gabriel [Atkin]'.

He took Lydia Lopokova to supper at the Savoy after the ballet, *The Sleeping Princess*, on Friday, 23 December, where they chatted till 1 a.m. They arranged to meet again after his return from Tidmarsh. From this point on, the progress of their affair was astonishingly rapid. 'I'm entangled – a dreadful business – and barely fit to speak to,' he wrote to Lytton on 27 December. 'What is to be done about it? I am getting terrified,' he wrote to Vanessa the next day. Vanessa wrote back on 1 January 1922, 'don't marry her. Flight to India may save you. However charming she is, she'd be a very expensive wife and would give up dancing and is altogether to be preferred as a mistress.' Vanessa seems to have been jumping to conclusions. Maynard replied on 6 January, 'You needn't be afraid of marriage, but the affair is very serious and I don't know in the least what to do about it. I begin to think it's a good thing I am going to India. However, she's very adorable.' And he followed this up on 9 January: 'I'm in a terribly bad plight, almost beyond rescue. Clive simply grins with delight at seeing me so humbled.' On 21 January Keynes informed Edwin Montagu that he would not be available to go to India after all.[8]

Maynard had first fallen under Lydia's spell in the autumn of 1918. Diaghilev's Ballets Russes had returned to London after an absence of five years, and Lydia, making her first appearance there, had captivated her war-weary audiences at the Coliseum as Mariuccia in Leonide Massine's new ballet, *The Good-Humoured Ladies*, a zany comedy set in seventeenth-century Venice. Keynes had not been impressed: 'She's a rotten dancer – she has such a stiff bottom,' he told Foxy Falk as they came away from his first visit. However, it was a different matter backstage where he unexpectedly found her charms more potent than those of the 'new Nijinsky', Stanislas Idzikovsky.[9] Her first letter to him, dated 29 December 1918, thanks him for a copy of *The Economic Consequences of the Peace* and wishes him a 'most happy New Year in which my husband joins me heartily'.

The critic Cyril Beaumont has described the impression Lydia made on him that autumn:

> Lopokova off the stage was very much like Mariuccia on it. Under medium height, she had a compact, well formed little body which would have delighted Théophile Gautier. Her hair was very fair, fluffed out at the forehead, and gathered in a little bun at the nape of her neck. She had small blue eyes, pale plump cheeks, and a curious nose, something like a humming-bird's beak, which gave a rare piquancy to her expression. She had a vivacious manner, alternating with moods of sadness. She spoke English well, with an attractive accent, and had a habit of making a profound remark as though it were the merest badinage. And I must not forget her silvery laugh.

They sometimes met for tea or dinner at the Savoy. Off stage, Lydia would relax:

> As soon as she had taken leave of those who came to pay her homage, she would wipe off her make-up – she never put very much on – and change into a simple short skirt, woolly jumper and tam-o-shanter, skipping home like a schoolgirl let out of school. She had an ingenuous manner of talking, but she was very intelligent and witty, and, unlike some dancers, her conversation was not limited to herself and the Ballet.[10]

While Maynard agonised over reparations in Paris, Lydia prepared for her forthcoming season at the Alhambra, taking daily lessons with the 'Maestro', Enrico Cecchetti, in his rooms in Wardour Street. Ninette de Valois, then twenty, first met her there, looking like 'an earnest tired child; her face had a grave sincerity, but when she laughed it was transformed . . . for when Lopokova laughed she willed that the whole world laughed with her'. She loved to draw attention to the individuality of her nose. But in the midst of her jumping, giggling and self-dramatisation, 'like a thunderclap she made one feel her capacity of direct thought'. Her strong individuality could be undermining, but she had no vanity or false pride, 'only a largesse of utter frankness and widespread generosity'.

> We students adored her, and she was particularly kind and helpful to me. Cecchetti would shout and scold at this diminutive dynamo and she would regard him, her oval face fairly drooping with the gravity of the situation . . . then suddenly the air would be rent by a peal of merriment that reduced the old Maestro to the growls of a distant ineffectual thunderstorm.[11]

Maynard was back from the Paris Peace Conference in time to see Lydia triumph in *La Boutique Fantasque* at the Alhambra Theatre in June 1919. This was another new Massine ballet, set in a toyshop, with music by

Rossini and costumes and scenery by Derain. 'Those who never saw the Can-Can in *Boutique* danced by Lopokova and Massine will never know that dance as it was, or appreciate how exhilarating it could be,' recalled Cyril Beaumont. Fred Ashton said her performance was 'like champagne corks popping'. Lopokova, Beaumont wrote, 'had an extraordinary resemblance to a doll, for which her rounded limbs, plump features, curved lips, and ingenuous expression were admirably suited'. The English adore a comedienne and *Boutique* established Lydia as London's favourite ballerina – a position she held as long as she went on dancing. Yet, at one moment, her expression did change. When the shop closed, and she was temporarily parted from her sweetheart, 'she gazed at him with a look of ineffable love, which seemed to light up her whole face'.[12]

But on 10 July 1919 she suddenly 'disappeared'. Beaumont had noticed a 'certain coolness between Lopokova and [her husband] Barocchi' after the production of *Boutique*. From the Savoy Hotel she wrote to Diaghilev that 'for reasons of a personal nature, I have had a nervous breakdown so serious that only with difficulty was I able to get through the performances . . .'. Barocchi wrote to Diaghilev on 16 July to say that he had 'been through Hell for a few weeks' because Lydia had acted 'totally out of character'.[13] It was clear that Lydia wanted to escape from Barocchi, and this she could not do while she remained with Diaghilev. No one knows what caused this sudden estrangement. There is a hint that it may have had to do with Barocchi's philandering.[14] She went to stay with Russian friends in north London. Nothing was seen or heard of her for eighteen months.

Where was she in this interval? We cannot be sure, but there is strong circumstantial evidence that she spent part of the time in Russia. In the Keynes Papers at King's, there is a copy of a letter from Lydia to Diaghilev dated 26 July 1919, in which she tells him that her 'decision to quit the stage is, of course, irrevocable. You probably know that I have applied for a divorce, and as soon as I receive it I shall marry General Martynov. We are soon to leave for Russia. . . .' Lydia's passport reveals that on 13 August 1919 she was granted permission by the Italian Consulate in London to travel to Batum in Georgia by way of Taranto in Italy. Georgia was at this time an independent republic (recognised as such by the Allies in January 1920), with a British naval presence at Batum. The passport establishes that Lydia was briefly in London in August 1920 on her way to France and also in January 1921 *en route* to the United States. She resurfaced in New York in February 1921 in a show called *The Rose Girl*.

The fact that there was no trace of Lydia for so long after her disappearance strongly suggests that she did go to Batum with the General. Polly Hill asks why her mysterious general should have taken her to this 'insalubrious naval base . . . of all places'.[15] The reason might be that it was an obvious point of entry from Britain to non-Soviet territory. The civil war was raging. The autumn of 1919 marked the high point of the advance of

the White Russian armies from the south, under General Denikin, towards
Moscow, and from the west, under General Yudenitch, towards Petrograd,
where Lydia's family were. She had not seen them for ten years; communications had been cut; no doubt she felt extremely anxious about their safety.
In other words, Lydia and the General would have left for Russia in the
expectation of an imminent White victory: Batum was merely a place to
wait for this to happen. However, Denikin and Yudenitch collapsed in the
winter of 1919–20; by the spring of 1920 the Red armies were at the frontiers
of Georgia. If Lydia and the General were still there, it was clearly time to
leave. Nothing is known about Martynov. They evidently did not marry,
and she probably left him behind in Russia. He may never have been more
than a means to get away from Barocchi. Lydia never referred to the missing
months. No one who knew her had any idea what she had done in that
time, except presumably Maynard himself, who kept silent. She simply put
the episode behind her.

By May 1921, Lydia was back in London with Diaghilev for a brilliant
season at the Prince's Theatre, where she repeated her triumph in *Boutique*,
and also danced the Bluebird *pas de deux* from Tchaikovsky's *Sleeping Beauty*.
Among the hearts she captured on her reappearance were those of the
artificial-silk manufacturer and picture collector Samuel Courtauld and his
wife Elizabeth ('Lil'), who became lifelong friends. But Keynes's engagement diary records only one visit to the ballet, on 27 June, in the company
of Gabriel Atkin. It was the opening night of Stravinsky's *The Rite of Spring*
and Lydia was not dancing. There is no record of his having renewed his
acquaintance with her at this time.

Lydia seems to have re-entered his life only after Diaghilev's *The Sleeping
Princess* opened at the Alhambra in November 1921, and then not immediately. He had moved back to 46 Gordon Square after the Cambridge term
ended on 5 December, but spent most of the time till Christmas finishing
off his new book, *A Revision of the Treaty*. He did not mention Lydia when
he wrote to Duncan in Paris on 21 December, only to Vanessa, still in St
Tropez, the next day. He may have felt embarrassed about telling an old
boyfriend about a new girlfriend.

Lydia Lopokova was then thirty, with an astonishingly varied life already
behind her. She was born Lydia Vasilievna Lopukhova, in St Petersburg,
on 21 October 1891. Her family name Lopukhov means burdock, a wild
plant. Her father Vasili, an usher at the Alexandrinsky Theatre, was of
Tatar origins. Her mother, Constanza ('Karlusha') Douglas, was a Balt,
with recent Scottish ancestry. (She always spoke German better than Russian.) Lydia was a sturdy survivor. Whim and events were to carry her to
far-off places; but in her life, as in her dancing, she always managed to land
securely.

She was the third of five children, four of whom – Evgenia, Fedor, Lydia
herself and Andrei – were educated at the Imperial Ballet School, graduated

to the Maryinsky Theatre and became professional dancers, Fedor eventually becoming the Maryinsky's director and chief choreographer. All except Lydia stayed in Russia and, after the Revolution, were stuck there. Lydia herself joined the *corps de ballet* of the Maryinsky in 1909. She danced in Paris with other members of the Imperial Ballet assembled by Diaghilev in 1910, her virtuosity and ingenuousness making a great impression in *Sylphides*. But instead of going back to St Petersburg, and before Diaghilev formed his permanent company in 1911, she left, with her brother Fedor and sister Evgenia, for the United States, lured by a contract to appear as a 'speciality act' in a touring vaudeville programme. She was only nineteen, and it was the first of those gambles with her career for which Lydia became famous.

Fedor and Evgenia soon went back to Russia, but Lydia stayed in America for seven years. 'Within that period,' writes Frank Ries, 'she appeared as dancer, cabaret artist, model, vaudeville performer, and even as a dramatic actress on the Broadway stage.'[16] It was a leap to freedom from the stuffy atmosphere of the Imperial Ballet. Outside New York, ballet scarcely existed in the United States. Lydia and her small troupe were often sandwiched between clowns and performing animals. Nevertheless, she, together with Pavlova and Mikhail Mordkin, with whom she often danced, put ballet on the map in the United States. Her charm, gaiety and naughtiness made her a favourite with audiences everywhere.

In 1913, Lydia decided that she wanted to be an actress, and a dramatic actress at that. She had acted Shakespeare as a child – in Russian of course – on the stage at the Alexandrinsky, and was an exceptionally expressive dancer, with an outstanding capacity for mime. Her acting ambitions were encouraged by the American actress Mrs Minnie Fiske, well known for her naturalistic style. But the language of speech, unlike that of the dance, is not universal. To perform Shakespeare successfully in English required muting the very Russian way she used the English language which made her so appealing off-stage. She never resolved this conflict. Her English was always so idiosyncratic that one learns with some surprise that she took English and drama lessons for nearly a year in preparation for her new career. (She even learnt the part of Nora in Ibsen's *A Doll's House*.) In February 1914 she announced she was giving up dancing for good, and appeared in a worthless comedy which collapsed soon after opening on Broadway in December 1914. Always a realist (and no doubt needing the money), Lydia took up dancing again, with her usual success, and at an increased salary. Then just as suddenly she switched back to straight acting. By the end of 1915 she was talking of settling permanently in the United States, and of marrying Heywood Broun, a giant of a sports writer on the *New York Herald Tribune*, who alternated his coverage of baseball matches with 'puffs' for Lydia's dramatic performances.

And she might have done all this (for a time) had not Diaghilev, stranded by the war in Switzerland with a skeleton company, managed to fix up an American tour. This opened in New York in January 1916. In engaging Lydia to be his *première danseuse*, Diaghilev shrewdly realised the value to him of her American connections; she worked indefatigably on and off stage to ensure the tour's success. She danced for the first time with Nijinsky in *Spectre de la Rose* at the Metropolitan in April 1916, earning a rare unfavourable comparison with Karsavina. In fact, she virtually saved the Ballets Russes single-handed. Diaghilev, understanding her value and realising her flightiness, sought to bind her to the company by getting her to marry Randolfo Barocchi, a wealthy backer, now his business manager – a very small Italian with well-trimmed beard and whiskers, an engaging charm and a gift for mimicry.

After a brief interlude in Spain, Lydia returned to America with the Ballets Russes in October 1916 on Nijinsky's ill-fated tour, dancing with the increasingly deranged genius in *Petrushka* and in the Bluebird *pas de deux* from *The Sleeping Beauty*. She left America with the company in February 1917.

> Very few dancers were as loved there as she was, and one cannot think of anyone who risked as much as she did to enter the dramatic profession, changing her career so radically in mid-stream. The fact that she was able to return to dance so triumphantly proves her inherent talent and discipline. Unlike the other Russian dancers who came to America, she accepted and welcomed its way of life; the people returned her love by applauding her talents, whether they were encased in a bad revue or in the glamour and prestige of the Russian ballet.[17]

Although she was a performer of great virtuosity and charm, Lydia was not a classical dancer like Pavlova or Karsavina, the outstanding ballerinas of the age. She lacked the grace and lyricism of the purest classical type. She was very short and rather dumpy; her head was often likened to a plover's egg; her personality, comic and pathetic, showed through everything she did. But she was more than a 'character dancer'. 'To one's astonishment,' wrote her friend Lydia Sokolova,

> everything she attempted came off. Few dancers have performed with such assurance or flown through the air as she did. Lydia had tiny strong feet, little hands and short arms. She had no idea of hairdressing and wore very little make-up on stage – what there was was usually still there the next morning – but when she stood looking up at Big Serge (which was what she called Diaghilev), with her screwed-up little bun of hair, the tip of her nose quivering, and an expression between laughter and tears, I defy anybody to say she wasn't worth her weight in gold.[18]

She was made for, and made by, the ballets of Leonide Massine, Diaghilev's post-Nijinsky protégé, whose jerky, puppet-like choreography was moulded round the expressive gifts of a few artists like himself, Lydia, Idzikovsky and Woizikovsky. His ballets were short, high-spirited, scintillating. They also fitted the post-war mood. Their speed and economy matched the pace of life; ultra-modern in choreography, they nevertheless recalled an elegant, witty, classical world, remote from the horrors of war. Later Lydia would come to see Massine as an inventor of 'wonderfully thought out steps and dances only', as someone who 'introduced symphony into dance', not a choreographic innovator like Fokine, Nijinsky or Balanchine.[19] In Lydia, Massine found the perfect instrument for expressing his art. But it was his art; he was the supreme egoist, and his ballets expressed only one side of Lydia's personality.

It was a bold gesture of Diaghilev to challenge post-war taste with a lavish revival of Tchaikovsky's *Sleeping Beauty*, reeking of nineteenth-century romanticism. It was a sign, perhaps, of his lack of faith in the revival that the Alhambra's proprietor, Sir Oswald Stoll, got Diaghilev to change the name to *The Sleeping Princess*.* Diaghilev's production, which opened on 2 November 1921, was the most magnificent account of this work which has ever been staged. Big Serge had given minute attention to every detail of the lavish spectacle. Bakst's costumes evoked the masques and entertainments of the eighteenth-century French nobility; his dresses were made of the finest materials; his opening scene, suggestive of Versailles at the time of Louis XIV, was inspired by the architectural conceits of the Bibienas. Stravinsky arranged Tchaikovsky's music; Sergeyev revived Petipa's choreography; Bronislava Nijinska added new dances. The complications of assembling all these bits of balletic machinery were enormous. The budget of £10,000 put up by Stoll was soon overspent, and another £10,000 reluctantly handed over.

For the leading role of Aurora, Diaghilev engaged three ballerinas of the old school – Olga Spesivtseva, Vera Trefilova and Lubov Egorova – but Lydia Lopokova also alternated the part. Her own special roles, though, were those of the Lilac (or Good) Fairy and the Enchanted Princess, danced in the Bluebird *pas de deux* with Idzikovsky, which was generally reckoned to have stolen the show. However, the critics were cool; and the public preferred their Christmas pantomimes. The ballet was considered too long and out of date. Amazingly, Tchaikovsky's music was also out of fashion. Lytton Strachey told Sacheverell Sitwell that it 'made him feel sick'.[20] Probably more important than any of this, the *Belle*, as Diaghilev called it, was put on in the depth of the post-war depression. The houses never recovered after the Christmas holiday. Instead of running into the early summer,

---

*Diaghilev mischievously told Lydia that he had changed the name to *The Sleeping Princess* because her nose was the wrong shape for her to be regarded as a Beauty.

which would have enabled Diaghilev to pay back Stoll, *The Sleeping Princess* was rudely bundled off the stage on 4 February 1922.

Keynes sat it out to the end, in the half-empty stalls. On him, at least, *The Sleeping Princess* made a lifelong impression. The Perrault fairy-tale, mingled with memories of the Victorian pantomimes and melodramas he had seen with his father as a child, merged in his imagination with his love affair with Lydia, itself a most fanciful conjunction. Its symbolism permeated his thoughts. It was *The Sleeping Beauty* which he chose for the gala reopening of Covent Garden on 20 February 1946; and in his last ever speech, at the Savannah Conference, he invoked the protection of the Good Fairy for his brainchild, the International Monetary Fund, against any lurking 'malicious Fairy or Carabosse' – a remark which the US Secretary of the Treasury, Fred Vinson, apparently took personally.

A few days before *The Sleeping Princess* closed, Diaghilev fled from his creditors to Paris, leaving his company stranded and penniless in London. Maynard quickly took control of Lydia's finances, persuading her to open a bank account rather than leave her earnings with the head porter at the Waldorf, where she was staying. With Vanessa still abroad, Maynard installed Lydia in her flat at 50 Gordon Square, where she started giving enormous tea parties for the hungry dancers. Maynard was spending most of the spring term in London anyway, working on his *Manchester Guardian Commercial* Supplements, so he was with her much of the time, 'to severe complaints from Sebastian' at Cambridge, he told Vanessa.[21] Being outside the English class system, Lydia had no inhibitions with servants, and was soon chatting away in the kitchen with Grace Germany, Vanessa's cook, who was looking after her younger son Quentin. Quentin remembers Keynes used to take both Lydia and him out for drives in a hired Daimler. They would visit Westminster Abbey, Hampton Court, the Tower of London and other monuments, Keynes talking brilliantly the while 'about English history, the Constitution, the Church, and Heaven knows what else'. Ostensibly these lessons were for Quentin's benefit, but Lydia 'could hardly dodge the splendid shower of information', and Quentin felt that Maynard was educating her for her future role as his wife.[22] They would also go to the pantomime, which they all loved: did Maynard ever think about St George?* By the beginning of March, Keynes was voicing his usual complaints to Vanessa: 'what with Lydia, the *Manchester Guardian* (which is very hard work) and moving about constantly in high financial international politics circles, I am rather exhausted'.

Maynard's infatuation with Lydia was at first a source of astonishment, rather than distress, to his closest friends. Duncan wrote to Vanessa on 25 January, 'As for Maynard, until I see him carrying on with L. I must

---

*St George, a pre-war Cockney boyfriend of Maynard's and Duncan's employed in the theatre. See Skidelsky, *Keynes*, i, 257.

give up trying to imagine what happens – it beggars my fancy.' Duncan's incredulity is understandable. It was not the fact of Maynard wanting to 'carry on' or 'settle down' with a woman which surprised him; other Bloomsbury homosexuals had taken this route, Duncan himself, even Lytton. It was his choice of woman, and the intensity of his feeling. Lydia came from right outside the circle of women whom Maynard's friends would have considered suitable or sensible for him. Had he settled down with one of the Cambridge or Slade School 'neo-pagans', few Bloomsbury eyebrows would have been raised. But what, at least partly, defined Keynes's homosexuality was his inability to enter into a loving relationship with women of this kind. His sexual and emotional fancy was seized by free spirits. The two great loves of his life, Duncan and Lydia, were both *uneducated*; their reactions were spontaneous, fresh, unexpected. Keynes was not looking for an inferior model of himself, but a complement, or balance, to his own intellectuality. And one must remember, too, that there was nothing earthbound about Keynes's brain. His fancy could leap and soar over all rational obstacles. He was a gambler, and Lydia was his greatest gamble.

Lydia, too, was a gambler. She was always breaking loose, doing the unexpected. To start life with a Cambridge don would be her biggest gamble yet. But there was a certain logic in it. Bloomsbury viewed her as a dancer, a chorus girl almost, suitable for a flirtation, hardly a marriage. Yet, if Maynard was more than an economist, Lydia was more than a ballerina. Outside Bloomsbury, there is unanimous testimony to her intelligence, though it was purely intuitive, not trained. While her roots were in the ballet, she was curious about other worlds, eager to learn. She appreciated the aesthetics of Maynard's mental life, its undercurrents of feeling and style, and was thus able to sustain an improbable dialogue with him, even about matters of which she knew nothing. Maynard was enchanted by his Fairy Princess; and Lydia, perhaps more slowly, came to love her Prince for his spaciousness of mind and spirit.

So the clever dog caught the wild duck. There was much that was as yet unresolved. Lydia was still married to Barocchi; Maynard had not yet given up Sebastian. 'We had a good deal of *éclaircissement* on Sunday,' he wrote to Vanessa on 9 February 1922, 'which was painful for a moment, but seems to have made no real difference to us all.' Was this when he told her about his past – and present? 'Maynard is rather mysterious,' Lytton wrote to Sebastian on 6 June 1922. 'I've only talked to him vaguely (and not very lately) about his states of mind, but I didn't at all gather that he likes you less. I think your Janus-diagnosis is the right one. . . .' But Sebastian, too, faded as a lover, though not as a friend. Slowly the gate closed on Maynard's past, never to be opened again.

III

THE RECONSTRUCTION OF EUROPE

Keynes's cancellation of his trip to India meant he could devote himself to planning the Reconstruction Supplements to the *Manchester Guardian Commercial*. The first one was now brought forward to April 1922. There were to be twelve issues altogether. Keynes was to be paid £200 an issue as general editor, one shilling a word for international rights to his signed articles, and further payments for his unsigned contributions. He eventually produced a dozen signed articles, some of substantial length; so his earnings for the venture approached £4000.

Although Keynes did not come cheap, he worked obsessively hard on his new assignment. Cambridge was confined to the shortest of weekends, with Gerald Shove taking over his teaching duties for the term. This left most of the spring term of 1922 free to prepare the Supplements, including his own contributions. They were billed as an 'exhaustive survey of European conditions, financial, economic, and industrial, written by the chief authorities in Europe', to be printed in five languages and 'based on more complete knowledge than is yet anywhere available'. Keynes, like Diaghilev, was the impresario of a complex project. He had to decide themes and topics for each issue; assemble contributors; fix scales of payment; calculate costs per issue; arrange translations. The *Manchester Guardian* provided an extensive back-up service. Keynes used its network of foreign correspondents, particularly P. A. Voigt (Berlin), Arthur Ransome (Petrograd), David Mitrany (Eastern Europe). At all times he collaborated closely with the *Manchester Guardian*'s editor, C. P. Scott, and his two sons, E. J. (Ted) and J. R. Scott, as well as with the assistant editor A. P. Wadsworth, who acted as liaison officer for the whole project. Being Keynes he had decided views not just about content, but about layout, design, photographic material. C. P. Scott developed mixed feelings about Keynes. He disapproved of his 'arid intellectualism', and wrote to the historian J. L. Hammond, 'Keynes is a brilliant and original thinker in his own subjects, but he is also about the most obstinate and self-centred man I ever encountered.'[23]

Salvation through Knowledge was the flag under which Keynes's ship sailed, and he was determined to assemble a glittering crew. He spent most of his London days with his new secretary, Miss Rees, dictating letters to discuss projects, propose articles, commission writers. His engagement diary for these months is crammed full of appointments, mainly connected with the Supplements. There was a trip to Amsterdam, for which he claimed £12 from Scott.

Keynes's wartime contacts stood him in good stead. He used his friend Carl Melchior to solicit German contributions, and the historian Lewis Namier, like Keynes a wartime civil servant, to commission in Central

Europe. Keynes had fixed a top rate for contributors of £100, but he soon discovered that the Germans would write for almost nothing, and was able to cut his estimated costs per issue by £300. The main Germans Keynes got, apart from Melchior himself, were Rudolf Hilferding, Hjalmar Schacht and Wilhelm Cuno, soon to be Chancellor. Walther Rathenau, the mercurial German Foreign Minister, was assassinated before he could deliver. Keynes got a delicate lesson in manners from Melchior. He had sent him sheets of blank writing paper, with a standard letter, for commissioning German authors. Melchior wrote to him, 'I should be very pleased if you would have the kindness to write direct to the gentlemen who have undertaken to write articles. . . . That is a little more personal nuance which, as I understand the physiology [sic] of men, will not fail to make a pleasant impression.'[24]

Keynes himself canvassed American, Italian and British contributors. Walter Lippmann was commandeered, as were American financial 'experts' like Paul Cravath, Oliver Sprague, Alonzo Taylor, John H. Williams, Thomas Lamont and Russell Leffingwell, who had all been involved with Keynes in Paris. Keynes must have been pleased by Leffingwell's acceptance – 'What others saw through a glass darkly, you saw vividly; what others lacked the courage or the skill to tell, you told clearly.'[25] He met Leffingwell in London that summer and liked him. He was less pleased, as we shall see, by his article.

Luigi Einaudi, Professor of Public Finance at the University of Turin and doyen of Italian economists, agreed to write on Italian public finance, as did Amedeo Giannini, commercial and financial attaché to the Italian Embassy in London. On 7 December 1921 and 20 March 1922, Einaudi's pupil, Piero Sraffa, came to 46 Gordon Square. Keynes commissioned an article from him on Italian banking which, when published in the Eleventh Supplement (7 December 1922), was to enrage Mussolini.

The British contributors form a cross-section of Keynes's worlds. Economists included Henry Clay, Walter Layton, Arthur Pigou, J. H. Richardson (a Cambridge graduate working at Geneva in the International Labour office) and Dennis Robertson. (Gustav Cassel of Stockholm University and Irving Fisher of Yale were Keynes's most distinguished foreign economists.) Nicholas Davenport, Sydney Russell Cooke, Basil Blackett (anonymously), Oswald Falk and Dudley Ward (friend of Rupert Brooke, ex-Treasury, banker) wrote about high finance. Politicians included Asquith, Lord Robert Cecil, Ramsay MacDonald, Philip Snowden and Sidney Webb; political writers, Goldie Lowes Dickinson and Harold Laski (Laski thought Keynes had 'a badly swollen head').[26] Bloomsbury, too, played a fleeting part in Keynes's enterprise. He asked Vanessa Bell and Duncan Grant to design a logo. Ted Scott rejected their first idea of two buxom mermaids holding up a banner 'Reconstruction in Europe', settling for their alternative motif of intertwining leaves and flowers. This was the masthead of the first issue. But even this proved too much for Scott. For the second and subsequent

Supplements, Bloomsbury aesthetics were discarded in favour of Futurist machinery, more symbolic of the New Age. Most of the politicians, British as well as foreign, were men of the centre-left: Blum, Herriot and Painlève from France, Nitti and Orlando from Italy. Keynes had few connections on the right. His one close Conservative associate was Bonar Law, his old Treasury chief, who refused an invitation to contribute in a charming letter: 'You know that I am not fond of writing at any time. I am sure it would be very bad business for the *Manchester Guardian* to pay me so much as £100 for it.'

Keynes understood the importance of psychology for European reconstruction, and enlisted writers and thinkers of the stature of Maxim Gorki, Henri Barbusse, Anatole France (whose contribution, however, never arrived), Benedetto Croce and Guglielmo Ferrero. Gorki wrote, of the Bolshevik Revolution, that a few hundred men had seized power to establish 'an empire of perfect equality and social justice' (Fourth Supplement). In 'A Philosopher's View of Population' (Sixth Supplement), Croce argued that conflict, rather than equilibrium, would be the dominant tendency of the twentieth century.

The French and the Russians gave Keynes most trouble. He used his French translator Paul Franck to commission articles from French notables. But Franck's contacts, like Keynes's, were with the left. When Franck got the promise of an article from the 'pro-German' Joseph Caillaux, a former Prime Minister who was also involved in a financial scandal, the Poincaré publicists boycotted the project, and Raymond Poincaré himself refused to join other Prime Ministers in sending a message of goodwill for the first number.

Keynes was determined to devote one Supplement to the Soviet Union, and personally solicited, without success, a contribution from Lenin. He soon discovered that Russian officials objected to the inclusion of any material not supplied by themselves. As Ivan Maisky, the chief of the Soviet Foreign Press Department, wrote to Keynes on 6 June 1922, 'We certainly do not want in the least to interfere with the editing of the Russian number because it is entrusted to you, but on the other hand we as representatives of the quite definitive philosophy and new ideals must be careful in all our social actions. We have to take into consideration the opinion of the masses who are standing behind us. . . .' This note led Arthur Ransome, the *Manchester Guardian*'s Russian correspondent, to describe Maisky as a 'wooden headed ass'.[27] No doubt Maisky was writing for the record: a compromise was fixed up, whereby the Fourth Supplement contained a Russian section 'expounded by themselves', with a critical comment by (of all people!) Samuel Gompers, the American trade union leader. Maisky and his wife became friends of the Keyneses when he came to London as ambassador in 1934.

It is noticeable that Maynard's affair with Lydia coincided with a dramatic increase in both his work load and his work plans. We see it now, slotted into the few vacant spaces in his engagement diary. Perhaps this was his way of coping with the terror it aroused in him. Not surprisingly, he started to feel exhausted. 'I am absolutely overwhelmed with work,' he told his mother on 27 March. The next day he explained to C. P. Scott that 'What has been rather breaking my back recently has been my own heavy contributions to the first two issues.' There were to be four substantial articles by him, which he planned to turn into a short book.

The first Supplement appeared on 20 April 1922, with 30,000 copies printed of the English edition. They then continued, at intervals of about three weeks, till 4 January 1923, priced at one shilling each. The first issue dealt with the problem of the foreign exchanges. Keynes had no less than three signed articles in it: versions of two of them went into his *Tract on Monetary Reform*.[28] Despite its forbiddingly technical aspects, the question being discussed was simple in outline and of immediate practical importance. Everyone agreed on the need for the world to get back to a fixed exchange-rate system as soon as possible. The question which Keynes posed under the heading 'Stabilisation or Deflation?' has not lost its relevance today. Should the disordered currencies of Europe be fixed at their existing depreciated values in terms of gold, or should an effort be made to restore them to their higher pre-war values? The monetary reformers, who now included most economists, answered, 'Stabilise' (or devalue); the 'sound money' men, who were mainly bankers, responded, 'Deflate.' Keynes was a monetary reformer. He insisted that it was 'far more important to fix the exchanges than to improve them'. This was to bring him into increasing conflict with the Bank of England and the British Treasury, who aimed to restore the pre-war gold value of the pound. The same day as his article appeared Keynes wrote to Luigi Einaudi, 'We both agree that the immediate problem is to persuade the world that a return to the pre-war parity is an absurdity. . . .'[29]

The Eleventh Supplement returned to the debate. 'Promises', Leffingwell insisted, 'are made to be kept.' The confidence requirements of businessmen could not be met by a monetary standard whose value was subject to the views of 'experts and politicians'. The cure for currency depreciation was 'for the Government to stop inflation at home and for the people to export more goods and services and import less – that is, to work and save'. This was the standard view from New York, but not from Yale. The economist Irving Fisher wrote, in support of Keynes, that deflation always and inevitably 'produces injustice to debtors, stockholders, enterprisers, and similar classes, and so causes depression of trade. No more insane policy for European reconstruction could be proposed than to restore greatly depreciated currencies to their original parities. . . .' Leffingwell's argument that 'Promises are made to be kept' assumed that an injustice would be done to holders of government debt if it were paid back in depreciated notes. Fisher pointed out that most of the money had been lent in depreciated notes to start with, since most of the debt was incurred late in the war *after* inflation had taken hold. Paying the debt back in full-value notes would provide many, if not most, bondholders with a massive windfall. Currency values should be stabilised at the 'centre of gravity of existing contracts'.[30]

An 'important and novel feature' of the First Supplement, which ran through all twelve issues, was the business 'barometer', based on an 'index' of business conditions. Compiled for Europe by the London School of Economics and for the United States by the Economic Research Department of Harvard University, these barometers claimed to be able to forecast changes in the economic weather. Keynes spent a great deal of time discussing with William Beveridge and A. L. Bowley at the LSE and Charles Bullock at Harvard the theory of the barometers and acquiring rights to publish them in the Supplements. He was normally quite sceptical about using inductive methods to forecast future events, but was for a while captivated by them. In fact, in a letter to Oswald Falk, dated 26 October 1921, he proposed developing special indexes to indicate 'strength of tendency' as distinct from 'tendency', which he called Accelerators or Accentuators.[31] Keynes helped start the London and Cambridge Economic Service – a regular survey of business conditions – in 1923, and produced for it for seven years an annual memorandum on stocks of commodities. The difference between Keynes and some of his fellow 'barometricians' was that he did not, in fact, believe that business conditions were like the tides – beyond human control. Rather he was looking for an adequate statistical basis for the 'scientific' control of credit which, in his view, was the key to the successful control of the business cycle.

IV

THE GENOA CONFERENCE

By the time the First Supplement appeared in April 1922 Keynes was comfortably ensconced in the Hotel Miramare in Santa Margherita, with two assistants, W. H. Haslam, a former King's man whom he had encountered in Rome two years before, and S. J. Buttress, the bursar's clerk at King's, as well as members of Britain's financial delegation. He had arrived on 8 April to cover the Genoa Economic Conference for the *Manchester Guardian*, the third and last of his journalistic coups, which added thirteen articles to his work load, and over £1000 to his income.[32]

It was a curious assignment, since Keynes must have known that the Conference, attended by twenty-nine countries, would accomplish little or nothing. It was the remnant of a far grander design by Lloyd George, the centrepiece of which was to have been a British guarantee of French security in return for French concessions on reparations, but which also included involving America and the leading European powers in an international consortium to finance the reconstruction of Soviet Russia. German participation in such a scheme would have the advantage of generating revenues for reparations without hurting British trade.

However, these larger elements had obstinately refused to fall into place. The French Prime Minister, Aristide Briand, had resigned after the Cannes Conference of January 1922, suspected of being under Lloyd George's thumb. His successor, Raymond Poincaré, a tenacious lawyer from Lorraine, with the mind of an accountant, came to power pledged to 'uphold firmly all France's rights under the Treaty of Versailles'. He refused to come to Genoa himself, and removed reparations from its agenda. This caused America to withdraw too, on the grounds that no real 'business' would be done.[33] All that was left was Lloyd George's hope of reviving Europe's economy (and Britain's flagging export trade) by financing the rebuilding of the Soviet Union, for which he had no money.[34] Lloyd George had clearly become a closet Keynesian, but too late. Had he been able to offer France a larger share of a smaller indemnity, as Keynes had suggested, he might have made progress. But this he was prevented from doing by his own misdeeds at Paris in 1919, and by America's insistence on full payment of the British debt. Nor could he offer France any British divisions for its defence: only paper promises. Meanwhile, Germany had virtually stopped paying reparations, and the mark (par value twenty to the pound) had fallen from 250 in March 1920 to over 1000 by March 1922.

Nevertheless, Genoa was not without interest for Keynes. There was a powerful Financial Commission, headed by the British Chancellor of the Exchequer, Sir Robert Horne; and Keynes moved in his familiar world of bankers and Treasury officials – Addis, Blackett, Brand, Hawtrey, Peacock and Strakosch from Britain; Cassel and Wallenberg from Sweden; Cuno and Melchior from Germany; Vissering from Holland; Frank Vanderlip (of the First National City Bank of New York) from the United States. Although Keynes came as a journalist, he would not have been Keynes had he not arrived with an ingenious plan. This was his scheme for stabilising the exchanges. Its appearance in the *Manchester Guardian* on 6 April was carefully calculated to make it the first talking point of the Conference; advance copies had also been circulated.

Keynes proposed that victors and neutrals should fix their exchange rates straightaway on the basis of their currencies' current gold values. These would be the permanent values of those currencies which had depreciated by over 20 per cent; stronger currencies like sterling would be allowed to 'crawl' up to their pre-war parities by no more than 6 per cent a year, if their prestige was thought to require it. Central banks should allow a 5 per cent difference or 'band' between the selling and buying price of gold to accommodate temporary fluctuations in the demand for their currencies. They should be allowed to borrow gold from the Federal Reserve Board of the United States at 10 per cent interest per annum up to a borrowing limit of $150m. for any country, and $500m. in total at any one time.[35] 'You will be interested to know', Keynes wrote to Ted Scott on 15 April,

> that my . . . articles on the exchanges have excited a good deal of interest here. . . . Soon after my arrival, I was summoned by the Chancellor of the Exchequer for a conference with him and the other official experts to consider whether the proposals of my first article ought to be formally laid before the Conference. In the end they decided adversely because of the weight of conservative opinion against Great Britain coming into any scheme. . . . [36]

Keynes kept producing such plans, with technical variations, for the rest of his life: the last of them led to the setting up of the Bretton Woods system in 1944. Their object was always to combine the advantages of the gold standard with a reasonable degree of national autonomy in the conduct of monetary policy. But, until the last one, they always foundered on the unwillingness of the United States to play its allotted role as lender of the last resort. Monetary reform at Genoa proceeded along different lines, with the adoption of resolutions recommending 'means of economising the use of gold by maintaining reserves in the form of foreign balances'.[37] This proposal for setting up a gold-exchange standard was the work of Ralph Hawtrey, then at the high point of his influence at the British Treasury.

What chiefly interested Keynes at Genoa was the presence of a Russian delegation, invited, for the first time since the war, to join the high priests of Europe in their deliberations. He denied – in an article published on 10 April – that 'the issue of the near future [is] between the forces of Bolshevism and those of the bourgeois states of the nineteenth century type'. Bolshevism was a temporary delirium like Jacobinism, 'bred by the besotted idealism and intellectual error of the sufferings and peculiar temperaments of Slavs and Jews'. He expected Russia and the West to converge in time on moderate socialism. Meanwhile, 'Soldiers and diplomatists – *they* are the permanent, the immortal foe.'[38] Keynes could not believe that the Soviet Union was a new form of power state which might be even more threatening to liberal values than 'soldiers and diplomatists'.

In his hopes for convergence he was undoubtedly influenced by his liking for Chicherin, an elegant homosexual of the old school, who came to Genoa as Soviet Russia's Commissar for Foreign Affairs. Keynes invited him to dinner on 12 April: 'The question whether or not the Conference is going to be no better than a bore depends almost entirely on yourself and Mr. Lloyd George between you.' In fact it was Chicherin who gave Keynes an interview in the Hotel Imperial in Santa Margherita on 13 April. Keynes developed an affinity for this 'rather amiable and agreeable snake',[39] who, however, was a mere executant of Soviet foreign policy.

Every day Keynes received an adoring letter from Lydia in London; except for two short notes, none of his to her have survived (in fact, none before September 1923). On 11 April she was 'very anxious to see your articles printed: to-day I went to three news stands, but not one . . . did . . . produce *Manchester Guardian*'. She added, 'I live simple working man's life, and you – do you go in the evenings to dissipated houses?' (Keynes had been gambling at the Casino in Rapallo.) Lydia had started dancing again at Covent Garden in a programme of *divertissements* organised by Massine: one of them featured her in a Scottish reel, another dressed as a negress. When, on 17 April, Keynes published his plan for a 'return to the gold standard', Lydia wrote, 'What you say now is dry and serious and enfluences [*sic*] the conference and a little later I see U.S. stepping into it by your idea. You are very famous, Maynard.' Lydia was finding it difficult to get rid of the black paint she had to put on to dance in *The Cockatoo's Holiday*: 'I have a feeling I ought not to wash myself for a week then easily I become the incarnation of a nigger.'

On 18 April Keynes turned again to Russia. Lloyd George, too, wanted to strike a sensible bargain with Chicherin, but was hamstrung by the French insistence that the Soviet Union should first acknowledge the tsarist debts. To Keynes this seemed like a dreadful rerun of Versailles and its 'rubbish about milliards'.

> We are pressing Russia to repeat words without much caring whether or not they represent sincere intentions, just as we successfully pressed Germany. . . . We act as high priests, not as debt collectors. The heretics must repeat our creed. . . . Genoa, instead of trying to disentangle the endless coil of impossible debt, merely proposes to confuse it further with another heap of silly bonds. The belief that all this protects and maintains the sacredness of contract is the opposite of the truth.[40]

Britain should write off the Russian war debt to itself. Russia should be allowed to compound with its other pre-war creditors for a modest annual sum, after a five-year moratorium. Wherever possible private properties held by foreigners 'should be restored to their original owners on the basis of partnership or profit-sharing arrangements between the owners and the Bolshevik government . . .'. This would open the way for a return of foreign capital to the Soviet Union. Inducements could take the form of *de jure* recognition and an export credit of £50m. to be spent by Russia buying British and German agricultural machinery and means of transport. 'If Russia exports food again one year earlier than she otherwise would, this may lower the price of wheat enough to save us a huge sum on our food bill alone.'[41]

None of this, of course, came to pass. The two pariahs, Russia and Germany, signed a separate treaty at Rapallo on 16 April, cancelling all claims on each other and making the debt-collectors look foolish. It did not lead to the reconstruction of Russia by German capital, because Germany had none. The question remains: could the Bolsheviks have been bribed to abandon their Revolution by Western credits? The Revolution had not yet been set in Stalinist concrete. Lenin was a supreme opportunist. He had embarked on a limited return to capitalism with the New Economic Policy in March 1921, which welcomed foreign capital. Rathenau's view was: 'Let private trading corporations go in individually. When they have got a sufficient number of contracts, the Soviet system will fall.'[42] Lloyd George and Keynes felt the same. We will never know, because the bribery was never attempted.

Maynard's articles on Russia excited Lydia very much. 'I see you have sympathy for Russia,' she wrote to him on 18 April. 'When Chicherin reads it he will follow your direction. . . .' And the next day: 'Your article for the Russian settlement can be only approved. I do want it to be adopted. It is clever. When I read what you write I feel bigger than I am.' And after reading him on 26 April on 'The Financial System of the Bolsheviks', she wrote, 'In your work to-day financially speaking Russians has only pessimistic roubles to offer of no value. But . . . after reading your article they must stabilise money.'

Lydia's commentaries can hardly be called profound. But that was not their purpose. They were designed to build up Maynard's self-esteem. He never got praise like this from his Cambridge or Bloomsbury friends. A year before he had confided to Virginia Woolf that 'he liked praise, & always wanted to boast. He said that many men marry in order to have a wife to boast to. "I want it [praise] for the things I'm doubtful about." '[43] He was particularly doubtful about his journalism, mistrusting his own facility. Lydia swept these doubts away. 'Do not speak against your articles in jornalism [sic],' she wrote on 22 April, 'just think how many people read, understand and remember it'; and on 28 April, 'You say you don't do much good. It is not true. . . . Do you not see how they need you?' Lydia's praise was unstinting. 'Your articles . . . *breathe* to me'; 'your plans . . . are like clear compact buildings'.

But it was not just his mind that Lydia wanted. Her early letters are full of expressions of sexual, mainly oral, endearment: 'I gobble you, my dear Maynard'; 'I retain infinitely your warm wet kisses'; 'I cover you with kisses full of flame'; 'With caresses large as sea I stretch out to you'; 'I want to wrap around you and give the [abundance] of my feeling.' She often signed herself 'your faithful dog'. To inspire such sexual devotion must have done wonders for the morale of someone who was convinced that he was unattractive to both sexes.[44] Keynes appeared to reciprocate: 'I want to be . . . gobbled abundantly,' he wrote from Genoa on 24 April. Sexual relations certainly developed, and by 1924 Lydia was appreciative of Maynard's 'subtle finger'. She had a childish sense of humour which suited him. 'Last night,' she wrote on 21 April, 'I had such a laughter I thought I could not finish from it – Miassin while dancing lost halph his shirt, collar, hat; when I saw that I immediately thought to have a decidedly funny disaster is to lose his trousers.'

Keynes left Genoa on 4 May, the day his last article appeared. It exuberantly praised Lloyd George for dragging his 'preposterous cargo of assembled statesmen to the point of presenting Russia in the fourth week a document which is a starting-point for reasonable negotiation' ('We are all amused that Keynes has taken to blessing the PM . . .' noted Tom Jones in his diary.)[45] To his mother, Keynes wrote, 'I have made the acquaintance of many great men. Even Ll.G. summoned me to him once! but we did not like one another any more than before.' One almost-great man who hunted Keynes down in the Hotel Miramare was Frank Harris, who proposed to publish an interview with him in *Pearson's Magazine*, which he was then editing. Harris was a great admirer, calling Keynes one of 'God's Spies'. But he was also a complete fantasist and, when he sent Maynard a copy of the interview, Maynard wrote back saying he hated it so much he couldn't possibly agree to its publication. Harris puts into Keynes's mouth words of utter banality mainly because, as he himself admitted, he was talking so much himself he never bothered to listen. The only thing worth rescuing is his memory of 'the mobility of those riotous eyes'.

V

THE PROPRIETIES

Maynard returned from Genoa to the growing complications of his affair with Lydia. He had installed her in Vanessa's flat at 50 Gordon Square. This worked perfectly well while Vanessa was away in Paris. But she returned at the same time as Maynard left for Genoa. Lydia, who had committed herself to Massine, stayed on as her lodger. There seems to have been little friction between them at this stage. In fact Vanessa told Roger Fry that she saw very little of Lydia, then only late at night, and that she was very charming, though 'there is some truth perhaps in Clive's complaint that she has only one subject of conversation, the ballet'.[46] It was in fact Clive, Vanessa's husband, who first turned against Lydia. Clive certainly loved the idea of Lydia. In fact he dedicated an excruciating poem 'To Lydia Dancing' ('Is it true? / Are Ariel's Whims / Embodied in your artful limbs?'). He also flirted with her, as he did with all pretty women. This apparently aroused the jealousy of his mistress Mary Hutchinson. At any rate it seems to have been Mary who 'set Clive against Lydia'.[47] He suddenly suggested to Vanessa that they spend their summer holidays in France, because a whole summer of Lydia at Charleston would be too boring.

There followed, Vanessa told Clive, 'one or two long & slightly painful . . . conversations with Maynard' on his return from Genoa. He agreed that it was probably impossible to have Lydia at Charleston all summer, and suggested that she might take Tilton Cottage, on the neighbouring farm, if the farmer could be bribed to let it. Vanessa had objected to this, saying that 'housekeeping for her would be so difficult & local cooking so bad that it would end in their really living at Charleston'. But Lydia disliked the idea of living with Keynes as his mistress. She thought it would be 'too scandalous' if she and Maynard lived together at Tilton, or at Charleston with the Bells not there. In any case, Vanessa thought, 'I don't see that we can go out of our way to consider proprieties for them – nor do I think we can start on the summer holidays with Lydia as part of the establishment. I get on with her perfectly well & like her very much – but I see that the introduction of anyone – especially female, for more than a week into such an intimate society as ours is bound to end in disaster.' Tilton Cottage proved unavailable, so Vanessa (who, it seems, was left by Clive to do his dirty work) finally wrote to Maynard on 19 May:

> Clive says he thinks it impossible for any of us, you, he, I, or Duncan, to introduce a new wife or husband into the existing circle for more than a week at the time. He himself is prepared (no wonder) to abstain from doing so & sooner than make one of such a party would prefer to go away alone. . . . Duncan and I feel that the whole question ought to be faced & that the only way is to talk quite frankly about it, only as it's almost impossible to see you in peace, I am writing to give you some rough idea of what we feel. . . . Don't think however that what I say is any kind of criticism of Lydia for it isn't. We feel that *no one* can come into the sort of intimate society we have without altering it (she has done so perhaps less than anyone certainly less than any other woman would have done). That's inevitable isn't it? I think you must realise it & I think it must be taken into account not only in its effect upon summer holiday plans but altogether. Clive says that if anyone else is to be permanently here [50 Gordon Square] he would have to leave the house [46 Gordon Square, where he still had rooms]. . . . I can't offer any solution to the summer problem. We were much rather you were at Charleston of course, but I'm afraid you may be forced to choose between us and Lydia. It all seems horribly complicated & I wish it weren't.

Clive Bell, always prickly about his 'Bloomsbury' rights, and always rather on edge with Keynes, was clearly the prime mover in all this. The problem was complicated by the fact that the Bells, Duncan, Maynard and

Lydia shared their meals together at Number 46. Keynes responded to Vanessa's ultimatum with spirit. As regards London, he wrote on 22 May,

> we must take Clive's leaving no. 46 as a fixed point. The psychological situation being what it is, and meals etc rather than beds being what count, that seems to me inevitable. . . . I must feel that there is no awkwardness at all in [Lydia] coming to the house whenever and as often as she wants; also it will be a great relief to get rid of Mary [Hutchinson] . . .

Other rearrangements, Keynes continued, could include Lydia going to live at Number 41, where Alix and James Strachey had a flat to let, Vanessa coming back to Number 46 and Clive going to live in Chelsea. 'A great deal depends on whether you can face Clive's leaving the Square. We all want to have and not to have husbands and wives.' As for the summer, the real problem was the uncertainty of Lydia's further ballet engagements. If she had only a short holiday, a compromise might be for her to come to Charleston for a week or so, and Clive go off to visit Mary. Otherwise two summer establishments were unavoidable, and the servant problem arose. He could surrender the servants (at 46 Gordon Square) to Vanessa for the summer, and take another house equipped with servants for the period of Lydia's holiday. 'But then the question of the proprieties will arise!' He concluded, 'Oh for a quiet and peaceful life with no crises.'

Nothing was settled immediately. Lydia sensed that all was not right. There is a very rare note of asperity in her letter to Maynard dated Monday, 12 June 1922: 'Clive gave a tea party – iced coffee was tasty; as usual great many boring people, including Ottoline, Mary, J. H. Smith and others.' For most of June and July Lydia danced at the Coliseum, while Maynard continued to work on the Supplements.

The second issue of 18 May 1922 contained a wonderful piece of economic metaphysics by Gabriel Hanotaux, a former French Foreign Minister of 'decidedly reactionary tendencies', which Maynard, tongue in cheek, had printed in French as well as in English 'for the benefit of those readers who will enjoy reading in the original so distinguished an example of French prose'. Hanotaux mentioned meeting the Mayor of Perngan (his own village on the Aisne) and the Mayor saying to him, 'M. Hanotaux, in spite of all the fine speeches of you fine gentlemen, here I am passing my eighth year in my cellar.' Hanotaux had replied, 'You really ought to write to Monsieur Keynes to tell him so.' Keynes advised Hanotaux 'to tell the mayor very confidently that his house will be rebuilt much sooner by my economics than by the sentimental miscalculations of M. Poincaré'.

The last week in June found Keynes staying with Falk at Lindisfarne Castle on Holy Island, just off the coast of Northumberland. There Lydia joined him, Falk and the puffins for three days on her way north to dance in Glasgow as part of a Massine 'quintette'. She had hesitated to come –

'I do not know your friend, perhaps he does not desire me, it is only in relation with you' – but wrote afterwards, 'how lovely the time was spent with you in the castle'. Keynes returned to London to work on the Supplements; on 17 July Lydia started a three-week season at the Coliseum, once more with Massine.

It was certainly one of the busiest times of Maynard's life. Tuesday, 11 July, a London day, was only mildly overcrowded by his standards. The earlier part of it was positively leisurely, with perhaps only telephone calls from his bed to his stockbroker. His speculations were going well, he told his mother about this time: 'half of them go up and half of them go down when the news is bad, and vice versa when the news is good; so I have what is called a "well-balanced position". . . . I understand, however, about father's unwillingness to go in for these terrifying adventures.'[48] The first engagement was a lunch with John Foster Dulles and Lewis Strauss, a New York banker. A meeting of the British Editorial Board (Beveridge, F. W. Hirst, Tom Jones, Keynes) of the Carnegie Endowment for International Peace followed at 2.30. Miss Rees, his secretary, came at four. At five o'clock there was an appointment with Asquith. At seven o'clock Keynes was seeing his Cambridge pupil J. V. Joshi. There was a party at H. G. Wells's at 9.30; then round to Christabel Aberconway, a great friend of the Asquiths and Courtaulds, at 10.30.

Keynes was living on a high, and his excitement communicated itself to Roy Harrod, who had just graduated from Christ Church, Oxford. He wanted to study economics in Cambridge under Keynes and was bidden to lunch at 46 Gordon Square on 27 July:

> I mounted the stairs to the drawing-room on the first floor, where the meal was served. The room itself made a strong impression. It seemed empty, devoid of the usual ornaments and appendages, in a style that was rapidly to come into fashion, but was strange to me. On the walls were two pictures only, and these were very modern, perhaps by Matisse or Picasso. The armchairs were exceedingly comfortable. There was nothing else except the small table at which we were to eat. This environment, with its assertion of modernity, itself provided a slightly exciting background. Keynes came quickly across to me and greeted the stranger with warmth. There were two others at lunch, one of whom was a young French economist on a brief visit.*
>
> The talk began without any pause; it was quick and animated. Keynes was discussing with the Frenchman the latest gossip about Continental statesmen, their mistresses, their neuroses, as well as their political manoeuvres. These seemed as exciting as fiction; I supposed they must be real. There was financial talk of the latest movements of

---

*Keynes's engagement diary for 27 July gives four guests: Franck, Harrod, Jacoby, Patterson. Perhaps one of them did not show up, or Harrod's memory is at fault.

the exchanges, budgetary positions, the international movement of money. This was still far beyond my ken. But then certain more familiar strands began to come into the pattern, for the three of them seemed able and ready to relate their items of financial intelligence to theoretical doctrine, the quantity theory of money, foreign exchange equilibrium. There were passing references to the latest ideas of Cassel and Fisher, and subtle points of criticism were made. Then I realised that I was in the presence of something quite unusual – this mixture of *expertise* in the latest theories with inside knowledge of day-to-day events. . . . The excitement was unbearable.[49]

Keynes travelled to Oxford on 4 August to address the Liberal Summer School on reparations. A day later Lydia's season at the Coliseum ended. On 8 August the two lovers travelled together to Ostend to see the Diaghilev ballet and gamble with Sheppard: the proprieties could be dropped for 'abroad'. On their return, Maynard went to stay for a few days with the McKennas in Menabilly in Cornwall, while Lydia danced in Manchester. 'I float rapidly between Cornwall, Hamburg, Sussex and Wiltshire,' Keynes wrote to Sebastian Sprott from Menabilly on 19 August. On 23 August Lydia danced the can-can before the rheumatic old ladies of Harrogate; three days later Keynes revealed his latest financial plan to the rheumatic old bankers of Hamburg.* Lydia stayed with her friends Vera and Harold Bowen from 27 August to 7 September; Maynard was at Charleston from 30 August to 5 September, dreaming about a commune on the Downs.

On 7 September they both moved into Parsonage House, Oare, near Marlborough, Wiltshire, which Maynard had rented from Geoffrey Fry, who had served under him in the Treasury. Here they finally spent three weeks together. Their neighbours were Desmond and Molly MacCarthy, their only visitors Sheppard and Cecil Taylor.† 'We are very happy here,' Maynard wrote to Vanessa on 17 September, 'and time flies by. We ride every day in most perfect country and by the end of the week the riding master thinks Lydia will be accomplished.' There survives a draft of a letter, in Keynes's hand, taken down from Lydia's dictation, refusing an invitation to a dinner in London in honour of Adeline Genée. 'But even gay dancers must have holiday sometime from being so gay; and I am now in country with a horse as a dancing partner.' Lydia left for London on 29 September to start rehearsals for a new ballet; Keynes had hoped to have Sebastian

---

*On 27 August, Keynes and Melchior met two German Foreign Office Officials at the home of Wilhelm Cuno, soon to be German Chancellor. Keynes 'advised the Germans to rather risk open conflict than to yield to French demands'. ('Note for the Diary' by Carl Melchior, 28.8.22, in Privat-Archiv Warburg, Hamburg; Carl Melchior/Max M. Warburg Papers MA 16.) I am indebted to Dorothea Hauser for bringing this document to my attention.

†Cecil Taylor was a schoolmaster at Clifton College. His nickname was 'Madame' – see Skidelsky, *Keynes*, i, 237–8.

Sprott for a few days after she left; he consoled himself with stag-hunting till his return to Cambridge.

In Bloomsbury the game of domestic musical chairs was finally concluded. Lydia moved from Number 50 to Number 41, Vanessa from Number 50 to Number 46, and Clive from Number 46, not to Chelsea, but only to Number 50. Blanche and Mr Bam had gone from Number 46, replaced by Mrs Harland, a 'jewel of a cook', and her husband, who had been a 'valet to nobility'. Lydia opened on 9 October with a three-week season of *divertisse-ments* at the Coliseum. This time, with Maynard's encouragement and under his direction, she started a ballet company of her own. Stoll paid her £175 a week, out of which she paid the other dancers. 'From the artistic point of view', Cyril Beaumont wrote to her, 'your attempt is miles above the Mas-sine show.' A new entertainment, *Mozart's Evening Music*, produced by her friend Vera Bowen, choreographed by Massine and designed by Duncan Grant, opened at the Coliseum on 19 November. On 29 October Vanessa had reported to Roger Fry, 'Maynard is in London for a few days. Then he's going to Berlin to help arrange their finances. Lydia & he seem to have settled down to married life & I'm not at all sure it won't end in real marriage as I think she's beginning to want a baby very badly & will soon insist on it. Well, if so I shall have to move once again. . . .'

VI

THE UNLUCKY EXPERTS

Keynes's appearance in Berlin on 2 November 1922 marked the return of the experts after the collapse of Lloyd George's grand political initiatives. Lloyd George's failure at Genoa not only doomed his premiership, but also marked the effective end of the Anglo-French entente. He was convinced that, had Briand stayed in power, a 'European appeasement from the Urals to the Rhine might have been reached in 1922'.[50] This is wishful thinking: Anglo-French differences were too great. After Genoa, London came to understand that the key to a European settlement lay in Washington, not Paris. The American objective, which reflected the views of both the new Republican administration of Warren Harding and the New York bankers, was to take financial questions out of politics, treating them as purely business matters. The administration's programme linked a resumption of private US lending to Europe to payment of the Allied war debts to the USA, settlement of the reparations question by financial experts, not poli-ticians, and currency stabilisation. Throughout the summer and autumn of 1922, experts and bankers met and produced plans: they all foundered on the rock of Poincaré's refusal to 'allow a committee of bankers to arbitrate the rights of France or influence her destiny'.[31] The Balfour Note of August 1922 announced Britain's intention of limiting its claim to reparations and the war debts it was owed to the net amount required to meet its obligations to the United States. Despite its hostile reception in both America and France, it was the opening move in the realignment of British policy.

Meanwhile, the Reparation Commission had to arrange the conditions for the moratorium Germany had asked for at the end of 1921. Sir John Bradbury, Britain's Treasury representative, favoured a two-year moratorium to give Germany time to balance its budget and stabilise the mark; Poincaré demanded *gages productifs* in return for any suspension of cash payments: taking over the German customs, seizing its mines and forests, taking majority shareholdings in prosperous firms. The British refused to entertain such proposals. Poincaré's attitude, wrote Lord D'Abernon, the British Ambassador in Berlin, 'is that of a teacher who is constantly rapping a pupil on the knuckles, not realising that he is moribund'.[32] The mark continued to plummet. Making their own currency absolutely worthless was the one way the Germans had of evading the insistent French demands. When the printers at the Reichsbank went on strike, Havenstein, the Bank's president, brought in strike-breakers to keep the supply of notes churning out.[33]

In his speech to the Liberal Party Summer School on 4 August 1922, Keynes rejected the Balfour Note's attempt to link the reparations problem and Britain's debt to the United States. 'We must abandon the claim for pensions and bring to an end the occupation of the Rhinelands.... If France would agree to this, which is in her interest anyway . . . it would be right for us to forgive her (and our other Allies) all they owe us . . . regardless of what the United States may say or do.'[34] This view was endorsed by Asquith; but no British government would unilaterally cancel the debts it was owed, with its own liabilities to America still undetermined. In trying to appease Paris, Keynes missed the importance of involving Washington. Basil Blackett at the Treasury, possibly advised by Keynes, had held up the Balfour Note 'against the whole Cabinet for a month'.[35] Keynes looked at America with his blind eye.

In more sombre mood, Keynes wondered whether all these debt-collecting plans, sensible or crazy, did not misunderstand the mechanisms of modern economic life. Writing in the Eighth *Manchester Guardian* Reconstruction Supplement of 28 September he noted that the nineteenth-century system of capital transfers was not tied to 'export surpluses'. Debtors paid interest out of fresh loans; creditors reinvested the proceeds of past loans, which accumulated at compound interest. National wealth was not built up by returns on foreign investment but by 'knowledge, skill, organisation and a proper balance between the factors of production'. The analogy between governments and business firms was wrong: if a state defaulted on its debts 'there is no legal process for dealing with it.... it is foolish, therefore, to

suppose that any means exist by which one modern nation can exact from
another a tribute continuing over many years'. European civilisation needed
German support to defend it against the 'dark forces' of Bolshevism. All
Keynes's old animosity against Lloyd George burst out: he had 'proved
himself the least capable of enduring and constructive statemanship of any
man who has long held power in England'. It was time, he concluded, for
'new men . . . to make the speedier progress which Europe's state impera-
tively now demands'.[56]

The day of the new men came at last. On 22 October 1922, Lloyd George
fell from power, victim of the Chanak crisis and the 'stench of the Honours
scandal'.[57] He was succeeded by Keynes's old Treasury chief Andrew Bonar
Law, who after a general election held in November, formed a purely
Conservative government. In Germany, Joseph Wirth was succeeded on 14
November by Wilhelm Cuno, a 'non-political' Hamburg shipowner and a
friend of Melchior: Keynes had negotiated with him at Versailles over the
handover of German shipping, and had met him subsequently in London
and Hamburg. The German economist Moritz Bonn thought he would have
been an excellent reception clerk in a luxury hotel. His support was limited
to shipping and banking circles. A new man of a rather different kind,
Benito Mussolini, seized power in Italy on 30 October 1922.

Lord D'Abernon had persuaded the Wirth government to invite Keynes
to Berlin as a member of a commission of experts to advise on currency
reform. The commission was made up of some 'very clever men' (Keynes,
Cassel, Brand and Jenks, an American professor) and 'the requisite ballast
of dull ones to lend respectability' (Vissering, Dubois and Kamenka).*
Keynes went across with Brand, who had given up a day's pheasant shooting
in the cause of European reconstruction. They were joined in Berlin by
members of the Reparation Committee – Barthou and Bradbury – still
quarrelling about conditions for a moratorium. The arrival of so many
currency doctors proved almost fatal for the currency – 'the moment they
appear the mark bolts: this time it has got quite out of control, in a headlong
flight towards the abyss'. Lord D'Abernon was amused by the relations
between the two sets of experts, noting in his diary of 6 November:

> In the early days the official experts looked askance at the free experts:
> they were jealous that their province had been invaded . . . they were
> alarmed at some fresh fashion in obsequies. But Berlin society has
> shown skill and tact, and has bridged the gulf. At first the free experts
> were invited to entertainments after dinner – like actresses with doubt-
> ful pasts. . . . then it was arranged for them to meet reparationists . . .
> at casual teas; to-day they are invited together to luncheon; to-morrow

*All three were bankers: Leopold Dubois, president of the Schweizerische Bankverein, Basel;
G. Vissering, governor of the Bank of the Netherlands, Amsterdam; B. Kamenka, president of
the Russian Asoff-Don Bank, in Brussels.

they will dine at the same official table at the American Embassy.[38]

Keynes was in Berlin for a week; Melchior provided him with a flat and secretary at the Hamburg-Amerika line's headquarters in Bellevuestrasse. 'The German problem is very difficult,' Brand wrote to his wife Phyllis, a sister of Nancy Astor, on 3 November. 'All they hope is that we shall lend them money & we shan't. If they can get off Reparations for the time being, they must dare themselves. . . . We have quite a good Committee. There is an American on it, Professor [Jeremiah] Jenks from Columbia Univ. He doesn't seem at all bad.' A day later Brand reported that the discussions had reached a critical stage and there was a good deal of difference of opinion among the free experts. The Reparation Commission was waiting for the German government's plans, and the German government was waiting for the free experts to advise them. 'It is a v. psychological moment. . . . These currency problems are the devil. I often feel out of my depth in them as indeed most bankers do.' That evening there was a huge dinner of captains of industry, bankers and professors. Keynes sat next to Max Planck, the German physicist and Nobel prize-winner. Planck told him that he had thought of studying economics early in his life but had found it too difficult! A couple of years later, Keynes recalled this conversation in his obituary on Alfred Marshall. Professor Planck, he wrote, could easily have mastered the 'whole corpus of mathematical economics in a few days'. What Planck meant was that economics was imprecise and intuitive, and therefore 'overwhelmingly difficult' for those whose gift was to imagine, and pursue the implications, of known facts.[59] The conviction that economics was not like a natural science dominated Keynes's own work.

By 5 November, Brand was complaining about overwork – and Keynes. '[He] is rather upsetting the other members of the Ctee. He is so arbitrary & critical . . . that he rather loses the effect of his extraordinary cleverness. They get distrustful of him. He always wants to rush everyone.' Brand thought the Committee would break up; he had to play the part of peacemaker.*

On 7 November the experts submitted their reports to the German government. 'One banker & 3 Professors' (Brand, Cassel, Jenks and Keynes) signed the majority report. Brand wrote,

*The main conflict was between Keynes and Dubois. Dubois wanted a report acceptable to the French. He spun out proceedings, hoping Keynes would leave Berlin before he had got a majority. Warned by the Committee's secretary, Ernst Kocherthaler, an employee of Warburgs, Keynes delayed his departure. Since he turned up to meetings with 'completely formulated drafts' while all the others were 'blithering' (beim Dibbern) he managed to stay a step ahead of Dubois. Keynes's aim was to enable Germany to break with France, with England's support. At a private meeting with the Chancellor, he said this could be achieved only if Germany coupled its demand for a moratorium with a pledge to use the gold of the Reichsbank to stabilise the mark. But such an act of daring was beyond the will of the tottering Wirth government.

The other 3 bankers are making up their own report. They think ours will anger the French so that they won't sign it. . . . I searched my conscience & decided to say *the truth*. So there it is. . . . Almost the Nordic races versus the Mediterranean & Slav. . . . There was some heat, as the other party thought Keynes had deliberately manoeuvred them into a tight corner. But he hadn't meant to.[60]

Back in London, Keynes briefed Montagu Norman. His Berlin trip had cost him £6 15s 8d.

The majority report, drafted by Keynes, called for the immediate stabilis-ation of the mark by Germany's own efforts, but emphasised that this required a two-year moratorium on reparations payments and a budget balanced 'by the utmost economy in government expenditure and the utmost of rigour in the collection of taxes'. A foreign loan would be useful, but not indispensable. Lord D'Abernon thought that the report was 'the most important document which has been drawn up in the recent course of the reparation controversy'; he added, 'it received not the smallest attention, either from the Allies or from Germany. Creditor and debtor – who agreed in nothing else – agreed in ignoring it.'[61]

The experts' report was not pro-German. The Germans argued that the reason for the collapse of the mark was an adverse balance of trade, so that stabilisation required, in the circumstances, a large foreign loan. Keynes completely rejected this reasoning. As he wrote in the Eleventh Reconstruc-tion Supplement on 7 December, 'If the quantity of a currency can be controlled, then sooner or later it can be stabilised. This simple truth still holds good. The quantity of a currency can be controlled unless the govern-ment is in financial difficulties.'[62] Thus the key to stabilisation, Keynes told Rudolf Havenstein, president of the Reichsbank, was to stop printing money:

If I felt confident I could control the budgetary position, I should not doubt my capacity, in Germany's present situation, to control the exchange. As soon as the supply of new currency is limited, I do not see how it is possible that the balance of trade should be adverse. I believe that the point of view which looks first to the balance of trade, and seeks for an improvement in that first of all, or alternatively to the support of a foreign loan, is deeply erroneous and has not penetrated to the true process of causation. . . . [63]

This is Keynes at his most orthodox, speaking in the accents of Hume and Ricardo. It was also the French position. What he insisted on, against the French, was that the strain a social system could take before it collapsed was very limited.

With Cuno, advised by Melchior, installed as the new Chancellor in Berlin, and Bonar Law as British Prime Minister, Keynes now had access to policymakers in two countries. In London he found he was being consulted 'almost as in the old Treasury days'.[64] He received from Bradbury successive drafts of the Treasury plan for settling reparations as it evolved up to 1 December. He thought it 'brilliant', though impossibly obscure, suggested technical improvements and tried to make it more favourable to France.[65] He saw Bonar Law on 19 December and offered him a scheme of his own, again designed to ensure that France got a larger share of scaled-down payments.[66] The previous day he had been consulted by Stanley Baldwin, the new Chancellor of the Exchequer, about the American debt, which Baldwin was about to go to Washington to settle. At the same time he had opened up a line of communication, through Melchior, to the new German government. 'I think you will find hardly a prominent politician in England', he wrote to Melchior on 1 December, 'who is not astonished and dismayed by the extraordinary weakness of the German government . . . in its perpetual attempts . . . to try and find out some useless formula which will not offend. . . . Is there no one in Germany capable of calling out in a clear voice . . . ?'[67] This was probably the moment he decided that he would be the clear voice. Melchior passed his comments on to Cuno. Keynes felt that at last he was where he wanted to be: helping to shape policy in both countries from both inside and outside.

Over the winter of 1922–3 his work load continued to be prodigious. Memoranda and articles poured from his pen almost every day. In November and December he gave four very meaty lectures to the Institute of Bankers. His telephone rang constantly, moving him to complain publicly in the *New Statesman*, 'at no time during the day can I rely on a quarter of an hour's uninterrupted work'.[68] The last issue of the *Manchester Guardian* Supplements came out on 4 January 1923. It contained an introduction by him in which he turned to a topic never far removed from his thoughts: the depleted moral legacy available for reconstruction. 'In our present confusion of aims,' he wrote,

> is there enough clear-sighted public spirit left to preserve the balanced and complicated organisation by which we live? Communism is discredited by events; socialism, in its old-fashioned interpretation, no longer interests the world; capitalism has lost its self-confidence. Unless men are united by a common aim or moved by objective principles, each one's hand will be against the rest and the unregulated pursuit of individual advantage may soon destroy the whole. There has been no common purpose lately between nations or between classes, except for war.

These judgements were premature. The discredit of communism had yet to come; that of socialism has (perhaps) only just come; fascism had hardly started. Keynes could offer no new faith, and only rather pallid 'objective principles': pacifism and population control – 'not as furnishing in themselves a good life, but as absolutely necessary prerequisites of any good life', and 'the prolegomena to any further scheme of social improvement'.[69] In ending thus, Keynes undersold himself and the Supplements. Keynesianism was already a gleam in his eye – not as an economic theory, but as the vision of an enlightened Middle Way. The economic principles of the Victorians were not to be discarded, but they needed to be applied with a new flexibility which reflected the fragile character of post-war societies. The high priests of the new Middle Way were to be not politicians but economic technicians, because it was not a new political settlement, but a new economic settlement which Europe needed. A few months earlier he had written, 'No!' the economist is not king; quite true. But he ought to be! He is a better and wiser governor than the general or the diplomatist or the oratorical lawyer. In the modern overpopulated world, which can only live at all by nice adjustments, he is not only useful but necessary.'[70]

VII

KEYNES–MELCHIOR

What followed over the next few months, and especially in May–June 1923, was certainly one of the strangest episodes in Keynes's life and one of the most curious in the hidden diplomacy of the inter-war years. Essentially he and the German banker Carl Melchior turned the 'curious intimacy' they had established at Spa in 1919[71] to the task of securing an Anglo-German agreement. The complicity of victor and vanquished on that occasion was re-enacted in a correspondence – parts of which are unfortunately missing – in which Keynes offered constructive criticism of German tactics which Melchior passed on to Cuno, and Melchior sent Keynes 'inside' political and financial intelligence which he would use in discussion with British officials. By these means the two friends hoped to attune their own governments to each other's wavelength.

Carl Melchior was one of Keynes's greatest friends; he and Marcel Labordère were his best foreign friends. 'In a sort of way I was in love with him,' Keynes had said after their meeting at Spa in March 1919. Yet Melchior remains elusive. Contemporaries spoke of his 'superhuman and almost impudent modesty'. Perhaps his extreme reserve was a sign of the suppressed homosexual he probably was, and this is what Keynes intuited. A fine collection of modern paintings was the only outward indication of at least some sensual quality in this otherwise withdrawn man.

Their friendship enabled, rather than caused, them to play a game which they conceived to be in the national interests of their own countries and of Europe as a whole. For Melchior the prize was to isolate France. Keynes believed that French policy under Poincaré disguised economic and territorial ambitions which threatened Britain's commerce. The risks in this amateur diplomacy were obvious. By encouraging the Germans to believe that, sooner or later, the British would come down on their side, Keynes encouraged German resistance to French demands. Like most Englishmen he also underestimated French resolve. The results were unexpected by both. By helping to crowd out direct Franco-German negotiations, the Keynes–Melchior initiative paved the way for eventual American intervention, which resulted in the Dawes Plan.

The occasion for this private initiative was France's resort to force to overcome the German default. The statesmen and experts had assembled once more with their plans – in London on 9 December 1922, in Paris on 2 January 1923. At the first of these conferences, Bonar Law, 'clear and acute, but ultra-pessimistic',[72] presented the British Treasury proposals, which implied 'a radical rethinking of reparations'.[73] There was to be a four-year moratorium. The Germans would then start to pay at the rate of 2 billion marks or £100m. a year. Provision for a complicated series of bond issues was designed to ensure that the more quickly Germany paid, the less its total liability would be: ideally, as little as 37 billion marks. In addition, Germany must stabilise the mark along the lines recommended by the Keynes–Cassel report of 7 November. The British plan provided for a supervision of German finance through a Foreign Finance Council with 'very wide powers' but a unanimity requirement. In return for French acceptance, Britain would write off the major part of France's debt to itself.

Keynes had hailed the plan as a 'very fine performance intellectually'.[74] So he might, for the performance was partly his. His influence is apparent in the writing off of the 'fictitious' part of the German debt; in the incentive and stabilisation proposals; and in addressing the question of sweeteners to France. What the British plan did not do was to provide for any reduction in the British *share* of the scaled-down bill; indeed, by demanding the repeal of Belgian priority and declaring that Britain would use French and Italian gold reserves in London if necessary to cover French and Italian debts it succeeded in isolating Britain. Keynes hoped that the published scheme would be a prelude to a British proposal of 'far more striking generosity' to France before the Conference ended.[75] But Bonar Law had nothing more to say. Poincaré, predictably, rejected the British ideas and prepared to act. Having persuaded a majority on the Reparation Commission to declare Germany in default on coal deliveries, he sent French engineers and troops into the Ruhr on 11 January 1923. The politicians and experts having failed to come up with an answer, the soldiers took over. 'France', Keynes declared, 'has chosen to tear up the Treaty and break the peace of Europe.'

While Keynes was gaining credit with the Treasury he was losing it with the Bank of England. Baldwin, the new Chancellor of the Exchequer, had sailed for Washington with Montagu Norman at the end of December to arrange for a settlement of the American debt. With the governor it was a matter of honour that Britain should pay back what it had borrowed. Honour coincided with the City's interests, Anglo-American co-operation to restore the gold standard, and the resumption of American lending in Europe, all of which were essential elements in Norman's grand design. Keynes had consistently advocated cancellation of inter-Allied war debts. He did not consider them moral obligations since they were incurred in a common cause. He feared that Britain would feel obliged to make one-sided payments even if it received nothing from its debtors. Moreover, the war debts raised the same theoretical and practical issues as did German reparations. They had created no profitable assets out of which to repay: payment could be made only by lowering living standards. In his *Revision of the Treaty* he predicted, rightly, that 'America will not carry through to a conclusion the collection of the Allied debt any more than the Allies will carry through the collection of their present reparation demands. Neither, in the long run, is serious politics.'[76] But in the long run, as he was himself to say, we are all dead; and in the short run American lenders wanted their bond. As President Calvin Coolidge was to say, 'We hired them the money, didn't we?'*

Keynes was shocked when Baldwin returned in January with his provisional settlement, stipulating annual British payments of between $161m. and $184m. stretching sixty-two years ahead. He and McKenna advised Bonar Law to reject the terms: let 'America discover that they are just as completely at our mercy, as we are at France's and France at Germany's', Keynes wrote to Baldwin's private secretary, J. C. C. Davidson, on 30 January.[77] Bonar Law threatened to resign if the Cabinet agreed to them; but McKenna, who had urged him to resist, now backed down. Norman was furious with Keynes for endangering his designs. In Washington he had been much impressed with the 'newly-found desire on the part of the Americans to come into Europe again'.[78] He now dismissed Keynes as a 'clever dilettante with an even greater potential for mischief than the irresponsible Beaverbrook' and never asked for his advice again.[79] But the point was that Keynes was not keen for 'the Americans to come into Europe again'. He wanted Europe to solve its problems by itself. America was not part of his grand design.

Meanwhile, there was a diplomatic impasse in Central Europe. Instead of capitulating when French troops marched into the Ruhr, as perhaps Poincaré expected, the German government called for a policy of passive resistance – non-work in the occupied areas – financed by an empty

*The American view on the debts was forcefully put to Keynes by John M. Micklin, a professor at Dartmouth College, New Hampshire, on 24 May 1928: 'If, as you say, Europe is disgusted at America for belying her lofty idealism by playing the international Shylock please remember that many Americans are disgusted with Europeans for obfuscating stern hard facts with an appeal to mawkish sentiment. You are practically asking this country to pay for the blunders, the stupidities and the age-old enmities of Europe. Is this "moral" . . . ?' (In *CW*, xviii, 301.)

exchequer to the final ruin of the mark. This drove the French and Belgians to commandeer the railways and mines of the Ruhr and work them with their own labour. The British balanced in the middle, 'unwilling to break with France or to discipline Germany.'[80] (D'Abernon likened Bonar Law to Pontius Pilate.)[81] The Americans would do nothing till the debt situation was finally resolved. The circumstances were made for 'a further series of individual initiatives, more or less detached from the position of the various governments'.[82]

It was not till 20 April that Lord Curzon, the francophile British Foreign Secretary, invited Germany to submit proposals for a settlement. The German reply of 2 May, in which Melchior collaborated, offered a little less than Bonar Law had asked for, to be paid for by means of an American loan. It did, however, offer to submit to impartial arbitration the question of German capacity to pay. The French and Belgians rejected the German offer on 6 May; the British followed suit on 13 May, but suggested that Germany 'reconsider and expand' its proposals, which at least kept open the door for further exchanges. Keynes's comments, launched from the *Nation*, over which he had just acquired control (see p. 134 below), are scathing about the performance of all three leading governments, though he adopted a different tone for each. From Germany one heard:

> the gramophone record of a muddled drafting committee. From the days of Versailles until now the Notes of the German government have lacked both passion and persuasiveness. . . . One might suppose her statesmen . . . were nourished exclusively on potatoes.
>
> Heaven knows that propaganda is a sinful thing! But there is nothing wrong in writing a short sentence. . . . The peace of Europe, almost, is menaced by prose style. Who, smiling at his German governess,* could have foreseen that this national peculiarity would have turned out so important!
>
> The faults of form are not only literary. . . . by making her proposal appear to depend on an international loan, impracticable in size and to be contributed by others, she has contrived to make it look a deception and an evasion at the same time.[83]

Sorrow rather than playfulness marked his comment on the British Note; he deplored, in particular, Curzon's omission of any reference to the German suggestion of an expert commission to assess German capacity:

> Lord Curzon's reply to the German Note indicates that the British government drifts, and is still without a European policy. The degree to which Mr. Bonar Law's Cabinet lacks both nerve and intelligence becomes painfully apparent in the face of big issues. The best that can be said of the reply is that in moderately polite language Germany is

*Keynes had two as a child.

invited to try again, and that its pompous and condescending phrases are quite free from menace.[84]

Bonar Law's illness, though not its terminal nature, was already public knowledge. When he resigned a few days after the above assessment appeared, Keynes wrote a friendly appreciation, which nevertheless dubbed his statesmanship as 'too pessimistic to snatch present profits and too short-sighted to avoid future catastrophe'.[85]

His vitriol was reserved for the French:

> The French reply, sent without consultation with her Allies, offends against more important things than tact or style. The small, malignant figure of Poincaré lacks even the grim, ingratiating quality of the old grey owl Clemenceau. One feels oneself in a black cavern, narrowing to a point through which nothing human can creep, nightmare narrowness.
>
> France demands her bond and her forfeit too – to cut out Germany's heart and to extract the utmost ducat at the same time; greed and fear and revenge, overreaching one another, until they end in a sort of nihilism. It is not well to invoke the majesty of law in the act of outraging it, or to raise the plea of justice untempered by truth or mercy. The sneering reply of France closes the door on everything. It does not even grasp at a tangible object.[86]

Keynes's letter of 10 May to Melchior is missing. But he evidently told his friend that he intended to 'come over to Germany and lift the veil'.[87] In preparation for this visit he wrote a private letter to the German Chancellor, enclosing 'A Suggested Reply to Lord Curzon'. He said to Cuno:

> I have of course been following the recent events with deep pessimism and profound sympathy for the efforts you have been making. Nothing, in my opinion, is of any utility at present, except something which makes clear to the average Englishman and the average American the true purposes of France and Germany respectively. It is hopeless to attempt to satisfy France. Any further reply you may make to Lord Curzon can have no object except to affect favourably British and American opinion. . . . I venture, very humbly, to enclose a suggestion of the line which a further reply might take. I have shown this sugges-tion to no one. The reply must be short and simple and dignified. . . . Please excuse my presumption in sending it. A foreigner naturally feels much delicacy in making a suggestion.

Keynes's suggested reply contained four short paragraphs. Germany would accept Bonar Law's 'general scheme' of January 1923, including the securities proposed in the event of a default, 'provided that the amount of the annuity commencing in 1927 (i.e. the rate of interest on the first series of new bonds) is determined in due course by an independent tribunal as proposed in her previous communication'.[88] By this ingenious formula Keynes hoped to align the German position with British proposals and American wishes, while preserving Cuno's room for domestic manoeuvre. But there was a snag. Melchior (deputed to reply to 'our mutual friend') explained that 30 billion marks was the German maximum. In his letter of 24 May (which went to Cuno) Keynes insisted that the German reply 'get away from the capital sum (which is bound to fall short of what people here expect) and from the loan (which is absurd), and to speak in terms of annuities'. Germany should declare its willingness to accept arbitration on the capital sum. Keynes considered the following two points important:

(1) If in fact the new Note is no advance on the old Note let this be proved plainly and even boasted about.
(2) Let Germany, instead of making moan about how badly she is being treated, insist rather on her capacity for indefinite resistance and even introduce a slight note of menace. Her present propaganda about how cruelly she is oppressed produces the impression that she will break down before long. *In the long run* firmness and a proud bearing will produce more effect on opinion than conciliation and moans.[89]

In his published comment in the *Nation* on 26 May, Keynes once more attacked the 'chimera' of the great international loan.[90] Through Melchior, he advised the Germans to delay their reply to the British Note pending government changes in Britain. Stanley Baldwin had replaced Bonar Law as prime minister on 22 May; Robert Cecil was definitely in the Cabinet, and Reginald McKenna was expected to be Chancellor of the Exchequer, so 'there are now two very influential figures [in the government] who do *not* believe in huge figures.'[91]*

Keynes had decided to slip over to Berlin on the weekend of 1 June. On 30 May he saw Baldwin and McKenna, explaining to Baldwin that he was going over to Germany to try to influence the German government into 'more fruitful paths'.[92] He was in Berlin from Friday, 1 June to Monday, 4 June, staying in Melchior's flat. Over the weekend the German reply was hammered out in conversations between Keynes, Cuno, Melchior and the German Foreign Minister, von Rosenberg. Keynes explained the conflicts of opinion within the British government. The Foreign Office was pro-French, the Treasury pro-German. Baldwin would not overrule Curzon, who had hoped to succeed Bonar Law as prime minister. Baldwin and McKenna thought Germany should not lay too much stress on an international conference of experts, because the French would not agree to it.

*Baldwin's plan to make McKenna his Chancellor fell through, and Neville Chamberlain became Chancellor of the Exchequer.

Keynes and Melchior discussed the German Foreign Office draft reply the evening Keynes arrived, Keynes suggesting some changes. On Saturday morning Keynes, Cuno and Rosenberg had detailed discussions, Melchior joining them later. Rosenberg, a quick drafter, produced a new draft giving figures on annuities; Keynes and Melchior opposed putting in figures on the ground that the French would reject them out of hand. A new draft without figures was prepared in the afternoon. On Saturday night Keynes, Melchior and Rosenberg were Cuno's dinner guests. The afternoon draft was approved, and Keynes made an English translation. Melchior relates that they were 'all aware that success was improbable'. Keynes returned to London on the morning of 4 June, the day after his fortieth birthday,

> to prepare public opinion. . . . The best that [Keynes thought] could be attained at present would be that Baldwin and McKenna would make some favourable remarks about the German Note and that the British Cabinet would then contact the other powers entitled to reparations with a view to convening an inter-allied conference at which England would propose a second conference which would include the participation of Germany.[93]

The absence of any reference to the United States in these discussions shows how little Keynes realised that America was, or wanted it to be, the key to the solution.

On his return, Keynes lost no time in communicating the draft German reply to Baldwin. It was seen and approved by McKenna and Norman, and favourably received by the British Treasury. By the time it was officially delivered on 7 June, 'Cuno and von Rosenberg were aware that it was not going to be rejected by the British government.'[94]

The German Note was much admired for its conciliatory character and tautness of style. Germany agreed to submit its 'capacity to pay' as well as the amount and method of payment to an impartial international body. If large-scale loans proved impracticable, it would substitute a scheme of annuities. It offered definite guarantees for payment. 'In a matter so vast and complicated', the Note concluded, 'real progress cannot be made by the exchange of written documents, but can only be achieved by word of mouth at the conference table.'[95] Keynes was in the fortunate position of being able to write an appreciative review of his own handiwork, praising the Note's 'tone and method of approach', its avoidance of 'irrelevant and controversial issues' and 'faults of manner and expression'.[96] He urged Baldwin 'to promote a settlement along the lines offered by Germany', but at the same time to 'woo France and be prepared to act by her with generosity in return for concessions to our point of view'.

The Keynes–Cuno initiative, which Roy Harrod failed to mention in his biography, was the high point of Keynes's involvement in reparations diplomacy. It failed to thaw the diplomatic ice. Baldwin responded to the

German *démarche* with a display of masterly inactivity; and events took their course as the economic collapse of Germany finally produced the diplomatic movement which Keynes had failed to secure. In September, the German mark reached 250 million to the pound. As no one would now accept its currency, the German government had to surrender. Cuno's successor, Streseman, called off passive resistance; Hjalmar Schacht, Havenstein's successor as president of the Reichsbank, introduced a new currency, the Rentenmark, in November. These developments opened the way to France's eventual acceptance of a committee of 'impartial experts', set up under the American banker Charles Gates Dawes, to work out a new reparation scheme. The experts' report, published in April 1924, managed to avoid mentioning a capital sum, suggested a year's moratorium, and thereafter proposed variable annuities related to the size of Germany's export surplus under a fixed-exchange regime. Acceptance of the Dawes report was eased by the replacement of Poincaré by Edouard Herriot in June 1924. General acceptance of the Dawes Plan in turn led to the Dawes Loan, through which private American money returned to Europe. All the stages of the nightmare, it seems, had to be gone through before the new financial hegemony of American banking could be established and Central Europe brought back to economic life.

In the 1920s bankers and financial experts filled the gap between the *laissez-faire* ideology of governments and stabilisation requirements. Instead of abolishing the wartime debts, as Keynes had wanted, the Dawes Plan made private bankers responsible for a recycling mechanism built on debt. It became the instrument for the phantom hegemony of the United States which Keynes had resisted. By these means the reparations question was 'solved'. Early in 1923 Keynes had started to write a new book in which he expounded his plans for a monetary remedy for Britain's unemployment problem. The fight against Britain's return to the gold standard had started.

CHAPTER FIVE

Monetary Reform

I

What started Keynes on the road to the Keynesian Revolution was the incomplete British recovery from the depression of 1920 to 1922. Nothing like the collapse of prices, output and employment had been seen since the end of the Napoleonic Wars. When the position was finally stabilised in 1923 it was on the basis of 10 per cent unemployment, which lasted for the rest of the decade. This is the observed basis of Keynes's later theoretical concept of 'unemployment equilibrium'. On top of this came the great depression of 1929–32 and the incomplete recovery from that. Over the whole inter-war period, lasting almost twenty years, Britain never experienced anything like full employment. Hitherto, large-scale unemployment had been seen as a problem of the business cycle. It now seemed that it might be endemic.

It turned out that economics had very little to say about all this. To the economist the labour market was much like the market in apples. If the supply of apples exceeds demand at the asking price, the price drops till the market clears. In theory the same thing should happen to the price of labour: the average wage would fall till everyone looking for work found jobs. If the supply of labour continued to exceed demand this could be due only to labour persisting in asking for a higher wage than made its full employment profitable to entrepreneurs. Economics did nothing to illuminate such persistence. It was held to reflect social practices, institutions, attitudes which had no foundation in economic logic. Economic reasoning could only point out their consequences. It is a sign of the poverty of economics that social practices were excluded from its domain. Even Keynes, as we shall see, was unable to think in terms of the influence of social conditions on behaviour, though his analysis took into account social facts.

Nevertheless, the emergence, and continuation, of large-scale unemployment in the British economy of the 1920s started a debate which has gone on ever since. Was it a sign of what was already starting to be called the 'British disease' – overpowerful unions, amateurish management, an obstinate refusal to adapt to changing conditions? Was it the result of avoidable policy mistakes, like going back to the gold standard at an over-valued currency? Or was it a symptom of some change in the environment of modern capitalism?

The most popular explanation of continuing British unemployment ran in terms of structural maladjustment. British employment was heavily dependent on the export demand for its products, and British exports failed to grow in the 1920s in line with world trade. The war, it was said, had disrupted Britain's established trading networks. Britain's pre-war export trade was dominated by coal, cotton, shipbuilding, and iron and steel. Their share of world trade declined in the 1920s; but also Britain's share of this trade fell as overseas countries, cut off from British supplies during the war, expanded their production of these goods, which then competed with Britain's on the basis of cheaper labour costs: the destruction of Lancashire's textile trade by Japan is the most dramatic example. In addition, a large proportion of Britain's exports went to slow-growing primary producing countries.

However, the real problem was Britain's failure to win a leading share in the export of new products. 'In nearly every major industrial category, whether expanding, declining or stable from the point of view of world trade, Britain's share in each case declined, especially between 1913 and 1929.'[1] Britain was finding it more difficult to compete all-round, and it is this which needs to be explained.

In retrospect, it seems clearer than it did at the time that between 1919 and 1922 the British economy suffered from two major 'shocks' from which it never recovered between the wars. The first was a 'real' shock – a once-and-for-all increase in British unit labour costs. In 1919–20 trade unions were able to win a 13 per cent reduction in the working week at unchanged weekly wages and productivity.[2] This meant a 13 per cent rise in the efficiency wage – the wage per unit of output. Labour was able to win, that is, a larger share of a given output. Superimposed on this was a 'monetary' shock – the savage deflation of prices – which left the real wage – the purchasing power of the money wage – higher at the end of the depression in 1922 than it had been in the boom of 1920. This was because money wages, though surprisingly flexible by later standards, still failed to fall as far as the fall in wholesale and retail prices. It was this deadly double-blow of a union-induced rise in the efficiency wage and a government-induced profit deflation which left profit expectations in the British economy too low to provide for full employment.

As we have seen, Keynes thought that most of the ensuing trouble could have been avoided had an attempt been made to stabilise the economy at the end of 1920, on the basis of zero inflation, 6–7 per cent unemployment and an exchange rate of 3.60 dollars to the pound. Instead deflation was allowed to continue unchecked. Real interest rates remained punitively high right through the period of falling prices, 1921–2. The authorities allowed the depression to gather force unchecked because they were determined to *improve* the sterling–dollar exchange so as to make possible the restoration of the gold standard at the pre-war sterling–dollar parity of 4.86 dollars to the pound. The deflation was eased up only when the pound rose to 4 dollars and above. Thus equilibrium was 'restored' by the end of 1922 on the basis of a much lower level of wages and prices and a much higher level of unemployment and exchange rate than at the end of 1920. (See Appendix 1 to this chapter.)

From this sequence it would appear that the British unemployment 'problem' of the 1920s was policy-induced, the crucial policy being the maintenance of 'dear money' right through the slump. (The budget surpluses of 1920 and 1921 were also deflationary.) This resulted in a maladjustment between costs and prices at the policy-induced exchange rate. The 'real' shock of the shorter working week might have been overcome had British industry been allowed to compete at a lower exchange rate.

Although Keynes was extremely critical of excessive deflation, no more than anyone else did he think it would create a permanent unemployment problem. Thus he looked forward, in September 1921, to 'trade recovery, tolerable employment, and a new equilibrium'.[3] What pulled him up short was that there was no return to 'tolerable employment' *after* prices had stopped falling in the last quarter of 1922. Unemployment in the spring of 1923 was almost as bad as it had been a year previously. It was this persistence of high unemployment which alerted him to the possibility that the costs of the deflation might be more than 'transitional'.

The appearance of this strand in his thinking, which was to become central in the development of the Keynesian Revolution, dates from a series of four lectures he gave to the Institute of Bankers from 15 November to 5 December 1922. We can see it clearest in a passage dealing with the relationship between the policy of improving the sterling exchange and the British trade depression. He argued that:

> the slowness of the revival of trade in this country, as compared with what is now going on in America, is due to an important extent to the course of the sterling exchange. The tremendous fillip that trade has had in America through the rise of prices has hardly been reflected here. The rise of prices in America has been counterbalanced here in the improvement in the rate of sterling, so that things are left here very nearly as they were. That is hindering our merchants, I think, partly because trade will never go ahead until people are certain they [prices] have touched bottom. They will never be certain that they have touched bottom unless they see them going up a little; so that I am in favour of a moderate rise in prices as the only way of getting out of the present period of depression, and I think the improvement of sterling towards par is a hampering influence on that. Indeed, it is

obvious it must be. In that connection . . . the more I study statistics the more convinced I am that we shall not be in equilibrium until wholesale prices have risen from [that is, by about] 15 to 20 per cent. The business of forcing down certain levels of wages, and so forth, into equilibrium is almost hopeless, or it will take a long time. The continuance of unemployment is to an important extent due to the fact that we have got the level of wages . . . out of gear with everything else. The only way in which they will get into gear will be by an increase in the level of prices.

Keynes estimated that the cost of living was 60 per cent above pre-war; imports were also costing about 60 per cent above their pre-war price. However, the average wage level was 80 per cent above pre-war; the unskilled labourer especially 'is now being overpaid in relation to the cost of living, and in relation to what the skilled labourer is getting'. Moreover, the wage index underestimated the overpayment. It was based on weekly earnings, 'but owing to the reduced hours of working, the wages that [are] paid per hour are probably double pre-war, that is to say, 200'. High wages, Keynes went on,

> are compelling us to ask double for our exports when the world level of prices, as measured by what we must pay for our imports, is only about 60 per cent up. It is clear that that is not a situation which can go on permanently. People will not pay us for our exports at so discrepant a price from what goods generally are worth in the world; and we see the fruits of high prices [for labour] in the diminishing volume of our exports, and in our complete incapacity to employ the whole body of labour.

There was little prospect of reducing money wages from 200 to 160; the only remedy was to raise the general level of prices to 200. 'Every hindrance in the way of that puts off the day when we shall be in equilibrium, and when we can employ our population.'[4] Although Keynes did not explicitly say so, such a policy logically implied a devaluation of sterling – abandoning the attempt to restore the pre-war sterling–dollar exchange rate of 4.86 dollars to the pound. On this analysis the equilibrium exchange rate with the dollar was certainly no higher than 3.50 dollars to the pound.

A key issue which emerged only later had to do with the character of wage behaviour. Money wages had fallen by a third during the slump – the last example in British economic history of downward flexibility. Yet they had not fallen enough to restore equilibrium, and for the rest of the 1920s remained rigid, despite further deflationary pressure. As we shall see, Keynes and the financial Establishment drew different lessons from this experience. Keynes concluded that the deflation of 1920–1 had brought Britain to the 'verge of revolution', and that, as a working assumption, wage rates should be regarded as too rigid in the short period to adjust to the 'ebb and flow of international gold credit'.[5] The Treasury and the Bank concluded that wage costs had shown themselves sufficiently flexible between 1920 and 1922 to justify one further deflationary push to restore the pre-war gold standard.

We have in these lectures an important early clue to what Keynes was to be saying in the years ahead. Wages were 'stickier' than prices. This observation was not novel. More novel was the conclusion that, as a practical matter, the price level and exchange rate should be adjusted to the going wage rate, rather than the other way round. The most novel observation of all was that it was 'almost hopeless' to try to bring about a general fall in real wages by cutting money wages. Was this just because of existing wage-fixing arrangements? Or was there a more fundamental, theoretical reason? Keynes was not yet ready to say.

II

A GREATER NATION

By 1923 Keynes had acquired a journalistic platform from which to mount his assault on the policy of deflation. In March of that year he became chairman of the board of directors of the Liberal journal, the *Nation and Athenaeum*, with Hubert Henderson as editor. The *Nation*, started in 1907 with Rowntree money, had been the bastion of the high-minded Liberalism which had flourished in Oxford and Hampstead before the war. Its galaxy of intellectuals, assembled at the regular *Nation* monthly lunches by its editor Hugh Massingham, included J. L. Hammond, L. T. Hobhouse, J. A. Hobson and H. W. Nevinson. Theirs was an attempt to update, not so much Liberal policy, as Liberal philosophy, which they tried to shift from belief in individual freedom and unfettered property rights towards concepts of 'positive' freedom and social justice. Keynes had no connection with this pre-war endeavour. He regarded 'New' Liberalism as a typical example of Oxford Idealist muddle. His own post-war efforts to update Liberalism stemmed from a different background, and a different intellectual style.

By the early 1920s, both the *Nation* and the Liberal Party were in a state of collapse. The Rowntrees were getting tired of financing the *Nation*'s losses. They were also getting tired of its increasingly eccentric editor, Hugh Massingham, who alternated between savage abuse of Lloyd George and support for the Labour Party, to which other New Liberals had also started to gravitate. (Leonard Woolf, who worked for him, noticed how people of strong pacifist convictions were prone to extreme verbal violence.) Liberalism was also intellectually and politically bankrupt. The dignified rump of

Asquithians who survived the slaughter of the 'coupon' election of 1918 had little contact with the new world of fluctuating currencies and organised business and labour. Lloyd George, the one dynamic force left to Liberalism, was busy trying to secure his own political future in a Centre Party with the Conservatives. The fall of the Lloyd George coalition in October 1922 cleared the way for reuniting the two wings of the Liberal Party. But this was stymied by bitter personal rivalry at the top, which was not, however, shared by the mass of Liberal activists, who wanted their party back.

It was in these circumstances that a number of Manchester-based Liberals started to meet in 1920 to discuss the party's future. Their leading members were E. D. Simon, a businessman and Liberal MP, C. P. and 'Ted' Scott (father and son) of the *Manchester Guardian* and Ramsay Muir, Professor of Modern History at Manchester University. Muir's *Liberalism and Industry* (1921) was a basic text. It 'included nationalisation of mines and railways, control of trusts and cartels, more public spending on housing and social services, more progressive taxation, a minimum wage and profit sharing in industry'.[6] The Manchester meetings led to a larger conference at Grasmere in the Lake District in 1921, where it was decided to start annual summer schools alternating between Oxford and Cambridge. These would work out a Liberal policy for the 1920s.

Keynes came into contact with the Manchester Liberals through his work with the Scotts on the *Manchester Guardian Commercial* Supplements. He spoke at the first Liberal Summer School at Oxford in August 1922 on reparations. The Summer School movement was predominantly Oxford-inspired, Keynes, Hubert Henderson and Walter Layton being the main Cambridge representatives. What Cambridge did was to place financial questions at the centre of updated Liberalism. The Summer School group had to balance not just between Oxford and Cambridge, but (after October 1922) between Asquith and Lloyd George. Although there were many cross-currents, the main tendency was to look forward to an eventual Lloyd George leadership of a united Liberal Party. The Scotts, especially, were fervent supporters of the Lloyd George cause. In associating himself with these developments, Keynes was starting on a painful personal transition from the Asquith to the Lloyd George camp.

By the end of 1922 the Rowntrees had decided to sell the *Nation*. This coincided with the Summer School Committee's search for a platform from which to expound modern Liberalism and Keynes's own desire for a regular journalistic outlet for his ideas on monetary reform. With his usual energy he started organising financial backing for a takeover bid. Together with Arnold Rowntree, L. J. Cadbury and E. D. Simon he formed a New Nation Company to buy the old *Nation* from the Rowntree Trust. The Rowntrees insisted that Massingham must be given first refusal as editor. Massingham tried to hold on. He regarded the summer school's plans as 'iniquitous', and wrote to tell Keynes that he 'would oppose them by every means in my power'.[7] However, he failed to raise the money, and the *Nation* was bought by the New Nation Company in March for £12,500, Keynes becoming chairman of a board of directors consisting of himself, Simon, Layton and Rowntree.

The plan was to have Ramsay Muir as editor. But Keynes soon made it clear that he had little sympathy with Muir's wishy-washy Liberalism. He imposed such strict conditions on Muir's editorship (including a reduction in salary, rationing of Muir's own contributions and supervision of contents by an editorial committee) that Muir withdrew, accusing Keynes (accurately) of wanting to reduce the Summer School group 'as near as possible to impotence in the conduct of the paper'.[8] The episode is a good example of Keynes's ruthlessness. Muir's withdrawal left him free to offer the job to his Cambridge colleague, Hubert Henderson, then Fellow of Clare College. Henderson objected that he 'had never edited anything; he had done very little journalism. Maynard, like a prancing steed, overrode all his objections. He wanted him as editor, and Hubert must not and could not refuse.'[9] Henderson accepted on terms (including the previous editorial salary) which Keynes had refused Muir. Layton foresaw that the journal would be dominated by the 'Cambridge School of Economics', but this could not be helped, as it was 'not our fault if all the best Liberals were trained in the Cambridge Economics School . . .'[10] Keynes had acquired virtually untrammelled freedom to shape the journal as he wished.

Keynes had told Muir that it was temperamentally impossible for him to be a 'sleeping partner' in any organisation he joined. Why did he take on this huge extra chore? First, during the period of his maximum involvement – from 1923 to 1925 – he was a man with a message, or rather a double message: to stop the return to the gold standard and to get a sane settlement of reparations. He was a preacher who needed a pulpit. He had no less than four pieces in the first issue under the new management. Over the whole period of the *Nation*'s life – from May 1923 to February 1931 – 155 items by him are listed in the *Collected Writings*. Very broadly, these include fifty articles on domestic policy, forty on debts and reparations, five book reviews, twelve anonymous contributions and fourteen letters. In 1923 he contributed regular features – 'Finance and Investment' (fourteen), 'Life and Politics' (six) and 'Events of the Week' (six) under his own name. Most of this output appeared in the *Nation*'s first two years. After 1925, his attention shifted to the *theory* of stabilisation policy, and the volume of his contributions declined.

Secondly, though Keynes's gospel was preached to all parties, its primary purpose was to equip the Liberal Party with a philosophy of government. This is not just because Keynes was a Liberal himself, or because the Liberals in 1923 could still be regarded as serious competitors for power. He believed that the Liberal temper was more readily attuned to his message than dynastic Conservatism or class-war Labour. 'Our own sympathies', he wrote in the first editorial of 5 May 1923, 'are for a Liberal Party which has its centre well to the Left . . . but with bolder, freer, more disinterested minds than Labour has, and quit of their out-of-date dogmas.' After the general election of 1929 it was clear that the Liberal Party was finished as a governing party. 'We are, so to speak, the manufacturing establishment of politics,' Hubert Henderson wrote on 15 June 1929, 'and, if we are compelled for a time to let others do the retailing, we must not try to deprive them of good salesmen and handsome shop-walkers.'

Thirdly, Keynes was attracted by the role of patron of Bloomsbury: Bloomsbury writers dominated the back part of the paper. Finally, the *Nation* presented a challenge to him as an entrepreneur. He actively involved himself in trying to restore its circulation and revenues. He made the critical appointments – of editor and literary editor – which determined the 'tone' of the front and back parts; and he decided both its pricing policy and its management structure. Most of his *Nation* work, including some at least of his writing, was crammed into the two days he spent in London in mid-week, where it had to compete with his City activities, his editorship of the *Economic Journal*, looking after Lydia, and an active social round. He had also started a book on monetary policy. The pace of his life continued as manic as ever.

Such a degree of proprietor involvement would not have been possible without an editor as compliant as Hubert Henderson. Keynes's collaboration with Henderson in the 1920s is as remarkable in its way as his theoretical collaboration with Dennis Robertson at Cambridge, for in temperament they were both totally unlike him. Henderson was an argumentative parsimonious Scot, cautious, sceptical, unheroic. 'I never knew anyone so instinctively protective of his habits,' Keynes told Lydia on 15 November 1925. He entirely lacked Keynes's facility in writing. His widow Faith Henderson recalled that his articles were a nightmare to him. After everyone had left the office on Wednesday, Hubert would settle down to write his leader. 'Hour after hour he would scribble and smoke, scratch out and tear up. Never did anyone write with such blood and sweat. Sometimes he would catch the last tube back to Hampstead, sometimes the first tube train on Thursday morning.'[11] Lydia's comment (27 November 1927) was terser: 'Every Wednesday Hubert comes home at 3 am preparing his appearance in Nation, with you it is one hour or 1½. Different glands, different speed, and different merits.' Henderson was more intellectually fastidious than Keynes, shunned popularity, mistrusted Keynes's flights of fancy and was adept at spotting weak points in his mentor's reasoning.

Faith Henderson recalls that 'Hubert & Maynard were in complete agreement in those days in general outlook. . . . Maynard was always in and out of the *Nation* office, & he was much much less overbearing then than he became in later years.'[12] Like other clever but unimaginative men, Henderson was highly susceptible to Keynes's intellectual charm. His mistrust of economic dogmas of all kinds made him hostile to the simple panaceas for Britain's ills being trotted out by the Treasury and the Bank of England. Thus he was willing for a long time to harness his scepticism to the chariot of Keynes's iconoclasm. Keynes in turn had a great respect for Henderson's brains – a necessary condition for their successful partnership. But there was never complete sympathy of outlook. Henderson's own analysis of Britain's economic ills placed much more weight on structural maladjustment than failure of monetary policy, which he regarded as an aggravating, not fundamental, factor. In the 1930s he came to mistrust Keynes's monetary panaceas as much as he had the Treasury's. The violence with which he spoke out against Keynes in the 1930s reflects something of the resentment he felt at having to subordinate his own views in the 1920s to those of his masterful proprietor.

Keynes's first choice as literary editor was T. S. Eliot, then languishing at Lloyd's Bank. But Eliot 'spun out the situation into endless complexities',[13] and Keynes approached Leonard Woolf, who was already working for Massingham. E. M. Forster warned Woolf of the danger of working for Keynes: 'Maynard, since I have seen him apart from the Cambridge haze that envelops one's friends, has always seemed to me a curious mixture of benevolence and school-boy selfishness. . . . I should work under him if you needed the money and were certain to get it – not otherwise.'[14] Woolf did need the money and took the job for £500 a year, half Henderson's salary. (This was later reduced to £400.) But he insisted on complete autonomy for his part of the paper.

If the Cambridge School of Economics dominated the front of the *Nation*, Apostolic Cambridge and its close connections reigned in the middle and back. Woolf brought in two groups of writers – members of Bloomsbury, old and young, and writers he published in the Hogarth Press – as well as contributing a weekly 'World of Books' page himself. (Lytton Strachey wrote eighteen signed articles altogether.) 'I doubt', Woolf later wrote, 'whether any weekly paper has ever had such a constellation of stars shining in it as I got for the *Nation*.' The resulting highbrow and coterie flavour was by no means to the liking of Henderson, who aimed to attract 'the Philistine' as well as 'the Chosen People'. Within a few months of taking over he was complaining to Woolf of the 'insolent tone' of reviews by Clive Bell, Bunny Garnett, Francis Birrell, Dadie Rylands and Raymond Mortimer – Mortimer had described a new play by A. A. Milne as 'degringolade, below which it would be impossible for anyone to fall' – and urged Woolf to choose reviewers more appreciative of 'the better type of non-Bloomsbury writing'. Woolf stuck his ground; Bell protested loudly that 'the best writers of the day were not to be ruled by financiers'; Keynes patched up a truce.[15] He sympathised with both sides, for in his personality, as in his writing, Cambridge utilitarianism and aestheticism clashed and mingled. Woolf and

Henderson managed to sustain their cramped, uneasy association at 38 St James's Street for six years.

Keynes himself received the usual complaints from eminent men aggrieved by what they considered unfair attacks. H. G. Wells and J. L. Garvin, editor of the *Observer*, were both pilloried by 'Kappa' (Samuel Kerkham Ratcliffe) in his 'Life and Politics Column'; in revenge Garvin described Keynes as an 'ungovernable soda-water siphon' in the *Observer* of 28 October 1928.

The *Nation* projected itself as 'the organ of a new school of Liberal thought which includes some of the most original economists and political thinkers in England' and also as 'the leading weekly review of Literature and the Arts'. Some famous readers felt it lived up to its billing. 'The impression of direct contact with the problems you are discussing amazes me,' wrote Walter Lippmann to Keynes on 9 November 1923. 'The *Nation* doesn't seem to have that characteristic fault of weekly reviews which comes from seeming to comment merely upon the comments that have already been made in the daily newspapers.' The financial journalist Nicholas Davenport still agreed in 1930. The *Nation* was 'the leading weekly for those who think. In the old days I suppose the *Nation* was read for its English and its personality – it is now read for its thinking on economic and political subjects and its English has not suffered. So it's a greater *Nation*.'[16]

However, the thinkers were not sufficiently plentiful to secure a buoyant circulation. Although Keynes cut the cost per issue from 9*d* to 6*d* and assiduously solicited foreign subscriptions by announcing that his communications to the press now appeared exclusively in the *Nation*, circulation fell from its Massingham level of about 8000 to between 6000 and 7000 – well below the *Spectator* and somewhat lower than the *New Statesman*. He effected substantial economies on the production and distribution side by changing printers and by appointing a business manager (F. W. Slaughter, later F. A. Hargreaves) to replace the existing external managing agents. By the end of the decade the *Nation* was just about breaking éven. Nevertheless, he had had to pay out £4000 of his own money over the period to keep it afloat, and other guarantees had also been called up.

The *Nation* was not just too highbrow; like the Liberal Party, it was being squeezed between right and left. Dmitri Mirsky, an acute Marxist observer of British intellectual life, wrote that it stood for 'Bloomsbury liberalism [which] can be defined as thin-skinned humanism for enlightened and sensitive members of the capitalist class who do not desire the outer world to be such as might be prone to cause them any displeasing impression'.[17] The limits on the *Nation*'s success paralleled those set to the Liberal revival by the social and economic forces of the time. Keynes's decision to merge the *Nation* with the *New Statesman* in 1931 symbolised the fact that historic Liberalism had run its course.

III

SECOND THOUGHTS ARE BEST

An appreciative, though discerning, reader of the *Nation* was Lydia Lopokova. 'With palpitations I demanded [it],' she wrote to Maynard on 5 May, the date of the first issue under the new management. 'The cover gives confidence of strength. The British Policy in Europe [Keynes's article] is powerful and reads with easiness. . . . Sarah B[ernhardt, by Lytton Strachey] is brilliant only I am confused how to take . . . serious or not serious, and when?' On 12 May: 'This week you are the *only* star . . . your mental energy with this cold fresh atmosphere is of Vesuvian dimensions. I . . . take a warm bath instead, as no mental powers exist in me.' A week later, Lydia thought Virginia Woolf was 'wasted on Misses Wilson and Richardson, who are full of romance and heart, but who cares for them?' On 26 May: 'The whole number looks alive, because it is touched by your flicker. . . .'

In Bloomsbury parlance, Lydia and Maynard were now 'married', which simply meant 'going steady'. Lydia lived at 41 Gordon Square; Clive at Number 50; Vanessa and Maynard shared Number 46, where Lydia also took her meals. Her latest engagement, in *Togo, A Noble Savage*, a feeble Massine ballet stuck into an even feebler variety show, *You'd Be Surprised*, played to half-empty houses at Covent Garden before expiring on 24 March 1923. After that she joined the ranks of the unemployed. But even when working she was free on Sundays. With Maynard in Cambridge, she often turned to Vanessa for company. Lydia had 'today spent 3 solid hours sitting in my room gossiping', Vanessa complained to Roger Fry after one session in February. 'This now happens every Sunday which is usually my one day at home for doing odd jobs, also as you know very often at tea time.'[18]

The idea that doing 'odd jobs' might interfere with chatter would have struck Lydia as absurd. As she later explained in an article, 'We Russians – You English':

> The English are not exactly dumb – I do not say that. They even make after-dinner speeches. But they do not talk as we do in the train, in the tram, in the café, endlessly, uproariously, just for its own sake. Very often we are unreasonable, we talk nonsense, we exaggerate and we lie. One remembers the heroine of *The Cherry Orchard* and the old Chekhov world; their conversation was their only outlet. When I ask an English lady to lunch she begins to put on her gloves . . . almost as soon as we leave the table. But when I ask Russian friends, they arrive, it is true, an hour late, but they stay on to tea, and to dinner if there is any encouragement, and will think it natural to spend the night on the drawing-room sofa.[19]

But it was a life-style as well as a culture clash. The Bloomsburyites worked hard during the day – painting, decorating, writing, reading – and relaxed in the evenings. Lydia worked in the evenings; exercises apart, her days were free. And there were long periods when she didn't work at all. There was also Vanessa's reserve:

> The chief difficulties no doubt [Vanessa wrote to Roger Fry on 18 February] lie in my character & hers. I suppose it's true, as you always tell me, and as Maynard said, that it's almost impossible to know what I am feeling – I don't show when I want Lydia to go & she can't be expected to know. On the other hand her character is such that if she had any suspicion she wasn't wanted she'd probably never come near me at all which would be absurd. So between us I don't see how one is to make her see the truth which is that I want to see her in moderation.

Both Duncan and Vanessa spoke about Lydia to Maynard, 'who had been quite sensible in the end but was rather helpless'. The situation was eased when Maynard returned to London for the Easter vacation, while Vanessa retired to Charleston to give Duncan a free run with 'Tommy' Tomlin in London. There was much talk at this time of Maynard buying a big house in Fitzroy Square where they could all live together – the last attempt to combine 'marriage' to Lydia with the collegiate life of old; but it came to nothing. Vanessa's unfriendly feelings towards Lydia come out in an unflattering portrait she painted of her at this time which she showed in the London Group Exhibition in April. Keynes did not buy it; on Duncan's advice, he purchased Matthew Smith's *Reclining Woman* instead; but, as Vanessa remarked, he 'never or hardly ever really likes my painting'.[20]

Maynard's friends were clearly hoping that he would tire of Lydia. They couldn't understand what he saw in her. The idea of sexual passion seemed to be too far-fetched; and, as Virginia Woolf frequently complained, Lydia had no 'head piece'. Virginia was the most forthright opponent of marriage. There was much about Keynes she disliked; but she venerated his brain and could not bear to see him hitched to a 'parrokeet'. On 28 April she wrote to her sister, 'We're dining with Maynard on Tuesday. What about Lydia? I hope to God Maynard has been restrained – a fatal and irreparable mistake.' And a month later: 'Unfortunately, talking to Lydia, I called Maynard "your husband". I see this is not the thing to do. Poor little parrokeet – there she sits in the window in a pink kimono awaiting him, I suppose. "Maynar liked your article so much Leonar . . ." I suppose she has to read the Nation now. What tragedies these parrokeets go through. . . .' To Barbara Bagenal, Bloomsbury's choice for Maynard's wife, Virginia wrote on 24 June,

> Lydia has got a new bed. Very tactlessly I asked her if it was a double one. No it isn't yet, she said; I saw that one must not make jokes

about beds [however many Russian Generals and Polish princes or
Soho waiters she's lain with]. Her respectability is something you
gamps would revere. But I find that talk about the Ballet has its
limitations. Not indeed that she dances anymore; unfortunately she
sometimes writes.[21]

Throughout 1923 the campaign to 'save' Maynard went on.

It was an awful year for Lydia. With her divorce proceedings from
Barocchi deadlocked between three sets of lawyers in three countries, her
marriage prospects were as uncertain as her career ones. Maynard's feelings
remained mysterious. His activities gave him little time for her. He had
proposed to spend his Easter holidays in North Africa – with Sebastian
Sprott! Lydia kicked up such a fuss about this that he abandoned the plan;
but the revelation of his continuing attempt to get the best of both worlds
must have been pretty disconcerting. Without dancing engagements, and
with her 'maestro' Cecchetti retiring to Italy, her thoughts once more turned
to acting. She immersed herself in *Rosmersholm*, remarking 'that it was very
difficult to play Ibsen, only action in the mind'. There was the usual London
gossip, and she reported Vanessa and Clive Bell 'oxygenating Angelica's
Cockney'. Vanessa's reserve, on the other hand, seemed to have been growing. She resented the loss of her old intimacy with Maynard. She now
saw him mainly in Lydia's company; he spoke only of the *Nation*, politics,
investments, business matters. Lydia's presence seemed to her to symbolise
the passing of the old order.

Throughout this difficult time, Lydia was sustained by her own circle of
friends. They were rich lovers of the arts, devoted to ballet, and to Lydia
in particular. They were grander and more conventional than Maynard's
Bloomsbury friends, ballet linking their world of money and chic to the
avant-garde in art, music and thought.

Vera Bowen was Lydia's greatest woman friend in the 1920s. Married
since 1922 to Harold Bowen, a Persian scholar, linguist and (unsuccessful)
playwright, she was a clever, vivacious, quarrelsome Russian who had
settled in England in 1914 and had the money and leisure to indulge her
passion (and talent) for producing ballets and plays. She had joined Maynard in relaunching Lydia's career after the fiasco of *The Sleeping Princess*; he
arranging the contracts, and she the productions, of the performances Lydia
gave at the Coliseum and Covent Garden in 1922–3. A fastidious woman,
she took in hand Lydia's 'education', trying to get her to dress elegantly, as
she did herself, and taking her round the concerts and art galleries. Lydia
was much more receptive to the latter than the former: off and on stage she
remained a mess.

Vera was the only friend Lydia could confide in about her affair with
Maynard; but their friendship experienced a distinct chill in the summer of
1923 as a result of Maynard's haggling with Vera over the financial terms of

the July/August production of *Masquerade* at the Coliseum.[22] 'Disagreeable', 'unpleasant' and 'amazingly rude' are adjectives Harold Bowen uses about Maynard in his diary for 1923–4. 'Talking him over afterwards,' Bowen wrote a year later, 'we [he and Vera] decided that it is his self-consciousness that makes other people feel so uncomfortable when in his company. His self-consciousness is overpowering, consequently other people feel very uncomfortable indeed.'[23]

After Maynard, the most important man in Lydia's life was Samuel Courtauld, the artificial silk manufacturer and picture collector. Courtauld's hospitality was as lavish as his benefactions: Lydia and the Bowens could often be found at the weekends in his grand house at 20 Portman Square, eating and drinking too much, and complaining afterwards of the excruciating dullness of the company. The Bowens considered the Courtaulds (especially Sam's wife Elizabeth or 'Lil') to be social climbers, Vera declaring that Sam's gift of £50,000 to the Tate Gallery in 1923 to buy nineteenth-century French pictures was 'an occult scheme of social advancement' aimed at a peerage.[24] Lil's real passion was the opera; she financed the Covent Garden seasons from 1925 to 1927; they both spent part of the year in the United States, where Samuel Courtauld owned the Viscose Company. Lydia loved Sam, a shy, dour man of exacting standards and submerged passions. 'I always feel a pact of friendship to Sam (without going to bed with him) and that is why it is so nice,' Lydia wrote to Maynard on 22 November 1924. And on 7 March 1925: 'Honesty, sincerity, competence, intelligence, modesty are Sam's feathers, but he can't soar, his little feet follow him' – unlike Maynard, whose mind was 'human and divine' (27 February 1925). For his part, Sam adored Lydia, thawed in her company, flirted with her and took her for long drives in his Rolls-Royce. He also got on well with Maynard. He was the kind of visionary businessman whom Maynard admired, belying his frequent dicta about the degeneration of family firms. A little later, Maynard persuaded him to back Duncan and Vanessa and other Bloomsbury painters in the London Artists' Association.

These were Lydia's mainstays. There were also Basil Maine, pianist and songwriter (her 'platonic lover'), and Florence ['Florrie'] Grenfell, a close friend of Diaghilev, married to the banker and Conservative MP Edward ('Teddy') Grenfell, with whom she lived in great opulence in Cavendish Square. Lydia skipped off to Paris with her and Muriel Gore, another woman friend, in mid-June 1923 to see a new Diaghilev ballet, *Les Noces*. 'Big Serge gave me outwardly friendly embrace,' she wrote to Maynard on 15 June; she saw Nijinsky in the box 'in a quiet state'.

Bloomsbury, whose snobberies were intellectual and aesthetic, feared that these rich friends of Lydia's would corrupt Maynard. Virginia Woolf foresaw 'Lydia, stout, charming, exacting; Maynard in the Cabinet; 46 [Gordon Square] the resort of the dukes and prime ministers'.[25] A little later she reflected on 'the limits of luxury: how far can the human soul stretch into rugs & rooms; at what point they suffocate its force. I have seen several rich people this autumn; & thought them, perhaps, dulled, coarsened, by it: Lady Cunard; two days ago Mrs. Bowen & Mrs. Grenfell at Lydia's.'[26]

Virginia was right to foresee that Maynard would escape from Bloomsbury's orbit. He moved increasingly in the company of 'thinking' or 'civilised' bankers, businessmen, politicians – people who, like him, straddled ideas and affairs, the arts and money-making. Lydia did not pull him into this world: public affairs did that. Nevertheless, Maynard and Lydia together were much more *socially* attractive than Maynard would have been on his own, or linked to a Bloomsbury blue-stocking. People like the Courtaulds or Grenfells, Bob Brand and Oswald Falk tended to *revere* him for his mind, but *love* Lydia for her gaiety and charm; and, in a world which prized social values, the combination became a valuable social asset. Nor should its importance in Maynard's political evolution be underestimated: if intellectually he was drawn to the left, socially he was increasingly tethered to the right.

The two worlds of Lydia and Maynard were neatly juxtaposed early in August. On Saturday, 4 August 1923, the Bowens went to the last performance of *Masquerade* at the Coliseum, Harold Bowen noting in his diary that 'Lydia had taken even less care than usual over her appearance and looked hideous. . . . Our depression was increased afterwards at the sight of the Chinese costumes, designed by Duncan, which she proposes to wear in the "Divertissement" [a week of which was to follow].' The same day Maynard had returned to Cambridge for the opening of the Liberal Summer School (see p. 149 below), at which he was to give an expensive entertainment, culminating in a performance of Euripides' *Cyclops*, produced and directed by Sheppard, and with Dennis Robertson cast as Silenus. Of course he took a busy part in the preparation, suggesting, and helping to select, 'a chorus of six sailors, a chorus of six satyrs, two sheep and two goats'.[27] Eight hundred turned up for the party in the Fellows' Garden on 7 August, including the Asquiths. Bertram Bulmer, a second-year satyr at King's, wrote that the play:

> went off quite well considering that we hardly rehearsed it at all. Daddy [Dr A. H.] Mann composed the music 2 days before the play was performed. [Boris] Ord was to have done it, but went away to Sicily & we found that he had not done it . . . There was a nonconformist at the back who went away because he disapproved, & one lady told Sheppard afterwards that she did not know there was such a lot of slang in Greek. . . . The Cyclops was a splendid sight, about 8 ft. high.[28]

The entertainment cost Maynard £130.

That summer there was no Charleston for Maynard and Lydia. Instead Maynard took a grand house, the Knoll, at Studland, Dorset, seaside home

of the Duke of Hamilton. As usual he filled it up with his friends: Raymond
Mortimer, Dadie Rylands, the Hendersons, the Woolfs. Hubert Henderson
and Leonard Woolf had a row about the *Nation*. Virginia Woolf, who 'wanted
to observe Lydia as a type for Rezia', a character in a novel she was writing,
has left two memorably nasty descriptions of her stay. In her diary for 11
September she wrote:

> Maynard is grown very gross & stout, especially when he wraps his
> leopard spotted dressing gown tight around his knees & stands in front
> of the fire. . . . He has a queer swollen eel like look, not very pleasant.
> But his eyes are remarkable, & as I truly said when he gave me some
> pages of his new book to read, the process of mind there displayed is
> as far ahead of me as Shakespeare's.

Lydia was another story. Ignorant 'of the most binding of all laws of female
life', she had thrown her sanitary towels into the empty grate.

> Imagine the consequences [Virginia wrote to Jacques Raverat on 4
> November 1923]. . . . The cook's husband, and Duke's valet, did the
> room. Soon the Cook herself requested to speak with the lady. There
> was such a scene, it is said, as shook the rafters, – rages, tears, despair,
> outrage, horror, retribution, reconciliation: and – if you knew Lydia,
> you'll see how naturally it follows – lifelong friendship upon a basis of
> – well, bloody rags. Really, there is a curious feeling about that
> menage, as well may be with such a foundation. Lydia has the soul of
> a squirrel: anything nicer you cant conceive: she sits by the hour
> polishing the sides of her nose with her front paws. But, poor little
> wretch, trapped in Bloomsbury, what can she do but learn Shakespeare
> by heart? I assure you its tragic to see her sitting down to King Lear.
> Nobody can take her seriously: every nice man kisses her. Then she
> flies into a rage and says she is like Vanessa, like Alix Sargent Florence,
> or Ka Cox . . . – a seerious wooman.[29]

This was the last holiday Lydia ever spent with Bloomsbury; it probably
put paid to Maynard's lingering hopes of a commune. Shocked by her
treatment, Lydia fled to Colworth, the Bowens' country pile in Bedfordshire,
to pour out her troubles to Vera, a ready listener, while Maynard went off
stag hunting in Devon. 'Vera in return ventured on the most outspoken
criticism of Bloomsbury and its ways. Loppie looks on the end of her
Maynard attachment as inevitable and not even out of sight.'[30] Back in
London Lydia had time on her hands. She tried to get J. M. Barrie to write
a play for her; she had her head sculpted by Frank Dobson; she joined
Muriel Gore in taking Spanish lessons. There was endless dinner-party
chatter, 1920s style:

> Psycho-analisis was the main light of the table talk. . . . Lil thought

that if one wanted to make a confession there was a chance as one would do to a priest; V[era] said that Freud had every chance to make a success, the facts were such that all his patients did not improve their condition one iota, the only man in nerves specialist that interested her was Dr. Head. . . .* Poor Sam was bored.[31]

On 19 November, 'Loppie came to dinner – and reduced V[era] to tears. . . . by remaining almost until 12 o'clock, discussing interminably the problem whether Maynard is to marry her or no. . . .'[32]

It is hard to know what to make of all this. Possibly Lydia felt the whole situation was impossible. On the other hand, she had no money and no work. As Polly Hill remarks, 'her own letters provide no clue to her real state of mind; and Maynard's letters retain their unruffled, affectionate aloofness'.[33] There is no hint that he ever intended to give her up. In the interval of writing an article on population, he wrote to Lydia, 'Shall you and I begin our works on population together and at the same time?' And: 'My dearest poet, I am sure that when you make your contribution to the population it will be a poet that comes out.'[34]

At 46 Gordon Square, Vanessa had taken further steps to insulate herself from Lydia by arranging a separate dining room for the Bells. On the evening of 8 October, Clive came to dinner 'and I couldn't help feeling horribly guilty in our really very nice little dining room with Grace [Germany] rushing in & out & delicious food & the thought of the chilly couple with Harland upstairs'.[35] By these means Vanessa gradually excluded Lydia, and hence Maynard, from her life. For Maynard too had to make a choice. And when the crunch came, he chose Lydia. His friendship with Vanessa did not end: it just subsided. Lydia's love, too, survived his emotional incapacity, and Bloomsbury's hostility. How near she came to giving him up can be guessed at from her inscription on the back of a photograph of them both she sent to Vera after their marriage: 'Second Thoughts Are Best'. There is no evidence, in Lydia's letters, of the hurt she suffered at Vanessa's hands. The evidence is in the way she and Maynard arranged their lives, and in how she lived after his death. Lydia reacted to her exclusion much as Vanessa had anticipated – by not wanting to see Vanessa any more. The two women spent their last years in Sussex a few hundred yards from each other, both with their memories of Maynard, almost strangers to each other.

---

*Sir Henry Head, the alienist, who was involved, with Geoffrey Keynes, in rescuing Virginia Woolf after her suicide attempt in 1914.

IV

THE THREE DEVILS: DEFLATION, POPULATION, PROTECTION

On 7 July 1923, with unemployment at 1.3m., or 11.4 per cent of the insured workforce, bank rate was put up from 3 per cent to 4 per cent. In the *Nation* on 14 July Keynes denounced the rise as 'one of the most misguided movements of that indicator which has ever occurred'. The Bank, he wrote, 'think it more important to raise the dollar exchange a few points than to encourage flagging trade'.[36]

This attack marked his public break with official policy. The confident tones in which it was delivered reflect the influence of the new book on monetary policy he had started to write at the beginning of the year. It was the start of his campaign against the return to the gold standard at the pre-war sterling–dollar parity. In a longer perspective, it was the start of the Keynesian Revolution. From 1923 till 1937 Keynes was the leading intellectual critic of the monetary, and increasingly the fiscal, policy actually pursued.

Bank rate was put up to correct the fall in sterling against the dollar – from $4.70 in March to $4.56 in June. The rise was not universally welcomed. In the Commons on 12 June Baldwin has said that 'there is no greater necessity for this country . . . than cheap money'. And Sir Charles Addis, chairman of the Hongkong and Shanghai Banking Corporation, and a director of the Bank of England, had written to Montagu Norman on 4 June, 'The first consideration in determining a change in Bank Rate should be the condition of trade and industry.' So Keynes was not without allies. On the other hand, Reginald McKenna told Norman on 20 June that 'our Rates are too low & diff[erence] between 3 & 4% cd not really affect trade . . .'.[37]

The issue Keynes was raising was of theoretical as well as practical importance. The rise in bank rate might temporarily correct the sterling–dollar exchange by bringing American money back to London. But it could bring about a 'real and lasting' improvement in the exchange only by producing 'some curtailment of credit and some fall of sterling prices'. In other words, the raising of bank rate was a signal that the government intended to 'produce a falling tendency in sterling prices', and that if a 4 per cent bank rate did not suffice to lower them they would be prepared to raise it to 5 per cent or more. 'This is the moment when the Bank of England chooses deliberately to add one more discouragement, one more warning sign to anyone who contemplates new business that he had better wait a bit and keep his hands in his pockets, even if it means that his workmen must keep their hands in their pockets, too.'[38] Even more than the actual it is the *expected* rate of interest which determines investment decisions.

Critics accused Keynes of being an inflationist. To this charge he made a robust reply:

A policy of price stability is the very opposite of a policy of permanently cheap money. During the last boom, the present writer preached vehemently in favour of very dear money, months before the Bank of England acted. But when employment is very bad, enterprise disheartened, and prices with a falling tendency, *that* is not the moment to raise the Bank Rate.[39]

The City editor of *The Times* made a shrewd thrust. 'As prices have remained stable within the past eighteen months,' he wrote, 'it is difficult to appreciate the force of many arguments employed by those who are avowedly in favour of stabilisation.' This raised a hornet's nest of problems which was to take years to sort out. What did one mean by the 'price level'? If there were several price levels, which of them was it important to try to stabilise? What caused any of these price levels to be what they were? In the *Nation* of 28 July Keynes admitted that wholesale prices had remained fairly stable. But he insisted that actual purchasing power had been 'silently and steadily' deflated for some time, and that this partly accounted for 'the failure of trade and employment in this country to keep pace with the revival in the United States . . .'. In support, he cited the shrinkage in bank deposits by about 10 per cent since January 1922, as well as the fall in the retail price index since that date. The Bank of England 'has been using its secret and enormous powers to *contract* credit by no less an amount than 10 per cent'. He demanded 'an authoritative enquiry into the methods of compilation of index numbers'.[40] Here was an early statement of Keynes's view, later to be developed in his *Treatise on Money*, that overall price indexes may hide movements of sectional price levels – wages, consumer goods, investment goods – crucial for the analysis of business cycles.

An important assumption underlying Keynes's criticism was that the price level (any price level?) depended on the credit policy of the Bank of England. 'Expert opinion' supported him in the belief that:

> it lies in the power of the Bank of England, and the Treasury, within wide limits, to determine in the long run how much credit is created. If the Bank of England had pursued a different policy, I believe that prices would stand at a different level. . . . the policy of the Cunliffe Committee assumes that the authorities have the power in the long run to fix the price level, just as much as the policy of price stabilisation assumes it.

He concluded that 'lack of confidence' in the price level was 'a considerable cause, and probably the only remediable one, of present unemployment'. This qualification is important. Keynes never claimed that *all* unemployment could be cured by monetary policy, only that part which was the result of deflation. If the Prime Minister and the governor of the Bank announced that they were determined to do 'all in their power to promote and preserve confidence in the existing level of sterling prices (letting the dollar exchange go hang, if necessary), great good would result'.[41]

Keynes's speech to the Liberal Summer School at Cambridge on 8 August 1923 gives a further insight into the thinking going in to the book he was writing. Modern capitalism, he said, could not stand a violently fluctuating standard of value. Only if the value of the currency was subject to conscious control could a capitalist society be defended against the 'attacks and criticism of Socialist and Communist innovators'. Keynes explained how falling prices, and even more a 'general expectation' of falling prices, must always be bad for business. The explanation must wait till later. But some comment is needed on the following passage: 'If they [economic agents] felt confident that the price would not fall, they would not hesitate to buy. They put off their purchases, not because they lack purchasing power, but because *their demand is capable of postponement* and may, they think, be satisfied at a lower price later on.' Keynes was later to identify this ability to 'postpone demand' as the distinctive feature of a 'money economy'. In his address, Keynes gave two hostages to fortune. Economists, he declared, were 'as united on the scientific theory of [how to maintain stable money] as they are about free trade'. Events were to prove otherwise in both cases. And he still insisted that the market system was self-correcting: 'Sooner or later a rising tendency of prices will spring up again . . . partly because postponed demands cannot go on being postponed indefinitely; partly because catastrophes tend to diminish the supply of goods and to increase, rather than to diminish, the supply of money. For this reason I am not so pessimistic as the President of the Board of Trade about the prospects of employment in the long run.'[42] Later, Keynes was to abandon this view also. The economy is not self-correcting. Demand postponed, he would say, is demand destroyed.

In his early discussions of unemployment, Keynes always insisted that 'the problem of unemployment is . . . in part, a problem of population'.[43] This argument had several strands, and was differently presented in different contexts. First, Keynes maintained that a British *employed* population equivalent to that of 1914 was producing 10 per cent less output than pre-war at the pre-war wage – this largely due to a shortening of the working week. Secondly, the *employable* working population was increasing by 100,000 to 200,000 every year. Keynes doubted whether '*on these terms*, we shall be able to employ the whole employable population except at the very top of periodic booms', without 'great improvement in the technique and intelligence of trade and industry', and in the longer run without the practice of birth control. Without improvements in efficiency or a lengthening of the working week, the real wage had to fall if greater employment was to be possible.[44]

The third strand concerned the terms of trade, or exchange, between primary and manufactured goods. As early as 1912 Keynes had pointed to

the re-emergence of the 'law of diminishing returns for raw products', leading to a shift in the terms of trade against industrial countries. Essentially,
Keynes was saying that the nineteenth-century era of cheap food and raw
materials was over.[45] This argument was reproduced in *The Economic Consequences of the Peace*, where Keynes pointed out that it was now costing Europe
more manufacturing output to buy the same quantity of food from America
and elsewhere which it had consumed before the war. The pre-war trend
was reinforced by the elimination of Russia's grain exports. Western Europe,
in the short run at least, had to 'tighten its belt' – accept a lower standard
of life or 'real wage' than before the war.

This then was the basis of Keynes's 'Malthusian' explanation of post-war
unemployment. Falling prices made unemployment greater than it might
otherwise have been by pushing the real wage still higher above the equilibrium real wage. In the *Economic Journal* of December 1923 he gave an example
of how equilibrium might be restored:

> Food prices . . . might rise 20 per cent, money wages might rise 10 per
> cent, other manufacturing costs might be reduced (with a larger output
> and more efficiency) sufficiently to compensate the rise in money wages
> leaving the money-price of manufactures unchanged; our real price of
> manufactured goods would then have returned to its pre-war level and
> this might encourage a sufficient increase in their volume to absorb
> an important proportion of our unemployed. But it must be observed
> that in this illustration the result would have been achieved at the cost
> of a reduction in real wages.[46]

In the autumn of 1923 Keynes found himself unexpectedly embroiled in
a debate about these matters with Sir William Beveridge, the new director
of the London School of Economics. In his Presidential Address to Section
F of the British Association, delivered on 18 September 1923, Beveridge
singled Keynes out as the leading exponent of the fallacious view that British
unemployment resulted from over-population. The question, said Beveridge,
was not whether the Malthusian Devil was loose, 'but whether Mr. Keynes
was right to loose this Devil . . . upon the public'. He produced statistics
showing that the terms of trade had not turned against the industrial countries. Britain's economic problem required no Malthusian explanation; it
was simply a problem of structural readjustment, since 'Providence had not
concentrated on these islands the coal and iron supplies of the world'. What
was needed was not birth control but free trade.[47] In his reply in the *Nation*
of 6 October Keynes conceded that his statistics on the terms of trade were
inconclusive, but insisted that 'unemployment may be a symptom of a
maladjustment very closely connected with population – namely, that which
results from an attempt on the part of organised labour, or of the community
as a whole, to maintain real wages at a higher level than the underlying
conditions are able to support'.[48] Keynes was simply wrong about the terms

of trade: they moved in favour of Britain throughout the inter-war years.*
But Keynes remained a neo-Malthusian. On several occasions in the 1920s
he called for a population policy. He believed that Britain would be better
off 'if we had fewer to employ and to feed' and that 'the greater part
of man's achievements are already swallowed up in the support of mere
numbers'.[49]

He soon had an opportunity to test his belief in free trade. Foiled of cheap
money, Baldwin announced at Plymouth on 25 October 1923 that protection
was the only cure for unemployment. On 12 November he decided to seek
a mandate to introduce protection and imperial preference, Bonar Law
having promised not to do so without a general election. Election day was
fixed for 6 December.

'Good bye Baldwin – he is finished now,' was Keynes's immediate reaction
to Baldwin's Plymouth speech. 'At least the days of praise from all are
finished; the old struggle of the parties begins again.'[50] The election was a
political watershed, though not quite as Keynes predicted. Most expert
opinion predicted a Baldwin victory. Montagu Norman advised Lydia Lopokova to get more dresses at the Galerie Lafayette to beat import duties.
Instead the election produced a large free-trade majority. Yet the main
beneficiaries were not the Liberals, reunited under Asquith's leadership, but
the Labour Party. With 191 MPs to the Liberals' 157 (the Conservatives
remained the largest party with 257), Ramsay MacDonald formed the first
Labour government with Liberal support. The nervously affluent locked
away their silver; some went abroad, never to return. The modern form of
two-party politics had arrived.

The Cambridge Liberal Association invited Keynes to stand for Parliament, unopposed by the Conservatives. Despite Lydia's urging ('One more
thing, can it matter to you?') he refused. But he took a moderately active
part in the campaign, speaking in Lancashire at Blackpool, Blackburn and
Barrow. He also wrote three articles on the election for the *Nation*. His object
was what would now be called a hung parliament, to prevent the 'quack
remedies' of both right and left. Against the 'mystical stupidities' of Conservatism he counterposed the no less mystical belief in free trade. 'If there
is one thing Protection can *not* do, it is to cure unemployment,' he wrote on
24 November. To claim otherwise 'involves the protectionist fallacy in its
grossest and crudest form'. But then he contradicted himself. It might
increase employment temporarily, but only by putting up prices and
depressing wages. Keynes forgot to mention that his own plan involved
doing just the same thing by cheap money and devaluation. To bolster up
a shaky case, Keynes claimed that Britain would soon be back at full
employment anyway.[51] His argument seemed to amount to this: Protection

*Taking the ratio of Britain's export to import prices in 1913 as 100, the average for 1921/9
was 127 and for 1930/7 was 138. (W. A. Lewis, *Economic Survey, 1919–1939*, 79.)

could not cure unemployment if there was no unemployment to be cured.

Keynes always had mixed feelings about the hustings. His new suit not being ready, he campaigned in an old shabby one, which he thought went down better with cotton operatives. He found his Blackburn audience of 3000 'serious and intelligent – a quite different type from London working classes. The interest they take in politics is extraordinary; and the more serious a speech is, the better they seem to like it. The Election was a big education for them; and I feel like a preacher – half enjoying it. If only my voice was different, I'd be in danger of enjoying it too much.' There was the rub: 'I hate my ugly voice more than ever,' he told Lydia after speaking in Blackpool's Opera house on 4 December. On Lydia, at least, Keynes's arguments had their usual gratifying effect. 'Free Trade,' she wrote to him, 'is admirable. So decisively clear. Protection as a cure for unemployment – ca n'existe pas! When you speak of our imports as incomes it seems to me a suicide not to trade free. Life without incomes is deplorable.'[52]

A lecture to the National Liberal Club on 13 December shows how far Keynes had come in his thinking over the previous twelve months. The political-economy note is sounded from the start: 'It is obvious that an individualist society left to itself does not work well or even tolerably. . . . The more troublous the times, the worse does a *laissez-faire* system work.' He enumerated the 'triple evils of modern society' as profiteering, precarious expectations and unemployment, all 'mainly due' to the 'instability of the standard of value'. However, he believed that as a result of one of the 'biggest jumps ever achieved in economic science', the control of the credit cycle was in sight. All that was needed was 'so to regulate the supply of Bradburies and of bank credit that their volume in terms of goods will be reasonably steady; i.e., that the index number of prices will never move far from a fixed point'. This could be done by the Bank of England, without the need for any legislation.

The issue was not one between collectivism and *laissez-faire* but between targeted state action and a socialism which was 'out of date and contrary to human nature'. But there was not much time to avoid the latter. Keynes declared,

> I would like to warn the gentlemen of the City and High Finance that if they do not listen in time to the voice of reason their days may be numbered. I speak to this great city as Jonah spoke to Nineveh. . . . I prophesy that unless they embrace wisdom in good time, the system upon which they live will work so very ill that they will be overwhelmed by irresistible things which they will hate much more than the mild and limited remedies offered them now.[53]

These remedies he was now ready to offer to the world.

V

'IN THE LONG RUN WE ARE ALL DEAD'

A Tract on Monetary Reform was published on 11 December 1923. It continued Keynes's habit of publishing his books on current affairs at the end of the year, a schedule which reflected the fact that he mainly wrote them in the university's long summer vacations. The *Tract* sums up what Keynes had been thinking and writing about the theory, practice and objects of monetary policy over the previous three years. Most of it was culled together from already published, or lecture, materials.* The result is the most sparkling but the least well organised of his economics books. In the opinion of Milton Friedman, it is his best.[54]

The central policy proposal of the *Tract* was that monetary policy should be used to stabilise the price level. Its central theoretical claim was that this should be accomplished by trying to stabilise the 'demand for money' for business purposes, rather than the supply of money. If the demand for money can be stabilised by policy, then, according to the quantity theory of money, the price level can be whatever the monetary authority decides.

The *Tract*'s personal intellectual ancestry can be traced back to Keynes's *Indian Currency and Finance* (1913), with its concern with seasonal fluctuations in the demand for rupees, as well as to his pre-war lectures on the theory of money. What did Keynes mean, then, when he talked about a scientific breakthrough? He meant a greater understanding of the theory of money, in particular the role of the banking system in creating credit. As a result of this gain in knowledge, a central bank would be able to control the demand for money. The central claim of the *Tract* is that by varying the amount of credit to the business sector, the banking system could even out fluctuations in business activity. The claim to have identified a controllable single variable – the supply of credit – capable of determining the level of prices and amount of activity in the economy as a whole is the start of macroeconomics.

This was not a theoretical revolution, still less one Keynes had pioneered. He drew freely not just on the Cambridge theory of money, but on the writings of monetary reformers like Irving Fisher and Gustav Cassel, as well as on his wartime experience. (See Appendix 2 of this chapter.) Keynes saw the new bits of theory he used as developing, rather than replacing, existing theory. The claim being made was for a greater understanding and control

*Chapter 1, 2, 3.2 and 3.4 are based on Keynes's articles in the 27 July and 20 April 1922 issues of the *Manchester Guardian* Reconstruction Supplements. But the articles of 27 July 1922 were themselves based on lecture material from the autumn of 1920. Chapter 3.1 on the quantity theory of money is based on lectures on money Keynes had been giving since 1911. All the material in chapter 4 had appeared in one form or another in the previous two years. Chapter 5 alone breaks new ground on policy, though not on theory.

of short-run or cyclical phenomena. The relationship between the 'short run' and the 'long run' (or indeed what these concepts meant) was left unexplored.

In the *Tract* it is hard to disentangle the scientific from the therapeutic. Keynes's belief that a breakthrough in the theory of money had occurred is genuine enough; but the claim for monetary management was also driven by the conviction that a modern economy, with its complex of more or less sticky contracts, 'could not stand' serious fluctuations in the standard of value. This is the context of Keynes's attack on the gold standard. The gold standard could not guarantee price stability, since no central bank had the power to determine the quantity of its gold stock.

Keynes's argument that price stability could only be secured by unshackling money from gold struck his critics as highly paradoxical. It failed to convince them then, and is not convincing now. Empirically they could contrast the relative stability of prices under the nineteenth-century gold standard with the experience of wild fluctuations in prices between 1914 and 1923, when currencies were under 'national' management and the gold standard suspended either *de facto* or *de jure*. And, whatever the state of the theory, they were convinced that without the 'discipline' of the gold standard, with its requirement that domestic currencies be convertible into gold at a fixed price, the quantity, and therefore the value, of money would be politically determined.

In fact, Keynes's proposals were not quite as radical as they sounded. His book has often been interpreted, and praised, as an argument for floating exchange rates. This is not so. His real concern was that sterling should not be pegged to other currencies in perpetuity. In other words he wanted the monetary authorities to accept the *de facto* devaluation of sterling which had occurred, and to be prepared to devalue (or revalue) the currency from time to time in the future. He wanted the best of both worlds – a monetary regime which could deliver stable domestic prices and relatively stable exchange rates.

What made his book shocking was its iconoclasm of expression rather than of theory or proposal. The tone was heavily ironic. Keynes was still very much the Cambridge Apostle blaspheming against conventional morality. He was writing, at least partly, for the reader who shared the values of Lytton Strachey. This made for entertaining reading, but bad advocacy. As in *The Economic Consequences of the Peace* he could not help mocking the 'sound men' he needed to persuade.

The *Tract on Monetary Reform* opened in a mood of scientific optimism. 'Nowhere is the need of innovation more urgent' than in questions of currency, he declared in his preface, and he dedicated his book to the Bank of England. 'Unemployment, the precarious life of the worker, the disappointment of expectation, the sudden loss of savings, the excessive windfalls of individuals, the speculator, the profiteer – all these proceed, in large measure, from the instability of the standard of value.' Specifically, currency reforms, based on 'sound monetary principles', would 'diminish the wastes of *risk*, which consume too much of our estate'.[55]

Chapter 1 is about the *effect* of a change in the value of money on the short-run distribution of wealth and the level of output. Although the discussion of the bad effects of a changing price level was not new,[56] Keynes was quite unusual in his stress on the 'stickiness of social and business arrangements' and the need it created for completely stable prices if capitalism was to be consistent with social stability. Inflation, he says, inflicts most injury by altering the distribution of wealth; deflation by retarding the production of wealth. In the first case, businessmen gain at the expense of savers and most workers whose incomes are fixed (in the short run), while their value falls. This is good for business, but undermines capitalism in the long run, by turning entrepreneurs into profiteers and drying up the supply of savings. Falling prices on the other hand injure output and employment by imposing windfall losses on businessmen, whose major costs of production (including wage costs) remain fixed in the short run, while the selling prices of their products fall. The most distinctive feature in Keynes's account is his stress on expectations. Orthodox theory held that only unanticipated price changes could have 'real' effects of the kind Keynes described. In Keynes's account it is the certain expectation that prices will rise or fall combined with uncertainty as to the extent of the movement which does the damage. In the deflationary case, 'the *fact* of falling prices injures entrepreneurs; consequently the fear of falling prices causes them to protect themselves by curtailing their operations'. Thus 'a comparatively weak initial impulse may be adequate to produce a considerable fluctuation'.[57]

In particular, one element in the cost of production – the money rate of interest on loans – is expectationally determined:

> For it is not the *fact* of a given rise of prices, but the *expectation* of a rise compounded of the various possible price movements and the estimated probability of each, which affects money rates; and in countries where the currency has not collapsed entirely, there has seldom or never existed a sufficient general confidence in a further rise or fall of prices to cause the short-money rate to rise above 10 per cent per annum, or to fall below 1 per cent. A fluctuation of this order is not sufficient to balance a movement of prices, up or down, of more than (say) 5 per cent per annum – a rate which the actual price movement has frequently exceeded.[58]

Interest-rate inertia in face of price fluctuations is thus seen as a leading cause of windfall profits and losses and thus of fluctuations in output and employment, and its cause – uncertainty about how much prices will move in one direction or another – identified.

Keynes concluded chapter 1 with a famous, carefully nuanced, passage:

'Thus inflation is unjust and deflation inexpedient. Of the two perhaps deflation is, if we rule out exaggerated inflations such as that of Germany, the worse; because it is worse, in an impoverished world, to provoke unemployment than to disappoint the *rentier*.'[59] The important qualifying phrase 'in an impoverished world' has been ignored by those who claim this passage as evidence of Keynes's indifference to inflation. In fact, as he makes clear, 'it is not necessary that we should weigh one evil against the other. It is easier to agree that both are evils to be shunned.'

Having dealt with the effects of changes in the value of money, Keynes turned in chapter 3 to the causes. These involved the famous quantity theory of money. According to the theory, the price level varies proportionately with the quantity of cash issued by the banking system – that is to say, the greater or fewer the number of currency notes, the higher or the lower is the price level in the same proportion.'[60] 'This theory,' Keynes writes, 'is fundamental. Its correspondence with fact is not open to question.'[61] But, having delivered himself of this judgement, he proceeds to show that it has little correspondence with fact in the short run.

Keynes wrote down a simplified version of Pigou's Cambridge equation: $n = p (k + rk')$, where n is currency notes, p is the cost-of-living index, k is the fraction of their assets people keep as cash in their pockets, k' the fraction they keep in checking accounts and r the fraction of these deposits which the banks keep in their vaults or with the central bank as reserves. Money is simply the stock of bank notes issued which are at any time partly in the hands of the public and partly in the hands of the banks – what Marshall called 'cash balances' held for spending. Provided these balances are being spent at the same rate from one period to another, there must be a constant relationship between money and prices, since things must cost what you pay for them. In the long run, Keynes wrote, 'this is probably true. . . . But this *long run* is a misleading guide to current affairs. *In the long run* we are all dead. Economists set themselves too easy, too useless a task if in tempestuous seasons they can only tell us that when the storm is long past the ocean is flat again.'[62]

What Keynes meant by this, the most famous of all his remarks, was that, in the short run, changes in the *speed* with which people spend their cash – what economists call the velocity of circulation – can change prices independently of changes in the quantity of cash. What happens according to Keynes is that they speed up their spending when prices rise or are expected to rise, and slow it down in the reverse cases. He produced figures on pp. 67–8 showing that roughly the same volume of currency had supported a price level 50 per cent higher in October 1920 than in October 1922, the difference being explained by the great shrinkage in bank deposits since the earlier date. So the task of a banking system which wants to keep prices stable is to keep the amount of deposits, not the amount of currency, constant.

Keynes had outlined his alternative. He favoured independently managed national monetary systems; these would be consistent with *de facto* exchange-rate stability over long periods. But he also understood that this was not practical politics; so he set himself the lesser aim of trying to ensure that the return to gold was brought about with the least disruption possible to the British economy. His general line in 1924 was one of 'wait and see'. He was not against fixing the pound at its pre-war parity with the dollar if circumstances justified; but he argued that it should not be an object of policy and was especially opposed to a deliberate policy of deflation to bring it about. Thus for tactical reasons he abandoned outright opposition to the return and pushed the case for delay. One explanation of Keynes's sometimes hesitating line in the run-up to the return is that his opposition to the policy was practical rather than theoretical. Thus in the final stages of the debate he oscillated between pointing out the practical difficulty of deflating money wages by the amount required to restore equilibrium at the pre-war parity and urging the authorities to attend to this before deciding to go back: another argument for delay, but inconsistent with his general anti-deflationary stance. All this twisting and turning can readily be understood in terms of the logic of the second-best: but it reinforced the impression that Keynes was 'too clever by half'.

The underlying fact was that Keynes's argument in the *Tract* against going back to gold had failed to convince. P. J. Grigg noted in his diary that 'the opponents of the policy advocated by the Cunliffe Committee were confined to a small number of those who were susceptible to the still small voice of Keynes, and this in spite of the fact that the still small voice was already beginning to be immeasurably amplified by the multiple organ of Lord Beaverbrook'. The resumption of gold payments might have come in 1923 or 1924 had it not been for financial uncertainty about the future political direction of both the Baldwin government and its Labour successor. These factors caused a 'flight from sterling' in mid–1923, and a low level ($4.30–$4.40) for most of 1924.* Not that Labour ministers shared Keynes's doubts about the wisdom of returning the pound to the gold standard: Philip Snowden, Labour's Chancellor of the Exchequer, was a strong supporter of gold, and in April 1924 appointed a Committee on the Note Issue, headed by Austen Chamberlain, to advise him on 'when and how the final step should be taken'.[34]

Expert opinion, as revealed in the evidence to the Chamberlain Committee, was almost unanimously in favour of restoring the gold standard. Three benefits were most commonly adduced. The first was that it would anchor the value of domestic money, or prevent inflation. Montagu Norman, in his

---

*In his evidence to the Chamberlain Committee, Montagu Norman attributed the 'flight from sterling' first to an incautious speech by the Conservative Minister of Labour, Sir Montague Barlow, in the summer of 1923, secondly to 'fears as to what the [Labour] government might do' in the way of taxation'. (TP, T.160.197/7528/02/1, pp. 33, 35.)

evidence, was quite explicit that the return to gold would prevent a 'great borrowing by public authorities'. Sir Felix Schuster, representing the clearing banks, was 'very much afraid of the inflationary theories' put forward by Keynes and socialists.[35] The Bank of England saw in a return to gold the chance to regain control over domestic monetary policy lost by Cunliffe to Bonar Law in 1917; the Treasury a chance to regain control of public expenditure from the politicians; employers saw it as a means to discipline the unions.[36]

Secondly, the return to gold was seen as an industrial policy. It was denied, most forcibly by Sir Felix Schuster, that there could be any long-run difference of interest between the City of London and the 'trade of the country', since 'traders lose much more by variations in the Exchange than by having to pay a little more for their banking'.[37] This was not a view shared by the Federation of British Industries, which nevertheless agreed that a '*general* return to [a] gold basis . . . would be greatly to our benefit'.[38]

Finally, the bankers were unanimous that a return to gold was necessary to restore the City of London to its position as the world's leading banker, and sterling to its position as the world's leading currency. In the absence of a resumption of gold payments, not just the US dollar, but even the German mark would become 'a far more popular currency than the British pound'.[39]

Two comments are in order. Keynes's argument in the *Tract* that the gold standard itself was an important source of price instability weighed much less heavily than the perception that inconvertible paper standards were inherently inflationary, since it cost almost nothing to manufacture bits of paper signed by a central bank's cashier.* To those who argued that the British experience of 1922–5 showed that a paper standard need not be inflationary, Montagu Norman pointed out in 1925 that 'These three years of "managed" finance have been possible only because they have been made up of steps – deliberate steps – towards a golden summer.'[40] Roy Harrod wrote that Keynes believed that 'England [was] a sufficiently mature country for it to be possible to assume that the authorities could be trusted . . . not [to] indulge in an orgy of feckless note issue.'[41] This is a feeble defence: monetary authorities are part of a political and social system and are bound to respond to its pressures. The gold bugs were right to point out the inflationary implications of 'managed currencies'.

Where Keynes was right was to distinguish between fixing the exchange and the rate at which it was fixed. 'I should simply aim', he wrote, 'at something as near as possible to what we are in fact adjusted to when the

---

*It is certainly a tenable argument that British inflation would not have been as great in 1919–20, nor would the deflation from 1920 to 1922 have needed to be so severe, had Britain remained on the gold standard in this period, since the much greater rise of British than American prices in the boom of 1919–20 would hardly have been possible had the pound been linked to the dollar.

change is made.'[42] He was alone of those experts regarded as reputable in being willing to contemplate devaluation. Devaluation, wrote Pigou in his draft report for the Chamberlain Committee in September 1924, 'has only to be mentioned to be dismissed'.[43] This is the point at which irrationality infected British financial decision-making. The policy of forcing up the level of sterling assumed away the problem of forcing down domestic money wages. It was the tacit assumption that wages would fall like magic to the wand of a higher bank rate which, more than anything else, convinced Keynes that the decision-makers had the wrong model of the economy in their minds. In practice,the gold-standard party was split between those who wanted Britain to go back to gold only after British costs were internationally competitive at $4.86 and those who were prepared to use the restoration of the gold standard to force domestic costs down. For tactical reasons, Keynes allied himself with the first position. But he weakened his case by arguing that sterling would probably regain parity with the dollar anyway because American prices were bound to rise sooner or later. This encouraged the hardliners to argue that not much readjustment in British costs would be needed. In theory, the hardliners wanted British costs lowered rather than American prices raised. In practice, they feared to attempt the first, and therefore hoped for help from the second. They lacked the ruthlessness of Mussolini, who in 1927 simply announced that the lira was at par and ordered all wages to be cut by 20 per cent. That is why Mussolini was so admired in certain British circles in the 1920s.

V

EFFORTS AT PERSUASION

Keynes gave his own evidence to the Chamberlain Committee on 11 July 1924. Since his turn towards insular capitalism he was no longer the Treasury's favourite son. But he still moved in the circles from which the Committee's membership – Austen Chamberlain, Otto Niemeyer, Bradbury, Pigou and Gaspar Ferrer (a banker) – and witnesses like Montagu Norman, Sir Charles Addis, Edwin Cannan, Sir Henry Goschen, Walter Leaf, Reginald McKenna, Sir George Paish and Sir Felix Schuster were drawn. He had his reputation to consider; he could not appear to favour a policy which smacked of inflation.

Before the Committee, Keynes repeated the arguments he had put forward in the *Tract* for preferring price stability to exchange stability. He repeated the point he had made in his argument with Cannan that it was difficult to operate credit control by currency control 'because you are acting on almost the *last* event in the causal train'. He was forced to face up to the objections to discretionary monetary management. Who would control credit in Keynes's system? Keynes's answer was: the Bank of England. Bradbury asked, 'Leave it to a private institution?' Keynes replied, 'I do not regard it as a private institution. I regard it as one of our Heaven-sent institutions by which through anomalistic methods we get the advantages both of a private and a public institution.' The Bank did not need the crutch of the gold standard.

Keynes was then pressed by Austen Chamberlain: could one trust the Chancellor of the Exchequer not to run budget deficits to finance his favourite schemes?

J. M. K.: 'I do not think there is any means of strapping down a really wicked Chancellor of the Exchequer.'

Chamberlain: 'Well, you could try to stop him as much as possible.'

J. M. K.: 'No. I should try to throw him out of office. On your assumption that there might be a Chancellor of the Exchequer who was borrowing by inflationary means, he would not do it by actually paying out currency notes. He would borrow on terms that led to an inflation of credit and did not represent real savings. My opinion is that if we had a Chancellor of the Exchequer with these wishes, the operation of the limitation of the currency note issue probably would not come into effect in his time anyhow.'

Gaspar Ferrer then intervened: 'Do you think we shall have to breed a superman to control credit?'

Keynes said: 'No. I am not changing the methods. If the directors of the Bank of England are as stupid as some people think they are, our currency will break down in any case. I do not regard my system as intrinsically more difficult. What is more difficult is to manage a credit regime under which gold plays no part in circulation as compared with the medieval [that is, pre-war!] system when it was otherwise. . . . I should not have the smallest hesitation in thinking that there would always be half a dozen persons in the City well competent to look after it.'[44]

There was something distinctly cavalier about the way Keynes sidestepped the problem of the Wicked Chancellor. The fact is that, as a result of the war, government expenditure was a much higher proportion of the national income, and government debt (especially short-term debt) a much larger part of all credit instruments than it had been before the war. Government policy was thus bound to have a controlling influence on monetary conditions, even if the Bank was nominally independent. This was the danger against which the return to gold was supposed to guard.

Keynes's practical objection to an immediate return was that it would require a 'drastic restriction in credit' – enough to bring about a fall in money wages of about 12 per cent. This was based on the fact that the sterling–dollar exchange at the time stood at $4.44, or 88 per cent of par. Deflation on such a scale 'would probably prove socially and politically impossible', Keynes said. He was not pressed on why a much greater deflation had been possible in 1920–2. Reginald McKenna, chairman of the

Midland Bank, put the point even more succinctly in his evidence: 'The attempt to force prices down when you have a million unemployed is unthinkable....'[45] However, in the longer term, linking sterling to gold would, Keynes thought, expose Britain to the opposite danger of inflation. In his evidence he chose to emphasise the *inflationary* rather than the deflationary danger. This was more than tactical, though tactics played a part. The Federal Reserve Board had been extremely successful in its King Midas policy of sterilising gold inflows, but Keynes did not see how this could last. American prices would have to rise: and the export of gold would bring inflation to Europe.

Keynes's policy recommendation was that the export and import of gold should be permanently subject to licence, though such licences might be given for long periods 'to all comers without question'. Then in answer to Chamberlain's question, 'Is it an essential part of your views that we ought not to attempt to restore the old parity of the sovereign?', Keynes replied:

> No, that is not an essential part of my views. My own belief is that the policy I advocate – price stability – would almost certainly lead to a restoration of the parity of the sovereign, because I find it hard to believe that American prices will not rise in time, unless they do improbable things. . . . The peculiarity of my policy is limited to this, that having got back to par I should like to accept the import of gold only by licence of the Treasury. That is to say, suppose there is a big wave of inflation in America which carries us back to par, I do not want to be carried on by that inflation.[46]

Keynes's evidence to the Chamberlain Committee was hardly a robust attack on the policy of restoring the gold standard. He was not against the pound regaining its pre-war parity with the dollar, but against deliberate deflation to bring this about. His idea of restoring gold payments by licence failed to meet the credibility argument and was not taken up. Nor did the Committee take seriously Keynes's fear that the inflationary movement in the United States might lift sterling above parity. The Committee could well conclude that Keynes expected parity to be regained, without deflationary exertion, in the not too distant future, by a rise in American prices. This was what the Committee and most of the witnesses believed anyway; and the advice of its report, drafted by Pigou, and submitted in September 1924 was, essentially, to wait for external events to waft sterling back to par. Keynes's testimony helped to crystallise the view that the pre-war parity could be regained and maintained without detrimental effect on the real economy.

A few days after Keynes had given his oral evidence, an interesting and rather modern-sounding debate developed between him and Sir Charles Addis. Addis was one of a number of bankers at this time who urged what would now be called a 'pre-commitment' to return to gold as a way of influencing expectations. Walter Leaf, chairman of the Westminster Bank, wanted to signal the intention to return in the near future by raising bank rate – a suggestion approved by Montagu Norman.[47] Keynes attacked this in an article in the *Nation* of 19 July 1924. 'In the early stages the excitement of the bulls might provoke a rapid upward movement. But before the final goal was reached, many other difficult and injurious things would have to come about.'[48] This produced a long letter from Addis (21 July), who argued that Britain should commit itself to resume the gold standard by 1 January 1926, when the embargo on gold exports was due to expire.

> The effect of such an announcement, if people really believed it, would tend to raise the sterling exchange . . . but, of course, the effect would not be permanent unless it were followed up by the appropriate action of the Bank. . . . Eighteen months is long enough as a warning to merchants to put their houses in order. . . . The whole thing is largely psychological. If we say that we are going to resume the free export of gold and say it in such a way that people will believe it, you can take it as good as done.[49]

Keynes wrote back on 25 July:

> Either the government's announcement is believed and the future is discounted immediately in the rate of exchange, in which case we suffer all the elements of a violent and sudden deflation; or else the Government's announcement is disbelieved, or only half believed, in which case we have a slow movement with the expectation of a further movement in the same direction, the effect of which on trade and employment hardly bears thinking about. As soon as the business world has good reason to believe that prices are likely to fall, no course is open to it except to contract its engagements, draw in its horns and go out of business as far as may be until the *funeste* process is over.

Such explicit discussion of the effects of expectations on events was rare at the time. Addis's argument was that the announcement of intention would cause a rise in the exchange, which in turn would produce a fairly painless adjustment of domestic costs. Keynes's counter-argument was that between the bulls on sterling and the bears on profits British industry and employment would have to shrink.

> The more I spend my thoughts on these matters [his letter to Addis continued], the more alarmed I become at seeing you and others in authority attacking the problems of the changed post-war world with . . . unmodified pre-war views and ideas. To close the mind to the idea of revolutionary improvements in the control of money and credit is to sow the seeds of the downfall of individualistic capitalism. Do not be the Louis XVI of the monetary revolution. . . . I am told

by a good many friends that I have become a sort of disreputable figure in some quarters because I do not agree with the maxims of City pundits. But you know I ought not to be considered so really! I seek to improve the machinery of society not overturn it.[50]

The general election of October 1924 found Keynes briefly on the hustings, hating his voice as much as ever. His letter of support to the Liberal candidate for Cambridge contains an interesting mixture of supply-side and demand-side policies to mitigate unemployment: 'we must increase the mobility of labour between one job and another, organise more skilfully the employment of credit, and direct more wisely the use of our annual savings. . . . By reason of their old fashioned dogmas and the class-interests they are compelled to serve, neither Socialists nor Tories are likely to do anything sensible and effective in the near future.'[51] As usual, he was wildly over-optimistic about Liberal prospects: gambling on Keynes's forecasts, Vanessa and Duncan lost £70 each, which he forgave them. (His total losses came to £350.)[52] The Conservative victory under Baldwin at last opened the door to a 'golden' age. Sterling, which had been in the $4.40–$4.50 range in the summer of 1924, rose to $4.70–$4.80 from December through to April 1925. This reflected foreign speculation on a rise, but also a compelling international conjuncture. The spread in wholesale prices between the USA and Britain, which had been estimated at about 10–12 per cent in the summer of 1924, narrowed substantially in late 1924 and early 1925 with a rise in American prices, as the Federal Reserve Board, under the leadership of Benjamin Strong of the Federal Reserve Bank of New York, pursued an easy-money policy, partly to offset a domestic recession, partly to ease the return of sterling to parity. The same policy – which involved holding interest rates in New York 1 per cent below those in London – also made it profitable to borrow money in New York and lend it to London.

Under these circumstances, the British authorities came under great pressure from Strong not to let the 'golden opportunity' slip. In Strong's view stabilisation of sterling was the key to ending currency disorganisation, which had been a 'withering influence' on international trade.[53] He and Norman, who went to New York in December 1924, agreed that the failure of Britain to take the opportunity to return to gold now would have consequences 'too serious really to contemplate'. Norman told Strong that it would mean 'violent fluctuations in the exchanges, with probably progressive deterioration in the values of foreign currencies vis-à-vis the dollar; it would provide an incentive to all those who were advancing novel ideas and expedients other than the gold standard to sell their wares; and incentives to governments . . . to undertake various types of paper money expedients and inflation'.[54] It is not difficult to imagine whom he had in mind. In New York, Norman assured himself of a 'cushion' of credit to defend sterling if it went back to gold in the near future. He cabled to the Bank on 6 January

1925: 'our return to gold is desired by responsible people here and opposed only by certain politicians and cranks'. March 1925 was the date he suggested.[35]

The pressure of the two governors for an early return was partly resisted by some in the Bank and the Treasury. Sir Charles Addis drafted a cable on 9 January, sent to Norman a day later by Cecil Lubbock, deputy governor of the Bank, which stated: 'In our judgement the restoration of the Gold Standard should follow and not precede the conditions of trade appropriate to the maintenance of a stable exchange.' The criterion should be a balance of international payments in favour of Britain 'tested by a period of comparatively stable exchange'. He favoured an announcement by the Chancellor that he would raise the embargo on the free export of gold 'when, in the opinion of the Government and after consultation with the Bank of England, it might be deemed advisable to do so'. Another director, Lord Revelstoke of Baring Bros., as well as Otto Niemeyer of the Treasury, had similar reservations.[36] Keynes's persuasion had clearly been having some effect. But such counsels of caution were overwhelmed by the pace of events. Not only was sterling being pushed back to parity by expectations of an early announcement, but with a string of foreign and Dominion currency stabilisations being planned for 1925 Britain was in danger of being pushed to the back of the line.

Keynes instinctively understood that the secret of persuasiveness was to stay within the limits of the possible. In an address to the Tuesday Club on 14 January he made his accommodation to the inevitability of sterling's *de facto* return to parity, and sought to narrow the gap between 'the Monetary Reformers and the Gold Standarders' to one simple point: 'Should the removal of the embargo [on gold exports] come first or last?' Keynes proposed that it should come at the end of the process of adjustment and not in order to force it: 'We must take steps to be at par first and *say* we are there after we are there.' He pointed out that the present value of sterling was the result of heavy speculation of the pound and of an American boom. To link the pound to the dollar at near the top of the boom would be to bear the brunt of the ensuing American deflation, plus the 8 per cent by which sterling was below par when the boom started. Keynes proposed to begin the 'necessary adjustments to parity' by a 'firm monetary policy here'. He would let the sterling–dollar exchange go to $4.86 and then keep it there by a tight monetary policy. When all internal adjustments seemed complete and there was no special boom in America or bull speculation in sterling, he would remove the embargo, but keep gold out of domestic circulation and restrict the right of mintage to the Bank of England. The alternative of removing the embargo immediately 'seems to me to involve wishing the end, but not the means. I think it is all the more dangerous because in the early stages it is perfectly feasible.'[37]

There is no record of who attended Keynes's talk. The active membership of the Tuesday Club at this time consisted, apart from Keynes, of Oswald Falk, Sir Charles Addis, Bob Brand, Sir Felix Schuster, Sir Josiah Stamp, Sir Henry Strakosch, Sir John Anderson (chairman of the Board of Inland Revenue), M. S. Spencer-Smith (a director of the Bank of England), Otto Niemeyer, Walter Layton and Dennis Robertson. The City, the Bank and the Treasury were probably all represented.

In the Bank of England, Addis, perhaps persuaded by Keynes not to be the Louis XVI of the monetary revolution, now fought for delay. The final meeting of the Chamberlain (now Bradbury) Committee took place on 28 January. The governor brought along Addis, so the Committee could hear both points of view. Norman argued that the 'rise in the Dollar exchange' was the decisive argument for an early return. In America, a Republican President and Congress assured political stability for several years ahead. Switzerland, Holland, Sweden, South Africa and Australia were anxious to get back to gold. Britain's return to gold was 'looked upon as an international question and not as national to this country only'. Addis countered that it was not just a question of 'capacity to return to the gold standard which nobody doubts, but of your capacity to maintain it after you have reached it'. This meant 'a reasonable prospect of something like equilibrium being maintained between the relative price levels'. One could not rely on calculations of purchasing power parity, as there were too many index numbers. There was no other test than 'an approximately steady rate of exchange round about parity during a continued period' – unsupported by borrowing or 'any artificial aids'. No attempt should be made to return on the basis of borrowing from the United States, because the temptation would then be to rely on borrowing to maintain the exchange as an alternative to more drastic remedies. He argued for a delay of six months at least.

It was Pigou who put the knife into Addis's testimony. How was Addis's view that the exchange should remain stable 'for some time before committing oneself' consistent with his view that the government should commit itself to return later? Would not that announcement itself keep the exchange stable? Would it not 'have destroyed the value of the test, the stability of the exchange as a test?'[38] The Committee agreed with Norman that the time had come, and reported accordingly. Niemeyer, one of the signatories of its report, immediately began the task of persuading the Chancellor of the Exchequer, Winston Churchill.

Churchill understood modern no better than old-fashioned economics, but he was worried about the domestic, and particularly the deflationary, implications of returning sterling to par. On 29 January, with the Bradbury Committee's report fresh in his hands, he produced an 'Exercise', setting out objections to a quick return to gold, which led Bradbury to think that 'he appears to have his spiritual home in the Keynes–McKenna sanctuary'.[39] Churchill was certainly familiar with Keynes's arguments, from the *Nation*.

Churchill's 'Exercise' was answered by Niemeyer, Bradbury, Norman and Hawtrey – and also by Keynes, who, of course, did not see it. In one of his best articles, in the *Nation* of 21 February 1925, he argued that the rise of sterling had been due to 'abnormal' factors and would be checked (as it had been in the past) when the Federal Reserve Board took steps to choke off the American boom, or when the boom, having got out of hand, collapsed. If Britain had meanwhile removed the gold embargo a 'stern deflation' would be forced on it 'in the effort to keep the exchange at parity'. Thus it would not be prudent to remove the embargo until 'the mean level of dollar prices appears to be *stabilised* at a somewhat higher level than in recent times'. But 'if we want to return to parity steps should be taken to achieve the *fact* by raising bank rate and checking foreign issues'. (The authorities took his advice, raising bank rate to 5 per cent and embargoing foreign issues early in March.) Keynes made the point that the American economy was much more flexible than the British: 'The slump of 1921 was even more violent in the United States than here, but by the end of 1922 recovery was practically complete. We still, in 1925, drag on with a million unemployed.' Of equal interest in the longer term was Keynes's acceptance of the fact that he had lost the political battle about the form of currency regime. Monetary reformers would have to 'expound their arguments more fully, more clearly, and more simply, before they can overwhelm the forces of old custom and general ignorance'.[60]

For a brief moment Keynes might have felt that his persuasion was starting to work. In reply to the 'Exercise', Charles Goodenough, chairman of Barclays Bank, had told Churchill 'not only that the pound ought to achieve parity by natural processes before the decision was taken, but that it should be maintained at par for several months without our being finally committed' – which was also Addis's position.[61] More importantly, Churchill himself was inspired by reading Keynes's *Nation* article to fire off a Sunday-morning salvo to Niemeyer, dictated from his bed, which contains perhaps the most savage indictment of the Treasury and Bank ever penned by a Chancellor of the Exchequer. The relevant passage starts, 'The Treasury have never, it seems to me, faced the profound significance of what Mr Keynes calls "the paradox of unemployment amidst dearth". The Governor allows himself to be perfectly happy in the spectacle of Britain possessing the finest credit in the world simultaneously with a million and a quarter unemployed,' and ends, 'I would rather see Finance less proud and Industry more content.'[62] It is nonsense to claim, as Moggridge does, that in passages such as these Churchill was merely putting forward objections in order to elicit cogent replies from his advisers.[63]

In their efforts to persuade Churchill, the Treasury and the Bank used two main arguments. The first was the negligible divergence between British and American prices. Niemeyer argued early in February that they were 'within 4½ per cent of each other, if not nearer', so that the 'extra sacrifice' to regain parity was hardly worth considering. Bradbury thought the price differential was not more than 2 to 2.5 per cent. These estimates were important in countering the critics' argument that the rise in sterling was largely capital-induced.[64] Opinion, though, was still divided about whether the remaining gap would be closed by American inflation or needed to be closed by British deflation.

The Treasury's other main argument was that the return to gold was an *employment* policy. British unemployment would only be mopped up by a worldwide trade recovery, for which stabilisation of the exchanges was a necessary condition. Thus there could be no contradiction between the interests of finance and industry, as Churchill had implied. 'The real antithesis', Niemeyer pointed out, 'is between the long view and the short view.'[65] In his reply to Keynes's article, Niemeyer wrote on 22 February, 'You may by inflation (a most vicious form of subsidy) enable, temporarily, spending power to cope with large quantities of products. But unless you increase the dose continually, there comes a time when, having destroyed the credit of the country, you can inflate no more, money having ceased to be acceptable as value.'[66]

Keynes continued to search for a point of agreement between himself and his opponents. In the *Nation* of 7 March 1925 he approved the rise in bank rate, arguing that it would not harm employment if no fall in the price level was anticipated. What influences enterprise is not the money rate of interest, but 'anticipated real rate of profit over the period of the productive process', compounded of bank rate and anticipated price movements. The important thing was to free the business world 'from anxiety lest their anticipated profit will be obliterated by a falling price level'.[67] As Moggridge points out, acceptance by the monetary reformers of the dear-money policy undercut their most popular argument against the return to gold.[68] In an address to the Commercial Committee of the House of Commons on 18 March, Keynes struck a populist note. It was wrong to have to turn the tap of credit on or off:

> merely because an investment boom in Wall Street had gone too far, or because of a sudden change of fashion among Americans towards foreign bond issues, or because the banks in the Middle West had got tied up with farmers, or because the American President was dead, or because the horrid fact that every American had ten motor-cars and a wireless set in every room of every house had become known to the manufacturers of these articles.[69]

One may wonder whether, in these months, Keynes did not regret having resigned from the Treasury in 1919. Would the decision have gone the other way had he stayed? Or would he himself have been singing a different tune? As it was, it was not till 17 March that he got his chance to confront the Treasury's arguments directly, by which time it was almost too late. His engagement diary for that day has a note: '8.30. Winston'. Churchill had arranged for the subject to be thrashed out one more time at a dinner party at 11 Downing Street, to which he had invited, as well as Keynes, Niemeyer, Bradbury and McKenna. The only record of what was said is contained in the memoirs of his private secretary, P. J. Grigg, who was present and who recalled that 'the Symposium lasted till midnight or after'. According to Grigg, Keynes and McKenna stuck to the point that the discrepancy between British and American prices was nearer 10 per cent than the 2.5 per cent indicated by the exchanges, and that domestic prices would therefore have to be deflated by something of that order. 'This meant unemployment and downward adjustment of wages and prolonged strikes in some of the heavy industries, at the end of which it would be found that these industries had undergone a permanent contraction.' It was much better, therefore, to try to keep domestic prices and nominal wage rates stable and allow the exchanges to fluctuate for the time being. Bradbury's main argument was that the gold standard was 'knave proof'. It could not be 'rigged for political . . . reasons'. Return to gold would stop Britain living in a fool's paradise, by ensuring a competitive basis for its export industries. The argument finally ended when Churchill asked McKenna, 'Given the situation as it is, what decision would you make?' McKenna, an ex-Chancellor himself, replied, 'There is no escape; you have to go back; but it will be hell.'[70] This is what Keynes meant about McKenna 'always letting one down in the end'.

It was the last argument. On 20 March Churchill decided to lift the gold embargo in his budget statement. In announcing Britain's return to the gold standard at the pre-war parity on 28 April, the Chancellor declared, 'If we had not taken this action the whole of the rest of the British Empire would have taken it without us, and it would have come to a gold standard, not on the basis of the pound sterling, but a gold standard of the dollar.'

VI

THE ECONOMIC CONSEQUENCES OF MR. CHURCHILL

In the weeks following the return to gold, Keynes developed three lines of attack on the decision.[71]

First, he pointed to the double-edged consequence of using bank rate to maintain the restored parity. A bank rate high enough to attract foreign funds to London but not high enough to enforce a 'deflation of credit', would secure the worst of both worlds: Britain could maintain the overvaluation of its currency, 'paying its way by borrowing instead of exporting', and leaving the economy locked into permanent unemployment. It was a prescient prediction of how policy actually worked in the gold-standard years.[72]

Secondly, he attempted a more precise way of analysing the extent of sterling's overvaluation. He distinguished for the first time between the price levels of 'unsheltered' and 'sheltered' goods. Unsheltered – or internationally traded – goods followed the law of one price: their selling prices had to conform to world conditions of supply and demand. The prices of sheltered goods and services – those sold mainly at home, like houses and transport – had no automatic tendency to adjust to the prices of unsheltered goods. To put the matter concretely: if the sterling proceeds from the sale abroad of a ton of coal were suddenly reduced by 10 per cent, there was no assurance that the sterling cost of producing that ton – which would include freight charges and interest payments – would also fall by 10 per cent. The true index of maladjustment between external and internal prices, therefore, showed itself in the difference between the prices of unsheltered and sheltered goods. This maladjustment was not revealed by comparing indices of wholesale prices, which were composed largely of internationally traded goods. A comparison between British and US cost-of-living indices in January 1925 showed a disparity of 18 per cent. This gave a more accurate indication of the extent of deflation required than a comparison of wholesale prices.[73]

The third point Keynes made was that labour was the main non-traded good. In assuming that domestic prices 'automatically' adjust to any given exchange rate, policymakers were assuming perfectly competitive wage rates. This ignored the 'deplorably inelastic conditions of industrial organisation today'. In his evidence, on 9 July 1925, to the Balfour Committee on Trade and Industry he pointed to the 'power of trade unions in preventing the cutting of rates [of pay] by competition from unemployed labour', to the effect of the dole in reducing 'the extreme pressure to find employment elsewhere', to the lack of a proper housing market. Keynes told the Committee that 'we are in something much more like the medieval conditions, in which it was so difficult to change the internal value of money that when you were in disequilibrium with the external value you had to have what was called a debasement of the currency . . .'. Keynes never neglected supply-side problems: he just thought that little could be done about them. More important was the change in demand conditions: in the nineteenth century 'everything was on a general crescendo'; the economy was never faced with the problem of reducing average costs by 10 per cent.[74]

Keynes had been asked to serve on the Balfour Committee, but declined. Members of the Committee probed what they saw as the weak points in his presentation. He had stated that 'whereas our cost of living and wages were in equilibrium with the United States last March [1924, when the pound was down to $4.29] they are now 10 or 11 per cent higher'. Sir Arthur Balfour pointed out that even then British trade was 'desperately bad'. Keynes had to admit that even then British costs had been out of line with those in France and Germany.[75] Nevertheless, 'I think that [in March

1924] . . . if we had kept the exchange adjusted to our position at that date and had not raised expectation of a return to the gold standard, and had had easy money, we could have gone a long way towards abolishing unemployment by now.'[76] But Keynes had not said this at the time. He told the Balfour Committee, 'I would like to stimulate in all sorts of unsound ways a general state of prosperity in the hope that I could get a cumulative wave of prosperity which would lap up the slack. I do not believe you can ever get straight by depressing things. I think there is always a lot of unused capacity in the country, and I would like to create unsound artificial prosperity in the hope that it would prove cumulative.'[77]

Before he appeared in front of the Balfour Committee Keynes had offered Geoffrey Dawson of *The Times* a series of articles on the effects of the return to the gold standard. When Dawson saw them, he turned them down: 'They are extraordinarily clever and very amusing; but I really feel that, published in *The Times* at this particular moment, they would do harm and not good.'[78] Beaverbrook was more receptive, and they appeared in the *Evening Standard* on 22, 23 and 24 July. A week later an expanded version was published by the Hogarth Press, entitled 'The Economic Consequences of Mr. Churchill'. Seven thousand copies were printed, priced at 1s. a copy. They sold out immediately; several more editions were printed over the summer. But the pamphlet flopped in the United States, with only 210 sold after six months, and 216 copies given away.

'The Economic Consequences of Mr. Churchill' was more than the echo of a name. Like its best-selling predecessor, Keynes's pamphlet combined a scorching analysis of policy with a passionate denunciation of injustice. He can be criticised, as at Versailles, for seeing the matter more clearly in retrospect than before the fateful decisions were taken. It needed the decision itself to crystallise the indictment.

'Our troubles' arose from the fact that sterling's value had gone up by 10 per cent in the previous year. 'The policy of improving the exchange by 10 per cent involves a reduction of 10 per cent in the sterling receipts of our export industries.' But they could not reduce their prices by 10 per cent and remain profitable unless all internal prices and wages fell by 10 per cent. 'Thus Mr. Churchill's policy of improving the exchange by 10 per cent was, sooner or later, a policy of reducing everyone's wages by 2s. [10p] in the pound.' He pointed out that there was 'no machinery' for effecting a simultaneous reduction. It meant 'engaging in a struggle with each separate group [of workers] in turn, with no prospect that the result will be fair, and no guarantee that the stronger groups will not gain at the expense of the weaker'. Those attacked first were 'justified in defending themselves' because they had no guarantee that they would be compensated later by a lower cost of living.

Why had Winston Churchill done it? He had 'no instinctive judgement in financial matters'; but mainly it was because he was 'gravely misled by his experts'. Keynes dismissed the Chamberlain–Bradbury Report as 'vague and jejune'. The experts used inappropriate price indices; they also misunderstood and underrated the difficulty of reducing domestic prices. Keynes never blamed Winston Churchill personally for the return to gold. Nor did Churchill take Keynes's attack personally: in 1927 Keynes was elected to The Other Club, the society started by Churchill and F. E. Smith in 1909 for 'dining and wagering'.

Keynes then posed what he took to be the crucial question: by what *modus operandi* does credit restriction reduce money wages and the cost of living?

> *In no other way* [he answered] *than by the deliberate intensification of unemployment.* The object of credit restriction, in such a case, is to withdraw from employers the financial means to employ labour at the existing level of prices and wages. The policy can only attain its end by intensifying unemployment without limit, until the workers are ready to accept the necessary reduction of money wages under the pressure of hard facts . . . Deflation does not reduce wages 'automatically'. It reduces them by causing unemployment. The proper object of dear money is to check an incipient boom. Woe to those whose faith leads them to use it to aggravate a depression![79]

Keynes understood that the Bank and government would shrink from applying the measures their decision entailed. They would try to borrow rather than deflate. Politics would cause them to do things which would defeat their economic objective. This in fact happened the very day Keynes's pamphlet appeared. On 30 June the coal owners had demanded a new agreement with the Miners' Federation which implied a substantial wage reduction. The miners, backed by the TUC, prepared for a general strike. The Prime Minister, Baldwin, declared bluntly that 'all the workers of this country have got to take a reduction of wages to help put industry on its feet',* but the next day (31 July) he agreed to give the coal industry a subsidy of £10m. to pay wages at the existing rate for nine months.

Keynes was too astute a publicist to ignore this early confirmation of his argument, and he inserted an extra chapter into the Hogarth pamphlet dealing with the coal industry. Churchill had unwisely said that the return to gold had no more connection with the troubles of the coal industry than did the Gulf Stream. Keynes showed that if British collieries were to compete with American and European coal they would have to lower their sterling prices by 1s 9d a ton. To achieve this the coal owners proposed to lower the standard of life of the coal miners. Warming to his theme, Keynes went on:

> It is a grave criticism of our way of managing our economic affairs, that this should seem to anyone to be a reasonable proposal . . . If

---

*This is what Baldwin was reported to have told the Miners' Federation executive; he denied it. (Middlemas and Barnes, *Baldwin*, 387.)

miners were free to transfer themselves to other industries, if a collier
out of work . . . could offer himself as a baker, a bricklayer, or a railway
porter at a lower wage than is now current in these industries, it would
be another matter. But notoriously they are not so free. Like other
victims of economic transition in past times, the miners are to be
offered a choice between starvation and submission, the fruits of their
submission to accrue to the benefit of other classes. But in view of the
disappearance of an effective mobility of labour and of a competitive
wage level between different industries, I am not sure that they are
not worse placed in some ways than their grandfathers were.

   Why should coalminers suffer a lower standard of life than other
classes of labour? . . . On grounds of social justice no case can be made
out for reducing the wages of the miners. They are the victims of the
economic juggernaut. They represent in the flesh the 'fundamental
adjustments' engineered by the Treasury and the Bank of England to
satisfy the impatience of the City fathers to bridge the 'moderate gap'
between $4.40 and $4.86. *They* (and others to follow) are the 'moderate
sacrifice' still necessary to ensure the stability of the gold standard . . .[80]

Even at his most bitter Keynes was always ready with a policy. Deflation
might just succeed if it was not openly avowed. 'A furtive restriction of
credit by the Bank of England can be coupled with vague cogitations on
the part of Mr. Baldwin (who has succeeded to the position in our affections
formerly occupied by Queen Victoria) as to whether social benevolence does
not require him to neutralise the effects of this by a series of illogical
subsidies.' Keynes adamantly rejected this course. His own remedy (within
the new constraints of the gold standard) was typically resourceful. Lower
bank rate, cheapen credit and encourage an exodus of gold to the United
States, in order to stimulate a rise in prices there. (Hawtrey at the Treasury
was urging the same policy.) At the same time, try for a 'social contract'
by which all wage-earners would be asked to accept a 5 per cent reduction
in money wages and all dividend-holders a 1*s* increase in income tax. Only
by a simultaneous reduction in all the main elements of cost could prices
be brought down without reducing living standards, without disturbance of
relativities and without outrage to the sense of fairness.[81]

We stand [Keynes wrote] mid-way between two theories of economic
society. The one theory maintains that wages should be fixed by
reference to what is 'fair' and 'reasonable' as between classes. The
other theory – the theory of the economic juggernaut – is that wages
should be settled by economic pressure, otherwise called 'hard facts',
and that our vast machine should crash along, with regard only to its
equilibrium as a whole, and without attention to the chance consequences of the journey to individual groups.

   The gold standard, with its dependence on pure chance, its faith in 'automatic adjustments', and its general regardlessness of social detail, is an essential emblem and idol of those who sit in the top tier of the machine. I think that they are immensely rash . . . in their comfortable belief that nothing really serious ever happens. Nine times out of ten, nothing really does happen – merely a little distress to individuals or to groups. But we run a risk of the tenth time (and stupid into the bargain), if we continue to apply the principles of an economics, which was worked out on the hypothesis of *laissez-faire* and free competition, to a society which is rapidly abandoning these hypotheses.[82]

Keynes's case was answered by a long letter from his friend Henry Strakosch in *The Times* of 31 July, which is perhaps the best summary of the orthodox position. Strakosch produced figures to show that the maladjustment in costs between Britain and America had persisted right through the period of 'managed currency' from December 1922 to April 1925, except in the single month of March 1924. A deflationary adjustment would have been required to restore the gold standard at any time in this period, 'unless indeed we had determined in March, 1924, as our national policy, permanently to debase sterling to a ratio of $4.29 to the £ by a process of devaluation – more appropriately called repudiation'. Repudiation 'pure and simple' was, to Strakosch, unthinkable. His second point was that throughout the period when both dollar and sterling prices were stable the dollar–sterling exchange had fluctuated substantially. Keynes's policy of keeping domestic prices stable was therefore no guarantee against speculative movements in favour of sterling which would have brought about exactly the same problem for the export industries allegedly caused by the return to the pre-war parity. 'No stronger argument', Strakosch wrote, 'in favour of . . . a return to the gold standard can be adduced. If during that period [1922–5] sterling had been so stabilized, there would have been (*except for the initial adjustment*) no disparity between our wages and cost of living on the one hand, and the American cost of living on the other . . .'(italics added). Keynes's reply to Strakosch was published in *The Times* the next day:

> I hold that in modern conditions wages in this country are, for various reasons, so rigid over short periods, that it is impracticable to adjust them to the ebb and flow of international gold-credit, and I would deliberately utilise fluctuations in the exchange as the shock-absorber. Sir H. Strakosch, believing that any other course is 'more appropriately called repudiation', would make exchange stability at 4.86½ the central object of policy and would leave price and wages to be the shock-absorbers. In this case he must put up from time to time with unemployment and trade disputes and worse; but looking as usual at the bright side of things, he will doubtless contrive to see even in these the final demonstration of 'the outstanding virtues of the gold standard'.

The arguments of the orthodox school were distorted by self-interest and delusions. The City wanted above all to get back to its foreign lending business, even if it meant borrowing short to lend long. The war had frightened financiers and Treasury officials with the revelation of unlimited government power. So they retreated to the fantasy of an 'unmanaged' monetary standard which had not even existed before the war. The chance was lost to restore the gold standard as a 'constitutional monarch', which is what Keynes really wanted.

VII

WAS KEYNES RIGHT?

Keynes's opposition to the restoration of the gold standard in 1925 can be summed up as follows. The decision to go back at the pre-war parity committed Britain to a reduction in the money costs of production. It was difficult to secure a reduction proportionate to an increase in the international value of sterling because of the 'stickiness' of money-wage rates and other costs. Under the circumstances, it would have been better to adjust the international value of sterling to domestic costs of production.

History's verdict has been on Keynes's side. Few economists now deny that sterling was overvalued between 1925 and 1931.* Subsequent defenders of the decision blamed its failure on events which could not have been foreseen: the 'stickiness' of wages (in contrast to the experience of 1921–2), the subsequent French and Belgian currency stabilisations at a small fraction of their par values. They do not defend the results. Nor do critics now claim that a lower exchange rate would itself have solved all Britain's economic problems. Rather it would have created a more buoyant climate for solving them.

In Moggridge's view, the overvaluation of sterling was much more striking in relation to the devalued European currencies than to the dollar.[83] Before the return, Keynes was as much American-centred in his calculations of purchasing-power parity as the others: a universal mindset stemming from the fact that in the war the sterling–dollar rate was the only one which mattered. By concentrating on the sterling–dollar rate Keynes ignored the strongest argument for not rushing the return to gold, which was to wait and see how other European currencies, particularly the franc, settled down.[†]

*However, some monetarist economists have questioned the whole notion of 'overvaluation': see K. C. P. Matthews, 'Was Sterling Overvalued in 1925?', *Economic History Review*, 2nd series, XXXI, 4, 1986, 572–87.

†The appreciation of the pound against foreign currencies between June 1924 and November 1925 was: franc 47 per cent; lira 22 per cent; mark 12 per cent; dollar 12 per cent; Belgian franc 12 per cent; Swedish krona 11 per cent; yen 10 per cent.

In retrospect, the strongest criticism of the return to gold in 1925 is that it was not part of a concerted move back to a fixed exchange-rate system, with the parities and 'rules of the game' agreed in advance. The inattention to *detail* which marked Britain's actual return was to cost it – and the world monetary system – dear in the years ahead.

Keynes's argument with the gold-standard party was practical, not theoretical. He said that its implicit programme of cutting money-wages could not be applied in the given social and political climate (at least in the absence of a 'national treaty'); so the pound would remain overvalued and unemployment unalleviated at the pre-war exchange rate. In this he proved quite right. In theory, a lower exchange rate of, say, 4.30 dollars to the pound would have helped exports, inhibited imports and allowed lower interest rates. The actual effect on employment would have depended on how the policy was viewed by financiers, businessmen, workers. An economic policy which makes no sense at all will never work. But a policy which makes sense on paper may not work in practice. In a free society, it has to be consistent with the beliefs of all the major social actors. The gold-standard party's programme did not meet with the required acquiescence of the working class, and therefore it failed as an employment policy. But it is not self-evident that devaluation would have met the confidence requirements of financiers and businessmen. People had to be persuaded by events and arguments that Keynes was right. And this took time.

VIII

MR AND MRS J. M. KEYNES

On 4 August 1925, at the Pancras Registry Office, Lydia Lopokova became Mrs J. M. Keynes. What she called her 'degree nisi' had been pronounced in January and made absolute in July. Maynard's last bachelor reading party had taken place in April, in the Lake District, where he had huffed and puffed up a hill, struggled through Aldous Huxley's *Those Barren Leaves* – 'one of the worst books I've ever read' – and talked theory of money with Dennis Robertson and Austin Robinson. Sebastian Sprott's exile to Nottingham, also in April, closed another chapter of the old life. At the end of July Lydia attended a reception for Franceso Nitti, a former Italian prime minister, at the Liberal Summer School. Maynard was formally introducing his future wife to Cambridge in his setting, not hers. 'What an ordeal to be "public property",' wrote Lydia to Florence.

The wedding ceremony was 'the simplest imaginable'. Vera Bowen and Duncan Grant were the witnesses; otherwise it was mainly family. Keynes's maternal grandmother, aged eighty-eight, was there, but not his father, aged seventy-three. Lydia, in a fawn-coloured outfit, 'looked like a little ghost – as scared of the newspaper people and photographers as if she had never faced the public before', wrote Florence to Neville. Afterwards there was a tea party at 46 Gordon Square with a 'lovely and delicious wedding cake given by Lydia's friend Mrs. Grenfell'. Maynard's old friend Gordon Luce opened his newspapers in Rangoon a fortnight later to 'gruesome pictures' of the famous couple: Maynard, at thirteen stone, had visibly entered prosperous middle age. Duncan described the nuptials to the absent friends at Charleston. 'My future prospects are blighted,' he told them without emotion. He had, hitherto, been Maynard's heir. Clive Bell bet Duncan a champagne dinner that Maynard and Lydia would not have children within a given period. 'Maynard is too fast on the trigger,' he announced.

Maynard and Lydia had planned to spend the first month of married life at Tilton, but the house was already let to tenants, who refused to budge. So they rented another house, Oaklands, in nearby Iford, just south of Lewes, where the usual stream of visitors arrived: his pre-war student Archie Rose (back from China), Hubert and Faith Henderson, Sheppard, Maynard's brother Geoffrey. Virginia Woolf fainted at a party held at Charleston on 19 August to celebrate both the marriage and Quentin Bell's fifteenth birthday. A disturbing guest at Iford was the philosopher Ludwig Wittgenstein, who landed from the Newhaven ferry on 20 August for a six-day stay. He had given up philosophy to teach in a village school in Austria because, he explained to Keynes, the pain it gave him overcame the pain of doing philosophy, as a hot-water bottle pressed against the cheek takes away the pain of a toothache.[84] He had also given up his huge inheritance, so Keynes had to send him £10 for the journey. Wittgenstein's conversational method was like a punch in the face. 'What a beautiful tree,' Lydia remarked, no doubt brightly. Wittgenstein glared at her: 'What do you mean?' Lydia burst into tears.[85] Keynes too was driven frantic by Wittgenstein's obsessive monologues. He had struggled to understand the *Tractatus*, but his mind was 'now so far from fundamental questions that it is impossible for me to get clear about such matters'.[86] When he tried to explain Wittgenstein's philosophy to the Apostles in Cambridge in November, he found that 'it escapes the mind – I could only half remember it'.[87]

On 3 September, Maynard and Lydia left for a fortnight's visit to the Soviet Union. Maynard adored train journeys: to be conveyed, reading masses of books and newspapers, in a travelling armchair, with no duties or responsibilities, was his idea of a perfect break. He went to meet Lydia's family in Leningrad, and also as the official representative of Cambridge University at the bicentennial celebrations of the Russian Academy of Sciences. They stayed a week in Leningrad and then went on to Moscow. There is no record of what Keynes made of Lydia's family, or they of him, beyond a brief 'I have got to love him already' from Lydia's mother Karlusha to Florence Keynes, dated 17 September.

In Moscow it was business as usual – meetings with GOSPLAN and the State Bank, concerts, *Hamlet* (presumably in Russian) at the Moscow Art Theatre, banquets. Maurice Dobb, who was also in Moscow, remembered Keynes 'instructing' the Gosplan economists 'in the virtues of financial rectitude and "Treasury control" '.[88] Keynes also met Preobrazhensky, who introduced himself as a 'professional revolutionary'. In between these surreal encounters, he gave two lectures on 'The Economic Position of England' and 'The Economic Transition in England' before audiences of Russian academics, the second based on the speech he had just given to the Liberal Summer School, 'Am I a Liberal?' His suggestion that a Liberalism remodelled on collectivist lines was the true alternative to both anarchical capitalism and Marxist communism predictably failed to win the assent of Soviet economists.[89] (These speeches are discussed in chapter 7 below.)

On their return to Iford, Maynard and Lydia walked over to neighbouring Rodmell to see the Woolfs – 'M. in Tolstoi's blouse & Russian cap of black astrachan – A fair sight, both of them, to meet on the high road', Virginia commented.

> An immense goodwill & vigour [she continued] pervades him. She hums in his wake, the great mans wife. But though one could carp, one can also find them very good company, & my heart, in this the autumn of my age, slightly warms to him, whom I've known all these years, so truculently pugnaciously & unintimately. We had very brisk talk of Russia: such a hotch-potch, such a mad jumble, M. says, of good and bad, & the most extreme things that he can make no composition of it – can't see yet how it goes. Briefly, spies everywhere, no liberty of speech, greed for money eradicated, people living in common, yet some, L[ydia]'s mother for instance, with servants, peasants contented because they own land, no sign of revolution, aristocrats acting showmen to their possessions, ballet respected, best show of Cezanne & Matisse in existence. Endless processions of communists in top hats, prices exorbitant, yet champagne produced, & the finest cooking in Europe, banquets beginning at 8.30 & going on till 2.30; people getting slightly drunk, say about 11, & wandering round the table. Kalinin getting up, & perambulating followed by a little crowd who clapped him steadily as he walked; then the immense luxury of the old Imperial trains; feeding off the Tsars plate; interview with Zinoviev who (I think) was a suave cosmopolitan Jew, but had two fanatical watchdogs with square faces, guarding him, & mumbling out their mysteries, fanatically. One prediction of theirs, to the effect that in 10 years time the standard of living will be higher in Russia than it was before the war, but in all other countries lower, M. thought might very well come true. Anyhow they are crammed & packed with sights & talks: Maynard has a medal set in diamonds, & L. a gold

sovereign wh. she was allowed to take from the bags at the mint.[90]

Keynes spent the rest of the summer vacation at Iford, turning the jumble into a composition: three articles under the title 'Soviet Russia' appeared in the *Nation* on 10, 17 and 24 October. They were published by the Hogarth Press in December as *A Short View of Russia*, one of his most eloquent productions. Lytton Strachey came to observe the new ménage and was not impressed. 'The Keynes visit was rather lugubrious, somehow or other,' he informed Carrington. 'For one thing the house was so hideous. Then Lydia is a pathetic figure, to my mind – and so plain. Maynard is engrossed as usual in his own concerns. He was very interesting on Russia and Wittgenstein; but there is a difficulty of some kind in one's intercourse with him – he seems rather far-off. . .'[91] This remark pinpoints the defect in Lytton's judgement, or sympathy. He could not imagine that Keynes's distraction had anything to do with his being 'in love' with Lydia.

The merits of Maynard's marriage continued to be sharply disputed by his friends. In 1928 Roger Fry reported a 'tremendous talk on Maynard and Lydia' with Sheppard and Clive Bell. Sheppard:

> gets on with them, likes to see them together, thinks they are a perfectly assorted couple and that it's our fault that we don't. But it's all much more complicated than he understands. We discussed whether Maynard had lost his soul or whether he'd ever had one . . . I seemed to get a clearer idea than I had of what has happened, but I see no way of mending things, though I think it's rather tragic for Maynard . . . [92]

In the light of what Keynes went on to achieve, Fry's judgement was spectacularly wrong. This is not to deny that there were grounds for it: the marriage was a gamble for both Maynard and Lydia. At the same time the judgement was rooted in a failure to understand the nature of Maynard's genius and the support Lydia could give it. Fry, Virginia Woolf, the Charlestonians saw only a conflict in his character between worldliness and unworldliness, with his marriage to Lydia as a capitulation to the former. They did not see that a revolution in economic statesmanship could not be launched from fortress Bloomsbury. It required a different attitude to the world and its concerns, a different location in that world.

Perhaps his marriage made Maynard more worldly, in the sense of being more at ease in the world; but that was no bad thing, if his mission was to save the world. Marriage softened his asperity, widened his sympathies, made him more 'human', less relentlessly brilliant.[93] It also gave him the physical and emotional security to build for the future. He acquired a stronger sense of direction. In 1921 he told Daniel Macmillan that he would 'never attempt anything again on so large a scale' as the *Treatise on Probability*. In the eleven years following his marriage to Lydia, he produced two books which rivalled it in scale and exceeded it in importance. In 1921 he had addressed the Apostles on the dilemmas of the brilliant but uncreative mind, suggesting that money-making was the only suitable sphere for its employment. After 1925 he seems to have understood that it might be possible to be creative in economics. It would be wrong to say that Lydia, or marriage to Lydia, planted the thought in him. But she certainly understood, and tirelessly pointed out, that he had the stuff of creation in him. 'The truth', she told him, 'lies in your eyes'; he came to understand how life with Lydia might give the truth he saw space and time to grow.

Virginia Woolf's prediction that 'age and familiarity . . . would entirely crush' his love for Lydia[94] proved the opposite of the truth. As his life became increasingly intertwined with hers, his love steadily deepened. His pleasure in being with her 'grew greater every year', he wrote in October 1925. In 1926 he was writing to her: 'How lucky we never bore one another. Can one go on being in love with someone who bores you? Your old hopes-he-never-bores M.' And in 1928: 'Why are we separated? – especially when the sun shines so warmly. I hate Cambridge, and am so homesick to be with you.'

A great part of Lydia's charm for Maynard, as we have seen, was her extremely individual use of the English language, or what Keynes called 'Lydiaspeak'. Her emphases, pronunciation and unerring choice of words and phrases were a constant joy. Her friend Sokolova recalls a toast she once gave to Florrie Grenfell: 'And let us not forget dear Florrie's mother who compiled her.' After attending a wedding party she spoke of 'Jesus fomenting wine out of water at Cannes.' Having seen a hostess's famous collection of birds, she reported, 'I had tea with Lady Grey. She has an ovary which she likes to show every one.' She once referred to the 'undeveloped arrestedness' of the Sitwells. She called Schumpeter, Stumpeter, and Lady Colefax, Lady Colebox. Her words, she told Maynard, were designed to 'enigmatise you', and, certainly to him, she remained an adorable enigma, a bubbling brook of surprises.

Marriage to Lydia also brought out Maynard's protectiveness. He understood that she was defenceless in the world of refined intellectual feelings on which his Bloomsbury friends prided themselves. A lesser man might have tried to mute her often embarrassing style. But Maynard accepted Lydia for what she was, and never indicated – in public at least – that he found her conversation foolish. When Clive Bell snubbed her for a remark she made about Proust, he was furious in her defence.[95] He regarded her utterance as privileged, beyond rational criticism. He made her know that, whatever Bloomsbury might think, she was his 'miele' or 'beloved', his 'dearest beautiful one', his 'dearest darling Lydochka', his 'dearest pupsik' – or 'little navel'. (She called him, less romantically, 'lanky', 'my dear long tree' or 'you dear musky one'.) Lydia felt keenly her lack of intellectual power. She hoped that, when she died, the *Nation* would write about her, as it had about Queen Alexandra, that 'she was fresh, radiant and simple', but would add that 'when she made conquest of J. M. Keynes, also all her life she longed for a university degree, which was of course outside her brain-province, but on the whole it was not a deficit in her character'.[96] When she wrote to him, 'Is it not sad for you that I am not a learned woman and never will be?', he immediately wrote back, 'Do not be sad and especially do not be a learned woman. Your Maynarochka.'[97] And she had pride, too, in being a star. When she headed the cast list for *Petrushka* she wrote to him, 'that is how it should be I think, first wrangler in your language'.

Lydia was aware of her tendency to 'blab in public' and vowed to be more like Lytton Strachey, unfortunately 'I have no beard attached to me.'[98] She acknowledged that she wrote 'absurdities' and was a 'chatter-box' – she signed off one letter 'Your trash bag L'. Clive Bell used to say that her spiritual home was Woolworths. She was full of prejudices against Jews and Negroes which the English educated classes no longer expressed so crudely. Maynard did not seem to mind. She herself defended her Lydia babble as 'from a different angle . . . good – because there is no one's tongue like that at Cambridge'.[99] Maynard called her his 'Lady Talky', his 'tender chatter-chatter'. Lydia, however, feeling that she was not appreciated 'for my own values' in the company of Maynard's friends, vowed 'to sit like a mouse and watch the conversation of the great'.[100] Fortunately she did not always succeed; but she schooled herself, with some success, to be the great man's wife – domestic, decorous, subdued, talking about housekeeping and buying fish at Selfridges; 'she does her trick, then goes under the table, and leaves before eleven . . .'[101]

Lydia's domestic concerns extended to Maynard's wardrobe. She opened his tallboy and was shocked to find what she called his 'pantalets' full of holes, hardly any socks, and masses of dress shirts; when she upbraided him for coming to bed looking like 'Christ in the last stages', he collapsed into helpless giggles.[102] Her attention to his underwear was closely allied with concern for his health. She constantly urged him to wear vests to protect him from the icy Cambridge blasts, though it was her firm belief that vests, unlike 'pantalets', must have 'little holes' to 'air' him properly. Maynard was, in fact, quite prone to colds. He frequently referred to his 'cycles', the low points of which, he playfully suggested, coincided with her monthly periods' – 'guests' in Lydiaspeak. 'I bleed exactly to suit your prediction,' Lydia wrote to him on one occasion, suggesting that her menstrual movements attracted his barometric interest. But his concern was more than statistical. When she complained of being unwell, he bombarded her with letters, telegrams and telephone calls from Cambridge.[103] Behind his fascination with the working of her body there was a practical object: for they planned to have children when Lydia gave up dancing.

Although she never claimed to be an intellectual, Lydia could occasionally astonish the critical Bloomsberries with her sureness of artistic judgement. 'How does her mind work?' Virginia Woolf once asked herself. 'Like a lark soaring . . . & direction at Maynard's hands,' she concluded.[104] On ballet, of course, Lydia needed no direction, except that Maynard tidied up her prose when she wrote for publication. She was a firm traditionalist. Although she could appreciate the cleverness of the new choreography, she preferred a good story line, 'tenderness', 'soul' and an opportunity for stars to shine, to the collectivised, intellectualised and abstract ballets of Balanchine. (She wrote in *Vogue* to this effect on 2 August 1926.) Her comments on dancers were forthright. Anton Dolin had a 'sort of silliness that you do not meet on the stage in great dancers'; Errol Addison 'has good legs, but oah God! what a face'.[105] Her judgements on books, films and pictures were acute and well expressed. 'Bonny [Garnett] must not lose his connection with animals, it is his chief attraction . . .'; 'Virginia's brain is so quick that sometimes her pen cannot catch it'; 'Lytton's intelligence is his strongest point'. After visiting a retrospective Roger Fry exhibition in February 1931, she wrote to Maynard, 'I put the portraits and the pictures of 1898 the best, the rest is intelligent, laboured, but always in imitation of somebody better'. One of Maynard's critics 'picks at words like a bilious sparrow'; a German film at the New Gallery cinema was so slow 'we were left with the empty slipper of Cinderella for hours and hours'; the Dutch artists 'knew what they wanted, they painted what they saw, and what they saw did not trouble them, so much splendid solidity'.[106] Lydia was educating herself. As she wrote to Maynard on 23 November 1925, 'You do develop my cranium, miely Maynarochka, and I am so very glad that I live with you and I'm intimate with your little holes (also cells) your soul your breath and your kisses. L.' Virginia Woolf's more balanced judgement on the marriage emerges in a diary entry she made after dining with the Keyneses in 1928:

> He & she both urbane and admirable. Grey comes at Maynard's temples. He is finer looking now: not with us pompous or great: simple, with his mind working always, on Russians, Bolshevists, glands, genealogies: always the proof of a remarkable mind when it overflows thus vigorously into byepaths. There are two royal stocks in England he says from which all intellect descends. He will work this out as if his fortune depended on it. Lydia is composed, & controlled. She says very sensible things.[107]

The biggest change which marriage made was to their living arrangements. Lydia moved out of 41 Gordon Square into Number 46; Vanessa moved out of Number 46 into Number 37. The break-up of the old ménage was not without friction. There were rows over rates and rents. Maynard claimed a picture of Duncan and screwed it to the wall: Vanessa arrived with a screwdriver and took it off triumphantly to Number 37.[108] Vanessa seemed to be saying: by marrying Lydia, you have given up your right to a share in Duncan. Soon Keynes was building a library and extra bathrooms in Number 46: the installation of bidets marked one break with the old order. The whitewashing of Duncan's and Vanessa's murals was another. Lydia was determined to create her own ambience. A sky-blue carpet of the thickest pile appeared in the old Bloomsbury drawing room, together with satin curtains picked up in a sale, a whitewashed ceiling obliterating Vanessa's decorations, and candelabras from Maples.[109] Here Lydia could dress and undress herself 'completely before the fire', no stray Bloomsberry wandering in; here too she could hold her own salon. Her favourite occasions were Russian-style Sunday lunches, which went on for most of the day. Ballet dancers would mingle with young men from Cambridge like Dadie Rylands and Douglas Davidson, who were renting rooms from Vanessa at 37 Gordon Square, friends like the Bowens, Frank Dobson and Boris Anrep, and the occasional highbrow, and high-born, 'Bolshie' from Russia. For such occasions she would shyly beseech Maynard for permission to raid his wine cellar. 'What do people do on Sunday?' she asked him. 'They talk and talk desperately, it is not necessary, yet it is clever for nature to endow us with the tittle-tattle.'[110] This was how Lydia liked to entertain, giving her guests 'the warmth, food, wine and sympathy of the house'. In her own circle, she was quick-witted, uninhibited and fun to be with. Like many people in the theatre, she was both conventional and unshockable; with her ballet background, she effortlessly straddled the chic and the camp. Boris Anrep told her that 'in all the years with Helen [his wife] there never happened frank conversation as took place with me'; Sam Courtauld 'confessed that he is never bored with me and I replied because we were unrestrained in our relations'.[111]

Arranging or attending the more frozen variety of banking/political dinner party in mid-week, when Maynard was in town, filled her with dread. He would carefully instruct her in the social art of extending, accepting and refusing invitations, but she hated doing it: 'All my "lingo" stops for those occasions, the pen droops out, I become illiterate and illegitimate.'[112] She did not much enjoy the event either. And she could also impose her wishes. After refusing yet another invitation from that importunate hostess Lady Colefax, she wrote, 'I do not want her in 46, yet I cannot diminish her energy; she is filled with desperate courage that has no use to you or me or the world.'[113]

On 3 March 1926 Keynes took possession of Tilton after complicated negotiations. Lord Gage had wanted to let it to him on a yearly basis, in order to keep open the option of living there himself if he decided to let his family home, Firle Place: a sign that he, like other landlords, had been hit by falling agricultural prices. But Keynes refused to put money into necessary improvements 'if I have not more than a year's security of tenure'. Instead he proposed a twenty-one-year lease at £120 a year, with improvements to the value of £600, of which he would pay £500 and the landlord £100. This eventually proved acceptable. By 1 October 1925 negotiations were sufficiently far advanced for Keynes to be able to write to his mother, 'I have definitely decided to take Tilton. But as regards the alterations, I am now inclining to something much more like your modified proposal and to spending the money so released on a new library at the bottom of the yard which looks southwards and Downwards.' It was only a couple of years later that he discovered that '1000 years ago Tilton was called Telitone . . . and that the tenant was called de Cahagnes – which is the same name as Keynes'.

The happiest, and most productive, months of the remainder of Keynes's life were to be spent at Tilton – a plain but surprisingly roomy two-storey farmhouse, beautifully situated, in its several acres of lawn, orchard and woodland, on the north edge of the South Downs. As he told his mother it was an ideal place for work, and his main early improvement was the construction of a library and 'loggia' from a group of outhouses at the end of the courtyard at the south of the house. They looked out on to an orchard, with the Downs rising up beyond, from the top of which one could see Newhaven and the Channel.

The conversion was entrusted to George Kennedy, for whom Keynes had secured the commission to rebuild King's College. Kennedy was a personal friend, a fellow Old Etonian and fringe Bloomsbery: his nephew Richard left an amusing account of working for Leonard and Virginia at the Hogarth Press. Kennedy had taken up architecture before the war to support a growing family: a gifted draughtsman, he relied on his partner Frederick Nightingale to make his buildings stand up. He was excellent company in the Desmond MacCarthy anecdotal style, specialising in commissions for the cultivated rich: he designed a house for Lytton Strachey which never got built, and a gazebo at Biddesden for Bryan and Diana Guinness, Lytton's neighbours at Ham Spray, which did.

Kennedy gave Keynes a spacious, formal library and an Italianate terrace with a vaulted ceiling, opening out to the orchard. Work started in the summer of 1926. It was in this rather damp annexe, approached from the main house by a covered pathway, that he wrote much of *A Treatise on Money* and most of *The General Theory*.

Tilton soon overflowed with indifferent furniture. Maynard bought indiscriminately for about a year after they moved in, mainly from a favourite Cambridge antique dealer, but also at auctions. Forty pieces were acquired on a single day, 26 October 1926, 'but I suppose Tilton will suck them in and show no difference'. Lydia tried to restrain him. 'As for your purchases,' she wrote to him, 'it's the box for studs that is so noticeable, as you have no studs; it's human nature that goes on almost necessarily acquiring the unnecessary.'[114] His buying was a mixture of lavishness and meanness. On one occasion he acquired 'a sound but ugly carpet, large enough to cover two servants' bedrooms, if cut, for £4'. Gradually Tilton filled up with fine pictures, fruit of Keynes's purchases in the 1930s.

It was never a grand house. Unlike Charleston it boasted a telephone and electric lights. But, despite the additional bathrooms, the water pipes burst, the boiler was often out of action and members of the household went for days without washing. A primitive central-heating system pumped hot air into the hall through a grille; elsewhere coal fires belched smoke profusely from the chimneys; there were large patches of damp, and the books in the library curled. Lydia was convinced that the English did not understand about chimneys. At Christmas, she and Maynard would huddle round the smoking fire with watering eyes and layers of extra woollens.

The modest staff of six would be considered astonishingly ample by today's standards. Tilton was looked after the year round by Ruby and Edgar Weller, installed in a cottage in the grounds, she as housekeeper, he as chauffeur/gardener. Ruby Coles, who came from Norfolk, had entered Lydia's service in London in 1923. When she arrived at 41 Gordon Square, Lydia had greeted her, 'You are Ruby, who is working for me,' shook her hand and immediately went upstairs. Ruby recalled Pavlova coming to Gordon Square: 'The front-door bell rang, and as I answered it I bent down to pick up a letter from the floor. I remember seeing a lovely pair of legs in black stockings looking, as I later said to Madame, like the legs of a Black Minorca chicken. She laughed and said, "Yus, but lays 'noer' eggs." '[115] Ruby stayed with Lydia fifty-five years; to the end she always called her 'Madame'. Lydia and Maynard brought her down to Sussex in 1924 and 1925, where she met her future husband Edgar Weller, a local man. She and Edgar married at the end of 1925, her farewell to maidenhood being greeted by Mrs Harland, the cook, with a 'begonia dress'.

Edgar Weller, who served at Tilton till the Second World War, was an ex-navy man who liked his drink. But Keynes had great confidence in him. He loved driving Keynes's cars, not always steadily. He created the gardens and kept them impeccably. By 1926 Tilton could boast blackcurrants 'dropping from every corner, and a kitchen garden 'proliferating' with beans and carrots.[116] With Maynard's encouragement, Edgar started a serious vegetable and fruit garden, which was soon producing for market. Pig farming was added, and Maynard and Lydia would take squealing pigs to the market in Lewes in the back of their Morris Cowley: by 1931 Tilton's pigs were showing a 'moderate profit'. These were preludes to the much more extensive farming operations Maynard started in the mid–1930s when he took over the whole of Tilton farm.

Edgar and Ruby had three children, Andrei, named after Lydia's brother, Sonia and Barry. Andrei remembers Lydia giving him a pullover and £1 on every birthday, without variation. He also recalled a story from his childhood told him by his father. He was doing somersaults outside Tilton Cottage when Keynes walked by. Andrei said to Keynes, 'You can't make somersaults, can you?' Keynes took some coins out of his pocket, 'No, but you can't make money, can you?'

When the Keyneses came down to Tilton they would bring the Harlands from Gordon Square, he as butler, she to cook. Then there was Edgar's aunt, Penny ('Auntie'), Lydia's sewer and dressmaker, as well as a succession of nameless maids.

Tilton was what would now be called a holiday home. Until Maynard's heart attack in 1937 and the outbreak of war in 1939 modified the routine, he and Lydia were in residence over part of the Christmas and Easter vacations and for about two and a half months in the summer. Like the Charlestonians, the Tiltonians were not integrated into the local community. They were friendly enough with their landlord, George Gage, who liked having artists and writers as tenants; but county society was anathema to them. Their company was the guests they asked down: in the 1920s, the Hendersons, Dennis Robertson, Frank Ramsey and his wife Lettice, Peter and Topsy Lucas, Sheppard, the Courtaulds (complaining about lack of wine and washing facilities), family, old friends of Maynard's like the Luces from Rangoon and Furness from Egypt. Alfred Marshall's widow Mary was a regular visitor, 'who digged with a little fork on the lawn, and in the evening knitted stockings'. She said to all that Maynard's marriage to Lydia 'was the best thing he ever did'.

The Tiltonians saw little of the Charlestonians, who in any case were spending an increasing part of the year at Cassis, in the South of France. In the summer of 1927, Vanessa had 'for the most part managed to forget the Keynes' existence';[117] this is typical of a mountain of dismissive comment. Vanessa's constant maliciousness about 'the Keynes'' has to be set against Maynard's 'doglike affection' for his old friend, which 'almost brought the tears' to Virginia's eyes,[118] and also against the financial backing he was providing Vanessa and Duncan. Duncan did not share Vanessa's malice – he was entirely without it – but he played up to it. It seemed to be the price he was willing to pay for his own freedom to have affairs; but perhaps he too found it hard to understand, or accept, Maynard's new-found heterosexuality. The Keyneses and the Woolfs visited each other regularly at Christmas, mainly, it seems, because they got into the habit of doing so. The visits do not seem to have given the Woolfs much pleasure. On 30 December 1929, Virginia wrote to her sister,

> What should we find at the gate, coming to tea Saturday in the rain, but a seedy grey Rolls [Maynard had bought it from the Courtaulds]; with the detestable Edgar and the Keynes. I don't see that one's friends have any right to mutilate one's life in this way. There I was forced to rake the cinders of Bloomsbury gossip with Lydia – it was an insult – a murderous act and one has no remedy. They had a bag of crumpets, which Maynard steeped in butter and made Lydia toast. It is this kind of tallow grease grossness in him that one dislikes. But of course I admit they were amiable in the extreme. But then, curse them, we have to lunch at Tilton tomorrow.

Although the old casual intimacy was gone, there were more formal gatherings of the Bloomsbury clan – parties and entertainments, sometimes with printed programmes and specially commissioned playlets, at both Tilton and Gordon Square, at which Lydia and Maynard sometimes performed their Keynes–Keynes, a parody of the can-can which Lydia had danced with Massine in *Boutique*. 'It was the common opinion of Bloomsbury', writes Nigel Nicolson, 'that the Keynes' were remarkably economical in their hospitality.' After going to their Christmas party at Gordon Square in 1927, Lytton wrote to Sebastian Sprott, 'The cold was complained of but I don't feel it and I had taken the precaution of eating a large dinner before hand, so that I remained unaffected by the grimness of the sandwiches at supper.' Virginia gossiped to Lytton on 3 September 1927 about 'a night at Tilton, when we picked the bones of Maynard's grouse of which there were three to eleven people. This stinginess is a constant source of delight to Nessa – her eyes gleamed as the bones went round.' Dinner was followed by a 'brilliant entertainment . . . in the new Loggia, with a rustic audience [seated in the orchard facing it]. Sheppard half naked . . . was Miss T[ettrazzini] to perfection: Maynard was crapulous and obscene beyond words, lifting his left leg and singing a song about Women. Lydia was Queen Victoria dancing to a bust of Albert. What did the yokels make of it?'[119] Russians are rather well known for their hospitality, so the stinting seems to have been Maynard's. Wine did not agree with him, and he drank it sparingly. He gobbled his food down without much attention. Perhaps the truth is that neither of them cared enough about food or drink – or more generally about domestic style – to give them much thought or time.

Despite their friends' apparent lack of pleasure in their company (except as a source of malicious gossip), Maynard and Lydia were wonderfully happy in their country house. They were far from heroic walkers, but would regularly tramp across the Downs or through the woodlands for a couple of miles with their dogs Patsy, Pushkin and Ross. They would pat balls inexpertly to each other on the lawn-tennis court (Lydia took lessons in London with a 'Mr. [Fred?] Perry', but never learnt to return more than one ball in ten). The scents and noises of the countryside enchanted them. 'What a melody of a morning,' Lydia wrote one early March, 'music in the air, smells of strength and softness, one squeaks, stretches and blinks in perfect bliss.' Although, as she remarked, 'the elements' were often 'atrocious', there were the long summers when she could sunbathe naked in the courtyard or loggia reading Tolstoy's *War and Peace*, while Maynard scribbled away happily on the theory of the bank rate in his library.

CHAPTER SEVEN

Keynes's Middle Way

I

Victorian governments believed that an economy prospers best when left to the free play of market forces. From this followed the golden rule of 'non-interference' or *laissez-faire*. Economic policy, in the sense of a commitment to certain outcomes for the economy as a whole, did not exist. The idea that the economy should be 'managed' to secure 'objectives' like full employment, stable prices, a healthy balance of payments, a satisfactory growth rate and so on would have struck the Victorians as incomprehensible or merely fanciful. Goods and capital were left free to flow where they would. The government raised taxes to pay for its own upkeep, including defence and law and order, but not to influence the volume of activity. There was no monetary policy, the supply of domestic currency being regulated by the 'automatic' mechanism of the gold standard. Governments made no attempt to prevent, and little to mitigate, unemployment. There was a business cycle, but the unemployed sooner or later seemed to disappear of their own accord – either back into jobs or on to ships taking them to North America or Australia. There were no attempts to 'restructure' British industry or agriculture to make them more competitive: the market system was supposed to take care of this. The *laissez-faire* consensus had started to break down by the end of the nineteenth century. The Right advocated protection of British industry against foreign competition; the Left called for higher income and inheritance taxes to pay for social services. Economists were hostile to the first, but accepted an economic case for the second. In general, there was little disposition to tamper with a system which had brought the British economy growing prosperity in the nineteenth century. *Laissez-faire* was validated by success, just as later it was ruined by failure.[1]

Keynes rejected *laissez-faire* as a policy before he developed a convincing economic theory explaining why *laissez-faire* would not work. Economists have taken this as a sign of his 'intuitions' running ahead of his theory, but this characterisation is too one-sided. From 1924 to 1929 Keynes developed a powerful critique of *laissez-faire*, but it was not specifically economic-theoretical, though it carried a strong theoretical charge. It was directed to showing that the presuppositions of *laissez-faire* – the psychological and organisational conditions which had made it work as a policy in the nine-teenth century – had passed away. The idea that the nineteenth century was a special case in economic history thus makes its appearance in Keynes's thinking before the idea that classical economics – the *theory* of the 'special case' – was itself a 'special case' of a more general theory of economic behaviour applicable to the more usual condition of mankind. Psychological and institutional *observation* was the foundation of Keynesian economics.

In chapter 2 of *The Economic Consequences of the Peace* Keynes explained the precariousness of the nineteenth-century achievement under four headings: 'population', 'organisation', 'the psychology of society' and 'the relation of the old world to the new'. The basic argument was that the increasing prosperity of Europe's growing population had depended on a worldwide system of free imports and capital exports made possible by peace and security, and on a social and moral equipoise which produced contented workers so long as the rich saved, and rendered the duty of saving 'nine-tenths of virtue'. This whole 'complicated and artificial' system depended on precarious balances which were already endangered before the war, and which the war had shattered: the class balance between capital and labour, the psychological or moral balance between saving and consumption, and the balance of trade and capital transfers between Europe and America. The epoch, that is, for which *laissez-faire* had been tolerable as a policy, and for which 'classical economics' had provided a tolerably accurate stylisation, was already doomed before the First World War delivered the knock-out blow. The question for thought and action was how Europe, including Britain, was to maintain its existing and still growing population when the mechanisms of fine and semi-automatic adjustment between global supplies of, and demands for, money, goods and labour had broken down. The older school of statesmanship and economics said: restore these mechanisms as quickly as possible. Keynes replied that they could not be restored, or could only be partially restored, and anyway the best chance of restoring them had been destroyed by the peacemakers at Versailles.

As the 1920s unfolded, Keynes shifted his emphases within this general approach. The problem of population remained a preoccupation till at least the late 1920s, demanding a 'population policy'. In the early 1920s he concentrated on the need for a monetary policy. Instability in the value of money was undermining the social contract on which capitalism was based. Workers' acquiescence in a modest reward depended on capitalists – entre-preneurs and investors – doing their duty of producing wealth. Inflation and deflation cut the moral link between effort and reward, leading to the unjustified enrichment of some and the unjustified impoverishment of others; hence the supreme importance of price stability for the virtue of the system. 'Any important change in the cost of living and general price level, whether up or down, will endanger industrial peace,' Keynes wrote just before Britain

Maynard Keynes and Lydia Lopokova, *c.*1922.

Lydia Lopokova as Mariuccia in *The Good-humoured Ladies*, London 1918, as Maynard Keynes would have first seen her.

Maynard Keynes with Virginia Woolf, Studland, Dorset, 1923.

Lydia Lopokova, John Sheppard and Cecil Taylor ('Madame') at Studland, 1923.

Peter Lucas, Dadie Rylands and Sebastian Sprott, Cambridge, 1922.

Reading party at Hawes End near Keswick, 1925; *from left*, Dennis Robertson, Ted Spencer, Roger Mynors, Austin Robinson and Fred Burgess.

'Second Thoughts Are Best . . .'
(see page 146), Lydia and Maynard
Keynes.

'Famous Economist Weds Ballerina',
1925.

Maynard Keynes in Russia, 1925.

Maynard Keynes in Petrograd for the
200th anniversary of the Russian
Academy of Sciences, 1925.

Vera Bowen

Maynard Keynes and Lydia in Berlin, 1928.

Samuel Courtauld stepping out of the
Rolls-Royce he sold to Maynard
Keynes.

Piero Sraffa, Maynard Keynes and
Dennis Robertson at Tilton, 1927.
Maynard Keynes is sitting on the
bird-bath.

From Hubert Henderson's copy of the
Liberal *Yellow Book*.

Robert Brand

Maynard Keynes and Lloyd George at the Liberal Summer School, Cambridge, 1927.

went back to gold. In 1924 he started questioning whether a mature economy like Britain could any longer provide enough investment opportunities to absorb the historically given rate of domestic saving. Should savings be allowed to drift abroad or should the government take active measures to provide for their employment at home? He also pointed to the increasing unwillingness of modern societies – Britain being the society he knew best – to adjust their internal structures to the ebb and flow of money and trade. Stability of internal economic conditions was the essential requirement of social stability; this precluded a *laissez-faire* attitude to the three chief determinants of the standard of life: population, money, and saving and investing.

Unlike Marx, Keynes did not regard the 'organisation' of society as determining its psychology: that is, its beliefs and expectations. They influence each other. Nor did he accept, or even understand, the core Marxist proposition that firms which covered their costs were exploiting the worker. But under capitalism there is a double problem of legitimacy. The first arises, as we have seen, from instability of money, which cuts off effort from reward. The second is more fundamental. In Keynes's view capitalism's driving force is a vice which he called 'love of money'. Material outcomes are the measure of its success – or failure. As long as it fulfilled its historic task of producing wealth for all it was reasonably secure. But, if wealth-creation faltered, capitalism was vulnerable to creed-based systems, which appealed to more worthy motives.[2] As a piece of social machinery for getting mankind from poverty to affluence capitalism was the best on offer. But its success was no more assured than its failure. To succeed it had to be able to take on new forms in new habitats. The economist's task was to discern the form or style suitable to the age – a matter of aesthetics and logic.

Keynes always stressed the crucial importance of 'vigilant observation' for successful theory-construction – theory being nothing more, in his view, than a stylised representation of the dominant tendencies of the time, derived from reflection on the salient facts. It is fascinating to observe how Keynes's imagination and logical power acting on the data of experience gradually yield a distinctive understanding of the *modus operandi* of modern economic life to which the adjective 'Keynesian' is correctly applied.

Implicit in all this is a crucial shift in view concerning the relationship between the economy and the polity. Nineteenth-century economists had looked to a liberal political system – one dominated by the business class – to underwrite economic prosperity. Keynes was the first economist to argue that economic prosperity was the only secure guarantee of a liberal political system.

II

THE LIBERAL CONTEXT

Keynes's understanding of the diseases of modern capitalism, and the remedies for them, was not developed in isolation. Michael Freeden has rightly
drawn attention to 'the context of the production and dissemination of
Liberal ideas that was taking place at the time he [Keynes] was developing
his own theories'.[3] Keynes and Henderson both understood that new theories
about controlling the business cycle might provide Liberalism with an alternative to the protectionism of the right and the redistributionism of the left,
especially if dramatised as an unemployment policy. Lloyd George seemed
to grasp this, Asquith did not. That is why the man of ideas was drawn,
despite the past, to the man of action.

The period 1924–9 marks Keynes's maximum involvement in the politics
of the Liberal Party. He quite explicitly set out to supply the Party with a
new philosophy of government. But, with the historical Liberal Party in
decline, Keynes also came to see his reconstructed liberalism as the common
ground of a two-party system, with the Liberal Party 'supplying Conservative governments with Cabinets, and Labour governments with ideas'.[4] In
the 1930s this Liberal context disappeared, and Keynes did not add importantly to the political philosophy he had developed in the 1920s.

What Freeden calls the 'production and dissemination' of Liberal ideas
took place through three overlapping institutional networks in each of which
Keynes played a leading part: the Liberal Summer Schools meeting alter-
nately in Oxford and Cambridge from 1922 onwards, the weekly journal
the *Nation*, and the Lloyd George-financed Liberal Industrial Inquiry, whose
report *Britain's Industrial Future* was published in 1928.

Keynes's involvement in the politics of Liberalism raises the question of
the relationship between Keynes's Liberalism and that body of ideas known
as the New or social Liberalism which flourished before 1914 and is distinguished from the classical or individualistic Liberalism which preceded it.
'From 1906 to 1914', wrote Hubert Henderson, 'a common economic policy
united the parties of the Left – the development of the social services
involving public expenditure, and the raising of the money by stiffer taxes
on wealth.'[5] To this tradition, Ramsay Muir and the 'Manchester Liberals'
added industrial democracy, as a way out of the class struggle, and also to
limit the growth of private and public power. Peter Clarke sees Keynes's
Middle Way as being continuous with this tradition, particularly with its
political goal of a Labour–Liberal partnership.[6] Michael Freeden, on the
other hand, sees Keynes as the intellectual progenitor of a new 'centrist
Liberalism', grafting technocratic solutions to specific problems on to an
individualist stem. By confining state intervention to spaces left vacant by
private enterprise, by 'jettisoning redistribution as a major field of socio-

economic policy' and by 'de-democratising' policymaking in favour of expert control, Keynes repudiated the distinctive features of the pre-war 'new' Liberalism.[7] This is also the interpretation of Maurice Cranston.[8]

Freeden and Cranston are more nearly right than Clarke. However, the matter is not quite straightforward. There were similarities as well as differences between Keynes's Liberalism and the tradition of social Liberalism. The issues can be summarised under four heads.

First, and most obviously, Keynes added macroeconomic stabilisation to the pre-war Liberal agenda and, in fact, gave it priority. Post-war Liberalism, he said, must address itself to new, not old, problems. The short-run instability of capitalism was a greater threat to the social order than any long-run inequity in the distribution of wealth and income. The greatest economic evils, Keynes proclaimed, were the fruits of 'risk, uncertainty, and ignorance'. The state's main economic duty was to offset the effects of these by monetary policy and capital spending. Keynes also understood that to emphasise social reform while business confidence was low would prevent the recovery of private investment needed to lift the economy out of the slump. Questions of social justice had to be shelved as long as businessmen lacked the confidence to invest. This is a clear line, though one to which the left has often been blind.

However, it was not just that Keynes downgraded social reform as a priority; it was never a passion with him. Elizabeth Johnson may exaggerate when she writes that, for Keynes, 'social injustice existed only in there not being enough jobs to go round',[9] but his rather complacent reflections on the pre-war social order – 'escape was possible, for any man of capacity or character at all exceeding the average, into the middle and upper classes . . .'[10] – hardly suggest a burning dissatisfaction with it. The truth is that Keynes's notion of inequity was largely limited to the existence of windfall or unjustified gains and losses. Justice to Keynes involved the maintenance of existing group norms and the fulfilment of settled expectations. His notion of it was contractual, or commutative, rather than substantive. He regarded as unjust the arbitrary shifts in wealth and incomes caused by avoidable business fluctuations – shifts unrelated to effort and beyond the control of ordinary prudence. That is why he sympathised so strongly with the miners at the time of the General Strike in 1926 – victims of the return to the gold standard in 1925. The insight that what groups of workers really feared was the loss of *relative* position would inform his discussion of wage behaviour in the *General Theory*. What Keynes did, in essence, was to transfer the problem of social justice from the microeconomy to the macroeconomy. Injustice becomes a matter of uncertainty, justice a matter of contractual predictability. Redistribution plays a minor part in his social philosophy, and then only as an adjunct to the machinery of macroeconomic stabilisation, not as a means to an ideal end.

Secondly, Keynes's emphasis on stabilisation policy is connected to what may be called his short-termism. Its philosophic basis was the principle of 'moral risk', which he got from Burke and Moore, and which tells us it is more rational to aim for a smaller good with a high probability of attainment than for a larger one with a low probability of attainment. This was the guiding principle of his statesmanship. It inoculated him equally against communism and the sacrificial thinking implicit in much of orthodox economics. It explains why Keynes tended to take the economic structure as given, and try to find a way round the rocks rather than try to pulverise them. Expediency is raised to a high principle of statecraft. 'It is fatal', he wrote, 'for a capitalist government to have principles. It must be opportunistic in the best sense of the word, living by accommodation and good sense. If any monarchical, plutocratic or other analogous form of government has principles, it will fall.'[11] Keynes's scepticism about the benefits of large-scale social change was matched by an extraordinary optimism about the possibility of intelligent management of short-run problems.

Thirdly, it was Keynes's statism and elitism which distanced him above all from the pre-war New Liberals. The New Liberals valued democracy as an end in itself and wanted to extend it to control private and public concentrations of power. Keynes's purposes required a managerial state. Moreover, since it was a state driven, in its economic functions, by updated economic theory, it was a technical or expert state. Thus Keynes welcomed the coming to power of a new class of Platonic Guardians. He wrote in 1925, 'I believe that the right solution [to the economic question] will involve intellectual and scientific elements which must be above the heads of the vast mass of more or less illiterate voters.'[12] Beatrice Webb could not have put it better.

A final point to note is the difference in intellectual style between Oxford and Cambridge. 'What a home of diseased thought Oxford is,' Keynes had written to his father in 1906 after reading a book on logic by the philosopher Horace Joseph.[13] Oxford was the centre of the New Liberalism of the pre-war era. Not only was Oxford (by Cambridge standards) ignorant of economics, but the Oxford-based attack on *laissez-faire* was couched in a mixture of Hegelian and biological language which Keynes and his generation at Cambridge found repellent. The epistemological assault on Bradley's doctrine of 'internal relations', led by Moore and Russell, carried over to the social ethics associated with T. H. Green, L. T. Hobhouse and J. A. Hobson. Against the view that the good of the individual and the good of the whole are organically connected, Keynes emphasised that good states of mind could be enjoyed by individuals in isolation from social states of affairs. Yet one must be aware of the connections as well as the differences. There was a large trace of Hegelianism in Moore's doctrine of 'organic unities'; and by the 1920s Keynes was willing to acknowledge that many processes of production and consumption were 'organic' rather than atomistic.

III

THE END OF *LAISSEZ-FAIRE*

Keynes's 1924 Sidney Ball lecture, 'The End of *Laissez-Faire*', delivered at Oxford on 6 November 1924 and published in 1926, provides the framework within which his arguments developed over the next five years. Like all his best work, it is full of sparkling prose and arresting ideas. He seems to have read, or at least delved, quite widely in the history of economic and political thought: the essay version is sprinkled with references to Locke, Hume, Rousseau, Paley, Bentham, Godwin, Burke and Coleridge, as well as to the nineteenth-century political economists. An important source was Leslie Stephen's *English Thought in the Eighteenth Century*. But no less characteristically its superb style hides a deal of hasty argument. As Schumpeter remarks, Keynes never gave himself the extra fortnight needed to perfect his occasional pieces.

Keynes traced the origins of *laissez-faire* thinking to the eighteenth-century view that social well-being resulted from individual calculations of self-interest. 'Suppose that by the working of natural laws individuals pursuing their own interests with enlightenment in conditions of freedom always tend to promote the general interest at the same time! Our philosophical difficulties are resolved. . . . The political philosopher could retire in favour of the businessman – for the latter could attain the philosopher's *summum bonum* by just pursuing his own private profit.'[14] The synthesis between the two received further powerful reinforcement in Darwin's theory of natural selection. 'The principle of the survival of the fittest could be regarded as a vast generalisation of the Ricardian economics. Socialist interferences became, in the light of this grander synthesis, not merely inexpedient but impious, as calculated to retard the onward movement of the mighty process by which we ourselves had risen like Aphrodite from the primeval slime.'[15]

The trouble is that Keynes fails to develop any sustained critique of this set of doctrines. This is the hole at the heart of the essay. He lumps together, in briefest summary, objections to *laissez-faire* which may be philosophical or merely practical ('the prevalence of ignorance over knowledge'), moral objections (the 'cost . . . of the competitive struggle' and the 'tendency for wealth to be distributed where it is not appreciated most'), and objections which stem from changed techniques of production (economies of scale) leading to monopoly. As a result we are left in the dark about whether the *laissez-faire* project cannot, as a matter of fact, be realised in given circumstances, whether it cannot be realised under any conceivable or probable set of circumstances, or whether it would be wrong to try to realise it, even if it could be.

Rather than pursuing these questions, Keynes explains the continued resilience of *laissez-faire* ideas by the 'poor quality of its opponent proposals

– protectionism on the one hand, and Marxian socialism on the other'. Protectionism is treated a little more gently than the year before; but 'Marxist socialism must always remain a portent to the historians of opinion – how a doctrine so illogical and so dull can have exercised so powerful and enduring influence over the minds of men and, through them, the events of history'. Keynes, as Donald Winch has remarked, was always 'notoriously tone deaf as far as Marx was concerned'. Nor did the war experience greatly increase the appeal of 'centralised social action on a great scale', since 'the dissipation of effort was . . . prodigious, and the atmosphere of waste and not counting the cost . . . disgusting to any thrifty or provident spirit'.[16]

The conclusion Keynes draws from all this is that the question of the proper sphere of individual and state action cannot be settled on abstract grounds. Each age, he implies, needs to distinguish for itself between what the state ought to do and what can be left to the individual; or, in Bentham's terms, between the Agenda and Non-Agenda of government. 'Perhaps the chief task of economists at this hour is to distinguish afresh the *Agenda* of government from the *Non-Agenda*; and the companion task of politics is to devise forms of government within a democracy which shall be capable of accomplishing the *Agenda*.'[17] This is a misleading way of stating the task. The Agenda of government cannot be laid down apart from considering what 'governments in a democracy' can successfully accomplish; political theorists, not just economists, have to work it out.

Keynes then develops what looks like a public-goods argument for state intervention. 'We must aim', he wrote, 'at separating those services which are technically social from those which are technically individual.' The most important items on the Agenda relate 'not to those activities which private individuals are already fulfilling, but to those functions which fall outside the sphere of the individual, to those decisions which are made by no one if the State does not make them'. Remedy for the evils arising from 'risk, uncertainty and ignorance' required 'deliberate control of the currency and of credit by a central institution, and . . . the collection and dissemination of . . . business facts'. He proposed in addition a 'coordinated act of intelligent judgement' concerning the aggregate volume of savings and their distribution between home and foreign investment, and a population policy 'which pays attention to innate quality as well as to . . . numbers'.[18] Keynes does not explain why the last two goods are *technically* social – that is, why private individuals cannot provide savings and children in the amounts they desire. We have here a good example of the difficulty of trying to build collectivist conclusions on individualistic premises.*

*The technical argument that markets cannot provide certain goods in the quantity they are desired rests heavily on the 'free rider' problem: the lack of incentive for individuals to pay voluntarily for goods in which there are no private property rights. Defence is a classic example. In the pure logic of the case, if a country's defence system had to be provided by voluntary contribution, expenditure on defence would be zero, since everyone would share in it whether they contributed or not. So it must be provided by compulsory contribution (taxes)

Keynes's public goods are to be provided by the state. But when he talks about the state the private–public distinction on which the argument hinges breaks down because of the existence of intermediate institutions. Keynes points to the growth of 'semi-autonomous bodies within the State' like the 'universities, the Bank of England, the Port of London Authority, even perhaps the railway companies', as well as to mixed forms of industrial organisation, such as joint-stock institutions, 'which when they have reached a certain age and size [tend] to approximate to the status of public corporations rather than that of individualistic private enterprise'. Echoing the ideas of the Managerial Revolution, soon to receive their classic exposition by James Burnham, Keynes pointed out that corporations of a certain age and size were owned by anonymous shareholders, but were actually run by managers increasingly sensitive to the public implications of their activities. The Bank of England, the rights of whose shareholders 'have already sunk to the neighbourhood of zero', was merely an extreme instance of institutions which were 'socialising themselves'. The growth of these 'semi-autonomous bodies', Keynes suggested, harked back to 'medieval conceptions of separate autonomies'.[19]

Most people, of course, do not think of the state as including private bodies. Keynes was suggesting that the rise of planning and administration within the private sphere pointed to the fracturing of sovereignty, *de facto* if not yet *de jure*, in reversal of the whole tendency since the Middle Ages for property to become fully privatised, with its public functions being taken over by the Crown. The classical liberal idea of a sovereign but limited state, and an untrammelled market was yielding to new corporatism, in which the state (in the narrow sense) was simply one – a *primus inter pares* – in the order of corporations or associations.[20]

What is striking is not Keynes's recognition that the growth of private power posed new questions for the relationship between the state and the economy – this recognition was widespread in the political thought of the time – but his way of resolving the issue. Old-fashioned liberals still aimed to pulverise private power by trust-busting; social liberals wanted to subject it to 'democracy' – whether by decision-sharing, profit-sharing or wider share ownership. Socialists saw it as furnishing a justification for nationalisation. These were all efforts to secure accountability, whether to consumers, workers or electors. Keynes had no real interest in them. He was no pluralist. He welcomed the 'aggregation of production' as tending to stabilise the economy; he accepted uncritically the view that captains of industry were

in amounts decided by collective choice. But this argument cannot be applied to saving or population, since individuals do not have to share their savings or children with anyone else. Keynes is saying something different: that there is an optimal quantity of population or saving different from the desired quantity as reflected in individual decisions. But do these optima exist? Later he was to say that the community as a whole cannot achieve its desired level of saving if its income is subject to large fluctuation. This *is* a technical economic argument, which was lacking from the 1924 statement.

constrained, by the size of their undertakings, to serve the public interest; and he assumed, without further argument, that an interconnected elite of business managers, bankers, civil servants, economists and scientists, all trained at Oxford and Cambridge and imbued with a public service ethic, would come to run these organs of state, whether private or public, and make them hum to the same tune. He wanted to decentralise and devolve only down to the level of Top People.

Keynes's anti-market, anti-democratic bias was driven by a belief in scientific expertise and personal disinterestedness which now seems alarmingly naive. This runs like a leitmotiv through his work and is *the* important assumption of his political philosophy. Economic progress, he emphasised, depends 'on our willingness to entrust to science those things which are properly the concern of science'; the principles of central banking, he was to say a little later, should be 'utterly removed from popular controversy and . . . be regarded as a kind of beneficent technique of scientific control such as electricity or other branches of science are'. He contrasted the 'scientific spirit' with the 'sterility of the purely party attitude'. He recognised the problem of combining 'representative institutions and the voice of public opinion with the utilisation by governments of the best technical advice', yet in economic policy he looked forward to the 'euthanasia of politics'.[21] Although his language was sometimes extreme, this, as Noel Annan has pointed out, was the authentic voice of 'Our Age'. It approximated to what actually happened in the 'consensus years' of the 1950s and 1960s. The consensus broke down only when the experts started to disagree, and it became apparent, as it always should have been, that policy is a handmaiden of politics.

With technical questions removed from party warfare, political debate would, Keynes suggested, largely revolve round the nature of the ideal society of the future. The basic divide, he felt, would be over the scope to be allowed 'to the money-making and money-loving instincts as the main motive force of the economic machine'. Capitalism could be made an efficient technique of production; but the motives it relied upon might still be felt to be morally objectionable. 'Our problem is to work out a social organisation which shall be as efficient as possible without offending our notions of a satisfactory way of life.'[22] If this was a problem for society, it was a personal problem for Keynes, the speculator who was also a disciple of G. E. Moore.

'The End of *Laissez-Faire*' is a flawed production; but it remains the most impressive short attempt on record to define a social and economic philosophy fit for the time of troubles framed by the two world wars. Nearly seventy years after it was written its spaciousness, humanity and sheer linguistic vivacity still shine brightly. Its faults are shortness and hastiness. Every proposition cries out for development, criticism, refinement. Had he lived longer, Keynes would surely have been tempted to embed his economic theory (which came later) in a culminating work of political and social philosophy to rival and confront Hayek's *Constitution of Liberty*. For the argument is not over. Capitalism may have vanquished socialism, but the debate between *laissez-faire* and Keynes's philosophy of the Middle Way is still fiercely joined.

Three themes following on from the Sidney Ball Lecture which Keynes was to develop in articles and lectures over the next five years are worth picking out: his characterisation of capitalist 'stages of development'; his attitude to Conservatism and socialism; and the way he relates economic life to the good life.

IV

THE POLITICAL ECONOMY OF STABILISATION

The second half of the 1920s is the period of Keynes's greatest interest in the institutions of capitalism. He was never interested in institution-building, whether creating markets or organs of state planning. He took existing institutions as given and tried to work with their grain. A new ideology was required for a capitalism evolving into more organised forms. This was quite different from the robust liberal or socialist approach of remoulding institutions to fit theory. The institutional shifts which Keynes observed were the eclipse of the independent entrepreneur, maximising his profits, by the joint-stock company, mainly interested in the general stability of trade; the organisation of the labour market by trade unions; the increasingly dominant role of the banking system in determining monetary conditions; and growing state responsibility for investment through the rise of the public corporation. In 'The End of *Laissez-Faire*' Keynes had talked about the growth of semi-autonomous bodies between the individual and the state. In two talks he delivered in the summer of 1925 – 'Am I a Liberal?' in Cambridge on 1 August, and 'The Economic Transition in England' in Moscow on 15 September – he tried to set this development in a historical framework, producing a non-Marxist theory of 'stages of economic development' suggested by the American John Rogers Commons. Commons, an institutional economist who taught at Wisconsin University, is an important, if unacknowledged, influence on Keynes. Indeed, Keynes wrote to him in 1927 that 'there seems to me to be no other economist with whose general way of thinking I feel myself in such general accord'.[23]

Commons distinguished three epochs, which he called the ages of scarcity, abundance and stabilisation. The first, lasting till the fifteenth or sixteenth century, was characterised by communistic, feudal or governmental control through physical coercion. The second era was associated with the triumphs of individualism. England, Keynes claimed, was:

> now entering on a third era, which Professor Commons calls the period of stabilisation, and truly characterises as 'the actual alternative to Marx's communism'. In this period, he says, 'there is a diminution of individual liberty, enforced in part by governmental sanctions, but mainly by economic sanctions through concerted action, whether secret, semi-open, open, or arbitrational, of associations, corporations, unions, and other collective movements of manufacturers, merchants, labourers, farmers, and bankers.
>
> The abuses of this epoch in the realms of government are Fascism on the one side and Bolshevism on the other. Socialism offers no middle course, because it also is sprung from the presuppositions of the era of abundance ... The transition from economic anarchy to a regime which deliberately aims at controlling and directing economic forces in the interests of social justice and social stability, will present enormous difficulties both technical and political. I suggest, nevertheless, that the true destiny of New Liberalism is to seek their solution.[24]

In Moscow, Keynes went on to say that the old economics depended on the 'principle of diffusion' – the principle that when any disturbance is introduced at any point in the economic organism it diffuses itself rapidly through the whole organism until a new position of equilibrium is reached. But the rate of diffusion was much less than before. It was easier to adjust when everything was expanding rapidly than in times of stagnation; the power of trade unions to maintain wages and exclude the entry of new workers into a trade had grown; humanitarian ideas had spread, too, exemplified by the more generous system of unemployment benefits. As a result the capitalist system had become rigid; but the authorities still acted on the assumption that it was flexible.[25]

> The idea of the old-world party [he continued in 'Am I a Liberal?'], that you can, for example, alter the value of money and then leave the consequential adjustments to be brought about by the forces of supply and demand, belongs to the days of fifty or a hundred years ago when trade unions were powerless, and when the economic juggernaut was allowed to crash along the highways of progress without obstruction and even with applause.
>
> Half the copybook wisdom of our statesmen is based on assumptions which were at one time true, or partly true, but are now less and less true by the day. We have to invent new wisdom for a new age. And in the meantime we must, if we are to do any good, appear unorthodox, troublesome, dangerous, disobedient to them that begat us.[26]

Keynes was describing what Mancur Olson in the 1980s called the 'sclerotic society':[27] one in which the accretion of powerful vested interests has robbed the economy of vitality. His own stylisation of this process is important for understanding the spirit of his economics. The great art of economics, he always believed, was to choose models relevant to the contemporary world. Organised producer groups were now in a position to resist large changes damaging to themselves. Hence the importance of stabilising prices: 'For the most violent interferences with stability and with justice, to which the nineteenth century submitted . . . were precisely those which were brought about by changes in the price level.'[28] so 'the first and most important step . . . is to establish a new monetary system . . . which will not ask from the principle of diffusion more than it can perform'.[29] But, in addition, a new partnership had to be established between the government and the private sector to match the growing corporatism of industry. 'Our task must be to decentralise and devolve wherever we can, and in particular to establish semi-independent corporations and organs of administration to which duties of government, new and old, will be entrusted – without, however, impairing the democratic principle or the ultimate sovereignty of Parliament.'[30]

V

THE POLITICS OF THE MIDDLE WAY

Although Keynes intended his 'new wisdom' to transcend party politics, there remained the question of which of the two main political parties was most likely to apply his conception of modern statesmanship. 'How could I bring myself to be a Conservative?' Keynes asked himself in 'Am I a Liberal?' 'They offer me neither food nor drink – neither intellectual nor spiritual consolation. I should not be amused or excited or edified . . . [Conservatism] leads nowhere; it satisfies no ideal; it conforms to no intellectual standard; it is not even safe, or calculated to preserve from spoilers that degree of civilisation which we have already attained.'[31]

For a Liberal of Keynes's generation, the Conservative Party was the historic enemy, and remained so throughout the inter-war years, despite the 'decency' of Stanley Baldwin. It was the party of stupidity, superstition and prejudice. It was also the party of protectionism and jingoism. It ought to be evolving a version of capitalism suited to the new circumstances: instead 'capitalist leaders in the City and in Parliament are incapable of distinguishing novel measures for safeguarding capitalism from what they call Bolshevism'.[32] The other problem with the Conservatives was they were guardians of the reactionary codes of morals against which Keynes's generation had rebelled. As part of the agenda of Liberalism he listed 'Birth control and

the use of contraceptives, marriage laws, the treatment of sexual offences
and abnormalities, the economic position of women, the economic position
of the family . . . drug questions'.[33] On all matters of special concern to
Bloomsbury and Hampstead, Conservatives – at least in public – upheld
positions which he habitually dubbed 'medieval'. He attributed the stupidity
of Conservatism to its attachment to the hereditary principle. This also
explained the inefficiency of British industry. British capitalism was dominated by third-generation men.[34] His initial respect for Baldwin rapidly
waned – 'There was an attraction at first that Mr. Baldwin should not be
clever. But when he forever sentimentalises about his own stupidity, the
charm is broken.'[35]

Yet it is easy to imagine Keynes at home, or as at home as he would ever
be, in the Conservative Party of Macmillan and Butler – both of whom
became personal friends, unlike any Labour leaders. He admired Conservatism's elitism: 'the inner ring of the party can almost dictate the details and
technique of policy', he remarked admiringly.[36] It was only to stupid elitism
he objected. Keynes believed that ability was innate, and deplored only the
fact that, in its attachment to the hereditary principle, Conservatism prevented natural ability from rising to the top. A Conservative Party led by
Oxford and Cambridge men would not have been so objectionable to him
as one which still stuffed Cabinets with dukes. And, as he became older and
started his own ascent to the peerage, the stupidity and class prejudice
associated with the hereditary principle came to seem less noxious to him
than parallel manifestations of these tendencies in the Labour Party. Starting
as a Liberal Keynes ended up as a Whig.

Nevertheless, in the circumstances he faced, Keynes undoubtedly saw the
Labour Party as more likely to execute the policies of the Middle Way. If
the Conservatives were the stupid party, Labour was the silly party. But at
least much of its heart was in the right place. What was needed, he suggested, was Labour's head of steam yoked to the programme of Liberalism.
In most of his political commentary Keynes is engaged in a dialogue with
the Labour movement. This sometimes involved him in very ambiguous use
of language as he tried, at one and the same time, to distinguish his position
from that of socialism and also to stress the compatibility of a range of
Liberal and socialist aspirations. This is true of his utopianism. He insisted
that 'the Republic of my imagination lies on the extreme left of celestial
space'.[37] But the ideal he sometimes chose to call socialist has much more
to do with ends such as leisure, beauty, grace, excitement, variety, which,
as Anthony Crosland rightly observed, are 'not to be subsumed under any
defensible definition of socialism',[38] than with equality, fraternity, democracy. Moreover, this socialism, Keynes thought, would come into its own
when further economic progress had rendered capitalism unnecessary – a
future remote enough to satisfy even the rhetorical requirements of Ramsay
MacDonald.

Keynes emphatically rejected socialism as an *economic* remedy for the ills of *laissez-faire*. Its doctrines were ideological, obsolete, irrelevant, inimical to wealth-creation, and likely to involve gross interferences with individual liberty. The inefficiency, as well as irrelevance, of socialism as an economic technique had been vividly brought home to him in Soviet Russia. He predicted (accurately) that the system would survive, though at a very low level of efficiency, but he could not see that it had made 'any contribution to our economic problems of intellectual interest or scientific value'.[39]

Secondly, Keynes objected to the revolutionary strain in socialism. He gave two reasons. He did not regard the existing order of society as so bad that it could not be reformed; and it was doubly wrong to have a revolution to establish a system worse than the one being overthrown. Reviewing a book by Trotsky in March 1926, he wrote, 'It is not necessary to debate the subtleties of what justifies a man in promoting his gospel by force; for no one has a gospel. The next move is with the head, and fists must wait.'[40]

Keynes recognised that the bulk of the Labour Party were not 'Jacobins, Communists, Bolshevists' – the 'party of catastrophe' he called them – but he thought their 'malignity, jealousy, [and] hatred of those who have wealth and power (even in their own body)' pervaded the whole party and consorted ill 'with ideals to build up a true social republic'.[41] In a debate with Thomas Johnston at the Liberal Summer School on 3 August 1929, Keynes argued that Labour had to 'put on an appearance of being against anyone who is more successful, more skilful, more industrious, more thrifty than the average. . . . This is most unjust and most unwise. It disturbs what is and always must be the strongest section of the community and throws them into the reactionary camp.'[42]

Keynes emphatically rejected the class basis of socialist ideology and politics. 'It [the Labour Party] is a class party, and the class is not my class. If I am going to pursue sectional interests at all, I shall pursue my own. . . . I can be influenced by what seems to me to be justice and good sense; but the *class* war will find me on the side of the educated *bourgeoisie*.'[43] Keynes's attitude was, of course, influenced by his social background and milieu, which, in Cambridge and London, were not anti-working class but non-working class: Eton Scholars, civilised bankers and industrialists, upper-middle-class writers and painters. Keynes did not hesitate to describe himself as a 'leveller': 'I want to mould a society in which most of the existing inequalities and causes of inequality are removed.' But he went on, 'I do not want to level individuals. I want to give encouragement to all exceptional effort, ability, courage, character. I do not want to antagonize the successful, the exceptional. I believe that man for man the middle class and even the upper class is very much superior to the working class.'[44]

That occasionally penetrating observer of inter-war British culture, Dmitri Mirsky, gave a Marxist gloss to Keynes's position in his book *The Intelligentsia of Great Britain*. The intellectual aristocracy – what Keynes called the

'educated bourgeoisie' – not being directly involved in the production process, could consider itself outside or above class. It criticised bourgeois
society from the point of view of the good life, but was anti-socialist too. In
economics, its demand was for more organisation, which it called socialism,
but in individual life it wanted more freedom. This was part of the 'cultural
contradictions' of capitalism – a theme later developed by both Schumpeter
and the sociologist Daniel Bell. The weakness of this sociological analysis
is not that it views ideas as social products, but that it is unwilling to
confront the question of their validity.

Finally, and significantly, Keynes objected to Labour's anti-elitism. He
felt that 'the intellectual elements in the Labour Party will [n]ever exercise
adequate control; too much will always be decided by those who do not
know *at all* what they are talking about'.[45]

Keynes admired three things about socialism: its passion for social justice
(even though he distanced himself from it);[46] the Fabian ideal of public
service; and its utopianism, based on the elimination of the 'money motive'
and 'love of money'. It was his utopianism which links up his work as an
economist with his commitment to the good life.

VI

THE LOVE OF MONEY

The most eloquent expression of his utopianism is found in his essay 'Economic Possibilities for Our Grandchildren', first delivered as a talk to the
Essay Society at Winchester College on 17 March 1928, and repeated and
revised on a number of occasions before its publication in 1930. Its context
is important. His visit to Soviet Russia in the late summer of 1925 had
triggered or, more accurately, reactivated reflections on the moral value of
capitalism, and he told Lydia on 6 November that he had written 'some
philosophical pages about Love of Money'. Another important influence at
this time was Freud. In June of that year, James Strachey had reported
Keynes 'engrossed in the Case Histories [of Freud].'[47] Keynes was fascinated
by Freud's reflections on the pathology of money, particularly its association
with the anal sadistic character, and by the Freudian mechanism of subli-
mation. Freud enabled him to build on his insight into the sacrificial nature
of capitalism, first expressed in *The Economic Consequences of the Peace*. Here
the price of economic progress is seen as the cultural deformation of the
'rentier bourgeoisie', who have sacrificed the 'arts of enjoyment' to 'compound interest'.[48] Was there any escape from the dilemma that economic
progress seemed to depend on motives condemned as immoral by religion
and neurotic by psychology?

For a brief moment Keynes toyed with the idea that the Soviet Union might have discovered at least the beginning of an answer. Admittedly, he produced, in 'A Short View of Soviet Russia', published in December 1925, one of the most searing attacks on Soviet communism ever penned:

> For me, brought up in a free air undarkened by the horrors of religion, with nothing to be afraid of, Red Russia holds too much which is detestable. Comfort and habits let us be ready to forgo, but I am not ready for a creed which does not care how much it destroys the liberty and security of daily life, which uses deliberately the weapons of persecution, destruction, and international strife. How can I admire a policy which finds a characteristic expression in spending millions to suborn spies in every family and group at home, and to stir up trouble abroad? . . . How can I accept a doctrine which sets up as its bible, above and beyond criticism, an obsolete economic textbook which I know to be not only scientifically erroneous but without interest or application for the modern world? How can I adopt a creed which, preferring the mud to the fish, exalts the boorish proletariat above the bourgeois and intelligentsia who, with whatever faults, are the quality of life and surely carry the seeds of all human advancement? Even if we need a religion, how can we find it in the turbid rubbish of the Red bookshops? It is hard for an educated, decent, intelligent son of western Europe to find his ideals here, unless he has first suffered some strange and horrid process of conversion which has changed all his values.[49]

Yet, although he found the system in many ways detestable, Keynes thought it just possible that Soviet communism might 'represent the first confused stirrings of a great religion', that beneath its cruelty and stupidity 'some speck of the ideal may lie hid'.[50] The significance of Bolshevism, he thought, lay not in its economics but in its attempt to construct a social system which condemned personal enrichment as an end and made it impossible for anyone to pursue it seriously. It was this, he thought, which gave communism the moral edge over capitalism. For 'modern capitalism is absolutely irreligious, without internal union, without much public spirit, often, though not always, a mere congeries of possessors and pursuers. Such a system has to be immensely, not merely moderately, successful to survive.'[51] In Soviet Russia, what all the great religions recognised as spiritually criminal, had been made legally and socially so. The characteristic thought here is that capitalism is bad, not because it exploits the worker, but because it creates 'bad states of mind' in capitalists. Capitalism was (or could be made) efficient, but lacked a creed; communism had a creed, but was grossly inefficient.

After a further visit to Russia in April 1928, Keynes reluctantly concluded that the price for the creed was too high. 'We enjoyed the ballet and the opera,' he informed Ottoline Morrell,

> and I adored Lydia's relatives (who talked so much that they almost talked her conversational head off), but came back very depressed about the Bolshies. I have a much less favourable impression than last time. It is impossible to remember, until one gets in the country, how mad they are and that they care about their experiment more than about making things work.[32]

The romance was clearly over. One could not enjoy good states of mind unless things worked. What Keynes's mild flirtation with Soviet communism shows is the need he had, in common with others of the non-believing generation, for a cause, a vision of the good life, to which he could hitch his worldly activities. It was to show how capitalism, despite its faults, might be evolving the conditions of the good life that Keynes wrote 'Economic Possibilities for Our Grandchildren'.[53]

Keynes's thesis was that the engine of capitalism was driven by a neurosis which he calls 'love of money'; but this neurosis is also the means to the good, because it is the means to the abundance which will make capitalism unnecessary. In no other piece of writing does Keynes's ambivalent attitude to capitalism come out so clearly; yet, as we have mentioned earlier, his utopia is not socialist, simply non-capitalist. That is because, like Max Weber, he defines capitalism as a spirit, not as a social system. Whatever happens to property relations, capitalism as such is self-liquidating. Thus beyond Commons's epoch of stabilisation stretches a new age of abundance, when individualism can flourish again, though shorn of the unlovely features associated with its first coming.

Keynes calculated that if capital increased at 2 per cent per annum, population growth levelled off and productivity rose at 1 per cent per annum, in one hundred years the prospective population of the 'civilised' world would have a standard of living between four and eight times as high as in the 1920s, obtainable at a small fraction of the effort currently being expended.[54]

With most wants satiated, the value of a particular psychological disposition (purposiveness) will become obsolete: specifically, the 'love of money' will be recognised as 'a somewhat disgusting morbidity, one of the semi-criminal, semi-pathological propensities which one hands over with a shudder to specialists in mental disease'.[55] People will be free to adopt once more the 'sure and certain principles of religion and traditional virtue', valuing today over tomorrow, ends over means, the good over the useful. 'We shall honour those who can teach us how to pluck the hour and the day virtually and well, the delightful people who are capable of taking direct enjoyment in things, the lilies of the field, who toil not, neither do they spin.' But for the time being 'we must go on pretending that fair is foul and foul is fair;

for foul is useful and fair is not. Avarice and usury and precaution must be our goods for a little longer still. For only they can lead us out of the tunnel of economic necessity into the daylight.'[56] Faust could then dispense with the services of Mephistopheles and say, 'Zum Augenblicke durft ich sagen: Verweile doch, du bist so schön.'

'Economic Possibilities for Our Grandchildren' has attracted little attention from economists, perhaps rightly. It is a provocation, a *jeu d'esprit*, aimed at clever young Wykehamists and Etonians. One of his students, A. F. W. Plumptre, who heard the talk in Cambridge, wrote,

> Here was Keynes at his best and his worst. His worst, because some of his social and political theory would not stand too close a scrutiny; because society is not likely to run out of new wants as long as consumption is conspicuous and competitive; and because . . . democratic government is more than a gathering of benevolent Old Etonians. His best, because of the roving, inquiring, intuitive, provocative mind of the man.[57]*

Keynes's little essay is typical, in its ratio of fancy to hard argument, of his table talk. These were the lines on which his mind instinctively, and habitually, ran, when not reined in by the requirements of formal treatment. So the talk gives a better idea of what went on in his own mind than his more academic or specialised pieces. In his disapproval of business pursuits he was a typical son of England's 'educated bourgeoisie': they despised money-making as a career or vocation, though they were not averse to a bit of it on the side. His utopia suggests an enlarged Bloomsbury at the top and bread and circuses for the masses. It is a paradise of leisure. But what will most people do? It is also typically parochial, in being confined to the 'civilised' world.[58] Keynes's idea of money-making as a neurosis was fed by the fashionable interest of his circle in Freud. 'Love of money' is rhetorically precise – capitalism is given a single neck ready to cut – but does Keynes really mean to say that all the activities of capitalism – enterprise, investment, saving – are driven by Avarice, Usury and Precaution? Was he not simply caricaturing one star in the capitalist constellation – the dividend-drawing bourgeoisie? And can he really have expected to be taken entirely seriously when he called all future-regarding motives foul?

'Economic Possibilities for Our Grandchildren' sums up many of the ambivalences in Keynes's own thinking and psychology. The qualities he admired were not typically those that make for effectiveness in practical life, but he was extremely effective. He did not much love the Victorian virtues even though they made for economic success, yet he possessed them. He

*Keynes admitted that within societies whose basic needs have been satisfied there remains the problem of relative needs – 'those that satisfy the desire for superiority', which Fred Hirsch later called 'positional goods'. Although he thought that such needs might be insatiable (*CW*, ix, 326), he did not allow the admission to complicate the argument.

loved generosity of spirit and life much more than shrewd calculation or prudent housekeeping, but he was 'remarkably economical' in his own hospitality. Economics was an ignoble science, praising what philosophers and moralists condemned, yet he was an economist. The solution of the economic problem was the end of economic calculation, yet he was a born calculator. Above all, the object of striving (the good life) is separated from the virtues necessary to bring it about.

Yet in the end there is some kind of reconciliation. His ethics and psychology do eventually link up dramatically with his economics. Whereas in the 1920s, they pulled in different directions – 'love of money' was morally and psychologically bad, but economically good – by the 1930s 'love of money' has become economically bad.* It could be said that Keynes changed his theory to suit his morals. To work well capitalism requires less puritanism, more hedonism. More likely, Keynes's dislike of exaggerated purposiveness – which he thought of as essentially irrational – alerted him to its possible role in the malfunctioning of capitalism.

VII

THE JEWS

In 'Economic Possibilities for Our Grandchildren' Keynes remarked, 'Perhaps it is not an accident that the race which did most to bring the promise of immortality into the heart and essence of our religions has also done most for the principle of compound interest and particularly loves this most purposive of human institutions.'[59] There are a few other references to Jews in Keynes's writings which would now be construed as anti-semitic. In 'A Short View of Russia' he had doubted whether communism 'makes Jews less avaricious'. After a visit to Berlin in June 1926, he depicted Germany as under the 'ugly thumbs' of its 'impure Jews', who had 'sublimated immortality into compound interest'. This was for a talk to the Memoir Club, published only posthumously; it was his most prejudiced utterance on the subject, but it falls a long way short of the murderously flip remarks which even someone like Dennis Robertson was capable of making.[60]

Stereotyping of Jews was common in Keynes's circle, and the stereotypes were usually unfavourable. Keynes's letters are mercifully free from personal abuse – not so Lydia's, or those of some Bloomsberries. Individual Jews

---

*Robert and David Schaeffer point out that the 'curious corollary' of Keynes's depreciation of thrift is the encouragement of 'conspicuous consumption' by the wealthy, which, as he had realised in *The Economic Consequences of the Peace*, would make economic inequality far more morally problematic. (In 'The Political Philosophy of J. M. Keynes', *Public Interest*, Spring 1983, 56.)

were exempted by the devices of exceptionalism or non-recognition of their Jewishness. Thus was decency reconciled to prejudice. But the occasion for decency did not often arise. Although Virginia Woolf married a Jew, and Sraffa and Wittgenstein were half-Jewish, there were very few Jews in Keynes's world in the 1920s. That came later – with the exodus from Central Europe. Meanwhile, stereotyping could flourish, and there was no need to mind manners.

Keynes's own stereotyping took place on the philosophical, not vulgar, plane. Much like Weber's disciple Sombart, he thought of Jews as embodying the 'spirit' of capitalism, which to him was an abstract 'love of money'. His fancy was seized by the idea of a nexus between immortality and compound interest – in the individual psyche, in the history of the Jews and in the history of capitalism. 'Compound interest' is the 'impure' form of immortal longing. And so Keynes distinguished between the 'pure' or religious or intellectual Jews like Einstein, or Melchior, or his favourite pupil Richard Kahn, and the money-loving Jews like Clemenceau's Finance Minister, Klotz. When 'Economic Possibilities for Our Grandchildren' was published, Professor Radin of the University of California pointed out the lack of congruence between Keynes's hypothesis and the facts. He told Keynes that 'the hope of immortality played an extremely unimportant part in Jewish theology' and that the Jews were 'not especially distinguished by their concern with compound interest or the accumulation of money' – rather the reverse: civic insecurity had made many Jews 'extremely extravagant' and prone to 'reckless gambling rather than painful accumulation'. In his reply, Keynes apologised for having been thinking along 'purely conventional lines'. But he was reluctant to give up his fancy: 'I still think that the race has shown itself, not merely for accidental reasons, more than normally interested in the accumulation of usury.'[61] This correspondence took place in the autumn of 1933. It has to be balanced by Keynes's condemnation of the 'barbarism' taking place in Germany at the time. (See p. 486 below.) Keynes's anti-semitism, if such it was, was little more than a theological fancy: the expression, perhaps, of some unresolved conflict about his own Nonconformist roots. There is no evidence that it influenced his personal conduct.

VIII

CONCLUSION

Keynes's politics of the Middle Way in the 1920s can be interpreted in two senses. It can be seen as an expression of an Aristotelian sense of balance, with both nineteenth-century individualism and twentieth-century communism being viewed as excesses of their virtues. Or Keynes can be seen as a prophet of capitalism on the defensive. The institutions of society have become like rocks which require the most skilful circumnavigation if the ship of state is not to be smashed up. There was no margin left for stupidity, silliness or obsolete ideas in government. Only the most generous and disinterested spirit, equipped with high intelligence and scientific policies, could save the social order from shipwreck.

Both perspectives are valid, the first reflecting Keynes's education, the second his experience. In 1926 there seemed little evidence of his spirit in high places. Baldwin's government and the trade unions were set on a collision course. And Keynes was depressed.

APPENDIX

Among Keynes's unpublished papers are some notes, dated 23 December 1925, on the theme of 'love of money' which shed further light on his train of thought, as well as exhibiting the curiosity and fertility of his mind. His argument is that 'modern scientific advertising' tends to appeal to those respects in which people are similar, and to ignore the 'valuable elements in individuals' which often turn on small differences. The result is an increasingly standardised product, which leads to an increasingly standardised consumer. Keynes produced figures to show that in the United States the number of types of glass bottles had been reduced from 210 to 20, cigars from 150 to 6, collars from 150 to 25, and so on.

The result of this standardising process has been to raise 'the economic price of idiosyncrasy', to 'disclose to us what profusion and variety cost in terms of money'. For example, 'it may be true that if we all consumed exactly the same things, the present prices of these things would be divided by two. The modern advertiser would express this by saying that variety costs England £2,000,000,000 a year.'

Keynes went on to argue that it was not good to know exactly what everything costs. It was right to weigh concrete things against each other, but not to weigh concrete things against abstract money, 'the ultimate object of which is vaguely conceived or not conceived at all'. In the example above, it is not reasonable to accept a programme of standardised consumption unless one has decided exactly how the £2,000,000,000 saved is going to be spent, and in the light of this to see whether it is worthwhile saving it.

Keynes comes to his main point:

> The ... test of money measurement constantly tends to widen the area where we weigh concrete goods against abstract money. Our imaginations are too weak for the choice, abstract money outweighs

them. The sanctification of saving tends dangerously on the side of abstract money. The growth of individual wealth does the same.

. . .

It is not right to sacrifice the present to the future unless we can conceive the probabilities of the future in sufficiently concrete terms, in terms approximately as concrete as the present sacrifice, to be sure that the exchange was worth while.

We ought more often to be in the state of mind, as it were, of not counting the money cost at all.

Abolition of inheritance would help by making it more difficult to shirk the problem of concrete comparisons.

We want to diminish, rather than increase, the area of monetary comparisons.

The fluctuations of history [are] due to the fact that the social system which is economically efficient is morally inefficient. The Babylonian economy raises states to great affluence and comfort and then leads to their collapse for moral reasons. The fundamental problem . . . is to find a social system which is efficient economically *and* morally.

CHAPTER EIGHT

Liberalism and Industry

RUN-UP TO THE GENERAL STRIKE

' "All the workers of this country have got to face a reduction of wages" murmurs Mr. Baldwin between a sermon and a subsidy.' This comment by Oswald Mosley, a rising Labour politician, neatly captures the state of mind of the Baldwin government following Britain's return to the gold standard. Commitment to the pre-war parity logically required an all-round reduction in industrial costs. But, stranded between *laissez-faire* and fear of social revolution, the government could not impose an industrial policy of its own, nor could it afford to stand aside to let employers fight it out with the trade unions. It was in the coal industry that irresistible logic first came up against immovable force. When the coal owners had demanded a 10 per cent wage cut from their workforce and the TUC had warned this would mean a general strike, Baldwin stepped in with a compromise: a temporary subsidy to the coal industry plus a Royal Commission, headed by Sir Herbert Samuel, to tell it how to reorganise itself. The subsidy was due to expire on 30 April 1926. The unions prepared their resistance; the government prepared for a general strike; men of goodwill hoped that the Samuel Commission would come up with a magic formula.

While this time-bomb was ticking away, there was nothing Keynes could do. He had made clear his opposition to a policy of 'intensifying unemployment' to bring down wages. Given the gold standard, the best that could be done was to curtail foreign investment, absorb the surplus labour in the export industries in a programme of capital development at home and ship gold to America to encourage a rise in prices there. This is what Keynes would have done had he been in power; but he was not. In a speech to the Manchester branch of the Federation of British Industries on 13 October 1925 he suggested an escape from the policy of cutting wages. A policy aiming at 'production up to capacity and full-time employment may enable us at the same time to pay present real wages and, nevertheless, reduce our costs'.[1] This seemed to put the problem in a new light. Might not a fuller utilisation of idle plant pay for itself by cheapening the cost to the employer of each worker employed? This was one of Keynes's thoughts that flickered and died. What remained was the idea that prosperity is 'cumulative', that what British industry needed was fattening up not dieting.

Churchill's remark that the return to gold had no more to do with the difficulties of the coal industry than had the Gulf Stream was returning to haunt him. His advisers tried to cheer him up by saying that there was no alternative. Realities, minuted Niemeyer on 4 August 1925, had to be faced; money wages would come down after a lag, removing the export handicap; Keynes's policy of 'letting exchange go hang' had 'never been tried in practice; and . . . has received no support from practical men . . .'. Bradbury was on firmer ground in criticising Keynes's proposal to export gold in order to force up American prices. 'The notion that we have control of any expedients which would force America to inflate is a chimera.' A year later Niemeyer had abandoned argument for rhetoric: 'At any rate we have descended from the clouds to terra firma . . . there is now none that is not desperately anxious to follow us to a safe anchorage.'[2]

The autumn of 1925 found Keynes, as usual, complaining of overwork ('too much to do, no leisure, no peace, too much to think about . . .'). He refused an invitation to go to Budapest to advise the National Bank of Hungary, and a suggestion by Mitrany that he become Finance Minister of Rumania; but he could not forgo offering advice to the new French Minister of Finance, M. Loucheur, on how to balance his budget.[3] A more substantial autumnal commitment was organising the London Artists' Association, in homage to both art and friendship. The idea was to give the leading Bloomsbury painters and their protégés – a group headed by Duncan, Vanessa and Roger Fry – a guaranteed income, so they could paint without worrying about money. Perhaps Keynes saw it as a way of compensating Duncan for the loss of his inheritance. He persuaded Sam Courtauld and two other businessmen, Hindley Smith and L. H. Myers, to join him in guaranteeing the members an income of £150 a year. The Association held their first London show, at the Leicester Galleries, in April 1926. It was hailed by their relentless publicist Clive Bell as 'an event of capital importance . . . no less than the reassertion of an English school'.* By 1929, 700 works of art, worth £22,000, had been sold.[4]

From the start tensions dogged the Association's life, which reflected those between Tilton and Charleston. Keynes wanted to bring in non-Bloomsbury painters like Matthew Smith and Paul Nash, partly to strengthen the financial basis; Duncan, Vanessa and Roger Fry objected to his interference.

*The original members were Bernard Adeney, Keith Baynes, Vanessa Bell, Roger Fry, Duncan Grant, Frederick Porter and Frank Dobson, who had sculpted Lydia. Fry, who was independently wealthy, renounced his right to an income. The Association was an artists' co-operative. It functioned as their sole showing and selling agent, deducting a commission of 30 per cent from the gross revenue from sales to pay a secretary, and topping up individual incomes from sales which came to under £150, the guarantors making up any shortfall. Any artist whose sales came to more than £150 plus the commission was allowed to keep the excess.

Keynes was right, for many reasons, not least because he foresaw that Duncan and Vanessa would get tired of subsidising the non-earners. But it was a fixed idea at Charleston that Keynes had no artistic judgement: his role should be to pay up and leave artistic policy to them. 'If one wants to make him do something,' Vanessa wrote to Roger Fry, '[the only way] is not to listen to a word he says, to let him talk, keeping one's attention firmly fixed to one's own ideas, & then repeat them regardless of what he's said.'[5]

Maynard's friends assumed that, when she married, Lydia would give up dancing. With only one three-week engagement in the year preceding her marriage (in a slight comedy called *The Postman*, in which she fell off her bicycle), this seemed a reasonable assumption. But in October 1925 Diaghilev offered her an engagement for his four-week autumn season at the Coliseum, with a chance to star in her favourite roles, *Boutique, Good-Humoured Ladies, Carnaval* and *Petrushka*. She was not in full training and found the Coliseum season hard work for her toes. In *Boutique* she repeated her triumphant can-can with Woizikovsky, but complained of feeling very tired in her legs.[6] By 14 November she was dancing *Carnaval* 'with one terrible water blister that will not burst yet but gives tooth ache in the toe'. Moreover, Diaghilev had persuaded her to take on yet another role, in *Cimarosiana*. 'I am afraid I dance my number badly. . . . Of course I could refuse but there is a devil residing in me and insisting on my performance, another case of public speaking, only with legs.' (This was a reference to Keynes's dislike of giving public lectures.) Nevertheless, the Diaghilev season was a great success, and Lydia was recalled again for the summer season in 1926. Earning ten guineas a performance, she was able to contribute to Maynard's furniture-buying. 'Think of that,' he wrote to her on 23 November. 'Every time you lift your toe a complete article of furniture drops out and in one week you fill the bedroom.'

Back in Cambridge after Christmas at Tilton, Maynard was again feeling overworked. On 24 January 1926 he complained to Lydia of a 'terrible excess of meetings and of work. . . . Why do I do it? Over-activity of the cells, I suppose – indeed a kind of cancer.' He had agreed to send the *Banker* a centenary article on Walter Bagehot: the editor required it to be long enough to enable its banking readership to get through three glasses of port. One passage in it reflects his current political preoccupations: 'Labour politicians demand the nationalisation of the Bank of England; Dr. Leaf predicts that appalling disasters would ensue from such an act. They both waste their words. Bagehot nationalised the Bank of England fifty years ago.'[7] On 5 February, he complained to Lydia that he was 'dulled with work'. No sooner was Bagehot finished than the economist Edgeworth died, on 13 February. Within a fortnight, Keynes had composed a 5000-word memoir, published in March in the *Economic Journal*, which he had co-edited with Edgeworth for fifteen years; Lydia thought it had 'the dignity of noble coolness'.[8] In that time, Maynard had done most of the editorial work, since, as the *Times* obituarist remarked, Edgeworth's remarkable powers as an economist were combined 'with a complete innocence of business and administrative affairs'.[9] Keynes offered the joint editorship to his old rival Edwin Cannan of the LSE; when Cannan refused, it went to David Macgregor, the business economist, who held it till 1937. But it remained very much Keynes's show. Wherever he went his briefcase bulged with manuscripts.

Early in 1926 the issue of the future of the Liberal Party came up again. Following the débâcle of 1924, Asquith (now the Earl of Oxford and Asquith) retained the Party leadership, with Lloyd George chairman of the Liberal rump of forty-two MPs in the House of Commons and controlling a vast fund dubiously accumulated in Coalition days.* The Party was starting to shed MPs to both right and left: Hilton Young and Sir Alfred Mond joined the Conservatives in protest against Lloyd George's ambitious land-nationalisation plans, Wedgwood Benn and Kenworthy were about to go over to Labour. There were rumours that Lloyd George had been trying to work out a deal with Ramsay MacDonald; in the *Nation*, Hubert Henderson ran the idea of a progressive alliance between the Labour and Liberal Parties.[10]

Keynes intervened in the discussion in a 'frank speech' on Labour–Liberal relations at the presidential dinner of the Manchester Reform Club on 9 February, an occasion sufficiently august for him to get his hair cut. It was published in the *Nation* on 20 February as 'Liberalism and Labour'. His argument has a contemporary ring. It starts, 'I do not wish to live under a Conservative government for the next twenty years.' He did not think that the Labour Party could win over half the seats in Parliament on its own. The Liberal Party would not disappear; but it would never again be a formidable parliamentary force. Sensible Liberals should start talking to sensible socialists. Keynes's defeatist mood annoyed Lloyd George. In a letter to C. P. Scott on 10 February he condemned as premature Keynes's desire to 'seek understanding with Labour'. The Labour leaders, he asserted, 'are suspicious, jealous, and, oddly enough for a semi-revolutionary party, they are above all timid. Snowden is the only man of first class courage amongst them, with the possible exception of J. H. Thomas.'[11] Lloyd George recognised that the Liberal Party had to be up and walking before Labour would talk to it.

The real trouble with Keynes's argument, as Keynes no doubt recognised,

---

*The sources of the Lloyd George fund are still disputed. It was subscribed originally to Lloyd George for political (anti-socialist) purposes when he was Prime Minister, allegedly in exchange for honours. The appreciation of the fund, though, seems to have been due to Lloyd George's investment in a group of newspapers, of which the chief was the *Daily Chronicle*. He sold his controlling interest in this group between 1926 and 1928, receiving £2m. in cash, a large part of which went into the fund. The Asquithians were less worried about the origins of the fund than that Lloyd George kept it under his own control, releasing only dribs and drabs to the Liberal Party after the 'reconciliation' of 1923.

was that the 'sensible' people on both sides had no ideas. Ramsay MacDonald had nothing to offer between utopia and Treasury finance; Philip Snowden was a socialist of the old Henry George type, sharing Lloyd George's passion for land reform, but in all other respects an orthodox Gladstonian. Similarly, the 'sensible', or Asquithian, Liberals by no means agreed with Keynes. They had all supported the return to the gold standard. As H. N. Brailsford, editor of the *New Leader*, wrote to Keynes on 26 February, 'I used to know Runciman fairly well, and like him as a human being, but surely his vision of life is nowhere near yours. And the same is true of other abler people like Wedgwood Benn and Pringle.'[12]* Lloyd George had both ideas and energy, but sensible people regarded him as the devil incarnate. In the Labour Party, his only friends were the Snowdens, who had a cottage at Churt in Surrey, where Lloyd George had a country house.

Neither would the most important Labour convert to Keynes's ideas, Oswald Mosley, have been widely regarded as a sensible socialist. 'Tom' Mosley's reputation at this time was that of a rakish young man about town, a seducer of both crowds and women. (Lydia one night dreamt she was kissing him.)[13] Yet his pamphlet, 'Revolution by Reason', published in 1925, was the first political attempt to apply Keynes's ideas to economic policy. Mosley squarely blamed unemployment on the lack of 'effective demand'. 'At present Socialist thought', he wrote, 'appears to concentrate almost exclusively upon the transfer of present purchasing power by taxation, and neglects the necessity for creating additional demand to evoke our unused capacity which is at present not commanded either by the rich or the poor.' He wanted an Economic Council to 'estimate the difference between the actual and potential production of the country' and to issue consumers' and producers' credits which would taper off towards full employment, at which point 'all payments by the State must be balanced by taxation'. He was prepared to abandon the gold standard to allow the currency to depreciate to its true purchasing-power parity.[14] Responding in *The Times* on 20 April 1925 to Keynes's friend Robert Brand, who argued that his proposals would be inflationary, Mosley claimed that inflation would become a problem only when the economy approached full capacity.

Keynes had met Mosley at dinner parties in London; there is no evidence that he read, or discussed, his pamphlet with him. He did read an enlarged, and more muddled, version of it, written by Mosley's friend John Strachey, and, he told Strachey on 5 January 1926, 'liked it very much'. But he could not appreciate Mosley's flash of intuition about a 'lack of effective demand'. (Mainly because it *was* a flash of intuition: had Mosley been able to explain properly how it could occur, he, and not Keynes, would have been the author of the new economics.) Strachey had talked about 'the surplus income

---

*The *New Leader* was the journal of the Independent Labour Party, the earliest constituent body of the Labour Party, now on its left wing.

[that is, savings] of the rich' exerting 'no influence towards increased production'. In his letter to Strachey of 9 January 1926 Keynes said the problem was that savings were going abroad, and 'it cannot be more than a change of use you are after, e.g., from foreign investment to home wages'.[15]

Keynes also responded sympathetically to the Independent Labour Party's pamphlet, 'The Living Wage', published in 1926, which was equally anathema to the Labour leaders. Heavily influenced by J. A. Hobson's 'underconsumptionist' theory, it aimed to increase working-class purchasing power through redistributive taxation and credit expansion. In a letter to Brailsford, one of its authors, dated 27 October 1926, Keynes condemned the second proposal as smacking of the 'inflationist fallacy', and insisted as he had done to Strachey 'that the end from which to start is the complex of questions connected with the amount and direction of saving, foreign investments, and the distribution of our plant and labour forces as between industries working for the foreign market and those working for the home market'. He went on:

> I don't think I quite subscribe to Hobson's doctrine of underconsumption. But I do agree with a notion, which is perhaps kindred to his, to the effect that prosperity is cumulative. If in existing circumstances we could do something, orthodox or unorthodox, to stimulate demand, from whatever quarter, that demand would call forth an increased supply, which in turn would maintain and intensify the demand, and so on. But all the same it is not quite what Hobson has in mind I think.[16]

At this stage in his own development, Keynes could see a leakage of demand occurring only through foreign lending unrequited by exports. He did not yet see thriftiness as such as a potential subtraction from demand.

Labour's leadership presented a depressing spectacle, but Keynes was discovering a new sympathy for the Fabians of the older generation. Beatrice Webb had written him a warm letter of appreciation when 'Liberalism and Labour' appeared in the *Nation* on 20 February 1926. She particularly liked the echo of the old Fabian idea of permeation, while admitting that 'the particular line of research which we in the Fabian Society started in the nineties . . . is now exhausted . . .'.[17] Before the war Keynes had mocked Beatrice Webb. But, after lunching with her and Bernard Shaw on 19 March, he took her *My Apprenticeship* (sent to him for a review which he never wrote) to Andalucia, where he and Lydia spent their Easter holiday. He was much moved by her account of her struggle to replace her lost Christian faith by a new 'religion of humanity'. On their return on 18 April 1926, Duncan Grant reported, 'Maynard almost became a Socialist owing to his reading Mrs. Webb on the train in Spain.' He added cattily, 'I see Socialism is going to become for them a moral excuse for meanness.'[18] Maynard and Beatrice now embarked on an improbable friendship based on mutual fascination, much incomprehension, but a shared belief in social science and public service.

Another friend from the mid–1920s was H. G. Wells. Maynard gave his novel *The World of William Clissold* an enthusiastic review in the *Nation* on 22 January 1927. His sense of elitism was attracted by Wells's idea that the motive force for change had to come from the men of power and knowledge – the business tycoons and the scientists – rather than from socialist intellectuals or workers. 'Clissold's direction is to the Left – far, far to the Left; but he seeks to summon from the Right the creative force and the constructive will which is to carry him there.' The great danger was, in Clissold's words, lest 'before the creative Brahma can get to work, Siva, in other words the passionate destructiveness of labour awakening to its now needless limitations and privations, may make Brahma's task impossible'. But what motive, Keynes wondered, have the captains of industry to give up making money to join the 'open conspiracy'? They lacked a creed, a religion, or – he would add later – an economic theory 'to which they can attach their abundant *libido*'. Similar themes impregnated the work of Bernard Shaw, another old Fabian whom Maynard and Lydia were starting to see in London. The men of power, represented in *Major Barbara* by the arms manufacturer Undershaft, lack ideals; the men of knowledge are impotent because they have no faith; the masses are potentially destructive because they have no knowledge. 'What a debt every intelligent being owes to Bernard Shaw!' Keynes wrote. 'What a debt also to H. G. Wells, whose mind seems to have grown up alongside his readers', so that, in successive phases, he has delighted us and guided our imaginations from boyhood to maturity.'[19]

Keynes returned from his Easter holiday in Spain to a Cambridge crisis. The Provost of King's College, Walter Durnford, grandson of the flogging Dr Keate of Eton, had died on 9 April. Should Keynes offer himself for election? Most of the younger Fellows wanted him to; most of the older ones favoured Clapham, the economic historian, who represented Nonconformity, mountaineering and convention. On 23 April Keynes told his 'dearest darling Provostess' that he was 'weakening', but that he felt it was a 'wrong inclination'. Virginia Woolf reported him to Vanessa, on 29 April, 'torn between the Provostry of King's and respectability; and Gordon Sqre and scalliwags'. In a letter to C. J. Gray, who represented the younger Fellows, Keynes put his doubts in different language which perhaps amounted to the same thing: 'I am much afraid . . . that the position of Provost may be in some ways unsuitable to a person of my activities and temperament.' By this time, it had become clear that, if Keynes stood, the College would be bitterly split. To avoid this, he threw his weight behind a compromise candidate, A. E. Brooke, an elderly divinity professor and uncle of Rupert Brooke, who was duly elected. The mixture of motives which led Maynard to withdraw is nicely, though unkindly, captured by Virginia Woolf:

'Maynard has decided not to stand. . . . He says he would always be called Provost and not Keynes; he would become respectable; he would sink and disappear. . . . So he is *not* lost to Bloomsbury. But as everyone agrees he would almost certainly have failed, the arguments do not convince me. Leonard said he seemed greatly depressed.'[20]

Maynard was out of humour for much of the summer term of 1926. The feasting and drinking which followed Brooke's election left him exhausted and with a 'bad complexion'. On 13 June he wrote to Lydia, 'Last night I was quite mad with patience – I sat cold and alone till nearly half past two determined to win it, but playing so badly from fatigue that it was impossible . . .' On 14 June: 'Nothing could have been slower or more boring than this morning's University Council – I must resign. Today I told my neighbours at the table that in future I would bring my knitting . . .' He was with Leonard Woolf and Gordon Luce for Lydia's first-night appearance on 17 June in *Pulcinella* at Her Majesty's Theatre, spoiling the evening for Leonard with his nervousness. The sensation of the Diaghilev summer season was Stravinsky's *Les Noces* – 'musically it is a wonderful orgy, but as a ballet it is more like mathematics,' Lydia wrote to him on 30 May. Lydia saw that her dancing days were coming to an end: she felt 'mentally shaky after my 6 months absence of legs', feared she was becoming a 'second hand dancer', and felt she would 'like to retire for ever after London season'. On 20 June she and Maynard left London for Berlin, where he was to give a lecture at the University.

II

THE BREAK WITH ASQUITH

The cause of Maynard's depression and irritability had less to do with his failure to get the provostship of King's than with the General Strike and the painful personal circumstances accompanying it. Throughout his life he complained that disturbing public events were bad for his nerves: one reason for the supreme importance he attached to peace and contentment as goals of statesmanship. But there was a further factor. The General Strike produced another upheaval in the Liberal Party, and this time Keynes backed Lloyd George against Asquith. His breach with old friends was not only distressing to him; it made many rub their eyes. The scourge of the Welsh Wizard now emerged as his champion. It was no good Keynes saying 'I support Mr. Lloyd George when he is right, and oppose him when he is wrong.' The Asquithians – Simon, Runciman, Phillips, Maclean, Pringle, Grey, Gladstone – who were bound together by personal loyalty and historic memory rather than by ideas, viewed his abandonment of their old leader as a betrayal. The mistrust which Keynes's policies inspired in sound quarters was now compounded by his cohabitation with sin.

The occasion of the break was the General Strike. The coal industry had finally run out of time. The Samuel Commission, reporting in March 1926, had recommended wage reductions now and reorganisation later. The Miners' Federation rejected the cuts, and the owners the reorganisation; the TUC promised to support the miners. Over-optimistic as ever, Keynes was convinced a bargain would be struck; and, with his usual confidence, told the *Nation*'s readers on 24 April what it should be. The coal-mining industry had to raise its net proceeds by 3s a ton. This could come only from lower wages, economies of production and higher prices to domestic consumers. Keynes suggested 1s from each of the three sources, with a temporary subsidy to help the second. If only life were so reasonable! Keynes thought that the miners would prefer a modest wage reduction to 'widespread unemployment'. He assumed that the government accepted the need for a further subsidy. He believed that the owners accepted the need for some concentration of production on the most efficient pits. All three suppositions were wrong.[21]

The subsidy ran out on Friday, 30 April. Baldwin, displaying a lethargy remarkable even for him, bestirred himself to seek a compromise only in the week it was due to expire. When the Cabinet rejected his proposal to extend it for a fortnight, he broke off negotiations with the TUC on a flimsy pretext: when the TUC delegation arrived at 10 Downing Street on Sunday evening, the Prime Minister had gone to bed.

Keynes blamed the strike on the lethargy and stupidity of the government. In a cable to the *Chicago Daily News* on 6 May, he said that subsidy and negotiations should have continued until the miners had a chance to accept or reject a 'fair and generous offer'. The forces of law and order were bound to prevail, he said, but the problem of 'evolving a better way of conducting our business' remained. He predicted, this time accurately, that the big gainer would be the parliamentary Labour Party. His next comment, written a day later, never appeared, because Leonard Woolf, out of solidarity with the strikers, refused to print the *Nation* on the Hogarth Press.[22] Its opening is Keynes at his best:

> Sir John Simon tells us that the Strike involves breach of contract. Lord Birkenhead declares that the quarrel must not be ended until it is recognised that there is 'one Government and one Government only in this country'. Everyone speaks of 'the attack on the Constitution'. All this is true or partly true. But those whose minds are filled with these ideas and phrases are not thinking or saying the things which it is important to think and say. The strikers are not red revolutionaries; they are not seeking to overturn Parliament; they are not executing the first move of a calculated manoeuvre. They are caught in a coil,

not entirely of their own weaving, in which behaviour, which is futile and may greatly injure themselves and their neighbours, is nevertheless the only way which seems to them to be open for expressing their feelings and sympathies and for maintaining comradeship and keeping faith. The strike is a protest, a demonstration, an expression. . . . Unlike Sir John Simon, it is inarticulate, unlogical, ill calculated. Certainly I cannot put it into words. But my feelings, as distinct from my judgement, are with the workers.[23]

The General Strike, in fact, was called off by the General Council of the TUC, which had never wanted it, on 12 May, after it had received a meaningless assurance from Baldwin that the government would 'consider' certain suggestions put forward by Sir Herbert Samuel. This figleaf barely disguised an unconditional surrender. The miners held out till the autumn, when starvation forced them back on the owners' terms. The government's strategy was vindicated. But in the longer run Keynes's analysis was the more percipient. His view was: one can run a modern industrial society either by conciliating the major interests or by exercising class power. He stood for the former; the government had adopted the latter, and won. But it did not know what to do with its victory. Significantly, Baldwin rejected the package of measures proposed by Lord Birkenhead for permanently weakening the trade unions. Of his proposals to end immunity for trade union funds, to require secret ballots on strike action, to impose restrictions on picketing and changes in the political levy, only the last was enacted.[24] The unions remained unappeased and unbowed. The industrial heartlands of Northern England, Scotland and Wales, already distressed and soon to be crippled by the great depression, were alienated from the Westminster system. The whirlwind was reaped only in the 1970s when, strengthened by decades of full employment and pro-union legislation, the trade unions paid back the government and the middle classes for the wrongs inflicted between the wars. In 1984 the miners rose again, in a conscious, but much more vicious, echo of 1926 and were crushed again. But by this time Keynes's Middle Way of class conciliation and full employment had been abandoned. *On those terms* Britain had proved to be ungovernable. But it might have been very different had it been tried in 1926.

Only one politician, Keynes thought, rose to the occasion. Before the General Strike started Lloyd George had urged the government to keep negotiating until a settlement was reached. After it had been called, he declared support for the government, but flayed it for its dilatoriness in starting negotiations, its precipitancy in breaking them off, its insistence on unconditional surrender and its refusal to print the appeal of the two Archbishops for a negotiated settlement in its strike newspaper, the *British Gazette*. His tone was in marked contrast to that of Asquith and Simon, who laid weight on the illegal and unconstitutional character of the strike.

(Asquith and Grey, in messages to the *British Gazette* on 8 May, insisted on unconditional withdrawal of the strike notices.) As Lloyd George's biographer Peter Rowland puts it, 'there was a distinct difference of opinion between Lloyd George and the other leaders of the Liberal Party as to how the Strike should be treated, for Lloyd George was basically sympathetic towards the miners while Asquith and his colleagues feared that a General Strike would pave the way to revolution'.[25]

Keynes's relations with Lloyd George had been thawing for some time. It was now seven years since he had declared, desperately, to Margot Asquith in Paris that he could not bear working for such a man for another day, another hour. Even then, though, his loathing was pierced by flashes of admiration. 'He can be amazing when one agrees with him,' he had told Bloomsbury's Memoir Club in 1920.[26] Now he was finding that he was agreeing with him more and more. Lloyd George might know nothing about economics and finance. But his expansionist instincts were now much more in tune with Keynes's views than the dreary negatives of the Treasury and the Bank of England, the straitlaced rectitude of Runciman and Simon. As early as 1920 he had declared, 'we must have more output'. He had favoured public works in 1924; in 1925 he had condemned Churchill's 'egregious recklessness' in returning Britain to the gold standard. Out of power, with his natural radicalism reasserting itself, with his energy unimpaired, and in the market for bold ideas, he was a much more attractive proposition than in his days of glory. Lloyd George, too, was an arch-seducer. 'I had a terrible flirtation with [him at a "tête-à-tête lunch party"] yesterday,' Keynes confessed to Lydia on 8 May 1925, 'and have been feeling ashamed of myself ever since! It ended in my promising to ask him to dinner at No. 46 to meet H. G. Wells and now I don't want to at all; – because it isn't really any good. . . . He was slightly pathetic and forlorn, without a friend or an intimate in the world – or so it seemed – and that helped to melt my heart. But one's heart should *never* melt. Don't you agree?' Lloyd George knew how to wait.

A College meeting had prevented Keynes from hearing Lloyd George's speech at Cambridge on the eve of the General Strike, in which he attacked the government for dawdling: 'all talking and no tackling'.

Apparently [Maynard informed Lydia on 2 May] he was brilliant. Dennis [Robertson], who was there, said he had never seen a better entertainment in his life. I saw him arrive in a large car looking just like a prima donna with the last dab of powder where it should be and every hair in place. Afterwards I had tea with him. He was very affable and invited you and me to spend a weekend with him. I accepted, but like your tea invitations, no date was fixed. . . . The coal business is a disgrace of mismanagement with old Baldwin a stuffed dummy. All the same I can't take the General Strike very seriously. Do you?

Lloyd George showed his disapproval of the Asquithian line on the strike by refusing to attend a meeting of the Liberal Shadow Cabinet on 10 May. Asquith, goaded, it is said, by his wife Margot and his daughter Violet Bonham-Carter, chose to make an issue of Lloyd George's non-attendance; after letters from both men to each other appeared in the national press on 26 May, Asquith, supported by the Old Guard, declared that Lloyd George had 'expelled himself' from the Shadow Cabinet, said he would not remain leader of the Party if Lloyd George returned, and called on his friends to support him.

Those friends were too few; and Keynes was no longer one of them. Like most Liberals he thought Lloyd George had shown the true Liberal temper during the strike, and was appalled that Asquith had handed the game to the Labour Party. On 22 May, the *Nation* had seen in the collapse of the strike a new chance for Liberalism to discredit Labour's 'class war' approach to industry and politics; now the opportunities opened up by Lloyd George's display of statesmanship had been lost. 'Who would have believed', Hubert Henderson wrote in the *Nation* of 29 May, 'that in a controversy between these two statesmen Mr. Lloyd George would be triumphantly and unmistakably in the right?' Lord Oxford, he said, had 'blundered'.

Letters attacking the *Nation*'s position now started flooding its correspondence columns; Asquith's family mounted its private bombardment. On 2 June, his son-in-law Maurice ('Bongie') Bonham-Carter wrote in pained terms to Henderson that, while Keynes's neglect of the distinction between a coal strike and a General Strike was explicable because 'he believes that all principles fade into insignificance before the indignity of the return to the gold standard', it was an 'essential part of the Liberal tradition to maintain the sovereignty of Parliament'. In his reply on 4 June, Henderson agreed that it was important to defeat the General Strike, but maintained that it was an equally important part of the Liberal tradition to resist 'Jingo hysteria'. This brought a wonderful letter from Bongie's wife, Violet Bonham-Carter, which poured out all the pent-up grievances, old and new, of the Asquithians against Lloyd George:

I *absolutely* understand your dislike of a Jingo attitude during the Strike – I think I shared it to the full – What I cannot understand is that you (& Maynard!!) – who are not credulous Baptist chaplains attending remote provincial chapels – can seriously acclaim LLG. – the executor of the 'Knock-out blow' & Dog-fight interviews, the organizer & defender of Irish Reprisals . . . the fosterer of every Jingo passion afterwards (you surely remember his inverted Limehouse period when Labour was 'the common enemy'?) – who as lately as last July twitted the Govt. when they gave the subsidy with 'not daring to face cold

steel' . . . *now* in all seriousness as the prophet of conciliation and
peace. . . .

You probably know that last autumn he was planning with
Garvin . . . to become head of a Govt. of Public Safety supported by
the anti-Baldwin Tories . . . the Guest 'Liberals' & . . . one or two
detachable Labour men of the Thomas breed. [When this plan col-
lapsed] LLG. began to seek a new orientation . . . [he] had been seeing
Ramsay with a view to joining them – pledging himself not to compete
for leadership but to content himself with the Ministry of Agriculture
provided he cld put his whole Green Book [on land nationalisation]
into operation. Then the Strike came – the thunder of the Right had
obviously been stolen . . . so he made a bid for the 'Christian' thunder
of the Left.

. . . Do you really & honestly think it possible for my Father – or
indeed any reasonably straight & sensitive man – to continue to work
in confidential relations with LLG. under these circumstances? . . .
The thing was cumulative. . . . Whatever you may think of my Father's
action . . . I cannot believe that you & Maynard (of all people!) genuinely think that LLG. has a fixed needle in his compass pointing Left
or Right or indeed consistently in any direction whatsoever. I think
of Maynard's unpublished chapter in the Economic Consequences of
the Peace in which he compares LLG.'s mind to glass – having no
colour of its own – but receptively catching any shade in the prism
which is thrown across it at a given angle. . . . The Party – led by him
– would cease to be 'Liberal' – it would become a mere subsidized
personal appendage – liable to be marched into any camp at any
moment – at the beck of the highest bidder. . . . LLG. has no
'colleagues' . . . he has not one unsalaried supporter in his immediate
entourage – & in the H.o.C. his backers are mainly . . . old Coalition
wreckage. . . .

That you & Maynard shd. bind yourselves to the chariot-wheels of
this most Protean but also *most* transparent Crook simply because
(apart from Runciman being unsound on the gold standard) he took
on one occasion a few steps down (what you felt to be) the right
turning in pursuit of a cat which had (as a matter of fact) jumped the
other way – wd. really be almost funny even to me – to who [*sic*] it is
also rather sad.[27]

Margot Asquith's assault on Maynard started on 22 May. A passionate
lioness she turned with desperate loyalty on those who hounded her
wounded, but Olympian, mate.

Dearest Maynard,
Nothing has so amazed me as yr. praising LL.G.'s conduct in the
Strike & saying it means 'Liberalism'. Poor LL.G.! his incapacity to

see an inch before his *own* nose & his Press, his lack of all public conscience, as well as his private treachery to his leader & colleagues have *finished* him. . . . On Monday 3rd, H. [Asquith], Grey & all our men told LL.G. the line they wd take in the most illiberal action ever known. LL.G. *entirely* agreed. Between [the] 3rd at noon & Tuesday night he saw a lot of his old friends Beaverbrook etc & changed his whole mind . . . & took up the idiotic line of pro-strike thinking to fish in troubled waters. . . . Till we rid ourselves of LL.G. not one honourable man will either work for us or give us money. H. can't give up *all* his convictions & *all* his friends for any man, not even a Welshman! – *No* one has ever been so generously patiently & humanely dealt with by a Chief as LL.G. but . . . he is a natural cheat & liar & wd blackmail his mother. The Gen. Strike has shown the difference between politicians & statesmen & was stopped by Liberalism and Liberals.

And on 28 April: 'Is this the man who represents Liberalism better than the blundering Oxford? . . . I wd rather be a tiny Party straight than a straggling Party crooked. I may be a fool but I prefer the Truth.' Keynes sent a reply on 30 May:

My dear Margot,

I have been wretched over this business since I heard last Tuesday what was going on. I know what LL.G. is like and so do most of those who feel as I do over this affair – we are under no illusions. But the split has come in such a way that any radical, who is not ready to subordinate his political ideas entirely to personalities, has absolutely no choice. I find a unanimous – astonishingly unanimous – feeling that this is so amongst every single leftish Liberal whom I have spoken to in the last week. A party which has to look forward to consisting mainly of Simon and Runciman seems to me about as gloomy and mouldering an affair as one can conceive. I couldn't breathe in that mortuary. Apparently their rival claims for leadership in the H. of C. depend on whether it is felt that Simon most effectively supported the Govt. in a speech which was bad law or Runciman in a speech which was bad economics.

I see nothing satisfactory in the outlook. But at least my feelings are unchanged. 'The Blundering Oxford' remains the one I should *like* to follow and whom I love and respect.

Yours ever,

J M Keynes

Margot Asquith returned on 31 May with 'It comes to this: LL.G. or H.? – those who prefer the former will not want to retain us as a friend.'[28]

Lloyd George was not slow to cement promising political alliances. On

6–7 June, Maynard and Lydia spent their first weekend at Churt. 'It can't do any harm,' Maynard thought, and 'why not?' They returned to Gordon Square with the gift of a fresh trout caught by a passionate Liberal land reformer. On Monday, Maynard wrote to Lydia, 'LL.G. doesn't taste very nice in the mouth when one smacks the tongue in retrospect. What do you think? However, it's life.' He attended a meeting called by Lloyd George in London on 29 June to discuss setting up a Radical League outside the Liberal Party.[29]

The painful switch of loyalties was made no easier by the fact that on 12 June Asquith had a stroke, which incapacitated him for three months. A letter by Keynes appeared in the *Nation* on the same day. While admitting Lloyd George's faults, he praised him as 'naturally and temperamentally a radical, happiest when his lot lies to the left, in spite of excursions in other directions', a 'great politician – an engine of power for the big public'. The Asquithians were at fault in raking up their old grievances, which preceded the reconciliation of 1924. Lloyd George's conduct during the strike had been admirable. If he left it, the Liberal Party would die of inanition. 'Lord Oxford is a whig. Mr Lloyd George is a radical. The Liberal Party is strongest when these two elements in it, which have always existed side by side, can work together.'[30]

This conciliatory letter brought a sad, but less angry, one from Margot, dated 20 June and written, as was her wont, at 4 a.m.:

> I can see you have *no* idea how ill Henry is. . . . I open all his letters but he only sees the ones I think will cheer him up so I cd not show him yours. When he read the 'Blunder of Ld O' before he was ill he said to me: 'This isnt Maynard, its Henderson; Maynard wd never approve of a Gen. Strike; he's far too clever! but I'm surprised he put it in his paper.' I cd see it hurt him. . . . Remember he is *very* unceltic . . . He is really dying of a broken heart & he is not at *all* sentimental.

Keynes replied on the 27th:

> I am touched by your letter of last Sunday. May he get well again as soon as possible, and above all recover his spirits. If there is one thing which has been apparent in the recent affairs, it has been the affection of *everyone* for Lord Oxford. . . .
>   Ever yours,
>   J. M. Keynes

Keynes never saw Asquith again. He died on 15 February 1928. Maynard's obituary notice in the *Nation* was warm, respectful and just: 'he was the perfect Whig for carrying into execution those Radical projects of his generation which were well judged'. Margot Asquith wrote to him, 'I know dear Maynard that you liked him *very* much once, & that you like me very much now. . . .'

III

THE LIBERAL INDUSTRIAL INQUIRY

Maynard made two weekend excursions from Tilton in the summer of 1926. On Saturday, 7 August he and Lydia went to stay with the Webbs at Passfield Corner in Hampshire, Maynard going on to Easton Lodge to address the ILP Summer School on 'The Future Balance of British Industry'. Beatrice Webb wrote down her impressions of him:

Hitherto he has not attracted me – brilliant, supercilious, and not sufficiently patient for sociological discovery even if he had the heart for it, I should have said. But then I had barely seen him; also I think his love marriage with the fascinating little Russian dancer has awakened his emotional sympathies with poverty and suffering. For when I look around I see no other man who might discover how to control the wealth of nations in the public interest. He is not merely brilliant in expression and provocative in thought; he is a realist: he faces facts and he has persistency and courage in thought and action. By taste an administrator, by talent a man of science, with a remarkable literary gift, he has not the make-up of a political leader. Not that he lacks 'personality' – he is impressive and attractive, he could impose himself on an audience and gather round him a group of followers and disciples; if he could tolerate a political party as God makes it, he could lead it. But he is contemptuous of common men, especially when gathered together in herds. He dislikes the human herd and has no desire to enlist the herd instinct on his side. Hence his antipathy to trade unions, to proletarian culture, to nationalism and patriotism as distinguished from public spirit. The common interests and vulgar prejudices of aristocracies and plutocracies are equally displeasing to him – in fact he dislikes all the common-or-garden thoughts and emotions that bind men together in bundles. He would make a useful member of a Cabinet, but would he ever get there? Certainly not as a member of one of the present Front Benches. I do not know which one . . . he would despise most. As for the rank and file! Heaven help them. What Keynes might achieve is a big scheme of social engineering; he might even be called in to carry it out, but as an expert and not as a representative.

As an ardent lover of the bewitching Lydia Lopokova this eminent thinker and political pamphleteer is charming to contemplate.[31]

On 25 September, Keynes was one of '14 professors' summoned to Churt. 'The occasion', Keynes reported to H. G. Wells, 'was a gathering of a few trying to lay the foundations of a new radicalism; and for the first time for years I felt a political thrill and the chance of something interesting being possible in the political world. But I have no trust yet. Ll.G. was as good as gold – it is scarcely conceivable that anyone could be so good. But how long it will last I don't know.'[32] Earlier in the year, the Liberal Summer School Committee (which included Keynes) had decided to set up an industrial inquiry. Lloyd George had promised to back it with £10,000 from his fund and the services of a secretariat. The events of the early summer cast doubt on the commitment. But on 15 October Asquith resigned the Party leadership, leaving Lloyd George in control. For the next three years he poured out his heart, energy, brains and money in an effort to revive a party dying at its roots. It was a glorious but forlorn battle. None of the top Liberal politicians – all, except Sir Herbert Samuel, Asquithian leftovers – really believed in him or his plans; they were, anyway, a colourless lot. The Liberal revival depended on one man's force and another man's brains. Lloyd George was the political tycoon; Keynes the thinker. Did Keynes now see himself as the Brahma to Lloyd George's Shiva?

On the Inquiry, Keynes served on an executive committee of a dozen, headed by Walter Layton. There were initially five specialist committees: state and industry (Ramsay Muir), labour and the trade unions (E. D. Simon), unemployment (Lloyd George), pay and status (E. H. Gilpin), industrial and financial organisation (Keynes), staffed by twenty-five supporting experts and politicians. Keynes's committee was responsible for covering 'the organisation of business' and 'national finance'. These reflected the interest of the author of the *Tract on Monetary Reform* and 'The End of Laissez-Faire' in stabilising a 'sticky' economy. Keynes was not given (or did not choose) the unemployment problem. One wonders what the result would have been had he and his fellow economists on the Inquiry – Layton, Henderson, Robertson, Stamp – had the unemployment brief.

While the Industrial Inquiry got down to business, Keynes was educating himself, for the first and last time, in the practical problems faced by a declining British industry. As readers of this biography will be well aware, Keynes's world was that of the ancient universities, Westminster politics, administration and finance, extended only by his involvement in the high culture of Bloomsbury. The world of *homo faber* was a closed book to him. Friends and correspondents the world over included economists, bankers, intellectuals, journalists; few manufacturers were numbered among them. One exception was Lydia's friend Samuel Courtauld, the artificial silk manufacturer, with interests in both Britain and the United States, and enlightened views on industrial management which he applied to his own businesses. There was some contact with the big Liberal Quaker business families – the Frys, Rowntrees and Cadburys. Apart from such links,

Keynes's knowledge of business life was theoretical and statistical; and theory and numbers were illuminated for him by some very characteristic prejudices.

Unlike Marshall, Keynes had little respect for the business vocation. Marshall wrote that 'the higher forms of mental activity, those which are constructive and not merely critical, tend to promote a just appreciation of the nobility of business work rightly done'.[33] Keynes was a much more typical product of the ancient universities in ranking business activity very low in his scale of values. 'Putting money making and capacity aside,' he had asked a meeting of the Apostles as a young man, 'is there any brother who would not rather be a scientist than a businessman, and an artist than a scientist?'[34] Keynes ranked business life so low partly because he considered that the material goods produced by entrepreneurs had less ethical value than the intellectual and aesthetic goods produced by dons and artists, partly because he despised the 'love of money' as a motive for action.

Under the influence of Shaw and Wells he began to take a more favourable attitude to the business tycoon as a type of social reformer; and to see the evolution of big business as providing a motivational Middle Way between profit-maximisation and public service. But these speculations remained essentially abstract: he could not, for example, make the link between Shaw's Undershaft and Sir Alfred Mond, chairman of Imperial Chemical Industries, who had opposed the return to the gold standard and who was actually trying to apply Keynes's ideas of industrial co-operation in the Mond–Turner conversations he started with the TUC in 1927. Keynes was put off by Mond's strong anti-socialism: but what else did he expect of a business tycoon?[35]

In any case, Mond was exceptional. What chiefly impressed Keynes about British businessmen was their stupidity and laziness. He was a firm believer in the three-generation cycle: the man of energy and imagination creates the business: the son coasts along; the grandson goes bankrupt. When friends asked his advice about which solicitor or stockbroker or estate agent to go to he told them to enquire carefully about when the firm had been established: this would tell them exactly which point in the cycle of decay it had reached. In 'Am I a Liberal?' he wrote:

> I believe that the seeds of the intellectual decay of Individualistic Capitalism are to be found in . . . the hereditary principle. The hereditary principle in the transmission of wealth and the control of business is the reason why the leadership of the Capitalist cause is weak and stupid. It is too much dominated by third-generation men. Nothing will cause a social institution to decay with more certainty than its attachment to the hereditary principle. It is an illustration of this that by far the oldest of our institutions, the Church, is the one which has always kept itself free from the hereditary taint.[36]

Keynes's remarks brought an appreciative letter from Laurence Cadbury, the 'youngest of the third generation' of the cocoa firm, who hoped that Keynes might allow 'a few exceptions to the general rule'. Cadbury made the point that a firm selling a proprietary line could carry on almost indefinitely 'by its own momentum'; he proposed a system of 'efficiency auditing' to be carried out by the Board of Trade.[37]* Cadbury served with Keynes on the Liberal Industrial Inquiry.

Despite his strictures on business competence, Keynes took with surprising levity the problem of training people for a business career. He rejected the notion of courses for business studies. It was a mistake for a university, he said in a radio discussion in 1927, to 'attempt vocational training. Their business is to develop a man's intelligence and character in such a way that he can pick up relatively quickly the special details of that business he turns to subsequently.'[38] He was about to apply the theory to himself.

Keynes was drawn into the problems of coal and textiles – Britain's two chief decaying industries – by the return to the gold standard and the General Strike. In 'The Economic Consequences of Mr Churchill' he had argued that going back to gold at the pre-war parity had put two shillings on each ton of coal, logically entailing a 10 per cent wage reduction. A year later, however, his emphasis had switched to reducing surplus capacity. In 'Coal: A Suggestion', published in the *Nation* on 24 April 1926[39] he attacked the coal owners for having no ideas except to reduce wages and extend hours – the latter being 'half-witted' in view of the surplus productive capacity in the industry. These proposals showed 'that we are dealing with a decadent, third-generation industry'. The main need was 'to transfer men out of the industry, to curtail production and to raise export prices'. He suggested that the owners form a cartel to restrict output.

In an article published in the *Nation* on 13 November 1926, Keynes contrasted the situation in two decaying industries, coal and cotton. Coal had ruined itself by uncontrolled overproduction, cotton by 'organised short-time extending over five years'.† He calculated that half of Lancashire's business in coarser cottons had gone permanently to Japan. But instead of concentrating production on its most efficient units – mainly those producing finer cottons – Lancashire had kept its capacity and workforce through short-time working which raised its costs of production above competitive levels by adding additional overhead costs to wage levels which were too high. Reduced sales, countered by short-time working, leading to higher

---

*Third-generation Cadbury's had amalgamated with seventh-generation Fry's in 1918, as the only alternative to absorption by the Swiss company Nestlé. Nestlé took over Rowntree in 1988.

†Short-time working was made possible by the fact that unemployment benefit could be claimed for the off-days. It was a disguised form of subsidy, which made sense only on the assumption that full-capacity working would soon be restored. It was kept going because no one could think of anything else to do.

costs was a 'cumulative road to perdition only limited by the rate at which other countries can erect new spindles'. The termination of short-time working was urgently needed through 'amalgamation, grouping, or elimination of mills'. Keynes partly blamed the banks, which had extended an endless overdraft line to the mill owners, but he soon reverted to his familiar theme:

> The mishandling of currency and credit by the Bank of England since the war, the stiff-neckedness of the coalowners, the apparently suicidal behaviour of the leaders of Lancashire raises a question of the suitability and adaptability of our business man to the modern age of mingled progress and retrogression. What has happened to them – the class in which a generation or two generations ago we could take a just and worthy pride? Are they too old or obstinate? Or what? Is it that too many of them have risen not on their own legs, but on the shoulders of their fathers and grandfathers?[40]

This was explosive stuff: here was a mere theoretician telling practical men how to run their affairs! However, there were some who were willing to listen. On 16 November 1926, the Short-Time Committee of the Federation of Master Cotton Spinners invited Keynes to Manchester to discuss the points raised in his article. Keynes came to Manchester on 22 November. His meeting with the Short-Time Committee was followed by a communiqué in which he advocated a cartel to fix minimum selling prices and assign quotas.[41] This rapid shift in Keynes's position is typical of his flexibility. The idea of permanently shutting down productive capacity was still too shocking to contemplate. So Keynes put his weight behind a more flexible and efficient scheme for market-sharing, with a provision for quotas to be transferred from weaker to stronger firms.

The plan matured at a three-hour meeting between Keynes and a deputation of spinners from the American section held in London on 16 December. The American section, which specialised in the coarser yarns, had been the hardest hit by Japanese competition. It was also the least organised, being divided into over 300 fiercely competing family firms. A committee of spinners, led by John Ryan, had been trying to organise it into a cartel – the Cotton Yarn Association. Ryan, a statistician who had read mathematics at Cambridge, was the real brains behind the attempt to reorganise the industry. Following the London meeting, Keynes accepted the position of consultant and publicist for this embryonic body.

On 4 January 1927, Keynes returned to Manchester to address a meeting of spinners of American cotton. After his speech, he met the masters and men in separate rooms. His first cousin Neville Brown, who had joined the family textile business, recalls Keynes remarking that the men were more intelligent than the masters. He did not feel his speech was a success. 'The pen, and not speech, is my weapon,' he told Neville Brown.

He knew nothing about Lancashire and asked me about the spinning trade. I remember telling him that whilst the spinning mills which had modernised themselves were going bankrupt, old fashioned family concerns like those in Royton, Oldham, which had spent nothing on plant, were surviving except when they cut prices against each other out of family pride. 'Montagues and Capulets' he said. I said I had not heard of mills of these names. . . . My abiding recollection is of the skill with which he saved my blushes.[42]

In his speech, Keynes presented the choice as between orderly marketing leading to gradual reorganisation; and neighbour-begging price-cutting, leaving widespread bankruptcy to do its work. He appealed to the bankers to provide working capital: 'I tell them to have courage, to rise from their beds and walk, to resume the functions of hearing and speech.'* A resolution supporting the formation of an association was passed with one dissentient vote.

The Cotton Yarn Association was launched on 18 February 1927, with Lincoln Tattersall as chairman and John Ryan as secretary. At first all went well: about 200 firms of the 350 firms in the American section joined, representing 20 million spindles, or 76 per cent of capacity. But by August 1927 'a point had been reached', Keynes wrote, 'at which the opportunities of the spinners outside the Association to obtain all its benefits without paying any part of the price are becoming intolerable'.[43] Efforts to stop free-riding by bringing in the minority failed. By November 1927, the Association was obliged to relieve its members of the obligation to observe the short-time rules and minimum selling prices. In the summer of 1928 Keynes tried to get financial backing for Ryan's proposal to form a combine of mills to rationalise production and buy up surplus capacity. Partly as a result of these efforts the Lancashire Cotton Corporation was formed, with Bank of England backing, early in 1929; much of the management came from the Cotton Yarn Association. Keynes commented, 'One is disposed to murmur with Galileo – It moves all the same.' John Ryan, whom Keynes described as 'far and away the best man' associated with Lancashire cotton,[44] went on to a successful career as chairman of the British Closures Manufacturers' Association.

Keynes used to come away from Manchester with feelings of 'intense pessimism', provoked by the short-sighted individualism of the Capulets and Montagues, the hostility and indifference of other elements in the industry to the problems of the American section, the unconstructive attitude of the unions, the sermonising of those who wanted to put the industry through the wringer, the ingrained dislike of any suggestion of monopoly.

*Cf. his reply to the City editor of the *Manchester Guardian Commercial* on 2 November 1925: 'So I appeal to him to step out of his coffin, discard his strait-laced shroud, and join the ranks of the living.'

'Thus and with these ingredients, good and bad and indifferent, phlegm and spleen and frog's brains, and rosemary for remembrance, is the witch's cauldron filled.'[45] All his prejudices against third-generation men were confirmed. Late in the Second World War he lamented that Hitler's bombers had not been able to destroy every factory in Lancashire 'at an hour when the directors were sitting there and no one else. . . . How else we are to gain the exuberant inexperience which is necessary, it seems, for success I cannot surmise.'[46] Immediately, Keynes's involvement with cotton reinforced his pessimism about curing unemployment by tackling the supply-side problems of British industry. The rocks could not be shifted; they had to be submerged in a rising tide of prosperity.

Keynes's education in the realities of British business life fertilised his contributions to the Liberal Industrial Inquiry. Specifically, they strengthened his conviction that the era of the individual family firm was over, and the day of the combine had arrived.

The day after his speech at Manchester on 4 January 1927, he addressed Liberal candidates on the theme of 'Liberalism and Industry' at the National Liberal Club. Keynes rarely told a joke, but this time he found one apposite to his theme. A friend of his had recently visited an asylum and had asked the warders how they managed to run the place with so few staff. 'Oh,' came the answer, 'lunatics never combine.' Keynes added, 'I wish I had heard that story soon enough to repeat it in Manchester yesterday.'

In his speech, Keynes once more staked out a Middle Way Liberalism based on 'the contrivings of science and constructive industry' against the 'anti-communist rubbish' of the right and the 'anti-capitalist rubbish' of the left. Both were remote from 'the actual nature of the economic world we live in', the 'new industrial revolution, a new economic transition . . .'.

In the world of feelings, the most important shift had been from the 'optimistic *Zeitgeist*' of the nineteenth century to the 'pessimistic *Zeitgeist*' of the twentieth. Neither businessmen nor workers had the same confidence that 'private ambition and compound interest' would carry them to paradise; in particular the working classes,

> now, as a delayed result of the franchise reforms of the last two generations, on the road to political power . . . no longer have sufficient hopes in the general trend of things to divert their attention from other grievances. . . . the great danger of today . . . is lest the immense destructive force of organised Labour should, in its blindness and ignorance, destroy the opportunity . . . to guide the transition along sound lines.

The small family firm was giving way to the large business run by salaried managers, partly for technical and marketing reasons, but also because 'methods which were well adapted to continually expanding businesses are ill adapted to stationary or declining ones. . . . Combination in the business world, just as much as in the labour world, is the order of the day; it would be useless as well as foolish to try to combat it. Our task is to take advantage of it, to regulate it, to turn it into the right channels.'

The main tasks of government in this 'age of transition' were: to diffuse knowledge of industrial conditions; to prepare policies to deal with industrial shocks; to guide savings into channels 'most conducive to national prosperity'; to experiment with 'all kinds of new partnerships between the state and private enterprise'; to have 'a wages and hours policy'; to promote industrial training and labour mobility.[47]

Little of the work of the Liberal Industrial Inquiry has survived in Keynes's papers. According to his engagement diary, his Committee met at his house in London several times in the winter of 1926–7. At a plenary session at Churt from 8 to 11 April 1927, two committees, Keynes's and Ramsay Muir's, were entrusted with preparing a complete draft of the report by 17 June. After a meeting of Keynes's original Committee at King's College, he wrote to Lydia on Sunday, 29 May, 'I am worn to death with food and talking and too much company. I entertained my Liberals royally until dinner time tonight. Now they have gone away. They were nice and sensible and we did good work spending hours going through drafts. But it is exhausting. I must try to rest my nerves and stomach for a bit.'*

However, 'readjusting and readorning' the 'Liberal blather' went on all through 1927. There were four more weekends at Churt – 24–26 June, 17–19 September, 28–30 October and 9–11 December – to hammer the report into final shape, Lloyd George providing a fleet of Daimlers to ferry members of the Inquiry to and from his house. On 31 July, Keynes introduced the Liberal Summer School at Cambridge to one of his main themes in a talk entitled 'The Private and the Public Concern', in which he declared that the demarcation between the two shifts 'in accordance with the practical needs of the day.'[48] At his now traditional garden party at King's, Lloyd George replaced Asquith as the guest of honour. More redrafting took place in October. In late November Keynes spent a day devising a new scheme 'for the rating reform of the country' after objections from E. D. Simon to the original draft.[49] Finally it was done. *Britain's Industrial Future* was published, in yellow covers, at the beginning of February 1928. '[It] has had rather a bad press,' Keynes wrote to Lydia on 5 February, 'but I daresay it deserves it. Long-winded, speaking when it has nothing to say, as well as when it has, droning at intervals "Liberals, Liberals all are we, gallant-hearted Liberals." It would have been so much better at half the length

---

*Attending at King's that weekend were Keynes, R. H. Brand, Sidney Russell-Cooke, H. D. Henderson, H. L. Nathan (a Liberal MP), D. H. Robertson and F. R. Salter (a Cambridge historian). The secretaries were W. McEagar and J. Menken. This was the eighth and last meeting of the original Keynes Committee.

splashing only what is new and interesting and important.' To H. G. Wells he wrote on 18 January,

> It has been a heavy piece of work to produce, and I am afraid it will be a heavy one to read. I hope never again to be embroiled in co-operative authorship on this scale. The parts with which I have been particularly concerned are Book II and Book V . . . But anyhow, it is a pretty serious effort to make a list of the things in the politico-industrial sphere which are practicable and sensible. It may therefore have a good deal of influence on future political programmes, whether or not there is a Liberal Party to put the matter through.[30]

Keynes was right: the report is heavy reading. 'How many people', it asks on p. 78, 'have any clear idea of the constitution of the Metropolitan Water Board?' and then goes on to expound it, with appropriate references to the 'great researches of Mr. and Mrs. Sidney Webb'. The report inhabits the world of means, not of ends. This suited Keynes: it was useless, he told Philip Kerr, to inscribe 'pious ideas on a political banner of a kind which could not possibly be embodied in legislation'.[51] Nevertheless it addressed the central political problems of the day: the role of the state in the economy (though, of course, without reference to the later Keynesian theory of demand management), and class conciliation in industry. On both these issues it tried to carve out a Middle Way between individualism and state socialism. Much of its Leger-like vision found expression in the machinery of the 'mixed economy' set up in the 1940s. Other proposals, more distinctively Liberal, fell by the wayside. The idea of two-tier boards for large companies, with the top tier containing employees' representatives, was taken up, without success, by the Bullock Report in 1976. Proposals for employee share-ownership and for a variable element in workers' pay, linked to their firm's profitability, started to find favour only in the Thatcherite 1980s. Keynes himself, though, was responsible for introducing profit-sharing at the National Mutual.

At the end of April 1927, Keynes had prepared a draft on 'The Financial and Industrial Structure of the State', based on his talk to Liberal candidates in January, which was intended to provide a general framework for the whole report. Little of it survives in the final version. But it is the most compact expression of his general approach at this time, though doubtless tailored to the needs of his Party. Its main theme is the contrast between the nineteenth-century world of small private firms operating in a continually expanding economy and the twentieth-century world of joint-stock compan-ies, run by salaried managers under the nominal control of anonymous, ignorant shareholders, faced with large-scale structural adjustment. The tendency towards cartel, merger and monopoly was driven not only by the technical conditions of production and the financial advantages of large-scale industry in raising money from the Stock Exchange, but by the menace of overproduction and surplus capacity. Adaptation had become both more necessary and more difficult. Thus the picture of society painted by the theoretical individualist no longer 'fits the facts as a whole'. Great businesses of vast scale, salaried management and diffused ownership had to be accepted as naturally evolved, containing elements of efficiency and inefficiency. Law and central organisation needed to be adjusted 'to the actual state of affairs'.

While the old individualism was passing away, conscious experiments were being made on social lines, some centralised, others semi-centralised, some decentralised, but all divorced 'from the pure private profit criterion which still characterises large-scale business of the modern type'. They were confronted with 'a great variety of intermediate types' between pure private profit and non-profit making concerns'. Keynes went on to give a list of 'the various types of socialised, semi-socialised, and other State-regulated enterprises'; claimed that they controlled two-thirds of the total capital of the country; suggested that 'evolution' was tending to convert private companies into public or semi-official boards, with capital in the form of fixed-interest bonds rather than shares; and argued that such boards would take over increasing parts of industry, that there was no reason to suppose that they would be less efficient than the boards of large private companies and that 'the choice between a Public Board and a Private Company' would 'resolve itself into little more than a question of the appointment of the Directors'.[52]

This draft brought strong criticism from the banker Robert Brand, whose Liberalism was distinctly more right-wing than Keynes's. (He had written a pamphlet 'Why I Am Not a Socialist' in 1925, in which he had defended profit as a reward for risk and argued that state enterprises would involve the community in vast losses because they were sheltered from the failure which private enterprise visits on the incompetent.) Brand argued that the idea that two-thirds of large-scale industry was no longer administered by private enterprise was definitely misleading. Apart from public utility enterprises, not a single manufacturing or commercial enterprise appeared on Keynes's list. The extension of the board principle was desirable in some areas – for example, where a natural monopoly existed – but definitely not over 'ordinary' industry. The spread of shareholding did not have any bad consequences which could not be remedied by greater publicity. Instead of turning the small shareholder into a holder of government bonds, wider share owning should be encouraged.

> I certainly hold strongly to the opinion that the world is essentially a 'chancy' and risky place, and will always remain so. . . . I would prefer the losses resulting from the risks inherent in almost every sphere of life coming out into the open . . . rather than being hidden and con-

cealed as they are where public or semi-public corporations can cover them up by a recourse to rates and taxes . . . [53]

The issues here split Liberalism straight down the middle. Although Keynes was a gambler by temperament, he was much less willing to take *social* risks than was Brand. This was connected with a different judgement on the link between efficiency and profit. Brand came to industrial problems from the side of business, or money-making. 'Knowledge of real life', he wrote in 'Why I Am Not a Socialist', showed that Courts of Efficiency, Audit and Professional Honour, such as the Webbs proposed, were no substitute for the Court of Profit. Keynes came to the same problems from the side of academic life, administration, public service. The necessity of profit as a spur to effort, he wrote in the report, was greatly exaggerated. 'It has never been even supposed to be true . . . of the soldier, the statesman, the civil servant, the teacher, the scientist, the technical expert.' And what was true of this group was true of most people: 'a certain salary, plus the hope of promotion or of a bonus, is what the generality of mankind prefers'.[54] Thus the trade-off between stability and efficiency could be made more favourable than Brand supposed. Perhaps Keynes was already starting to idealise his youthful period in the India Office: at the time he had complained of 'government by dotardry'.

Brand's objections proved decisive. Most of Keynes's evolutionary speculations were omitted from Book II; a strong section on the virtues of individualism was inserted;[55] the suggestion that the public concern might become the typical unit of industrial organisation was dropped; and proposals for reorganising business structure largely limited to making the various existing forms of public concern more 'lively and efficient'.[56]

However, there is a further theme in Keynes's section of the report, which throws light on his later proposal for the 'somewhat comprehensive socialisation of investment.'[57] *Britain's Industrial Future* proposed that the investment funds of the public concerns, whether borrowed or (as with the road fund) raised by taxation, should be pooled, and segregated into a capital budget, to be spent under the direction of a national investment board. Keynes estimated that the board would influence or control the spending of £100m. p.a., or one-fifth of annual national savings, using it to finance 'new capital expenditure by all central, local, or *ad hoc* official bodies . . .' as well as to make advances for new capital improvements to railways, or even to private companies, on the lines of the Trade Facilities Acts.[58] In addition, the state should pay off £100m. of debt a year instead of the £40m. it was currently doing, and attract new savings through the issue of national investment bonds for capital development, thus slowly replacing dead-weight debt by productive debt without increasing the outstanding amount of loans. 'We have here, with the least possible disturbance, an instrument of great power for the development of the national wealth and the provision of employment. An era of rapid progress in equipping the country with all the material adjuncts of modern civilisation might be inaugurated, which would rival the great Railway Age of the nineteenth century.'[59] Like most political manifestos, the report did not mention that such a sinking-fund policy would mean an extra 1s on the income tax. The more important flaw was that Keynes could not give a convincing theoretical answer to the question why the modern equivalent of the Railway Age could not be built on private savings privately employed as the original had been. His only reply was lamely institutional: 'the existing machinery for investment [does not necessarily preserve] the correct balance between expenditure on Public Utilities at home and loans for similar purposes abroad . . .'.[60] He touched briefly on the point that increased Treasury competition for funds might raise the interest rate; but remarked only that to forgo a public investment programme for this reason would be 'desperately misguided'.[61]

There were a few typical Keynes touches in the remaining chapters of Book 2. Ignorance, chapter XI proclaimed, is the root of the 'chief political and social evils of the day'. It fostered class suspicion, made possible the acquisition of great fortunes through insider knowledge, bred 'risk, uncertainty, and precariousness of business, from which spring, on the one hand, unemployment, bankruptcies, and waste, and on the other hand, those great fortunes which fall to the not specially deserving individuals who are lucky in the lottery', and made the lot of the economist truly pitiable. 'How can economic science become a true science, capable, perhaps, of benefitting the human lot as much as all the other sciences put together, so long as the economist, unlike other scientists, has to grope for and guess at the relevant data of experience?' It concluded, 'The nationalising of knowledge is the one case for nationalisation which is overwhelmingly right.'[62] There was a call for an economic general staff to utilise expert knowledge, and the now familiar attack on the hereditary principle.[63]

Book 5 on national finance added little of interest to the student of Keynes. In a striking phrase, the process of revaluing the currency was likened to the 'once fashionable medical policy of "bleeding" . . . [it] is infallibly accompanied, whenever taken, by severe trade depression'.[64] The Bank of England should be more accountable and less secretive in its operations;[65] the national accounts should be reformed to distinguish between the capital and current account, and between national and local taxes and expenditure. There was an interesting suggestion for a separate, or earmarked, social services budget.[66] The report took no view on the desirable burden of taxation, but was clear that any economies in expenditure should come from defence and not the social services.[67]* It emphasised the 'disastrous effects' of the business rate: extracting contributions from industries in proportion not to their profits but to fixed capital was a 'vicious principle'.[68]

Book 4 of the report, drafted under the direction of Lloyd George rather than Keynes, makes the important distinction between 'normal' (that is, pre-war) and 'abnormal' (post-war) unemployment, which dominated the thinking of the times. Roughly half of the 10 per cent unemployment of the 1920s was regarded as 'abnormal'.[69] This distinction was the basis of Lloyd George's famous pledge in the 1929 general election to reduce unemployment 'in the course of a single year to normal proportions'.

IV

CONCLUSION

What can we now say about the patterns forming in Keynes's mind? Central to his thought is the attempt to define the character of his age. Economics as a guide to policy was useless unless it grasped the 'nature of what is happening'. 'What is happening' referred not just to events in the material world but also to people's perceptions of those events, and the expectations about the future to which those perceptions gave rise. Combination, or collective organisation, which Keynes identified as the dominant trend of his period, reflected both technical developments in production and marketing – the advantages to be had from economies of scale – and a defensive reluctance to pay the price of change – this in turn reflecting both the growth of social conscience and a shift to a more pessimistic *Zeitgeist*, the latter an inevitable product of the First World War and post-war disorganisation. Both sides of politics failed to grasp 'the significance of what is happening'. The left mistook the defensive organisations of the workers as revolutionary vanguards; the right continued to mouth the platitudes of individualism,

---

*The report argued that, in the era of disarmament, Britain was arming itself almost as vigorously as in 1913. The following passage bears such a family resemblance to a passage Keynes wrote at the time of the Boer War (see Skidelsky, *Keynes*, i, 90) that it seems plausible to attribute it to him:

> There is no automatic standard of reasonableness in this connection [desirable level of armaments]; but we may find comparatively firm ground if we regard our expenditure on defence as an insurance premium incurred to enable us to live our lives in peace and consider what rate of premium we have paid for this privilege in the past. During the last quarter of the nineteenth century we were in no imminent danger of war. . . . Our defence expenditure was £25 millions – a premium of 2 per cent. [of national income]. In 1913 . . . the premium had jumped to 3½ per cent. To-day it is still 3 per cent., though we see no reason for regarding this country as in greater peril than in the last quarter of the nineteenth century. (*BIF*, 428)

Notable in this period is Keynes's use of images of life and death. He called on the leaders of thought and action to join the 'ranks of the living', to resume the functions of 'hearing and speech', to step out of their coffins, mortuaries, shrouds, to stop 'bleeding' the patient to death – an imagery that goes back to his description of Woodrow Wilson as the 'blind and deaf Don Quixote'. Most politicians could 'hear' the voice of the people, but they could not 'see' what was happening; and so they too were allies of the forces of death, not of life.

'Vigilant observation' was thus the first quality Keynes demanded of those in the business of human betterment. An indispensable tool for the dispersal of fog was adequate statistics. Ignorance of the 'facts of the situation' was the chief mechanical barrier to the making of wise policy. But Keynes never believed that statistical facts could tell one what was happening, or what to do. They were data for making patterns in the mind. It was in this sense that he wanted policymakers to 'see' what was happening. The task of statesmanship was to understand, and work with, the grain of the times, the task of 'science' to maximise the constructive possibilities which the times offered. There was no single 'wisdom' for all ages; the frontier between the private and the public shifted with changes in technology, changes in standards of comfort, changes in political and industrial organisation, changes in international relations and the interaction between these and other things and the psychology of society. People who give mechanical replies to the question of what Keynes would have done in the 1980s or 1990s ignore the supreme importance he attached to getting the character of the age right as a first step to theorising and policymaking. Vigilant observation should direct theoretical and practical endeavour; political economy comes before economics.

With economics proper, a more specialised gift of sight was needed. Economics spoke in models, or logical constructs. It was not enough to show that such models failed to 'fit' the facts. One had, somehow, to tease out their tacit assumptions, which themselves were highly abstract distillations of empirical messiness. The key tacit assumption underlying orthodox economics which Keynes identified in the 1920s was what he called the principle of diffusion, the view that the economic organism was sufficiently fluid and mobile to allow any disturbance to work itself out rapidly through marginal adjustments to a new position of satisfactory equilibrium. This assumption was obsolete. Not only had the growth of monopoly and humanitarian feelings made the economic system more rigid; but the 'continuous crescendo' of the nineteenth century which made marginal adjustments relatively easy had come to an end.

In the 1920s most of Keynes's work was policy-oriented; he took it for granted that the principle of diffusion was too impaired to guarantee an economy, subject to the kind of shocks Britain's had been, a rapid return to a satisfactory state of equilibrium. So he plotted and planned different types of state intervention – stabilising monetary interventions to offset shocks, and public-works types of interventions to 'submerge' the 'rocks' in a 'rising tide of prosperity'. But he did not seriously consider what might be the theoretical, or logical, consequences of abandoning a principle of diffusion which worked through small changes in relative prices. How, in fact, does a 'stationary or slowly progressive community' adjust to shocks? What form does the principle of diffusion take under those circumstances? What is the theoretical account to be given of it? In the coal and textile industries he had experienced local examples of the actual mechanism: output and employment fall, surplus capacity develops. But he was not yet in a position to show how localised contractions of activity might work, through the principle of diffusion, to generalise depression rather than recovery. For he had not yet challenged, or perhaps even sought to challenge, another building block of the orthodox theory, bound up with the classical principle of diffusion: Say's Law, which stated the impossibility of *general* – as opposed to local – gluts.

In the 1920s Keynes sketched in much of the institutional background to the vision which would inspire his *General Theory*. It is the picture of a sluggish economy, which having fallen into a rut needs the helping hand of the state to pull it out of it. The great depression, though, had not happened, and that affected an economy – the American – far less sclerotic than the British economy. In the *General Theory*, purely psychological factors play the dominant role: industrial topography is taken as given, and not further analysed. Yet the fickle psychologies of investors and entrepreneurs wreak their havoc on whole economies only because the expanding frontier of nineteenth-century capitalism has come to an end. The state emerges in Keynes's thought as the last frontier, the last unused psychological resource. So much was already clear to him. The task of translating the vision into economic theory was to prove immeasurably more difficult.

CHAPTER NINE

The Case of the Missing Savings

In politics and economic policy Keynes worked closest with Hubert Henderson; in economic theory his main partner was Dennis Holmes Robertson. From 1913 to 1930 it is almost impossible to say which ideas were Keynes's and which Robertson's. They started sparking each other off when Robertson was writing his dissertation on business cycles in 1912 and 1913. Robertson's textbook *Money* (1922) expounded the same theory of money as Keynes's *Tract on Monetary Reform* in 1923. In *Banking Policy and the Price Level* (1926) Robertson linked changes in the demand for money to changes in saving relative to investment. Keynes's *A Treatise on Money*, developing this saving–investment analysis, followed in 1930, although it diverged significantly from Robertson's 'forced saving' thesis. In their published work, Robertson was the trail-blazer, Keynes followed, though Robertson always acknowledged the 'immeasurable debt' which he owned to Keynes. Their open divergence started only in 1931. It is a tribute to Cambridge's 'passion for truth' that they worked together harmoniously for so long, despite the great difference in their methods and characters; and even though they fell out in 1930s, there was a partial reconciliation during the Second World War.

Keynes's great respect for Robertson's ability was reinforced by personal affection. Also much in their background and training was the same: both were scholars at Eton, though Robertson was a classical scholar and had no mathematics; both were pupils of Marshall and Pigou at Cambridge; both had artistic leanings; both were excellent stylists; and both had a Victorian sense of duty. But Keynes was much more of a gambler, in private life and in ideas – and, at the highest level, more creative.

Born in 1890, Dennis Robertson was the sixth and youngest child of a schoolmaster and parson of Scottish origin. By the time he arrived on the scene, the Revd James Robertson's family, like that of Mr Quiverful, had much need of fortune's helping hand. His father had just resigned as headmaster of Haileybury, under some sort of cloud.[1] Dennis Robertson grew up in straitened circumstances at Whittlesford parsonage in Cambridgeshire. His father taught him the classics so successfully that he gained a scholarship to Eton the year Keynes left. This parsonical and parsimonious background clung to Robertson all his life. In 1928 he wondered 'whether it is sensible for a person of my habits and fortune (about £5000)' to have three-fifths of his savings in equities.[2] He hung on and lost most of his investment in the Crash of 1929. Thereafter 'Dennis Prefers Bonds' became a Cambridge joke.

Robertson was Eton's top scholar and became Captain of the School; he came up to Trinity College, Cambridge in 1908 as a classical scholar, gained a top first in Part I of the Classical Tripos in 1910, and then switched to economics because he wanted to help the poor, gaining another first in Part II of the Economics Tripos in 1912. He followed Keynes as president of the Liberal Society and president of the Union; and Keynes was his director of studies. But he was not part of the Apostolic circle, becoming, unusually, an Apostle only in 1926, at the age of thirty-six. Robertson volunteered at the outbreak of war, serving as a transport officer in the 11th Battalion, the London Regiment, mainly in the Middle East, where he gained the Military Cross. He had just become a Fellow of Trinity College, Cambridge, and lived there from 1919 to 1938.

Steven Runciman, an undergraduate, and then a young colleague of Robertson's, at Trinity in the 1920s remembers him as 'a cosy avuncular bachelor who, in some ways I suppose, had never quite grown up: which made him very approachable to undergraduates'. Unlike the relentlessly brilliant Keynes, he had a gift for putting the young at their ease.[3] He was one of Cambridge's repressed bachelor dons, much given to romantic love affairs with handsome young men – in the mid–1920s he became infatuated with Dadie Rylands. He was an excellent amateur actor, often being seen in Cambridge in productions of the Marlowe Society, the Amateur Dramatic Club and the Greek play, and excelling in such Shakespearian parts as Justice Shallow. In 1928 he described to Maynard a cosily academic domestic scene: 'Dadie is correcting a school certificate paper on King Lear, one of which, in answer to a question on the character of Cordelia, began "The three daughters of King Lear can be divided into two sections." There's the scientific spirit.'

As this letter shows, humour kept breaking through Robertson's reserve. His textbook *Money* was full of playful touches. Each chapter was headed by a quotation from Alice in Wonderland; the question of what money is was discussed by a 'Bradbury' and its interrogator. Robertson on the velocity of money was delightful: 'Some pieces of money are very agile, like pieces of scandal, and skip easily from one person to another; others are like an old lady buying a railway ticket – one would think they had lost the power of locomotion altogether.' He was already inventing his own special vocabulary: he called a person's bank deposit his 'chequery', 'because it is both a breeding ground and a homing-place for cheques, as a rookery is for rooks'.

If Robertson's puritanism went with a donnish playfulness, Keynes's playfulness was combined with a vestigial puritanism. In this area of overlap was room for fruitful economic collaboration; but in the end personality differences pulled their economics apart. And this was nowhere more evident than in their attitudes to the present and the future. The sacrificial nature of Victorian economics – 'Jam yesterday, jam tomorrow, but never jam today' – was alien to Keynes's spirit; he mocked it from the outside, even when he understood what it had made possible. For Robertson the struggle for a better tomorrow – 'the procreant urge of the world' – was at the heart of the moral, as well as the economic, battle. He worried that people would not save enough to keep investment going, and called on the banking system to remedy this defect in human nature, or foresight. Keynes disagreed. His attitude to saving was always elusive, but he came to see it as excessive in relation to the investment opportunity available in an 'old' economy like Britain's.

There was a further difference. For Robertson industrial fluctuations were inseparable from the use of fixed capital, in turn inseparable from progress: 'out of the welter of industrial dislocation the great permanent riches of the future are generated'.[4] He was a civilised man and wanted to limit turbulence without destroying vitality. Keynes thought that industrial instability subjected modern society to too much strain. He was a stabiliser, and looked to the banking system to maintain economic activity on an even keel. Robertson came to see in Keynes's successive stabilisation schemes a deep reluctance to pay the price of progress.

Robertson's vision explains his approach to the analysis of economies. If industrial fluctuations were part of the machinery of progress, it followed that economic theory should be dynamic, not static, concerning itself with the analysis of processes in time, not (temporary) states of rest. By the same token, economic policy should have regard to 'maximising the community's aggregate of net satisfaction through time', rather than maximising it at a single point in time.[5] Keynes's method was more static. He was less interested in processes than in outcomes. He typically asked: how can we get the best from the possibilities of the present? His economics were built for the short haul, Robertson's for the marathon.

Keynes's approach facilitated much more clear-cut policy objectives for government than Robertson's: price stability and full employment rather than 'appropriate' fluctuations in both. Here the temperament of the civil servant, the Treasury official, came into conflict with that of the ivory-tower academic, eager to understand economic phenomena in their full complexity and not much concerned with policy measures. Robertson was writing for Cambridge; Keynes for the world.

In all this there was much room for agreement. Robertson conceded that actual industrial fluctuations were excessive or inappropriate, and could go some way towards Keynes's objective of stabilisation. Thus while he wanted measures to increase saving in the upswing of the cycle, he favoured policies to increase consumption in the downswing. And Keynes was as alive as was Robertson to the need to maintain a high level of investment. It was in their overlapping but differently shaped time-frames that the two men found their points of agreement and disagreement.

Robertson, it will be seen, had a great deal of the Marshallian in him: much more, really, than Keynes. But his vision of economic progress was also powerfully influenced by an almost unknown Frenchman, Marcel Labordère, one of whose phrases, 'la crise est venue parce qu'on a voulu faire trop vite trop de choses à la fois', he was fond of quoting. Labordère's essay, 'Autour de la crise américaine de 1907 ou capitaux-réels et capitaux-apparents', published in the *Revue de Paris* on 1 February 1908, made a great impression on both Robertson and Keynes. Robertson writes: 'I owe my acquaintance with [Labordère's] article . . . to Keynes, whom he used to visit from time to time in London.'[6] But it is not clear at what point the Labordère article came into Keynes's hands, or when he showed it to Robertson. Robertson's basic argument in *A Study of Industrial Fluctuation* (1915) is independent of Labordère. Keynes's critique of Robertson's dissertation in 1913 is, on the other hand, analytically very similar to Labordère's essay. So it may be that we have here a line of influence running jointly from Keynes and Labordère to Robertson.[7] Although Keynes was more immediately influenced by Labordère, Labordère's was one of the 'skins' he was able to slough off. Labordère, on the other hand, got inside Robertson's skin and stayed there: in particular, his poetic evocation of disappointed business hopes left a permanent trace on Robertson's thinking.

Labordère was an eccentric French financial journalist who had first got in touch with Keynes in 1911 after reading his article on Indian prices in the *Economic Journal* of March 1909. He described himself to Keynes as an 'amateur of monetary statistics', who had fallen under the spell of money when reading Xenophon as a boy. He was then fourteen years older than Keynes, unmarried, and lived in Paris with his mother, who loved her securities as much as her children, from which Labordère inferred 'that I was loved as a beloved bond'. After the war he acquired a property in the Jura, part of which he let out at a rent based on an index-number heavily weighted with the price of Gruyère cheese. Robertson remembers him on a visit to Cambridge in the 1930s as 'a very likeable old man, rather deaf and with a long white beard, much absorbed in a religion strangely compounded of Buddhism and Islam'.

When Keynes got to know him he had just been ruined in the American Stock Exchange crash of 1907; he wrote to Keynes later, that it was like 'the rending and taking away of my own flesh'. This forced him to make his living from journalism. But he could write only if he could travel by taxi, to pay for which indulgence he lived on bread and water for five months in the year. There are over sixty letters from Labordère to Keynes in the Keynes Papers at King's, running from 1911 to 1945. Most of

Keynes's letters to Labordère have disappeared. But one can see that it was a remarkable correspondence, between two men who had the highest regard for each other. The best parts of it date from the mid–1920s when they are discussing 'love of money' and the psychology of investment – topics which always fascinated Keynes. 'Be convinced, Dear Mr. Keynes,' Labordère wrote on 16 December 1928, 'that although I have practically always adhered to a technical standpoint exactly opposite to yours . . . I highly revere your moral qualities and so many graceful shades of your sensibility.' Labordère was the one Frenchman Keynes grew to love, as he loved Melchior, addressing him towards the end as 'My dear Alchemist'.

Labordère had seized the favourable opportunity afforded by his own ruin in 1907 to philosophise about the causes of financial crises. The result was a brilliantly suggestive set of parables in the style of Xenophon. In the first the 'country gentleman' overinvests in relation to his stock of consumer goods (savings); the latter runs out before the investment begins to pay – 'the vine planted will not give fruit until four years' time'. The crisis is brought about by a 'shortage of real capital'. In the second parable, Labordère considers the case of a single enterprise (the city corporation) which has access to the savings of the whole community. The crisis comes about, again, because too large a proportion of savings has been transformed into 'fixed capital' and not enough left over for 'circulating capital'. In both cases, the crisis, poetically considered, is 'one episode in the struggle between the future and the present, of the future which wants to come too quickly . . . and of the present which must first create enough to eat but desires enjoyment'. In the city, the hubris of the isolated property owner is magnified by the 'contagious impulses called crowd psychology, which increases errors much more than proportional to the number of individuals'.

In the final 'realistic' section, Labordère divides up the loanable funds into two parts 'capitaux réels' and 'capitaux apparents' – the first made up of 'real' savings (stocks), the second of money created by the banks against the security of shares, factories, properties: 'this is the birth of money. Money is born in a deposit.' The crisis is precipitated by a rise in interest rates, reflecting the shortage of 'real capital'. 'Crisis breaks out like a clap of thunder, the scenery falls down. It is the real available capital which could not be seen anywhere, the very existence of which we were beginning to doubt, which suddenly erupts into our perception . . . It is like waking from a dream, a dream of available apparent capital.' The loans are called in, assets are forcibly sold, inflated share prices collapse, the slump is at hand. Labordère has his imaginary American banker saying, 'If we look at it closely, we invest our savings before we have made them. You in Europe invest your savings after you have made them; that is more down to earth. Despite appearances, we are not a down-to-earth people. We work on fantasy.'[8]

By 1913 Robertson had finished his dissertation, *A Study of Industrial*

Fluctuation. His was a 'real' theory of the business cycle, in which the cycle is started by genuine investment opportunities (such as new inventions, agricultural abundance or the demand for new capital) but then collapses, because the lumpiness and long gestation period of large fixed capital multiplies the chances for miscalculation and leads to more investment being undertaken than is profitable. Monetary factors play a subordinate, almost insignificant, role. Almost simultaneously, Ralph Hawtrey, by no means overworked at the Treasury, had produced the first English 'monetary' theory of the business cycle, in his book *Good and Bad Trade*. Here the investment boom is triggered off by a change in the quantity of bank credit. The trade cycle, according to Hawtrey, is a 'purely monetary phenomenon' – a view from which he never subsequently deviated. Keynes wrote to Hawtrey on 26 October 1913, 'Your reasoning seems to me in most parts impeccable. But all the same I don't agree that money has so great an influence . . . very often . . . the initial facts are not as you posit them.'[9] A month previously he had written to Robertson, 'Your work has suggested to me what appears at first sight a superb theory of fluctuations. I believe it synthesises an enormous amount of your facts.'[10] What Keynes produced in a talk entitled 'How Far Are Bankers Responsible for the Alternation of Crisis and Depression?', delivered in London to the Political Economy Club on 3 December 1913, was a synthesis of the Fisher–Hawtrey 'monetary' and the Robertson 'real' theories of the business cycle, though only Fisher is mentioned by name.

Contrary to Fisher and Hawtrey, Keynes accepted Robertson's contention that the investment boom is usually triggered off by 'real' factors, such as new inventions or the rundown of existing capital equipment. But he denied that 'overinvestment', leading to crisis and collapse, was necessarily connected to the use of fixed capital, as Robertson thought. Specifically, Keynes denied that 'more capital can be invested than really exists' and that in most cases 'more investment is made than really pays'.[11] In other words, he accepted Labordère's contention – which derives from Ricardo – that investment is necessarily limited by the availability of 'real' capital.

How then can it be carried to the point of overinvestment, leading to crisis and downturn? Keynes argued that the seeds of disaster lay in the ability of the banks to create credit in excess of what the community voluntarily wished to save – by encroaching, as he put it, on the 'community's reserve of free resources' held in the banking system 'to be spent or saved as future circumstances may determine'. It was the bankers' ability to create credit which explained the failure of the cost of borrowing to keep up with the profit rate during the upswing; the equalisation of the market rate of interest and the profit rate at the top of the boom explained why the expansion goes into reverse: 'If in any year the amount invested exceeds the amount saved, this establishes a scale of investment from which there must necessarily be a reaction.' Thus the business cycle is really a credit cycle, characterised by fluctuations in the flow of investment round a fixed stock of 'voluntary' saving. Keynes wrote, 'One of the characteristics of the boom period . . . as distinguished from the period of depression is . . . that in the former period investment exceeds saving while in the latter period investment falls short of saving. And it is the machinery of banking which makes this possible.'[12]

In Keynes's critique of Robertson's *A Study of Industrial Fluctuation* is to be found the origins of their later divergence. For Robertson the business cycle is a 'real' phenomenon; for Keynes it is inherently connected with the operations of the banking system and can be prevented by 'credit control'.[13]

It was the inflation of the First World War and the post-war boom which got the idea of 'forced saving' into the textbooks, though it is really an extension of Labordère's 'capitaux apparents'; its ancestry goes back much further, to Joplin and Bentham. In his book *Money* (1922), Robertson clearly identifies it as a source of loanable funds for investment. Credit creation forces up consumer prices. All those who could not increase their money incomes in line with inflation (to some extent wage-earners but particularly bondholders or 'old widows') were 'forced', by having to reduce their consumption, to 'pay' for the increased spending of entrepreneurs or government. Inflation was a forced levy on some parts of the community to pay for the spending of others. Keynes's chapter on the 'inflation tax' in his *Tract on Monetary Reform* discusses how inflation enables a government to spend what the private consumer has to forgo. To obviate 'forced saving' Keynes wanted the Bank of England to keep prices stable. Robertson, on the contrary, stressed the need for monetary accommodation to cyclical forces which originated outside the sphere of money. This set the scene for the Keynes–Robertson debate. Keynes denied that inflation as such could create additional resources for investment: it could only redistribute resources between different sections of the community. Robertson believed that inflation provided an important source of loanable funds to businessmen, leading to the building up of new capital assets. His *Banking Policy and the Price Level* was conceived as a critique of Keynes's stress on preventing any fluctuations in the price level. 'I do not feel confident', Robertson wrote, 'that a policy which, in the pursuit of stability of prices, output, and employment, had nipped in the bud the English railway boom of the forties, or the American railway boom of 1869–71, or the German electrical boom of the nineties, would have been on the balance beneficial to the populations concerned.'[14]

Keynes was heavily involved in the gestation of Robertson's book, even while he was working on his own sequel to the *Tract on Monetary Reform*. His purposeful discussions with Robertson started at Tilton in the summer of 1924. 'If you have nothing better to do come back here for a few days,' he wrote to Robertson on 14 September. 'I am working at Credit Cycle theories which I think you may like – they go half way to meet you: and would much like to talk them over.'[15] Helping to 'hatch Dennis's egg' occupied him for much of 1925. After reading the proofs, he wrote to Lydia on 22 May 1925, 'It won't do at all – I'm sure it's wrong; so afterwards I went round to bully him some more and almost to say he ought to tear it up and withdraw it from publication. It's dreadful. When I've finished this letter, I shall write to him about it.' There was an exchange of letters, including a reply from Robertson, on 24 May, which was 'almost a second book'.[16] In his letter of 28 May, Keynes, as was his wont, went straight for the jugular: 'The point is the following: . . . an act of inflation unaccompanied by any change in the amount of hoarding represents a mere transference of existing wealth without any necessary effects on the volume of consumption.'[17] This is highly classical – money as such cannot affect the volume of real demand. On 1 June, Keynes reported to Lydia that 'Dennis and I have at last come practically to agreement about what is right and tasty in the egg and what not – which is a relief.' On 18 October, Robertson deposited the 'last and final version of his egg'; and on 12 November Keynes reported him happy because he had handed it back 'at last with my full benediction, approval, and praises'. Keynes had written to him two days previously: 'I think that your revised chapter v. is splendid, – most new and important. I think it is substantially right and at last I have no material criticism. It is the kernel and real essence of the book.' *Banking Policy and the Price Level* was published in January 1926.

The technical aspects of the argument between the two men are too obscure to go into here: the fact that Robertson had invented a rather witty new language to express his ideas, which, on the whole, remained private to him, did not help clarity. (See Appendix 1 at the end of this chapter.) But it is hard to accept Presley's conclusion that there was a real meeting of minds.[18] Looking at the debate now, one is puzzled how they could have thought there was. Basically, Robertson believed that voluntary saving was insufficient for the capital needs of a growing economy and that 'appropriate' credit creation by the banks (or what was then called inflation) might be necessary to plug the gap.[19] Keynes denied both parts of the proposition. The problem was one of the right distribution of existing saving – between foreign and home investment – rather than of its level. But in correspondence with Robertson he also denied, on technical grounds, that inflation 'automatically' generated more saving, or 'lacking' as Robertson called it. Inflation could produce new 'lacking' only by *inducing* the community as a whole to save a higher proportion than formerly out of its money income. Some people might do this; more likely people would spend more, running down their cash balances. He later concluded that any 'induced lacking' was 'too precarious a source of additional savings to deserve separate notice'.[20] Robertson accepted Keynes's 'induced lacking' as a possible effect of a rising price level, but he refused to regard it as the only source of additional funds.[21]

Keynes's criticism of Robertson does not bear out the view of those who see him as one of nature's inflationists. The idea of inflating in order to get people to save more struck him as counter-intuitive. 'On balance,' he wrote to Robertson, 'there may quite likely be something to the credit of inflation. But this is not the whole story: and the policy of inflation cannot be recommended until we have weighed the above credit against the many familiar items to the debit of inflation.'[22]

It is also clear, from reading the surviving fragments of correspondence between the two men, that they were interested in different things. Keynes's main policy object was to stabilise prices. Robertson's discussion chiefly interested him as demonstrating the complications this involved, without changing his goal. Robertson, on the other hand, wanted 'appropriate' fluctuations in order to maintain growth. His opinion that the banking system could not achieve both growth and price stability 'wholly ignored bank rate' in Keynes's view.[23] They might have come together on the short-term problem of mitigating depression. But here their analyses pulled in different directions. Robertson thought of the problem as one of insufficient voluntary saving. Keynes thought the problem was, as he was to put it a little later, one of 'more saving than we can use at home' at existing interest rates. For Robertson, the way out of the slump was to create 'new' saving, for Keynes to 'mobilise' existing saving. Robertson, however, seemed to have a clearer appreciation of one part of the problem when he wrote, 'For . . . while there is always *some* rate of money interest which will check an eager borrower, there may be *no* rate . . . in excess of zero which will stimulate an unwilling one.'[24] Keynes's praise for the final result was qualified by the thought that 'the whole thing can be put *much* simpler and shorter' and that Robertson had left 'practical applications' in the air.[25]

Nevertheless, his engagement with Robertson at this point in his life was crucial in the development of his own ideas. Later he was to tell him that 'I certainly date all my emancipation from the discussions between us which preceded your *Banking Policy and the Price Level.*'[26] In retrospect, Keynes's rejection of Robertson's 'forced saving' doctrine, as an equilibrating mechanism, seems a vital negative decision. It made it possible for him to see saving as a function of level of income rather than quantity of money, and thus opened the way to the theory of effective demand.

But Robertson's book also marked a positive step in the unravelling of orthodoxy. In the early 1920s, economics at Cambridge had been largely 'glosses on Marshalliana'.[27] Marshall was mainly concerned with the forces determining 'long period' or 'normal' prices. He did not regard temporary disturbances to these forces as theoretically interesting. Robertson's was the first serious attempt to work through the economics of what Fisher called 'transition periods'. In doing so he showed up the limitations of the quantity theory of money, both as a tool of analysis and as an instrument of policy.

II

Keynes had written to Lydia from Cambridge on Sunday, 30 November 1924, 'I have begun the new book! – today, and have written one page. This is the first sentence: – "I begin this book, not in the logical order, but so as to bring before the reader's mind, as soon as possible, what is most significant in what I have to say." ' If only he had stuck to this intention! Early drafts of the tables of contents show that Keynes's intention was to study the theory of money in relation to the 'credit cycle' for the practical purpose of devising an optimum banking policy. In the first draft chapter, which he started on 30 November, he took up the unfinished business of his 1913 talk to the Political Economy Club. The analysis was broadly the same. Banks cause business cycles by lending greater or smaller amounts of 'bank money' than is represented by the 'real' savings of the public deposited with them. They do this in response to fluctuations in the demand for 'working capital'. The banks can only *transfer* as much purchasing power from savers to borrowers as the public are willing to save. But they can *lend* more or less than this: for their 'main criterion of how much to lend is a totally different one, – namely the proportion of their cash reserves to their money liabilities'. This distinction between lending money and transferring resources was to remain central to the *Treatise on Money*: it links up, as we shall see, with Keynes's discussion of the reparation problem. The policy conclusion was that the Bank of England should use its control over the money supply to keep bank money a constant fraction of real balances. The new task Keynes set himself was of analysing the causes of fluctuations in 'real balances', particularly in relation to 'fluctuations in the demand for circulating capital'.[28]*

We need to follow the main thread. In a credit-money economy decisions to save and decisions to invest are independent of each other, and there is nothing to harmonise them except banking policy. However, the banking system needed a new criterion to govern its lending policy, and this, Keynes suggested, should be stability of the price level. If fluctuations in bank lending round the available volume of 'real credit' caused both inflation and deflation and boom and slump, a policy of price stabilisation would simultaneously avoid both phenomena. We can see here why Keynes was

---

*Some translation of terms is needed. Keynes used the terms 'real credit' and 'real balances' to mean the real value (purchasing power) of bank deposits held in current and savings accounts. The real value of these deposits would fluctuate with changes in prices. 'Circulating' or 'working' capital is the *liquid* capital required to carry on production – that is, all capital not represented by plant and equipment (for example, stocks of partly finished goods, cash in hand, bank loans). Business borrowing from the banks arose mainly from the demand for this type of capital.

so reluctant to abandon the quantity theory: it could be used both to explain and to cure the diseases of the macroeconomy. Economists always prefer to economise on the number of policy instruments needed to achieve a desired goal.

The train thus set going in 1924 did not change direction much over the next three years: it simply became longer and filled up with passengers. Unlike the *General Theory, A Treatise on Money* was composed in solitude and was not circulated for comment until it was too late to change. Robertson was away for almost a year from 1926–7. Ralph Hawtrey was at Harvard in 1928–9. The criticisms he made on his return were fundamental, but were too late for Keynes to use. The Prof. (Pigou) was no help. He hated discussing economics anyway, and by 1928 was seriously unwell with heart trouble. Keynes found his book on *Industrial Fluctuations* (1927) 'rather miserable – perhaps Mrs. Marshall is right that he should have married, his mind is dead, he just arranges in a logical order all the things he knew before'.[29] Most important of all, although Keynes gave lectures from successive drafts of his book, he had no graduate students able or willing to engage with him on points of theory. This was in strong contrast to the powerful support group which assisted in the birth of the *General Theory*.

Keynes started on the second chapter in February 1925; on 8 March he is reporting to Lydia that he wasted two whole mornings on 'mathematical rubbish' which he tore up. Possibly these are early shots at the 'Fundamental Equations'. Back at Cambridge in April, he felt free 'to go plodding on', spoke the first chapter as a lecture and began a third. However, little more was done in 1925, and it was not till April 1926 that he was back at work. By the end of August he had drafted about 55,000 words of Book I entitled 'The Theory of Money'. This now included a 'fundamental equation of price', together with the 'variability of its elements' (though the drafts suggest this was still the old Fisher quantity equation). By 31 August 'the plurality of price levels' and the problem of index numbers (which he had dealt with in his Adam Smith Prize Essay in 1909) had appeared; as well as the chapter on 'the *modus operandi* of bank rate'. By 12 September he had evidently started work on Book II, 'The Theory of Credit'. He had made sufficient progress to write to Daniel Macmillan on 22 September, 'I am now at work on a serious treatise to be entitled "The Theory of Money and Credit", for publication about a year hence or a little later.' At this stage, all that Keynes contemplated was the two sections – Money and Credit – running to between 100,000 and 120,000 words, and nineteen chapters.[30] A ledger entry at R. and R. Clark, his Edinburgh printer, dated 28 September 1926, reads: 'On the basis of 120,000 words, with 300 to the page, the extent will be about 400 pp. . . .'

A couple of indications can be given of Keynes's thinking at this time. In an address to the Tuesday Club of 13 October 1926, he urged an embargo on capital exports – a consistent proposal from 1924.[31] In a comment on the speech of McKenna to the Midland Bank shareholders on 28 January 1927 he argued that disaggregation of *the* price level was necessary to distinguish between 'prices' and 'costs'. His central contention was that credit restriction had deflated 'prices', but not 'costs', producing a situation of 'pseudo-equilibrium' which left 'trade depressed and a million unemployed'. His specific criticism of McKenna was that he underestimated the difficulty of expanding credit under the gold standard.[32] In a letter to Keynes on his piece, McKenna wrote, significantly, 'possibly I attach more importance than you do to the economies of full-scale production. Overheads are a very big item in cost.'[33]

Keynes had got back to writing again at Cambridge on 21 January 1927. On Friday, 28 January he looked forward to three peaceful writing days – 'A happy country has no history' – and had redrafted one of the chapters. He went down to Tilton to collect some others, and forgot to bring them back. By 27 May he was 'rewriting successfully one of the bits I was troubled about at Tilton'. Work went on through the summer of 1927, Keynes resisting an invitation from the Courtaulds to join them in Greece. (Lydia said she had told Sam that 'if you were searing about your book, no one could sway you the other way'). Three tables of contents from this period show an alarming tendency for the book (now renamed *A Treatise on Money*) to expand. There were now five Books (or sections) and twenty-six chapters. Keynes seemed to be aiming at a completeness appropriate to a full-blown Treatise rather than splashing what was new and important. In retrospect, this decision to expand the book into a Treatise can be seen as a mistake. Too much of his intellectual capital was being locked into a fixed investment, at a time when circumstances and his own ideas were exceptionally fluid.

On 18 January 1928 Keynes reported the arrival of a large packet of proofs from Clark's in Edinburgh. But now there was a major derailment. Dennis Robertson had returned from a trip to Asia in April 1927, looking 'only moderate – rather older, *very* bald, with the bones of his skull showing more than they did . . . very Chinese'.[34] He started to revise his textbook on *Money* and talk on theory started up again, at Tilton and Cambridge. On 23 January 1928, Keynes wrote to Lydia, 'Dennis came in last night and we had a long talk about the new theory. I think it will do, and that it is very important. But it owes a great deal to him.' By 30 January he had finished the first draft of 'The Pure Theory of the Credit Cycle' on sixty pages of Basildon paper, 'so I felt very cheerful and free and didn't care tuppence one way or the other about the speculations'. By 5 February the Basildons had grown to eighty-two, and were sent off to the typist. In the 1928 edition of *Money* Robertson too had a new chapter, 'The Question of the Cycle', 'which ought scarcely . . . to see the light of day over any signature than [Keynes's]'.[35]

Keynes's book now seems to have entered a Robertsonian phase. Dynamic analysis has appeared, with the credit cycle being driven by 'profit inflations' which impose a 'forced abstinence' on the working class and by 'profit deflations' which follow. Keynes added four chapters of historical illustrations. Frank Ramsey wrote, after a visit to Tilton that summer, 'How exciting your quantity equation seemed . . . I could see it was a great advance.'[36] Keynes was influenced at this time by Ramsey's theory of the 'optimal rate of saving' required to achieve 'Bliss', to which he contributed, but which was closer to Robertson's technique than his own.[37]

The major impact of 'the new theory' was to cause Keynes to abandon his notion that the sole aim of monetary policy should be to stabilise the price level. For a rise in the price level might be required to reverse the previous profit deflation. An important additional impetus to this line of thought came from Reginald McKenna. Keynes reviewed a collection of his annual speeches to shareholders as chairman of the Midland Bank on 2 November 1928.[38] McKenna's central contention was that a policy of credit restriction to avoid inflation *when there were large unemployed resources* was tantamount to policy of 'continuous deflation'.[39] A correct criterion for banking policy would, in other words, need to have regard to appropriate credit policy for different phases of the cycle, and not just to the situation of full employment.

Keynes's new line of thinking is contained in a draft of the *Treatise* which seems to date from the autumn–winter of 1928:

> Nevertheless, it must be admitted that the advocates of price stability, amongst whom I number myself, have erred in the past when their words have seemed to indicate price stability as the sole objective of monetary policy to the exclusion of the right adjustment of the supply of bank credit to the business world's demands for it – or at least as an objective which, if reached, would necessarily involve the simultaneous attainment of all associated objectives. To speak or write in this way is unduly to simplify the problem by overlooking the dual character of the functions of the banking systems [to achieve price stability and equilibrium between saving and investment] . . . Mr D. H. Robertson's acute and profound criticisms (in his *Banking Policy and the Price Level*), emphasising the other side of the problem, have therefore been calculated to exert a most salutary influence on contemporary thought (and have done so on mine). On the other hand, Mr. Robertson . . . seems to me, in that book, not to state the problem clearly enough as a problem of reconciliation of purposes – and, if necessary, of compromise.[40]

To his American publisher, Alfred Harcourt, Keynes wrote on 26 September 1928: 'I have devoted the whole of this summer to my Treatise on Money, thus completing four years' work on it. . . . I should say that four-fifths is now completely finished. I am hopeful that I shall have finished it before Easter [1929], and that it may be published in this country about May.'[41]

On 10 December 1928 Keynes still thought that there was a reasonable chance of the *Treatise* appearing in 'the first half of 1929' in its single volume, five-book form.[42] By 18 February 1929, he was postponing publication till 1 October. But the autumn publication plan was abandoned too. The book had been derailed once more by the intellectual controversies surrounding the general election of May 1929. 'I am ashamed to say', Keynes wrote to Daniel Macmillan on 20 August, 'that after I had got more than 440 pages into paged revise I had to come to the conclusion that certain chapters must be drastically rewritten, and the whole very considerably rearranged.' January 1930 was to be the new publication date, and there were now to be two volumes. The *Treatise* appeared in October 1930.

III

ASPECTS OF KEYNES

Like most authors, Keynes complained endlessly about interruptions to his work of his own devising. Apart from his fixed commitments in Cambridge and London, there were what the edition of his Collected Writings calls his 'Activities' – hundreds of pages of them for this period. Gold and Russia took up his time and energy in 1925. Much of 1926 and 1927 was taken up with his Liberal Party and cotton work. There was an endless succession of one-off events. For example, he contributed an article to the *Nation* on 12 March 1927 on the problems of the book trade;[43] in October 1927 he had to give a lecture to 'all the bank clerks in Cambridge. It took me most of the morning to prepare it. Why do I do such things? I am mad. Still, it's a long time since I have had such an appreciative audience – one which laughed so loud at my jokes and clapped so loud at my sentiments. Very different from Manchester.'[44] On 13 May 1928 we find him writing to Winston Churchill: 'What an imbecile Currency Bill you have introduced!'[45] Despite his efficient work habits, it is small wonder that he lost the thread of his ideas, left chapters mouldering for months unread at Tilton. By the end of 1928 the complaints of tiredness grow more insistent. These circumstances, quite as much as the changing tack of his own ideas, explain why the different parts, or phases, of the *Treatise* fit so ill together.

In February 1927, Keynes finally resigned from the 'Chinese torture' of University Council, but he was as heavily involved as ever in College business. In June 1928, the Governing Body approved the next instalment of Kennedy's rebuilding plan, providing for a 'new and swanky' Combination Room, to much buzzing from W. H. Macaulay, a very senior mathematics Fellow, who understood about engineering. 'Hours of my life', he complained to Lydia in May 1929, 'are spent hearing arguments from

Macaulay (dressed in mourning and a top hat) whether it is proper to pour washing-up water and "little" water [Lydia's code for urine] down the same pipe. That is when I feel I am living my life in vain.' But it was Macaulay's brother Reginald who put up the £20,000 needed to go ahead.[46]

The Annual Audit dinner of 1927 provided Keynes, as Bursar, with a chance to test one of his favourite theories:

> The most interesting part [he wrote to Lydia on 18 November 1927] was the negotiation with a farmer who has been in a state of violent quarrel with the College for 7 years. I had never seen him before but had been led to believe he was an impossible character. But he came up for the dinner last night, and as soon as I cast eyes on his *hands* I knew that all this was a complete mistake – that he was very nice, absolutely honest and capable, and that the only thing wrong with him was a violent temper which we had managed somehow to arouse. So I proceeded to . . . behave to him as though he were perfectly sensible and nice with the result that we came to a complete settlement. . . . Hands! Hands! Hands! Nothing else is worth looking at. In 10 seconds I had completely revised my idea of his character.

Then there were family obligations. At Sunday lunches with the 'starychki' at Harvey Road a sense of torpor was likely to be induced, not just by Neville Keynes's excellent claret, but by the heavy mass of Browns: Uncle Kenneth with his 'mirthless jokes'; Uncle Walrus (Walter Langdon Brown) huge of frame and moustache and endlessly anecdotal; Aunt Walrus (Frances, his wife) 'in a dress which made her look like an absolute monster'; the seventeen-stone 'bearded' Aunt Jessie and her daughter Muriel, and many others. After such luncheon parties, F.i.l. would retire to his study to listen to his favourite gramophone records, while Maynard staggered back exhausted to King's.

While the *Treatise* meandered on its rather solitary way, Cambridge economics was coming to life after its long war-induced slumber. These were the days before the great Cambridge schism of the 1930s. Keynes, according to H. M. Robertson, was looked up to 'as a particularly bright star in a constellation in which an almost celestial harmony reigned'. To Robertson, a postgraduate from Leeds who came to Emmanuel College in 1926 to continue his economic studies, Keynes appeared 'rather more like a stockbroker than a don' with his City suits and City gossip. His conversation was full of the iniquities of the Bank of England, the Treasury and 'those City interests which seemed prepared to allow industry and employment to suffer for the benefit of . . . international fiance'. His hero in this world was Reginald McKenna, chairman of the Midland Bank. If he could only replace Montagu Norman as governor of the Bank, the unemployment problem would be solved! Robertson recalls that Pigou, known as 'the Professor', was 'virtually inaccessible, recovering slowly from a severe cardiac ailment, but . . . treated with an almost exaggerated respect . . . as Marshall's anointed successor'. This bears out what Austin Robinson says. When he first attended his lectures in the early 1920s, Pigou was still 'the tall, powerfully built, athletic player of all ball games . . . the keen climber, with his cottage among the mountains in Cumberland where he led his friends up the climbs'; an excellent lecturer, 'very clear, very systematic, but at the same time very rooted in the Marshall tradition – "it's all in Marshall" '. But by the mid to late 1920s, he had become 'remote and aloof', his misogyny ever more pronounced, the discussion of economics 'taboo'.

Cambridge's main monetary theorist, apart from Keynes and Robertson, was Frederick Lavington, of Emmanuel, who 'had done so much to round out Marshall's monetary theory' and who carried a full load of teaching till his early death in 1927. At the Political Economy – or Keynes – Club, which Robertson, like most other students, found 'delightful – and frightening', the main faculty attenders were Gerald Shove, shy and withdrawn, who gave 'inordinately dull lectures on trade union organisation', J. R. Bellerby, of Gonville and Caius, who was 'close to Keynes', the Marxist Maurice Dobb, at Pembroke, and Marjorie Tappan (later Holland) of Girton.

However, a younger cohort of economists, which was to play a central part in Keynes's story, was moving into position. Of the coming stars, Joan Maurice and Austin Robinson, married in 1926, returned to Cambridge at the end of 1928, after a spell in India, he to a lectureship in economics. Austin Robinson was more an academic politician and administrator than a theorist, but his wife Joan, who joined the faculty in 1931, was a woman of outstanding brains, personality and looks, to whom the word 'bluestocking' applies in its best sense. Photographs show a serious young woman with intense, questioning eyes, and hair plaited into two buns, rather like ear muffs. She brought to economics 'the extraordinary ability to zero in on the heart of the matter and in a few well-chosen words to convey its essence. She had an irritating penchant to dismiss as nonsense ideas with which she did not agree.' In the 1930s she was to be intimately involved in the Keynesian Revolution, which she later tried to generalise into a long-period theory of employment.[47] Keynes had had good economics students before – notably Frederick Harmer, Eton Colleger, excellent mathematician and Apostle, who obtained a first-class degree in economics in 1927, before going off to become a banker. But Richard Ferdinand Kahn was the first who was able and willing to help him in his own work. Kahn had come up to King's in 1924 to read mathematics and physics. An indifferent degree persuaded him to shift to Part II of the economics tripos in 1927: Schumpeter later told him that 'many a failed race-horse makes quite a good hack'. He was taught by Gerald Shove, and, once a fortnight on Saturday, with three others, was supervised by Keynes. 'I actually trembled as I was about to enter Keynes's rooms in College for my first supervision . . .', Kahn recalled. Kahn went to his lectures in the autumn of 1927 on 'The Pure Theory of

Money' – read from the galley proofs of his book – which he found 'extremely puzzling, based, as they were, on the Quantity Theory'.[48] On 29 April 1928, Keynes wrote to Lydia, 'Yesterday my favourite pupil Kahn wrote me one of the best answers I have ever had from a pupil – he must get a first-class.' And on 20 May, 'In a few minutes my favourite pupil Kahn comes in to discuss whether he shall stay on here next year as a student or try to earn money.'

When Kahn first met Keynes at the age of twenty-two he was a slight, serious, rather beautiful young man, with masses of thick black hair. He spoke with an air of quiet authority, which contrasted oddly with extreme nervousness about his health – a lifelong obsession. His ancestry was German; his father, Augustus Kahn, was a peppery schoolmaster and amateur economist; he was educated at St Paul's School, London. He remained an orthodox Jew all his life, more faithful to the letter than the spirit: he would get his gyp (college servant) to open his letters on the sabbath, even though he wasn't allowed to himself. Keynes, who could never resist classification, took to referring to him as 'the little Rabbi'. To friends of his own age he was Ferdinand, which somehow seemed more appropriate than Richard. He was a much better mathematician than most of those in Keynes's circle; he recalled Keynes himself as being a poor mathematician by 1927; his ability to think mathematically was to be of crucial help to Keynes in the early 1930s. His mind was remarkably meticulous and he took great pains to help his friends. His relationship with Keynes was a prototype of the other important relationships of his life, particularly with Joan Robinson. He was the self-effacing backroom boy rather than the star of the show; an excellent listener, with a hard core of analytic power. Schumpeter wrote perceptively that he was the type of scholar 'that Cambridge produces much more readily than do other centres of scientific economics. . . . They throw their ideas into a common pool. By critical and positive suggestion they help other people's ideas into definite existence. And they exert anonymous influence – influence as leaders – far beyond anything that can be definitely credited to them from their publications.'[49]

Kahn duly got his first, and stayed on at King's to compete for a College fellowship. Keynes hoped to 'kill two birds with one stone', by getting him to do some empirical work on bank deposits for his dissertation; but all his personal influence with McKenna failed to get him access to the Midland Bank's confidential statistics. 'McKenna always lets one down in the end, as I knew already,' Keynes commented sourly.[50] Contrary to Keynes's belief, this was rather a relief for Kahn. He was never interested in monetary economics, his prejudice against the quantity theory of money having started in 1923 on a family holiday on the Baltic Sea when he noticed that, despite the shortages of banknotes, prices doubled every twenty-four hours. He turned with relief to an examination of Marshall's theory of the short period.

This led him into another area of criticism of Marshall then opening up at Cambridge under the influence of Piero Sraffa.

It was Sraffa who gave Cambridge economics its shot in the arm in the late 1920s. Robertson's *Banking Policy and the Price Level* was considered largely incomprehensible by the young. Keynes's *Treatise on Money* had not yet appeared. Sraffa's ideas filled the gap. 'Sraffa is established here and in a terror of nerves over his lecture,' Keynes reported to Lydia on 9 October 1927. 'He asked me yesterday whether he could not suddenly become ill and run away.'

Sraffa, armed with a letter from Salvemini, had first introduced himself to Keynes in London in December 1921, when doing some research at the London School of Economics. He was then twenty-three, a tall, erect law graduate of Turin University, who had written a thesis on Italian monetary management during the war. Keynes was sufficiently impressed by him to ask him to write an article for the *Economic Journal* on the current Italian banking crisis, and another for the Eleventh Reconstruction Supplement of the *Manchester Guardian Commercial*, on the same subject, which appeared on 7 December 1922. Mussolini, who had just come to power, sent two telegrams to Sraffa's father, the Rector of the Bonconi University in Milan, denouncing Sraffa's article as 'an act of true and real sabotage of Italian finance' and calling on Angelo Sraffa to get him to write a second article to 'dissipate the . . . pessimistic impression' caused by the first. Sraffa's father wrote back, with spirit, that his son had 'nothing to rectify and nothing to add'.[51] Keynes thought that Mussolini was 'making an ass of himself', but, as it seemed that Sraffa might get into trouble, suggested he come to Cambridge for a short time. He was stopped at Dover and deported as an undesirable alien. An enraged Keynes wrote to J. C. C. Davidson, Bonar Law's Parliamentary Private Secretary, 'it surely cannot be the business of our Home Office to abet the more outrageous stupidities of Mussolini';[52] but Sraffa was not let in till 1924. Although he was to become professor of economics at the University of Cagliari in 1926, his well-known socialist sympathies and his friendship with the communist leader Antonio Gramsci made life difficult for him in fascist Italy. At this time, his intellectual interests overlapped with Keynes's, and he produced the Italian translation of *A Tract on Monetary Reform*. But Sraffa had already started to work on problems of classical value theory bequeathed by Ricardo – a lifetime obsession which led him away from the monetary problems which preoccupied Keynes.

After 1924, Sraffa started coming over to England regularly. There is a note to Keynes written from Nevern Square, London on 6 November 1924: 'But above all I was honoured and pleased by being among the first to hear from your own mouth your great new theory of the credit cycle and the outline of the social policy which, I hope, will direct progress in the near future.' On 6 June 1926 Sraffa sent him a précis of an article on 'the relations between cost and quantity produced' which he had just published in Italian, asking him 'whether there is anything on these lines which might be usefully developed for the Economic Journal'. It was his article, 'The Laws of Return under Competitive Conditions', appearing in the *Economic Journal* of December 1926, which caused so much excitement in Cambridge. The question which Sraffa posed, in his letter to Keynes of 6 June 1926, was how Marshall's assumption of increasing returns to scale could be reconciled with orthodox value theory, based on perfect competition. If a firm's costs of production fall as its output rises, there is no stable equilibrium between supply and demand, and nothing to stop its size expanding indefinitely. The problem, then, is how equilibrium is reached under conditions of falling cost curves and 'imperfect competition'.

If Sraffa's ideas gave Cambridge its second (that is, post-Marshallian) wind,[53] it was not a wind which filled Keynes's sails. Although he found Sraffa's work 'very interesting and original'[54] – and indeed got him his University lectureship and rooms and high-table rights at King's – he was too absorbed in his own project to see its relevance to his concerns. Sraffa never himself considered the possible bearing of 'increasing returns' on the unemployment problem. And Keynes did not think the theoretical problems for value theory raised by Sraffa of serious practical importance – an attitude he was to take to the whole of Sraffa's work. Any tendency towards monopoly, he thought, would be offset by the well-known tendency of long-established firms to decay. More helpful, he felt, was a two-hour discussion he had with Sraffa on the Pure Theory of the Credit Cycle on 2 March 1928, leading to the correction of a few 'small mistakes'. Still, it remains a puzzle that the two escape routes from Marshallian orthodoxy – the one associated with Sraffa and imperfect competition, the other with Keynes and effective demand – never converged in Keynes's lifetime, though leading disciples like Kahn and Joan Robinson were heavily involved in both 'revolutions'.

Sraffa gradually took root in Cambridge and became one of Keynes's best friends. 'Pottering with Piero' round the antiquarian bookshops on Saturday afternoons became his substitute for riding with Sebastian Sprott, or buying indifferent furniture. Sraffa was someone Keynes liked to worry about. He was negligent about his clothes, had a horror of lecturing and took drastic action to evade it: 'Piero *was* ... to have given his lecture to-morrow,' Keynes wrote to Lydia on 16 January 1929. 'He sat next to me in hall talking in high spirits and came to the combination room afterwards, then he rose from the table, delivered the whole of his dinner on the mat, lay on the ground almost fainting with no pulse at all, was doped with brandy – and so won't lecture to-morrow after all! I am having (once more) to make the necessary announcement.' His aversion to teaching became so profound that Keynes had to invent a number of jobs to keep him in Cambridge – including the editorship of the Royal Economic Society's edition of Ricardo's papers. Sraffa was addicted to Sherlock Holmes stories, and he now followed every clue to new caches of Ricardo papers with a persistence which the great detective would have envied. But he took much longer to solve his cases. In 1933 Keynes puffed the 'forthcoming complete and definitive edition of the works of David Ricardo . . . to be published in the course of the present year'. In fact the first four volumes of the eleven-volume edition appeared in 1951. By 1928 Sraffa had already prepared a manuscript of a slim theoretical volume. It appeared only in 1960, under the title *Production of Commodities by Commodities*, and fuelled a famous debate on capital theory.

Someone who took thirty-two years to publish an eighty-seven-page 'prelude to a critique' was clearly not inspired by any great sense of urgency. Sraffa felt much the same about public writing as Keynes did about public speaking: 'I confess that always, when I read something which I have written, I feel such a deep disgust that I cannot resist the temptation to destroy it, unless I have a definite engagement to deliver it.'[55] This neurotic fastidiousness, as well as his great subtlety of mind, endeared him to Keynes. Passionately devoted to his mother, Sraffa was a lame eagle, to be protected from an unkind world.

A year after Sraffa's arrival, the Divine Fool started knocking at the gate. 'A letter from Ludwig', wrote Keynes to Lydia on 28 November 1928. 'He . . . wants to come and stay with me here for a fortnight. Am I strong enough? Perhaps if I do no work between now and then, I shall be.' Wittgenstein had given up teaching in his Austrian village in 1926, returning to Vienna to build an obsessively functionalist house for his sister. Now the house was finished, and Wittgenstein turned again to philosophy to cure his intellectual and emotional headaches. On 17 January 1929 Keynes wrote, 'Ludwig . . . arrives to-morrow . . . Pray for me!' And the next day: 'Well, God has arrived. I met him on the 5.15 train. He has a plan to stay in Cambridge permanently.' While God whistled Bach in the drawing room, Keynes crept to his study to write his letter to Lydia. 'I see that the fatigue is going to be crushing. But I must not let him talk to me for more than two or three hours a day.'

> My dearest, darling Lydochka [he wrote on 20 January 1929],
> I would willingly exchange my guest for yours! ['guests' were Lydia-speak for her periods] – though we are really getting on very well and I must not complain. Sometimes it is almost unbearable – the fatigue and, I think that is it, his tremendous self-centredness. . . . However, we have established a good regime – he has a fire in his little attic room and leaves me free in my rooms for most of the morning. Now the poor creature has got a very bad cold or influenza, and is mostly in bed, but he won't stay there long. . . . His idea is to come and live in Cambridge for a year as a research student.

Keynes fled to London a day earlier than usual. He returned to find God in very good spirits, because the authorities had agreed to let him become a research student under Frank Ramsey. (In June 1929 he successfully submitted the *Tractatus* for a Doctorate of Philosophy.)

Complaining that he 'was not born to live permanently with a clergyman', Keynes gave Wittgenstein notice to quit on 2 February; Wittgenstein moved in with Frank Ramsey and his wife, then with Maurice Dobb; though not before Keynes had caught a savage cold from him which required ten days' absence from University. 24 February: 'He is coming to dine with me to-night. Will he give me a relapse?' 25 February: 'Last night Ludwig came to dinner. He was more "normal" in every way than I have ever known him. One woman at last has succeeded in soothing the fierceness of the savage brute – Lettice Ramsey, under whose roof he stayed in the end for nearly a fortnight. . . .'

In May, Maynard asked Ludwig to tea, 'which only brought a long letter (quite mad . . .) saying that the reason why I was cross with him last time we met was because I had a grudge against him based on the fear that he wanted to get some money out of me! So now I have to write a long letter asking him to dine with me in hall to-night. Sweet, humble Pigou is, anyhow, less exacting. But I love them both! – if I will not see them too much.'[56]

What did they talk about for two or three hours a day – or rather, what did Wittgenstein talk about, for he disliked interruptions to his monologues? Much of the conversation must have been philosophical. Keynes's interest in philosophy had been kept alive by Frank Ramsey, a seventeen-stone presence at King's, still, incredibly, only twenty-five, as well as by Richard Braithwaite. Ramsey, Braithwaite and Wittgenstein had rejected the central contention of Keynes's *Treatise on Probability* – that probability is a logical relation. The intellectual current of the time – and one must add here the overwhelming influence of Freud – was running strongly against the pre-war rationalism of Keynes's generation. Ramsey himself had been psycho-analysed in Vienna, to cure him of his unsettling passion for married women; what is rational, he said, is what works. For Wittgenstein, philosophy was a kind of inspired madness. There is talk of a famous lunch at which Ramsey, Wittgenstein and Sraffa discussed probability with Keynes. It is hard not to believe that Keynes's intercourse with the most powerful philosophical minds of the day shook him out of his comfortable pre-war certainties, which, of course, were bound up with the belief in 'automatic' progress. Who could now credibly assume that people behaved rationally? Or that, even if they tried to, logical intuition could tell them what was rational to do or believe?

The work leading to nuclear fission had already started in Cambridge's Cavendish Laboratory, pinpointing the contrast between the weakness of philosophy and the power of experimental science. Keynes knew the brilliant young Russian atomic physicist Peter Kapitsa, though not well, shrewdly predicting that he would go back to the Soviet Union, 'because he is a wild, disinterested, vain, and absolutely uncivilised creature, perfectly suited by nature to be a Bolshie'.[57] The obsession with the power of science had, by the late 1920s, produced the first communist 'cell' at Cambridge. They were mainly young scientists, who knew nothing about politics, but saw Marxism as the first true 'science of society' and Stalin's Russia as the first experimental laboratory for testing out its theories.[58] The main link between Keynes's circle and the Marxist scientists round Kapitsa and the crystallographer J. D. Bernal was Alister Watson, 'a very clever mathematician', later physicist, who came up to Trinity College from Winchester in 1926.[59] Watson became the leading Apostle of the late 1920s; Anthony Blunt, also at Trinity, learnt his Marxism from Watson and was 'born' into the Society in May 1928. Both stayed on at Cambridge in the 1930s.

Keynes was never in the least influenced by Marx, but he too was infected with a spirit of boldness, a new willingness to experiment in social and economic policy. The switch in allegiance from Asquith to Lloyd George was symbolic of this: from the man of balance to the man of power. Everything had to be questioned, nothing deserved to be taken on trust. If something seemed likely to do good – try it out, even though Ricardo and Mill and Gladstone had proved it to be nonsense; for to where did their 'proofs' point except to the grave? Thus was Keynes's ingrained Edwardianism undermined by the facts and spirit of the age. But, even as he accommodated to them, he never surrendered to them. His ultimate aim was to control the new forces at the behest of the Edwardian ideal of rational, civilised living.

Largely through his continuing connection with the Apostles, Keynes's life remained balanced between the pre-war and post-war generations: a mixture which enabled him to be both *enfant terrible* and authority figure. Disconcertingly, the young now included the children of his best friends: Julian Bell and Molly MacCarthy's nephew Francis Warre Cornish both arrived at King's in 1927, Julian a 'great lumbering lion-like creature, with thick tawny curls, a ridiculous nose and eyes . . . a big babyish joyful aesthete.'[60] At forty-five, Keynes was finding contact with the young increasingly difficult. He was always kind to them. He loved talking to them, in the way students enjoy talking about everything, but found that his reputation intimidated them. Lunch in January 1928 for Julian and four of his friends which went on till 4 p.m. was 'hard work', with himself having to introduce all the topics of conversation.[61] On 25 November 1928, his 'party of young boys' ('rather hard work') included Michael Redgrave, Anthony Blunt, Julian Bell and Charles Gifford: the last, a mathematician, had just come up to Trinity from Winchester, having asked Keynes down to give his talk on 'Economic Possibilities for Our Grandchildren' earlier in the year. A more relaxed occasion was the mingling, a month earlier, of the Bloomsbury generations at a party in Dadie Rylands's rooms: Vanessa Bell up to see Julian, Virginia Woolf to read her paper ('A Room of One's Own') to the

young ladies of Girton, Lytton Strachey, the wicked uncle, Julian and
Angelica. In December Julian succeeded where his father had failed by
being elected an Apostle. A talented poet, he contributed a wickedly funny
poem in Drydensque couplets to the avant-garde literary magazine, the
Venture, called 'An epistle on the subject of the ethical and aesthetic beliefs
of Herr Ludwig Wittgenstein (Doctor of Philosophy) to Richard Braithwaite
Esq. MA (Fellow of King's College)'. One stanza of it goes:

> In every company he shouts us down
> And stops our sentence stuttering his own;
> Unceasing argues, harsh, irate and loud,
> Sure that he's right and of his rightness proud.

Young Cambridge in the late 1920s was poetical and theatrical rather
than political. Keynes had got the theatre-going habit from his father. His
education, love of language and natural sense of style had given him a
discriminating appreciation of drama, both classical and Elizabethan. For
someone of his tastes, King's was a congenial place to be. Not only were
the classics and literature taught as 'part of life' – and Greek drama translated with a view to live performance – but, with its reputation for eccentricity and homosexuality, King's attracted young men who loved dressing
up. Sheppard, Dadie Rylands – after his return to King's as a Fellow in
1927 – Frank Birch (a history don) and Donald Beves, all King's men, were
the pillars of King's theatrical life. Keynes talked classics and literature to
his friend Peter Lucas and also to George Thomson, an Apostolic scholar
from Eton. And a succession of talented young undergraduates connected
with the stage flitted through his life: Alec Penrose, Dennis Arundell, Tom
Marshall and Michael Redgrave.

A great theatrical event at this time was the Marlowe Society's production
of *King Lear* on 2 March 1929, 'the most wracking play ever put on the
stage – my throat was full and choking', Maynard told Lydia. His letter
continued,

> I liked Dadie's production very much. It was much less definite than
> Frank's [Frank Birch had produced *Lear* earlier in the 1920s for the
> Amateur Dramatic Club], the producer was invisible . . . so Shake-
> speare had a chance for once to be himself. Lear was, on the whole,
> astonishingly well done [by Peter Hannen]. (Dennis sat by me rather
> sadly.) Several of the other characters good. Michael Redgrave brilli-
> ant as Edgar, a very difficult and important part. . . . Dadie himself
> was terrific and gigantic as one of the wicked daughters [Regan],
> Molly's nephew [Francis Cornish] as Cordelia was very pretty but
> rather a failure. I think you will enjoy it very much. The play is the
> furthest point that Shakespeare's language ever reached. But it is
> rather difficult. So you ought to begin to read it over at once. The

question is – Do you want to see it *twice*, that is on Friday night as well as Saturday?

It was Keynes's links with the theatre which now brought Cambridge into Lydia's orbit. Lydia was thirty-five in 1927. She had steered clear of any further ballet engagements in order to have a child. The letters she and Maynard exchanged give only vague hints of what happened. There is some suggestion that she aborted in May 1927, Keynes assuring her that 'we shall have in the end what we so much long for'.[62] In June Lydia went butterflying with Neville Keynes in Switzerland; she put in a guest appearance with Diaghilev's company at the Prince's Theatre in July 1927, at a gala performance of the Polovtsian Dances before King Alfonso of Spain, who had especially asked for her. Then apparently she became pregnant again. On Monday, 10 October 1927, Keynes wrote, 'Dearest Lydochka, Well, I have had the telegram – the sad deed is done and my dear little bun has had its throat cut. No more to be said until I see it [you?], except a tender touch where the sweet bun was.' It is hard to know exactly what these words mean, since there was no trace on Lydia's body of a hysterectomy. At any rate, there seem to have been no further plans to have a child. Family folklore is that Lydia's pelvis was too narrow to hold a baby.

Deprived of baby and career, Lydia pottered around rather aimlessly in the winter of 1927–8. She helped Angus Davidson with the printing at the Hogarth Press ('it is a neat craft to put letters so near each other that they cannot breathe only kiss'); she started doing Dalcroze eurythmics; she took tennis lessons; she wrote newspaper articles on such subjects as 'Tea'; her Russian lunches sprawled even more abundantly over the whole of Sunday. In June 1928 she appeared in a worthless show called *Hiawatha* and had trouble with her knee. But Maynard had a plan. In October 1928 we find him coaching her by letter: 'Sorrow, borrowed, owed. Can you hear me pronouncing them?' Lydia's o's, pronounced 'oah' in the Russian style, were always a problem for her. A triple bill had been arranged at the ADC Theatre, in which Lydia was to dance in Stravinsky's narrative ballet *The Soldier's Tale*, and also to appear in Shakespeare's *A Lover's Complaint*, as the rustic maiden bewailing her seduction by the young Michael Redgrave. Duncan Grant was commissioned to do the sets and costumes, and Maynard undertook to guarantee the occasion against loss. It was the first staging of Shakespeare's poem, and Lydia's public debut in England as a straight actress.

Keynes, of course, knew all about her acting in America. 'Out of the charades and other nonsense at the parties at Gordon Square'[63] the thought had come to him that her piquant charm in dance might transfer to speech; and early ambitions regained take the place of lost motherhood. The problem was the way she spoke her lines. Dennis Arundell, who arranged the music for *A Lover's Complaint*, was surprised, at a trial reading, 'not only by her accent but also by the ultra-regular rhythm of her speech', like the ticking of a clock. When he suggested a more human approach, 'Maynard authoritatively approved her accentuation as being according to the mechanical scansion.' As for her pronunciation, 'My dear Dennis, it doesn't matter, they haven't heard the piece before.'[64]

Lydia charmed everyone at rehearsals, the box office was sold out, the performances in early November went well, and Frankie Birrell loyally praised her in the *Nation*. Keynes had launched her on a new career. She did not become a continuous part of his Cambridge life till much later. She still 'visited', staying with his parents in Harvey Road; he continued to live in his bachelor rooms. But she had established a presence in Cambridge which was to grow with the years. More improbably, her willingness to extend her range was to make her a central figure in forging a new English style out of the traditions of the Elizabethan masque and the Russian classical ballet, leading to the birth of the Camargo Society in 1930. In setting much of this machinery in motion Keynes was not only bringing his different worlds together, but guilefully fertilising his marriage.

On 28 April 1929 he gossiped to Lydia in a relaxed frame of mind. Would she be bold enough to do Cressida if Frank Birch put on *Troilus* at the ADC next term? He confessed to 'sinning' at Glyphoon's, an antique dealer, by buying a collection of dishes which 'would be very suitable for wedding presents if you don't like them'. There had been a 'terrific hullabaloo' at the starychki's lunch party, with Geoffrey and his Margaret, their four sons, Vivian (Hill), Helen (Dimsdale), himself, M.i.l. and F.i.l.

> Dennis [Robertson] seems exceptionally well this term. In the hotel in the Tyrol, his mother fell down stairs. This distracted his thoughts and greatly improved his health! Peter [Lucas] seems a very gay bachelor. [He and his wife 'Topsy' had parted.] George Thomson [classicist Fellow of King's, Marxist, devotee of Sinn Fein] leaves us after this term to teach Irish to tramps. Piero's mother is here. Ludwig and Piero canoe together on the river. Michael Redgrave is the Editor of the Cambridge Review and Julian writes rather good poems for it. Vivian [Hill] was in hall last night and we talked all the time about whales. Very amusing. [He had invested in a whaling company formed by Rupert Trouton in which Keynes had an interest.] So this is my Budget of 'News in Brief.'

IV

THE ECONOMICS OF INERTIA

Peter Clarke has compellingly argued that the final derailment of the *Treatise on Money* came about as a by-product of Keynes's involvement with Lloyd George, and his resulting confrontation with the Treasury view.[65] A general election was due in 1929. Lloyd George was planning his political come-back on the basis of a great programme of public works to mop up 'abnormal' unemployment. This policy received Keynes's enthusiastic endorsement. Addressing the National Liberal Federation on 27 March 1928 he declared, 'Let us be up and doing, using our idle resources to increase our wealth. With men and plant unemployed, it is ridiculous to say that we cannot afford new developments. It is precisely with these plants and these men that we shall afford them. When every man and every factory is busy, then will be the time to say that we can afford nothing further.' At the Cambridge Union on 16 October 1928 Keynes said, 'We have the savings, the men and the material. The things are worth doing. It is the very pathology of thought to declare that we cannot afford them.' One of those present recalled that he spoke for fifty-five minutes without notes. 'I could hardly believe it. . . .'[66]

On 31 July 1928 Keynes flew Lloyd George's kite in an *Evening Standard* article, 'How to Organise a Wave of Prosperity'. This started a discussion, both within the Treasury and within the government, which also had its eye on the coming election. As the debate became public in the run-up to the election in early 1929, Keynes was forced to sharpen his analytical tools in order to meet objections, crystallised in what became known as the Treasury view. As a result of this debate, Keynes felt he had to restructure his book and 'drastically rewrite' certain chapters. This is what held up its publication till the autumn of 1930.

The 1928 article, in itself, said little new. Keynes pointed to the depressed condition of much of industry, with unemployment 200,000 higher than the previous spring. This was because 'we have deflated prices by raising the exchange value of sterling and by controlling the volume of credit; *but we have not deflated costs*'. 'The fundamental blunder of the Treasury and of the Bank of England has been due, from the beginning, to their belief that if they looked after the deflation of prices the deflation of costs would look after itself.' The General Strike had shown that a frontal assault on wages would be 'socially and politically inexpedient'. The best industries were trying to reduce costs by 'rationalisation', but this would take time and produce extra unemployment in the interval. But there was a way to break the deadlock: a programme of national development to start a 'cumulative' upward movement; working plant to full capacity, which would itself reduce costs; and some rise in prices to reduce the cost-price gap. 'Unemployment will not decline unless business men have the incentive of plentiful credit, high hopes and a slightly rising level of prices – a slight inflation of prices *but not of costs.*'

Keynes wrote, 'When we have unemployed men and unemployed plant and more savings than we are using at home, it is utterly imbecile to say that we cannot *afford* these things. *For it is with the unemployed men and the unemployed plant, and with nothing else, that these things are done.*' The whole subsequent history of the Keynesian Revolution was not able to improve substantially on this rationale for state action to get an economy out of depression.[67]

It was the emergence of a political challenge to the prevailing economic consensus that forced both the Treasury *and* Keynes to sharpen their analytic tools. The old debate about whether Britain should or should not go back to the gold standard was over. The exchange rate had been fixed, and unemployment had not gone away. Given that the interest rate could not be lowered while Britain remained on the gold standard, the problem as it presented itself to the Liberals was how to get more investment at the ruling interest rate. Lloyd George, prompted by Keynes, said: the government must borrow the money itself. But this raised, or rather highlighted, the issue of where the money was to come from. If the government taxed, or borrowed, private savings, this would surely "crowd out" private investment. Keynes himself had advocated mobilising savings 'going abroad', but had not explained why this would increase employment. Either, it seemed, there must be some cache of unused savings, or the banks would have to create 'new' money, which it was then thought would be inflationary.

It was along these lines that the Treasury developed its response to the Liberal initiative. Following the publication of Keynes's article, Churchill asked Richard Hopkins, Frederick Leith-Ross and Hawtrey to comment on it. Sir Richard Hopkins had just succeeded Otto Niemeyer as controller of finance, Niemeyer having gone to the Bank of England; Leith-Ross ('Leithers') was his deputy. But it was Hawtrey, director of financial enquiries, and the Treasury's sole professional economist, who put his finger on the weak spot in Keynes's argument. Basing himself on an article he had published in *Economica* in 1925, he simply said that with a fixed money supply, any loan raised by the government for public works would be at the expense of existing 'consumer outlay'.* This became the basis of the Treasury view that any additional expenditure must be at the expense of something already being done, unless it was inflationary.[68] Leith-Ross commented, 'What Keynes is after, of course, is a definite inflation of credit.'

---

*In his article in *Economica*, March 1925, p. 40, Hawtrey wrote that 'The money borrowed is genuine savings. In other words, it must come out of consumers' income. The effect of this diversion of a part of the consumers' outlay into the hands of the government is to diminish by that amount the effective demand for products'. Hawtrey's view that only an expansion of credit will increase the demand for unemployed labour led him to condemn public works as a 'piece of ritual'.

Hawtrey's abstruse formulation was simplified for Baldwin's speeches: 'we must *either* take existing money *or* create new money',[69] and, of course, 'new money' meant the dreaded inflation. The problem was not excess, but insufficient, capital: there must be more saving before there could be more investment. This was the position that Keynes had to shake.

As Peter Clarke has shown, the Treasury was fighting a battle on two fronts: against Keynes and Lloyd George, on the one side, and against expansionist government ministers like the Home Secretary, Joynson-Hicks, and the Minister of Labour, Steel-Maitland, on the other. In February 1929 both had submitted proposals for large public works programmes: the Treasury's arguments against these could readily be turned against Lloyd George.[70] There was some contact between Hubert Henderson and Steel-Maitland, and it was possibly to give the latter ammunition in his own battle against the Treasury that Keynes either inspired, or wrote, an unsigned article, 'The Objections to Capital Expenditure', in the *Nation* on 23 February 1929. In this it is, for the first time, suggested in print that the savings available for the Liberal programme included not just savings being lent abroad but savings which 'dissipate' themselves in forcing up the prices of Stock Exchange securities thus promoting the deflationary trend. 'For, of course, money savings that do not find their way into real investment represent so much purchasing-power withdrawn from the demand for goods and services.'[71] At about the same time, Clarke argues, Keynes was chopping up the page proofs of the *Treatise on Money* to accommodate the new thought that an expansion of credit by the banking system need not be inflationary if its aim is to 'restore equilibrium between saving and investment'.[72]

Between the summer of 1928 and the early months of 1929 the concept of a 'disequilibrium between saving and investment' became Keynes's main personal answer to the Treasury view that all savings were being invested. Keynes had first identified the leakage of savings into the Stock Exchange in a paper dated 1 September 1928.[73] It arose out of an acrimonious debate he was having with Falk. Falk believed there was a serious inflation in the United States; that the Fed would deal with it by tightening credit, which would reduce share prices; and that the National Mutual, of which he was a director and Keynes chairman, should sell the bulk of its American securities. Keynes replied that the real danger in the United States was not overinvestment but underinvestment, given the huge level of US savings. The Stock Exchange boom was not evidence of the former: all that was happening was swops in share ownership.

A little later Keynes identified a second source of leakage, through the balance of payments. In 1924 he had argued that the export of British capital (savings) did not automatically create a matching export surplus. He had earlier used the same argument to challenge French estimates of Germany's capacity to pay reparations. In both cases it was being suggested that the export of savings, whether in the form of a tribute or a loan, automatically enlarged the market for the export of goods from the paying country. Purchasing power was simply being transferred from A to B. There was no leakage.

Keynes's answer to this argument came in two bites, which enables us to pinpoint the shift in theory. In an article in the *Economic Journal* of December 1927 entitled 'The British Balance of Trade, 1925–7', Keynes claimed that foreign loans from Britain and the United States had been 'hoarded in liquid form in the foreign centre where the borrowing had occurred', thus exerting a strong deflationary influence. 'We and the United States have been continually creating purchasing power for foreigners on a very generous scale in relation to our surpluses, but they have not been using it.'[74] This goes back to arguments Keynes had used in the *Tract* and even earlier. If a central bank sterilised gold inflows in order to prevent price changes, purchasing power in the system was reduced.

By the start of 1929 he had developed a new ground on which to challenge the orthodox doctrine, which had nothing to do with savings being 'hoarded'. In an article published in the *Economic Journal* in March 1929 under the title 'The German Transfer Problem' he argued that each country had a 'natural' rate of exports, or competitiveness, determined by its level of money wages. He wrote:

> My own view is that at a given time the economic structure of a country, in relation to the economic structures of its neighbours, permits of a certain 'natural' level of exports, and that arbitrarily to effect a material alteration of this level by deliberate devices [for example, reducing wage costs] is extremely difficult. Historically, the volume of foreign investment has tended, I think, to adjust itself... to the balance of trade, rather than the other way round, the former being the sensitive and the latter the insensitive factor. In the case of German reparations, on the other hand, we are trying to fix the volume of foreign remittance and compel the balance of trade to adjust itself thereto. Those who see no difficulty in this – like those who saw no difficulty in Great Britain's return to the gold standard – are applying the theory of liquids to what is, if not a solid, at least a sticky mass with strong internal resistances.[75]

This article gave rise to a famous controversy with Bertil Ohlin and Jacques Rueff on whether or not a transfer problem existed. (See Appendix 2 at the end of this chapter.) The question is this: what happens if a country tries to lend or transfer abroad more than its 'natural' export surplus? Keynes supplied the answer not in his *Economic Journal* article, but in an article he wrote for the *Evening Standard* on 19 March 1929. 'If... we lend the money abroad on a scale disproportionate to our export surplus at the present level of wages, the Bank of England loses gold and raises the Bank rate.'[76] In other words, the attempt to invest abroad savings in excess of investment demand at home or foreign demand for British exports fails to conserve purchasing power in the system because bank rate has to be raised in order to protect the exchange. The problem would not arise if the exchange was free to fall or if wages were perfectly flexible and labour perfectly mobile. In either case the balance of payments would adjust to the capital flow without any leakage of purchasing power.

Keynes was certainly being inventive. He had discovered two leaks from the flow of saving into investment, which did not rely on the familiar possibility that savings might be being 'hoarded'. In this way he was assembling bits and pieces of the 'new theory' of the *Treatise on Money*. This theory seemed to reveal a treasure trove of savings waiting to be claimed by the Liberal bounty hunters. But had Sherlock Holmes really solved his case? For in what sense could these savings actually be said to exist once the leakages had caused the level of the national income to drop?

Keynes's involvement in the Liberal battles of early 1929 sharpened his ideas while diverting him from his book. He had refused yet another invitation to stand as Liberal candidate for Cambridge University. ('I don't know when I have vacillated more about making a decision,' he wrote to the Liberal agent, F. A. Potts.) However, he was a member of a special committee, chaired by Seebohm Rowntree, charged with turning the report of the Liberal Industrial Inquiry into the campaign document, *We Can Conquer Unemployment*, and he endorsed Lloyd George's decision to issue his famous pledge, of 1 March 1929, 'to reduce the terrible figures of the workless in the course of a single year to normal proportions . . .' by means of a large scheme of national development.[77]

The Liberals proposed to finance their public works programme by activating 'idle balances'. This line owed more to McKenna than to Keynes. Using the statistics he had denied Richard Kahn, McKenna calculated that between 1919 and 1928 the ratio of 'time deposits' to 'demand deposits' had risen from 28.6 per cent to 44.7 per cent; although the total volume of money had risen, the proportion 'actively engaged in trade' had shrunk.[78] This was the old 'velocity of circulation' approach: money had become arthritic, like Robertson's old lady; it was being hoarded, not being invested. J. A. Hobson took up the same line in the *Nation* of 30 March, when he talked of the Liberal road-loan policy as a way of 'melting . . . frozen savings'. The Treasury's riposte, in one of six *Memoranda on Certain Proposals Relating to Unemployment*, published by Stanley Baldwin's government on 13 May, denied that demand deposits were 'idle'. The were regarded by industry as an essential liquid reserve, and were employed in loans to the short-term money market. Commenting on the Treasury's case, Keynes said, 'Mr. Baldwin has invented the formidable argument . . . that you must not do anything because it will mean that you will not be able to do anything else.'[79]

It is important to note that Keynes did not mean by 'dissipated' or 'wasted' savings what McKenna meant by 'idle balances' or Hobson by 'frozen savings'. Whether they were being 'hoarded' or being used in some way was a secondary issue. The main point was their non-use in adding to the capital equipment of the country – which was what was relevant for employment. And this was the crucial *cause* of 'bad trade' and not just the result, as McKenna seemed to imply. But the new theory, as Keynes himself recognised, was still too undeveloped to be extensively used in public controversy. So on the whole his defence of the Liberal policy proceeded along more familiar, and more intuitive, lines.

Keynes visited the Treasury on 7 March 1929 for discussions with Hopkins and Leith-Ross. The idea which he put to them on this occasion was that bank rate might be raised to attract capital from abroad. This would improve the balance of payments, thus allowing a public investment programme to be undertaken without endangering the gold standard. 'This novel theory', Leith-Ross commented, 'represents a complete volte face from his former doctrine that our troubles are all due to Bank Rate.'[80] As usual, the Treasury took time to adjust to Keynes's endless ingenuity. Nevertheless this meeting marks the first cautious step towards a *modus vivendi* between Keynes and his old department. Leith-Ross was persuaded that Keynes was 'no longer an advocate of inflation'; he also accepted, for the first time, that wage adjustment was much more difficult than the Treasury had believed in Niemeyer's heyday.

In his *Evening Standard* article of 19 March Keynes projected Lloyd George as a man of sober thought, masked by vivid rhetoric. The Liberal schemes had all been suggested by Royal Commissions and had simply been pigeonholed by the Treasury 'under the influence of what I can only describe as a mental affliction'. Using his favourite device of *reductio ad absurdum* Keynes proceeded:

> They have believed that, if people can be induced to save as much as possible, and if steps are then taken to prevent anything being done with these savings, the rate of interest will fall. . . . Indeed, if all forms of capital enterprise were to be rendered illegal, the rate of interest would sink towards zero – while the rate of unemployment would mount towards heaven.
>
> . . .
>
> It will be time enough for prudence when we see prices tending to rise and the demand for labour in excess of the supply.
>
> The orthodox theory *assumes* that everyone is employed. If this were so, a stimulus in one direction would be at the expense of production in others. But when there is a large surplus of *unused* productive resources, as at present, the case is totally different.
>
> The notion that saving and investment are always exactly balanced – i.e., that whenever I save £100 some entrepreneur sets on foot a new capital enterprise for £100 – is an unfounded delusion. So is the view

that our exports will increase by £2,000,000 because last week we lent £2,000,000 to Chile.

Moreover, if the above were true, it would be just as true that the building of a new factory by Sir Herbert Austin or Mr Samuel Courtauld would add nothing to employment – which nobody believes. In short, the fatalistic belief that there can never be more employment than there is is altogether baseless.[81]

Keynes continued his electioneering when he replied, on 19 April, to an article in the *Evening Standard* by Sir Laming Worthington-Evans, the Secretary for War, attacking his own article of 19 March. Worthington-Evans had been properly briefed in the Treasury view. Keynes now said there were three sources from which savings could be drawn: saving on the dole, a reduction of foreign lending, and those savings which have not 'materialised' in investment.[82] There were further exchanges, when Worthington-Evans accused him of inconsistency and being more a politician than an economist. To Lydia he wrote on 24 April, 'I couldn't help sitting down and writing an answer. But what a bore it is! What does it matter anyhow what I said in 1925?' Lydia, on the other hand, was delighted when Worthington-Evans called her husband a 'mad Mullah'. 'That is what you are when you dance with me . . . but he does not know that it is poor of him to not allow you to be more than economist, all your "walks of life" make a piquant personality. . . .'

Keynes's main defence of the Liberal programme, written jointly with Hubert Henderson, was published as a Hogarth Press pamphlet on 10 May. It was called 'Can Lloyd George Do It?' and was mainly cobbled together from pieces Keynes and Henderson had been writing in the *Nation* over the preceding months. The answer was a resounding yes delivered with all the panache and elegance one had come to expect of Keynes's popular writing. The pamphlet was based on a paradox which Keynes was to repeat at the end of the *General Theory*: the so-called practical men were so enslaved by obsolete theory – 'venerable academic inventions' – that they could not see the 'common sense of the problem' which was, quite simply, 'There is work to do; there are men to do it. Why not bring them together?'

Keynes and Henderson considered the government's case that the Liberal programme of £100m. a year (for three years) would provide negligible additional employment. This was based on the view that for every £1m. spent less than 2000 jobs would be provided, so that the spending of £100m. would put under 200,000 to work – and probably far fewer in the first year, given the practical difficulties in getting the schemes started. This calculation ignored the indirect effects of the expenditure: for every man put to work on building a road or a house, at least another would find a job supplying the inputs required. Moreover, these jobs would be in ordinary industry. So a 'safe average' for the Liberal programme as a whole would be 5000 men for each £1m.; or 500,000 a year altogether – the extent of the 'abnormal' unemployment.

But beyond this there was the 'cumulative force of trade activity'. Keynes and Henderson said, 'The fact that many workpeople who are now unemployed would be receiving wages instead of unemployment pay would mean an increase in effective purchasing power which would give a general stimulus to trade. Moreover, the greater trade activity would make for further trade activity; for the forces of prosperity, like those of a trade depression, work with a cumulative effect.' They added: 'It is not possible to measure effects of this character with any sort of precision.' But they were 'of immense importance' and would make 'the effects on employment of a given capital expenditure . . . far larger than the Liberal pamphlet assumes'. Moreover, these effects would start even before the programme was fully operational, for the *expectation* of large schemes coming on line would give 'an immediate fillip to the whole trade and industry of the country'.[83]

This is a key passage in the pamphlet, and indeed in the history of the Keynesian Revolution. It prompted Keynes's 'favourite pupil' Richard Kahn to attempt to sum these cumulative (but diminishing) effects over successive rounds of spending. The result was the 'employment multiplier'. The other point has to do with expectations. Keynes and Henderson assumed that the announcement of the public works programme would cause businessmen to increase their investment in working capital to meet the forthcoming orders. But suppose businessmen thought, instead, that the government had gone mad, that they had started a dangerous inflation, that public works were merely a prelude to socialist confiscation, and so on. Would they not in that case want to hoard their money or send it abroad rather than invest it? Which way, in other words, would the business community jump? This was to become another key issue in the Keynesian Revolution.

Next Keynes and Henderson trained their guns on those 'mysterious, unintelligible reasons of high finance and economic theory' (that is, the Treasury view) which claimed that the Liberal programme would 'merely substitute employment on State schemes for ordinary employment': 'abra would rise, cadabra would fall'. There were three sources of funds available for new investment. First, there were the savings now used for government consumption – maintaining men on the dole. Secondly, savings could be found by a net reduction of foreign lending: it would be foreign governments and municipalities who would be 'crowded out' by a loan-financed public works programme.[84] Thirdly, there were 'the savings which now run to waste through lack of adequate credit'.[85] Mysteriously, the three sources became four when Keynes and Henderson slipped in the phrase 'something [that is, fresh savings] will be provided by the very prosperity which the new policy will foster'.[86] The suggestion was that the investment would create part of the saving needed to finance it.

Keynes and Henderson addressed themselves to another point: if savings were surplus to investment demand why did not the rate of interest fall to adjust the two? In their answer substance and style are mixed together with notable effect:

> The rate of interest can fall for either of two opposite reasons. It may fall on account of an abundant supply of savings, i.e. of money available to be spent on investments; or it may fall on account of a deficient supply of investments, i.e. on desirable purposes on which to spend the savings. Now a fall in the rate of interest for the first reason is, obviously, very much in the national interest. But a fall for the second reason, if it follows from a deliberate restriction of outlets for investment, is simply a disastrous method of impoverishing ourselves.
>
> A country is enriched not by the mere negative act of an individual not spending all his income on current consumption. It is enriched by the positive act of using these savings to augment the capital equipment of the country.
>
> It is not the miser who gets rich; but he who lays out his money in fruitful investment.
>
> The object of urging people to save is *in order* to be able to build houses and roads and the like. Therefore a policy of trying to lower the rate of interest by suspending new capital improvements and so stopping up the outlets and purposes of our savings is simply suicidal. . . . But this, is in fact, what the Treasury has been doing for several years. . . .
>
> The futility of their policy and the want of sound reasoning behind it have been finally demonstrated by its failure even to secure a fall in the rate of interest. For . . . if outlets for investment at home are stopped up, savings flow abroad on a scale disproportionate to our favourable balance of trade, with the result that the Bank of England tends to lose gold. To counteract this position, the bank rate has to be raised.
>
> So in the end we have the worst of both worlds. The country is backward in its equipment, instead of being thoroughly up to date. Business profits are poor, with the result that the yield of income tax disappoints the Chancellor of the Exchequer and he is unable either to relieve the taxpayer or to push forward with schemes of social reform. Unemployment is rampant. This want of prosperity *actually diminishes the rate of saving* [italics added] and this defeats even the original object of a lower interest rate of interest. So rates of interest are, after all, high.[87]

The pamphlet concludes with Keynes's familiar contrast between the forces of life and death:

Negation, restriction, inactivity – these are the government's watch-
words. Under their leadership we have been forced to button up our
waistcoats and compress our lungs. Fears and doubts and hypochon-
driac precautions are keeping us muffled up indoors. But we are not
tottering to our graves. We are healthy children. We need the breath
of life. There is nothing to be afraid of. On the contrary. The future
holds in store for us far more wealth and economic freedom and
possibilities of personal life than the past has ever offered.

There is no reason why we should not feel ourselves free to be bold,
to be open, to experiment, to take action, to try the possibilities of
things. And over against us, standing in the path, there is nothing but
a few old gentlemen tightly buttoned-up in their frock coats, who only
need to be treated with a little friendly disrespect and bowled over
like ninepins.

Quite likely they will enjoy it themselves, when once they have got
over the shock.[88]

It was exhilarating stuff.

Lifted up by his own rhetoric, Keynes was extremely optimistic about the
electoral prospects of the party he supported. He was convinced that Hubert
Henderson – whom he had persuaded to stand in his place – would get in
at Cambridge, and that the Liberal Party nationally would get over 100
seats. Lydia, wandering in Hyde Park, thought most of the people there
would vote Conservative 'with their blank dopy empty expressions; the club
footed or armless were the more attractive, and no doubt will vote something
else'. In fact, the general election of 30 May 1929 produced 287 Labour
MPs, 260 Conservatives and 59 Liberals. Henderson was not one of them,
and Keynes lost £160 on his bets, though he won £10 from Winston Churchill. Although the Liberals got 23 per cent of the vote (as against 38 per cent
for the Conservatives and 37 per cent for Labour) they obtained only 10
per cent of the parliamentary seats. Lloyd George's last fling had failed.
MacDonald formed his second Labour government, with the Liberals holding the balance of power. 'I can't see that anything satisfactory can possibly
result from it,' Keynes wrote gloomily to Lydia on 3 June.

APPENDIX I

Robertson's Economics

The aim of *Banking Policy and the Price Level* was to suggest monetary policies
for moderating industrial fluctuations. Robertson believed that investment
booms were brought to a premature halt by a shortage of 'real capital', as
consumption encroached on voluntary saving. In such circumstances, bank-

ing policy should aim to 'force' the public to save more and consume less. This required action to raise the price level, or counteract any tendency for it to fall, as the least disruptive method of bringing about the required shift from consumption to saving. Monetary policy should be designed to maintain equilibrium, this equilibrium being defined as 'appropriate' fluctuations in the production of capital goods. Equilibrium was thus defined in dynamic terms – in terms of the needs of a 'progressive' or 'growing' economy – rather than in static terms, or stability at any single moment in time.

Fluctuations, Robertson argued, were inseparable from the use of 'fixed capital', in turn inseparable from progress. They were related to 'cycles of demand' for new instruments of production, changes in labour productivity and inter-sectoral shifts in demand. There was no absolute measure of what is 'appropriate' – indeed workers and employers are likely to have divergent views on this. In an owner-dominated economy workers are 'overworked' in the boom and 'condemned to walk the streets' in a depression.[89] So what is 'appropriate' depends on the community's 'time preference' map, resulting from the balance of power in industry. This determines the degree of 'sacrifice' the community will tolerate to keep progress going.

Given agreement on what is 'appropriate', 'inappropriate' fluctuations are nevertheless endemic in a decentralised economy (even without money) for three main reasons: (1) the indivisibility of investment, (2) the interdependence of psychology, magnifying 'errors of optimism and pessimism', and (3) 'the stress of competition, aggravated by the length of time which is required to adjust production to changing demand': if 10 per cent increased output is required by changed demand conditions, anarchic competition will probably produce 25 per cent, so the greater the contraction eventually needed to restore equilibrium.[90] Monetary policy can superimpose a further set of 'inappropriate' fluctuations, magnifying both boom and bust. Nevertheless the aim of monetary policy should be not to prevent all fluctuation 'but to permit those which are necessary to the establishment of appropriate fluctuations in output and to repress those which tend to carry the alterations in output beyond the appropriate point'.[91]

Robertson invented a whole new vocabulary to distinguish between different kinds of saving by motive and different kinds of capital by function. Capital is provided by 'lacking': Spontaneous, Automatic, Induced, the last two being 'imposed' by the rise in prices. If a saver does not apply his lacking to producing new capital he is said to hoard (Abortive Lacking). There is a correlative vocabulary for spending, also distinguished by motive: Spontaneous and Automatic Splashing, and Induced Dis-Lacking, the last two also being imposed by falling prices.

Lacking is used to provide capital. Spontaneous Long Lacking provides society with its fixed capital. Spontaneous Short Lacking provides it with its circulating or 'working' capital, but the banks can also provide circulating capital by transforming Spontaneous New Hoarding into Short Lacking, and by 'imposing' Lacking on the community.

The main duty of the banking system is to offset a developing shortage of Spontaneous Short Lacking in the upswing. It does this (1) by preventing an 'increased desire to hoard' from withdrawing funds from the provision of circulating capital, and (2) by making additional loans to counteract the rise in the value of hoards due to increased productivity, which would otherwise lead to a fall in the price level.

The aim Robertson stresses above all others is to prevent the boom being prematurely extinguished by a fall in the price level or in the rate of inflation, because this stimulates consumption (the real value of money balances rising as prices fall), and thus deprives industry of the 'lacking' necessary to complete the investment. But it is also very difficult to establish the 'appropriate' price level, because the quantity theory of money is not a reliable guide in the short run. An expansion in credit could produce a rise in the price level smaller or greater than the amount of new credit, depending on whether it produces hoarding or dishoarding. The banking system can offset these secondary tendencies by fine-tuning interest rates. In other words, the banking system must organise some rise in the price level, but prevent secondary effects without choking off the expansion itself.

On the downward path of the business cycle, the banking system's main duty is to ensure that the 'justifiable' decline in output does not beget an unjustifiable one. But this is much harder, Robertson pointing out that when output is contracting the banking system has much less control over the volume of credit than when it is rising – that is, it may not be able to make an unwilling borrower borrow unless the interest rate falls to zero.

Banking Policy and the Price Level concentrates mainly on fluctuations in Short Lacking. But Long Lacking too might need to be imposed on the public in a progressive community. The duty of the banking system is to ensure a complementary provision of both kinds of Lacking to get a proper 'balance of industrial production' as the economy moves forward through time.

The main differences between Robertson and Keynes (1920s model) are:

1 Stabilisation (Keynes) versus Appropriate Fluctuations (Robertson) as policy goal.
2 Preference for static and aggregated (Keynes) rather than dynamic and disaggregated (Robertson) analysis.
3 Undersaving (Robertson) versus oversaving (Keynes) as cause of depression.
4 Even if undersaving is the problem, 'forced saving' is too precarious a source of funds to make inflation worth trying.
5 Duty of banking system to keep saving and investment equal (Keynes, *A Treatise on Money*) versus duty of banking system to keep 'lacking' and

investment equal (Robertson, *Banking Policy and the Price Level*).

Points of agreement:

1 Separation of decisions to save from decisions to invest.
2 No automatic adjustment between the two.
3 Central role of banking system in adjustment process.
4 Unreliability of quantity theory of money as guide to policy.

APPENDIX 2

The Transfer Problem

Keynes's 1929 debate on the German transfer problem with the Swedish economist Bertil Ohlin and the French economist Jacques Rueff[92] is notable mainly for the classical, or pre-Keynesian, way he analysed the problem, concentrating on relative price movements and ignoring demand effects.

Keynes had continued to comment on the reparation problem. He praised the Dawes Report of April 1924 (Josiah Stamp was its chief author) as 'the finest contribution hitherto to this impossible problem'.[93] The novelty of the report lay in separating the budgetary from the transfer problem. It assumed that what the German government raised in taxes for reparations purposes could not necessarily be 'transferred' across the exchanges. It therefore provided that the money should be paid into a special account, and only so much paid to Germany's creditors in a given year as would not cause the mark to fall. The theory behind this was that Germany's 'capacity to pay' was limited by its trade balance.

This was the doctrine Keynes was to uphold in his March 1929 article in the *Economic Journal*. Its occasion was the setting up of a new committee of experts under the American Owen D. Young to recast the machinery of reparation payments started by the Dawes Plan of 1924. It had long been apparent that Germany had been paying no 'real' reparations (that is, goods and services) at all, even though, every year, it religiously transferred money to its creditors. As Keynes commented in 1926, 'the United States lends money to Germany, Germany transfers its equivalent to the Allies, the Allies pay it back to the United States government. Nothing real passes – no one is a penny the worse off'.[94] Nor, he might have said, were the Allies a penny the better off. The French and Italians, the two chief claimants, argued that Germany could pay much larger annual sums if it wanted to. Keynes could not resist the chance to take on his old adversaries. Against the 'French School', he asserted that 'You do not automatically create an export surplus merely by collecting taxation within Germany.'[95]

Keynes claimed that any money raised by taxes in excess of Germany's existing trade surplus could be transferred only by cutting German money wages to make its industries more competitive on world markets.[96] His main supporting argument was that Germany did not in fact have a trade surplus, even though the German government was raising the necessary taxes for reparations. It could pay such reparations as it did only by borrowing from the Americans.

In his rejoinder to Keynes in the June 1929 issue of the *Economic Journal*, the Swedish economist Bertil Ohlin pointed out that the reason Germany did not have an export surplus was that it was borrowing almost twice as much as it was paying out in reparations, such borrowing expanding its imports and encouraging production for the home market rather than for export. Germany did not borrow because it lacked an export surplus: its borrowing prevented an export surplus from developing. The transfer problem was created by the borrowing. Ohlin argued that the collection of taxes in Germany would cause demand in Germany to fall. The transfer of this demand to (say) American would lead to an increased American demand for German goods. The increase in Germany's exports to America was thus independent of changes in relative wage rates. The crucial mechanism was transfer of purchasing power. 'Is it not obvious', Ohlin wrote in a rejoinder to a rejoinder, after several fruitless exchanges of letters with Keynes, 'that the buying power of a country, like that of an individual, will exceed its (his) income by the amount of gifts and loans, quite independently of any change in the price levels?'[97]

Jacques Rueff, who entered the fray in the September issue of the *Economic Journal*, relied on a classic price-adjustment argument which went back to David Hume. Any increase in the supply of marks in the foreign-exchange market would cause their value to fall relative to other currencies', which automatically involved the relative cheapening of goods whose price was expressed in terms of marks; in other words, it would stimulate German exports and hinder imports. So here too there was no problem.

Keynes rejected this argument. 'For it is not simply a case of changing the value of money all round, but of changing the terms of international trade in a direction unfavourable to Germany, so that a larger quantity of exports than before will have to be offered for a given quantity of imports.'[98]

This led him to the point at issue with Ohlin. He asserted that the payment of reparations imposed a primary and a secondary burden on Germany. First, it had to tax its citizens by the amount of the payment. Secondly, its export prices had to fall relatively to its import prices, so that a larger volume of exports was required to pay for a given amount of imports. The size of the second burden depended on the responsiveness of world demand to a reduction in the price of German exports. If the elasticity of demand was less than one, competition would tend to turn the terms of trade indefinitely against Germany. The payment of reparations thus involved a double loss of German real income: x in respect of the actual payment, and y in respect of the deterioration in the terms of trade necessary to effect the transfer. Keynes's argument was that this second burden, which involved cutting money wages, would be resisted and that transfer therefore could not take place.

According to Ohlin, the act of reducing German private incomes by taxation and transferring the proceeds abroad led to an adjustment of the trade balance, without the second burden coming into play. German 'buying power' would fall, American 'buying power' (say) would rise. Germany would import less and export more; the United States would import more and export less. Relative volumes would change at unchanged relative prices. Ohlin accepted that the price-elasticity argument had force and might require relative wage or efficiency adjustments, but he thought it of minor importance.

If we stick to the pure theory of the matter, Keynes was wrong and Ohlin was right. Keynes's argument would be correct only if the transfer of capital left demand conditions in one or other or both countries unchanged.

Nevertheless, he was intuitively right to believe that there were severe difficulties in effecting transfers in the actual state of the world. An obvious difficulty arose if the recipient of the transfer put up tariff barriers against the import of the transferer's goods, or hoarded rather than spent the extra purchasing power. In such cases there would be a shrinkage of effective demand over the whole system. What makes the debate difficult to follow was that Keynes kept muddling up the theory with applications to the particular case. For example, he wrote at one point, 'I am quite unable to see how untransferred reparation payments lying in Berlin are going to cause an expansion of credit in this or any other country.' But they were only lying in Berlin because of the transfer-protection clauses of the Dawes Plan. Ohlin's argument presumed that they were in the hands of the creditors. Misunderstandings of this kind prevented any meeting of minds. Keynes finally wrote to Ohlin, 'the whole question of the theory of international transfers . . . is in a most muddled condition'.[99]

The transfer problem debate fits into Keynes's thought as part of a wider argument. It was simply an illustration from geography of the principle that decisions to save and decisions to invest were made by two different sets of people. If saving was unmatched by investment, demand would run down. This was irrespective of whether the savings were being hoarded or being used to buy existing securities. What Keynes failed to explain was why this process of rundown should not go on for ever – until there were no more savings left. He was being grimly earnest when he said that the strict application of orthodox principles led to the mortuary.

The reparation issue links up with his economic theory in another way. An 'old' country tended to increase its foreign lending as investment opportunities at home dried up. This required more exports. More exports could be 'forced' on the world only by turning the terms of trade against the lending country, that is, by producing more exports for a given quantity of imports. This could not be done because 'efficiency wages' were fixed. Thus the attempt by an old country to maintain a policy of free capital exports would lead to growing unemployment over time.

APPENDIX 3

Labordère

A flavour of the Labordère–Keynes correspondence is given by the letter Labordère wrote to Keynes on 1 September 1928:

> It is self-evident that man will never be able to know what money is no more than he will be able to know what God is, or the spiritual world. Money is not the infinite but it is the indefinite, an astounding complex of all sorts of psychological as well as material reactions. . . . Such being the case, the borrowers, as are termed such people as think they are warranted in undertaking to pay at a certain time a certain amount of an unknown thing called 'cash', should be taxed of sheer folly. As a sequel a market where the brokers' loans have reached a high water level is a market where lunatics abound and may run loose at any time and play havoc.
>
> The frame of mind of a borrower is tantamount to the frame of mind of a speculator. He pictures to himself a vivid image of the future, for him a glowing certainty: he is harnessed in faith, he is passionate and obstinate, he is a loser. . . . However a principle always holds good: 'Never keep a security which you would not buy under present circumstances; never keep liquid assets at a time when you would not feel inclined to realise your investments. . . .' But there is another principle which stands in the way of the first: 'Never change your investments, be faithful.' . . . Life is contradictory, we are and have to be ever in doubt. All the fun in life is in this contradiction because it makes for anxiety and anxiety is at the bottom of movement which is life. We have an instinct which propels us to barter our securities for cash and our cash for securities and to shift from one security to another. Whilst another instinct propels us to adhere fondly to our cash or to a given security, as we are apt to adhere to a pet dog.
>
> When we are in doubt as to which way to go . . . we should first of all inquire from ourselves which way are our dominant leanings, which way the temptation is more acute . . . and, if in the light of reason chances appear to be equal both ways, we should unhesitatingly decide the other way. Such is the advice given by Cartesius.

If we have made up our mind, if we have sold a genuinely good security . . . because the price was apparently far too high for the time being . . . we should never part with all of it. Why so? For the sake of faithfulness – a most paying virtue – in order to keep a link alive between the security we parted with and ourselves . . . so that we may step in again at the proper time and buy back.

Keynes's reply is missing. He obviously received this letter with great excitement, Labordère confessing that on the day he wrote it he was 'in a splendid mood' quite unrepresentative of his normal state.

CHAPTER TEN

Summing Up the 1920s: A Treatise on Money

I

INTRODUCTION

A Treatise on Money was published on 24 October 1930. After Keynes finished the preface on 14 September, he wrote his usual statistical summary for his parents: 'It has occupied me seven years off and on, – and so one parts from it with mixed feelings . . . . Artistically it is a failure – I have changed my mind too much during the course of writing it for it to be a proper unity. But I think it contains an abundance of ideas and material. It is nearly twice as long as Probability and four times the length of my other books.' Schumpeter, on reading it, was amazed that he had been able to accomplish it at all 'among all the multifarious calls on your time and force'.[1]

Although it was published during the great depression, it is pre-depression in atmosphere. It is an attempt to theorise about economic instability – its causes and its phases, with the aim of suggesting a cure, or at least mitigation. Its main, though not exclusive, reference point is the British economy of the 1920s, with the evidence it supplied of the extreme difficulty in adjusting the level of costs to movements in prices, especially downwards. Its method is dynamic as befits an economics of what Fisher called 'transition periods'. Its object, Keynes declared in the preface, was to find a method useful in describing not just the characteristics of static equilibrium but the 'dynamical laws' governing the passage from one position of equilibrium to another. He confessed that the ideas with which he ended up were very different from those with which he began.

His initial ideas were those of the monetary reformers as he had expressed them in the *Tract on Monetary Reform*. The familiar theme is the monetary mismanagement of a credit-money economy. Its issues are those raised by the great inflation and deflation of 1919–23, the debates surrounding the return to the gold standard in 1925 and the subsequent problem of the imperfect British adjustment – as it seemed – to the restored parity.

To these ideas we must add the method Keynes and Robertson had jointly developed, starting in 1913 but continuing in the mid–1920s, for discussing short-run problems. Theirs was a first shot – at least in Anglo-Saxon economics – at integrating monetary and 'real' factors in the analysis of the business cycle. Changes in monetary conditions could cause saving to diverge from investment; this divergence was the efficient cause of business fluctuations. The distinction between forced and voluntary saving followed, as did the view that the difference between saving and investment was exactly equal to a prior change in the 'effective' quantity of money – the supply of money multiplied by its velocity of circulation.

By the time he had finished the *Treatise on Money* Keynes had broken away from this range of ideas. Saving and investment could diverge without any prior change in monetary conditions, and without leaving any trace on the statistics of monetary aggregates. Decisions to save and invest were made by different sets of people; an act of saving does not necessarily lead to an act of investment, and vice versa. In a sense the *Treatise on Money* had started at the wrong end. It had tried to use the quantity theory of money as a tool for analysing fluctuations which Keynes had come to feel originated outside the sphere of monetary circulation – in business psychology, which ought to be the true focus of investigation. Monetary conditions reflected these fluctuations, but did not necessarily cause them.

The idea that saving and investment could diverge spontaneously was deeply heretical for it suggested that there was no spontaneous balancing mechanism. In what Keynes had not yet started to call classical theory, there was a price – the rate of interest – which would always equalise the two. Keynes did not yet doubt that this was so. Following Wicksell he called this price the 'natural' rate of interest. But there is no connection in his system between the market rate of interest and the 'natural' rate. Nothing brings them into equality *except banking policy itself*, and the banking system was not obliged to follow a particular policy. The rate of interest – the price of credit – is already a purely monetary phenomenon. This was the consequence of having a credit-money economy. The criteria governing credit-creation had no reference to the quantity of credit required to keep saving and investment equal. In such a system there was no automatic thermostat: nothing to stop it spiralling out of control except the 'traditions and principles' of the banking system itself.

Keynes tells two stories in the *Treatise* about what happens once an existing equilibrium is disturbed. The first is a 'credit cycle' story in which an initial disequilibrium corrects itself through a mixture of banking policies and lagged shifts in class income shares. This business-cycle story goes back to the Keynes–Robertson discussions of the 1920s: in the upswing we have a sequence of commodity inflation, profit inflation and income inflation, which then reverses itself. In the second story, a deflationary shock can produce a cumulative downward movement with no 'point of return'. This story is told in his famous banana parable. The first story is replete with rebalancing mechanisms (though these might be 'sticky'). In the second story, which abstracts from banking policy, there is no adjustment mechanism. Keynes regarded the second story as his real contribution, the kernel of his message. It points to the *General Theory*. Did Keynes already feel, by the time he had finished the *Treatise*, that cyclical phenomena were less significant than the fact that the cycle was taking place at such a reduced level of activity?

An important, and neglected, source of Keynes's arguments in the *Treatise* is his involvement in the reparation controversy, and the distinction it led him to make between the transfer of money abroad and the transfer of real resources. In 1924 he applied this idea to British foreign lending. British savings which could not be profitably invested at home were drifting abroad without setting up an equivalent demand for British exports. By 1928, reflection on the New York Stock Exchange boom had suggested to him a theoretical explanation of why this might be so: savings could be used to buy titles to shares without setting in motion any new acts of production: this was the nature of a speculative bull market. As he put it in the *Treatise on Money*, savings could be withdrawn from the industrial into the financial circulation, from investment into speculation. Saving used for speculative purposes was just as deflationary in its effects as savings 'kept idle' or 'hoarded', even though the 'effective' quantity of money showed no change. It was equally that part of a community's current income not being spent on buying things capable of being produced.

These, then, were the ideas, suggested by 'vigilant observation' of the facts, which fed into the *Treatise on Money*. The formal analysis, represented by the Fundamental Equations, was still conducted in terms of price levels. But the dynamic analysis – what caused the price levels to fluctuate – was rooted in decisions to save and invest. Technically, these, together with the decision of the banking system about how much credit to supply, are the short-run *independent variables* of Keynes's new system, the price levels the *dependent variables*. The result is a hybrid. Its appearance is that of some version of the quantity theory of money; but what gives it locomotion are decisions independent of monetary conditions.

The equality of saving and investment was the stability condition of the economic system; it was when they diverged that you got boom or slump. In the *Treatise* Keynes still thought that the normal object of monetary policy should be to stabilise the purchasing power of money, specifically the consumer price index. This is because he thought that changes in the desire to save or invest had their first effects on the price level of output: effects on volume followed. Thus the task of the banking system was still, as in the *Tract on Monetary Reform*, to offset fluctuations in the price level by varying the supply of credit.

Carried over from the *Tract on Monetary Reform* is the theme of conflict between price stability and exchange-rate stability. An exchange rate fixed by law has to be maintained by policy; the policy may bring about economic depression. But the argument has shifted somewhat. The complaint of the *Tract* against the gold standard was that it did not guarantee the quantity of money (or gold) needed to maintain stable prices. In the *Treatise* a new complaint is added: the gold standard prevents the monetary authority from adjusting the rate of interest so as to secure or maintain equality between saving and investment.

The *Treatise* was not radical enough for the critics of capitalism, though it offered them a few crumbs. The idea that a capitalist economy thrives best in periods of 'profit inflation' (with investment running ahead of saving) hints at a Marxist theory of exploitation. Explanation of depression in terms of 'excess saving' nods in the direction of J. A. Hobson and his theory of underconsumption. The suggestion that capitalism might lack an automatic pilot was certainly heretical. But this is as far as it goes. The *Treatise* is a glorification of the banker as economic therapist.

> Those who attribute sovereign power to the monetary authority in the governance of prices do not, of course, claim that the terms on which money is supplied is the *only* influence affecting the price level. To maintain that the supplies in a reservoir can be maintained at any required level by pouring enough water into it, is not inconsistent with admitting that the level of the reservoir depends on many other factors besides how much water is poured in . . . [2]

By the 1930s, the banker as therapist had faded from the scene. The full resources of the state are required to restore capitalist economies to health, and by implication to keep them healthy.

'I feel', Keynes wrote in the preface, 'like someone who has been forcing his way through a confused jungle. Now that I have emerged from it, I see that I might have taken a more direct route and that many problems and perplexities which beset me during the journey had not precisely the significance which I supposed at the time.' By the time he had finished rewriting the theoretical parts of the *Treatise* linguistic exhaustion had plainly set in. Books III and IV are full of dreadfully convoluted sentences.[3] They are also replete with pages of dismal algebra (the Fundamental Equations) in which one identity is transformed into another with the help of an increasing pile of symbols until the reader has forgotten where he started from or what they mean.

On the other hand, in volume two, *The Applied Theory of Money*, where Keynes is under less theoretical pressure, things go much better. Chapter 30 on 'Historical Illustrations' is full of fancy, sparkle and paradox, especially when Keynes is expounding his favourite theme, that it is the virtuous who are damned and the sinners who are blest. 'When you're not too esoteric,' Sir Frederick Leith-Ross of the Treasury wrote to him, 'the artist in you is so fascinating that I often wish you wouldn't confine yourself to economics.'[4] Keynes is always at his brightest when he can bring his economics into line with his 'religion'. Much of the uncertainty as to what he was about might have been avoided had he allowed the following shaft of sunlight to play on his argument earlier than the 458th page:

> It has been usual to think of the accumulated wealth of the world as having been painfully built up out of the voluntary abstinence of individuals from the immediate enjoyment of consumption which we call thrift. But it should be obvious that mere abstinence is not enough by itself to build cities or drain fens . . . It is enterprise which builds and improves the world's possessions . . . If enterprise is afoot, wealth accumulates whatever may be happening to thrift; and if enterprise is asleep, wealth decays whatever thrift may be doing.
>
> Thus, thrift may be the handmaid and nurse of enterprise. But equally she may not. And, perhaps, even usually she is not. For enterprise is connected with thrift not directly; but at one remove; and the link which should join them is frequently missing. For the engine which drives enterprise is not thrift, but profit.[5]

The idea that abstinence is no guarantee of wealth; that it is the profiteer and not the abstainer who brings life into a capitalist economy, and inescapably so, since investment is an uncertain business, is the vision behind the algebra, and imperfectly captured by it.

Few students of Keynes now bother with the *Treatise*; they have accepted Keynes's own view that anything of value in it was better and more briefly expressed in the *General Theory*, which, in addition, produced the genuinely 'new theory' for which Keynes is remembered. Such views have contributed to widespread misinterpretation of Keynes's work as a whole.

It is always wrong to concentrate on one part of a thinker's thought to the exclusion of others – and this despite Keynes's own image of himself as 'sloughing skins' like a snake. Two problems claimed his analytic attention over his professional lifetime: (1) the problem of fluctuations in prices and output, and (2) the problem of persisting mass unemployment. These problems can occur together, in the sense that fluctuations can take place round a lower rather than a higher level of employment. Over Keynes's life the focus of attention gradually shifted from the first to the second – in line with what was actually happening – and this led to a shift in analytical method.

A Treatise on Money is at the tail-end of a literature concerned with economic fluctuations. It was a conceptualisation of an historical experience stretching from the last quarter of the nineteenth century through to the start of the great depression. Unemployment is conceived as fluctuating round some 'norm'. It is not the 'norm' which is the problem, but the fluctuations. By the 1930s, the 'norm' rather than the fluctuations has come to be seen as the problem. This is associated not just with the experience of the 1930s, but with Keynes's growing feeling that 'mature' economies are more stagnant than immature ones. But what is, in fact, the 'normal' state of a mature capitalist economy? It is not clear that the 1930s gave a conclusive answer. The *Treatise* reminds us that modern economic history includes both the nineteenth century and the post–1945 epoch. If the fluctuation in prices and output rather than persisting mass unemployment is the main focus of practical interest, the *Treatise* is likely to be more fruitful than the *General Theory*. To read off 'Keynesian' policy prescriptions from a single book can give, and has given, rise to systematic errors in applying his ideas.

A focus on fluctuations rather than on stagnation highlights the role of monetary, rather than fiscal, policy. Fiscal policy is the most direct means of lifting an economy out of a semi-permanent slump. Active monetary policy is advocated in the *Treatise* for all states short of gross and prolonged enfeeblement. That Keynesian policy after the Second World War came to be identified so exclusively with 'fiscalism' was a misreading of the times fostered by a 'single book' approach to Keynes.

The *General Theory* is much more abstract than the *Treatise*. With one exception, it shuns institutional detail. It is about an 'economy', not about a world of economies. For Keynes's views on international money, exchange-rate policy, monetary policy, cost-inflation – many of the problems besetting 'open' economies running at near full employment – one needs to go to the *Treatise* rather than the *General Theory*.

Finally, it may be considered a virtue of the *Treatise* that it brings out much more clearly than the *General Theory* the role of changes in relative prices and income shares in a dynamic adjustment process: either to a new equilibrium or to a new growth path. Abnormal profits, forced saving, dishoarding as sources of investment funds have disappeared from the *General Theory*, obliterated by the assumption that 'normally' the factors of production will be heavily unemployed. But it is useful to be reminded that, over a wide range of possibilities, a capitalist economy prospers when profits are growing faster than wages and slumps when wages are increasing faster than profits; and that there are limits to how far everyone can march forward harmoniously in step.

II

DEFINITIONS

The big ideas of the *Treatise on Money* are so deeply embedded in an insti-tutionalised monetary framework and a formal apparatus of special terms and definitions that they rarely emerge into the daylight. This fact, as well as the lack of harmony between the parts, is what makes it such a difficult book to understand. The briefest sketch of the conceptual apparatus follows.

Books I and II introduce three important ideas. The first is that the deposit-creating power of the banking system gives it complete control over a community's credit conditions. There is a circular flow of money in and out of the banking system, all the active (bank-created) deposits flowing back into the system as passive (customer-created) ones. The banking system's cash reserves are never run down, so there is no limit to the amount of credit it can create. Secondly, Keynes distinguishes between income and business deposits held for the purpose of making current payments on the one hand, and savings deposits held for the purpose of making investments on the other. Thirdly, he discusses the plurality of price levels and the question of which one most accurately measures the purchasing power of money.

The main point which emerges from all this is that aggregate concepts like the quantity of money, velocity of circulation and 'the' price level give no adequate indication of changes in the public's propensity to save, hoard, invest or speculate, the total quantity of deposits and the price level of total transactions quite possibly remaining the same. Thus business deposits include speculative balances. 'The pace at which a circle of financiers, speculators and investors hand round one to another particular pieces of wealth, or titles to such, which they are neither producing nor consuming but merely exchanging, bears no definite relation to the rate of current production' and is subject to 'great and incalculable fluctuations', depending on such factors as the state of speculative sentiment.[6] Similarly, the object of stabilising purchasing power required the choice of the right price level. 'I do not believe', Keynes wrote, 'that Great Britain would have returned in 1925 to the gold standard at the pre-war parity had it not been for the habit of regarding the wholesale standard as a satisfactory index of general purchasing power'; the prevalence of the idea that all price levels 'come to much the same thing in the end' has retarded the study of short-period fluctuations 'for the failure of different price-levels to move in the same way is the essence of such fluctuations'.[7] The best measure of purchasing power is the consumer price index, and the object of monetary policy should be to stabilise this, since it was the amount of income spent on consumption goods which 'sooner or later' dictated other kinds of expenditure.[8] Distinguishing between the different types of deposit by motive, between different kinds of expenditure by object, and between costs of production and selling prices is designed to enable the economist to explain, and the banking system to offset, tendencies towards expansion and contraction in the economic system, unrevealed by the aggregate variables of the standard 'quantity of money' equation. As Keynes explained to Pigou, 'The old-fashioned quantity-theory tutor, who only looks at the quantity of the kitchen-bills, has ... nothing to learn from the new theories about the causes of dyspepsia!'[9]

The *Treatise* is dominated by Marshall's concept of 'normal' or long-run prices and seeks to explain deviations from them in either direction. Thus it is an analysis of the causes of disequilibrium – seen initially in the emergence of disequilibrium prices. This emphasis on dynamics explains

Keynes's choice of definitions. The key concept is the community's money income and how it earns and spends it over a period of time. The community's income is equal to its factor earnings, or costs of output, cost including the 'normal' reward to entrepreneurs as well as to workers. In equilibrium its money income will equal the value of its output, which is simply a way of saying that everything earned in a period will be spent on buying something produced in that period. In disequilibrium the prices at which entrepreneurs sell output diverge from the prices at which they buy 'factors of production'. This divergence is expressed by Keynes's notion of 'profit', positive or negative – profit being 'the difference between the cost of production of the current output and its actual sales proceeds'.[10] Keynes's object in excluding profit from income was to segregate the 'normal' from the 'abnormal' factors, static from dynamic conditions. But it got him, as we shall see, into great trouble, because it made it more difficult for him to see (or at least say) that fluctuations in business activity lead to fluctuations in income, and to draw certain conclusions from this about what happens to saving. Definitions suitable for explaining the divergence of the system from some more or less satisfactory 'norm' turn out to be unsuitable for explaining its tendency to converge to some less satisfactory one.

The story unfolds as follows. The community's income is earned producing both consumption (finished) and investment (capital) goods. Part of this income is saved. The price level of consumption goods is equal to that proportion of its earnings which the community spends buying consumption goods – that is, its total earnings minus what it saves. The central proposition then emerges that, if in a period of time people spend less on buying consumption goods than they have earned in producing them, the consumer price index falls, involving the businessmen producing these goods in losses (or negative profits). This is identical to saying that saving runs ahead of investment, since in this case people are saving more out of their incomes than they have earned in producing investment goods, and therefore spending less than they have earned in producing consumption goods. It follows that, unless the excess of saving over the cost of investment is spent buying new capital goods, its only effect is a fall in the price level of output as a whole. Given the price level of investment goods, the price level of output is determined by the price level of consumption goods. All this is true by definition and would not be in the least remarkable but for the fact that Keynes takes the amount of investment to be independent of the proportion of their income which the community has decided to save.*

This is a technical way of saying that it is not abstinence which builds

---

*The condition of equilibrium in the capital-goods market is that the cost of investment equals the value of investment. A rise in the price of capital goods could mean either that the businessmen producing them are making abnormal profits, or that there is a speculative bull market in securities which could be consistent with saving 'running ahead' of investment, that is a prelude to depression.

cities or drains fens, but enterprise, and if enterprise is lacking, all that saving does is to reduce output and employment. For entrepreneurs will not invest more, whatever people save, unless they see a profit in it.

The materials of this story are contained in Keynes's Fundamental Equations. In equilibrium costs of production are equal to the value of production; 'profits' are zero; saving is equal to investment. The economy is in equilibrium – the price level of output as a whole showing no tendency to change – if the cost of new investment equals the volume of current savings. All this is true by definition. The fun begins when, starting from this position, people decide to save more or invest less, and vice versa.

III

EXCESS BEARISHNESS AND EXCESS SAVING

A fall in output can come about either through 'excess bearishness' or through 'excess saving'. A few months before the *Treatise* was published Keynes had tried to explain its plot to his colleagues on the Macmillan Committee (see pp. 343–62 below) and we may imagine him doing so to a reader with limited economic understanding:

Q: Your main point is that saving can run ahead of investment, and vice versa?

J.M.K.: No, that's not really the main point. I had said as much in 1913. My theory has more to do with the causes and effects of such a divergence. When Mr Robertson was writing his *Banking Policy and the Price Level* in 1925, and we were discussing it, we both believed that inequalities between saving and investment could arise only as a result of what one might call an act of inflation or deflation by the banking system. I worked on this basis for quite a time, but in the end came to the conclusion that this would not do. I found that the salient phenomena could occur without any overt act on the part of the banking system.

Q: You mean, through what Mr Robertson calls Hoarding and Dishoarding?

J.M.K.: That's certainly part of it. The great weakness of the quantity theory of money is that it assumes that people acquire money only to get rid of it as quickly as possible. But money is also a store of value.

Q: Could you explain this?

J.M.K: The orthodox theory assumes that the only reason people save money – refrain from consumption – is in order to invest it. This seems reasonable enough – after all you can't consume bits of paper or gold. But then you have the King Midas problem. I don't think he was completely mad, though he certainly seems to have been an extreme case of an anal-sadistic personality. When other forms of wealth become too insecure, hoarding money can be a rational alternative to investing it, because although it doesn't earn any interest, or very little, this may be a minor consideration compared with the risk of losing your savings altogether in an investment which turns out badly. If for some reason or other people choose to keep an increased proportion of their savings in the form of hoards, then the purchasing power of the community falls. I call this situation one of 'excess bearishness', and I think this is part of the explanation of our troubles.

Q: Could you explain this further?

J.M.K.: In deciding what to do with his savings a person has to balance the advantages of keeping money in a savings deposit – interest earned, plus the advantages of liquidity – and buying investments – capital appreciation and dividends. He may refrain from buying securities now in the hope of making a profit or avoiding a loss by buying them later. His 'propensity to hoard' thus depends on what I call his 'bullishness' or 'bearishness' – on whether he thinks the market in shares will go up or down. If the price of securities is generally expected to fall, savings will be redistributed from 'securities' to 'hoards' and vice versa if they are expected to rise. A state of 'excess bearishness' exists when those who prefer at the moment to avoid securities – the bears – outnumber those who prefer to hold them – the bulls. The price of securities *will* then fall in line with expectation, and this means that the demand for new investment will fall as well. This is one source of what I call saving 'running ahead' of investment.

Q: Is this your new theory?

J.M.K.: No, only a part of it. Much of this is already in Mr Robertson's book, though I am the first economist, I think, to emphasise the speculative motive in investment decisions, arising from uncertainty as to the future price of securities. Given this uncertainty, investment is very much a matter of animal spirits. It has little or nothing to do directly with what the community decides to consume and save. I know what I am talking about because I have been playing this game myself for the last ten years. The theoretically novel part of my theory is the assertion that, even without any change in hoarding habits, saving and investment can diverge. Acts of hoarding and dishoarding are one of the ways this divergence can come about, but by no means the only one.

Q: What are the others?

J.M.K.: Well, let me give you a parable which I have found helpful, with some people who have not had the benefit of attending my lectures at Cambridge, in getting my theory down to its simplest terms. Imagine a community, initially in a state of equilibrium, which produces only bananas. A thrift campaign is started, as a result of which people start saving more and consuming less, the rate of investment in banana plantations initially staying the same. The price of bananas then falls by the amount of the increased saving. Virtue is rewarded: people get the same amount of bananas as before for less money, and they have 'saved' as well. But the producers of bananas have now made an unexpected loss, since they have been forced to sell their bananas at below cost price. They cannot, of course, 'hoard' them, because they will rot. The increased saving has not increased the aggregate wealth of the community at all: it has simply transferred part of it from the producers to the consumers of bananas. So nothing has happened to reduce their excess saving.

Q: What happens next?

J.M.K.: In the next phase, the loss-making businessmen try to protect themselves by reducing their wage bills, which means, in practice, throwing workers out of jobs. But this does not help, since the income of the community will be reduced by just as much as the aggregate costs of production. Thus the entrepreneurs continue to make losses so long as the community continues to save more than it invests and the output of bananas to decline until either all production stops and the population starves to death, or the thrift campaign is called off or peters out as a result of growing poverty, or the government starts investing the excess savings itself in new banana plantations.

Q: But there is no use the government starting a new banana plantation for the fun of it?

J.M.K.: If you have more banana plantations, or mechanical banana cutters, than you want, for heaven's sake stop saving. But that is not our position. There are always plenty of things to do at a price if you can borrow cheaply enough.

Q: You say, 'for heaven's sake stop saving', but does that simply mean eating more bananas?

J.M.K.: If we have eaten all the bananas that are good for us and should merely have indigestion if we ate more, we can have a slacker time – not work so hard, as I pointed out in my 'Economic Possibilities for Our Grandchildren'. But we have not reached that point.

Q: What I don't understand is what happens to my increased savings. Suppose they are invested in mechanical banana-cutters. This will bid up the price of the current output of these machines, the losses of the banana-growers being exactly balanced by the abnormal profits of the makers of banana-cutters. Labour will be transferred from growing bananas to making banana-cutters, so there need be no unemployment either.

J.M.K.: You are missing a step in the argument. Unless the attractiveness of investment is going up *independently* the additional savings will not provide a fund for new investment. The fact that you do not spend that money means that some businessman has to accept a lower price for what he sells you and is, therefore, poorer by the exact amount that you are richer. And very likely, without knowing it, you as a shareholder in a banana plantation are that much poorer as well. Why on earth, with producers of consumption goods making a loss, should anyone think it worth while investing in new facilities for making these goods? The process so impoverishes the community that in the end it cannot save at all and so you reach equilibrium.

Q: But surely the rate of interest falls as a result of the increased saving?

J.M.K.: Another illicit assumption. What has happened to make the rate of interest fall? Why on earth should it fall if the fund of saving available for investment – as opposed to swopping titles to existing wealth – is no larger than before? Of course, I agree with you that you could always cure the trouble by lowering the rate of interest. But that is a matter for the banking system. In a closed economy, like banana-land, there would be no problem about doing this. But as things now are in Britain, if the Bank of England were to lower the interest rate, money would go abroad and we would lose gold, forcing up the rate of interest again. That is the price we pay for being on the gold standard. And, as long as we are in that position, the business world will go on losing a sum of money equal to the difference between what we save at home and the sum of what we invest at home and our export surplus.

Q: So the solution to our problems is either to save less or invest more.

J.M.K.: Exactly. I would prefer the second, since we have hardly reached a condition of indigestion.

Spotting the flaw in Keynes's banana parable was to occupy both him and his ablest critics for two years or more.[11]

IV

THE *MODUS OPERANDI* OF THE BANK RATE

The purpose of credit operations by the banks is to alter the relative attractiveness of saving and investing, as well as hoarding and buying securities, by bringing about changes in the rate of interest. Equilibrium requires not only that saving equals investment, but that, with a given volume of saving, the demand for cash balances be kept in equilibrium with the demand for securities.

'The attractiveness of investment', Keynes writes, 'depends on the prospective income which the entrepreneur anticipates from the current investment relatively to the rate of interest which he has to pay in order to be able to finance its production.'[12] The price of capital goods can change, therefore, either because the prospective yield has changed, or because the rate of interest has changed. Long-term expectation of profit is rooted in non-monetary factors. Keynes followed both Schumpeter and Robertson in holding that innovations come in waves; but he had no real theory of profit.[13] His book is concerned with the deterrent or stimulating effect on investment of banking operations. The banking system can act on both yield and cost. By buying and selling securities it can directly raise or lower their price and thus affect the prospective yield of investment; by altering its terms of lending, it can change the cost of borrowing.* Keynes does not exclude a vigorous resort to the first method, especially when 'excess bearishness' is endemic; but normally it is by varying the price of credit that the banks will be able to control the rate of investment.

Following Wicksell, Keynes distinguished between the 'natural' (that is, equilibrium) and the market rate of interest. The market rate is what actually prevails; the natural rate is the notional rate 'at which saving and the value of investment are exactly balanced'.[14] Unlike Wicksell, Keynes had no theory of what determines the 'natural' rate – the rate of return on physical capital. The banking system's duty is to keep the two rates equal. To say that saving is running ahead of investment is the same thing as to say that the 'natural' rate is below the market rate, either because of a rise in the latter or because of a fall in the former; to boost the rate of investment, the banking system will have to lower the market rate. Moreover, it is the long-term, or bond, rate to which the banks will need to pay attention, since it is the prospective income over the whole life of an investment which is important to the investor.[15] 'Booms and slumps', Keynes writes, 'are simply the expression of an oscillation of the terms of credit about their equilibrium position.'[16]

By keeping the two rates equal, Keynes meant, in practice, stabilising the purchasing power of money. The main practical difficulty of doing this lay in the fact that monetary policy under the gold standard was directed towards a different, and possibly conflicting, end – maintaining equilibrium in the balance of payments. This might require an interest-rate policy different from that needed to maintain domestic equilibrium. If the condition of domestic equilibrium is that saving equals investment, the condition of external equilibrium is that there be no net movement of gold in or out of the country. In order to maintain overall equilibrium in an open economy, the rate of interest has to do two jobs which may be incompatible.

Here the *Treatise* recapitulates matter which has already been discussed in the previous chapter. Keynes distinguishes between a country's 'foreign lending' and its 'foreign balance' in a manner partly corresponding to the distinction between saving and investment,[17] external disequilibrium being a state of imbalance between the first two. The foreign balance is the balance of trade on income account (visible and invisible), which may be positive

---

*Open-market operations tend to do both. Since the purchase of securities by the central bank automatically 'creates deposits', it will have the effect not only of raising the price of securities but also of lowering the price of credit.

or negative (confusingly he calls this balance 'foreign investment'). Foreign lending is the unfavourable balance of transactions on capital account. To avoid a loss of gold foreign lending must be equal to foreign investment: there must be a surplus on income account just sufficient to cover the loss on capital account. The transfer of capital abroad (foreign lending) no more automatically improves the foreign balance (that is, results in a sale of goods of equal value) than does an act of saving result in an equivalent act of domestic investment. Foreign investment would go up only if the exporting country's costs of production were lowered. Otherwise, gold would be exported, which the monetary authority would have to offset by raising the interest rate. The argument is put forward at length in chapter 21, which is mainly a reworking of Keynes's debate with Bertil Ohlin on the 'transfer problem'.

Here then is the mechanism by which the external constraint can cause domestic disequilibrium, or prevent its cure. In the nineteenth century, the conflict for Britain was less acute. The Bank of England was 'the conductor of the international orchestra';[18] it could influence the international situation to suit itself.[19] But this was entirely the result of a favourable international conjuncture; there was no binding obligation on the Bank to maintain domestic equilibrium. Raising bank rate in response to a loss, or threatened loss, of gold was supposed to restore both short-run and long-run equilibrium on external account. In the short run, it would increase the relative attraction of holding sterling. But, assuming an initial position of domestic equilibrium, with saving equal to investment, raising bank rate also had the effect of raising the 'market' above the 'natural' rate, increasing the attraction of saving relative to investment. The argument applies equally to the case where the monetary authority is prevented from lowering the market rate to the level of the 'natural' rate to correct a previous disequilibrium. The long-run effect of a rise in the interest rate is to lower domestic costs relative to foreign costs, thus improving the foreign balance. Bank rate can then come down again, having done its work of enlarging the foreign balance sufficiently to sustain the given volume of foreign lending.

> The dilemma of modern banking [Keynes writes] is satisfactorily to combine the two functions. As a purveyor of representative money, it is the duty of the banking system to preserve the prescribed objective standard of such money. As a purveyor of loans on terms and conditions of a particular type, it is the duty of the system to adjust, to the best of its ability, its supply of this type of lending to the demand for it at the equilibrium rate of interest, i.e. at the natural rate. Moreover, the preservation of the objective standard is bound up . . . in a peculiar way, the precise character of which has generally escaped notice, with the rate at which the banking system in its capacity of lender is facilitating the investment in new capital. Since, for this

reason, the complete attainment of one of its duties is sometimes incompatible with the complete attainment of the other, those in control of the banking system have to make up their minds which objective is to prevail, or, if neither is to prevail, to achieve a just compromise between the two.[20]

Keynes claimed to have given the first complete account of the *modus operandi* of bank rate, and it remains a classic of its kind. However, it is open to the same criticism as his saving–investment analysis – as Ohlin had pointed out. The ultimate effect of a rise in bank rate was held to be an enlargement of the foreign balance through a decline in 'efficiency wages', making possible a greater volume of exports. Keynes ignored the consideration that the reduction in domestic incomes would tend *automatically* to improve the foreign balance by reducing the amount of both imports and foreign lending. As in the closed-economy case, he ignored the possibility that equilibrium might be restored through output, rather than relative-price, adjustment.

V

WAGES

In Keynes's Fundamental Equation, there are two terms which determine the price level of output, efficiency earnings, or per-unit costs of output, and the savings–investment relationship, governed on the one side by the propensity to save, and on the other by the propensity to hoard. The first term determines long-run or equilibrium prices; the second, short-run or disequilibrium prices.[21] If saving equals investment, the price level would be determined by long-run costs. In Hicks's language, efficiency earnings are the rigid prices – the 'costs of production' or the 'community's money income' – the prices of consumption and investment goods the flexible prices.[22] It is the fluctuation of the flexible prices about the rigid prices, brought about by changes in the second term, which is the essence of the business cycle; it is the induced adjustment of the rigid prices which brings the upward and downward phases of the cycle to an end. Thus the upward phase will be marked by what Keynes called a commodity inflation – prices running ahead of costs – leading to a profit inflation; this will cause earnings to catch up with a lag–income inflation. The boom will normally break – for reasons to be discussed below – the downward sequence being commodity deflation, profit deflation and income deflation. It is when prices are changing, and particularly when profit inflations and deflations are being experienced, that output and employment change.

Income inflation can thus mean two different things: an 'induced' (though lagged) response to a profit inflation, and a 'spontaneous' rise in money wages relative to efficiency – what we now call cost or wage inflation. Patinkin denies that the *Treatise* was concerned with the second phenomenon because, he says, 'Keynes's income inflation is not a "spontaneous", exogenous labour-union-monopoly phenomenon, but the "induced", endogenous result of the increased demand for the factors of production generated by the excess profits.'[23] This is not entirely so. One of the key problems for monetary management posed in the *Treatise* is whether monetary policy should seek to accommodate a spontaneous upward tendency in unit costs – due to 'the power of trade unions or the mere human inclination to think in terms of money' or to stabilise the purchasing power of money.[24] As a practical policy, Keynes generally favoured the second; but he thought that ideally monetary policy should be adapted to the 'natural tendencies of spontaneous change which characterise the earnings system as it actually is', especially in a declining society, where efficiency may be decreasing. The worst of all possible worlds is one where 'spontaneous changes in earnings tend upwards, but monetary changes, due to the relative shortage of gold, tend downwards, so that . . . we have a chronic necessity for induced changes sufficient not only to counteract the spontaneous changes but to reverse them. Yet it is possible that this is the sort of system which we have today.'[25] In modern parlance, long-run equilibrium requires the supply of money to accommodate cost inflation.

This is a severe limitation on the power of the banking system, as Keynes acknowledges: 'If there are strong social or political forces causing spontaneous changes in the money rates of efficiency wages, the control of the price level may pass beyond the power of the banking system.'[26] In practice, Keynes did not think this was an important problem: union power was measured by an ability to resist 'induced' downward changes in money-wages, rather than to force 'spontaneous' upward changes. He favoured a policy of stabilising prices and letting money wages rise to absorb productivity gains. This was his reading of the 1920s. The problem arguably became acute from the 1960s onwards, though the question whether wage inflation is best described as autonomous or induced is still much debated.

The important point is that spontaneous income changes have no tendency in themselves to produce disequilibrium prices, 'because – so long as the currency authority allows the change without attempting to counteract it – entrepreneurs will always be recouped for their changed outlay by the corresponding change in their receipts, which will result from the proportionate change in the price level'.[27] Only if the spontaneous changes require a supply of money incompatible with for example, the gold standard or the 'traditions' of the banking system can disequilibrium prices – and therefore business losses – develop, as the monetary authority puts up interest rates to protect its reserves.

This leads Keynes to classify the initiating cause of price disturbances under the two heads of monetary factors and investment factors. Monetary factors are more likely to be the disturbing cause in an open economy with fixed exchange rates. In the typical case, the monetary authority reduces the quantity of money in order to secure an income deflation to improve the foreign balance, but only succeeds in producing a profit deflation, the income deflation coming only later as a result of business losses and unemployment. The distinguishing feature of this kind of disturbance is that it leads to equilibrium at a new price level – that is, it is a one-way price movement, with no cycle.

In returning Britain to the gold standard in 1925, bankers and economists ignored the fact that the currency authority had no direct control over the wage system and could only affect earnings indirectly by causing business losses:

> It must be considered a defect that the central banking authority has in most modern economic systems no means . . . directly [to] influence the level of efficiency earnings. In Bolshevist Russia or Fascist Italy it may be possible by decree to change the money rate of efficiency earnings overnight. But no such method is available in the systems of capitalist individualism which prevail in most of the world. It was not open to the British Treasury when at the time of the return to the gold standard the standard of value was by its decree raised 10 per cent to decree at the same time that efficiency earnings should be reduced all round by 10 per cent. On the contrary, the first term of the equation can only be influenced indirectly – raised by stimulating entrepreneurs with abundant credit and abnormal profits; lowered by depressing them with restricted credit and abnormal losses. When bank rate is raised, not in the interests of equilibrium to keep the second term from rising, but in order to bring the first term down, this means that the object of the higher bank rate is to involve entrepreneurs in losses and the factors of production in unemployment, for only in this way can the money rates of efficiency earnings be reduced. It is not reasonable, therefore, to complain when these results ensue.[28]

The conclusion is that monetary policy should be run in such a way as to avoid 'induced' changes in earnings. This may or may not be compatible with price stability, depending on the 'spontaneous' characteristics of the wage system.

The business cycle proper is characterised by changes in investment relative to saving, without any prior change in the quantity of money. Something has happened to raise the 'natural' rate of interest – a new invention, a war, a return of business confidence, a Stock Exchange boom – but nothing to raise the market rate. If factors are fully employed, their money wages are bid up as producers adding to capital compete for the services of workers producing consumption goods. However, prices will rise more than incomes as the output of consumption goods falls – Keynes calls this a 'commodity inflation' – thus generating windfall profits. Where the boom starts with unemployed factors (the more usual case), aggregate earnings rise without any increase in consumption goods or in efficiency earnings, leading equally to a commodity inflation which produces a profit inflation.

It is the next stage which carries the seed of collapse. Under the stimulus of windfall profits, businessmen increase the output of all types of goods employing factors of production. Income inflation will gradually catch up with commodity inflation, eroding the windfall profits. The increased supply of consumption goods which the additions to capital will have made possible will now come on to the market causing a 'commodity deflation'. The fall in prices will cause some entrepreneurs, who have been producing at subnormal efficiency under the stimulus of windfall profits, to cease production. Financial opinion will turn 'bearish'. And the marginal productivity of capital goods (or the 'natural' rate of interest) will fall 'with the increased supply of certain kinds of capital goods'.[29] The point will come when the banking system, which has accommodated to the boom, 'is no longer able to supply the necessary volume of money consistent with its principles and traditions'. The market rate will rise above the natural rate. The onset of a profit deflation will induce sooner or later an income deflation. Wage reductions, following on mass unemployment, will bring down the rigid prices to the level reached by the flexible prices, which will be the new position of equilibrium.

> Thus the collapse [Keynes writes] will come in the end as the result of the piling up of several weighty causes – the evaporation of the attractions of new investment, the faltering of financial sentiment, the reaction in the price level of consumption goods, and the growing inability of the banking system to keep pace with the increasing requirements, first of the industrial circulation and later of the financial circulation also.[30]

In Book IV, dealing with these matters, Keynes is telling what we have called Story I rather than Story II. For the point of Story II, as illustrated by the banana parable, is that, as consumption falls, there is no tendency whatever for an 'income deflation' to develop. In banana-land 'the spending power of the public will be reduced just as much as the aggregate costs of production. By however much entrepreneurs reduce wages and however many of their employees they throw out of work, they will continue to make losses . . . Thus there will be no position of equilibrium . . .'[31]

The Austrian School, represented by Ludwig von Mises and Hayek, wanted to abolish the credit cycle by abolishing credit: banks were to be required to keep 100 per cent gold reserves against notes. Keynes wanted to abolish the credit cycle, too: if the banking system managed the currency successfully 'the credit cycle would not occur'.[32] Robertson, on the other hand, thought the credit cycle ought to be allowed, since its upward – commodity inflation – phase causes real wealth to grow faster than it would have done, owing to 'imposed' lacking. Keynes conceded something to this view. He distinguished between a 'virtuous' and a 'vicious' inflation – the first designed to correct a previous commodity deflation – and also conceded that it is in times of disturbance that new men and new methods get resources which, in placid times, are controlled by 'third-generation' businesses. Against this, though, must be set the losses of the deflationary phase of the cycle, particularly 'involuntary unemployment which is a greater evil than the overtime of the boom is a benefit'.[33] Keynes implicitly accepted that an investment boom must fail owing to a fall in the marginal productivity of capital; therefore it should not be allowed to develop. On the other hand, he thought that a climate of moderate commodity inflation, brought about by the steady increase of the money supply, allowing prices to rise a little ahead of money wages was healthy for business and might be maintained without ill-effects almost indefinitely, any resulting social injustice being remedied through the tax system.[34] The world of inflationary expectations was still far away.

VI

THE USES OF HISTORY

The purpose of volume two, *The Applied Theory of Money*, was to provide a statistical and historical account of the fluctuations in the monetary and investment factors as an introduction to the proposals for 'managing money'. In this, Keynes was handicapped by the 'present deplorable state of our banking and other statistics'.[35] For example, there was no single set of figures 'which measures accurately what should be capable of quite precise measurement – namely, the rate at which the community is adding to fixed capital'.[36]

Nevertheless, by dint of much writing round to bank chairmen, Keynes got statistical support for some hypotheses, which perhaps aroused in him an echo of the excitement he first experienced in 1909 when he told Duncan Grant, 'Here are my theories – will the statistics bear them out? Nothing except copulation is so enthralling and the figures are coming out so much better than anyone could possibly have expected that everybody will believe I have cooked them.'[37]

Keynes had argued in volume one that an unchanged quantity of money could conceal important changes in circulation as holders transferred money between the cash and savings deposits, and between the income and business deposits. His main statistical find was that the proportion of deposit (that is, savings) to total accounts had risen in Britain from 38 per cent to 46 per cent between 1920 and 1926, the 'continual transference from current to deposit accounts' acting as a 'concealed measure of deflation' sufficient to explain a drop in the price level of 20 per cent over the period.[38] Turning to investment factors, he found (on p. 91) that fluctuations in employment were highly correlated with fluctuations in working capital. Basing himself on Wesley Mitchell's statistics, he estimated that the fluctuation of working capital and employment over a cycle will be about 10 per cent between peak and trough on average.[39]

The *Treatise*'s liveliest chapter, 'Historical Illustrations', is intended to exhibit the great movements in economic history as being driven forward by abnormal profits and reversed by abnormal losses. Contrary to the nineteenth-century stereotype, the Profiteer not the Saver emerges as mankind's benefactor. The attack on the abstinence theory of progress, or indeed of any kind of achievement ('Were the seven wonders of the world built by thrift? I doubt it'), here achieves its most striking expression.*

Keynes's 'monetary' interpretation of world history was based on periodic redistributions of the precious metals between the continents – an idea which clearly fascinated him. The most famous application in chapter 30 is to Western Europe's commercial revolution in the sixteenth and seventeenth centuries. To Keynes, the 'origins of capitalism' are to be found pure and simple in Spanish treasure, specifically in the influx into Western Europe of precious metals from Spanish America: an idea that links economic progress to the animal spirits of buccaneers and pirates rather than to the abstinence of secular monks. 'Never in the annals of the modern world', Keynes writes, 'has there existed so prolonged and so rich an opportunity for the businessman, the speculator and the profiteer. In these golden years modern capitalism was born ... It is unthinkable that the difference between the amount of wealth in France and England in 1700 and the amount in 1500 could ever have been built up by thrift alone.'[40]

And not just wealth: Roger Fry reported him, over lunch at this time, 'full of his own ideas about financial history which are rather fascinating. He thinks he can show exactly how much inflation of currency is necessary to produce an outburst of artistic creation. He says that if Shakespeare had been born fifty years earlier England could not have afforded him.'[41]

By contrast, the price fall between 1890 and 1896 produced a 'very thrifty period' – there has been no other case where one can trace so clearly the effects of a prolonged withdrawal of entrepreneurs from undertaking the production of new fixed capital on a scale commensurate with current savings'.[42] Keynes was able to use statistics to good effect to show that the cause of this price decline was not a reduction in the quantity of gold – gold

*Both Marshall and Robertson would have replied: by involuntary thrift.

was plentiful – but a state of 'excess bearishness' triggered off by the Baring crisis of 1890.

The inflationary war finance of 1914–18 was a classic case of 'forced saving'. There are discussions of the post-war booms and slumps in terms of profit and income inflations and deflations.[43] On the failure of the return to gold in 1925 to produce the expected income deflation, Keynes wrote:

> It may be that in earlier periods the pressure of subnormal profits and the unemployment of the factors of production may have operated more rapidly than they do now to achieve the necessary object of an income deflation. I believe that the resistances to a severe income deflation, which is not merely a reaction from a previous inflation, have always been great. But in the modern world of organised trade unions and a proletarian electorate they are overwhelmingly strong.[44]

Keynes pointed out that the average money-wage rate was almost as high in 1930 as in 1924, after six years of deflation.

The reason for the abnormal unemployment in Britain in the late 1920s was the interaction between the failure to achieve an income deflation and the excess of saving over investment. Business losses from the profit deflation made foreign lending more attractive, forcing up interest rates and 'so riveting still more firmly on our necks the profit deflation'.[45] This was one of the very few occasions in the *Treatise* when Keynes urged a policy of public works and even tariffs to raise the level of investment if 'social and political forces' stand in the way of the money-wage reductions required by the maintenance of the existing sterling exchange rate.[46]

Keynes's 'amateur' economic history has not found much favour with economic historians or economic theorists. For his account of the sixteenth-century price revolution he relied heavily on the researches of an American historian, Earl J. Hamilton, who had found a significant correlation between the price of grain in Andalucia and imports of gold and silver from South America. Ironically, Hamilton was accused by later 'Keynesian' economists of relying on the 'obsolete' quantity theory of money. The causal chain, they argued, went the other way: the increase in economic activity increased the demand for gold, which stimulated gold mining. On the other hand, the wage-lag hypothesis is generally accepted, especially for England. It is estimated that the real wage rate of the English carpenter (1721–45 = 100) fell from 122.4 in 1501–50 to 83.00 in 1551–1600, and 48.3 in 1601–50. This is explained by money illusion, wages fixed by contract and delays in payment – all a result, to a lesser or greater degree, of lack of labour organisation.

Against Keynes there is also Schumpeter's weighty argument that gold imports and wage lags don't necessarily produce investment. It depends on who gets the money and on what purposes it is spent. In India gold was routinely hoarded. In Spain, the profits of business were creamed off by the

Habsburgs to support their dynastic wars; France, too, remained capitalistic-ally backward, despite a large influx of precious metals. Influx of gold is simply an alternative to depreciating the coinage, by which the medieval monarchs had financed their wars. Historians and theorists of economic development would now accept that certain institutions (for example, well-defined property rights, a certain kind of international order) and/or certain 'psychic' conditions, whether this be Weber's 'capitalist ethic' or Keynes's 'spirit of enterprise', have to be in place if windfalls are to lead to growth and not be hoarded in fear or squandered in religious or warlike ecstasies.[47]

Keynes's historical chapter pointed forward to his endorsement of mercan-tilism in the *General Theory*. It is important to recognise that for all its 'amateurishness' it does embody his vivid vision of how capitalist economies actually work. What is lacking is any explicit reference to uncertainty. As Keynes saw it, throughout history there has been a perennial weakness in the inducement to invest – to embark money on slowly maturing projects – because the future is unknown. Under most circumstances rational calcu-lation produces a rate of investment below the normal volume of saving (uncertainty stimulating the second and retarding the first); periods of high investment therefore need to be explained by special events – gold influxes, inventions, wars – which are 'good for the nerves' of the entrepreneur. His vision of the capitalist process, as one lurching forward by fits and starts, while opportunities for exceptional profit cause, briefly, the gambling spirit to swamp the counsels of prudence, is an important corrective to the stan-dard neo-classical growth models in which uncertainty plays no part.

VII

CENTRAL BANKS TO THE RESCUE

The policy proposals with which Keynes ended his *Treatise* are much what one would have expected from the author of the *Tract*. The premiss of the argument is that, provided a central bank has control over its own assets, it can control the quantity of money and credit, and therefore the rate of interest; through varying the rate of interest as well as through its open-market operations it can control the rate of investment; by controlling the rate of investment it can keep investment in line with what the community wants to save; through keeping saving and investment equal it can keep prices equal to costs and thus prevent the emergence of profit.

By its open-market operations (buying and selling securities) it can control the volume of savings deposits by creating credit to balance the demand for them, and thus prevent them stealing money from the industrial circulation. The banking system can also control the long-term rate of interest – the

bond rate – crucial to investment, by its control over the short-term rate.
Keynes produced statistical evidence for his argument that short-term rates
have a predominant influence over the long-term rate: cheap money drives
down the rate on bonds, mainly because of the movement of funds between
short and long-dated securities, which tends to equalise their yield. Much
of the discussion hereabouts[48] concerning the psychology of investors – 'they
do not possess even the rudiments of what is required for a valid judgement,
and are the prey of hopes and fears easily aroused by transient events and
as easily dispelled' – anticipates the well-known chapter 12 of the *General
Theory*.

Keynes recognised that the banking system had more power to maintain
a pre-existing equilibrium than to restore one by forcing an income deflation.
However, as we have seen, he did not feel he had to worry about cost
inflation. He also accepted that it would be difficult for the central bank
unaided to lift an economy out of a slump, since the policy of buying
securities *à l'outrance* in order to raise their price may involve it in losses if
bearishness is too deeply entrenched. In such a situation 'the choice may
conceivably lie between assuming the burden of a prospective loss, allowing
the slump to continue, and socialistic action by which some official body
steps into the shoes which the feet of the entrepreneurs are too cold to
occupy.'[49] But this was a limiting case. In general, Keynes thought the
central bank could do the stabilising job. He had a high regard for both the
Bank of England and the Federal Reserve Board of the United States as
examples of semi-socialised enterprise whose policies were guided by 'general social and economic advantage'. The successful management of the
dollar by the Fed. between 1923 and 1928 was 'a triumph'.[50] Keynes preferred mandarins to be in charge.

The Fed. had a better record than the Bank of England because the
United States, being a net gold importer, did not have to face a conflict
between domestic stability and exchange stability: it could just sterilise the
gold. Keynes accepted the *fait accompli* of the gold standard, so as not to
divide the 'forces of intelligence and goodwill',[51] but he did not speak in the
accents of a true believer. The gold standard was 'part of the apparatus of
conservatism'; the defence of gold 'a furtive Freudian cloak' for repressed
infantile anality.[52] For the sake of ensuring that everyone keeps in step the
gold standard prevents 'pioneer improvements of policy the wisdom of which
is ahead of average wisdom, and does nothing to secure either the short-
period or long-period optimum if the average behaviour is governed by
blind forces such as the total quantity of gold . . .'.[53] More radically, Keynes
wondered whether it was wise to have a 'currency system with a much
wider ambit than our banking system, our tariff system and our wage
system', especially one which allowed 'a policy of unmitigated *laissez-faire*
towards foreign loans . . .'[54] – remarks which foreshadow his articles on
national self-sufficiency in 1933. To ease the external constraint Keynes

advocated a number of devices for controlling foreign lending, like taxing income from foreign securities more highly than standard income tax, and widening the gold points so as to create doubts about the future terms of exchange between currencies.[55] Diminishing London's international business was not too high a price to pay for domestic stability.

Was there any escape from the choice between 'national autonomy' and 'the advantages of the stability of local currencies . . . in terms of the international standard'? The essential condition was to ensure that countries never had to deflate because of a relative or absolute shortage of gold reserves. As a 'minimum step' towards co-ordinated management of the gold standard, Keynes proposed that all central banks be allowed to hold at least half of their legal reserve requirements in foreign currencies.[56] As a 'maximum' he urged the creation of a fiduciary reserve asset (forerunner of the Special Drawing Right provision of the IMF) to be advanced by a 'supranational bank' to the central banks of countries in temporary balance-of-payments difficulties.[57]

In the longer run Keynes wanted the world banking system to stabilise a wholesale index of sixty 'of the standardised foods and raw materials of world-wide importance'.[58] This would have the advantage of allowing local currencies to depreciate in line with the 'spontaneous' tendencies of earnings (since Keynes expected the prices of commodities to fall relatively to those of services) which would also lighten the burden of debt. Keynes ignored the contradiction involved in trying to combine currency depreciation with the elimination of windfall profits: it was a matter of compromise.

The *Treatise* is Keynes's great essay in intellectual compromise. Its twists and turns, its contradictory stories, its conflicting policy prescriptions start to make a coherent pattern at a higher level if we recall – as perhaps he did – the Chorus's lines in the *Oresteia*:

> A middle course is best,
> Not poor not proud; but this,
> By no clear rule defined,
> Eludes the unstable, undiscerning mind,
> Whose aim will surely miss.

From this point of view, the *Treatise* and not the *General Theory* was Keynes's classic achievement. But the world was about to go mad again for the second time in his life, and the middle course became much more difficult to hold.

CHAPTER ELEVEN

The Slump

I

DID HE FORESEE IT?

No one in the summer of 1929 suspected that the world economy was about to collapse. With shares on Wall Street rising ever more dizzily, Americans believed they had discovered the secret of permanent prosperity. As long as the United States boomed, the rest of the world felt secure. There was little hint of trouble in international politics either. Under Stalin Soviet Russia had turned from exporting revolution to terrorising its own people. The Locarno Treaty of 1925 had lulled French fears and seemingly tamed German ambitions: Hitler, wrote Lord D'Abernon in 1929, had 'fad[ed] into oblivion.'[1] Mussolini appeared to have settled down too; in 1928 he delighted sound finance by overvaluing the lira. There were, of course, disturbing signs for the augurs to read: the diversion of US savings into the Stock Exchange boom from 1928 onwards made it more difficult for primary producers to finance their debt, for Germany to pay reparations, for Britain to maintain the gold standard. In retrospect one can see that demand was being switched from production to speculation. But the worry of a few was drowned by the chorus of optimism.

After the excitements of electioneering, Keynes's life reverted to its normal routine. Most of the summer of 1929 was spent rewriting the *Treatise* at Tilton. It was interrupted by a ten-day Continental outing, from 19 to 29 July, during which he had to 'transit his mental faculties' to two days of lectures in Geneva at the invitation of the Financial Section of the League of Nations, followed by a holiday with Lydia in Burgundy. 'This sort of trip in spite of its positive qualities', Lydia wrote to Florence, 'one could only perform once a year, as one's liver reserves cannot survive.'[2]

The returning travellers plunged into ballet rehearsals at Tilton and in London. Lydia had agreed to dance with Anton Dolin and George Balanchine in a five-minute ballet inserted into one of the first British 'talkies', *Dark Red Roses*, the idea being that, as in *Hamlet*, the 'play within the play' would mime the main story and have a great effect on one of the characters. Keynes, of course, was in charge of all the practical arrangements. Balanchine arrived at Tilton on 9 August to practise the score, taken from Moussorgsky's *Khovanshina*, on a grand piano specially bought from the Courtaulds.

'With Keynes', writes Balanchine's biographer,' he got on beautifully, for Keynes loved to talk about ballet, and Balanchine loved to talk about economics . . .'[3]

While the filming took place at Wembley on 19 and 20 August, news came through of Diaghilev's death in Venice. 'The dancers crouched on the floor in a little group,' Maynard wrote to his mother, 'talking memories of him hour after hour. It was an extraordinary scene – with masses of machinery all round, the crowds of supers in dress clothes with jaundiced made up faces (supposed to be watching the ballet) and they in their central Asian costumes.' While Diaghilev lived he *was* ballet. With his death, the struggle for the inheritance started. A year later Lydia, with Maynard's backing, would assist Ninette de Valois in starting the Camargo Society, forerunner of the English National Ballet.

Dark Red Roses had bad luck. In the ballet the music was slightly out of synchronisation with the dance. Soon after the first showing in October, a fire destroyed the film studio and almost all the copies of the film. It was the only time Lydia danced before the cameras.[4]

Filming and a weekend with the McKennas out of the way, Maynard got down to his book again, taking the odd afternoon off to beat Lydia at tennis. Friends and relations came and went: the Hendersons, Sebastian Sprott, Peter Lucas, Sheppard, his mother Florence (approaching seventy and just about to become Mayor of Cambridge) and his brother Geoffrey (now an established and increasingly eminent surgeon). Frances Marshall, down to stay at Charleston, found that 'the feud with Tilton' was still going strong. Lydia spent all day 'bowling for the pig' at the Firle fair, and 'horrified the village by bursting into tears' when she failed to win it. However, all was 'honey' when she dropped into Charleston one morning in white trousers, a red shirt and a large straw hat trimmed with poppies to borrow some eggs.[5] The feud was absent from Cambridge, where Julian Bell – 'a very lovable old bear' – was often in Maynard's company, though he found his girlfriend, Helen Souter, 'too plain'. Sam and Lil Courtauld came to lunch on 29 September, Sam being shocked, but 'inwardly pleased' when Maynard argued for protection. There was a BBC broadcast, a night at Churt with Lloyd George and a meeting in London with the new Chancellor of the Duchy of Lancaster, Oswald Mosley, who had been appointed to ginger up the Labour government's public works programme.*

A fortnight after Maynard's return to Cambridge, the painfully constructed edifices of the post-war world started to collapse. 'Wall Street did have a go yesterday. Did you read about it?' he wrote to Lydia on 25 October. 'The biggest crash ever recorded. Falk's voice on the telephone this morning rather worried and uneasy, I thought.' The *New York Evening*

*Keynes met Mosley in London on 4 September. On 11 September, Mosley proposed that the government should take direct control over an enlarged road-building programme. This was turned down in November, after objections from the Ministry of Transport.

Post had asked him for a short message, and he had spent half an hour writing it and twenty-five minutes dictating it down the telephone, which gave him a headache. 'Thus I've been in a thoroughly financial and disgusting state of mind all day.'

Keynes's telephoned prophecy about the consequences of the Wall Street crash proved spectacularly wrong. There would be a 'bad winter of unemployment in Britain' as the result of the 'dear money' which had recently prevailed; but he looked forward to 'an epoch of cheap money ahead [which] will be in the real interests of business all over the world'. With low interest rates, 'enterprise throughout the world can get going again . . . commodity prices will recover and farmers will find themselves in better shape.'[6]

As we know, the Wall Street crash triggered the greatest world depression of all time. The collapse of wholesale prices in 1930 completely swamped any effect of cheap money: real interest rates rose sharply even as nominal interest rates fell. These events were to shake Keynes's belief in the efficacy of monetary policy during a severe slump. However, till well into 1930 few believed that anything worse was happening than a cyclical downturn, which would soon correct itself. Indeed there was some recovery of both share prices and activity in the spring of 1930.

Keynes has been accused of not predicting the depression. 'There will be no further crash in our lifetime,' he is reported as saying in 1926.[7] Also, if the value of an economist's theory is judged by the state of his portfolio, Keynes comes off badly: by the end of 1929 he was almost wiped out, for the second time in his investing career.

The truth is more complicated. Keynes's analysis of US business prospects was coloured by his admiration for the stabilisation policies of the Federal Reserve Board. He assumed that the Fed would be able and willing to prevent a serious slump from developing. However, he never succumbed to the widespread belief that the US had 'learnt the secret of perpetual prosperity'.[8] And by 1928 he felt he had good reason for worry.

That year, his business partner Oswald Falk came to the conclusion that credit conditions in the USA were 'unsound', and that the National Mutual, the Independent Investment Company and other companies which he and Keynes controlled should get out of Wall Street in particular and equities in general. This was also the position of Keynes's Harvard correspondent Charles Bullock, and most 'sound' banking opinion in the United States, alarmed by the great rise in collateral loans following the cut in the discount rate to 3.5 per cent in August 1927.

These apprehensions in 1927–8 became the basis of the subsequent orthodox explanation of the US slump. In his book *Sailors, Statesmen and Others*, published in 1935, Commander Kenworthy recalled that Oliver Sprague had told Labour MPs in 1931 that 'the Federal Reserve Board had desired to break the American boom in 1927, but that the wicked politicians had brought pressure to bear against this plan, because of the forthcoming

presidential election campaign of Mr Hoover'.[9] Writing in 1934, Lionel
Robbins likewise argued that the slump originated in the credit expansion
started by the Federal Reserve Board in 1927, partly to offset a mild
recession in the United States, mainly to help Britain stay on the gold
standard. This unleashed an orgy of speculation which could not be checked
by the dear money imposed subsequently.[10] The slump was the punishment,
as well as the cure, for the reckless extravagance of the previous years.

So powerful was this image of nemesis that it outlived the Keynesian
Revolution, returning to taunt the world with its misdeeds in the 1970s and
1980s. The boom was the fantasy, the slump the reappearance of reality.

Keynes never took the view he attributed to 'some austere and puritanical
souls' that slumps were an 'inevitable and desirable nemesis on . . . man's
speculative spirit', that it would be 'a victory for the mammon of unright-
eousness if so much prosperity was not subsequently balanced by universal
bankruptcy'.[11] Nor did he agree that America was on the booze in 1927.
The test of inflation, he repeatedly said, was the 'test of prices'. Judged by
the commodity price index, there was no danger of inflation in 1927. Hence
by raising the discount rate from 3.5 per cent in January 1928 to 5 per cent
by July 1928 in order to choke off speculation, the Federal Reserve Board
was imposing an act of deflation on a thriving US economy. This was the
basis of Keynes's commentary on the American situation in 1928. In July
and September he argued that the danger facing the US was not inflation,
but deflation.[12] 'The difficulty will be', Keynes wrote in September 1928,
'to find an outlet for the vast investment funds coming forward – particularly
if central banks resist the tendency of the rate of interest to fall'. 'Why is
the Federal Reserve Board so disturbed about what appears to be a reasonably healthy situation?' he asked the American economist Allyn Young on
15 August 1928.[13] And in reply to Professor Bullock he wrote on 4 October
1928, 'I cannot help feeling that the risk just now is all on the side of a
business depression . . . If too prolonged an attempt is made to check the
speculative position by dear money, it may very well be that the dear
money, by checking new investments, will bring about a general business
depression.'[14] So by 1928 Keynes thought a slump was likely if policy was
not changed.

In the *Treatise on Money* Keynes retracted one part of this analysis. He
conceded that the stability of the price index in 1928 and 1929 concealed a
'profit inflation'. However, he insisted that the profit inflation, particularly
in real estate, concealed a more general tendency to underinvestment in
relation to corporate saving. Both sides, in other words, accused the other
of looking in the wrong place. Orthodox banking opinion saw in the speculative boom a clear indication of unsound credit conditions; Keynes, on the
other hand, believed that the inflated share prices on Wall Street were an
inaccurate indicator of the total position. 'Thus I attribute the slump . . .
primarily to the effects on investment of the long period of dear money

which preceded the stock-market collapse, and only secondarily to the collapse itself.'[15] Had Benjamin Strong not been ill in 1928 (he died in October), the Fed might have acted more quickly and resolutely to break the Stock Exchange boom in 1928, thus avoiding the *prolonged* period of dear money which led up to the investment collapse of 1929.

Keynes's expectations in 1928 were influenced by his own business dealings. He was not wiped out on Wall Street, since he owned no shares there. The origin of his difficulties lay in the commodity markets, in which he had been speculating with mixed success for six years. By the end of 1927 his net assets totalled £44,000, or nearly a million pounds in 1992 prices. But in 1928 he was long on rubber, corn, cotton and tin, when the markets suddenly turned against his position. His losses on commodities forced him to sell securities to cover his position, by the end of 1929 on a falling market. This left a security portfolio dominated by 10,000 shares in the Austin Motor Company, whose value fell from 21s in January 1928 to 5s by the end of 1929. By that date his net worth had slumped from £44,000 to £7815.[16]

Here in microcosm is an important clue to the 'unsoundness' of the prosperity of the 1920s. There was a persistent tendency to excess supply in primary products. Savings were absorbed in accumulating stocks to maintain prices. When savings were switched to the New York bull market in 1928, the cost of holding stocks rose, the stocks were unloaded and prices started to sag. As in banana-land, virtue was rewarded: the consumer got his food more cheaply, but the producers of these and other primary products suffered a loss of income; and the fall in prices led to further disinvestment in working capital, and so on.

Keynes's picture of what was happening in the United States is thus in part a generalisation of his own speculative experience in 1928. Plentiful savings, as he saw it, were combined with an underlying tendency to underinvestment, offset by the pumping out of credit by the Federal Reserve System. When the pumping slowed down, the economic balloon shrivelled up. Keynes was to build on this analysis in explaining the deepening depression. The second of his personal financial setbacks also ended the speculative phase of his financial operations. Thereafter he adopted what he called a policy of 'faithfulness' – investing in a few favoured shares and sticking to them through thick and thin. A decade spent in trying to 'beat the market' had convinced him that this was the only rational response to uncertainty. (See Appendix at end of this chapter.)

The intimate phase of Keynes's collaboration with Oswald Falk now came to an end. There was not just the dispute over the future course of US prices, but also Falk's increasingly dictatorial behaviour on the companies which he and Keynes ran. On the PR ('All is flux') Finance Company, which engaged mainly in commodity speculation, Keynes and Falk agreed to split responsibility following the losses of 1928, Keynes handling the

capital subscribed by his family and friends (Walter Langdon Brown, Geoffrey Keynes, Neville Keynes, A. V. Hill, Clive Bell, David Garnett, Roger
Fry and Lytton Strachey), and Falk the rest. After one year of the new
arrangement – during which Wall Street had collapsed – the Keynes-con-
trolled share of the capital had gone down from £28,000 to £24,000, the
Falk share from £56,000 to £20,000.[17] Falk's poor showing was due to his
impetuous decision, reversing his 1928 arguments, to 'bull' New York in
the summer of 1929. The same decision, taken against Keynes's advice,
involved the Independent Investment Company in heavy losses in 1929–30,
as a result of which Falk had to agree 'to pay attention to the opinion' of
members of an enlarged board.[18] Early in 1930 Lydia noted, with a rare
touch of malice, that Falk had been obliged to put up his country house,
Stockton, for sale. Keynes's falling out with Falk was the first of a number
of close friendships which cooled as the depression hotted up – with Sam
Courtauld, Hubert Henderson and Dennis Robertson. Worst of all, his
former pupil, later co-director of the Natural Mutual Assurance Society,
Sidney Russell-Cooke, shot himself on 3 July 1930, victim of the financial
reversals he and his firm, Rowe and Pitman, suffered in the long bear market
which started with the Wall Street crash.

II

THE MACMILLAN COMMITTEE

'As you said, I am becoming more fashionable again,' Keynes wrote to
Lydia on 25 November 1929, following his appointment as a member of the
Macmillan Committee on Finance and Industry. A wide-ranging inquiry
into how the banking system affected the economy, it was not intended to
influence immediate policy. This was to be the job of the Economic Advisory
Council, a brainchild of the Prime Minister, Ramsay MacDonald, to which
Keynes was also appointed, after attending three luncheon parties hosted
by MacDonald in November and December. The idea for an 'Economic
General Staff' had been in MacDonald's mind since 1924 and had been
strongly urged both by Beveridge and in the Liberal Yellow Book on *Britain's
Industrial Future*. Baldwin had set up a Committee on Civil Research on his
return to power in 1925, but it had been quickly marginalised by the
Treasury.

A full account of these luncheons, attended, in addition to Keynes, by
such luminaries as Lord Weir, Sir Andrew Duncan, Walter Layton, G. D.
H. Cole, Henry Clay, Sir Josiah Stamp, J. A. Hobson, Walter Citrine and
Sir Kenneth Stewart is given in Tom Jones's *Whitehall Diary*, edited by Keith
Middlemas.[19] After much floundering by MacDonald, a council was set

up on 22 January 1930 under his chairmanship, to 'advise His Majesty's
Government in economic matters', and consisting of senior ministers and
fifteen outside experts, including Keynes. Hubert Henderson joined the
secretariat, thereby relinquishing his editorship of the *Nation* to another
Cambridge economist, Harold Wright, in what was to be its last year of
life.

In the intervals between these luncheons, Keynes sent in two memoranda
to MacDonald. In the first, on the industrial situation, he urged a co-
operative solution to Britain's industrial difficulties; in the second he said
that government policy should be influenced by expert opinion. MacDonald
agreed with both: this does not mean he intended to do much.[20]

Keynes was not quite as fashionable as he thought, or hoped. Politicians
rarely look to economists to tell them what to do: mainly to give them
arguments for doing things they want to do, or for not doing things they
don't want to do. The immediate political purpose of the Macmillan Committee was to placate the Labour Party after bank rate had been raised to
6 per cent in September to stop the drain of funds to New York. Its report
would be long delayed, and would then, no doubt, quietly gather dust.*
The Economic General Staff was a device to accommodate the impatient
Mosley and to take the heat off his political chief, J. H. Thomas, the
Lord Privy Seal, who faced mounting criticism over his failure to relieve
unemployment. Keynes's words about co-operation and expert advice fitted
the political realities faced by MacDonald, heading a minority government
and with a rebellious left wing. The new Prime Minister had himself talked
about a 'council of state'. Expert inquiries were a way of heading off the left
and strengthening MacDonald's position against Snowden, his Chancellor of
the Exchequer. Keynes's inclusion on these committees was designed to give
the appearance, not reality, of radical movement. In fact, as the depression
deepened, the movement was all the other way: back to orthodoxy. Policy
which started off as open, and reasonably flexible, gradually narrowed to a
single point: defence of confidence, which included defence of the pound.
Nevertheless, between 1929 and 1931 Keynes directed his persuasive efforts
at MacDonald, rather than Lloyd George, and in fact dropped out of Liberal
Party politics altogether.

Keynes was not a political animal, but he was a political economist. He
invented theory to justify what he wanted to do. He understood that his
theory had to be usable for politicians and administrators: easily applied,
offering political dividends. But he also understood that, before he could
win the political argument, he had to win the intellectual argument. However great the political advantages may seem, politicians will rarely be

---

*However, Keynes may have originated the idea. In a letter to J. Conway Davies, secretary
of the Mond–Turner Conference, dated 29 March 1928, he had urged the conference to pass
a resolution calling for a full inquiry into credit policy. This suggestion was adopted by the
TUC and the inquiry was promised by the Labour Party in the 1929 election.

induced to do things which the government machine regards as hopelessly impracticable or unsound. (Mrs Thatcher's governments of the 1980s were a notable exception.) The Macmillan Committee and the EAC gave Keynes the direct access to 'inside opinion' which he had been denied since the early 1920s. Specifically, he was given a chance to confront the Treasury and the Bank of England; and to argue his case before leading businessmen, bankers, civil servants and economists. The result was a two-way flow of ideas. Keynes won considerable ground, but he was forced to retreat on specific issues. Moreover, the differences which opened up on the EAC's Committee of Economists in the autumn of 1930 determined him to write another major book of theory 'to bring to an issue the deep divergences of opinion between fellow economists which have for the time being almost destroyed the practical influence of economic theory'.

In accepting appointment to the Macmillan Committee, Keynes had promised Snowden that it would be 'a first charge on my time'. He was as good as his word. Weekly meetings of his Currency Committee were fitted into his already crowded mid-week London life. 'Keynes dominated the proceedings of the Committee, both in examining witnesses and shaping the report'[21] in over forty-nine days of taking evidence and over a hundred meetings. In addition, he spent five sessions in February and March 1930 outlining his own thoughts on monetary theory and policy, and a further three days in November. His exposition enthralled the Committee. It was a masterpiece of sustained logical thinking, which also shows him fully in command of both language and mood. The chairman, Lord Macmillan, a judge, who was ignorant of finance but open-minded and sympathetic, said that he lost track of time when Keynes was speaking. Keynes's two main allies were McKenna and Ernest Bevin. McKenna was sharp, cocky and well informed throughout. Keynes went out of his way to woo Bevin, the powerful general secretary of the Transport and General Workers' Union, taking him as a guest to a meeting of the Political Economy Club in London early in December 1929. Bevin, besides being a quick learner, spotted Keynes as an economist sympathetic to the working class. His exposure to Keynes's ideas at this point, as well as his previous participation in the Mond–Turner conversations, helped lay the industrial foundations of the wartime and post–1945 'consensus'. Idiosyncratic support for the Keynes line came from the ex-communist Labour MP, J. Walton Newbold, 'a strange fellow who sometimes has an interesting idea, but more often is too rambling to be easily intelligible'.[22] The other economist on the Committee, Theodor Emmanuel Gregory, who held the Cassel Chair in Banking and Currency at the London School of Economics, proved a surprisingly ineffective critic. Bob Brand, as always, was swayed, but not converted, by Keynes's brilliance. Lord Bradbury represented the Treasury and Cecil Lubbock the Bank of England. There were a couple of businessmen.

Keynes's exposition to the Macmillan Committee, based on his *Treatise on Money*, reflected the experience of the 1920s, not the 1930s. It was an analysis, not of a world in deep depression, but of the problems of an arthritic economy in an otherwise moderately prosperous world. For Nicholas Kaldor, its value for today lies precisely here: for, although the world depression was overcome, the arthritic condition of the British economy was not. Keynes's testimony, says Kaldor,

> put forward a macroeconomic 'model' of the British economy which in certain respects was superior to that put forward six years later in the *General Theory*. This is because his analysis specifically referred to Britain and examines the *modus operandi* of the British economy in the context of her peculiar institutions. Exports, the trade balance, the flow of overseas lending, the nature of the adjustment mechanism in foreign trade, the instruments employed by the Bank of England, are brought into relationship one with another to show how the system generates a low employment trap, as a result of the high interest rates enforced by the Bank of England which are made necessary by the need to limit overseas lending to the amount that the level of net exports . . . permits.[23]

Keynes's exposition of 'the general character of the theory which mainly influences my mind in considering the practical issues which are before us' started on 20 February 1930, with an account of the *modus operandi* of bank rate under the gold standard. He started with what he called the 'orthodox' theory of the bank rate, because he believed that the Bank of England had the power to regulate the quantity of credit and that the amount of credit controlled the working of the macroeconomy, determining, within broad limits, the level of prices, investment and employment. His testimony is a paean of praise to the beauty and efficacy of bank-rate policy. In this he was expressing genuine aesthetic pleasure. But he also wanted to give the Bank of England a sense of its power and grandeur.

The great virtue of the bank rate was that it acted simultaneously to correct both a country's capital and income account imbalance. In the short run, raising bank rate attracts extra foreign funds to London; in the long run, it lowers internal costs. 'So the bank rate', he told the Committee, 'sets in motion rapid forces to diminish the calls on us to lend abroad, and slow forces which will have the effect of increasing our ability to lend abroad by reducing our price level to a competitive level with the outside world.' In saying this, he was restating what he took to be 'traditional doctrine'.[24] But there was an implication which was not so well understood. Domestic costs can be reduced only by paying factors 'less for their efforts' – by lowering profits or wages. Bank rate's only direct power was to reduce profits by increasing the cost of borrowing.[25] Thus 'there is no other way by which bank rate brings down prices except through the increase of unemployment.'[26] It is the increase in unemployment which brings down wages, makes exports more competitive and increases our ability to invest abroad, enabling bank rate to be lowered, 'having done its work' – with foreign lending equal to the export surplus, and full employment restored.[27] That, Keynes concluded, 'is the beginning and end of traditional sound finance in this country'.[28] 'An extraordinarily clear exposition,' declared the chairman. 'An extraordinarily clear exposition, and thoroughly understood by us,' echoed Reginald McKenna.

However, the working of this equilibrating mechanism depended 'on the assumption that money wages are not fixed, that they are reasonably fluid and responsive to unemployment'. The orthodox adjustment theory denied, that is, that there could be any divergence – except possibly in the very short term – between selling prices and costs of production. However, if, as a matter of fact, selling prices are flexible, and wage costs fixed, all raising bank rate does is to reduce profits and increase unemployment. The adjustment process jams at this point. 'Since 1924 money wages have remained for all practical purposes fixed.'[29]

The question of why British wages were, or had become, so 'sticky' provoked some of the most interesting exchanges on the Committee. It was a puzzle to Keynes; it has remained a puzzle to this day. In his Ludwig Mond Lecture at Manchester University on 7 November 1929, Keynes had given a reason: wage rates were fixed by 'social and historical forces', not by the marginal productivity of labour.[30] However, in a broadcast conversation with Josiah Stamp, in February 1930, he gave a more concrete reason:

> The existence of the dole undoubtedly diminishes the pressure on the individual man to accept a rate of wages or a kind of employment which is not just what he wants or what he is used to. In the old days the pressure on the unemployed was to get back somehow or other into employment, and if that was so to-day surely it would have more effect on the prevailing rate of wages . . . I cannot help feeling that we must partly attribute to the dole the extraordinary fact . . . that, in spite of the fall in prices, and the fall in the cost of living, and the heavy unemployment, wages have practically not fallen at all since 1924.[31]

Before the Macmillan Committee, Keynes reverted to his Manchester lecture position. He denied that money wages had ever been downwardly flexible. 'My reading of history is that for centuries there has existed an intense social resistance to any matters of reduction in the level of money incomes. I believe that, apart from the adjustments due to cyclical fluctuations, there has never been in modern or ancient history a community that has been prepared to accept without immense struggle a reduction in the general level of money income.' The last attempt to force one in England, in the 1820s and 1830s, had brought the country to the 'verge of revolution'.[32] Thus it was not true that money wages had become less flexible over time, due to the growth of trade unions, unemployment benefit and so on.

Secondly, according to Keynes the nineteenth-century gold-standard system had never required the degree of downward wage adjustment called for in 1925:

> prices were on the whole tending upwards, and allowing for the very sharp increase in efficiency which was going on all the time there was never any occasion to use bank rate to bring about a downward adjustment of wages. It was sufficient to use it as the regulator of the rate of the upward movement. Efficiency was itself sufficient to allow wages to rise quite materially year by year, and all the bank rate did was to regulate the rate at which we could afford to pay higher wages.

Thus the return to gold in 1925 set bank rate 'a task it had never been asked to do before in the economic history of this country'.[33]*

This allegation brought a sharp response from Bradbury, the second chairman of the Committee which had recommended the return to gold:

BRADBURY: Yes, of course, we did not know that wages were going to prove anything like as stubborn as they have proved . . . The previous history was that adjustments of money wages were comparatively easy both before the War and after.

J.M.K.: You cannot quote any case in which they had gone down.

BRADBURY: We had very considerable reductions in the export industry.

J.M.K.: Apart from the fall in 1921 during the reaction from the boom, if you go back to pre-War history there was no case in which it ever occurred.

BRADBURY: No, but we had the post-war reductions.

J.M.K.: You were thinking that 1920–1 was a good precedent, and you had not analysed to see why it was not.

BRADBURY: There was no reason, I think, why it should not have been a good precedent . . . Why do you think that that last 10 per cent was more difficult than the preceding 20?

J.M.K.: Because the whole economic body was adjusted to this new level, whereas before it had not been. During the boom there were all kinds of advantages which had been enjoyed only for a matter of days or weeks or months which were quite easily swept away. When you got to the level of 1924 you practically got to the level which people had enjoyed continuously . . . from about 1916 . . .[34]

---

*Keynes calculated that 'efficiency' had been increasing at 1.5 per cent p.a. since 1925, that is 7.5 per cent in total over five years. 'To get back to equilibrium with the gold standard would have meant [a] 10 per cent [cut in money wages], but with the subsequent fall of world prices it has meant 20 per cent, so while we were 10 per cent out in 1925 we are 12.5 per cent out now.' (CW, xx, 58.)

His statement that 'for 60 years prior to the War the long-period movement of prices was always upward, with the exception of some 10 to 12 years from the middle 80's to the middle 90's' (CW, xx, 55) is wrong. It would be more accurate to describe British price experience in the mid-Victorian period as one of price stability. However, money wages showed a persistent tendency to rise, resulting in a doubling of real wages between 1860 and 1914.

Keynes's argument was supported by Bevin. The tremendous fluctuations in prices during and after the war had been regarded as abnormal, aberrant and temporary, and therefore it had been possible to index wages to the cost of living. In 1919–20 8m. workers were covered by 'sliding scale' agreements: wages were indexed to the cost of living or the selling price of a commodity (for example, coal): 'every five points [movement of the relevant index] meant 1s on or off wages'. However, this came to an end once prices had stopped falling, and in 1930 there were not more than a million workers covered by such agreements. 'There has been a gradual conversion into a stabilised wage.' The 'stop-point', Bevin suggested, had come when workers felt they had got back to their pre-war standard of living.[35] Bevin omitted to say that the hours worked for the weekly real wage had, in 1919–20, fallen by 13 per cent without any corresponding gain in productivity, implying a rise in the 'efficiency wage' – the wage per hour worked. Workers were defending not just their 1914 position but the 'gain' of a shorter working week. This was the reason for the maladjustment of prices and costs as Britain came out of the depression in 1922–3.

However, although the shorter working week may explain the origin of the maladjustment, it does not explain why workers were able to 'hold on' to their gains of 1919–20 in face of high and persisting unemployment. Why did not a surplus of labour drive down its price, as orthodox theory suggested? The French economist Jacques Rueff provided an answer which echoed Keynes's remarks in his conversation with Stamp:

> In actual fact the wages level is a result of collective contracts, but these contracts would never have been observed by the workmen if they had not been sure of receiving an indemnity which differed little from their wages. It is the dole, therefore, that has made trade union discipline possible . . . Therefore we may assume that the dole is the underlying cause of the unemployment which has been so cruelly inflicted on England since 1920.[36]

This argument was taken up by two American economists, Benjamin and Kochin, in 1979.[37] Lord Macmillan made very much the same point when he suggested to Keynes that social security benefits had prevented 'economic laws' from working. Keynes replied tartly, 'I do not think they are sins against economic law. I do not think it is any more economic law that wages should go down easily than that they should not. It is a question of facts. Economic law does not lay down the facts, it tells you what the consequences are.' Unemployment benefits were not the cause of unemployment. 'I think we are forced by the use of the wrong weapon to have a hospital because it has resulted in there being so many wounded.'[38] There the argument rests.

Keynes ended the first part of his testimony:

I conclude, for these various reasons, that bank rate policy, whilst theoretically intact, has broken down as a practical instrument for restoring true equilibrium. It leaves us in a chronic position of spurious equilibrium, and in that spurious equilibrium the brunt falls on profits. As long as we have a form of society in which profit is the driving force of enterprise you will have a gradual decay if you have a situation in which it is impossible to earn profit. The choice then is between accentuating bank-rate policy until it does do its work or falling back on some alternative method. The worst thing is to have a bank-rate policy which is not severe enough to bring about equilibrium by that method, and yet diverts our minds from any alternative policy.[39]

The heart of Keynes's exposition, which occupied most of the second session, Friday, 21 February, was his saving–investment analysis. He reported to Lydia on 23 February, 'On Friday they found my speech much more perplexing, as I thought they would. I think I did it all right. But it was unfamiliar and paradoxical, and whilst they couldn't confute me, they did not know whether or not to believe . . . I got back to Cambridge very tired.'

What Keynes provided was a summary of the *Treatise* theory, replete with banana parable. If saving exceeds investment, the remaining income for consumption is not sufficient to buy consumption goods at prices which cover their costs: hence unemployment. Keynes showed how this could happen, and had happened, in Britain. Investment consisted of home and foreign investment. If bank rate were too high relative to the expected yield of domestic investment, savings were lent abroad. But net foreign investment could not be greater than the surplus on income account, which could be increased only by lowering British money (and to a lesser extent real) wages. 'If you had complete fluidity there would always be a point where our wage system would allow our foreign investment to be equal to the surplus of our savings over home investment; but if our wage system is rigid the amount of our foreign investment is rigid also.'[40] In that case, saving is 'spilled on the ground, and becomes business men's losses'.[41] Keynes added that in a closed system this problem would not arise.

CHAIRMAN: In a self-contained state bank rate would function perfectly?
J.M.K.: Yes, because in a self-contained state you could keep wages fixed; you could reconcile yourself to that fact and keep your investments always equal to the savings, and let the price level adjust itself to the level of income.[42]

Keynes's view that in a 'closed system' one could simply reduce the bank rate to that level where savings and investments were equal was to be strongly challenged by the Bank of England, which denied that the banking system had the power over credit conditions which Keynes attributed to it.

Keynes summed up the logical relationship between his bank-rate expo-sition and his savings–investment analysis in the following taut sequence:

> The way prices are forced down is this. You put the bank rate at a level at which savings are in excess of investments. Business men make losses, prices fall, and then at long last the business man forces down the remuneration of the factors of production and prices [wages?] are then lower. But if you jam the machine halfway through so you have a chronic condition in which business men make losses, you also have a chronic condition of unemployment, a chronic condition of waste; and the excess savings are spilled on the ground.[43]

Some evidence of the perplexity Keynes's 'new theory' caused is revealed by a couple of exchanges:

BRAND: The . . . point I do not quite follow is this; I have always assumed that if I save money those savings go in some form, either by my own investment or by the banker's investment, back into industry.

J.M.K.: In a fluid system they always would, because the rate of interest as a result of your savings would fall, and, therefore, there would be more demand for investment; but as the rate of interest cannot fall for foreign reasons, your savings can only flow into investments if it takes the form of increased exports.

BRAND: What happens to my savings?

J.M.K.: The fact that you do not spend that money means that some business man fails to sell you something he hoped to sell you and has to accept a lower price, and is, therefore, poorer by the exact amount that you are richer . . . And very likely, without your knowing it, you yourself as a shareholder find that you are that much poorer. One of the remedies that eventually comes, is that this process so impoverishes the community that in the end it cannot save at all and so you reach equilibrium.

CHAIRMAN: That is a strange doctrine to a Scotsman.[44]

Keynes was supremely confident that he had cracked his case: that his analysis of the disequilibrium between saving and investment did actually provide a theoretical explanation of why Britain was caught in a low employ-ment trap. In correspondence with Brand and Montagu Norman, Keynes claimed that his theory was a 'mathematical certainty', not 'open to dis-pute'.[45] Keynes tried to elucidate the point which worried Brand: 'Thus . . . the savings which are spilt on the ground are the savings which . . . he [the businessman] *would* have had if his business income [from profits and shares] had been normal. So you will see that the spilling of savings on the ground is . . . practically the same as business losses.'[46] As long as Keynes persisted (as a result of his *Treatise* definitions) in calling non-existent savings 'excess savings' he was bound to confuse his audience. However, Keynes chose his *Treatise* definitions to illustrate the process by which savings are destroyed or created, rather than the outcome of the process. As he put it, 'I want to study what happens during the process of disequilibrium [not what happens in a position of equilibrium].'[47]

Of course, Keynes did understand that the fall in income would itself reduce saving:

> In actual fact . . . we do get some relief . . . insofar as the growing impoverishment of the community is leading to diminished savings; it is the route by which in the long run you would – failing any other – bring about equilibrium. The continuation of the present state of affairs would in the end so impoverish the community that they would not have a sufficient margin of income to save, and when that had gone far enough we should find unemployment disappear . . . in fact, if there were not some reduction of savings going on I think the position would be very much worse than it is from the point of view of employment.[48]

There is a clear hint here of the idea that the process of depression itself eventually rebalances saving and investment at a lower level of income. The interesting point, in the light of Keynes's later theory of 'unemployment equilibrium', is that he believed that this low-income equilibrium would nevertheless be a full-employment equilibrium. His idea was that as the machinery of production shrinks the unemployed find low-paid service jobs outside the industrial system – as 'gardeners and chauffeurs'.[49] This passage is evidence of the fact that Keynes continued to cling to the notion of balance or equilibrium as one involving full employment. However, this kind of rebalancing of the economy, as well as being retrogressive, would clearly take a long time, so not unsurprisingly Keynes put it 'very low' on the list of remedies he started advocating to the Committee on his third day of testimony, 28 February.

He started by ruling out devaluation, except as a last resort.[50] A second type of remedy was 'an agreed reduction of the level of money incomes in this country', as he had recommended in 1925. The sacrifice would apply to *all* 'wages, salaries, and emoluments of every kind', and would be balanced 'to a considerable extent' by the resulting fall in the cost of living. Bevin was quick to point out the difficulty: 'What guarantee of that is there?'[51] This has plagued all subsequent attempts to develop 'incomes policies'. Trade unions have some control over the wage bargain: they have none over the price level.

Keynes next mentioned the possibility of 'bounties to industry in general or to particular industries', raised by taxation and enabling relief of particular taxes on employers. General taxes were a lesser deterrent to employers than 'imposing a poll tax on the number of men employed [through national insurance contributions]. The taxes fall on [the employer] in a different way. They only fall on him after he has made his profit, and they fall on a much wider area.' Here Keynes was repeating a point he had made in his Ludwig Mond Lecture about the design of social policy: 'if [on the ground of humanity – or justice] you want to give the poorer part of the community £100,000,000 more income you would be wiser to do that out of taxation than by fixing the wages of individuals at a higher figure than it pays their employers to give them'.[52] This argument against minimum-wage legislation has lost none of its force. Fourthly, costs of production could be lowered by 'rationalisation', leading to a long-run increase in efficiency.[53]

The remedies so far were all directed towards lowering production costs. A fifth remedy, protection, could give direct relief to the business community by raising prices at unchanged costs of production.[54] The virtue of protection is that 'it does the trick, whereas in present conditions free trade does not'.[55] Free-trade policy was part of 'the bank-rate policy argument'. It presupposed a 'fluid' system in which employment would always be distributed in line with comparative advantage. However, 'as soon as that link in the chain is broken the whole of the free-trade argument breaks down'. It was better for Britain to produce motor cars inefficiently under protection than to produce nothing at all. Keynes was not yet ready to endorse protection publicly. He disappointed the Committee's tariff reformer, Sir Walter Raine, by saying that he was 'frightfully afraid of protection as a long-term policy'. It was like 'drug-taking': once tariffs were put on 'you will never get them off again'.[56] He would prefer his sixth remedy, which he postponed till the fourth session on 6 March.

This was the Liberal policy of loan-financed public investment. The 'Treasury view' that additional investment would be at the expense of existing investment was 'pure logical delusion'. It ignored the distinction between saving and investment; it 'only demonstrates that home investment is not a cure for unemployment, by first of all assuming . . . that there is no unemployment to cure'.[57]

Against the Treasury view, that the loan-financed public expenditure would draw on savings already being invested, Keynes argued that the new expenditure would itself create the fund to repay the loans: half from saving on the dole, another half from restoring 'normal profits'.[58] He next disposed of the Treasury objection that it was difficult to find sufficiently attractive new investment opportunities. If the rate of interest is fixed by bank-rate policy at 5 per cent, it is true that investments which bring 4 per cent are unproductive. But that is not the real choice: the choice may be between investing £100 at 4 per cent and losing £100; so 'new investment yielding four per cent or in special cases three per cent would be nationally preferable to unemployment and business losses'.[59] The Treasury view assumed full employment. 'If investment in a four per cent proposition . . . were to prevent money going into a six per cent investment, this would be a very foolish thing to do . . . I am arguing that that is not the situation.'

Two points of theoretical interest arise in this section of Keynes's exposition. First, he argued that increased investment (however brought about) would set up beneficial 'repercussions' because 'the consumption of the men thus employed will lead to more employment'.[60] This is an advance on the vaguer notion of 'cumulative prosperity' Keynes had used in his 1929 defence of the Lloyd George proposals. Secondly, Keynes admitted that the 'new investment' would be 'a substitute for existing investment and not a net addition' unless the Bank of England increased the supply of credit or the public became more 'high spirited' (that is, hoarded less).[61] By introducing the idea of 'repercussions', especially repercussions on expectations, Keynes was giving the Treasury a chance to reformulate its view as a confidence argument – an opportunity which, as we shall see, Sir Richard Hopkins was too clever to miss.

Keynes suggested a number of technical devices for stimulating domestic investment: separating the market for home and foreign securities by 'gadgets', though this would be 'enormously difficult'; discouraging overseas investment by taxing foreign investment income; creating machinery for long-period credit to small borrowers, like the French *credit mobiliers*. The most direct route, though, was central government spending on telephones and roads; and allowing local authorities, public boards and public utilities to borrow at below market rates. The following burst of passion is a good example of Keynes's favourite techniques of paradox and *reductio ad absurdum*:

> It seems to me we have got into quite a desperate habit of thinking in separate compartments; the Treasury will reject something on the ground that it will cost money regardless of what they could hope to save on the 'dole' or from increased revenue. We get into a vicious circle, we do nothing because we have not the money; but it is precisely because we do not do anything that we have not the money. The buoyancy of the revenue gets less and less. There is also the idea of keeping down home investment with a view to getting the interest on the national debt down as low as possible. That is one of the most desperate muddles the human mind has ever entertained. If you were to push it to its logical conclusion, the right thing would be to prohibit house building, for example, altogether. If you absolutely prohibited any outlet for investment and if you could control the foreign situation, we might all be dead, but at any rate the rate of the interest which it would be necessary to pay on consols would have fallen to zero. The whole object of having a low rate of interest is in order to do something. But if you think that it is wise to stop doing things in order to lower the rate of interest, you are standing upside down.[62]

Government action to stimulate domestic investment was needed to break the 'vicious circle' of deflation and restore business profits to normal; after that it should be possible 'gradually to diminish the amount of Government intervention', subject to the proviso of not allowing foreign lending at will. Keynes developed this point with all his customary force and lucidity:

> ... I believe that *laissez-faire* in foreign lending is utterly incompatible with our existing wages policy. For if individuals are entirely free to lend their savings without discrimination in whatever quarter of the world they obtain the greatest reward, this means, broadly speaking, that the proportion of the joint product which we award to labour as compared with the proportion which we award to capital cannot be greater here than it is in other parts of the world ... relatively to its efficiency. Assuming that labour and capital are equally efficient in Germany and England, and in England our wages policy awards three-fifths of the value of the product produced to labour and two-fifths to capital, and in Germany it awards three-fifths to capital and two-fifths to labour the rate of profit must be 50 per cent higher in Germany than it is in England and they will be able to offer 7½ per cent when the English borrowers only offer 5 per cent. If that is allowed to go on freely we are bound to get back into the position we are now in, that is to say, either we shall be in a state of chronic disequilibrium ... or we shall have to force down wages in England until capital gets the same proportion of the product as in Germany.
>
> We have now reached this point, that our wages policy is definitely set to a more liberal remuneration of the worker relatively to his efficiency than prevails in a good many other countries ... this ... is definitely incompatible with the policy of *laissez-faire* towards foreign investment.[63]

Keynes's seventh remedy, introduced on 7 March, was for 'concerted policy between the leading central banks of the world not only to prevent a further fall in international prices, but ... also to raise prices to a parity with the international level of money incomes and with the international level of money costs of production'.[64] Deflation, in other words, was a world problem, caused, as he had said earlier, by 'the return to the gold standard in many other countries which caused them to behave just as we have'.[65] The problem of the sagging commodity price index was a problem of under-demand rather than overinvestment; 'world-wide encouragement of invest-ment and of capital development generally would help.'[66] Standing in the way were the 'gold hoarding propensities' of the Bank of France – it was hardly an exaggeration to say that economic science was 'non-existent' there – and the tendency of the Federal Reserve System to be dominated by domestic considerations. In his concluding remarks, Keynes registered, for the first time, the onset of the world depression:

> it is now fairly obvious that we are on the downward slope of an international credit cycle ... The intensity of our own problem today

is due to the fact that we now have the influence of this international
depression superimposed on our own pre-existing domestic
troubles . . . A year or two ago our troubles were primarily domestic;
now the international problem is at least equally important.[67]

In the coming months he would deploy these suggestions, in different combinations, in his successive plans to counter the slump.

Keynes's nine-hour 'private' testimony to the Macmillan Committee was
a magnificent performance, intellectual and stylistic. It not only greatly
influenced its hearers. It was immediately recognised as of first-rate importance by Bank of England and Treasury officials: the confident simplicities
of their reasoning were shattered, never to be revived. But this does not
mean that Keynes had 'won' the argument. The Bank and Treasury were
reserving their fire. When it came, Keynes did not emerge unscathed. He
was forced to reconsider his position in two crucial respects.

First in the field was the Bank of England. The Bank went into the
hearings in confident mood: after giving his testimony in November 1929,
Sir Ernest Harvey, the deputy governor, had received a 'charming letter'
from Keynes which led him to believe that 'we at any rate have nothing to
fear' from the Macmillan Committee.[68] This confidence was shattered after
the cross-examination of the governor. Montagu Norman's testimony, on
26 March 1930, was a disaster for the Bank. He was ill at ease, ill-informed,
vague, contradictory, resentful and unforthcoming. He hated the game of
consequences which Keynes, McKenna, Bevin and others forced him to
play; being forced back, time and again, on such phrases as 'I do not know',
'I would not like to say', 'I am not sure' or 'I don't remember'. He eventually
remarked to Bevin, 'It is a curious thing, the extent to which many who
inhabit the City of London find difficulty in stating the reasons for the faith
that is in them . . .' Keynes remembered him as 'an elf; an artist, sitting
with his cloak round him hunched up, saying "I can't remember – " thus
evading all questions, & triumphing – going away disguised – going mad.'[69]
His deputy, Harvey, was given the unenviable task of 'doctoring' his evidence for the printed record, 'so threadbare and deliberately negative had
been the Governor's contribution'.[70]

Nevertheless, Norman's strategy was perfectly clear. He wanted to shift
responsibility for unemployment from the Bank's shoulders to others. First,
he denied that the level of employment was the Bank's responsibility. The
Bank was responsible for maintaining external equilibrium. This it had
done, despite the unanticipated difficulty of the subsequent undervaluation
of the French franc. It was up to industry to make itself competitive. 'I have
never been able to see myself why for the last few years it should have been
impossible for industry starting from within to have readjusted its own
position.'[71] More importantly, he denied that the Bank had the power over
credit conditions which Keynes claimed for it. Bank rate affected only 'short

money', leaving the 'whole mass of credit' little changed.[72] Primed by its three resident economists, Henry Clay, Walter Stewart and Oliver Sprague[73]* the Bank developed these two interconnected points. In doing so it revived the Real Bills doctrine of the nineteenth century: the view that the banking system responded to the needs of trade; it did not cause the needs of trade to be what they were.

According to Clay, it was the supply side of the British economy, not banking policy, which was at fault. The 'dislocation of pre-existing economic relations [between industries and their markets] by war' would have produced a British unemployment problem, whatever the monetary policy pursued.[74] Credit was not short: it was being used up in financing loss-making industries instead of creating new ones – a point with which Keynes would have agreed.[75] The use of capital, Clay told the Committee, 'is conditioned by the existing organisation of industry; if your employers and work people and market connections are all specialised to an industry in which there is no possibility of expanding there will be no demand in it for capital . . .'.[76] Recovery, Clay said, required 'reducing costs; or finding new outlets for the employment of labour, on which prices can be obtained which will cover the costs'. This would take a generation.[77]

The Bank of England's evidence raised a crucial theoretical point. Clay was asserting that the supply of credit was endogenous not exogenous. The banks cannot create credit in excess of the demand for it. 'The truer view', Clay wrote, 'seems to me to be, that while the conditions of sound banking impose a limit on the extension of credit, the *origin* of credit is to be found in the action of the businessman, who approaches his bank for assistance with a business transaction, and the *basis* of credit in the probability that the transaction can be done at a profit.'[78] This amounted to a denial of the agenda of the monetary reformers. As Keynes put it in his cross-examination of Stewart: 'what you are saying is that there is always the right quantity of credit?'[79] Stewart doubted whether 'the expansion of bank credit in quantity was a determining factor in prices and trade activity';[80] 'there are a great many things that people can do with money besides buying commodities. They can hold it.'[81] All that meant, Keynes rejoined, was that you 'would have to dose the system with money', 'feed the hoarder' in order to bring down money rates.[82] Echoing Norman, and denying the central policy assumption of the *Treatise*, Stewart remarked, 'I should not have thought that bank credit determines the long term rate.'[83] Keynes admitted that when a depression had got too deep a 'negative rate of interest' might be required to bring about an industrial revival, but that normally 'a reasonably abundant supply of credit would do the trick'.[84] Stewart persisted: 'Only if borrowers saw a prospect of making a profit and of repaying debts.' Keynes

*Henry Clay, a professor in economics at Manchester University, was economic adviser to the Bank of England from 1930 to 1944; Walter Stewart and Oliver Sprague, American economists, were special advisers to Norman from 1928 to 1930 and 1930 to 1933 respectively.

was driven back to arguing that 'though [the supply of credit] may be only a balancing factor, it is the most controllable factor'.[85]

STEWART: As an economist I cannot believe that all the ills of business can be cured simply by an increase or decrease in the volume of Central Bank credit.

J.M.K. It may be that the weather has much more influence on business than the matter of the bank rate; but nevertheless, when one is discussing what should be done, it would not be useful to keep on saying it is the weather which really matters. In a sense it is true it may be the biggest factor?

STEWART: It may be the only thing that the Central Bank can do; but it does not strike me as the only thing that business men can do . . . I regard wage adjustments as ever so much more important in industry than . . . anything bankers can do.[86]

Keynes's belief in monetary manipulation was shaken, but not shattered. He still believed that when interest rates were lowered investment projects became profitable at the margin which were not profitable before. But he admitted that bank rate was a weaker instrument than he had believed. In an article he wrote for the *Nation* of 10 May, before his cross-examination of Stewart and Clay in front of the Committee, but after Dennis Robertson's appearance,* he noted that although money was 'now cheap beyond dispute' at 2.5 to 3 per cent, 'the results must be relative to circumstances. What would attract borrowers when prices are rising or are stable, may be far too dear when they are falling.' For the first time, Keynes acknowledged that what is important for recovery is falling *real* interest rates. Moreover, 'cheap money does very little by itself to mend matters. In the main it creates an environment in which enterprise is more likely to lift its head again.'[87] But the policymaker was not faced with an exclusive choice between monetary policy and 'the weather': the other controllable element in the situation was the volume of investment. If businessmen would not invest, the government always could. At this point, the Treasury view came into Keynes's sights, in the person of Sir Richard Hopkins.

Keynes thought he knew what the Treasury view was and that he was in a position to refute it. The Treasury had claimed that additional loan-financed public spending could not add to investment and employment,

---

*Dennis Robertson really echoed the Bank's view in his evidence, given on 8 May 1930. (Keynes would already have seen his Statement of Evidence before he wrote his *Nation* article.) Cheap money might not succeed against the 'unwillingness of business men to borrow even at very low money rates of interest if prices are falling, or expected to go on falling, rapidly' even in a 'closed system'. In such a situation, public works were the only remedy. Keynes found Robertson's position 'more pessimistic' than his own. (Minutes of Evidence, Committee on Finance and Industry, i, Statement of Evidence, paras 4, 10, 4834, 4877, 4922.) Robertson later complained that this train of thought 'woke no response' in Keynes at the time. (*CW*, xxix, 167.)

only divert them from existing uses. This was true, Keynes was prepared
to say, only on the assumption of a fixed money supply and full employment.
But Hopkins had foreseen this. He too had a political motive. He did not
want to make it seem that the Treasury was against action to help the
unemployed, especially as there had been a change of political masters. An
argument designed for use by Churchill and Baldwin in defending the
Conservative government's record needed to be modified for the use of
Labour ministers committed, however haltingly, to public works schemes.

The Treasury was not opposed to government spending in principle,
Hopkins declared at the outset. Its objection was to a particular plan, that
put forward by Lloyd George in 1929. This plan, far from 'setting up a
cycle of prosperity' as Keynes had hoped, would much more probably
'produce a great cry against bureaucracy' and a suspicion of 'extravagance
and waste', so that the loans would have to be 'put out at a very high price',
with 'despondency on the part of general business'. The more distrusted the
plan was, the higher the rate of interest would have to go.[88] This new version
of the Treasury doctrine would later be labelled 'psychological crowding
out'. It showed how, even with less than full employment, loan-financed
government expenditure might make no difference to the level of
employment.

There was another, more subtle strand in the Treasury's new line. Keynes
had consistently argued that 'cheap money' was the main requirement for
recovery. He had advocated public works as an alternative to it. Following
the Wall Street collapse, interest rates were starting to tumble. Was not
Keynes's advocacy of new expenditure likely to retard the fall in interest
rates?

The reformulation of the Treasury view took Keynes by surprise. He tried
to pin down Hopkins to his original understanding. Was it the Treasury
position that 'schemes of capital development are of no use for reducing
unemployment'? That was going 'much too far', Hopkins replied. Did the
Treasury not hold that 'any capital that could be found for their schemes
would be diverted from other uses?' That, said Hopkins, was 'a much too
rigid expression of any views that may have come from us'. It was the
'atmosphere in which schemes may be undertaken' which conditions their
consequences.

'You mean', said Keynes, 'if the schemes are very unpopular they may
have other reactions of an adverse kind?'

'Yes.'

'But that would not affect the amount of employment which the scheme
would create?'

'Not the amount which the particular scheme will create at the time while
it is in being, but it immediately alters its dynamic effect.'

'So the issue', Keynes went on, 'between those who are in favour of these schemes and those who are against them, is not whether they cure unemployment?'

'Do you wish me to agree?'

'What is the point where we differ?'

'If . . . a scheme of this type is undertaken under different conditions [from those you assume] it is not in itself a dynamic force towards a great renewal of activity and prosperity . . . it does [then] make a hole in the capital which is available for the purposes of the community . . . It might lead people to think that this country was a much worse place in which to invest.'

'Is it your view that all the capital which is available is used?'

'No, I should say very likely that may not be so now.'

'Nearly all of what you have been saying today comes to this, that it is difficult to find good schemes.'

'Yes.'

'And that bad schemes are open to indirect objections. That is quite different from what I previously thought to be the Treasury view. It was not that kind of view, but a theoretical view, that the objection to these schemes was that they caused diversion on theoretical grounds. That was a misunderstanding on my part . . . ?'

'Yes . . . the Treasury view . . . is not a rigid dogma. It is the result of the view that we take as to the practical reactions of the scheme.'

'It bends so much that I find difficulty in getting hold of it.'

'Yes; I do not think these views are capable of being put in the rigid form of a theoretical doctrine.'[89]

The discussion turned to the criterion of a 'good scheme' – one that would have a favourable effect on business confidence. Hopkins said the 'ultimate test' was: 'Is it on a reasonable view economically justified?' This gave Keynes another chance: was it Hopkins's view, that 'schemes which yield 4 per cent cure unemployment whereas schemes which yield 3 per cent do not cure unemployment'? But Hopkins was not to be drawn. 'We have already agreed before', he said, 'that both good schemes and bad schemes benefit unemployment.' The difference was that 'if you had to get it [the loan for a particular scheme] taken up at a very high rate [of interest] and accompanied by an adverse public sentiment you would very quickly lose what you gained by that from the number of people who would think it better to invest the next lot of money that they had to invest in America'. Keynes had one more try. Suppose, instead of borrowing the money from the public, the government simply printed it; 'it would not make the slightest difference to its economic effect?' That was 'fantastic', Hopkins replied. 'If I am right in thinking that a great loan directly raised in the ordinary way would carry with it a bad public sentiment, and . . . adverse repercussions, what would happen if it were raised by what is ordinarily called plain inflation I cannot imagine.'[90] The chairman concluded: 'I think we may

characterise it as a drawn battle.'[91] Keynes wrote to his wife (18 May 1930):
'I had a rather exciting cross-examination . . . Sir R. Hopkins . . . was very
clever; but he did not understand the technique of what we were discussing;
– so the combination made a good hunting. But it proved that the Treasury
don't know any more than the Bank of England what it is all about –
enough to make tears roll down the eyes of a patriot.'

The question posed by Hopkins was: could Lloyd George's policy have
worked if the market judged it unsound? Or to put it more generally: was
the aggregate amount of investment in a free society any more 'controllable'
than was the rate of interest? Keynes was not shaken in his conviction that
the state could and should maintain employment at a high level. But for
the first time he started to pay explicit attention to the role of 'confidence'
in influencing the 'dynamics' of an expansionary policy. As we shall see,
this led him to place increasing emphasis on protection, his fifth remedy, in
the coming months.

Emmanuel Goldenweiser, an official of the Federal Reserve Board who
visited Europe in the summer of 1930, took away an interesting impression
of the state of play on the Macmillan Committee, to which he also gave
evidence:

> Lord Macmillan, the Chairman, is a judge and a very able presiding
> officer. Reginald McKenna of the Midland Bank and John Maynard
> Keynes are the two most active members . . . [They] take the general
> view that Great Britain's troubles are due to a large extent to a
> premature return to the gold standard at the old parity, and to a
> policy of credit restriction pursued by the Bank of England. They are
> inclined to take these dogmas as conclusive, and not to consider any
> material or evidence that does not support the general view. It is hard
> to say whether the majority of the Committee agrees with them. I
> know Gregory holds a great many qualifications and reservations on
> this viewpoint. It is generally understood that Walter W. Stewart gave
> brilliant testimony in refuting the charges that the present situation is
> due to any extent to Bank of England policy. His general position was
> that the one thing that functions most nearly perfectly in England is
> the money market and that the causes of troubles experienced by
> English industry are found in other fields.[92]

Keynes had further chances to expound his views, on 27 and 28 November
and 5 December 1930. By this time he had joined the chairman and Brand,
Gregory and Lubbock in a drafting committee. The tide of reaction was
flowing strongly as unemployment rose inexorably, threatening the government's own finances. 'I feel this is a bad moment for any changes,' Brand
wrote to Keynes on 7 November, 'because the world is in such a frightfully
nervy state.' Walter Newbold, on the other hand, having seen the draft
report, protested that, if workers were told they would have to accept wage

cuts, it would lead to revolution. Caught between the collapse of business confidence and rigid money wages, Keynes had little room for manoeuvre. His suggestions before the full Committee were designed to improve the technique – for example, widening the gold points – and increase the resources, of the Bank of England, so that Britain could 'combine with adherence to an international standard the maximum of domestic autonomy . . .'[93] Keynes's view was still that 'if . . . our economic life is to be regulated at the source, there can be no possible instrument of this except the Bank of England'.[94] But monetary policy must not be given tasks it could not do. He was clear it could not, and should not, be used to adjust the economy to a declining price level. But he was less clear about the alternatives. At one moment we find him saying, 'If we wish to have our money incomes move differently from the rest of the world, but nevertheless want to remain on an international standard, we may be able to do it by handling our foreign trade on the Russian model.'[95] His more considered conclusion was that 'we have got a system which simply does not work when there are large changes in the value of money in an upward direction. We must therefore avoid large changes [in the value] of money in an upward direction . . .' if capitalism was to be saved from socialism.[96]

Keynes's appearance before the Macmillan Committee marks the start of the Keynesian Revolution in policymaking. No policymaker after 1930 made the mistake of assuming that all prices were flexible and that, by fixing the exchange at any level one wanted, one secured an automatic adjustment of costs. When the gold standard was abandoned in 1931, it was abandoned for good: 'cheap money' was the slogan of the 1930s. This was Keynes's victory. But the influence did not flow all one way. The Bank was not shaken out of its belief that monetary policy was less powerful than Keynes was suggesting. This was Clay's victory. The Treasury had brought the confidence issue to the forefront of the public works discussion. This was Hopkins's victory. Keynes was influenced by both arguments. The main conclusion he drew from all this is that his theory had to go back to the drawing board before it could hope to overcome the 'model' of the economy lodged in the minds of the 'practical men'. The *General Theory* was, in part, a response to the objections of the Bank and the Treasury to his proposals.

Keynes's own policy agenda had not changed since 1922 when he first noticed that it was 'almost hopeless' to try to force down wages in line with prices, and suggested the alternative aim of forcing up prices to the level of the 'going' wage rate. Less clearly, Keynes was coming to see that public spending was needed as a complement to cheap money in order to raise prices and thus restore 'normal' profits. The question of 'confidence' might be met by a policy of protection. Finally, Keynes was looking to a 'social contract' to prevent British 'efficiency wages' from rising faster than elsewhere in the long run. This was the drift of his thinking on policy by the autumn of 1930.

III

THE COMMITTEE OF ECONOMISTS

On the Macmillan Committee, Keynes tried to get bankers, civil servants and economists to rethink their principles. As a member of the Economic Advisory Council he had a chance to persuade the government to do something. The EAC met once a month: MacDonald presided, Snowden and Thomas also attended. Keynes soon realised he was back in the 'monkey house', as he liked to call committee meetings at which no business could be done. The agendas were cluttered up with a ragbag of issues hived off by the departments – some of them carried over from the Committee on Civil Research. The Council spawned sub-committees to inquire into miscellaneous topics like the training of biologists, the Channel Tunnel (on which Keynes sat), migration, the sugar-beet industry and so on. MacDonald's analogy with a 'brain' was defective: there were too many brains chasing too many hares.

From Keynes's point of view, the most important result of the first meeting, held on 17 February 1930, was the setting up of a Committee on the Economic Outlook, to 'diagnose the underlying situation' created by the slump. Keynes as chairman was joined by Sir Arthur Balfour, Sir John Cadman (both businessmen), G. D. H. Cole and Walter Citrine, general secretary of the TUC (soon replaced on the Committee by Bevin). At its second meeting on 13 March, the EAC authorised the Committee to 'inquire into the desirability of more intensified State action for the purpose of increasing employment by capital expenditure on loans, or otherwise . . .' But there the harmony ended. Keynes and Cole argued in favour of 'a programme of productive and useful home development'; the businessmen wanted to reduce costs, including taxes.[97]

Predictably, Snowden found the businessmen's report 'weightier' than that of the economists, though he could hardly have relished the hints of protection in both. His real objection was to the Council discussing such matters at all. After dining with Colin Clark (a statistician on the staff of the EAC) on 1 June, Hugh Dalton wrote in his diary, 'It [the Council] wanted to enquire into Free Trade . . . but Snowden wouldn't have this. Nor would he agree to an enquiry into monetary policy, since the Macmillan Committee was sitting. Nor into the function of the state in relation to unemployment policy, which Keynes wanted. Keynes hurts the P.M.'s feelings by describing himself at one meeting as "the only socialist present".'[98]

In an effort to bypass the Chancellor's veto, Hubert Henderson persuaded MacDonald, on 10 July, to circulate questions designed to 'enable the [non-Ministerial members of the] Council to concentrate on large questions of public policy'.[99]* Given the Council's composition, Keynes thought this would only add to the confusion. As a means of silencing the businessmen, he urged MacDonald to abandon the method of proceeding by questionnaire and appoint instead a small committee of economists 'to closet themselves together and try to produce, say by the end of October, an agreed diagnosis of our present problems and a reasoned list of possible remedies'.[100] MacDonald set up the Committee on 24 July with Keynes as chairman and Pigou, Henderson, Stamp and Lionel Robbins as the other members. The secretaries were A. F. Hemming, joint secretary with Henderson of the EAC, and Keynes's pupil, Richard Kahn, now a prize Fellow at King's. Its brief was 'to review the present economic condition of Great Britain, to examine the causes which are responsible for it and to indicate the conditions of recovery'. The Committee met for the first time on 10 September.

This 'small but significant victory for the economists' point of view'[101] was made possible by the damage the government had suffered through Mosley's resignation on 19 May. ('The article of O. Mosley in the *Daily Express* was good,' Lydia wrote to Maynard on 25 May. 'I did not feel any humbug about it.') In a powerful resignation speech on 28 May Mosley had attacked not only the policy of inaction but also the institutional machinery for dealing with unemployment. Mosley's resignation strengthened MacDonald's position against Snowden. He now took over the chairmanship of a panel of ministers to deal with unemployment, shifting the discredited J. H. Thomas to the Dominions Office. Over the Treasury's objections, more money was made available for local authority spending on public works. The advice MacDonald now sought from the EAC Committee of Economists was a further direct challenge to Treasury control. It gave Keynes his best chance since the war to change the direction of economic policy – if he could carry his fellow economists with him. As Howson and Winch say, his main hope of producing an agreed diagnosis rested explicitly on the 'assumption of a common language' and implicitly on 'confidence in his powers of persuading his fellow economists to accept the diagnostic framework of his *Treatise*'.[102]

Keynes produced a short list of questions for the second meeting of the Committee on 11 September. He asked his fellow economists to estimate the effects on unemployment, prices and real wages of an increase in investment (at home and abroad), or a tariff, or a reduction in British money wages. In the second part of his questionnaire, he asked them to estimate 'how much too high (in order of magnitude are) (a) real wages, (b) money

---

*MacDonald's questions were: (1) What in your view are the chief causes of our present industrial position? (2) What in your view should be the trade policy adopted by HMG to restore trade? (3) How in your view can the home market be developed thus enabling more people to command effective power to consume? (4) How in your opinion can the volume of exports be increased? (5) What in your opinion would be the framework of a definite Imperial Trade policy? Replies were received, but were not discussed.

wages at the existing level of world prices?', continuing, 'If your estimate
of the excess of real wages is greater than your estimate of the increase of
real wages per unit of productivity [since 1910–14], how do you explain
this?' When the doctors assembled at Stamp's house, Shortlands, on 26–28
September, to compare their diagnoses of the sickly British economy, they
soon found themselves at loggerheads.

In theory the Keynes–Henderson axis should have been the pivot on
which everything turned; but, as Dalton noted, Henderson's 'positive side'
had wilted since his appointment as joint secretary to the Economic Advisory
Council. It was Henderson, not Keynes, who had become MacDonald's
favourite economist. MacDonald liked to needle Snowden by setting up
committees, but was happy to accept excuses for inaction delivered in a
Scottish accent. Henderson's reports to the EAC had been getting steadily
more gloomy and alarmist. He was increasingly worried about the effects
of a budget deficit on business confidence. In an article for the *Nation* of 2
November 1929, entitled 'The Limits of Insular Socialism', he had warned
that increased taxes to pay for social services would produce a capital flight
– at the very time Keynes, in his Ludwig Mond Lecture at Manchester,
was advocating just this to keep down wage pressure. Business fears, Henderson told MacDonald on 12 March 1930, were shrinking domestic investment at the very moment the slump was reducing exports. Henderson's
advice was not completely passive. He proposed an Industrial Reorganisation Fund based on a temporary 10 per cent import duty to support
rationalisation schemes and reduce the deficit on the unemployment
insurance fund by £10m. a year. This would promote industrial efficiency
while providing an assurance against increased taxation.[103] However, even
this timid idea – total expenditure was to be limited to £25m. p.a. for three
years – was 'very disturbing' to the Treasury.[104]

The change in Henderson's views was partly the result of a change in
position: Henderson was now inside the government machine, Keynes outside it. But Henderson also thought the slump had drastically curtailed the
field for national manoeuvre. Unorthodox experiments carried a higher
economic and political risk. Henderson's shift is symptomatic of a wider
movement of opinion. Historians have exaggerated the support which
existed for radical solutions to unemployment.[105] The fair-weather radicalism
of the 1920s, unbacked by intellectual conviction, was the first casualty of
the slump. Everywhere hard times were met by retrenchment.

Henderson's defection from the joint position of 'Can Lloyd George Do
It'? was signalled in a letter to Keynes of 30 May 1930. The gist of it was
that, with the slump gathering force, nothing should be advocated, or done,
which would lead businessmen to expect heavier taxation. Given the world
depression, the budgetary cost of public works schemes was bound to shoot
up, as the projects financed became progressively less remunerative ('parks
and playing grounds'). Business would expect higher taxes, and:

the alarm might quite easily serve to counteract fully the employment benefits of the programme, and you would then be in the vicious circle of requiring a still bigger programme, still more unremunerative in character, with an increasing hole in the Budget, and increasing apprehension, until you were faced with either abandoning the whole policy or facing a real panic – flight from the pound and all the rest.[106]

Economists will recognise the Ricardo equivalence theorem: deferred taxation is no different from current taxation in its effects on willingness to invest.

Keynes countered: 'As regards psychology, I maintain that if I am right that a large capital programme would increase the profits of businessmen, this would, after the first blush, have more effect on them than anything else. Moreover, if it is true that the capital programme would increase the wealth of the country, it follows that the dangers of insular socialism would be diminished rather than increased.'[107] He accused Henderson of 'lack of fundamental diagnosis in your present attitude. After all, the budgetary problem is largely a by-product of unemployment. To avoid an increase of taxation is not to remedy unemployment, whilst a decrease of taxation is scarcely to be hoped for. The main question is, therefore, to diagnose unemployment.' He admitted that 'psychological factors and high taxation' played a part in keeping home investment low. But more important was that interest rates were 50 per cent higher than before the war, despite the fact that we had more capital equipment per head. 'Therefore I twist and turn about trying to find some reasonable means of permitting investment of a fairly sensible kind to take place in spite of its not yielding the current market rate of interest. The necessity for this is increased, and not diminished, by any deterrent effect on private effort which may result from high levels of taxation and of wages which are beyond remedy.'[108] The argument soon became *ad hominem*. Henderson accused Keynes of being unable to accept a conservative conclusion as 'inconsistent with your self-respect'; Keynes wondered whether Henderson had become 'a Conservative under the influence of reading the Iron & Steel Committee Report' – one of the leftovers from the Committee of Civil Research, whose conclusion Keynes described as one of 'utter impotence'.

In his reply to Keynes's questionnaire of 11 September, Henderson stressed that, given the depth and severity of the depression, against the background of Britain's heavy burden of debt and taxation, it would be 'utterly wrong under present circumstances to embark on anything in the nature of a gamble . . . in view of the present state of business confidence, I am very doubtful whether anything which is clearly calculated to make things worse a little later on would yield any immediate advantages on balance'. He favoured tariffs for revenue, balance-of-payments and protective purposes, but they were no alternative to lower money wages, though they might make the reduction needed less. Unemployment benefit should be examined: it was an 'essentially new phenomenon', affecting both labour mobility and the budgetary balance, 'thus creating a new vicious circle in the history of the trade cycle'.[109]

At fifty-three, Arthur Pigou, Professor of Political Economy at Cambridge, was the senior economist on the Committee. His fellow member Lionel Robbins described him as a 'recluse', who 'hated oral discussion of technical subjects'.[110] Partly because of these habits, he was also by this time an isolated figure at Cambridge. Heart trouble in the late 1920s had given him a shambling, unkempt appearance. He wrote to Keynes in 1929, 'My heart is nearly as good as new; I plan to renovate my head next.' But both Keynes and Kahn feared the Prof. might have gone 'gaga'. Keynes was fond of Pigou, and they agreed about policy more often than not; it was to Pigou's way of doing economics that Keynes chiefly objected. 'My main hesitation', he wrote to him on 5 January 1930, '. . . arises out of a doubt as to whether the method of abstraction by which you first of all deal with the problems in terms of a barter economy, and then at a later stage bring in monetary considerations, is a legitimate means of approach in dealing with a short-period problem of this kind, the characteristics of which are, or may be, hopelessly entangled with features arising out of monetary factors.'[111] Inasmuch as the *General Theory* was a methodological revolution, it was chiefly directed against Pigou's method of economic analysis.

Before the Macmillan Committee, and also in reply to Keynes's questionnaire, Pigou had explained the unemployment problem in terms of shifts in demand unaccompanied by shifts in people, leaving real rewards to sections of labour wrongly distributed. In addition, the decline in prices following the return to gold, uncompensated by reductions in money wages, had left real wages ahead of the real aggregate demand for labour. Money-wage rigidity in face of shifts in demand and falling prices had been promoted by the dole. Pigou's analysis suggested that if money wages were completely flexible there would be no unemployment problem. Like Keynes, Pigou assumed that wages were fixed in the short run. Thus he had a letter in *The Times* of 6 June 1930 supporting Mosley's proposals for a big programme of public works. In favouring 'unsound devices' to increase employment, he told the Macmillan Committee, 'A man ordered to walk a tight-rope carrying a bag in one hand, would be better off if he were allowed to carry a second in his other hand, though, of course, if he started bagless, to add a bag would be to handicap him.'[112] Pigou laid chief stress on the short-term psychological effects of 'devices'. Thus public investment might increase employment if 'it bamboozles wage earners into not claiming money-wage increases equivalent to price increases'; a tariff would increase employment 'insofar as it removed errors of pessimism or created errors of optimism in businessmen's minds'. Keynes commented, 'Must they always be errors?' Monetary cures, Pigou implied, could affect real events only if workers and businessmen were subject to 'money illusion'. The debate on this question has gone on to this day.

Keynes's most intransigent opponent was the thirty-two-year-old Lionel Robbins, who had just been made Professor of Economics at the London School of Economics. He was jealous of Cambridge's prestige and was determined to build up the LSE as a rival centre of power and influence. A powerful and passionate man, anti-collectivist, pro-free trade, with a temper as quick as Keynes's, he alone had the intellectual conviction to resist Keynes's consensual embrace. Perhaps Keynes did not realise the strength of Robbins's *laissez-faire* convictions when he suggested him; or perhaps he simply overestimated his own powers of persuasion. Two years after his experience with Robbins on the Economists' Committee he refused to debate unemployment with him on the wireless: 'He is so difficult and queer! Also his reasons for differing are so eccentric and so totally different from the ordinary man's, that it may be difficult to bring out the real points which are perplexing the public.'[113]

What made their disagreements non-negotiable was that they had diametrically opposite *theories* of the causes of the slump. Robbins's derived from Austrian economics. For Robbins the slump was not the disease which needed cure: it *was* the cure for the previous disease of over-expansion of credit. The wasting away of the patient was simply the removal of layers of blubber caused by years of riotous living. If this might seem an odd way of describing Britain's experience in the 1920s, Robbins had an ingenious answer: Britain was suffering from the effects of having consumed its capital during the war without having adjusted its standard of living to its reduced circumstances. The cure would be rendered far less painful if wage flexibility were restored. Here Robbins agreed with Pigou. Unlike Pigou, though, Robbins was fundamentally opposed to Keynes's 'remedies', which, he thought, could only retard the healing forces of the slump. In the *General Theory*, Keynes would write ironically, 'It is the distinction of Prof. Robbins that he, almost alone, continues to maintain a consistent scheme of thought, his practical recommendations belonging to the same system as his theory.'[114] Robbins later regretted his quarrel with Keynes. He conceded that, whatever the validity of his explanation of the origins of the slump, in terms of overinvestment, its '*sequelae* . . . were completely swamped by vast deflationary forces'; his cure was 'as unsuitable as denying blankets and stimulants to a drunk who has fallen into an icy pond, on the ground that his original trouble was overheating.'[115]

Josiah Stamp, the most respected public servant of his day, was indifferent to theory, but most of his instincts were 'Keynesian'. Although a director of the Bank of England, he found Norman 'impulsive, rigid, and depressing.'[116] He testified to the Macmillan Committee that the return to gold had depressed British industry, and argued that deficit finance could lift the economy from a low- to high-employment equilibrium.[117] In a notably relaxed broadcast conversation with Keynes in February 1930 – 'he slightly towards the "right" and you slightly towards the "left" '[118] – and marked by friendly exchanges starting 'My dear Stamp', and 'Hush, Maynard', Stamp had worried that Keynes went too far in his attack on foreign lending, but conceded graciously, 'I never can answer you when you are theorising.' His role on the Committee was to keep the peace.

Keynes's answer to his own questionnaire, dated 21 September, was so congested, and the terms so complicated, that he had to plead for the charity of his fellow economists. Nevertheless his 'prolegomena', derived from the disequilibrium model of the *Treatise*, provided a framework for analysing the link between unemployment and the level of real wages which his foremost critic, Robbins, conceded to be of 'great aesthetic beauty'.

Real wages are in equilibrium, Keynes wrote, when full employment coexists with 'normal' profits. Disequilibrium real wages might arise either because of a change in labour productivity or because of a change in the terms of trade, since movements in either will affect the real value of output to firms. Keynes defined 'equilibrium terms of trade' as those which prevail when 'the level of money wages at home relatively to money wages abroad is such that the amount of the foreign balance (i.e. of foreign investment) *plus* the amount of home investment at the rate of interest set by world conditions (i.e. which just prevents gold movements) is . . . equal to the amount of home savings . . .'.[119]

Keynes denied that British real wages had been increasing ahead of British per-capita output.* Only one-ninth of 'abnormal' unemployment could be attributed to this cause. Most unemployment was due to the rise of sterling in 1924–5 having turned the terms of trade against Britain 'without this being compensated by a reduction of money wages to correspond to the new equilibrium terms of trade'.[120] Sterling's overvaluation thus narrowed the export surplus available for foreign investment while imposing a high bank rate which forced British savings abroad. As Keynes put it, 'the foreign balance is tending to decline at a time when foreign lending is

---

*This somewhat reversed the position he had taken up on the Macmillan Committee and in his Ludwig Mond Lecture, when he seemed to accept the view that British labour was claiming 'a larger share of the product of industry than formerly' and than abroad. (*CW*, xx, 7, 13, 147–8.) This was akin to the Marxist view that the real wage level, and hence the rate of profit in any country, is determined, in the long run, by the state of the class struggle. Recent research suggests that Keynes, in his 1930 paper, underestimated the extent of the divergence between real wages and productivity by ignoring the sharp fall in labour productivity (due to a reduction in hours worked), uncompensated by a decline in the real wage, which occurred in 1919–20. (S. Broadberry, *The British Economy between the Wars: A Macroeconomic Survey*, 86–91.) In fact, Keynes subsequently accepted Robbins's argument that 'in 1924 real wages had run 10 per cent ahead of productivity as compared with pre-War' and restricted his own conclusion to the period 1924–9. (Note, 25 September 1930, *CW*, xx, 406.) This implied, though, that more than one-ninth of 'abnormal' unemployment was due to 'real wages running ahead of productivity'.

trying to increase'.[121] Thus total investment was falling short of domestic savings – whence business losses and unemployment.

Beneath Keynes's technical drapery a fundamental question was being asked. How much could workers *do* about their unemployment? In the *General Theory* Keynes would distinguish between 'voluntary' and 'involuntary' unemployment, the former resulting from labour-market practices, the latter from demand 'shocks'. Pigou and Henderson, while recognising the importance of such shocks, emphasised the inflexible response of the industrial system to them as the *cause* of the higher unemployment which had prevailed since the war. The shocks would not have been nearly so disruptive if money wages had been flexible or, which partly came to the same thing, if the dole had not existed to increase the incentives to idleness. Keynes recognised that the industrial system was inflexible; to him this was a reason for switching economic analysis to the causes of shocks, and economic policy to methods of preventing them. As regards the situation in 1930, Keynes admitted that excessive real wages were correlated with unemployment, but he denied that the causation ran from wages to employment, as the analytical method of the other economists forced them to argue. It was not that excessive real wages caused 'abnormal' unemployment: rather, 'abnormal' unemployment and excessive real wages were joint effects of the fall in prices and loss of export markets due to sterling's overvaluation. It was the fall in output which caused the employed workers' share of output to rise, not workers' efforts to encroach on profits. Thus 'Real wages seem to me to come in as a by-product of the remedies which we adopt to restore equilibrium. They come in at the end of the argument rather than at the beginning'.[122] Keynes accused economists like Pigou of treating the wages question solely as 'part of the long-period theory of distribution' in a closed system, while keeping the 'short-period theory of money and international trade' in a separate compartment of their minds.[123]

The policy alternatives suggested by Keynes's analysis were to *meet* the worsened equilibrium terms of trade by cutting money wages or *improve* them by reducing the pressure to lend abroad or enlarging the foreign balance at the given terms of trade. Of the latter, the first pointed to the stimulation of home investment, the second to protection. All three remedies implied some fall in the 'real wage' – employed workers' standards of living – since they all involved a decline in money wages relatively to cost of living. But in the case of the second and third remedies the real wage reduction comes about as a 'by-product' of an exogenous stimulus to demand. It is not a requirement of increased employment, but an effect of it. Keynes rather muddied the waters, though, by treating the wage-cutting and output/price-raising strategies as equally valid policy alternatives, differentiated only by degree of difficulty and considerations of equity.

Thus he wrote, 'It is better, if possible, to raise prices than to reduce money wages', for three reasons: (1) 'Because there is less social resistance to keeping money wages unchanged when cost of living rises x per cent, than to reduce money wages x per cent with prices unchanged.' (2) 'Because, although a reduction of x per cent in money wages will mean a smaller reduction in real wages, this will not be believed.' (3) 'Because the method of raising prices throws the burden over a much wider area. In particular, it throws a due share on the *rentier* class and other recipients of fixed money incomes. Thus, from the point of view both of justice and of self-interest, the trade union leaders are right in preferring a rise of prices to a reduction of money wages as a means of restoring equilibrium.'[124] This is what Keynes had believed since 1922. Here for the first time he marshalled the arguments against a policy of wage-cutting. However, no new point of theory is involved. There was no hint of the argument he used in his cross-examination of Pigou on the Macmillan Committee,[125] later developed in the *General Theory*, that there might be no way that workers could get their real wages down by making revised money-wage bargains with employers, because prices might fall by an equal amount.

In developing his familiar case for increased home investment Keynes made use of a 'primitive draft' of the 'employment multiplier' worked out by Richard Kahn, joint secretary to the Committee, helped by Colin Clark. In his 1929 pamphlet with Hubert Henderson, 'Can Lloyd George Do It?', Keynes had suggested that an initial expenditure on public works sets up a 'cumulative effect' through an 'increase in effective purchasing power'. Kahn had worked out a formula for calculating the net addition to employment produced by the consumption of the newly employed. (For a fuller account of the multiplier theory, see pp. 449–52 below.) Following Kahn, Keynes assumed that 'a given amount of primary employment gives rise to an approximately equal amount of secondary employment'. He emphasised that 'the amount of secondary employment . . . does not depend on how the primary employment has been brought about' – thus brushing aside the Treasury's warning about possible repercussions of the initial expenditure on the state of business confidence. He reckoned that £150m. of extra investment (enough to employ 750,000 for a year) would 'substantially' cure the unemployment problem through its repercussions on consumer spending. Keynes denied that the additional spending would be inflationary; but he failed to grasp the real significance of Kahn's work, which was that the investment programme would create the saving required to finance it.[126]

The most contentious feature of Keynes's paper was his espousal of protection. Tariff protection was put forward as a way of increasing the foreign balance, thus satisfying 'the pressure to lend abroad at existing relative rates of interest'.[127] Beyond this Keynes stressed its effects on increasing capital wealth, business confidence and home investment, and enabling real wages to be reduced by raising prices rather than cutting money wages. A more fundamental attack on the free-trade case comes with the argument that 'any manufacturing country is probably just about as well fitted as any other to manufacture the great majority of articles'. Further, he would preserve 'essential industries' like British agriculture, even at the expense of some inefficiency, rather than have the rural population 'driven to live in Birmingham making screws'. This marshalling of the arguments for a tariff shows that Keynes had come to regard it as the only policy option, short of the unthinkable devaluation, left open to a British government, to protect the people from the full severity of the slump. This was a correct political judgement, but one that stuck in Robbins's gullet.

What would happen if the slump were allowed to run its course? Keynes admitted that 'certain mitigations' might come to the rescue:

> The gradually increasing impoverishment of the country will diminish saving, and the lower money wages will make us steadily more independent of imports; – a point may come, for example, if we stick to *laissez-faire* long enough, when we shall grow our own vines. Provided there is a residue of British exports (e.g., peers and old masters) which America is glad to have, and we can reduce our necessary imports *plus* our surplus savings to equality with this residue, equilibrium will be restored.[128]

Keynes concluded:

> I suspect, therefore, that the correct answer along austere lines is as follows: A reduction of money wages by 10 per cent will ease unemployment in five years' time. In the meanwhile you must grin and bear it.*
>
> But if you can't grin and bear it, and are prepared to have some abandonment of *laissez-faire* by tariffs, import prohibitions, subsidies, government investment and deterrents to foreign lending, then you can hope to get straight sooner. You will also be richer in the sense of owning more capital goods and foreign investments five years hence. You may, moreover, have avoided a social catastrophe. But you may also have got into bad habits and ten years hence you may be a trifle worse off than if you had been able to grin and bear it.
>
> The worst of all, however, will be an attempt to grin and bear it which fails to last through. The risk of this is perhaps the biggest argument against the 'grin and bear it' policy.[129]

High thinking at Shortlands left little time for relaxation. Keynes did not even have time to scribble a note to Lydia. But he did manage a joke. 'Here comes a man who has ruined his health with manly exertion,' he remarked to Robbins, as they sat in the garden watching Pigou return from his self-imposed duty walk. Over the weekend Keynes produced three papers of

*With this important qualification, that if the policy of reducing money wages 'helps to set [a] fashion, as it well might, world prices will never recover, and we shall be no further forward, but, on the contrary, faced with the prospect of having to repeat the process'. (*CW*, xiii, 199.)

comments on the other questionnaire replies, and also a suggestion for
'tariffs plus bounties' around which he hoped the economists could unite.
'My proposal is for a uniform tariff of, say, 10 per cent on all imports
whatever, including food, and a bounty of the same amount on all exports
whatsoever.' Imported raw materials would pay the tariff, but when they
were worked up into exports the money would come back to exporters to
correct the resulting rise in export prices.[130]

The economists dispersed on 28 September, to meet again in London on
7–8 October. For this meeting, Keynes circulated a draft report which is
perhaps the most balanced statement to come from his pen of what a
Keynesian unemployment policy at the time might have looked like, both
in terms of the modesty of what could be achieved by demand expansion
and because of its attention to supply-side factors. It gives an excellent,
though incomplete, insight into the conditions of effectiveness of Keynesian
measures to reduce unemployment. The balance was forced on Keynes by
the need to accommodate the differing analyses of his fellow economists.
But this strengthened rather than weakened it, by forcing him to take into
account the psychological repercussions set up by government action.

He started by arranging in a coherent pattern the various causes which
the economists had adduced for the heavy post-war British unemployment.
Basically he combined the other economists' 'real' story of the early 1920s
with his own 'monetary' story of the later 1920s, on to both of which was
superimposed the collapse in world prices since 1929, which had left 'all
economic arrangements made in terms of gold standard money . . . seriously
and perhaps disastrously inappropriate. . . . Consequently producers lose
money; they are unable to maintain their former labour forces; and unemployment ensues on a colossal scale.'[131] Therefore 'nothing can be a remedy
or even a palliative for the evils set forth above which does not restore
business returns to a more normal level, increase the inducements to entrepreneurs to engage labour, and bring the value of what the employment of
additional workers can produce back to equality with the wages which they
expect to receive'.

He rejected a policy of cutting money wages on the grounds set forth in
his first paper. But to satisfy Henderson, Pigou and Robbins, he urged a
number of labour-market reforms including the reform of restrictive practices, removal of obstacles to labour mobility and a 'drastic amendment of
the conditions of eligibility of unemployment benefit' which 'immobilises'
labour in declining industries 'in a state of subsidised unemployment'.[132] He
also inserted a section on rationalisation. Of price-raising measures, those
were to be preferred which 'are likely to have a large effect on employment
and a relatively small effect on real wages'. He now made much more
effective use of Kahn's multiplier to define the conditions under which
additional 'primary' employment could give rise to 'secondary' employment,
and to distinguish the different sources which would be available to finance

the investment associated with both. In particular, Keynes used the *Treatise* model to distinguish between what he called 'anti-deflationary' and 'inflationary' amounts of investment: the first restoring business profits to 'normal', the second producing 'windfall' profits at the expense of wages and debts. How much inflation would be needed to restore full employment depended 'on the responsiveness of the volume of output to the stimulus of a small change in price', but he thought it a reasonable hope, 'having regard to the surplus capacity which now exists for the production of almost every class of goods – that a fairly large increase of output could be obtained to a fairly small improvement in prices'.[133]

Throughout this discussion Keynes assumes that economic groups have firm expectations of what is 'normal', which will govern their response to government policy. If they see expansionary measures as being directed to restoring 'normal' conditions ('normal' prices, profits, real wages, employment levels) they will not resist the modest redistribution of their real rewards which comes about as an effect of increased output and employment. Only if they believe that expansionary measures will result in 'abnormal' conditions (for example, continuing inflation) will workers demand compensating wage increases, or will businessmen believe the policy to be unsound. This was Keynes's attempt to answer the revised Treasury view. But it did imply that Keynesian policy will only work up to the limit of workers' willingness to accept a lower real reward for effort. This limits its efficacy to the reversal of cyclical downturns or deflationary shocks – something which post-war Keynesian managers often ignored, and which Keynes's *General Theory* did not explicate nearly as clearly as the disequilibrium analysis of the *Treatise*. The tragedy of post-war Keynesian demand-management was that, by relying increasingly on inflation to boost employment, it obliterated the distinction between 'normal' and 'abnormal' conditions on which Keynes's own machinery of action depended.

The next matter to consider was 'how, in practice, increased investment can be brought about'. The task was to restore business confidence. Keynes took on board Hubert Henderson's suggestions for confidence-raising measures like balancing the budget and drastic reform of the dole – which as it operated might be seen as 'symptomatic of a general unwholesomeness in the body politic'; but 'in the long run we do not see how business confidence is likely to be maintained otherwise than by an actual recovery of business profits'. Emergency measures of a temporary character to restore business profits would improve business confidence, after which business confidence might take the place of the emergency measures as providing the necessary stimulus. A tariff on manufactured imports emerges as the residual 'emergency' solution: the only measure which could raise output, employment and profits, without damaging business confidence, thus bypassing the Treasury objection to public works.[134]

Discussions of Keynes's draft occupied the meetings of 7–8 and 15–16

October, both in London. On 7 October Henderson produced a note rejecting Kahn's multiplier argument on the ground that it ignored the 'essential
tendency for new demands for capital to raise the rate of interest'. It was
agreed on 8 October that Henderson should rewrite the section on rationalisation and Pigou should redraft the sections on investment. Keynes had two
meetings with him in Pigou's new rooms at King's – 'all done in pale blue
and white in the modern style with Heal-like curtains and no superfluous
objects' – following which 'I am making a try to draft the Economists'
Memorandum all over again on different lines. Your very weak lamb.'[135]
Discussion in London on 15 October continued on the basis of Keynes's
revised draft. By this time, Henderson and Robbins were in open revolt.

Henderson felt verbal amendments were not enough to bring out his
'serious disagreement' with the 'practical gist and tenor' of the draft report.
He accused Keynes in his draft of running away 'by complex sophistication'
from the 'plain moral of the situation, as plain as a pikestaff . . . [which is]
the disagreeable reactionary necessity of cutting costs (including wages) in
industry and cutting expenditure in public affairs'. Rejecting the even more
'disagreeable necessity' of agreeing with 'the ordinary, conservative unintel-
lectual businessman', Keynes had invited the Duke of Wellington's retort:
'All the clever fellows were on the one side, and the damned fools were on
the other; and, by God! all the damned fools were right.' Some of Keynes's
remedies were not remedies at all but 'aggravations of the fundamental
maladjustment which has got to be put right'. They rested unduly on the
hope that world conditions would improve. While some proposals might be
useful as palliatives they were not *alternatives* to reducing costs. He accused
his former mentor of not minding 'if there was a flight from the pound and
a real *dégringolade* of British currency and credit'. His policy was like advising
a man who is suffering from toothache not to go to the dentist but to take
some whisky instead. Henderson used the language of metaphor deliberately, 'because it seems to me that the really important issues which divide
the Committee are of a broad and almost temperamental nature and are
merely obscured by disputes about investment and secondary employment
or even about the increase in physical productivity since 1913'. Henderson
thought that devaluation might become inevitable but that 'the attempt to
reduce money costs must be made first'. However, he threw out a lifeline
to Keynes: 'I can see no adequate reason for depriving ourselves, at a very
critical time, of the great relief which a moderate general tariff would afford
in many ways – relief to the Budget position, relief to the exchange position,
some slight direct assistance to employment, and a much-needed stimulus
to business confidence.'[136]

Henderson's outburst coincided with Robbins's revolt. Robbins was
passionately opposed to any version of a tariff. It was incredible, he burst
out, that the finest minds in England were joining company with Beaverbrook and Rothermere in an 'Eldorado banal de tous les vieux garçons'. He

presented an alternative draft report, which he said he would issue on his own rather than accept Keynes's draft. Keynes announced on 16 October that he could insert much of Robbins's draft into his section of diagnosis, which kept Robbins on board, though not quiet or happy, through a further weekend meeting at Cambridge on 18–19 October.

By this time Keynes was 'so tired and in such a bad cycle that I hardly know what to do with myself'.[137] Strain from overwork no doubt partly explains what Robbins called his 'ungovernable rage' at the weekend meeting in Cambridge when Robbins demanded the right to a separate report. 'He denounced me before the others and laid it down that, as a minority of one, I was not entitled to a separate report.'[138] Henderson would not, of course, support Robbins on free trade. Pigou and Stamp wanted a consensual report. Pigou, representing the Cambridge establishment, told the young LSE upstart, 'One never does that . . . one tries to reach the greatest possible measure of agreement and then, if necessary, adds a minute of dissent on particular points.'[139] Precedents were hunted up to show that what Robbins proposed was inadmissible. Keynes read out a letter from Hemming, the Committee's joint secretary, commenting 'very adversely' on Robbins's emotional condition. The row continued at a further final meeting in London on 22–23 October. Eventually, on Hemming's advice, Keynes allowed Robbins a separate report, at the end of the main report, but before the statistical appendices.[140] Dalton, who had had a blow-by-blow account from Robbins, a former student, noted in his diary, 'The tariff stuff is pitiable. I was taught to despise Protectionists at Cambridge. I do still.' He added, 'Lord Oswald [Sir Oswald Mosley] is much with Keynes at present. But, of course, he can only take in the cruder arguments [for protection].'[141] The economists' report was initialled on 24 October.

Redrafted and reshaped within Keynes's original framework by Pigou, Henderson and Robbins, it was 'a surprisingly coherent document'.[142] Keynes conceded on diagnosis to maximise support for protection. The diagnostic section follows the Pigou–Henderson–Robbins line on the genesis of British unemployment: adjustment to war and post-war shocks had been impeded by labour-market rigidities. Pigou's drafting can be seen in the phrase 'Since the War, a series of policies has been fashionable, each capable of ingenious defence in itself, but the whole tending cumulatively to industrial ossification and the diminution of the National Dividend.' There was no mention of Keynes's saving–investment analysis, and the return to the gold standard was given a subsidiary role. The remedial sections were headed by discussions on trade union restrictive practices, steps which could be taken to improve industrial efficiency and the possibility of money-wage reductions. The economists recommended 'a systematic reform of the whole system of unemployment insurance', but the main emphasis was on the difficulties of doing anything in these areas. In the section on business confidence, Henderson's embargo on any increase in direct taxation was accepted. His objections also helped mute any advocacy of public works, which could be justified only 'if they are of a useful and productive character' (the revised Treasury view). Kahn's multiplier argument for public works did not survive. Keynes thus secured majority support for protection, he, Henderson and Stamp advocating a temporary 10 per cent tariff on imports for revenue purposes, plus a protective tariff on iron and steel, on condition 'that the industry should rationalise itself in accordance with an approved plan'. Pigou admitted the theoretical case, but dissented from the actual proposals. He said that the rationalisation condition could not be enforced, and tariffs were never temporary. Keynes's proposal for an all-round tariff with bounty was supported by Stamp, but rejected by Henderson and Pigou, on the ground that bounties on exports would be countered by foreign countries under anti-dumping laws and 'would be generally regarded as a serious offence against international economic comity'.

These objections to protection were voiced much more strongly by Robbins and formed the core of his dissenting report. While he later saw his quarrel with Keynes on public spending as 'the greatest mistake of my professional life', he believed he was right on the tariff question. When he argued that it was easier to put on tariffs than get them removed, Keynes apparently replied, 'How can you say the public will show reluctance? I have not yet spoken on the problem.'[143]

The economists' report – and more so the discussion which preceded it – is important biographically and intellectually, but left no immediate mark on policy. After reading it, Snowden spoke 'with withering scorn of Keynes and Stamp'; he found Robbins's dissent 'a most trenchant reply', Robbins having meanwhile 'alerted Labour ministers to the intensity of expert opposition to Keynes'.[144] Mosley tried to rally the Labour Party behind a policy of protection and imperial 'insulation', but though this gained him the support of some young Tories (and encouraged him a little later to start the New Party) it got little response from the predominantly free-trade Labour Party. The report's five-month discussion by the Economic Advisory Council 'cannot be regarded as a success'.[145] The Cabinet Committee set up to consider it dismissed it as a 'disappointing document', lacking unanimity and too general to be of use.[146] With these words it was buried. But the political-economy case for protection was too compelling to disappear, though it needed a change of government for it to be accepted. In deciding to drop public works and go all out for a tariff Keynes once more showed his uncanny ability to anticipate what would soon be politically acceptable. His own public conversion to protection in March 1931 helped create the political climate for the Import Duties Act six months later.

While the politicians, businessmen, bankers and economists talked, the slump had been getting steadily worse. 'Stimulated by the sense of impoverishment resulting from Stock Exchange losses, the "vicious circle" of reactions which characterises the typical trade depression is now in full play. . . .

The fall in the prices of primary products during the last few months . . . is a movement of the first order of magnitude comparable with the fluctuations which have ushered in the most severe depressions in economic history.' This was how Henderson presented the gathering world depression to the Economic Advisory Council in May 1930. He was still hopeful that trade depression, 'though for some time cumulative in its operation, sets forces in motion which ultimately effect a cure; notably cheap money'.[147] However, the cumulative forces continued to gather strength. After noting the 'catastrophic fall' in prices since September 1929, the economists' report declared that 'there is no recorded case in recent economic history of so violent and rapid a collapse in the prices of staple commodities'.[148] After a temporary recovery, Wall Street broke again in May and again in October 1930. Keynes was still expecting a recovery of prices in September and advised John Ryan, secretary of the Lancashire Cotton Federation, to buy large supplies of Indian and American cotton as a speculation on a rise.[149] By 10 October he was writing to Lydia, 'Very bad smash on Wall Street, revolution in Brazil, coming collapse in Germany – means that nothing is safe.' Unemployment surged relentlessly ahead. 'The Great Depression', as Henderson presciently predicted it would be known to posterity, 'has engulfed almost every country, whether free trade or protectionist, agricultural or manufacturing, backward or forward. . . .'[150] It formed the crucial background to the generalisation of Keynes's theory from the 'open' to the 'closed' economy, as well as his radical re-evaluation of the prospects of unmanaged capitalism.

Throughout 1930 Keynes had expended a huge amount of energy to no avail. Under the impact of the depression, the government's hopeful inquiries were wound up. A decisive moment, as A. J. P. Taylor writes, was Labour's rejection of Mosley's New Deal in May 1930: 'the moment when the British people resolved unwittingly to stand on the ancient ways'.[151] At the Labour Party's Conference in October, MacDonald shuffled off responsibility for the slump on capitalism: 'So, my friends,' he cried in his melodious Scottish baritone, 'we are not on trial; it is the system under which we live. It has broken down, not only in this little island; it has broken down in Europe, in Asia, in America; it has broken down everywhere *as it was bound to break down* . . .' (italics added).[152] There was nothing more Keynes could do except urge on from the sidelines as the depression moved to its culmination.

IV

MAYNARD'S CHEERFULNESS

Keynes's analysis of the slump is remarkable for its buoyancy. He utterly rejected the idea of Lydia's 'Bolshie' friend Dmitri Mirsky that this was the final crisis of capitalism. But equally he rejected the orthodox view, with its powerful moral overtones, that the slump, being the cure for previous excess, had to be allowed to run its course. Partly this was a matter of natural optimism, partly it was the result of his conviction, rooted in analysis, that capitalism was not sick but unstable. Keynes's activism, which drew him so strongly to short-term problems, made him utterly opposed to the doctrine of nature's cure – whether it came from Marx or Hayek. That is why he was so resistant to structural analyses of the slump. For such analyses pointed to the need for vast, and possibly catastrophic, changes in the 'structure of production', whereas his own analysis suggested that the cure lay in a revival of cheerfulness or, as he was to call them, 'animal spirits'. To be sure, Keynes was not simply applying the doctrine of Coué to economics. Businessmen's sagging spirits would not revive spontaneously, though he did believe the slump would level out – 'the mere lapse of time tends to bring about some degree of recovery'.[153] Things had to happen which would cause businessmen to see the world in a more confident way. But, before the right things could be made to happen, the slump had to be seen as a man-made catastrophe, not as a visitation from God or nature. It had to be seen as *manageable*, robbed of its cosmic significance, presented in a frame that made technical solutions seem feasible. Keynes's paradox, which few could grasp and which many would find unacceptable today if expressed in ordinary language, is that horrendous events may have trivial causes, and trivial remedies. When our world collapses, we want to believe that something is greatly wrong; and we mistrust someone who says it was all the result of avoidable policy mistakes.

Keynes's cheerfulness comes out in his choice of 'Economic Possibilities for Our Grandchildren', which he had first given to the Winchester Essay Society in 1928, for a public lecture in Madrid on 9 June 1930. He had been invited over by the Anglo-Spanish Friendship Society. 'The prevailing world depression,' he declared,

> the enormous anomaly of unemployment in a world full of wants, the disastrous mistakes we have made, blind us to ... the true interpretation of the trend of things. For I predict that both of the two opposed errors of pessimism which now makes so much noise in the world will be proved wrong in our own time – the pessimism of the revolutionaries who think that things are so bad that nothing can save us but violent change, and the pessimism of the reactionaries who consider the bal-

ance of our economic and social life so precarious that we must risk no experiments.[154]

The ten days he and Lydia spent in Spain were a particularly welcome break for both of them. Maynard was exhausted by the Macmillan Committee hearings, the EAC and trying to finish his book. A shattering blow was the death, on 19 January, of Frank Ramsey, at Guy's Hospital, following an operation for jaundice. He was only twenty-six, 'in a way the greatest genius in College and such a dear creature besides', Maynard wrote to Lydia. 'Poor Lettice and the two babies.' Ramsey's death not only impoverished economics – to which he had started to make notable contributions – but broke up the powerful intellectual circle, formed when Sraffa and Wittgenstein arrived in Cambridge, which had rekindled Keynes's love of philosophy. Keynes had been left 'saddened and nervous' by the shooting of 'Sandy' Wollaston, the Tutor at King's College, by a disturbed student just before he left for Spain, as well as by a quarrel with Vanessa, Duncan and Roger Fry over the hanging of pictures at a forthcoming exhibition of the London Artists' Association. To cap it, Lydia had forgotten her lines in a play, *The Searcher*, in which she was appearing in London. Spain provided a rest and a tonic. Following numbing entertainments given by the British Ambassador and Spanish grandees in Madrid, the visitors slowly wended their way home through the Romanesque cities of Old Castile.

Maynard continued to buzz and fuzz while putting the finishing touches to his *Treatise* at Tilton that summer. He engaged in a long correspondence with H. B. Lees-Smith, the Postmaster-General, on the quality and range of telephone appliances supplied by the Post Office. The Liberal plans for reducing unemployment had included the modernisation of the telephone system, so Keynes was able to link up his own demand for brackets with an appeal to the public good. 'Obviously such a development as I have been suggesting', he wrote to Lees-Smith on 25 September, 'ought to be entered upon in a spirit of enterprise and cheerfulness, or not at all. The objections you mention to me are those which I should expect from people to whom innovation is distasteful and from whom cheerfulness would be absent.'[155]

Country life, Bloomsbury style, remained as inharmonious as ever:

Duncan [Clive Bell reported to Lytton Strachey on 6 September] seems to have been pressing on his affair with George Bergen, an Eastside Jew boy from New York . . . Vanessa is rather unhappy I'm afraid . . .

Also the Keyneses have fallen into the deepest disgrace . . . Virginia, suffering a good deal from the heat, having entertained Vita and her children to breakfast, & Ethel Smythe in the forenoon, received a visit from the Keyneses at tea-time; and showing them over the hot-house fell down in a swoon. The Woolves, either on principle or from economy, were without a servant, so Maynard and his chauffeur [Edgar Weller] helped to carry her into the house and lay her down on the floor. Whereupon the Keyneses and chauffeur made off. As Virginia had a second and worse attack a few minutes later this conduct was generally condemned, although Maynard says that he could tell by her colour that it was not a swoon but a touch of the sun. She is getting better but is not yet perfectly recovered.

Cheerfulness, or some would say foolhardiness, was very much to the fore in Keynes's enthusiastic backing of Lydia's plans for a new ballet venture. Lydia had started on her career as a straight actress at the ADC Theatre in Cambridge in November 1929.* But she eagerly seized the chance of a second ballet career offered by a scheme to produce ballets in London and provide work for ballet dancers and choreographers living there. In the autumn of 1929 she began taking lessons with Madame Zanfretta – 'good old Italian School, more strict than Checchetti' – and joined Arnold Haskell, Philip Richardson, Edwin Evans and Ninette de Valois in founding the Camargo Society at the end of 1929, named after the stage name of the eighteenth-century Belgian dancer Anne Cuppi. The idea was to put on original and classical ballets four times a year before subscription audiences in the West End, using the dancers of the Mercury Theatre Club and the Vic-Wells School. Lydia joined its Committee as 'choreographic adviser' and spoke at its luncheon launch at the Metropole Hotel on 16 February 1930. The luncheon was hosted by Adeline Genée, whose Swanilda had so entranced Maynard in 1906.

Ninette de Valois, Fred Ashton and Constant Lambert now became regular guests at Lydia's all-day Sunday lunches, discussing their projects with much consumption of Maynard's excellent claret. 'My Lankiest, it is extraordinary how much human beings talk,' Lydia told Maynard on 13 October 1929, after Ninette had stayed five hours. She had to tell Ashton, then a competent young dancer in Marie Rambert's Mercury Theatre Club, that his future lay in choreography, not dancing, and that he could not expect leading roles in Camargo's productions. 'So you see, it is all delicate, but we are facing frank grounds,' she explained to Maynard.[156] Ashton recalls that 'she could be extremely nice at first, but then extremely outspoken and frank'.[157] He remembers visiting Tilton with Lambert in the summer of 1930 to discuss the programme they were putting on at the Arts Theatre Club, London, in December.

We arrived on Friday, and Constant, who loved his drink, found nothing but water. Then Saturday came and Maynard arrived and with him was a full symphony of wonderful wines from Cambridge. He told us about the pedigree of each, and the ensuing evening was

*Appearing in *Life's a Dream* by the seventeenth-century Spanish dramatist Calderón, and in Joe Ackerley's *The Prisoners of War*. She also performed the Lady in *Comus* for the first time, and with great success, with Dadie Rylands in his rooms at King's on 7 December, repeating it at the Keyneses' Christmas party on 19 December.

one of great gaiety and laughter. On Sunday it was back to water, and Constant went off to the pub, which was a long way away, saying he must go for a walk.[158]

Karsavina, living in London, was also recruited to help the new venture. 'She would love to talk to you about home industries,' Lydia wrote to Maynard.

The Camargo Society was a new addition to Maynard's role as patron of the arts. He had backed the London Artists' Association out of friendship for Duncan and Vanessa; he backed Camargo, as he was later to build the Arts Theatre at Cambridge, to give his beloved Lydia an appropriate stage for her genius. 'Using my tongue more than my legs', Lydia appeared at the Arts Theatre Club from 10–16 December 1930 in a masque of poetry and music, *Beauty, Truth, and Rarity*, produced by Dadie Rylands, with a cast of Cambridge undergraduates. She repeated her 1928 performance as the Afflicted Fancy in *A Lover's Complaint*, acted the Lady in *Comus* for the first time in public, and danced a pavane by Dowland with Fred Ashton. She danced in Camargo Society productions of *Cephalus and Procris* in January 1931; Wiliam Walton's *Façade*, with Fred Ashton, in April; Constant Lambert's *Rio Grande* as the Queen of the Whores in November; *The Origin of Design* in 1932; and *Coppelia* in 1933. Arnold Haskell thought Lydia 'wonderful both in her acting and dancing' in the masque,[159] but in his more considered judgement her career in the English ballet – which ended in 1933 – fell short of her Diaghilev days 'for a very understandable reason: the choreography assigned to her was insufficient in complexity to extend a dancer of such wide experience. She forced her effect and earned applause through over-acting, where before she had been subtle and restrained. . . . This mixture of an old tradition with a new development can never succeed.'[160] Maynard's family connection with Camargo extended to Geoffrey Keynes, whose adaptation of William Blake's designs for his poem *Job*, set to music by Walton, choreographed by de Valois and with décor by his sister-in-law Gwen Raverat, became the Society's most important original work.

Patronage mingled in Maynard's mind with larger purposes. The attempt to start an English ballet company in the depth of a depression was a considerable act of faith, Maynard's support for it a conspicuous sign of the cheerfulness he failed to find in the Post Office. The depression was a time to be doing things, not closing them down. 'The patient does not need rest. He needs exercise,' he declared in a radio broadcast in January 1931. Of course, they soon ran out of money. Lydia appealed to Maynard for help on 29 January 1931: 'Oh Lank! Committee for ever, one could run "Camargo" without a committee, only with cash, instead we all meet, and we are all different like Liberals'. Maynard agreed to become Hon. Treasurer. Their attempts to raise money from the Courtaulds brought what Lydia called a 'frigidaire' in her relations with Sam, who had subscribed a mere £25 to the Society. Lydia was not the only one to come away empty-handed. Mosley had been to solicit funds for his New Party. Sam 'liked Mosley very much, he does not think him big enough to rule the country'.[161] To Lydia Sam wrote with dignity that 'we should be able to differ amicably on artistic matters'.[162] The Courtaulds' coolness towards the Camargo Society was not just artistic: Maynard noted in January 1931 that shares in Sam's company were worth £54m. less than they had been eighteen months before.[163] After a 'shocking' meeting with Lil and Sam in May, he seems to have got a promise of support.[164]

Maynard continued to press for action in his public pronouncements. On 13 December he was praising Oswald Mosley's Manifesto, signed by seventeen Labour MPs, for 'offering a starting point for thought and action'.[165] 'Is the [man in the street] now awakening from a pleasant dream to face the darkness of facts? Or dropping off into a nightmare that will pass away?' he asked in the Nation on 20 December 1930. In his reply, he directly challenged the pessimists. 'The other was *not* a dream. This *is* a nightmare. For the resources of nature and men's devices are just as fertile and productive as they ever were . . . We were not previously deceived.' The world was suffering 'magneto trouble'. He urged the three central banks of the United States, Britain and France to act together to restore confidence in the 'international long-term loan market'.[166]

In a radio broadcast on 15 January 1931 Keynes urged the British housewife to spend, not save. 'What is the use of cheapness when incomes are falling?' he asked. Private and public saving was the worst remedy for the slump. The object of saving was to release labour to produce capital goods. But, if there was already a large unemployed surplus, it simply added to unemployment. When a single man was thrown out of employment in this way, his diminished spending power caused further unemployment among those who would have produced what he could no longer afford to buy. The following passage shows Keynes at his populist best:

> The best guess I can make is that whenever you save five shillings, you put a man out of work for a day. . . . On the other hand, whenever you buy goods you increase employment – though they must be British, home-produced goods if you are to increase employment in this country. . . . Therefore, O patriotic housewives, sally out tomorrow early into the streets and go to the wonderful sales which are everywhere advertised. You will do yourselves good – for never were things so cheap, cheap beyond your dreams. Lay in a stock of household linen, of sheets and blankets to satisfy all your needs. And have the added joy that you are increasing employment, adding to the wealth of the country because you are setting on foot useful activities, bringing a chance and a hope to Lancashire, Yorkshire and Belfast . . . For

what we need now is not to button up our waistcoats tight, but to be
in a mood of expansion, of activity – to do things, to buy things, to
make things.

(Lydia took him at his word and went out to buy blankets in a big department store. The shop assistants, she said, 'want Conservatives back; with
such blankets Labour people never cover themselves, not even Mrs. Snowden, who is interested in Camargo by the by . . .'.)

He urged the same attitude on the local authorities:

I read a few days ago of a proposal to drive a great new road, a broad
boulevard, parallel to the Strand, on the south side of the Thames, as
a new thoroughfare joining Westminster to the City. That is the right
sort of notion. But I should like to see something bigger still. For
example, why not pull down the whole of South London from
Westminster to Greenwich, and make a good job of it – housing on
that convenient area near to their work a much greater population
than at present, in far better buildings with all the conveniences of
modern life, yet at the same time providing hundreds of acres of
squares and avenues, parks and public spaces, having, when it was
finished, something magnificent to the eye, yet useful and convenient
to human life as a monument to our age. Would that employ men?
Why, of course it would! Is it better that the men should stand idle
and miserable, drawing the dole? Of course it is not.[167]

The forty leading articles, the cartoons and the sheaves of letters which
followed this broadcast made Keynes feel very 'prima donnish'. 'Never such
publicity in my life,' he told Lydia. Yet in fact he had never been so isolated.
The clamour for retrenchment, particularly on the dole, was reaching a
crescendo. Henry Clay records that the first reports to reach the Bank of
England 'of distrust of sterling' started coming in after the middle of October
1930, following a widely publicised speech at the Guildhall by Snowden in
which he had said that 'there is one item of national expenditure which is
distressing me almost beyond measure, and that is the cost of unemployment'. On 29 January 1931, the Treasury memorandum to the Royal Commission on Unemployment Insurance – prepared by Hopkins – had declared
that 'continued state borrowing on the present scale without adequate provision for repayment . . . would quickly call in question the stability of the
British financial system'. On 11 February, Snowden agreed to set up an
Economy Committee (headed by an actuary, Sir George May), remarking
in the House of Commons that expenditure which may be 'easy and tolerable' in good times, 'becomes intolerable in a time of grave industrial
depression'. The only resistance in the debate came from Mosley, who
argued that the government's plans of putting 'the nation in bed on a
starvation diet are the suggestions of an old woman in a fright', and from

Lloyd George, who, recalling the opposition of bankers to expenditure on munitions in the war, delivered a slashing attack on the City.[168] Lydia reported her charwoman, Mrs Turtle, firmly anti-Labour: 'would stop the dole of the young unmarried women at once'.[169]

> I have no doubt you read Hopkins' statement before the Dole Commission [Brand wrote to Keynes on 31 January]. . . . Our real strain is coming . . . in the Budget. . . . In fact I am beginning to regard the situation as a dangerous one . . . partly because a really serious budgetary position will frighten everybody with capital here, and partly because foreigners with capital here are already showing signs of nervousness. . . . This is the reason why I, personally, am all for economy – both in Municipal and Government affairs. The trouble is that democracies seem unable constitutionally to make budgets balance. It is impossible to get candidates for Parliament not to promise to spend money. In one country after another drastic economies can only be made by suspending the constitution, and I am not at all sure that our time isn't coming.[170]

Henderson thought Keynes had gone mad:

> My complaint against the tenor of all your public writings or utterances . . . [he wrote on 14 February] is that in not a single one of them has there been a trace of a suggestion that the Budget situation is one which is really very serious and must be treated seriously. On the contrary, over and over again you have implied that it doesn't matter a bit, that expenditure is a thing you want to press on with, whether by the Government or by anybody else, and that the question of whether it involves a Budget charge is a minor matter which is hardly worth considering. . . . The effect is to convey the impression to all people, however intelligent and open-minded, that you have gone completely crazy, and impairing all the influence you have with them, while pleasing and encouraging only those who say that you mustn't lay a finger on the dole.[171]

No reply by Keynes is recorded. But in a letter to the New York banker Walter Case, of Case Pomeroy Inc., Keynes refused to join the 'bears' on sterling. 'My own view,' he wrote on 21 February, 'is that all this pessimistic prognosis is complete moonshine. . . . The introduction of a tariff which is a resource for both the Budget and for general business confidence which we still have up our sleeves . . . may quite suddenly reverse sentiment when it will be discovered that the market is completely bare of stock. . . . I may perhaps add that it is not by any means off the map for the present Labour Government to have recourse to a revenue tariff.'[172]

Once more, Keynes seems to have been relying on his powers of persuasion. His public response to the looming financial crisis was given on

7 March, seven weeks before the budget, when his 'Proposals for a Revenue Tariff' were published in the newly merged *New Statesman and Nation* (see p. 388 below.) The argument is taken from his draft report for the Committee of Economists. Keynes conceded that an expansionist policy based on public works would frighten businessmen too much unless steps were taken to neutralise its effects on the trade balance, the budget and business confidence. The only instrument available was a revenue tariff. He proposed 'no discriminating or protective tariffs' but a couple of flat rates each applicable to wide categories of goods: £50m.-£75m. worth of revenue might be achieved by import duties of 15 per cent on manufactured and semi-manufactured goods and 5 per cent on foodstuffs. By substituting home production for foreign production they would add to employment. By relieving pressure on the balance of trade they would 'provide a much-needed margin to pay for the additional imports which a policy of expansion will require and to finance loans by London to necessitous debtor countries'. By relieving the strain on the budget they would restore business confidence. By restoring confidence in London they would enable Britain to resume 'the vacant financial leadership of the world'.

> Free traders may, consistently with their faith, regard a revenue tariff as our iron ration, which can be used once only in emergency. The emergency has arrived. Under cover of the breathing space and the margin of financial strength thus afforded us, we could frame a policy and a plan, both domestic and international, for marching to the assault against the spirit of contractionism and fear.
>
> If, on the other hand, free traders reject these counsels of expediency, the certain result will be to break the present government and to substitute for it, in the confusion of a crisis of confidence, a Cabinet pledged to a full protectionist programme. I am not unaccustomed to being in a minority. But on this occasion I believe that 90 per cent of my countrymen will agree with me.[173]

It was one of Keynes's most powerful pieces. 'As the recantation of an avowed free trader, it caused a sensation.'[174] At Lord Rothermere's request he provided a more popular version for the *Daily Mail*. 'What do you think? Is it loss of virtue – to write for Lord R. in exchange for 10 eiderdowns?'[175] (Keynes was paid £100, the equivalent of well over £2000 today.) In the columns of the *New Statesman*, free traders sprang to the defence of their cherished dogma. In a passionate and vituperative reply, Lionel Robbins said Keynes had overestimated the yield of his tariff by £20m. to £30m. There were 'half a dozen ways of meeting [the budget problem] each better both administratively and economically than this stale and dreary expedient of a tariff'. The only solution was to reduce costs; tariffs never came down, they simply grew.[176] Beveridge and E. D. Simon also weighed in on the free-trade side. Keynes replied realistically, 'Now free trade, combined with great mobility of wage-rates, is a tenable intellectual proposition. . . . The practical reason against it, which must suffice for the moment, whether we like it or not, is that it is *not* one of the alternatives between which we are in a position to choose. We are not offered it. It does not exist outside the field of pure hypothesis. The actual alternative is the policy of Negation.' He rejected the argument that tariffs were never removed. 'Joseph Chamberlain's campaign was engendered in the falling price level of the 'nineties and was entombed in the rising price level of the nineteen-hundreds. When prices are falling, we all welcome a measure which will hold some of them up; and when they are rising we all welcome what will cause a reduction.'[177]

The controversy raged for several weeks and was taken up by other journals. The *Economist* complained that a tariff would raise the working-class cost of living – 'crocodile tears', Keynes said, as its own policy was to reduce wages by 10 to 15 per cent.[178] Increasingly the discussion got bogged down in arguments about the yield of the proposed tariff, or its effect on Britain's exports. Keynes kept hard down on the main issue. 'For never before have we had to consider what it is best to do in face of an enduring and large-scale disequilibrium. We have been generally concerned, not with the problem of how to get out of a very tight place, but with what will be the best long run policy *assuming conditions of equilibrium.*' His critics, he wrote, had ignored the most important matter:

> the analysis of our present state, which occupied most of my original article and led up to the tariff proposal in the last paragraph. Is it the fault of the *odium theologicum* attaching to free trade? Is it that economics is a queer subject or in a queer state? Whatever may be the reason, the new paths of thought have no appeal to the fundamentalists of free trade. They have been forcing me to chew over again a lot of stale mutton, dragging me along a route I have known all about as long as I have known anything, which cannot, as I have discovered by many attempts, lead one to a solution of our present difficulties – a peregrination of the catacombs with a guttering candle.[179]

Politically, Keynes's new departure had little effect in the quarters where it mattered most. Conservatives welcomed his conversion and added his arguments, somewhat inconsistently, to their own proposals for protection. The Liberals regretted his new stand and recalled his brilliant articles in defence of free trade in 1923. Copies sent in advance to MacDonald, Snowden and Lloyd George produced no result. Mrs Snowden, replying on behalf of the Chancellor, who was ill, wrote, 'I dare say he will feel as sad as I do that you should think it necessary to take this line, for we are as strongly convinced that it is wrong (taking the long view) as you are that it is right.' Snowden's budget of 27 April had no revenue tariff: Keynes commented in the *Evening Standard*, 'The Budget That Wastes Time'. When he republished his *New Statesman* article in *Essays in Persuasion*, he wrote, 'Mr. Snowden, endowed with more than a normal share of blindness and obstinacy, opposed his negative to all the possible alternatives until at last natural forces took charge and put us out of our misery.'[180] Lydia was more direct. Having read a report of a speech by Ethel Snowden, she wrote to Maynard, 'She probably drinks, otherwise she couldn't speak such idiocies.'[181] Garvin of the *Observer* was more enthusiastic: 'If you could only make Ll.G. adopt it . . .'. But Lloyd George was tethered to his crumbling free-trade party.

Maynard was again working flat out in the winter of 1930 and spring of 1931, in mainly atrocious weather. To his writing, broadcasting, corresponding, teaching, bursarial work, committee work, City work, ballet work, drafting the Macmillan Report, 'arguing out the *Treatise*' with Hawtrey, Robertson, Kahn and the 'Circus' (see p. 446 below) was added the chore of winding up the *Nation* and transferring its titles to a new company, of which he remained chairman. The *Nation*'s death was not due to financial problems. Losses were reduced to £250 a year in the last three years of its life, following ruthless cost-cutting and a large increase in advertising revenue. What caused Keynes to call it a day was the departure of Hubert Henderson in 1930, the impending loss of Leonard Woolf and the failure of the Liberal Party to break through in the 1929 general election. The political balance of the left-centre had shifted decisively to the Labour Party. The *New Statesman* board, for its part, was determined to get rid of its long-standing editor Clifford Sharp, by now an alcoholic. Keynes had first proposed a merger in the summer of 1929, the two papers combining to form a 'Liberal' journal. This was turned down. In the autumn of 1930 he put together a new merger package. What decided him to try again was that he knew Kingsley Martin was available to take over the editorship of the *New Statesman*. Keynes had known Martin at Cambridge and, though he failed to get a fellowship at King's College, was so impressed by his thesis on Lord Palmerston that he got him a reviewing job in the *Nation*. When Martin, languishing at the *Manchester Guardian*, told Keynes that he was in the job market, Keynes suggested him to Arnold Bennett, chairman of the *New Statesman* board, as a possible editor of the magazine.

The push for the merger certainly came from the *Nation* side. Keynes looked for an amalgamation on equal terms, but was worsted in the negotiations by the *New Statesman*'s acute business manager, John Roberts. Roberts was clear that this was to be an acquisition, with the *New Statesman*'s staff running the new show. His financial position was stronger, and anyway Keynes was too busy to give the negotiations his full attention. Keynes explained to an anxious Lloyd George that 'it would be difficult or impossible to make a real success of both papers separately since we appeal to almost identical politics. But the combined paper should be capable of establishing itself securely and being an important organ of opinion.'[182]

The first issue of the *New Statesman and Nation* appeared on 28 February 1931. It styled itself as an independent organ of the left, without special affiliation to a political party. Many of the *Nation*'s contributors continued to write for it, including Keynes, who, as we have seen, produced one of his most notable articles for its second issue. Keynes continued to interfere in editorial policy, objecting particularly to the paper's growing sympathy for Soviet communism; but whereas the *Nation* bore the stamp of Keynes, the *New Statesman* was unmistakably Kingsley Martin's.

With hindsight one can see that from this period of intense strain date the first signs of the breakdown of Keynes's health. He complained of a bad toothache at the end of January, and spent over an hour with the dentist, who dragged out a tiny fragment of nerve. Lydia kissed his 'corrected teeth', but by the end of February he was ill with tonsillitis and influenza. After taking a week off (during which he presumably wrote his article on protection), he was back in time for a six-hour College Council on 7 March: 'like being with lunatics each of whom sees very small rats and mice running in every direction, but no two of them see the *same* rats and mice'. On top of this there were servant problems. In January, the Harlands suddenly left the Keyneses' service after ten years, Alice Brown replacing Mrs Harland as cook. Lydia acquired a maid, '14 years of age, small, one crossed eye, glasses, no man would snatch her, only disadvantage Roman Catholic', who had to be dismissed in May. She appealed to Maynard to write 'a little note to her Mama saying that she is a good girl, with the best will, but somehow results are bad, untidy, sloppy, and vacant in her mind, the last three adjectives should not be mentioned to her mother'. Macmillan Committee drafting took up an enormous amount of time, with twenty-three meetings recorded in Keynes's engagement book in April and May. Something of Maynard's lassitude emerges from his letter to Lydia of 4 May: 'Last night an evening squash at Dadie's, but such a party needs too much surface vitality. I was sleepy and inactive. Sat down next to Lettice [Ramsey] and could find nothing to say to her. Was introduced to a Siamese Prince, half Russian, and could find nothing to say to him. Found myself next to Michael Redgrave, and had nothing to say to him. So I must come back to my dearest Countess of Talkie.'

V

AMERICAN INTERLUDE

On 30 May, Maynard and his Countess embarked at Southampton for New York on the SS *Adriatic*, his first visit since 1917. He had been invited by Quincy Wright, an economist at Chicago University, to take part in a symposium on unemployment organised by the Harris Memorial Foundation. It was an opportunity to study American conditions first-hand. They travelled out in some style, with two bedrooms with 'real beds' in them, a bathroom and a sitting room. Each morning Maynard worked on his lectures; Lydia observed their fellow passengers: 'rich humbuggers, adventurers, music teachers from Arizona, fat ladies, thin ladies, and young girls'.

They spent two weeks in New York at the Ambassador's Hotel, Maynard seeing columnists, Federal Reserve Bank officials and other bankers, to whom he was introduced by Walter Case. Part of the first weekend was spent with Eugene Meyer, president of the Federal Reserve Board, at his country house in Long Island. Before Keynes left for the United States, the European financial crisis had started with the collapse of Vienna's Credit-Anstalt Bank on 11 May. This led to a drain of short-term funds from Germany. On 17 June, Keynes wrote to Hubert Henderson of his visit to Meyer:

> The German question was, of course, boiling, and he was constantly on the telephone with the President, Morgans, etc. I was alone with him and he talked to me with astonishing freedom . . . so much so, that I can't but think he wanted me to pass something on. He . . . was opposed to the Federal Reserve System having anything to do with any patching up scheme [for German and other debt] . . . his own policy if he could persuade the President [was] to cut down all War Debt payments by 50% for a period of five years, the benefit to be passed on to Germany. . . . The President . . . had discussed on his own initiative the question of a total remission (not suspension) for two years. . . . Will you hand on to the P.M. any part of the above which you think will interest him?[183]

Three days later, President Hoover announced his plan for a one-year moratorium (that is, suspension, not remission) of all inter-governmental payments, including reparations, arising from the war. For a week there was a boom on the Stock Exchange. It collapsed once it became clear that France was making difficulties. Keynes praised the Hoover initiative as 'a *first* step of the greatest practical value'. It was the effective end of the miserable reparations saga. But it came too late to save the world financial system. As for the American situation, Keynes reported to Falk that he had not realised how insolvent the banking system was: 'They have purchased great quantities of second-grade bonds which have depreciated in value and their advances to farmers and against real estate are inadequately secured.' So nervous were depositors that safe deposit boxes were no longer obtainable: there must have been $400m.–$500m. actually hoarded in boxes.[184] To Henderson he wrote; 'At any moment bank runs are liable to break out almost anywhere in the country. All this tends towards a mania for liquidity by anyone who can achieve it.' 'Barmy' opposition from some New York banks was inhibiting the Fed. from open-market operations to push up bond prices. 'They do not in the least question . . . that everything possible must be done to persuade the banks and public to exchange their enormous liquid funds for bonds.'[185] This shows how highly Keynes still rated the Fed. and the possibilities of monetary policy.

At the request of Alvin Johnson, he gave two lectures to the New York New School of Social Research: 'Do We Want Prices to Rise?' and 'What Can We Do to Make Prices Rise?' They were mainly an attack on Sprague's view – which Keynes later reported was shared by 'most of the so-called "economists" attached to the leading New York banks'[186] – that recovery depended on reducing manufacturing costs and prices to the collapsed level of agricultural prices. Not only would the whole financial structure be deranged by adopting Sprague's proposal, he said, but it completely ignored the need to 'cause business receipts to rise relatively to business costs. . . . If a reduction of business costs means cutting down business receipts by an equal amount, business will be no more profitable than before.' The depression must be fought by price-raising, not price-cutting. Prices could be raised only by increasing spending, preferably investment spending. If government spending was ruled out the banks must act 'to increase the quantity and reduce the cost of banking credit'.[187]

In Chicago, Keynes gave three lectures to the economists, on 22 and 26 June, and on 2 July, as well as a talk to the Chicago Council on Foreign Relations on the Hoover moratorium. The lectures are his most complete explanation on record of the causes of the great depression. They are also the last occasion when he deployed an unmodified *Treatise* model to explain what was going on.

The leading characteristic of the 1925–8 boom was an 'extraordinary willingness to borrow for purposes of new real investment at very high rates of interest'. The resulting prosperity, based on 'building, the electrification of the world, and the associated enterprises of roads and motor cars', spread from the United States to the rest of the world, except Britain. The part played by inflation was 'surprisingly small'. The slump which followed was due to 'extraordinary imbecility', not overinvestment producing an inevitable reaction. Business conditions required interest rates to fall; but instead the Federal Reserve System pushed up interest rates to check Wall Street. Very dear money in the United States had contractionary effects elsewhere. Also speculation was attracted to Wall Street away from foreign bonds. Once the decline started it gathered cumulative force. This was 'the whole of the explanation for the slump'.

His argument admittedly rested on the 'tacit assumption' that a 'fall in investment produces a fall in the level of profits'. Keynes used the *Treatise* model to show that the difference between the costs and receipts of entrepreneurs is equal to the difference between saving and investment. Thus 'the whole matter may be summed up by saying that a boom is generated when investment exceeds saving and a slump . . . when saving exceeds investment'. Keynes assumed that savings vary less than the amount of investment over the cycle, 'except . . . towards the end of a slump [when the country] is very impoverished indeed'.[188] 'Negative saving' by government on the dole eventually reduces the 'net volume of saving' to equality with reduced investment, thus allowing an 'equilibrium point of decline' to be reached. A little later Keynes described this automatic unbalancing of the budget in face of declining revenues as 'Nature's way' of halting the rundown of the economy. There can, however, be no permanent recovery till fixed investment has recovered to the level of full-employment savings.

There is a peculiarity in this analysis which escaped the Chicago economists. The full-employment condition in the *Treatise* is that saving equals investment. If saving and investment, therefore, are equalised by the 'impoverishment' of the community, the resulting situation is by definition one of full employment. Employment is only a proxy for income in the short run. In the long run, a low-income equilibrium need not mean an unemployment equilibrium. This distinction, which had already emerged in Keynes's evidence before the Macmillan Committee, disappeared from the *General Theory*, which was a short-period employment theory.

The decline in investment had not yet been fully compensated by 'diminished savings or by government deficits', so he foresaw 'dragging conditions of semi-slump' lasting a long time, unless the authorities acted to increase investment. Keynes went on to argue that cheap money had a big part to play in raising investment in housing, public utilities and transportation. 'Every fall in the rate of interest will bring a new range of projects within the practical sphere.' Keynes ended with hints of 'secular stagnation': as countries get richer they are likely to find it 'more and more difficult to find outlets for investment'.[189]

Keynes also took part in a number of round-table discussions with the economists to whom he had lectured. The main point of interest is that the Chicago economists were much keener than he was on public works as a remedy for American unemployment. Keynes remained true to his *Treatise* analysis that in a closed system (to which America approximated more than Britain) a reduction in the rate of interest would do the trick.[190] Although the Chicago economists seemed more Keynesian than Keynes on this point, the truth is that none of them had the confidence to carry out a theory-based policy of public works, because bits of the theory were missing. Specifically, the multiplier was unknown in Chicago.

The visitors spent their last weekend in the United States staying with the Walter Cases at Bald Peak Country Club in New Hampshire. Lydia reported it heaven after Chicago, 'where we were boiled in the day time and fried at night, when I walked like Eve without garments into the passages of the hotel to get the draft, and could have been arrested, [while] Maynard with better manners lied in bed and sweated quietly . . .'. In New Hampshire Maynard played golf in the day and bridge in the evenings, with equal lack of proficiency.

VI

DÉGRINGOLADE

They arrived back in Southampton on 18 July to the onset of the British financial crisis. While they were on the high seas, Montagu Norman received a cable from Harrison, governor of the Federal Reserve Bank of New York: 'We are concerned and surprised at the sudden drop in sterling exchange today. Can you throw any light on this?' Norman could throw no light. The Macmillan Report had been published on 13 July. Most of it was a sophisticated account of the technique of monetary control, with a long-term recommendation that monetary policy should be directed much more to the control of domestic prices than to the exchange rate. It marked belated acceptance of Keynes's position in the *Tract on Monetary Reform*. On the question of immediate remedies for the slump, the Committee predictably divided into warring groups. The largest group of those who published addenda attached themselves to Keynes's advocacy of capital development under cover of a tariff (Keynes, Thomas Allen, Ernest Bevin, McKenna, Frater Taylor, A. A. G. Tulloch). Bevin added a separate addendum advocating devaluation, which the Keynes group rejected 'in the special circumstances of Great Britain'. The report was generally regarded as a triumph for Keynes. However, this mattered less than a small section of figures showing that in March 1931 London owed £407m. and was owed £153m. of short money – a net short-term debtor position of £254m. Everyone knew that the City had been borrowing short and lending long. But with London's short-term assets being immobilised by foreign moratoria – Germany defaulted on 15 July – the question of the City's solvency was posed. This was shortly followed by doubts about the government's solvency. The May Report of 31 July forecast a budget deficit of £120m. and demanded economies of £97m., including a 20 per cent cut in the standard rate of unemployment benefit. (The projected deficit turned out to be £170m.) Thus the *dégringolade* which Henderson had long foreseen came to pass. Britain was seen by investors as an unsafe place in which to hold money. Within a month the Labour government had been swept away, to be followed shortly by the gold standard itself.

Unlike in the financial crisis of 1914, when he was summoned to London, Keynes passed the 1931 crisis fretting at Tilton. True enough, MacDonald wrote to him on 2 August from Lossiemouth asking for his reactions to the May Report. Keynes replied on the 5th that they were not fit to be published. But he strongly urged MacDonald not to attempt to carry out the report, for reasons he had long given but more especially because 'it is now clearly *certain* that we shall go off the existing parity at no distant date . . . when doubts, as to the prosperity of a currency, such as now exist about sterling, have come into existence, the game's up . . .'. As always, he was ready with a plan for converting disaster into success. 'I should seek forthwith to win the hegemony of a new Currency Union' embracing the empire, but including 'anyone who felt inclined to come in', and based on a gold currency, devalued by at least 25 per cent.[191] He soon changed his mind about making public his view on the May Report, writing in the *New Statesman* of its authors: 'I suppose that they are such very plain men that the advantages of not spending money seem obvious to them. They may even be so plain as to be unaware of the existence of the problem which I am now discussing.' The problem was that the reduction in purchasing power which would follow the recommended economies would add 250,000–400,000 to the unemployed and diminish tax receipts, thus reducing the budget 'saving' from £120m. to £50m. 'At the present time,' Keynes continued, 'all governments have large deficits. [They are] nature's remedy, so to speak, for preventing business losses from being . . . so great as to bring production altogether to a standstill.' His policy would be to 'suspend the Sinking Fund, to continue to borrow for the Unemployment Fund, and to impose a revenue tariff'. Nevertheless, the report was valuable because 'it invites us to decide whether it is our intention to make the deflation effective by transmitting the reduction of international prices to British salaries and wages'.[192]

There was no reference in his published article to the 'certainty' of devaluation. Indeed, in another letter to MacDonald, enclosing the proof of his article, he backtracked by saying that 'it probably still lies within our power' to keep on the gold standard, and that he personally 'would support for the time being whichever policy was made, provided the decision was accompanied by action sufficiently drastic to make it effective'. Keynes's hesitations were seen by MacDonald as reinforcing the Bank's advice to carry out the May Report's recommendations.[193] Perhaps Keynes was held back by an ingrained patriotism from actually urging, or even positively wanting, devaluation. When Falk suggested that the Independent Investment Trust, of which they were both directors, should exchange its dollar for sterling liabilities, he wrote back, 'What you suggest amounts in the present circumstances to a frank bear speculation against sterling. I admit that I am not clear that this would be against the national interest. . . . All the same I am clear that an institution has no business to do such a thing at the present time.'[194] As a result, the Trust lost £40,000 when sterling was devalued. But another attitude emerges which contradicts his general bias to moderation: his demand that whatever action is taken should be 'made effective'. He had had too much experience – going back to reparation – of decisions which wound, but do not heal. This reaction is understandable, but once more, at the critical moment, his counsel was clouded. This was a great pity. When the gold standard was abandoned a month later, one of the former Labour ministers, Thomas Johnston, said, 'No one ever told us we could do that.'

The Bank of England having obtained temporary credits from the Bank of France and the Federal Reserve Bank of New York, the Labour Cabinet tried to agree an economy package as a condition for a further loan to be arranged by its New York broker, J. P. Morgan. The New York requirement was a programme to balance the budget which would be supported by 'all three parties'. The Conservative and Liberal leaders (minus Lloyd George, recovering from a prostate operation) told MacDonald that they would support him only if he carried out the May Report. The political advantage of having 'unpalatable measures' implemented by the Labour government had not of course escaped them.[195] The Cabinet supported – by fifteen votes to five – Keynes's suggestion that a revenue tariff be used to help balance the budget. Had the government adopted this strategy, the Conservatives would have been hard-pressed to withhold their support. But Snowden's veto left the government with no counter-play. When MacDonald could not persuade a large minority of his Cabinet to go beyond £56m. of economies, with the balance met by taxation, and leaving the dole largely untouched, he went to Buckingham Palace, on 24 August, to resign, only to emerge as head of a 'national government' to 'defend the pound'. It contained three (later four) of his Labour colleagues, including Snowden, but, with the bulk of the Labour Party in opposition, it relied on Conservative and Liberal support in the House of Commons. Failing to saddle a Labour government with unpopular measures, the Opposition had achieved the next best thing – to detach MacDonald from the party he led. The new Cabinet agreed a programme of cuts on 27 August. Two days later it raised loans totalling £85m. in New York and Paris.

Keynes hated what was happening, but took comfort from the fact that at least the issue between deflation and reflation had finally been joined.[196] In the *Evening Standard* of 10 September, he continued to urge import controls, though he personally believed that devaluation was now desirable.[197] Two days later he was writing in the *New Statesman* that 'the "economy" policy can only delay, it cannot prevent, a recurrence of another crisis similar to that through which we have just passed'. If the new government was serious about preserving the gold-standard system it should immediately summon an international conference 'to reverse the whole trend of deflation'. Meanwhile, Britain should impose controls on the export of capital.[198] 'The budget and the Economy Bill [introduced on 8 and 10 September] are replete with folly and injustice,' he wrote in the *New Statesman*.[199] He explained to Walter Case on 14 September that 'every person in this country of super asinine propensities, everyone who hates social progress and loves deflation, feels that his hour has come and triumphantly announces how, by refraining from every form of economic activity, we can all become prosperous again'.[200] On 16 September, at the invitation of a small group of politicians including Mosley, he addressed a meeting of MPs in the House. His notes are remarkable for the passion which he generally expunged from his public utterances:

I should like to say a word first on social justice [of the budget]. Can scarcely trust myself to speak. The attacks on the schoolteachers seem to me to be a most foul iniquity.

. . .

As regards employment every single effect adverse. . . . In order to prove perfectly mad, increase of industrial contribution[s]. Stop housing, roads, telephone expansion – simply insane. Flagellate ourselves so that foreigners will say at any rate these Britons take their problems seriously – we might lend them some money.

. . .

I speak from a full heart. The course of policy pursued so far has reduced us to a point of humiliation one could not have conceived. During the last 12 years I have had very little influence, if any, on policy. But in the role of a Cassandra, I have had considerable success as a prophet. I declare to you, and I will stake on it any reputation I have, that we have been making in the last few weeks as dreadful errors of policy as deluded statesmen have ever been guilty of.[201]

The only person in the House of Commons who understood and supported Keynes was Oswald Mosley, soon to vanish into the political wilderness. In a powerful speech on the reassembly of Parliament on 8 September, he said:

Perhaps my views can be briefly summarised if I say that I believe it is vastly more important to deal, and deal quickly, with the industrial situation than it is to deal with the Budget. And for this reason: the continual decline and collapse of the industries of this country makes completely illusory any attempt to balance the Budget. You may balance the Budget on the present basis of revenue, but there is no one in the House who can say with any confidence that this basis of revenue will be long maintained. . . . Suppose that we adopted the view that it is far more important to have industrial recovery than to balance our Budget. . . . We should then adopt the method of balancing our Budget advocated by Mr. Keynes and other economists which is simply to continue to borrow – I know that it shocks hon. Members – to continue to borrow to provide for the Unemployment Insurance Fund, or I would prefer to say, borrow to provide constructive works to give employment in place of it, to suspend the Sinking Fund, and to raise the remainder by a revenue tariff or, as I should say, a protective tariff.[202]

The crisis Keynes had predicted came much sooner than he had foreseen. A mutiny of naval ratings at Invergordon on 16 September, suggesting that the empire itself was crumbling, led to another run on the pound. On 18 September, the Bank of England told the government it could not hold the exchange beyond the weekend. On Monday, 21 September, Philip Snowden reversed Winston Churchill's decision of six years before and suspended convertibility. The cross of gold had been lifted, this time for good. 'At one stroke, Britain had resumed the financial hegemony of the world,' Keynes announced. Graham Hutton remembered him 'chuckling like a boy who has just exploded a firework under someone he doesn't like'.[203]

The restored international gold standard had collapsed, never to be revived. Why had it failed the second time round? Keynes's views were given in an article he wrote in April 1932:

> By the return to the gold standard in 1925, at an unsuitable parity, the Bank had set itself a problem of adjustment so difficult as to have been well-nigh impossible. On the one hand, it was obviously impracticable to enforce by high Bank rate or by the contraction of credit a deflation sufficiently drastic to bring about a reduction in internal costs appropriate to the parity adopted. On the other hand, the maintenance of a low Bank rate, which would have rendered London unattractive to foreign short-term funds, would, in the actual circumstances of our trade balance and readiness to lend abroad, have led to a rapid loss of gold by the Bank and a much earlier collapse of the gold standard. . . . the policy actually adopted was to preserve a middle course – with money dear enough to make London an attractive centre for foreign short-term funds but not dear enough to force an adjustment of internal costs. In this way we tided over the immediate situation by exploiting London's immense reserves of credit and prestige. We were even able to continue lending abroad on a scale almost commensurate with our former strength, in spite of the increasingly adverse balance on account of current business. But the inevitable price of this temporary ease was the accumulation of a heavy burden of short-term liabilities. . . . Sooner or later, for good reasons or for bad, some loss of confidence might arise; and then . . . the insecure structure had to tumble.[204]

It is important at this point to present an opposite view of the collapse and Keynes's role in it, as seen by New York bankers of the old school, because the issues involved continue to divide people to this day, being much more to do with temperament and attitude to life than with economic theory in its narrow sense. On 29 August 1931 Russell Leffingwell wrote to Thomas Lamont:

> You will remember that when Monty [Norman] came over to discuss with us plans for the return to the gold standard, I asked him whether it was politically possible for the Bank of England to raise the bank rate from time to time to defend her gold and complete the operation. He assured me that it was. He was mistaken about this. The general

strike soon followed and instead of Monty's defending the gold standard and completing the deflation on classical lines by making money dearer in England, he called upon Ben [Strong] to defend it by making it cheaper in America. This Ben did for Monty consistently and persistently, and successfully until the return of France to the gold standard in 1927 and her adoption of a definite deflation policy. This seemed to make it necessary for Ben to adopt an active (instead of passive) inflation policy in the latter part of that year. Ben's long illness in 1928, and the stupidity and stubbornness of the Washington Federal Reserve Board in 1929, left the inflation policy uncorrected until it was too late to correct it without the disaster of . . . October 1929.

Thus it is an ironical fact that Ben and Monty, although they expressed themselves as bitterly opposed to Keynes's managed money inflation theories, did in fact themselves . . . pursue Keynes's policies, not quite wholeheartedly to be sure, but with sufficient vigor to create a first-rate disaster in this country. . . . I hold Ben and Monty and Keynes, a strange trio, responsible for the disaster. . . . Without the managed money inflation which Ben and Monty deliberately created from 1925 to 1929 in this country, in pursuance of Keynes's ideas, this country would not have had the great boom nor the great disaster.[205]

This view became the conventional wisdom in the New York banking community:

I do not think [Lamont wrote to Louis Wiley on 4 November 1931] England made a mistake in restoring the pound to its pre-war value in 1925. The mistake was in permitting the trade-unions, after the general strike, to impose a rigid wage scale on British industries and subsidising the resulting unemployment by the dole.[206]

Leffingwell wrote to Walter Lippmann on 30 December 1931:

The Macmillan Report demanded inflation. To men generally inflation meant the abandonment of the gold standard by England. Fear of the abandonment of the gold standard by England led to a flight from the pound, internal and external. The flight from the pound caused the abandonment of the gold standard. . . . Nothing has done so much as the abandonment of the gold standard by Great Britain to aggravate, intensify and prolong the crisis of confidence, to enhance the value of gold, to lead to the hoarding of gold, to aggravate the depression and the deflation. Thus the economic paradox is exemplified. Keynes and his school in the effort to get inflation . . . contributed more than the Credit Anstalt, more than war debts and reparations, more than Hitler, more than anything to aggravate the deflation which was in progress . . .

Now the lesson is that Keynes and all his school, which means all

the Treasury civil servants who to a greater or less extent follow him
and think with him, have not the judgment of practical men. They
are mathematical tripos men. They are civil servants. They are professors of political economy. They are not bankers and they are not
business men. The one thing that bankers and business men in England know is that confidence is based on keeping one's promises. That
is something that Keynes will never know.

There is another thing that Keynes and his school (all of them,
Strakosch, Blackett, Salter, Hawtrey, etc are to a greater or less extent
disciples of Keynes, although some of them would deny it) do not
seem to realize, and that is that the gold standard is not something
that economists, politicians and bankers have thought up and devised
as a convenient expedient for the welfare of mankind. The gold standard is something deeply rooted in the appetites of men. The love of
gold is instinctive in men like their love of land and women. The
harder you try to substitute price index money or paper money for
the gold they want, the worse they want the gold.[207]

VII

THE END TO CHAMPAGNE

The day the pound went off gold, Beatrice and Sidney Webb stayed the
night with Maynard and Lydia in what Beatrice called 'their ramshackle
old farmhouse under Firle Beacon'. 'What frightens me about the future',
Beatrice had written to Keynes on 3 September, 'is the emergence of class
war in its most insidious form; the sabotage of the standard of living . . . by
an organised Capitalist Party, and, on the other hand, unintended sabotage
of Capitalist enterprise by a Trade Union Labour Party. . . . But what
is the moral of the sorrowful tale . . . a Creed Dictatorship?'[208] Keynes,
accompanied by Walter Citrine, joined them before dinner 'in a great state
of inward satisfaction at the fulfilment of his policy of . . . inflation. . . . He
had lunched with Winston, who said he had never been in favour of the
return to the gold standard.' Lydia noticed that:

> Beatrice was very much alive with Royal Commissions and Labour
> party conversations, she drank wine, smoked cigarettes and altogether
> till 12 o'clock, kept the termometre of society going. The husband was
> nice too, but much older, rather sad to be out of office. . . . Then we
> had Mr. Citrine . . . flirting with Maynard. However all night long I
> heard the steps and the banging of the doors. Mr. Citrine was ill with
> indigestion and Beatrice as usual was making tea at 4 o'clock in the
> morning, dragging Sidney out of bed to provide the company. At 8

o'clock everyone was dressed, before the water was given, although I was careful not to encourage them about the bathroom, as our boiler refuses to boil this summer.

Beatrice had lunch next day with Beveridge, 'who heartily dislikes Keynes and regards him as a quack in economics'.[209] Keynes and Lydia returned to London on 27 September. There was 'too much going on now for me to stay away any longer'.

The gold standard, and therefore the occasion of the national government, having gone, the Conservatives were eager for a general election to give them a mandate for protection, which was now no longer necessary. Keynes did his best to stiffen MacDonald against the clamour, urging that the national government should stay in office for six months to deal with 'the currency question, the Indian Conference, and the Disarmament Conference' before leaving the parties to return to their normal alignments.[210] On 5 October he lunched with the Prime Minister at Chequers, before going on to Lloyd George, now recovered, at Churt. He told him of his hope that 'if this ridiculous Government does force things to an election . . . you will lead the Liberal party – or what is left of it – into the fight in an honourable alliance with Labour'. He continued:

> I do not think that those who are pressing for an election probably realise the extraordinary critical character at this moment of the international financial situation. Our own problems are more or less solved for the moment. The reports I hear about the stimulus to British exports and the buzz of business which is going on are quite extraordinary. But abroad things are still crashing to destruction. I doubt if there is now a solvent bank in the whole of the United States. Some considerable disasters cannot be far off. . . .[211]

Whatever Keynes said to MacDonald, the die was cast. On 6 October Parliament was dissolved. Laski predicted Labour would get 240 seats, the Liberals 50 and the Conservatives 320.[212] Cambridge is 'democratic more than fascist, but chiefly perplexed', Maynard wrote to Lydia on 11 October. 'Pigou will vote for Labour. Adcock and Clapham ("for the first and last times in their lives, of course") will vote for the National Govt. JTS[heppard]. speaks against the National Govt. We discuss whether we ought to give Feasts and if so should wine be consumed. The decision is to give Feasts but without ostentation substituting beer and cheaper claret for champagne! So you see that we too are patriots. . . .' Lydia told Sam and Lil that she would vote Labour. 'I have rolled my eyes on the manifestoes of Ramsay and Stanley, but they close instantaneously with dreariness.' On 27 October the national government, appealing for a 'doctor's mandate' and aided by a vitriolic broadcast from Snowden denouncing Labour's programme as 'Bolshevism run mad', swept to the greatest electoral victory in British history, winning 552 seats to Labour's 46.

APPENDIX

The shift in Keynes's attitude towards investment policy is signalled in a letter he wrote to Oswald Falk on 3 September 1931 discussing the future policy of the National Mutual.

I completely agree [Keynes wrote] that the prospect seems to be for still more deflationary pressure. Yet, all the same, I believe that a drastic clearance would be a mistake. My chief reasons are these:

1. The tendency of a deflation will be sooner or later towards very cheap money.
2. I am convinced that we shall have a tariff within 6 months and that will make a great difference to prices.
3. Many individual prices already much more than discount anything that has happened up to date. Markets are even worse for panic reasons bred out of uncertainty than they ought to be on reasoned grounds.
4. Many of the things one would pick out to sell are not saleable at all on any reasonable terms.
5. It is so difficult to predict what is ahead, though there *might* be a complete turn-about for reasons at present quite unforeseeable.
6. Some of the things which I vaguely apprehend are, like the end of the world, uninsurable risks and it is useless to worry about them.
7. If we get out, our mentality being what it is, we shall never get in again until much too late and will assuredly be left behind when the recovery does come. If the recovery never comes, nothing matters.
8. We must keep up our income yield. For we cannot afford to suffer heavy depreciation and a heavy drop of income.
9. From the point of view of our credit etc., a recovery which we failed to share would be the worst thing conceivable.
10. I hesitate before the consequences of the doctrine that institutions should aggravate the bear tendency by hurrying each to be in front of the other in clearing out, when a general clearing out is by the nature of things impossible. General action along these lines, which are dangerously near, would bring the whole system down. I believe that there are times when one has to remain in the procession and not try to cut in.[213]

PART THREE

THE ECONOMIST TO THE RESCUE

He had one foot on the threshold of a new heaven, but the other foot . . . in the Benthamite calculus. (J. M. Keynes on G. E. Moore)

You certainly have an amazing gift for making your discontent with the traditional ideas 'get you somewhere' instead of landing you in a maze of general carping and dissatisfaction. (H. O. Meredith to J. M. Keynes, 15 May 1936)

CHAPTER TWELVE

Portrait of
an Unusual Economist

I

Keynes was an applied economist who turned to inventing theory because the theory he had inherited could not properly explain what was happening. Like the other Cambridge economists of his day, he was drawn to economics chiefly by the prospect it held out of making the world better. They were interested in what Pigou called 'fruit', or results. The 'light', or illumination, which guided their steps, had been supplied by Marshall. Marshall, in their view, had left an *'organum* of thought', powerful, comprehensive and flexible enough to explain how modern economies behaved. They believed it to be much superior to that to be found anywhere else: a view partly based on ignorance, partly on the belief that Marshall had mined, sifted, restated and synthesised all that was valuable and true in economic thought up to his day. The Cambridge economists were improvers, not scholars. Their belief that the theory they needed for action was 'all in Marshall' survived into the 1920s. In 1922 Keynes wrote that 'important improvements' to the 'existing method of thinking' were becoming rare, and the main task of economists was to exercise 'skill in the application' of existing principles to the facts. By 1928 he acknowledged that 'controversy and doubt are increased', but thought that further research should clear it up. Most Cambridge economics in the 1920s is accurately described as 'glosses on Marshalliana'.[1]

From the start 'scientific' economics had been strongly normative. By increasing understanding of 'economic laws' it hoped to shift actual economic arrangements towards the competitive ideal which would maximise the creation of wealth; hence the strong association between nineteenth-century economics and the policy of *laissez-faire*. Adam Smith and his followers were chiefly preoccupied with the failures of government. Their idea was that government should keep law and order, and get out of economic life.

By the last quarter of the nineteenth century the mood had changed. The failures of *laissez-faire* were palpable; the competence and integrity of governments were much improved; the growth of democracy had increased pressure on the state to 'solve' or at least alleviate social problems. What Dicey called 'the age of collectivism' dawned. Feeding the growth of collectivism was the growth of the social sciences, and the parallel emergence of an activist intelligentsia, claiming a right of direction, vacated by the aristocracy and the clergy, by virtue of superior intellectual ability and expert knowledge of society. The central claim which emerged from the confluence of these two tendencies was that society was a machine whose working could be improved by deliberate action, with unintended side-effects being equally amenable to correction and control, much as a mechanic fine-tunes an engine.[2] It was the vision of a Corbusier, applied to society as a whole. Indeed, there are parallel movements in the arts and in politics. Noel Annan talks of modernism and collectivism as the two movements in whose shadow his generation grew up.[3] In their different spheres, usually in conflict with each other, they boldly proclaimed that we can make of our lives and the world what we wished. There were no supply constraints, only constraints of imagination and demand.

An inescapable conundrum of biography is to know what allowance to make for the *Zeitgeist* in directing one's subject's thought and life. People are children of their times, as well as of their parents; their works are both idiosyncratic and representative; they reflect their times and affect them. At all points the social invades the personal, helping to shape preferences, tastes, life-choices, ideals. But the implicit biographical assumption is that for most explanatory purposes the *Zeitgeist* can be held constant; that it changes more slowly than the individual life; and that, therefore, family, education and class are the main systemic external influences the biographer needs to consider. Roy Harrod's recourse to the 'presuppositions of no. 6 Harvey Road' to explain some of Keynes's characteristic attitudes – his sense of duty, for example – is a characteristic use of this familiar biographical technique. The assumption here is that biographical subjects are much more frequently products of their *backgrounds* than of their *times*. This method works perfectly well in many cases. It breaks down when the *times* become turbulent, when the mentality or sensibility of society – using those terms as approximations for more precise concepts – starts to shift. Lytton Strachey was recognisably the son of a Victorian general (though not to the porter of Trinity College, Cambridge) and a formidable, eccentric literary mother; growing up with so many sisters no doubt increased his own stock of eccentricities. But *Eminent Victorians* was the product of a new age. Something had to have changed in people's attitude to themselves and to the world for such a book to have been conceived and written. It is in periods of transition that generational history and group biography come into their own as mapping such changes. The 'children of the 1960s' carry with them to this day the stigmata of the decade in which they grew up; and so did the children of Edwardian England.

Keynes's relationship to the twin movements of modernism and collectivism is both extraordinarily important in understanding his work as a whole and extremely difficult to say anything sensible about. He was linked to modernism through his membership of Bloomsbury; and to collectivism through his philosophy and economics. Bloomsbury's aesthetic theory – insofar as it was expressed in the writings of Roger Fry and Clive Bell – located beauty not in the subject matter or 'narrative' of a work of art, but in its formal structure, intuitively apprehended; the shift from flow of narrative to flow of thought is the distinguishing mark of Virginia Woolf's novels. A parallel shift towards formalisation, or model-building, was taking place in economics. It is harder to relate this to a change in perception; nevertheless, the general effect of the move to abstraction in economics was to place the mind of the economist rather than the narrative of the market at the source of economic reasoning. Modernism in the arts and collectivism in politics and economics thus came together in the assertion that the interpretation of reality is a creative act. The claim to direction on behalf of those gifted with a special insight into the nature of reality becomes indistinguishable in practice from the claim that reality can and should be constructed by powerful minds.*

The normal impatience of the clever young with the bungling of their elders is not in itself a sign of a generational shift, and is generally replaced by growing tolerance as the young become in their turn middle-aged. In the 1930s, as we shall see, Keynes's attitudes and life-style became steadily more conservative, even as his economic theory became more radical. Other characteristic traits of impatience are more obviously attributable to temperament than anything else. Keynes always had supreme confidence in his own practical abilities. C. R. Fay recalls his remark as a freshman of King's: 'I've had a good look round the place and come to the conclusion that it's pretty inefficient.'[4] When he and Duncan Grant visited Versailles in 1907, he talked 'about nothing except the management of the water works . . .' and, no doubt, about how they might have been improved.[5]

Keynes's confidence was also cultural. His was the last generation which claimed to direct human affairs in the name of culture rather than expertise. He addressed the world as a priest, not as a technician. And though he rearranged its theology, economics spoke, through him, as a church, not as a branch of the differential calculus. After the First World War, culture, as the nineteenth century had known it, disintegrated. The disciplines turned

---

*Not epistemologically indistinguishable. As we have seen in chapter 3, Appendix 1, Moore, Russell and Keynes believed themselves to be attacking the Idealist doctrine that 'reality is mental' in the name of an intuitively known order of ethical, aesthetic and/or logical truths, akin to Platonic Ideas. However, since people's intuitions differ, this doctrine rapidly degenerates into the claim that some intuitions are privileged – that is, that the expert in intuitions should be on top. For a lively discussion of this point, see Alastair MacIntyre, *After Virtue*, esp. chs 2 and 3.

inwards; their practitioners talked to each other, not to the world. This had less to do with the explosion of knowledge than with the breakdown of the larger frameworks of thought which had proportioned knowledge to the purposes of human life. And, indeed, with the breakdown of – for want of a better word – religion, what obstacle was there to the cancerous growth of academic pedantry on the one side, and what Keynes called 'love of money' on the other?

The generational shift with which Keynes was associated is properly called avant-garde. His generation saw itself as the front line of the army of progress. It took the Victorian achievement for granted; its world-view contained no hint of dark forces lurking just below the surface. As Keynes put it in 1938: 'we repudiated all versions of the doctrine of original sin. . . . We were not aware that civilisation was a thin and precarious crust erected by the personality and will of a very few, and only maintained by rules and conventions skilfully put across and guilefully preserved. We had no respect for traditional wisdom or the restraints of custom. We lacked reverence. . . .' In place of reverence there was the revelation embodied in G. E. Moore's *Principia Ethica*, of which Keynes could say in 1938 that it 'is still my religion under the surface'. Moore substituted a religion of personal relations and aesthetic and intellectual enjoyments for the twin Victorian religions of Christianity and Humanity. It was a religion, as Keynes put it, of 'unsurpassed individualism', premissed on the notion of automatic progress, moral and material, 'by virtue of which the human race already consists of reliable, rational, decent people, influenced by truth and objective standards, who can be safely released from the outward restraints of convention and traditional standards and inflexible rules of conduct, and left, from now onwards, to their own sensible devices, pure motives and reliable intuitions of the good'. Political goals such as justice or equality did not feature in Moore's list of things 'good in themselves': they might or might not be good as means. For Keynes the generations were divided into Before and After Moore, in consciously blasphemous imitation of the Christian calendar. In 1906 he wrote to Lytton Strachey, 'It is impossible to exaggerate the *wonder* and *originality* of Moore; people are beginning to talk as if he were only a kind of logic chopping eclectic. Oh why can't they see. How amazing to think that only we know the rudiments of a true theory of ethic; for nothing can be more certain than that the broad outline is true.' And he wondered at 'this colossal superiority that we feel . . . most of the rest never see anything at all. . . .'[6]

In 'My Early Beliefs' Keynes said, 'We entirely repudiated a personal responsibility on us to obey general rules. . . . We repudiated entirely customary morals, conventions and traditional wisdom':[7] which ranks with 'in the long run we are all dead' as the most provocative of his many famous pronouncements. Yet one cannot agree with Norman Barry that this view of life led straight to the doctrine of the philosopher king, to the 'social philosophy of impatience'.[8] What Barry calls Keynes's 'personalised, anthropomorphic' view of life was formed against a backdrop of rules, conventions, institutions, wealth-creating mechanisms, political philosophies which were taken for granted. The partial transfer of such a view to the public realm required the pulverising effect on creeds and morals of the First World War. This produced a generational rupture much more profound than that between the Victorians and the Edwardians; because, as we have seen, it was the idea of progress itself, based on reasonableness, which the war shattered.

To this we must add that Keynes's doctrine of means was always far more cautious than his doctrine of ends. Ends were taken to be self-evidently good or bad. Judgement of means took place in the 'twilight of Probability'. Rational action was constrained by two further principles, the 'weight of argument' and the doctrine of 'least risk'. Here again Moore's influence was crucial, though Keynes found the same message in Burke.[9] Probability might be the 'guide of life'; but the guide had to make his way through the fog of uncertainty. Keynes's decision to connect 'ought' to 'probability' was a decisive event in his intellectual formation. It limited his respect for tradition and 'rules of thumb', while immunising him from the appeal of revolutionary socialism. It provided the philosophic basis of his politics of the Middle Way. A. F. W. Plumptre, one of his students in the 1920s, put the matter perfectly accurately. Keynes:

> saw clearly that in England and the United States in the nineteen-thirties, the road to serfdom lay, not down the path of too much government control, but down the path of too little, and too late. Continued unemployment meant socialism, complete government control, unlimited government intervention. He tried to devise the minimum government controls which would allow free enterprise to work. The end of *laissez-faire* was not necessarily the beginning of communism.[10]

Monetary theory provided an ideal vehicle for the kinds of limited, compact projects of amelioration and reform which appealed to Keynes's temperament and understanding. The theory of money, in the modern, 'Cambridge' form bequeathed by Marshall and developed by Pigou, might be applied to controlling price fluctuations which Keynes, together with Wicksell and Fisher, regarded as the chief cause of business fluctuations. Keynes used the theory of money before the war to suggest measures to stabilise the seasonal purchasing power of the rupee; after the First World War, he saw the management of money as the way to stabilise the British price level. For Keynes, the key breakthrough to a 'scientific' theory of money was the realisation that its quantity, in a credit-money economy, was controlled by the banking system, while the demand for it, in the short period, was unstable. Both of these propositions were stated in his *Tract on*

Monetary Reform. When we add the proposition that the volatility of the demand for money was largely caused by disturbances to the saving–investment relationship, and that the duty of the monetary authority was so to regulate the stock of money as to keep saving equal to investment, we have the *Treatise on Money*. In the interval between these two books Keynes came to the conclusion that there was nothing except banking policy itself to keep economies stable. We have moved, that is, from a world of regularities – like the tides of the sea – to a world of potential chaos, notably encapsulated in the banana parable, where the smallest shock is sufficient to set off vast cumulative reactions. Order has to be created; it is not natural. This was part of the modernist/collectivist mindset. However, Keynes did not deny that much of economic life was non-chaotic and self-regulating. State intervention was eventually – after a refinement of theory in the 1930s – limited to one point only: ensuring a level of investment consistent with full employment.

The charge, therefore, that Keynes substituted an economics of power and will for the self-regulatory mechanisms of civil society, including the market system, is vastly exaggerated. Uncertainty pervades both private and public calculations of means to achieve given ends. The uncertainty which imposed mediocre performance on unmanaged market economies applied equally to the effects of government policy. Keynes's disciples, the policymakers of the 1960s and 1970s, could not hold this balance in their minds. They actually did start to act as though they believed that the power of economists over economies was virtually unlimited. This is because they had inherited Keynes's machinery, but not the philosophy which sets limits to the scope and effectiveness of that machinery. Their hubris was inevitably succeeded by nemesis.

II

THE PERSONALITY OF AN ECONOMIST

Like many who aspire to it, Keynes thought a lot about greatness – how it came about, what it consisted of. As an admirer of Galton, he believed in the importance of hereditary connections; but he also understood how tradition shapes achievement, and discovered (or perhaps invented) a Cambridge tradition of economics, stretching back to Malthus, 'the first Cambridge economist'. Keynes used his biographical essays to ponder and delineate the character of economic and scientific genius. (He never felt confident enough to attempt a biographical sketch of an artist.) 'An easy subject, at which few excel!' he wrote of economics in his essay on Marshall. 'The paradox finds its explanation, perhaps, in that the master economist must possess a rare combination of gifts. . . . He must be mathematician, historian, statesman, philosopher – in some degree . . . as aloof and incorruptible as an artist, yet sometimes as near the earth as a politician.' In a striking phrase, he tells of Marshall's ambition to observe business life 'with the eyes of a highly intelligent angel'.[11] Keynes claimed for Malthus 'a profound economic intuition and an unusual combination of keeping an open mind to the shifting picture of experience and of constantly applying to its interpretation the principles of formal thought': an ideal combination, in his view, of the necessary intellectual qualities of a great economist.[12] What he picked out from Jevons was his 'unceasing fertility and originality of mind', his 'divine intuition', his 'inductive curiosity' and delight in statistics, closely linked to his antiquarianism, his electrifying style of exposition, his showmanship, his single-mindedness. He noted of Jevons what Schumpeter was to notice about him: that he left no perfect work, that he always attempted 'what he could not quite succeed in doing', that he was 'a man of parts – parts which he could not put together as a whole'.[13] And in Keynes's essay on Isaac Newton we have that extraordinary characterisation of the first modern scientist as 'the last of the magicians'. Keynes wrote of Newton, 'I fancy his pre-eminence is due to his muscles of intuition being the strongest and most enduring with which a man has ever been gifted,' and quoted de Morgan's verdict: 'so happy in his conjectures as to seem to know more than he could possibly have any means of proving'.[14]

The qualities which Keynes repeatedly singles out – 'divine intuition', 'unusual powers of continuous concentrated introspection', logical capacity, a feel for the salient facts, style, many-sidedness, theoretical and practical gifts in combination – are the qualities he most admired, aspired to and thought were required for great achievement in economics. All these qualities describe, to some extent, Keynes himself – as he certainly knew.

In 1912 Keynes first made a crucial distinction between Jevons and Marshall which was equally self-referring: 'Jevons, perceiving some one part of the theory with penetrating clearness and illuminating to the utmost possible extent; Marshall, exhaustively aware of the whole theory and its interconnections, but discarding, in his attempt to take in the whole stage at once, the limelight which, presenting some parts in a more brilliant aspect, must necessarily leave others in a greater obscurity.'[15] (The contrast was less kind to Marshall after Marshall's death: Jevons 'chisels in stone, where Marshall knits in wool'.) In this respect, Keynes was like Jevons. Jevons was in the tradition of the pamphleteer: he wanted to 'spill his ideas, to flick them at the world'; Keynes, too, urged his fellow economists to 'leave to Adam Smith alone the glory of the quarto . . . pluck the day, fling pamphlets into the wind, write always *sub specie temporis*, and achieve immortality by accident, if at all'; to this, Marshall had already replied that 'if the economist reasons rapidly and with a light heart' his economics is likely to suffer from 'bad connections'.[16]

Robertson's criticism of Keynes was precisely anticipated by Marshall's criticism of Jevons: 'His success was aided even by his faults . . . he led many to think he was correcting great errors; whereas he was really only adding important explanations.'[17] Keynes, however, went one better than Jevons: the pamphlets are the 'ghosts in the machine' of his treatises; and his distinctive ideas come out better in his shorter pieces written for a purpose. The battle between the splashers and the synthesisers continues unabated in economics, as it always has. In the next generation, Kaldor is the great example of the first, Hicks of the second. Both, one might say, are necessary to the organised development of the discipline. The first breaks new ground, the second consolidates the breakthrough into a more general statement, which includes the previous doctrine as a special or possible case, or as a partial statement. The splashers are more intuitive than logical; the synthesisers, more logical than intuitive; though elements of both must be present in any scientific achievement. In modern economics, scientific breakthroughs have been frequent, scientific revolutions almost non-existent. Keynes came closest to the latter; but even he was absorbed, as we shall see.

In another respect, Keynes was closer to Marshall, even more so to Foxwell, the two outstanding Cambridge economists of his youth. Comparing Marshall to Edgeworth, Keynes wrote, 'Edgeworth wished to establish *theorems* of intellectual and aesthetic interest, Marshall to establish *maxims* of practical and moral importance.' He perceptively noticed that Marshall was good at mathematics, but Edgeworth thought mathematically.[18] Like Marshall, Keynes believed that mathematics was useful as a check on one's thoughts; he did not think his thoughts mathematically. He allowed his mathematics to rust away because, unlike Edgeworth, he was not interested in 'mathematicising' the social sciences. He believed with Foxwell that 'economics . . . belongs to the art of managing public affairs by the application of sound reasoning to the whole *corpus* of experience', though he would never have claimed, as Foxwell did, that it was not a branch of logic.[19] Good economic performance, he thought, required an amalgam of intuition and logic applied to a wide range of facts, not to simplified and artificial hypotheses. But he was great and perceptive enough to appreciate types of mind utterly unlike his own, and he leaves Edgeworth seated, as a boy, aloft in a heron's nest reading Homer. 'So, as it were, he dwelt always, not too much concerned with the earth.'

Keynes's scepticism about the use of mathematics in economics grew rather than diminished with age, though it was present from the start. It has to do with his growing understanding of the complexity, and reflexive nature, of social life. A fundamental statement is in his essay on Edgeworth:

> Mathematical Psychics has not, as a science or study, fulfilled its early
> promise. In the 'seventies and 'eighties of the last century, it was

reasonable, I think, to suppose that it held great prospects. When the young Edgeworth chose it, he may have looked to find secrets as wonderful as those which the physicists have found since those days. But . . . this has not happened, but quite the opposite. The atomic hypothesis which has worked so splendidly in physics breaks down in psychics. We are faced at every turn with the problems of organic unity, of discreteness, of discontinuity – the whole is not equal to the sum of the parts, comparisons of quantity fail us, small changes produce large effects, the assumptions of a uniform and homogeneous continuum are not satisfied. . . . Edgeworth knew that he was skating on thin ice; and as life went on his love of skating and his distrust of the ice increased, by a malicious fate, *pari passu*.[20]

Keynes, however, did not retreat from the attempt to capture important elements of this complexity in models – the hallmark of economic procedure since Ricardo's time. On the contrary: the greater the complexity and uncertainty of human life, the more important it was to build lean, spare models suitable for the explanatory purpose in hand. In the deductive– inductive debate, he was on the side of the deductive school, unlike Beveridge, who believed that 'laws' could be discovered by accumulating facts. He criticised both Marshall and Malthus for trying, later in life, to make their theories more realistic by burdening them with historical detail. The approach to realism should be achieved by choosing a type of abstraction which can explain the salient characteristics of the epoch or problem to be investigated. Thus Keynes would criticise the classical economists of his day for using models which assumed full employment instead of constructing models which tried to explain why unemployment was endemic. The counterpart of this was Keynes's own willingness to change his model or – in popular perception – his mind, when the facts or problem changed. There is a paradox here, for he ended up constructing a theory 'general' enough to be applied 'in different circumstances according to the different sets of realistic assumptions . . . to flexible economies, inflexible economies, and intermediate conditions'.[21]

The fluctuating nature of the data requires that economists not only 'think in models' (which is fairly easy) but be imaginative and creative (which is very difficult). Progress in economics consists of theory invention. Good economists, Keynes told Roy Harrod in 1938, were scarce because 'the gift of using "vigilant observation" to choose good models . . . appears to be a very rare one'. Intuition thus controlled both the deductive and inductive sides of the economic enquiry. From the almost limitless data of experience, the economist had to discern those facts which constitute the important causes of the phenomenon he is trying to explain. The good economist's crucial gifts are the power of introspection and a 'sense of magnitudes'. Keynes consistently championed the cause of better economic statistics, but his purpose was to provide material not for the regression, or correlation coefficient, but for the intuition of the economist to play on. He told Austin Robinson that his best ideas came to him from 'messing about with figures and seeing what they must mean'. He was not the first of the modern statisticians, but the last of the magicians of number. For him numbers were akin to those mystic 'signs' or 'clues' by which the necromancers had tried to uncover the riddles of the universe. This is the aspect of Newton which most attracted him: 'He regarded the universe as a cryptogram set by the Almighty. By pure thought, by concentration of mind, the riddle, he believed, would be revealed to the initiate.'[22] Keynes would not have denied that the inductive testing of a hypothesis should be attempted; but he doubted the usefulness of the method, except under highly restricted conditions. For some purposes at least, Keynes thought that the distinctions between magic, science and art were less interesting than the similarities.

Keynes's insistence that successful economic reasoning is based on intuition and argument rather than on induction does not mean that he thought himself any less of a scientist. He believed that the scientist's intuitions deserved the same respect as the artist's. They were a privileged form of knowledge, reached by 'direct acquaintance' with reality. They must not be shrivelled prematurely by devastating criticisms on points of fact or logic, as academics are too wont to do. This attitude, when carried into practice, made Keynes a wonderful teacher: his habit of claiming the same latitude for himself as he accorded his students annoyed his critics. What he has to say about Freudian theory is extremely interesting in this context:

> Professor Freud seems to me to be endowed, to the degree of genius, with the scientific imagination which can body forth an abundance of innovating ideas, shattering possibilities, working hypotheses, which have sufficient foundation in intuition and common experience to deserve the most patient and unprejudiced examination. . . . But when it comes to the empirical or inductive proof of his theories, it is obvious that what we are offered in print is hopelessly inadequate to the case. . . . I venture to say that at the present stage the argument in favour of Freudian theories would be very little weakened if it were to be admitted that every case published hitherto had been wholly invented by Professor Freud in order to illustrate his ideas and to make them more vivid to the minds of his readers. That is to say, the case for considering them seriously mainly depends at present on the appeal which they make to our own intuitions as containing something new and true about the way in which human psychology works, and very little indeed upon the so-called inductive verifications. . . . [23]

Today we are much more reluctant to give intuitions such privileged epistemic status. The scientific furore which erupted when it was suggested that the educational psychologist Professor Cyril Burt had 'cooked' his data to fit his hypotheses is a good example, though much less transparent instances abound in all scientific enquiry. We are more likely to say that Keynes, like Freud, or any great thinker, was a master of persuasive utterance. His intuition persuades, not so much because it corresponds to our own intuition of reality, but because we are very susceptible to persuasive language. To the extent that we are persuaded, and modify our behaviour, there is a new reality. Great masters of thought and utterance, we are likely to say, do not discover reality, they create it. Keynes did not believe this to be so: but we do not quite believe Keynes's denial.

By now we will not be surprised to learn that Keynes attached high value to eccentricity and what he often called 'crankiness'. For example, he noted that Jevons's prediction, in his first book, *The Coal Question*, of the exhaustion of coal supplies was influenced 'by a psychological trait, unusually strong in him, which many people share, a certain hoarding instinct, a readiness to be alarmed and excited by the idea of the exhaustion of resources'. He tells the story of how Jevons, alarmed by the approaching scarcity of paper, laid in such vast stores of writing and packing paper that fifty years after his death it had still not been used up; though 'his purchases seem to have been more in the nature of a speculation than for his personal use, since his own notes were mostly written on the backs of old envelopes and odd scraps of paper, of which the proper place was the waste-paper basket'.[24] He detected a similar hoarding instinct in Foxwell's bibliomania, which he associated with his 'passion for orderliness and classification'. Keynes's own 'propensity to hoard' – a family trait, really, for which, as we have seen, he gave a Freudian explanation – alerted him both to its existence in others and to its neglected importance in explaining unemployment.*

By a crank Keynes meant someone whose curiosity, obsession, flair or intuition is, in varying degrees, stronger than his logic or intellect, or runs ahead of it. The founder of eugenics, Francis Galton, with his habit of counting the number of fidgets in his audience as he lectured, was clearly a borderline case. 'His original genius', Keynes wrote, 'was superior to his intellect, but his intellect was always just sufficient to keep him on the right side of eccentricity.'[25] As Keynes's respect for orthodox economics waned, his respect for 'economic heretics' increased. They appear in the *Treatise*; they stalk chapter 22 of the *General Theory*: 'the army of heretics and cranks, whose numbers and enthusiasm are extraordinary', with a 'fierce

---

*Keynes view of Jevons's hoarding of paper as a 'speculation' seems to be based on a false analogy with ordinary speculation in commodities, that is with the desire to make a profit on expected price fluctuations by buying now and selling later. The hoarding instinct is a psychological tendency which exists independently of the profit motive. The fact that Jevons wrote letters on old scraps of envelopes by no means confirms Keynes's hypothesis. In a similar way, Keynes's identification of the 'propensity to hoard' money with the 'speculative motive' in the *General Theory* seems to mix up two separate motives for economic action. Keynes might have been saying that Jevons's hoarding of paper would be rational only if *intended* as a speculation, but this is a different point.

discontent . . . far preferable to the complacency of the bankers'.[26] Although
Keynes tended to use the word 'crank' indiscriminately in conversation, he
distinguished between the 'great Trinity of crankdom', consisting of John
Taylor Peddie, A. W. Kitson and Major Douglas, for whom he had little
time (though he made amends to Douglas in the *General Theory*), and people
who got in touch with him like P. Larranaga, a Basque mining engineer,
who struck Keynes as a brilliant amateur, but not a crank, M. C. Rorty,
an American engineer with a plan to raise investment, A. G. MacGregor,
also an engineer, who wanted to raise wages in the slump and lower them
in the boom, and Ian Sutherland, an Australian, whose pamphlet, *The
Monetary Puzzle*, he thought had a 'touch of genius'.[27] Engineering to most
of these 'cranks' (Major Douglas was an engineer as well) was clearly more
than a metaphor. As Keynes himself got more heretical, he became more
interested in heretics of the past, as he tried to establish an anti-Ricardian
lineage for his own ideas. Reading a book by Werner Stark, a Czech refugee,
on *The Histories and Historians of Political Economy*, he wrote that '[Thomas]
Hodgskin is a lot more interesting than I had realised. Here again a man
who perceives ideas of the future very obscurely and imperfectly is much
more interesting to posterity than to his contemporaries. The former, in the
light of subsequent knowledge, can interpret the significance of his thought,
whilst to the latter it would be no more than a hopeless and boring muddle.'[28]

But Keynes's favourite economist of all was undoubtedly Thomas Malthus. In the final version of Keynes's essay on Malthus we are treated to
the two faces of Malthus – the Malthus of Population and the Malthus of
Effective Demand. These are astonishingly like the two faces of Keynes.
Keynes never wrote a treatise on population. Yet putting the economic
problem in a historical setting meant, for much of Keynes's life, putting it
in a Malthusian setting.

Keynes's fascination with Malthus goes back to an early age. His learned
biographical essay dates only from 1922 and was frequently read, revised
and added to, before its publication in *Essays in Biography* in 1933. But
Keynes included some biographical remarks on Malthus, based largely on
Bishop Otter's *Life*, in an unpublished lecture on population he gave at
Oxford in 1914. (See Appendix at the end of this chapter.) Apart from his
published essay, and variants on it, he directly addressed the personality
and thought of Malthus on many occasions, notably in a speech of 2 April
1924 to the Political Economy Club in London and, for the last time, in the
Cambridge Review of 8 March 1935, on the occasion of the centenary of
Malthus's death.

Malthus interested Keynes for a number of reasons. There is more than
a trace of ancestor worship in his frequent tributes to the 'first Cambridge
economist'. Malthus's father Daniel, a man of intellectual distinction and
notable friendships who nevertheless allowed 'diffidence to overcome
ambition', reminded Keynes of his own father; and his account of a delightful

father–son relationship mirrors his view of his own relationship with Neville Keynes. With part of his mind at least Keynes was attracted by what he saw as Malthus's peculiarly English combination of adventurous thinking and conventional living. As he told the Malthusian League in 1927: 'It is not necessary in England to lead a bold life in order to have bold ideas.' Keynes never sympathised much with the radical intelligentsia of the Continent whose intellectual iconoclasm had to express itself existentially. Though his own private life was far from conventional he kept up appearances and valued them. Of the first edition of Malthus's *Essay on the Principle of Population*, Keynes wrote, 'It is profoundly in the English tradition of human science . . . a tradition marked by love of truth and a most noble lucidity, by a prosaic sanity free from sentiment and metaphysic, and by an immense disinterestedness and public spirit.'[29] That this was a tradition Keynes admired is clear from this passage. But he only fitfully managed to attach himself to it. His temperament was only partially suited to it, and in any case the tradition itself had been fractured by the collapse of belief in a divine order.

Keynes increasingly saw Malthus as the founder of the 'true' tradition in British economics, derailed by the abstractions of Ricardo. In his 1935 tribute he praised Malthus's attempt to 'penetrate . . . events . . . by a mixture of intuitive selection and formal principle'. Keynes's own identification with Malthus is even clearer when he writes in the same essay:

> In the closing years of the eighteenth century the misery of the labouring class presented itself to Malthus as chiefly consisting in their low standard of life. In the years after Waterloo . . . it presented itself to him as chiefly a problem of unemployment. To these two problems his work as an economist was successively directed. As the solution of the first he had offered his principle of population. . . . In the second half of his life, he was pre-occupied with the post-war unemployment, and he found the explanation in what he called insufficiency of effective demand: – to cure which he called for a spirit of free expenditure, public works and a policy of expansionism.[30]

As Keynes's own interest shifted from the problem of insufficient resources to that of their under-use so the emphasis in his often reworked essay on Malthus shifted from the Malthus of Population to the Malthus of Effective Demand. As early as 1924 he was quoting Malthus's letter of 9 October 1814 to David Ricardo in which Malthus denied that 'consumption and accumulation equally promote demand'.[31] (Keynes quoted a longer extract from this letter on that occasion – his speech to the Political Economy Club mentioned above – than appears in his 1933 essay.) So there must at least be a possibility that Keynes was himself influenced by the Malthus of Effective Demand, rather than, as has hitherto been supposed, discovering him after he had developed the principle independently himself.

III

'IT'S ALL IN MARSHALL'

Keynes and his fellow Cambridge economists were men of a single book, Marshall's *Principles*, published in 1890, supplemented by a few other published fragments and 'oral tradition', mainly about his theory of money. When Keynes published his *General Theory* in 1936, the strongest reproaches of his fellow Cambridge economists, notably Pigou and Robertson, were directed against his alleged disloyalty to the 'Old Master'. The house that Marshall built, they implied, was sufficiently capacious to accommodate the extra furniture Keynes wanted to bring into it. This is partly true; it is also true that Keynes remained unmistakably a Marshallian. His greatest criticism of Marshall was that he fudged crucial analytical issues in his quest for peace, influence and accessibility. 'You can't find much truth in him, and yet you cannot convict him of error,' Keynes said to his students in a lecture in 1933.[32]

It is also true that Marshall left his house unbuilt. The analysis of money and business cycles was left out of the *Principles*. Marshall completed his trilogy with *Industry and Trade* in 1919, and *Money, Credit, and Commerce* in 1923. But the latter two were an old man's books, of little interest, by then, to the younger generation. They were not considered to have added anything to his 'system'. *Industry and Trade* was mainly historical and institutional; his theory of money was already part of oral tradition. There was a gap between his theory of value and his theory of money: all the interesting and urgent economic problems of the 1920s and later seemed to fall down that hole.

Nevertheless, Keynes was deeply influenced by Marshall. He wholly endorsed his view of economics as 'not a body of concrete truth, but an engine for the discovery of concrete truth', a view based on Marshall's perception that the 'habits and institutions of industry' do not stay constant.[33] The theory of money he taught at Cambridge till the early 1930s was Marshall's. He never abandoned it, but came to restrict its applicability to conditions of full employment. Moreover, he developed it creatively with Dennis Robertson. The great advantage, from Cambridge's point of view, of Marshall's quantity-theory equation over Fisher's, was that it concentrated attention on people's motives for holding money. As Kahn has put it, Fisher and his successors thought of money 'as a means of effecting transactions', Marshall and his successors as 'a form of holding wealth necessary for effecting the ordinary transactions of life without trouble'.[34] Marshall left tools, here, for integrating the theory of money with the theory of value, though he did not use them. Finally, Keynes was permanently influenced by Marshall's technique for dealing with time.

There is a famous Cambridge joke. In the 1960s a group of Cambridge economists were discussing Bergson's aphorism that time is a device to stop everything happening at once when one of them, Dharma Kumar, quipped, 'And I suppose space is a device to stop everything happening in Cambridge.'[35] The idea that things don't all happen simultaneously and that economic theorising has to take account of this is the hallmark of the Cambridge way of doing economics. In the preface to the first edition of his *Principles*, Marshall wrote that 'the element of Time . . . is at the centre of the chief difficulty of almost every economic problem'; on p. 30 of the eighth edition comes the sentence, 'the condition that time must be allowed for causes to produce their effects is a source of great difficulty in economics'. Marshall felt passionately that the major disagreements in economics arose from not specifying the time-period in which the causes in dispute were supposed to determine outcomes. He introduced the idea of time, therefore, as a way of making theorising more able to take account of complex and shifting reality. One of his favourite devices was to allot different theories to different time-periods. Thus he reconciled the Jevonian and Ricardian value theories by asserting that utility governed value in the short period, but cost of production determined it in the long period.[36] The chief debates about Keynes's theory of employment would revolve round the question: in what kind of period is it meant to be true?

As Keynes himself pointed out, the problem of time lay at the heart of the quarrel between Malthus and Ricardo. Ricardo wrote to his friend on 24 January 1817:

> It appears to me that one great cause of our difference in opinion on the subjects we have so often discussed [Ricardo was thinking especially of the possibility of the failure of 'effectual demand'] is that you have always in your mind the immediate and temporary effects of particular changes, whereas I put these immediate and temporary effects quite aside, and fix my whole attention on the permanent state of things which will result from them.

To this, Malthus replied 'with considerable effect' on 26 January:

> I certainly am disposed to refer frequently to things as they are, as the only way of making one's writing practically useful to society, and I think also the only way of being secure from falling into the errors of the taylors of Laputa, and by a slight mistake at the outset arrive at conclusions the most distant from the truth. Besides I really think that the progress of society consists of irregular movements, and that to omit the consideration of causes which for eight or ten years will give a great *stimulus* to production and population or a great *check* to them, is to omit the causes of the wealth and poverty of nations – the grand object of all enquiries in Political Economy.[37]

Keynes sided wholeheartedly with Malthus. He never admired Ricardo's cast of mind, and by 1933 could write that 'the obliteration of Malthus's line of approach and the complete domination of Ricardo's for a period of a hundred years has been a disaster to the progress of economics'.[38] Ricardian economics abstracted from time (as well as space) in a double sense: it dealt, as Ricardo implied, with the permanent, rather than temporary, effect of causes, leaving the intervening landscape flattened and devoid of incident; and, by assuming that man was the same everywhere and at all times, it claimed universal validity for its laws.*

Marshall, as usual, compromised. The *Principles* was a Ricardian construction. It investigates the causes of long-run 'normal' or 'natural' values: that is, of the prices which 'would ultimately be obtained, if the economic conditions under view had time to work out undisturbed their full effect', as distinct from the causes of market or 'actual' prices 'on which the accidents of the moment exert a preponderating influence'.[39†] 'Normal' prices in this sense are the prices which equilibrate the long period flows of supply and demand. They are associated with the notion of persistence. However, Marshall recognised that the forces affecting prices work at different speeds, and invented 'period' analysis to deal with the problem. Periods in Marshallian economics are not discrete slices of chronological time. They have reference to the time it takes for different forces affecting the price of a commodity to establish a dominance. They overlap, rather like the distances on a racetrack, with runners, starting at the same time, covering the different distances at different speeds.‡ In the period under consideration, the non-dominant (faster- or slower-moving) forces are segregated 'into a pound called *caeteris paribus*'. Their activity is not denied, Marshall says, 'but their disturbing effect is neglected for a time'. Marshall's time-period technique is an example of a more general approach known as comparative static, or partial equilibrium, analysis, the static method arising from the impossibility of discussing at once the effects of all the causes at work.

Marshallian period analysis is designed to exhibit the different stages of the adjustment of the supply price of a commodity to changes in the demand for it. In the 'market' day, the supply of the commodity is fixed; in the 'short period', supply is variable but the capital equipment for producing it is fixed; in the 'long period', the capital equipment can be expanded or contracted; in a shadowy 'secular' period, population and knowledge are variable. All these forces act on 'price' simultaneously; which one treats as

---

*One must not ignore the element of racial stereotyping in the Cambridge response to Ricardo. Marshall wrote, 'He is often spoken of as a representative Englishman: but this is just what he was not . . . his aversion to inductions and his delight in abstract reasonings are due . . . to his semitic origins.' (*Principles*, 8th edn, 629.) Keynes, too, preferred the 'aristocratic clergyman' to the 'Jewish stockbroker'. (*CW*, x, 95.)

†Marshall is characteristically evasive (on pp. 28–30 of the *Principles*, 8th edn) on whether 'normal' prices and the equilibrium resulting from them are in some sense 'optimal'.

‡The informal expressions 'short run' and 'long run' give a better idea of what Marshall meant by 'periods'. We can imagine the 'forces' as sprinters, middle-distance and long-distance runners.

fixed or variable depends on the period in view – that is, on whether one is trying to explain 'market', 'short period', 'long period', or 'secular' prices.[40] The crucial distinction is between the 'short period' when existing capital equipment is worked more or less intensively and the 'long period' when the capital stock has been fully adjusted to the changed conditions of demand.

No more than any other economist of his day did Marshall believe that demand could be deficient for *all* commodities. His time-period method was designed to explain the adjustment experience of a single industry. It was Keynes who first thought of applying it to the adjustment of a whole economy to a change in demand.

The time-period method sets Cambridge economics apart from the market-clearing simultaneity of the general equilibrium tradition. As John Vaizey put it, 'This idea of three sorts of period [he omitted Marshall's fourth period] is fundamental to Cambridge economics; no Cambridge economist can think in any other terms. . . .'[41] For Richard Kahn, who wrote his dissertation, under Keynes's direction, on the 'Economics of the Short Period', 'the whole usefulness of the device of the Short Period is based on the fact that the life of fixed capital is considerably greater than the period of production, greater that is to say than the life of working capital'.[42] However, Marshall's is a tricky instrument to use. Variables held constant for analytical purposes can easily be mistaken as constant (unchanging) in fact; and logical time-periods can be confused with chronological ones.

Keynes himself wrote in 1929:

> there has always seemed to me to be a confusion in the Marshallian distinction between long and short periods. Sometimes he means by a long period something where time is the essence of the matter, as for example the wearing out of a durable instrument or the length of period of production. In other cases he merely means by the long period what happens when everyone correctly foresees the situation, and by the short period what happens when mistakes of forecasting have been made.[43]

Keynes extended the Marshallian time-period method in two ways. First, he applied it to the analysis of the general price level, rather than to the prices of particular commodities. He was one of the first economists to state clearly that the quantity theory of money was a long-period theory, and that in the short period the 'demand for money' was the 'disturbing' influence on the price level. Secondly, in the 1930s, Keynes applied it to the analysis of output as a whole, rather than the output of a single industry. In chapter 18 of the *General Theory* he offered a short-period theory of output determination, showing how a fall in demand with a given capital stock can result in 'unemployment equilibrium'.

Economists of Marshallian persuasion accused Keynes of breaking off his analysis prematurely. His short-period method, they said, ignored forces tending to restore full employment. He was guilty of treating as inactive in fact influences on employment which he excluded on purely methodological grounds. The debate has gone on interminably ever since. Keynes could no doubt have invoked the principle of indifference which justifies the theorist in sterilising the influence of those things about which nothing certain can be said. The real issue is different. In this intellectual Olympiad economists could not agree on the speeds of the different 'runners'. This is what makes economics such a fascinating, and dangerous, game.

IV

THE MASTER-ECONOMIST?

How did Keynes measure up to his ideal of the 'master-economist'? He was not interested in being anything but a 'great' economist. Why should he be? He knew himself to be a member of the intellectual aristocracy. His own intellectual career had been an almost unbroken success story. He was one of Marshall's anointed successors. (Was there a feeling here that he had to make up for his father's failure to satisfy Marshall's hopes?) But he had also been a member of Pop at Eton, president of the Cambridge Union, a member of the Apostles. In four years he had risen to control of a key department of the Treasury, created, it almost seemed, for the exercise of his particular talents. His *Economic Consequences of the Peace* was a bestseller and the most influential book to come out of the war. Keynes's life as it unfolded was continuing confirmation to him of his supreme talent in a variety of fields. He had every reason to be colossally self-confident, and so he was. The only obvious areas of mistrust had to do with his physical appearance and his speaking voice. His eyes were riotous; his lips lascivious; his aspect somewhat irregular. He did his best to turn himself into a normal-looking member of the Establishment, with military moustache, and City suits which he wore even in the country. In the 1930s he enjoyed the role of squire of Tilton. About his voice he could do nothing. It was the voice of a scholar, a man of taste and erudition, slightly precious, without much resonance or range, deficient in rhetorical quality. He made music with his pen. But where an argument had to be put, he was a brilliant advocate, as his testimony to the Macmillan Committee shows.

Much in Keynes's life was coded, hidden from the prying outsider. His extreme reluctance to give interviews testifies to his self-protectiveness. He was not as he seemed, in appearance, habits or thought. In thought, the tension arises at precisely the points where heart and head failed to fuse. This poses a problem for the interpretation of both his philosophy and his economics. He left a huge corpus of guarded utterances, which includes three treatises. He chose to play the academic game, because he enjoyed it, and because he knew that his influence depended on his playing it. He accepted the conventions of economics, especially the convention of rationality. Yet scattered through his writings are clues to the fact that he regarded the intellectual technique he practised as a surface technique only, and public life as a world of appearance; that he realised that beneath the knowledge in which he publicly dealt there lay an esoteric knowledge open only to a few initiates, the pursuit of which fascinated him as it did Newton. His writings, like those of Ibsen, are full of 'overtones' which may be 'felt and heard by the sensitive', but 'which will be out of proportion and almost vulgar if . . . sufficiently emphasised to be obvious and inescapable'.[44] But he knew perfectly well what he was about, for the stability of the public sphere was necessary to protect the secret places where disguises are not needed, and things can be assessed at their true worth.

The thought that he was saying something new seems to have been with him from the start, coupled with the conviction that his elders were too stupid or conventional to understand it: for example, his comments on his examiners at Eton and later. Throughout his life, though decreasingly as he got older, he seemed to Hubert Henderson to be an *enfant terrible*, anxious above all to avoid stating a conventional opinion. This was not just the arrogance of an individual, but the arrogance of a place, Cambridge. Keynes proclaimed himself a rebel against Marshallian orthodoxy. But for most of his life Cambridge economics, like Cambridge philosophy, saw itself as far in advance of anything being done elsewhere. Marshallians in the 1900s, even in the 1920s, saw themselves as pioneers, blazing new intellectual trails. It was also the arrogance of a group, Bloomsbury. Both combined to give Keynes that sense of 'colossal superiority' of which he wrote to Strachey in 1905.

Keynes displayed an awesome array of talents, without being pre-eminent in any. He was not a genius in the sense of being a Divine Fool as was Mozart or Wittgenstein – extraordinary at one thing, babyish in everything else. He was a wonderful all-rounder, with a superbly efficient thinking machine. At Eton he had excelled at mathematics *and* classics, and throughout his life he effortlessly bridged the two cultures. He was not a remarkable mathematician. Nor was he a great philosopher. As a historian he was an inspired amateur. He had a theory of politics, but it never saved him from the charge of being politically naive.

Keynes was great in the combination of his gifts. His achievement was to align economics with changes taking place in ethics, in culture, in politics and in society – in a word, with the twentieth-century spirit. But, like Jevons, his qualities never quite jelled. That, rather than too great a haste, is why he failed to produce a work of art, although his writings are full of artistry. As a stylist he was the best economics has ever had, but his best stylistic achievements were in his shorter pieces – notably his biographical essays. In his big books he was the pamphleteer trying to rein in his imagination, school himself to the demands of a formal treatise. He had powerful intuitions of logical and historical relationships, but was not at his happiest in sustained argument. Like Marshall, his concentration came in short bursts. His temperament was too restless, his mind too constantly active, and bursting out with ideas and plans, for thinking in solitude.

Everyone agrees that Keynes was 'the most intuitive of men',[45] using intuitive as people talk, or used to talk, of 'feminine' intuition – as something apart from rationality. One of his biographers, Charles Hession, erects a theory of creativity on the supposed synthesis of the two. To Hession, the creative personality is 'androgynous' – one who combines female intuitions with masculine logic. Keynes was androgynous, his androgyny being rooted in his homosexuality, which in turn was caused or facilitated by having a masculine mother (she rode bicycles!) and a feminine father (he liked the theatre!). But it does not seem to add anything to the argument to call a combination of exceptional qualities androgynous.[46] More interesting is the privileged epistemic status Keynes claimed for intuition in general, and his intuitions in particular. This does tell us something about the way he worked with colleagues and critics. His view of how knowledge in economics was obtained had profound implications for his strategy of argument and persuasion. He regarded an economic argument (or 'conversation' as Donald McCloskey would say) as, in the first instance, a way of exposing the 'intuitions' of those taking part. At this stage, Keynes always pleaded for 'charity' towards factual or logical mistakes or obscurities, since much the most important thing was to get the drift of the argument, to consider whether it had value. Keynes's most acid controversies after the publication of his *Treatise on Money* were with critics like Hayek who, he felt, missed what he was driving at in order to trip him up on logical points. But it followed, secondly, that argument or conversation could not be fruitful once opposing intuitions came to light, unless or until a conversion took place from one camp to another. Good conversation, in economics as in other subjects, started from shared sympathies and could not survive a falling out of sympathy. In the 1920s Keynes's good conversations in economics were with Robertson, Hawtrey, Henderson, Gerald Shove, less frequently with Pigou: all Cambridge men, within the Marshallian tradition. These good conversations (except with Shove) came to an end in the 1930s, to Keynes's regret, because his intuitions had started to diverge too seriously from theirs. In the 1930s his good conversations were with disciples like Richard Kahn, Joan and Austin Robinson, though he continued to have bad ones with his older colleagues.

As with all original minds, Keynes's intuitions were never fully captured by his analytical system. His books are full of historical generalisations which are not 'modelled' at all. And his theory of liquidity preference hardly captures the richness and passion of his informal speculations concerning the psychology of hoarding or his view that 'love of money' was the cancer of economies.

Arthur Smithies has written that Keynes's 'analytical achievement was always in response to the practical situation that confronted him'.[47] Moggridge has noted Keynes's 'immense practicality and almost complete absorption in questions of policy', adding that 'he used traditional methods of analysis for policy problems until they broke down and then proceeded to fashion new tools to fill in the gaps'.[48] To this we may add that the key to Keynes's effectiveness as a policy adviser, both inside and outside the government machine, was his speed and skill in drafting. His wont was to come to meetings with completely formulated drafts while the others 'blathered'. These drafts inevitably became the basis of discussion. Throughout his life Keynes had a plan ready for any occasion or problem. It was part of his colossal self-confidence; it was also a sign of the quality of his mind.

All this is true, but incomplete. Although it is clear that a practical challenge was the spur, Keynes always had intellectual ambitions, or tastes, surplus to the requirements of the problem. The 'tool-maker' view of Keynes is the view of those who have been mainly interested in expounding or using the tools. The idea that he was basically an extraordinarily clever civil servant can be overdone. After all, he had spent ten years working on and off on his *Treatise on Probability*. The truth is that a problem got Keynes interested in a subject, but that very soon he became fascinated in developing it for its own sake. Many of the chapters in the *General Theory* are not needed for the tool-box. They are there because he wanted to say something about the nature of economic life.

A number of intellectual and personal characteristics stand out. One of Keynes's favourite and most effective techniques was the use of the *reductio ad absurdum* to ridicule the reasoning of his opponents. Many of the examples which can be cited of his use of this technique involve the paradox of thrift. 'For take the extreme case,' he says in a broadcast in 1931. 'Suppose we were to stop spending our incomes, and were to save the lot. Why, everyone would be out of work. And before long we should have no incomes to spend . . . and the end would be that we should all starve to death.'[49] Similarly, if money wages kept on being cut in a depression, as the classical economists suggested, one could show that the wages bill would be reduced to zero, with the same result. The King Midas legend was the imaginative source of chapter 17 of the *General Theory*, in which it is suggested that a *laissez-faire* economy ends up with the last person expiring on a heap of gold. These conclusions, which all depend on *ceteris paribus*, illustrate the fact that Keynes used the Marshallian technique of partial equilibrium to explain total situations, not partial ones, as Marshall intended. He never, that is, saw the economic system as a system of interdependent variables. His striking results were always obtained by concentrating attention on a single factor, or small group of factors, and working out the consequences of changes in them on the total situation, while ignoring the repercussions of these changes on other elements in the initial position. (Malthus proceeded in much the same way in his theory of population.) A good example was his stance on reparations in the debate with Ohlin when he ignored income repercussions on the recipients of transfers. As Robertson would say, Keynes's mind was a powerful searchlight, rather than a glow-worm, lighting up a path, rather than a landscape. There is some reason to believe that the marginalist revolution, which exhibits, among other things, the rewards to different factors of production as aspects of a general theory of pricing, never really got under his skin. Was this a flaw in his equipment as an economist? If so, it was a creative flaw. That pre-eminent theorist Professor Frank Hahn of Cambridge University certainly believes that had he been a better theorist he would not have been such a great economist, which is surely something to ponder.[50]

In his attitude to his fellow humans, Keynes was a mixture of benevolence and intolerance. He had a great capacity for affection, and was always loyal to his friends. There was no trace of malice in him, or jealousy. He was appreciative of mental quirks, oddities, obsessions, which he often saw as containing interesting possibilities. He revered genius, a word which he used in its original sense of a 'free spirit', and which he used generously. He loved his French friend, Marcel Labordère, whom he hardly ever saw, for the sheer poetry of his mind, and addressed him as 'My dear Alchemist'; Labordère saw the same quality in him. Like many intellectuals, he had immense respect for practical expertise, even of the humblest. He was quick to excuse the faults of youth and inexperience. His social sympathies were not as highly developed as his personal ones, but as he grew older these expanded too; and at all times he could be angered by specific acts of injustice, whether to individuals or to groups. In general, he was not a patient man, but he could take enormous trouble with the affairs of his friends, and those he thought deserving of it.

At the same time, he could be devastatingly rude – especially to those he thought ought to know better. Stories of his rudeness are legion. On one occasion at a board meeting of the National Mutual, he broke out at Francis Curzon, brother of the marquess, 'Really, Curzon, you have all the pomposity of your brother and none of his intelligence.' On another occasion he snapped at an auditor at some board meeting, 'We all know, Mr X, that auditors consider that the object of accounts is to conceal the truth, but surely not even you can believe that their object is to conceal the truth from the directors.' Another snub was fully deserved. A Conservative MP, Waldron Smithers, secretary of the House of Commons Finance Committee, wrote to him in 1933, asking whether he would put his name to a pamphlet he (Waldron Smithers) had written for his constituents. Keynes wrote back,

'If you want someone to furnish you with a name, I suggest that you might perhaps advertise in the "Personal Column" of "The Times"!' Keynes was by no means easy company for the slower-witted. He was almost invariably the cleverest person in any gathering, knew it and showed it. Kenneth Clark, who served with him on CEMA (the Council for the Encouragement of Music and the Arts) during the Second World War, complained that he used his brilliance 'too unsparingly . . . he never dimmed his headlights'. Alternatively, he could be inattentive to the point of rudeness. Isaiah Berlin, himself a memorable conversationalist, has left a painful account of sitting next to him in hall at King's in 1930. It was not till the last course that Keynes turned to him. 'Why are you here? What are you doing?' Berlin answered, 'I am reading a paper to the Moral Sciences Club later this evening.' 'What about?' 'Pleasure.' 'Really? What a ridiculous subject.' Then, picking up the menu: 'Now, what are we eating? Potage de something or other. Why don't you read about that? Just as good a subject.' After a silence: 'What do you think about Whitehead?' Berlin said that he found the early chapters on *Science and the Modern World* interesting. After a much longer silence: 'I don't agree with you.' After which, Berlin remembers, 'he turned away from me'. The philosopher A. J. Ayer had a similar experience.

Keynes admired artists above all others and had well-developed aesthetic tastes of his own, especially for poetry, Shakespeare in particular. His own ability to find fit words for themes and occasions was incomparable. He loved the dramatic arts best of all, and might have been a keener opera-goer had he been exposed to opera earlier. But music in all its forms came late to him, though often on a Sunday evening he would slip into a concert in the College Chapel. How much he really enjoyed pictures, as opposed to the idea of having them, and supporting those who painted them, is disput-able. Although he built a fine collection, he often bought dross – out of loyalty to his friends. He had little taste in furniture, though he spoke, as a young man, of the need to work in beautiful rooms. As he grew older, the coarseness which comes out in his letters to Lytton Strachey, and the comments of his Bloomsbury friends, vanished; those who knew him only in later life would have been amazed to learn that his 'mind was like a sewer', which is probably why he was known as Pozzo. He was not a fastidious man, but he had fastidious sides to him. He had his collars specially made for him at Cambridge, till his tailor stopped making them. He always wore silk underwear, though sometimes till it was in tatters. He liked well-kept hands and fingernails, and used these as a test of character. A great hoarder of letters, he threw away Goldie Lowes Dickinson's, because he could not stand their messiness. His personal, as well as work, habits were as orderly as the processes of his mind. He was as economical in his use of time as he was in his entertainments. He composed his essays and books in long-hand, often in pencil, on a writing board, sitting in an arm-chair, before sending off drafts to be typed. He rarely rewrote his short pieces; his big books, though, went through many drafts, and he left none of them completely satisfied. Whether he worked so hard from a sense of duty, a sense of pleasure or an incapacity to relax is difficult to say. He dominated any committee he was on, and did most of the work. Gradually he cut down his commitments to protect himself.

He had his full share of the foibles, some amiable, others less so, which he so admired in his biographical subjects. His fanciful mind made him a great 'sounder off'. He tended to lecture people on their own expertise, taking up some point, playing with it, developing it into a fantastic theory. A typical *obiter dictum* was his assertion before the Lottery Commission in 1932 that stock-market gambling was so prevalent in the United States because not enough grass grew to encourage horse-racing.[52] Some people thought there was a touch of charlatanry about him. He could be as credulous as any alchemist, and in the same way, investing money in 1930 in a process which guaranteed to turn base metal into gold, and speculating that the discovery might solve the world's unemployment problem.[53] He had the utmost confidence in his predictions of specific events, which were rarely justified by the outcome, though he was excellent at spotting general trends. He consistently lost money (his own and his friends') on the results of general elections. Quentin Bell tells the story of how he assured his friends in Sussex that a neighbouring, and highly polluting, cement factory would soon go bust, because its finances were wrongly constructed. It pollutes to this day. He almost invariably refused to sign circulars, write introductions to other people's books and allow his speeches to be printed, having decided views on why these things should not be. He had a profound mistrust of solicitors and accountants, and thought of their employment as a disagreeable necessity, to be avoided wherever possible. He had a great capacity for 'buzz and fuzz', bombarding ministers with letters, not just about great failings in national policy, but about tiny lapses in the running of their departments. Almost any matter, however small, was capable of arousing his indignation – as when he fulminated for several months to the Lewes Borough Council over a small mistake he alleged them to have made in charging him a tiny sum for summoning the fire brigade to Tilton.

Keynes was a man of endless fascination, not altogether lovable. That he mellowed as much as he did was due, in no small measure, to the influence of Lydia, the enduring love of his life. He was, in his own sense, a great genius and a great thinker, stamped by some of the less attractive qualities of family, place and time. His supreme effort of imagination and intellect was yet to come.

In Keynes's papers is a thirty-nine page manuscript on 'Population', omitted from the published *Collected Writings*, with which he opened a discussion at the Political Philosophy and Science Club, Oxford, on 2 May 1914. The topic was: 'Is the Problem of Population a Pressing and Important One Now?'

The title is indicative of concerns. In the years leading up to the war, population was regarded as a problem not because of its absolute excess but because of the relative excess of certain populations. Imperialists lamented the decline in the numbers of whites relative to Asians. Eugenicists like Galton and Pearson lamented the decline in the quality of the whites as the educated classes abandoned their procreative duties. The imperialists called for prodigies of patriotic procreation; the eugenicists wanted the wealthy and educated to have more children and the poor and uneducated less. All this registers a considerable collapse of confidence by the governing class in the permanence of European dominance abroad and class rule at home.

Against this background Keynes's talk was fairly optimistic. He was one of a 'small minority', he said, who welcomed the fall in the birthrate 'as one of the most hopeful signs of the times'. He was interested in the differential birthrate between rich and poor not chiefly for its supposedly deleterious effect on the quality of the population but as showing that Malthus was wrong to believe that the birthrate went up with prosperity. Rather the reverse was true, as the expense to parents of having children relative to their economic utility increases with affluence. What this suggested was that in the very long run the economic problem would be solved. As for those who worried about the effect on the population's quality of the class difference in the birthrate, the remedy was obvious: abandon Victorian morals and spread the knowledge and practice of contraception to the poor. To 'put difficulty in the way of checks' merely served to 'increase the proportion of the population born to the drunk, the ignorant, and the imprudent'.

Keynes was less pessimistic about population than about resources. The second factor which had falsified Malthus was the opening of overseas markets for food, which had postponed the operation of the law of diminishing returns in agriculture. But, Keynes averred, 'it must be plainest to the meanest intelligence' that this factor was temporary only. He then went on, in a passage which he reproduced almost verbatim in *The Economic Consequences of the Peace* (*Collected Writings*, ii. 5) to argue that Europe's favourable balance of trade with the United States had reversed itself. From the point of view of Keynes's post-war preoccupations this is the most important passage in the 1914 talk. He approached post-war problems with a sense of a secular decline in Europe's ability to wrest a living from the world, which the war had speeded up. Given this decline, population growth was excessive, even though the growth rate had slowed.

Keynes's conviction that Europe would have to pay more for its food was directly linked to the demographic shift which so worried the imperialists. The Malthusian law had never been suspended in the east. 'Three quarters of the world', Keynes concluded, 'has never ceased to live under Malthusian conditions.' And, with that world's increasing pressure on the world food supply, 'the period of postponement for the rest may be coming to an end'.

Keynes's 1914 paper is of particular interest as representing the last, as well as the only, time he tried to see the future of Europe and the United States in relation to what is now called the developing world. There is a typical Edwardian Yellow Peril coda to these reflections. Keynes believed that the differential rate of increase between whites and non-whites posed a potential conflict for the whites between happiness and security. But he rejected the militarist remedy of increased fecundity. Rather the white nations would need to protect their living standards against the more prolific races by stringent immigration controls and restriction of access to food supplies. This was quite likely to provoke 'racial wars'. But at least, he concluded with misplaced satisfaction, 'such wars will be about substantial issues' – as opposed, no doubt, to what he later called 'the projects and politics of militarism' which obsessed Europe's leaders.

CHAPTER THIRTEEN

The Practical Visionary

I

Early in October 1931, Vanessa and Duncan went to the cinema in London, when:

> suddenly Maynard appeared on the screen enormously big, in a well-appointed library blinking at the lights & speaking rather nervously & told the world that everything was now going to be all right, England had been rescued by fate from an almost hopeless situation, the pound would not collapse, prices would not rise very much, trade would recover, no one need fear anything. In this weather one can almost believe it. . . . [1]

Keynes was clearly in an up-beat mood. On 16 October 1931, he sent off the manuscript of his 'Essays in Prophecy' to Daniel Macmillan. They were published a month later under the title *Essays in Persuasion*. In the preface he wrote,

> We are standing at a point of transition. It is called a national crisis. But that is not correct – for Great Britain the main crisis is over. There is a lull in our affairs. We are, in the autumn of 1931, resting ourselves in a quiet pool between two waterfalls. Scarcely any one in England now believes in the Treaty of Versailles or in the pre-war gold standard or in the policy of deflation. These battles have been won – mainly by the irresistible pressure of events and only secondarily by the slow undermining of old prejudices. But most of us have, as yet, only a vague idea of what we are going to do next, of how we are going to use our regained freedom of choice.[2]

The essays were a collection of his chief non-theoretical writings of the previous decade – 'the croakings of a Cassandra', he called them, 'who could never influence the course of events in time'. In saying that his prophecy had been more successful than his persuasion, Keynes was selling himself short. The drip of his pen had played its part in undermining old prejudices. That there was no serious attempt to revive the gold standard is a tribute to Keynes's persuasion in the 1920s. *The Times*, champion of monetary orthodoxy, wrote *finis* on that episode by saying that in 1925 'honour was at stake and worth an effort', but that 'British industry failed to make the necessary adjustment.'[3] From now on Keynes found *The Times* open to him, and his most important policy suggestions in the 1930s appeared in its columns.

Keynes's persuasive methods came in for critical scrutiny. Leonard Woolf thought he displayed his cleverness too recklessly; Harold Laski accused him of being an eighteenth-century rationalist who ignored the fact that capitalism was unreformable, a criticism echoed by John Strachey. Oswald Falk regretted that he was not a 'practising fatalist'.[4] Keynes was never a fatalist, whether of the Marxist or sceptical kind; his most attractive quality was his optimism. One eighteenth-century rationalist was beyond the pleasure Keynes's book would have given him. On 21 January 1932, Lytton Strachey died of cancer. Keynes had not seen much of his old friend of late, although they had continued writing to each other and sending each other their books. Lydia had refused to go to Ham Spray, apparently because she disapproved of Carrington's immorality.[5] On Carrington, Lytton's death had a devastating effect. 'Nothing seems to me worth anything in comparison with that perfection of jokes and intelligence,' she wrote to Sebastian Sprott in March, a few days before shooting herself. The letter Maynard must have written to Carrington on Lytton's death has not survived, destroyed perhaps in one of the bonfires Carrington made of their possessions before she died. Lytton was part of Maynard's life which Lydia could not, and did not want to, share – the friend who had had a decisive influence over his style and sense of values. The memorial of their friendship is their letters, nearly a thousand of them, mostly dating from before the First World War, when they had openly discussed their feelings, joked about their friends and fought each other for the love of Duncan Grant. 'The letters? – for God's sake, lock them up for years yet,' Maynard told Lytton's brother James after Lytton's death.[6] Death started taking its toll of other pre-war friends: Goldie Lowes Dickinson in 1932, Roger Fry in 1934, Frankie Birrell and Brynhild Popham (née Olivier) in 1935. 'I am an idealist', Maynard told Virginia Woolf, '& therefore on the whole I suppose I think that something may continue. Clearly the brain is the only exciting thing – matter does not exist. It follows therefore . . . but one is very vague.'[7]

Keynes's own health collapsed in the autumn of 1931, for the second time that year. 'I *am* after all having my days in bed and in horrid circumstances,' he scribbled to Lydia on 25 October 1931. 'I woke up yesterday with the most dreadful pains in my chest, so bad that I telephoned at once for a doctor. It turns out to be a sort of rheumatism, and inflammation of the sheaths of the small muscles which encircle the lungs (intercostal). Not at all dangerous or serious but horribly painful.' He was nursed by Richard Kahn and his bedmaker, Mrs Taylor, his bed being moved from his bedroom, where icicles had formed, to his study. Lydia (rightly) suspected pleurisy. The fever persisted for several days, the illness dragged on for several weeks. 'My health is respectable but not quite perfect yet,' he reported on 15 November. 'I occasionally have a rheumatic twinge; my eyes are not quite so strong – just like last November; and my teeth are tender. And I still walk slowly, but I make progress. . . .' He was feeling 'very broken' at the end of November. That winter and early spring Keynes complained repeatedly of bronchitis, of lumbago, of rheumatic pains 'flying about the body'. He underwent periods of daily massage and treatment from Lydia's sun-ray lamp. Keynes had never looked robust; he had started to look unwell. He had put on a lot of weight. Vanessa Bell found him 'incredibly white and fat' in Lewes in the summer of 1930.[8] A portrait painted by William Roberts in the winter of 1931 shows a portly-looking Keynes, cigarette clutched in spatula-like fingers, with a no-longer birdlike Lydia beside him.

In the 1930s, Keynes was never as active in public life as he had been up to 1931. Partly, and certainly at first, this was because economic policy had caught up with his prescriptions. The deflationary constraint of the gold standard had ended, the decade of cheap money was at hand. The Keynesian agenda of the 1920s, applied in the 1930s, enabled Britain to escape the worst of the world depression. He endorsed, and partly inspired, the cheap-money policy and its corollary, managing sterling at a low rate of exchange with the dollar (that is, at about \$3.50), which followed the end of the gold-standard era.[9] He applauded Chamberlain's conversion of £2b. of 5 per cent war loan to 3.5 per cent as 'a constructive measure of the very first importance', not on budgetary-saving grounds, but for its effect on the long-term interest rate.[10] All this had its expected results. The balance of payments improved. Cheap money (bank rate stayed at 2 per cent from June 1932 to 1939) facilitated a boom in private house building, which helped revive economic activity. But recovery was slow in coming and it was seriously incomplete. Unemployment did not fall below 20 per cent till the middle of 1933.

Keynes found other things to applaud. Reparations were finally cancelled at the Lausanne Conference in July 1932. Keynes congratulated MacDonald, who presided: 'It is a long time since June 1919 when I resigned from the British delegation in Paris in an enraged and tormented state of mind. The waste over the intervening years has been prodigious. But it is a comfortable feeling that at last it is cleaned up. For whatever America may do, this is necessarily the end so far as Germany is concerned.'[11] Britain made a last token payment of its war debt to America in December 1933, and after that paid no more. (Its debt currently stands at \$14b.)* After the

---

*The last payment in fact was made on 24 March 1949, when the US Treasury received \$4,480.65 under the terms of a will made by a British subject.

Second World War, the victorious Allies declined to repeat their mistakes of 1919. Keynes's persuasion prevailed.

Keynes did not so much oppose the government's tariff and imperial-preference policy as regard it as a distraction from the more important task of general currency realignment. Free traders like Lionel Robbins argued that 'exchange-rate flexibility provided a complete solution to Britain's problem of external balance'.[12] Keynes agreed that the case for a tariff had lost its urgency, and that anything a tariff could do 'currency depreciation is doing and . . . better'.[13] However, he believed in a managed, not floating, currency, and he did not recover his free-trade faith. In fact he developed a case for combining tariffs with limited currency depreciation;* in April 1933 he would advocate protection as part of his argument for 'national self-sufficiency'.

Keynes had always tried to balance price and exchange stability. He applauded the devaluation of sterling not on narrow nationalistic grounds, but as providing a non-deflationary standard of value for the sterling bloc – the group of over twenty nations, mainly primary producers, who had devalued their currencies in line with sterling in order to preserve their entry to the British market. This collective devaluation had also freed the debtor group of nations from the thrall of the creditor nations, led by the United States and France, which remained on the gold standard. The spontaneous emergence of a sterling bloc, or club as Keynes called it, suggested to him 'a reputable sterling system for the Empire . . . managed by the Bank of England and pivoted on London', with sterling stabilised in terms of a basket of commodities, and the Bank of England keeping its exchange as steady as possible with the dollar.[14] Eventually equilibrium would be reached between the two clubs – largely through the destruction of the creditor position of the USA and France – which would allow the restoration of a single international monetary system. He hoped such ideas might be pursued at the Imperial Conference held at Ottawa in July 1932, with Britain being prepared to bargain the value of sterling against the level of Dominion tariffs.[15] But he rightly suspected that the 'ultra-conservative' Neville Chamberlain and Montagu Norman would 'nip anything constructive in the bud'.[16] Chamberlain duly obliged by stopping any discussion of currency questions.[17]

Meanwhile, the departure of some countries from the gold standard had only tightened the grip of deflation on those countries which remained on

---

*In a letter to Cyril Asquith, dated 5 December 1931 (KP: CO 6.34) he argued that the theoretical case for a tariff was not completely destroyed by exchange depreciation. A fall in the exchange below a certain optimum point (for example, owing to capital flight) tends to be cumulative, as interest owed by foreigners as well as exports of goods pay for a diminishing proportion of imports. Thus 'a situation may arise in which further currency depreciation will lead to our giving our exports away too cheap, and the best hope of stopping the rot is to be found in restricting imports without giving any further bounty to exports'.

it, hindering global recovery. After a visit to Hamburg in January 1932, Keynes reported the situation there as 'truly appalling . . . business . . . is almost at a standstill. The shipping people are suffering impossible losses.'[18] 'Can we,' he asked in his lecture to the International Economic Society in Hamburg on 8 January 1932, 'prevent an almost complete collapse of the financial structure of modern capitalism?' In Berlin he spent an hour with the Chancellor, Heinrich Brüning. Piling misery on his own people was an essential part of Brüning's strategy of convincing the Allies that Germany could no longer pay reparations. It would be folly to give up 'a hundred yards from the finishing post', he declared. His policy certainly finished off the Weimar Republic.

Nearly half the banks in the United States failed in the depression, depriving their depositors of spending power. The problem, Keynes explained in *Vanity Fair* in January 1932, arose from the 'slow and steady sapping of the real resources of the banks as a result of the progressive collapse of [the] money values [of the real assets against which loans had been made] over the past two years'.[19] While failing banks were bringing down the economy, the economy was bringing down the banks.[20] Not that Keynes had much sympathy for the sufferings of the rich. When the American financier Frank Altschul lunched with him in Cambridge in May 1932 and told him about the panic on Wall Street, he rudely replied that 'they were all sub-normal and even sub-human; also that he and his friends were of gangster mentality'.[21] The one financier for whom Keynes retained unbounded admiration was the Swedish match king Ivar Kreuger, who committed suicide in March 1932 after his business empire crashed to ruin. Calling him the 'greatest constructive intelligence of his age', Keynes used his death to illustrate the 'helplessness of the individual . . . crushed between the ice-bergs of a frozen world which no individual man could thaw and restore to the warmth of normal life'.[22]

Keynes, like Milton Friedman subsequently, blamed the Federal Reserve Board for its failure to prevent a collapse of the US money stock. It did not start to buy securities on any scale till 1932. By then it was too late. The banks which survived became safety-deposit institutions, refusing to lend. This was the context in which Keynes was to develop his proposals for international public works to raise the price level in 1933.

The question of the right budgetary policy for recovery had been continually debated between Keynes and the Treasury between 1929 and 1931. It was sidelined by the collapse of the gold standard and the start of cheap money, but re-emerged early in 1933 when Keynes published his 'Means to Prosperity'. Keynes appreciated that 'sound finance' was necessary at a time of financial crisis, to boost confidence and to make possible the transition to easy money; but no policy which did not aim directly at increasing total expenditure was likely to bring recovery. He reckoned that the national government's policies had had a neutral effect on demand: devaluation and cheap money had just about compensated cuts in public expenditure and increased taxes. ' "Sound" finance may be right psychologically, but economically it is a depressing influence,' he commented on Chamberlain's budget of April 1932. 'There is nothing in this Budget to hasten the recovery of ourselves or of the world from the slump.'[23] With the conversion operation over, he started fretting for an expansionary fiscal policy. To Harold Macmillan he wrote on 6 June 1932: 'There are enormous psychological advantages in the *appearance* of economy. It prepares the way for the conversion of the Debt and it tends to lower the long-term rate of interest. The opposite would also be bad for business sentiment. But that does not prevent economy from being deflationary and probably injurious to business profits.'[24] The debate was a repeat of his tussles with Hubert Henderson and Sir Richard Hopkins in 1930. They stressed the adverse effects on confidence and therefore interest rates of unbalancing the budget; Keynes the beneficial effects on activity. But it was not till he was confident enough to use Kahn's multiplier theory that he felt he could clinch the argument.

The relative meagreness of Keynes's public activities in the early 1930s is also explained by the collapse of his networks of persuasion. Politically he was homeless. The Liberal Party virtually ceased to exist in October 1931, the ageing Lloyd George heading a family group of four MPs. The parliamentary Labour Party was reduced to a rump. Its leading Keynesian, Mosley, was out of Parliament and had started the British Union of Fascists. Keynes's intellectual networks had also collapsed. Kingsley Martin's *New Statesman* could not give him the platform he had had in the *Nation* under Hubert Henderson. Its politics was too left-wing for his liking, and it was not interested in economics. The old liberal-minded world of clubs and committees, of civil servants and of bankers, politicians, economists and do-gooders, on which Keynes had cast magic spells till 1931, had also lost influence, as business Conservatism, headed by Neville Chamberlain, seized power from the nerveless grasp of MacDonald and Baldwin. The Tuesday Club, which Keynes had used to such effect as a sounding board in the 1920s, met less and less frequently: Keynes did not address it once between 1930 and 1934. He still had access to MacDonald, both privately and as a member of a number of expert advisory committees which the Prime Minister appointed to strengthen him politically. Keynes thought that MacDonald had 'given up thinking nonsense'.[25] But, whatever he thought, the ex-Labour Prime Minister was a prisoner of his huge 'national' majority of right-wing Conservative MPs. The depression had anyway caused rifts in the old mandarin circle – over free trade, over unbalanced budgets and, increasingly, over economic theory. It would regroup at the end of the 1930s. Meanwhile, Keynes fell back on a new support group of Cambridge disciples headed by his 'favourite student' Richard Kahn. He appears a more isolated figure in the 1930s than in the 1920s, but his very isolation gave him the breathing space to write his great book.

The depression radicalised Keynes intellectually, but not politically or socially. Politically, he still thought of himself as a liberal, a believer in individual freedom and its corollary of limited government. He never embraced socialism. In the 1930s, he insisted as he had in the 1920s that the state should not try to take over the functions of private enterprise, merely fill its gaps. His political economy thus shows great continuity with his Middle Way notions of the 1920s. Socially, indeed, he was growing more conservative. He 'is the most crusted tory of my acquaintance', Sam Courtauld remarked in September 1932 after spending a 'happy' weekend at Tilton, during which Keynes had told him that 'the age of institutions is the best criterion of their worth, & progress is only admissible if it is so slow as to be imperceptible . . .'.[26] This was, as we shall see, at the precise moment when his economic theory was being radicalised. The paradox is only apparent, for ever since 1919 he had preached that radical thought was the only antidote to radical change.

While privately conceding that 'one could not possibly have wished the Labour Government to be returned' in October 1931,[27] Keynes continued his dialogue with the Labour Party. Addressing a socialist group on 13 December 1931 on the 'Dilemmas of Modern Socialism', he delivered his retrospective judgement on Labour's two years in office. The problem with the Labour Party was that it lacked a viable philosophy of government. Committed to a socialist utopia it failed to interest itself in the problem of running capitalism. As a result it combined redistributionary threats which depressed businessmen with slavish adherence to financial orthodoxy which depressed the economy. It had been 'totally out of sympathy', Keynes said, 'with those who have had new notions of what is economically sound . . . such as Mr. Lloyd George or Sir Oswald Mosley or Mr. Bevin or myself'. Yet starting, Keynes suggested, from a different intellectual perspective – that of a general deficiency of purchasing power – his own policies could be shown to be consistent with a range of socialist policies, notably central controls on investment and measures of income redistribution not to knock capitalism out but to raise purchasing power.[28]

When he reviewed the Labour Party's policy on banking, in the *New Statesman* of 17 and 24 September 1932, he supported nationalisation of the Bank of England, but attacked the Party's demand for 'democratic interference' in its working. It was the policy, not the structure, of the Bank which was at fault, and care should be taken to protect its 'autonomy' and 'independence and prestige' which were national assets. He accepted Labour's proposal for a national investment board, but rejected the idea of 'qualitative control' over investment. The task of such a board should be to maintain the aggregate rate of investment high enough 'to ensure the optimum level of employment', not to choose between investment projects. Keynes emphasised the 'smallness of the part [in investment] which purely private enterprise now plays'. If the state could determine 'the rate of aggregate investment' of 'public and semi-public bodies', it could 'safely leave industry to raise what funds it needs as and when it chooses'.[29]

The left was by no means receptive to Keynes's way of analysing the economic problem. After 1931, its favoured remedy was the physical planning of production, in the belief that 'socialist' planning and public ownership would themselves be sufficient to restore full employment. The main intellectual input into Labour's economic theory, apart from Marxism, came from the London School of Economics. Hugh Dalton upheld Cannan's old-fashioned quantity theory of money on Labour's Finance and Trade Committee; younger socialist economists from the LSE like Evan Durbin and Hugh Gaitskell were much influenced by Lionel Robbins's and Hayek's pessimistic 'Austrian' analysis, which seemed to reinforce the view that slumps were inevitable under capitalism. In addition, 'the Labour Party was highly suspicious of Keynes' both because of his association with Lloyd George and Mosley and 'for his unfortunate manner'.[30] Keynes himself steered well clear of such Labour Party think tanks as the New Fabian Research Bureau or the XYZ Club, the latter started in 1932 by his friend Nicholas Davenport. The historian A. L. Rowse wanted Keynes to join the Labour Party. His ideas, Rowse argued, could succeed only if they were in the 'right relation' with the organised working class.[31] But Keynes remained suspicious of Labour. 'I should officially join that party', he wrote to Rowse in 1936, 'if it did not seem to be divided between enthusiasts who turn against anything if there seems a chance that it could possibly happen, and leaders so conservative that there is more to hope from Mr. Baldwin.'[32] Even after the *General Theory* was published, the Labour Party 'remained too firmly committed to socialism even to heed the younger Keynesians within its own ranks'.[33] A more promising search for a Middle Way was taking place within the ranks of the 'national' majority – in organisations such as Political and Economic Planning, initially directed by Keynes's friend Basil Blackett, and the Next Five Years Group, started in 1935 by Harold Macmillan and Clifford Allen. Keynes was especially attentive to the ideas of Harold Macmillan, younger brother of his schoolfriend and publisher Daniel. But, till the later 1930s, Macmillan was more of a corporatist than an expansionist. In the 1930s new thinkers on both left and right were obsessed with developing a machinery of planning to replace failed market forces, whereas Keynes wanted to supply the market system with enough demand to maintain full employment. His revolution in theory was designed to replace the first route out of capitalist crisis by the second.

Keynes had already started to feel that practical persuasion had to be based on a new theory. 'I have begun again quietly in my chair writing about monetary theory,' he told Lydia on 22 November 1931. The passionate rows between the economists in 1930 had shocked him, and, as he later put it in the preface to the *General Theory*, 'almost destroyed the practical influence of economic theory'. When the *Treatise* was published in October 1930, he recognised that it was an artistic failure. He did not immediately see it as an intellectual failure. The adverse comment it got, as well as changes in the total situation since it was conceived, persuaded him otherwise. Perhaps the two failures are connected. A new explanation of prolonged depression was needed, which the formal apparatus of the *Treatise* could not supply.

II

INFLUENCES

Keynes's return to theory was inherent in his analysis of the slump. He refused to think of it as the final crisis of capitalism. In his preface to his *Essays in Persuasion* he emphasised his 'central thesis throughout – the profound conviction that the economic problem . . . is nothing but a frightful muddle, a transitory and *unnecessary* muddle'. The obstacles to recovery, he told his audience in Hamburg in January 1932, were not material but 'reside in the state of knowledge, judgement and opinion of those who sit in the seats of authority'.[34] In his Halley-Stewart Lecture on 4 February 1932, he said that in the United States 'it is almost inconceivable what rubbish a public man has to utter today if he is to keep respectable'.[35]

If the cause of the slump lay in intellectual error, its cure lay in right reasoning. This was Keynes's answer to Marx. The economic problem started to look different if one dropped all those practical maxims which were true and useful only at full employment. What Marx had diagnosed as a distributional struggle to be settled by power, Keynes saw as a problem of insufficient demand to be remedied by expertise. If the leaders of capitalism insisted on treating problems of demand as though they were problems of supply, and on screwing down the wages of workers in order to restore profits, then a class war could easily arise which would vindicate Marx's prophecy. But such a result would be correctly attributable to error or stupidity: it was not necessary to the survival of the capitalist system that it should act in such a way as to precipitate its own downfall. Keynes came to doubt the rhetorical and analytic power of the *Treatise* to expel the 'rubbish'. So he returned to theory with the aim of planting a different model of the economy in the minds of 'those in authority' so as to clinch the case for a different kind of policy.

Peter Clarke has argued that, unlike the composition of the *Treatise*, the development of the *General Theory* 'must . . . be understood in "internalist" terms. It was the outcome of a process of intellectual discovery rather than of political invention.'[36] John Hicks, too, accepts the 'internalist' explanation of the transition between the two books, arguing that no change in world conditions between 1930 and 1936 can explain the change in focus from prices to output.[37] This ignores the fact that the *Treatise*, dating from the mid–1920s, was inspired by the great price fluctuations of the early 1920s, whereas the *General Theory*'s background was the great output collapse of the early 1930s. The *General Theory* was certainly not tied to a political campaign, as the revised *Treatise* partly was. But Clarke's alternatives ignore the impact on Keynes's theorising of the changing economic and political environment.[38] A theory designed to save the world can never be wholly 'internalist' in inspiration.

The *General Theory* was projected against the background not just of the world depression, but of its political and social repercussions: specifically, the spread of communism and fascism. The flight of the intelligentsia from democracy had started. 'Stephen [Spender] is going bolshy like most of my friends,' noted Harold Nicolson in his diary of 24 September 1931. In January 1933, Adolf Hitler became Chancellor of Germany. Keynes wrote to save the world from the 'two opposed errors of pessimism – the pessimism of the revolutionaries who think that things are so bad that nothing can save us but violent change, and the pessimism of the reactionaries who consider the balance of our economic and social life so precarious that we must risk no experiments'.[39]

The *Treatise* was constructed with the British problem very much in mind. The *General Theory* was designed to supply a theory for a world in depression. This is one of the many ways in which the new theory is more 'general' than the old. But there was a special reason for the shift. Keynes was particularly impressed by the scale of the American collapse. Here was no sclerotic economy like Britain, but one which still bore many of the traces of the nineteenth-century 'fluidity'. The US collapse spurred Keynes to think more generally about the predicament of modern economies. The older emphasis on 'rigidities' gives way to a new attention to 'uncertainty', the ravages of speculation and the shrinkage of investment opportunities, as America replaces Britain as the example *par excellence* of the distressed economy.

Formally, the switch is from a model of an 'open' to that of a 'closed' economy. Here again, the American example may have been influential, as foreign trade was far less important for America than for Britain. But, in addition, analysis of unemployment in terms of maladjustments between different countries seemed to make much less sense when unemployment was truly 'general'. As Keynes noted in the *New Statesman* of 24 December 1932, 'The course of exchange, as we all know, moves round a closed circle. When we transmit the tension, which is beyond our own endurance, to our neighbour, it is only a question of a little time before it reaches ourselves again travelling round the circle.'[40] By 'closing' the economy Keynes is in effect saying: there is no solution within the system; it has to come from outside. The government becomes the last frontier. Another effect of the depression can be seen in the gradual switch from dynamic to static analysis. What needed to be explained was not the business cycle, but the persistence of a low level of business activity.

The generality and depth of the depression damaged Keynes's never very robust faith in the two 'classic' adjustment mechanisms, wage and interest-rate cuts. He had proposed a national treaty to reduce British money incomes in 1925, and supported a similar scheme implemented in Australia in 1931. Now, in June 1932, he told the Australian economist Giblin, 'if wages are reduced prices are sure to go down too . . .'.[41] This is a 'closed economy' idea. If a firm reduces its costs it can sell more of its output; and the same is true of a country heavily involved in international trade; but wage reductions applied all-round simply destroy purchasing power. Clarke is right to suggest that Keynes's new stress on the 'fallacy of composition' was 'continually prompted by the experience of the world slump'.[42]

Experience of the great depression also reinforced Keynes's doubt about the efficacy of cheap money. 'It may still be the case', he said in his Halley-Stewart Lecture of 4 February 1932, 'that the lender, with his confidence shattered by his experience, will continue to ask for new enterprise rates of interest which the borrower cannot expect to earn. . . . If this proves to be the case there will be no means of escape from prolonged and perhaps interminable depression except by direct state intervention to promote and subsidise new investment.' He hoped the world economy would not have to wait for a new war to lift it out of the slump.[43] The notion of a 'liquidity trap' had its origins in the severity of the depression.

The world slump was the indispensable background; its existence penetrated every thought Keynes had. Yet at the same time the new theory emerged through a process of intellectual argument, marked by a sense of high responsibility from all concerned to get the logic of the argument right. This argument is extremely well documented. In the period 1931–2 Keynes engaged in intermittent, but intense, correspondence on points of theory with Hawtrey, Robertson and Hayek. There are the 'pooled memories' of the so-called Cambridge Circus. There is the evidence of early drafts of the new book and other of Keynes's writings, as well as fragments of lectures, and complete sets of the lecture notes of some of his students, which run from 1932 to 1935. The historian and biographer is therefore well placed to piece together the stages in the intellectual construction of the *General Theory*.

Arguments about interpretation are more difficult to resolve. In what sense is the *General Theory* different from the *Treatise on Money*? What is distinctively new about the second book? When did Keynes first come to understand the new theory?

Certain matters can be cleared up. Samuelson writes, 'With respect to the level of total purchasing power and employment, Keynes denies that there is an *invisible* hand channelling the self-centred action of each individual to the social optimum. This is the sum and substance of his heresy.'[44] If this is so – and there are excellent grounds for believing it to be so – the heresy dates from at least Keynes's 1924 lecture, 'The End of Laissez-Faire', when he denied that 'individuals acting independently for their own advantage will produce the greatest aggregate of wealth'; and cited 'risk, uncertainty, and ignorance' as 'the cause of the unemployment of labour'.[45] This is too vague to be a theory. But even if we take as our yardstick the narrower form of the heresy as enunciated by Samuelson – the assertion that there is no 'internal efficacious economic process' to ensure that 'whatever people try to save will always be fully invested', this is already present in the Treatise on Money. In the Treatise, there is nothing to balance saving and investment except banking policy. If someone, that is, had asked Keynes in 1930, 'What determines the rate of interest?' he would have replied, 'The monetary authority.' Other 'innovations' of the General Theory also seem to have been in Keynes's mind much earlier. That a slump can stabilise itself at a low level of activity was already apparent to Keynes in 1930.[46] On 29 November 1934, he wrote to a Spanish correspondent, Luc Beltram, who had been studying the Treatise on Money, 'in a work of mine which will probably come out in about a year's time I deal with the under-lying theory on what, at any rate on the surface, would appear to be lines rather different from those adopted in my Treatise on Money. Under the surface, however, the essential ideas are the same.'[47]

One important reason economists did not register the heretical nature of the Treatise was that its theory was not presented as an explicit challenge to the orthodox way of doing economics. Formally, he presented a short-run disequilibrium model, which did not impugn the conventions of 'normal' science. The theoretical ambitions of the General Theory were much larger. Keynes openly attacked the methodology of economics. Economists, he said, were precluded from understanding the behaviour of modern economies by their habit of 'abstracting' money from their analysis, which ruled out all the problems created by money's existence. Monetary forces were not temporary disturbances to placid waters: they entered fundamentally into the determination of equilibrium states. All economic values were monetary values, which meant that the theory of money and the theory of production could not be separated. It was not a matter of replacing a bad economic theory by a better one. It was a matter of 'doing' the subject in a different way. This was the problem evaded in the Treatise, but faced up to in the General Theory.

Little of this aspect of Keynes's novelty emerges from the standard schol-arly accounts of the 'origins' of the General Theory. These are mainly devoted to showing two things: how Keynes switched the emphasis in his analysis from a theory of price adjustment to a theory of output adjustment; and how he corrected the 'logical mistake' in the banana parable in which output is allowed to run down to zero. The basic shift involves using the saving–investment relationship to determine the volume of output and employment rather than the price levels of consumption and capital goods; and showing how changes in output and employment keep saving and investment equal. The main 'moments' in this story are Keynes's redefinitions of saving and income, and his grasp of the 'psychological law' that when income changes consumption changes in the same direction but less than income, both of which lead up to the 'theory of effective demand'. The switch in attention from price to output changes is genuine enough; but too much attention has been paid to Keynes's discovery of the 'equilibrating' effect of output changes. There are all kinds of passages from the 1930–2 period which show that Keynes was perfectly aware that downturns were not cumulative, that they levelled off and were followed by recoveries, though these need not get far. One may say he was looking for something like his 'psychological law' to explain this 'levelling off' before he found it.

That this is part of the story of the change from the *Treatise* to the *General Theory* is undeniable. But it is not the whole part. In particular, it ignores the fact that much of Keynes's efforts in 1932 and 1933 were devoted to analysing the differences between a monetary and a real-exchange economy – that is, developing a critique of the methodology of classical economics. So there are two elements in the story which we have to keep in mind: Keynes's attempt to develop a 'monetary theory of production' and his attempt to develop a short-period theory of output determination, which includes the equilibrating role of quantity adjustment. The second is the distinctive technical accomplishment of the *General Theory*, the part most relevant for policy, the part on which attention has been focused; but it is not the *General Theory*. As we shall see, the first reaction of senior economists to the *General Theory* was not to attack Keynes's arguments, but to attack him for putting at risk their discipline.

Much ink has been spilt over the secondary question of when exactly the 'theory of effective demand' – the theory of how aggregate supply adjusts to aggregate demand – entered Keynes's mind. Peter Clarke would put 'understanding' of the new theory in 'the summer of 1932'. Don Patinkin puts 'full understanding' 'sometime in 1933'; Dimand agrees with him. Milgate believes it was not till 1934.[48]

This scholarly obsession with timetabling the *flow* of intellectual invention partly reflects genuine disagreement about the 'tests' appropriate to establishing understanding of a theory. Whereas Clarke looks for 'initial insights', 'disjointed flashes of illumination', Patinkin demands that we distinguish between the 'signal' and the 'noise' – or the 'systematic' and 'random' components of Keynes's thinking.[49] For Patinkin an economic theory exists only when it can be written down as a model or a set of equations. But economic theories are not born fully clothed. Despite his mathematical competence, Keynes did not think original thoughts in mathematics. In one of his lectures in 1933, he said that creative thought begins as a 'grey, fuzzy, woolly monster in one's head'. Precision comes later. Specifically, one can think 'accurately and effectively' long before one can formalise one's thought.[30] The point at which ideas become interlocking parts of a new theory is always a fuzzy one, as is the question of when the language being used is sufficiently like the final language to be sure that it contains the final thought. When does an embryo become human? The usual criterion is the capacity for self-sustaining life outside the womb of its creator. We need to ask ourselves what would have happened to the Keynesian Revolution had Keynes himself died in 1932 or 1933.

The obsession with dating also reflects an agenda which is not purely historiographical or methodological. Involved are the linked questions of the relative value of *Treatise* and the *General Theory*; the degree of continuity between these two books, and indeed between the *General Theory* and the whole corpus of Keynes's writings; the relationship between Keynes's work and that of the other monetary economists of his day; and what the 'main point' of the *General Theory* was. The wisest words on all these matters were said by Axel Leijonhufvud: 'The usual approach to the analysis of a man's life-work, whether it belongs to the arts or to science, rests on the assumption that his thought will show a consistency and continuity of development which, once grasped, make it possible to view his work as a coherent whole'.[51]

Ralph Hawtrey

Keynes's revision of the theory of the *Treatise* was prompted by criticisms he started receiving from his fellow economists. First in the field was Ralph Hawtrey, who dusted himself down from the Treasury shelf to deliver a painstaking critique of Keynes's ideas. Hawtrey's comments on the *Treatise* start before the book appeared, with Keynes's oral evidence to the Macmillan Committee, which was the subject of a memorandum, 'Mr. Keynes's Theory of the Bank Rate', written in February/March 1930. Keynes then started sending Hawtrey proofs of the *Treatise* as they became available. Hawtrey began composing a long commentary, 'Mr. Keynes's Treatise on Money', finished by the end of 1930. A revised version of this eventually appeared as chapter 6 of his *The Art of Central Banking* in 1932.[32] He sent Keynes instalments of this memorandum and also shorter proof corrections throughout the summer of 1930. However, Keynes made little use of them. Hawtrey wrote exhaustively, but not concisely; if he ever thought of an arresting phrase, he failed to commit it to paper. It was not till the publication of the *Treatise* in October 1930 that Keynes turned his attention to Hawtrey's fundamental criticisms.

Hawtrey's main objection to the *Treatise* was the failure of Keynes's Fundamental Equations to capture the output effects of a decline in consumer demand. 'If anything occurs to affect the demand for goods . . . the first result is an increase or decrease in sales at *existing prices* . . . There is always some interval of time before prices are adjusted, and the interval may be considerable.'[33] This observation followed directly from his own theory, which stressed the pivotal role of middlemen and dealers, who, when their inventories rise, curtail their orders to manufacturers, who cut their production runs and lay off workers. Hawtrey was also the first to point out that the 'excess of saving over investment' was simply another name for business losses.[34] On a normal definition of income, saving and investment are necessarily equal at all levels of income.

This does not mean that Hawtrey had in mind an equilibrating mechanism: the equality was simply an accounting identity, increased saving having its counterpart in an accumulation of unsold stocks (or 'working capital'), and vice versa. As we shall see, Keynes's failure properly to distinguish between the accounting identity of saving and investment and the process by which they are equalised was to be a source of great confusion in his *General Theory*. However, in his earlier comment, 'Mr. Keynes's Theory of the Bank Rate', Hawtrey had written, 'It is obvious that as soon as the consumers' income and outlay [expenditure] begin to decline, the portion destined for savings is likely to decline at least in proportion. This decline of savings will do nothing to relieve the depression, even if it goes so far as to wipe out the discrepancy between savings and capital outlay altogether.'[35] And in section vi of his memorandum on the *Treatise*, omitted from the published version in *The Art of Central Banking*, he put his insight to work to show how a change in investment changes saving by an equivalent amount – an independent discovery of the multiplier theory.*

At this point in time (1930) Hawtrey was nearer to understanding the role of output in adjusting to shocks than was Keynes himself. Specifically, he claimed that quantities adjust to a fall in demand before retail prices; that this 'wipes out the discrepancy between savings and capital outlay'; and that, in these circumstances, additional capital outlay creates the saving to pay for it. However, he never accepted Keynes's fundamental theoretical intuition that the economy lacked any internal mechanism to balance demand and supply at full employment. Output adjustment produced only 'temporary equilibrium': eventually prices would adjust to restore full employment. This is a good example of how a clever theorist could work

---

*Given in a numerical example in RGHP: 11/3, Section vi, paras 60–2, where he supposes that if investment be increased by £5m. a month, the increase in income will be divided between spending and saving over successive rounds, working itself out so that £5m. of additional saving is left to balance the £5m. of additional investment. 'Similar calculations' would apply to a reduction in investment. This multiplier, unlike Kahn's, incorporated both an explicit personal-savings function and price as well as output effects. The general idea that 'when industry is under-employed . . . the rise of prices and the increase of production are, to a great extent, *alternatives*' had been part of Hawtrey's thought since at least 1927. (Hawtrey, *Currency and Credit*, 1928 edn, 49–50; N. Cain, 'Hawtrey and Multiplier Theory', *Australian Economic History Review*, March 1982.)

out something very like a 'Keynesian' adjustment process, without accepting Keynes's intuition that an entrepreneur economy had no other method of adjustment open to it.

These criticisms hit home, reinforcing Keynes's dissatisfaction with the story he had told in the *Treatise*. Three passages are worth quoting from his letter to Hawtrey of 28 November 1930. First, he specified a 'normal order of events' in the cycle as: (1) 'a decline in fixed investment relative to saving'; (2) a fall in prices less than necessary for adjustment; (3) 'a fall in output, as a result of falling prices and accumulating stocks on the minds of entrepreneurs'; (4) a fall in prices greater than needed for adjustment as a result 'not of a low level of output but a declining level of output'. As soon as output stops declining, therefore, 'there will be some kick-up of prices'. He believed it 'impossible to understand the life history of the credit cycle' without relating disturbances in demand to 'prices and profits'. This was a restatement of the credit cycle of the *Treatise*. Keynes added, 'It would lead me too far afield to examine the causes which prevent output from declining to zero. Amongst other things one must not neglect the effect of all these events on the volume of savings.' Keynes continued, secondly, 'The question of *how much* reduction of output is caused, whether by a realised fall of price or an anticipated fall of price, is important, but not strictly a monetary problem. I have not attempted to deal with it in my book, though I have done a good deal of work at it.' Thirdly, 'I repeat I am not dealing with the complete set of causes which determine the volume of output. For this would have led me on an endlessly long journey into the theory of short period supply and a long way from monetary theory; – though I would agree that it will probably be difficult in future to prevent monetary theory and the theory of short-period supply from running together.'[36] This set his agenda for his new book.

Keynes started rethinking his own theory in the summer of 1931, with Hawtrey's memorandum before him. 'I could further re-express my theory in your language,' he wrote to him on 1 October 1931, 'by saying that . . . whenever there is increased capital expenditure then, other things being equal, consumers' income is increased by an equal amount. And again, whenever anyone saves money, other things being equal, that has the effect of reducing consumers' income by an equal amount.'[37] Keynes wrote to Hawtrey on 1 June 1932 that in rewriting the *Treatise* he was placing less reliance on price changes and more on changes in expenditure, or effective demand. To this Hawtrey replied, 'Undoubtedly it will be an improvement to base it on Expenditure. . . . In a . . . theory . . . dealing with short-period movements price levels are merely symptomatic. The only alternative to price levels is Expenditure. That governs demand, and its fluctuations are felt in the threefold effect on stocks, output and prices. I am eager to know more of the changes you are making.'[38]

The Cambridge Circus

While Keynes was discussing the *Treatise* with Hawtrey, the Circus was arguing it out in Cambridge. The Circus was the name retrospectively given to a group of Keynes's younger colleagues who started meeting after the *Treatise* was published in October 1930: Richard Kahn, Piero Sraffa, Austin Robinson, Joan Robinson and James Meade. The first four were teachers at Cambridge; James Meade had just graduated in PPE at Oxford and was spending a postgraduate year at Trinity College, Cambridge before taking up a fellowship in Oxford: it was through him that Keynes's ideas passed to the New Fabian Research Bureau. Informal discussions started in Richard Kahn's rooms in November 1930; what would now be called a 'seminar' consisting of the original five, and a few selected graduate and third-year students, met regularly in Trinity College in the Lent term of 1931; there was a wider seminar in April, which discussed the conclusions of the smaller group. Keynes did not attend, nor did the other senior Cambridge economists, Pigou and Robertson.

Despite much 'pooled memory' to the contrary, the Circus seems to have played a relatively minor part in the development of the *General Theory*. A point emphasised by Patinkin is that it came to an end several months before Keynes himself started thinking along *General Theory* lines. Nevertheless, the Circus was profoundly educative for those who took part in it; and it is not impossible that at various times individual members of the Circus, more particularly James Meade, grasped the logical implications of some of the new ideas circulating more quickly than did Keynes.

Most of the collective discussion revolved round the so-called 'widow's cruse' fallacy of the *Treatise*. As the Bible tells it, God ensured that the widow's jar was always full of water however much the prophet Elijah drank from it; by contrast, the Danaides of Greek legend had to carry water to the city of Argos in broken jars. These stories suggested to Keynes a striking analogy with the cumulative processes which might be set in train by the emergence of windfall profits and losses. Profits were like the widow's cruse: however much of them were spent on consumption, they would remain undepleted, because their spending would cause prices to rise, creating profits for other entrepreneurs. Conversely, losses, once they had developed, could not be staunched; however much the loss-making entrepreneurs refrained from consumption, total losses would continue, because their 'saving' would cause prices to fall, inflicting losses on other entrepreneurs. Thus profits are a widow's cruse 'which remains undepleted however much of them may be devoted to riotous living', whereas when entrepreneurs try to save more 'the cruse becomes a Danaid jar which can never be filled up'.[39] Keynes's delight in this analogy was not lessened by the Biblical authority he could invoke on behalf of 'riotous living'; between them, the two stories from Antiquity overturned the Puritan order of things. Riotous living paid for itself, while saving simply increased misery all round.

It did not take long for the Circus to puncture these striking paradoxes. They pointed out that they depended on entrepreneurs continuing to supply a fixed quantity of consumption goods despite the emergence of profits and losses. According to Joan Robinson, it was her husband Austin who 'immediately spotted the fallacy in the widow's cruse at a time of unemployment. If businessmen increase consumption when profits rise, there will be an increase in the output of goods and services, with not necessarily any rise in prices at all.'[60] The way Austin Robinson put it was this: if an entrepreneur loaded with profits decided on his way home to have a shoeshine, was the effect solely to raise the price of shoeshines rather than affect the number of shoes shone?[61] Equally, the emergence of losses causes output and not just the price level of output to fall.

However, it is not clear exactly when the 'fallacy' was spotted. Evidence comes from an article which Joan Robinson is supposed to have written in the 'summer of 1931', though it was not published till February 1933.[62] But there is no firm evidence it was written as early as then. The only surviving correspondence on the topic dates from April 1932, when Mrs Robinson sent a draft of the article to Keynes, who denied he had committed the 'fallacy' complained of:

> I think you are a little hard on me [Keynes wrote on 14 April 1932] as regards the assumption of constant output. It is quite true that I have not followed out the consequences of changes in output in my earlier theoretical part. I admit that this wants doing. But in my *Treatise* itself, I have long discussions [on] the effects of changes in output; it is only at a particular point in the preliminary theoretical argument that I have assumed constant output, and I am at pains to make this absolutely clear. Surely one must be allowed at a particular stage of one's argument to make simplifying assumptions of this kind. . . . [63]

Assuming that collective memory has not erred, the most important effect of the Circus discussions was to reinforce the impetus Hawtrey gave Keynes to working out a short-period theory of output. This was bound to conflict with the 'quantity theory–price level' approach of the *Treatise*. A theory which assumed fixed output could not explain what caused output to vary.

Much more important than the Circus's collective contribution to Keynes's progress was Kahn's personal contribution. Kahn was someone who liked to work behind the scenes, and advance his ideas through others. He also published very little. So his own ideas tended to be invisible. He was almost certainly the creative force behind *The Theory of Imperfect Competition* by Joan Robinson, with whom he started an affair during or soon after the end of the Circus. (Early in 1932 Keynes surprised them on the floor in Kahn's study, 'though I expect', he told Lydia, 'the conversation was only on The Pure Theory of Monopoly'.[64])

However, the nature of Kahn's contribution to Keynes's thinking is much disputed. Everyone agrees on the importance of his multiplier theory, in which James Meade also played an essential part. This greatly strengthened the theoretical case for public works. However, Patinkin's conventional view that the multiplier represented a 'major step toward the *General Theory*' and was 'logically equivalent to the theory of effective demand', though neither Kahn nor Keynes at first realised this,[65] has been challenged by Neville Cain, who points out that the first published version of Kahn's multiplier lacked a personal-saving function. 'Kahn's great service to Keynes lay on the side of supply; exploring the interrelations of output elasticity, employment and prices, he rendered with a cogent formality ideas to which Keynes had previously given only partial and intuitive expression. On the side of demand, however, it is Warming to whom we look for potential significance.'[66]

Kahn's multiplier article, 'The Relation of Home Investment to Unemployment', was published in June 1931 in the *Economic Journal*. It was an attempt to answer the three main objections to loan-financed public works as a remedy for unemployment: the meagreness of the employment produced; the budgetary burden entailed; and the crowding out of private borrowing. The inability of Keynes and Henderson to meet these objections in their 1929 pamphlet *Can Lloyd George Do It?* turned the balance of the argument against large-scale public works under the Labour government and led to their cessation in the aftermath of the fiscal crisis of 1931. Hubert Henderson abandoned Keynes and sided with the Treasury.

Kahn started work on the multiplier theory while on holiday in the Tyrol in August 1930. When he returned he was helped by Colin Clark, a statistician on the staff of the EAC. Keynes, as we have seen, used a first draft of the argument on the Committee of Economists to estimate the employment effects of an expansionary programme. Kahn's starting point was the Keynes–Henderson assertion, in 'Can Lloyd George Do It?', that a public works programme would provide 'primary' employment (on the job and making materials for the job) and also 'secondary' employment resulting from the newly employed spending their wages, but that these secondary effects were incalculable.[67] As Kahn later said, there was no obvious reason why 'the multiplier is not infinite'.[68] This can be illustrated by the simplified account Keynes gave to his mother at the end of 1932:

But imagine [he wrote on 11 December] that [initial] sum of money passing from hand to hand, perhaps twenty times in the course of a year, in exchange for the production of goods and services, which would have gone otherwise without a buyer. Each recipient in turn can become a purchaser and create fresh employment. For one man's expenditure is another man's income; and whenever we cut off expenditure and substitute nothing for it, we cut off someone's income and someone's employment.

The question was: what was to stop an extra £1 of purchasing power from raising incomes to infinity? The obvious intuitive answer is that it will not all be spent buying goods and services. If over each successive spending round a fraction of the original spending power was saved, the total of secondary employment created could be summed to a finite number, which would be a ratio or multiple of the employment created by the initial expenditure. This is the simplest form of the multiplier theory.

This is not the way Kahn set out the argument. He achieved his finite number by making two deductions ('alleviations') from the enlarged expenditure stream: saving on the dole (that is, what the unemployed were already spending) and spending on imports. These represented those fractions of the newly employed's wages which did not go to increasing spending on home-produced goods. From this he concluded that 'the more a country approximates to a closed system and the smaller the dole in relation to a full wage, the greater is the ratio of secondary to primary employment'.[69] It was arithmetical child's play to calculate that secondary employment would increase, over successive rounds of spending by the newly employed, to the point when the fractions of extra income unspent at home (saving on the dole, and spending on imports) equalled the initiating expenditure by the government. Kahn's estimate of a British multiplier of 2 assumed that the whole of the increased spending would go to raising output and employment, and none to raising prices. James Meade generalised the calculation by allowing the increased spending to be divided between raising output and raising the price of output. This would create a third 'leakage' – 'unspent profits' minus any 'diminution in rate of saving due to rise in prices'.[70] 'Mr. Meade's Relation' showed that, whatever assumptions were made about elasticity of supply, the offsets added up exactly to the cost of the investment; – that is, the public works programme would 'pay for itself'.* But the bite of the demonstration lay in the claim that, with unemployed resources, most of the extra spending would raise employment, not prices.

It is easy to see why Keynes was so enthusiastic about the multiplier theory. 'Unbalancing the budget' – the great sin of orthodox finance – promised more employment at less cost to the government than the Treasury calculations of 1929 allowed. And the beauty of it was that the expenditure would miraculously provide the savings to pay for it, without taking them

*In saying that a loan-financed public works programme would 'pay for itself' Kahn and Meade were not claiming that the government would immediately recover the cost of the investment; simply that, in a closed economy, the increased saving of the community would add up to the cost. At unchanged rates of taxation and public spending, the budget deficit would eventually disappear, as a result of increased revenue coming from a higher national income.

from other uses. That he was quick to grasp the possibilities of the new analysis is shown in a letter he wrote to a Cambridge colleague, Harold Jeffreys of St John's College, on 18 December 1931. This, his first recorded use of Kahn's article, is not included in the *Collected Writings*:

> For example, if the Cunard were to spend three million pounds on a new ship, the money would be found partly from savings on the dole . . . partly out of additional business profits which would be saved; and partly out of the increased yield of taxation from these increased profits. If one includes in one's calculations the complete train of events arising, not out of an initial expenditure of three million pounds, but out of the increased employment given by the increased expenditure out of the increased wages of the men employed by the ship-builders, then the accrued sums forthcoming under the three heads I have indicated can be shown to add up exactly to three million pounds, minus the increased expenditure on imports resulting from the complete train of events. . . . Thus, assuming that there are unemployed productive resources available of a suitable kind, the only net cost to the community as a whole is the cost of the additional imports.[71]*

The Kahn–Meade story established the identity of 'aggravations' and 'alleviations' (to use their terms for increased investment and increased saving). It offered no behavioural theory to explain how this identity came about. The nearest they came was in the notion of 'unspent profits', or corporate saving. But this 'leakage' depends on a distributional effect which is not specified by the theory. If the only source of additional private sector saving is 'unspent profits' this must mean that the newly employed spend the whole of their additional incomes. As Cain says, Meade's notion of 'unspent profits' did not 'point to the *General Theory* but rather to the class-based saving function which Kalecki was to deploy in his own particular approach to effective demand.'[72] It was Keynes (in a letter to Kahn of 28 September 1931) who first broached the idea of a personal-saving function with 'each level of aggregate output' having 'an appropriate proportion of saving to incomes attached to it'.[73] But the personal-saving or consumption function first came into the multiplier literature with an article by the Danish statistician Jens Warming in the *Economic Journal* of June 1932. Warming 'combined an exclusively income-related personal saving function with Kahn's own multiplier algebra to render neatly the income adjustment mechanism by which saving is equilibrated with an initiating change in investment'. Keynes probably saw Warming's article when it was first submitted to the *Economic Journal*, of which he was co-editor. As we shall see, he started to make use of a consumption function in the spring of 1932. So

---

*In fact this was not necessarily a net cost. As in his argument over German reparations Keynes ignored the income repercussions on those countries whose exports had risen as a result of the Cunard programme.

the theoretical influence may have run more directly from Warming to Keynes than from Kahn to Keynes at this point. Kahn, influenced in turn by Warming, presented a 'multiplier derived from marginal propensities to save and import' in a paper on 'Public Works and Inflation' to the American Statistical Association in Cincinatti in December 1932; Keynes's 'The Means to Prosperity', published three months later, presented this revised version of Kahn's theory.[74]

The multiplier is the most notorious piece of Keynesian magic, the speed of the movement deceiving the eye. What it did was to telescope all the beneficial repercussions in a single moment, thus abstracting both from the confidence issue emphasised by the Treasury* and from the problem of raising the finance for the new investments. But the trick was spotted by Henderson and Robertson, who never accepted the multiplier analysis as a valid basis for calculating either the employment or revenue effects of a public works programme or as obviating the need for the banking system to provide a major source of funds.

Dennis Robertson

Keynes and Robertson engaged in a copious, exhausting, intermittently playful correspondence between 1931 and 1933 mainly about whether Keynes meant the same thing by saving and investment as Robertson meant by 'lacking' and ordering new 'machines'. Specifically, did Keynes mean by excess saving what Robertson did by increased hoarding? They argued the matter by correspondence in May 1931, and in the *Economic Journal* in September. This discussion overlapped with Keynes's debate with Hayek, fought out in the *Economica* (August, November 1931; March 1932 – 'a 3-cornered debate, all of us talking different dialects' Robertson called it) with an intervention from Nicholas Kaldor, a research student of Hayek's at the London School of Economics.[75] They went on arguing into 1933.

At issue was the usefulness of the quantity theory of money for analysing short-period disturbances to the saving–investment relationship. Keynes insisted that saving and investment can stay equal even if the quantity of money changed, and can diverge even if the quantity of money stayed the same. Savings need not be spent buying new investments – they could be used to speculate or finance business losses. Demand might be deficient even if all savings were being 'spent'. This situation he characterised as 'saving running ahead of investment'. Robertson argued, as did Hayek, that voluntary saving and investment could not diverge if the 'effective' quantity of money – its supply multiplied by its velocity of circulation – was held

---

*"Towards the end of my article I was careful to state that it was based on the assumption that "the state of general confidence [was] not affected". I did not mean that this was at all probable – but merely that in the study of one type of causation it is necessary to abstract from others.' (R. F. Kahn, *The Making of the General Theory*, 93).

constant. Thus in his review of the *Treatise* in the September 1931 issue of the *Economic Journal* Robertson said that new savings would always be used to buy new 'machines', unless people were simultaneously adding to their cash balances. What Keynes called excess saving was simply an increase in hoarding, or decline in velocity, due to the decline of business profitability. The fact that loss-making businessmen were consuming less did not mean that they were adding to their savings, as Keynes's definitions implied. (See pp. 321–2 above for the *Treatise* definitions.) 'How many of those', he wrote, 'who have taken up the cry that a slump is due to the excess of Saving over Investment realise that the savings which are so deplorably abundant during a slump consist largely of entrepreneurs' incomes which are not being spent, for the simple reason that they have not been earned?'[76]

Keynes had now received three criticisms – from Hawtrey, the Circus and Robertson – of his *Treatise* definitions, as obscuring the fact that when businessmen, for whatever reason, made losses the national income, and therefore the amount saved, fell. In a memorandum Keynes sent Robertson on 22 March 1932 he 'bowed the knee' by acknowledging that 'excess savings' were simply incomes which had not been earned. They had no existence. This is a key moment in his emancipation from the definitions and ideas of the *Treatise*. He proposed a new definition of income to include profits and losses, hitherto segregated by his special definition of income as 'normal' earnings. It followed from this that investment and saving were 'the same concept looked at from opposite points of view.'* People, he began to say, save what they want to save out of the incomes they have, though these may not be the incomes they expected to have.[77]

A further implication is that 'S[aving] always and necessarily accommodates itself to I[nvestment]. Whether I consists in housing schemes or war finance, there need be nothing to hold us back, because I always drags S along with it at an equal pace.' Saving 'is no longer the dog . . . but the tail'.[78] James Meade was later to use this image (which he perhaps thought original to himself) as the 'quintessence of Keynes's intellectual innovation'.[79] The classical economists said that saving determines investment; Keynes was to say that investment determines saving.†

What Keynes had done was to dispense with the old monetary aggregate, the 'quantity of money', in favour of a new aggregate, 'total money income'. Now he could say that income depends on expenditure, and 'economy' or 'saving' varies with income: a much neater way of modelling what actually

---

*Y [community's income] = C[onsumption] + I[investment]; therefore I = Y − C. But S[aving] = Y − C; therefore I = S.

†'the total volume of saving ceases to be a factor having any independent existence . . . it solely depends on what the value of current investment happens to be'. (*CW*, v, xxiii. Written on 5 April 1932.) Keynes thought this 'paradoxical' at the time, but this was the view he came to hold.

happens in booms and slumps. Monetary changes then become effects, not causes, of changes in expenditure. The classical economists, he said, were wrong to think that if people decided to save more out of income (consume less) they would succeed in doing so. For if expenditure governs output, and income governs saving, decreased expenditure on consumption may lead not to increased saving but to reduced output and therefore reduced income.[80]

So much was (moderately) clear to Keynes on 22 March 1932. What he yet had to do was to integrate a multiplier theory with a personal-saving 'leakage' into his analysis.

With the publication of Keynes's 'The Means to Prosperity' in March 1933, the debate between Keynes and Robertson took a new turn. Criticising the multiplier theory, here publicly deployed for the first time, Robertson accused Keynes of fudging the question of where the finance was to come from. Credit-creation by the banking system would still be required to produce the necessary investment funds without increasing the national debt. Here Robertson was harking back to his old idea that increased investment required 'forced saving' – imposed restriction on consumption brought about by a rise in prices. Keynes's reply was coldly dismissive. 'You are addressing yourself to one of the deader of my dead selves. . . . All the versions of the quantity theory, which make no distinction between swops and intermediate transactions and genuine production–consumption transactions, seem to me to tell one nothing.'[81] The correspondence meandered on a little longer.

The hoarding–saving debate was not entirely fruitless. Keynes rejected Robertson's idea that the quantity of hoards was a measure of economic failure. This was part of his rejection of the 'quantity theory of money' approach to economic instability. But in the *General Theory* 'the propensity to hoard' or 'liquidity preference' plays a vital part in the mechanics of an economy's rundown, once something has happened to make investment less attractive. And this links up with Keynes's sense that, at some level too deep to be captured by mathematics, 'love of money' as an end, not a means, is at the root of the world's economic problem.

Friedrich Hayek

One of Keynes's favourite *reductiones ad absurdum* was of a world perishing from starvation, in which the last economist alive proclaimed with his dying breath that he had always had the courage of his convictions about saving being too low and he was right. Perhaps Keynes had Hayek in mind. Of all his critics Hayek was the most intransigent defender of the non-interventionist order. It was Hayek, too, who spotted the revolutionary character of Keynes's *Treatise on Money*. 'Mr. Keynes's assertion that there is no automatic mechanism in the economic system to keep the rate of saving and the rate of investing equal', he wrote in his review of the *Treatise*, 'might with equal justification be extended to the more general contention that there is no automatic mechanism in the economic system to adapt production to any other shift in demand.'[82]

As John Hicks has said, Keynes's debate with Hayek in the early 1930s was quite a drama. When the thirty-two-year-old Hayek came from Vienna to London in 1931 he brought with him a belief in the market system as a spontaneously evolved and self-adjusting order far more fervent than anything to be found in Cambridge. This belief was grounded in three characteristics of the Austrian school: a profound disillusionment with interventionist politics; a relentless methodological individualism; and, most immediately relevant to Hayek's debate with Keynes, a theory of capital and interest which was largely lacking from the Anglo-Saxon tradition. Derived from the work of Böhm-Bawerk, this showed how the market system secured an optimal distribution of resources not just at any moment in time but over time. This intertemporal theory of value rounded off neo-classical value theory and was intended to make it invulnerable to attack.

According to the Austrians, decisions to save were simply decisions to give up a certain amount of goods now in order to secure the consumption of a greater quantity of goods in the future. They were thus signals to producers to switch from the production of consumption to the production of what Keynes called investment, but Hayek called intermediate, goods. The rate of interest is the 'natural' rate of exchange between present and future goods. The fact that decisions to save and invest were done by different sets of people was quite irrelevant to Hayek. Changes in the structure of production, reflecting changes in intertemporal preferences, take place smoothly if money is kept 'neutral' – in the absence of inflation or deflation by the banking system. This is a crucial point in Hayek's theory. Unless the 'effective' amount of money is kept constant, the market rate of interest diverges from the 'natural' rate, so that producers get price signals which do not reflect the wishes of consumers. Hayek agreed with Robertson on analysis, but took a diametrically opposite view on policy. Whereas Robertson saw credit expansion as a way of 'forcing' the saving necessary to finance investment. Hayek condemned it as distorting the structure of production and bringing about an eventual collapse.

According to Hayek it is monetary incontinence which causes things to go wrong. The crisis which produces the slump is a crisis of overinvestment – overinvestment in relation to the amount of consumption people want to postpone – financed by credit-creation by the banking system. This, as we have seen, was Hayek's explanation of the boom and bust in the United States, accepted by Lionel Robbins, who brought him to the London School of Economics. The slump was merely the process of eliminating the unsustainable investments, those not financed by genuine savings. Government intervention would only prolong the agony; the quickest cure would be for people to save more, to bring about a recovery in investment.

This was the theory Hayek was expounding in his first lectures at the LSE in the spring of 1931 at the same time that the Circus in Cambridge was puzzling over the *Treatise of Money*, which, of course, drew completely opposite conclusions to Hayek: the slump was due to underinvestment, not overinvestment; the cure lay in increasing spending, not saving. Hayek came to Cambridge in January 1931 to give a one-lecture version of his theory to the Marshall Society before starting on his LSE lectures. His exposition was greeted with complete silence. Keynes was in London, but Richard Kahn, who was in the audience, felt he had to break the ice. 'Is it your view', he asked Hayek, 'that if I went out tomorrow and bought a new overcoat, that would increase unemployment?' 'Yes,' replied Hayek, turning to a blackboard full of triangles, 'but it would take a very long mathematical argument to explain why.'[83] The contrast with Keynes's 'Whenever you save five shillings you put a man out of work for a day,' uttered on the wireless the same month, could not have been starker.

At the LSE Hayek was much more successful. His lectures there created a 'sensation', the excitement afforded by 'a work of art seen almost in the process of composition'.[84] On one LSE student, Ronald Coase, the effect was 'magical. . . . After hearing these lectures we knew why there was a depression.'[85] Beveridge, the LSE's director, immediately offered Hayek the Tooke professorship, which he accepted. For three or four years afterwards, Hayek's theories disputed those of Keynes to the succession of classical economics. Many famous later Keynesians like Nicholas Kaldor and A. P. Lerner started off as Hayekians. Whether, when he accepted the London appointment, the courteous Hayek realised that his function was to be the LSE's chief weapon in a power struggle with Cambridge is unclear.

In his review of Keynes's *Treatise* for the LSE-based journal *Economica*, Hayek accused Keynes of lacking a theory of capital and interest. Keynes's account of a change in the direction of money flows (as between consumption and saving) impinged on a rigid structure of production. But the decision to save implies, and sets in motion via a fall in the interest rate, a transfer of factors into more roundabout processes for making consumption goods. An analysis of the reasons which made different stages of production more or less attractive would have shown that changes in saving habits can never of themselves give rise to total profits and losses in Keynes's sense, or a divergence between saving and investment. Only a change in the 'effective' quantity of money can do that. Keynes's conclusion that saving and investment can diverge depends on the banking system departing from monetary 'neutrality'. If his 'mistake' were eliminated, his theory was simply a version of a forced-saving theory.

Keynes was not at all pleased: his copy of Hayek's twenty-six-page review has thirty-four pencilled marks or comments, and at the end he scribbled, 'Hayek has not read my book with that measure of "good will" which an author is entitled to expect of a reader. Until he can do so, he will not see what I mean or whether I am right. He evidently has a passion which leads him to pick on me, but I am left wondering what this passion is.' Keynes wrote this in almost total ignorance of what Hayek's own theory was. He came to understand more of Hayek's 'passion' when he read Hayek's LSE lectures, published in September 1931 under the title *Prices and Production*. His own rejoinder to Hayek's review in the *Economica* of November 1931 soon 'drifted' into an attack on Hayek's book, which he called 'one of the most frightful muddles I have ever read. . . . It is an extraordinary example of how, starting with a mistake, a remorseless logician can end in Bedlam.'[86]

In *Prices and Production* Hayek provided a parable to rival Keynes's banana parable:

> The situation [following an injection of money by the banking system] would be similar to that of a people on an isolated island, if, after having partially constructed an enormous machine which was to provide them with all necessities, they found they had exhausted all their savings and available free capital before the new machine could turn out its product. They would then have no choice but to abandon temporarily the work on the new process and to devote all their labours to producing their daily food without any capital.[87]

Interestingly enough Hayek's version of 'Nature's cure' is very similar to what Keynes described before the Macmillan Committee – a return to less capitalistic methods of production, with unemployed workers taking jobs as gardeners and chauffeurs. The difference, of course, is that given his analysis of the causes of the slump, Hayek did not believe the government could improve on 'Nature's' remedy. He was wholly opposed to the method of overcoming depression by a policy of cheap money (inflation) which would only perpetuate the maladjusted structure of production. There was nothing a government could do to get an economy out of a depression before its 'natural' end had come.[88] Hayek, like Keynes, hoped to prevent a slump from developing by preventing the credit cycle from starting. But his method was very different. It was to forbid the banks to create credit, something which could best be achieved by adherence to a full gold standard. He was quite pessimistic, though, about this being practical politics, so his conclusion, like Keynes's, was that a credit-money capitalist system is violently unstable – only with this difference, that nothing could be done about it. One can understand why Hayek's doctrines attracted a certain kind of socialist: they seemed to reach Marx's conclusions by a different route. Because of the Austrian school's close attention to the institutional and political setting of a credit-money economy, Hayek's picture of the capitalist system in action was altogether more sombre than that of conventional Anglo-Saxon economics, with its story of easy adjustments to 'shocks'.

The Keynes–Hayek exchanges were the opening shots in the battle of the journals. Keynes now asked Piero Sraffa to review *Prices and Production* for the *Economic Journal* of March 1932. Sraffa dismissed Hayek's book as a model of unintelligibility, a 'maze of contradictions'. Both Hayek's reply and Sraffa's rejoinder were published in the *Economic Journal* of June 1932. Goodwill was plainly in short supply all round. Joan Robinson joined in on the Cambridge side; Hayek was not without his supporters.

In his review, Sraffa singled out for attack Hayek's claim that a structure of production built on credit was less stable than one built on voluntary saving. Those consumers who had been 'forced to save' had no way of getting back their 'lost' consuming power. The transfer of consuming power was permanent; so, therefore, was the new structure of production. 'One class has, for a time, robbed another class of part of their incomes; and has saved the plunder.' The forced savings of the losers became the voluntary savings of the gainers; and if wage-earners benefit in due course from the increased flow of consumption goods made possible by the roundabout processes, the gainers do not thereby lose the additional real capital they have created. Thus Hayek's account of the genesis of the slump collapses. Sraffa's criticism seems less penetrating in the light of the inflationary experience of the 1970s and 1980s. Of more interest to Keynes was Sraffa's suggestion that Hayek's notion of monetary 'neutrality' was theoretically impossible because 'there is no such thing as an equilibrium (or unique natural) rate of interest', rather a multiplicity of 'commodity rates of interest' all of which can diverge from each other in disequilibrium. Thus a non-monetary economy would also be subject to cyclical fluctuations. Keynes would appropriate Sraffa's construct of commodity rates of interest for his own purposes in chapter 17 of the *General Theory*.[89]

There seemed to be a complete intellectual gulf between the two men. But Keynes was undoubtedly stung by Hayek, as well as by Robertson, to attempt to justify his assertion that, after a shock, the system does not automatically adjust back to its previous level of employment. He conceded in his rejoinder to Hayek (November 1931) that the *Treatise* lacked 'any satisfactory theory of capital and interest' and promised to remedy this. He made the interesting suggestion that his and Hayek's theories occupied different terrains: Hayek's being a theory of dynamic equilibrium, marked by fluctuations of the 'natural rate' of interest; his (Keynes's) dealing with the case where the market rate departs from the 'natural rate'.[90] Keynes would develop a distinction between interest as the 'price of money' and the 'natural rate' (though he abandoned the term) as the 'price of capital'. Hayek's role in the Keynesian Revolution was thus to force out of him the logical distinction between a money and a 'real exchange' economy.

The public polemics between the two men did not prevent them exchanging 'an inconclusive series of letters . . . on definitions' in the winter of 1931–2. There is no support in this exchange for Hayek's later claim that 'after the appearance of the second part of my article [in February 1932], Keynes told me that in the meantime he had changed his mind and no longer believed what he said [in the *Treatise*]'.[91] What Keynes actually wrote to Hayek, on 29 March 1932, was that he had not yet studied the second part of Hayek's review 'as closely as I shall', but that he doubted whether he would reply to it. 'I am trying to re-shape and improve my central position, and that is probably a better way to spend one's time than in controversy.'[92] It is important to be clear about this, because Hayek later repeatedly claimed that he did not review Keynes's *General Theory* because he feared that 'before I had completed my analysis he would have changed his mind'. More likely, Hayek did not want to expose himself to another mauling from the Keynesians. But the decisive reason, as he himself later suggested, was that 'my disagreement with that book did not refer so much to any detail of the analysis as to the general approach followed in the whole work. The real issue was the validity of what we now call macro-economics. . . .'[93]

Keynes was too pregnant with his own ideas to have much time for Hayek's. 'The wildest farrago of nonsense yet', he scribbled on a draft copy of Hayek's article, 'Capital Consumption', published in German in 1932.[94] On the other hand, he had no personal animus against him. 'Hayek has been here for the weekend,' Keynes wrote to Lydia on 5 March 1933. 'I sat by him in hall last night and lunched with him at Piero's to-day. We get on very well in private life. But what rubbish his theory is – I felt to-day that even he was beginning to disbelieve it himself.' This seems to have been the last occasion when they discussed economic theory. Thereafter they corresponded amiably enough about their various antiquarian discoveries. Keynes befriended Hayek during the war, and it was he who proposed him for a fellowship of the British Academy in 1944. He made an unforgettable personal impression on Hayek – 'the magnetism of the brilliant conversationalist with his wide range of interests and bewitching voice'. But Hayek never ceased to believe that Keynes's influence on economics was 'both miraculous and tragic'.[95] Hayek remained a bystander as the Keynesian Revolution unfolded; and only started to organise a resistance after Keynes's death.

III

HALF-FORGED WEAPONS

Putting together all the correspondence and argument it can be seen that the critical stages in refashioning the theory of the *Treatise* occurred in the early spring and summer of 1932, and that the key move was the shift of analysis in terms of prices to analysis in terms of income and expenditure.

We have the evidence from two of the eight lectures Keynes gave in the summer term of 1932 on 'The Pure Theory of Money', and from the eight lectures on 'The Monetary Theory of Production' in the autumn term of 1932, which followed a period of book-drafting at Tilton in the summer vacation, four fragments of which survive. There are a few other texts.

In the two lectures of 25 April and 2 May the chrysalis of a short-period theory of output has emerged. Aggregate income and output depend on aggregate expenditure. Investment, not saving, is the volatile element in expenditure – there is a 'stable propensity to save'. When income goes down, expenditure goes down, but not by as much. Quantities expressed in money – income, output, expenditure – have replaced values – costs, prices, profits – as units of analysis.

At Tilton that summer, Keynes wrote 'nearly a third of my new book on monetary theory' as well as piecing together some 'Essays in Biography' as a complement to his *Essays in Persuasion*.[96] A visitor was the Swedish economist Per Jacobsson, head of the monetary department of the newly formed Bank for International Settlements. He recorded that 'Keynes was occupied by some difficult theoretical problems on the rate of interest which absorbed him fully. It was not enough . . . to lower interest rates, it was too slow a process. . . . in the future a great deal more of the utilisation of savings had to be done through the Treasuries. . . . large amounts were employable for the rebuilding of London by the aid of public authorities.'[97] This account tends to confirm the supposition that it was at this time that Keynes arrived at his liquidity-preference theory of the rate of interest.

'Gentlemen, the change in the title of these lectures' – from 'The Pure Theory of Money' to 'The Monetary Theory of Production' – 'is significant.' 'With these words on 10 October 1932,' recalled Lorie Tarshis, 'Keynes began the first of his eight lectures . . . and in effect announced the beginning of the Keynesian Revolution.'[98] Tarshis was a postgraduate from Toronto, where he had studied the *Treatise on Money* under Keynes's former pupil, Plumptre. He attended all the four lecture series between 1932 and 1935 which led up to the publication of the *General Theory*. His lecture notes, together with those of his fellow Canadian Robert Bryce and other students like Alec Cairncross, Martin Fallgatter, Walter Salant and David Champernowne, who attended one or more of the lecture series, are a unique record of the evolution of Keynes's ideas and interests over the period.[99] 'I attended that first lecture, naturally awed but bothered,' recalled Tarshis. 'As the weeks passed, only a stone would not have responded to the growing excitement [the lectures] generated.' The following summary is pieced together not only from the lecture notes, but also from typed fragments from which Keynes appeared to have lectured, and from the chapters of the book surviving from the summer of 1932. An important source for his ideas at this time is also his essay 'A Monetary Theory of Production' written 'in late 1932' for the *Festschrift* for the German economist Spiethoff.

The subject of Keynes's enquiry was: what determines the volume of output in a monetary economy? The new approach was based on the conceptual distinction between the economics of a monetary economy, in which money affects 'motives and decisions and expectations and predictions', and that of a neutral or 'real exchange' economy, where money has no influence on production, saving and investment are equal, relative prices reflect the 'real exchange values' of goods, and booms and slumps are ruled out by assumption. The point Keynes wanted to make was this. Those economists, like Marshall and Pigou, who believed that a monetary economy behaved like a 'real exchange' economy, assumed a certain policy by the monetary authority, namely, the policy of keeping money 'neutral'. But there was no unique long-period monetary policy which the monetary authority was bound to follow. Classical economics dealt with a special case – that is, with a long-period position corresponding to a 'neutral' monetary policy. But saving and investment may be equal at different levels of output. The fact that optimal output cannot be assumed required the development of both a short-period and a long-period theory of output.[100]

Here we have the premise on which the theory of effective demand rests. At first glance, it is not so startling. The older economists had certainly talked rather loosely of money as a 'veil', but in practice had assumed that money had to be *kept* 'neutral' by the banking authority: this was the point of Bagehot's doctrine of 'lender of the last resort'. The more profound point Keynes is making is that there may be no way money *can* be kept neutral by banking policy; it was in this sense that there was no 'automatic' stabilising mechanism.

Keynes then develops his new theory of output. The level of output is determined by aggregate 'disbursement', the forerunner of 'effective demand' in the *General Theory*. Changes in output are produced by changes in the relationship between disbursement and earnings (defined as in the *Treatise*). If disbursement on currently produced output goes down relatively to earnings (because people try to save more), entrepreneurs make losses, and output and total income (earnings plus profits) fall together.[101] What is to stop output running down 'until production was at a total standstill'? Keynes suggests an equilibrium condition verbally identical to the 'psychological law' of the *General Theory*: 'The simplest condition for stable equilibrium is that when aggregate income changes, the change in aggregate expenditure should be the same in direction but smaller in absolute amount. And there are reasons for expecting that this condition will normally be satisfied.'[102] However, he envisages that this will happen only after the decline in output has gone a certain way (similar to the 'impoverishment' of the Harris Lecture the previous year).[103] Also the context of most statements of this condition at this time shows that it depends as much on changes in the *distribution* of income which accompany rising and falling prices as on a stable propensity to consume.* These two things lead Patinkin to believe that Keynes had not yet achieved a 'full understanding' of the theory of effective demand.[104] However, none of this is very different, at least verbally, from what he said in the *General Theory*.†

The equilibrium above, Keynes makes clear, is a short-period equilibrium. Tarshis has him saying on 14 November 1932 that there is 'no inherent tendency for the economic system to react back to the optimum output . . .';[105] in the fragment from which he lectured he says that the 'decline in output may be itself one of the factors which had, by reason of its retarding effect on saving, produced the new equilibrium, so that the fact of the level of output being below the optimum may be in itself one of the conditions of the maintenance of equilibrium'.[106] There is, nevertheless, at this level, some tendency for the rate of interest to fall, as the ratio of money stock to income rises, and this will turn the economy round. But the 'increase in investment . . . may not be as rapid as the increase in savings as output begins to rise again', unless the interest rate is deliberately lowered even further, leaving the boom to peter out before full employment is reached.[107] All this is very characteristic of the disequilibrium method Keynes is still using. The basic idea is that, following a slump in output, the economy is likely to oscillate round a low level indefinitely unless 'something is done' to improve investment prospects. This gives a more succinct idea of Keynes's views than he managed in the *General Theory*, dominated as it is by a static analysis.

In order to understand how Keynes reached these conclusions, we need to bring in his discussion of wages and his new interest-rate theory. According to the pre-Keynesian theory of the self-equilibrating economy, tendencies to depression automatically generate reductions in costs tending to restore profits to 'normal', unless interfered with by trade unions, legislation or policy. 'The first of these is the reduction of the rate of wages; and the second is the automatic tendency in such conditions for a reduction in the rate of interest. The two are sometimes connected, because the reduced

CW, xiii, 401; also Bryce on Keynes's lecture of 24 October: 'The old idea that adjustment [of saving to investment] must be made by prices neglects possible adjustment by distribution of income.' Yet consider Bryce on 21 November: 'Simplest condition for stable Eq[uilibrium] is that the state of time preference is such [that] the change in expenditure [sic] is [in the] same direction but not as great in amount – this is the time preference effect. It is necessary to know or assume human nature qualities.'

†Compare the passage from chapter 8 of the mid–1932 draft, quoted by Patinkin on pp. 19–20 of *Anticipations*, and p. 98 of the *General Theory*: 'Thus, when employment falls to a low level, aggregate consumption will decline by a smaller amount than that by which real income has declined.' This implies that until employment has fallen to a 'low level' the marginal propensity to consume is unity. On Patinkin's test of 'full understanding' of the consumption function, Keynes has not achieved it even in the *General Theory*. Keynes also believed that changes in the propensity to consume as income rose and fell affected the level of equilibrium attained. (*GT*, vii, 97.)

demand for money, consequent on a fall in wages, may be one of the forces relied upon to produce the reduction in the rate of interest.'[108] In order to establish his alternative construction Keynes had to show why cost/price adjustment would not take place *before* being overwhelmed by income/output adjustment.

Two fragments written in the summer of 1932 called 'Effects of Changes in the Rate of Earnings' and 'The Long-Run Adjustability of the Rate of Interest', together with the first of the autumn lectures, anticipate several of the themes of chapters 2 and 19 of the *General Theory*. Taking first the case where money wages are fluid, Keynes denies that an all-round reduction in the real wage (money wages falling further than prices) will stimulate consumption, even if it improves profits, since the gains will accrue to those with a lower propensity to consume. But this reduction in the real wage is unlikely to happen anyway since, if wages are reduced all-round, prices will fall by as much.* If entrepreneurs *believe* that wage reductions will increase their profits, this will stimulate investment, and the 'mere prevalence of a belief will in itself make it partly true'. However, if wage reductions lead consumption to fall off by the same amount or more, 'the above belief being based on precarious foundations may collapse before its effect on [Investment] has gone far enough to balance the increase in [Saving]'. He admits, as we have seen, that wage reductions may put downward pressure on the rate of interest in the long run, by increasing the proportion of money stock to income, but argues that this will not produce full recovery unless the rate of interest is deliberately lowered further. The effect of wage reductions on 'disbursements' is therefore indeterminate. So long as demand is insufficient, entrepreneurs will make losses, however fluid wages are.[109] But wages are not in practice perfectly fluid. The short-period supply price of a machine 'drops like a stone' when there are too many of them. But labour's supply price includes the disutility of work, and maintenance when not working. So its short-period supply price is more nearly horizontal; the wage-cutting route to recovery is not open.[110] This was Keynes's fall-back position and has been perhaps the main reason for the general acceptance of Keynesian economics.

The most difficult problem Keynes had to face was: why, when investment fell off relative to saving, did not the interest rate fall immediately to remove the discrepancy between the two? His answer was the liquidity-preference theory of the rate in interest, stated in his fourth lecture (31 October): the rate of interest is determined by 'liquidity preference' *independently* of the

---

*Keynes, that is, accepts the argument that rising employment must be accompanied by a falling real wage. But money-wage reductions can bring this about only if the unemployment has been due to a change in the direction of demand not if the unemployment has been 'due to deficient disbursement in the aggregate'. For 'where there is a *general* falling off of demand for all purchasable things alike . . . if everyone accepts a reduced money income, no one . . . need suffer a reduction of real rates of income'. (*CW*, xxix, 52–3.)

expected return on investment; but, so determined, it may reduce the amount of investment below the level necessary to ensure full employment. The argument hinges on a sharp distinction between interest as the price of exchanging money for a debt and Marshall's 'quasi-rent', the expected capitalised stream of income accruing over the life-time of a 'machine'. The rate of interest is fixed by the banking system in conjunction with the relative preference of the public for holding and parting with money. (In his lecture, Keynes wrote $p = A(M)$, where p is the rate of interest, A is liquidity preference and M the quantity of money.) Then, 'Rate of interest being price of a debt fixes [the] basis of capitalisat[ion] of quasi-rents'.[111] Keynes would add to this the thought, already present in his Halley-Stewart Lecture, that 'circumstances can arise, and have recently arisen, when neither control of the short-rate of interest nor control of the long-rate will be effective, with the result that direct stimulation of investment by government is the necessary means'. But such a liquidity trap arises only in a 'very abnormal situation'.[112]

In his sixth and seventh lectures Keynes outlines 'the parameters of a monetary economy' as (1) the quantity of money, (2) the factors of market psychology: liquidity preferences, time preferences, expected quasi-rent, and (3) the supply schedule of output – these become the independent variables of the *General Theory*. Given the state of time preferences, the amount of output is determined by the amount of investment; given the quantity of money the rate of interest is determined by the state of liquidity preference; given the rate of interest, the amount of investment is determined by 'the expectation of quasi-rent'.[113] The practical significance of the parameters 'is to tell what state of output would ensue from given parameters & how the parameters would have to be influenced to get the desired output'.[114] The duty of the monetary authority is to 'maintain a rate of interest which leads to an optimum level of investment.'*

Keynes's last autumn lecture, 'Historical Retrospect', given on 28 November, partly reflects the thoughts inspired by his reworking of his essay on Malthus. As the begetter of a radical theory in flaming opposition to orthodoxy, he felt for the first time the need to place himself in a tradition, or perhaps to invent a tradition in which he could place himself. Malthus, whom he had always admired, fitted the bill. It was Sraffa's discovery of the Malthus side of the Ricardo–Malthus correspondence in 1930 which inspired Keynes to proclaim Malthus as the precursor of the theory of

---

*A flavour of Keynes's exposition is given by Bryce's notes: 'He [Keynes] says all can be deduced from M [the supply of money], A [equal to] the amount of liquidity preferred in given conditions, B [equals] the state of expectation of quasi-rents, G [equals] the state of time preference, J [equals] the supply function, and L equals the earnings reaction – what the state of costs will be for any condition of these. If these are known he [Keynes] thinks the rest can be obtained but that all are needed. In particular, if these are known, output, price level, what income [etc.] will be [known].'

effective demand in terms which very much reflect his mood in 1932: Ricardo is 'investigating the theory of *distribution* of the product in conditions of equilibrium', Malthus with 'what determines the *volume* of output day by day in the real world'; Malthus deals 'with the monetary economy in which we happen to live; Ricardo with the abstraction of a neutral money economy'.[115] No matter that Keynes got Malthus's theory wrong – he was an underconsumptionist not a primitive Keynesian. He admired his compassion and his refusal to sweep short-period problems under the carpet of abstraction. He wrote to Lydia on 30 October 1932 that he had become 'completely absorbed' in rewriting his life of Malthus, 'and sit by the hour at my desk copying bits out and composing sentences and wanting to do nothing else with stocks of books round me. What a relief not to be writing arguments. What an easy and agreeable life fanciful writers must have.' He was still working at it on 20 November 'with much enjoyment'. 'If only Malthus,' Keynes wrote, 'instead of Ricardo, had been the parent stem from which nineteenth-century economists proceeded, what a much wiser and richer place the world would be today!'[116]

His lecture, in which, at his most paradoxical, he relates his ideas to 'popular convictions' of the past held by those 'traditionally uncultured at Cambridge economics'[117] is a first sketch for chapter 22 of the *General Theory*. In sharp contrast to his remarks to H. M. Robertson in the 1920s about intellectual history being for the incipiently senile,[118] he now says it is a mistake to neglect past thoughts and relegate them to book collecting, or antiquarianism. Specifically he commends the medieval usury laws, mercantilism, extravagant consumption and the labour theory of value.[119]

Adam Smith had realised that, if interest rates were too high, money would flow into debts and speculation, not investment. Mercantilism made sense with a fixed (metallic) currency. If liquidity preference was increasing, there was no way to lower interest rates except by trying to attract a greater proportion of the world's gold, or depreciating the currency. Cairncross scribbled, 'If in the Middle Ages money was fixed, mercantilism, depreciation and direct attack on rates of interest [through usury laws] were the only ways of restoring prosperity.' Keynes further commended Mandeville's *Fable of the Bees*, whose theme was that private vices produced public benefits, and to be personally virtuous was to land the kingdom in ruin. 'Only economists believed that saving would be good.' Bryce penned, 'O economists!' The commonsense view that it was right to reduce incomes when labour was scarce and increase them when it was abundant, upheld by Malthus, was destroyed by Ricardo, who ignored the fact that wages are an essential source of effective demand. Economists have generally been wrong, popular convictions right. Throughout history saving had tried to run ahead of investment, reducing output to far below optimum. Business enterprise has been a losing game. The only reason it had gone on at all, Keynes remarked in anticipation of chapter 12 of the *General Theory*, was the gambling instinct. The risk was unknown. Business, Keynes concluded, is a roulette wheel with a zero – only the 'house' makes a profit.

In a letter Keynes wrote to Harrod in August 1936, he looked back on this period:

> You don't mention *effective demand* or, more precisely, the demand schedule for output as a whole. . . . To me, the most extraordinary thing, regarded historically, is the complete disappearance of the theory of the demand and supply for output as a whole, i.e. the theory of employment, *after* it had been for a quarter of a century the most discussed thing in economics. One of the most important transitions for me, after my *Treatise on Money* had been published, was suddenly realising this. It only came after I had enunciated to myself the psychological law that, when income increases, the gap between income and consumption will increase, – a conclusion of vast importance to my own thinking but not apparently, expressed just like this, to anyone's else's. Then, appreciably later, came the notion of interest as being the meaning [measure?] of liquidity-preference, which became quite clear in my mind the moment I thought of it. And last of all, after an immense lot of muddling and many drafts, the proper definition of the marginal efficiency of capital linked up one thing with another.[120]

To this author, the embryo of the *General Theory* seems very well formed by the end of 1932, on the very verge at least of sustaining a life outside the womb of its creator. Fundamental was the argument, only implicit in the *Treatise*, that in a monetary, unlike a 'neutral money', economy there is no mechanism which *automatically* ensures full employment, either in the short period or in the long period. This is why we need a theory of aggregate output. The main building blocks of a theory of output are also in place: Keynes has identified 'the state of time preference' (later the consumption function) relating saving to income; 'quasi-rents' or the prospective yield on investment; the rate of interest as the measure of liquidity preference; and supply schedules for the main components of output. Missing was the multiplier, not yet incorporated into the output-adjustment process (but in the process of being so); the 'link up' between the theory of interest and the theory of capital is also underdeveloped. Nor is there any very clear statement that economic activity is driven by uncertainty, which gives money its special role. Although static elements – like the necessary equality between saving and investment – have been introduced, the emphasis of the analysis is still dynamic, with divergences between 'disbursements' and earnings setting up a chain of indeterminate repercussions. What we have is a preliminary sketch of the final picture, blurred and incomplete, but perfectly recognisable.

IV

THE MEANS TO PROSPERITY

With increasing confidence in his analysis, Keynes started to propound his policies for the 1930s. By the autumn of 1932 the brief British recovery had fizzled out. Real interest rates had come down dramatically, but, following a flurry of activity after devaluation, output fell to its lowest point in August/September 1932 (though the fall was nothing as severe as in 1921) and unemployment remained above 20 per cent of the insured labour force from January 1931 to May 1933. And this was despite the 'confidence' generated by the national government with its balanced budget and huge Conservative majority. Here was Keynes's unemployment equilibrium in real life. He now had a much firmer theoretical basis for arguing that increased government spending was the only way to full employment: for, with private spending so depressed by the fall in national income, where were the spontaneous forces to bring recovery?

Keynes posed the important question at the end of 1932: 'Will it be apparent by the middle of 1933 that this slump is the same in kind as past slumps though more violent in degree, and is gradually working itself off by the operation of natural forces and the economic system's own resiliency? Or shall we find ourselves after a modest upward reaction and dubious hopes of recovery, plunged back again into the slough?'[121] He had little doubt of the answer. His policy advice from this time onwards is dominated by the belief that there was no way out of the slump unless governments took action to raise world demand. He did not, of course, discount the possibility of 'some accidental event' turning up to 'put speculators in funds and spirits'.[122] But this was not the 'internal efficacious mechanism' which classical economists relied on. Yet the verdict on the 1930s remains open. The depression in Britain reached its trough in the last quarter of 1932. There *was* a predominantly market-led recovery in Britain and some other countries which was deeper and longer than Keynes expected (it did not collapse till 1937). It is at least an open question whether Keynesian policies in Britain could have achieved much more, given the pre-Keynesian climate of expectations and the decentralised character of economic decision-making. The American recovery under the New Deal was rather less successful than Britain's. Hitler's Germany alone provided triumphant vindication of Keynesian economics, but only in semi-war conditions, backed by terror.

Keynes's main inside influence was exerted through the Committee on Economic Information, effective residuary of the Economic Advisory Council. Stamp was its chairman, and its members, apart from Keynes, were Citrine, Cole, Sir Alfred Lewis (of the National Provincial Bank), Hubert Henderson, Sir Arthur Salter (who had just retired as director of the Economic and Finance Section of the League of Nations) and Sir Ernest Simon. Two Treasury officials attended: Sir Frederick Leith-Ross from 1932 and Sir Frederick Phillips from 1935. The first of its regular 'Surveys of the Economic Situation' appeared in March 1932. Arthur Salter recalled that:

> Some twenty reports (almost all unanimous), each of about twenty pages, were laboriously discussed and drafted. . . . Of the policy urged on the Government I will only . . . say that it bore the impress of Keynes, that it was basically different from the official policy actually being pursued on the joint advice of the Treasury and the Bank of England, and that there would now, I believe [1967], be a general consensus that, where they differed, the committee was right and the official policy wrong.[123]

MacDonald had set up another committee of the EAC in February 1932 to advise him on economic policy. Consisting of Stamp (chairman), Henderson, Robbins, Blackett and Simon, it produced an 'atavistic document' advocating the 'habit of thrift' and supporting wage and public expenditure cuts.[124] Almost simultaneously a Committee on Unemployment, stuffed with industrialists, concluded that the public works programme of the Labour government had been a waste of time.[125] This was the background against which Keynes's persuasion had to be carried out. The first of these reports shows what even Keynes's friends were likely to say when he was not there. They found it much easier to advocate 'unsound' experiments in good times than when businessmen were panicking. Keynes wrote the *General Theory* to demonstrate the reverse: that what was unsound in good times was sound in a depression.

Keynes's influence was soon felt. The first of his Committee's surveys on the internal situation in November 1932 criticised the balanced-budget policy, curtailment of the public works programme and cuts in wages and unemployment benefit as deflationary, and said that, while they might have been necessary to get over the financial crisis, the time had come 'to back up the cheap money policy with a more liberal budgetary policy'.[126] But how much more liberal was not specified. The Treasury objected on four grounds: budget deficits to pay for public works would damage confidence; if they were a means of creating credit they were unnecessary because cheap money would do this just as well (Hawtrey's old point), and without destroying confidence, while directing money to 'normal trade and not hothouse schemes'; public works took too long to get started; and they had never done more than 'touch the fringe' of the unemployment problem in the past.[127]

Keynes had also begun his public campaign. He felt intuitively that the psychological moment had come to strike. A correspondence in *The Times* in October shows the economic profession lining up into two camps based on Cambridge and the LSE. Pigou, D. H. McGregor, Keynes, Layton,

Salter and Stamp signed a letter on 17 October which said that economising on consumption led to unemployment. Saving did not automatically flow into investment when confidence was low but led to a reduction in national income. So public investment should be encouraged. Of the critical letters which followed, the chief one came from the LSE under the signatures of T. E. Gregory, Hayek, Arnold Plant and Lionel Robbins, supporting the balanced-budget policy. Keynes and his co-signatories replied on 21 October that it was an illusion to think that money saved today represents money available to be spent tomorrow when confidence returns. 'Insofar as labour and capital are idle, the resources available for paying income to their owners are not conserved; they simply do not come into existence.'[128] The influence of Keynes's ideas on these collective statements is palpable.

The New Year brought a flurry of activity. His article in the *Daily Mail*, headed 'Some Hopeful Portents' as befits a New Year message – 'Slumps, like booms, do come to an end; at least, they always have . . .' – nevertheless warned that the improvements taking place were 'partial and precarious, relative and not absolute' and needed the support of public works.[129] In a broadcast conversation with Stamp on 11 January he delivered two good *mots* – 'Look after unemployment, and the Budget will look after itself' and 'We must save if spending is to be healthy, and we must spend if saving is to be healthy' – and produced a structural argument which is an underestimated part of his thinking: private enterprise could no longer absorb the whole of private saving due to the relative growth of the public or quasi-public sector, so it is 'loan expenditure I am wanting'. On 31 January came a public attack on the Ministry of Health, headed by his old friend Hilton Young – the 'sphinx without a riddle' – for cutting down on municipal house-building. He inspired the Committee of Economic Information to send MacDonald a letter, dated 9 February, backing up their recommendations of November.[130]

While the campaign of persuasion was hotting up, Keynes froze in Cambridge. 'Ugh! How cold it is here!' he wrote to Lydia on 20 January. 'I wear the new woolly all day long. Last night I had two of the pipes on in my bedroom *all night through*. In my study I keep the electric fire going all the time, whether I am there or not. . . . So praise me!' He read his revised essay on Malthus to his economic club on 23 January, and included it in a new book of essays he sent off to the printers – his *Essays in Biography*. 'I mustn't write any more articles for a long time,' he told Lydia on 5 February, and next day: 'A return to virtue in the morning, since I wrote a little at my book.' But he sensed it was time to go on to the offensive. On 22 February he wrote to Geoffrey Dawson, 'I have felt very strongly moved in the last day or two to write two or three articles on the present situation, which I would offer you for *The Times* and then perhaps expand shortly afterwards into a pamphlet.' His purpose in writing was to influence the budget in April and the World Economic Conference due to assemble in

London in June. Dawson offered £60 for four articles, double the standard rate of payment (though Keynes got paid £100 per article from the *Daily Mail*). On 27 February the Reichstag in Berlin went up in flames. Newspaper attention being concentrated on this outrage, the publication of Keynes's articles, designed to suggest a 'means to prosperity' which did not involve burning down parliaments, was delayed till 13–16 March. But, even before this, an advanced set of the articles had reached the new American President, Franklin Roosevelt. Keynes's pamphlet, 'The Means to Prosperity', was published later that month. An American edition, published in April, incorporated additional material on 'The Multiplier' which had appeared in the *New Station* (Cambridge's nickname for the recently merged journal) on April Fool's Day.

The articles had a sensational impact, despite being more sombre in mood, more solid in style than similar productions in the 1920s. Gone was the linguistic vivacity, the delight in paradox, which had marked 'The Economic Consequences of Mr. Churchill' or 'Can Lloyd George Do It?' Perhaps Keynes had taken to heart Leonard Woolf's criticisms of his previous efforts at persuasion. At any rate Bloomsbury wit, digs at stupid bankers, mad politicians and so on were put aside in favour of a wholly serious, unadorned development of his case; perhaps he felt, too, that the world depression was too serious a disease to be treated by wit. At fifty, the *enfant terrible* was acquiring gravitas. From now on he would display his iconoclasm much more sparingly, at least in public. Macmillan, not the Hogarth Press, published the pamphlet, symbolising the shift in desired audience. 'The Means to Prosperity' was also much less parochial than the two earlier series, as befitted a *world* in depression. Remedies for Britain were explicitly linked to the recovery of world demand, and the argument culminated in a plan for world reflation. The articles marked, that is, the emergence of Keynes as a world statesman; or rather, the re-emergence of a much more mature Keynes than in 1919 when he had first tried to legislate the world back to prosperity. There was also a new search for consensus. Although the multiplier theory was his own special contribution, his international plan built on the work of Henderson and others and was close to becoming the Treasury view. Keynes had also emerged from the tunnel of the *Treatise*. Theory was kept in the background, but the work he had done over the previous year enabled him to put simple ideas directly.

The start of the pamphlet was, however, characteristic. The world's troubles were due not to material destruction, but to 'failure in the immaterial devices of the mind' – more plainly, 'clear thinking'. What was needed to cure them 'was a blend of economic theory with the art of statesmanship . . . political economy'.[131] He then applied the multiplier theory (which was for the first time labelled as such) to confute the two main arguments against 'loan expenditure' by government: 'the meagreness of the employment created' and the 'strain on national and local budgets'.[132]

To obtain the magnitude of the multiplier 'we have simply to estimate . . . what proportion of typical expenditure becomes someone's income and what proportion of this income is spent. For these two proportions, multiplied together, give us the ratio of the first repercussion to the primary effect. . . . we can then sum the whole series of repercussions. . . .'[133] Keynes calculated a British multiplier of 2; the American multiplier would be more than 2, for reasons which Kahn had given.[134] Suppose additional government loan expenditure of £100m. gives 500,000 workers direct employment – say building houses and the materials necessary to produce them. If the multiplier is 2, the net employment, over several rounds of spending, will work out at one million. Saving on the dole and the increase in tax revenue will reduce the budgetary charge to £50m. over the life of the repercussions. Keynes added a number of refinements to Kahn's article. The exposition is worked out in terms of changes in national income as well as employment, the two coming to 'much the same thing'.[135] He emphasises favourable international repercussions: Britain's beneficent action will be 'twice blessed' since out of an increased national income it will be able to buy more foreign goods, setting up a foreign-trade multiplier for other countries.[136] He came to the rescue of Kahn (who had abstracted from time-lags) by suggesting that 'seven-eighths of the total effects come from the primary expenditure and the first two repercussions, so that the time-lags involved are not unduly serious'.[137] He simplified the calculation by ignoring repercussions on prices until 'our remedy was becoming very successful'.[138] He suggested dividing the budget into a capital and income account and balancing it over the cycle.[139] And he argued that the same principle which multiplies an initial expenditure multiplies any reduction. 'Just as an initial impulse of modest dimensions has been capable of producing such devastating repercussions, so also a moderate impulse in the opposite direction will effect a surprising recovery. There is no magic here, no mystery; but a reliable scientific prediction.'[140] On the other hand, Keynes had come to feel curiously insecure in doing even simple arithmetic calculations. 'I hope I don't make any bloomers,' he wrote to Kahn, who was in America lecturing on the same subject. 'I wish you were here to look over my shoulder.' But Kahn thought his exposition of the multiplier 'beautiful'.[141]

The second and third articles introduce and expound his plan to raise world prices. This aspect of the plan was put forward mainly for relieving debt burdens, something of particular importance to primary producers: in much of the world, recovery of profits had to lead recovery of demand. His international recovery plan was worked out with Hubert Henderson and Basil Blackett on one of MacDonald's endless advisory committees.[142] He had been plugging variants of it for a couple of months and managed to express its rationale more vividly in the *New Statesman* of 24 December 1932 than in his *Times* articles:

What is the charm [he wrote] to awaken the Sleeping Beauty, to scale
the mountain of glass without slipping back? If every Treasury were
to discover in its vaults a large *cache* of gold proportioned in size to
the scale of its economic life, would not that work the charm? Why
should not that *cache* be devised? We have long printed gold nationally.
Why should we not print it internationally? No reason in the world,
unless our hands are palsied and our wits dull.[143]

Conceding to orthodoxy, Keynes proposed to revive a modified gold
standard. To relieve the anxiety of central banks an international authority
should create additional world reserves by a fiduciary issue of gold certificates up to $5b. which all participating countries would accept as a means
of international payment. They would receive a quota equal to their gold
reserves in 1928. In return for their *caches* of gold certificates they would be
required to agree to return to the gold standard, though within wider bands
(Keynes suggested 5 per cent) and at adjustable parities; they would have
to renounce exchange restrictions, reduce their tariffs, eliminate import
quotas and embargoes on foreign lending, write down their debts. Keynes
was relaxed about having described the gold standard as a 'barbarous relic'.
He now wrote, 'A barbarous relic, to which a vast body of tradition and
prestige attaches, may have a symbolic or conventional value if it can be
fitted into the framework of a managed system of the new pattern. Such
transformations are a regular feature of those constitutional changes which
are effected without revolution.'[144]

The fundamental purpose of the plan was psychological: to free central
banks from anxiety about their reserves 'which is a condition of freely
encouraging the increased loan-expenditure without which world prices
cannot rise'.[145] He wrote, 'We cannot, by international action, make the
horses drink. That is their domestic affair. We can provide them with water.
To revive the parched world by releasing a million rivulets of spending
power is the primary task of the World Conference.'[146] Countries could use
their *cache* as they pleased. 'Some would discharge pressing foreign obligations; some would restore budgetary equilibrium; some would re-establish
commercial credit; come would prepare for conversion schemes; some would
organise schemes of national development; and so on. But all uses alike
would tend in the desired direction.'[147] Keynes already had a vision of a
permanent system: 'there should be an elasticity in the quantity of the
additional reserves outstanding, so that they would operate, not as a net
addition to the world's monetary supply, but as a balancing factor to be
released when prices are abnormally low as at present, and to be withdrawn
again if prices were rising too much.'[148] All this, of course, looked forward
to the International Monetary Fund and the Bretton Woods system. Did
Harry Dexter White read the American edition of 'The Means to
Prosperity'?

Keynes's emollient mood continues to the end. There is a pat on the back for both Labour and Conservatives. The Labour government had started public works, but wouldn't take measures to strengthen the foreign balance; the national government had improved the foreign balance but shunned public works. The two policies needed to be combined. In his reply to critics in *The Times* of 5 April, Keynes argued that the Labour government's modest public works programme had been swamped by a much larger deterioration in the balance of payments, which it failed to counter by devaluing or putting on a tariff. (This led Hawtrey to conclude that an 'obvious and easy alternative to the whole elaborate programme of capital outlay' would be a deliberate reduction in 'the gold value of the pound'.)[149] And the final, now habitual, warning: if measures like this were rejected, 'we must expect the progressive breakdown of the existing structure of contract and instruments of indebtedness, accompanied by the utter discredit of orthodox leadership in finance and government, with what ultimate outcome we cannot predict.'[150]

Keynes's articles marked the start of public understanding of the Keynesian Revolution. They begat an enormous debate which went on in several countries. Economists and politicians started to bandy the concept of 'repercussions' around as though they had known about it all their lives. Sharp divisions emerged between the Expansionists and those who Wanted to Sit It Out. An editorial in *The Times* of 13 March was cautiously supportive; masses of letters appeared in the following days, mainly in favour of Keynes, including one drafted by Roy Harrod and signed by thirty-seven university teachers of economics. There was no signatory from the LSE. Sir Josiah Stamp threw his weight behind unbalancing the budget. Cassel in Sweden supported him. Sir Arthur Salter, in the *Manchester Guardian* of 21 March, wrote that Keynes 'has expressed the strong, and now almost overwhelming, mass of opinion, lay and expert alike, that the time has come for expanding public investment . . .'.

Keynes's articles as usual received close scrutiny by the Treasury and the Bank of England. The new generation of Treasury officials – particularly Sir Richard Hopkins and Sir Frederick Phillips – were much more sympathetic to Keynes than Sir Otto Niemeyer had been in the 1920s, but they still felt bound to reject his suggestions. 'The one gilt-edged argument', minuted Phillips, who orchestrated the scrutiny, 'is *delay*. Keynes's whole point is the urgency of immediate action, whereas we know perfectly well that public works don't get started in a year and don't get in full working order for three years.'[151] In his reply to critics in *The Times* of 5 April, Keynes tried to meet this line of attack by switching the emphasis in his proposals from increasing government spending to remitting taxes. This would have the great advantage of avoiding delay, and also energising expenditure through 'numberless normal channels'. Phillips queried Keynes's budgetary calculations. 'Perhaps the process he intends would be better described as a speculative balancing of the Budget over a long term of future years without regard to the deficit produced in the early years of the period.' Phillips also reiterated the Treasury's earlier objection that Keynes's argument was only right 'if there were large unused savings and if they can be attracted into investment by issuing gilt-edged stock without raising the long-term rate of interest.'[152] It was Henderson who finally scotched this, pointing out correctly that Keynes's proposal did not assume idle bank deposits. The main objection to Keynes's plan, Henderson said, was 'that any substantial increase of internal trade activity in England, unless accompanied quickly by a corresponding movement elsewhere, would tend to increase imports and to render the balance of trade adverse . . .'.[153] Henderson was now in favour of 'reversing the engines in regard to public works programmes; and I think that the beneficial repercussions would probably be fully as great as you claim'. But he still rejected the multiplier approach. It dealt 'with great minuteness with certain qualifications to the repercussion argument' but ignored two others which might be of 'crucial importance': (1) that centrally organised public work may to some extent take the place of existing work of the same kind; and (2) that the possibly damaging effects on confidence would come before the beneficial effects of expenditure. The first objection was urged strongly by Sir Arthur Robinson, permanent secretary at the Ministry of Housing, who said that, if the government spent more on housing, local authorities would spend less.[154]

> You often say [Henderson wrote to Keynes on 28 February] 'It's nonsense to talk about confidence; confidence depends on orders.' Very likely. But I maintain that if you were to announce that you were going in for a large £200 million programme, you would not get a single order under that programme for at least a year, whereas the effects on the gilt-edged market and the like of the announcement of your intention would be immediate. You might thus easily get a vicious circle wound up before your virtuous circle had begun to operate at all. Speaking generally, therefore, I am very much off the idea of public works as a major constructive remedy for our present troubles.[155]

Scrutiny of Keynes's proposals went hand in hand with preparations for the budget. Chamberlain asked to see Keynes on 17 March: 'Could it be that the Walls of Jericho are flickering?' Keynes asked Richard Kahn. He tried hard to give them a final push. Resuscitate the national income, he advised Chamberlain on 5 April, and the revenue will flow in; allow it to fall and there will always be a budgetary problem. 'Unfortunately, the more pessimistic the Chancellor's policy, the more likely it is that pessimistic anticipations will be realised and vice versa. Whatever the Chancellor dreams, will come true.'[156] Chamberlain still dreamt of economy. In his budget speech of 25 April, he condemned 'those speaking as having authority' who proclaimed that unbalancing the budget leads to salvation. The proposal to aim for a budget balance over time involved a great optimism that tax cuts would bring increased revenues. But what would happen to private spending 'if the public realised, as they certainly would do, that what was spent to-day, had presently to be paid for'? Britain had stood the strain better than any other country because its budget was balanced. It was now being asked to throw away the advantage gained just when the benefits were about to be reaped and other governments were following suit. 'No Finance Minister', Chamberlain declared bleakly, 'ever deliberately unbalanced his Budget.' Keynes criticised the budget 'for making no attempt to bring about better times by anticipating them'.[157] There were only two things wrong with Keynes's arguments. Chamberlain did, in fact, balance the budget in 1933/34. And post-war Keynesian chancellors consistently failed to make their dreams come true![158]

The Bank of England's reaction focused on international repercussions: 'There is a rather marked absence of comment by Keynes on the probable effects of his proposals on the sterling exchange.'[159] Predictably the Bank objected to vesting management of a restored gold standard in an international board. But its main fear was that a reflation, undertaken by Britain alone, would cause a drop in sterling. This was Brand's view. In private and public, he insisted that the key to recovery lay in the United States.[160] Keynes had countered this in his original articles by arguing that if Britain imported more it would also sell more abroad. But this part of the argument was undeveloped and made little impact. Keynes replied in *The Times* of 7 April: 'I wish I could move Mr. Brand out of his passivity. Though he himself realises the magnitude of the world's present catastrophe, his article shows no sign of it. There may be a gloomy satisfaction in going to perdition according to the rules. But I hate to sit back, hoping for something to turn up in America, whilst abject poverty consumes the possibilities of life and civilisation crumbles.' In fact, Franklin Roosevelt turned up in America and within days of Keynes's rejoinder to Brand, changed the whole framework of the discussion.

'The Means to Prosperity' is a key document in the history of the Keynesian Revolution. At this level, the level of practical policy, grounded for the first time in the multiplier analysis, the Keynesian Revolution was on the way to being won. And it was thus won during and after the war. The abstract argument whether the economy possessed long-run self-stabilising properties was relegated to academic discussion. The substantial remaining doubts concerned practicability and psychological repercussions.

There are the points that have been taken up by later historians. They estimate the multiplier in the early 1930s as much lower than 2 – nearer 1 – and argue that the kinds of fiscal deficits and adverse trade flows needed to make any substantial impact on the employment figures would rapidly have brought on a major financial and political crisis requiring either the reversal of the policy or the move to a completely state-controlled economy like in Nazi Germany.[161]

V

On 17 April 1933 Keynes arrived in Dublin on a two-day visit, his first since 1911, to deliver the first Finlay Lecture at University College. He chose as his subject 'National Self-Sufficiency'. Composed almost immediately after his *Times* articles, it seemed to swing the full circle from Adam Smith to Friedrich List, German founder of economic nationalism; or, for the contemporary-minded, to Dr Schacht, Nazi Germany's economic overlord. Keynes had in fact been pursuing both lines of thought – internationalism and nationalism – for some time past without bringing them together. It would be easy to say that protectionism was for him a second-best option, to be adopted if the international reflationary package he had put forward for the World Economic Conference failed; he did not allow the printed version of his Dublin lecture to appear till after the conference was over – in the *New Statesman* on 8 and 15 July. But his advocacy of national self-sufficiency was painted in much more winning colours than that. He had trailed it in a broadcast talk at the end of 1932: national self-sufficiency promised a 'well-balanced' or 'complete' national life, allowing English people to display the full range of their national aptitudes in mechanical invention and in agriculture, as well as preserving traditional ways of living. It would be 'a shocking thing if we were to be without a prosperous and inventive motor industry'; 'I wish to see the blast furnaces of the north-east coast roar again and ships of British steel sail out of the Clyde'; another type of Englishman 'needs as his pursuit in life the care and breeding of domestic animals and contact with the changing seasons and the soil'. If all this cost a bit more, so be it. 'To say that the country cannot afford agriculture is to delude oneself about the meaning of the word "afford". A country which cannot afford art or agriculture, invention or tradition, is a country in which one cannot afford to live.'[162] Here was Keynes the patriot rather than the balancer of economic advantages; and something more: Keynes the squire of Tilton, who was farming on an increasing scale; Keynes the paternalist protesting against the economic juggernaut which rooted up people from their homes and associations in the interest of cheapness; Keynes the artist seeking perfection in harmony and proportion. Addressing the Cambridge Chamber of Commerce on 17 February 1933, he paraded his local roots. Speaking as the son of a registrary of the University and mayor of the town, he praised Cambridge as a place where one could spend an afternoon strolling round 'talking to one's lifelong friends' and shopping in 'shops which are really shops and not merely a branch of the multiplication table'.[163]

In his Dublin lecture Keynes tried to give these musings a more solid rationale. He now adduced four main arguments for a greater degree of national self-sufficiency. First, he was:

Cartoon by Vanessa Bell, 1927, of Lydia and Maynard dancing a version of the can-can from *Boutique-Fantasque* (the 'Keynes-Keynes').

'An Extra One', the resignation of Sir Oswald Mosley, 19 April 1930.

Punch, February 1931.

Hubert Henderson

Richard Kahn and Lydia sitting on the
bird-bath at Tilton, *c.*1931.

F. Hayek, 1931.

Oswald Falk

LYDIA LOPOKOVA AND GEORGE RYLANDS

(in " Comus ")

Lydia and G. Edwards in *A Doll's House*.

Lydia and Dadie Rylands in *Comus*
(from the programme).

Arts Theatre Logo

Maynard Keynes and Bertil Ohlin at Antwerp, 1935.

Maynard Keynes and General Jan Smuts at the World Economic Conference,
July 1933.

Maynard Keynes,
Beatrice and Sidney
Webb at Passfield
Corner, *c.*1928.

George Bernard Shaw
and Maynard Keynes,
Fitzwilliam Museum,
Cambridge, 1936.

Maynard Keynes' letter of condolence to Reginald Macaulay on the death of his brother, William Herrick Macaulay, Fellow of Kings.

Copy

KING'S COLLEGE,
CAMBRIDGE.

Nov 29 1936

Dear Macaulay,

Low caricature of Maynard Keynes.

not persuaded that the economic advantages of the international division of labour to-day are at all comparable with what they were . . . Over an increasingly wide range of industrial products, and perhaps of agricultural products also, I become doubtful whether the economic cost of national self-sufficiency is great enough to outweigh the other advantages of gradually bringing the producer and the consumer within the ambit of the same national, economic and financial organisation. Experience accumulates to prove that most modern mass-production processes can be performed in most countries and climates with almost equal efficiency . . . Moreover, as wealth increases, both primary and manufactured products play a smaller relative part in the national economy compared with houses, personal services and local amenities which are not the subject of international exchange. . . .[164]

Secondly, Keynes stated bluntly that free trade, combined with international mobility of capital, was more likely to provoke war than keep peace. In times of stress, particularly, the ownership of national assets by foreigners was likely to 'set up strains and enmities' which, he implied, had led to war in 1914. So: 'I sympathise . . . with those who would minimise rather than with those who would maximise economic entanglement between nations. Ideas, knowledge, art, hospitality, travel – these are the things which should of their nature be international. But let goods be homespun whenever it is reasonably and conveniently possible; and, above all, let finance be primarily national.'[165]

Thirdly, Keynes urged the case for 'politico-economic' experiment: 'We each have our own fancy. Not believing we are saved already, we each would like to have a try at working out our salvation. We do not wish, therefore, to be at the mercy of world forces working out, or trying to work out, some uniform equilibrium according to the ideal principles of *laissez-faire* capitalism.'[166]

Finally, the system of economic calculation which made 'the whole conduct of life . . . into a sort of parody of an accountant's nightmare' is seen to have failed in its own terms. In a High Victorian outburst Keynes declared:

> We have to remain poor because it does not 'pay' to be rich. We have to live in hovels, not because we cannot build palaces, but because we cannot 'afford' them. . . . We destroy the beauty of the countryside because the unappropriated splendours of nature have no economic value. We are capable of shutting off the sun and the stars because they do not pay a dividend. London is one of the richest cities in the history of civilisation, but it cannot 'afford' the highest standards of achievement of which its own living citizens are capable, because they do not 'pay'.
>
> If I had the power today I should surely set out to endow our capital cities with all the appurtenances of art and civilisation on the highest

standards . . . convinced that what I could create, I could afford – and believing that money thus spent would not only be better than any dole, but would make unnecessary any dole. For with what we have spent on the dole in England since the War we could have made our cities the greatest works of man in the world.

. . . We have until recently conceived it a moral duty to ruin the tillers of the soil and destroy the age-long human traditions attendant on husbandry if we could get a loaf of bread thereby a tenth of a penny cheaper. There was nothing which it was not our duty to sacrifice to this Moloch and Mammon in one; for we faithfully believed that the worship of these monsters would overcome the evil of poverty and lead the next generation safely and comfortably, on the back of compound interest, into economic peace.

Today we suffer disillusion, not because we are poorer . . . but because other values seem to have been sacrificed . . . and sacrificed unnecessarily. For our economic system is not, in fact, enabling us to exploit to the utmost the possibilities for economic wealth afforded by the progress of our technique . . . leading us to feel we might as well have used up the margin in more satisfying ways.

But once we allow ourselves to be disobedient to the test of an accountant's profit, we have begun to change our civilisation.[167]

Having delivered this Ruskinian denunciation of capitalist civilisation, Keynes ended with some words of caution against silliness, haste and intolerance. But the balance was not well held. Perhaps defending himself, he wrote, 'Words ought to be a little wild, for they are the assault of thoughts upon the unthinking. But when the seats of power and authority have been attained there should be no more poetic licence.' Like a gazelle, Keynes leapt from one mode to another. Did he not see that duller spirits might not be able to make the transition? Or did he think the gazelles would always be in power? It was the nearest he ever came to endorsing communist, or fascist, economics. The fascist leader Oswald Mosley congratulated him on his conversion. Keynes replied that he wrote as he did 'not to embrace you, but to save the country from you'.[168]*

---

*Nicholas Kaldor wrote to the *New Statesman* on 15 July, 'And granted that with the increase in wealth, holiday amenities, personal services, etc., become relatively more important than commodities, would he [Keynes] deny that the Riviera can provide these things much better than Blackpool?' Kaldor acted on his theoretical conviction by acquiring a house in the south of France in the early 1960s, though this did not prevent him from espousing protection for manufacturing industry. Cf. G. L. Schwartz, *New Statesman*, 22 July 1933: 'Let the high table at King's restrict itself to Empire wines and grow witty on Trinidad burgundy (*asphalte mousseux*). . . . Mr. Keynes, who stands in the great tradition of Adam Smith, aligns himself with the crass idiots who advocate the exclusion of foreign produce on the ground that the earlier ripening of fruits in lower latitudes constitutes unfair competition.'

A vivid account of Keynes's lecture has been left by James Meehan in his biography of George O'Brien, who had invited him:

> Keynes gave the first Finlay lecture, on 'National Self-Sufficiency', in the Physics Theatre in Earlscourt Terrace . . . Finlay lectures have usually been well attended but this first one surpassed them all. Almost all the members of the new government were present. Headed by Mr de Valera, they sat on one side of the theatre as far removed as possible from the members of the government they had replaced. It was assumed, for some reason which is lost to memory, that the lecturer would denounce the pursuit of protection by high tariffs which had contributed to the Great Depression. The smiles and self-confidence were therefore much more obvious on one side of the theatre than on the other. But as Keynes proceeded to show himself unexpectedly friendly to the erection of economic defences, above all when he declared that 'were I an Irishman, I should find much to attract me in the economic outlook of your present Government towards greater self-sufficiency', the smiles faded from one side and appeared on the other.

As Meehan implies, Keynes's Dublin lecture, indeed the Irish visit, was a political event. He had arrived in the middle of the so-called trade war between Britain and Ireland. When De Valera replaced Cosgrave in 1932, he renounced the oath of allegiance and packed off the Governor-General to a suburban villa, shorn of powers and dignity; he also withheld payment of land annuities owed to the British government. Britain retaliated by imposing economic sanctions in the form of agricultural duties; Ireland countered with duties on British coal and manufactures. For Keynes to appear in Dublin as an economic nationalist pleased the Irish government, but annoyed the British. Naturally enough Keynes saw himself as a peacemaker. He wrote to Stamp on 29 April:

> the general tenor of my remarks was in the main an apology for contemporary movements to greater self-sufficiency. Since, however, De Valera has been considering doing some foolish things, I feared that this might be taken as giving him undue encouragement. I therefore interpolated a passage of warning relating to Irish conditions.

The interpolated passage ended with a quotation from Paul Valéry: 'Political conflicts distort and disturb the people's sense of the distinction between matters of importance and matters of urgency.' Keynes had a long private talk with De Valera, 'who impressed me distinctly favourably. . . . I was very glad to find that his mind was moving from his insane wheat schemes to peat proposals which are at any rate harmless and might quite conceivably turn out well.' Cosgrave, on the other hand, was 'such a nineteenth century liberal!'.[169] Would Stamp do his best to get the negotiations out of the hands of J. H. Thomas, the bellicose Colonial Secretary, and into Runciman's control at the Board of Trade? Stamp, who followed Keynes to Dublin, and found De Valera 'very charming', promised to 'work him into Runciman's hands on some sort of trade agreement'. This duly came to pass in 1934.[170]

Keynes had the usual round of exhausting engagements: lunch with the Lieutenant Governor; press conference; dinner with the Governor of the Bank of Ireland, and so on. He had time to see his friend George Thomson of King's. His lecture on 19 April was followed by a dinner given by O'Brien to which he had 'invited', on Keynes's prompting, some of the best wits of Dublin. It was, by O'Brien's account, a total failure. There were too many wits and Gogarty* talked too much. Worse still, Keynes was called to the telephone in the middle of the meal. When he came back, he said, 'You may be interested to know that the United States has just left gold.' The short silence that was felt to be appropriate was broken by Gogarty: 'Does that matter?'[171]

VI

FAREWELL TO THE CONFERENCE

On 29 June 1933 Lydia Lopokova graced the dismal obsequies of the World Economic Conference with her final appearance on the ballet stage. It was a gala performance of *Coppelia* at Covent Garden, organised by her husband Maynard Keynes. At forty, Lydia had decided it was time to hang up her shoes. The gala performance was also the last event staged by the Camargo Society. The Society had not only prolonged Lydia's dancing career, but had given a focus to her life after her failure to have a child in 1927. She loved her 'Russian lunches' at 46 Gordon Square, at which ballet gossip, plotting new productions and political chatter, stimulated by Maynard's wine, went on all day. On these occasions she sometimes acted as an eccentric conduit for Maynard's ideas, repeating parrot-like that 'higher prices create more employment' but 'I do not know why.'[172] Vera Bowen had largely dropped out of her life; Sam Courtauld, whose wife Lil had died of cancer at the end of 1931, remained a dogged admirer. But her constant companions of this period were Camargo's mainstays Ninette de Valois, Fred Ashton and Constant Lambert. With her ballet career finally over, she and Maynard prepared for her next gamble, her appearance as Olivia in Shakespeare's *Twelfth Night*.

The gala, on which Maynard netted £314, was more profitable than the

---

*Oliver Joseph St John Gogarty, Irish poet and notorious bore; the inspiration of 'stately, plump Buck Mulligan' in Joyce's *Ulysses*.

conference, the most futile gathering of the inter-war years. The delegates from sixty-six countries who had assembled at the South Kensington Geological Museum on 12 June, and now thronged the grand tier boxes at Covent Garden, had done their mechanical dances like the wound-up dolls in Coppelius' workshop, but there was no force to kick them into life. In his opening address MacDonald talked vaguely about reducing war debts, which they had all agreed not to discuss. This was attributed to senility rather than bad faith. The British had a plan, a watered-down version of the Keynes–Henderson proposals called the Kisch Plan, to redistribute gold from America and France to the rest of the world so they could trade. Not surprisingly the Americans and French objected, and it was never produced. The French, who headed a gold bloc in Western Europe, wanted to restore the international gold standard, which not surprisingly the British, and now the Americans who had just left it, rejected. The Americans supported a scheme for international public works, which the British rejected. The Conference was left with no agenda. Its programme had expired.

Keynes tried to give it the kiss of life with a plan of his own. America's decision to leave the gold standard had taken him by surprise. 'My little proposals are too modest and moderate for this lunatic world', he told his mother on 23 April. 'There seems to be nothing between a Government which does nothing whatever and one which goes right off the deep end'. But he was ever resourceful. He was covering the Conference for the *Daily Mail*, and he published his new plan in the issue of 27 June, sending copies to Neville Chamberlain and Montagu Norman. It involved an all-round devaluation in terms of gold of the world's leading currencies of between 20 and 33 per cent, as a prelude to *de facto* stabilisation. The Treasuries of the participating countries would appropriate the windfalls accruing to the banks and put them into circulation by public works or immediate relief of taxation. Owing to the increase in effective gold reserves, exchange and import restrictions would be abolished. Five per cent of the profit of countries with large gold holdings would be put into a pool to help debtor countries. These revamped ideas were designed to give Britain and America a common basis for action, but had something to offer the gold bloc and the debtor nations too.[173] Meanwhile, Roosevelt had been on a fishing trip and was having ideas of his own. On 3 July the appalled delegates, who included his own, received his 'bombshell', rejecting attempts to stabilise currencies as 'the fetishes of so-called international bankers'. Despite the fact that Roosevelt's message scuppered his own plan, Keynes proclaimed that 'President Roosevelt is Magnificently Right' in choosing the path of national currency management, though he hoped he would not reject reasonable co-operation between the Federal Reserve Bank of New York and the Bank of England. Britain should ignore the threats of the gold bloc to leave the conference, and throw in its lot with the United States in a 'sterling–dollar bloc committed to economic progress and the restoration of economic health'. For the United States:

> invites us to see whether without uprooting the order of society which we have inherited we cannot, by the employment of common sense in alliance with scientific thought, achieve something better than the miserable confusion and unutterable waste of opportunity in which an obstinate adherence to ancient rules of thumb has engulfed us. Nor is the prescription alarming. We are to put men to work by all means at our disposal until prices have risen to a level appropriate to the existing debts and other obligations fixed in terms of money; and thereafter we are to see to it that the purchasing power of our money shall be kept stable.... We are offered, indeed, the only possible means by which the structure of contract can be preserved and confidence in a monetary economy restored.[174]

Ever optimistic, Keynes was inventing Roosevelt's programme for him. He was soon to say, quite accurately, that Roosevelt had about as much idea of where he would land as a pre-war pilot.

The Conference lingered on in a coma for the best part of a month. Keynes dined with the Prime Minister on 4 July and helped concoct an American statement designed to keep it alive. But, unlike the world economy, it was beyond resuscitation. On 27 July it adjourned *sine die*. There was, after all, 'no cat in the bag, no rabbits in the hat – no brains in the head'. In his last article, Keynes pointed out that a pow-wow of sixty-six nations would never agree. Only 'a single power or a like-minded group of powers' could force through a plan. It was not a lesson he would forget.[175]

CHAPTER FOURTEEN

New Deals

I

SOCIAL EXPERIMENTS

The rhythms of the 1920s and 1930s are curiously similar. Both decades were bounded by catastrophe; their middle years promised well only to deceive. In both decades, the world seemed to be recovering from war and depression respectively, only to collapse back into depression and war respectively. Such disasters discredited the cosmopolitan, non-interfering principles which had governed economic affairs in the nineteenth century: the idea that capitalist market economies, left to themselves, would deliver jobs for all who wanted to work and increasing prosperity for all – the latter removing at the same time the main causes of war. As Keynes noted in his 'National Self-Sufficiency' articles, social experiments were in fashion; all of them, whatever their political provenance, envisaged a much enlarged role for government, and a greatly restricted role for free commerce.

These social experiments were influenced more by morals, geopolitics and political ideology than by new economic thinking. The economic crisis of the twentieth century was met by nineteenth-century ideas funnelled through the experience of the First World War. It was the critics of the nineteenth century – all those who rejected *laissez-faire* capitalism on religious or moral or strategic or social or aesthetic or tribal grounds – who got their chance between the wars. The war itself was plausibly attributed to the worldwide 'struggle for markets'; it had shown what governments could achieve by mobilising the resources of their communities. If they could do this for war purposes, why not for peace purposes – in building a 'land fit for heroes'?

Keynes has often been placed in the tradition of these nineteenth-century critics of capitalism. Thus Mini locates him in the romantic, anti-Benthamite movement, represented by Coleridge, Carlyle, Arnold, Ruskin and other opponents of Victorian capitalism.[1] Some have seen him as heir to the socialist revolt against intolerable industrial conditions. There have been persistent attempts to reconcile him to Marx. The 'National Self-Sufficiency' articles seem to hark back to eighteenth-century mercantilism. Keynes has been identified with the machinery of central control – planning, corporatism, rule by technocrats – arising out of the war. All these readings have their place, if only because any critic of the nineteenth century was bound to sound, in some respects, like any other critic. And Keynes did not disdain the support of the older traditions in his campaign of persuasion, because persuasion, to be effective, has to link up to something already in people's minds. At the same time, it is important to understand that he felt himself to be saying something completely new about the behaviour of economies, something which had never been said or thought before – except possibly by Malthus; and which, if accepted, would make most of these other traditions redundant, or at least remove them from centre stage.

None of the critics of nineteenth-century capitalism had been able to mount an effective challenge to the central *economic* theory of *laissez-faire*, namely that, left to itself, a competitive exchange economy tends to produce more output and allocate it more efficiently than any alternative system. It continually enlarges individual incomes and thus aggregate wealth by discovering more efficient ways of producing goods, and continually directs the flow of income towards preferred patterns of consumption. All that is produced is consumed, directly or through exchange. Money makes no difference: it facilitates the exchange process by removing the need to trade in specific commodities. Interference by the state in this self-regulating system is bound to produce inferior (less preferred) outcomes. Critics lacked the intellectual tools to challenge the internal logic of this set of arguments. They attacked the market system from outside: as being inconsistent with tradition, morals, social health or the security of the nation. Marx produced the most sustained economic critique of capitalism. But even he could not show convincingly why the 'robbery' of working-class 'holdings' by a capitalist class – even if this could be demonstrated – should impede either wealth-creation or optimal employment.

All these critics, Keynes said, lacked a theory of effective demand. The fatal flaw in the system, he pointed out, lay in the variability of spending relative to earnings; and this was rooted in the use, and purposes, of money. The result was that the market system was liable to collapse into prolonged depression. If the logical flaw in classical reasoning which 'proved' this was impossible could be corrected, and communities induced by policy to consume what they can produce, the existing system could be saved. Thus Keynes was radical in his economics, 'moderately conservative' in his social aims. The points of contact between Keynes and the nineteenth-century critics lay in the very restricted area opened up by Keynes's theory of deficient aggregate demand. But the kind of intervention required to fill this gap in *laissez-faire* fell very far short of the social revolutions on offer in Europe and elsewhere; its purpose was to make the capitalist market system work better, not destroy it.

This then is the standpoint from which to understand Keynes's reactions to the various contemporary attempts to overcome the inter-war crisis of capitalism. In Europe the characteristic form of such attempts was fascism, the root idea behind which was geopolitical, not economic. Europe, it was claimed, was being dwarfed by the rise of America and Russia. Spengler's *Decline of the West* (1917) was an obituary of old Europe's culture of competing city, later nation, states. The future seemed to lie with continental-scale empires. Europe must be united, by force if necessary, to preserve both its way of life and its means to life. The economic reasoning behind this, if it can be so called, was that to allow the means of life to be traded across political frontiers was to put yourself at the mercy of more powerful states. Only a very large state could be securely self-sufficient. If you did not have enough territory you must grab it. Hence the fascist drive for empire, which in the case of Germany meant continental empire. It is easy to understand how such ideas got their chance with the breakdown of the world economy. But they were by no means a rational response to such a breakdown, since they were held independently of whether the world economy was working well or not.[2]

In Britain, European unification, political or economic, voluntary or forcible, was seen as a threat rather than a promise. Britain's own empire was fading but still intact; imperial economics, in Britain, meant regrouping British trade on the British empire. Keynes was not interested in this, but he no more felt part of Europe than did most of his fellow countrymen. His French was always poor; his German had rusted away to dust; he never spoke or wrote either language and soon stopped trying to follow any serious argument in them. 'England still stands outside Europe,' he had written in 1919. 'Europe's voiceless tremors do not reach her. Europe is apart and England is not of her flesh and body. But Europe is solid with herself.'[3] In the 1930s, Europe acquired a dreadfully raucous voice, but this increased Keynes's alienation from the Continent.

Keynes, of course, had good liberal friends in Europe, dating from his Treasury and Peace Conference days. The trouble was that European liberals were against social experiments, while those who favoured them were anti-liberal. Economics might have tried to bridge this divide. But, although the main European countries had economists, they lacked an economics profession organised for theoretical research in the Anglo-Saxon sense. The exceptions were the Swedes and the Austrians, who, however, were largely cut off from the dominant Continental traditions, though not from each other. Keynes regarded French economists as antediluvian.[4] In Germany, there was no professional opinion he could get in touch with. He had admirers outside the economics profession, like Wladimir Woytinsky, adviser to the German trade union movement, who sent him a copy of his proposals to raise prices in December 1931. Keynes replied with what John Garraty describes as 'polite indifference'.[5] At this time, Melchior and Bonn advised him to turn down an invitation to address a group of economists and industrialists in Berlin, as these were 'not quite the right people' for Keynes to be talking to.[6] But there were no 'right' people with the 'right' ideas. Nevertheless, by October 1934 three million workers had been re-employed in Germany over two years, half the previous total of unemployed, and Keynes's silence on Hitler's New Deal was deafening.

The reason is that Hitler's recovery programme was too mixed up with imperialist aims and terroristic methods for it to hold any attraction for him. Keynes was trying to save liberal society, not destroy it. He would give no comfort to its enemies. Garraty has noted the similarities between Hitler's and Roosevelt's programmes; even their rhetoric, with its invocation of the war spirit, sounded the same. But, whereas Roosevelt was the scion of the American ruling class, Hitler was nurtured on the hatreds of Central Europe and the agony of Germany's defeat; for him war was the purpose, not the symbol, of the effort to restore Germany's industrial might. Keynes understood this from the start. 'Germany is at the mercy of unchained irresponsibles,' he wrote on 15 July 1933. And on 19 September: 'Broken in body and spirit, [they] seek escape in a return backwards to the modes and manners of the Middle Ages, if not of Odin.'[7] Anti-semitic though Keynes occasionally seems by the standards of our day, he was outraged by the officially sponsored outbreaks of Jew-baiting in Nazi Germany. On 25 August 1933, he wrote to Professor Spiethoff, who was arranging the publication of a German translation of 'National Self-Sufficiency':

> Forgive me for my words about barbarism. But that word rightly indicates the effect of recent events in Germany on all of us here . . . It is many generations in our judgement since such disgraceful events have occurred in any country pretending to call itself civilised . . . If you tell me that these events have taken place, not by force, but as an expression of the general will . . . that in our view would make some of the persecutions and outrages of which we hear . . . ten times more horrible.[8]

When Germany withdrew from the World Disarmament Conference on 14 October, he wrote to Lydia, 'Everyone must soon be faced with the alternative of simply allowing Germany to rearm when she likes, or of attacking her as soon as she begins to do so. Hideous!' Keynes never went to look at the 'new' Germany. Carl Melchior, subjected to anti-semitic attack, died in December 1933. When the Mayor of Hamburg visited King's College in 1934 and invited Keynes over, he replied, 'After the death of my friend . . . there is nothing left that could attract me to Hamburg.'[9]

Keynes served on the Academic Assistance Council set up to help German scholars fleeing the persecution, and contributed to its fund. Yet he was far too intelligent not to seek a deeper meaning in the outrages he condemned. This is well brought out in a short comment he wrote on the exiled Einstein, published (reluctantly)[10] by Kingsley Martin in the *New Statesman* on 21 October 1933 and written long before he could have any inkling of the Holocaust. He started with a quotation in German from Einstein's 'Essay on the Special and General Theory of Relativity': 'Assuredly you too, dear reader, made acquaintance as boy or girl with the proud edifice of Euclid's geometry ... Assuredly by force of this bit of your past you would treat with contempt anyone who casts doubts on even the most out of the way fragment of any of its propositions'; and continued:

> It is so indeed. The boys, who cannot grow up to adult human nature, are beating the prophets of the ancient race – Marx, Freud, Einstein – who have been tearing at our social, personal and intellectual roots, tearing with an objectivity which to the healthy animal seems morbid, depriving everything, as it seems, of the warmth of natural feeling. What traditional retort have the schoolboys but a kick in the pants? ...
>
> Thus to our generation Einstein has been made to become a double symbol – a symbol of the mind travelling in the cold regions of space, and a symbol of the brave and generous outcast, pure in heart and cheerful of spirit. Himself a schoolboy, too, but the other kind – with ruffled hair, soft hands and a violin. See him as he squats on Cromer beach doing sums, Charlie Chaplin with the brow of Shakespeare ...
>
> So it is not an accident that the Nazi lads vent a particular fury against him. He does truly stand for what they most dislike, the opposite of the blond beast – intellectualist, individualist, super-nationalist, pacifist, inky, plump ... How should they know the glory of the free-ranging intellect and soft objective sympathy and smiling innocence of heart, to which power and money and violence, drink and blood and pomp, mean absolutely nothing? Yet Albert and the blond beasts make up the world between them. If either cast the other out, life is diminished in its force. When the barbarians destroy the ancient race as witches, when they refuse to scale heaven on broomsticks, they may be dooming themselves to sink back into the clods which bore them.[11]

This subtle piece of writing makes uncomfortable reading. Keynes identified up to a point with the violent reaction against the deconstructionist tendencies in modern science and art, in the name of 'the warmth of human feeling'. Heaven, he seems to be saying, has to be 'scaled on broomsticks', and it is the fate of the Jews to be persecuted because mankind's guides and instructors necessarily appear to the 'blond beasts' as witches and devils. To interpret this passage as anti-semitic would be the crudest vulgarity. Its meaning, and possible sense, lies in the symbolic world, which Keynes never disdained; and here he turns the metaphor of witches against the anti-semites. Keynes's identification with Einstein is also too clear to miss. Keynes was writing a 'General Theory' of employment, in which he called classical economics a 'special case' and classical economists. 'Euclidean geometers in a non-Euclidean world'. But the identification was not complete. At Eton Keynes had made his peace with the 'healthy animals'. He knew how to get on with their middle-aged embodiments, the conservative bankers and businessmen. His mission was not to destroy them, but to persuade them into paths of righteousness.

In the early 1930s what would now be called Keynesian methods of fighting the depression were tried out in Japan and Sweden. It is unlikely that Takahashi, the Japanese Finance Minister, drew much inspiration from Keynes; but Ernst Wigforss, Sweden's Finance Minister, did; more so perhaps than from the younger Swedish school of Lindahl, Myrdal and Ohlin, who were themselves in touch with Keynes, but who never made the transition from the monetary disequilibrium approach of Wicksell (or indeed the Keynes of the *Treatise*) to the *General Theory* position. Keynes kept a watching brief on Swedish developments, but Sweden was too small to be a centre of attraction. In a letter to Markus Wallenberg of Stockholm's Enskilda Bank, he advised going slow on public works and urged a conservative budget 'if... this would be helpful as a transitional measure towards much lower interest rates'. For 'in the long run ... nothing on earth will save the capitalist regime except the steady lowering of long-term rates of interest to a level at which in contemporary conditions current savings can still be profitably absorbed along normal lines'.[12]

Britain's intellectual class was more susceptible to the appeal of Soviet Russia, especially in the 1930s, when capitalism seemed on the verge of shipwreck. Soviet Communism a New Civilisation? asked the Webbs in their last massive tome, published in 1935. (The second edition dropped the question mark.) Reformist hopes had depended on the success of capitalism in creating wealth. Its failure in the early 1930s convinced many on the left that it could be kept going only by methods of barbarism; that progress had come to depend on its abolition; that the Soviet experiment of central planning of a publicly owned economy pointed the way forward for all. Keynes had flirted with Soviet communism as a 'new religion', but, unlike the Webbs, he could never think of Soviet Russia as a serious intellectual resource for Western civilisation. In the 1920s he had said that Marxism and communism had nothing of scientific interest to offer the modern mind. The depression did not alter his view. Russia 'exhibits the worst example which the world, perhaps, has ever seen of administrative incompetence and of the sacrifice of almost everything that makes life worth living ...'; it was a 'fearful example of the evils of insane and unnecessary haste'; 'Let Stalin be a terrifying example to all who seek to make experiments.'[13] He found Kingsley Martin too 'pro-Bolshie' in the *New Statesman*.[14]

These strictures were probably influenced by Lydia's report of her visit to her family in Leningrad at the end of 1932 in the company of her friend Lady Muriel Paget. She was depressed to find her mother and sister sharing a tiny flat with her sister's ex-husband, forcing her mother into '7 years of waiting in a chair at night' for the ex-husband to leave.[15] Fyodor Lopukhov, now chief teacher of character dancing at the Maryinsky Theatre, wrote Keynes fulsome letters of thanks, on what appeared to be rolls of lavatory paper, for the money and clothes regularly sent from London. To poverty and incompetence, terror had been added as Stalin's dictatorship took hold. Lydia was advised to keep both private and public comments on Russia circumspect for fear of reprisals on her family. Both she and Maynard cultivated the Russian Ambassador to London, Ivan Maisky, partly in an effort to get Fyodor and Andrej out (on the pretext of ballet engagements), but Maisky was unable to arrange it. In 1934, Keynes sent a guarded message to the Russian journal *Za Industrialitsu* to mark the 'success' of the first five-year plan. 'It is, however, certainly true that the growth of industrial production is much facilitated in a state which starts from a very low level and is prepared to make great sacrifices to increase industrial production without making a close calculation as to whether it is strictly speaking profitable and advantageous for the existing generation of workers.'[16]

This left the United States. Keynes was not notably pro-American. He shared all the usual cultural prejudices of his class against American materialism; he also resented the passing of British power and influence to the United States. But he was more intellectually at home with Americans than with any other group of foreigners. And the Americans at least were making attempts to tame, manage and regulate the rampant individualism of their system. In the 1920s Keynes had found much to admire in the way the Federal Reserve Board set out to stabilise the purchasing power of the dollar; in the 1930s it was the New Deal which excited his interest. Disillusion with *laissez-faire* at home thus led Keynes not to Berlin or Moscow but to Washington. From the 1930s onwards his efforts at persuasion were increasingly directed towards the United States. For Keynes remained convinced that in economic thinking, if no longer in business life, the British still enjoyed a comparative advantage over everyone else. But equally he understood that America, not Britain, held the key to the survival of capitalist civilisation.

II

AN OPEN LETTER TO THE PRESIDENT

Herbert Hoover's departure from the White House on 4 March 1933 ended the paralysis at the centre of American government. Felix Frankfurter described the outgoing President as 'a man of over-weening ambition yoked to fear'. His successor Franklin Delano Roosevelt proclaimed, 'The only thing we have to fear is fear itself.' Likening the depression to war, he claimed emergency war powers to fight it; he promised to expel the money-lenders from the temple. His inaugural speech sent waves of hope throughout the world. The party at Churt, Lloyd George's country house, which heard it over the wireless, was 'magnificently and completely bowled . . . over . . . LL.G. was terrifically excited . . . and said it was the *most remarkable* utterance by a man . . . *not* on the eve of an election but on taking up his job *after* the Election.'[17]

America certainly needed action. 'Even I would hardly think that I could know what to do if I were President,' Keynes wrote to Lydia, 'though I expect I should when it came to it.'[18] As Arthur Schlesinger tells it:

> The national income was less than half of what it had been four short years before. Nearly thirteen million Americans – about one-quarter of the labour force – were desperately seeking jobs. The machinery for sheltering and feeding the unemployed was breaking down everywhere under the growing burden. And a few hours before, in the early morning before the inauguration, every bank in America had locked its doors. It was now not a matter of seeing whether a representative democracy could conquer economic collapse. It was a matter of staving off violence, even (at least some thought) revolution.[19]

Roosevelt responded with his 'Hundred Days', 'a presidential barrage of ideas and programmes unlike anything known to American history'. Eager young lawyers, college professors, economists, sociologists flooded into Washington as the New Deal gathered pace.[20] Congress enacted a hotchpotch of recovery measures, culled from different strands of America's political tradition, inspired by no coherent plan, certainly not one of Keynesian provenance, but by the conviction that 'something had to be done' to stave off collapse and start the wheels of industry rolling. The banking system had money pumped into it; bank deposits were guaranteed and the Stock Exchange regulated; the gold standard was suspended, internally and externally; a national scheme of unemployment relief was set up; acts were passed to refinance agricultural and housing mortgages. The President was authorised to inflate the currency; the Tennessee Valley Authority became America's first experiment in state socialism; organised efforts to raise wages and prices and plan (or restrict) production were authorised in the Agricultural Adjustment and the National Industrial Recovery Acts. Although these measures pulled in different directions, there was a political logic to them. Everyone in the President's entourage got something. On fiscal policy Roosevelt played a cagey game, balancing economies in current spending with a $3.3b. public works programme. As Herbert Stein notes, he understood that business confidence required the appearance, not the reality, of a balanced budget.[21] The immediate result of this frenetic activism was a tremendous upsurge in confidence. Wall Street started booming, much to Keynes's benefit. Industrial production almost doubled between March and July. Government was in charge again, not events.

Keynes followed Roosevelt's experiments with genuine, but baffled, admiration. 'Your President has persuaded Congress to provide him with some lovely blank sheets of writing paper and some beautifully sharp pencils, but what part of his powers he really means to rely on, we, over here, simply don't know,' he told Lippmann in his transatlantic broadcast conversation on 11 June.[22] Particularly mysterious was the almost immediate revival of business activity, long before the expansionary measures in the President's programme could have had time to work.

> One fears your President is depending far too much on psychological as distinct from real factors [Keynes wrote to an American correspondent, M. C. Rorty, on 4 July 1933]. The operation of the psychological factors is . . . being flattered by the fact that it began at a point when you were entitled to a strong upward reaction, even without adventitious aids. On the other hand, real factors, such as open-market operations and public works, are being tackled much too timidly. There is a risk of a hiatus when the psychological stimulus will have exhausted itself before the real factors, which are slow moving, will have come into effective operation.
>
> At any rate that is the risk. On the other hand, one must not underestimate – and I am always quarrelling with Kahn about this – the cumulative effect of a recovery in working capital due to an upward movement, however engendered . . . What I call the Multiplier . . . may in the United States to-day be very large indeed. Thus it is not impossible that the programme may carry through successfully.
>
> At any rate your country is making so much better an effort than any other to mend things, that in spite of my grave hesitations I am more disposed to sympathise than to criticise.[23]

The immediate results of Roosevelt's measures also troubled the Prime Minister: 'If Roosevelt has really brought something like normality,' Mac-Donald wrote to Hubert Henderson on 30 June, 'it looks as though our policy has been altogether wrong . . .'[24] The collapse of the boomlet in the autumn ended Roosevelt's honeymoon period. It also marked the start of hard analysis on the future direction of the New Deal. Some urged greater public spending; others wanted balanced budgets. The *Herald Tribune*'s columnist Walter Lippmann, primed by Keynes on his trip to London that summer, was one of the first to warn Roosevelt against the danger of muddling up spending with planning, recovery with social reform.[25]

This was the theme taken up by Keynes himself at the end of 1933. He had not yet tried to intervene in the New Deal. Now he was urged to do so by Felix Frankfurter, Professor of Administrative Law at Harvard University, future Supreme Court justice and an unofficial member of Roosevelt's 'brains trust'. Frankfurter was spending the academic year 1933–4 at All Souls College, Oxford, where, Robert Hutchins, president of Chicago

University, warned him, 'the port . . . is very good, but the claret . . . dates from the Crimean War'. A small, captivating, manipulative man (friends addressed him as 'Horns and Tail'), with 'an uncommon capacity for melting reserve, breaking through inhibitions, and generally emancipating those with whom he came into contact',[26] Frankfurter had an unbounded admiration for the English, and for Keynes, whom he had first met at the Paris Peace Conference. 'Why did we not have anybody, even remotely comparable to Keynes in guts and insight?' he had asked Jacob Viner the previous year.[27] Frankfurter wanted Keynes to tell Roosevelt what to do – and what not to do. As a trust-buster in the Progressive tradition (he had voted for La Follette in 1924), he wanted to wean the President from the corporatist National Recovery Administration (NRA) codes, which exempted industry from the anti-trust laws. Those who wanted to restore the free market increasingly looked to Keynes's spending theories to support their aims.

Frankfurter had dined as Keynes's guest at the Founder's Feast at King's on 6 December 1933, 'the gayest and most gracious experience this visit to England has so far furnished'. On 11 December Frankfurter wrote to him, 'You might like to know that . . . I have had American news indicating that there will be considerable sentiment in the Senate for heavy increases in public works appropriations. The President is, I believe, receptive. I write because I think that a letter from you with your independent arguments and indications would greatly accelerate the momentum of forces now at work in the right direction – however much time may have been lost already.'

Keynes's 'Open Letter to the President' was published in the *New York Times* on 31 December, after Roosevelt had received a private copy. It started:

Dear Mr President,
    You have made yourself the trustee for those in every country who seek to mend the evils of our condition by reasoned experiment within the framework of the existing social system.
    If you fail, rational change will be gravely prejudiced throughout the world, leaving orthodoxy and revolution to fight it out.
    But if you succeed, new and bolder methods will be tried everywhere, and we may date the first chapter of a new economic era from your accession to office.

Having opened encouragingly, Keynes did not pull his punches. The President was engaged on a 'double task, recovery and reform – recovery from the slump, and the passage of those business and social reforms which are long overdue'. But 'even wise and necessary reform may . . . impede and complicate recovery. For it will upset the confidence of the business world and weaken its existing motives to action before you have had time to put other motives in their place . . . And it will confuse the thought and aim of yourself and your Administration by giving you too much to think about all at once.' This passage clearly brings out Keynes's order of priorities, while deliberately leaving open the question of the long-term future of the capitalist system. It was his characteristic way of talking to right and left at the same time.

The NRA should be put into cold storage. It was a programme of reform, disguised as recovery, which probably impeded recovery. But Keynes also attacked faults in Roosevelt's technique of recovery. Recovery meant increased output. Rising prices were a natural counterpart of increasing output. Trying to raise prices by restricting output was exactly the wrong way round. Trying to raise output by inflating the currency was also the wrong way round: 'it is like trying to get fat by buying a larger belt'. This was a dig at Roosevelt's gold-buying policy: the 'gold standard on the booze' Keynes called it.*

What Roosevelt should aim to do was to keep the dollar–sterling exchange as stable as was consistent with an accelerating programme of loan-financed public expenditure and open-market operations to reduce the long-term rate of interest. Although Keynes favoured both policies, he acknowledged the practical difficulties in the way of the former and attached 'great importance' to the latter. 'The United States is ready to roll toward prosperity, if a good hard shove can be given in the next six months.'[28] Herbert Stein complains that Keynes's letter was ill-timed and badly argued. There was 'no hint of the multiplier, no consideration of popular concerns about where the money was coming from . . .' But all this was in 'The Means to Prosperity', which Keynes had sent the President earlier in the year. Stein says it 'sounded like a letter from a school teacher to the very rich father of a very dull pupil'.[29] This is a matter of taste, but there is no doubt that Keynes's intellectual style, then and later, antagonised many Americans. It is unlikely that it made any difference to his persuasiveness. He could not hope to run the New Deal by sea mail.

The Roosevelt programme certainly needed intellectual stiffening. Although in 1931 Keynes had found considerable support in Chicago for countercyclical public works policy, the New Deal was undertaken in defiance of the professional views of most American economists.[30] Schumpeter at Harvard favoured a federal loan to be spent on 'additional unemployment relief', but he feared that reflation would lead to an inflationary

---

*Under the influence of an agricultural economist, George F. Warren, Roosevelt had adopted a plan to inflate crop prices quickly. The idea was that if the government bought gold at rising prices, domestic commodity prices would soar as the gold value of the dollar fell. The price of gold was gradually raised from $20 an ounce in March 1933 to $35 an ounce by January 1934. Keynes acknowledged the possible benefit to America's exports, but insisted that 'exchange depreciation should follow the success of your domestic [recovery] policy as its natural consequence, and should not be allowed to disturb the whole world by preceding its justification at an entirely arbitrary pace'.

'catastrophe'; nor could he regard the depression as an 'unmixed evil' since it had liquidated 'unsound and untenable' investments and adjusted the economy to the 'objective situation'.[31] In reply to criticism from Professor Harwood of the Massachusetts Institute of Technology, Keynes argued that 'the theory of a *fixed loan fund*, so to speak, is in my present belief a complete fallacy'.[32] But Jacob Viner of Chicago probably summed up mainstream American professional opinion best when he wrote, 'Most remedies have dangerous possibilities and the degree of the danger as well as the degree of probability that they will work are both very much matters of judgement . . . After all social psychology is a vital element in the situation.'[33]

Keynes is nowadays credited with having had little influence on the New Deal – except right at the end of the 1930s. And this is true in the sense that Roosevelt refused to come down decisively in favour of Keynes's ideas. He preferred to keep all balls in play, with a disregard for logic 'which drove logical men to despondency'.[34] But Keynes had considerable influence on specific policies, and the Open Letter is an example. Lippmann wrote to Keynes on 17 April 1934:

> I have been on the point of writing you for sometime to urge you to write another article, following up your letter to the President last December. I don't know whether you realize how great an effect that letter had, but I am told that it was chiefly responsible for the policy which the Treasury is now quietly but effectively pursuing of purchasing long-term government bonds . . .
>
> Our greatest difficulty now lies in the President's emotional and moral commitments to the NRA and to the various other measures which he regards as the framework of a better economic order. As they are being administered, they are a very serious check to our recovery, for the obvious reason that they have raised costs faster than production has increased.
>
> Nobody would make so great an impression upon the President as you could if you undertook to show him the meaning of that part of his policy.[35]

But, by the time he got Lippmann's letter, Keynes had decided to go to the United States to see for himself what was happening.

III

SHARPENING THE TOOLS

By April 1934, Keynes's new theory for recovery had taken final shape. He had worked at it in his greatest effort of concentrated intellectual energy since his dissertation on probability in 1906–7. He felt he was racing against time. Hitler had become German Chancellor, Mosley had started the British Union of Fascists, communism had captured student politics at Cambridge. Keynes was convinced that another great depression was due in three or four years' time. Could the new system of thought be in place by then?

He had worked well on his book in the 'heavenly' summer of 1933, despite the considerable distraction of Bunny Garnett's arrival at Charleston piloting his own aeroplane, and despite rumours of war, which worried him so much he couldn't sleep.[36] He now thought it might be published 'in the first half of next year'.[37] This was wildly over-optimistic, but unlike the *Treatise* there was to be no change of direction. Three chapters were turned over to Richard Kahn for inspection when he returned to Cambridge; most of the others were in draft.

As always, when Keynes was fired up he worked at a tremendous pace. On Friday, 20 October 1933 he reported to Lydia from Cambridge a '*tremendous* burst of activity at writing my book this morning – scribble, scribble, scribble for 3½ hours, which, of course, left me as weak as a rag'. With the writing went the arguments. Hawtrey, he told Lydia on 30 October, was:

> very sweet to the last but quite mad. One can argue with him a long time on a perfectly sane and interesting basis and then, suddenly, one is in a madhouse. Are all the economists mad except Alexander [Kahn]* and me? It seems so, yet it can't be true. I have just been having a hopeless debate with Dennis. His mind, though frightfully ingenious, seems to me to be maliciously perverse. Again it is like arguing with a madman. But when I talk with Alexander, it's all so quite different.

Once again he had found Kahn on the floor of his inner room with Joan Robinson, unshaved and bare-footed. 'But you mustn't suppose wrongly,' he told Lydia. 'They were on the floor because that is the only convenient way of examining mathematical diagrams and there is a Jewish Feast on to-day during which to wear socks or to shave is against the law of Moses.'[38]

In October 1933, he met a very different kind of Jew, Victor Rothschild, an undergraduate at Trinity College, soon to be an Apostle, '*very* handsome . . . full, dominating and victorious . . . not at all a Rabbi like Leonard [Woolf] or Alexander'.[39] Rothschild was a scientist, more interested in driving fast cars and collecting books and pictures than in politics. Maynard was soon dining with Victor and his wife Barbara, daughter of St John and Mary Hutchinson, at their family residence, Palace House, in Newmarket, full of pictures of horses, sometimes in the company of Aldous

*Lydia's nickname for Kahn, to distinguish him from the other Richard – Braithwaite.

Huxley. One evening, he was arrested as a burglar as he approached the house. The Rothschilds were evidently well guarded. Over dinner, he had 'a violent argument about Communism with Alister Watson and Co.'.[40]

Two events on Armistice Day, 11 November 1933, crystallised the problem of the 1930s as Keynes saw it. Sheppard was elected Provost of King's, the subversive old Apostle looking 'very ecclesiastical as he came into chapel to accept office, with silk gown, white hair and reverently bowed head!'[41] Keynes was genuinely, and increasingly, moved by such ceremonies, which reminded him of his own initiation into the brotherhood of 'research, religion, and education' in 1909, of the vows he had then made to preserve 'the laws and traditions' of his College.[42] On the same day young Cambridge erupted in a great anti-war demonstration which marked the start of communism's capture of student politics. Two Apostles, Julian Bell and Guy Burgess, used Julian's beaten-up Morris as a battering ram to break through a barricade outside Peterhouse.[43] The juxtaposition of the two happenings, the first symbolising what Keynes meant by civilisation, the second the destructive forces ranged against it, could only have strengthened his resolve to save the heritage of the past from its wreckers.

Six sets of students' notes have survived of the lectures Keynes gave in the Michaelmas (autumn) term of 1933. They show that the lectures were much sharper than those of the year before, the theory in much better focus. Had they been published as delivered, the world would have got a pretty clear idea of what it later received as the *General Theory of Employment, Interest, and Money*. All that remained was tidying up – a matter of proper formalisation and filling in gaps in the exposition.

The world would also have got a more vivid idea, because in lecturing Keynes was less restrained in his expression. In the *General Theory* the iconoclasm was largely covered up by technical drapery. Here it can be grasped more directly. Keynes had to fit his vision of how economies behaved into the straitjacket of concepts and terms agreeable to economists who did not, and never would, accept it. His genius led him to suspect the whole tradition of Western economics. But his training inhibited him; and also his sense of duty: for though his inspiration was radical, his purpose was conservative. It was in the fourth lecture that he delivered his remarkable outburst against formalisation. 'When you adopt perfectly precise language,' he said, 'you are trying to express yourself for the benefit of those who are incapable of thought.' He went on to attack 'mechanical logic' in economics. 'Scholasticism' may be useful, though, as a check on the logic of one's thinking. Keynes's appeal as a theoretician has always been to those who love inspiration above models, and prefer fertile thinking to elegant proofs.

The structure of the lectures is given by the December 1933 draft table of contents of his book. Book I deals with 'The Relation of the General

Theory of Economics to the Classical Theory'. Book II contains the 'Funda-
mental Concepts' of quasi-rent, income, disbursement and saving. In Book
III, employment is said to be a 'Function of the Motives to Spend and
Invest'.[44]

Keynes started by showing how classical theory eliminated the problem
of 'involuntary unemployment' and deficient demand by assumption. The
two wage 'postulates' of the *General Theory*'s second chapter appear as in the
final version, as does the attack on Say's Law. The classical economists –
and he now brings Pigou, whose *Theory of Unemployment* had just been published, into the discussion – had argued that employment was a function of
the real wage and could expand only if real wages fell. Keynes accepted this
argument, but turned it against Pigou by saying that workers bargain for
money wages, that the money wage is the key price in the system,
and that a fall in money wages would not necessarily lower the real wages:
thus 'there may be no escape for labour from high real wages in a
slump'.[45]

Next he turned his attack on Say's Law, the idea that 'supply creates its
own demand', which he identified as the key macroeconomic proposition of
classical economics – one that made macroeconomic policy redundant. He
developed this attack by distinguishing, as he had the previous year, between
an idealised 'co-operative' or 'neutral' and a real-world 'entrepreneur' or
'money wage' economy. In the former 'the factors of production are
rewarded by dividing up in agreed proportions the actual output [in kind
or money] of their co-operative efforts',[46] whereas in the latter they earn
money incomes which they are *free to spend or not as they wish*. People's freedom
not to spend is thus the logical crux of Keynes's denial that 'supply creates
its own demand' and his assertion that deficiency of demand is possible.
Instead he proposes that 'expenditure creates its own income'.[47] An entrepreneur or 'money wage' economy could be *made* to behave like a co-operative
or neutral economy, but the classical economists were wrong to assume that
it did so automatically.*

Keynes plays with this central idea in his one complimentary reference
to Karl Marx, also dropped from the *General Theory*.[48] He credits Marx with
having pointed out that in a capitalist economy money transactions cannot
be reduced to barter transactions. Businessmen pay out money in order to
make more money; they don't pay out commodities to make more commodities. The problem for policy is precisely to ensure that $M–C–M'$ equals
$C–M–C'$; or that the production and use of money is consistent with all
currently produced output being bought. One way of doing this, Keynes
suggests, echoing Silvio Gesell, is to make money go bad. 'The trouble with

---

*'the classical theory . . . as exemplified in the tradition from Ricardo to Marshall and Professor
Pigou, appears to me to presume that the conditions for a Neutral Economy are substantially
fulfilled in general; – though it has been a source of great confusion that its assumptions have
been *tacit* . . .'. (*CW*, xxix, 79.)

this . . . is that if we were clever enough to have such money, we would be clever enough to do without it.'[49]*

Keynes's tauter 1933 version brings out more sharply than in the published account his view that expenditure is driven by expectations, and that capitalists may be too scared to embark their money on new machinery, preferring to hoard it. Deficiency of demand thus originates in the fears of capitalists, their fear of making a capital loss. This is a non-Marxist theory of depression. Keynes agrees with Marx that capitalists are ruled by the profit motive. But it is not what he calls the 'post-mortem' failure of profits which produces unemployment; it is the fact that profit expectations may be too low to get capitalists to invest on a sufficient scale. Capitalists do not adjust their production mechanically to results. Rather the results are forced to adjust to their state of mind – their hopes and fears. So you get a level of output corresponding to every set of such hopes and fears: 'Income is the expectation that induces you to do what you are doing.' Expenditure, the psychological factor, is in the driving seat, and income, output and employment have to adjust to 'validate the equations'. All this is in Keynes's fourth and fifth lectures.[50]

Effective demand – the expected sales proceeds which cause production to be what it is – is made up of two components, consumption demand and investment demand. Keynes relates consumption demand to the 'psychological law' that 'normally the change in consumption is less than the change in income'.[51] The multiplier theory follows, relating changes in investment to changes in income, saving and employment. The consumption function was the part of the new theory which proved most accessible (and acceptable) to orthodox economists. That is why it is conventionally seen as the 'kernel' of Keynes's theory. For it is the one genuine *function* in Keynes's system, a *stable* short-term relationship which prevents radical disorder and guarantees a finite multiplier. Yet there is a hidden radicalism lurking here. For what Keynes has implicitly done is to make *workers* (those who normally save only a tiny fraction of their incomes) the saviours of the capitalist system, businessmen its wreckers. While capitalists are febrile creatures, whose nerves can cause economies to go wild, the workers go on stolidly consuming according to slowly changing habit, their 'demand' giving output such stability as it has. They lack the margin, perhaps the imagination, to be nervous; the deadly thought is that the capitalist system will become

---

*It should be noted that the conditions of a money-neutral economy would be satisfied if money were a commodity, like gold. For then the community as a whole could not decide to spend less than it earned. Any increase in the demand for money would merely divert employment into digging up more money. But, although there would be no unemployment, there would certainly be a King Midas problem. Hoarding of commodity money, as we have seen, was Keynes's explanation for the poverty of Asia. This illustrates a point which has generally been missed. Unemployment was, for Keynes, only one (short-run) consequence of the more general *underperformance* of entrepreneur economies in relation to their potential.

more unstable as workers get richer and start to behave more like capitalists.

It was part of the Say's Law approach that a decision to save was a decision to consume later: it was simply a way of redistributing spending through time. It therefore automatically set up a demand for productive facilities (Robertson's 'machines') to produce a larger supply of consumption goods in the future. Keynes's central point was that the logic of a barter economy (in which storing corn now was obviously a decision to use it later) could not be transferred to an economy in which savings are held in money. In a monetary economy, he said, a decision not to have dinner today was not a promise to have dinner next week, an image he reproduces in the *General Theory*. The saver gives no indication of his future consumption plans. 'You diminish sales expectations of entrepreneurs preparing today's dinner and you don't increase expectations of those preparing next week's dinner.' In practice, the effect on entrepreneurs' expectations was worse than this. Investment, Keynes argued, was carried on by means of a 'social convention' that present facts were accurate predictors of events in the far future. By spoiling the immediate prospect of consumption, saving worsened long-term expectations on which current investment depends, and thus influenced demand the wrong way: entrepreneurs conclude that a decision not to have dinner today is a decision never to have it.[32]

A decision to save was thus a subtraction from effective demand, not part of it; bringing about, other things being equal, a fall in aggregate income, and thus output and employment: unemployment is due to uninvested savings. This is Keynes's famous 'paradox of thrift', the central point of his assault on the evangelicised economics of the Victorians, which he expounded in a 'rather good' sixth lecture on 20 November. He believed he was simply strengthening the central contention of his *Treatise on Money*. 'On my view a decrease in consumption will not alter the rate of interest, and hence it will not alter investment. For several years I have argued this position without much effect. Here is a new and perhaps more convincing argument. It takes the lurking fallacy in the classical view to be its implicit identification of deferred consumption, i.e. Savings, with actually expected consumption.'[33] This was his answer to the Hayek/Robertson criticism of his banana parable. They had said: if the price of bananas goes down, the price of machines automatically goes up. But Keynes's economy is not a see-saw; it is more like a leaky balloon, in which the escaping air has nowhere to go back to.

Given the propensity to consume, the income and employment of the community depends on the amount of investment. Investment demand is the most unruly element in the capitalist universe. It is governed by the future expected return on investment goods discounted at the current rate of interest. Aggregate investment will be pushed to the point where the expected net yield (Keynes still uses the Marshallian term 'quasi-rents') equals the market rate of interest – the income which could be obtained from lending money rather than buying capital assets. Given the cost of producing investment goods, investment can increase only if prospective quasi-rent increases, or if the rate of interest falls. Investment is unstable because estimates of future yield are uncertain. 'It is hard to see', Keynes says, 'how any rational man can ever invest, the difficulty of making these estimates is so great. Fortunately, it is the habit of human beings to make guesses on very inadequate evidence. People go right on making these guesses, even though there is no recorded instance of one of them ever being right.' In practice, current yields exercise an 'irrational' influence on estimates of future fields, so that investment fluctuates with every change in the news. In America, irrationality has gone so far that railway property is valued on last week's receipts. 'You must estimate not what the security is intrinsically worth, but what a prospective buyer is likely to take it to be worth according to the conventions of valuation which the complex and irrational psychology of speculation induces. I sometimes think I'd like to . . . [make] investment something like marriage, which is terminable only by death or grave cause.'[54] All of this foreshadows Keynes's depiction of the 'casino' aspects of the stock market in chapter 12 of the *General Theory*; his 'marriage' proposal is also a remarkably accurate statement of the investment philosophy he developed for himself in the 1930s.

To answer the question what determines the rate of interest, Keynes elaborates on liquidity preference – 'the demand which exists for money rather than another form of wealth' – which he had introduced the previous year. Analysing the decision to hold money in terms of *motives*, he identifies for the first time a 'speculative' demand for money. Keynes's theory of interest is tautly summarised: 'It is the rate of interest which brings the quantity of money into alignment with the state of liq[uidity preference] having regard to the state of the news.'[55] The interest rate, being determined in the market for money, cannot be the price which equilibrates saving and investment. Given from the outside, it fixes the scale of investment activity, and thus the amount of saving, output and employment for any set of business expectations.

Keynes had difficulty in explaining what the classical theory of the rate of interest was. Marshall thought the rate of interest was the same thing as quasi-rent, then realised that it entered into the capitalisation of quasi-rents and skated about the problem 'most beautifully'. That was characteristic of Marshall: 'You can't find much truth in him, and yet you cannot convict him of error.' Keynes himself had taught that the interest rate is determined at the point of intersection of the two curves of saving and investment. But this 'doesn't hold one drop of water', because 'Investment and Saving are merely two names for the same thing. You cannot find where a point lies merely by having two names for it. The curves rise and fall together, not in opposite directions.'[56] This way of disposing of the classical theory of interest was, as we shall see, to be strongly attacked by Roy Harrod.

In his retrospective account of the development of his ideas (quoted above, p. 466) Keynes said the theory of investment gave him most trouble. The problems had to do with the way expectations are formed and the 'periods' over which they apply. By the 'state of the news' is meant the influence on people's economic actions of such things as 'Roosevelt's unpredictable character'.[57] But slower-changing forces like the quantity of existing capital goods also enter into profit expectations, giving an expected long-run 'normal' profit. In a draft chapter dating from this period Keynes calls the 'marginal *efficiency* of capital . . . the equilibrium concept about which quasi-rent oscillates, quasi-rent being, so to speak, the short-period version of m.e.c.'.[58] The policy implications of this formulation are pretty obscure. If deficient investment is seen as a 'state of the news' problem, deficit spending by the state might be regarded simply as a jump start, with the private investor returned to the driving seat as soon as the car gets moving. If capitalist economies are doomed to permanent 'underperformance', the case for making the state the chauffeur is much stronger. But what then determines the long-period marginal efficiency of capital?

These have not been lectures about policy, but Keynes outlined three expedients open to government to raise effective demand: it could increase its own expenditure out of loans, increase the quantity of money to force down the long-term rate of interest, or redistribute income in favour of those classes with the highest propensity to consume. The question of the state's permanent role is not addressed.

By the time he gave the lectures, Keynes had come to doubt that monetary manipulation would be enough in existing circumstances:

> My proposals for the control of the business cycle [he wrote in the *American Economic Review*, December 1933] are based on the control of *investment*. I have explained in detail that the most effective ways of controlling investment vary according to circumstances; and I have been foremost to point out that circumstances can arise, and have recently arisen, when neither control of the short-rate of interest nor control of the long-rate will be effective, with the result that direct stimulation of investment by government is a necessary means.

But the problem was not just confined to recent circumstances. Keynes believed that the yield of investment 'in the epoch we are now entering' would be much lower than in the nineteenth century as *opportunities* for investment dried up, requiring a 'rate of interest appreciably below . . . the nineteenth century level' if full employment was to be maintained.[59] This 'secular stagnation' thesis, to which Keynes became increasingly attracted, pointed to a permanently higher level of government spending, combined with measures of income redistribution.

He ended his autumn lectures with some historical reflections along these lines, as taken down by his student Martin Fallgatter:

We might play with the idea that the inability of the interest rate to fall has brought down empires. In the building up process, the population was in a condition of 'natural' poverty to which they were adjusted, and which is steadily being mitigated. There is ample employment, and the abundance of both capital goods and consumption goods increases. With the increase in capital goods towards the saturation point, the risk increases that the interest rate will not fall fast enough, unemployment will appear and rapidly rise. The rapid rise of riches falters. All classes suffer. Social discontent is much greater than under the 'natural' poverty, and there is destructive social disorder.

Thus it is of overwhelming importance that the optimum interest rate be determined by institutions and banking practice. And the bad effect of saving must be recognised. All past teaching has (if my view here given is correct) been either irrelevant, or else positively injurious. We have not only failed to understand the economic order under which we live, but we have misunderstood it to the extent of adopting practices which operate most harshly to our detriment, so that we are tempted to cure ills arising out of our misunderstanding by resort to further destruction in the form of revolution.[60]

So much for the dismal science! Has any major economist so affronted the method and style of his discipline? Only his genius and the desperate character of the times enabled him to get away with it – and then only to a minor extent. For today, in truth, there is little left of Keynes's vision, only some crumbling bones of scholasticism, disinterred for first-year macro-economics students.

Keynes had a ruthless power of concentration. He kept his activities in separate compartments of time, but his feelings pointed them to the same end, which he would have called 'the good life'. It is not surprising therefore that, as pressure of theoretical work lifted, a new, or rather very old, dream should have come into his mind. The idea of a repertory theatre for Cambridge had occurred to him as early as 1913. Now he became obsessed by the thought of creating a stage for Lydia. On 18 September 1933 she had made her professional acting debut at the Old Vic as Olivia in Shakespeare's *Twelfth Night*. Over the summer Keynes had carefully gone through her part with her, but, as she herself recognised, 'I do not always pronounce ideally.' The performance was a critical disaster. *The Times* cruelly mocked her 'Illyrian accent'; the *Daily Telegraph* critic (W. A. Darlington) called her 'the most humourless female in literature'; Virginia Woolf thought it (privately) a 'dismal farce', though her notice in the *New Statesman*, written at Lydia's request, was relatively kind.[61] As the three-week run ended, Keynes wrote to her (on 15 October), 'Don't be too sad about the acting. I swear we will have another go. Dadie to whom I talked about it again presses Nora [in

Ibsen's *A Doll's House*]. He says it is the perfect part for you . . .'

Lydia never tried to act Shakespeare again. While she consoled herself with her 'Russian lunches' at Gordon Square, Maynard plotted his theatre for her at Cambridge. On 20 November he was:

> thinking out a plan to build a small, very smart, modern theatre for the College. Will you agree to appear in the first production of it if it comes off? The argument is this. The ADC has been burnt down. Our Peas Hill site [opposite the College across King's Parade], upon which we intend to build soon, is of ideal size and position. Why should we not join with the ADC? – build a really good theatre to hold 400 to 500, give them Club rooms and certain rights over the theatre (say four weeks in the year) and have the theatre to let as we choose for the rest of the year? The project fascinates me and I already begin to draw up plans of my own for it.

'Everyone thinks Nora very suitable for you and wants you to do it here,' Keynes wrote to Lydia on 21 January 1934, 'but *until* we build the theatre is a difficulty.' On 18 February he reported terrible exhaustion after 'fighting through the Building Scheme [to reconstruct the Provost's Lodge] and the first stages of the theatre scheme' through College Council. 'I made eight speeches altogether, one lasting nearly half an hour and another three-quarters of an hour . . . But the scheme went through.' Although Sheppard was an inspiring Provost, he was a hopeless chairman of committee, and Keynes was to complain even more bitterly than before of fruitless hours wasted on College Council.

Lydia was determined to succeed as an actress. On 4 March 1934, she appeared as Nora in an Arts Theatre Club production in London, Maynard putting up a £125 guarantee. This time the critics were much more friendly; 'Dear Old Maynard was – and this is true – streaming tears,' wrote Virginia Woolf to her nephew Quentin Bell, 'and I kissed him in the stalls between the acts; really she was a marvel, not only a light leaf in the wind, but edged, profound, and her English was exactly what Ibsen meant – it gave the right aroma.'[62]

The building project at Cambridge, together with his writing, was to be Maynard's main occupation over the next two years. On 25 March 1934 he wrote to his mother from Tilton that 'the weather is fine, water plentiful and pigs fat. Kahn is with us and we are discussing the MS of my next book, now nearing completion.' To Lydia he sent a couplet written by a Fellow of King's in the reign of King James I: 'Only in love they happy prove/Who love what most deserves their love.' Maynard said, 'I think it is true.'

IV

Maynard and Lydia sailed for New York on 9 May 1934. Shortly before they docked on 15 May, their ship, the SS *Olympic*, rammed and sank a lightship in the fog, killing seven people.[63] The occasion of Maynard's visit was to receive an honorary degree from Columbia University, New York, on 5 June 1934; its motive was 'inquisitiveness'. He cut down his speech-making and social life to a minimum. He wanted to find out what was happening, and exercise private persuasion in the quarters which mattered.

His visit coincided with a crisis in the New Deal. 'The Skipper's personal machine . . . has physically broken down.'[64] Wall Street was ferociously opposed to the Securities Exchange Bill, which aimed to restrict stock-market speculation by limiting trading on the margin. The banks, fearing a state takeover, were refusing to lend to industry.[65] Business hated the wage-raising labour codes of the NRA. Neville Brown, travelling round America in 1934, briefed his cousin that 'Educated people . . . have a philosophic doubt and antipathy for the whole conception [of the New Deal]. They allege interference with "Economic Laws"; unsuitability for the lawless and individualistic American temperament and tradition; excessive "Regimentation". They fear that the monetary position will eventually become uncontrollable. They constitute a very powerful body of opinion.'[66]

Maynard and Lydia stayed nine days in New York at the Ambassador's Hotel. Walter Case had provided him with an office at Case Pomeroy & Co. in Wall Street, gave a dinner in his honour at the Council for Foreign Relations on 21 May, and fixed up appointments for him with leading bankers, businessmen and banking economists from whom he learnt first-hand the depth of business hatred of the New Deal. Sandwiched at one lunch between Alfred Sloan, president of General Motors, and Walter Chrysler, Keynes understandably found 'much pessimism prevalent because costs [were] increasing faster than incomes and fear [of] inflation causes hoarding of money'. Sam Courtauld, who dined with Maynard and Lydia on 17 May, wrote to Christabel Aberconway:

> Business is at a standstill again – one of those sudden drops which seem to happen so often here from some rapid & unexplained wave of nervousness. Roosevelt is meeting every kind of factional obstruction – partly brought about by all the graft & place-hunting among his own party. The old gang are getting their heads up & working for reaction – everyone is disappointed because miracles don't happen; & the air is full of wild talk about fascism and communism.
>
> . . . I got some of this from Maynard who has spent three days 'downtown', & seems appalled at the tone of mind in financial circles.

He thinks, as I do, that Roosevelt by any comparative standards has done a great deal in a very short time... I must say I admired Maynard for the views he expressed.[67]

Keynes went on to Washington on 24 May, where he stayed at the Mayflower, 'Washington's finest hotel', leaving Lydia to spend the weekend of 26–28 May with the Walter Cases in New Jersey. Felix Frankfurter stage-managed the Washington part of Keynes's trip, supplying him with a sheaf of introductions. 'I am sure a lot of his Wall Street friends will pump him full of poison,' he wrote to Tom Corcoran at the Reconstruction Finance Corporation. 'He is as keen as a lynx, but even he doesn't know the stuff that's buried in the tomes of the Senate Committee [on Banking and Currency], and so even he has hardly an idea of the piracies and greed of American finance or of the huggermuggery and abuses of the Stock Exchange.'[68] Frankfurter asked Roosevelt to see Keynes, to counteract the poison.

On 25 May there were ten hours of conferences, and Maynard found 'life too strenuous for comfort'. In the morning he saw Roosevelt's Secretary of Labour, Frances Perkins, 'the American Susan [Lawrence] but streets above Susan'. According to Perkins's own account, Keynes gave a simple exposition of the multiplier in terms of grocery purchases, which left her baffled.[69] He lunched with Rexford Tugwell, leader of the planning group in Roosevelt's brains trust and 'Walter [Case]'s bête-noire'. There was a meeting with William Phillips, Assistant Secretary of State, 'to discuss War Debts, German debts etc', followed by tea with Supreme Court Justice Brandeis 'to talk legal side of Securities Act, Utilities etc'. Brandeis and Tugwell were at opposite poles of the New Deal – trust-busting versus central planning – and significantly Keynes had more sympathy with the former, not least because he regarded planning as a distraction from recovery. The day finished with a dinner given by Herbert Feis, an old friend from Treasury days and economic adviser to the State Department. It was 'awful hard work trying to be at the top of one's form, to put oneself over the blighters, *all* day', Maynard told Lydia.

On 26 May, 'feeling most lonely', he had lunch with Bewley, of the British Embassy, tea with Morgenthau, Secretary of the Treasury, and dinner with Calvin Hoover, agricultural economist and minor brains-truster, for whose book on Russia he had found an English publisher. (Hoover had also written on Hitler's New Deal, Lydia remarking that 'he always gets into an upheavaled country and scribbles its effects'). Using Keynes's bathroom to wash his hands, Hoover was careful to take a clean towel from the pile, without disturbing the others. Entering the bathroom after him, Keynes swept the whole pile to the floor in lordly fashion, explaining, as he crumpled them up, that his methods of using towels would do more to stimulate employment than Hoover's.

There were more appointments on Sunday and Monday. 'I'm still fright-fully busy, seeing people continuously and now know much more than one small head can hold! It's a very difficult picture to get hold of, but I can't but believe that Walter [Case] has got hold of it all wrong.' Keynes finally saw Roosevelt for an hour at 5.15 p.m. on Monday, 28 May. No one knows what they talked about. Keynes found the tête-à-tête 'fascinating and illuminating'; Roosevelt told Frankfurter that he had had a 'grand talk with Keynes and liked him immensely'.[70] As always, Keynes paid particular attention to Roosevelt's hands – 'Rather disappointing. Firm and fairly strong, but not clever or with finesse.'[71] On Tuesday, his last full day in Washington, he addressed a luncheon meeting of nine leading senators on his recovery plan, and a dinner meeting at the Commerce Department of over fifty NRA organisers; he also saw Lewis Bean of the Agricultural Adjustment Administration. He wrote to Lydia, 'I've had enough I can tell you, and must come away as I'm incapable for the time of absorbing any more information or impressions.'

In many of these meetings, Keynes was 'more of an admiring observer than . . . an instructor',[72] but he was also quoted as saying on several occasions 'that if federal recovery expenditures, then running around $300 million a month, were raised to $400 million a month, the United States would have a satisfactory recovery'.[73] His letter to Frankfurter, written from the Mayflower on 30 May, indicates his state of mind as he prepared to return to New York:

> . . . I must send you a line to thank you for those letters. You chose well and I have been able to use my time here comprehensively and enjoyably. Indeed it has been a great experience. Here, not in Moscow, is the economic laboratory of the world. The young men who are running it are splendid. I am astonished at their competence, intelli-gence and wisdom. One meets a classical economist here and there who ought to be thrown out of [the] window – but they mostly have been.
>
> I wish I were in the job myself, and I can't imagine how you can bear to be away another hour.[74]

Away from Washington, Keynes was again subjected to conservative influ-ences, at a weekend session of the National Industrial Conference Board, an employers' organisation, held near New York. But he refused to be shaken from his belief in the New Deal. At the Commencement Day luncheon, given in his honour by Columbia University on 5 June, he commended Washington's efforts to New York. The New Deal, he said, had aroused his 'deepest sympathy' because it represented an attempt to make the economic system work without destroying the 'free play of individual initiative' and the 'inestimable liberty of thought and speech'. The 'experimental and empirical method' was inevitable because there was 'no one to whom the

President could look for infallible advice'. The atmosphere in Washington reminded him of Whitehall in the early days of the war, with youth being given its head. The contrast with Whitehall in the 1930s must have flashed through Keynes's mind. There were no new faces there: only the same old sceptical faces which had been turning down his proposals for the last ten years. Some movement was certainly taking place under those masks, but it was far from having reached the level of conviction; and the convictions of Whitehall's political masters were all on the side of 'sound finance'.

Keynes went on to appeal to the 'Master Builders' of old America – the tycoons of the past – not to 'turn a deaf ear to the younger generation knocking at its door'. The problem was no longer one of how the individual firm could produce most, but of ensuring that 'a sufficient effective demand will be forthcoming to furnish the inducement to the individual firm to produce what it is capable of producing'. He concluded with his familiar warning that 'If the new problem is not solved, the existing order of society will become so discredited that wild and foolish and destructive changes will become inevitable.'[75]

In his last big engagement, a speech to the American Political Economy Club the next day, Keynes gave a précis of his 'theory of effective demand' to an audience of economists. This had been the basis of his discussions with officials in Washington. America thus received Keynesian economics ahead of England, because there was more to hope for in America than in England.

'In a given situation,' Keynes said, 'output and employment cannot increase unless entrepreneurs anticipate an increased effective demand and prepare to meet it.' In American conditions this anticipation depended on the scale of government loan expenditure. On his estimate of the American multiplier, $400m. a month would do the trick; $300m. was too little. He said a number of other interesting things. All government loan expenditure, including spending on relief, should be treated as equivalent to investment 'at least when . . . considering short-run effects'. This was to prove a danger-ous doctrine when applied mechanically after the Second World War. He explained that a part of the increased expenditure would be taken up by increased production, a part would go to raising prices. The price effect would become greater as recovery proceeded and bottlenecks were encount-ered. Anticipating chapter 19 of the *General Theory* he argued that 'true' inflation was not possible till full employment occurred. 'When a point has been reached at which the whole of the labour and capital equipment of the community are employed, further increases in effective demand would have no effect whatever except to raise prices without limit.' At this point the precepts of sound finance would apply again.[76] Having delivered himself of these pronouncements, Keynes sailed back to England on 8 June, once more on the *Olympic*.

Before leaving he had sent Walter Lippmann, with whom he had dined in New York, an 'Agenda for the President', published in the *New York Times* on 10 June, again after an advance copy reached the White House. This tried to balance the mingled impressions he had received in New York and Washington. He acknowledged that some aspects of the New Deal had created a crisis of confidence in the business community, but turned this into an argument that the government should increase its emergency expenditure to $400m. a month, while trying to reassure business that 'they know the worst' and discontinuing some of the objectionable policies of the National Recovery Administration. In the 'second chapter of the story' government expenditures could be run down as private enterprise took up the slack.[77]

Keynes was once more credited with magical powers over the New Deal. Winfield Riefler of the Federal Reserve Board thought his meeting with the senators on 29 May would ensure the pasage of new housing legislation.[78] Opponents attributed the continuing deficit in the federal budget (a modest $4b. a year!) to 'the advice that Mr John Maynard Keynes the English economist gave the President in June'.[79] On 9 January 1935, Lippmann reported Roosevelt's policy to be 'far more in accord with what you advised last spring' than with the NRA phase.[80] But Roosevelt, incensed by business and judicial opposition to the NRA, and with his re-election prospects threatened by populists like Huey Long and Father Coughlin, was about to swing the New Deal off into a radical, non-Keynesian orbit.

Keynes, like Roosevelt, left different people with different impressions. Some thought he regarded loan-financed public spending as mere pump-priming to get out of a deep slump; others as a permanent part of the machinery for maintaining demand. Keynes explained to Victor von Szeliski, chief statistician of the Research Planning Division of the NRA, that 'My *theory* is the same whether the expenditure is by government or by private capitalism . . . Only in the event of a transition into Socialism would anyone expect government expenditure to play a predominant part year in year out.' But people did not so easily separate theory from political intention.

Szeliski asked another pertinent question. Why was Keynes advocating increased government loan expenditure in the United States when Britain was recovering from the depression with a balanced budget? Keynes wrote back:

> In the case of England our progress has been much slower and on a smaller scale than it would have been if there had been more government loan expenditure. Such improvement as we have, however, is almost entirely attributable, in my judgement, to increased private loan expenditure due to the great fall in the rate of interest. We are in fact in this country in the middle of a building boom. In the case of the United States I see no likelihood of private investment developing on an adequate scale for some considerable time to come.[81]

Keynes objected to people playing politics with his economics; but his own theory held that politics enter expectations, and therefore economics. Government loan expenditure would always leave more to (capitalist) fear than to hope if it was seen as a prelude to socialism. The bankers' strike in the first phase of the New Deal is a good example. These psychological imponderables make it almost impossible to assess the New Deal's contribution to recovery. In Britain, a Conservative government, with a huge majority and two years of sound finance behind it, might reasonably have taken greater risk with business sentiment. But it is hard to know whether unbalancing the budget would have accelerated or retarded recovery in the absence of a well-specified Keynesian theory understood and accepted by businessmen and policymakers alike.

As always, Russell Leffingwell offered an interesting commentary on the different situation in the two countries from a conservative standpoint. In a letter to Lippmann, dated 25 March 1935, he wrote:

> You can lead the horse to water (cheap money) but you cannot make him drink . . . Now the water is there and the thirst is there. Why doesn't the horse drink? It is against nature that he does not drink.
>
> I can tell you why the English horse doesn't drink. First, because English industry has been moribund ever since the war. Their mines are too deep, their plant is obsolescent, and their costs are too high. And, as was pointed out by . . . the Macmillan Committee, their capital market like ours is demoralized and lacks issuing houses to handle domestic capital issues.
>
> Here in America, by contrast, we have a continent still inadequately developed and still underpopulated, and, having been relieved of the monetary obstacle to recovery, there is nothing to prevent recovery, except lack of business profits, and the closing of the capital market by the Banking Act and the Securities Act.[82]

V

STILL WORKING

Keynes returned from the United States with a violent toothache. He had to have his wisdom teeth out – 'a wise routine at my time of life' – chafing at the verbose attentions of the matron in his nursing home. But Virginia Woolf found him 'very fertile' at Tilton in August, speculating about the effects of the American climate on work, the effect of Jewish emigration on the German balance of payments, and other such topics. It was 'that queer imaginative ardour about history, humanity' which Virginia found so attractive about him; 'able to explain flints & the age of man from some book he has read', but 'amused too by little scenes . . .'. He complained that 'great men, Shaw & Wells, are not serious; they do their stunt. Why cant they be simple, & do no stunt? He said Shaw never said anything new, but Charlotte [Mrs Shaw] does. He has a ranging adventurous mind, which I enjoy.'[83]

Keynes was in full flow again with his book. He had been hard at work drafting chapters in the Easter vacation and summer term. He wrote and rewrote on his return from America. He hoped that 'The General Theory of Employment, Interest, and Money' would be ready 'some time next year'.[84] Dennis Robertson stayed, and argued; Kahn came for a long stay and was 'extraordinarily helpful'.[85] 'I think I've solved the riddle of how to define *income* in some sort of *net* sense', Keynes reported to Kahn on 18 September.[86] But ordinary life kept breaking in. Old Mrs Marshall came round for tea, saying she hadn't had sugar in it since the Crimean War. George Kennedy came to discuss the Cambridge theatre project. He attended Roger Fry's funeral. More distracting was Edgar Weller's trial for drunken driving, at which Maynard had to appear as a character witness – Edgar got off with a caution – and an invasion of wasps. 'Tilton is becoming *the* curse of my life', he complained to Sheppard.[87] Nevertheless, chapters 2–14 were in proof for his autumn lectures.

They were much more like the new book than those of the previous year. The 'co-operative – entrepreneur economy' distinction is replaced by the contrast between the 'special case' of full employment represented by the classical theory, and Keynes's own theory in which demand is a problem and the economy can be in equilibrium at any level of employment. 'Therefore, it is essential to discover what determines demand. This . . . is my real subject matter.'[88] There is now a long 'digression' on terms (covering the ground of Book II of the *General Theory*), in which the classical theory is criticised for applying precise methods to vague concepts, and which involves Keynes in specifying appropriate units of quantity (amounts of money value and employment), and defining expectations, income and the marginal efficiency of capital. He restates his old point that the quantity theory of money is useless for causal analysis of changes in output. Definitions of saving and investment follow, with the motives for saving fully spelt out. Keynes then gets on to the theory. Effective demand depends on 'expected consumption' and 'expected investment', and Keynes explains why investment may be insufficient to secure full employment, bringing in the psychology of specu-lation, and his theory of the rate of interest as the 'reward for not hoarding'. At one point when Keynes remarks that the rate of interest has nothing to do with people's desire to save, Bryce, by now a veteran at Keynes's lectures, scribbles 'But oh this is too damn much'.[89]

Michael Straight, in his first year at Trinity College, remembers going to the 1934 lectures. 'The largest lecture hall in Cambridge was crowded . . . It was as if we were listening to Charles Darwin or Isaac Newton. The audience sat in hushed silence as Keynes spoke. Then, in small circles, he was passionately defended and furiously attacked.'[90] Keynes disliked lecturing, and Lydia, as always, bolstered his confidence. 'To-morrow is your ordeal, My Lank,' she wrote to him on 18 November. 'I know you will do it as ever interestingly, as you always give a new twist to everything you say.'

The flavour of Keynes's 'general theory' at this stage is given by his second lecture on 'The Theory of Effective Demand'. The aggregate demand function is the money proceeds employers expect to receive from employing N men; the aggregate supply function, 'the sum which will just make it worthwhile to employ N men'.

> Say's Law [holds that Demand equals Supply] for all values of N. However many men you employ there is no danger of [Supply] being greater than D[emand]. There is therefore never any obstacle to full employment . . . All classical theory is based on this vital assumption, that the demand price of output as a whole is always equal to its supply price. If we question that, the classical results only follow sometimes, in special cases; they are not universal truths. Malthus opposed this classical assumption, and said the trouble arose because effective demand was deficient, which Ricardo said was impossible. Malthus was swept out of the way and Ricardo was completely victorious. The controversy disappeared from economic discussion or was ignored, except by the underworld of Marx, Gesell, and Major Douglas. This has given an unreality to economics . . . hence the lack of respect of the common man . . . The Marxists have become the ultra-orthodox economists. They take the Ricardian argument to show that nothing can be gained from interference. Hence, since things are bad and mending is impossible, the only solution is to abolish [capitalism] and have quite a new system. Communism is the logical outcome of the classical theory.[91]

In a broadcast, published in the *Listener* on 21 November 1934, Keynes explained why he thought effective demand *is* a problem.

> Now the school which believes in self-adjustment is, in fact, assuming that the rate of interest adjusts itself more or less automatically, so as to encourage just the right amount of production of capital goods to keep our incomes at the maximum level which our energies and our organisation and our knowledge of how to produce efficiently are capable of providing. This is, however, pure assumption. There is no theoretical reason for believing it to be true.[92]

As he explained to Alick de Jeune, president of the Antwerp Chamber of Commerce, 'In the past we have been opposing the orthodox school more by our flair and instinct than because we have discovered in precisely what respects their theory was wrong.'[93]

Thus the validity of Keynes's 'general theory' rests on his assertion that the classical theory of the rate of interest is, as he put it in his lectures, 'nonsense'. If it were true, the classical 'special case' would, in fact, be the 'general theory', and Keynes's aggregative analysis not formally wrong, but empty, redundant. It is worth noting, at this point, that mainstream economists after the Second World War treated Keynes's theory as a 'special case' of the classical theory, applicable to conditions where money wages and interest rates were 'sticky'. Thus his theory was robbed of its theoretical bite, while allowed to retain its relevance for policy.

These were, in fact, the main criticisms made by Robertson when Keynes sent him the proofs from which he had been lecturing at the end of 1934. In the long run, Robertson said, the propensity to save of ordinary people had more effect on the rate of interest than 'shifts along the liquidity curve' of professional speculators; and he saw little evidence in nineteenth-century history to persuade him that 'failure to get up to a norm' was 'chronic and endemic' in the modern world.[94] He appended a mass of detailed comments, which Keynes found useful, but which did not prevent him breaking off the correspondence.

Keynes's autumn lectures were delivered in a not untypical term of activity. On Friday, 12 October, he wrote to Lydia, 'I had a heart to heart with Hugh [Durnford] last night and he was very sweet. But the upshot is that he gives up the [domus] bursarship.' Richard Kahn replaced him, without, however, relieving Keynes of the usual autumnal overwork. 'I never seem to get a minute of peace and quiet by myself in the chair with eyes half closed,' he told Lydia on Sunday, 28 October. 'But the worst is over – I went through a mass of Buttress's [bursar's clerk] results to-day, and they are in good order . . . A pack of undergrads. to lunch.'

The following day he wrote to her again:

It's 7.15, my first free moment since daybreak with my Club still to come after Hall. I am too weak to write in ink . . . Gerald [Shove] . . . came to my lecture and said it was the best lecture he had ever heard in his life . . .

I went to a very nice concert in hall last night – Haydn, Brahms variations and songs in Welsh by a choral scholar . . . The theatre project groans along slowly but surely. I feel rather chippy, but it's really overwork. I have too much on my shoulders at this time of year. But I think I'm through the worst.

Your weary lank, M.

On Friday, 2 November:

Frightfully busy, but it has been a peaceful and pleasant day all the same. In the morning I finished my article 'Shaw on Wells on Stalin' and wrote some things which will warm your cockles, I hope. . . . I begin to think about next week. Shall I ask Victor and Barbara [Rothschild] to dinner on Saturday. Or whom would you like to see most?

On 4 November:

Still very busy, but also fairly peaceful. Joan and Austin [Robinson] came to lunch . . . I enjoyed their company. Last night I feasted at Caius, overate, and talked to other Bursars about tithes. On Saturday I had some nice refujews to lunch. I even write my book, and between times I sit in the College Office – so I never walk in the streets. Pipes in bedroom and electric blazers in sitting rooms are necessary, and are on at full strength.

The next day:

This afternoon I finished my College accounts, thank God! My head aches from it, but it is done for another year, and then, perhaps, I can make Alexander do it for me. I was rather pleased with my lecture this morning, – thought it was a good one and better put than in the MS of my book. . . . Walter Case for dinner tomorrow.

On Thursday, 15 November:

Conferences all day [about the theatre]. Lots of little improvements thought out, and now George [Kennedy] has been finally instructed to prepare finished plans for the builders. So you can count the nights until your first night.

 . . .

Duncan has done a record even for him! It appears that he is coming to the Feast here tonight as the guest of George Barnes. A few minutes ago I heard D's voice on the telephone. He was at Peterborough, having got into the wrong train! and would not arrive here until 9.30. All right, I said, have dinner in the train, for by that time there will be nothing but drink here, no food. I can't, came the voice back, for I lost all my money at King's Cross and have only fivepence in my pocket – I had to borrow from the stationmaster to telephone to you.

The following day:

I am half dead with fatigue from over-work and over-eating . . . and will scarcely attempt to write you a letter – I must go and sit in my chair. . . . Stock Exchange still so busy that I am rung up ten or a dozen times a day, and *that* is tiring too – however, great fun and I am enjoying life.

On Friday, 23 November:

Though still a little stupid and muddy in my insides . . . staggered with Piero in the afternoon and visited Glyphoon. [They bought silver to the value of £18.] They turned out to be Hugh Durnford family heirlooms, the silver of Dr. Keate [the famous flogging headmaster of Eton]. As the initial letter is K they will do alright for Keynes.

On 25 November:

Sebastian [Sprott] was in hall last night and enquired after relations in Leningrad – he would like to go there again; meanwhile, poor boy, he lectures 19 hours a week in Nottingham.

On Monday, 3 December:

My last lecture was nearly a disaster. My watch stopt just before I was due to start, and I didnt discover the right time until ten minutes after I ought to have begun. So I rushed down the street and began so breathless that I could hardly speak. . . . I am frightfully tired this evening. But this, I think, is my last heavy day for a long time.

On the 4th:

I was thoroughly overtired yesterday and didn't sleep well. So to-day I am very chippy and in a cycle. However life is peaceful. I worked all day in my office, except for an hour's stagger with Piero in the afternoon; and there Alexander sits too, trying to understand everything more clearly than is possible.

And on the 5th:

The Board of the Theatre has just finished, sitting 4½ hours, and accomplished much business satisfactorily. But I am still pretty tired – for again I didn't sleep properly and am in a heavy cycle (though quite cheerful). I suppose it will pass in a day or two, but I shall be glad to be back at 46.

VI

KEYNES VERSUS MARX

Keynes's conviction that Washington, not Moscow, was the economic laboratory of the world was not widely shared in Cambridge. Anthony Blunt, returning in October 1934 from a year in Rome to a fellowship at Trinity College, found that 'all my friends . . . almost all the intellectual and bright young undergraduates who had come up to Cambridge . . . had suddenly become Marxists under the impact of Hitler coming to power'. Marxism was embraced by the 'brightest and the best' as the cure for war, fascism and unemployment. Membership of the University's Socialist Society and Labour Club, both Marxist-dominated, rose to about 1000 – a fifth of the undergraduate total – by the time of the Spanish Civil War.

Julian Bell's conversion to Marxism affected Keynes personally, for not only was he part of his 'family', but it challenged the whole credo of Bloomsbury, with its separation of art from politics, its combination of ethical idealism and political quietism. Keynes, of course, was not a quietist; but he, too, portrayed the life of action as a necessary chore; the 'crisis of capitalism' as a 'transitory and unnecessary muddle' to be solved by thinking. This cool tone separated him from the young *enragés*. Julian's dissertation on Alexander Pope had failed to get him a fellowship in 1932; its successor, on ethics, which also failed, started with conventional homage to Moore. But Julian, like Rupert Brooke before him, recoiled from Moore's contemplative ideal; he hailed action as the 'most potent of drugs' and embraced 'battlefields and revolutions' as the cure for 'romantic despairs – and other diseases incident to life'.[95] In a letter published in the *New Statesman* a month after the Armistice Day demonstration in 1933, Julian had written:

> In the Cambridge that I first knew, in 1929 and 1930, the central subject of ordinary intelligent conversation was poetry. As far as I can remember we hardly ever talked or thought about politics. For one thing, we almost all of us had implicit confidence in Maynard Keynes's rosy prophecies of continually increasing capitalist prosperity. Only the secondary problems, such as birth control, seemed to need the intervention of the intellectuals.
>
> By the end of 1933, we have arrived at a situation in which almost the only subject of discussion is contemporary politics, and in which a very large majority of the more intelligent undergraduates are Communists, or almost Communists. As far as an interest in literature continues it has very largely changed its character, and become an ally of Communism under the influence of Mr Auden's Oxford Group. . . . Communism in England is at present very largely a literary phenomenon – an attempt of a second 'post-war generation' to escape from the Waste Land.

Julian conceded the 'very large element of rather neurotic personal salvation in our brand of Communism', but said this was only one side of the picture.

> If Communism makes many of its converts among the 'emotionals', it appeals almost as strongly to minds a great deal harder. It is not so much that we are all Socialists now as that we are all Marxists now. The burning questions for us are questions of tactics and method, and of our own place in a Socialist State and a Socialist revolution. It would be difficult to find anyone of any intellectual pretensions who

would not accept the general Marxist analysis of the present crisis.[96]

Bell's claim that Marxism was a hard-headed reaction to the 'crisis of capitalism' does not stand up to serious scrutiny. Hardly any of those involved knew any economics; they just repeated John Strachey's line that nothing could be done to reform capitalism, because any suggested reforms, including Keynes's, were against the objective interests of the dominant class. What Marxism supplied was a language of moral disgust against bourgeois softness and Britain's decadence dressed up as science; communism, a call to action which fused personal and social salvation. The moral and psychological satisfactions being offered were not unlike those of Buchmanism, or even fascism, as Bell recognised. There was also the 'burning question' of 'our own place', as Bell put it, in a social order which no longer generated the 'surplus value' to sustain a leisured class.

Marxism invaded and captured the Apostles, the citadel of Keynes's Cambridge. According to Noel Annan, who came up to King's College in 1935, fifteen of the thirty-one Apostles elected between 1927 and 1939 were 'communist or *marxisant*'. By contrast, only five of the forty-four inter-war elections could be called 'lifelong homosexuals': a question-begging phrase.[97] 'We talk endlessly in the Society about Communism, which is dull,' reported Victor Rothschild to Keynes.

> Guy [Burgess], Alister [Watson] and Richard [Llewellyn] Davies speak with shiny eyes and sweaty foreheads . . . vehemently but somewhat illogically it seems to me. . . . Hugh Sykes Davies prates endlessly about Sadism and Swinburne, while Guy, [William Grey] Walter and I content ourselves with obscene jokes about electric currents. In fact an atmosphere of decadence is appearing and we need your presence.[98]

The Society was, in fact, peripheral to the student politics of the 1930s; its notoriety stems from the fact that four of the eight Cambridge men known to have been recruited to spy for the Soviet Union – Blunt, Guy Burgess, Leo Long and Michael Straight – were Apostles. The psychology of the spies differed from that of the open communists. If contempt for an effete Establishment was common to both, the spies were drawn to the game of conspiracy and deception, to the charms of the clandestine, for its own sake. And here the link with the Apostles is not fortuitous. The spies, like the Apostles, were a secret elite within the elite. The role of such secret elites is to leaven the lump; treachery becomes possible if arrogance turns to hatred and contempt; when 'the country I love is no longer the country I know'. Under particular historical circumstances the machinery of the Society could be captured, and its intense emotional attachments suborned, for service of a foreign cause. As Andrew Boyle says, the full extent of the treachery, with all its shades between passing information to controllers, collusion and covering up for friends, will probably never be known.

Blunt and Burgess were part of Keynes's Cambridge circle – he sat next to Burgess at a College Feast on 24 February 1934 – but what he thought of them is not recorded. The cold-eyed aesthete and the dissolute cherub were no doubt attractive, clever and amusing enough to pass the time with.

Keynes had his own way of analysing and combating the Marxism that gripped the young. He could never take it seriously as a science. But he did take it seriously as a sickness of the soul, for which his generation was partly responsible. For had not Marx – as well as Freud – invaded the spaces left vacant by his own generation's demolition of Christianity? Virginia Woolf has left a fascinating account of having Keynes and T. S. Eliot to dinner in April 1934. Eliot had just published some lectures, *After Strange Gods: A Primer of Modern Heresies*, greatly admired by Keynes, in which he attacked the absence of moral and religious judgements in literary criticism. Keynes had followed Eliot's tortured road back to Christianity with sympathy, starting with a note of appreciation of his *Fragment of an Agon* in 1927. At dinner Keynes said to Eliot, 'You have brought up again one of the primal questions, & nobody has even tried to consider it.' No, replied Eliot, looking, according to Virginia, 'much like a great toad with jewelled eyes'. Keynes told Eliot that 'he would be inclined not to demolish Xty if it were proved that without it morality is impossible'. He said to Virginia, 'I begin to see that our generation – yours & mine . . . owed a great deal to our fathers' religion. And the young, like Julian, who are brought up without it, will never get so much out of life. Theyre trivial: like dogs in their lusts. We had the best of both worlds. We destroyed Xty & yet had its benefits.' Then Julian Bell came in and Keynes turned to 'the economic question: the religion of Communism'. Marxism was 'the worst of all & founded on a silly mistake of old Mr Ricardo's which M[aynard]. given time will put right. And then there will be no more economic stress, & then – ? How will you live, Julian, you who have no moral strictness?' Julian replied that the absence of the old morality had landed his generation in psychoanalysis, but that 'I prefer my life in many ways.'[99]

If morals depend on religion, the question is: which religion? Keynes could never follow Eliot all the way back to Christianity. For his own religion of sweetness and light and optimism, based on Moore's *Principia Ethica*, had inoculated him and his Cambridge friends from that experience of moral chaos which fuelled Eliot's quest for moral authority. Keynes's French correspondent Labordère added the 'self-evident' thought that 'King's men are a religious order and their home a monastery'.[100] Keynes never needed a Jehovah, because he had never experienced despair. It was not his atheism, but his faithfulness to Moore's revelation, embedded in the life of a secular religious order, which kept him out of the Christian camp, just as it immunised him against the appeal of communism. The question of the 'leap of faith' which troubled so many would-be believers did not worry him unduly: for Keynes's religion, too, depended on a direct judgement of what was good, and could no more be proved or disproved than could the existence of God. But he could see that the religion of Bloomsbury and King's had no appeal to someone like Julian Bell when the world was ablaze. And so putting out the fire was a necessary condition for a return to the paths of true religion. Thus far he agreed with Julian. But he could not stomach Marxism as an analysis, or communism as a method. And so he could both love the communist generation for their idealism, and despise them for their muddle-headedness.

If Keynes could not solve the 'primal question' of how to live, he felt he could solve the secondary question of what to do. His assault on the scientific pretensions of Marxism and the horrors of the Soviet system was unremitting, and needed no revelation of mass murder. He insisted on the supreme importance of 'preserving as a matter of principle every jot and tittle of the civil and political liberties which former generations painfully secured . . .'. He was outraged when London University tried to silence the loquacious Professor Laski of the LSE, writing in the *New Statesman* to defend Laski, but adding, 'Too many of the younger members of the Left have toyed with Marxist ideas to have a clear conscience in repelling reactionary assaults on freedom.'[101]* In November 1934 he wrote an article for the *New Statesman* in which he developed his critique of Marxism in the wonderfully good-natured way he had acquired in dealing with sages of the older generation. Its occasion was the publication of an interview H. G. Wells had had with Stalin, on which both Shaw and Keynes were asked to comment. Wells had suggested that in the West the planned economy would be brought about by an intermediate class of technicians and engineers, not by the class struggle between capitalists and workers. Stalin, at his suavest, replied it was impossible to plan the economy without getting rid of private property; the technical intelligentsia could not play an 'independent historical role'. Shaw dismissed Wells's observations as 'Clissoldism', and accused him of instructing Stalin, not listening to what Stalin had to say. Shaw had evidently not felt himself to be under any such limitation in his own two-and-a-half-hour conversation with Stalin in 1931, reducing the monster to silence except for simulated laughter at Shaw's jokes. Stalin thought Shaw a buffoon.

Keynes performed a delicate balancing act between the two socialist gurus. He tried to defend Wells, though he could hardly have enjoyed his feeble performance. 'Wells', he told Virginia Woolf, 'is a little squit. . . . Shaw feels it. Shaw wd. never write of anyone he respected as he wrote of Wells.'[102] But he did not say this in public. As against Stalin and Shaw, Keynes accepted the Wells doctrine of the intermediate class, as he had when he first reviewed 'Clissold' in 1927. The trouble was that Wells had

---

*Laski tried to have it both ways, one side of him deeply rooted in the constitutional legalism of Brandeis and Frankfurter, the other playing with revolutionary violence.

no instruction to give. This was Keynes's summary of the whole 'planning' movement. It was all machinery; no ideas to animate it. Shaw and Stalin ignored the possibility that 'mere intellectual cogitation may have something to contribute to the solution, and also that their traditional interpretation does not fit the present facts'. Shaw was as much a slave to obsolete economics as Asquith and Dean Inge. 'Th[at] system bred two families – those who thought it true and inevitable, and those who thought it true and intolerable. There was no third school of thought in the nineteenth century. Nevertheless, there is a third possibility – that it is not true'; and this will allow us to escape without revolution or socialism.

Had Shaw kept up with the newspapers since the death of Queen Victoria, he would know that capitalists were no longer the self-assured Titans of the nineteenth century. 'Their office-boys (on salaries) rule in their mausoleums. . . . Time and the Joint Stock Company and the Civil Service have silently brought the salaried class into power.' The present order suited them no more than it did the workers. 'When Wells has succeeded in discovering the right stuff, the public will swallow it in gulps – the Salatariat quicker than the Proletariat.' The parochialism of this analysis was pointed out by P. J. M. Larranaga, one of Keynes's favourite monetary 'cranks'. He wrote,

> As you are careful to say . . . your remarks applied to England, where capitalism has taken a semi-paternal responsibility, no doubt under the influence of the 'salatariat'; but in the outside world . . . your hopes and remarks do not apply. . . . England is a country with people and institutions *sui generis*, where every paradox and illogicality is possible, and increasing latent conflict can exist without, at any rate, too frequent violent explosions.[103]

Keynes offered Stalin a crumb of comfort. Communism enormously overestimated the significance of the economic problem. 'The economic problem is not too difficult to solve. If you will leave that to me, I will look after it. But when I have solved it, I shall not receive, or deserve, much thanks. For I shall have done no more than disclose the real problem.' Here he reverts to the ideas of his 'Short View of Russia' in 1925. Communism as an economic system is 'an insult to our intelligence'. Its 'subtle, almost irresistible, attraction' is that it promises to make the situation *worse*. It is a protest against the 'emptiness of economic welfare, an appeal to the ascetic in us . . .'. It is the curate in Wells which draws him to Moscow. 'When Cambridge undergraduates take their inevitable trip to Bolshiedom, are they disillusioned when they find it all dreadfully uncomfortable? Of course not. That is what they are looking for.'

Dora Russell – Bertie's third wife – asked what was intended as the killer question: Why hadn't the world adopted Keynes's plans if nobody was exerting power to prevent it? Keynes was modest, but consistent, in his reply: 'Because I have not yet succeeded in convincing either the expert or the ordinary man that I am right. If I am wrong, this will prove to have been fortunate. If, however, I am right, it is, I feel certain, only a matter of time, before I convince both; and when both are convinced, economic policy will, with the usual time-lag, follow suit.'[104]

Shaw, by his own account, dropped down dead on 24 November, only to be miraculously resuscitated, clearly for the purpose of writing Keynes two spry Shavian letters, putting him right on Marx, the Koran, Ricardian economics, Jevonian economics, Fabian economics, Shaw's own contributions to economics, the horrors of academic life, and much more, before calling Maynard 'a bright and promising youth, frightfully handicapped by the Cambridge nullification process, with some inextinguishable sparks of culture in you which make you interesting'. Keynes read the second one out delightedly to Virginia Woolf. His reply to Shaw's first letter is dated 2 December:

My feelings about *Das Kapital* are the same as my feelings about the *Koran*. I know that it is historically important and I know that many people, not all of whom are idiots, find it a sort of Rock of Ages and containing inspiration. Yet when I look into it, it is to me inexplicable that it can have this effect. Its dreary, out-of-date, academic controversialising seems so extraordinarily unsuitable as material for the purpose. But then, as I have said, I feel just the same about the *Koran*. How could either of these books carry fire and sword round half the world? It beats me. Clearly there is some defect in my understanding. . . . But whatever the sociological value of [*Das Kapital*] I am sure that its contemporary *economic* value (apart from occasional but inconstructive [sic] and discontinuous flashes of insight) is *nil*. Will you promise to read it again, if I do?

Keynes's second letter is dated 1 January 1935:

. . . I will try to take your words to heart. There must be *something* in what you say, because there generally is. But I've made another shot at old K.M. last week, reading the Marx–Engels correspondence just published, without making much progress. I prefer Engels of the two. I can see that they invented a certain method of carrying on and a vile manner of writing, both of which their successors have maintained with fidelity. But if you tell me that they discovered a clue to the economic riddle, still I am beaten – I can discover nothing but out-of-date controversialising.

To understand my state of mind, however, you have to know that I believe myself to be writing a book on economic theory, which will largely revolutionise – not, I suppose, at once but in the course of the next ten years – the way the world thinks about economic problems.

When my new theory has been duly assimilated and mixed with politics and feelings and passions, I can't predict what the upshot will be in its effects on actions and affairs. But there will be a great change, and, in particular, the Ricardian foundations of Marxism will be knocked away.

I can't expect you, or anyone else, to believe this at the present stage. But for myself I don't merely hope what I say, – in my own mind I'm quite sure.

Although Keynes's new theory had little impact as yet beyond the circle of Cambridge's 200 economics students, they at least could not doubt its central message: that there was nothing in the unemployment problem which *required* a revolutionary solution. This itself must have helped limit the political radicalisation of Cambridge in the 1930s. But he knew well enough that good ideas can prevail against political passion only in the long run. In a paper to the Apostles read before the First World War, he had asked, 'How are we to gather unto ourselves the necessary fire and flame if we have no charm of incantation . . . how is intellect ever to hold its own against the force and fury of those who think they have a panacea?'[105] Keynes's greatness as an economist was his combination of intellect and 'charm of incantation' in the service of moderation.

Apart from his lectures, Keynes's direct influence was felt by the pupils who came to him for supervisions, and those who attended the meetings of his Political Economy Club. Of the lecture note-takers, only two, David Champernowne and Bryan Hopkin, were tutorial pupils of Keynes, the latter, exceptionally, not a student at King's. In Keynes's supervisions of the early 1930s are to be found names of those who later achieved fame as economists and public servants. In addition to Champernowne and Hopkin, Bensusan Butt, P. J. Gifford and Brian Reddaway stand out. (Keynes considered Reddaway, who came up with Champernowne in 1931, 'by far the best economist of his year'.)[106] As always, the essays Keynes set his students reflected both the important questions of the day and his own theoretical preoccupations. In December 1931 Crosfield, Cuthbertson, Reddaway and Blair-Cunynghame were invited to 'Compose a communication to the United States on the question of War Debts, writing as an economist, not as a rhetorician, using no bad arguments and making no false appeals, and *sharply distinguishing* between (1) the economic issues, (2) the political issues, and (3) the general problems of relations between nations which are involved.' The same Part I class was asked in April 1933 to 'Outline a policy for the World Economic Conference in the light of the latest developments in the USA'. In November 1933 Champernowne, Cuthbertson and Reddaway, now in Part II of the tripos, were asked to define, and state the conditions for, 'short-period equilibrium' and 'long-period equilibrium' respectively. On 10 February 1934, Champernowne and

Reddaway were required to 'Summarise and criticise the theory of the Rate of Interest as it is to be found in the works of Marshall and his contemporaries' and to 'Consider the relation of the Rate of Interest to the Marginal Efficiency of Capital'. In the following academic year Keynes teased Alexander Henderson, Christopher Simon and Bryan Hopkin with another topic close to his heart: ' "Prices depend on the marginal cost of production." "Prices depend on the quantity of money." How, if at all, would you reconcile the two orders of ideas which lie behind these two statements respectively?'

Keynes's Political Economy Club of dons, postgraduates and the best Part II students continued to meet weekly in his rooms on Monday evenings. One of those who attended was Michael Straight, the son of Dorothy and Willard Straight. Michael's father had died in 1918, and Dorothy, a Standard Oil heiress with ideals, married another idealist, Leonard Elmhirst, in 1925. They bought Dartington Hall, a Tudor manor in South Devon, from the Champernownes, and started a utopian community, based on an arts college, progressive school, textile plant, sawmills, cider press and two modern farms. Keynes had got to know Dorothy through the Lippmans, and his journalistic connection with *New Republic*, which she owned. He was planning to bring the Kurt Jooss ballet, established at Dartington Hall after it left Germany – he thought Jooss one of the two greatest living choreographers, the other being Massine – to his new theatre at Cambridge; he also kept an eye on the handsome, but troubled Michael when he came up to Trinity. Michael Straight has left two impressions of Keynes in action in the autumn of 1935. The first, in a letter to his mother dating from mid-October, describes a meeting of Keynes's club addressed by an Italian postgraduate, Zampart Lambardi, on 'The Price Level and Stabilisation', at which he was drawn to speak ninth, before Keynes. 'I felt my stomach contracting continually, in fact almost shrinking through my back. I couldn't understand one word of his wretched paper.' Three other second-year students had to speak before him.

> [Peter] Bauer, the Austrian, spoke so fast that no one could understand what he said, so that he got away with it. Stamp, the son of Josiah Stamp, made a long and intricate analogy about a traveller and a map in which he never mentioned economics – so he got away with it; and [Alexander] Henderson trotted out some phrase from Joan Robinson which he'd obviously just learnt beforehand and sat down before anyone could ask him what he meant – so he got away with it.
>
> I tried to say something about the price level and stabilization and didn't get away with it. After I had finished a halting pointless speech I turned to Lambardi and put in a form of a question. But he looked up with a perplexed face and said quite justifiably that he couldn't see the point of what I'd said.

I turned round and asked in a despairing strangled voice if *anybody* could see the point in what I'd said.

But needless to say none of them could and Keynes nobly rescued me by saying 'I think I know what you mean . . .' and then explaining a long and difficult theory which of course had never entered my mind but with which I fervently agreed.

Then he wound up brilliantly and I sneaked out before anyone had a chance to pin me down. . . .

In his published recollection of this event, Straight says that after Keynes had finished speaking he glanced at him without even a smile, so as not to lay claim on his gratitude. The occasion is a good example of his winning way with the young.[107]

A fortnight later, on 28 October, Champernowne had to speak on Marx. Straight, then a fervent Marxist who, characteristically, had opened *Das Kapital* for the first time only the evening before, fielded the first question addressed to Champernowne, when Keynes got up.

He stood like a great bear in front of his fireplace. He rocked back and forth. Marxism, he said, was even lower than social credit as an economic concept. It was complicated hocus-pocus, the only value of which was its muddleheadedness. He had read Marx, he said, as if it were a detective story, trying to find some clue to an idea in it and never succeeding.

It was the first time, Straight recalls, that a leading Cambridge intellectual challenged the 'new orthodoxy that had fastened itself upon the minds of the undergraduates. . . . David was crushed. Sraffa was silent as we walked at night along Kings Parade. I was shaken, but my political allegiance was unchanged. Intellectually, I was a follower of Keynes; emotionally, I was dependent upon James [Klugman] and John [Cornford].'[108]

Michael Straight gained first-class honours in both parts of the economics tripos, and became an Apostle and president of the Union in 1937. Through the influence of Keynes, whom he loved and admired, he lost his belief in Marxism, but not his emotional dependence on his communist friends. That is why he allowed himself to be recruited as a Soviet agent by Anthony Blunt, though he never spied for the Soviet Union.

VII

'MODEST PREPARATIONS FOR THE GOOD LIFE'

The depressed condition of capitalism in the 1930s did not stop Keynes
from becoming 'horribly prosperous'. In 1929 he had lost practically all his
money; in 1931 he even tried to sell two of his best pictures, his Matisse
Déshabillé and his Seurat *Study*, but found no buyers at his minimum price.
By 1936 his net worth came to over £500,000, or about £13m. in today's
values. His capital had appreciated by twenty-three times, in a period when
Wall Street's stock prices had only trebled, and London's had hardly moved
at all. Most of Keynes's gains came from New York. He entered Wall Street
for the first time in 1932, and dollar shares made up 40 per cent of his
portfolio by 1936. Over his life Keynes was a spectacularly successful investor, though he suffered three major setbacks – in 1920–1, 1928–9 and 1937–8.
Practically all his durable gains came after 1932. Keynes's annual income
was large, but not stupendously so. Between 1930 and 1936 it averaged just
over £6000 a year (gross) – the equivalent of about £150,000 today. In the
two tax years 1936–7 and 1937–8 it shot up to over £16,000 a year (or
£400,000) but never got as high again. His academic income came to about
a third of the total from 1930–6; the rest was from dividends and fees. He
and Lydia lived very comfortably, but not extravagantly.

Keynes was also partly responsible for the investment policies of a number
of companies, and of King's College, Cambridge. The PR Investment Trust
for friends of Keynes and Falk was wound up in 1935. The Independent
Investment Trust also suffered in the depression. Falk and Keynes again
fell out, Keynes playing little part in the 1930s. This left the National
Mutual and the Provincial Insurance Companies (the latter a family trust
managed by Francis Scott). The more directly under Keynes's control the
investments were, the better they performed. The outstanding example is
his management of the College Chest. Unlike the other College funds, it
was his sole responsibility. Its capital increased sevenfold from 1920 to 1936
– from £30,000 to £200,000 – again mostly in the 1930s. The National
Mutual and the Provincial, whose investment decisions were decided by
boards on which Keynes sat, did less well, but still 'gave a good thrashing'
to the indexes.[109]

Keynes's personal investment philosophy changed with his economic
theory, the symbiotic connection between the two being most apparent in
chapter 12 of the *General Theory*, when he sharply distinguishes between
investment and speculation. In the 1920s Keynes saw himself as a scientific
gambler. He speculated on currencies and commodities. His aim was to
play the cycle. This was the height of his 'barometric' enthusiasm, shared
with Falk, when he believed it was possible, by forecasting short-term
rhythms, to beat the market. The gambling instinct was never quite extingu-

ished. There is a famous occasion in 1936 when he was forced to take delivery of a month's supply of wheat for England from Argentina on a falling market. He planned to store the wheat in King's College Chapel, but was told it was too small. Ever resourceful, he proposed to object to its quality: the cleaning took a month, by which time its price had risen sufficiently for him to escape without loss. There were loud complaints that some 'infernal speculator' had cornered the market![110]

By the 1930s he was prone to dismiss this kind of activity as a mug's game. 'I was the principal inventor of credit cycle investment,' he told Richard Kahn in 1938, 'and I have not seen a single case of a success having been made of it.' Credit cycling meant valuing shares relative to money, rather than to their worth relative to other shares;[111] or, as he put it in his 1933 lectures, valuing them by last week's results, rather than by their long-term prospects. His new philosophy can be summed up as fidelity to a few carefully chosen stocks: his 'pets', as he called them. The investor should *buy*, not sell, on a falling market; the expectation of picking up bargains was more rational than yielding to the panic psychology of the crowd. Thus his personal investment philosophy came into line with his increasing theoretical emphasis on the need to stabilise investment. The investor, like the government, should fight the mania for liquidity. The realisation that, as he put it in his 1938 Memoir Club paper, 'My Early Beliefs', civilisation was a 'thin and precarious crust' also pointed to the investor's rational interest in social stability. A new form of the equation between long-run self-interest and the public good had formed in Keynes's mind.

He acted on his principles, despite frequent attacks of 'nerves'. In 1932 he started buying preferred shares of the big American public utility holding companies 'which are now hopelessly out of fashion with American investors and heavily depressed below their real value'.[112] When South Africa left the gold standard, he bought shares in a South African gold-mining company, Union Corporation, whose managing director was his old friend Henry Strakosch.[113] He was unrepentant at being caught out by the crash of 1937–8. As he told Francis Curzon, one of his fellow directors of the National Mutual, in 1938, to hold on in a falling market was more than self-interest; it was an obligation:

> I feel no shame at being found still owning a share when the bottom of the market comes. I do not think it is the business of . . . [a] serious investor to cut and run on a falling market. . . . I would go much further than that. I should say that it is from time to time the *duty* [italics added] of a serious investor to accept the depreciation of his holdings with equanimity and without reproaching himself. Any other policy is anti-social, destructive of confidence, and incompatible with the working of the economic system. An investor is aiming or should

be aiming primarily at long period results and should be solely judged by these.[114]

Keynes offered a lighter-hearted piece of wisdom to Marcel Labordère. They had been discussing the differences between the 'slow-going' and 'quick-going' investor.

> But whether for the slow-going or the quick-going [Keynes wrote on 28 September 1937], is not the rule to be in the minority? It is the one sphere of life and activity where victory, security and success is always to the minority and never to the majority. When you find any one agreeing with you, change your mind. When I can persuade the Board of my Insurance Company to buy a share, that, I am learning from experience, is the right moment for selling it.

Athol Fitzgibbons is right to say that Keynes blamed the instability of capitalism on the bad faith of investors.[115]

A sign of Keynes's growing social conservatism was his commitment to the countryside. To the young Keynes, as to any bourgeois of his time and place, rural life (though not owning a country house) was synonymous with ancient prejudice and superstition. In the 1920s he had poured scorn on land as an investment, and had liquidated as many as he could of the College's land holdings. This attitude started to change when the agricultural depression at the end of the 1920s faced King's with the choice of selling a large estate, Elsham, in north Lincolnshire, which it had bought in 1925, or farming it itself. Keynes emerged as the unlikely champion of the second course. 'There was something expiatory in this,' wrote Hugh Durnford, the domus bursar at the time. Keynes, whose attitude to farming had been that of a hard-headed accountant, now succumbed to the romanticism of the soil. Nor was this an abstract fancy. He took his duties as an improving landlord seriously, visiting the estate frequently, and learnedly discussing points of stock and the dietary habits of pigs with the labourers. This, his first serious contact with an admittedly untypical segment of the English working class, humanised rather than radicalised him. It also brought out a latent paternalism. In 1930 he started a piggery with Edgar Weller at Tilton, contracting to deliver pigs of a certain quality to a local bacon factory. They acquired a huge boar, Tilton Beau; Keynes congratulated Weller on his white sow's 'huge progeny'. He began to see himself as the Squire of Tilton. In 1934 he acquired shooting rights over Tilton Wood. At the end of 1935, he took out a new twenty-one-year lease on the house and the whole farm – about 3000 acres in all – and appointed a bailiff, Logan Thompson, to manage it. Lydia started distributing presents to the farm workers at Christmas. At the same time, as we have seen, he began lauding national self-sufficiency, and talking about the dignity of manual labour. All this was part of an evolution in his character, and outlook, for which his economics provided a sophisticated rationale. Critics would say that the *General Theory* marked an intellectual retrogression. More justly it can be seen as a spiritual and moral adaptation to the realities of the 1930s.

Keynes was not one of those who averaged out his consumption over his life-time. He was not extravagant, but when he had money he spent it, not on good living, but on the good life. Thus the scale of his benefactions rose in the 1930s with increasing wealth, this despite the fact that two of his good causes succumbed to the depression. The Camargo Society, as we have seen, was wound up in 1933, after putting on two seasons of ballet in the depth of the slump. The London Artists' Association came to an end the same year. There had been fierce quarrels with Duncan, Vanessa and Roger Fry about enlarging the Association in 1930, with Keynes championing the claims of the younger painters; Duncan and Vanessa resigned from it in 1931 after receiving an offer from Agnew's Gallery 'too good to be refused'. Maynard was wounded both by the withdrawal of his oldest friends and by their refusal to tell him what Agnew's had offered. Their defection doomed the Association, since they were its best-selling painters. With sales slumping, Keynes was forced to tell the remaining painters, in October 1933, that 'the results were no longer justifying the expenditure and that the Association should be wound up'. He and the two other guarantors, Samuel Courtauld and Frank Hindley-Smith, agreed to go on supporting Edward Wolfe and William Roberts – Wolfe, probably for old times' sake, Roberts because he was the young English painter Maynard most admired. He bought several paintings of his at the LAA exhibitions, including Roberts's portrait of himself and Lydia, for £50, in July 1932, which he hung in his study at Tilton; he believed that Roberts 'will really live'.[116] For a few years after the rupture with the LAA, relations between Tilton and Charleston became distinctly chilly. Leaving the Association proved a false move for both Duncan and Vanessa. They lost touch with the younger painters, and their own individuality was not strong enough to impose itself on contemporary taste. Their reputations went into rapid decline. The rejection in 1936 by the Cunard line of Duncan's decorative panels for the *Queen Mary*, which it had commissioned from him, was a devastating blow to his confidence from which he never really recovered. Maynard intervened with the chairman, Sir Percy Bates, but to no avail.

Keynes used his wealth to buy both pictures and books. He added two Cézannes and two Delacroixs to his collection in 1935–7. He also bought his first painting from Ivon Hitchens, another young English artist who became a favourite in the late 1930s. The picture which escaped him was the finished painting of Seurat's *La Grande Jatte*, of which he owned one of the three studies. He had a chance to buy it from the family in 1935: it is now the jewel of Chicago's Art Institute. The mid–1930s also saw the start of large book and manuscript purchases. He had 'evolved the plan of forming a really comprehensive collection to illustrate the history of thought'.

Starting with the purchase of thirty-six titles from Gibbon's Lausanne Library auction in December 1934 he systematically pursued it for the rest of his life. His book and manuscript collecting increasingly absorbed energies earlier devoted to the stock market, but it was governed by the same principle of buying stock which he thought underpriced relative to its intrinsic worth.[117] From this time, too, he started making substantial donations to charities, settling annuities on Bunny Garnett, Duncan Grant and younger relations, and giving lavish presents, mainly of rare books, to his friends.

But his main capital spending in these years went on his building programme. Having secured his new lease at the end of 1935, he commissioned Kennedy to rebuild Tilton, with a new wing and a big new main staircase. Kennedy had also submitted plans, costing £42,000, for a new theatre and hostel for King's College students at Cambridge, on a site facing Peas Hill and St Edward's Passage. The project was proving extremely complicated, not just because of the rabbit-warren character of the site, and the need to buy out and relocate shops (including Gustave David, his old bookseller) but also because the College Council refused to finance the theatrical part of the rebuilding programme. Keynes submitted a memorandum on 25 July 1934, in which he undertook to accept financial responsibility for building and running the theatre, on a long lease of part of the site. This broke the deadlock. 'I believe', he wrote,

> that a good small theatre, equipt with all the contrivances of modern stagecraft, is as necessary to our understanding of the dramatic arts, with their complicated dependence on literature, music and design, as a laboratory is to experimental science. It is the outstanding characteristic of our own generation that we have gone far to restoring the theatre . . . to the place in the serious interests of the University which it held at the beginning of the seventeenth century.[118]

Kennedy submitted a new plan for a theatre costing £15,000. In October 1934, Keynes appointed Norman Oppenshaw Higgins, who ran the 'excruciatingly uncomfortable' Cosmopolitan Cinema, as secretary, at £400 a year, of a company of which he would be chairman, to build 'The Cambridge Arts Theatre'. The other members of the Board were Dadie Rylands and Miss J. M. Harvey, who had been secretary of the Camargo Society and now ran the London Film Society. Higgins would manage the theatre, which would also show films. When Higgins protested that he knew nothing of theatrical management, Keynes assured him that 'we shall learn by experience unencumbered by notions which may prove inappropriate to the present venture'.

The plan was for a theatre to seat 500–600, with the College providing a ninety-nine-year lease. Soon a restaurant was added to the plan, Keynes insisting that a civilised theatre-goer 'must be able to dine within the building'. He got a £5000 mortgage from his friend and co-director Francis Scott of Provincial Insurance, giving the company a capital of £20,000 with 7500 ordinary and 7500 £1 preference shares. Building started in March 1935. But despite a circulation of prominent Cambridge residents, few preference shares were bought. Costs, including provision for working capital, escalated to £30,000. Keynes ended up paying £20,000 himself (about £500,000 today), to build the theatre, half in the form of an interest-free loan to the company, his sister Margaret and Miss Harvey putting up much smaller sums. 'The greatest comfort of all, I think, from having some money,' he wrote to Lydia on 17 January 1935, 'is that one does not need to badger other people for it.'

As he was providing most of the money, Keynes naturally kept a tight control over costs. But, being Keynes, he developed an insatiable interest in every aspect of the work. 'You can't imagine the details which have to be attended to,' he told Lydia on 10 February 1935. 'We have to get permission for all plans from the Chief Constable, the Fire Brigade, the Borough Surveyor, the County Surveyor, the licensing justices, and the Vice-Chancellor.' There were endless conferences with Dadie and Higgins, the latter 'a jewel of the highest price, – flawless, perfect and serene'. The whole of Saturday, 23 February 1935 was spent going through criticisms of the plans made by Frank Birch, King's Fellow and ADC producer: Kennedy emerged victorious, because 'he had so much more genius than Frank', Keynes told Lydia. Keynes himself corresponded with Professor Inglis of the Engineering Laboratory on lighting and electrical problems. He fussed about the position of the wind and string instruments in the orchestra pit, and weighed the acoustical effects of separating the under-stage from the orchestra by curtains or 'some sort of wooden contraption'. He approved the design and positioning of the seats. He worried about the colour of the panelling, while admitting to George Kennedy that 'I always find it difficult to visualise such things.' Influenced by his experience of Lydia's backstage conditions, he worked with Higgins to get the dressing rooms 'as large and convenient as possible'. Finding the right people to run the restaurant proved a nightmare without end. An offer to a Mrs Burton had to be hurriedly withdrawn when her own restaurant went bust. Dadie produced a 'rich young baronet with social connections'. Kahn offered a lady with the right 'nuance'. Higgins proposed a butler married to a Hungarian cook. Eventually a Mrs Hooper and a Mrs Travers were appointed at £3 a week. More satisfying was the decision of the Board that 'the Chairman and Mr. Rylands should proceed with the purchase of wines at their discretion'. But the restaurant never did work properly. To Keynes also fell the task of organising the programme for the first season. He wrote round to playwrights to send him plays, to theatre managers to exchange productions; he tried to link up with pre-London runs. The Irish dramatist Sean O'Casey was highly sceptical of the whole idea. 'Is it out of his mind he [Keynes] is?' he asked David Garnett, whom Keynes had used as an intermediary.

'Better by far to build a convalescent Home for the English Dramatic Critics.'[119] An opening season was cobbled together, its highlights being a gala opening by the Vic–Wells ballet, and an Ibsen cycle of four plays, featuring Lydia as Nora in *A Doll's House* and Hilda Wangel in *The Master Builder*. The original plan was to open in October. But this had to be postponed as the building took longer to finish than anticipated.

Early in January 1936 Keynes was still inspecting the 'designs for matchboxes, uniforms for the page boys, cork floors for dressing rooms, etc, etc'. Men worked all through the night to get everything ready for the opening. At last, on 17 January, Keynes could tell Lydia that the 'fundamentals are finished'. He was well satisfied with the theatre's final appearance, except that 'its curious pentagonal shape [which symbolised the five arts of drama, opera, ballet, music and cinema] makes it look to my eye a little lopsided'. The theatre, which has no frontage of its own, being approached from under the student hostel, is still in use. It illustrates Kennedy's particular skill in conjuring spacious interiors out of nothing, and in adapting his designs to other buildings already there.[120]*

Lydia was both nervous and excited about the career she and Maynard had mapped out for her. 'Hilda Wangel is a wonderful part, I do want to be good in it,' she told him on 17 January 1935. She became a regular theatre-goer and play-reader, taking lessons in intonation, and avidly discussing with Maynard the plays they had both seen. Keynes thought Gielgud's Hamlet was 'too much on top of the situation and was fully capable, from the beginning to the end, of doing in the whole lot of them . . .';[121] she thought Wendy Hiller, a 'most attractive young actress', who was 'not praised enough' for her performance in Greenwood's *Love on the Dole*.[122] In Cambridge, Maynard had been to see Dadie's production of Pinero's *The Second Mrs Tanqueray* at the rebuilt ADC theatre. 'It was very amusing, much too amusing,' he wrote,

> but there was no attempt to reconcile the two hopelessly divergent keys. There was no disguising that it was a brilliantly constructed 'strong' period drama verging on serious tragedy, frightfully important in the history of the theatre. But there was also no avoiding its being played as a screaming farce, with the period costumes guyed, an undergraduate playing Mrs Pat's part, Dadie's George Alexander, and

*In 1938, Keynes transferred control of the Arts Theatre Company to a board of Trustees representing the University. He handed over all his shares to the new board, covenanted to pay it £5000, and obtained a £12,000 mortgage from Barclay's Bank to repay the loan to himself. After just over two seasons, the theatre had put on performances under the auspices of bodies like the Greek Play Committee, the University Musical Society and the ADC and Marlowe Societies. It had itself produced plays by Shakespeare, Molière, Goldoni and Ibsen, and operas by Mozart, Arne, Handel and Vaughan Williams. It had given seasons of performances by the Vic–Wells ballet and opera companies, Dublin's Abbey Theatre, the Westminster Theatre, the Mercury and so on.

lots of lines in the play worthy of 'Young England'. So we all howled with laughter – it *was* frightfully funny. But the serious side in me rebelled a little, and it would in you even more. I've never been so *cold* as I was in the ADC.[123]

Lydia's letters to Maynard continue to be full of ballet comment, uncharitable to Alicia Markova ('wobbling Jewish feet'), interested in Margot Fonteyn ('possibilities with her body; but I wonder if she [has] something of her own'), sad about the failure of Jooss in London ('his ballets cannot reach Croydon'), hopeful about Fred Ashton ('out of the ballet world, he is the one who is interesting . . . I always feel he might yet do something great . . .'). She gossiped affectionately about Sam Courtauld, with his indigestion but undiminished appetite; less affectionately about the Bowens, with whom relations had cooled. She had taken to ending her letters to Maynard with curious Italian and French phrases: 'Addio, Lank', 'Au demain'. She referred to her private parts as 'rendez-vous' after a new ballet by Fred Ashton; but perhaps, by now, more in hope than expectation, slyly telling Maynard that her occasional orgies of cream cakes and clothes-buying 'were sexual, weren't they?'

Lydia accepted an invitation from the BBC to read Hans Christian Andersen's fairy tale, 'The Red Shoes', on Christmas Eve in 1934. It is a story about a little girl whose obsession with her appearance, symbolised by her beautiful red shoes, brings on her the curse to dance in them till she dies. Eventually, she repents of her sin, and has her shoes and feet cut off, and her soul flies up to heaven. Maynard congratulated Lydia on her broadcast with a strange little fairy tale of his own, about some red shoes made for an accountant's son.

> Now the little boy's name was Maynar. Beautiful specking shoes. And when Maynar specked to the right, the shoes specked to the left, and when Maynar sold a speck, the shoes bought a speck . . . Until he came to the Solicitor's house in the forest. And the solicitor said, 'Do you know who I am? I cut off wicked people's fortunes.' And Maynar said, 'Do not cut off my fortune for then I could not make recompense. But cut off my shoes with the specking feet in them.' And he confessed all his sin . . . [124]

Was not his recompense for the sin of speculation the Arts Theatre which he built for his Princess?

VIII

FINAL TOUCHES

By May 1935, Maynard's book was in a 'retouching' state. [125] This meant some fairly drastic rewriting, mainly shortening and simplifying. 'What I have to say is not really so terribly complicated,' he wrote to Harrod, 'but there is some evil genius which sits at the elbow of every economist, forcing him into all sorts of contorted and unnecessary complications.'[126] He took his new theory to Oxford in February 1935; the result was a notable duel with Hubert Henderson, now a Fellow of All Souls. In June, Bryce, the veteran note-taker, expounded the new doctrine at the LSE, where Hayek courteously opened his seminar to him. The chief problems his audience found were with the definitions of income and investment. Keynes found Bryce's summary 'excellently done'; that the chief difficulties at the LSE should be with definitions illustrated 'the appalling state of scholasticism into which the minds of so many economists have got . . . in writing economics one . . . is trying to arouse and appeal to the reader's intuitions; and, if he has worked himself into a state when he has none, one is helpless!'[127]

Galley proofs went out to Harrod, Hawtrey, Kahn and Joan Robinson in mid-June. The exchanges with Robertson were not resumed, by mutual agreement. Keynes had found Dennis's commentary earlier in the year 'most painful'; his state of mind 'pathological'. Dennis, he told Lydia, was 'dangerously near trying to prevent [Joan Robinson] from lecturing . . . *Why* are economists all mad?' Robertson was going through a troubled time. His mother, from whom 'he was never properly separated', had died in January, and 'the morbid madness of her old age used to affect him very much'.[128] His inability to accept the Keynesian revelation was starting to make him feel a 'back number' at Cambridge. Neither Henderson nor Pigou received proofs. Thus, of his own generation, Keynes thought only Hawtrey was sufficiently sympathetic to help him in his last stage. The battle-lines were forming up.

In fact, the Keynes–Hawtrey exchanges, which meandered on through the summer and autumn, ended with Keynes feeling that 'on certain points we are still further apart than you think'.[129] Hawtrey's letters grew longer and longer; Keynes was extraordinarily patient in his replies. As Joan Robinson, to whom he handed over the correspondence at one point, told him, 'I certainly don't think an archangel could have taken more trouble to be fair and to be clear. I darkly suspect that Hawtrey hasn't really taken in the theory of the rate of interest. His sudden relapse into talking about "idle savings" seems to give him away.'[130] Hawtrey thought Keynes's obscure chapter 17, relating 'own-rates' of interest to the marginal efficiency of capital, 'brilliant and original',[131] but otherwise he was mostly critical. Keynes accepted some points. He dropped the word 'quasi-rent' after Hawtrey persuaded him that his use of it was inconsistent with Marshall's and added nothing to the idea of 'expected profit'.[132] Other points, on which Keynes did not yield, were to be taken up by subsequent critics. Hawtrey thought Keynes's 'investment' confused a number of separate activities, subject to different motives; for example, he accused him, in his chapter 12 on long-term expectations, of not distinguishing between 'the state of mind of the promoter of a capital enterprise and that of the purchaser of shares'.[133] He objected to the definition of effective demand in terms of expected rather than actual sales.[134] He thought Keynes greatly exaggerated the importance of liquidity preference.[135] He was troubled (as many others have been) by the relationship between saving and investment as an identity and the process by which saving and investment are adjusted to each other.[136] Hawtrey did succeed in obtaining one important elucidation. 'But whilst my theory of the rate of interest is essentially based on uncertainty,' Keynes wrote to him on 8 November, 'my theory of prospective yield is not. Prospective yield must take account of uncertainty, but uncertainty is merely a complication, not the essence of the matter.'[137] But what, then, was the essence?

Harrod's criticism had more effect; Keynes wrote to him on 10 September that he had 'gained a great deal from your hard knocks, and would like some more'. Harrod was by then teaching economics at Christ Church, Oxford. Though he had not been involved in the Circus, he and Meade were the chief Keynesians at Oxford. This had not stopped Harrod from calling Pigou's *Theory of Unemployment* a 'supreme intellectual achievement' when he reviewed it in the *Economic Journal* in 1934. Harrod's criticism of Pigou showed that he was essentially a 'Book I' Keynesian: he thought Pigou had failed to clinch his argument that money-wage reductions would bring about a fall in the real wage, and he made this point in his letter to Keynes of 30 August 1935:

> Your really important and effective criticism of the classical view occurs in Book I. It is implicit in the classical view that any given level of output is uniquely correlated with a given level of *real* wages . . . Once you knock that on the head, as you do most effectively, the level of output is either indeterminate, or has to be determined by some new equation not provided for in the classical system. Thus the way is clear for a radical reconstruction. Your new equation is the liquidity preference schedule . . . No further criticism of the classical system is required. All your subsequent criticism is fussy, irrelevant, dubious, hair-splitting and hair-raising.[138]

Harrod criticised Keynes's attack on the classical theory of the rate of interest partly on grounds of controversial manners, but also because he thought Keynes had misunderstood the classical theory. On the first point, he urged Keynes to 'minimise and not maximise the amount of generally

accepted doctrine that your views entail the scrapping of. A general holocaust is more exciting. But . . . you no longer require these artificial stimulants to secure attention.'[139]

Keynes replied on 27 August:

> But the general effect of your reaction . . . is to make me feel that my
> assault on the classical school ought to be intensified rather than
> abated. My motive is, of course, not in order to get read. But it may
> be needed in order to get understood. I am frightfully afraid of the
> tendency, of which I see some signs in you, to appear to accept my
> constructive part and to find some accommodation between this and
> deeply cherished views which would in fact only be possible if my
> constructive part has been partially misunderstood. That is to say, I
> expect a great deal of what I write to be water off a duck's back. I
> am certain that it will be water off a duck's back unless I am sufficiently
> strong in my criticism to force the classicals to make a rejoinder. I
> *want*, so to speak, to raise a dust . . . [140]

Harrod's substantive criticism was stated as follows on 12 August 1935:

> . . . I hold there is sense in saying that interest equates the demand
> for investment to the supply of saving. And I also hold that the fact
> that S must be equal to I does not itself invalidate the proposition
> that interest is the price which makes them equal. I further hold that
> if there was some other mechanism for securing constancy of income,
> which the *old* classical doctrine assumes (i.e. it implicitly assumes
> constancy of income and does not envisage the rate of interest as the
> mechanism for keeping incomes constant) then the classical doctrine
> that it is the rate of interest which equates the propensity to invest to
> the propensity to save would not only make sense but also be true.
>
> The essence of your point I feel to be that the *cet. par.* clause of the
> supply and demand analysis, which in this case includes the level of
> income, is *invalid*. The classical theory [therefore] is invalid but not
> nonsense.[141]

Harrod's criticism amounted to saying that, if the level of income were
kept constant by (fiscal) policy, there would be no objection to the classical
view that the rate of interest is the price which equalises saving and investment. However, Keynes insisted that the classical theory of the rate of
interest made no sense on any assumption at all about level of income. 'It
has to be discarded in toto, and is incapable of rehabilitation in any shape
or form.'

> The fault of the classical theory [he wrote on 10 September] lies, not
> in its limiting its terrain by assuming constant income, but in its failing
> to see that, if either of its own variables (namely propensity to save

and schedule of marginal efficiency of capital) change, income must also *cet. par.* change; so that its tool breaks in its hand and it doesn't know and can't tell us what will happen to the rate of interest, when either of its own variables changes.

I say, therefore, that it is *nonsense* to assume at the same time that income is constant and that the propensity to save and the schedule of the marginal efficiency of capital are variable.[142]

Keynes did not shift from his position that the classical rate of interest theory was a 'nonsense theory',[143] though he did drop the argument that what made it nonsense was the identity of saving and investment. He also used a suggestion by Harrod to draw a diagram – which became the only diagram in the *General Theory* – of intersecting curves, the first showing how much investment will take place at each rate of interest, the second showing how much will be saved out of income at each rate of interest. Keynes accepted the diagram suggestion because it showed 'most elegantly' the relation 'between the rate of interest and the level of income, given the schedule of the marginal efficiency of capital and the propensity to consume', *not* because he believed, as Harrod did, that saving is *simultaneously* determined by the rate of interest and the level of income: the interest rate, he insisted, has 'nothing whatever to do with saving'.[144]

In his historical chapter, Keynes was determined to make amends for the savage review he had written of one of J. A. Hobson's books in 1913.[145] Kahn did a lot of the mugging up; but Keynes himself had been in correspondence with Hobson in 1935, and he took advantage of this both to apologise to him and to restate his own theory succinctly:

The essence of my argument is that no more savings can come into existence than is provided for by the outlet in current investment. If the inducement is weak relative to the propensity to save, the result is a deficiency of effective demand which leads to diminished employment; and the unemployment is increased by whatever figure is necessary so to impoverish the community as to reduce the amount people desire to save to equality with the amount they are willing to invest.[146]

However, Keynes himself read Heckscher's book on mercantilism, which he thought 'magnificent', using – or misusing – it, in chapter 23 of the *General Theory*, to construct his own intellectual lineage.

Apart from a short visit to Antwerp with Lydia in July 1935 to discuss exchange stabilisation, Maynard spent the summer and early autumn at Tilton working on his revisions. Once more, he was not in the best of health. Influenza in June was followed by a 'furious bilious attack' in August. Florence and Neville Keynes came to stay, Neville miraculously recovered from a serious illness. Rupert and Billie Trouton spent the night and they all went up to the top of the Downs in Rupert's car and 'at night it looked most wonderful, with Newhaven lights, electric trains sparkling and almost glow worms'. In August Kahn stayed, and also Maynard's niece Polly Hill, reading economics at Newnham, and longing to be supervised by her uncle. Kingsley Martin was another visitor. Maynard had recently persuaded him to stay on at the *New Statesman* and not take the chair in Aberystwyth which tempted him; he had also had to sort out the vexed matter of literary editorship (claimed by both Raymond Mortimer and Bunny Garnett); he had been much taxed, too, in fixing up a job to enable Piero Sraffa to stay at Cambridge. But it was his fate, and desire, to solve other people's problems. On 15 September Lydia reported to Florence that she had been reading a book on Abyssinia: 'What a country to live . . . no one has w.c. except for the King of Kings . . .' The Abyssinian crisis was about to erupt, shortly followed by the general election in which Maynard, for the first and only time in his life, voted Labour, though he still looked forward to evolutionary progress under 'good King Baldwin'.

On Christmas morning Lydia carried 'sacks of merchandise' to the villagers. She and Maynard looked over their 'black-pink piglets' from the 'most handsome and expensive sow in England . . . with such gloss on them that any film star would envy'. Duncan Grant, Duncan's mother and Kahn were guests at their lunch of turkey, ham, cheese and celery, and they all chatted so long they missed the King's (last) speech. (A few days earlier in Cambridge Keynes had surprised Kahn and Joan Robinson sitting in their easy chairs at 11.30 a.m. drinking sherry. 'I think it may happen every morning,' he told Lydia.) Maynard, Lydia reported to Florence, was 'quite well'. Every day they would be conveyed by Edgar to the top of the Downs, 'then we descend, droop into chairs, drink tea, and drop our senses into somnambula'.[147]

The General Theory of Employment, Interest, and Money was published on 4 February 1936. The Arts Theatre had opened the previous day: two projects, linked by a common feeling, converging at a single moment in time.

CHAPTER FIFTEEN

Firing at the Moon

Never did a book fall more quickly and more completely into the hands of summarisers, simplifiers, boilers-down, pedagogues and propagandists. To get at what it seemed like at the time (and perhaps to what it really was and is) one has to fight one's way through a cloud of commentators, and try to see it in a more empty landscape. (D. M. Bensusan-Butt)

I

THE VISION

There are many different ways of telling the story of *The General Theory of Employment, Interest, and Money*, and many different stories to be told about it. The stories pour out to this day, in books, articles, comments, lectures; new stories are constantly being discovered. So far, at least, Keynes's masterpiece has escaped the fate of every other great tome in economics: to be an unread classic. Like Cleopatra, it exhibits the spirit of eternal youth: 'age cannot wither her, nor custom stale/Her infinite variety'. Even those who reject its central reasonings have loved it for its often arresting phraseology, its wide-ranging speculations on the history and fate of capitalism, its brilliant account of the stock market, its philosophical, even poetic, pages on money.

In its refusal to stale, the book reflects its author. Keynes was a magical figure, and it is fitting that he should have left a magical work. There has never been an economist like him: someone who combined so many qualities at such a high level, and allowed them all to fertilise his thought. He was an economist with an insatiably curious mind; a mathematician who could dazzle people with the most unmathematical of fancies; a logician who accepted the logic of art; a master-builder who left monuments in stone as well as words; a pure theorist, an applied theorist and a civil servant all in one; an academic intimate with the City. Even his sexual ambivalence played its part in sharpening his vision. He was, above all, a buoyant and generous spirit who refused to despair of his country and its traditions, and offered the world a new partnership between government and people to bring the good life within reach of all. The book attracts, as well as repels, because the personal qualities, foibles, interests and passions of the man shine through it so clearly.

To read the book in an empty landscape is no longer possible; indeed it was not possible then. It appeared at the tail-end of the greatest depression in modern history, and straightaway became a central part of the argument about what caused it and what could be done to cure it, and prevent further depressions in the future. This was not an abstract argument, but seemed a matter of desperate urgency, especially by those who accepted Keynes's teaching: he had himself been involved in it for years before his *General Theory* appeared. Within four years another world war broke out, and Keynes's theory was turned to the problems of financing a 'total war'.

So it was not surprising that the earliest 'Keynesians' saw his book as a machine for policy, and interpreted it primarily as providing a rationale for public spending. The earliest 'policy' versions of the *General Theory* took the form of income–expenditure models. The IS–LM diagram, first drawn by John Hicks in 1936, *is* the *General Theory* as it has been taught to economics students ever since: 384 pages of argument whittled down to four equations and two curves. Hicks, Harrod, Meade and Hansen in America, the leading constructors of 'IS–LM' Keynesianism, had a clear motive: to reconcile Keynesians and non-Keynesians, so that the ground for policy could be quickly cleared. These early theoretical models incorporated features which were not at all evident in the *magnum opus*, but which conformed more closely to orthodox theory. The constructors of these models also thought they were improving the original building. Joan Robinson, no slouch with insults, would later label the result 'bastard Keynesianism'. But Keynes was the bastard's father.

Today there is no need to follow in these particular footsteps. The useful bits of Keynes's theory have long been extracted, 'modelled', put to work, improved, popularised, shown to have succeeded or failed. Economists still pursue research programmes based on models they call 'Keynesian', in the hope of one day being able to explain things more clearly than is possible. Today we can see the *General Theory* as a work of art and imagination as well as economic logic, and can treat it as an invitation to thought rather than as a machine for solving crises.

Just as Keynes was more – and perhaps less – than an economist, so the *General Theory* is both more and less than a book of economics. It paints a picture of the pathologies of a particular social system – what Keynes called 'present-day capitalistic individualism' – and explains why it works badly. It thus stands comparison with Marx's *Das Kapital*, another classic which will outlive the fate of its plumbing. Although Keynes had little time for Marx – intellectual style being the main barrier – their starting point was very similar: a perception that economies did not behave in the way economists said they did, that something vital had been left out of their accounts, and it was this missing element which explained their malfunctioning. Marx accused economists of his day of abstracting from the class struggle; Keynes accused economists of his day of abstracting from the existence of uncertainty. For Keynes, most of the things which go wrong – and right – in decentralised market economies stem from the central fact that human beings take decisions in ignorance of the future. Ignorance enters into all the motives for forward-looking action, investing them, at the limit, with the character of dreams and nightmares; more usually, shaping them into patterns of conventional behaviour which cause 'economies' to perform well below the 'peak' performance of which they would be capable – and in 'moments of excitement' achieve – were the future consequences of actions not hidden.

It may be argued that this is too general to be useful. To say that social performance is inescapably mediocre is not to say anything very interesting. Nor does the notion of economic underperformance lead directly to a theory of employment – the subject of Keynes's book. It may mean nothing more than that societies are poorer than they might be. The analytic power of the *General Theory* comes from showing how underperformance in modern capitalist societies can, and usually does, take the form of persisting mass unemployment. This demonstration is independent of whether anything can be done about it. But Keynes did believe that something could, and should, be done about it, and his demonstration is set up in such a way as to show which of the causes of a particular kind of unemployment – 'demand-deficient' unemployment – could be favourably influenced by government or central bank action.

Today we can more clearly see the *General Theory* as a many-layered work, reflecting not only the intellectual history and multifarious interests of its creator, but the different phases of creation. Inspiring any scientific revolution is what Schumpeter calls a Vision – the 'preanalytic cognitive act that supplies the raw material for the analytic effort'. It is intuitive – seeing things in a light 'of which the source is not to be found in the facts, methods, and results of the pre-existing state of the science'. It is what Keynes called the 'grey fuzzy woolly monster' in one's head. Economics was, largely still is, built up from the logic of choice under conditions of scarcity. Keynes's vision, which one can trace back to his youth, has to do with the logic of choice, not under scarcity, but under uncertainty; with its daring corollary that the desire for goods is more easily satisfied than the desire for money, or liquidity. The second stage in the scientific achievement is the stage of theorising, working out the logical consequences of this change in perspective. It involves 'conceptualizing the contents of the vision . . . the fixing of its elements into precise concepts that receive labels or names in order to retain their identity, and in establishing relations (theorems or propositions) between them'. Keynes calls this the stage of 'making precise' the 'grey fluffy matter'. The third stage, not clearly distinguished by Schumpeter, but of central importance in economics, is the production of a 'scientific model', usually mathematical, which is close to what Keynes called 'scholasticism', or the attempt to be 'perfectly precise'. A model is a tight-jointed version of a theory, which differs from it by rigorous exclusion of variables other than those specified in the model, and a precise specification of the form of the relationships between the interlocking parts. The question of the appropriate 'degree of precision', or level of abstraction, is one to be settled by the nature of the problem or material under investigation. Keynes believed economics was over-addicted to 'specious precision' – making perfectly precise what was in reality vague and *complex*. It is significant that he refused to present the 'model' of the *General Theory* in mathematical form, even though he assembled its (verbal) elements in chapter 18. The final choice is of a method of analysis most suitable to one's theoretical, practical or persuasive object. Once uncertain expectations enter into the content of a theory, the problem of how to 'model' time becomes both overwhelmingly important and pretty intractable. Keynes asks us to imagine an apple which changes its mind as it falls to the ground. What definite statement can one make about the outcome of its flight? He had to find some way of allowing uncertainty to determine outcomes, while suspending its effect over a time-period long enough for a definite result to establish itself. His final choice of analytic method – a short-period equilibrium rather than disequilibrium model – came fairly late in the day.[1]

Difficulties in selecting the 'central story' of the *General Theory* arise from the fact that the four elements in the total structure are to some extent independent of each other. The vision is not perfectly captured by the theory, the theory not perfectly captured by the model. Neither the vision nor the theory logically requires the analytic method Keynes actually adopted. For example, Keynes's vision of the investment process in chapter 12 is very different from his theory of the investment process in chapter 11. Similarly, his vision of the rate of interest as the 'own rate on money', introduced in chapter 13 and developed in chapter 17, is quite different from his formal statement of the theory in chapter 15: it was this difference which caused the bitter 'liquidity preference' versus 'loanable funds' battle with Dennis Robertson. Finally, the equational system extracted from the *General Theory* simply tells you what the machine can do, not why you need the machine.

This double character of the *General Theory* – enquiring into the nature of economic life and providing a tool of policy – has divided interpreters of the book into what Alan Coddington happily calls 'fundamentalist' and 'hydraulic' Keynesians.[2] During Keynes's life-time and for many years afterwards, the hydraulic Keynesians were in the ascendant. A Keynesian machine was actually built at the LSE showing the circular flow of purchasing power, equipped with injections and leakages. As faith in Keynesian hydraulics waned, attention shifted to Keynesian kaleidics. The latest interpreter of the *General Theory* ends on a nihilistic note: 'Given the hopeless distortion of Keynes's message we might perhaps do better to abandon his *General Theory* as a guide to policy and look for inspiration to Keynes's life.'[3]

The *General Theory* is no one's property. The account which follows tries to convey the impression the book makes on a contemporary biographer, who has tried to understand the way Keynes's mind worked. It tries to follow the argument in the way he set it up. Readers should be aware of my biases, if they are not already. I am much less of an economist and mathematician, much more of a historian, than was Keynes. We share, I think, a curiosity to understand how social systems work. The probability is that I overestimate the weight he gave to his speculative fancies. But before embarking on what Keynes called the 'meaty stuff', here are some remarks on the book as a whole.

At its most 'general' it can be seen as a work of social reflection, ranging widely over time and space, though of course reflecting the particular experiences of his own time and his own kind of society. As Keynes tells it, it is the 'psychology of society' as fashioned by the need to act in face of an unknown future which sets mankind its fundamental economic problem. Because the future is unknown, and often thereby feared, the 'good life' which is the only rational object of striving is postponed by systematic underperformance. Keynes cites the United States and Britain as examples of societies in which there is a growing gap between capacity and performance – between the power to produce and the willingness to consume – measured by the depth and duration of depressions.[4] It is up to governments to close the gap. Inspiring his approach were the ethical doctrines of G. E. Moore, his own early reflections on probability, and his understanding of the purpose of government, as influenced by his early study of Burke. This was part of his Edwardian inheritance.

What he offers the reader is a complex psychological drama, in which it is the urge to consume which pushes economic activity forward, and the urge to not-consume which holds it back: his own version of Mandeville's *Fable of the Bees*, which he cites twice with approval. In his third lecture in 1933 he gave a fable of his own about a 'scientific experiment recently conducted at this university'. A scientist had removed part of the brain of a hen on which depended its instinct to consume. The hen acted normally enough except that in the presence of a pile of wheat it proceeded to starve to death.[5] An ambivalence to saving, and thus to one of the central doctrines of economics – the abstinence theory of progress – runs right through Keynes's work. This long antecedes his objection to excessive thriftiness in conditions of unemployment, and arises from a moral distaste for the character of the saver, whom he frequently identifies (in his non-economic writings) with the hoarder and the miser. He accepts up to a point the economic rationality of saving – both for the individual and for society – yet believes that, on the whole, progress would be faster, and employment fuller, if people were less thrifty. The reason is that it is the urge to consume, not the urge to save, which drives investment demand; so any weakening in the urge to consume slows down, other things being equal, the rate of investment. The clue to Keynes's attitude is that he linked part of the desire to save not to individual 'plans' for a more secure or prosperous future, but to a generalised anxiety about the future as well as to a lack of capacity to enjoy the present. Thus the community's propensity to save – the primitive expression of which is the propensity to hoard – is surplus to its future consumption requirements. Although he never mentions Weber, and probably never read him, the psychological picture he paints is recognisably that of nineteenth-century Western, and more particularly, Puritan society, in which control over accumulation was vested in the non-consuming class. It is seen most boldly in *The Economic Consequences of the Peace*, where Keynes depicts a society whose capacity for enjoyment is crippled by the duty of non-consumption, and in his 'Economic Possibilities for Our Grandchildren' where the psychological structure of modern society makes the 'good life' which science had made possible the object of fear, not longing.

However, there is also a play within a play, on which most attention focused, because it was this play which seemed to throw most light on current economic disorders. Here the two main characters are the Entrepreneur and the Hoarder. They are the disturbed, and disturbing, characters; it is their decisions which cause economies to collapse as well as to boom. They are anxious characters, though it is not their anxiety which causes the problem, but their instability. The Entrepreneur swings from the heights of optimism to the depths of gloom; the Hoarder accumulates money to satisfy his feelings of panic – or to make a quick killing on the Stock Exchange. In fact, the Entrepreneur can turn into the Hoarder or Speculator if his anxiety or greed becomes sufficiently great. At any particular time it is the battle between the 'inducement to invest' and the 'propensity to hoard' – a battle often raging in the mind of the same person – which exercises a dominating influence over the level of economic activity. It is Keynes's contention that, in the circumstances of contemporary capitalism, the propensity is likely to be greater than the inducement. The particular conjuncture which Keynes thought typical of his time was one in which investment opportunities have shrunk at existing levels of non-consumption, while the propensity to hoard savings, or speculate with them, has grown as the prospects of the system appear increasingly uncertain. A full employment rate of investment invariably depends on the triumph of hope over reason; when hope is disappointed (as it must be) investment collapses. It is the instability of an investment 'function' based on dreams and nightmares, which brings about catastrophes like that of the great depression.*

The *General Theory* is a drama, not just about people, but about things. If Marx is the poet of commodities, Keynes is the poet of money. The struggle between consumption and non-consumption, between investment and hoarding, is fought with the weapons of goods and money, and it is money ultimately – in chapters 15 and 17 – which controls the outcome. Money for the classical economists is primarily a facilitator of transactions, a means of exchange, even an over-generous one. For the purposes of Keynes's drama it is first and foremost a store of value, an alternative to consumption and investment, a 'subtle device' through which the fear of the future takes its revenge on the hopes of the present. 'Money is the root of all evil' is almost a sub-text of the *General Theory*; the idea that money keeps better than goods, and therefore the desire for it cannot be choked off, runs like a *leitmotiv* through it. It is not the inflationary, but the deflationary, effects of money which Keynes fears, and this sets Keynes's vision off against that of his most eminent contemporary economist, Friedrich Hayek, whose fear of the incontinence of money dominated his life-work.

The social landscape of the *General Theory* thus exhibits a life-denying *rentier* class which practises non-consumption in order to postpone the day of enjoyment; a business class driven by fantasies of triumph and disaster; a working class victimised not by calculated oppression but by the unsteady commitments of their controllers; and, on the other side of the divide, a radiant vision of cities beautified and marshes drained, and the good life brought within reach of all under the benevolent guidance of a Platonic state.

Much of the appeal of the *General Theory* has been that it can be interpreted as a morality play. Theology and economics have always been closely connected in the Anglo-Saxon tradition. What has been missing is history and sociology. The *General Theory* is no exception. The psychological 'propensities' are data. They are the equipment which 'agents' bring to their decisions. Their roots in events or social systems are unexplored. There is no mention of the Great War, political and currency disorders, the changing balance between capital and labour, all of which might plausibly be called *causes* of the great depression. The social system, as Keynes puts it, is 'given' – outside the model. Ethics and science have always given Anglo-Saxon

---

*This account is deliberately over-dramatised to bring out the emphasis Keynes places on the instability of investment. He does not deny that strategies, based on 'reasonable calculation', are available which are compatible with greater stability of investment than occurs in practice. His own later investment philosophy, based on 'faithfulness', is an example of such a strategy. But he did not write the *General Theory* to show how well reasonable people coped with an uncertain environment, but to show how easily attempts to be reasonable could be overwhelmed by delusion and panic.

economics its cutting edge: they are the two blades of its scissors. They are responsible for its greatest achievements and also its single biggest blindspot: neglect of the institutions through which people act. Keynes was in this tradition.* His breach with orthodoxy at the level of vision was twofold. First, he did for economics what Nietzsche did for morals. He transvaluated values, so that thriftiness becomes (under the most usual circumstances) a pathology, not a sign of health, and virtue brings catastrophe on the societies which practise it. Secondly, by introducing the a-historical device of 'uncertainty' he seriously weakened the nexus between economic decision-making and rational calculation. This was an essential part of his denial that *laissez-faire* capitalism possessed an efficacious self-adjusting mechanism. The behaviour disclosed by the *General Theory* seems to be either mechanical or unstable. It seems to have little to do with the Benthamite or Jevonian calculator maximising his flow of utilities over time. Economists could live with the transvaluation of values (in the standard model, preferences are 'given') but not with the disappearance of economic man. Keynes, by making expectations such an important influence on behaviour, posed a challenge to mainstream economics which was eventually met by the 'rational expectations' revolution, by means of which uncertainty was reduced to the same epistemological status as calculable risk.

Keynes calls his theory the 'theory of output and employment as a whole' as distinguished from the orthodox theory of what causes the output of an 'individual industry or firm' to be what it is and of what causes 'the rewards and the distribution between different uses of a given quantity of resources' to be what they are.[6] So Keynes changed the question which economics asked; or, rather, he introduced a new question: what causes the output of an economy as a whole to be what it is? He was the first economist to visualise an economy as an aggregate quantity of output, resulting from two streams of demand: consumption demand and investment demand. This new way of seeing the architecture of an economy is perhaps the *General Theory*'s most enduring legacy.

The main reason for asking the new question was that the 'given quantity of resources' whose allocation between different uses it was the object of orthodox value and distribution theory to explain seemed to be, for long periods of time, or even normally, well below the capacity of society to produce resources. Keynes was the first leading modern economist to focus

*More in the *General Theory* than in his writings of the 1920s, in which economic malfunction was rooted more concretely in the working of particular institutions – particularly the labour market. Keynes's explanation of the great depression looks very different from a historical, political or sociological explanation chiefly because, like all economic work in the Anglo-Saxon tradition, it abstracts from the extra-economic framework which plays such a large part in determining the shapes of the particular curves in any period of time. The question of whether the great depression was *sui generis* or an ever-possible outcome of the normal working of a capitalist social system is a historical-cum-sociological question, and cannot be answered by an a-historical, a-sociological economics.

analytic attention on the level of demand, or spending, as the determinant of the level of activity.* His book is an attempt to show how consumption and investment demand in any period can fall short of potential supply, or capacity to produce, resulting in mass unemployment. The demonstration must wait, but the idea itself is not difficult to grasp, and is widely familiar.† Formally, the principle of effective demand, the cornerstone of Keynes's theory, states that the level of employment depends on the level of aggregate demand for goods and services; if demand falls short of supply, supply – the society's level of income – has to adjust downwards to bring it back to equality with demand; this equality being the condition of a 'stable equilibrium at . . . a level below full employment'.[7] The revolutionary thought was that people could be unemployed due to a 'lack of effective demand', and not because they had 'priced themselves out of jobs'.

We all recognise that this is what happens in a depression. Once demand falls off, the economy deflates like a punctured tyre, leaving a large fraction of the workforce out of jobs. Keynes says that the economy will stay in this deflated condition until something happens to improve businessmen's sales prospects. The message of the *General Theory*, in its simplest form, is that things capable of bringing about a revival do not happen automatically, or at any rate quickly. They have to be produced by policy. The government has to do things to encourage spending like reducing interest rates, cutting taxes, or increasing its own spending to get the wheels of industry turning again. Thus Keynes's theory sets out to explain two things: how business expectations of profitable sales can collapse, leading to mass unemployment; and why, demand having collapsed, 'automatic' forces cannot be relied on to restore the original position.

Such ideas were intuitively acceptable and also wanted by the late 1930s. Commonsense was with Keynes. Economies had been sputtering all through the inter-war years, with a couple of large collapses into extreme depression: a third was to follow a little over a year after the *General Theory* was published. It was plainly irrational to have unemployed workers, idle machines and unsatisfied wants all together. It was absurd to say that in a depression mass unemployment was the fault of the unemployed: it was obviously caused by forces beyond the control of any individuals. Equally it was contrary to commonsense to say there was nothing government could do to

---

*Keynes (in chapter 23 of the *General Theory*) recognised precursors, of whom the chief were Malthus and Hobson. To these Patinkin would add Nicholas Johannsen's *Neglected Points in Connection with Crises* (1908), mentioned by Keynes in the *Treatise on Money*, though not in the *General Theory*. (See Patinkin, *Anticipations of the General Theory?* 6 and n., 191.)

†As a worker in Britain's shrinking motor-car industry put it on BBC Television's *Nine O'Clock News*, 7 February 1992, 'When no one's buying cars there's no point in making them.' Applied to aggregate output, rather than to the output of a single industry, this is an excellent one-line summary of Keynes's doctrine.

prevent or reverse collapses which left labour out of work, factories deserted, regions devastated. What were governments for?

Just as there was a theory embedded in the vision, so there was a model embedded in the theory. Keynes often said he preferred to be vaguely right than precisely wrong; but like all economists he was prone to the fallacy of misplaced precision. Above all, he wanted to influence policy. The *General Theory* was built for use. The policymaker needed a determinate model 'both to bring about change and affect its form'.[8] So key propensities of a *laissez-faire* economy like the 'inducement to invest' and the 'propensity to hoard' which are presented as inherently unruly have to be made sufficiently tractable to be acted on by the policymaker.

Keynes's key move was to assemble a model capable of determining an equilibrium position short of full employment. He combined in a single argument two kinds of analyses which had split economics asunder – the analysis of long-period stationary states and the analysis of fluctuations. In the *Treatise on Money* Keynes had tried to construct a theory of an economy which is out of equilibrium with its long-run 'normal' position. He signalled his change of approach in his 1932 lectures, 'The Monetary Theory of Production', in which money enters into the determination of the equilibrium itself, and is not merely a veil behind which 'real' exchanges take place. In the *General Theory* he distinguishes between 'the theory of stationary equilibrium and the theory of shifting equilibrium – meaning by the latter the theory of a system in which changing views about the future are capable of influencing the present situation. *For the importance of money essentially flows from it being a link between the present and the future.*'[9]

The *General Theory* exhibits a static model in which changes in expectations determine an equilibrium position, not just 'deviations' from it. This is made possible by treating expectations as given, or unchanging, in the relevant unit of time. Keynes can then say that there is a level of output and employment corresponding to each set of expectations, though in the real world of time everything is changing. The psychological factors which determine the action (the propensities to consume and hoard, the inducement to invest) become stable mathematical functions of variables (the level of income, the rate of interest) 'which can be deliberately controlled or managed by central authority in the kind of system in which we actually live'.[10] (Formally, Keynes takes expectations as exogenously given in working out particular relationships or curves. Changes in expectations establish new positions for the curves with consequent changes in output and employment.) However, this does raise the question of the time-unit appropriate to the assumption of fixed expectations. If expectations fluctuate all the time, while there is theoretically an equilibrium implied at each moment in time, this is not much *operational* use.

John Hicks was the first to notice the revolutionary character of this 'method of expectations' – while correctly pointing out that it had been anticipated by the Swedish economists Lindahl and Myrdal in their analysis of price fluctuations. He wrote, 'The point of the method is that it reintroduces determinateness into a process of change. The output of goods and the employment of labour, together with the whole price-system, are determined over any short period, once the stock of goods (. . . including capital goods) existing at the beginning of the period, is given *and once people's expectations of future market conditions are given too*'. (italics added).[11]

The advantage of this approach is threefold: it established the possibility of 'unemployment equilibrium'; it gave policy the task of determining the equilibrium, by detaching the equilibrium concept from any 'norm' to which the system 'naturally' tended; and it made policy seem simple, by abstracting from any effect of policy on the psychology of society. The disadvantage of the method was that it made the concept of unemployment equilibrium highly dependent on the shortness of the time-unit chosen, by excluding slower-moving 'repercussions' which tend to change expectations.

Thus his model excludes two important parts of both vision and theory: it abstracts from the omnipresence of uncertainty which is forever altering the mathematical 'functions' that determine the model; and it provides no explanation of the oscillations of the economy round a chronically 'subnormal' level which Keynes takes to be the 'outstanding' feature of the 'economic system in which we live'.[12] These sacrifices were made for the sake of persuasive and policy effectiveness.

The *General Theory* consists of both Keynes's positive theory and an attack on something he calls 'the classical theory'. Stalking his book is what Robertson called 'a composite Aunt Sally of uncertain age' and what Keynes called the Classical Economist. Keynes's method of attack on this mythical figure was annoying, but highly effective. He said to his fellow economists: 'For you to believe that, you must believe this. Do you believe this?' Thus both the quantity theory of money and the 'classical' theory of wages, Keynes said, depended on Say's Law (that supply creates its own demand). Economists could believe Say's Law, he said, only if they believed that the rate of interest was the price which adjusted the supply of saving to the demand for investment. If this theory of the rate of interest was wrong, the whole 'classical' edifice collapsed. Economists were forced either to abandon their belief in the self-regulating economy or to deny that their belief in it depended on believing the things Keynes said they needed to believe, or to invent new arguments to justify their belief in it. It was the explicit attack on the belief-system of orthodox economics which created the greatest fuss when the book came out. This was deliberate. As Keynes told Roy Harrod, he wanted to 'raise a dust'. Whether he was wise to raise such a dust is questionable. Certainly it forced on him a couple of years of increasingly arid disputation which might have been better spent developing his own theory.

The difficulties Keynes encountered in forcing his vision/theory into the straitjacket of his model/method makes the *General Theory* very difficult to digest. Much of Book II dealing with the definitions, concepts and units of measurement appropriate to uniform time-periods is as much a nightmare to read as it was for Keynes to write. The uncertainty about whether his 'unemployment equilibrium' is to be thought of as temporary or persisting or purely logical makes it very hard to relate it to 'classical' discussions which assume a tendency to full employment. Once the *General Theory* was published Keynes repeatedly warned against the dangers of premature formalisation of his theory. But the reduction of theory to model was inseparable from its triumph as a tool of policy.

All of which makes it easier to understand why the 'simple' ideas of *The General Theory of Employment, Interest and Money* are apt to get lost in a maze of logical puzzles and mathematical conundrums. The economist's mingled sense of admiration and frustration on first encountering the *General Theory* is well brought out in a comment made by Paul Samuelson ten years after the book appeared. Samuelson wrote:

> It is a badly written book, poorly organised; any layman who, beguiled by the author's previous reputation, bought the book, was cheated of his 5 shillings. It is not well suited for classroom use. It is arrogant, bad-tempered, polemical, and not overly-generous in its acknowledgments. It abounds in mares' nests and confusions: involuntary unemployment, wage units, the equality of savings and investment, the timing of the multiplier, interactions of marginal efficiency upon the rate of interest, forced savings, own rates of interest, and many others. In it the Keynesian system stands out indistinctly, as if the author were hardly aware of its existence or cognizant of its properties; and certainly he is at his worst when expounding its relations to its predecessors. Flashes of insight and intuition intersperse tedious algebra. An awkward definition suddenly gives way to an unforgettable cadenza. When it is finally mastered, we find its analysis to be obvious and at the same time new. In short, it is a work of genius.[13]

Pigou said, 'We have watched an artist firing arrows at the moon. Whatever be thought of his marksmanship, we can all admire his virtuosity.'[14] Once the *General Theory* was mastered, glimpses of the moon disappeared, as inappropriate matter for an economics textbook.

II

THE *GENERAL THEORY*

Keynes's attack on the classical theory of wages, in chapter 2, is all that is left of his earlier distinction between the behaviour of a 'co-operative' and that of a 'money-wage' economy. It is extremely convoluted. But it is also very important because, together with chapter 19, it contains the gist of what he wanted to say about the behaviour of the labour market in relation to employment and unemployment.

The best way into it is to assume an economy-wide demand 'shock' which leaves the average real wage too high to employ all those looking for work. The 'classical' economists, and here Keynes has mainly Pigou in mind, argued that it was in the power of workers to maintain their full employment by accepting a lower real wage – a reduced amount of goods measured by what money can buy. Keynes said that this ignores the fact that wage-bargains are made in terms of money; and that a reduction in the average money wage is likely to reduce prices proportionately. 'In assuming that the wage bargain determines the real wage the classical school have slipt in an illicit assumption. For . . . there may exist no expedient by which labour as a whole can reduce its *real* wage to a given figure by making revised *money* bargains with employers.'[15] Thus even in an economy with perfectly flexible money wages, 'involuntary' unemployment is possible. Formally, Keynes accepts the first 'classical postulate' that the level of employment is inversely correlated with the real wage. But he rejects the second – that the real wage is always what workers want it to be, that is, equal to the marginal disutility of work. Involuntary or unwanted unemployment exists if a small rise in consumer prices relative to money wages increases the amount of employment.[16] So the level of employment, together with the real wage, must be seen as the resultant of the general demand for goods and services in the economy. It follows that the effect of a cut in money wages on employment depends on its effect on the determinants of aggregate demand – a topic he postpones till chapter 19 when his own theory has been developed.*

---

*The first fifteen pages of chapter 2 are mainly an attack on *The Theory of Unemployment* (1933) by Pigou, an Aunt Sally of certain age but uncertain heartbeat, though Keynes states Pigou's theory as the 'classic' theory of employment. Keynes gives what he takes to be the 'classic' position on p. 5 of the *General Theory*. The level of employment is uniquely determined by two fundamental 'postulates': (a) the wage is equal to the marginal product of labour, and (b) the wage measures the marginal disutility of labour. Given diminishing returns to labour in the short period, there is an inverse relationship between employment and the real wage, a larger volume of employment being associated with a lower real wage. Assuming perfect competition, employment is maximised at the point where the real wage claimed by the last worker employed just equals the value of his 'marginal product' to the employer. By definition there can be no involuntary unemployment, only voluntarily chosen leisure together with some 'frictional' unemployment. Keynes omitted to say that Pigou's was a long-period theory. Pigou accepted that a shock to demand could generate unwanted unemployment. What he denied was that this could be an equilibrium position since a price at which unsold supplies existed could not be an equilibrium price. The competition of the unemployed for jobs would bring down the price of labour sooner or later, though it might take an awfully long time.

It is important to note that Keynes's refutation of Pigou does not depend on money wages being 'fixed' by trade unions. He recognises that, in practice, money wages are resistant to downward revision, which he thinks makes for stability rather than otherwise, by keeping up

Keynes had shown to his own satisfaction that 'classical' theory cannot prove the impossibility of unwanted unemployment by Pigou's methods. *Therefore* it needs Say's Law – the doctrine that 'supply creates its own demand' – whether it likes it or not. The attack on Say's Law starts on p. 18; and the rest of the *General Theory* is devoted to showing that Say's Law is false: that is, that demand can fall short of potential supply, because there is no necessity for all income earned in a period to be spent. The crux of his attack is on the 'classical' theory that saving is the same thing as spending. He quotes Marshall's 'familiar economic axiom' that 'a man purchases labour and commodities with that portion of his income which he saves just as much as he does with that he is said to spend'. This doctrine 'still underlies the whole classical theory, which would collapse without it.'[17] Nevertheless, it is false, since there is no 'nexus' which 'unites decisions to abstain from present consumption with decisions to provide for future consumption'. There is, that is, no 'market' for saving and investment, and therefore no 'price' which matches them to each other. This is the nub of Keynes's critique of orthodox economics. An alternative mechanism is needed to show how demands and supplies in the economy are equated to each other. This is his theory of effective demand, which is developed in Books III and IV.

Chapter 3 is a preliminary statement. Effective demand is defined as entrepreneurs' expected sales proceeds (incomes, which include payments to workers) from the amount of employment they decide to give. Employment will be in equilibrium when the proceeds entrepreneurs expect from selling a quantity of output equal the expected costs of producing that output. This is the 'point' of 'effective demand'. When expected proceeds exceed expected costs, businessmen have an incentive to expand production; when they fall short, to curtail it. Keynes contends that the economy can be in equilibrium, with expected proceeds equal to expected costs, at less than full employment. This is the essence of the *General Theory*. Most of the rest of the book is devoted to showing how this can be.*

---

money demand and therefore prices: it is fortunate, he says, that workers, though unconsciously, 'are more reasonable economists than the classical school' (p. 14). He even has a theory of why money wages are rigid: groups of workers resist a reduction in their real wage relative to other groups, not a reduction in the real wage which affects all alike. No group will therefore be the *first* to agree to a reduction in its money wage. The main institutional rigidity of the 1920s – the stickiness of money wages in face of heavy unemployment – is here given for the first time a theoretical explanation in terms of uncertainty about the behaviour of other groups. That is why it is reasonable to suppose that there will be no resistance, in conditions of heavy unemployment, to a real wage reduction brought about by a small increase in the price level which affects all groups alike (pp. 13–14). But Keynes's theoretical case against the 'classical' theory does not depend on this set of arguments.

*Keynes's 'aggregate supply function' (pp. 24–6) has been the subject of exhaustive discussion. Alvin Hansen in his *A Guide to Keynes* (pp. 30–1) gives this simple illustration. In order to make it worth their while employing 60m. workers at current wages, employers in the aggregate require $300b. worth of sales; 50m. workers, $240b. of sales; 40m. workers, $200b. of sales.

Book II, unfortunately, can no longer be regarded as a 'digression' on concepts and definitions; for this is where the properties of the model are set out. Three points may be picked out, each of which has spawned a vast literature. First, employment, output and income are all measured in wage-units, or money payments to workers per hour worked.[18] That all three move in the same direction in response to a change in demand is clear enough. But how adjustment is shared between output, employment and prices is not clear. The elementary textbook presentation of the income–expenditure model, that adjustment is done entirely by output and employment, depends on fixed costs (prices) in the labour and goods markets, which Keynes only assumed at a preliminary point in the discussion. The standard Keynesian view is better represented by the proposition that adjustment is made by nominal income, with the division between quantity adjustment and price adjustment dependent on the circumstances, particularly the level of employment.

Secondly, saving is made necessarily equal to investment at all times by the following formula: Income = Value of Current Output = Consumption + Investment. Saving = Income – Consumption. Therefore Saving = Investment.[19] But if they are always the same, how can they be adjusted to each other by changes in income? As Michael Stewart has written this 'baffled even the experts when the *General Theory* appeared, and was responsible for some of the most eminent economists of the 1930s never really understanding what Keynes was getting at'.[20] The answer is that the desire to save and the desire to invest may diverge, but the amounts saved and the amounts invested are always equal, because any divergence immediately produces an equalising adjustment of income.*

Finally, Keynes makes current employment depend on both short-term and long-term expectations. The former is concerned with the sales proceeds from producing finished goods with given capital equipment, the latter with the profits from producing with new capital equipment. New equipment takes time to install; considerable time may elapse between the decision to install and the start of sales. Long-term expectations are, therefore, much

How many will actually be employed, and how much output produced, depends on the employers' actual expectation of sales from employing these different quantities of labour. If, with 60m. employed, sales-proceeds are expected to be $240b., employment will be reduced to 50m. For problems connected with Keynes's aggregate supply function, see Patinkin, *Anticipation of the General Theory*, chapter 5.

*Bafflement was increased by Keynes giving two different definitions of investment, on pp. 52 and 62. In the first inventories are included in 'capital equipment', leading to the paradoxical result that when unsold stocks are piling up owing to the increased desire to save, investment is increasing simultaneously, and vice versa. But it is clear from context that this has nothing to do with the necessary equality between saving and investment in the sense Keynes intended, the latter being defined on p. 62 as 'the current addition to the value of the capital equipment which has resulted from the productive activity of the period'.

more uncertain than short-term expectations, and 'liable to sudden revision'.[21] The fluctuating expectations of investors form part of the short-term expectations of producers of capital goods, tending to drive down the expected sales proceeds of output as a whole to below what they would be if they depended only on short-period expectations. This is what Keynes means when he says demand in any short period may fall below the supply represented by the potential output of a quantity of labour applied to existing capital equipment.

Books III and IV dealing with consumption demand, investment demand and the rate of interest are the analytical kernel of Keynes's theory, because these are what determine the level of employment. Keynes states the economic 'riddle' as follows. 'Consumption . . . is the sole end and object of economic activity.' Investment demand is a derived, or induced demand. It can take place only if 'future expenditure on consumption is expected to increase.' A diminished propensity to consume today:

> can only be accommodated to the public advantage if an increased propensity to consume is expected to exist some day. We are reminded of [Mandeville's] 'The Fable of the Bees' – the gay of to-morrow are absolutely indispensable to provide a *raison d'être* for the grave of to-day . . . Any weakening in the propensity to consume regarded as a permanent habit must weaken the demand for capital as well as the demand for consumption.[22]

In chapter 8, the first of three chapters dealing with 'the propensity to consume', Keynes make consumption in a given period a 'fairly stable' proportion of current income.[23] The shape of the function is given by the famous 'psychological law' that 'when aggregate real income is increased aggregate consumption is increased but not by so much as income'.[24] This means that people do not spend all of their increased incomes. Expansions peter out, so do contractions. The fact that consumption fluctuates less than income gives the system a stability which it would otherwise lack, limiting the range of fluctuations upwards and downwards. On the other hand, if people consumed the whole of their incomes there would never be an employment problem to start with: expected prices would be realised, Say's Law would hold. Given a 'propensity to consume' of less than one, any increase of employment requires an amount of investment sufficient to fill the gap between consumption and income.[25]

In disclosing the problem a society sets itself by not consuming all it produces Keynes stands the classical thesis on its head. The classical economists praised 'parsimony' or 'thrift' as increasing the supply of capital, and thus the wealth of nations. Its fruits were the penny-pinching individual and the penny-pinching Treasury. Keynes argued on the contrary: every decision to save depresses investment demand; it depresses the business of preparing today's dinner, without stimulating the business of preparing tomorrow's; in fact 'since the expectation of future consumption is so largely based on current experience of present consumption' it depresses the business of preparing for tomorrow's dinner too.[26] This was Keynes's 'paradox of thrift'. Moreover, since Keynes thought that the marginal propensity to save rose in line with income, the problem of securing an adequate amount of investment worsened over time. 'Each time we secure to-day's equilibrium by increased investment we are aggravating the difficulty of securing equilibrium to-morrow.'[27] A rich society will have to invest an increasing proportion of its income even as the profitability of investment declines, unless special measures are taken to discourage saving. This was the basis of Keynes's view that under *laissez-faire* recoveries peter out before they reach full employment, and economies normally oscillate round a mediocre employment position.

All these paradoxes depend on a single point: that an increase in the propensity to save does little or nothing to reduce the rate of interest. Keynes writes that the 'influence of moderate changes in the rate of interest on the propensity to consume is usually small'.[28] The influence of the rate of interest on the amount saved, however, is very great, and in the opposite direction to that usually supposed; for a rise in the rate of interest, by causing a fall in investment (other things being equal), 'must have the effect of reducing incomes to a level at which saving is decreased in the same measure as investment'. Thus 'the more virtuous we are, the more determinedly thrifty, the more obstinately orthodox in our national and personal finance, the more our incomes will have to fall when interest rises relatively to the marginal efficiency of capital. Obstinacy can bring only a penalty and no reward. For the result is inevitable.'[29] The aggregate amount saved is a 'mere residual. The decisions to consume and the decisions to invest between them determine incomes.'[30]

No more striking example can be found in the *General Theory* of Keynes sharpening to a point his difference from the orthodox school. As we shall see this sharpness disappeared, both later in the book and in the subsequent controversy. But he never doubted that the interest-inelasticity of saving was the right assumption to make for the purposes and time-period he had in mind. But he also believed something else, which is that the classical economists had got the psychology of action wrong. He did not think there had ever been a close *psychological* connection between decisions to save and decisions to invest. While thriftiness, for the classical economists, represented a desire for greater consumption in the future, Keynes saw much of it as flowing from a lack of capacity to enjoy the present – that is, from the Puritan instincts. Thus the 'propensity to save' is the psychological inverse, not complement, of the 'propensity to consume'. A high propensity to save keeps society poorer than it might be, justifying the virtue of thriftiness. In the *General Theory* for the first time Keynes manages to link up his intuition about the psychology of the saver with the economic argument more virtuous we are, the more our incomes will have to fall'.*

The 'psychological law' is also vital for the working of Keynes's model. It establishes a definite multiplier: expansions and contractions converge to a fixed position. Suppose the government spends an extra £100m. on public works. The community's income will increase by a multiple of the propensity to consume so that at the higher income saving has increased by exactly £100m. The reverse will happen if the government cuts its programme by £100m. There is thus a determinate relationship between income, employment and government spending. Economists who are mainly concerned with macroeconomic policy tend to be 'consumption function' Keynesians, because the consumption function is the one stable function in the Keynesian model. It establishes an adjustment variable (income) alternative to the rate of interest. This is the principle of 'effective demand'. It establishes the multiplier as the adjustment *mechanism*. And it makes the question of where the finance for the additional investment is to come from, as well as the fear of inflation, seem irrelevant, at least in the short period. From the point of view of overturning the orthodox mindset, the consumption function is Keynes's greatest tactical coup.

If it all sounds too simple, it is. Keynes admits that though the 'logical theory of the multiplier . . . holds good continuously, without time-lag, at all moments of time', actual results will be by no means as definite as the model suggests.[31] For example, an unforeseen expansion of the capital-goods industries may produce no immediate corresponding increase in output from the consumption goods industries. In this case, consumer prices rise, profits increase, and the additional investment has to be financed by something suspiciously like the 'forced saving' of the workers as the marginal propensity to consume falls.[32] However, he does not consider the opposite case, where the government's spending programme is foreseen, but disliked. Let us take Keynes's own famous variant:

If the Treasury were to fill old bottles with bank-notes, bury them at

*It would be interesting to trace the evolution of Keynes's attitude towards saving. The idea that part of the saving instinct was ethically irrational seems to have been in his mind from the start, as a reaction against Victorian values. The idea that it was economically irrational came later. Non-consumption is described as a cause of wealth accumulation in *The Economic Consequences of the Peace* (1919) and also in 'Economic Possibilities for Our Grandchildren', published in 1930, but dating from two years earlier. (JMK, *CW*, ii, 11; ix, 330-1). But by the time of the *Treatise on Money* it had shed its function as an engine of economic progress. 'If enterprise is afoot, wealth accumulates whatever may be happening to thrift; and if enterprise is asleep, wealth decays whatever thrift may be doing.' (*CW*, vi, vol 2, 132). In the *General Theory* the high propensity to save is a drag on investment, and Keynes now considers it has been so at all times, though in some periods the spirit of optimism has been sufficiently strong to overcome this drag. The idea in the *General Theory* that 'enterprise' produces its own 'saving' has a clear precursor in his often expressed view that most of the capital development of the West was financed by 'enterprise' in the form of piracy and plunder. None of this is to deny that Keynes thought that some voluntary saving is both rational and desirable.

suitable depths in disused coal-mines which are then filled up to the surface with town rubbish, and leave to private enterprise on the well-tried principles of *laissez-faire* to dig the notes up again . . . there need be no more unemployment and, with the help of the repercussions, the real income of the community, and its capital wealth also, would probably become a good deal greater than it actually is.[33]

Assume that this expedient is tried in a strongly religious community whose priests rise up and tell the people that the notes have been planted by the Devil to tempt them from the paths of righteousness. Now the notes stay in the bottles, or are secretly hoarded, the multiplier is one, and unemployment stays the same. Admittedly this is as unlikely a 'repercussion' as is the fancy which inspired it. The point is that the effects of a Keynesian policy depend on expectations. The algebra of the multiplier assumes that no intervening agency interferes with the working of the 'psychological law'. This robs the multiplier analysis of part of its practical usefulness.

Keynes next turns to the 'inducement to invest'. The general idea is that the rate of investment is governed by prospective profits compared to the rate of interest. Entrepreneurs produce investment goods, like consumption goods, for profit. With investment goods, it is profits expected to accrue some time after the investment is made. Expected profits depend on a collection of knowns and imponderables. Most of them are determined exogenously – outside the model. In chapter 11, Keynes constructs an orthodox-looking investment–demand schedule relating the expected yield from additional capital goods to the cost of producing them. The rate of return over cost is the 'marginal efficiency of capital'. Then 'the rate of investment will be pushed to the point on the investment demand-schedule where the marginal efficiency of capital in general is equal to the market rate of interest'.[34] Keynes makes the quite orthodox point that, as capital goods become more plentiful, their expected yield falls, so there is less demand for them. Therefore the continued expansion of investment as income rises depends on a corresponding reduction in the rate of interest. Here the unorthodoxy comes in. Investment is a function of the rate of interest; but the rate of interest is not a function of investment. When it falls below what people wish to save, the rate of interest does not fall in sympathy. Thus there is no guarantee that the volume of investment consistent with a given rate of interest will be enough to secure full employment; indeed Keynes believes it will do so only by accident.

It is in chapter 11 that the rate of interest first seriously enters the *General Theory* story as a joint influence on the volume of investment. But it is a fairly minor influence on the total pattern of events, as chapter 12, 'The State of Long-Term Expectations', suggests.

In chapter 12, the instability of investment demand emerges as the crucial factor in economic fluctuations. The curve relating the marginal efficiency of capital to the rate of interest is liable to rapid shifts. This is because the expectations which govern the decisions to invest today are necessarily based on forecasts of events which, in large part, are inherently uncertain. Because of this, the impact of 'shocks' is enormously magnified. The investor is a febrile person, rather like a politician, overloaded with 'news' pulling him in different directions, unable to maintain a steady course. But the instability of the investment function cannot be explained within the model, where each short-period position is already determined. Chapter 12 is on a 'different level of abstraction from most of this book' in being based on the 'actual observation of markets and business psychology'.[35]

Keynes's contention, in chapter 12, is that the uncertainty attaching to expectations of the future yield of investment has given birth to a particular institution through which much of investment is channelled in a capitalist society – the stock market. His starting point is 'the extreme precariousness of the basis of knowledge on which our estimates of prospective yield have to be made'.[36] The organised investment market (or Stock Exchange) reduces the riskiness of investment by making 'liquid' for the individual investments which are 'fixed' for the community,[37] and supplying the investor with conventional share valuations (stock-market prices) on which he can place some degree of reliance as measuring the marginal efficiencies of different pieces of capital. The 'convention' promises that 'the existing state of affairs will continue indefinitely, except insofar as we have specific reasons to expect a change', thus limiting the risk to the investor to 'that of a genuine change in the news over the *near future*'.[38] But a conventional valuation thus established will have 'no strong roots of conviction to hold it steady' in face of sudden panics.[39] Suddenly everyone wants to become 'liquid': but 'there is no such thing as liquidity of investment for the community as a whole'.[40] What Keynes is saying is that much of investment in a modern capitalist society is driven by the fallacy of misplaced precision. As investors, we perform our calculations as though we know better than we actually do what the future will bring. When something happens which disturbs this spurious certainty, there is nothing firm to hold on to. Chapter 12 is the best account in the economic literature of the psychology of panics; it can be applied with profit to an electoral process dominated by opinion polls.

The inherent instability of the convention gives large scope to the play of speculation and 'animal spirits'. 'The social object of skilled investment should be to defeat the dark forces of time and ignorance which envelop our future. The actual, private object of the most skilled investment today is to "beat the gun"', that is, guess better than the crowd. 'We have reached the third degree where we devote our intelligences to anticipating what average opinion expects the average opinion to be. And there are some, I believe, who practise the fourth, fifth and higher degrees.'[41] In a well-known passage Keynes wrote, 'Speculators may do no harm as bubbles on a steady stream of enterprise. But the position is serious when enterprise becomes a bubble on a whirlpool of speculation. When the capital development of a country becomes a by-product of the activities of a casino, the job is likely to be ill-done.'[42] But, equally, 'a large proportion of our positive activities depend on spontaneous optimism rather than on a mathematical expectation, whether moral or hedonistic or economic'.[43] 'Reasonable calculation' has to be supported by 'animal spirits', so that the fear of eventual loss 'is put aside as a healthy man puts aside the expectation of death', if individual initiative is to provide enterprise adequate to the community's needs. Dependence of enterprise on animal spirits means not only that slumps tend to be exaggerated by reason of 'errors of pessimism', but that economic prosperity is excessively dependent on 'a political and social atmosphere which is congenial to the average business man'. The advent of a Labour government or a New Deal could upset the 'delicate balance of spontaneous optimism'. The volume of investment depends in part on 'nerves', 'hysteria', 'the weather' or 'digestions'.[44] It is our 'innate urge to activity which makes the wheels go round . . .'[45] When 'animal spirits' dim, investment falters. Animal spirits come into play not only because mathematical expectation is defeated, but because Keynes thinks that calculated expectations of future returns are not in any case the mainspring of business psychology.

The only radical cure for 'crises of confidence' was to give the individual no choice between 'consuming his income and ordering the production of [a] sp[ecific] capital-asset'.[46] The relationship between the investor and his share should be like that of husband and wife. (This was before the days when marriage started to approximate to the stock market!) Nevertheless, Keynes believes that a conventional basis of share valuation is compatible with 'a considerable measure of continuity and stability in our affairs'.[47] The prospective yield of many investments was legitimately dominated by fairly stable short-period expectations. For very large classes of investments – notably building, public utilities and investments of public authorities – 'the influence of short-period changes on the state of long-term expectations' was not so important. Thus the rate of interest could normally be expected to exercise 'a great, though not decisive, influence on the rate of investment'. But Keynes remained sceptical that 'a purely monetary policy directed towards influencing the rate of interest' would suffice to offset fluctuations in market estimates of yield. So 'I expect to see the State, which is in a position to calculate the marginal efficiency of capital-goods on long views and on the basis of the general social advantage, taking an ever greater responsibility for directly organizing investment.'[48]

Chapter 12 is the most vivid and realistic in the *General Theory*. Mainline Keynesians have not thought it theoretically fundamental, Harrod noting that 'the stress he lays on expectations . . . might be incorporated in traditional theory without entailing important modifications in its other parts'.[49] At the level of vision it is fundamental. It is closest to Keynes's own life: the chapter where autobiography meets economics. Its intellectual debt to his early work on probability is obvious; also to his subsequent correspondence with Marcel Labordère. It also reflects his own ambivalence as an investor. Keynes himself stalks its pages, as financial philanderer and latterly as faithful husband. The writing conveys to the full the excitement of the chase, the attractions of gambling, the lure of the quick profit; and more soberly and perhaps regretfully an appreciation of its often anti-social consequences. Meltzer comments, not unfairly, 'It is consistent with Keynes's approach to a problem that he would criticise severely those who continued to pursue the portfolio strategy that he had once considered promising but now had abandoned.'[50] We can go further: the change in investment philosophy between the early and the late Keynes is mirrored in the contrast between his chapter on forward exchanges in the *Tract on Monetary Reform*, where he praises currency speculation, and his advocacy of fidelity in the *General Theory*.

The contrasting spirit of chapters 11 and 12 has given rise to radically different interpretations of the *General Theory*. Very broadly, chapter 11 Keynesians, by assuming 'given' expectations, believe that short-run stabilisation of a capitalist economy by policy is fairly easy, even mechanical. Chapter 12 Keynesians, emphasising the role of uncertainty, regard it as inherently difficult, emphasising the effects of policy on the 'state of confidence'.

As we have seen from his comments on the New Deal, Keynes himself was torn between these perspectives. It was an essential part of his purpose to present the total volume of investment as controllable by the central authority in a society in which the responsibility for investment remained largely in private hands. However, he also recognised that the outcome of policy – whether this involves forcing down the rate of interest or increasing government spending – depends crucially on the 'state of confidence'. The two chapters, taken together, amount to no more than the assertion of the need at all times for the most careful judgement, general commonsense and 'vigilant observation' on the part of the policymaker. But this kind of balance, which came naturally to Keynes, was rarely attained by his followers. The 'hydraulic' Keynesians made the 'correction' of capitalism sound too easy, the 'fundamentalist' Keynesians too difficult; between them, the Keynesian Revolution eventually came unstuck.

As the *General Theory* progresses, the rate of interest becomes steadily more important; indeed it ends up, by a sort of chain logic, taking control of the plot in chapter 17. Given the propensity to consume, income is determined by the level of investment. Given the state of expectations, the level of investment is determined by the rate of interest. We don't know what the level of investment will be till we know what the rate of interest is. In this logical sequence, the rate of interest is the final independent variable.

In chapters 13 to 15, Keynes set himself three tasks: to show that the 'classical' interest-rate-adjustment mechanism was wrong; to show that the rate of interest is determined in the market for money, specifically by 'liquidity preference'; and finally to prove that the rate of interest could remain too high to allow a full employment volume of investment. To anticipate an exceedingly complex set of reactions to this interlocking demonstration: the critics, and even some of the supporters, of the *General Theory* accepted the third proposition, while rejecting the first two in the form they were stated. That is, Keynes's 'liquidity preference' theory of interest was accepted as modifying the orthodox theory of interest-rate determination, not replacing it. We can see how the *General Theory* itself laid the basis for this 'reconciliation'.

In chapter 14, Keynes sets out to construct 'The Classical Theory of the Rate of Interest'. He was not interested in what economists at the time actually believed. As he told Hawtrey after the book's publication: 'the essential point is that my discussion of the classical theory of the rate of interest is merely an attempt to make an hypothesis as to what the classical theory must be if it is to be consistent with their general views'[51] – that is, with the imputed dependence of classical theory on Say's Law. So the classical theory of interest is the belief that it is 'the rate of interest . . . which brings the demand for investment and the willingness to save into equilibrium with each other'.[52] From this follows the belief in the self-adjusting economy: a fall in investment relative to saving will bring down the rate of interest, discouraging thriftiness and encouraging both investment and consumption at an unchanged level of income.

It seems that at first Keynes considered it a sufficient refutation of this theory to say that it could not be true if saving and investment were necessarily equal, that is if 'it is impossible to name a rate of interest at which the amount of saving and the amount of investment could be unequal'.[53] Thus he wrote to the Swedish economist Gunnar Myrdal on 16 June 1937, 'it is not the rate of interest which makes saving and investment equal, since they are equal *ex definitione* whatever the rate of interest'.[54] If the further assumption is made that investment is not sensitive to small interest-rate charges, the interest rate is not actually needed to explain anything: the two independent variables are simply the 'propensity to consume' and the 'inducement to invest'. The determination of the rate of interest is left over as a small piece of unfinished business, 'hanging in the air', so to speak, after the main work was done. And some Keynesians would have liked it to stay there. But this is not the final form of the *General Theory*. Harrod insisted that Keynes produce an *argument* to show why the interest rate does not adjust saving and investment. The liquidity-preference theory of the rate of interest became that argument. It was logically impossible for the rate of interest to adjust saving to investment *because* it was determined in the market for money.

Let us trace the causal chain. In chapter 14, Keynes introduced the *General Theory*'s only diagram (on p. 180), an orthodox supply and demand diagram with two intersecting curves, the first showing the amounts which will be invested at different rates of interest, the second showing the amounts which will be saved out of a given income at different rates of interest. The formal error of the classical theory, thus portrayed, was to commit a 'fallacy of composition': to ignore the fact that a shift in the aggregate investment–demand schedule would change society's income, and thus the amount it saved as well – as the theory of effective demand said. But now we do not know what the propensity to consume out of a given income will be until the rate of interest is known, and therefore we do not know how much income will have to change. We require, that is, a theory of the rate of interest to establish a determinate equilibrium.[55]*

Keynes's concession to Harrod has always been regretted by the 'hydraulic' Keynesians, partly becomes it brings the *General Theory* more into line with the *Treatise on Money* and Keynes's outlook in the 1920s, in which the interest rate (and more generally monetary management) was seen as the 'balancer' of the economic system. Robertson, who of all the economists knew him longest, would explain this shift in the analytical balance of the *General Theory* by what he called Keynes's habit of 'successive overemphasis'. His mind was like a powerful searchlight casting its beam on one object after another, with everything else in temporary darkness. It was almost as if he 'got to' the rate of interest at the tail-end of his new analytical journey and then realised that it complicated things. What economists call partial equilibrium analysis – holding part of the landscape in darkness to concentrate on the problem in hand – came naturally to him; what did not come naturally to him was simultaneous equilibrium analysis. His mind did not work that way.

What then determines the rate of interest? Keynes says that the rate of interest 'cannot be a return to saving or waiting as such. For if a man hoards his savings in cash, he earns no interest, though he saves just as much as before.' But why should anyone outside a lunatic asylum want to hoard money when it earns no interest? His general answer is better given in an article he wrote after the *General Theory* was published than in the book itself:

> Because, partly on reasonable and partly on instinctive grounds, our desire to hold money as a store of wealth is a barometer of the degree of our distrust of our own calculations and conventions concerning the

---

*Keynes did not regard this concession to Harrod as important, since he continued to believe that, as stated on p. 95, 'in a given situation the propensity to consume may be considered a fairly stable function [of real income]', with changes in the rate of interest on the short-period propensity to save 'relatively unimportant' (p. 94). Even this, however, may be compared with his much more emphatic statement in a 1934 lecture, 'The rate of interest has nothing at all to do with the propensity to save . . .', which as we have seen, led Bryce to remark, 'But oh this is too damn much.' (T. K. Rymes, *Keynes's Lectures, 1932–5: Notes of a Representative Student*, p. 158.)

future. Even though this feeling about money is itself conventional or instinctive, it operates, so to speak, at a deeper level of our motivation. It takes charge at the moments when the higher, more precarious conventions have weakened. The possession of actual money lulls our disquietude; and the premium which we require to make us part with money is the measure of the degree of our disquietude.[56]

This 'premium' was the rate of interest. The rate of interest is 'the reward for parting with liquidity for a specified period . . . and [thus] the measure of the unwillingness of those who possess money to part with their liquid control over it'.[57] It is the price or 'inducement' for not-hoarding.[58] His most dramatic formulation – in chapter 17 – is that it is the 'own rate of interest on money itself', a measure of the value it has as a 'store of wealth'. More generally, it is the price which 'equilibrates the desire to hold wealth in the form of cash [liquidity preference] with the available quantity of cash'.[59] It is only by accident that a rate of interest thus determined will be consistent with full-employment level of income. Keynes's 'general theory' is thus completed by his showing how the rate of interest can remain above the 'rate of return to capital' necessary to secure full employment.

Liquidity preference had already featured – as 'bearishness' – in the *Treatise on Money*. People will want to hoard money if they expect the price of securities to go down. In the *General Theory* he also has his division between the 'bulls' and the 'bears', but it now determines not the price of securities, but the rate of interest. The basic reason for the shift seems to be that in the *Treatise* Keynes had not realised (or at least said) that buying bonds is an alternative to buying equities; so that an expectation of a fall in the price of equities cannot itself be a motive for 'liquidity preference', but merely a motive for buying another type of security. By linking liquidity preference to the price of bonds, Keynes has found a way of linking it directly to the rate of interest.

The 'necessary condition', indeed the 'sole intelligible explanation' of the existence of liquidity preference is 'the existence of *uncertainty* as to the future of the rate of interest, i.e. as to the complex of rates of interest for varying maturities which will rule at future dates'.[60] Given this uncertainty, there will always be a 'speculative motive' to hold cash in preference to bonds. Any rise in the price of bonds will lower the interest rate. If speculators believe the interest rate will go up they have a motive to sell bonds for cash, which lowers the price of bonds, and raises the interest rate.* Normally, the

---

*This can be illustrated by an example. Consols are a government security which give their owners (say) £2.50 interest for every block nominally worth £100. Suppose that the price of Consols rises to £200. The owner of Consols now has to pay £200 in order to obtain an income of £2.50 a year: the rate of interest on his Consols has fallen to 1.25 per cent. Now, if he thinks the rate of interest will be 2.5 per cent in six months' time, he will hold cash rather than buy Consols; if everyone agrees with him, the price of Consols will fall by exactly the amount needed to establish the expected rate of interest.

speculators will be divided into 'bulls' and 'bears' – those who believe that interest rates will go lower and those who believe they will go higher. The market price of bonds – and therefore the interest rate – will be fixed at the point where the sales of the 'bears' and purchases of the 'bulls' balance.[61] At any time, the 'propensity to hoard' (the alternative phrase for liquidity preference) exerts a much more powerful pull on the interest rate than the 'propensity to save'. The sting in the tail is that if investment demand falls relative to the propensity to save, the rate of interest will not fall as the 'classical' theory supposed. Investors will switch from securities to bonds. This will drive up the price of bonds. Speculators will sell bonds for cash, and the fall in the interest rate will be aborted, or retarded. The liquidity-preference theory of the rate of interest thus clinches Keynes's refutation of Say's Law. The only 'natural' adjustment to a fall in investment is a fall in income.

All this is on the assumption of a fixed money supply. The monetary authority can step in and try to lower the interest rate by buying bonds itself. But this can also generate speculative forces. Keynes does not suppose that, typically, purchases of bonds by the Bank of England will be exactly balanced by the sales of the public. If this were so, open-market operations designed to lower the interest rate would be wholly ineffective. However, it is possible under some circumstances that even a small reduction in the rate of interest may cause a 'mass movement into cash' if opinion is 'unanimous' that the rate is too low.[62] Inactive balances pile up as wealth-holders sell both securities and bonds. This can happen in a deep depression. This is Keynes's famous 'liquidity trap', when monetary policy is wholly ineffective in lowering the interest rate beneath a minimum set by the fear of illiquidity. It typically occurs when the rate of interest falls to a low figure. The lower the rate of interest, the smaller the 'earnings from illiquidity' available 'as a sort of insurance premium to offset the risk of loss on capital account'. This, says Keynes, is the 'chief obstacle to the fall in the rate of interest to a very low level'. A long-term interest rate of 2 per cent 'leaves more to fear than to hope, and offers, at the same time, a running yield which is only sufficient to offset a very small measure of fear'.[63] Liquidity preference may then become 'virtually absolute' in the sense that almost everybody prefers cash to holding a debt which yields so low a rate of interest. It is the 'pure' case, when fear of investment of any kind becomes total. In this event the monetary authority would have lost effective control over the rate of interest.[64] However, the flight into cash might occur at a higher rate of interest, as in the United States in 1932.[65]

Ultimately, then, the rate of interest, like the volume of investment, depends on the state of confidence. A monetary policy which strikes the public as being 'experimental in character or easily liable to change' may cause liquidity preference to shoot up; the same policy may succeed if it 'appeals to public opinion as being reasonable and practicable and in the public interest, and promoted by an authority unlikely to be superseded'.[66] The same considerations apply, of course, to a policy of public works, though Keynes does not say this. If government policy strikes the business community as unsound, the state of confidence goes down, and liquidity preference goes up. It will then require an increasing quantity of money pumped into the economy to prevent the rate of interest from rising, which increases lack of confidence, liquidity preference and so on. This brings us back to the ultimate independent short-period variable, the 'state of the news'.

Keynes rounds off the discussion by calling the rate of interest 'a highly conventional, rather than a highly psychological, phenomenon'.[67] It may 'fluctuate for decades about a level which is chronically too high for full employment' – especially if it is thought to be self-adjusting. Thus the difficulty of maintaining full employment lies in 'the association of a conventional and fairly stable long-term rate of interest with a fickle and highly unstable marginal efficiency of capital'. Keynes does not enquire into what causes the expected rate of interest to be expected: as Robertson has elegantly put it, all his theory tells us is that 'the rate of interest is what it is because it is expected to become other than it is'.[68] But he does say that because 'the convention is not rooted in secure knowledge, it will not be always unduly resistant to a modest measure of persistence and consistency of purpose by the monetary authority'.[69] There is nothing to determine the convention except the convention itself. The monetary authority, in other words, may be able to supply the monetary 'convention' needed to maintain full employment.

The implications of Keynes's discussion of the interest-rate problem go deep. His denial of the 'classical' interest-rate adjustment mechanism clinches, in his view, his theoretical assault on Say's Law: he has shown that the rate of interest cannot be expected to be naturally adjusted so as to provide continuous full employment. The rejection of the idea that interest is a reward for saving makes the 'encouragement of thrift ... no longer a virtue but a vice in a depressed economy' since it 'does not bring a lowering of the rate of interest and a subsequent encouragement to invest'.[70] The possible inefficacy of monetary policy to secure the same result reinforces the case for fiscal policy in combating depression.

The fundamental unity between Keynes's liquidity-preference theory of interest and the rest of his ideas in the *General Theory* lies at the instinctive, or visionary, level. It has to do with the role of money or liquidity in satisfying deep-seated elements in the human psyche. As we have seen, he was not uninfluenced by Freudian explanations of the 'love of money', for which he was able to give an economist's rationale in terms of uncertainty about the future. Thus it was almost certain that he would make the desire to hoard the dominating factor in situations of great uncertainty or trouble.

He was able to do this all the more readily because he had already detached the psychological desire to save from the desire to consume more in the future. The desire for liquidity is, in fact, the primitive form of the saving urge; it takes over when uncertainty becomes too great to bear. It is through money's role as a 'store of wealth' that 'changing views about the future are capable of influencing the present situation'. The liquidity-preference theory of interest must therefore be regarded as an integral part of Keynes's *vision* of economic behaviour, however late it comes in the analytical development of the *General Theory*.

However, Keynes had not provided a complete theory of interest, as was pointed out after the *General Theory* was published; it is best seen as a theory of the dominant influences on the rate of interest, in line with his assumptions about human psychology, and suitable for the purposes in hand. Left out of the story so far are two motives for holding money other than the 'speculative' motive, what Keynes calls the 'transactions' and the 'precautionary' motives. He rightly discusses all three in chapter 15 under the heading 'incentives to liquidity', but it is a misuse of language to call the transactions and precautionary motives part of 'liquidity preference', because they have nothing to do with the desire for liquidity as such. The transactions demand for money is to facilitate business and personal transactions (for example, keeping money to pay wages); the precautionary demand stems from 'the desire for security as to the future cash equivalent of a certain proportion of total resources'. Keynes regarded money held for these two motives as a fairly stable proportion of income, and as having little effect on, or being little affected by, the interest rate. However, this ignores an important repercussion which works through changes in the 'income velocity' of money. Changes in investment redistribute money between the active and inactive balances, leading, other things being equal, to changes in interest rates. Thus it is the total demand for money and not just the demand for 'hoards' that determines the interest rate. Keynes regarded such variations in the 'income velocity of money' as explaining the observed fact that interest rates rise in a boom and fall in a slump. The congestion in the money market, taken in conjunction with the rise in saving, explains why booms tend to peter out before full employment is reached. It can, however, be relieved by the monetary authority, subject, of course, to the speculative motive. Thus he allows an interest-rate adjustment mechanism, but it works *through* changes in income, rather than by adjusting saving to investment at an unchanged level of income, as the 'classical' story told. It is a secondary adjustment mechanism, which serves to counteract the consumption-function mechanism. This set of arguments is implicit in the *General Theory*. It was left to critics to bring them out afterwards. Robertson's charge that Keynes originally approached his interest-rate theory from a 'one-sided standpoint' (liquidity preference proper) for 'dramatic' purposes has some foundation.[71]

The purely static part of the *General Theory* is now done. The Say's Law proposition that all income earned, including non-consumed income, is spent in any period is false. Supply at any time may be limited by demand, because the propensity to save sets an upward limit to consumption, and liquidity preference a lower limit to the rate of interest, while there is no comparable limit to the fall in the marginal efficiency of capital. Involuntary unemployment can be an equilibrium outcome, because the unsatisfied demands of the unemployed for work have no power to influence the real wage at which they could be employed: they do not constitute 'effective demand'.

The rest of the book (chapters 16 to 24, excluding the summary of the model in chapter 18) is devoted to applying the organised body of thinking Keynes has developed to situations and conjectures outside the static framework. He believed that 'the economic system in which we live' was liable to fluctuate round a 'chronic condition of sub-normal' activity.[72] There are discussions on the business cycle, prices, and what Pigou called 'day of Judgement' topics. Many Keynesians, repelled by the hydraulic aspects of the basic model, have found this part of the book (together with chapter 12) the most appealing part, as exhibiting to the full the fertility, curiosity and fancy of the artist–mathematician.

What would happen, he asks us to imagine in chapter 16, to a society where capital is so plentiful that its prospective yield is zero, yet in which people still hoard money, so the rate of interest is positive, and save at full employment? Starting from full employment, the stock of capital and level of employment would shrink till the community became so poor that there was no aggregate saving. Equilibrium would fluctuate round this low point, as uncertainty would still bring booms and slumps. This might seem too fanciful to be plausible, but Keynes suggests that a foretaste of such an 'equilibrium' was seen in the post-war experiences of Britain and the United States. Such an outcome would represent the triumph of the death instinct. Assuming, on the other hand, state action to ensure a rate of interest which corresponds to a full-employment rate of investment, a 'properly run community' with modern technique and stationary population should achieve capital abundance in a single generation, reaching a quasi-stationary state in which change and progress would result only from changes in technique, taste, population and institutions. This would be the most sensible way of getting rid of the objectionable features of capitalism. For 'enormous social changes' would result from the disappearance of a return on capital. People would still be free to accumulate earned income, but their accumulations would not grow. They would 'simply be in the position of Pope's father, who, when he retired from business, carried a chest of guineas with him to his villa at Twickenham and met his household expenses from it as required'.[73] The mood and language recall Keynes's 'Economic Possibilities for Our Grandchildren'.

Chapter 17 may be seen as Keynes's central dramatic statement of the conflict between the Investor and the Hoarder, which fails for precisely the reason that economics is not a good vehicle for conveying drama. Here he presents a vision of the Day of Judgement in which the desire to accumulate money knocks out all other forms of production, so that wealthy societies, like King Midas, drown in a sea of gold. The technical idea behind it, which Keynes owed to the debate between Piero Sraffa and Hayek in 1931–2, is that the marginal returns to money, not just in any period, but over time, fall less than those to capital.[74] This is because money has a unique liquidity premium, allied to a small elasticity of production, and negligible carrying costs. It is the combination of the fixed supply of money (excluding the monetary authority's action) and the insatiable demand for it, which keeps up its 'own rate' of interest, whereas 'if money could be grown like a crop or manufactured like a motor car, depressions would be avoided . . . because, if the price of other assets was tending to fall in terms of money, more labour would be diverted into the production of money'.[75] Even if the quantity of money is increased the interest rate might not fall 'to anything approaching the extent to which the yield from other types of assets falls when their quantity is comparably increased' because of its unique liquidity premium.[76] In the absence of money the 'own rates' of commodities would reach equilibrium only at full employment. Instead societies grow rich in money and poor in goods:

> Unemployment develops, that is to say, because people want the moon: men cannot be employed when the object of desire (i.e. money) is something which cannot be produced and the demand for which cannot readily be choked off. There is no remedy but to persuade the public that green cheese is practically the same thing and to have a green cheese factory (i.e. a central bank) under public control.[77]

If chapter 17 is taken to be an integral part of the *General Theory*, the complete doctrine of the book may be summed up in the words of Keynes's student Reddaway: 'Money causes a difficulty because the entrepreneurs argue that if they increase production, they will not "get their money back" because people won't spend the whole increase on consumption, whilst investment is held up because there is no asset whose prospects would tempt people to part with money . . . at a rate they (the entrepreneurs) could pay.'[78]

A few economists have found chapter 17 the most original in the whole book; it is brilliantly suggestive, a pure flight of fancy, with mathematics at the service of art. Keynes stands the classical verities on their head by making resources abundant, money scarce. Unfortunately, the paradox has lost much of its suggestiveness, for since the war the monetary authorities have amply proved their ability to make money go as bad as cheese, and private enterprise has managed to stimulate new wants apparently without limit.*

Keynes has not so far talked much about wages and prices. The argument has been conducted on the assumption of fixed money wages. (This is consistent with prices rising in line with marginal costs, thus allowing a fall in the real wage.) Book V on 'Money-Wages and Prices' relaxes the fixed-wage assumption. In chapter 19, Keynes returns to the discussion broken off in chapter 2 by considering the effect of money-wage reductions on investment, saving and liquidity preference. The conclusion is that the only way an all-round reduction in money wages can improve employment in a closed system is if the reduction in the transactions demand for money balances causes the rate of interest to fall, and if falling wages improve businessmen's expectations of profit. A better policy would be to aim for this result by increasing the quantity of money.[79] Chapter 21, 'The Theory of Prices', allows for a 'condition of prices rising gradually as employment increases' as a result of the misallocation of labour, which, together with a tendency for workers to press for money-wage rises as employment improves, produces positions of 'semi-inflation' short of full employment.[80] These chapters make it clear that the familiar summary of the *General Theory*'s message, 'quantities adjust, not prices', is seriously incomplete. In particular it is not true that Keynes believed that wages will start rising only when full employment is reached. Both quantities and prices adjust the national income upwards and downwards; output is not the sole adjustment variable. The relative parts played by each depend on the institutions of the labour market and the state of expectations. This is a much more sensible way of looking at things than the hydraulic income–expenditure version of Keynesianism. Had the message of these two chapters been properly digested, the stagflation of the 1970s might have been avoided.†

Book VI, a section of three chapters headed 'Short Notes Suggested by

---

*It is odd to speak of the marginal productivity of something (money) whose yield is purely psychic. There is a strange passage at the top of p. 242 in which Keynes attributes the poverty of the world after 'several millennia of steady individual saving' to the 'high liquidity-premiums formerly attaching to the ownership of land and now attaching to money'. Land is not usually thought of as liquid, and, though it cannot be manufactured, it has a non-psychic yield. Keynes subsequently admitted he would alter this passage and 'I am not quite clear what it is I am trying to say.' (KP: p. 145, JMK to Labordére, 7 May 1937.)

†Keynes, however, was to some extent to blame for postponing the 'flexible price' story till chapter 21. He wanted to drive home the message that 'quantities adjust, not prices', in order to distance himself from orthodoxy, and also to maximise the value of the employment multiplier. Orthodoxy was thereby given a comeback by being able to say that Keynes's output-adjustment story depended on fixed wages. Chapters 19 and 20 are therefore essential to understanding the full argument which, incidentally, cannot be accommodated within Keynes's 'short period'.

the General Theory', relates Keynes's theory to other theories, past and present, to history, and to his hopes for the future. To most economists they are literary embellishments. But chapter 22 is important for the theory, for here Keynes steps back from his short-period method, turns on the projector and exhibits the 'propensities' which determine the position of the economy at any moment in time themselves moving through time.

Perhaps the most popular misconception to which Keynes's static method gave rise was the idea that the system had no self-adjusting properties: that the rate of unemployment associated with any short-period position went on for ever. But Keynes did not believe this. Booms and slumps continue in his system, but the static method cannot exhibit this. So chapter 22, 'Notes on the Trade Cycle', drops it for a more 'realistic' sequence analysis. The great depression was the slump phase of a cycle; when the *General Theory* was published, the boom phase had been going for two years. Unemployment rose in the slump and fell in the boom: to that extent the market economy was obviously self-adjusting, and Keynes did not deny this.

The point Keynes wants to make is that 'normal' conditions are not normally 'optimal' conditions. The slump is brought about by the collapse of the marginal efficiency of capital relative to the 'normal rate of growth [of capital] in a given epoch'. It is caused partly by the growing abundance of the particular set of capital goods fuelling the boom and their rising costs of production, but above all by over-optimistic expectations generated by the mass psychology of investment markets and excited animal spirits. A boom, Keynes writes, 'is a situation in which over-optimism triumphs over a rate of interest which, in a cooler light, would be seen to be excessive'.[81] It is not surprising that when disillusion falls on an 'over-optimistic and over-bought market . . . it should fall with sudden and even catastrophic force'.[82] The collapse is aggravated, rather than caused, by a rise in interest rates, due to increased liquidity preference. The collapse in the marginal efficiency of capital may be so complete that 'no practicable reduction in the rate of interest' will be enough to offset it.[83] That is why an interval of time has to elapse before the 'return of confidence'.[84] Confidence does not spring out of thin air. It returns, essentially, when 'the shortage of capital through use, decay and obsolescence' becomes sufficiently obvious. Keynes particularly emphasises the relationship between the phases of the cycle and the 'average durability of capital in a given epoch'.[85]

There is nothing, in short, to stop the rundown; but the appearance of scarcities in stocks, working capital and above all durable capital, provides the basis of recovery and subsequent overshoot. In other words, although income runs down to adjust saving to the level of investment given by a particular set of expectations, expectations do sooner or later improve for the definite reason that the decay of the existing capital stock makes it profitable once more to employ more labour to replenish it. 'Unemployment equilibrium' is just that: the position corresponding to the 'existing quality and quantity of available equipment'.[86] There is nothing permanent about it.

Keynes rejects both the overinvestment and underconsumptionist explanations of the business cycle. 'The situation, which I am indicating as typical, is not one in which capital is so abundant that the community as a whole has no reasonable use for any more, but where investment is being made in conditions which are unstable and cannot endure, because it is prompted by expectations which are destined to be disappointed.' The remedy for the cycle is 'not to be found in abolishing booms and thus keeping us permanently in a semi-slump; but in abolishing slumps and thus keeping us permanently in a quasi-boom'.[87] Underconsumptionists like Hobson were right in their practical recommendations if investment was left to fluctuate 'according to speculative fevers' and the rate of interest never fell below a conventional level. But it would be better to 'advance on both fronts at once' by means of a 'socially controlled rate of investment' and policies designed to increase the propensity to consume.[88]

In chapter 22, Keynes stakes out an anti-Ricardian lineage for his own ideas, endorsing the anti-usury laws of the medieval schoolmen, finding 'fragments of practical wisdom' in the mercantilist obsession with accumulating precious metals (interpreted as an attempt to drive down the rate of interest), commending Mandeville and Malthus for their praise of extravagant consumption, honouring 'the strange, unduly neglected prophet Silvio Gesell' for proposing 'stamped' money ('the future will learn more from the spirit of Gesell than from that of Marx'), making handsome amends for his previous neglect of J. A. Hobson, and even enrolling the founder of Social Credit, Major Douglas, in the 'brave army of heretics'. Harrod deplored this chapter as 'a tendentious attempt to glorify imbeciles';[89] Schumpeter, who declared himself no Marxist, recognised Marx's greatness sufficiently 'to be offended at seeing him classed with Silvio Gesell and Major Douglas'.[90] The discussion confirmed critics in their view that Keynes's theory, by rehabilitating old fallacies, marked regression, not progress, in economic science; but it was his way of honouring the 'cranks' who 'have preferred to see the truth obscurely and imperfectly rather than to maintain error, reached . . . by easy logic . . . on hypotheses inappropriate to the facts'.[91]

The last chapter, 'Concluding Notes on Social Philosophy', may be seen as an updating of Keynes's politics of the Middle Way, first developed in the 1920s. 'The outstanding faults of the economic society in which we live are its failure to provide for full employment and its arbitrary and inequitable distribution of wealth and incomes.'[92] The much greater prominence now given to the second of these 'faults' was not just a tactical concession to socialist sentiment; it was a direct implication of his view that 'thriftiness' or 'abstinence' retards the growth of wealth in any situation short of full employment. Excessive thriftiness could be tackled in two ways: by redistributing spending power to those with a high propensity to consume (the workers); and by reducing the rewards of thriftiness by fixing a low interest rate. This would remove the power of the savers to exploit the scarcity value of capital. It is in this context that Keynes advocated the 'euthanasia of the rentier'.[93] This double-squeeze on the saver is balanced (though not very fervently) by the endorsement of 'significant inequalities of incomes and wealth', though not of 'such large disparities as exist to-day'.[94]

Because banking policy was unlikely to be able to maintain an 'optimum rate of interest', Keynes proposed a 'somewhat comprehensive socialisation of investment'. Beyond this, there was no 'obvious case' for state socialism or other forms of interference; his theory was 'moderately conservative' in its implications.[95] With deficient demand removed from the picture, the full benefits and promise of the 'Manchester System' could for the first time be realised domestically and internationally: efficiency, freedom and variety of life at home, mutual harmony and peace abroad.[96]*

Keynes ends with a too-often quoted passage about ideas being more powerful in the long run than 'vested interests'.

> Indeed the world is ruled by little else. Practical men, who believe themselves to be quite exempt from any intellectual influences, are usually the slaves of some defunct economist. Madmen in authority, who hear voices in the air, are distilling their frenzy from some academic scribbler of a few years back. I am sure that the power of vested interests is vastly exaggerated compared with the gradual encroachment of ideas.[97]

The last sentence of the book is: 'But, soon or late, it is ideas, not vested interests, which are dangerous for good or evil.' Stalin and Neville Chamberlain, Marx and the classical economists all fall under this double condemnation. And, since Keynes always had one eye on the young, it can be read as a repudiation of the doctrine of the Marxist generation, that it was 'capitalism' which stood in the way of social and economic reform. A more sober summing up of the mood and argument of the *General Theory* is the less quoted passage on p. 381:

> The authoritarian state systems of today seem to solve the problem of unemployment at the expense of efficiency and freedom. It is certain that the world will not much longer tolerate the unemploy-

---

*Keynes lauded, in almost Hayekian vein, individualistic capitalism as embodying 'the most secure and successful choices of former generations', and being 'the most powerful instrument to better the future'. (*CW*, vii, 380.)

ment which, apart from brief intervals of excitement, is associated –
and, in my opinion inevitably associated – with present-day capitalistic individualism. But it may be possible by a right analysis of the
problem to cure the disease whilst preserving efficiency and freedom.

CHAPTER SIXTEEN

Whose General Theory?

I

REACTIONS

This chapter is about economic theology. The publication of the *General Theory* was followed by a war of opinion among economists. The broad division into Keynesians, anti-Keynesians and Reconcilers conceals not only varying degrees of acceptance or rejection of the new dispensation, but the start of the argument about what the central message of the *General Theory* was, and what one needed to accept to be a 'Keynesian', which has gone on ever since. The complexity of the doctrine itself, and its ambiguous relationship to 'orthodox' economics, meant that it was never a simple question of taking it or leaving it, rather of degrees of mutual accommodation and assimilation. In the course of the argument, much that was unique to Keynes himself – especially his Vision of the mainsprings of economic action – got lost. The two things which survived were the idea that, for one reason or another, unmanaged capitalist economies were liable to collapse into slumps, and an efficient machine for action, waiting to be used when rulers were ready.

The *General Theory* was immediately perceived to be an immensely disturbing work. It was subjected to extensive review in the leading learned journals as well as the popular press all over the world. Although reactions to it were sharply divided, there is no case of outright dismissal.* Even the most hostile critics recognised that Keynes had a case to be answered. Opinion ranged from those at one end (his Cambridge disciples) who set out to spread the gospel to those at the other who argued that all Keynes's revolutionary claims were wrong, and his valid points could be assimilated into modified classical theory. In between were those like Hicks, Harrod and Meade, more mathematically inclined than either of the wings, who were intent on developing a formal structure which could incorporate Keynes's doctrine as a 'special case' of a generalised theory of employment. The generational pattern in the reactions is most obvious at either extreme,

*Professor Benjamin Haggot Beckhart of Columbia University may claim the dubious distinction of being the exception to this rule. The *General Theory*, he wrote, 'is likely to remain for the academician but an interesting exhibit in the museum of depression curiosities'. (In the *Political Science Quarterly*, December 1936.)

economists of Keynes's own age and seniority being the most opposed to his new doctrine, the youngest ones the most enthusiastic. As Paul Samuelson put it, 'The *General Theory* caught most economists under the age of thirty-five with the unexpected virulence of a disease. . . . Economists beyond fifty turned out to be quite immune to the ailment.'[1] But it was the intermediate generation which accomplished the translation of the *General Theory* into the new orthodoxy. Economists of all ages read Keynes's book in the light of the doctrines of their own 'schools'. Keynes claimed no monopoly of radicalism. Twentieth-century events had plunged economics into crisis long before Keynes: Cambridge, Chicago, Stockholm and Vienna offered their own deviant branches from the orthodox stem, and Keynes's panaceas were contrasted with theirs. Chicago and Stockholm upheld their own theories in face of Keynes's onslaught. The Austrian outpost at the LSE crumbled. Hayek and Robbins offered no reply: the younger members of the economics faculty – Lerner, Kaldor, Hicks – deserted to the Keynesian camp. In the Anglo-Saxon world some version of Keynesianism triumphed in the end, because it offered to resolve the crisis in economics, much as Marshall's *Principles* had done in the nineteenth century. John Hicks was the first to find a pedagogically effective way of doing this; and it is with his name that the Keynesian Revolution is imperishably associated.

Keynes took an active, even heroic, part in the controversies which followed his book's appearance, despite Lydia's advice. 'I expect you are right – you always are,' he wrote to her on 17 May 1936. 'But I have such a dreadfully controversial temperament that it is difficult for me to keep away from it.' To Dennis Robertson he wrote on 2 December 1936, 'I am trying to prevent my mind from crystallising too much on the precise lines of the *General Theory*. I am attentive to criticisms and to what raises difficulties and catches people's attention – in which there are a good many surprises'.[2] What caught the attention of young students of economics was very different from what caught the attention of their professors. Bensusan-Butt, who came up to read economics at King's in 1933, offers a typical retrospect of the effect of the *General Theory* on his Cambridge generation of economists:

> What we got was joyful revelation in dark times. We thought that Keynes had . . . found the 'flaw in the capitalist system', and had proclaimed its remedy. He had demonstrated that this flaw lay in the absence of any mechanism for the maintenance of full employment, in the possibility that the system could drift along in various degrees of slump forever. He had shown that the fact that the level of employment had generally been high before 1914 had been essentially a temporary and accidental fact, and that the horrors we had seen throughout our young post-war lives were more natural to and typical of an ill-controlled modern capitalism . . . The mystery of contemporary iniquity had been unveiled by a masterpiece of sustained intellectual effort. All the other

tangled turgid stuff which lesser men were producing to rationalise the
mess around us simply faded away. Now we all knew why.

Further he had gone on to examine the cures, and these, flowing by
a kind of inexorable logic from the analysis, were of the kind to
revive the idealism even of a disenchanted socialist. Keynes's reformed
capitalism had everything and more the Fabian generation had looked
for in socialism: it was morally speaking egalitarian, it was fully
employed, it was generous and gay; it was a very new sort of capitalism
controlled not by the greedy votaries of Mammon but by the intellect
and joie de vivre of an intelligent and robust democracy. It had no
more place for the dull, mean and fearful parrots of Birmingham and
the City then in charge of affairs at home than for the suicidal tyrannies
of the Left and the bestialities of the Right then boiling up abroad.

Thus the *General Theory* was to us less a work of economics theory
than a Manifesto for Reason and Cheerfulness, the literary embodi-
ment of a man who, to those who ever saw him, remains the very
genius of intellect and enjoyment. It gave a rational basis and moral
appeal for a faith in the possible health and sanity of contemporary
mankind such as the youths of my generation found nowhere else. We
took as our religion that short and now classical peroration about the
power of ideas, and, in the very doubtful hope of surviving the impending war, off we went to spread the light as clerks in Whitehall.[3]

Lorie Tarshis, who attended all four years of Keynes's lectures between
1932 and 1935, remembers his experience in much the same terms:

What Keynes supplied was the excitement of a new beginning as the
residue of Classical economics was swept away. He supplied too that
measure of impatience the situation called for and the opportunity for
all of us to be a part of a great adventure. And finally what Keynes
supplied was *hope*: hope that prosperity could be restored and maintained without the support of prison camps, executions and bestial
interrogations . . . In those years many of us felt that by following
Keynes . . . each one of us could become a doctor to the whole world.[4]

The reviews by Brian Reddaway, David Champernowne and A. P.
Lerner, all in their twenties, were by followers.[5] They consisted, in the
main, of expositions of the new theory. However, Champernowne, who was
influenced by Robertson and Pigou as well as Keynes, took a more heterodox
line. The classical theory and Keynes's theory were not opposites, but
appropriate to different situations. Thus the classical theory would be of
'no avail if outlets for investment are so scarce or if the employers are so
nervous of any increase in the supply of money that they hoard, and it is
impossible to lower the rate of interest sufficiently to cause sufficient investment to keep prices and money wages from falling'. The practical import-

ance of Keynes's structure depended on the behavioural characteristics of the period.[6] Champernowne was also the first 'Keynesian' to emphasise that the possibility of increasing employment by demand expansion depended heavily on workers not asking for higher wages as prices rose.[7] Abba Lerner, a temporary assistant lecturer at the London School of Economics, had been converted to the doctrine of the necessary equality between saving and investment in August 1933, and never subsequently deviated from it. 'There is only one curve,' he wrote in his review, 'which is both the supply curve and the demand curve for savings, so that the rate of interest remains unexplained.'[8] Harrod's first review appeared in the *Political Quarterly* of April 1936. He was the only reviewer to point to the political importance of the book in heading off extremists. If Keynes's diagnosis was accepted, 'the prospect is opened before us of keeping the existing system running without any drastic upheaval'. This was really the point of the *General Theory* for Harrod. It coloured his interpretation of the theory itself, and his treatment of Keynes's life when he came to write the official biography. Socialist reviewers included Douglas Jay (in the *Banker*, April 1936), A. L. Rowse, who wrote another of his pleas for Keynes to join the Labour Party, and Evan Durbin (in *Labour*, April 1936). Rowse said, 'It is my contention, as it is my belief, that there is little or no divergence between what is implied by Labour policy and by Mr. Keynes . . . Rather than trying to charm Montagu Norman, Keynes should put behind his ideas the interests of the Labour movement.'[9] By contrast, Durbin, a lecturer at the LSE, was unimpressed by Keynes's social philosophy. 'It is difficult for me to understand,' he wrote to him on 29 April 1936, 'how the author of the *Economic Consequences of the Peace* . . . can argue that one advantage of a *laissez-faire* system lies in the freedom it gives to certain privileged persons to exercise their sadistic impulses in the control of industrial workers.'[10] Henry Douglas went one better in the communist *Daily Worker* of 9 April 1936: 'Which "reality" does Keynes want – Olympia and the poison gas of Abyssinia, the end of Bloomsbury and all culture – or the flowering of a new life (and full employment . . .) in the Soviet Union?'

Hicks, who had moved from the LSE to Cambridge in 1935, reviewed the *General Theory* for the *Economic Journal* in June 1936. He and Keynes were not, nor did they ever become, particularly close, and Keynes underestimated Hicks as a theorist, describing his *Theory of Wages* (1932) as 'the serious and careful work of an unoriginal but competent mind.'[11] It is ironic that Hicks, who played no part in the genesis of the *General Theory*, and was at best an incomplete Keynesian, became by far the most influential interpreter and seller of the Keynesian Revolution. Hicks's review in the *Economic Journal* of June 1936 set the scene for his famous article, 'Mr. Keynes and the Classics' in *Econometrica*, April 1937, which transformed the *General Theory* into its famous IS–LM form. Hicks's enthusiasm is reserved for the 'method of expectations', 'the most revolutionary thing' about the book from the standpoint of 'pure theory'. Keynes's achievement was to capture 'the changing, progressing, fluctuating economy' in a determinate short-period framework. It is to this revolution that the term 'general' may be applied; apart from that there is Keynes's 'special theory' (that is, the theory of effective demand) whose usefulness is 'mainly a matter of judgement, depending upon our estimates of the relative importance of particular causes in particular situations'. Hicks inclined to the 'loanable funds' theory of the rate of interest. He found no adequate justification for Keynes's 'fundamental law' of diminishing returns to capital, which assumes gluttability of wants and nil invention.[12]

The American reviews greeted the *General Theory* with a mixture of hostility and incomprehension, though not without a sense that they were dealing with a work of historical importance. The *Quarterly Journal of Economics* devoted a (mainly) critical issue to it in November 1936. However, conversion came rapidly, though patchily.

The four main American reviewers were Hansen, Schumpeter, Knight and Viner, all established economists of distinction, the last two at Chicago. They pinpointed Keynes's emphasis on liquidity preference as his essential contribution, but saw it as a modification of, not an alternative to, the classical theory of interest, capable (perhaps) of explaining mass unemployment, though not of determining a position of 'underemployment equilibrium'. American interpretations of persisting unemployment laid more stress than did British ones on imperfections in the goods markets. This reflected a strong institutionalist tradition, from which few American economists at the time were immune, itself the product of the political battles to control trusts and monopolies.

Alvin Hansen, who came to Harvard University from Minnesota in 1937, and was soon to become Keynes's leading American advocate, is typical here. The *General Theory* is not 'a landmark in the sense that it lays a foundation for a "new economics" . . . [it is] more a symptom of economic trends than a foundation stone on which a new science can be built'. Hansen argued that 'stable unemployment equilibrium' could not occur without rigidities in the wages and goods markets; he feared that Keynes's partial socialism would lead to the full-blooded variety. Although Hansen thought that 'economic progress tends towards equilibrium full employment', he recognised that the 'closing of the frontier' for investment combined with rigid costs and a static population made 'secular unemployment' possible. This was the foretaste of the 'secular stagnation' thesis which became the basis of his (and much American) acceptance of the Keynesian revolution.[13]

Hansen's depiction of the *General Theory* as a 'reversion to the economic doctrines of mercantilism' was echoed by his Harvard colleague Joseph Schumpeter, for whom the book marked a scientific regression. Aiming for realism, it exhibited the worst features of the 'Ricardian Vice' of excessive abstraction, with its use of artificial definitions, specialised assumptions and 'paradoxical-looking tautologies' to invest 'special cases' with a 'treacherous generality'. One such is the theory of 'underemployment equilibrium', which rests on the assumption of 'fixed production functions'. Interestingly, Schumpeter's attack on this doctrine does not depend on Say's Law, or the classical theory of interest. Indeed, he welcomed Keynes's monetary theory of interest, 'which is . . . the first to follow my own'. It rests much more on a theory of long cycles which are deepened by all the usual elements of rigidities, lags and so on, and which prevent the equilibrating mechanism from functioning properly. Schumpeter accuses Keynes of treating his 'propensities' as causes: Keynes does not explain 'why people expect what they expect'. His book mixes up science and politics: 'on every page, the ghost of [policy] . . . frames his assumptions, guides his pen', with his advice expressing 'the attitude of a decaying civilization'.[14] Schumpeter, with his Continental background, was unusual, in all his comments on Keynes, in fitting him into a British context, and in interpreting the *General Theory* as a sociological as much as an intellectual phenomenon.

The review of Frank Knight, the dominating influence in inter-war Chicago economics, appeared in the *Canadian Journal of Economics* in February 1937. Knight said that Keynes had not solved the mystery of 'what blocks employment'. 'Men get control of capital through borrowing money, but there is never any connection between saving money and the offer of funds in the loan market.' Socialising investment meant 'taking it out of business and putting it into politics'; pumping money into the system to maintain an artificially low interest rate would unbalance the capital structure. But Knight's strongest criticism was reserved for Keynes's procedure, which led to a caricature of classical doctrines and reinvention of old fallacies. Instead of starting with a simplified, abstract model which is then brought closer to reality, Keynes treated propositions true in context as general, and attacked classical propositions as untrue which were related to a simplified stage of analysis that abstracted from disturbances. Thus Keynes's theory was, after all, a 'special case', and 'the argument . . . requires extensive re-interpretation and integration with a general theory running in terms of equilibrium with full employment before it can be accepted as sound or useful'.[15]

There should have been some points of sympathy between Knight and Keynes. Knight was the first to point to the pervasiveness of uncertainty in economic affairs, and to distinguish properly between 'uncertainty' and 'risk'. (Not surprisingly he liked chapter 12 of the *General Theory* best.) He devoted much attention in his writings to the ethical foundations of capitalist society. But, like Hayek, he regarded the market system, and the reasoning which supported it, as the best defence against political barbarism. Keynes refused the offer to reply to Knight's review, writing: 'Indeed with Professor Knight's two main conclusions, namely, that my book had caused him intense irritation, and that he had great difficulty in understanding it, I am in agreement.'[16] In Knight's 'passionate, expiring cries' there is the feeling, common to many of the older economists, that Keynes had committed a *trahison des clercs*. This feeling was, no doubt, particularly strong in 1936. A few days after the *General Theory*'s appearance, Hitler marched into the Rhineland, tearing up the Treaty of Versailles as Keynes had torn up classical economics.

But Knight's was not the only voice from Chicago. Jacob Viner was both more favourable and more constructive than Knight, calling parts of the *General Theory* 'an outstanding intellectual achievement', and Keynes thought it alone of the American reviews – it appeared in the *Quarterly Journal of Economics* in November 1936 – merited a reply. Viner was careful throughout his review to compare Keynes's doctrine, not with the 'Aunt Sally' he had erected, but with 'current' doctrine in Chicago and elsewhere, and found a large measure of agreement, concealed by Keynes's method and polemical style of argument. Viner accepted Keynes's analytical framework, but was 'unable to accept some of Keynes's account of how these "propensities" operate in practice or his appraisal of their relative strength'.[17] Noting the widespread aversion to holding 'dead' cash, Viner thought liquidity preference was far less important in determining the interest rate than the transactions demand for cash, related to income, saving and investment. The demand for capital and the propensity to save can be restored as determinants of interest, 'though, I admit, in somewhat modified and improved fashion'.[18] Viner, like Pigou, criticised Keynes's view that a cut in money wages caused prices to fall equiproportionally, and thought he had accepted too uncritically the perfect-competition assumption in product markets: if plants are working only at 30 per cent capacity, diminishing returns to labour may not hold.[19]

Reviewing his review twenty-seven years later, Viner wrote:

> My appreciation of the quality and originality of its analysis as short-run analysis has grown since rather than shrunk . . . On its adequacy as long-run analysis, and especially on its denial that (in a truly competitive economy) there exist powerful automatic forces which in the long run, if not counteracted by perverse governmental intervention, will restore 'equilibrium', I still remain sceptical at least, with some propensity to be hostile . . . What we should concede, with acknowledgements to Keynes, is that in counting our putative long-run blessings we should not disregard as trivial the short-run woes that they may have involved merely because they were, or may have been, present for a period substantially short of infinity . . . [20]

The Chicago School combined a robust belief in the market system with advocacy of stabilisation policy, both monetary and fiscal. As we have seen, the Chicago economists found Keynes rather conservative on fiscal policy when he visited them in 1931. Milton Friedman was a graduate at Chicago in the early 1930s. Recalling his debates with Lerner in the 1940s, Friedman asked himself why Lerner was such an enthusiastic convert to Keynes, while he, Friedman, remained 'largely unaffected, and, if anything, somewhat hostile'. His answer is that Keynes's remedies for slump were no great novelty in Chicago in the 1930s:

Lerner had been trained at the London School of Economics where the dominant view was that the depression was an inevitable result of the preceding boom; that it was deepened by the attempts to prevent prices and wages from falling and firms from going bankrupt; that the monetary authorities had brought on the depression by inflationary policies before the crash and had prolonged it by 'easy money' policies thereafter; that the only sound policy was to let the depression run its course, bring down money costs, and eliminate weak and unsound firms.

In contrast to this dismal picture, the news emerging from Cambridge about Keynes's interpretation of the depression and of the 'right' policy to cure it must have come like a flash of light on a dark night . . . It is easy to see how a young, vigorous, and generous mind would have been attracted to it.

The intellectual climate at Chicago had been wholly different from that at the LSE. My teachers regarded the depression as largely the product of misguided government policy. They blamed the monetary and fiscal authorities for permitting banks to fail and the quantity of deposits to decline. Far from preaching the necessity of letting deflation and bankruptcy run their course, they issued repeated calls for government action to stem the deflation.

There was nothing in these views to repel a student, or to make Keynes attractive. On the contrary, so far as policy was concerned, Keynes had nothing to offer those of us who had sat at the feet of Simons, Mints, Knight and Viner.[21]*

*These recollections of Friedman should be taken with a pinch of salt, for reasons which Patinkin points out in 'The Chicago Tradition, the Quantity Theory, and Friedman', *Journal of Money, Credit and Banking*, February 1969, and 'Friedman on the Quantity Theory and Keynesian Economics', *Journal of Political Economy*, September/October 1972. However, Patinkin's presentation of the views of Henry Simons (on pp. 50–1 of his *JMCB* article) is so similar to Keynes's quantity-theory approach in his *Tract on Monetary Reform* (1923), that it would be interesting to know whether there was a line of influence running from Keynes (1923) to Chicago (1934). Simons argued that the extreme instability of V (velocity of circulation) required countercyclical policy to offset fluctuations in V by changes in M, which is identical to Keynes's proposal (*Tract*, *CIV*, iv, 68). Friedman, as we have already noted, considers the *Tract* Keynes's best book. (See p. 153 above.) The Chicago School was less keen than Keynes was on discretionary policy; and favoured automatic variations in tax receipts as providing built-in stabilisers. Patinkin shows that Friedman's recollections of the Chicago tradition were unconsciously influenced by the impact of the *General Theory*. But the concentration of scholarship on charting the influence of this book has led to two errors in the study of the transmission of Keynes's ideas: (a) that the *Tract* and the *Treatise* had no independent influence of their own; and (b) that there was little continuity between the earlier and later books. The Keynesian 'flavour' can be got from all three of them, and no doubt there were economists throughout the world in the inter-war years as 'Keynesian' as Keynes was himself before the *General Theory* was written.

The situation was very different at Harvard, which soon became the centre for the diffusion of Keynes's ideas through the profession and government. Pre-Keynesian Harvard, where Taussig was the dominant influence, was much more 'classical' than Chicago, as witnessed by the book of essays, *The Economics of the Recovery Programme*, published in 1934 by its Economics Department and replete with classical nostrums about the need for saving and wage flexibility. Robert Bryce arrived at Harvard from Cambridge at the beginning of 1936 'to start the indoctrination of Harvard before the *General Theory* appeared'.[22] Lorie Tarshis arrived at neighbouring Tufts University soon after. Paul Samuelson, a fellow student of Milton Friedman's at Chicago, who had come to Harvard in 1935, became the most notable convert of the younger generation. He retained his Chicago microeconomics, but embraced Keynes's macroeconomics. Alvin Hansen's seminar in macroeconomic policy provided a centre for discussion from 1937 onwards. John Kenneth Galbraith, who joined Samuelson at Harvard, recalled, 'The old economics was still taught by day. But in the evening and almost every evening from 1936 onwards almost everyone in the Harvard community discussed Keynes.'[23] Most of the leading American names associated with the Keynesian Revolution – Samuelson, Galbraith, James Tobin, Robert Solow, Seymour Harris – passed through Harvard. A Tufts–Harvard Keynesian manifesto was issued in October 1938.[24] The recruitment of the young Harvard Keynesians to Washington gave a kick-start to the languishing New Deal. 'By the end of the 1930s,' Galbraith has written, '[Lauchlin] Currie [Roosevelt's main economic adviser] had established an informal network of converts extending into all the fiscally significant agencies.'[25] Columbia, however, remained relatively immune to the new doctrines. What took hold in America were Keynes's tools, not his 'general theory'. He made it possible to stick macroeconomic policy on to traditional microeconomics. Classical economics was perfectly all right, but there were rigidities in the labour, goods and capital markets which could lead to quantity effects swamping price effects. As Samuelson later put it, 'Had Keynes begun his first few chapters with the simple statement that he found it realistic to assume that modern capitalistic societies had money wage rates that were sticky and resistant to downward movements, most of his insights would have remained just as valid . . .'[26] So Keynes's theory was a special case of the classical theory, with particular relevance for policy.[27]

The *General Theory* did not break the hold of Wicksell among the younger economists of the Stockholm School, whose leading members were Bertil Ohlin, Gunnar Myrdal and Erik Lindahl. There was some reciprocal influence between Stockholm and Cambridge, and Keynes had arranged to have Wicksell's *Interest and Prices* translated into English by Richard Kahn, but the Swedish economists stuck to the disequilibrium approach which Keynes had briefly espoused in the *Treatise*. Ohlin, who had studied at Cambridge in the 1920s, and clashed with Keynes on German reparations, published a two-part statement of the Stockholm method in the *Economic Journal* of February 1937, which introduced British economists to the Swedish *ex ante* and *ex post*, or 'looking forward' and 'looking backwards', concepts, later incorporated into some versions of Keynesian theory. The Swedish economists were particularly concerned with adjustment as a *process* which reconciles inconsistent plans. The divergence between *planned* saving and investment gives rise to dynamic changes which equalise *realised* saving and investment. The Swedish disequilibrium method gets rid of Keynes's awkward 'identity' of saving and investment; it more naturally brings out the role of both output *and* prices in adjusting the economy to shocks, without implying a cleavage between them.[28] Myrdal wrote later, 'the Keynesian revolution . . . was mainly an Anglo-American occurrence. In Sweden, where we grew up in the tradition of Knut Wicksell, Keynes' works were read as interesting and important contributions along a familiar line of thought, but not in any sense as a revolutionary breakthrough.'[29] Sweden's successful recovery programme in the 1930s, like Germany's but under a very different kind of government, suggests that successful 'Keynesian' policy can be based on theoretical constructions quite different from that of the *General Theory*.

The *General Theory* was published in German by Duncker and Humblott at the end of 1936, with an unfortunately worded preface from Keynes, claiming the peculiar applicability of macroeconomics to the 'conditions of a totalitarian state' with strong 'national leadership'.[30] It received enormous coverage in both learned journals and the popular press, with many of the reviewers showing a commendable independence of the official policies of the regime: for example, the (anonymous) reviewer in the *Frankfurter Handelsblatt* of 14 June 1936 criticised the 'closed-economy' approach of the *General Theory* for its autarkic implications. On the other hand, Carl Brinkman of Heidelberg University, an apologist of the regime, welcomed the *General Theory* as a vindication of National Socialism. 'What might English theory and German practice have been able to contribute to each other if Keynes had taken the latter as the basis for the induction and, in turn, the verification of his theory?'[31]

The German economic tradition was much more historically minded than the British. Economists like Werner Sombart, Wilhelm Röpke and Alexander Rustow (the two latter, after the war, leading architects of the 'social market economy') tried to get at the social roots of capitalist malfunction, in a way foreign to Keynes and the British economists, who took their inherited institutions for granted, and relied on technical solutions to economic problems.[32] To central European economists like Sombart and Ropke – and for that matter Schumpeter – prosperity in the nineteenth and depression in the twentieth, centuries were the result not of 'accidents', but of systematic changes in the social conditions of capitalism. Sombart emphasised the growth of a 'corporatist', cartelised structure of capitalism, much as Keynes, influenced by Commons, had done in the 1920s. To Wilhelm Lautenbach, the 'German Keynes', the crisis of twentieth-century capitalism was due to the removal of the 'exogenous balancing factor' (that is, expanding foreign trade) which had sustained prosperity in the nineteenth century.[33] Alfred Weber attributed the upward movement in interest rates which had started at the turn of the century to the growth of protection, the ability of trade unions to force wage increases through the political process, and the role of armaments expenditure in crowding out private investment. These comments do not go very far, but they testify to a sociological curiosity which was largely lacking in the Anglo-Saxon tradition of economics. This kind of historical–sociological analysis pointed to the enhancement of the state's role as both planner and entrepreneur. The German recovery programme of the 1930s was thus built on a mixture of native traditions and specific imports from Keynes's work from the period 1929–33, injected into the Economics Ministry by Lautenbach.[34]

In contrast to Nazi Germany, the *General Theory* was neglected in the Soviet Union, no doubt because the problem to which it was addressed – mass unemployment – seemed irrelevant to an economy in which all physical inputs and outputs were centrally planned. The first proper review, by I. G. Blyumin, appeared only in 1946. It was on classical Marxist, scholarly lines. Blyumin accused Keynes of underestimating the danger of inflation; omitting the labour theory of value from his discussion of profit and interest; ignoring the role of monopoly in its relation to capitalist crisis; and proposing utopian solutions. By the time the first (expurgated) Russian translation appeared in 1948, the Cold War had started, and the same Blyumin, in 1952, called Keynes a 'cynical intriguer, the worst enemy of the working class and the toiling masses, and the trusted servant of contemporary imperialism'. But, even without the Cold War, the *General Theory*, as Letiche notices, 'gave rise to fear of a formidable, intellectual–political challenge. Its conclusions contravened the Stalinist predictions that capitalist countries are inherently unable to promote national economic planning. By formulating the contrary view, Keynes had in effect disputed the inevitability of Socialism in the form of Communist-ruled centrally planned economies.'[35]

For different reasons, the *General Theory* had little impact in France. The French translation, by Jean de Largentaye, an inspector of finance, had to wait till 1942, and there was almost no discussion of the book in the 1930s. Pierre Rosanvallon has explained the powerful obstacles to the progress of Keynes's ideas in France. There was hostility to Keynes personally, going back to *The Economic Consequences of the Peace*. French economics was underdeveloped, and there was strong doctrinal resistance from France's established economists like Charles Rist and Jacques Rueff, whose views closely resembled those versions of the 'classical' theory which Keynes had caricatured in the *General Theory*. Rueff, the one French economist who had crossed swords with Keynes (over German reparations), published his polemic against Keynes's ideas in 1948. He never deviated from his view that the *General Theory* 'legitimises the creation of buying power... without savings ... [which] lies behind the tendency towards inflation which is the decisive trait of all post-Keynesian economies'. Keynes's ideas were associated with fascism by the left, and with communism by the right. (Largentaye's translation was held up because his publisher thought the *General Theory* 'communist in tendency': ironically it was the Nazis who allowed publication, 'on paper rather better than usual and the price not much higher than usual ...' Keynes remarked.) There was what Rosanvallon calls a 'contextual misalignment'. France had remained on the gold standard, so till the autumn of 1936 the policy debate was stuck at the point it had reached in Britain by 1931: devaluation versus deflation. With Léon Blum's Popular Front government in power, and devaluation finally accomplished, the focus of policy debate switched to the attempt by his government to establish a forty-hour week, which economists unanimously condemned as raising business costs. Finally, public works were part of the Colbertian tradition, and needed no doctrinal justification. In any case, economists had little influence on French public life. For these reasons the *General Theory* made no impact in the universities, and was taken up only by a few civil servants like Largentaye, Robert Marjolin and Georges Boris (who introduced its ideas to Mendès-France).[36]

The one exception to the indifference, or hostility, from across the Channel came from Keynes's old friend Marcel Labordère, whose eleven-page letter of appreciative comment reached him in January 1937. Labordère was not really a convert, and accepted Rueff's view that the attempt by a state agency to push investment ahead of voluntary saving would, barring 'Soviet commandeering', lead to a progressive debasement of the currency. But as always he was full of admiration for Keynes's aesthetic qualities and penetrating insights into the psychology of business behaviour. Keynes was delighted with his letter, remarking that 'something seems to have inspired your own incredibly accomplished use of English, the best yet in the time, now nearly a quarter of a century, that we have been corresponding'. He took trouble with his reply, sending five typed pages on Labordère's comments. Three points are worth noticing. He admitted that the 'whole question' of the relationship between saving and investment 'needs a little more thinking about', and accepted Labordère's statement that 'saving ... tends to lower the prevalent rate of interest... on a certain kind of investment':

> Other things being equal, I am sure that an increased propensity to save does not diminish the rate of interest; on the other hand, increased saving will not occur, again other things being equal, unless there is a reduction in the rate of interest. Apart from this, not all forms of saving and investment being homogeneous, increased willingness to

save by individuals might, for example, reduce the rate of interest of ordinary investment relatively to the rate of interest of bank loans.

Labordère had argued that in the long run the structure of production adjusts to lower prices. This produced a characteristic Keynes response: 'Certainly this seems the natural conclusion. But it is, I should say, a *very* long run . . . It is rather like saying that, even if the currency policy of Julius Caesar had been different, prices to-day would be the same as they are. Every separate influence becomes absorbed in the long course of history.' Labordère did not appreciate Keynes's remarks about the 'euthanasia of the rentier', and feared the effect of inflation on a *rentier* like himself:

> The rentier is useful in his way [Labordère wrote] not only, or even principally, on account of his propensity to save but for deeper reasons. Stable fortunes, the hereditary permanency of families, and sets of families of various social standings are an invisible social asset on which every kind of culture is more or less dependent. To entirely overlook the interests of the rentier class which includes benevolent, humanitarian, scientific, literary institutions and groups of worldly interests (*salons*) may, viewed in a historical perspective, turn out to have been a shortsighted policy. Financial security for one's livelihood is a necessary condition of organised leisure and thought. Organised leisure and thought is a necessary condition of a true, not purely mechanical, civilisation.

To this Keynes replied, 'I fully agree with this, and I wish I had emphasised it in your words. The older I get the more convinced I am that what you say here is true and important. But I must not allow you to make me too conservative.'[37]

The four senior British economists closest to Keynes – Pigou, Hawtrey, Robertson and Henderson – all produced detailed, and mainly critical, reviews or commentaries on the *General Theory*. These were supplemented by extensive personal correspondence between Keynes, Hawtrey, Henderson and Robertson; the last three also exchanged copious communications with each other. This circuit was largely, though not completely, independent of the younger economists who were transforming the *General Theory* into a usable model, Harrod being the main link between the two groups. None of the senior economists was converted by Keynes's theory, though Pigou acknowledged Keynes's contribution with great generosity in 1949.[38] They resented the fact that Keynes's disputatious method challenged them to choose between his theory and something he called orthodox theory, whereas they had been content to qualify and extend inherited theory to explain 'lapses' from full employment, and allow a place for vigorous recovery policies during a depression. However, they also had strong doctrinal objections to Keynes's equilibrium method, especially as it affected his wages and interest-rate theory; and they argued that Keynes's neglect of the long-run stability properties of the system opened the door to accelerating inflation.

Keynes had severely mauled Pigou in his book, and Pigou struck back in a 'most dreadful' and 'profoundly frivolous' review in the *Economica* of May 1936. Keynes read it not without a touch of sadness: 'I wish all the same, that I had succeeded in conveying to him what my argument is; for I should be intensely interested to know what he thinks of it. But it is no use whistling a new tune to an organ grinder, when the organ builder and the musician one knew once are no longer alive.'[39]

Like other senior Cambridge economists, Pigou deplored Keynes's sarcastic sallies at the totems of his profession, especially Marshall – a technique, he suggested, he had learnt with *The Economic Consequences of the Peace*. 'Einstein actually did for Physics what Mr Keynes believes himself to have done for Economics. He developed a far-reaching generalisation, under which Newton's results can be subsumed as a special case. But he did not, in announcing his discovery, insinuate, through carefully barbed sentences, that Newton and those who had hitherto followed his lead were a gang of incompetent bunglers.'[40] Pigou deplored Keynes's habit of lumping together all economists who disagreed with him as 'classical' and attributing to them conclusions inconsistent with their theories. Keynes had accused Marshall and Pigou of abstracting from monetary disturbances: but this was simply part of the well-recognised technique of starting with simplifying assumptions. Keynes's own abandonment of it in order to 'reach a stage of generality so high that everything must be discussed at the same time', led to loose and inconsistent use of terms and the muddling up stationary and moving states.

On the substance of the theory, Pigou rejected Keynes's view that the rate of interest is independent of the supply of saving or the demand for capital. If the demand for real capital increases, the rate of interest is bound to rise, unless kept artificially low by monetary policy. Pigou has a curious analogy between saving and the extraction of teeth:

> A decision to have one's teeth extracted is not in itself a decision to buy false ones. But few people in fact make the first decision without also making the second. Since false teeth are only wanted some months after the extraction, an increase in the number of extractions does not at once entail an addition to the capital stock of false teeth. But, none the less, a low propensity to retain one's natural teeth is 'conducive to the growth' of that capital stock.

Perhaps temporary toothlessness was a familiar part of English life in the 1930s: it would certainly explain the low propensity to consume of which Keynes complained! Pigou rejected Keynes's stagnationist thesis, or what he called the Day of Judgement: 'An era that has witnessed the development of electrical apparatus, motor cars, aircraft, gramophone and wireless, to say nothing of tanks and other engines of war, is not one in which we can reasonably forecast a total disappearance of openings for new investment.' Pigou agreed that employment could and should be much fuller than it had recently been, but warned that, as employment improves, wage-earners regain control over their own level of employment – that is, their own real wage. Any attempt by banking policy to force a higher level of employment than was desired, Pigou implied, would simply lead to inflation.[41]

Pigou's irritation is obvious, as is its cause. He had tried to refute the *General Theory* before it appeared, and thought he had: Keynes had simply ignored his argument. Pigou thought he had proved that when money wages fell, prices fell, but not in the same proportion, since nothing had happened to change non-wage-earners' income. This leads to an 'automatic' increase in employment because, with the old volume of employment there would be a disequilibrium, prices being above marginal costs.[42] Keynes had not countered this directly, merely asserting that changes in money wages can affect employment only through their influence on cash balances and expectations. When Pigou restated his position in an article in the *Economic Journal* in 1937, it was denounced by Keynes and his disciples as 'outrageous rubbish', the product of incipient senility, and Pigou retracted. (See p. 597 below.) But Pigou went on gnawing at the problem and finally came up in 1941 with the 'Pigou effect', which *was* a theoretical answer to Keynes. But by this time Keynes's theory had taken hold and no one was listening to Pigou. In fact, no one was really listening to Pigou in 1936. Attempts to salvage the old doctrines by adding arguments which no one had thought of before fell on deaf ears. Keynes's devastating charge that the old doctrine was *no use* in the circumstances fitted the intellectual and popular mood of the day.

Keynes had little correspondence with Pigou, since Pigou preferred to work out his ideas in isolation – unlike Hawtrey, who loved nothing better than to write huge nit-picking memoranda. As he had done with the *Treatise on Money*, Hawtrey began preparing a commentary on the *General Theory* for internal circulation in the Treasury as soon as he got proofs from Keynes in 1935; as he and Keynes discussed it, it grew longer and longer and was eventually published as a chapter in his book, *Capital and Employment*, in 1938. It was as dry and critical as a civil service paper can be, and Keynes was a saint to put up with it after his book was published, since Hawtrey made few positive statements of his own, and nothing of interest emerged. However, Hawtrey made one point which was to crop up time and again in the disputes which followed. 'So far as the essentials of your argument are concerned,' he wrote to Keynes on 1 February, 'your criticisms of the classical theory might have been confined to the single point that the theory assumes the effects of the speculative motive on cash balances to be negligible.' 'My dear Ralph,' Keynes wrote to him on 15 April 1936, 'I find your

[last] letter . . . rather shattering. For, after reading it, I am now convinced that nothing that I can say will open your eyes – I do not say to the truth of my argument – but to what the essence of my argument, true or false, actually is. I doubt if we ought, either of us, to continue this correspondence any longer.'[43] But they did.

The breach between Keynes and Hubert Henderson, opened up over public works in 1930–1, was widened by the *General Theory*. Henderson had resigned as secretary of the Economic Advisory Council in 1934 to take up a research fellowship at All Souls College, Oxford. He had written a short review of Keynes's book for the *Spectator* of 4 February 1936, but he reserved his main attack for a meeting of the Marshall Society at Cambridge on 2 May. Following this meeting, Keynes wrote to Lydia:

> Hubert came to the Marshall Society yesterday, with Dennis in the chair, to read his paper against my book. I was astonished at the violence of his emotion against it; he thinks it a poisonous book; yet when it came to the debate there was very little of the argument he was really prepared to oppose. He came off badly in the debate with Joan and Alexander and myself barking round him. The undergraduates enjoyed the cock fight outrageously. One got the impression that he was not much interested in pure economic theory, but much dislikes for emotional or political reasons some of the practical conclusions to which my arguments seemed to point. As a theoretical attack there was almost nothing to answer.[44]

Keynes's view was not shared by the chairman, Dennis Robertson. 'Of course, I think you have much the best of it,' he wrote to Henderson after reading his summary of the argument at the meeting, prepared immediately after.[45] Henderson had taken great trouble with his presentation, sending earlier drafts to Harrod and Robertson. The strength of his feeling can be gauged by a letter he wrote to Harrod on 2 April 1936:

> I have allowed myself to be inhibited for many years from publishing many things by a desire not to quarrel in public with Maynard . . . but it is impossible to accept the position that Maynard is to be allowed to deliver the most extravagant attacks upon the main body of orthodox economic theory, conveying the impression that everything that has been said hitherto is nonsense and that here is a great new light to which the heathen must be converted, and that others must abstain from effective reply to avoid the impression of economists quarrelling. You see, I don't believe there is a great new light at all. I regard Maynard's book, as I say in my paper, as a farrago of confused sophistication, and I find intensely exasperating the tacit assumption that prevails in certain circles that those who do not accept its general doctrine are to be regarded as intellectually inferior beings.

Harrod urged him to tone down the ferocity of his assault, shrewdly surmising that Henderson's hostility was in part the result of pent-up feelings of resentment against his former mentor and patron.[46]

Henderson's attack was directed against what he saw as the two main fallacies of the *General Theory*: its theory of employment and its theory of interest. His method was largely historical and institutional, which is perhaps why Keynes and his supporters felt that 'as a theoretical attack there was almost nothing to answer'. Henderson upheld the value of Marshall's short-period/long-period distinction. Natural forces worked clumsily and in the long run, and *laissez-faire* was therefore unviable. But that was no reason for dismissing the classical theory as nonsense. Because Keynes's theory took no account of natural forces, policies based on it would be a recipe for inflation. Specifically, he denied that 'in the ordinary working of the economic system there is a chronic and general deficiency of effective demand, and that in this is to be found the main explanation of unemployment'. He said there was a 'minimum' (what would later be called 'natural') rate of unemployment (which he estimated at 6 per cent) on which was superimposed structural and cyclical unemployment. Keynes's attempt to create boom conditions 'stronger and more prolonged than almost any of which we have experience' would lead to inflation followed by an inevitable reaction.[47]

Secondly, Henderson denied that the rate of interest was unaffected by the propensity to consume or the demand for capital, citing the fact that interest rates fall in depressions and rise in booms. Conversely, even large changes in the quantity of money had had no lasting effects on interest rates. This suggested that interest-rate behaviour was adequately explained by the 'classical' forces of productivity and thrift; it also cast doubt on Keynes's contention that 'the rate of interest can be brought down to as low a level as is desired and kept down by increasing the quantity of money sufficiently'. Henderson summed up the orthodox theory as follows: 'The actual movements of the rate of interest are determined by the relations of demand and supply in what is sometimes called the capital market. Orthodox economic theory asserts that the fundamental factors that lie behind supply and demand in the capital market are savings and investment.'[48]

The Cambridge meeting was followed by a painful exchange of letters between the two economists, which Keynes broke off. Henderson wrote, 'Your mood nowadays seems to be of saying "I am not interested in the long run: it never happens." Whereas it seems to me essential to any clearness of economic thought to distinguish between the immediate and the ultimate consequences of any change.' This, of course, is a rerun of the Malthus–Ricardo argument, with Henderson giving Ricardo's reply. Keynes's real crime, in Henderson's eyes, was to have destroyed the defences which classical theory, in separating out monetary from real factors, had built up against inflation. Like Ricardo before him, he seemed curiously unworried about the huge scale of unemployment.[49] Of the four senior economists, Henderson most explicitly upheld what Friedman was to preach in the 1960s: that monetary forces have no (long-run) real effects.

Robertson was himself brooding about how to respond to the *General Theory*. On 19 February 1936, he informed Henderson that he had 'cravenly' refused to review it for the *Economist* (Austin Robinson did it instead), but might write 'one or two articles later on the points of substance, eschewing the need to assess the thing as a whole'. He concluded his letter by saying that 'the whole thing is of course a devastating nuisance, personally and pedagogically, especially in Cambridge: and the difficulty is not to let that affect one's intellectual judgement'.[50]

Robertson's draft article was criticised by both Sraffa and Henderson. As a result he had decided to rewrite it from the start. 'It's a disaster', he told Henderson, 'that the case for relative sanity here should be in such stale & incompetent hands.' Henderson had sent him the correspondence he was having with Keynes:

> The whole business [he continued on 21 June] is of course devastating educationally, – but I suppose if they really think they have saved the world by finding that missing equation they are entitled to ignore that! . . . It appears to me that since, as is admitted [on pp. 248–9 of the *General Theory*], the 'liquidity' curve becomes unanchored as well as the savings curve when income increases, we aren't really any further on! i.e. 'equilibrium' may never be reached, and if it is, as you say, it will only be transitory . . . But I suppose that only means I'm not a mathematician!

The intermittent bouts of correspondence between Keynes and Robertson in 1936–8, in turn reproachful and joking, reveal the wreckage of their friendship. On his way to America in September 1936 Robertson wrote to Keynes, 'it's no use pretending I like it [the *General Theory*] much better, or that I don't agree more or less with most of the Prof.'s review . . .' He was preparing some notes which he hoped would be published. 'Whether afterwards you will feel that the sort of tabu which has arisen between us can profitably be removed, I don't know . . . perhaps we could meet rather oftener than we have done this year, and talk about drama and foreign policy . . . and even ephemeral economic situations?'[51]

Keynes wrote:

> It's awfully difficult to keep off Economics but *I* don't, dear Dennis, feel differently, and we must try to come to closer touch again. But indeed it is easy for *me*! For whilst, putting it at its worst, I only think you very obstinate, you and Hubert think me very wicked! – for being so cocksure and putting all the driving force I know how behind arguments which for me are of painfully practical importance.[52]

They had a long talk at King's on 11 October, Dennis 'very sweet and charming and rather well, I think, though also dotty'.

Robertson's 'Some Notes on Mr Keynes' General Theory of Employment' were published in the November 1936 issue of *Quarterly Journal of Economics* as part of the symposium on the *General Theory*. As always Robertson relies on subtle fencing to conceal what he felt were deadly thrusts. First, he uses Keynes's 'method of anticipations' to suggest that Keynes's equilibrium was as indeterminate as the classical one. Suppose, he says, that 'entrepreneurs (perhaps having heard at their last Rotary Club luncheon a lecture on J.B. Say) expand output in the *belief* that' their proceeds will justify giving more employment. Would this not become a self-fulfilling prophecy even though that belief was mistaken at the existing level of demand?[53] The idea that the (short-run) level of activity depends on expectations knocks out 'natural' forces; it also knocks out Keynes's theory of the determinate multiplier.

Robertson rejects the notion that the multiplier theory makes 'the finance of the process of investment . . . self-solving'. This is achieved only by abstracting from an 'explicitly temporal process of analysis'. While income is *expanding* it cannot 'at all times be an identical multiple of a given rate of investment'.[54] Not only is the multiplier indeterminate, but some source of 'new' money is required to finance the investment. This takes Robertson back to his old idea of forced saving as providing the funds for additional investment.

Finally, Robertson argued that Keynes had drawn the wrong conclusions from an initially 'one-sided' statement of the theory of liquidity preference. If correctly stated, it was simply a version of the classical 'loanable funds' theory of interest. Keynes had written as if only liquidity preference was sensitive to interest-rate changes. But a fall in the interest rate also stimulates the demand for loans, which enters into the 'transactions demand' for cash. Once Keynes admits (in chapter 15) the sensitivity of the 'transactions demand' for money to changes in the rate of interest he is 'readmitting by the backdoor the influence on the rate of interest of . . . the productivity [of] investment'. In turn, the supply of saving is influenced by the productivity of past saving. 'If, in the world of causation, today's [supply schedule of] saving is the great-grandchild of last year's rate of interest, surely that does not prevent it from being also a parent of today's rate.'[55]

Robertson's first published reaction to the *General Theory* expresses his two main criticisms of it, from which he never deviated: the static nature of Keynes's analysis, which re-established the classical dichotomy in a new form; and Keynes's ignoring any influence on the rate of interest of the forces of productivity and thrift. Keynes's denial of the second was a direct consequence of the first.[56] Keynes's 'monetary' theory of interest was as incomplete as the 'real' saving–investment theory he imputed to the classics. 'Loanable funds' was Robertson's reconciliation between the two.*

The publication of Robertson's 'Notes' prompted Keynes to write to him on 13 December 1936: 'there is not a great deal that is fundamental which divides us – even less perhaps than you think. For I agree with a greater proportion of what you say than you give me credit for.' Not surprisingly, Keynes accepted Robertson's 'expectational' conditions for a 'natural' recovery. He accepted Robertson's critique of the instantaneous multiplier, while remaining convinced of 'the extreme importance and utility of the idea . . .' However, he vehemently denied that his interest-rate theory was simply a 'backdoor' statement of the classical theory. By accepting that the rate of interest is determined by 'the demand for cash relatively to its supply', it was Robertson, rather, who had 'come right over to the liquidity theory of the rate of interest'.[57] Keynes ended his letter on a note of playful reproach:

> I see you are saying that [what I am saying] all makes no difference, that Marshall related it all to a Royal Commission in an affirmative sigh, that it has been well known to Pigou for years . . . that Neisser's bunk† comes to the same thing, and the like; though, in truth, *you* are the only writer where much of it is to be found in embryo and to whom acknowledgements are due . . . I certainly date all my emancipation from the discussions between us which preceded your *Banking Policy and the Price Level*. The last thing I should accuse you of is being classical or orthodox. But you won't slough your skins, like a good snake! You walk about with the whole lot on from the earliest until the latest, until you can scarcely breathe, saying that, because your greatcoat was once your vest, your present vest and your greatcoat are the same.[58]

Robertson's reply to Keynes on 29 December reveals the depth of his dissatisfaction with Keynes's controversial *method*:

> I do venture to think that with each new skin you are apt to put on a pair of blinkers, which makes it hard for you to see what other people, especially Pigou, are at . . . Both over the *Treatise* and this book I have gone through real intellectual torment trying to make up my mind whether, as you often seem to claim, there is some new piece on the board or rather a rearrangement, which seems to you superior, of existing pieces.
>
> . . .
>
> To begin with, may we not, for purposes of serious discussion, abandon the (journalistic) practice of labelling *authors* as 'classical' or

---

*The essence of the difference was whether one should analyse the determination of the rate of interest in the market for loans or in the market for money.

†Keynes had found Dr Neisser's 'bunk' 'particularly sympathetic' in his *Treatise on Money*, CW, v, 178.

the reverse, and use the word 'classical', if at all, to signify an analysis which assumes the rewards, real and money, of factors to be plastic and consequently all resources to be employed.

Robertson went on to say that the abandonment of these assumptions in the study of dynamic situations did not require the abandonment of 'the concept of the rate of interest as the *price* of the use of a certain factor of production per unit of time, that factor being what Marshall calls "free or floating capital" [and] what I call "loanable funds" '. When income is stationary 'the supply of loanable funds is, on my definitions, identical with the supply of savings; when income changes they diverge by the amount of bank money, or hoarding or dishoarding.' In both types of situation 'the rate of interest *is* the price at which the quantity of loanable funds demanded is equal to the quantity supplied', though the disposition to hoard must be taken into account as an influence on it.

> Your main purpose, as I read it, is to emphasise (a) the high elasticity of th[e liquidity preference] schedule in certain circumstances, (b) its great variability. I maintain that in order to fulfil this purpose there is no need whatever to cast discredit on the ordinary concept of the rate of interest as *being* the price of the use of loanable funds: and that there is great methodological disadvantage in doing so, since it involves going back on what I regard as one of the cardinal achievements of modern economic theory, viz. the exhibition of the rewards of the several factors of production as special cases of a general principle of pricing.[59]

After conceding to Robertson (and also to Ohlin) in June 1937 that 'planned investment . . . may have to secure its "financial provision" *before* the investment takes place'[60] Keynes now had reason to feel that 'the strictly intellectual differences between us are probably very small indeed at bottom. But I am trying all the time to disentangle myself, whilst you are trying to keep entangled. You are, so to speak, bent on creeping back into your mother's womb; whilst I am shaking myself like a dog on dry land.'[61] But this was too optimistic. Articles and rejoinders flowed continuously in the *Economic Journal*. 'As regards . . . terminology,' Robertson wrote to him on 1 January 1938, 'it seems to me to be *you* who are tumbling into pot-holes under the weight of your home-made greatcoats!' Robertson went on:

> On the broader question of our respective attitudes to the work of our predecessors (and contemporaries of other schools) there *is* of course a difference of temperament, as there was between Marshall and Jevons . . . may I suggest that I – managing to keep throughout in touch with all the elements of the problem in a dim and fumbling way – have been a sort of glow worm, whose feeble glimmer lands on all objects in the neighbourhood: while you, with your far more powerful

intellect, have been a light-house casting a far more penetrating, but sometimes fatally distorting, beam on one object after another in succession.

Keynes's method of 'successive over-emphasis' was no doubt 'very productive of knowledge and enlightenment', but should not exclude an occasional return 'to our mother's womb . . . which often reveals objects of surprising beauty and interest'.[62]

Keynes found Robertson's restatement of his loanable funds theory in the *Economic Journal* of June 1938 'completely worthless and, what is more, intolerably boring'.[63] Pigou decreed that the controversy must cease and that Robertson must get on with 'constructive work of his own', rather than spend all his time criticising 'Mr Keynes on this and that'.[64] Robertson was starting to feel a 'back number' at Cambridge. Research students, he told Hubert Henderson, wanted to work with Kahn and Joan Robinson, not him. In 1938 he left Cambridge to take up a chair at London University, driven out by the increasing hostility of Keynes's Cambridge disciples.

The debate between Keynes, Hawtrey, Henderson and Robertson kept coming back to the role of the rate of interest in adjusting the economy to 'shocks'. They all seemed to agree that, in practice, an increased desire to save, or a decreased desire to invest, would lead to a fall in income. But the senior economists (particularly Robertson) insisted this was *only* because classical theory had paid insufficient attention to the short-run variability of liquidity preference. Keynes said that no primary interest-rate adjustment mechanism existed; it was the level of income which adjusted to changed conditions of demand, with the rate of interest moving only in response to changes in the 'cash balances'. The senior economists wanted to preserve some adjustment role for 'natural' forces in order to limit government intervention and block off inflation. This explains Henderson's passionate insistence that the rate of interest is not a purely monetary phenomenon. Keynes wanted to remove 'natural' forces from the picture entirely so as to put the government, and monetary authority, in the driving seat. Amid the wreckage of orthodox economics the senior economists clung to the notion of the self-adjusting market because they mistrusted Keynes's theory of the self-adjusting politician.

II

KEYNES AND THE CLASSICS

Most of the important questions about the *General Theory* were raised within three years of its publication. The discussion that went on was of two kinds, the first concerned with the relationship between Keynes's theory and orthodox theory, the second with the interpretation, internal development and presentation of Keynes's own theory. The two discourses overlap, since the question of whether the *General Theory* was a revolutionary break with classical theory or a rearrangement of its pieces concerned both critics and followers. Keynes was involved in both discussions, but as we shall see he lost control over the disposal of his own property.*

Everyone understood that the chief questions raised by the *General Theory* were why the inter-war economy was so violently unstable, and why economies got stuck in deep slumps. Keynes's answer was that there was nothing to keep economies stable, and no 'natural' forces to revive them when they had collapsed. The classical answer was that 'natural' stabilising and/or recuperative forces existed but had been interfered with by politics. This seemed a reasonable view to take. It hardly seemed likely that the great depression would have been so severe had it not been for the First World War and the disturbances which followed it. On this view, Keynes's theory was useful for explaining a single set of events, not a chronic condition. Against this was the fact that the great collapse had started in the United States, the heart of *laissez-faire* capitalism, little dependent on world trade, run by staunchly Republican governments, and for purely internal reasons. The United States seemed to offer the ideal test for the self-adjusting hypothesis. It had failed.

The simplified division between Keynes and the 'classics' conceals important differences and similarities. It seems better to reserve the label 'classical' for the main Anglo-American tradition and use the term Continental for the Austrian and Swedish schools. We then get three kinds of understanding of macroeconomic misbehaviour, the Keynesian, Classical and Continental.

The problem may be stated as follows. If consumption is the sole rational purpose of production; if people are rational; if wants exceed availabilities, how can it be that society's productive capacity is chronically, or periodically, under-used?

Keynes's answer is based on the role of money as a store of value. He identified a particular want, the want for money as such, ignored by conventional economics. He explained it in terms which might make sense to the economist – as a rational response to uncertainty about the future. But there is no doubt he believed it to be partly irrational. A crucial twist to his theory was to see saving, and not just hoarding, as an expression of

---

*Put to one side are priority questions which only emerged later. Had the *General Theory* been anticipated, in whole or in part, by earlier or even contemporary economists? The claims of Michal Kalecki, a Polish economist, have been championed by Joan Robinson. (See Joan Robinson, *Contributions to Modern Economics*, where she writes (p. 55): 'Michal Kalecki's claim to priority . . . is indisputable.' This is challenged by Patinkin, *Anticipations of the General Theory*, chapter 3.) At the time, no one who mattered in economics or public life in Britain or the United States had heard of Kalecki, but everyone had heard of Keynes. Similarly it was Kahn's multiplier, not Johansson's or Hawtrey's or Giblin's, which became the influential policy tool.

this want. People saved money not to *do* something with it, but because they felt anxious about the future. That is why he could regard saving as a subtraction from demand rather than part of demand, and the rate of interest as the price of parting with money rather than the price for 'postponing' consumption. At this level Keynes felt he had overturned the classical paradigm. It was the hunger for money, not the hunger for goods, which controlled macroeconomic outcomes, much as the mercantilists believed. And the object of metallic standards was not to keep money stable, but to keep it costly, by keeping it scarce.

This 'normal' weakness in the 'propensity to consume' undermines the 'inducement to invest'. Decisions to save send no signals to producers to add to capital equipment; if anything, the reverse. In these circumstances, Enterprise, which *is* concerned with adding to real wealth, is left unduly dependent on stimulating events. But a productive structure created in 'moments of excitement' like the nineteenth century is likely to languish and decay once the stimulus has passed and the psychology of society reverts to its more normal state. Thus an undue tendency to save keeps societies poorer than they might be. An increase in the propensity to hoard registers the collapse of misplaced hopes. Keynes's vision embraces a theory of economic history as well as an explanation of current disturbances. In a single audacious sweep of ideas he explains the interwar depression, the nineteenth century boom, the rationale of the gold standard, and, for most of recorded history, the flat economic trajectory of Europe and Asia.

Both the Classical and Continental schools start from the opposite idea of non-consumption as providing the fund for capital development, with interest – greater future consumption – as the motive, and reward, for saving. The disposition to save is linked, that is, to a positive desire to consume more at some date in the future, which desire implies a release of real resources for the construction of capital facilities to increase the production of consumption goods. The classical economists' endorsement of capitalism was based on their belief, which Marx shared, that it was the first wealth-creating system in history. It placed, for the first time, responsibility for accumulation in private hands. The function of money as a store of wealth is ignored, except at moments of crisis. In this world-view, the poverty of mankind, as well as the instability of economies, is linked to inadequate saving, or inadequate incentives to save, largely due to discouraging social and political institutions or events. The medieval usury laws limiting interest on loans (which Keynes praises) would be one example. Similarly, wars, inflations or similar disturbances can upset the psychological and social balance needed for steady accumulation. (For Marx, the class war plays this role.) Keynes in his more classical days had hinted at one such possible consequence of the First World War: it had, he wrote, 'disclosed the possibility of consumption to all and the vanity of abstinence to many'.[65]

Great wars destroy not only savings, but, if, as is normal, they are financed by inflation, the incentive to save too.

It is fair to say that the Classical tradition saw much less difficulty than did the Continental in achieving a smooth flow of saving into investment. Given that people save in order to invest, the realisation of their aims depends on the existence of a saver-friendly set of institutions and political practices: a stable legal order, a responsible monetary authority, adequate competition, absence of social conflict, and so on. Classical theory proceeded to describe individual economic behaviour on the assumption that such institutions were in place, and need not, therefore, be referred to again. This was a predominantly Anglo-Saxon form of social analysis. It rested on long experience of institutional stability. Keynesian 'uncertainty', from this point of view, appears as a *deus ex machina* when he realises that this stability cannot be taken for granted.

The Continental view diverged from the Classical view in two important respects. The institutional structure appropriate to steady-state wealth-creation was regarded as inherently difficult to achieve and sustain. And much greater attention was paid to the *process* of transforming saving into investment, involving changes in the composition of the capital stock. Severe fluctuations could result from institutional frailties, technical change, sectoral disequilibria, and so on. Thus the Continentals viewed the capitalist system as much less stable than did the mainstream Anglo-American economists. Dennis Robertson and Lionel Robbins were the leading English economists most influenced by this point of view: Robertson from his study of industrial fluctuations before the First World War, Robbins by his study of Austrian capital theory after it. Robbins was always interested in the political basis of capitalism.

From these differences in social imagination came three different versions of the adjustment process. In the Classical view adjustment of saving to investment proceeds smoothly, quickly and without severe disturbance to the 'real' economy, in the absence of political 'shocks'. That is why, in the Classical view, the long-period equilibrium method is the best method of analysis, since disturbances to the full-employment equilibrium are shallow and transient. In Keynes's system, the only 'natural' adjustment mechanism following a collapse of investment is a decline in income sufficient to restore equality between saving and investment. Since there is no natural recovery mechanism, the short-period equilibrium position thus established may continue indefinitely. In the Continental view, too, regress is possible, though for different reasons. The coexistence of central banking with credit money makes 'monetary neutrality' impossible. Impoverishment is a necessary consequence of the malinvestments made temporarily possible by the previous credit expansion. The severe oscillations of the economy round a 'natural' rate of profit, resulting from monetary expansions and contractions, is best captured by a disequilibrium analysis.

When it comes to policy, there is much less disagreement than the differences in vision and analytic method would suggest. That is why Keynes so often accused 'classical' economists of holding conclusions inconsistent with their premises. The *General Theory* analysis suggested pretty unambiguously that it was the state's responsibility to improve the equilibrium yielded by *laissez-faire*. Economists like Pigou and Henderson, while attributing economic collapses to political interferences in the working of markets, supported policies to raise demand in actual situations of collapsed demand, though Pigou in particular warned that their success was highly dependent on creating 'errors of optimism'. ('Money illusion' was one such 'error'.) Hayek and Robbins believed depressions had to be allowed to run their course: out of suffering wisdom might emerge. But Robertson and also the Swedish economists believed that monetary manipulation could be used to dampen fluctuations in the 'natural' business cycle.

It is in this broad context that the issues between Keynes and 'the classics' were fought out. The single most contentious topic concerned Keynes's theory of the rate of interest. For all those engaged in arguing out, or arguing about, the *General Theory*, this seemed, at the time, to be the main point of *theory* involved. Keynes had foisted on 'classical' economists the belief that a rate of interest determined in the market for saving and investment was the crucial mechanism on which their theory relied to ensure a tendency to full employment. If, in fact, the rate of interest was determined in the market for money, it could not logically do the job given to it in the classical system, and economists were logically bound to accept this alternative theory of effective demand. The 'classic' counterattack then took the form of denying that Keynes had provided a correct theory of the rate of interest. Liquidity preference was admitted as a factor complicating the adjustment process, possibly requiring offsetting banking policy, but not overturning the basic classical position. Pigou was one of the few senior economists who refused to fight the battle on Keynes's chosen ground. He denied that the classical system depended on the rate of interest being the price of saving: wage flexibility was all that was needed to secure full employment. But Pigou lost this battle in what was seen as one of the earliest triumphs of the Keynesian school.*

*Pigou's attempted refutation of the *General Theory* along these lines appeared in the *Economic Journal* in September 1937. It was this article that convinced Keynes and his immediate followers that he was 'gaga'. The decisive refutation was by Nicholas Kaldor. (*Economic Journal*, December 1937.) Pigou argued that a cut in money wages cut prime costs and thus led to an expansion of employment. Kaldor argued, as Keynes had in chapter 19 of the *General Theory*, that a cut in wages leads to increased employment only if it lowers the interest rate via a reduction in the demand for money. But the adjustment mechanism is the fall in money income, and its effect on the interest rate, not the cut in money wages. Pigou retracted. (See David Collard, 'A. C. Pigou', in D. P. O'Brien and John R. Presley (eds), *Pioneers of Modern Economics in Britain*, 127–130.) For the controversy from Keynes's and Kaldor's point of view, see *CW*, xiv, 234–68.

The issue was not that Keynes had produced a monetary theory of interest. As Kohn puts it:

> All the neoclassicals, at least since Wicksell, had held a monetary theory of the rate of interest, believing the market rate of interest to be proximately determined by the supply of and demand for loans of money (the 'loanable funds' theory). What was new about Keynes's liquidity preference theory was not, therefore, that it was a monetary theory, but rather that it denied the existence of any 'normal' or 'natural' rate relative to which the market rate moved.[66]

The rate of interest, Keynes insisted, is monetary 'in the special sense that it is the *own rate* of interest . . . on money itself',[67] and therefore had no connection with the 'demand for loans', or productivity and thrift. This was the core of his Vision that he upheld in all the debates with his critics.

Keynes wrote four articles to do with the rate of interest between 1936 and 1938, mainly in reply to attacks by Robertson and Ohlin. He was on a sticky wicket, because his own 'demand for money' equation included a 'transactions demand' for money, which implied that the rate of interest was determined by the demand for loans as well as the demand for liquidity. In his June 1937 article 'Alternative Theories of the Rate of Interest' and his December 1937 article 'The "Ex Ante" Theory of the Rate of Interest' (both in the *Economic Journal*) he conceded that, if the demand for investment runs ahead of saving, forward-looking 'finance' or bank credit may be required to bridge the gap.[68] 'Finance' is 'credit required in the interval between planning and execution'.[69] Pressure for increased finance may, by causing 'congestion' in the loan market, 'easily affect the rate of interest', in the absence of accommodation by the banking system (overdrafts are an 'ideal system').[70] But he continued to deny that movements in the rate of interest as a result of a change in the demand for loans reflected any change in saving or investment, since at the 'financial' stage of the proceedings no new investment had happened. His vehemence in defending his more narrow interpretation of the 'demand for money' is striking evidence of the tenacity with which he hung on to his Vision of the role of money, since formally, of course, he had already conceded Robertson's point in the *General Theory*.

Keynes summed up the issue on 4 April 1938 in a letter to the American economist E. S. Shaw:

> I am inclined to agree with you that the whole controversy is becoming about very little indeed, and largely a question of expression. But you must remember that it did not begin that way. When my book first came out, the theory of liquidity preference was entirely repudiated by practically all my critics; and whilst many of them were already holding theories not really consistent with the classical idea of the rate of interest being fixed by the interplay of the demand for new capital

with the supply of savings, they were nevertheless clinging to that idea as having substantial validity. By a long series of easy stages a point has now been reached when there is indeed very little in it . . . Substantially my theory is exactly what it was when I first published the book.[71]

Keynes repeatedly said after his book was published that he had made a mistake in attacking what he called 'the classical theory', rather than concentrating on his own.[72] He had enormous trouble in placing his own theory against classical theory, and explaining why his theory was 'general' and the classical theory 'special'. Classical theory, he wrote, 'requires (1) . . . a state of definite and constant expectation and (2) . . . a state of full employment. These limitations mean that it is a particular theory applicable only to certain conditions; and this is my justification for calling my own theory a *general theory*, of which the orthodox theory is a limiting case.'[73] But orthodox economists would have denied these requirements for their theory to be true. They would have replied in the spirit of Ricardo, as Henderson did, that theirs was an analysis of long-run tendencies. Their counterattack took the form of asserting that Keynes's 'general theory' was a 'special case' of a more generalised classical theory, applicable to certain short-period circumstances ('sticky' labour markets, 'liquidity traps', political disturbances, and so on). Which theory is regarded as more 'general' would then seem to depend on which state of the world is regarded as more 'normal'. As Pigou remarked, the classical thought machine had not disgraced itself in the nineteenth century, because the conditions of the time had suited it. (See p. 607 below.)

This debate about the degree of generality of the two theories was intertwined with a debate about the right way of doing economic analysis. The correct method, as stated by Pigou and Knight, was to start with simplified assumptions, and then add in complicating factors. This, for Pigou, meant discussing unemployment first on the basis that money was 'neutral', and then adding a consideration of the effect of monetary happenings on the 'real supply schedule of labour'. On this view the classical method yielded more 'general' results than Keynes's, for the simplified model dealt with the more persistent or 'real' causes of outcomes, with the monetary complications being concerned with the transient causes. In this view, the generality of a theory is identified with the long-period method of analysis; Keynes's theory is a theory of complications only.

Keynes might not have disagreed with the method as stated by Pigou. But he would certainly have disagreed with Pigou's starting assumptions. The methodological habit of abstracting initially from the existence of uncertainty (and the role of money as a hedge against this) left intact the basic axiom that monetary happenings do not affect real events: they are held only to complicate, or delay, the working out of the new position of equilibrium.

Thus, according to Keynes, a 'Monetary Theory of Production' is the more general form of the classical theory of production. The relevant distinction is not between long-period and short-period analysis, since monetary factors enter both, but between theories which abstract from the influence of money at any stage in the analysis and theories in which 'money enters motives' at all stages; for it is through the decisions about how much money to invest and hoard that changing expectations about the future influence activity in the present. Monetary influences are not transient; they are always embedded in decisions to act, and determine what happens at all times.

Thus Keynes's 'general theory' applies equally to the short and long periods. Nevertheless, it is hard to find an explicit long-period theory in the *General Theory*. The model is concerned with short-period equilibrium. Then the question arises whether the concept of 'unemployment equilibrium' is a useful one.

The monetary disequilibrium theorists argued that a short-period equilibrium theory was bound to be a 'special case' of a more general theory of fluctuations. They wanted to make economics the study of dynamics, not statics. In this light, Keynes's methodology was as regressive as that of the long-period 'classical' school.

We get no picture, these critics of Keynes's method said, of an economy moving through time, merely an album of snapshots. As Dennis Robertson put it, 'You seem too easily satisfied – in your pure theory – if you have shown that a given position is determinate, and not concerned enough to enquire if it is also in any significant sense an equilibrium position, and not a mere point of transit in a process which is both cumulative and reversible.'[74] Ohlin wrote in 1937:

> The idea of an 'under-employment equilibrium' is unfortunate for two reasons. The equilibrium concept is apt to be misleading, as it indicates a stability of the state of large unemployment which does not exist. Secondly, how strong the tendencies towards increased employment, under the stimulus of adjustments in wages and interest rates, will be under different conditions can only be explained through an investigation into the business cycle, and general statements are apt to be more misleading than illuminating.[75]

This debate finds Keynes ranged against Robertson, Hawtrey and economists of the Swedish and Austrian schools. It partly explains the paradox that Keynes's fiercest arguments were with those closest to him in spirit, and most critical of the 'classical' apparatus he himself had attacked. He acknowledged this rather touchingly in a footnote to one of his controversial pieces:

I must, however, take this opportunity to apologise at once if I have led any reader to suppose that, as Professor Ohlin seems to think, I regard Mr Hawtrey and Mr Robertson as classical economists! On the contrary, they strayed from the fold sooner than I did. I regard Mr Hawtrey as my grandparent and Mr Robertson as my parent in the paths of errancy, and I have been greatly influenced by them. I might also meet Professor Ohlin's complaint by adopting Wicksell as my great-grandparent, if I had known his works in more detail at an earlier stage in my own thought and also if I did not have the feeling that Wicksell was *trying* to be 'classical'. As it is, so far as I am concerned, I find, looking back, that it was Professor Irving Fisher who was the great-grandparent who first influenced me towards regarding money as a 'real' factor.[76]

Keynes's copper-bottomed argument for the use of the equilibrium method was that disequilibrium analysis failed to yield precise concepts and tools of policy. He told Lindahl in 1934 that 'your way of dealing with time leads to undue complications and will be very difficult either to apply or to generalise about'. In 1937 Keynes put the matter clearly to Bertil Ohlin:

> As regards the *ex post* and *ex ante* method, I shall certainly give further thought to its advantages. This is in fact almost precisely on the lines that I was thinking and lecturing somewhere about 1931 and 1932, and subsequently abandoned. My reason for giving it up was owing to my failure to establish any definite unit of time, and I found that that made very artificial any attempt to state the theory precisely. So, after writing out many chapters along what were evidently the Swedish lines, I scrapped the lot and felt that my new treatment was much safer and sounder from the logical point of view.[77]

The short-period equilibrium method cleared the ground of all the fancy concepts which Robertson, the Swedes and the Austrians had invented to deal with situations of monetary instability: forced saving, loanable funds, *ex ante* and *post hoc* saving and so on, which according to Keynes had led to far worse muddles than those perpetrated by the 'classical' school. The strongest argument of the monetary disequilibrium theorists was that the implicit denial of *any* tendency to adjustment via movements of relative prices and income shares would lead to mistakes in policy; in particular, it would open the door to inflationary government finance. Keynes, of course, saw his downplaying of this possibility as an essential advantage of his method. The fact that he abandoned the fixed-price assumption in Book V of the *General Theory* was considered less significant than the fact that he assumed fixed prices in the specification of the formal model. This made it easy to say that Keynesian 'results' depended on particular features of the labour market.

These considerations dominate the debate on the validity of Keynes's concept of 'involuntary' unemployment. As we have seen, Henderson raised this issue; but so did Jacob Viner when he wrote in his review that Keynes's recipe for getting rid of involuntary unemployment pointed to 'a constant race between the printing press and the business agents of the trade unions, with the problem of unemployment largely solved if the printing press could maintain a constant lead . . .'[78]

Keynes wanted to show that the economic system 'may find itself in *stable* equilibrium . . . at a level below full employment' (italics added).[79] Involuntary (unwanted) unemployment was thus demand-deficient unemployment, the fraction of total unemployment existing at any time which could be got rid of only by expanding demand. Full employment is achieved when output becomes wholly unresponsive to any further expansion in demand, that is, when the number of job vacancies equals the number of unemployed. However, Keynes coupled this analysis with acceptance of the first 'classical' wage postulate – that the real wage equals the marginal product of labour. As more labour becomes employed, its marginal productivity falls, so that rising employment has to be accompanied by a falling real wage.

Keynes did not think this an onerous condition. There is no doubt that he associated a situation of demand-deficient employment with stable money wages. This was not just an analytic assumption. He thought it a valid historical induction.[80] He thought that money wages start to move only under fairly extreme pressure of deflation and inflation. Thus demand expansion could proceed a long way before money wages started to rise. However, his acceptance of the first classical postulate did make the success of employment policy peculiarly dependent on what Russell Brent Jones calls the 'acquiescence postulate': the assumption that while workers usually resist a cut in money wages they will not withdraw labour when there is a rise in consumer prices, except when an inflation-induced fall in real wages proceeds to an extreme degree.[81]

Keynes did not assume complete price stability. As employment increased prices would rise in line with marginal costs. This is what would produce the fall in the real wage. Nor, in chapter 19, did he assume complete wage stability. Since labour was not always available in the right place and with the right skills, an increase in demand would expose labour shortages in various sectors, so that employers would bid up money wages to attract labour, and this would raise prices further. Nevertheless, even in his less formal treatment, he assumed that wage and price movements would be small relative to movements of output and employment in the earlier phases of recovery. As full employment approached they would gradually overtake output effects until at full employment the whole of any further expansion of demand would be felt in rising prices – a position of 'true' inflation. Keynes thought there was no need to worry about this eventuality in the middle of a depression. But he did respond to the criticism of the socialist (but Hayekian) E. M. F. Durbin that his policy would lead to inflation:

> ... I agree that our methods of control are unlikely to be sufficiently delicate or sufficiently powerful to maintain continuous full employment. I should be quite content with a reasonable approximation to it, and in practice I should probably relax my expansionist measures a little before technical full employment had actually been achieved.[82]

Critics of Keynes emphasised the crucial importance of the 'acquiescence postulate'. Pigou, in his review of the *General Theory*, said that Keynes had underestimated the tendency of workers to bargain in real terms. Hayek in 1937 argued that the working class would 'soon learn' that an engineered rise in prices was no less a reduction in wages than a deliberate cut in money wages 'and that in consequence the belief that it is easier to reduce by the round-about method of depreciation the wages of all workers in a country than directly to reduce the money wages of those who are affected by a given change, will soon prove illusory'.[83] Henderson also thought money wages would start rising long before full employment was achieved. Robertson's position was more complex. Commenting on Keynes's chapter 2 in draft he wrote to Keynes on 3 February 1935:

> I am not persuaded that all this is good history or working-class psychology. What about the big series of strikes in 1910–12 for higher money wages in face of the rising cost of living? Were the railwaymen really only thinking of their position *relatively* to the coal miners and vice versa? – I should have thought that custom, the novelty and unreliability of index numbers etc. were quite sufficient reasons for the admitted tendency of workpeople (and others) to think, within limits, in terms of money, – which, I agree, is a most fortunate fact for enabling recovery from depression.[84]

Robertson seemed to be saying that money illusion was likely to be sufficiently pervasive for demand expansion to work, at least in the short run, though only for that reason.

Keynes's disciples tended to dismiss inflationary fears. In her 'baby-book' account of Keynes's ideas in 1937, Joan Robinson wrote as if the only effect of demand expansion in conditions of heavy unemployment would be to get rid of unwanted leisure. 'Wars and revolutions have frequently led to violent inflation, but in times of peace with a stable government and a competent monetary authority it is little to be feared.'[85] However, it was Keynes's pupil David Champernowne who most fully worked out the consequences of Keynes's acceptance of the marginal productivity theory of wages. Reviewing the *General Theory* in June 1936, he asserted that the failure of labour to respond immediately to a rise in the cost of living depended on (i) the existence of a definite contract based on the expectation of a stationary cost of living, (ii) a reluctance to incur the inconvenience involved in frequent demands for changes in money wages, (iii) a failure to notice immediately that the real wage had fallen (money illusion), and (iv) the habit of thinking in terms of the price level of a former date. In time all these causes would recede and the money-wage rate would in time fully compensate for price increases. The employment meanwhile created was 'monetary employment', which contained 'the seeds of its own destruction'. Moreover, wage contracts would be revised ever faster as wage-earners became accustomed to inflation. The policy of full employment would become progressively less potent and necessarily associated with accelerating inflation. Champernowne believed that the inflationary effects of 'monetary employment' would mean that periods of full employment would be brief and interspersed with 'monetary unemployment' or deflation, which would last longer, as workers' resistance to downward adjustments in money wages is much more potent than their 'acquiescence' in upward movements of the price level – a point recognised by Robertson.*

Champernowne made it clear that much of his analysis of wage behaviour was based on discussions with Pigou and Robertson. According to Brent Jones, post-war experience has borne out Champernowne's predictions except that, because of 'political pressures, optimistic forecasts, and an often seemingly blind faith in the power of a combination of demand expansion and an incomes policy to secure full employment without too high a price in terms of inflation, deflationary periods have not been of sufficient length or severity to eradicate an underlying and expanding "core" of inflation in the economy'.[86]

Keynes's acceptance of the first classical wage postulate was criticised at the time by both Keynesians and non-Keynesians. Ohlin wrote, 'When reading his book one sometimes wonder whether he never discussed imperfect competition with Mrs. Robinson,' to which Keynes replied, 'I have always regarded decreasing physical returns in the short period as one of the very few incontrovertible propositions in our miserable subject.'[87] Under conditions of imperfect competition, labour productivity might be expected to increase rather than decline as output expanded, owing to the greater utilisation of plant capacity, thus allowing an increase in real wages as employment rose. Keynes partially acknowledged this possibility in 1939, in a comment on articles by Dunlop, Tarshis, and Kalecki, after strong resistance on the way. As he rightly perceived, 'If we can advance farther on the road towards full employment than I had previously supposed without seriously affecting real hourly wages or the rate of profits per unit of output, the warning of the anti-expansionists need cause us less anxiety.'[88] Keynes's hopes of what policy might achieve were further boosted during the war,

---

*Cf. Robertson's subtle comment: 'It can, of course, be answered that acceptance of a cut in money wages argues a more deliberate and durable acquiescence in a cut in real wages than does acceptance of a raised cost of living.' (*CW*, xiv, 253n.)

when quasi-permanent boom was achieved at very moderate inflationary cost. This fuelled the dangerous belief of some of his post-war disciples that a peacetime economy can be driven at the same pace as a wartime economy, provided that the appropriate price and cost controls are in place.

There was no resolution of this question in Keynes's life-time. What Keynes would certainly have rejected was any attempt to apply his tools mechanically. A minimalist Keynesian policy might be directed to preventing or removing cyclical unemployment. The achievement and sustaining of 'maximum possible' employment would depend not on nominal wage stability but on what Hansen called 'stable productivity wages' – wage increases strictly related to productivity gains, with prices stable. But Keynes had no confidence that this was possible. What he meant by a 'reasonable approximation' to full employment can perhaps be inferred by reference to some historical 'norm' of unemployment, in Britain's case about 4 to 5 per cent. From everything he wrote, one can say that Keynes aimed not for the maximum possible employment, but for the maximum employment possible in a given situation, and taking into account the psychology of the business community, including the effect of policy on business expectations. In practice he was extremely cautious indeed, as is shown by his 1937 articles in *The Times*. (See p. 629 below.)*

It is obvious that the *General Theory* is far from being exclusively concerned with short-period equilibrium. Many passages, as well as sections of chapters 16, 17 and 23, raise 'Day of Judgement' questions – the long-term fate of a *laissez-faire* economy. Alvin Hansen fashioned his 'secular stagnation' theory from hints in the *General Theory*. On the other hand critics were unanimous in rejecting Keynes's doomsday scenario.

There is almost no history in the *General Theory*, unlike in the *Treatise on Money*. But Keynes's theory may, nevertheless, be regarded both as a reflection on history and as a thought machine designed to improve historical performance. His conceptual construction was obviously seen by him as more useful than the classical one, because he conceived of the 'economic

---

*Allan Meltzer has noted that, outside a very short period, there is no equivalence between output and employment. A situation of sub-optimal output persisting over any length of time may be consistent with full employment. (In *Keynes's Monetary Theory: A Different Interpretation*, 203.) Keynes might not have disagreed. In the first and second proofs of chapter 2, he wrote, 'This does not imply that labour, which is suffering involuntary unemployment, is idle. It may be employed as a *pis aller* in some occupation where it earns a real wage less than the wage potentially available. And, of course, a man who is not "out of work" may prefer to be occupied for a longer working week even at a lower hourly real wage than he is actually earning.' (*CW*, xiv, 364.) Thus Keynes would not regard an economy in which university graduates were employed as gardeners, or in part-time jobs, or had dropped out of the labour market, as fully employed, until the state of abundance was such that these occupations and leisure were voluntarily chosen. He would undoubtedly have viewed the job-creation statistics of the 1980s with considerable scepticism. Conceptually, that is, there is a distinction between 'unemployment equilibrium', relating to a short-period position, and 'underemployment equilibrium', relevant to a long-period position of sub-optimal output.

problem' as being more difficult, and the classical view too Panglossian. It was built to be used by central authority to improve economic performance beyond what the unaided market could achieve. The *General Theory* can thus be seen as an essay in historical generalisation, embracing in a single sweep of ideas its current predicament, the past experience of mankind and its future prospects.

Keynes's critique of classical theory clearly stems from his own experience of the great monetary upheavals of the immediate post-war years, which convinced him that monetary happenings have prolonged 'real' effects, and that no theory of employment which made any sense could start by abstracting from such disturbances. He had observed that the fall in prices in 1920-2 had left real wages too high – like the shoals on an ebbing tide – independently of any desire of workers to increase their 'share' of the national product; and as early as 1922 had said that the only way to lower real wages was to raise prices (see pp. 132-4 above). In both the *Tract* and the *Treatise* he had showed how changes in the value of money arbitrarily (that is, involuntarily) shifted class shares in the national income; or, to put it differently, how real wages oscillated round a conventional 'norm' during the business cycle. He had observed in the mid–1920s how a low state of business confidence (images of death were often on his lips) combined with a high rate of interest kept investment low and unemployment high even when prices were stable; and the experience of the great crash of 1929 and subsequent depression (as well as his own experiences in the market) provided the historical backcloth to his account of the volatility of investment and the relative inefficacy of monetary policy to lever an economy out of a deep slump. Keynes's *General Theory* is logically independent of these historical experiences, but its structure reflects them.

Keynes knew little history, but his vivid imagination more than made up for his lack of knowledge. Throughout his life he asked pertinent historical questions, though he may not have provided a framework for answering them which historians would consider satisfactory, or at least complete. Why was there so little economic change for the thousands of years before the seventeenth and eighteenth centuries? Why did Asia stagnate while Europe grew? His view that the marginal efficiency of capital has normally been too low relative to the 'conventional' interest rate has proved to be very fertile here, though needing to be filled in with institutional data. Modern economic historians like North and Thomas have emphasised the importance of well-specified property rights in creating an inducement to invest. Similarly the high liquidity premium attaching to gold, to which Keynes, following Jevons, attributed Asia's long secular stagnation, would need to be set in some ecological context, as Eric Jones has done.[89]

Running through large parts of the *General Theory* is the conviction that the 'economic problem' at all times has derived from the weakness of the inducement to invest and the strength of the motives towards saving and hoarding, coupled with the idea that economic progress takes place in bursts of energy, when optimism temporarily overcomes prudence.

> It is impossible to study the notions to which the mercantilists were led by their actual experiences [he wrote on pp. 347–8 of the *General Theory*] without perceiving that there has been a chronic tendency throughout human history for the propensity to save to be stronger than the inducement to invest. The weakness of the inducement to invest has been at all times the key to the economic problem. To-day the explanation of the weakness of this inducement may chiefly lie in the extent of existing accumulations; whereas, formerly, risks and hazards of all kinds may have played a larger part. But the result is the same.

His view that 1914 marked the end of a golden epoch from which retro-gression was inevitable was a not untypical reaction of the pre-war gener-ation to the betrayed hopes of automatic progress. But Keynes was unique among economists in investing the 150 years ending in 1914 with theoretical significance; for, as he saw it, it provided the data which validated the classical theory, overcame the theoretical hesitations of economists like Mal-thus and emboldened the classical economists to think of their theory as universal. Keynes's view of the nineteenth century as a 'special case' in economic history was the historical analogue of his view of the classical theory as a 'special case' of his own general theory.

For the historically minded there is an obvious question which rarely occurs to economic theorists: why, after all, was the macroeconomic problem so much less severe in the nineteenth century than in the inter-war years? What was it that caused the economic machine to push forward so vigorously then and stutter later? Or to put it another way; why did economies seem to require a jump-start from government in the 1930s when in the nineteenth century they never stalled?*

Pigou did think about these questions. Like Mancur Olson much later, he started with the assertion that wages had been much more rigid since the war, and that this was due to the greater role of trade unions and unemployment insurance. Pigou claimed that significant wage flexibility had existed before 1914 and this explained the fairly stable level of unemploy-ment over the cycle of about 4–5 per cent in the latter part of the nineteenth century. In such circumstances the classical view had 'not done badly'. But 'If . . . post-war policy is in fact responsible for adding some 5 per cent to the volume of unemployment which is normally brought about by other factors the country is confronted with a problem of a type which pre-war economics never found itself called upon to study.'[90]

---

*I used to put this question to my friend the late Nicholas Kaldor. It was evident he had never thought about it. He did not regard it as an interesting question.

Keynes had some sympathy with this view in the 1920s, but he had largely abandoned it by the 1930s, telling the Macmillan Committee that there had always been 'intense social resistance' to downward revision of money wages, that such revisions had rarely been required, and never on a large scale, and that it was conditions of demand, not supply, which had kept the nineteenth century economy buoyant.

Keynes's own notion of economic progress (it would be too much to call it a theory) relied heavily on the influence of stimulating events exciting the 'animal spirits' of businessmen. In the *Treatise on Money* he emphasises the stimulating effects throughout history of 'windfalls', in the form of treasure seized from foreigners, or 'booty' falling into the laps of entrepreneurs through domestic currency inflation. But, despite such passages, Keynes never had a monetary or mercantilist interpretation of economic history: his fascination with the King Midas legend should warn us against this. Asia was the 'sink of the precious metals', but Asia stayed poor, and Europe prospered. The power of gold and silver to unleash enterprise depended on the presence of a spirit of enterprise, or risk-taking; otherwise they would simply be hoarded. Money-creation is useless unless the spirit of enterprise stirs.

Keynes's view of the causes of nineteenth-century prosperity may be contrasted with Pigou's approach given above:

> During the nineteenth century [he wrote in the *General Theory*, p. 307] the growth of population and of invention, the opening-up of new lands, the state of confidence and the frequency of war over the average of (say) each decade seem to have been sufficient, taken in conjunction with the propensity to consume, to establish a schedule of the marginal efficiency of capital which allowed a reasonably satisfactory average level of employment to be compatible with a rate of interest high enough to be psychologically acceptable to wealth-owners.

Keynes's emphasis on population growth as a stimulus to prosperity would be developed in his Galton Lecture in 1937. It marked his break with his own neo-Malthusian past and the last vestige of Adam Smith's 'parsimony' theory of wealth-creation. The thrust of the argument is that what he called in 1919 that 'extraordinary episode in the economic progress of man ... which came to an end in August 1914' was highly dependent on fortuitous or non-repetitive events. His conviction that the inducement to invest would weaken, while the propensity to save and hoard strengthened, as societies grew more affluent inspired his futuristic vision of secular stagnation, and the policies for income redistribution and socialised investment to counter it which he puts forward in the last chapter of his book.

Keynes's historical logic thus led him to interpret the depression of the 1930s as a premonition of the fact that the richer societies become the more they were prone to remain in conditions of semi-slump. J. R. Commons's theory of the three stages to which he had alluded in 1925 – stagnation, explosive energy and stabilisation – was reworked in the light of his new ideas to yield the conclusion that the richest societies would stagnate like the poorest as they approached the point of want saturation, unless the state stage-managed the final ascent into paradise. Population growth would stop; as capital became more abundant the prospective yield from investment would fall. The marginal propensity to save would rise; as would money's 'own' rate of interest relative to the 'own' rates of capital.

Keynes's fear that economies would simply stagnate under *laissez-faire* now seems as spectacularly wrong as his idea that most wants would be satisfied if economies could be kept in a quasi-boom for a few years longer. Critics rejected it; even his own followers were split on how to treat it. For Joan Robinson, the end of population growth in the West, the closing of the frontier and a consequent decline in the rate of inventions meant that 'powerful stimulants will have to be applied to the economic system if chronic unemployment is to be avoided'.[91] On the other hand, Reddaway wrote to Keynes from Melbourne on 15 April 1937, 'there seems to me to be no *a priori* reason why the increased real income which is brought about by using increased capital should not raise the schedule of the marginal efficiency of capital by opening up quite new avenues of investment'.[92]

Keynes's stagnationist *obiter dicta* remained part of the mindset of most Keynesian economists, who expected another great depression to follow the temporary excitement of the Second World War. What he underestimated was humanity's ingenuity in inventing ways to keep capital scarce. In the *General Theory* saving and hoarding were the main enemies of capital abundance. He did not imagine that unrestrained population growth outside the West and rampant consumerism, combined with politician-induced 'earthquakes' – wars, civil disturbances, ideological fantasies – would achieve the same effect and keep most of the world's population poorer in true wealth than it needed to be. He would not have regarded armaments expenditure as a rational means of keeping the world booming. For Keynes quantity of demand always had reference to quality of life. To cite the huge numbers of people, television sets, drugs, armaments as proofs that mankind was solving its economic problem would have struck him as bizarre.

The ultimate irony is the obsolescence of the largest part of the capital equipment of Eastern Europe and the former Soviet Union – which, of course, reopens the West's frontier, long considered closed by the secular stagnationists of the twentieth century. In all this he would have found sombre confirmation of mankind's terror in confronting its 'real problem – how to live wisely, and agreeably, and well'.

The main issue endlessly revolved in the Keynes versus Classics debate is about which analytic method best captures the way an entrepreneur economy works. Specifically, is the existence of money as radically disturbing as Keynes claimed, or does the classical method of abstracting from monetary events remain a good 'first approximation'? If monetary influences do have a pervasive effect on outcomes, short or long, is this mainly in the direction of inflation or deflation? Is a method which excludes (or abstracts from) any self-correcting forces the best guide to policy? Against the critics of his central proposition that stable equilibrium could exist at less than full employment, Keynes had one extremely cogent argument: that its denial encouraged an attitude of passivity to slumps, not only or mainly on the part of economists, but of 'practical men' who were 'slaves' of defunct popularisers of the old theories. No doubt he had in mind the 'Treasury view' as he first encountered it in 1928–9. A point he repeatedly made was that the maxims of behaviour, or rules of thumb, associated with imperfectly understood and half-remembered nineteenth-century doctrines had a paralysing and perverse effect on public policy in times of depression: encouraging saving, cutting public spending, cutting wages and so on. Keynes understood that to undermine the orthodox mindset he had to attack it head-on, not envelop it in qualifications and methodological mazes. That is why he was so hostile to those nearest him in spirit – the monetary disequilibrium theorists. He believed he had cracked classical economics wide open; but it was just as important to be perceived as having done so. As the more recent career of monetarism shows, economic theories, presented at the right time and in the right way, can become powerful political myths, widening the scope of public action. This was always part of Keynes's intention.

III

VISION INTO ALGEBRA

The most important question facing Keynes after the publication of the *General Theory* was how he was to manage his own revolution. He had aimed to capture economic reality in all its richness and complexity; to supply a precise way of thinking about employment and unemployment; to provide a tool for policy. All three were elements in his persuasive strategy. He wanted to appeal to the intuitions, realism and also expertise of his audience of economists and policymakers. But the last two were especially important for conversion (in the technical sense) and action (by government). From this set of aims which Keynes held in balance in his own thought and character, two types of theory eventually emerged, both children of Keynes's *General Theory*. The first is what Shackle calls an 'economics of disorder', dominated by unruly, uncertain and fluctuating expectations and relationships. The second is an economics of given expectations and mathematical functions fit for policy manipulation. Keynes acquiesced in the mathematicisation of the *General Theory* for pedagogical and policy purposes, while at the same time warning that 'as soon as one is dealing with the influence of expectations and of transitory experience, one is ... outside the realm of the formally exact'.[93]

The way Keynes himself might have liked his revolution to go is indicated in a single sheet of chapter headings he scribbled down at Tilton in the summer of 1936 for a sequel entitled 'Footnotes to the General Theory'. It was to be in six chapters. Chapter 1 would consist of the 'Four Parts of the Theory': effective demand, the multiplier, the theory of investment and the theory of interest. Chapter 2 would be the 'Analysis of Effective Demand'. Chapter 6 was 'Statistical Notes'. Chapters 3, 4 and 5, which were plainly intended as the core of the book, were to be headed: 'The Theory of Interest Regarded as the Marginal Efficiency of Money', 'The Analysis of Liquidity Preference Regarded as Constituting the Demand for Money' and 'The Limitations on the Demand for Capital Goods'. The book was never written, but the proposed structure indicates that Keynes would have liked to give greater emphasis to the long-period aspects of his theory.

The mathematicisation of the *General Theory* started immediately it was published but it was left to Hicks to map the mathematics on to a two-curve diagram which became the accepted form of the *General Theory*. His famous paper 'Mr. Keynes and the Classics: A Suggested Reinterpretation' was published in *Econometrica* in April 1937. What Hicks does is to turn Keynes's logical chain of reasoning designed to expose the causes which drive the economy towards a low employment trap into a generalised system of simultaneous equations, devoid of causal significance, with the behavioural characteristics of the propensities to be filled in according to assumption. The 'generalised' system has room for Keynes's 'special theory', but also, for example, for the Treasury view, which Keynes wrote the *General Theory* to refute.[94] In this form Keynes's theory became more acceptable to Robertson, but only because it seemed to retreat from the 'one-sided' *General Theory* positions.[95] Keynes's closest disciples, Kahn and Joan Robinson, later felt it was a betrayal of the Keynesian Revolution; Kahn regretted that Keynes had not spoken out against it.[96] The interesting question is why Keynes conceded to Hicks what he had refused to Robertson: a way of reconciling this theory with orthodox economics.

Hicks starts out by constructing a 'classical' theory of employment (which he admitted 'cannot easily be found in the textbooks') in a form 'similar to that which Mr. Keynes sets out in his own theory'. In this model total money income depends on the quantity of money, aggregate employment depends on total income, saving and investment are adjusted to each other by the rate of interest, and income shares determined by the money-wage rate. This was 'probably more or less the theory that was held by Marshall. But with Marshall it was already beginning to be qualified. . . . What Mr. Keynes has done is to lay enormous emphasis on the qualifications, so that they almost blot out the original theory.'[97] Keynes's chief qualification is to make the demand for money a function of the rate of interest. 'It is the liquidity preference doctrine which is vital. For it is now the rate of interest, not income, which is determined by the quantity of money.' With the quantity of money and the investment-demand schedule given, the volume of investment is determined by liquidity preference; then the volume of employment *at given wage rates* is determined by the value of investment and by the consumption function. This amendment to the classical scheme:

> yields the startling conclusion, that an increase in the inducement to invest, or in the propensity to consume, will not tend to raise the rate of interest, but only to increase employment. In spite of this, however, and in spite of the fact that quite a large part of the argument runs in terms of this system, and this system alone, *it is not the General Theory*. We may call it, if we like, Mr. Keynes' *special theory*. The General Theory is something appreciably more orthodox.[98]

Hicks then 'generalises' Keynes's 'special theory'. He notices that Keynes makes the 'demand for money' depend not just on the interest rate, but also on money income, via the 'transactions balances'. This takes him 'a big step back to Marshallian orthodoxy', so that his theory becomes 'hard to distinguish' from the 'revised and qualified' Marshallian theories which 'are not new'. But Hicks adds some generalising of his own. 'Mathematical elegance would suggest that we ought to have I[ncome] and i[nterest] in all three equations [in saving and investment, as well as money] if the theory is to be really General.'[99] The 'generalised' General Theory is presented graphically in the form of two curves, with income and the interest rate as the co-ordinates, in a system of mutual dependency.*

What Hicks did was to finesse the debate about whether Keynes's theory or the classical theory was more 'general'. Both could be regarded as 'special cases' of a generalised short-period theory of employment, which, in fact, Hicks himself constructed. In this generalised theory, which was, however, based on the architecture of the *General Theory*, either 'classical' or 'Keynesian' solutions were possible, depending on the behavioural characteristics of the propensities. If investment and consumption demand is strong, 'the classical theory will be a good approximation . . .'. If there is a faltering in demand the limit to the fall in the rate of interest arising from the 'speculative motive' can determine a position of unemployment equilibrium. Keynes's 'general theory' is the 'Economics of Depression'. The 'generalised' general theory is consistent with either depression or boom or intermediate positions. One did not have to choose.

The story of the development of Hicks's IS–LM apparatus has been told in fascinating detail by Warren Young. According to Young, Hicks's unique

---

*See Appendix at the end of this chapter for the IS–LM diagram.

contribution was the IS–LM diagram itself. 'Having a picture is very important, since a picture is worth a thousand words.'[100] But Young sees Harrod as the 'driving force behind the determinate simultaneous equation approach'.[101] Hicks, Harrod and Meade all presented mathematical versions of the *General Theory* at the Econometric Conference held at Oxford in September 1936. Hicks saw both the other papers before the meeting, and Young believes it was Harrod's system of equations which inspired his own paper. Harrod, in making saving a function of both income *and* interest, wrote, 'However, there is no need to pick a quarrel here. The rate of interest may be brought back into this part of the picture without affecting the main argument.' 'Probably', too, the level of income should be inserted into the money equation, but no 'final pronouncement' is necessary. By means of such amendments, Harrod finds that 'Keynes has not affected a revolution in fundamental economic theory but a readjustment and a shift of emphasis.'[102] The Oxford meeting, which Young claims to be 'perhaps the most important meeting in the history of economics',[103] crystallised what he calls a split in the 'General Theory Group' over 'whether the approach they were developing was a determinate system which could be expressed in the form of simultaneous equations or a system fraught with uncertainty and animal spirits'. Kahn and Joan Robinson (who did not attend the Oxford meeting) saw the *General Theory* as a revolutionary break with orthodoxy, the Oxford economists 'as not unreconcilable with the orthodox mainstream . . .'. The triumph of the 'mathematically elegant' approach was due to the fact that working economists did not know how to digest the *General Theory* until Hicks's diagram told them how to see it, and also that Hicks's model 'was the conceptual manifestation of the quest for continuity and certainty . . .'.[104] Hicks, or perhaps ultimately Keynes, reconciled revolution and orthodoxy in a double sense: in terms of the discipline of economics, and in terms of the continuity of political and social institutions. The determinate system in which the 'authority' could act on the multiplier either by monetary or by fiscal policy also gave economists a potentially key position at the centre of government.

After the Oxford meeting, Kahn and Joan Robinson, who had played such a large part in the genesis of the *General Theory*, were edged out of the development of the Keynesian Revolution. Kahn later regarded the reduction of the *General Theory* to 'diagrams and bits of algebra' as a great tragedy. Keynes's 'insistence on the overwhelming importance of expectations, highly subject to risk and uncertainty, was one of his biggest contributions. This completely undermines the prevalent idea – for which Keynes' attempt at simplification is responsible – that [his] schedules can be regarded as stable relationships handed down from heaven.'[105] However, it has to be said that there is no evidence that Kahn and Joan Robinson protested *at the time* against the reduction of the *General Theory* to 'diagrams and bits of algebra', or to the apparent 'capture' of the revolution by Hicks,

Harrod and Meade. Kahn's lack of public involvement in these discussions is striking. Perhaps he felt inhibited by the Master's own position.

What was Keynes's attitude? He saw Meade's and Harrod's papers before they were presented at the Oxford meeting. He had no criticism of Meade's presentation.[106] Harrod sent him his paper with a disarming cover note. He would emphasise that Keynes was in 'no way responsible' for Harrod's interpretation and that 'my paper . . . stress[es] what to me seems important and not what might seem to you, not even what *I think* would seem to you, important in your contribution . . .'. Further, he felt a 'restatement in a different terminology' was needed to 'make some people (e.g., Pigou . . .) appreciate that there is more in the formal theory for them to cogitate upon than they have yet tumbled to'. Keynes wrote to Harrod affectionately on 30 August 1936: 'I think that you have reoriented the argument beautifully,' though he was not clear how, at full employment, 'my theory merges into the orthodox theory'. He accepted Harrod's implicit case for pursuing a different strategy from his own in developing his doctrine:

> You don't feel the weight of the past as I do. One cannot shake off a pack one has never properly worn. And probably your ignoring all this is a better plan than mine. For experience seems to show that people are divided between the old ones whom nothing will shift . . . and the young ones who have not been properly brought up and believe nothing in particular. The particles of light seen in escaping from a tunnel are interesting neither to those who mean to stay there nor to those who have never been there! I have no companions, it seems, in my own generation, either of earliest teachers or of earliest pupils; I cannot in thought help being somewhat bound to them. . . .[107]

It is as though he was saying: if this is where the young wanted to take his ideas, so be it. If he resented Harrod not sharing some of his deepest intuitions, he did not show it.

A copy of Hicks's paper reached Keynes in October 1936. He replied on 31 March – *six months* later, a rather astonishing lapse of time for such a punctilious correspondent: 'I found it very interesting and really have next to nothing to say by way of criticism.' But then, of course, he did: putting income into all the equations overemphasised current at the expense of expected income; it was important to insist that an increase in the induce-ment to invest *need* not raise the rate of interest. But these were quibbles, as though Keynes was not very interested. He gave no hint of realising the seminal importance of Hicks's paper.

Hicks replied on 9 April:

> . . . I remain impenitent about including income in the marginal efficiency of capital equation. Of course I agree that it is expected

income that logically matters; but the influence of current events on expectations (admittedly a loose and unreliable connection) seems to me potentially so important, that I feel much happier if it is put in and marked unreliable, than if it is merely talked about, and not . . . put into the formula, which [the student] will take down in his notes.[108]

The difference is between expectations being 'talked about' (as Keynes did in chapter 12) and being 'put into the formula' as Hicks did.

Two issues concerning Keynes's reaction to the efforts of Meade, Harrod and Hicks need to be distinguished. The first concerns the presentation of his system as a determinate model, the second its generalisation into a system of simultaneous equations. To take the second first: Keynes's Vision is surely quite different from Hicks's generalisation, which is purely a statement of logical possibilities, with no one more likely than the other. The *General Theory* was written to exhibit the pathology of capitalism, not its possibility of health. Nor did Keynes himself believe that some 'modification' of the classical system of thought was all that was needed. He thought that 'in the world we actually live in' it did not apply. Therefore it is highly unlikely that he thought of his *General Theory* as a 'special theory' in Hicks's sense, or that he believed its generality was the property only of its architecture. He thought that a state of unemployment or underemployment was the general condition of mankind, rooted in uncertainty; that intervals of full employment were rare, and depended on special conjunctures (including delusions). Moreover, Keynes never liked the general equilibrium method. There is a revealing letter to Hicks on 9 December 1934, in which he writes that 'Walras's theory and all others along those lines are little better than nonsense.'[109] So Hicks's generalisation is not something Keynes would have done himself, and it imported elements alien to the original conception, though not formally inconsistent with it. On the other hand, Keynes was passionately concerned with policy; so were most of those who took up the *General Theory*. Embedded in his book was an operational model. Keynes was not opposed to its being extracted, formalised, made determinate by assumption. To have bequeathed an organised method of thinking about aggregate output and employment – was not this, in the end, worth the sacrifice of a particular Vision? And to get the younger generation like Hicks, Harrod, Meade, Reddaway, Lange and others on his side in the battle against unemployment – was this not also more important than his doubts about their way of doing economics? If Keynes thought much about his response to Hicks perhaps his thoughts ran along some such lines. But perhaps he did not. In his long letter to Hicks there is not a single word of praise, hardly of criticism; no appreciation at all of the very singular feat Hicks had accomplished. Was he too tired to realise its importance? Was he too personally remote from Hicks to find the right words? Whatever the answer, he let the Hicks 'generalisation' of the *General Theory* through on the nod.*

What he did was to go on fighting on behalf of his own Vision, and the appropriate method it suggested of doing economics. Three examples may be given. In the published version of his Stockholm address in August 1936 he wrote:

> For the rate of interest and the marginal efficiency of capital are particularly concerned with the *indefinite* character of actual expectations; they sum up the effect on men's market decisions of all sorts of vague doubts and fluctuating states of confidence and courage. They belong, that is to say, to a stage of our theory when we are no longer assuming a definite and calculable future.[110]

Keynes's famous paper, 'The General Theory of Employment', which appeared in the *Quarterly Journal of Economics* in February 1937, became the basis of the 'Post-Keynesian' interpretation of the *General Theory*. Ostensibly his answer to criticisms by Taussig, Leontief, Viner and Robertson, it may also be seen as a warning to his mathematical interpreters – a warning completely ignored. It is significant that this restatement of the 'essence' of the *General Theory* is concerned particularly with the effects of uncertainty on investment demand and the rate of interest. It is prefaced by Keynes saying he is 'more attached to the comparatively simple fundamental ideas which underlie my theory than to the particular forms in which I have embodied them'. This reinforces a point he made in one way or another many times, to the effect that 'it is necessary in writing economic theory for one's language to be less generalised than one's thought'.[111]

His objection to the orthodox theory rests on its assumption of a calculable future in which 'risks were capable of an exact actuarial computation'. Actually, he says, 'we have, as a rule, only the vaguest idea of any but the most direct consequences of our acts'.

> Thus the fact that our knowledge of the future is fluctuating, vague and uncertain, renders wealth a peculiarly unsuitable subject for the methods of classical economic theory. . . . By 'uncertain knowledge' . . . I do not mean merely to distinguish what is known

---

*See D. Patinkin, 'On Different Interpretations of the *General Theory*', *Journal of Monetary Economics*, 26, 1990, for the most recent presentation of his view that Keynes and all Keynesians at first unambiguously accepted 'IS–LM' as an accurate representation of the *General Theory*, and that the 'Post-Keynesian' critique of this interpretation came only in the 1960s. Patinkin is right to say that the public challenges to the IS–LM approach came much later. But he does not, to my knowledge, try to explain Keynes's lack of *interest* in what Hicks was doing, or why he abandoned the 'systematic and mathematically elegant' formulation of the theory of effective demand which he used in his own lectures and which persisted into the 1934 drafts of his book. (See Patinkin, 'The Process of Writing the General Theory', in D. Patinkin and J. Clark Reith (eds), *Keynes, Cambridge and The General Theory*, pp. 16–17.)

for certain from what is only probable. . . . The sense in which I am using the term is that in which the prospect of a European war is uncertain, or the price of copper and the rate of interest twenty years hence, or the obsolescence of a new invention, or the position of private wealth holders in the social system in 1970. About these matters there is no scientific basis on which to form any calculable probability whatever.[112]

The need to act forces people to adopt a variety of 'techniques' or strategies which 'saves our faces as rational, economic men'. The three most important are (i) the belief that present conditions will continue indefinitely into the future; (ii) the assumption that 'the *existing* state of opinion as expressed in prices and the character of output is based on a *correct* summing up of future prospects'; (iii) conventional judgement – we endeavour to fall back on the judgement of the rest of the world'. Expectations are thus essentially *static*. They also reflect, to a great extent, the state of public opinion, or the state of confidence. They generate forecasts which may be couched in mathematical form, but to the extent that they pretend to certainty they are liable to be swept away by any change in the 'news'. 'The practice of calmness and immobility, of certainty and security, suddenly breaks down. New fears and hopes will, without warning, take charge of human conduct. The forces of disillusion may suddenly impose a new conventional basis of valuation.'[113]

Classical economists have also overlooked uncertainty in their treatment of money. 'We are told [it is a store of wealth] without a smile on the face. . . . But in the world of the classical economy, what an insane use to which to put it! For it is a recognised characteristic of money as a store of wealth that it is barren; whereas practically every other form of storing wealth yields some interest or profit.'

> The possession of actual money lulls our disquietude; and the premium which we require to make us part with money is the measure of the degree of our disquietude. . . . fluctuations in the degree of confidence [therefore] are capable of . . . modifying . . . the amount of the premium which has to be offered to induce people not to hoard. . . . This, expressed in a very general way, is my theory of the rate of interest.[114]

It is hardly surprising that the volume of investment should 'fluctuate wildly' for 'it depends on two sets of judgements about the future, neither of which rest on an adequate or secure foundation – on the propensity to hoard and on opinions of the future yield of capital assets'. Moreover, the two judgements tend to pull in the same direction – 'for the same circumstances which lead to pessimistic views about future yields are apt to increase the propensity to hoard'.[115] In a few pages Keynes has managed to concentrate his vision in a way he never managed in the more dispersed treatment of the *Genere! Theory*.

Keynes goes on to say that were 'our knowledge of the future calculable' there would be no need 'to work out a theory of the demand and supply of output *as a whole*', because demand would never be a problem. He then summarises his theory of effective demand. 'The theory can be summed up by saying that, given the psychology of the public, the level of output and employment as a whole depends on the amount of investment. I put it in this way, not because this is the only factor on which aggregate output depends, but because it is usual in a complex system to regard as the *causa causans* that factor which is most prone to sudden and wide fluctuation. . . . This that I offer is, therefore, a theory of why output and employment are so liable to fluctuation.' His remedies 'which, avowedly, are not worked out completely, are on a different plane from the diagnosis. They are not meant to be definitive; they are subject to all sorts of special assumptions and are necessarily related to the particular conditions of the time.'[116]

The relation of this argument to Hicks's 'little apparatus' might seem to be this. Keynes is saying that his own theory is what the classical theory would have had to be had it taken uncertainty seriously. Hicks's 'generalised' *General Theory* was, in other words, redundant, unless it was attached to 'Mr. Keynes's special theory'. The 'new classical' economists of our own time have taken Keynes at his word. By abolishing 'unreliable' expectations they have pronounced Keynes's *General Theory* abolished, leaving a little mathematical toy for students to play with if they want.

Finally there is Keynes's debate with Tinbergen in 1938 on the value of econometrics, in which Harrod also joined. The League of Nations had sponsored a book by the Dutch economist Jan Tinbergen to test hypotheses about the trade cycle produced by Haberler in his book *Prosperity and Depression*. Keynes was sent it in proof for comment. Going through it ruined his summer holiday in 1938, as he made clear to Kahn: 'I think it all hocus – *worse* than Haberler. But every one else is greatly impressed, it seems, by such a mess of unintelligible figurings. There is not the slightest explanation or justification of the underlying logic.'

Keynes attacked Tinbergen's efforts with an astonishingly fierce barrage of arguments (and some excellent jokes) on statistical philosophy, most of them too specialised to consider here, some harking back to his debates with Karl Pearson in 1908 on the influence of parental alcoholism on children; some culled from his *Treatise on Probability*; others perhaps influenced by his own flirtation with 'credit cycle' investment policies in the 1920s, which had left him ruined. The main thread running through the discussion is Keynes's insistence that economics, because of the nature of its material, is a 'moral science', requiring the constant exercise of judgement by the economist in choosing and applying models, supplemented by raw, and not 'cooked', data. Examples of Keynes's impatience can be seen in his initial response to the League's enquiry. He queried Tinbergen's logic in applying 'the method of multiple correlation' to non-homogeneous material and his assumption of fixed coefficients for long series.

> Is it claimed that there is likelihood that the equations will work approximately *next* time? . . . One can always cook a formula to fit moderately well a limited range of past facts. But what does this prove? . . . What place is left for expectation and the state of confidence relating to the future? What place is allowed for non-numerical factors, such as inventions, politics, labour troubles, wars, earthquakes, financial crises?

The root of the trouble, as Keynes saw it, was the 'false precision beyond what either the method or the statistics actually available can support. It may be that a more rough and ready method which preserves the original data in a more recognisable form may be safer.'[117]

Following an exchange of letters with Tinbergen, further thoughts were stimulated when Keynes saw Harrod's draft of his Presidential Address to Section F of the British Association on 'The Scope and Method of Economics'. Writing to Harrod on 4 July 1938 he insisted that economics was 'a branch of logic, a way of thinking', not a 'pseudo-natural science'. It was of the essence of model-building not to 'fill in real values for the variable functions' as Tinbergen had tried to do. Keynes continued, 'Economics is a science of thinking in terms of models joined to the art of choosing models which are relevant to the contemporary world.' This is because its material is 'in too many respects, non homogeneous through time'. Good economists are scarce 'because the gift for using 'vigilant observation' to choose good models, although it does not require a highly specialised intellectual technique, appears to be a very rare one'. Finally 'as against Robbins [whose *Essay on the Nature and Significance of Economic Science* was published in 1932] economics is essentially a moral and not a natural science. That is to say, it employs introspection and judgements of value'.[118] Keynes's objection to econometrics which emerges here and in his letter to Harrod of 16 July was that it tended to freeze models by filling in figures which 'one can be quite sure will not apply next time'. The specialist in model-manufacture will fail 'unless he is constantly correcting his judgement by intimate and messy acquaintance with the facts to which the model has to be applied'.

> I want to emphasise strongly the point [Keynes continued] about economics being a moral science. I mentioned before that it deals with introspection and values. I might have added that it deals with motives, expectations, psychological uncertainties. One has to be constantly on guard against treating the material as constant and homogeneous. It is as though the fall of the apple to the ground depended on the apple's motives, on whether it is worth while falling to the

ground, and whether the ground wanted the apple to fall, and on mistaken calculations on the part of the apple as to how far it was from the centre of the earth.[119]

A new aspect of debate opened up when Keynes sent Harrod a copy of the letter he had written to the League on Tinbergen's work. Keynes had told Tinbergen that his way of dealing with unmeasurables 'amounts to the fact that these are to all intents and purposes neglected'. Harrod defended him by saying that the random unmeasurables were not left out but come in as 'shocks'. 'Naturally they are not taken into account specifically, for if you insisted on doing that you would have to abandon all hopes of a cycle theory and lapse into cycle history.' Keynes was not persuaded: he would have been very hostile to the frequent current method of dividing up behaviour of economies into measurable variables and random shocks. He feared that economists and policymakers would become slaves of past statistical series, fitted out with the spurious precision given by regression coefficients, multiple correlations and so on. Harrod, who was developing a dynamic growth model, was much more sympathetic to Tinbergen's approach.

In private, Keynes continued to call Tinbergen's method 'charlatanism'. In his review, he toned down his criticisms but insisted that the next instalment of his work 'should be primarily devoted to the logical problem, explaining fully and carefully the conditions which the economic material must satisfy if the application of this method [econometrics] is to be fruitful'. Tinbergen 'so clearly prefers the mazes of arithmetic to the mazes of logic, that I must ask him to forgive the criticisms of one whose tastes in statistical theory have been, beginning many years ago, the other way around'. Keynes repeats that Tinbergen's method leaves out any causal role for psychology, expectations and unexpected events, depends on inadequate statistics, ignores the need for judgement in specifying the variables and neglects the possible mutual reactions among the variables themselves. He concludes with the 'strange reflection' that Tinbergen's work is likely to be 'the principal activity and *raison d'être* of the League of Nations' in 1939.[120]

Econometrics emerges from these diatribes, like classical economics itself, as one of those 'pretty, polite techniques' referred to in his *QJE* article, 'which tries to deal with the present by abstracting from the fact that we know very little about the future'.[121] Yet Tinbergen and others found it all very strange, because Keynes's own policy purposes required some attempt to quantify the consumption, investment and liquidity-preference functions, as well as to measure national income. He was also on the Council of the Econometric Society. Keynes, it may be said, objected not to econometrics as such, but to the method of econometrics. But the conditions he imposed on the fruitful application of the method were so strong as virtually to eliminate its usefulness.[122]

Only one of Keynes's correspondents, Hugh Townshend, a pre-war pupil, thought of linking the discussion of uncertainty in the *General Theory* to Keynes's pre-war concepts of non-numerical probabilities and 'weight of argument'. This led him to identify 'risk . . . without uncertainty' as the key postulate of the classical system, the only rational basis for its denial of the existence of inactive balances.[123] Keynes was sufficiently interested to write to Townshend (on 7 December 1938):

> I think it important to emphasise the point that all this is not particularly an *economic* problem, but affects every rational choice concerning conduct where consequences enter into rational calculation. Generally speaking, in making a decision we have before us a large number of alternatives, none of which is demonstrably more 'rational' than the others, in the sense that we can arrange in order of merit the sum aggregate of the benefits obtainable from the complete consequences of each. To avoid being in the position of Buridan's ass, we fall back, therefore, and necessarily do so, on motives of another kind, which are not 'rational' in the sense of being concerned with the evaluation of consequences, but are decided by habit, instinct, preference, desire, will, etc. All this is just as true of the non-economic as the economic man.[124]

By the end of the 1930s, the Keynesian Revolution was on the offensive, the classical system in retreat. Some theoretical honours they had salvaged, but there was a growing conviction that the world was more like that of Keynes than of the Classics, the unmanaged propensities of a capitalist system more likely to generate large-scale unemployment than continuous full employment. The collapse of 1937–8 long before full employment had been restored in Britain or the United States seemed to vindicate Keynes's view that unmanaged capitalism could not even secure a reasonably satisfactory average of activity over the cycle. But Keynes had not won in any clear-cut way. In Britain the critics, the sceptics, the agnostics remained in place and power: it would take another war and the entry into government of the younger generation to push them to one side, and then not completely. And the version of Keynesianism which came out of the debates following the publication of the *General Theory* was by no means wholly Keynes's. In the work of the reconcilers there was more than a hint that his revolutionary assault on the orthodox framework had failed. Perhaps Joan Robinson was right to call it 'bastard Keynesianism'. But only in that form could the Keynesian Revolution survive and grow.

In his article 'Mr Keynes and the Classics: A suggested reinterpretation' (*Econometrica*, April 1937), Hicks distinguished between 'classical theory', Keynes's 'special' theory, Keynes's 'general' theory, and the 'generalised' general theory respectively. In doing so he invented his 'little apparatus', a system of diagrams amounting to a technical extension of some aspects of the *General Theory*. Known as IS/LM, the model continues to be a highly influential representation of Keynes's ideas.

According to Hicks, Keynes stood the classical system on its head. He made saving depend on the level of income rather than on the rate of interest. And he made the demand for money depend on the rate of interest rather than on the level of income. Hicks said, however, that the case when the demand for money is determined solely by the rate of interest is not a true representation of the *General Theory*. This case is Keynes's 'special' theory. In his 'general theory' the demand for money depends on both the rate of interest and the level of income. By reinstating the level of income as a factor determining the demand for money 'Mr Keynes takes a big step back . . . to Marshallian orthodoxy'. In the 'generalised' general theory Hicks inserted the level of income into the investment function and the rate of interest into the saving function, yielding a system of simultaneous equations.

The 'generalised' General Theory can be represented diagramatically as follows:

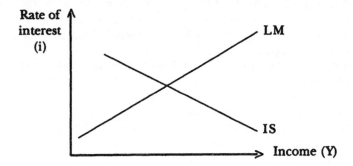

The curve LM shows the loci of combinations of income and interest at which the 'demand for money' (L) equals an exogenously given supply (M). Its upward slope reflects the fact that the demand for money is a declining function of interest but an increasing function of income. The IS curve maps the loci of combinations of income and interest at which saving (S) equals investment, its downward slope suggesting that more will be invested at lower rates of interest, and less at higher levels of income. The intersection of the two curves determines the equilibrium level of income and of interest rate for a given quantity of money.

The shapes and positions of the two curves are yielded by assumption, that is, by what are taken to be the dominant influences on saving, investment, and the demand for money. Take the 'classical' case, where the 'demand for money', being mainly a transactions demand, is largely determined by income, and saving and investment are increasing and decreasing functions of the rate of interest respectively. The LM curve will be almost vertical and the IS curve almost horizontal. With a fixed money supply, any shift in the 'demand for capital' causes the interest rate to go up or down, leaving total money income (or 'effective demand') almost unchanged:

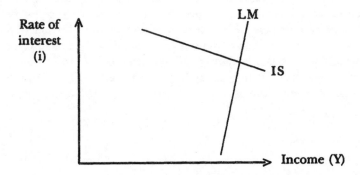

This is a good approximation to the 'Treasury View' of 1929. Money supply is fixed by the gold standard. A loan-financed public works policy (aiming to shift the IS curve to the right) 'crowds out' an equivalent amount of private investment. Macroeconomic policy is powerless to improve the pre-existing equilibrium. In modern language, unemployment is at its 'natural' rate.

Now take what is often called Keynes's theory, but is more accurately called the theory of a severe slump. The 'demand for money' is mainly determined by liquidity preference; saving mainly by level of income. The LM curve is almost horizontal, the IS curve almost vertical:

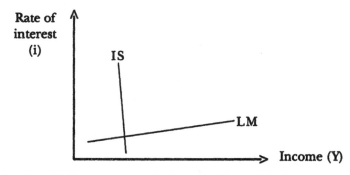

An increase in the money supply has no effect on the interest rate. Even if it did, a change in the interest rate would have little or no effect on investment. But here a loan-financed public works policy leads to a shift in the IS curve to the right, raising income and employment, the increased investment being financed by the increased saving out of the income it produces.

Keynes's 'special theory' is really intermediate between these two. He believed that the equilibrium of the economy, and the shapes of the curves, are normally such that a monetary policy can improve the equilibrium by bringing about a lower rate of interest, producing a higher volume of investment and saving, and a rise in both prices and output.

Hicks's 'little apparatus' can be used to illustrate many possible situations, but, as he said, his 'curves' are 'not really determinate', since the assumption of given expectations is not realistic. Specifically, the attempt to shift one curve might have unexpected repercussions on the other. Keynes's book, as Hicks says, 'was neither the beginning nor the end of Dynamic Economics'. If uncertainty is taken seriously, Keynesian results are bound to be mediocre. This does not mean that Keynesian policies cannot improve on a pre-existing equilibrium.

CHAPTER SEVENTEEN

'My Breathing Muscles
Were So Wonky . . .'

Keynes spent the fortnight before the publication of the *General Theory* in bed with influenza. On Tuesday, 28 January 1936 he wrote to his mother from Gordon Square, 'On Sunday I was normal all day, but (as usual) the second bout began on Monday when I went to 100 again and I'm above 99 to-day. There is a slight tendency for the poison to lodge in the muscles – otherwise nothing. I still hope to get back to Cambridge on Saturday.' On Monday, 3 February he and Lydia were in their box with the Vice-Chancellor for the opening of the Arts Theatre; his parents were in the front row of the dress circle, together with the Heads of House and their wives. In the Ibsen cycle which started on 17 February, Lydia played Nora Helmer in *A Doll's House* and Hilda Wangel in *The Master Builder*, while the 'mysteriously submerged passion of Jean Forbes-Robertson' dominated *Hedda Gabler* and *Rosmersholm*.[1] These were the best of Lydia's stage performances, the critics favourable, even Bloomsbury enthusiastic. No one had doubted her ability to play a pretty doll: Virginia Woolf had used the same word, 'squirrel', about her as did Nora's husband, Torvald Helmer. The revelation was her ability to conjure up terror and steel behind the songbird façade of Nora; and the nobility she brought to the character of Hilda. 'Never before', Clive Bell wrote to her, 'have I seen an actress who contrived not to give Nora's tirade something of the air of a suffragette speech.'[2] For Lydia 'feminism is really an outside problem with Ibsen. . . . What he was really struggling with was the *internal* clashing of human wills. It happened at the moment to be between men and women. . . .'[3] On 2 March the programme transferred to the Criterion Theatre in London, where it ran till 11 April.[4] As soon as it ended Lydia and Maynard went off for a few days' holiday in the south of France, staying at Cavalière in Var.

Keynes was now spending most of his time on his two creations, his mind clicking like a camera from Hawtrey's enormous memoranda to the apparently insuperable problem of getting decent food and service in the theatre's restaurant. His Saturday afternoons were taken up with meetings of the theatre board. On one occasion the chief electrician, the fireman, the box-office men, the chef and the 'Trojan women' Dadie Rylands had acquired for the restaurant were all sacked. He had also started a long essay on Jevons, which he read before the Royal Statistical Society on 21 April.

Jevons was, after Malthus, his favourite economist, and his life stimulated him to one of his most accomplished essays in biography. In May, the Arts Theatre put on *Murder in the Cathedral* and T. S. Eliot spent the weekend at King's. He and Tom 'got on beautifully'; unfortunately they had to spend most of the weekend hiding from Eliot's deranged wife Vivien, who had pursued her husband to Cambridge.[5] Maynard felt well enough, 'except that I have rheumatism flying about which is seasonal, I suppose'. Stimulated by Eliot's visit, he wrote a letter to Raymond Mortimer, literary editor of the *New Statesman*, telling him how much he had liked a piece by Cyril Connolly on A. E. Housman and disliked one by Rebecca West on Kipling. 'In the case of Kipling the interesting problem is how, in spite of everything . . . he can be so good; . . . in the case of Housman . . . how, in spite of everything . . . he could be so bad.'[6] There was not much wrong with his taste in either writers or critics.

Meanwhile, Tilton was being rebuilt 'on a magnificent scale, the landing, the staircase, the servants' quarters and a bath room to each guest are most enjoyable improvements'. On a weekend visit in May, Lydia had rubbed Keynes's head with oil for obscure medicinal purposes 'and he smells like a sardine, and looks like a Plantagenet with new tortoise spectacles'.[7] Such was his prosperity that a flat had also been acquired for Lydia in St Edward's Passage, opposite the Arts Theatre, to stay in when she came to Cambridge.

Keynes spent most of July and August at Tilton, by his standards in considerable idleness. Lydia had opted for idleness as well, refusing an invitation to make a guest appearance with the Russian ballet, 'as I felt I wasn't old enough as a museum piece, nor young enough as contemporary article'. Geoffrey's wife Margaret came early in August with her two sons, Milo and Stephen, who were great favourites. Margaret Hill's daughter Polly was there too; she seemed to be 'so content', despite narrowly failing to get a first in the economics tripos.[8] Kahn and Sraffa came. Keynes's health was moderately good apart from his 'gold bladder', which always played up when the barometer was low.[9] By 16 August Maynard could report to his mother, 'No visitors. No book to write. Just keeping level with my duties and correspondence and a few odds and ends. You'll have seen that I've written a third letter to the N.S. and N.; I also have something forthcoming in the Listener; and two short articles in the Economic Journal. Newton still absorbs more time than he should; but that is a hobby.'

Maynard had bought forty lots at a sale of Newton's papers at Sotheby's on 13/14 July, including his death mask (for £34) and several of his manuscripts on alchemy. He started preparing notes for the biographical study, which he read after dinner one night to the Royal Society in 1942, but which was published only after his death. His letters to the *New Statesman* were written in protest against that journal's peculiar combination of anti-fascism and resistance to rearmament. The suggestion that a Britain rearmed by the Conservatives would throw in its lot with the 'brigand powers' was 'insane', he declared. He advocated rearmament and collective security, but especially the first. 'It is better to have strong forces and no clear-cut foreign policy than to advocate no armaments one week and warlike alliances the next.'[10] However, the myopia of the left on foreign policy was proof against his efforts at persuasion. He tried to cheer up his father, who was 'very low about the European situation':

> The real difficulty about our making up our minds about our own foreign policy is that . . . our immediate interests are *not* threatened by any early ambitions either of Germany or of Italy. Italy wants to master the Mediterranean and, apart perhaps from Egypt (and even this is 'perhaps'), it would not matter truly very much if she does. In the same way, Germany's ambitions are all to the East, and certainly not towards us . . . [also] at sea we are much too powerful for them to want to try conclusions in that way.
>
> . . .
>
> There is very little likelihood indeed of any direct attack by the brigand powers on our own immediate interests. The question for us is how far we are prepared to go to the assistance, if at all, of other victims. I imagine it is almost certain that any thing we do will be guarded and we shall really wait for circumstances. . . . But this, as you will see, makes it all moderately remote.[11]

In late September Maynard and Lydia went to Leningrad to visit Lydia's family, stopping off in Stockholm, where Keynes gave a 'wonderful talk' to the Economic Club. Lydia's mother was well; when her blood pressure rose, leeches were sent from Moscow 'to get lyrical and drunk on my mother's back'. Maynard's reticent report of his visit was mainly about the extreme slowness of the trains, which he loved as it gave him a chance to read the proofs of Joan Robinson's new book.[12]

By the autumn the food at the Arts Theatre restaurant was no better: there was no tinge, Keynes informed Lydia, 'of French cooking from the alleged elderly French chef'. Kahn was doing 'wonders' with the College accounts, but he still had to do one horrid table of figures for himself: after three hours he was 'so exhausted that I cooked it and made it come right by cheating. I simply couldn't go on any longer looking for the mistake.'[13] His forgetfulness was becoming a problem. He had left his glasses in London; he forgot his cigarettes when he went to dine with Victor and Barbara Rothschild. 'I was convinced that I had stuck them in my pocket – I was so looking forward to smoking after B[arbara's] beautiful coffee out of Venetian cups – and then nothing! I was so disappointed that I searched in my pockets for ten minutes in vain.' There were other signs of time passing. His Cambridge tailor, 'The Bodger', no longer made his special socks; the Avoca collars he had worn since childhood were extinct. 'It is dreadful to be so antediluvian.' On the other hand, he was sleeping well, feeling much less tired, and 'full of bright ideas, scribbling away and having at last made a beginning on my Foxwell' – another biographical essay he had undertaken following Foxwell's death.[14] He sat next to W. H. Auden at dinner in hall:

> He was most charming, intelligent, straightforward, youthful, a sort of senior undergraduate; altogether delightful, but but but – his finger nails are eaten to the bones with dirt and wet, one of the worst cases ever, like a preparatory schoolboy. So the infantilism is not altogether put on. It was most disconcerting. For all other impressions so favourable. But those horrid fingers cannot lie. They must be believed. I talked to him about F.6 [*The Ascent of F.6*, the play he had written with Christopher Isherwood]. He has re-written the last part and would like us to look at it again.

Auden's fingernails, Keynes thought, explained 'something unsatisfactory in his work'.[15]

On 16 November, Bertil Ohlin came to give a talk to Keynes's Political Economy Club; by 22 November the Foxwell essay was finished, and *The Times* had accepted his proposal to write two articles on 'The Problem of the Next Slump'. He told Lydia that he was 'going to take trouble about it'. W. H. Smith, he gossiped, 'spend all their time tearing pages out of American magazines to keep secret the King's affair' (with Mrs Wallis Simpson). Keynes was solidly for Edward VIII. 'I thought to-day's leader in *The Times* absurd,' he wrote to Lydia on 4 December. 'Won't sympathy gradually increase for the King against the Archbishops oozing humbug? If the government offered him a morganatic marriage, that would be all right. But apparently – I don't know why – they refuse this.'

Maynard's mind was as bright as ever, but his body had started to deteriorate. For some years he had suffered from what he called his 'intercostal' pains, which shot all round his chest. He interpreted them as rheumatic, and connected them with his attack of pleurisy in October 1931. There was a history of tooth and gum trouble. He started to complain of breathlessness, not only after exertion, but when lying in bed, as he had experienced as a boy when winded at football, though not so acute. He had a severe attack of influenza with fever at Tilton over the Christmas vacation. 'Maynard is better,' wrote a worried Lydia to Florence on 5 January 1937. 'To-day he walked beautifully in the morning, slept for ¾ of an hour afterwards – lately he seems like his old self, perhaps he works a little less.' From Cambridge, he wrote to Lydia on 22 January, 'My health is progressing, though I feel very tired about six o'clock and my breath is terribly short and painful if I run upstairs or walk fast (which probably means that rheumatism in the chest is not far below the surface).' These were tell-tale signs of coronary artery insufficiency, with resulting anginal pains. 'My beloved girl,' he wrote two days later,

My breathing muscles were so wonky to-day that I only just managed to walk to Harvey Rd. So Fil in a loud voice, strong with power, and a most tyrannical manner insisted on sending for his favourite doctor to see me. He has given me two kinds of tablets to swallow and an ointment and recommends the lamp. I am perfectly well so long as I sit in a warm room, and the weakness only comes on when I walk in the cold East wind. So don't worry. The complaint is exactly what I thought it was – rheumatism in the little muscles of the chest *plus* post-influenza. . . . My head is in good form.

Keynes's articles – expanded to three – on 'How to Avoid a Slump' were published in *The Times* on 12–14 January 1937; a follow-up appeared on 11 March. They were his first attempt to apply the *General Theory* to policy. That another slump was coming was a straightforward deduction from his view that recoveries are aborted as saving grows ahead of investment opportunities. Moreover, the idea that the state should do something to prevent 'the recurrence of another steep descent' was, he thought, common ground. 'We have entirely freed ourselves – this applies to every party and every quarter – from the philosophy of the *laissez-faire* state.' Here he was being too optimistic. What is striking about the articles is the cautious nature of Keynes's proposals. With unemployment still at 12 per cent, Keynes thought Britain was approaching boom conditions. The industrial structure was 'unfortunately rigid'; labour dreadfully misallocated. With unemployment now largely confined to the 'distressed areas', the risk was that a further expansion in demand from the centre would cause inflation to take off. 'We are in more need today of a rightly distributed demand than of a greater aggregate demand; and the Treasury would be entitled to economise elsewhere to compensate for the cost of special assistance to the distressed areas.'

The second of Keynes's articles was headed 'Boom Control'. This, as he had admitted to Hubert Henderson, was a neglected topic in the *General Theory*. The most important requirement was to avoid 'dear money' like 'hell-fire'. If investment had to be curtailed, 'we must find other means of achieving this than a higher rate of interest. For if we allow the rate of interest to be affected, we cannot easily reverse the trend.' The rationale for this argument was, of course, his liquidity-preference theory of interest. 'A low enough long-term rate of interest cannot be achieved if we allow it to be believed that better terms will be obtainable from time to time by those who keep their resources liquid. The long-term rate of interest must be kept *continuously* as near as possible to what we believe to be the long-term optimum. It is not suitable to be used as a short-period weapon.' This left three other boom-control policies: repayment of government debt, postponement of local authority projects, and allowing the exchange rate to rise. Specifically, the Chancellor should meet the 'main part of the cost of armaments out of taxation, raising taxes and withholding all reliefs for the present as something in hand for 1938 or 1939, or whenever there are signs of recession'.

The task was to 'stabilise' the 'moderate prosperity we now enjoy'. In the longer run we should be 'slowly reconstructing our social system' to encourage a greater propensity to consume. Meanwhile, a 'board of public investment' should be set up to 'prepare sound schemes [of investment] against the time when they are needed'. When private investment turned down, the maintenance of a low rate of interest plus the expansion of public investment would be enough to prevent a slump from developing. 'Is there the slightest chance of a constructive or a fore-thoughtful policy in contemporary England? Is it conceivable that the Government should do anything in time? Why shouldn't they?'[16]

In February 1937 Neville Chamberlain announced that he would be borrowing £400m. over five years for rearmament. The Labour Party, combining pacifism with orthodox finance, opposed the loan. In his last speech as chairman to the annual meeting of the National Mutual Keynes said it should be possible to borrow this amount without driving up the rate of interest.[17] On 3 March he wrote to Labour's Pethick-Lawrence: 'The Chancellor says that £80m. is not inflationary. You say that it is . . . neither of you appear to me to give any detailed justification of your views.'[18] Keynes's article, which appeared in *The Times* on 11 March, was designed to 'assist the discussion'. It was based on an application of the multiplier. Inflation existed, he wrote, 'when increased demand is no longer capable of materially raising output and employment and mainly spends itself in raising prices. . . . The question is, therefore, whether we have enough surplus capacity to meet the increase in demand likely to arise out of an expenditure of £80,000,000 raised by loans. . . .' He thought the national income multiplier lay between 2 and 3, implying a growth of 5.5 per cent a year. Output could not grow by this amount. But various offsets might bring down 'the increase in the national output (apart from exports) necessary to avoid inflation to a figure of between 3½ to 4½ per cent', and spare capacity might allow for an output growth of about 3 per cent if armaments orders were placed in the Special Areas (of high unemployment). So 'the Chancellor's loan expenditure *need* not be inflationary. But, unless care is taken, it may be rather near the limit.' Keynes insisted that his guesses needed to be supplemented by proper statistics.

> It is essential to set up at the centre an organisation which has the duty to think about these things, to collect information and to advise as to policy. Such a suggestion is, I know, unpopular. There is nothing a Government hates more than to be well-informed; for it makes the process of arriving at decisions much more complicated and difficult. But, at this juncture, it is a sacrifice which in the public interest they

ought to make. It is easy to employ 80 or 90 per cent of the national resources without taking much thought as to how to fit things in. . . . But to employ 95 to 100 per cent . . . is a different task altogether. It cannot be done without care and management; and the attempt to do so might lead to an inflation. . . . [19]

Terence Hutchison, basing himself on the January articles, has argued that Keynes's rejection of further demand expansion with unemployment at 12 per cent suggests that he might have regarded this as Britain's 'natural' rate of unemployment at the time. He points out that the Committee of Economic Information, of which Keynes was a leading member, was concurrently taking a similar view.[20] In his reply to Hutchison, Richard Kahn argued that Keynes's suggestion that a further £80m. a year could be pumped into the economy without inflation rebutted Hutchison's suggestion. Keynes did not think a serious danger of inflation would arise till unemployment had fallen to 6 or 7 per cent. He did not advocate public works in his January 1937 articles because 'he wanted the "public works" to take the form of expenditure on arms growing as rapidly as possible'.[21] The resolution of the difference does not seem that difficult. What could be done to stimulate employment in the context of war preparations might clearly differ from what could be accomplished by ordinary public works, since the reactions of business and trade unions to the location of production, control of wages and prices, and so on might be very different in the two cases. Keynes was modest about policy because he was acutely aware of the importance of the 'state of expectations'.*

Keynes had accepted an invitation from the Eugenics Society to give the address at their thirtieth-anniversary dinner on 16 February 1937, suggesting as a title 'Some Economic Consequences of a Declining Population'. It is a sketch of a long-period extension of the *General Theory*. He started with a charming tribute to Francis Galton, the Society's founder, omitted from the published version. He could surely have been the subject of one of Keynes's biographical essays for, as Keynes says,

> For me the peculiar quality of his mind has always had a special fascination. I possessed all his books when I was still an undergraduate. There was no one who has possessed in purer essence than he the spirit of universal scientific curiosity. It was not the business of his particular kind of brain to push anything far. He had a rare and delicious scientific fancy. His job was, so to speak, to put all of us on enquiry. . . . His original genius was superior to his intellect, but his intellect was always just sufficient to keep him on the right side of eccentricity.[22]

*The question of whether a Keynesian policy could have succeeded in pre-*General Theory* Britain has been interestingly discussed by Roger Middleton in his book *Towards the Managed Economy* (1985).

Up to the *General Theory* Keynes had regarded a stationary or declining population as an unmixed blessing. He was a neo-Malthusian, who saw the increase in numbers as the main obstacle to universal felicity. That is why he had espoused policies of birth control since 1913. However, with demand now seen as a problem, he changed his mind. He came to see population growth as a major source of demand, and an explanation for nineteenth-century prosperity. Further, as societies become richer, consumption demand is directed increasingly to services which make fewer demands on capital. 'Now, if the number of consumers is falling off and we cannot rely on any significant technical lengthening of the period of production, the demand for a net increase of capital goods is thrown back into being wholly dependent on an improvement in the average level of consumption or on a fall in the rate of interest.' Assuming that people go on saving 8 to 15 per cent of their income, the capital stock has to increase, Keynes calculated, between 2 and 4 per cent a year to maintain full employment. 'And this will have to continue year after year indefinitely.' Then Keynes calculated that what he called inventions would absorb only about half of what people planned to save at full employment.

> It follows, therefore, that to ensure equilibrium conditions of prosperity over a period of years it will be essential, *either* that we alter our institutions and the distribution of wealth in a way which causes a smaller proportion of income to be saved, *or* that we reduce the rate of interest sufficiently to make profitable very large changes in technique or in the direction of consumption which involve a much larger use of capital in proportion to output. Or, of course, as would be wisest, we could pursue both policies to a certain extent.

There followed a fanciful play of ideas between the young Malthus, who told the world about the devil of population, and the old Malthus, who revealed to it the devil of unemployment. When Malthusian devil P is chained up, Malthusian devil U breaks loose, and vice versa. Unless we pursue with 'set and determined purpose' a policy of more equal incomes and low interest rates 'we shall be cheated of the benefits which we stand to gain by the chaining up of one devil, and shall suffer from the perhaps more intolerable depredations of the other'. According to taste, this authoritatively gloomy conclusion, based on a series of audacious guesses, may be considered Keynes at his best or his worst.[23]

Lydia was once more on stage, as Célimène in Molière's *The Misanthrope*. It opened at the Arts Theatre on 8 February, and on 23 February transferred to the Ambassadors Theatre in London for a two-week run. Raymond Mortimer in the *New Statesman* noticed that her voice had 'improved enormously, both in power and variety', but that 'the particular power of her acting must always be in the flash of her eyes, the poise of her elbows, the carriage of her head. Her whole body talks, and how happy we are to listen!'

Once more, Keynes had involved himself heavily in all the details: he corresponded with Derain about decor and costumes; asked Robert Atkins to produce; discussed choice of composer for the accompanying ballet ('Harlequin in the Street') – should it be Rameau, Lully or Couperin? – with Derain and Constant Lambert; arranged complimentary tickets: 'The Countess of Oxford, for example, will, I am sure, come,' he wrote to Sydney Carroll, 'but many thousands of years must have passed since she paid for a ticket!' Before the transfer to London, Keynes sacked Stanley Judson, who had played the Harlequin, 'since he seemed unable to dance', substituting for him a youth of sixteen, Hedley Briggs, 'of great beauty and piquancy'. The London season was a financial flop nevertheless, Keynes having to pay out £200 to make up the shortfall in takings.

Maynard had been taking Florence's advice and eating less. He didn't feel the 'intercostals' until he walked, but still couldn't walk more than a quarter of a mile without pain. Maynard 'only needs a little rest and a little gambling at the Casino', Lydia told Florence as they left for Cannes on 13 March, Maynard, of course, with a briefcase full of work, including his Stockholm lecture, which he was preparing for publication. But his chest was no better, and he could not walk more than a few hundred yards. There were spasms of two or three minutes, and two days after arrival he had an attack lasting three-quarters of an hour. From the Carlton Hotel, Lydia wrote to Florence that the 'rich are not lovable'. The news from Spain was good; she hoped 'the Italians will run like mice back to Rome. . . . it's in their blood, in spite of Mussolini . . .'

> Maynard is obeying your orders on the diet, hardly touches sugar, very little wine, mostly water and no honey, at the moment he is at the Casino, I hope he will come back with full hands as we have an agreement, that what he gains I get half, and what he loses, I give half, of course it is all morale, as I have no money, only words. He is just back, he found a flaw in [his] systeme aided and abetted by Rupert Trouton, but not until he has lost. . . . We must inspect Maynard's chest in London.

As soon as they returned, Maynard wrote to Uncle Walrus (Florence's brother, Sir Walter Langdon-Brown) with a detailed account of his symptoms and their history:

> Mother wants me to consult you about my chest. . . . Some four years ago [it was five and a half years] I had an acute attack of intercostal rheumatism with a slight temperature, and remained in bed for some time, being attended by L. B. Cole of Cambridge.* At that time I had a good deal of pain from time to time simply lying in bed. After I had recovered from that, I had no noticeable trouble before, say, six months

*Dr Leslie Cole was a physician at Addenbrooke's Hospital, Cambridge.

ago. At the end of the summer, however, and during the winter I was rather liable to an attack of breathlessness and discomfort in the chest on starting a walk. If, however, I rested a little and persevered, this would pass off. . . . The pain, however, such as it was, was exactly the same in quality as that which I now have more acutely.

Early the previous term (in January) he had had an attack of 'flu without temperature, but when he recovered he found that if he walked more than fifty yards he suffered 'great distress' in the chest. Then the 'flu came back much more acutely, with a high temperature. So long as he lay in bed he had no chest 'rheumatism' but it started as soon as he got up. This continued. Both in Cannes and on the way back he had had these attacks in bed. They left him winded, without having appreciable panting or rapid heart beat. 'At present I can only potter about in the neighbourhood of the house and cannot possibly manage a walk.' Four years before 'the pain seemed to be in the neighbourhood of the heart', but this time the position was 'high up in the middle of the chest between the tips of the lungs'. At Cannes he had drunk a 'bottle of quack medicine' obtained by Lydia. He had been using infra-red heat on his chest ten minutes each night and morning followed by rubbing with an unguent.

Uncle Walrus examined him on 31 March and had an X-ray of his chest taken next day. He reported on 8 April that Maynard's recent influenza 'has had a slightly poisonous effect on certain muscles in the heart or on the chest wall, but there is no evidence of any organic change'. Every precaution must be taken not to overtax the heart muscle 'while it is being given time to recover from the infection'. He prescribed daily doses of 'an improvement on luminal . . . in conjunction with a heart tonic . . . called protheonal'. A few days later Maynard complained to Langdon-Brown that the medicine was making him dopey and unfit for work. What Uncle Walrus failed to discover were the streptococcal bacteria swarming around in Maynard's mouth.

Keynes returned to Cambridge, where, after lunch on 4 May, he had five spasms of a different character. But he carried on until he collapsed, apparently at Harvey Road, on Whit Sunday, 16 May. On 20 May, Langdon-Brown reported to Florence that 'his heart muscle is somewhat damaged and it is vital that he should have a complete investigation and a long rest however difficult it may appear to be'. But he still had no idea of the extent of the problem. Keynes, he wrote, had suffered a 'pseudo angina'; the 'prognosis is a good one, sudden death not occurring'. This was too reassuring. Maynard stayed in bed in Harvey Road for over a month, nursed by Florence and Lydia: he still managed to write a letter to *The Times* on the gold problem. Friends commiserated, Virginia Woolf writing to Lydia on 6 June, 'I hope he won't get stronger *mentally* as his normal strength is quite enough for me.'

On 19 June he was taken by ambulance to Ruthin Castle in Wales, a sanatorium for the wealthy. F. C. Scott, his colleague on the Provincial, had recommended it as 'supreme in diagnosis' if rather primitive in its methods of treatment. There, the throat specialists discovered, as he told his brother Geoffrey, that his tonsils were in a 'shocking condition, covered with pus to the naked eye and creeping apparently with animals called fusillaria. . . . I gather that [Paterson, his physician] took the view . . . that there was enough poison distilling the system here to account for all the other symptoms. They have been tackling this by painting the tonsils ten times with a preparation of organic arsenic.' Bacterial endocarditis was the official diagnosis, a complication of rheumatic heart disease. Today this diagnosis seems unlikely. Subacute bacterial endocarditis is a sequel to damage of a heart valve from previous rheumatic fever, when *streptococcus viridans* settles on the scarred valve. But the symptoms of which Maynard complained were the classic symptoms of 'angina of effort', as a result of the narrowing of the coronary arteries, with coronary thrombosis as a possible outcome. His collapse in May seems to have been due to such an attack. No one at the time would have picked up Maynard's smoking as a possible cause.[24]

Keynes could not remain quiet. Soon his secretary had arrived with vast piles of correspondence. Lydia moved in to the neighbouring 'widows' hotel'. 'I fancy the embargo on movements of the mind may be removed before the embargo on movements of the body,' he scribbled to her on 29 June.

At least I hope so! For my mind is terribly active. They can take away drink from patients who drink too much and food from those who eat too much. But they can't take my thoughts away from me. When the Great White Chief comes round this afternoon, I shall have to confess that I have written a letter this morning to the Chancellor of the Exchequer.

At the end of June news reached Vanessa that her son Julian had been killed in Spain. From Ruthin Castle Keynes wrote to her by hand:

My dearest Nessa,
    A line of sympathy and love from us both on the loss of your dear and beautiful boy with his pure and honourable feelings. It was fated that he should make his protest, as he was entitled to do, with his life, and one can say nothing.
    With love and affection,
    Maynard

Bibliography and Sources

The literature, primary and secondary, on the Keynesian Revolution is immense. There is a case for trying to make the bibliography exhaustive, if only for reference purposes. However, I have decided to include only those sources which I have cited, or which in other ways helped me tell the story I have told. The bulk of them, that is, whether contemporary or later, refer to the events which took place between the years 1920 and 1937, and not to the subsequent history of the Keynesian Revolution. D. E. Moggridge's *John Maynard Keynes: An Economist's Biography*, Routledge, 1992, appeared after this volume was completed.

(1) MANUSCRIPT COLLECTIONS CONSULTED

I have followed the procedure adopted in the first volume of this biography of listing the manuscript collections consulted by location. Where I have cited papers consulted, the reference is to the collection alone; for example, references to the Keynes Papers, located at King's College, Cambridge, will be to KP. Abbreviations are given only for collections cited.

KING'S COLLEGE, CAMBRIDGE

The bulk of the manuscript sources consulted for this volume are in the Modern Archives of the King's College Library. Originally, Keynes's 'personal papers' were housed at King's College, while his 'economic papers' were deposited at the Marshall Library, Cambridge. Much of the latter material has been published in the *Collected Writings of John Maynard Keynes* (see next section). In 1986, following the completion of the *Collected Writings* edition, the 'economic papers' were transferred to King's College. A start was made by the then Modern Archivist, Michael Halls, on reclassifying the 'personal papers', which are now listed as PP. This has been carried further by the present Modern Archivist, Ms Jacqueline Cox. In particular, all the correspondence previously found in Boxes 17–19, 20–1, 22–4, 30–2, 34–6, most of that in Box 38 envelopes 1–6 and other items not previously listed were amalgamated in a new 'Correspondence' file, PP/45. References to these items will not, therefore, be consistent with those given in volume 1 of this biography. In all cases, I use the classification system in the current catalogue.

There will be no reference to source in citations from three important 'runs' of correspondence from the Personal Papers: (1) JMK and his parents, hitherto in Boxes 34–6, (2) JMK and Lydia Keynes, hitherto in Boxes 22–4, and (3) JMK and Lytton Strachey, hitherto unlisted. They are all in PP/45. All other citations from the Keynes Papers are referenced KP.

The King's College Library houses several other collections which I have consulted: the Charleston Papers (copies only); the E. M. Forster Papers; the J. T. Sheppard Papers; the Sebastian Sprott Papers; the Nathaniel Wedd Papers; and Miscellaneous Correspondence.

BANK OF ENGLAND

Norman's Diary is filed under ADM 20; Governor's papers under G1; Sir Charles Addis's papers under ADM 16; Otto Niemeyer's Papers under OV9. File EID 1/2 is on the Macmillan Committee; EID 4 is on Home Finance.

UNIVERSITY OF BIRMINGHAM

Austen Chamberlain Papers.

BODLEIAN LIBRARY

R. H. Brand Papers; J. L. Hammond Papers; MSS of the Society for the Protection of Science and Learning.

BRITISH LIBRARY

The most important collection for the purposes of this volume is the Strachey Papers, Add. MSS 60655–734. In addition, there are (1) the JMK and Duncan Grant correspondence, 1908–46, Add. MSS 57930–1; (2) JMK and Macmillan & Co., Ltd., Add. MSS 55201–4; (3) JMK's letters to O. T. Falk, Add. MSS 57923; (4) the Christabel Maclaren Papers (letters from Samuel Courtauld), Add. MSS 52432–5; and (5) the C. P. Scott Papers, Add. MSS 50906–9.

CHURCHILL COLLEGE, CAMBRIDGE

Ralph Hawtrey Papers.

COLUMBIA UNIVERSITY, RARE BOOK AND MANUSCRIPT LIBRARY

There are letters from JMK to Frank Altschul (Herbert H. Lehman Papers), J. M. Clark, M. A. Copeland, Albert H. Hart, Lewis L. Lorwin, Allan Nevins, Marie M. Meloney, Wesley C. Mitchell, E. R. A. Seligman and F. A. Vanderlip. The Seligman correspondence is the most substantial, relating mainly to the period 1914–15.

HARVARD UNIVERSITY

Thomas Lamont Papers; J. A. Schumpeter Papers.

HOUSE OF LORDS

Lloyd George Papers; J. C. C. Davidson Papers.

HUMANITIES RESEARCH CENTER, AUSTIN, TEXAS

Contains letters from JMK to Barbara Bagenal, Dora Carrington, J. L. Garvin, Mary Hutchinson and Ottoline Morrell.

UNIVERSITY OF ILLINOIS

H. G. Wells Papers.

LIBRARY OF CONGRESS

Felix Frankfurter Papers; Emmanuel Goldenweiser Papers.

LONDON SCHOOL OF ECONOMICS, BRITISH LIBRARY OF POLITICAL AND ECONOMIC SCIENCE

Edwin Cannan Papers; Dalton Papers; Durbin Papers; Meade Papers.

NUFFIELD COLLEGE, OXFORD

Hubert Henderson Papers; Sir Stafford Cripps Papers.

PRINCETON UNIVERSITY

Bernard Baruch Papers; John Foster Dulles Papers.

PUBLIC RECORD OFFICE, KEW GARDENS

Treasury Papers. The most important Treasury files are the general class T 160, including T 160/197 on the proceedings of the Chamberlain–Bradbury Committee, and T 160/463 on the return to the gold standard, and the miscellaneous papers T 172, which include T 172/1208 on the unemployment situation in 1921, and T 172/1499B on the gold standard (containing Churchill's famous Memorandum of 22 February 1925). Sir Otto Niemeyer's Papers, T 176, include T 176/16 on the consequences of the return to the gold standard; Sir Richard Hopkins's Papers, T 175, include T 175/26 on the unemployment situation 1928–30, and T 175/17 on JMK's 'Means to Prosperity' and the Kisch Plan for the World Economic Conference of 1933. Sir Frederick Phillips's Papers, T 177, include T 177/7 on gold problems, 1932.

FRANKLIN D. ROOSEVELT LIBRARY, HYDE PARK, NEW YORK

Franklin D. Roosevelt Papers.

SUSSEX UNIVERSITY

Monk's House Papers include copies of seven letters from JMK to Leonard Woolf, 1914–30, and five copies and one original from JMK to Virginia Woolf, 1912–38.

TRINITY COLLEGE, CAMBRIDGE

F. Pethick Lawrence Papers.

TATE GALLERY, LONDON

Vanessa Bell's letters to Roger Fry, 1920–32.

WISCONSIN UNIVERSITY LIBRARY

J. R. Commons Papers.

YALE UNIVERSITY, STERLING MEMORIAL LIBRARY

Irving Fisher Papers; Russell C. Leffingwell Papers; Walter Lippmann Papers; Paul M. Warburg Papers; Edward House Papers. The papes of the *Yale Review* in the Beinecke Rare Book and Manuscript Library contain eight JMK letters for the period 1931–3, mainly dealing with his 'National Self-Sufficency' articles.

PRIVATE COLLECTIONS

Duncan Grant's letters to Vanessa Bell are owned by Miss Henrietta Garnett; Harold Bowen's Diary by Mrs Clarissa Heald; O. T. Falk Papers by Mrs Roland Falk; R. H. Brand's letters to his wife by the Hon. Lady Ford; Miss Naomi Bentwich's 'Lucifer by Starlight: A Human Document depicting a Spiritual Adventure' by Mr Edward Birnberg.

OTHER

Professor T. K. Rymes of Carleton University, Ottawa, has assembled the lecture notes taken by Keynes's students between 1932 and 1935 in a single manuscript volume, 'Keynes's Lectures, 1932–35: Notes of Students', which can be purchased directly from him. These constitute the raw material for a published volume of lecture notes (see next section).

(2) PUBLISHED PRIMARY SOURCES

The main published source is *The Collected Writings of John Maynard Keynes*, 30 vols, including Bibliography and Index, published by Macmillan/CUP for the Royal Economic Society, 1971–89. Volumes XV to XVIII were edited by Elizabeth Johnson, the remainder by Donald Moggridge. They include practically all Keynes's published writings, including journalism, as well as a generous proportion of his unpublished economic correspondence, notes, memoranda, lectures and speeches. They do not include his personal correspondence, except for a few excerpts from his letters to his parents and his wife, nor his unpublished philosophical writings. All references to Keynes's published writings are to this edition, although the text is not always identical to the originals – for example, capital letters are used more sparingly. References are also given to the published versions of the manuscript material. Where references are given to the Keynes Papers themselves, this is to material which has not been published.

The volumes which have been most relevant to the writing of this book are:

II. *The Economic Consequences of the Peace* (1919) 1971
III. *A Revision of the Treaty* (1922) 1971
IV. *A Tract on Monetary Reform* (1923) 1971
V. *A Treatise on Money*, i: *The Pure Theory of Money* (1930) 1971
VI. *A Treatise on Money*, ii: *The Applied Theory of Money* (1930) 1971
VII. *The General Theory of Employment, Interest, and Money* (1936) 1973
VIII. *A Treatise on Probability* (1921) 1973
IX. *Essays in Persuasion* (1931) 1972. Full text with additions
X. *Essays in Biography* (1933) 1972. Full text with additions
XI. *Economic Articles and Correspondence: Academic* (1983)
XII. *Economic Articles and Correspondence: Investment and Editorial* (1983)
XIII. *The General Theory and After: Part I, Preparation* (1973)
XIV. *The General Theory and After: Part II, Defence and Development* (1973)
XVII. *Activities 1920–2: Treaty Revision and Reconstruction* (1977)
XVIII. *Activities 1922–32: The End of Reparations* (1978)
XIX. *Activities 1922–9: The Return to Gold and Industrial Policy*, 2 vols (1981)
XX. *Activities 1929–31: Rethinking Employment and Unemployment Policies* (1981)
XXI. *Activities 1931–9: World Crises and Policies in Britain and America* (1982)
XXVIII. *Social, Political and Literary Writings* (1982)
XXIX. *The General Theory and After: A Supplement (to vols XIII and XIV)* (1979)
XXX. *Bibliography and Index* (1989)

The other main published primary sources are:

The First Interim Report of the Committee on Currency and Foreign Exchanges after the War [Cunliffe Committee], Cmd 9182, 1918
Report of the Committee on the Currency and Bank of England Note Issues [Chamberlain–Bradbury Committee], Cmd 2993, 1924–5
Memoranda on Certain Proposals Relating to Unemployment, Cmd 3331, May 1929
Report on the Committee on Finance and Industry [Macmillan Committee], Cmd 2897, 1931. Minutes of Evidence, 2 vols, Treasury, 1931
Polly Hill and Richard Keynes (eds), *Lydia and Maynard: The Letters of Lydia Lopokova and John Maynard Keynes*, André Deutsch, 1989, is an edited version of the correspondence covering the years 1922–5 only. I have aligned my own quotations from the letters for this period as far as possible with those of this edition, though sometimes I have preferred my own transcriptions of Lydia Lopokova's idiosyncratic prose

Otherwise the main runs of published primary sources are:

Anne Olivier Bell (ed.), assisted by Andrew McNeillie, *The Diary of Virginia Woolf*, vols i–v, Hogarth Press, 1977–84
Lord D'Abernon, *An Ambassador of Peace: Pages from the Diary of Viscount D'Abernon*, 3 vols, Hodder & Stoughton, 1929
Max Freedman (ed.), *Roosevelt and Frankfurter: Their Correspondence 1928–1945*, Bodley Head, 1968
Joseph P. Lasch, *From the Diaries of Felix Frankfurter*, W. W. Norton, 1975
Norman and Jeanne MacKenzie (eds), *The Diary of Beatrice Webb*, 4 vols, Virago/LSE, 1982–5
Perry Meisel and Walter Kendrick (eds), *Bloomsbury/Freud: The Letters of James and Alix Strachey 1924–1925*, Chatto & Windus, 1986

Keith Middlemas (ed.), *Thomas Jones, Whitehall Diary 1916–1930*, 2 vols, OUP, 1969
N. Nicolson (ed.), *Harold Nicolson, Diaries and Letters 1930–1939*, Collins, 1966
——, (ed.) assisted by Joanne Trautmann, *The Letters of Virginia Woolf*, 6 vols, Hogarth Press, 1975–80
Ben Pimlott (ed.), *The Political Diary of Hugh Dalton, 1918–1940, 1945–1960*, Jonathan Cape, 1986
Elliott Roosevelt (ed.), *FDR, His Personal Letters 1928–1945*, 2 vols, Harrap, 1949
T. K. Rymes (ed.), *Keynes's Lectures 1932–1935: Notes of a Representative Student*, Macmillan Press, 1989
David Scrase and Peter Croft, *Maynard Keynes, Collector of Pictures, Books and Manuscripts*, Fitzwilliam Catalogue, 1983
Frederic Spotts (ed.), *Letters of Leonard Woolf*, Weidenfeld & Nicolson, 1989
Denys Sutton (ed.), *Letters of Roger Fry*, 2 vols, Chatto & Windus, 1972
G. H. von Wright (ed.), with an intro., assisted by B. F. McGuinness, *Ludwig Wittgenstein: Letters to Russell, Keynes and Moore*, Basil Blackwell, 1974

(3) SECONDARY SOURCES

BOOKS

Peter Ackroyd, *T. S. Eliot*, Hamish Hamilton, 1984
Derek H. Aldcroft, *From Versailles to Wall Street 1919–1929*, Allen Lane, 1977
——, *The British Economy between the Wars*, Philip Allan, 1983
Edward J. Amadeo, *Keynes's Principle of Effective Demand*, Edward Elgar, 1989
Noël Annan, *Our Age: Portrait of a Generation*, Weidenfeld & Nicolson, 1990
Pier Francesco Asso, *The Economist behind the Model: The Keynesian Revolution in Historical Perspective*, Quaderno di Ricerche, No. 18, 1990
A. J. Ayer, *Part of My Life*, Collins, 1987
Geoffrey Barraclough, *An Introduction to Contemporary History*, Penguin Books, 1967
Norman Barry, *Hayek's Social and Economic Philosophy*, Macmillan, 1979
Bernard Baruch, *The Public Years*, Odhams, 1961
Bradley W. Bateman and John B. Davis (eds), *Keynes and Philosophy: Essays on the Origin of Keynes's Thought*, Edward Elgar, 1991
C. W. Beaumont, *Diaghilev Ballet in London: A Personal Record*, Putnam, 1940
Clive Bell, *Civilisation*, Chatto & Windus, 1928
——, *Poems*, Hogarth Press, 1921
Quentin Bell, *Bloomsbury*, 1968
D. M. Bensusan-Butt, *On Economic Knowledge: A Sceptical Miscellany*, Australian National University, 1980
Michael Bentley, *The Liberal Mind 1914–1929*, CUP, 1977
Michael Bentley and John Stevenson (eds), *High and Low Politics in Modern Britain*, Clarendon Press, 1983
Isaiah Berlin, *Personal Impressions*, Hogarth Press, 1980
Robert John Bigg, *Cambridge and the Monetary Theory of Production*, Macmillan, 1990
Mark Blaug, *Great Economists before Keynes*, Wheatsheaf, 1986
——, *Great Economists since Keynes*, Wheatsheaf, 1985
——, *John Maynard Keynes: Life, Ideas, Legacy*, Macmillan Press, 1990
Andrew Booth and Melvyn Pack, *Employment, Capital and Economic Policy: Great Britain 1919–1939*, Basil Blackwell, 1985
John Bowle, *Viscount Samuel*, Gollancz, 1957
Andrew Boyle, *The Climate of Treason*, Hutchinson, rev. edn, 1980
——, *Montagu Norman*, Cassell, 1967
S. Broadberry, *The British Economy between the Wars: A Macroeconomic Survey*, Basil Blackwell, 1986
Neville Brown, *Dissenting Forbears: The Maternal Ancestors of J. M. Keynes*, Phillimore, 1988
J. M. Buchanan, John Burton and R. E. Wagner, *The Consequences of Mr. Keynes*, IEA, 1978
Richard Buckle, *Diaghilev*, Weidenfeld & Nicolson, 1978
A. Bullock, *The Life and Times of Ernest Bevin*, i, William Heinemann, 1960

John Burton (ed.), *Keynes's General Theory: Fifty Years On*, IEA, 1986

John Campbell, *Lloyd George: The Goat in the Wilderness 1922–1931*, Jonathan Cape 1977

Anna M. Carabelli, *On Keynes's Method*, Macmillan Press, 1988

Hugh and Mirabel Cecil, *Clever Hearts: Desmond and Molly MacCarthy: A Biography*, Victor Gollancz, 1990

A. Chandavarkar, *Keynes and India: A Study in Economics and Biography*, Macmillan Press, 1989

Kenneth Clark, *The Other Half: A Self-Portrait*, vol. 2 of his autobiography, John Murray, 1977

Peter Clarke, *The Keynesian Revolution in the Making 1924–1936*, Clarendon Press, Oxford, 1988

S. V. O. Clarke, *Central Bank Cooperation 1924–1931*, CUP, 1971

Henry Clay (ed.), *The Interwar Years and Other Papers: A Selection from the Writings of Hubert Douglas Henderson*, Oxford, 1955

Alan Coddington, *Keynesian Economics: The Search for First Principles*, George Allen & Unwin, 1983; reviewed by John Fender, *EJ*, December 1983, 914–16

Douglas Cooper, *The Courtauld Collection*, with a memoir of Samuel Courtauld by Anthony Blunt, Athlone Press, 1954

B. A. Corry, *Money, Saving and Investment in English Economics 1800–1850*, Macmillan, 1962

Maurice Cowling, *The Impact of Labour 1920–1924*, CUP, 1971

Derek Crabtree and A. P. Thirlwall (eds), *Keynes and the Bloomsbury Group*, Macmillan Press, 1980

C. A. R. Crosland, *The Future of Socialism*, Jonathan Cape, 1956

Nicholas Davenport, *Memoirs of a City Radical*, Weidenfeld & Nicolson, 1974

——, *The Split Society*, 1964

Joseph S. Davis, *The World between the Wars 1919–39*, Johns Hopkins University Press, 1975

Richard Deacon, *The Cambridge Apostles*, Robert Royce, 1985

R. W. Dimand, *The Origins of the Keynesian Revolution*, Edward Elgar, 1988

Ian M. Drummond, *British Economic Policy and the Empire 1919–1939*, George Allen & Unwin, 1972

Bruce Duffy, *The World as I Found It*, Secker & Warburg, 1987

Elizabeth Durbin, *New Jerusalems: The Labour Party and the Economics of Democratic Socialism*, Routledge, 1985

John Eatwell and Murray Milgate (eds), *Keynes's Economics and the Theory of Value and Distribution*, Duckworth, 1983

John Eatwell, Murray Milgate and Peter Newman (eds), *The New Palgrave: A Dictionary of Economics*, 4 vols, Macmillan Press, 1987

Barry Eichengreen (ed.), *The Gold Standard in Theory and Practice*, Methuen, 1985

Eprime Eshag, *From Marshall to Keynes: An Essay on the Monetary Theory of the Cambridge School*, Basil Blackwell, 1963

Keith Feiling, *The Life of Neville Chamberlain*, Macmillan, 1946

Herbert Feis, *1933: Characters in Crisis*, Little, Brown & Co., Boston, Toronto, 1966

George R. Feiwel (ed.), *Joan Robinson and Modern Economic Theory*, i, Macmillan Press, 1989

Carole Fink, *The Genoa Conference: European Diplomacy, 1921–1922*, Chapel Hill, 1984

Irving Fisher, assisted by Harry G. Brown, *The Purchasing Power of Money: Its Determination and Relation to Credit, Interest and Crises*, Macmillan, NY, 1911

Athol Fitzgibbons, *Keynes's Vision: A New Political Economy*, Clarendon Press, 1988

H. E. Fraser, *Great Britain and the Gold Standard*, Macmillan, 1933

Sir James Frazer, *The Golden Bough*, Macmillan, abr. edn, 1924

M. Freeden, *Liberalism Divided*, Clarendon Press, Oxford, 1986

Milton Friedman and Anna Jacobson Schwartz, *The Great Contraction 1929–1933*, Princeton University Press, 1965

J. K. Galbraith, *A Contemporary Guide to Economics, Peace, and Laughter*, Houghton Mifflin, 1971

——, *The Great Crash 1929*, André Deutsch, 3rd edn, 1973

——, *A Life in Our Times: Memoirs*, André Deutsch, 1981

——, *Money: Whence It Came, Where It Went*, André Deutsch, 1975

Angelica Garnett, *Deceived with Kindness: A Bloomsbury Childhood*, Chatto & Windus, 1984

David Garnett, *Great Friends*, Macmillan, 1979

John A. Garraty, *The Great Depression*, Harcourt, Brace, Jovanovich, 1986

J. C. Gilbert, *Keynes's Impact on Monetary Economics*, Butterworth Scientific, 1982

Sean Glynn and Alan Booth (eds), *The Road to Full Employment*, George Allen & Unwin, 1987

Robert Graves and Alan Hodge, *The Long Weekend: A Scoial History of Great Britain 1918–1939*, Faber & Faber, 1950

Martin Green, *Children of the Sun: A Narrative of 'Decadence' in England after 1918*, Constable, 1977

P. J. Grigg, *Prejudice and Judgment*, Jonathan Cape, 1948

G. Haberler, *Prosperity and Depression*, Lake Success, 1946 edn

Ian Hacking, *The Emergence of Probability*, CUP, 1975

Frank Hahn, *Money and Inflation*, Basil Blackwell, 1982

Peter A. Hall (ed.), *The Political Power of Economic Ideas: Keynesianism across Nations*, Princeton University Press, 1989

O. F. Hamouda (ed.), *Controversies in Political Economy: Selected Essays of G. H. Harcourt*, Wheatsheaf Books, 1986

Alvin H. Hansen, *A Guide to Keynes*, McGraw-Hill, 1953

G. H. Harcourt (ed.), *Keynes and His Contemporaries*, Macmillan Press, 1985

——, *The Microeconomic Foundations of Macroeconomics*, Macmillan Press, 1977

José Harris, *William Beveridge*, Clarendon Press, 1977

Seymour Harris, *John Maynard Keynes*, Scribners, 1955

R. F. Harrod, *The Life of John Maynard Keynes*, Macmillan, 1951; Penguin Books, 1972

Arnold Haskell, *Balletomania: The Story of an Obsession*, Victor Gollancz, 1934

R. G. Hawtrey, *The Art of Central Banking*, Longmans, 1932

——, *Currency and Credit*, Longmans, 1919; reviewed by JMK, *EJ*, September 1920, *CW*, xi, 411–14

F. A. Hayek, *Money, Capital, and Fluctuations*, Routledge, 1984

——, *New Studies in Philosophy, Politics, Economics and the History of Ideas*, Routledge & Kegan Paul, 1978

——, *Prices and Production*, Routledge, 1931

——, *A Tiger by the Tail*, IEA, 2nd edn, 1978

Charles H. Hession, *John Maynard Keynes: A Personal Biography of the Man Who Revolutionized Capitalism and the Way We Live*, Macmillan, NY; Collier Macmillan, London, 1984

J. R. Hicks, *Critical Essays in Monetary Theory*, Clarendon Press, Oxford, 1979 edn

Michael J. Hogan, *Informal Entente: The Private Structure of Cooperation in Anglo-American Economic Diplomacy 1918–1928*, University of Missouri Press, 1977

Martin Hollis, *The Cunning of Reason*, CUP, 1987

Michael Holroyd, *Bernard Shaw*, 4 vols, Chatto & Windus, 1988–92

——, *Lytton Strachey*, 2 vols, William Heinemann, 1967–8; Penguin edn repr. with revs, 1979

Calvin Hoover, *Memoirs of Capitalism, Communism, and Nazism*, Duke University Press, 1965

Alistair Horne, *Macmillan 1894–1956*, Macmillan, 1988

T. E. B. Howarth, *Cambridge between the Wars*, Collins, 1978

Susan Howson and Donald Winch, *The Economic Advisory Council 1930–1939: A Study in Economic Advice during Depression and Recovery*, CUP, 1977

David Hubback, *No Ordinary Press Baron: A Life of Walter Layton*, Weidenfeld & Nicolson, 1985

Terence W. Hutchison, *Keynes and the 'Keynesians' . . . ?*, with commentaries by Lord Kahn and Sir Austin Robinson, IEA, 1977

——, *On Revolutions and Progress in Economic Knowledge*, Cambridge University Press, 1978

——, *The Politics and Philosophy of Economics*, Basil Blackwell, 1981

Geoffrey Ingham, *Capitalism Divided? The City and Industry in British Social Development*, Macmillan Education, 1984

Erin E. Jacobsson, *A Life for Sound Money*, Clarendon Press, 1979

Harold James, *The German Slump: Politics and Economics 1924–1936*, Clarendon Press, 1986

Roy Jenkins, *Asquith*, Collier, 1964

——, *Baldwin*, Collier, 1987

Elizabeth S. Johnson and Harry G. Johnson, *The Shadow of Keynes: Understanding Keynes, Cambridge, and Keynesian Economics*, Basil Blackwell, 1978

E. L. Jones, *The European Miracle: Environments, Economics and Geopolitics in the History of Europe and Asia*, CUP, 1981

J. H. Jones, *Josiah Stamp, Public Servant: The Life of the First Baron Stamp of Shortlands*, Pitman, 1964

Richard Kahn, *The Economics of the Short Period*, Macmillan Press, 1989

——, *The Making of Keynes' General Theory*, CUP, 1984; reviewed by A. P. Thirlwall, *TLS*, 20 July 1984

J. M. Kenworthy, *Sailors, Statesmen – and Others: An Autobiography*, Rich & Cowan, 1933

Daniel J. Kevles, *In the Name of Eugenics, Genetics, and the Uses of Human Heredity*, A. A. Knopf, NY, 1985

J. N. Keynes, *Studies and Exercises in Formal Logic*, Macmillan, 1906 ed.

Milo Keynes (ed.), *Essays on John Maynard Keynes*, CUP, 1975

—— (ed.), *Lydia Lopokova*, Weidenfeld & Nicolson, 1983

Charles P. Kindleberger, *The World in Depression 1929–1939*, Allen Lane, 1977

King's College Cambridge, *John Maynard Keynes 1883–1946: A Memoir*, CUP, 1949

E. D. Klemke, *Studies in the Philosophy of G. E. Moore*, Quadrangle Books, Chicago, 1965

Leszek Kolakowski, *Positivist Philosophy: From Hume to the Vienna Circle*, Penguin Books, 1972 edn

F. Lavington, *The English Capital Market*, Frank Cass, 1921

——, *The Trade Cycle*, P. S. King, 1925

Tony Lawson and Hashem Pesaran (eds), *Keynes' Economics: Methodological Issues*, Croom Helm, 1985

Melvin P. Leffler, *The Elusive Quest: America's Pursuit of European Stability and French Security 1919–1933*, University of North Carolina Press, 1979

Axel Leijonhufvud, *On Keynesian Economics and the Economics of Keynes*, OUP, NY, 1966

Sir Frederick Leith-Ross, *Money Talks: Fifty Years of International Finance*, Hutchinson, 1968

Robert Lekachman, *The Age of Keynes: A Biographical Study*, Penguin Books, 1967

—— (ed.), *Keynes's General Theory: Reports of Three Decades*, St Martin's Press/Macmillan, 1964

W. Arthur Lewis, *Economic Survey 1919–1939*, George Allen & Unwin, 1949

D. Lloyd George, *The Truth about Reparations and War-Debts*, William Heinemann, 1932

F. L. Lucas, *Tragedy in Relation to Aristotle's Poetics*, Hogarth Press, 1927

Nesta MacDonald, *Diaghilev Observed*, Dance Horizons, NY/Dance Books, London, 1975

Walter A. McDougall, *France's Rhineland Diplomacy 1914–1924*, Princeton University Press, 1978

Alasdair Macintyre, *After Virtue: A Study in Moral Theory*, Duckworth, 1981

R. M. MacIver, *The Modern State*, Clarendon Press, 1926

R. McKenna, *Post-War Banking Policy*, William Heinemann, 1928

Harold Macmillan, *Winds of Change 1914–1939*, Macmillan, 1966

Charles S. Maier, *Recasting Bourgeois Europe: Stabilization in France, Germany, and Italy in the Decade after World War I*, Princeton University Press, 1975

Étienne Mantoux, *The Carthaginian Peace or The Economic Consequences of Mr. Keynes*, OUP, 1946

Sally Marks, *The Illusion of Peace: International Relations in Europe 1918–1939*, Macmillan Press, 1976

David Marquand, *Ramsay MacDonald*, Jonathan Cape, 1977

A. Marshall, *Industry and Trade*, Macmillan, 1919

——, *Money, Credit and Commerce*, Macmillan, 1923

——, *Principles of Economics*, Macmillan, 8th edn, 1920

Kingsley Martin, *Editor*, Hutchinson, 1968

——, *Father Figures*, Hutchinson, 1966

Léonide Massine, *My Life in Ballet*, Macmillan, 1968

James Meade, *An Introduction to Economic Analysis and Policy*, OUP, 1936

Robert Medley, *Drawn from Life: A Memoir*, Faber & Faber, 1983

James Meenan, *George O'Brien: A Biographical Memoir*, Gill and Macmillan, 1980

Carl Melchior, Ein Buch des Gedenkens und der Freundschaft, with a foreword by Dr Jurt Seiveking, J. C. B. Mohr (Paul Siebeck) Tübingen, 1967

Allan H. Meltzer, *Keynes's Monetary Theory: A Different Interpretation*, CUP, 1988

Keith Middlemas and John Barnes, *Baldwin: A Biography*, Weidenfeld & Nicolson, 1969

Roger Middleton, *Towards the Managed Economy: Keynes, the Treasury and the Fiscal Policy Debate of the 1930s*, Methuen, 1985

Murray Milgate, *Capital and Employment: A Study of Keynes's Economics*, Academic Press, 1982

Piero V. Mini, *Keynes, Bloomsbury, and The General Theory*, Macmillan Press, 1991

H. P. Minsky, *John Maynard Keynes*, Macmillan Press, 1976; reviewed by B. A. Corry, *EJ*, June 1977, 335–6

Dmitri Mirsky, *The Intelligentsia of Great Britain*, trans. Alec Brown, Victor Gollancz, 1935

D. E. Moggridge, *British Monetary Policy 1924–1931: The Norman Conquest of $4.86*, CUP, 1972
——, *Keynes*, Macmillan Press, 1976; paperback, Fontana Great Masters Series, 1976; reviewed by B. A. Corry, *EJ*, June 1977, 335–6
——, *The Return to Gold, 1925: The Formulation of Economic Policy and Its Critics*, CUP, 1969
—— (ed.), *Keynes: Aspects of the Man and His Work*, Macmillan Press, 1974
Sir Alfred Mond, *Industry and Politics*, Macmillan, 1927
Ray Monk, *Wittgenstein*, Jonathan Cape, 1990
G. E. Moore, *Philosophical Studies*, Routledge & Kegan Paul, 1922
——, *Principia Ethica*, CUP, 1971 edn
——, *Some Main Problems of Philosophy*, George Allen & Unwin, 1953
E. V. Morgan, *Studies in British Financial Policy 1914–1925*, Macmillan, 1952
K. O. Morgan, *Consensus and Disunity: The Lloyd George Coalition 1918–1922*, Clarendon Press, 1979
Sir Oswald Mosley, *My Life*, Nelson, 1968
C. L. Mowat, *Britain between the Wars 1918–1940*, Methuen, 1955
J. H. Muirhead, *The Platonic Tradition in Anglo-Saxon Philosophy*, George Allen & Unwin, 1931
Harold Nicolson, *Some People*, Constable 1927
Douglass North and Robert Paul Thomas, *The Rise of the Western World: A New Economic History*, CUP, 1973
D. P. O'Brien and J. R. Presley (eds), *Pioneers of Modern Economics in Britain*, Macmillan Press, 1981
R. M. O'Donnell, *Keynes: Philosophy, Economics and Politics*, Macmillan Press, 1989
—— (ed.), *Keynes as Philosopher-Economist*, Macmillan Academic, 1991
C. K. Ogden and I. A. Richards, *The Meaning of Meaning*, Kegan Paul, 1923
Mancur Olson, *The Rise and Decline of Nations: Economic Growth, Stagnation, and Social Rigidities*, Yale University Press, 1982
Frances Partridge, *Memories*, Victor Gollancz, 1981
Don Patinkin, *Anticipations of the General Theory*, Basil Blackwell, 1982; reviewed by Susan Howson, *EJ*, December 1983, 912–14
——, *Keynes's Monetary Thought: A Study of Its Development*, Duke University Press, 1976; reviewed by Edward Nevin, *EJ*, June 1977, 333–4
Don Patinkin and J. Clark Reith (eds), *Keynes, Cambridge, and the General Theory*, Macmillan Press, 1977
D. Pears, *Wittgenstein*, Fontana Modern Masters, 1971
G. C. Peden, *British Rearmament and the Treasury 1932–1939*, Scottish Academic Press, 1979
Frances Perkins, *The Roosevelt I Knew*, Hammond, 1947
A. C. Pigou, *Aspects of British Economic History 1918–1925*, Macmillan, 1947
——, *Economics in Practice*, Macmillan, 1935
——, *Keynes's 'General Theory': A Retrospective View*, Macmillan, 1950
——, *The Theory of Unemployment*, Macmillan, 1933
——, *Unemployment*, Home University Library, 1913
Ben Pimlott, *Hugh Dalton*, Jonathan Cape, 1985
——, *Labour and the Left in the 1930s*, CUP, 1977
Sidney Pollard (ed.), *The Gold Standard and Employment Policies between the Wars*, Methuen, 1970
J. R. Presley, *Robertsonian Economics*, Macmillan Press, 1978
Frank Plumpton Ramsey, *The Foundation of Mathematics and Other Logical Essays*, ed. R. B. Braithwaite, with a preface by G. E. Moore, Macmillan, 1931
Lionel Robbins, *Autobiography of an Economist*, Macmillan, 1971
——, *The Great Depression*, Macmillan, 1934
——, *The Theory of Economic Policy in English Classical Political Economy*, Macmillan, 1952
D. H. Robertson, *Banking Policy and the Price Level: An Essay in the Theory of the Trade Cycle*, P. S. King, 1926
——, *Lectures on Economic Principles*, Fontana Library, 1963
——, *Money*, Nisbet, 1923; rev. edn, 1928
——, *A Study of Industrial Fluctuation*, P. S. King, 1915; rev. edn, LSE, 1948
Joan Robinson, *Collected Economic Papers*, Basil Blackwell, 1960
——, *Contributions to Modern Economics*, Basil Blackwell, 1979
——, *The Economics of Imperfect Competition*, Macmillan, 1933

——, *Introduction to the Theory of Employment*, Macmillan, 1937
——, *The Rate of Interest and Other Essays*, Macmillan, 1952
C. H. Rolph, *Kingsley: The Life, Letters and Diaries of Kingsley Martin*, Victor Gollancz, 1973
W. Ropke, *Crises and Cycles*, William Hodge, 1936
——, *International Economic Disintegration*, William Hodge, 1942
E. Rosenbaum and A. J. Sherman, *M. M. Warburg & Co., 1798–1938, Merchant Bankers of Hamburg*, Hamburg, 1979
S. P. Rosenbaum, *Victorian Bloomsbury: The Early Literary History of the Bloomsbury Group*, i, Macmillan Press, 1987
—— (ed.), *The Bloomsbury Group: A Collection of Memoirs, Commentary and Criticism*, Croom Helm, 1973
Henry Roseveare, *The Treasury: The Evolution of a British Institution*, Allen Lane, 1969
Peter Rowland, *Lloyd George*, Barrie & Jenkins, 1975
A. L. Rowse, *Glimpses of the Great*, Methuen, 1985
——, *Mr. Keynes and the Labour Movement*, Macmillan, 1936
Herman J. Rupieper, *The Cuno Government and Reparations 1922–1923*, Martinus Nijhoff, 1979
B. Russell, *My Philosophical Development*, George Allen & Unwin, 1959
——, *Our Knowledge of the External World*, George Allen & Unwin, 1914; 5th imp. 1969
——, *The Principles of Mathematics*, George Allen & Unwin, 1903, 1937
——, *The Problems of Philosophy*, Williams & Norgate, 1913
Alan Ryan, *Bertrand Russell: A Political Life*, Allen Lane, 1988
Arthur Salter, *Slave of the Lamp*, Weidenfeld & Nicolson, 1967
P. Sargant Florence and J. R. L. Anderson (eds), *C. K. Ogden: A Collective Memoir*, Elek: Pemberton, 1977
R. S. Sayers, *The Bank of England 1891–1944*, 2 vols, CUP, 1976
Arthur M. Schlesinger, Jr, *The Coming of the New Deal*, William Heinemann, 1960
P. A. Schlipp (ed.), *The Philosophy of Bertrand Russell*, 19?
Stephen A. Schuker, *The End of French Predominance in Europe*, University of North Carolina Press, 1976
J. A. Schumpeter, *Capitalism, Socialism, and Democracy*, George Allen & Unwin, 3rd edn, 1952
——, *History of Economic Analysis*, George Allen & Unwin, 1954
——, *Ten Great Economists*, George Allen & Unwin, 1952
G. L. S. Shackle, *The Years of High Theory: Invention and Tradition in Economic Thought 1926–1939*, CUP, 1967
Andrew Sinclair, *The Red and the Blue*, Weidenfeld & Nicolson, 1986
Osbert Sitwell, *An Autobiography*, 5 vols, Macmillan, 1947–50
R. Skidelsky, *John Maynard Keynes: Hopes Betrayed 1883–1920*, Macmillan, 1983; Elisabeth Sifton Books, Viking, 1986; Papermac, 1992
——, *Oswald Mosley*, Macmillan, 1975; 3rd edn paperback, 1990
——, *Politicians and the Slump*, Macmillan, 1967; Penguin Books, 1970
—— (ed.), *The End of the Keynesian Era*, Macmillan Press, 1977
Mark Skousen (ed.), *Dissent on Keynes: A Critical Appraisal of Keynesian Economics*, Praeger, 1992
Lydia Sokolova, *Dancing for Diaghilev*, ed. Richard Buckle, John Murray, 1960
Felix Somary, *The Raven of Zurich*, Hurst, 1960
Frances Spalding, *Roger Fry: Art and Life*, Granada Publishing, 1980
——, *Vanessa Bell*, Weidenfeld & Nicolson, 1983
P. Stansky and W. Abrahams, *Journey to the Frontier*, Constable, 1966
Ronald Steel, *Walter Lippmann and the American Century*, Bodley Head, 1981
Herbert Stein, *The Fiscal Revolution in America*, University of Chicago Press, 1969
Michael Stewart, *Keynes and After*, Penguin Books, 3rd edn, 1986
John Strachey, *The Coming Struggle for Power*, Victor Gollancz, 1932
——, *Revolution by Reason*, Leonard Parson, 1925
Michael Straight, *After Long Silence*, Collins, 1983
B. Taper, *Balanchine, A Biography*, University of California Press, 3rd edn, 1984
A. J. P. Taylor, *English History 1914–1945*, OUP, 1965
Arthur J. Taylor, *Laissez-Faire and State Intervention in Nineteenth-Century Britain*, Macmillan Press, 1972
Peter Temin, *Did Monetary Forces Cause the Great Depression?*, W. W. Norton, 1976

A. P. Thirlwall (ed.), *Keynes and Laissez-Faire*, Macmillan Press, 1978
——, *Keynes as a Policy Adviser*, Macmillan Press, 1980
Marc Trachtenberg, *Reparation in World Politics*, Columbia University Press, 1980
Rexford Tugwell, *The Democratic Roosevelt: A Biography of Franklin D. Roosevelt*, Doubleday, 1957
Marjorie S. Turner, *Joan Robinson and the Americans*, M. E. Sharpe Inc., 1989
Ninette de Valois, *Come Dance with Me: A Memoir 1898–1956*, Hamish Hamiliton, 1957
Immanuel Wallerstein, *The Modern World-System, Capitalist Agriculture and the Origins of the European World-Economy in the Sixteenth Century*, Academic Press, 1974
G. J. Warnock, *English Philosophy since 1900*, OUP, 1958
Simon Watney, *The Art of Duncan Grant*, John Murray, 1990
Sidney and Beatrice Webb, *The Decay of Capitalist Civilisation*, George Allen & Unwin, 1923
Antony West, *H. G. Wells: Aspects of a Life*, Hutchinson, 1984
Knut Wicksell, *Interest and Prices: A Study of the Causes Regulating the Value of Money*, trans. from the German by R. F. Kahn, with an introduction by Bertil Ohlin, Macmillan, 1936 (published in Swedish, 1898)
L. W. Wilkinson, *A Century of King's 1873–1972*, KCC, 1980
——, *Kingsmen of a Century 1873–1972*, KCC, 1980
Philip Williamson, *National Crisis and National Government: British Politics, the Economy and Empire 1926–1932*, CUP, 1992
Donald Winch, *Economics and Policy: A Historical Study*, Collins/Fontana, 1972 edn
Ludwig Wittgenstein, *Note-Books 1914–1916*, ed. G. H. von Wright and G. E. M. Anscombe, Basil Blackwell, 1969
——, *Tractatus Logico-Philosophicus*, trans. from the German by C. K. Ogden, assisted by F. Ramsey, Routledge & Kegan Paul, 1922
John Cunningham Wood (ed.), *John Maynard Keynes: Critical Assessments*, 4 vols, Croom Helm, 1983
Neal Wood, *Communism and British Intellectuals*, Victor Gollancz, 1959
Leonard Woolf, *Downhill All the Way, 1919–1939*, Hogarth Press, 1968
David Worswick and James Trevithic (eds), *Keynes and the Modern World*, CUP, 1983
Harold Wright (ed.), *Cambridge University Studies*, Nicholson & Watson, 1933
Q. Wright (ed.), *Unemployment as a World Problem*, University of Chicago Press, 1931
Warren Young, *Interpreting Mr. Keynes: The IS–LM Enigma*, Polity Press, 1987
A. J. Youngson, *The British Economy 1920–1957*, Allen & Unwin, 1960

ARTICLES, MONOGRAPHS, CHAPTERS

James W. Angell, 'Monetary Theory and Monetary Policy: Some Recent Discussions', *Quarterly Journal of Economics*, February 1925, 267–99
Denise Artaud, 'À Propos de l'Occupation de la Ruhr', *Revue d'Histoire Moderne et Contemporaine*, January–March 1970, 1–21
Jürgen Backhaus, 'Die "Allgemeine Theorie": Reaktionen deutscher Volkswirte', in Harald Hazemann and Otto Steiger (eds), *Keynes' General Theory nach funfzig Jahren*, Duncker & Humblot, Berlin, 1988, 61–81
Giacomo Beccattini, 'L'Acclimatamento del Pensiero di Keynes in Italia: Invito ad un Dibattito', *Passato e Presente*, April 1983, 85–104
D. K. Benjamin and L. A. Kochin, 'Searching for an Explanation of Unemployment in Interwar Britain', *Journal of Political Economy*, 87, 1979, 441–78
William Beveridge, 'Mr. Keynes's Evidence for Overpopulation', *Economica*, February 1924, 1–20
R. D. Collison Black, 'Ralph George Hawtrey 1879–1975', *Proceedings of the British Academy*, vol. 63, 1977, 363–98
Alan Booth, 'The "Keynesian Revolution" in Economic Policy-Making', *Economic History Review*, 2nd series, 36, 1983, 103–23
Knut Borchardt, 'Keynes' Nationale Selbstgenügsamkeitp von 1933', *Zeitschrift für Wirtschafts- und Sozialwissenschaften*, January 1988, 271–84
R. H. Brand, 'A Banker's Reflections on Some Economic Trends', *Economic Journal*, December 1953, 761–70
Karl Britton, 'Recollections of Cambridge 1928–32', *Cambridge Review*, ciii, no. 2270, 1982

S. Broadberry, 'Aggregate Supply in Interwar Britain', *Economic Journal*, June 1986, 467–81

Kathleen Burk, 'Economic Diplomacy between the Wars', *Historical Journal*, 4, 1981, 1003–15

——, 'The House of Morgan in Financial Diplomacy 1920–1930', in B. J. McKercher (ed.), *The Struggle for Supremacy: Anglo-American Relations in the 1920s*, Macmillan Press, 1988

Neville Cain, 'Cambridge and Its Revolution: A Perspective on the Multiplier and Effective Demand', *Economic Record*, June 1979, 108–17

——, 'Hawtrey and the Multiplier Theory', *Economic Record*, June 1981, 68–78

E. Cannan, 'The Meaning of British Bank Deposits', *Economica*, January 1921

George Catephores, *Keynes as a Bourgeois Marxist*, Discussion Paper No. 91–23, University College London Discussion Papers in Economics

J. H. Chau and R. S. Woodward, 'John Maynard Keynes' Investment Performance: A Note', *Journal of Finance*, March 1983, 232–5

Peter Clarke, 'The Politics of Keynesian Economics, 1924–1931', in Michael Bentley and John Stevenson (eds), *High and Low Politics in Modern Britain*, 1983, Clarendon Press, 154–81

Tim Congdon, 'Are We Really All Keynesians Now?', *Encounter*, April 1975, 23–32

F. C. Costigliola, 'Anglo-French Financial Rivalry in the 1920s', *Journal of Economic History*, December 1977, 911–34

Maurice Cranston, 'Keynes: His Political Ideas and Their Influence', in A. P. Thirlwall (ed.), *Keynes and Laissez-Faire*, Macmillan Press, 1978, 101–16

Paul Davidson, 'Sensible Expectations and the Long-Run Non-Neutrality of Money', *Journal of Post-Keynesian Economics*, Fall 1987, 146–53

E. G. Davis, 'The Correspondence between R. G. Hawtrey and J. M. Keynes on the *Treatise*: The Genesis of Output Adjustment Models', *Canadian Journal of Economics*, November 1980, 716–24

Sir Piers Debenham, 'The Economic Advisory Council and the Great Depression', Oxford Economic Papers Supplement, *Sir Hubert Henderson*, 1953, 28–47

Maurice Dobb, 'A Sceptical View of the Theory of Wages', *Economic Journal*, December 1929, 506–19

J. T. Dunlop. 'The Movement of Real and Money Wage Rates', *Economic Journal*, September 1938, 413–34

Barry Eichengreen, 'The Capital Levy in Theory and Practice', in Rudiger Dornbusch and Mario Draghi (eds), *Public Debt Management: Theory and History*, CUP, 1990, 191–220

——, 'Sterling and the Tariff 1929–1932', *Princeton Studies in International Finance No. 48*, September 1981

W. Fellner, 'Saving, Investment and the Problem of Neutral Money', *Review of Economic Statistics*, November 1938, 185–93

Giuliano Ferrari Bravo, ' "In the Name of Our Mutual Friend . . .": The Keynes–Cuno Affair', *Journal of Contemporary History*, January 1989, 147–67

Geoffrey Fishburn, 'Keynes and the Age of Eugenics', *The Age Monthly Review*, June 1983

W. R. Garside, 'The Failure of the "Radical Alternative": Public Works, Deficit Finance and British Interwar Unemployment', *Banco di Roma*, Winter 1985, 537–55

D. A. Gillies, 'Keynes as a Methodologist', *British Journal for the Philosophy of Science*, 39, 1988, 117–29

Sean Glynn and Alan Booth, 'Unemployment in Interwar Britain: A Case for Re-Learning the Lessons of the 1930s?', *Economic History Review*, 2nd Series, 36, 1, 1983, 329–48

A. G. Gruchy, 'The Philosophical Basis of the New Keynesian Economics', *Ethics*, July 1948, 235–44

Gottfried Haberler, '*The Great Depression of the 1930s: Can It Happen Again?*', American Enterprise Institute, Reprint No. 118, January 1981

Bjorn Hansson, 'Keynes's Notion of Equilibrium in the *General Theory*', *Journal of Post-Keynesian Economics*, Spring 1985, 332–40

R. F. Harrod, 'Mr. Keynes and Traditional Theory', *Econometrica*, January 1937, 74–86

A. G. Hart, 'An Examination of Mr. Keynes's Price Level Concepts', *Journal of Political Economy*, October 1933, 625–38

R. M. Hartwell, 'Can We Escape?', in Ralph Harris and Arthur Seldon (eds), *The Coming Confrontation*, IEA, 1978, 119–36

R. G. Hawtrey, 'Public Expenditure and the Demand for Labour', *Economica*, March 1925, 38–48

——, review of *A Traction Monetary Reform*, *Economic Journal*, June 1924, 227–35

F. A. Hayek, 'The London School of Economics 1895–1945', *Economica*, February 1946, 1–31

——, review of *A Treatise on Money*, *Economica*, August 1931, 270–95, February 1932, 22–44

——, 'A Rejoinder to Mr. Keynes', *Economica*, November 1931, 398–403

Faith Henderson, 'Editing the Nation', Oxford Economic Papers Supplement, *Sir Hubert Henderson*, 1953, 7–27

J. R. Hicks, 'Dennis Holme Robertson 1890–1963', *Proceedings of the British Academy*, vol. 50, 1964, 305–16

—— 'Mr. Keynes and the "Classics": A Suggested Interpretation', *Econometrica*, April 1937, 147–59

——, 'Mr. Keynes's Theory of Employment', *Economic Journal*, June 1936, 238–53

Susan Howson, 'A Dear Money Man? Keynes on Monetary Policy, 1920', *Economic Journal*, June 1973, 456–64

——, 'The Origins of Dear Money, 1919–20', *Economic History Review*, 2nd series, 27, 1974, 88–107

Elizabeth Johnson, 'John Maynard Keynes: Scientist or Politician?', in Elizabeth S. and Harry G. Johnson, *The Shadow of Keynes*, Basil Blackwell, 1978

Bill Jordan and Mark Drakeford, 'Major Douglas, Money and the New Technology', *New Society*, 24 January 1980

R. F. Kahn, 'The Relation of Home Investment to Unemployment', *Economic Journal*, June 1931, 173–98

——, 'Some Aspects of the Development of Keynes's Thought', *Journal of Economic Literature*, June 1978, 544–58

N. Kaldor, 'Keynes as an Economic Adviser', in A. P. Thirlwall (ed.), *Keynes as a Policy Adviser*, Macmillan Press, 1980, 2–27

——, 'Professor Pigou on Money Wages in Relation to Unemployment', *Economic Journal*, December 1937, 745–53

William Kingston, 'Ideas, Civil Servants and Keynes', *Economic Affairs*, January 1985

Meir Kohn, 'Monetary Analysis, the Equilibrium Method, and Keynes's "General Theory" ', *Journal of Political Economy*, 94, 1986, 1191–1224

J. A. Kregel, 'Monetary Production, Economics, and Monetary Policy', *Économies et Sociétés*, April 1984, 221–32

Paul Lambert, 'The Evolution of Keynes's Thought from the *Treatise on Money* to the *General Theory*', *Annals of Public and Cooperative Economy*, 1969, 243–63

Tony Lawson, 'Keynes and the Analysis of Rational Behaviour', in R. M. O'Donnell (ed.), *Keynes as Philosopher–Economist*, Macmillan Press, 1991, 184–226

——, 'Keynes and Conventions', *Review of Social Economy* (forthcoming)

——, 'Probability and Uncertainty in Economic Analysis', *Journal of Post-Keynesian Economics*, Fall 1988, 38–63

——, 'Realism and Instrumentalism in the Development of Econometrics', *Oxford Economic Papers*, 91, 1989, 236–58

——, 'Uncertainty and Economic Analysis', *Economic Journal*, December 1985, 909–27

Axel Leijonhufvud, *Keynes and the Classics*, IEA, 1969

Bruce Littleboy and V. Mehta, 'Patinkin on Keynes' Theory of Effective Demand', *History of Political Economy*, Summer 1987, 311–28

Rodney Lowe, 'The Erosion of State Intervention in Britain, 1917–1924', *Economic History Review*, 2nd series, 21, 1978, 270–86

Donald M. McCloskey, 'The Literary Character of Economics', *Daedalus*, Summer 1984, 97–119

——, 'The Rhetoric of Economics', *Journal of Economic Literature*, June 1983, 481–517

Andrew MacDonald, 'The Geddes Committee and the Formulation of Public Expenditure Policy, 1921–1922', *Historical Journal*, 32, 2, 1989, 643–74

Walter A. McDougall, 'Political Economy versus National Sovereignty: French Structures for German Economic Integration after Versailles', *Journal of Modern History*, March 1979, 56–67

Sally Marks, 'Reparations Reconsidered: A Reminder', *Central European History*, December 1969, 356–65

K. P. G. Matthews, 'Was Sterling Overvalued in 1925?', *Economic History Review*, 2nd series, 39, 1986, 572–87

Allan H. Meltzer,'Keynes's *General Theory*: A Different Perspective', *Journal of Economic Literature*, March 1981, 34–65

Murray Milgate, 'Keynes and Pigou on the Gold Standard and Monetary Theory', *Contributions to Political Economy*, March 1983, 39–48

Lawrence Minard, 'The Original Contrarian', *Forbes*, 26 September 1983

D. E. Moggridge, 'From the *Treatise* to *The General Theory*: An Exercise in Chronology', *History of Political Economy*, Spring 1973, 72–88

——, 'Keynes: The Economist', in D. E. Moggridge, *Keynes: Aspects of the Man and His Work*, Macmillan Press, 1974, 53–74

D. E. Moggridge and Susan Howson, 'Keynes on Monetary Policy 1919–1946', *Oxford Economic Papers*, July 1974, 227–47

G. Mongiovi, 'Keynes, Hayek and Sraffa: On the Origins of Chapter 17 of *The General Theory*', *Économique Appliquée*, tome XLIII, 1990, 131–56

O. Mosley, 'Revolution by Reason', ILP, 1925

Bertil Ohlin, 'The Reparation Problem: A Discussion: I. Transfer Difficulties, Real and Imagined', *Economic Journal*, June 1929, 172–8; 'Mr. Keynes' Views on the Transfer Problem: II. A Rejoinder', *Economic Journal*, September 1929, 400–4

R. M. O'Donnell, 'Continuity in Keynes's Conception of Probability', in D. E. Moggridge (ed.), *Perspectives on the History of Economic Thought*, iv, Edward Elgar, 1990, 53–72

——, 'Keynes on Mathematics: Philosophical Foundations and Economic Applications', *Cambridge Journal of Economics*, March 1990, 29–47

Redvers Opie, 'Marshall's Time Analysis', *Economic Journal*, June 1931, 198–215

D. Wayne Parsons, 'Keynes and the Politics of Ideas', *History of Political Thought*, Summer 1983, 367–92

——, 'Newton the Man and Keynes the Economist', *Papers in Public Policy*, Series I, Number 3, 1991, Public Policy Research Unit, Queen Mary and Westfield College, London University

Don Patinkin, 'The Chicago Tradition, the Quantity Theory, and Friedman', *Journal of Money, Credit and Banking*, February 1969, 46–70

——, 'The Collected Writings of John Maynard Keynes: From the *Tract* to *The General Theory*', *Economic Journal*, June 1975, 249–69

——, 'Friedman on the Quantity Theory and Keynesian Economics', *Journal of Political Economy*, September/October 1972, 883–905

——, 'In Defence of IS-LM', *Banca Nazionale del Lavoro Quarterly Review*, March 1990, 119–34

——, 'In Search of the "Veil of Money" and the "Neutrality of Money": A Note on the Origin of Terms', *Scandinavian Journal of Economics*, 91, 1989, 131–46

——, 'On Different Interpretations of the *General Theory*', *Journal of Monetary Economics*, 26, 1990, 205–43

George Peden, 'Keynes, the Economics of Rearmament and Appeasement', in Wolfgang J. Mommsen and Lothar Kettenadker (eds), *The Fascist Challenge and the Policy of Appeasement*, Parsons, 1983

——, 'Keynes, the Treasury and Unemployment in the Late 1930s', *Oxford Economic Papers*, March 1980, 1–18

——, 'Sir Richard Hopkins and the "Keynesian Revolution" in Employment Policy, 1929–1945', *Economic History Review*, 2nd series, 36, 1983, 281–96

A. F. W. Plumptre, 'Keynes in Cambridge', *Canadian Journal of Economics*, August 1947, 366–71, repr. in J. C. Wood (ed.), *John Maynard Keynes: Critical Assessments*, i, Croom Helm, 1983, 147–53

J. R. Presley, 'J. M. Keynes and D. H. Robertson: Three Phases of Collaboration', *Research in the History of Economic Thought and Methodology*, 6, 1989, 31–46

——, 'J. M. Keynes and the Real Balance Effect', *Manchester School*, March 1986, 22–30

——, 'Marcel Labordère: A Neglected French Contribution to Trade Cycle Theory', *Kyklos*, vol. 2, 1979, 803–11

Pier Luigi Porta, 'Piero Sraffa 1898–1983', *Rivista Internazionale di Scienze Economiche e Commerciali*, January 1984, 14–20

Frank Ramsey, 'Note on J. M. Keynes's *Treatise on Probability*', *Cambridge Magazine*, Decentennial Number 1912–21, 3–5

D. H. Robertson, Review of JMK's *Economic Consequences of the Peace*, *Economic Journal*, March 1920, 77–84

——, 'Mr. Keynes's Theory of Money', *Economic Journal*, September 1931, 395–411
——, 'Some Notes on Mr. Keynes' General Theory of Employment', *Quarterly Journal of Economics*, November 1936, 169–91
H. M. Robertson, 'J. M. Keynes and Cambridge in the 1920s', *South African Journal of Economics*, September 1983, 407–18
E. A. G. Robinson, 'John Maynard Keynes 1883–1946', *Economic Journal*, March 1947, 1–68. Reproduced in John Cunningham Wood (ed.), *John Maynard Keynes: Critical Assessments*, i, Croom Helm, 1983, 86–143
——, *John Maynard Keynes: Economist, Author, Statesman*, British Academy Lecture, Oxford University Press, 1971, 3–20
Joan Robinson, 'A Parable of Saving and Investment', *Economica*, February 1933, 75–84
W. W. Rostow, 'The Terms of Trade in Theory and Practice', *Economic History Review*, 2nd series, 3, 1950, 1–20
Roy J. Rotheim, 'Interdependence and the Cambridge Tradition', in B. Gerrard and J. Hillard (eds), *The Philosophy and Economics of J. M. Keynes*, Edward Elgar, 1992, 32–58
——, 'Keynes and the Language of Probability and Uncertainty', *Journal of Post-Keynesian Economics*, Fall 1988, 82–99
——, 'Marx, Keynes and the Theory of a Monetary Economy', in G. A. Caravale (ed.), *Marx and Modern Economic Analysis*, Edward Elgar, 1991, 240–63
Bertrand Russell, Review of JMK's *Treatise on Probability*, *Mathematical Gazette*, July 1922
Jacques Rueff, 'Mr. Keynes's Views on the Transfer Problem', *Economic Journal*, September 1929, 388–408
Roberta and David Schaefer, 'The Political Philosophy of J. M. Keynes', *Public Interest*, Spring 1983, 45–61
Stephen A. Schuker, 'American Policy Toward Debts and Reconstruction at Genoa, 1922', in Carole Fink, Axel Frohn and Jurgen Heideking (eds), *Genoa, Rapallo and European Reconstruction in 1922*, CUP, 1991
——, 'The Collected Writings of John Maynard Keynes, volumes 17 and 18', *Journal of Economic Literature*, March 1980, 124–6
R. Skidelsky, 'The American Response to Keynes', in A. P. Thirlwall (ed.), *Keynes and Laissez-Faire*, Macmillan Press, 1978, 79–99
—— 'El Festeig de Lydia', in Marta Pessarrodona (ed.), *El Grup de Bloomsbury*, Fundacio Caixa de Pensions, 1988, 57–66
—— (with Marcus Miller and Paul Weller), 'Fear of Deficit Financing – Is It Rational?', in Rudiger Dornbusch and Mario Darghi (eds), *Public Debt Management: Theory and History*, CUP, 1990, 293–310
——, 'Keynes and Bloomsbury', the Joyce Brown Memorial Lecture, in Michael Holroyd (ed.), *Essays by Divers Hands*, Royal Society of Literature, 1982, 15–27
——, 'Keynes and His Parents', in Stephen R. Graubard (ed.), *Generations*, W. W. Norton, 1978, 71–80
——, 'Keynes and the Reconstruction of Liberalism', *Encounter*, April 1979, 29–39
——, 'Keynes and the State', in Dieter Helm (ed.), *The Economic Borders of the State*, OUP, 1989, 144–52
——, 'Keynes and the Treasury View: The Case for and against an Active Unemployment Policy 1920–1939', in W. J. Mommsen (ed.), *The Emergence of the Welfare State in Britain and Germany*, 1981, 167–87
——, 'Keynes e Sraffa: un caso di non-communicazione', in Riccardo Bellofiore (ed.), *Tra Teoria Economica e Grade Cultura Europea: Piero Sraffa*, Franco Angeli, 1986, 73–84
——, 'Keynes's Philosophy of Practice', in R. M. O'Donnell (ed.), *Keynes as Philosopher-Economist*, Macmillan Press, 1991, 104–23
——, 'Keynes's Political Legacy', in A. Kilmarnock (ed.), *The Radical Challenge*, André Deutsch, 1987, 72–96
——, 'Keynes's Political Legacy', in Omar F. Hamouda and John N. Smithin (eds), *Keynes and Public Policy after Fifty Years*, Edward Elgar, 1988, i, 3–28
——, 'The Political Meaning of the Keynesian Revolution', in R. Skidelsky (ed.), *The End of the Keynesian Era*, Macmillan Press, 1977, 33–40
——, 'Les possibilitats economiques per als nostres nets', in Marta Pessarrodona (ed.), *El Grup de Bloomsbury*, Fundacio Caixa de Pensions, 1988, 45–55

——, 'The Reception of the Keynesian Revolution', in Milo Keynes (ed.), *Essays on John Maynard Keynes*, CUP, 1975, 89–107

——, 'The Revolt against the Victorians', in R. Skidelsky (ed.), *The End of the Keynesian Era*, Macmillan Press, 1977, 1–9

——, 'Some Aspects of Keynes the Man', in Omar F. Hamouda and John N. Smithin (eds), *Keynes and Public Policy after Fifty Years*, Edward Elgar, 1988, i, 157–61

——, 'A Tale of Two Houses', in Hugh Lee (ed.), *A Cézanne in the Hedge and Other Memories of Charleston and Bloomsbury*, Collins & Brown, 1992, 140–9

——, 'Verdicts on Versailles', review of vols 17 and 18 of JMK's Collected Writings, *Times Literary Supplement*, 15 September 1978

Gregor W. Smith and R. Todd Smith, 'Stochastic Process Switching and the Return to Gold 1925', *Economic Journal*, March 1990, 164–75

Arthur Smithies, 'Keynes Revisited', *Quarterly Journal of Economics*, August 1972, 463–75

——, 'Schumpeter and Keynes', *Review of Economics and Statistics*, May 1951, 163–9

P. Sraffa, 'Dr. Hayek on Money and Capital', *Economic Journal*, March 1932, 42–53; F. A. Hayek, 'Money and Capital: A Reply', *ibid.*, June 1932, 237–49; P. Sraffa, 'A Rejoinder', *ibid.*, 249–51

——, 'The Laws of Return under Competitive Conditions', *Economic Journal*, December 1926, 535–50

George Steiner, 'Reflections: The Cleric of Treason', *New Yorker*, 8 December 1980

Richard Stone, *Keynes, Political Arithmetic and Econometrics*, Seventh Keynes Lecture in Economics, British Academy, 1978

L. Tarshis, 'Changes in Real and Money Wages', *Economic Journal*, March 1939, 150–4

Jens Warming, 'International Difficulties Arising out of the Financing of Public Works during a Depression', *Economic Journal*, June 1932, 211–24

Paul Wells, ' "Mr. Churchill" and the *General Theory*', in J. S. Cohen and G. C. Harcourt (eds), *International Monetary Problems and Supply Side Economics: Essays in Honour of Lorie Tarshis*, Macmillan Press, 1986, 9–27

Norbert F. Wiley, 'The Congruence of Weber and Keynes', in Randall Collins (ed.), *Sociological Theory*, Jossey-Bass, San Francisco, 1983, 30–51

Philip Williamson, 'A "Bankers' Ramp"?: Financiers and the British Political Crisis of August 1931', *English Historical Review*, October 1984, 770–806

——, 'Financiers, the Gold Standard and British Politics, 1925–1931', in John Turner (ed.), *Businessmen and Politics: Studies of Business Activity in British Politics 1900–1945*, William Heinemann, 1984

E. G. Winslow, 'Keynes and Freud: Psychoanalysis and Keynes's Account of the "Animal Spirits" of Capitalism', *Social Research*, Winter 1986, 549–78

——, 'Bloomsbury, Freud and the Vulgar Passions', *Social Research*, Winter 1990, 785–819

——, ' "Human Logic" and Keynes's Economics', *Eastern Economic Journal*, Autumn 1986, 413–30

——, 'John Maynard Keynes's "Poetical Economy" ', *Journal of Psychohistory*, Fall 1989, 179–94

UNPUBLISHED PAPERS

Peter Barberis, 'The Keynesian Revolution in Whitehall: An Assessment', Manchester Polytechnic, September 1987

Ingo Barens, 'From the "Banana Parable" to the Principle of Effective Demand', Bergische University, Wuppertal, Germany, undated

Russell Brent Jones, 'The Wages Problem in Employment Policy 1936–48', M.Sc. (Bristol University), 1983

N. Brown, 'Reminiscences of Keynes', speech at the University of Essex, 14 December 1971

Toshiaki Hirai, 'A Study of Keynes: From A Treatise on Money to the General Theory', 1988

Jesper Jesperson, 'Introduction to the Papers on New Interpretations of Keynes' Economic Theory and Method', Roskilde University, November 1990

Bruce Littleboy, 'Conventions: Their Role in Keynes's System and their Broader Significance', 1990

——, 'Why Economists Disagree about Keynes', 1989

Marcus Miller and Alan Sutherland, ' "Speculative" Anticipations and the Return to Gold in 1925' University of Warwick and Centre for Economic Policy Research, February 1991

R. M. O'Donnell, 'Keynes: Philosophy and Economics: An Approach to Rationality and Uncertainty', D.Phil., Cambridge University, 1982

T. J. O'Shaughnessy, 'Short-Period and Long-Period Interpretations of the Principle of Effective Demand', King's College, Cambridge, 1984

Don Patinkin, 'On the Chronology of the General Theory,' Hebrew University of Jerusalem, March 1992

Lorie Tarshis, 'The Keynesian Revolution: What It Meant in the 1930s', undated

Richard Wright, 'On "Madmen" and "Defunct Economists" ', Cambridge University, June 1987

References

These reference notes are intended to be used in conjunction with the Bibliography. Books and articles referred to are cited by author and short title. The following abbreviations have been used:

MANUSCRIPT SOURCES

BE: Bank of England
VBP: Vanessa Bell Papers
HBD: Harold Bowen's Diary
RHBP1: Brand Papers (in Bodleian)
RHBP2: Brand Papers (in possession of the Hon. Lady Ford)
ECP: Edward Cannan Papers
ACP: Austen Chamberlain Papers
CP: Charleston Papers
CW: *Collected Writings*, followed by relevant volume
JRCP: J. R. Commons Papers
OTFP1: O. T. Falk Papers (British Library)
OTFP2: O. T. Falk Papers (in possession of Mrs Roland Falk)
IFP: Irving Fisher Papers
EMFP: E. M. Forster Papers
FFP: Felix Frankfurter Papers
JLGP: J. L. Garvin Papers
EGP: Emmanuel Goldweiser Papers
DGP: Duncan Grant Papers
JRHP: J. R. Hammond Papers

RHP: Ralph Hawtrey Papers
HDHP: Hubert Henderson Papers
KP: Keynes Papers
TLP: Thomas Lamont Papers
RLP: Russell Leffingwell Papers
WLP: Walter Lippmann Papers
LGP: Lloyd George Papers
CMP: Christabel Maclaren Papers
MPP: Macmillan Publishers' Papers
MHP: Monk's House (Woolf) Papers
OMP: Ottoline Morrell Papers
PLP: Pethick Lawrence Papers
FDRP: Franklin Delano Roosevelt Papers
JASP: J. A. Schumpeter Papers
JTSP: J. T. Sheppard Papers
SSP: Sebastian Sprott Papers
SP: Strachey Papers
TP: Treasury Papers
TC: Tuesday Club
NWP: Nathaniel Wedd Papers
HGWP: H. G. Wells Papers

JOURNALS, REFERENCE WORKS

AER: American Economic Review
CAMJE: Cambridge Journal of Economics
CR: Cambridge Review
CJE: Canadian Journal of Economics
CEH: Central European History
DNB: Dictionary of National Biography
EcHR: Economic History Review
EJ: Economic Journal
ER: Economic Record
HPE: History of Political Economy
IJE: Indian Journal of Economics
ILR: International Labour Review
JASA: Journal of the American Statistical Association
JEL: Journal of Economic Literature
JF: Journal of Finance
JMH: Journal of Modern History
JPE: Journal of Political Economy

JRSS: Journal of the Royal Statistical Society
LBMR: Lloyds Bank Monthly Review
MS: Manchester School
MG: Mathematical Gazette
NP: New Palgrave Dictionary of Economics
OEP: Oxford Economic Papers
PQ: Political Quarterly
PSIF: Princeton Studies in International Finance
PBA: Proceedings of the British Academy
PI: Public Interest
QJE: Quarterly Journal of Economics
RHETM: Research in the History of Economic Thought and Methodology
RES: Review of Economic Studies
RSE: Review of Social Economy
SR: Social Research
SAJE: South African Journal of Economics
TLS: Times Literary Supplement

Prologue: What Is One to Do with One's Brains?

1. KP: UA/36.

2. Skidelsky, Keynes, i, 103.

Chapter 1: The Lives of Keynes

1. E. A. G. Robinson, an ex-RAF pilot who had come up to Christ's College to read economics, recalled the 'burning sense of the world's stupidities which animated the lecturer'. In 'John Maynard Keynes 1883–1946', EJ, March 1947, 1; repr. Wood (ed.), John Maynard Keynes, i, 102.

2. Steel, Walter Lippmann, 40.

3. Martin, Father Figures, 101.

4. See Sargant Florence and Anderson (eds), C. K. Ogden, 97.

5. Interview with RB, 22 October 1982.

6. H. G. Durnford in King's College Cambridge's John Maynard Keynes, 16.

7. Brown, Dissenting Forbears, 143–4.

8. Keynes deemed him 'far and away the most brilliant of the younger Classics up here'. MPP: Add. MS. 55201. JMK to D. Macmillan, 9 February 1921. For V. Woolf, see A. O. Bell (ed.), The Diary of Virginia Woolf, i, 305.

9. Brown, Dissenting Forbears, 113.

10. JMK, 'The Great Villiers Connection', CW, x, 63.

11. JMK to BB, 13 November 1920; CW, xvii, 191; JMK to LK, 12 November 1925.

12. Durnford, in King's College Cambridge's John Maynard Keynes, 16.

13. GLS to VW, 28 September 1919; q. Holroyd, Lytton Strachey, ii, 372.

14. VW to Barbara Bagenal, 23 December 1920; Letter 1160 in N. Nicolson (ed.), The Letters of Virginia Woolf, ii.

15. SP: Add. MS. GLS to JBS, 10 September 1921.

16. Rosenbaum (ed.), The Bloomsbury Group, 331.

17. KP: PP/45, Clive Bell to JMK, 16 January 1919.

18. CP: DG to VB, 10 April 1919.

19. See Skidelsky, Keynes, i, 380; CP: DG to VB, 26 July 1919.

20. Mirsky, The Intelligentsia of Great Britain, 113. Cf. Raymond Williams, 'The Significance of "Bloomsbury" as a Social and Cultural Group', in Crabtree and Thirlwall (eds), Keynes and the Bloomsbury Group, 51, 59. Williams sees Bloomsbury as an intellectual and artistic fraction of the British upper class, defined by 'their significant and sustained combination of dissenting influence and influential connection'.

21. David Garnett, Great Friends, 138.

22. Angelica Bell, *Deceived with Kindness*, 48.
23. CP: JMK to VB, 8 January 1919.
24. In Crabtree and Thirlwall, *Keynes and the Bloomsbury Group*, 69–70.
25. A. O. Bell (ed.), *The Diary of Virginia Woolf*, ii, 48.
26. *Ibid.*, 65, 126.
27. Holroyd, *Lytton Strachey*, ii, 391.
28. GLS to Carrington, 31 May 1920; q. Holroyd, *Lytton Strachey*, ii, 387.
29. SP: GLS to JBS, 26 November 1921.
30. A. E. Bell (ed.), *The Diary of Virginia Woolf*, ii, 33.
31. *Ibid.*, 69.
32. *Ibid.*, 120.
33. q. Q. Bell, *Virginia Woolf*, ii, 137.
34. JMK, 'My Early Beliefs', *CW*, x, 447, 450.
35. Harrod, *The Life of John Maynard Keynes*, 283.
36. OTFP2: OTF to his father Eugene Falk, 4 January 1920.
37. RLP: File 103–15.
38. WLP: File 1312.
39. *CW*, ix, p. xvii.
40. For details see *CW*, xvii, 148f.
41. Roseveare, *The Treasury*, 261f.
42. Bernard Baruch's *The Public Years* is a compendium of complaints against Keynes.
43. *CW*, xvii, 7–8.
44. See *CW*, xx, 17.
45. Hubback, *No Ordinary Press Baron*, 64.
46. TC: OTF, 'The Tuesday Club', 23 May 1950.
47. See *CW*, xii, 2.

48. Davenport, obituary in *The Times*, 20 November 1972.
49. Davenport, *Memoirs of a City Radical*, 50.
50. *CW*, xii, 107.
51. *CW*, ix, 329.
52. OTFP2: OTF Diary of the Paris Peace Conference, esp. 22 May 1919: 'Francs have reached 31 to the £ and the views Keynes and myself have always held are proving correct. . . . I think both Keynes and myself are surprised by the Swedish exchange. I certainly never expected the £ to be at a premium in Stockholm by this date. Keynes and I both expect francs and lire to depreciate further and we also expect sterling to depreciate in New York.'
53. OTFP1.
54. It was Brand who suggested OTF to F. S. Oliver, chairman of Debenhams, as the person to advise him on his and his wife's investments. Falk suggested Keynes as well.
55. Steel, *Walter Lippmann*, 75.
56. KP: L/21.
57. *Ibid.*
58. See Skidelsky, *Keynes*, i, 84.
59. Roger Fry told Margery Fry on 21 June 1923 that Vanessa and Duncan 'always inspire his [Maynard's] picture purchases'. (Sutton (ed.), *Letters of Roger Fry*, ii, 453.) Keynes later said that he bought his Seurat from a 'bird of passage dealer' who told him it came from a Swiss or German collection. KP: PP/45, JMK to Félix Féneon, 1 June 1936.
60. D. H. Robertson in *EJ*, March 1920, 77–84.
61. *CW*, ii, 170, 188.

Chapter 2: The Transition to Peace

1. *CW*, ii, 186–7.
2. *Ibid.*, 23.
3. *CW*, xx.
4. *CW*, xxi, 98–9.
5. *Ibid.*, 94.
6. *Ibid.*
7. *CW*, xx, 171, 179f.
8. See McDougall, *France's Rhineland Diplomacy*, 1978. The theme emerges more clearly in his article 'Political Economy versus National Sovereignty', *JMH*, 1979, 56–7.
9. *CW*, ii, 187.

10. KP: PS/2. Notes of a Talk to Shrewsbury School, 11 July 1920.
11. Trachtenberg, *Reparation in World Politics*, 78, 109; for Keynes's view, see Skidelsky, *Keynes*, i, 357.
12. *CW*, ii, 126.
13. GLS to Carrington, 4 September 1920; q. Holroyd, *Lytton Strachey*, ii, 389.
14. CP: DG to VB, 6 October 1920.
15. JMK to GLS, 20 May 1920.
16. The letters are in KP: PP/45.
17. CP: DG to VB, 20 September 1920.

18. A. O. Bell (ed.), *The Diary of Virginia Woolf*, ii, 317–18.

19. C. H. Broad has written that 'we owe the publication of Johnson's great work to his pupil Miss Naomi Bentwich. It is unlikely that he would ever have brought himself to undergo the drudgery of preparing his scattered manuscripts for the press had she not relieved him of the labour, and almost driven him to face the task.' *PBA*, January 1931.

20. FFP: Reel 45.

21. *CW*, vii, 181n. Austen Chamberlain, the Chancellor of the Exchequer, minuted: 'K[eynes] would go for a financial crisis. . . . Would go to . . . perhaps 10% and keep it at that for three years.'

22. *CW*, xvii, 184–5.

23. E. V. Morgan, *Studies in British Financial Policy*, 297.

24. q. Howson, 'The Origins of Dear Money, 1919–20', *EcHR*, 1974, 89.

25. JMK, 'The Economic Chaos of Europe' from *Harmsworth's Universal History of the World*, 25 June 1929, q. *CW*, xi, 354.

26. BE: ADM 20, Montagu Norman Diary.

27. Howson, 'The Origins of Dear Money, 1919–20', *EcHR*, 1974, 92.

28. *First Interim Report of the Committee on Currency and Foreign Exchanges after the War*, Cmd 9182, 1918.

29. *CW*, ii, 148–9.

30. Original in ACP: 35/1/8; also in *CW*, xvii, 179. Keynes wrote: 'I believe that the Treasury Minute, if it is maintained, must logically end in a very high bank rate and corresponding rate for Treasury Bills.'

31. *CW*, xvii, 179. This doesn't identify the talk as being to the Tuesday Club.

32. KP: OC/2, repr. *CW*, xvii, 184–5.

33. BE: Sir Charles Addis Papers, ADM 16/

2. Minutes of Committee of the Treasury, 4 August 1920; Norman to Pierre Jay, chairman, Federal Reserve Bank of New York, 6 September 1920.

34. Pigou, *Aspects of British Economic History*, 191.

35. OTFP1, OTF to JMK, 30 March 1920. In his letter Falk cited Blackett's 'optimism' about getting bank rate up, but thought this would be delayed.

36. VBP: VB to RF, 29 April 1920.

37. Basil Blackett, the controller of finance at the Treasury, had already invested £400 with Keynes outside the Syndicate. There was obviously a potential clash of interest here.

38. *CW*, xii, 7.

39. JMK to FAK, 23 December 1920. The story of the speculation can be followed in KP: File SY.

40. E. V. Morgan, *Studies in British Financial Policy*, 209.

41. Pigou, *Aspects of British Economic History*, 191.

42. KP: UA/6.

43. Lloyd George, *The Truth about Reparations and War-Debts*, 33–53.

44. *CW*, iii, 2.

45. *CW*, xvii, 89–90.

46. Lloyd George, *The Truth about Reparations and War-Debts*, 41.

47. *CW*, xvii, 208–12.

48. *Ibid.*, 219–20, 216.

49. J. F. Dulles writing in the *New Republic*, 12 March 1921.

50. *CW*, xvii, 224.

51. Lloyd George, *The Truth about Reparations and War-Debts*, 62.

52. q. Marks, 'Reparations Reconsidered: A Reminder', *CEH*, 1969, 358.

53. Lord D'Abernon's diary, 29 June 1921, q. *CW*, xvii, 240. Lord D'Abernon was British Ambassador to Germany.

Chapter 3: Keynes's Philosophy of Practice

1. KP: TP1/1, JMK to DM, 19 August 1920.

2. MPP: Add. MS. 55201.

3. See Skidelsky, *Keynes*, i. 152–4.

4. R. M. O'Donnell, 'Keynes: Philosophy and Economics: An Approach to Rationality and Uncertainty', D.Phil., Cambridge University, 1982, 2.

5. Skidelsky, *Keynes*, i, 147–8.

6. JMK, 'My Early Beliefs', *CW*, x, 446.

7. KP: UA/19. JMK, 'Ethics in Relation to Conduct', unpublished paper read to the Apostles, 23 January 1904. Moore's argument is on pp. 152–4 of his *Principia Ethica*. Keynes reproduces the gist of his 1904 paper in *Treatise on Probability*, 341–2. In the first volume of my biography, I was under a promise not to reveal

the source of the dating of the 1904 paper. It was supplied to me, from the record of meetings of the Apostles, by Mr G. Lloyd, then Fellow and tutor in classics at King's College, Cambridge.

8. See also O'Donnell, *Keynes: Philosophy, Economics and Politics*, 117-18.
9. JMK, *CW*, viii, 103-4.
10. *Ibid.*, 32.
11. *Ibid.*, 356.
12. *Ibid.*, 348.
13. *Ibid.*, 285.
14. *Ibid.*, 428.
15. For this need, see JMK, 'The End of *Laissez-Faire*', *CW*, ix, 288.
16. KP: UA/20. JMK, 'The Political Doctrines of Edmund Burke'. A brief summary was provided in Skidelsky, *Keynes*, i, 155-7. I hope this is an improved one. This section, and also the next, is based on material which appeared in Skidelsky, 'Keynes's Philosophy of Practice', in O'Donnell (ed.), *Keynes as Philosopher-Economist*, 104-23. See also Suzanne Helburn, 'Burke and Keynes', in Bateman and Davis (eds), *Keynes and Philosophy*, 30-54. Helburn's interpretation differs somewhat from mine in that she believes that Keynes took Burke to hold that the duty of government was to promote ethical principles (p. 38).
17. 'The Political Doctrines of Edmund Burke', 17-18. All the quotations are from Keynes's unpublished manuscript.
18. *Ibid.*, 8.
19. *Ibid.*, 41.
20. *Ibid.*, 93.
21. *Ibid.*
22. *Ibid.*, 16-17, 95. This is very similar to Moore, *Principia Ethica*, 167, from whom Keynes probably got the idea of 'moral risk'.
23. *CW*, iv, 65.
24. 'The Political Doctrines of Edmund Burke', 14.
25. *Ibid.*, 14-15.
26. *Ibid.*, 60-9.
27. *Ibid.*, 49.
28. *CW*, iv, 56-7.
29. Moore, *Principia Ethica*, 188-9.
30. *Ibid.*, 208f.
31. Keynes's 1910/1921 paper to the Apostles, 'On the Principle of Organic Unity', is in KP: UA/35. JMK's letter to F. L. Lucas of 19 March 1928 is in KP: PP/45. In fact Keynes's 'solution' was suggested by Moore, *Principia Ethica*, 219.
32. C. D. Broad, *Mind*, 1921, 73.

33. B. Russell, *MG*, xi, July 1922.
34. C. P. Sanger, *New Statesman*, 17 September 1921; *Spectator*, 24 September 1921.
35. KP: TP/1. JMK to C. D. Broad, 31 January 1922. KP: TP contains a collection of material relating to his TP.
36. *Ibid.*
37. Ramsey, *The Foundations of Mathematics*, 289.
38. Russell, *Principles of Mathematics*, intro. to 2nd edn, 1937, ix.
39. JMK, *CW*, viii, 6.
40. A. Wood in Russell, *My Philosophical Development*, 260-1.
41. *CW*, viii, 266.
42. G. von Wright (ed.), *Wittgenstein: Letters to Russell, Keynes, and Moore*, 12.
43. Pears, *Wittgenstein*, 61.
44. Wittgenstein, *Tractatus Logico-Philosophicus*, 41.
45. Wittgenstein, *Note-Books*, 91e.
46. Duffy, *The World as I Found It*, 150. Duffy has written an interesting 'faction' on the relations between Wittgenstein, Moore and Russell.
47. Ramsey, *The Foundations of Mathematics*, 161.
48. *Ibid.*, 186.
49. *Ibid.*, 182.
50. Hollis, *The Cunning of Reason*, 106.
51. Ramsey, *The Foundations of Mathematics*, 192-9.
52. Braithwaite in Wright (ed.), *Cambridge University Studies*, 25.
53. Kolakowski, *Positivist Philosophy*, 237.
54. *CW*, xviii, 448-9.
55. *CW*, x, 336-9.
56. *Ibid.*, 445. Keynes made a mistake here: *Principia Mathematica*, written jointly by Russell and A. N. Whitehead, was published in 1911. The Russell book to which Keynes referred was his *Principles of Mathematics*, published in 1903, the same year as Moore's *Principia Ethica*.
57. Russell, *Principles of Mathematics*, 96. Russell's book was an attempt to derive the whole of mathematics from a small number of logical axioms.
58. *Ibid.*, 159f.
59. Russell, *The Problems of Philosophy*, 59.
60. For the most accessible statement of these ideas, see G. W. Hegel, introduction to his *Philosophy of History*.
61. Russell, *Our Knowledge of the External World*, 157.
62. Russell, *The Problems of Philosophy*, 92.
63. Hacking, *The Emergence of Probability*, 12-14.

64. *Ibid.*, ch. 4.
65. *CW*, cviii, 89, 92.
66. *Ibid.*, 93.
67. *Ibid.*, 103–4.
68. O'Donnell, *Keynes: Philosophy, Economics and Politics*, 30.
69. Russell, *MG*, xi, July 1922.
70. *CW*, viii, 56.
71. *Ibid.*, 7.
72. *Ibid.*, 16.
73. *Ibid.*, 4.
74. *Ibid.*, 11–15.
75. *Ibid.*, 121.
76. *Ibid.*, ch. 4.
77. *Ibid.*, 22.
78. *Ibid.*, 39, Cf. Russell, *Principles of Mathematics*, 171.
79. *CW*, viii, 41.
80. *Ibid.*, 18, 35.
81. *Ibid.*, 19.
82. *Ibid.*, 285.
83. *Ibid.*, 291.
84. *Ibid.*, 295.
85. *Ibid.*
86. *Ibid.*, 468.
87. E.g. Harrod, *The Life of John Maynard Keynes*, 133–4, 651–6; Hession, *John Maynard Keynes*, 176, 182. Moggridge, *Keynes*, has a more extensive discussion of probability (pp. 20–2), but does not attempt to link it to the economics.
88. See Stewart, *Keynes and After*; Lekachman, *The Age of Keynes*; Gilbert, *Keynes's Impact on Monetary Economics*; Patinkin, *Keynes's Monetary Thought*.
89. Shackle, *The Years of High Theory*. The quotations are from the late Professor Shackle's letter to the author, 28 March 1986.
90. O'Donnell, *Keynes: Philosophy, Economics and Politics* (1989); Carabelli, *Keynes's Method* (1988).
91. In Bateman and Davis (eds), *Keynes and Philosophy*, 55. This, together with Lawson and Pesaran (eds), *Keynes's Economics* (1985), and O'Donnell (ed.), *Keynes as Philosopher–Economist* (1991) give a good introduction to contributors and the range of issues in the discussion.
92. Mini, *Keynes, Bloomsbury, and The General Theory* (1991) is excellent.
93. Carabelli, *Keynes's Method*, 99–100, 145–8. Carabelli says Keynes 'dropped rationalism during his early work on probability' but provides no evidence. She sets the TP in the context of the revolt against positivism, but ignores the revolt against Idealism.
94. *Ibid.*, 134; see also 40f. on the comparison with Wittgenstein.
95. *CW*, viii, 11; Carabelli, *Keynes's Method*, 25–6, 81.
96. Carabelli, *Keynes's Method*, 91–3.
97. KP: UA1, 'Modern Philosophy'.
98. *CW*, viii, 273. Frazer states the two principles of magic as the Law of Similarity and the Law of Contagion, the first assuming that an effect resembles a cause, and the second, that something may act on something with which it was once in contact, even after the contact has been removed – as in the superstition of the inhabitants of Mecklenburg that if you drive a nail into a man's footprint he will go lame. (*The Golden Bough*, 44.) Keynes was fascinated by magic, increasingly so as he grew older.
99. *CW*, viii, 18, 35; O'Donnell, *Keynes: Philosophy, Economics and Politics*, 65. For Ramsey's views, see Ramsey, *Foundations*, 163–4; for Braithwaite's, *CW*, viii, xii.
100. O'Donnell, *Keynes: Philosophy, Economics and Politics*, 64–5.
101. Fitzgibbons, *Keynes's Vision*, 19–23.
102. Carabelli, *Keynes's Method*, 148–50.
103. Fitzgibbons, *Keynes's Vision*, 37.
104. Letter to author, 28 March 1986.
105. See Winslow, 'Keynes and Freud: Psychoanalysis and Keynes's Account of the "Animal Spirits" of Capitalism', *SR*, 1986; Mini, *Keynes, Bloomsbury, and The General Theory*, 114.
106. O'Donnell, *Keynes: Philosophy, Economics and Politics*, 261.
107. Carabelli, *Keynes's Method*, 161.
108. Lawson, 'Uncertainty and Economic Analysis', *EJ*, 1985, 916–17; see also his 'Keynes and the Analysis of Rational Behaviour' in O'Donnell (ed.), *Keynes as Philosopher–Economist*, 204–22, and 'Keynes and Conventions', *RSE* (forthcoming).

Chapter 4: Russian and German Affairs

1. *CW*, xvii, 245, 248–9.

2. JNK to JMK, 11 September 1921.

3. *CW*, xvii, 263.
4. *Ibid.*, 274.
5. CP: JMK to VB, 26 October, 2 November 1921.
6. JMK to C. P. Scott, 14 September 1921; *CW*, xvii, 319.
7. JMK to VB, 12 December 1921.
8. Chandavarkar, *Keynes and India*, 49–50, is clearly pained by Keynes's last-minute withdrawal from the Commission, and explains that Keynes had been required to stay in India longer than he had planned. In fact, *CW*, xvii, 331–3, makes it plain that Keynes had asked to be released from the Commission before any extension of his service was mooted. Harrod, *The Life of John Maynard Keynes*, 308–9, rightly surmised that the main motive for his withdrawal was that he had fallen in love with Lydia.
9. See Skidelsky, *Keynes*, i, 252–3; also OTF to Cuthbertson, 6 June 1967 in TC.
10. Beaumont, *Diaghilev Ballet in London*, 115–16.
11. Ninette de Valois, *Come Dance with Me*, 40–1.
12. Beaumont, *Diaghilev Ballet in London*, 141, 139.
13. q. Milo Keynes (ed.), *Lydia Lopokova*, 4–5.
14. Beaumont, *Diaghilev Ballet in London*, 117, 140.
15. In Polly Hill and Richard Keynes (eds), *Lydia and Maynard*, 26.
16. In Milo Keynes (ed.), *Lydia Lopokova*, 54.
17. *Ibid.*, 70. For reviews of Lydia's performances in the US, see MacDonald, *Diaghilev Observed*, 137–211.
18. Sokolova, *Dancing for Diaghilev*, 74.
19. LK to JMK, 25 November 1933. This recounts a conversation with Fred Ashton on Léonide Massine as a choreographer.
20. q. Buckle, *Diaghilev*, 392.
21. JMK to VB, 24 February 1922.
22. Q. Bell in Milo Keynes (ed.), *Lydia Lopokova*, 88.
23. JRHP: V.1.34, C. P. Scott to J. L. Hammond, 11 March, 24 January 1923.
24. KP: GS/1/5, W. Cuno to JMK, 25 February 1922.
25. RCLP: Box 4, Folder 89, RL to JMK, 5 April 1922.
26. FFP: Reel 45, H. Laski to FF, 29 November 1922.
27. Maisky's letter is in KP: GS/1/3; A. Ransome to JMK, 7 June 1922, is in GS/1/2.
28. 'The Theory of the Exchanges and Purchasing Power Parity' and 'The Forward Market in Foreign Exchanges'.
29. KP: GS/1/2.
30. This debate can be followed in the Eleventh Supplement, 7 December 1922.
31. OTFP1, Add. MS. 57923, JMK to OTF, 26 October 1921.
32. His articles were also carried by the *Daily Express* in London, by the *New York World* and by a number of European newspapers.
33. Hogan, *Informal Entente*, 44–5.
34. Schuker, *The End of French Predominance in Europe*, 16; Rupieper, *The Cuno Government and Reparations*, 9–10.
35. *CW*, xvii, 363–9.
36. *Ibid.*, 369.
37. Eichengreen (ed.), *The Gold Standard in Theory and Practice*, 202–3.
38. *CW*, xvii, 372–3.
39. D'Abernon, *An Ambassador of Peace*, ii, 91.
40. *CW*, xvii, 388.
41. *Ibid.*, 390–4.
42. D'Abernon, *An Ambassador of Peace*, i, 255.
43. A. O. Bell (ed.), *The Diary of Virginia Woolf*, ii, 26 May 1921, 120.
44. On this, see Skidelsky, *Keynes*, i, 169.
45. Middlemas (ed.), *Thomas Jones, Whitehall Diary*, 5 May 1922, 199.
46. VBP: VB to RF, 11 April 1922.
47. A. O. Bell (ed.), *The Diary of Virginia Woolf*, 19 July 1922, 183.
48. JMK to FAK, 2 September 1922.
49. Harrod, *The Life of John Maynard Keynes*, 317–18.
50. Lloyd George, *The Truth about Reparations and War-Debts*, 66–7.
51. Leffler, *The Elusive Quest*, 78.
52. D'Abernon, *An Ambassador of Peace*, ii, 86.
53. *Ibid.*, 56–7.
54. *CW*, xviii, 17.
55. KP: GS/1/3. BB to JMK, 17 August 1922.
56. *CW*, xviii, 39–43, 34.
57. Rowland, *Lloyd George*, 586.
58. D'Abernon, *An Ambassador of Peace*, ii, 123.
59. JMK, *Essays in Biography*, *CW*, x, 186.
60. I am grateful to James Fox for letting me see the correspondence between R. H. Brand and his wife. Dorothea Hauser has drawn my attention to a detailed account of the Berlin Experts' Commission by its secretary, Ernest Kocherthaler, appointed to the job on Keynes's initiative. Kocherthaler's account is in

the Privat-Archiv Warburg, Hamburg: Carl Melchior/Max M. Warburg papers MA16, 'note for the diary' by EK, 10 November 1922.

61. D'Abernon, *An Ambassador of Peace*, ii, 122–3, 126–9. KP: F1/31.

62. *CW*, xviii, 71.

63. *Ibid.*, 66: JMK to Havenstein, 17 January 1923.

64. JMK to FAK, 22 December 1922.

65. *CW*, xviii, 93–6.

66. *Ibid.*, 97–9.

67. *Ibid.*, 86.

68. Letter to the *New Statesman*, 18 December 1922.

69. *CW*, xvii, 448–54.

70. *Ibid.*, 432.

71. See Skidelsky, *Keynes*, i, 360–1.

72. D'Abernon, *An Ambassador of Peace*, ii, 140.

73. Trachtenberg, *Reparation in World Politics*, 287.

74. *CW*, xviii, 110: JMK to G. Dawson, 3 January 1923.

75. Rupieper, *The Cuno Government and Reparations*, 74–5; *CW*, xviii, 111.

76. *CW*, iii, 113.

77. *CW*, xviii, 103.

78. Grigg, *Prejudice and Judgment*, 101; q. Boyle, *Montagu Norman*, 156–7.

79. Boyle, *Montagu Norman*, 160.

80. Marks, *The Illusion of Peace*, 50.

81. D'Abernon, *The Ambassador of Peace*, ii, 160.

82. Ferrari Bravo, *Economic Diplomacy*, 11.

83. *CW*, xviii, 136.

84. *Ibid.*, 140.

85. *CW*, x, 35.

86. *CW*, xviii, 138.

87. *Ibid.*, 143.

88. *Ibid.*, 143–4.

89. *Ibid.*, 148.

90. *Ibid.*, 150.

91. *Ibid.*, 156.

92. Middlemas and Barnes, *Baldwin*, 180–1.

93. Melchior's Diary as summarised and quoted in *CW*, xviii, 158–60.

94. Ferrari Bravo, *Economic Diplomacy*, 52.

95. *CW*, xviii, 165.

96. 'Events of the Week', *Nation*, 16 July 1923; *CW*, xviii, 165.

Chapter 5: Monetary Reform

1. Aldcroft, *The British Economy between the Wars*, 74–5.

2. Broadberry, 'Aggregate Supply in Interwar Britain', *EJ* 1986; Pigou, *Aspects of British Economic History*, 63, 81. Pigou thought 'efficiency' had fallen since 1913 owing to 'war weariness'.

3. *CW*. xvii, 265.

4. *CW*, xix, 65–7.

5. *Ibid.*, 423.

6. Hubback, *No Ordinary Press Baron*, 67.

7. KP: NS/1/1. H. Massingham to JMK, 5 January 1923.

8. *Ibid.*, Ramsay Muir to JMK, 9 February 1923.

9. Henderson, 'Editing the Nation', 8.

10. KP: NS/1/1, Walter Layton to JMK, 17 February 1923.

11. Henderson, 'Editing the Nation', 8.

12. KP: Faith Henderson to Austin Robinson, 9 March 1955.

13. Ackroyd, *T. S. Eliot*, 132.

14. MHP: E. M. Forster to Leonard Woolf, 15 May 1923. I am indebted to S. P. Rosenbaum for drawing my attention to this.

15. For the 'row' see HDHP: Box 21 for Leonard Woolf to Hubert Henderson, 26 September 1923, and Henderson's reply on 29 September 1923; also DGP for Vanessa Bell to Duncan Grant, 8 October 1923.

16. HDHP: Box 21. Nicholas Davenport to Hubert Henderson, 28 January 1930.

17. Mirsky, *The Intelligentsia of Great Britain*, 113.

18. VBP: 80.10.8.352, VB to RF (undated).

19. *News Chronicle*, 13 March 1929.

20. This portrait, now missing, is reproduced in Milo Keynes (ed.), *Lydia Lopokova*, between pp. 110–11, illustration 23. Duncan Grant 'touched it up'. See also DGP for VB to DG, 27 April 1923.

21. The three Virginia Woolf letters are nos 1383, 1395, 1405, in N. Nicolson (ed.), *The Letters of Virginia Woolf*, iii. The passage in brackets, another example of Virginia Woolf being nasty, was omitted from the published edition.

22. The quarrel is recounted in HBD; see also KP: LLK1/1 for Vera Bowen to JMK 9 August 1923, and JMK's reply

12 August 1923. The gist of it was about whether Vera should pay Lydia a salary, or whether Lydia should pay Vera one.

23. HBD: 21 May 1924.

24. *Ibid.*, 11, 17 June 1923.

25. VW to VB, 23 December 1922; Letter 1335 in N. Nicolson (ed.), *The Letters of Virginia Woolf*, ii.

26. A. O. Bell (ed.), *The Diary of Virginia Woolf*, iii, 8 December 1928, 210.

27. JTSP: 6.13, JMK to J. T. Sheppard, 23 June 1923.

28. NWP: iii, Correspondence, Bertram Bulmer to Nathaniel Wedd, 8 August 1923.

29. The two quotations are from A. O. Bell (ed.), *The Diary of Virginia Woolf*, ii, 266, and N. Nicolson (ed.), *The Letters of Virginia Woolf*, iii, Letter 1432.

30. HBD: 22 September 1923.

31. Lydia Lopokova to JMK, 2 November 1923.

32. HBD: 19 November 1923.

33. Polly Hill and Richard Keynes (eds), *Lydia and Maynard*, 101.

34. LL to JMK, 28 October 1923; JMK to LL, 28 October, 2 November 1923.

35. DGP: VB to DG, 8 October 1923.

36. *CW*, xix, 100, 101

37. BE: ADM 16/3. On the other hand, Reginald McKenna, one of Keynes's staunchest allies, told Montagu Norman on 20 June that 'our Rates are too low & diff[eren]ce between 3 and 4% cd not really affect trade . . .'. (Montagu Norman's Diary, BE ADM 20/10.) *The Economist* under Walter Layton also thought the rise in bank rate would make little or no difference to actual interest rates.

38. *CW*, xix, 100.

39. *Ibid.*, 104.

40. *Ibid.*, 107–12.

41. *Ibid.*, 111, 112.

42. *Ibid.*, 116.

43. Letter to *The Times*, 14 February 1923; *CW*, xix, 79.

44. *CW*, xvii, 270.

45. *EJ*, December 1912; repr. *CW*, xi, 220–1.

46. *CW*, xix, 134.

47. W. Beveridge, *Economica*, February 1924.

48. *CW*, xix, 121.

49. *Ibid.*, 134, 124.

50. JMK to LL, 26 October 1923.

51. *CW*, xix, 151–2, 153, 155.

52. JMK to LL, 4 December 1923; LL to JMK, 24 November 1923.

53. *CW*, xix, 158–62.

54. *The Economist*, 4 June 1983.

55. *CW*, iv, xiv.

56. The discussion of the effects of a changing price level was not novel in Cambridge. See Lavington, *The English Capital Market*, 54; D. H. Robertson, *Money*, 9.

57. *CW*, iv, 34.

58. *Ibid.*, 20.

59. *Ibid.*, 36.

60. *Ibid.*, 63.

61. *Ibid.*, 61.

62. *Ibid.*, 65.

63. *Ibid.*, 68.

64. *Ibid.*, 65–7. Cf. Kahn, *The Making of Keynes' General Theory*, 54.

65. *CW*, iv, 148–9.

66. *Ibid.*, 142–6.

67. *Ibid.*, 126.

68. *Ibid.*, 128.

69. *Ibid.*, 132–4.

70. *Ibid.*, 121.

71. KP: PP/45, M. Labordère to JMK, 1 July 1924.

72. *CW*, iv, 155.

73. *Ibid.*, 149–53.

74. *Ibid.*, 158–9.

75. R. G. Hawtrey, *EJ*, June 1924, 227.

76. *CW*, iv, 138.

77. *Ibid.*, 16.

78. *Ibid.*, 56–7.

79. Harrod, *The Life of John Maynard Keynes*, 339.

80. Basil Blackett to JMK, 31 December 1923; *CW*, xix, 153–4.

81. Both the Brand and Pigou letters (the latter undated) are in KP: MR 1/2. Brand's later comment is in 'Why I Am Not a Socialist', 1925, issued under the auspices of the Liberal Summer School, 26.

82. J. C. Stamp in *JRSS*, 24 May 1924.

83. *TLS*, 17 January 1924.

84. *Statist*, 22 December 1923.

85. See *Manchester Guardian*, 22 December 1923; *Westminster Gazette*, 19 January 1924.

86. *CW*, iv, 122–3.

87. KP: L/23.

88. BE: EID 4. In his address to the Institute of Bankers on 10 December 1923, Addis stated that 'Prices have fallen much more rapidly than the volume of purchasing power.' His argument, as that of J. A. C. Osborne of the Bank, who commented on Addis's address, was identical to Keynes's.

89. Robbins, *Autobiography of an Economist*,

83; KP: L/43, Josiah Stamp to JMK, 10 July 1943.

90. E. Cannan, 'The Meaning of British Bank Deposits', *Economica*, January 1921.

91. EC to JMK, 20 October 1917; JMK to EC, 28 January 1918. The correspondence between the two men can be followed in KP: EJ/1/2, and in ECP, Box 20c.

92. EC to JMK, 20 October 1917, 7 February 1918.

93. *Manchester Guardian Commercial*, 20 December 1923.

94. *CW*, xi, 414–19.

95. EC to JMK, 9 February 1924; see also *CW*, xix, 206–15 for JMK's criticism of Hawtrey.

96. JMK to LL, 27 January 1924.

97. KP: NS/1/1. JMK to Prof. Kurt Singer, 23 April 1925.

98. *CW*, xi, 375–81.

99. KP: L/25, JMK to IF, 14 May 1925.

100. Wicksell, *Interest and Prices*, 102. See esp. ch. 8, 'The Natural Rate of Interest on Capital and the Rate of Interest on Loans'. Wicksell's clear distinction between the rate of profit and the rate of interest, and the lack of any automatic adjustment between them, was to influence Keynes in the *Treatise on Money* and beyond. Wicksell's paper 'The Influence of the Rate of Interest on Prices' was published in *EJ*, xvii, 1907, but before Keynes became editor, or indeed an economist, and he seems to have missed it.

101. Fisher, *The Purchasing Power of Money*, 330; Wicksell, *Interest and Prices*, ch. 7, maintained that in a pure credit economy the rise in prices would be cumulative, the upward movement 'creating its own draught'.

Chapter 6: Gold and Marriage

1. LL to JMK, 19 January 1924.
2. JMK to LL, 2 May 1924.
3. *CW*, xviii, 255, 253, 227.
4. JMK to LL, 10 February 1924.
5. KP: PP/45: G. L. Keynes to JMK, 16 February 1923.
6. LL to FAK, 21 February 1924.
7. LL to JMK, 14 January 1924.
8. HBD, 1 April 1924.
9. LL to JMK, 5 May 1924.
10. JMK to LL, 14 May 1924.
11. JMK to LL, 15 May 1924.
12. JMK to LL, 1 June 1924.
13. LL to JMK, 31 May 1924.
14. HBD, 15 June 1924.
15. KP: A/24/1.
16. JMK to LL, 24 October 1924.
17. Schumpeter, *Ten Great Economists*, 271–2n.
18. GLS to JMK, 21 October 1924.
19. N. Nicolson (ed.), *The Letters of Virginia Woolf*, iii, VW to J. Raverat, 8 June 1924, 115.
20. A. O. Bell (ed.), *The Diary of Virginia Woolf*, ii, 15 August 1924, 310–11.
21. N. Nicolson (ed.), *The Letters of Virginia Woolf*, iii, VW to J. Raverat, 26 December 1924, 149.
22. A lecture on 'The State and Foreign Investment', delivered before the University of Cambridge on 11 February 1924, was shortened and amended for a talk to the Liberal Summer School at Oxford on 2 August 1924; it was published in the *Nation* on 9 August, with a further comment in the *Manchester Guardian Commercial* Supplement on 21 August. The series concluded with a lecture on foreign investment to the Edinburgh Chamber of Commerce on 12 December 1924. The two unpublished lectures are in KP: PS/2.

23. *CW*, xix, 285–8. In his Cambridge lecture Keynes said, 'In short, the nineteenth century, as in so many other respects, came to look on an arrangement as normal which was really most abnormal. To lend vast sums abroad for long periods of time without any possibility of legal redress if things go wrong, is a crazy construction; specially in return for trifling extra interest.'

24. *Ibid.*, 283.
25. KP: PS/2; *CW*, xix, 275–84.
26. KP: PP/45, C. R. Fay to JMK, 1 February 1925; JMK to C. R. Fay, 19 February 1925.
27. *CW*, xix, 224.
28. *Ibid.*, 219–23, 225.
29. *Ibid.*, 224.
30. *Ibid.*, 228–9.

31. Harrod, *The Life of John Maynard Keynes*, 349.
32. Eichengreen, *The Gold Standard in Theory and Practice*, 3–4.
33. The cruelty of the British ruling class has been the main thesis of Nicholas Davenport, then City editor of the *Nation*, in e.g., *The Split Society* (1964), and *Memoirs of a City Radical* (1974). He attributes it to fox-hunting. Keynes's references to Freud are to be found in *A Treatise on Money*, ii, 258–9, in a section headed 'Auri Sacra Fames' – Sacred Hunger for Gold.
34. Grigg, *Prejudice and Judgment*, 182, 185.
35. TP: T 160/197, File 7528. Governor's Evidence before the Chamberlain Committee, 27 June 1924, 13. Schuster's Evidence is on 68.
36. Ingham, *Capitalism Divided?*, 181–2. See also Rodney Lowe, 'The Erosion of State Intervention in Britain 1917–1924', *EcHR*, 2nd series, 21, 1978. Lowe's thesis is that after the war the Treasury reasserted its control of economic policy over the more interventionist 'social ministries' (Health, Labour and so on) set up as a result of the war.
37. TP: T 160/197, File 7528. Evidence of Sir Felix Schuster, 75–6; see also Norman's Evidence, 15.
38. *Ibid.*, Written Evidence of the Federation of British Industries, 29 July 1924.
39. *Ibid.*, Norman's Evidence, 6.
40. *Ibid.*, T 172/1499B. M. Norman, 2 February 1925 in reply to Churchill's 'Exercise'.
41. Harrod, *The Life of John Maynard Keynes*, 345.
42. KP: PS/6. JMK notes for a lecture, 1924, undated, but wrongly filed.
43. TP: T 160/197, File, 528, 10.
44. JMK's Evidence to the Chamberlain Committee, 11 July 1924; *CW*, xix, 257.
45. q. Moggridge, *The Return to Gold*, 30.
46. *CW*, xix, 239–61.
47. BE: ADM 20/10. Montagu Norman's Diary, 13 June 1924.
48. *CW*, xix, 263.
49. *Ibid.*, 268–9.
50. *Ibid.*, 267–72.
51. *Ibid.*, 324. JMK to F.L. Salter, 18 October 1924.
52. JMK to LL, 31 October 1924; see also Meisel and Kendrick, (eds) *Bloomsbury Freud*, JS to AS, 2 November 1924.
53. q. S. V. O. Clarke, *Central Bank Cooperation*, 71.
54. Memorandum of 11 January 1925, q. Moggridge, *The Return to Gold*, 41.
55. BE: ADM 16/3.
56. *Ibid.*; see also S. V. O. Clarke, *Central Bank Cooperation*, 79–80.
57. KP: PS/3.
58. BE: ADM 16/3.
59. TP: T 172/1499B, Bradbury to Niemeyer, 5 February 1925.
60. *CW*, ix, 192–200.
61. TP: T 172/1499B, WSC to ON, 6 February 1925.
62. *Ibid.*, WSC to ON, 22 February 1925.
63. See Moggridge, *British Monetary Policy*, 66, 67n.
64. TP: T 172/1499B, ON to WSC, 2 February 1925.
65. *Ibid.*
66. *Ibid.*, ON to WSC, 22 February 1925.
67. *CW*, xix, 335–7.
68. Moggridge, *British Monetary Policy*, 67.
69. *CW*, xix, 341–2.
70. Grigg, *Prejudice and Judgment*, 184.
71. Keynes made a rare mistake, in his immediate published account on Churchill's decision, of supposing that the Bank of England would not be required to import gold, only export it. This 'prudent' provision led him to mitigate his criticism of the return to gold. A week later he had to admit he had made a mistake: the Bank of England was obliged, as before, to buy gold in unlimited quantities which 'strips away most of the reasons for consolation I found last week'. *Nation*, 2 and 9 May 1925; *CW*, xix, 357–65.
72. *CW*, xix, 359–40.
73. *Ibid.*, 365, 373–4, 436–7.
74. *Ibid.*, 396–7.
75. *Ibid.*, 390, 393.
76. *Ibid.*, 390.
77. *Ibid.*, 405.
78. *Ibid.*, 419.
79. *CW*, ix, 218–20.
80. *Ibid.*, 222–3.
81. *Ibid.*, 225–8.
82. *Ibid.*, 223–4.
83. Moggridge, *The Return to Gold*, 79–80.
84. KP: PP/45, L. Wittgenstein to JMK, 18 October 1925; see also JMK to LK, 23 October 1925.
85. LK to JMK, 26 May 1929, recalling the incident.
86. KP: PP/45, JMK to L. Wittgenstein, 29 March 1924.
87. JMK to LK, 15 November 1925.
88. M. Dobb, *New Statesman*, 18 June 1971.

I am indebted to Mr Brian Pollitt for bringing this reference to my attention.

89. For JMK's speeches see *CIV*, xix, 434–42. Also KP: A/25.

90. A. O. Bell (ed.), *The Diary of Virginia Woolf*, iii, 24 September 1925, 43–4.

91. GLS to D. Carrington, q. Holroyd, *Lytton Strachey*, ii, 516–17. The house was not Tilton, as Holroyd says.

92. Sutton (ed.), *Letters of Roger Fry*, ii, RF to H. Anrep, 23 December 1928.

93. E. M. Forster was not the only one to notice JMK 'much softened & nicened by his marriage'. EMFP: Gen. Corr., EMF to Ada Borchgrevink, 15 November 1925.

94. N. Nicolson (ed.), *The Letters of Virginia Woolf*, iii, VW to VB, 25 April 1924, 101.

95. VBP: VB to RF, 13 August 1927.

96. LK to JMK, 28 November 1925.

97. LK to JMK, 18 January 1926; JMK to LK, 18 January 1926.

98. LL to JMK, 10 November 1924.

99. LL to JMK, 19 January 1925.

100. KP: LLK/5, LK to FAK, 3 March 1926.

101. N. Nicolson (ed.), *The Letters of Virginia Woolf*, iii, VW to VB, 15 May 1927, 12 May 1928, 376, 499.

102. LK to JMK, 2 November 1925, 24 April 1926.

103. LK to JMK, 25, 26 October 1925.

104. A. O. Bell (ed.), *The Diary of Virginia Woolf*, iii, 9 May 1925, 18; for LL's comment, see LL to JMK, 9 May 1925.

105. LK to JMK, 17 October, 8 December 1925.

106. LK to JMK, 17 January 1926, 9 May 1925, 26 November 1928, 27 February 1926, 27 November 1925, 4 March 1927.

107. A. O. Bell (ed.), *The Diary of Virginia Woolf*, iii, 21 April 1928, 181.

108. VBP: VB to RF, 25 September 1925.

109. N. Nicolson (ed.), *The Letters of Virginia Woolf*, iii, VW to VB, 20 March 1927, 349.

110. LK to JMK, 1 November 1925.

111. LK to JMK, 28 February 1926, 27 February 1928.

112. LK to JMK, 26 November 1928.

113. LK to JMK, 29 January 1928.

114. LK to JMK, 8 December 1925.

115. q. Milo Keynes (ed.), *Lydia Lopokova*, 34.

116. KP: LLK/5, LK to FAK, 8 September 1926.

117. VBP: VB to RF, 13 August 1927.

118. N. Nicolson (ed.), *The Letters of Virginia Woolf*, iii, VW to VB, 15 May 1927, 376.

119. *Ibid.*, 418.

Chapter 7: Keynes's Middle Way

1. For a good summary of nineteenth-century attitudes to *laissez-faire* see A. J. Taylor, *Laissez-Faire and State Intervention in Nineteenth-Century Britain*. The *locus classicus* of Victorian economists' views on economic policy is Robbins, *The Theory of Economic Policy in English Classical Political Economy*.

2. For an interesting discussion, see George Catephores, *Keynes as a Bourgeois Marxist*.

3. Freeden, *Liberalism Divided*, 155.

4. *CIV*, ix, 310.

5. Hubert Henderson, editorial, *Nation*, 5 May 1923.

6. P. Clarke, 'The Politics of Keynesian Economics, 1924–1931', in Bentley and Stevenson (eds), *High and Low Politics in Modern Britain*, 177–9.

7. Cranston, 'Keynes: His Political Ideas and their Influence', in Thirlwall (ed.), *Keynes and Laissez-Faire*, esp. 110–12.

8. Freeden, *Liberalism Divided*, 166–71.

9. Johnson and Johnson, *The Shadow of Keynes*, 28.

10. *CW*, ii, 6.

11. KP: PS/6. Unpublished fragment, dating from 1925–6, wrongly catalogued.

12. *CW*, ix, 295.

13. q. Skidelsky, *Keynes*, i, 172.

14. *CW*, ix, 274–5.

15. *Ibid.*, 276.

16. *Ibid.*, 285–6; for Donald Winch's comment, see his *Economics and Policy*, 346.

17. *CW*, ix, 288.

18. *Ibid.*, 291–2.

19. *Ibid.*, 288–90.

20. Associational theories of the state flourished at the time. See MacIver, *The Modern State* (1926).

21. *CW*, ix, 331; xx, 263, 27. The phrase 'euthanasia of politics' comes from Roberta and David Schaefer, 'The Political Philosophy of J. M. Keynes', *PI*, 1983, 59–60.

22. *CW*, ix, 293, 294.

23. JRCP: JMK to JRC, 26 April 1927. For Keynes's observations on 'organised' capitalism see Richard Wright: 'On "Madmen" and "Defunct Economists"', unpublished paper, Cambridge University, 1987.
24. CW, ix, 303–5.
25. CW, xix, 440–1.
26. CW, ix, 305–6.
27. Olson The Rise and Decline of Nations (1982).
28. CW, ix, 306.
29. CW, xix, 441.
30. CW, ix, 302.
31. Ibid., 296–7.
32. Ibid., 299.
33. Ibid., 302–3.
34. Ibid., 299.
35. KP: PS/6. Unpublished fragment, undated, but wrongly catalogued.
36. CW, ix, 295. This passage was left out of Essays in Persuasion.
37. In the Nation of 20 February 1926; CW, ix, 309.
38. Crosland, The Future of Socialism, 353.
39. CW, ix, 263.
40. CW, x, 67.
41. CW, ix, 299–300.
42. KP: PS/4.
43. CW, ix, 297.
44. KP: PS/4.
45. CW, ix, 299.
46. Ibid., 311.
47. JBS to Alix Strachey, 18 June 1925, q. Meisel and Kendrick (eds), Bloomsbury/Freud, 289.
48. CW, ii, 12–13.
49. CW, ix, 258.
50. Ibid., 269, 271.
51. Ibid., 267.
52. OMP: JMK to Ottoline Morrell, 2 May 1928.
53. The first version of 'EPOG' was read to the Chameleon Club in Cambridge on 10 February 1928. JMK then took it to the Essay Society of Winchester College on 17 March 1928, having been asked down by its secretary, Charles Gifford, who later read economics at Cambridge. The paper had another airing at the Political Economy Club in Cambridge on 22 October 1928, where Plumptre probably heard it, and Keynes read it to the Apostles on 31 May 1930. He then undertook a major revision for a lecture in Madrid in June 1930, which was published in the Nation on 11 and 18 October 1930. It was substantially this version that appeared in Essays in Persuasion. The main revision was to incorporate a reference to the great depression, which had started in 1929.
54. CW, ix, 322–6.
55. Ibid., 329.
56. Ibid., 330–1.
57. Plumptre is q. Wood (ed.), John Maynard Keynes, i, 153.
58. 'It seems to us', wrote D. R. Gadgill, reviewing Essays in Persuasion in IJE April 1933, 'that in his forecasts about the future Mr. Keynes has too exclusively confined his attention to Western Europe and the USA and has especially neglected the heavily congested tracts of China, India, and Japan. Is the economic problem going to be solved for the whole world only or only for the most fortunate countries of the West? And would it be possible to have any stable position with the economic problem solved for only half the world?' This is fair comment, but it is interesting that the world, even for Indians in the 1930s, did not include Africa.
59. CW, ix, 330.
60. CW, x, 382–4. See also KP: L/R2, DHR to JMK, 30 August 1929. 'I ran into the Prof. [Pigou] and Tom Gaunt on the way to Zermatt, and also made acquaintance with the latter's attractive negroid wife and her overdressed mama. They are a curious party. How hard it seems to be not to murder Jews.'
61. KP: L/33, Max Radin to JMK, 12 September 1933; JMK to MR, 2 October 1933.

Chapter 8: Liberalism and Industry

1. CW, xix, 446.
2. TP: T. 176/16, ON, Bradbury to WSC, 4 August 1925; ON to WSC, ? May 1926.
3. KP: L/25, H. A. Siepmann to JMK, 14 December 1925; D. Mitrany to JMK, 10 October 1925. For his advice on the franc see CW, ix, 76–82; KP L/26. 'The solution [to the budgetary problem]', he wrote to Loucheur on 3 December, 'ought to come about through internal

prices rising, with consequent relief to the budget, without any considerable further fall of the franc, thus avoiding any further shocks to confidence.' These ideas were elaborated in an article 'The French Franc: An Open Letter to the French Minister of Finance (whoever he is or may be)', published in the *Nation* on 9 January 1926, which itself gave rise to a considerable correspondence.

4. KP: PP/74, JMK 'History of the London Artists' Association' (?1929).
5. VBP: VB to RF, 8 September 1926.
6. LK to JMK, 31 October 1925.
7. *CW*, xix, 468.
8. Keynes's essay appears in *CW*, x, 256-71.
9. *The Times*, 16 February 1926.
10. HDH's four articles ran between 19 December 1925 and 9 January 1926.
11. LGP: G/17, LG to CPS, 10 February 1926.
12. KP: L/26, HNB to JMK, 26 February 1926.
13. LK to JMK, 16 October 1926.
14. Mosley, 'Revolution by Reason', 16-17, 14-15, 26.
15. Strachey, *Revolution by Reason*, 93-4; KP: L/26, JMK to JS, 5 January 1926.
16. KP: L/26, JMK to HNB, 27 October 1926.
17. KP: PP/45, BW to JMK, 22 February 1926.
18. CP: DG to VB, 18 April 1926; V. Woolf confirmed the effect of *My Apprenticeship* in a letter to Margaret Llewellyn Davies on 2 September 1926, repr. in N. Nicolson (ed.), *The Letters of Virginia Woolf*, iii, 289.
19. Keynes's review is in *CW*, ix, 315-20.
20. N. Nicolson (ed.), *The Letters of Virginia Woolf*, iii, VW to VB, 19 May 1926, 265.
21. *CW*, xix, 525-9.
22. N. Nicolson (ed.), *The Letters of Virginia Woolf*, iii, VW to VB, 12 May 1926, 260.
23. *CW*, xix, 530-2.
24. For Birkenhead's proposals, see the *Nation*, 26 June 1926.
25. Rowland, *Lloyd George*, 623.
26. In 'Dr. Melchior: A Defeated Enemy', *CW*, x, 419.
27. HDHP: Box 21.
28. The JMK-Margot Asquith correspondence is in KP: PP/45.
29. KP: L/26, Thomas T. Tweed to JMK, 23, 28 June 1926.
30. *CW*, xix, 540.
31. MacKenzie and MacKenzie (eds), *The Diary of Beatrice Webb*, iv, 93-4.
32. HGWP: HG 10, JMK to HGW, 11 October 1926.
33. Marshall, *Principles of Economics*, 8th edn, 250.
34. q. Skidelsky, *Keynes*, i, 158-9.
35. See Keynes's disobliging remarks on Mond in *CW*, ix, 320.
36. *Ibid.*, 299; cf. JMK, *Essays in Persuasion*, 327, for a more accurate text.
37. KP: L/25, L. T. Cadbury to JMK, 25 August 1925.
38. *CW*, xix, 654-60.
39. *Ibid.*, 525-9.
40. *Ibid.*, 578-85.
41. *Ibid.*, 585-8.
42. Brown, 'Reminiscences of Keynes' (unpublished).
43. *CW*, xix, 611, 613.
44. KP: C/1, JMK to OTF, 28 June 1928.
45. *CW*, xix, 627.
46. *CW*, xxiv, 261.
47. *CW*, xix, 538-48.
48. *Ibid.*, 695.
49. JMK to LK, 27 November 1927. Keynes's November draft is on pp. 440-9 of the report.
50. HGWP: HG 10.
51. JMK to PK, 31 August 1927, q. Freeden, *Liberalism Divided*, 118.
52. RHBP: Liberal Inquiry, Files 118(ii), 119(i); also *Britain's Industrial Future*, chs vi and vii.
53. RHBP: Liberal Inquiry, Files 118(ii), 119(i).
54. *Britain's Industrial Future*, 66.
55. *Ibid.*, 64-5.
56. *Ibid.*, 64.
57. *CW*, vii, 378.
58. *Britain's Industrial Future*, 112-13.
59. *Ibid.*, 114.
60. *Ibid.*, 110.
61. *Ibid.*, 115.
62. *Ibid.*, 122, 123.
63. *Ibid.*, ch. xii.
64. *Ibid.*, 410.
65. *Ibid.*, 414-15.
66. *Ibid.*, 422-5.
67. *Ibid.*, 428, 430-2.
68. *Ibid.*, 433.
69. *Ibid.*, 271.

Chapter 9: The Case of the Missing Savings

1. J.R. Hicks, 'Dennis Holme Robertson', *PBA*, i, 1964, x–xi.
2. KP: L/R/2, DHR to JMK, 27 July 1928.
3. Letter to author, 17 August 1990.
4. D. H. Robertson, *A Study of Industrial Fluctuation*, 254.
5. *Ibid.*, 241–2.
6. *Ibid.*, 1948 edn.
7. See the discussion in Presley, *Robertsonian Economics*, 93–5.
8. The quotations are from the English translation of Labordère's essay, which is reproduced in French in the 1948 edn of *A Study of Industrial Fluctuation*. I am grateful to Prof. Presley for providing me with the translation. The Keynes–Labordère correspondence is in KP: PP/45.
9. KP: PP/45, JMK to RGH, 26 October 1913.
10. JMK to DHR, 27 September 1913; q. *CW*, xiii, p. i.
11. *CW*, xiii, 4.
12. *Ibid.*, 6.
13. In 'Keynes on Monetary Policy, 1910–1946', *OEP*, 1974, 228, Moggridge and Howson write that Keynes moved 'briefly to an overinvestment view of the trade cycle' under Robertson's influence. But in fact Keynes explicitly attacked overinvestment theories of the Robertsonian type. Presley's view that Keynes came 'close to a theory of forced saving' (Presley, *Robertsonian Economics*, 77) is more accurate, though Keynes does not consider the effect of bank advances on prices and income distribution, which is necessary for 'forced saving' to occur. The 'forced saving' mechanism was last seriously noticed by Thomas Joplin in the early nineteenth century. On this, see Corry, *Money, Saving and Investment in English Economics 1800–1850*, 77.
14. D. H. Robertson, *Banking Policy and the Price Level*, 23.
15. *CW*, xiii, 16.
16. *Ibid.*, 30–3.
17. *Ibid.*, 34.
18. Presley, 'J. M. Keynes and D. H. Robertson: Three Phases of Collaboration', *RHETM*, 1989, 40.
19. D. H. Robertson, *Banking Policy and the Price Level*, 71.
20. *CW*, v, pp. i, 269.
21. D. H. Robertson, *Banking Policy and the Price Level*, 49, 50n, ch. v generally. The

Keynes–Robertson exchanges on induced lacking can be followed in *CW*, xiii, 29–41. Keynes wrote on 28 May 1925: 'In assuming that the public as a whole has to reduce its current consumption when inflation takes place you overlook the fact that whilst some depositors may as a result of the inflation have less real resources at the bank, other depositors have more.' Inflation cannot create extra resources for investment, Keynes was led to insist, unless or until 'someone is induced . . . to do *some new* hoarding out of current income'. This might come about either because those hit by inflation were more interested in maintaining the 'real' value of their cash balances than in maintaining the 'real' value of their consumption; or because inflation has redistributed income into the hands of those 'whose incentive and ability to hoard is greater than those from whom it is taken'; or because 'a higher bank rate may increase the incentive to hoard'. On the other hand, inflation produces some powerful incentives to dishoard, or dissave. 'The new equilibrium of prices, as a result of a given percentage of inflation, depends upon the resultant of these forces.' Keynes thought that prices would go on rising until one of the 'incentives to new hoarding' came into play. But, he told Robertson, the decision to increase the money value of his cash balances was by no means *forced* on the individual: 'it remains just as voluntary as any other form of saving; it is the result of individual decisions balancing the advantage of maintaining hoards at certain levels as against those of maintaining consumption at a certain level'. In June 1925, Robertson capitulated: 'I think I am now convinced on the point of substance, viz. that the new real Hoarding and the new Short Lacking are the same (like Mrs. Do-as-you-would-be-done-by and Mrs. Be-done-by-as-you-did in the Water Babies!).' Presley, in 'J. M. Keynes and the Real Balance Effect', *MS*, 1986, 28, holds that 'Robertson, and by implication Keynes, was using the real balance effect to explain the nature of the adjustment to a new equilibrium position when the absolute price level deviated from its equilibrium value.'

This is confirmed in *CIV*, xiii, 36–7. But it cannot be said that Keynes got very far in his 'stability analysis'. His discussion with Robertson was really about something else: whether inflation might be a way of increasing saving.

22. *CIV*, xii, 39.
23. *Ibid.*, 32–3.
24. D. H. Robertson, *Banking Policy and the Price Level*, 81.
25. *CIV*, xiii, 40, 41.
26. *CIV*, xiv, 94–5.
27. Moggridge, *Keynes*, ch. 3; see also R. J. Bigg, 'Cambridge Monetary Theory and the Degeneration of the Marshallian Research Programme 1900–1929', Ph.D. 1983, Cambridge, published as *Cambridge and the Monetary Theory of Production*, 1990.
28. *CIV*, xiii, 19–22.
29. JMK to LK, 21 February 1927.
30. MPP: JMK to DM, 22 September 1926.
31. KP: PS/3, 1925–7.
32. *CIV*, ix, 200–6.
33. KP: A/27, RMcK to JMK, 3 February 1927.
34. JMK to LK, 27 April 1927.
35. D. H. Robertson, *Money*, 2nd edn, 1928, ix.
36. FR to JMK, 3 August 1928, in *CW*, xiii, 78.
37. On Ramsey's 'optimal saving' theory see JMK's correspondence with Ramsey, *CW*, xii, 784f.
38. *CW*, xiii, 770–2.
39. McKenna, *Post-War Banking Policy*, 122, 129–31.
40. *CW*, xiii, 90–1.
41. *Ibid.*, 51.
42. MPP: JMK to DM, 10 December 1928.
43. *CW*, xix, 664.
44. JMK to LK, 14, 16 October 1927; *CW*, xix, 724–5.
45. *CW*, xix, 749.
46. JMK to LK, 20, 22 January 1928.
47. For reminiscences of Cambridge in the 1920s see H. M. Robertson, 'J. M. Keynes and Cambridge in the 1920s', *SAJE*, 1983, 407–18, and E. A. G. Robinson, 'Keynes and His Cambridge Colleagues', in Patinkin and Clark Reith (eds), *Keynes, Cambridge, and the General Theory*, 25–37. The quotation about Joan Robinson comes from George R. Feiwel in 'Joan Robinson Inside and Outside the Stream', in George R. Feiwel (ed.), *Joan Robinson and Modern Economic Theory*, 2.

48. Kahn, *The Making of Keynes' General Theory*, 170–1.
49. Schumpeter, *History of Economic Analysis*, 1152. Schumpeter couples Shove with Kahn. But Shove never achieved the 'anonymous power' at Cambridge which Kahn later did.
50. JMK to LK, 11 October 1928.
51. KP: L/S, PS to JMK, December 1922.
52. *Ibid.*, JMK to JCCD, 29 January 1923.
53. E. A. G. Robinson, 'Keynes and His Cambridge Colleagues', in Patinkin and Clark Reith, *Keynes, Cambridge, and the General Theory*, 26.
54. JMK to LK, 28 November 1927.
55. KP: L/S, PS to JMK, 23 November 1924.
56. JMK to LK, 26 May 1929.
57. JMK to LK, 31 October 1925.
58. See Annan, *Our Age*, 179–80; Sinclair, *The Red and the Blue*, 26–30; N. Wood, *Communism and British Intellectuals*, 150–5.
59. From Alethea Graham's diary, 9 May 1930, published in the *Charleston Magazine*, Summer/Autumn 1992, 24. Alethea Graham was up at Girton College from 1927 to 1930.
60. JMK to LK, 14 November 1926.
61. JMK to LK, 29 January 1928.
62. JMK to LK, 6 May 1927.
63. Harrod, *The Life of John Maynard Keynes*, 400.
64. q. Milo Keynes (ed.), *Lydia Lopokova*, 122–4; interview with the author, 8 September 1984.
65. P. Clarke, *The Keynesian Revolution in the Making*, esp. chs 3 and 4.
66. Notes of Keynes's speech in KP: OC/2. The comment is by Karl Britton in 'Recollections of Cambridge 1928–32' in *CR*, ciii, no. 2270, 1982, 273.
67. *CW*, xix, 761–6.
68. P. Clarke, *The Keynesian Revolution in the Making*, 51–4. In his article in *Economica*, March 1925, Hawtrey wrote, 'The money borrowed is genuine saving. In other words it must come out of the consumers' income. . . . The effect of this diversion of a part of this consumers' outlay into the hands of the Government is to diminish by that amount the effective demand for products.'
69. *Ibid.*, 64; see also TP: 175/26, Memorandum by Sir Frederick Leith-Ross, 3 August 1928.
70. P. Clarke, *The Keynesian Revolution in the Making*, 54–8.
71. *Nation*, 23 February 1929, 711.

72. See *CW*, xiii, 94, 108n.
73. *Ibid.*, 52–9.
74. *CW*, xix, 721.
75. *CW*, xi, 458.
76. *CW*, xix, 805.
77. Williamson, *National Crisis and National Government*, ch. 1, argues that the 'hastily produced' Lloyd George pledge was designed to 'pre-empt' similar schemes being canvassed in the Conservative and Labour Parties, and in fact inhibited both Conservative and Labour radicalism on unemployment. He cites the Joynson–Hicks and Steel–Maitland plans, as well as the fact that Snowden approved of a big public works programme 'early in 1929' (p. 40). But these plans – speculations really – which remained private, were similar to the Liberal one only in phraseology. The Conservative ministers' suggestions collapsed the moment the Treasury got to work on them, and Labour's would have as well, whereas the Liberal pledge was a public commitment, with administrative detail and intellectual guts behind it. There is simply no comparison with the vague proposals floating round the two other parties. Also the timing is wrong. The Lloyd George pledge was first mooted in a speech by Seebohm Rowntree in York in October 1928. Far from being 'hastily produced' it was a political crystallisation of the Liberal Industrial Inquiry, the work by the Rowntree Committee and estimates of both primary and secondary employment. Rowntree wrote to JMK on 31 January 1929, 'I am coming to the opinion that if it were possible for the Liberal Party to make a specific pledge with regard to the reduction of unemployment the results might be surprising. I propose to suggest to the Conference at Churt that such a pledge should be given. . . . We have the schemes ready, and we have what nei-

ther of the other Parties has, a leader with the imagination and drive to put a great scheme of this kind through.' (KP: L/29.)
78. McKenna's annual speech to the shareholders of the Midland Bank, as reported in the *Nation*, 26 January 1929, 599. See also *We Can Conquer Unemployment*, 55.
79. *Memoranda on Certain Proposals Relating to Unemployment*, 51. Keynes's comment is quoted in *The Times*, 29 May 1929.
80. q. P. Clarke, *The Keynesian Revolution in the Making*, 91.
81. *CW*, xix, 804–8.
82. *Ibid.*, 808–12.
83. *CW*, ix, 106–7.
84. Dimand, *The Origins of the Keynesian Revolution*, 98–9.
85. *CW*, ix, 116–19.
86. *Ibid.*, 120; also *CW*, xix, 821, 822.
87. *CW*, ix, 123–4.
88. *Ibid.*, 125.
89. D. H. Robertson, *Banking Policy and the Price Level*, 22.
90. *Ibid.*, 37–8.
91. *Ibid.*, 39.
92. This can be followed in *EJ* of March, June, September 1929; also in *CW*, xi, 451–80, which includes the Keynes–Ohlin correspondence.
93. *CW*, xviii, 241.
94. *Ibid.*, 281. JMK wrote to O. T. Falk from the Adlon Hotel in Berlin, 3 April 1928, that the general view in Berlin was that 'nothing can happen so long as the US goes on lending, and there is not the least sign of that stopping – Germany is full of American agents trying to find excuses to lend. There is also a very large amount of foreign short money here.' All this was to change after the middle of 1928.
95. *CW*, xviii, 316.
96. *CW*, xi, 454.
97. Ohlin *EJ*, September 1929, 400.
98. *CW*, xi, 476.
99. *Ibid.*, 474.

Chapter 10: Summing up the 1920s: A Treatise on Money

1. KP: L/30, J. A. Schumpeter to JMK, 29 November 1930.
2. *CW*, vi, 304. The *Treatise* is in vols v and vi in the *CW* edn; only volume numbers will be used below.
3. For example, *CW*, vi, 193.
4. KP:TM 1/3, F. Leith-Ross to JMK, 4 November 1930.
5. *CW*, vi, 132.
6. *CW*, v, 42.
7. *Ibid.*, 79, 81.
8. *Ibid.*, 121.

9. JMK to A. C. Pigou, 11 May 1931; *CW*, xiii, 216.
10. *CW*, v, 111.
11. 'Excess saving' and 'excess bearishness' are dealt with in *ibid.*, 154–60 and 127–9, 222–30.
12. *Ibid.*, 138–9.
13. *Ibid.*, 254; vi, 85–6.
14. *CW*, v, 139.
15. *Ibid.*, 315.
16. *Ibid.*, 165.
17. *Ibid.*, 118.
18. *CW*, vi, 274.
19. *CW*, v, 148.
20. *Ibid.*, 192–3.
21. *Ibid.*, 137.
22. Hicks, 'A Note on the Treatise', in *Critical Essays in Monetary Theory*, 191–2.
23. Patinkin, *Keynes's Monetary Thought*, 37.
24. *CW*, v, 152.
25. *Ibid.*, 153.
26. *CW*, vi, 314.
27. *CW*, v, 150.
28. *Ibid.*, 244–5.
29. *Ibid.*, 273.
30. *Ibid.*
31. *Ibid.*, 160.
32. *Ibid.*, 262.

33. *Ibid.*, 264.
34. *Ibid.*, 267–8.
35. *CW*, vi, 78.
36. *Ibid.*, 87.
37. Skidelsky, *Keynes*, i, 220.
38. *CW*, vi, 8–9.
39. *Ibid.*, 98–9.
40. *Ibid.*, 141, 154.
41. Sutton (ed.), *Letters of Roger Fry*, ii, RF to Helen Anrep, 5 May 1930, 648.
42. *CW*, vi, 150, 149.
43. See esp. the table at *ibid.*, 161.
44. *Ibid.*, 164.
45. *Ibid.*, 166.
46. *Ibid.*, 167–9.
47. For a good summary of the debate initiated by Hamilton, see Wallerstein, *The Modern World-System*, i, 70–85.
48. *CW*, vi, 322–4.
49. *Ibid.*, 334–5.
50. *Ibid.*, 243, 231.
51. *Ibid.*, 302.
52. *Ibid.*, 258–9.
53. *Ibid.*, 256.
54. *Ibid.*, 299.
55. *Ibid.*, 274f.
56. *Ibid.*, 356.
57. *Ibid.*, 358–61.
58. *Ibid.*, 351.

Chapter 11: The Slump

1. D'Abernon, *An Ambassador of Peace*, ii, 51–2n.
2. LK to FAK, 1 August 1929.
3. Taper, *Balanchine*, 126.
4. See JMK to FAK, 20 September 1929. The film, directed by Sinclair Hill, is about David, a sculptor (Stewart Rome), who believes his wife Laura (Frances Doble) has taken as a lover Anton, a musician (Hugh Eden). He sees the ballet, given as an entertainment in a country house, in which the husband (Dolin) returns while the wife (Lydia) is with her lover (Balanchine), and cuts off her hands with an axe. Laura has asked her husband to take a cast of Anton's beautiful hands, and the ballet gives the sculptor the idea of embedding the supposed lover's hands in plaster and telling him he will cut them off unless he goes away for ever. Even without the fire, the film would not, one suspects, have achieved immortality. The only extant copy was tracked down by the ballet writer Deirdre McMahon in the attic of a film buff in Co. Galway, Ireland, in 1984.
5. Partridge, *Memories*, 163.
6. *CW*, xx, 2–3.
7. Somary, *The Raven of Zurich*, 146–7; q. Skousen, 'Keynes as a Speculator', in Skousen (ed.), *Dissent on Keynes*, 163. Skousen is an able critic of Keynes from the 'Austrian' viewpoint.
8. Davis, *The World between the Wars*, 136.
9. Kenworthy, *Sailors, Statesmen – and Others*, 304.
10. Robbins, *The Great Depression*, 52–3.
11. *CW*, xiii, 349.
12. JMK, 'Is There Inflation in the United States?', 1 September 1928.; repr. in *ibid.*, 52–9.
13. KP: L/28.
14. *CW*, xiii, 71.
15. *CW*, vi, 170–7.
16. See *CW*, xii, 11, 15–17.
17. JMK to LK, 2 March 1930.
18. JMK to LK, 3 May 1930.

19. Middlemas (ed.), *Thomas Jones, Whitehall Diary*, ii, 218–28.
20. *CW*, xx, 18–27.
21. Editorial comment, *ibid.*, 38.
22. MPP: JMK to Daniel Macmillan, 23 July 1931.
23. N. Kaldor, 'Keynes as an Economic Adviser', in Thirlwall (ed.), *Keynes as a Policy Adviser*, 8–9.
24. *CW*, xx, 41–2.
25. *Ibid.*, 46.
26. *Ibid.*, 49.
27. *Ibid.*, 50–1.
28. *Ibid.*, 53.
29. *Ibid.*, 67.
30. *Ibid.*, 3–16. This followed a suggestion by Maurice Dobb, Cambridge's resident Marxist economist, whose 'A Sceptical View of the Theory of Wages' appeared in the *EJ*, December 1929. The talk was first given at Bedford College, London, on 24 October 1929. It was published as 'The Question of High Wages' in *PQ*, January–March 1930.
31. *CW*, xx, 318.
32. *Ibid.*, 64.
33. *Ibid.*, 56.
34. *Ibid.*, 59–60.
35. *Ibid.*, 58–61, 68.
36. *Ibid.*, q. Skidelsky, *Politicians and the Slump*, 291 Cf. Dimand, *The Origins of the Keynesian Revolution*, 112–13. Rueff first produced this argument in 1925.
37. Benjamin and Kochin, 'Searching for an Explanation of Unemployment in Inter-war Britain', *JPE*, 1979, 441–78.
38. *CW*, xx, 83–4.
39. *Ibid.*, 71.
40. *Ibid.*, 79–80.
41. *Ibid.*, 95.
42. *Ibid.*, 84–5.
43. *Ibid.*, 75.
44. *Ibid.*, 80.
45. RHBP: File 198, JMK to RB, 12 March 1930; JMK to Montagu Norman, 22 May 1930, in *CW*, xx, 350–6.
46. RHBP: File 198, JMK to RB, 12 May 1930.
47. *CW*, xx, 72.
48. *Ibid.*, 127.
49. *Ibid.*
50. *Ibid.*, 99–102.
51. *Ibid.*, 102.
52. *Ibid.*, 108–9.
53. *Ibid.*, 109–13.
54. *Ibid.*, 113, 117.
55. *Ibid.*, 115.
56. *Ibid.*, 116, 120–1.
57. *Ibid.*, 130.
58. *Ibid.*, 130–1.
59. *Ibid.*, 138.
60. *Ibid.*, 126.
61. *Ibid.*, 133–4.
62. *Ibid.*, 144–5.
63. *Ibid.*, 147–8.
64. *Ibid.*, 151.
65. *Ibid.*, 157.
66. *Ibid.*, 153.
67. *Ibid.*, 156.
68. BE: G1/426. E. M. Harvey to Montagu Norman, 19 December 1929.
69. Macmillan Committee, Minutes of Evidence, Q3516. For JMK's description of Montagu Norman see A. O. Bell (ed.) *The Diary of Virginia Woolf*, iv, 208.
70. Boyle, *Montagu Norman*, 258.
71. Macmillan Committee, ME 3339.
72. *Ibid.*, 3382.
73. For the construction of the Bank's brief, see P. Clarke, *The Keynesian Revolution in the Making*, 131–5.
74. Henry Clay, Memorandum on Unemployment since the War, prepared for the Macmillan Committee, para. 20, in Minutes of Evidence, p. 255.
75. Macmillan Committee, ME 8615.
76. *Ibid.*, 8733.
77. *Ibid.*, Memorandum by Henry Clay, paras 25, 26, 28, p. 255.
78. See Clay's Memorandum 'Bank Rate, Credit, and Employment', 17 May 1930, in BE: EID 1/2.
79. Macmillan Committee, ME 7690.
80. *Ibid.*, 7783.
81. *Ibid.*, 7647.
82. *Ibid.*, 7653, 7836.
83. *Ibid.*, 7662.
84. *Ibid.*, 7835.
85. *Ibid.*, 7841.
86. *Ibid.*, 7842–3, 7847.
87. *CW*, xx, 345.
88. Macmillan Committee, ME 5565.
89. *Ibid.*, 6500–24.
90. *Ibid.*, 5650, 5654, 5684–6.
91. *Ibid.*, 5690.
92. EGP: 4, Memorandum to the Federal Reserve Board, 8 October 1930.
93. *CW*, xx, 180.
94. *Ibid.*, 265.
95. *Ibid.*, 184.
96. *Ibid.*, 223.
97. Both reports are reprinted in Howson and Winch, *The Economic Advisory Council*, 174–80.
98. Pimlott (ed.), *The Political Diary of Hugh Dalton*, 115.

99. Howson and Winch, *The Economic Advisory Council*, 40.
100. KP: EA/4, JMK to JRM, 10 July 1930.
101. Howson and Winch, *The Economic Advisory Council*, 40.
102. *Ibid.*, 48.
103. HDHP: Files 17, 17a, 'Economic Outlook: Memorandum to the PM', 13 March 1930; 'Memorandum on Industrial Reconstruction', 30 May 1930.
104. *Ibid.*, File 22a, W. Eady to HDH, 16 May 1930.
105. For a discussion of such proposals see especially Booth and Pack, *Employment, Capital and Economic Policy*; Pollard (ed.), *The Gold Standard and Employment Policies between the Wars*; and Glynn and Booth (eds), *The Road to Full Employment*.
106. *CW*, xx, 359. HDH wrote (p. 358), 'where there are solid grounds for expecting that a certain event will happen, and the grounds are of a kind which the business community can understand, then the results of that event begin to take effect in advance'.
107. *Ibid.*, 361.
108. *Ibid.*, 362, 366.
109. Clay (ed.), *The Interwar Years*, Memorandum to the Committee of Economists, 18 September 1930, 69–70.
110. Robbins, *Autobiography of an Economist*, 134–5.
111. KP: PP/45.
112. Macmillan Committee, ME 6481.
113. KP: BR 2, JMK to C. A. Siepmann, 4 January 1933.
114. *CW*, vii, 30n.
115. Robbins, *Autobiography of an Economist*, 154.
116. J. H. Jones, *Josiah Stamp*, 222. Stamp to his wife, 11 March 1924.
117. Macmillan Committee, ME 3716–18, 3972–3.
118. LK to JMK, 14 February 1930. The broadcast is repr. in *CW*, xx, 315–25.
119. *CW*, xiii, 178.
120. *Ibid.*, 179.
121. *Ibid.*, 183.
122. *Ibid.*, 180.
123. *Ibid.*, 181.
124. *Ibid.*, 186.
125. Macmillan Committee, ME 6147.
126. *CW*, xiii, 187–9.
127. *Ibid.*, 192.
128. *Ibid.*, 185.
129. *Ibid.*, 199.
130. *CW*, xx, 416–19.
131. *Ibid.*, 325–6.

132. *Ibid.*, 431–2. Robbins had used Rueff's correlation between changes in unemployment and changes in the dole to persuade the Committee. See Dimand, *The Origins of the Keynesian Revolution*, 113.
133. *CW*, xx, 437–43; quotations from 441–2.
134. *Ibid.*, 443–8.
135. JMK to LK, 9 October 1930.
136. HDH, 'Drift of the Draft Report', 13 October 1930; repr. *CW*, xx, 452–6.
137. JMK to LK, 9 October 1930.
138. Robbins, *Autobiography of an Economist*, 151.
139. Pimlott (ed.), *The Political Diary of Hugh Dalton*, 123.
140. Robbins, *Autobiography of an Economist*, 151; *CW*, xx, 463–6.
141. Pimlott (ed.), *The Political Diary of Hugh Dalton*, 124.
142. Howson and Winch, *The Economic Advisory Council*, 72.
143. Robbins's dissenting report is repr. in *ibid.*, 227–31; the Keynes remark is from his *Autobiography of an Economist*, 155.
144. Pimlott (ed.), *The Political Diary of Hugh Dalton*, 124; Williamson, *National Crisis and National Government*, 68.
145. Howson and Winch, *The Economic Advisory Council*, 76.
146. *Ibid.*, 78.
147. *Ibid.*, 166–7.
148. *Ibid.*, 148.
149. KP: CO/1, JMK to Ryan, 7 September 1930.
150. Economists' Report, para. 5, q. Howson and Winch, *The Economic Advisory Council*, 180.
151. A. J. P. Taylor, *English History*, 286.
152. q. Skidelsky, *Politicians and the Slump*, 241.
153. OTFP1: JMK to OTF, 9 September 1930, 'A Note on This Phase of the Credit Cycle'.
154. *CW*, ix, 332.
155. KP: L/30.
156. LK to JMK, 25 May 1930.
157. Milo Keynes (ed.), *Lydia Lopokova*, 117.
158. *Ibid.*, 120.
159. KP: LLK1/1, AH to JMK, 12 December 1930.
160. Haskell, *Balletomania*, 185.
161. LK to JMK, 6 March 1931.
162. KP: LLK/5, LK to SC, undated, February 1931; SC to LK, 27 February 1931.
163. JMK to LK, 19 January 1931.
164. JMK to LK, 10 May 1931.
165. *Nation*, 13 December 1930; *CW*, xx, 474.
166. *CW*, ix, 126–34.
167. *Ibid.*, 137–9.

168. Skidelsky, *Politicians and the Slump*, 288–9, 297–300.
169. LK to JMK, 20 February 1931.
170. KP: L/31, RHB to JMK, 30 January 1931.
171. *CW*, xx, 484.
172. *Ibid.*, 486. Keynes was sending him regular financial appreciations at this time.
173. *CW*, ix, 231–9; q. 238.
174. Editor's comment, *CW*, ix, 231.
175. JMK to LK, 9 March 1931.
176. *New Statesman*, 14 March 1931.
177. *Ibid.*; *CW*, xx, 495–7.
178. *New Statesman*, 4 April 1931; *CW*, xx, 500.
179. *New Statesman*, 11 April 1931; *CW*, xx, 502.
180. *CW*, ix, 231n. Corr. in *CW*, xx, 489.
181. LK to JMK, 7 February 1931.
182. LGP: G 10/15, JMK to LG, 13 January 1931.
183. HDHP: File 21, JMK to HDH, 17 June 1931.
184. OTFP1: JMK to OTF, 22 June 1931.
185. HDHP: File 21, JMK to HDH, 17 June 1931.
186. *CW*, xx, 563.
187. *Ibid.*, 544–53.
188. *CW*, xiii, 354.
189. For the whole of the lectures, *CW*, xiii, 343–67.
190. Wright (ed.), *Unemployment as a World Problem*: Reports of Round Tables, vol. 1.
191. *CW*, xx, 591–3.
192. *New Statesman*, 15 August 1931; repr. in *CW*, ix, 141–5.
193. Marquand, *Ramsay MacDonald*, 610–11; Williamson, *National Crisis and National Government*, 294, cites MacDonald's letter to D'Abernon of 10 September 1931, showing that the Prime Minister thought Keynes had fallen in line with the other advice he was getting.
194. *CW*, xx, 611–12.
195. Feiling, *The Life of Neville Chamberlain*, 191; Bowle, *Viscount Samuel*, 271.
196. *CW*, xx, 598.
197. *CW*, ix, 238–42.
198. *CW*, xx, 598–602.
199. *CW*, ix, 145.
200. *CW*, xx, 605.
201. *Ibid.*, 609–11.
202. q. Skidelsky, *Oswald Mosley*, 268.
203. q. Rolph, *Kingsley*, 164; see also *New Statesman*, 27 September 1931; *CW*, xx, 245–6.
204. *LBMR*, April 1932; *CW*, xxi, 68–9.
205. TLP: Box 103–15.
206. TLP: Box 104–29.
207. WLP: File 1312.
208. KP: PP/45.
209. MacKenzie and MacKenzie (eds), *The Diary of Beatrice Webb*, iv, 260; LK to FAK, 22 September 1931.
210. JMK to JRM, 1 October 1931; *CW*, xx, 619.
211. LGP: G/10/15/16, JMK to LG, 1 October 1931.
212. FFP: Reel 45, Harold Laski to FF, 3 October 1931. Laski's comment on the crisis (6 September 1931): MacDonald and his followers 'have merely completed an evolution which is, in its way, just like that of Walter Lippmann; you cannot live with the aristocracy and avoid their ways of thought'.
213. OTFP2.

Chapter 12: Portrait of an Unusual Economist

1. This is the title of ch. 3 of Moggridge's *Keynes* (1976). Moggridge writes that when Marshall retired in 1907 he thought that 'the fundamental principles of the subject were fixed beyond dispute' (p. 46). In 1915, Keynes described the Cambridge school of economics as combining 'general agreement on principles with much variety of outlook, sympathies, and methods' (q. Skidelsky, *Keynes*, i, 209). For the Cambridge Economic Handbooks, see *CW*, xii, 855–60.
2. See the illuminating essay by R. M. Hartwell in Harris and Seldon (eds), *The Coming Confrontation*.
3. Annan, *Our Age*, 10.
4. In King's College Cambridge's *John Maynard Keynes*, 15.
5. q. Skidelsky, *Keynes*, i, 191.
6. JMK to GLS, 18 October 1905; see also Skidelsky, *Keynes*, i, 134.
7. *CW*, x, 446.
8. Barry, *Hayek's Social and Economic Philosophy*, 173.
9. Moore, *Principia Ethica*, 167.
10. A. F. W. Plumptre, 'Keynes in Cam-

bridge', *CJE*, August 1947, repr. in Wood (ed.), *John Maynard Keynes*, i, 153.

11. *CW*, x, 173, 187.
12. *Ibid.*, 108.
13. *Ibid.*, 110, 114–16, 121–2, 139, 146, 155.
14. *Ibid.*, 365.
15. In his review of the 4th edn of S. Jevons's *Theory of Political Economy*, *EJ*, March 1912; *CW*, xi, 516.
16. *CW*, x, 131.
17. Marshall, *Principles of Economics*, 8th edn, 85; for JMK on Jevons, see *CW*, x, 198; the JMK remark is quoted in Pigou, *Economics in Practice*, 22.
18. *CW*, x, 256.
19. *Ibid.*, 272.
20. *Ibid.*, 262–3.
21. *Ibid.*, 195–9.
22. *Ibid.*, 366.
23. JMK letter in the *Nation*, 29 August 1925; *CW*, xviii, 392–3.
24. *CW*, x, 117.
25. Introduction to JMK's Galton Lecture, 1937. For reference see chapter 17, n. 22.
26. *CW*, vi, 193.
27. KP: CO/2, JMK to D. Macmillan, 1 March 1932; see also JMK's correspondence with Larranaga in L/32. JMK to M. C. Rorty, 3, 29 February 1932, is in CO/6. See CO/2 for JMK to D. Macmillan on McGregor; L/35 for JMK to D. B. Copland, 14 January, 1 May 1935, and to I. M. Sutherland, 14 January 1935, on Sutherland.
28. KP: CO/1, JMK to W. Stark, 9 April 1942.
29. *CW*, x, 86.
30. *Cambridge Review*; *CW*, x, 107.
31. KP: PS/2. This speech was to the annual dinner of the Political Economy Club at Gatti's Restaurant, London, 2 April 1924. Keynes must have got the letter from *EJ*, 1907, 274, where it had been printed by Foxwell. The fact that Keynes was aware of the Malthus of 'effective demand' as early as 1924 casts further doubt on the idea of the editor of *CW*, x, 71n. that Keynes picked up this side of Malthus only 'when his own thinking about these issues had already taken final shape'.

32. Rymes (ed.), *Keynes's Lectures*, 121.
33. Marshall's Inaugural Lecture, q. *CW*, x, 196.
34. Kahn, *The Making of Keynes's General Theory*, 28–9.
35. As told in Hamouda (ed.), *Controversies in Political Economy*, 194 n. 2.
36. Marshall, *Principles of Economics*, 291.
37. *CW*, x, 97–8.
38. *Ibid.*, 98.
39. Marshall, *Principles of Economics*, vi.
40. *Ibid.*, 314–15.
41. In Skidelsky (ed.), *The End of the Keynesian Era*, 11.
42. Kahn, *The Economics of the Short Period*, xiii.
43. KP: EJ/1/2. JMK to F. W. Ogilvie, 2 October 1929.
44. *CW*, xviii, 328.
45. Moggridge, 'Keynes: The Economist', in Moggridge (ed.), *Keynes: Aspects of the Man and His Work*, 62. See also E. A. G. Robinson, 'John Maynard Keynes 1883–1946', *EJ*, 1947; repr. in Wood (ed.), *John Maynard Keynes*, i, 89; and his 'John Maynard Keynes: Economist, Author, Statesman', 8–9.
46. Hession, *John Maynard Keynes*, 17–18.
47. In *QJE*, August 1972, 463–4.
48. Moggridge (ed.), *Keynes: Aspects of the Man and His Work*, 57.
49. *CW*, ix, 138.
50. Letter to the author, 9 July 1986. See also Hahn, *Money and Inflation*, x: 'I consider that Keynes had no real grasp of formal economic theorising (and also disliked it), and that he consequently left many gaping holes in his theory. I none the less hold that his insights were several orders more profound and realistic than those of his recent critics.'
51. In Milo Keynes (ed.), *Lydia Lopokova*, 170; Ayer, *Part of My Life*, 124.
51. *CW*, xxviii, 399.
53. See *CW*, xx, 157–65. It must be said that McKenna emerges from this tale far more credulous than Keynes. The 'discovery' turned out to be a hoax, but who was fooling whom is not clear.

Chapter 13: The Practical Visionary

1. CP: VB to Clive Bell, 10 October 1931.

2. *CW*, ix, xix.

3. *The Times*, 4 December 1931.
4. Comments and reviews are collected in KP: P/1/3. Leonard Woolf, *New Statesman*, 19 December 1931; Strachey, *The Coming Struggle for Power*, 201–2; Harold Laski, *Time and Tide*, 19 December 1931; OTF to JMK, 29 November 1931.
5. A. O. Bell (ed.), *The Diary of Virginia Woolf*, iv, 27 December 1931, 56.
6. SP: Add. MS. 60672, JMK to JBS, 19 November 1933.
7. A. O. Bell (ed.), *The Diary of Virginia Woolf*, iv. 27 December 1931, 56.
8. DGP: VB to DG, 7 August 1930.
9. Howson and Winch, *The Economic Advisory Council*, 100–5.
10. In *EJ*, September, 1932, repr. in *CW*, xxi, 114.
11. JMK to J. R. MacDonald, 12 July 1931; *CW*, xviii, 379.
12. q. Eichengreen, 'Sterling and the Tariff 1929–32', *PSIF*, 1981, 32.
13. In *The Times*, 28 September 1931; *CW*, ix, 243; cf. Howson and Winch, *The Economic Advisory Council*, 98. JMK called tariffs a 'first-class curse' on 19 April 1932, *CW*, xxi, 103.
14. JMK, Memorandum to F. Leith-Ross, 16 November 1931; *CW*, xxi, 17.
15. In JMK's 'Report of the Australian Experts', *Melbourne Herald*, 27 June 1932, but written on 17 April 1932; *CW*, xxi, 98.
16. KP: A/32, JMK to Clive Baillieu, 14 July 1932.
17. Drummond, *British Economic Policy and the Empire*, 98–9.
18. KP: CO/6, JMK to Alexander Shaw, 13 January 1932.
19. JMK, 'The Consequences to the Banks of the Collapse of Money Values'; *CW*, ix, 151.
20. Galbraith, *Money: Whence It Came, Where It Went*, 192.
21. JMK to LK, 15 May 1932.
22. In a BBC broadcast on planning, 14 March 1932; *CW*, xxi, 90.
23. In the *Evening Standard*, 20 April 1932; *CW*, xxi, 107.
24. *CW*, xxi, 110.
25. *Ibid.*
26. CMP: Add. MS. 52432, Samuel Courtauld to Christabel Aberconway, 1 September 1932.
27. JMK to Walter Case, 2 November 1931; *CW*, xxi, 9–10.
28. JMK's talk, on 11 December 1931, was to the Society for Socialist Inquiry and Propaganda, started by G. D. H. Cole. A version of his talk was printed in *PQ*, April–June 1932, of whose board he was a member. The phrase in inverted commas was from the talk but was left out of the published essay: see KP: A/32.
29. *CW*, xxi, 135.
30. Booth and Pack, *Employment, Capital and Economic Policy*, 144.
31. A. L. Rowse, *Adelphi*, April 1932.
32. KP: GTE/1/5, JMK to A. L. Rowse, 12 May 1936; see Durbin, *New Jerusalems*, ch. 7.
33. Booth and Pack, *Employment, Capital and Economic Policy*, 66–7. For Keynes and the Labour Party see also Pimlott, *Labour and the Left in the 1930s*, ch. 4.
34. *CW*, xxi, 45.
35. *Ibid.*, 62.
36. P. Clarke, *The Keynesian Revolution in the Making*, 230.
37. Hicks, *Critical Essays in Monetary Theory*, 192.
38. Patinkin makes this point on pp. 18–19 of his *Anticipations of the General Theory*.
39. *CW*, ix, 322.
40. *CW*, xxi, 213.
41. JMK to L. F. Giblin, 2 July 1932; *CW*, xxi, 99: 'it may be that prices are related to costs after the same fashion as a cat to her tail'. He turned down an invitation at this time to visit Australia for six months for £2500, all expenses paid.
42. P. Clarke, *The Keynesian Revolution in the Making*, 272.
43. *CW*, xxi, 59–60.
44. P. A. Samuelson, 'The General Theory' (1946) in Lekachman (ed.), *Keynes's General Theory*, 321.
45. *CW*, ix, 284, 291.
46. OTFP1, JMK to OTF, 9 September 1930, where JMK says that those who argue in favour of automatic recovery forget 'that the reduction of output is reducing incomes and consuming power by just the same amount'; because of this the 'secondary recovery' from the bottom of the slump which takes place after an appropriate lapse of time will peter out well short of a 'real recovery'. In broad outline, this is the *General Theory* story; what is lacking is the consumption function.
47. KP: L/34, JMK to Lluc Beltram, 29 November 1934.
48. P. Clarke, *The Keynesian Revolution in the Making*, 263; D. Patinkin, 'Keynes' in

NP, 23b; Dimand, *The Origins of the Keynesian Revolution*, 167; M. Milgate, 'The "New" Keynes Papers', in Eatwell and Milgate (eds), *Keynes's Economics and the Theory of Value and Distribution*, 197–8. Moggridge's careful account 'From the *Treatise* to *The General Theory*: An Exercise in Chronology', *HPE*, 1973, 73, which antedates some evidence later available, says that Keynes had 'virtually completed the development of his analytical system' by 1932. Littleboy and Mehta, 'Patinkin on Keynes's Theory of Effective Demand', *HPE*, 1987, 311, argue that the banana parable of the *Treatise* does not involve Keynes assuming that the marginal propensity to consume is unity, though they recognise that he lacked a consumption function. This raises the question whether Keynes saw the banana parable as a logical device – a *reductio ad absurdum* – or as a 'realistic' narrative.

49. P. Clarke, *The Keynesian Revolution in the Making*, 258; Patinkin, *Anticipation of the General Theory*, 16.

50. M. Fallgatter's notes of Keynes's 4th lecture, 6 November 1933, in T. K. Rymes (ed.), 'Keynes's Lectures 1932–5: Notes of Students' (hereafter, Rymes, 'NOS'). This typed collection of students' notes, which is available from Professor Rymes, must be distinguished from T. K. Rymes (ed.), *Keynes's Lectures 1932–1935: Notes of a Representative Student* (hereafter, *Keynes's Lectures*), a published book, where the phrase does not appear on p. 101.

51. Leijonhufvud, *On Keynesian Economics and the Economics of Keynes*, 15.

52. The earlier version is in RGHP: 11/3.

53. *Ibid.*, para. 22.

54. *Ibid.*, para. 66.

55. RGHP: 11/2.

56. *CW*, xiii, 143–5.

57. RGHP: 11/5. Omitted from *CW*.

58. JMK to R. G. Hawtrey, 1 June 1932, *CW*, xiii, 172; Hawtrey's reply (omitted from *CW*) is scribbled on Keynes's paper, which he returned to him.

59. *CW*, v, 125.

60. Joan Robinson, *Contributions to Modern Economics*, xii–xiii.

61. *CW*, xiii, 340n.

62. Joan Robinson, 'A Parable of Saving and Investment', *Economica*, 1933.

63. *CW*, xiii, 270.

64. JMK to LK, 1 February 1932.

65. Patinkin, *Keynes's Monetary Thought*, 71.

66. Cain, 'Cambridge and Its Revolution', *ER*, 1979, 114. Cain's account is exemplary.

67. *CW*, ix, 106–7.

68. Kahn, *The Making of Keynes's General Theory*, 101–2.

69. Kahn, 'The Relation of Home Investment to Unemployment', *EJ*, 1931, 84.

70. *Ibid.*, 88.

71. KP: L/31.

72. Cain, 'Cambridge and Its Revolution', *ER*, 1979, 114.

73. *CW*, xiii, 374–5.

74. Cain, 'Cambridge and Its Revolution', *ER*, 1979, 113. Warming's article, 'International Difficulties Arising out of the Financing of Public Works during a Depression', appeared in *EJ*, June 1932.

75. *CW*, xiii, 238–45.

76. D. H. Robertson, 'Mr Keynes's Theory of Money', *EJ*, September 1931, 402n., 407.

77. JMK, 'Notes on the Definition of Saving', 22 March 1932; *CW*, xiii, 275–6, 278. Keynes gave up his *Treatise* definition reluctantly, not just because it brought out the main causes of disequilibrium situations, but because he wanted, in Bryce's words, to retain a 'moral quality' for saving. A. Cairncross: 'if shares rise . . . we do not speak of increase in saving'. Lecture notes of 24 October 1932, A21, D12, in Rymes, 'NOS'.

78. *CW*, xiii, 276.

79. In Milo Keynes (ed.), *Essays on John Maynard Keynes*, 82.

80. *CW*, xiii, 277–8.

81. DHR to JMK, 1 April 1933; JMK to DHR, 3 May 1933; *CW*, xxix, 16–18.

82. F. A. Hayek, *Economica*, November 1931, 401.

83. Kahn, *The Making of Keynes's General Theory*, 182.

84. G. L. Shackle in O'Brien and Presley (eds), *Pioneers of Modern Economics in Britain*, 236.

85. q. Durbin, *New Jerusalems*, 136.

86. JMK, 'A Pure Theory of Money: A Reply to Dr. Hayek', *Economica*, November 1931; *CW*, xiii, 243, 252.

87. Hayek, *Prices and Production*, 58.

88. *Ibid.*, 98.

89. P. Sraffa, 'Dr Hayek on Money and Capital', *EJ*, March 1932, 48, 49–51. See also G. Mongiovi, 'Keynes, Hayek and Sraffa: On the Origins of Chapter 17 of

The General Theory', *Économique Appliquée*, tome XLIII, 1990, no. 2.

90. *CW*, xiii, 252–4.
91. Hayek, *New Studies*, 284.
92. *CW*, xiii, 266.
93. Hayek, *New Studies*, 284.
94. The article is reprinted in Hayek, *Money, Capital and Fluctuations*.
95. Hayek, *New Studies*, 283, 287.
96. JMK to FAK, 18 September 1932.
97. P. Jacobsson's diary, 2 August 1932, q. in Erin E. Jacobsson, *A Life for Sound Money*, 107.
98. L. Tarshis, 'The Keynesian Revolution: What It Meant in the 1930s', unpublished typescript.
99. See n. 50 above.
100. Sources for the distinction between the two types of economy are: *CW*, xxix, 54–7, containing a 'Typed and handwritten fragment' from which Keynes appears to have lectured, 14 November 1932; Lectures 1 and 6 from Rymes's 'NOS', or his *Keynes's Lectures*; and from Keynes's contribution to the Spiethoff *Festschrift*, *CW*, xiii, 408–11.
101. Rymes, *Keynes's Lectures*, 17 October 1932, 59.
102. This is from a chapter of JMK's book, 'The Parameters of a Monetary Economy', written before the end of 1932, but after the summer vacation at Tilton: *CW*, xiii, 401.
103. *Ibid.*, 385–7. From ch. 8 of the summer's 'connected treatment'.
104. Patinkin, *Anticipations of the General Theory*, 20–1.
105. Rymes, 'NOS', 14 November 1932, I 19; see his *Keynes's Lectures*, 73.
106. *CW*, xxix, 57; also xiii, 387.
107. *CW*, xiii, 388–9, 395–6.
108. *Ibid.*, 389.
109. *Ibid.*, 390–6.
110. *CW*, xxix, 50–4; Rymes, *Keynes's Lectures*, 10 October 1932, 50.
111. Rymes, 'NOS', Cairncross notes on Lecture, 7 November 1932, D16.
112. JMK note in *AER*, December 1933, 675; *CW*, xiii, 396; for the whole argument see *CW*, xxix, 54–5; xiii, 394–6.
113. *CW*, xiii, 404; xxix, 54–7; Rymes, *Keynes's Lectures*, 14 November 1932, 76–7.
114. Rymes, 'NOS', Bryce's notes on Lecture, 14 November 1932, A39.
115. *CW*, x, 97. The revised essay dates from October/November 1932, not from the 'beginning of 1933' as the editor of *CW*, x, states (p. 71).

116. *Ibid.*, 100–1.
117. Rymes, 'NOS', Bryce's notes on Lecture, 28 November 1932, A48.
118. 'Indeed, he once told me that I had no business, at my age, to be immersing myself in such antiquarian pursuits. I protested how interesting a study they made. He did not deny their interest, he replied. When he was old and no longer alert enough for difficult and exact analysis, he, too, would like to give his time, as a refuge and diversion . . . to . . . economic history and the history of economic thought. But they were, he said, "too easy".' H. M. Robertson, 'J. M. Keynes and Cambridge in the 1920s', *SAJE*, 1983, 412.
119. JMK had taken part in an *Economic Journal* colloquium on 'Saving and Usury' earlier in the year; *CW*, xxix, 13–16.
120. JMK to R. F. Harrod, 30 August 1936; *CW*, xiv, 85.
121. *New Statesman and Nation*, 24 December 1932; *CW*, xxi, 210–11.
122. See his article on the 'Kaffir Boom', *Daily Mail*, 7 February 1933; *CW*, xxi, 228.
123. Salter, *Slave of the Lamp*, 87–8.
124. Howson and Winch, *The Economic Advisory Council*, 124–5.
125. *Ibid.*, 125–6.
126. *Ibid.*, 122.
127. *Ibid.*, 122–3.
128. *CW*, xxi, 138–40.
129. *Ibid.*, 141–5.
130. *Ibid.*, 145–62.
131. *CW*, ix, 335–6. The introduction was added for the pamphlet. This is the American version, with the multiplier.
132. *Ibid.*, 339.
133. *Ibid.*, 342.
134. Kahn, *The Making of the Keynesian Revolution*, 97.
135. *CW*, ix, 347.
136. *Ibid.*, 356.
137. *Ibid.*, 343.
138. *Ibid.*, 348.
139. *Ibid.*, 358 and n.
140. *Ibid.*, 349.
141. JMK to R. F. Kahn, 24 March 1933; RFK to JMK, 30 March 1933; *CW*, xiii, 413–14.
142. *CW*, xxi, 203–4.
143. *Ibid.*, 215–16.
144. In the *Daily Mail*, 17 February 1933; *CW*, xxi, 229–30.
145. *CW*, ix, 364.
146. *Ibid.*, 357.
147. *Ibid.*, 361.

148. *Ibid.*, 358.
149. *CW*, xxi, 179–80; RGHP: 11/5: 'The Means to Prosperity: Mr. Keynes's Articles in The Times' (undated).
150. *CW*, ix, 365–6.
151. TP: T 175/70 Pt 1, 21 March 1933.
152. *Ibid.*, T 175/17, 14 March 1933.
153. HDHP: Suppl. Box 68, HDH to Sir F. Phillips, 16 March 1933; see also Howson and Winch, *The Economic Advisory Council*, 129.
154. See JMK's correspondence with Sir Arthur Robinson, 10, 25 April 1932; *CW*, xxi, 191–3.
155. HDHP: Box 8.
156. *CW*, xxi, 184.
157. In the *Daily Mail*, 26 April 1933; *CW*, xxi, 195.
158. See Buchanan, Burton and Wagner, *The Consequences of Mr. Keynes*. The table on p. 39 shows that, between 1951 and 1976, a budget surplus was recorded only in two years – 1969 and 1970 – when Roy Jenkins was Chancellor.
159. BE: EID 4/103: J. A. C. Osborne to H. C. B. Mynors, 6 April 1933; cf. BE: G1/15 for R. N. Kershaw's Note on Keynes's Reply.

160. RHBP1: File 198, R. H. Brand to JMK, 20, 29 March 1933; article in *The Times*, 7 April 1933.
161. For a summary see Middleton, *Towards the Managed Economy*, 176–80.
162. JMK, 'Pros and Cons of Tariffs', *Listener*, 30 November 1932; *CW*, xxi, 204–10.
163. KP: PS/5/1930–3.
164. *CW*, xxi, 238.
165. *Ibid.*, 236.
166. *Ibid.*, 240–1.
167. *Ibid.*, 242–3.
168. Mosley, *My Life*, 247–8n.
169. JMK to FAK, 23 April 1933.
170. For the Stamp–Keynes correspondence, see KP: PS/5; L/33.
171. Meenan, *George O'Brien*, 170–1.
172. LK to JMK, 27 May 1933. See also the transatlantic broadcast discussion between JMK and Walter Lippmann, published in the *Listener*, 13 June 1933; *CW*, xxi, 251–9.
173. *CW*, xxi, 264–8. This closely followed the proposals adopted by the Committee on Economic Information, 16 May 1933. See Howson and Winch, *The Economic Advisory Council*, 120.
174. *Ibid.*, 273–7.
175. *Ibid.*, 281–2.

Chapter 14: New Deals

1. Mini, *Keynes, Bloomsbury, and The General Theory*, ch. 1.
2. This interpretation of the 'meaning' of fascism has been influenced by Barraclough, *An Introduction to Contemporary History*, esp. 30–33.
3. *CW*, ii, 2.
4. See e.g. JMK's comment on French economists in a letter to M. Pierre Jerome, 7 October 1932, in KP: CO/6.
5. Garraty, *The Great Depression*, 141.
6. KP: PS/5. The auspices were the journal *Der Deutsche Ökonomist* and the Studiengesellschaft für Wahrungstragen. One of the organisers, Dr Dahlberg, was an advocate of devaluation, which was apparently enough to damn him in the eyes of JMK's ultra-respectable liberal friends.
7. *CW*, xxi, 244, 285.
8. KP: L/33. JMK to A. Spiethoff, 25 August 1933. The German translation omitted the passage criticising totalitarian regimes.

9. KP: MM/19 'Melchior', L. Rosenbaum to Đ. E. Moggridge, 13 November 1971.
10. JMK to LK, 16 October 1933.
11. *CW*, xxviii, 21–2.
12. KP: L/33, JMK to Wallenberg, 12 April 1933.
13. *CW*, xxi, 243–4, 245, 246.
14. JMK to LK, 22 October 1933; cf. *CW*, xviii, 16–19.
15. KP: LLK/5, LK to FAK, 11 December 1932, 14 August 1934.
16. KP: L/34, JMK to editor of *Za Industrialisui*, Moscow, 20 October 1934.
17. Cynthia Mosley to FDR, 5 April 1933, q. Skidelsky, *Oswald Mosley*, 296.
18. JMK to LK, 3 March 1933.
19. Schlesinger, *The Coming of the New Deal*, 3.
20. *Ibid.*, 17, 19.
21. Stein, *The Fiscal Revolution in America*, 43.
22. *CW*, xxi, 252.
23. KP: L/33.
24. HDHP: Box 22A/1.
25. In his speech at Amherst, 11 November

1933, q. Steel, *Walter Lippmann and the American Century*, 307.

26. Berlin, *Personal Impressions*, 85.
27. FFP: Reel 66, FF to Jacob Viner, 6 June 1932.
28. *CW*, xxi, 289–97; an extended version of the Open Letter was published in *The Times*, 2 January 1934.
29. Stein, *The Fiscal Revolution in America*, 147–8.
30. Dimand, *The Origins of the Keynesian Revolution*, 61f.
31. JASP: HUG (FP) 4.8, Box 1, JAS to Irving Fisher, 10, 25 February 1933.
32. KP: A/34.
33. FFP: Reel 66, JV to FF, 1 June 1932.
34. Schlesinger, *The Coming of the New Deal*, 188.
35. KP: AV:1.
36. KP: LLK/5, LK to FAK, 13 August, 14 September 1934.
37. *CW*, xiii, 420.
38. JMK to LK, 13 October 1933.
39. JMK to LK, 29 October 1933.
40. JMK to LK, 22 April 1934.
41. JMK to LK, 12 November 1933.
42. A. O. Bell (ed.), *The Diary of Virginia Woolf*, iv, 209.
43. Stansky and Abrahams, *Journey to the Frontier*, 211.
44. *CW*, xiii, 421.
45. Rymes, 'NOS', Bryce, B8; Rymes, *Keynes's Lectures*, 88.
46. *CW*, xxix, 66.
47. Rymes, *Keynes's Lectures*, 92.
48. See also *CW*, xxix, 81–2; Rymes, *Keynes's Lectures*, 93–4.
49. Rymes, 'NOS', Fallgatter, G5; Rymes, *Keynes's Lectures*, 98.
50. Rymes, *Keynes's Lectures*, 104, 106.
51. Ibid., 112; Rymes, 'NOS', Fallgatter, G20.
52. Rymes, *Keynes's Lectures*, 115–16; Rymes, 'NOS', Tarshis, J26.
53. Rymes, *Keynes's Lectures*, 115; Rymes, 'NOS', Fallgatter, G20.
54. Rymes, *Keynes's Lectures*, 119–20; Rymes, 'NOS', Fallgatter, G26–7, Salant, M17.
55. Rymes, *Keynes's Lectures*, 125; Rymes, 'NOS', Bryce, B57.
56. Rymes, *Keynes's Lectures*, 121–2.
57. Ibid., 124.
58. *CW*, xxix, 112.
59. *CW*, xxi, 316.
60. Rymes, 'NOS', Fallgatter, G37.
61. See Milo Keynes (ed.), *Lydia Lopokova*, 219–23.
62. q. ibid., 223.
63. A. O. Bell (ed.), *The Diary of Virginia Woolf*, iv, 235. JMK blamed the captain, John W. Binks.
64. FFP: Reel 66, Tom Corcoran to FF, 22 April 1934.
65. Schlesinger, *The Coming of the New Deal*, pt 7, esp. 413f.
66. KP: AV:1, NB to JMK, 9 May 1934.
67. Ibid., telegram from JMK to R. F. Kahn, 23 May 1934; CMP: Samuel Courtauld to Christabel Aberconway, 18 May 1934.
68. FFP: Reel 66, FF to Tom Corcoran, 7 April 1934.
69. Perkins, *The Roosevelt I Knew*, 183.
70. FDR to FF, 11 June 1934, in Freedman (ed.), *Roosevelt and Frankfurter*.
71. q. Harrod, *The Life of John Maynard Keynes*, 20.
72. Tugwell, *The Democratic Roosevelt*, 275.
73. Stein, *The Fiscal Revolution in America*, 150.
74. FFP: Reel 66.
75. KP: PS/6.
76. *CW*, xiii, 456–68.
77. *CW*, xxi, 322–9.
78. Ibid., 321.
79. FDRP: OF 264, David King to Louis Howe, 27 September 1934.
80. WLP: M5 326, Box 82, Folder 1217, WL to JMK, 9 January 1935.
81. *CW*, xxi, 321–2, for Szeliski's letter; KP: AV:1, JMK to Szeliski, 2 June 1934, for the reply, not in *CW*.
82. WLP: File 1314.
83. A. O. Bell (ed.), *The Diary of Virginia Woolf*, iv, 236–7.
84. MPP, MP, JMK to DM, 7 September 1934.
85. JMK to FAK, 7 September 1934.
86. *CW*, xiii, 484.
87. JTSP: 6113, JMK to JTS, 13 September 1934.
88. *CW*, xiii, 516, JMK to DHR, 20 February 1935.
89. Rymes, 'NOS', Bryce, C51.
90. Straight, *After Long Silence*, 185.
91. Rymes, 'NOS', amalgam of notes of Bryce (C8) and Bryan Hopkins (H8–9).
92. *CW*, xiii, 490.
93. KP: A/34, JMK to A. de Jeune, 22 November 1934.
94. *CW*, xiii, 499–500.
95. Stansky and Abrahams, *Journey to the Frontier*, 94–5.
96. *New Statesman*, 9 December 1933, q. Stansky and Abrahams, *Journey to the Frontier*, 108–9.
97. Annan, *Our Age*, 235–6.
98. KP: PP/45.

99. A. O. Bell (ed.), *The Diary of Virginia Woolf*, iv, 19 April 1934, 208.

100. KP: PP/45, ML to JMK, 31 December 1937.

101. Letter, 11 August 1934; *CIV*, xviii, 25–7.

102. A. O. Bell (ed.), *The Diary of Virginia Woolf*, iv, 272.

103. KP: EJ/1/3, JML to JMK, 18 March 1935.

104. *CIV*, xxviii, 38–41. See also JMK's correspondence with Susan Lawrence, on NEC of Labour Party, 15 January 1935, in KP: L/35.

105. KP: UA/37, 'Have We a Panacea?'

106. KP: A/35, JMK to DM, 8 February 1935.

107. KP: PP/45, Dorothy Elmhirst to JMK, 19 October 1935, in which she quoted these passages from her son's letter. The published version is in Straight, *After Long Silence*, 66.

108. Straight, *After Long Silence*, 67.

109. *CW*, xii, 97.

110. *Ibid.*, 10–12.

111. *Ibid.*, 101.

112. *Ibid.*, 61.

113. *Ibid.*, 51–7.

114. *Ibid.*, 38.

115. Fitzgibbons, *Keynes's Vision*, 84–6. Apart from the exemplary summary provided by Moggridge in *CW*, xii, Keynes's investment activities have been the subject of a number of discussions – by Chau and Woodward, 'John Maynard Keynes's Investment Performance: A Note', *JF*, 1983, 232–51; Minard, 'The Original Contrarian', *Forbes*, 26 September 1983; Skousen, 'Keynes as a Speculator', in M. Skousen (ed.), *Dissent on Keynes*, ch. 10.

116. KP: PP/73, JMK to Hindley Smith, 27 October 1933.

117. A. N. L. Munby, 'The Book Collector',

118. KP: PP/80

119. *Ibid.*, Sean O'Casey to David Garnett, 25 October 1935.

120. For details of the Cambridge Arts Theatre, see KP: PP/80; also Norman Higgins's account in Milo Keynes (ed.), *Essays on John Maynard Keynes*, 272–9.

121. JMK to LK, 17 January 1935.

122. LK to JMK, 9 February 1935.

123. JMK to LK, 19 May 1935.

124. JMK to LK, 27 January 1935.

125. KP: LLK/5, LK to FAK, 26 May 1935.

126. JMK to RFH, 9 August 1935; *CW*, xiii, 538.

127. *CW*, xxix, 149–50.

128. These comments on DHR are in JMK to LK, 11 February, 4 March, 28 January 1935.

129. JMK to RGH, 6 January 1936; *CW*, xiii, 627.

130. J. Robinson to JMK, 2 December 1935; *CW*, xiii, 612.

131. *CW*, xiii, 574.

132. *Ibid.*, 570, 577–8, 580.

133. *Ibid.*, 571–2, 575, 578–80, 583–4.

134. *Ibid.*, 567–8.

135. *Ibid.*, 573–4.

136. *Ibid.*, 584–5.

137. *Ibid.*, 600.

138. RFH to JMK, *ibid.*, 550.

139. *Ibid.*, 537.

140. *Ibid.*, 548.

141. *Ibid.*, 540.

142. *Ibid.*, 552, 559.

143. *CW*, vii, 179.

144. *CW*, xiv.

145. See Skidelsky, *Keynes*, i, 218. The book was *Gold, Prices, and Wages*.

146. JMK to J. A. Hobson, 31 July 1935

147. KP: LLK/5, LK to FAK, 25 December 1935.

Chapter 15: Firing at the Moon

1. For a discussion of these questions see Schumpeter, *History of Economic Analysis*, 41–7; Rymes, *Keynes's Lectures*, 101–3; Milgate, *Capital and Employment*, 5–15.

2. Coddington, *Keynesian Economics*, ch. 6.

3. Mini, *Keynes, Bloomsbury, and The General Theory*, 210.

4. *CW*, vii, 219.

5. Rymes, 'NOS', G33; Rymes, *Keynes's Lectures*, 98.

6. *CW*, vii, 293.

7. *Ibid.*, 30.

8. R. F. Harrod, q. Young, *Interpreting Mr. Keynes*, 16.

9. *CW*, vii, 293.

10. *Ibid.*, 247.

11. Hicks, 'Mr. Keynes's Theory of Employment', *EJ*, 1936, repr. in Wood (ed.), *John Maynard Keynes*, ii, 40.

12. *CW*, vii, 249.

13. q. Lekachman (ed.), *Keynes's General Theory*, 318–19. This obituary is reproduced from *Econometrica*, June 1946, where it first appeared.
14. Pigou's review in *Economica*, May 1936, repr. in Wood (ed.), *John Maynard Keynes*, ii, 30.
15. *CW*, vii, 13.
16. *Ibid.*, 15.
17. *Ibid.*, 19.
18. *Ibid.*, 41.
19. *Ibid.*, 63.
20. Stewart, *Keynes and After*, 2nd edn, 85.
21. *CW*, vii, 51.
22. *Ibid.*, 104–6.
23. *Ibid.*, 95.
24. *Ibid.*, 27; for alternative formulation, see 96.
25. *Ibid.*, 97–8.
26. *Ibid.*, 210.
27. *Ibid.*, 105; see also 31.
28. *Ibid.*, 110; see also 94.
29. *Ibid.*, 110–11.
30. *Ibid.*, 64.
31. *Ibid.*, 122.
32. *Ibid.*, 123–4.
33. *Ibid.*, 129.
34. *Ibid.*, 136.
35. *Ibid.*, 149.
36. *Ibid.*
37. *Ibid.*, 153, 160.
38. *Ibid.*, 142–3.
39. *Ibid.*, 154.
40. *Ibid.*, 155.
41. *Ibid.*, 155–6.
42. *Ibid.*, 159.
43. *Ibid.*, 161.
44. *Ibid.*, 162.
45. *Ibid.*, 163.
46. *Ibid.*, 161.
47. *Ibid.*, 152.
48. *Ibid.*, 163–4.
49. Harrod, 'Mr. Keynes and Traditional Theory', *Econometrica*, January 1937, 74–86, q. Lekachman (ed.), *Keynes's General Theory*, 127.
50. Meltzer, *Keynes's Monetary Theory*, 121.
51. *CW*, xiv, 25.
52. *CW*, vii, 175.
53. *CW*, xiv, 476, variorum draft of *The General Theory*.
54. *CW*, xxix, 262–3.
55. *CW*, vii, 181.
56. JMK, 'The General Theory of Employment', *QJE*, February 1937, repr. in *CW*, xiv, 116.
57. *CW*, vii, 167.
58. *Ibid.*, 174; xiv, 116.
59. *CW*, vii, 167.
60. *Ibid.*, 168, 201.
61. *Ibid.*, 170.
62. *Ibid.*, 172.
63. *Ibid.*, 202.
64. *Ibid.*, 207.
65. *Ibid.*, 207–8.
66. *Ibid.*, 203.
67. *Ibid.*
68. q. Presley, *Robertsonian Economics*, 297, n. 35.
69. *CW*, vii, 204.
70. Presley, *Robertsonian Economics*, 182.
71. DHR comment on JMK's letter of 13 December 1936; *CW*, xiv, 91n.
72. *CW*, vii, 249–50.
73. *Ibid.*, 217–21.
74. *Ibid.*, 229.
75. *Ibid.*, 230–1.
76. *Ibid.*, 233.
77. *Ibid.*, 235.
78. W. K. Reddaway to JMK, 23 July 1936; *CW*, xiv, 66–7.
79. *CW*, xvii, 263–9.
80. *Ibid.*, 299–30.
81. *Ibid.*, 322.
82. *Ibid.*, 316.
83. *Ibid.*
84. *Ibid.*, 317.
85. *Ibid.*, 318.
86. *Ibid.*, 245.
87. *Ibid.*, 321–2.
88. *Ibid.*, 324–6.
89. JMK to Joan Robinson, 3 September 1935; *CW*, xiii, 650.
90. Schumpeter, 'The General Theory of Employment, Interest, and Money', repr. in Wood (ed.), *John Maynard Keynes*, 128, n. 2.
91. *CW*, vii, 371.
92. *Ibid.*, 372.
93. *Ibid.*, 376.
94. *Ibid.*, 374.
95. *Ibid.*, 377–8.
96. *Ibid.*, 379–83.
97. *Ibid.*, 383.

Chapter 16: Whose General Theory?

1. P. A. Samuelson, 'The General Theory', in Lekachman (ed.), *Keynes's General Theory*, 316.
2. *CW*, xxix, 185.
3. Bensusan-Butt, *On Economic Knowledge*, 34–5.
4. Tarshis, 'The Keynesian Revolution: What It meant in the 1930s', unpublished.
5. W. B. Reddaway, *ER*, June 1936; D. Champernowne, *RES*, June 1936; A. P. Lerner, *ILR*, October 1936. The Reddaway and Lerner reviews appear in Wood (ed.), *John Maynard Keynes*, ii, 32–8, 55–70; the Champernowne review in Lekachman (ed.), *Keynes's General Theory*, 153–73.
6. q. Young, *Interpreting Mr. Keynes*, 85.
7. Champernowne, in Lekachman (ed.), *Keynes's General Theory*, 154–7. This is implicit, but not explicit in *The General Theory*; see *CW*, vii, 173, 249, 253, 296, 301.
8. Wood (ed.), *John Maynard Keynes*, ii, 67; see also Joan Robinson, *Contributions to Modern Economics*, xv.
9. Rowse's *Mr. Keynes and the Labour Movement* was published as a pamphlet in 1936.
10. *CW*, xxix, 234. This point also worried Rowse: *Mr. Keynes and the Labour Movement*, 50.
11. KP: CO/2, JMK to D. Macmillan, 27 April 1932.
12. J. R. Hicks, *EJ*, June 1936, repr. in Wood (ed.), *John Maynard Keynes*, ii, 42, 45, 49.
13. A. H. Hansen, *JPE*, October 1936, repr. in Wood (ed.), *John Maynard Keynes*, ii, 83, 79–80.
14. J. A. Schumpeter, *JASA*, December 1936, repr. in Wood (ed.), *John Maynard Keynes*, ii, 125–8.
15. F. M. Knight, *CJE*, February 1937, repr. in Wood (ed.), *John Maynard Keynes*, ii, 141.
16. JMK to V. W. Bladen, 13 March 1937; *CW*, xxix, 217–18. The correspondent was the editor of the journal, who asked Keynes whether he wanted to reply. Keynes refused. On the question of the priority of Keynes's and Knight's theory of uncertainty, see O'Donnell, *Keynes: Philosophy, Economics and Politics*, 262–3.
17. Jacob Viner, *QJE*, November 1936, repr.

18. in Wood (ed.), *John Maynard Keynes*, ii, 88.
18. *Ibid.*, 93.
19. *Ibid.*, 87.
20. In Lekachman (ed.), *Keynes's General Theory*, 256.
21. In Burton (ed.), *Keynes's General Theory*, 48–9.
22. Robert Bryce in Patinkin and Clark Reith (eds), *Keynes, Cambridge, and the General Theory*, 40–1.
23. Galbraith, *A Contemporary Guide to Economics, Peace, and Laughter*, 48.
24. Lekachman, *The Age of Keynes*, 132.
25. Galbraith, *Money: Whence It Came, Where It Went*, 229–30.
26. In Lekachman (ed.), *Keynes's General Theory*, 332.
27. See the illuminating discussion in Turner, *Joan Robinson and the Americans*, 57–61.
28. Patinkin, *Anticipations of the General Theory*, ch. 2. Patinkin claims that the Swedish school's emphasis on price adjustments disqualifies it as an independent precursor of the theory of effective demand, that is, the equilibrating role of changes in the level of output. But Patinkin's own interpretation of the Keynesian Revolution – roughly 'quantities adjust, not prices' – has often been challenged, most recently by Amadeo, *Keynes's Principle of Effective Demand*, 21–3, 117f.
29. Patinkin, *Anticipations of the General Theory*, 37.
30. See B. Schefold, 'The General Theory for a Totalitarian State? A Note on Keynes's Preface to the German Edition of 1936', *CAMJE*, June 1980, repr. in Wood (ed.), *John Maynard Keynes*, ii, 416.
31. In the *Münchner Neueste Nachrichten*, 10, 1936.
32. See Wilhelm Ropke, *Crises and Cycles* (1936), and *International Economic Disintegration* (1942). The appendix in the second book by Alexander Rustow, 'General Sociological Causes of the Economic Disintegration and Possibilities of Reconstruction', gives an excellent flavour of the Continental approach, in which the great depression is seen as a 'symptom of a general social and psychological decomposition' (p. 267).
33. Lautenbach's review of *The General Theory* appeared in *Die Bank*, Berlin, 28

April 1937. Keynes had it translated and summarised for him. KP: GTE/1/5.

34. A. Weber, *Bankarchiv*, 15 March 1937. I have benefited from seeing Jürgen Backhaus's paper, '1936–1986: Fifty Years' Discussion of the General Theory in German Literature: A Curious Case' (unpublished). See also his 'Keynesianism in Germany' in Lawson and Pesaran (eds), *Keynes' Economics*, 209–53, which is particularly illuminating on the 'historical' method of Sombart.

35. J. Letiche, 'Soviet Views on Keynes', *JEL*, June 1971, repr. in Wood (ed.), *John Maynard Keynes*, iii, 461.

36. q. Pierre Rosanvallon, in Hall (ed.), *The Political Power of Economic Ideas*, 173, 181.

37. KP: PP/45.

38. In his 'Keynes's General Theory: A Retrospective View', published in 1950, but based on two lectures given in 1949. See esp. 65–6.

39. In a letter to DHR, 20 September 1936; *CW*, xiv, 87.

40. A. C. Pigou, *Economica*, 3 May 1936, repr. in Wood (ed.), *John Maynard Keynes*, ii, 18.

41. *Ibid.*, 26, 28, 29–30.

42. Pigou, *The Theory of Unemployment*, 100f.

43. See the exchanges between Hawtrey and Keynes, February–April 1936, in *CW*, xiv, esp. 6, 23.

44. JMK to LK, 3 May 1936, repr. in *CW*, xxix, 218.

45. HDHP: Box 10, DHR to HDH, 21 June 1936. For the summary together with Keynes's reply see *CW*, xxix, 219–24.

46. HDHP: Box 10, HDH to R. F. Harrod, 2 April 1936; RFH to HDH, 9 April 1936.

47. Henderson's (much revised) paper is reprinted in *The Interwar Years and Other Papers*, ed. Henry Clay. The quotation is from p. 167.

48. Clay (ed.), *The Interwar Years and Other Papers*, 170, 173.

49. *CW*, xxix, 218–31.

50. HDHP: Box 22B.

51. DHR to JMK, 28 September 1936; *CW*, xxix, 63–4.

52. JMK to DHR, 20 September, 1936; *CW*, xiv, 88.

53. D. H. Robertson, 'Some Notes on Mr. Keynes's General Theory of Employment', *QJE*, November 1936, repr. in Wood (ed.), *John Maynard Keynes*, ii, 100. Robertson refers to 'Marshall's famous account of the automatic forces of trade

recovery, with its suggestion of the need for, and ultimate occurrence of, a sort of plot'. The reference is to Marshall's *Principles of Economics*, 8th edn, 592.

54. Wood (ed.), *John Maynard Keynes*, ii, 101–2.

55. *Ibid.*, 107, 109.

56. See Presley, *Robertsonian Economics*, 181–2.

57. *CW*, xiv, 91.

58. *Ibid.*, 94.

59. *Ibid.*, 98.

60. *Ibid.*, 207. In his article 'Alternative Theories of the Rate of Interest', published in *EJ*, June 1937.

61. JMK to DHR, 6 December 1937; *CW*, xxix, 165.

62. *Ibid.*, 166–8.

63. JMK to Austin Robinson, 22 March 1938; *CW*, xxix, 168.

64. *Ibid.*, 179.

65. *CW*, ii, 13.

66. Meir Kohn, 'Monetary Analysis, the Equilibrium Method, and Keynes's "General Theory"', *JPE*, 94, 1986, 1224.

67. *CW*, vii, 213; xiv, 206.

68. *CW*, xiv, 207–9, 229.

69. *Ibid.*, 216n.

70. *Ibid.*, 222.

71. *CW*, xxix, 280.

72. E.g. in his letter to Hugh Townshend, 23 April 1936; *CW*, xxix, 246–7.

73. In 'The Theory of the Rate of Interest'. *CW*, xiv, 106.

74. DHR to JMK, 29 December 1936; *CW*, xiv, 95.

75. This is from the third instalment of his two-part article on the Stockholm theory in *EJ*, June 1937, not published. The passage is reproduced in *CW*, xiv, 198.

76. *Ibid.*, 202–3.

77. KP: L/34, JMK to E. Lindahl, 8 December 1934; JMK to B. Ohlin, 27 January 1937; *CW*, xiv, 184.

78. In Wood (ed.), *John Maynard Keynes*, ii, 83.

79. *CW*, vii, 30.

80. *Ibid.*, 336.

81. Brent Jones, 'The Wages Problem in Employment Policy', M.Sc. (Bristol University), 7.

82. JMK to E. F. Durbin, 30 April 1936; *CW*, xxix, 235.

83. F. A. Hayek, 'Monetary Nationalism and International Stability', 52–4, repr. in Hayek, *A Tiger by the Tail*.

84. *CW*, xiii, 501–2.

85. Joan Robinson, *An Introduction to the Theory of Employment*, 96.

86. Brent Jones, 'The Wages Problem in Employment Policy', 13–15. For this argument of Champernowne's, see Lekachman (ed.), *Keynes's General Theory*, 155–60. Another Keynes convert, A. P. Lerner, anticipated Friedman's 'natural rate' theory of unemployment in his *Economics of Employment* (1951).

87. *CW*, xxix, 192, 190. So did Joan Robinson, despite her work on imperfect competition: see Joan Robinson, *Contributions to Modern Economics*, 48–9.

88. J. G. Dunlop's article, 'The Movement of Real and Money Wages' appeared in *EJ* in September 1938; L. Tarshis's note, 'Change in Real and Money Wages', appeared in *EJ* in March 1939, together with Keynes's comment on both articles. Keynes's article is reproduced in *CW*, vii, 394–412, see esp. 403, 401. He also refers to Kalecki's *Essays in the Theory of Economic Fluctuations*. However, Kaldor is wrong to say that Keynes 'retracted his earlier views concerning real wages and employment' as the result of these studies. (Kaldor in Worswick and Trevithick (eds), *Keynes and the Modern World*, 14.) Keynes remained agnostic on the question.

89. See North and Thomas, *The Rise of the Western World*; E. L. Jones, *The European Miracle*. For an appreciative view of Keynes's 'intuitive' economic history, see Charles Wilson in Milo Keynes (ed.), *Essays on John Maynard Keynes*, 230–6.

90. Pigou's assessment of the nineteenth century is analysed in Hutchinson, *On Revolutions and Progress in Economic Knowledge*, 171, 190–1.

91. Joan Robinson, *Introduction to the Theory of Employment*, 98.

92. KP: KC/2.

93. JMK to G. F. Shove, 15 April 1936, *CW*, xiv, 2.

94. Middleton, *Towards the Managed Economy*, 155–64, produces an IS–LM model of the Treasury view.

95. For Robertson's sympathy with the IS–LM approach see Presley, *Robertsonian Economics*, ch. 12; also Young, *Interpreting Mr. Keynes*, 15, 159, 175.

96. Kahn, *The Making of Keynes's General Theory*, 160, 249.

97. Hicks, 'Mr. Keynes and the "Classics" ', *Econometrica*, April 1937, repr. in Wood (ed.), *John Maynard Keynes*, ii, 164–5.

98. *Ibid.*, 166–7.

99. *Ibid.*, 169.

100. Arthur Brown, q. Young, *Interpreting Mr. Keynes*, 89.

101. *Ibid.*, 15–16.

102. Harrod, 'Mr. Keynes and Traditional Theory', January *Econometrica*, 1937; quotations are from Lekachman (ed.), *Keynes's General Theory*, 129, 137.

103. Young, *Interpreting Mr. Keynes*, 10.

104. *Ibid.*, 14, 17, 18.

105. Kahn, *The Making of Keynes's General Theory*, 159.

106. Young, *Interpreting Mr. Keynes*, 34.

107. *CW*, xiv, 85.

108. *Ibid.*, 79–82.

109. KP: MM/19. Keynes's letter is to thank Hicks for his note on Walras for the *Economic Journal*. Keynes writes: 'There is one small point which perhaps I can help clear up. . . . You enquire whether or not Walras was supposing that exchanges actually take place at the prices originally proposed when those prices are not equilibrium prices. The footnote which you quote convinces me that he was assuredly assuming that they did not take place except at the equilibrium price. For that is the actual method by which the opening price is fixed in the Paris Bourse even to-day. His footnote suggests that he was aware that the Agents de Change used this method and he regarded that as an ideal system of exchange to which others were approximations. . . . In all these cases there is an application of Edgeworth's principle of re-contract, all those present disclosing their dispositions to trade and the price which will equate offers and demands is arrived at by an independent person, known in New York as the "specialist".'

110. *CW*, xiv, 107.

111. *Ibid.*, 111; JMK, 'Notes on Fundamental Terminology', *CW*, xxix, 36.

112. *CW*, xiv, 113–14; for a similar list see *CW*, vii, 149.

113. *CW*, xiv, 114–15.

114. *Ibid.*, 116.

115. *Ibid.*, 118.

116. *Ibid.*, 121.

117. *Ibid.*, 285–9.

118. *Ibid.*, 295–6.

119. *Ibid.*, 299–300.
120. *Ibid.*, 307, 309, 318.
121. *Ibid.*, 115.
122. For Keynes's attitude to econometrics, see O'Donnell, *Keynes*, 191f.; Mini,

Keynes, Bloomsbury, and The General Theory, 112–22.
123. Hugh Townshend to JMK, 7 April 1939; *CW*, xxix, 257.
124. *Ibid.*; *CW*, xxix, 294.

Chapter 17: 'My Breathing Muscles Were So Wonky . . .'

1. D. Arundel, in Milo Keynes (ed.), *Lydia Lopokova*, 131.
2. KP: LLK/5. Clive Bell to LK (undated).
3. KP: LLK/3. Lydia's notes for a talk on Ibsen – for the BBC? – corrected by JMK, with pauses and emphases underlined.
4. On 1 February 1936 an agreement was signed between the Tilton Company Ltd and Wyndham Theatres Ltd, whereby the former received a licence to use the Criterion Theatre from 2 March to 11 April 1936. The Tilton Company paid £350 on signature, £175 for each of the three subsequent weeks, and £125 for the fourth week.
5. JMK to LK, 24, 25 May 1936.
6. KP: PP/45, JMK to Raymond Mortimer, 29 May 1936.
7. KP: LLK/5, LK to FAK, 9 May 1936.
8. *Ibid.*, 1, 19 August 1936.
9. *Ibid.*, 9 August 1936.
10. Letter to the *New Statesman*, 8 August 1936; repr. in *CW*, xxviii, 48–50.
11. JMK to JNK, 15 July 1936.
12. KP: LLK/5, LK to FAK, 6 October, 2 November 1936.
13. JMK to LK, 9, 11 October, 2 November 1936.
14. JMK to LK, 18, 25 October 1936.
15. *Ibid.*, 15, 16 November 1936.
16. Repr. in *CW*, xxi, 384–94.
17. *Ibid.*, 402.
18. PLP: PL 2/213.
19. *CW*, xxi, 404–9.
20. For the EAC's view see Winch, *Economics and Policy*, 346; also Howson and Winch, *The Economic Advisory Council*, 139–40. The relevant EAC Report is No. 22, 'Report on Economic Policy and the Maintenance of Trade and Activity', EAC (E.1) 171, 15 February 1937, repr. in Howson and Winch, *The Economic Advisory Council*, 343–53.
21. Hutchinson, *Keynes and the 'Keynesians'* . . . 1977, 10–14, 48–50.
22. KP: PS/6.
23. *CW*, xiv, 124–33.
24. I am grateful to Dr Milo Keynes for his comments on JMK's medical symptoms. Regrettably, I have not been able to do justice to his plea that biographers should be medically literate! It is noticeable, though, how interested Maynard himself was in his health all through his life, a sign of the strong medical tradition in his family, without, however, having much idea of how to maintain it.

Dramatis Personae

This section should be read in conjunction with that at the end of the first volume of this biography, pp. 421–31. *DNB* stands for the *Dictionary of National Biography*; KCC for King's College, Cambridge; LSE for London School of Economics. Titles have been omitted where awarded after the years covered by this volume. I have included only those who play some part in JMK's story or in his mental life.

ADDIS, SIR CHARLES (1861–1945), banker. A surprising omission from the *DNB*. Joined Hong-kong and Shanghai Bank, 1880, London manager, 1905–21. Director of the Bank of England 1918–25. Jousted with Keynes at the Tuesday Club, and over the return to the gold standard, but sympathetic to JMK's argument for delay. First to make use of the modern idea of 'pre-commitment' in relation to exchange-rate policy.

AFTALION, ALFRED (1874–1956), French business-cycle theorist, who influenced D. H. Robertson. Keynes (in 1932) called him 'hopelessly old-fashioned on the theoretical side . . .'. This was typical of JMK's view of French economics.

ALTSCHUL, FRANK (1887–1981), American investment banker, philanthropist and bibliophile. JMK met him at the Paris Peace Conference in 1919, and in 1932 called him an 'early Victorian curio'.

ANREP, BORIS (1883–1969), a mosaicist, responsible for the floors at the Tate and National Galleries. His wife Helen, *née* Maitland (1885–1965), left Anrep for Roger Fry, with whom she lived till his death in 1934. Boris Anrep was a friend of Lydia Keynes.

ASQUITH, HERBERT HENRY, Lord Oxford and Asquith (1852–1928), Liberal statesman. Prime Minister, 1908–16. JMK's break with Asquith in 1926 was the most painful political rupture of his career.

ASQUITH, EMMA MARGARET ('Margot') (1864–1945), Asquith's second wife. After Asquith's death, the friendship between Margot and JMK started up again, and he was attentive to her in her impoverished old age. Margot continued to write him characteristically vivacious letters in the early hours of the morning. 26 July 1934: '*How* right you were when we discussed Henry's attitude over the General Strike. He never minded what view you took . . . he always delighted in yr society, & said you had *real genius*: (rare praise from a man of *no* extremes).' 8 December 1935: '[The Prince of Wales] *loved* our evening with you & Lydia was a dream of original and incomparable beauty.'

ASHTON, FREDERICK (1904–88), choreographer and ballet dancer. JMK and Lydia got to know him well from 1929 when he started to choreograph for the Marie Rambert dancers, then for the Camargo Society, for whom he created *Façade* in 1931. Often at Tilton, but found JMK rather frightening.

ATKIN, GABRIEL (1897–1937), songwriter, painter. Great-nephew of Leigh Hunt. Boyfriend of Sebastian Sprott, Siegfried Sassoon and JMK. Married Mary Butts (1893–1937). Rupert Hart-

Davis called him 'half-frivolous and wholly pleasure-loving', a 'talented drunken freak without strength of character to steer him through the shoals of intellectual Bohemia'. JMK bought two of his paintings, and sent him money in the early 1920s.

BAGENAL, BARBARA (*née* Hiles) (1891–1984), painter. Had affairs with a large number of Bloomsbury men, including JMK. The Charlestonians thought JMK should have married her, or at least have had children by her, but she married Nicholas Bagenal in 1918, by whom she had a daughter and two sons.

BALANCHINE, GEORGE (1904–83), choreographer. Invented the choreographic equivalent of 'stream of consciousness' in fiction. Became Diaghilev's ballet-master and choreographer in 1925, settled in USA 1934. Visited JMK at Tilton in 1929, in connection with the filming of *Dark Red Roses*, for which he composed the ballet sequence.

BALDWIN, STANLEY, Earl Baldwin of Bewdley (1867–1947), Conservative statesman. Prime Minister, 1923, 1924–9, 1935–7. A monument to inaction. According to Middlemas and Barnes (p. 1075), he 'believed it was rarely possible to solve problems'. JMK said that he 'sentimental-ises over his own stupidity'. But he liked him, and, according to Beatrice Webb (Diary, 19 June 1936) 'was always citing Baldwin as a model statesman who could bring about a modified socialism if his party would let him'.

BALFOUR, ARTHUR, EARL OF (1848–1930), Conservative statesman. President of the Council, 1919–22, 1925–9. The Balfour Note of 1922 started negotiations for the American debt settle-ment in 1923.

BARUCH, BERNARD (1870–1965), American financier prominent supporter of the Democratic Party. Famous for getting out of Wall Street just before the crash. Never forgave JMK for his attack on Woodrow Wilson, and limited his influence in USA.

BEAUMONT, COMTE ÉTIENNE DE (1883–1956), French impresario who tried to imitate Diaghilev. He put on *Les Soirées de Paris* in 1924, in which Lydia Lopokova danced.

BEAVERBROOK, LORD, Max Aitken (1879–1964), Canadian-born newspaper proprietor and politician. His newspaper, the *Evening Standard*, published some of JMK's most important articles in the 1920s, notably 'The Economic Consequences of Mr. Churchill' in 1925.

BELL family. CLIVE (1881–1964), the art critic, was married to the painter VANESSA, *née* Stephen (1879–1961), though after 1914 it was a marriage of convenience. They had two sons, JULIAN (1908–37) and QUENTIN (*b.* 1910). JMK was godfather to ANGELICA (*b.* 1918), the daughter of Vanessa and Duncan Grant. After the First World War, Clive, Vanessa and Duncan divided their time between Bloomsbury, Charleston and (after 1928) Cassis in Provence. JMK's taking Lydia as his mistress, later his wife, broke up the wartime Charleston 'family'. Vanessa Bell resented Lydia, initially prompted by Clive. The feud was incomprehensible to the younger generation, JMK establishing warm relations with Julian, when Julian came up to KCC in 1927.

BELLERBY, JOHN RUTHERFORD (1896–1977), economist. Fellow of Gonville and Caius College, Cambridge, 1927–30. A curious case. Much involved in early discussions of Keynes's monetary theory, he faded out of the Keynesian Revolution, and is now virtually unknown.

BENTWICH, NAOMI (1891–1988). Read moral sciences at Newnham College, Cambridge, 1915–17, and helped W. E. Johnson prepare the three volumes of his *Logic*. JMK's secretary from October 1920 to May 1921, she believed he had 'kindled' love for him in her, and suffered a mental breakdown. She recovered in 1927, and married Jonas Birnberg.

BERENSON, BERNARD (1865–1959), art historian. JMK, Vanessa Bell and Duncan Grant stayed with him in I Tatti in 1920, scene of the famous prank in which JMK and Grant switched identities.

BERGSON, HENRI (1859–1941), French thinker, whose theories of the mind influenced 'stream of consciousness' fiction. His doctrine of the *élan vital* influenced Bernard Shaw. A central cultural figure of the early twentieth century. JMK thought 'there's nothing in Bergson's logic, but something quite interesting in his ideas, if only one could get at them clearly' (JMK to Sebastian Sprott, 3 October 1920).

BEVERIDGE, SIR WILLIAM (1879–1963), statistician and administrator. One of Liberalism's 'social experts' between the wars, his famous report of 1942 laid the foundations of the post-war welfare state. Director of the LSE, 1919–37. Although he and JMK met frequently, they had little intellectual contact or personal sympathy, disagreeing about population (1923), tariffs (1931) and method in economics, but sharing the Edwardian idea of reform 'above class' introduced by a benevolent state staffed by technocrats. Beveridge was interested not in people, but in society, and hoped parliaments and dictators alike would be succeeded by 'enlightened professional administrators who would control the psychological and physical conditions'. José Harris has written an outstanding biography of this unlovable man.

BEVES, DONALD HOWARD (1896–1961), lecturer in French literature. Fellow of KCC. Produced and acted in many plays in Cambridge and elsewhere – 'the Beves–Rylands alliance . . . was to be the life and soul of Cambridge dramatic activity for more than three decades' (Wilkinson).

BEVIN, ERNEST (1881–1951), trade unionist and Labour politician. General secretary of the Transport and General Workers' Union, 1921–40; Minister of Labour in Churchill's wartime coalition, 1940–5; Foreign Secretary, 1945–50. JMK furthered his economic education as co-member of the Macmillan Committee in 1930–1. Bevin was a quick learner. The most powerful character and practical intellect produced by the twentieth-century British Labour movement. 'A turn-up in a million' was how he described himself.

BIBESCO, PRINCESS ELIZABETH (1897–1945), daughter of Asquith by his second wife, Margot. She married the Rumanian diplomat Prince Antoine Bibesco in 1919, but hankered after JMK. 'Her suffisance and utter idiocy are only fit for a Restoration comedy,' wrote Lytton Strachey to Mary Hutchinson on 21 October 1921, after lunching with her at the Savoy. 'She insisted on stuffing herself and unfortunately also me with pâté de fois gras and some very thick and sugary white wine, which she declared was Maynard's favourite.'

BIRRELL, FRANCIS (1889–1935), writer. An old boyfriend of JMK. In his Founder's Day Speech at King's in 1926, JMK said, 'nothing but financial stringency ever brought Birrell's parties to an end'.

BLACKETT, SIR BASIL (1882–1935), civil servant. JMK's closest associate in the Treasury, and partner in speculation. As controller of finance at the Treasury, 1919–22, Blackett's 'work . . . gave rise to criticism' and he went to India as finance member of the Viceroy's Council, where he 'effected a rigorous retrenchment of expenditure', but earned the hostility of Indian politicians. Became a director of the Bank of England in 1931. A City career, started in 1931, failed, perhaps due to his 'impulsive temperament'. He was killed in a motoring accident. JMK's influence at the Treasury declined when Blackett went to India. In the early 1930s Blackett publicly supported JMK's reflationary ideas.

BLUNT, ANTHONY (1907–83), art historian. Apostle; Fellow of Trinity College, Cambridge, 1932–6. Revealed as a Soviet spy, 1979.

'BOLSHIES', LYDIA'S. Three Russians, who apparently moved easily between the USSR and England, were often to be found at Lydia's Sunday lunches in the late 1920s. Paul Haensel, an economist, whom JMK had met in Moscow in 1925, tried, unsuccessfully, to get his 'Short View of Soviet Russia' published in the USSR. JMK described him (in a letter to Falk, 9 October 1926) as 'Financial Adviser to the Bolshie Treasury, but very anti-Bolshie himself. He has, rather oddly, written a standard treatise on English Death Duties.' Schumpeter eventually got him a job in the United States. Prince Dmitry Mirsky was a convinced Marxist. He used to refer to his 'beloved Stalin'; his study of the British intelligentsia seems to have been largely conducted at 46 Gordon Square. The third guest was P. Kupalov, a scientist.

BONAR LAW, ANDREW (1858–1923), Conservative statesman. Prime Minister, 1922–3. An improbable mutual affection existed between the pessimistic, sceptical Bonar Law and JMK, dating back to the wartime Treasury when Bonar Law was Chancellor of the Exchequer. Bonar Law was influenced by JMK on reparations and the American debt during his short premiership.

BONHAM-CARTER, VIOLET (1887–1969), daughter of Asquith, married Sir Maurice Bonham-Carter ('Bongie'). Rallied to defence of her father when *Nation* attacked him in 1926.

BOWEN, VERA (1889–1971), choreographer and producer of plays and ballets. Lydia's closest woman friend in the 1920s. Born in the Ukraine, she finished her studies in Switzerland, where she married her first husband, a Swiss doctor called Victor Donnet, who divorced her on the ground that she 'read too much, to the detriment of her marital duties'. She moved to Paris, where she met Diaghilev, and settled in London in 1914, marrying Harold Bowen (1896–1959) in 1922. He was a fine Arabic scholar and younger son of a tycoon who had made a fortune in South America. A woman of many talents, with a good sense of humour and excellent taste in clothes, she was Lydia's artistic as well as personal mainstay before her marriage to JMK in 1925. Later their friendship cooled, Lydia complaining that Vera was too critical of everything. Belgravia, not Bloomsbury.

BOWLEY, ARTHUR (1869–1957), statistician. Professor of Statistics, London University, 1919–36. The main source of the data on which JMK relied for his 'intuitions'.

BRADBURY, SIR JOHN (1872–1950), civil servant. Permanent secretary to the Treasury, 1913–19; British delegate to the Reparation Commission, 1919–25. Treasury notes issued in the First World War were known as 'Bradburies'. One of the main architects of the return to the gold standard; JMK clashed with him about the logic of this on the Macmillan Committee, 1930.

BRAILSFORD, HENRY NOËL (1873–1958), socialist writer. As editor of the *New Leader*, journal of the Independent Labour Party, 1922–6, he familiarised its readership with JMK's ideas on monetary reform, to no avail, though he himself was a follower of J. A. Hobson. Though Brailsford and JMK corresponded in the mid-1920s, there was no meeting of minds – too much socialist baggage on one side, too much Cambridge baggage on the other.

BRAITHWAITE, RICHARD (1900–86), philosopher. Apostle, 1921; Fellow of KCC, 1924; Knightbridge Professor of Moral Philosophy, 1953. A good, but not close, friend of JMK. He had a barking voice, and Lytton Strachey found his conversational method 'rather trying'.

BRAND, ROBERT HENRY (1878–1963), banker and public servant. His *Times* obituary (24 August) called him 'an outstanding example of a species which has dwindled in numbers over the years – the London private banker who is also economist, philosopher, and, within a certain range, a statesman, too'. The son of Viscount Hampden, he got a first in history at New College, Oxford, 1901, became a Fellow of All Souls, a member of Milner's 'Kindergarten' in South Africa, and in 1909 joined Lazard Bros, of which he remained a director till 1960. JMK first got to know him at the Paris Peace Conference in 1919, where he was financial adviser to Lord Robert Cecil. A 'man of the utmost charm, with a soft voice and a mild, short-sighted appearance' (*DNB*), he was 'uniquely fitted to find a meeting point' between JMK and City orthodoxy on the Macmillan Committee.

BRIAND, ARISTIDE (1862–1932), French statesman. Prime Minister of France eleven times between 1909 and 1929, including 1921–2, when he and Lloyd George came close to pulling off a reparation settlement.

BROAD, CHARLES DUNBAR (1887–1971), philosopher. Knightbridge Professor of Moral Philosophy, Cambridge, 1933–53. The 'stockbroker' of Cambridge philosophy between the wars, he reviewed JMK's *Treatise on Probability*.

BROOKE, REV. ALAN ENGLAND (1863–1933), clergyman. Provost of KCC, 1926–33. The 'compromise' candidate between JMK and Clapham.

BROWN, NEVILLE (*b.* 1904), businessman. JMK's first cousin, son of Florence Keynes's brother, John Harold Brown. Secretary of the Keynes Club at Cambridge, 1923–4, he provided JMK with useful information about conditions in the cotton industry in 1926, and in the USA on the occasion of his visit in 1934.

BROWN, SIR WALTER LANGDON (1870–1946), physician. JMK's uncle, brother of Florence Keynes, and known to the Keynes children as Uncle Walrus. After he was made Regius Professor of Physic in 1932, he and his wife Freda often attended the family Sunday lunches at 6 Harvey Road, to which JMK came.

BRÜNING, HEINRICH (1885–1932), German statesman. Chancellor, 1930–2. JMK saw him in Berlin in 1932, when he told JMK that he could not give up deflation 'within a hundred yards of the finishing post'.

BRYCE, ROBERT (*b.* 1910), economist. His lecture notes from 1932–5 are an important source of the genesis of JMK's *General Theory*. His own paper 'An Introduction to the Monetary Theory of Employment' brought JMK's new theory to the LSE in 1935. Canadian Ministry of Finance, 1938–45. JMK complained to him (10 July 1935) about the 'appalling state of scholasticism' of economists 'which allow them to take leave of their intuitions altogether' (*CW*, xxix, 150–1).

BURGESS, GUY (1910–63), Apostle, diplomat, spy. Defected to the USSR, 1951.

CAIRNCROSS, SIR ALEC (*b.* 1911), economist and civil servant. Attended JMK's lectures, 1932–3. Cambridge University lecturer in economics, 1935–9.

CANNAN, EDWIN (1861–1935), economist. Professor of Political Economy, LSE, 1907–26, who combined socialist beliefs with old-fashioned monetary theory, making him a leading opponent of 'monetary reformers' like JMK. His correspondence with JMK during and after the First World War is an important source of JMK's monetary ideas, for example JMK's letter to Cannan of 13 October 1917, which implied that the Treasury had no control over the money supply, but that it increased automatically in response to the requirements of the public.

CARRINGTON, DORA (1893–1932), painter. She met Lytton Strachey in 1915, and, soon after, they set up house together, first at the Mill House, Tidmarsh, after 1924 at Ham Spray, near Hungerford, though this did not stop her marrying Ralph Partridge in 1921, and having numerous affairs with men and women. Soon after Strachey's death, she committed suicide. At the Mill House 'one of her favourite visitors was Maynard Keynes and although she was completely ignorant of economics and politics . . . she loved listening to him talk about the affairs of the great world when she took up his breakfast' (J. H. Doggart).

CASE, WALTER (1885–1937), American investment banker. Founder, 1916, president and director of Case, Pomeroy & Co., Inc, a private New York investment company with a specialised research organisation. JMK sent him regular reports on the economic situation in the early 1930s, and he used the firm's office as his New York base on his US trips in 1931 and 1934. Critic of Roosevelt's New Deal.

CASSEL, SIR ERNEST (1852–1921), financier. Helped rescue JMK from his currency speculations with a loan of £5000 in 1920.

CASSEL, GUSTAV (1866–1945), Swedish economist. His textbook, *Theory of Social Economy* (1918), which presented the Walrasian system of general equilibrium in highly simplified form, was 'probably the most widely read textbook on economics in the interwar years' (Blaug). Inventor of the 'purchasing-power parity' theory of the exchanges. Cassel served with JMK on the Committee of Experts in Berlin in 1922, but later became a critic of Keynes's economics.

CECCHETTI, ENRICO (1850–1932), Italian ballet dancer and famous teacher. He opened a ballet school in London in 1918, at which Lydia Lopokova, who had trained under him before the war, took private lessons, till he retired to Italy in 1923.

CHAMBERLAIN, SIR AUSTEN (1863–1937), Conservative politician, eldest son of Joseph Chamberlain. Chancellor of the Exchequer, 1919–21; first chairman of the Chamberlain–Bradbury Committee on the Currency and Bank of England Note Issue, 1924–5; Foreign Secretary, 1924–9. JMK's connection with him goes back to his service on the Royal Commission on Indian Finance and Currency, 1913–14, of which Chamberlain was chairman. He liked him, though having a low opinion of his brainpower. So did Asquith, who wrote to Christabel Maclaren, 17 August 1921, 'Austen C is a curious mixture – woolly brained, wooden tongued, with a quick & rather malignant temper, and unattractive manners. But he is not a bad-hearted creature, and is at times quite an effective Parliamentary performer. He is not even a chip off the old block.'

CHAMPERNOWNE, DAVID (*b.* 1912), economist. Fellow of KCC, 1937–48; Professor of Economics and Statistics, Cambridge, 1969–78. One of the most eminent of JMK's students, whose notes on his lectures of 1934 have survived. His family sold Dartington Hall to the Elmhirsts.

CHICHERIN, GEORGI VASILEVICH (1872–1936), Soviet diplomat. Foreign Minister when JMK met him at the Genoa Conference in 1922. His old-world courtesy gave spurious respectability to Soviet aims.

CHURCHILL, WINSTON SPENCER (1874–1965), Liberal and Conservative statesman. Chancellor of the Exchequer, 1924–9; Prime Minister, 1940–5, 1951–5. Put Britain back on the gold standard, 1925, despite his doubts, a decision he subsequently regretted. JMK did not blame him personally, and the relations between the two men were friendly. JMK was elected to the Other Club in 1927, founded by WSC and F. E. Smith, 1911, a very English institution which combined political enmity with personal friendship, and met monthly for the purpose of dining and wagering.

CITRINE, SIR WALTER (1887–1983), trade union leader, general secretary of the Trades Union Congress, 1926–46. He stayed at Tilton in 1931, 'flirting' (politically!) with JMK.

CLAPHAM, JOHN (1873–1946), economic historian. Vice-Provost of KCC, 1933–46. Attacked 'empty box' method of formal economics, which JMK said was based on a misunderstanding.

CLARK, COLIN (1905–89), Australian statistician. Educated at Oxford, he was on the staff of the Economic Advisory Counci, 1930–1, and helped Richard Kahn with the first sketch of the multiplier theory. Lecturer in Statistics, Cambridge, 1930–7. JMK thought him 'a bit of a genius – almost the only economic statistician I have ever met who seems to me quite first-class'.

CLAY, HENRY (1883–1954), economist. Joined the Bank of England in 1930, and became its economic adviser in 1933. He was 'gentle, scholarly, sensitive, and undogmatic' (*DNB*). Partly responsible for the Bank's defence before the Macmillan Committee. Although his economic views were orthodox, Clay typified the search for a middle way and avoidance of extremes. In his contribution to JMK's *Manchester Guardian* Reconstruction Supplements, Clay wrote (in issue no. 9, August 1922), 'The mistake the Government made in the winter of 1920–1, when the depression became obvious, was to check and reduce production in all the services under its control.' The analogy between the individual and the state was 'profoundly wrong'. The individual had to curtail expenditure in bad times, but, if the state did so, it did not 'save' money, because the unemployed consumed its 'saving'. JMK first started saying this in 1929!

COLE, GEORGE DOUGLAS HOWARD (1889–1959), socialist writer and economist. Member of the Economic Advisory Council, and Committee on Economic Information, 1930–9. JMK called him 'a writer of great ability, but a prolific journalist who does not exercise much self-criticism'.

COMMONS, JOHN ROGERS (1862–1945), American institutionalist economist. Professor of Economics, University of Wisconsin, 1904–34. Foremost American critic of *laissez-faire*, who influenced JMK in the 1920s. Commons's writings were an attempt to give 'collective action', conceived as a set of controls (or laws) on conflicting private interests, its due place in economic theory. A monetary reformer, he believed, with JMK, that economics should combine statistical data with 'insight', defined as 'Illumination, Understanding, and an Emotional Sense of the fitness of things'.

COOKE, SIDNEY RUSSELL (1895–1930), stockbroker with Rowe and Pitman. Committed suicide in 1930. Had been one of JMK's closest friends as an undergraduate at KCC before the war, and was a co-director with him of the National Mutual Life Assurance Company in the 1920s. JMK was 'much upset by poor Cookie's death'.

COOLIDGE, CALVIN (1872–1933), American statesman. President of the United States, 1925–9. Opposed forgiving Allied war debts: 'We hired them the money, didn't we?'

COUÉ, ÉMILE (1857–1926), French psychologist, whose theory of auto-suggestion enjoyed a vogue between the wars. He had his patients say, 'Every day, in every way, I am getting better and better.' Among converts were the insomniac Lord Curzon and JMK's friend Robert Brand.

COURTAULD, SAMUEL (1876–1947), industrialist, patron of the arts. His family were Huguenot silversmiths, who came to England in the seventeenth century. Became chairman of the family firm of artificial silk manufacturers (by the viscose process) in 1921, introducing enlightened industrial practices. A great friend and admirer of Lydia, he was JMK's closest friend in the business community, and with JMK co-guarantor of the London's Artists' Association. Collected Impressionist paintings, but disliked Post-Impressionism. Gave £50,000 for the purchase of French paintings to the Tate Gallery in 1923, and founded the Courtauld Institute of Art. He and his wife ELIZABETH (d. 1931), daughter of Edward Kelsey, financed three seasons at Covent Garden, 1925–7, and started the Courtauld-Sargent Concert Club in 1929. Lydia frequently dined at the Courtaulds' house at 20 Portman Square, complaining of heavy meals.

CUNLIFFE, LORD (1855–1919), banker. Governor of the Bank of England, 1913–18, he chaired the Cunliffe Committee which advocated the restoration of the gold standard.

CUNO, WILHELM (1876–1933), German Chancellor, 1922–3. Cuno's and JMK's connections with Melchior enabled JMK to play role of unofficial go-between between the British and German governments in 1923.

CURZON, MARQUESS OF (1859–1925), British statesman. Foreign Secretary, 1919–24.

D'ABERNON, VISCOUNT, EDGAR (1857–1941), financier and diplomat. British Ambassador in Berlin, 1920–6, when JMK went there as a member of the Committee of Experts. A bold thinker, he was a strong supporter of JMK's views on reparations, and left one of the cleverest, must amusing records of a diplomatic mission in his *An Ambassador of Peace*, 1929–30.

DALTON, HUGH (1887–1962), economist and Labour politician. As reader in economics at the LSE (1923–36) he combined a fervent belief in redistributive taxation with strict adherence to free trade and the quantity theory of money. He and JMK did not much like each other.

DAVENPORT, ERNEST HAROLD ('Nicholas') (1893–1979), stockbroker and financial journalist. First in history at Queen's College, Oxford. Co-director with JMK of the National Mutual Life Assurance Society from 1930. Founded the XYZ Club in 1932 to educate the Labour Party in economics and finance. His book, *Memoirs of a City Radical*, is the best account of JMK in the City. Davenport thought that in his speculations JMK was more interested in testing out his theory of probability than in making money. When JMK 'carried you away on his flights of fancy or argument, it was as exhilarating as listening to a Mozart symphony' (p. 48).

DAVIDSON, JOHN COLIN CAMPBELL (1889–1970), politician. JMK got to know him at the Treasury in the war when Bonar Law was Chancellor, and used him as a conduit to Bonar Law and Baldwin afterwards.

DAVIDSON brothers. There were five of them altogether, four of whom were at Cambridge in the early 1920s. Dadie Rylands writes, 'The eldest was a Scottish laird; ALISTAIR had a career in the Navy – possibly a vice-admiral; MALCOLM was a singer – not very successful; the two Bloomsbury ones ANGUS and DOUGLAS were at Cambridge with me (Magdalene) and my friends – Douglas a close friend always. Angus [1898–1980] wrote a life of Edward Lear and translated from the Italian. . . . he worked briefly (like the rest of us) at the Hogarth Press. Douglas was a protégé of Vanessa and Duncan – a painter and designer, who decorated my South room [at King's]. We lodged in Gordon Square when we went down. We gave a memorable summer party with Philip Ritchie . . . attended by Bloomsbury entire, Russian ballet, Margot Asquith, Ottoline, Mary Pickford and Douglas Fairbanks.'

DAWSON, GEOFFREY (1874–1944), journalist. Editor of *The Times*, 1923–44. Refused to publish articles by JMK on economic topics in the 1920s. *The Times* was, as always, the weathercock of the British Establishment under his editorship.

DE VALERA, EAMON (1882–1975), Irish statesman. Prime Minister of Ireland in 1933 when JMK visited Dublin, hoping to talk him out of his 'insane wheat schemes'.

DE VALOIS, NINETTE (*b.* 1898), ballerina and choreographer. Helped organise the Camargo Society in 1930, subsequently started the Vic-Wells Ballet Company. Great friend of Lydia.

DIAGHILEV, SERGE (1872–1929), Russian ballet impresario. A major cultural influence on JMK's generation. Lydia Keynes and JMK always referred to him as 'Big Serge', and JMK met him in both London and Monte Carlo.

DICKINSON, GOLDSWORTHY LOWES (1862–1932), humanist and philosopher. JMK wrote to E. M. Forster (26 August 1933), 'I had a lot of letters from Goldie at different times, but was apt to throw them away out of dislike for the paper and the typing.'

DOBB, MAURICE (1900–76), economist. Lecturer in economics, and Fellow of Trinity College, Cambridge, 1924–67. A Marxist, he played little part in the Keynesian Revolution, but JMK was influenced by his article 'A Sceptical View of the Theory of Wages', which appeared in the *Economic Journal*, December 1929.

DOBSON, FRANK (1888–1963), sculptor. Sculpted a bust of Lydia Keynes in 1924.

DOGGART, JAMES HAMILTON (1900–89), ophthalmic surgeon. Sheppard's first post-war protégé, he was elected an Apostle in 1919, but preferred rugger to philosophy. His recollections of the Cambridge Apostles of his day are in the Miscellaneous Papers at KCC.

DOLIN, SIR ANTON (1904–83), born Sydney Francis Patrick Chippendall Healey-Kay, ballet dancer and choreographer. Joined Diaghilev ballet at Monte Carlo in 1923, where JMK and Lydia watched him rehearsing *Daphne and Chloë*. Partnered Lydia, and danced with the Camargo Society. Lydia thought him too silly to be a truly great dancer.

DOUGLAS, MAJOR CLIFFORD HUGH (1879–1952), engineer turned economist, founder of Social Credit. The most famous 'crank' of the inter-war years, his A + B theorem inspired a passionate political following in the farming communities of Australia, Canada and New Zealand, by promising a cure for the deflation of credit.

DUNLOP, JOHN THOMAS (*b.* 1914), American economist. His article 'The Movement of Real and Money Wage Rates', *Economic Journal*, September 1938, attracted a reply from JMK. The *New Palgrave* entry on Dunlop is wrong to say that this article 'caused Keynes to admit that the *General Theory* was wrong on the relation between them over the cycle'. JMK only suggested the need for further study of the relationship.

DURNFORD, SIR WALTER (1847–1926), Provost of KCC, 1918–26. His nephew, HUGH DURN-FORD, was made domus bursar in 1919. JKM liked him, but had to pension him off in 1935, as he kept making a mess of his accounts.

EDGEWORTH, FRANCIS YSIDRO (1845–1926), economist. Drummond Professor of Political Economy at Oxford, 1891–1922. JMK's co-editor of the *Economic Journal*, 1911–26, and the subject of one of his best 'essays in biography'.

EINSTEIN, ALBERT (1879–1955), German-born physicist, Nobel prizewinner. His theory of relativity shook the certainties of the Victorian world by suggesting that the universe was unstable. JMK met him in Berlin in 1926, and described him in 1933 as 'Charlie Chaplin with the brow of Shakespeare'. JMK's economic language of the 1930s, in which the classical theory of employment is a 'special case' of a 'general theory' of employment, is consciously modelled on Einstein's distinction between the special (Newtonian) and general theory of relativity, as is JMK's analogy between classical economists and 'Euclidean geometers' in a non-Euclidean world. These parallels, together with their cultural significance, are worth further investigation.

ELIOT, THOMAS STEARNS (1888–1965), American-born poet. His poem, *The Waste Land* (1922) expressed the mood of the post-war generation. He was JMK's first choice as literary editor of the *Nation*, and JMK, although an atheist, developed increasing sympathy for Eliot's social criticism, and defence of culture, from a High Anglican position.

ELMHIRST, DOROTHY (1887–1968) and LEONARD (1893–1974). He was a mystic, agricultural economist, and chairman of Political and Economic Planning (PEP), she a wealthy idealist. She and her first husband, Whitney Straight (*d.* 1918), financed the liberal weekly, the *New Republic*, started, with Herbert Croly as editor, in 1914, which took many of JMK's articles between the wars. Dorothy and Leonard Elmhirst founded a utopian community at Dartington, in Devon, which they bought from the Champernownes in 1925, and which housed the avant-garde Jooss ballet company after it left Germany. Dorothy's son, MICHAEL STRAIGHT (*b.* 1916), attended the Keynes Club while reading economics at Trinity College, Cambridge, 1934–7 (he got a first), was an Apostle, and was torn between JMK's economics and his friends' communism.

FALK, OSWALD TOYNBEE (1881–1972), stockbroker and actuary. JMK's closest associate in the City, a major influence on his understanding of the psychology of businessmen, and one of the most perceptive judges of his mind and character. His grandfather, Eugene Falk, a timber merchant, came from Danzig to England in 1839, and married into the Hadfield family, who owned salt mines in Cheshire. His mother was Arnold Toynbee's sister. Founder of the Tuesday Club, JMK's co-director in the National Mutual Life Assurance Society and several investment trusts, and a partner in the stockbroking firm of Buckmaster and Moore, 1919–1932. In 1930 he circulated a memorandum which received wide publicity saying British industry was finished, and investors should sell their British securities and buy American ones. JMK disagreed publicly in *The Times* of 11 March 1930. In 1933 started his own firm of merchant bankers, O. T. Falk & Co., to which he recruited bright young men like the economist Thomas Balogh and the physicist Lancelot Law Whyte. 'Their brains make them dangerous, for they arrive at their errors more rapidly' (*Fortune*, September 1933). Falk was fond of quoting, 'Genius does not consist in an infinite capacity for taking pains, but in the power to survive the taking of infinite pains with zest undiminished and sensitiveness unimpaired.'

FAY, CHARLES RYEL (1884–1961), economic historian, fellow undergraduate of JMK at KCC, Professor of Economics, Toronto University, 1921–30, before returning to Cambridge as reader. Described JMK in 1927 as 'the wizard, part medicine man, part devil of the economic world'.

FISHER, IRVING (1867–1947), American economist. Professor of Political and Social Science at Yale University, 1898–1935. Founder of the modern quantity theory of money and much else, his 'compensated dollar' was designed to eliminate price fluctuations. JMK regarded him as 'the true leader and pioneer' of the movement for monetary reform. Fisher's reputation and fortune (made from patenting a card-index system) both collapsed with the stock-market crash in 1929, which he had declared was inconceivable.

FORSTER, EDWARD MORGAN (1879–1970), writer. His *A Passage to India* (1924) helped shape post-war attitudes to colonialism, but had no effect on JMK. JMK helped get him a super-numerary fellowship at KCC in 1927.

FOXWELL, HERBERT SOMERTON (1849–1936), economist. JMK's favourite personality among the economists of Marshall's generation, and the subject of an affectionate obituary.

FRANKFURTER, FELIX (1882–1965), American jurist and legal philosopher. Met JMK at the Paris Peace Conference, developing for Woodrow Wilson 'the scorn that the tough-minded have for the high-minded' (Joseph Lasch, 23). In a letter to Walter Lippmann (11 July 1919) he referred to 'some brave like Keynes . . . who resigned because of the utter breach of faith the Treaty involved'. A member of Roosevelt's 'Brain Trust' and, in the early 1930s, the main conduit for JMK's ideas to Roosevelt.

FREUD, SIGMUND (1856–1939), founder of psychoanalysis. A central influence on the twentieth-century consciousness, he undermined JMK's belief in rationality. Members of JMK's circle, notably James Strachey and Frank Ramsey, went to Vienna for psychoanalysis. Strachey was analysed by Freud himself, subsequently producing an English edition of his writings. He was particularly struck by Freud as 'a dazzling artistic performer. . . . Almost every hour is made into an organic aesthetic whole.' His brother Lytton Strachey wrote to him on 24 November 1920, 'I wish to God he could have analysed Queen Victoria. It's quite clear, of course, that she was a martyr to anal eroticism: but what else? what else?'

FRY family. SIR GEOFFREY STORRS (1888–1960), Kingsman and barrister, served under JMK at the Treasury, 1917–19 and accompanied him to Paris as secretary in 1919. As private secretary to Bonar Law and then Baldwin he gave JMK access to both. JMK rented Oare House, Marlborough, from him in 1922. His cousin ROGER (1866–1934), was the painter, art critic and friend of JMK, famous for his formalistic theory of aesthetics. Scientific about pictures, but extremely credulous about everything else.

FURNESS, ROBERT (1883–1954), civil servant. JMK's undergraduate friend from KCC. Visited JMK in the inter-war years when on leave from Egypt.

GAGE, VISCOUNT, HENRY RAINALD (1895–1982), landlord of Tilton, which JMK rented in 1925. Member of the East Sussex County Council, 1924–74, becoming one of the country's leading experts on drains. 'Many of the Bloomsbury Group were his tenants. . . . He received them all at Firle and touched their diverse activities with his tolerance, and his own informal, but strong Christian beliefs, fortified by a considerable knowledge . . . of the Scriptures'. (obituary in *The Times*, 3 March 1982).

GARNETT, DAVID ('Bunny') (1892–1981), writer. The only Bloomsberry with a scientific training, and one of JMK's closest friends. In 1919, after the end of his affair with Duncan Grant, he and Francis Birrell started a bookshop in Taviton Street, which moved to Gerrard Street in 1923. His best novel, *Lady into Fox*, which made use of his knowledge of biology, was published in 1922. In 1924 he acquired Hilton Hall in Huntingdonshire. JMK paid for the education of his two sons by Ray Marshall, whom he married in 1921. In 1933 he visited Tilton flying his own aeroplane.

GARVIN, JAMES LOUIS (1868–1947), journalist. Editor of the *Observer*, 1908–42. Strong supporter of Lloyd George, and admirer of JMK. Called him (aptly) an 'ungovernable soda-water siphon', but this was in response to an attack on him, not by Keynes as he thought, but by 'Kappa' in the *Nation*.

GIANNINI, AMEDEO (1886–1960), Italian lawyer and diplomat. JMK met him at the Paris Peace Conference in 1919, and they were in frequent contact in the period leading up to the Genoa Conference of 1922.

GIBLIN, LYNDHURST FAULKNER (1875–1951), Australian economist, who read mathematics at KCC, and with whom JMK corresponded in the early 1930s. An independent inventor of the (foreign trade) multiplier in the late 1920s.

GOLDENWEISER, EMMANUEL (1883–1953), statistician. Director, Division of Research and Statistics, Federal Reserve Board, 1926–45.

GOODENOUGH, FREDERICK (1866–1934), banker. Chairman, Barclays Bank, during debate on the return to the gold standard.

GRANT, DUNCAN (1885–1978), painter. The charmer of Bloomsbury, he was lover (1908–11) and subsequently best friend of JMK. In 1922 he and Vanessa decorated JMK's rooms at KCC, and he designed a number of ballets in which Lydia appeared. JMK supported the London Artists' Association, which he and Vanessa Bell dominated. His reputation declined in the 1930s, and JMK settled an income on him in 1937.

GREGORY, SIR THEODORE (1890–1970), economist. Cassel Professor of Economics, LSE, 1927–37. Served with JMK on the Macmillan Committee. Supported the gold standard, and doubted JMK's view that the banking system could eliminate trade fluctuations.

GRENFELL, EDWARD ('Teddy'), the banker (1870–1941) and his wife FLORENCE ('Florrie'), *née* Henderson (1888–1971) were among Lydia's closest friends in the 1920s.

GRIGG, PERCY JAMES (1890–1964), civil servant. PPS to Winston Churchill at the time of the return to the gold standard, he left the only account of the famous dinner given by Churchill before the return for JMK, McKenna, Niemeyer and Bradbury.

HABERLER, GOTTFRIED (b. 1900), Austrian-born economist. He attempted to synthesise the main business-cycle theories in his book, *Prosperity and Depression* (1937). JMK, who had seen an early draft, wrote to him (31 October 1934), 'My essential point is that the method you have adopted forces you to a high degree of superficiality. . . . I cannot believe that the solution can be reached by bringing together in selected packets excerpts from the views of a large number of writers, each differing from the other more or less in fundamentals. The answer must lie somewhere much deeper down. . . .' After publication of the *General Theory*, JMK and Haberler clashed over the concept of the 'identity' of saving and investment.

HALDANE, J. B. S. (1892–1964), geneticist. In 1925 he was dismissed from his readership in biochemistry at Cambridge for 'immorality' (that is, being cited as co-respondent in a divorce case). JMK supported him and he was reinstated. A noted Cambridge communist in the 1930s, he resigned from the Party in 1950 'because of Stalin's interference with science' (*DNB*).

HANSEN, ALVIN (1887–1975), American economist, Professor of Political Economy, Harvard University, 1937–62. An early American convert to Keynes's *General Theory*, tirelessly promoted Keynesian theory in the United States, especially in its 'secular stagnation' form.

HARMER, FREDERIC (b. 1905), businessman and Treasury official. An Eton scholar, and Apostle, who read mathematics and economics at KCC, 1924–7, obtaining a first in both parts of the tripos. Lytton Strachey found his face a cross between a Pre-Raphaelite painting and wicked sheepdog.

HARRIS, FRANK (1856–1931), writer, journalist and (by his own account) prodigious lover. Interviewed JMK at Genoa for *Pearson's Magazine*, but JMK hated Harris's account so much that he refused to allow publication.

HARROD, ROY (1900–78), economist and philosopher. Student (that is, Fellow) of Christ Church, Oxford, 1924–67. After his graduation from Christ Church in 1922 (with first-class honours in both Greats and modern history), he studied economics (money and international trade) at Cambridge under JMK in the autumn of 1922. His main contribution to Keynes's *General Theory* came in 1935, with his comments on drafts of Keynes's book. His concept of the 'warranted rate of growth', a dynamic extension of Keynes's theory (1938), was an attempt to define an equilibrium growth path at which a community's saving would be continually absorbed into investment. Keynes thought him (in a letter to Harold Macmillan, 21 February 1939) 'the best man at Oxford . . . both as a pure economist and as a publicist', but 'a little inclined to over-write . . .' His official biography of Keynes (1951) 'said much more about the works of Keynes than about his life and must be credited as a major element in the rapid dissemination of Keynes' ideas in the 1950s' (Blaug). Harrod 'increasingly . . . regarded himself as being not only a disciple of Keynes, but the disciple on whom the responsibility for continuity had especially fallen' (obituary in *The Times*, 10 March 1978). A great economist, but not a great biographer.

HAWTREY, RALPH (1879–1971), economist. The only professional economist at the Treasury for most of his time there (1904–45). Anticipated Keynes in seeing changes in prices as symptomatic of changes in income and output. JMK called him one of his 'grandparents in errancy' (the other being Dennis Robertson). He said of him in 1930 (*CW*, xiii, 127), 'There are very few writers on monetary subjects from whom one receives more stimulus and useful suggestion than from Mr. Hawtrey, and I think there are few writers on these subjects with whom I personally feel in more fundamental sympathy and agreement. The paradox is that, in spite of that, I nearly always disagree in detail with what he says.'

HAYEK, FRIEDRICH (1899–1991), Austrian-born economist and Nobel prizewinner. Tooke Professor of Economic Science and Statistics, LSE, 1931–50. In a cultural and historical, rather than technical, sense JMK's outstanding opponent. He wrote, 'If I have succeeded . . . in building up something like a fairly systematic body of opinion on economic policy that is not least due to the circumstance that all this time I had to be content with the role of a spectator and had never to ask what was politically possible. . . .'

HENDERSON, HUBERT (1890–1952), economist and civil servant. A pupil of JMK before the First World War, his main inter-war association with JMK was as editor of the *Nation*, 1923–30, and as joint secretary of the Economic Advisory Council, 1930–4. He became a Fellow of All Souls College, Oxford, in 1934. The high point of their intellectual partnership was the pamphlet 'Can Lloyd George Do It?' (1929). Thereafter they fell out over theory and policy. Isaiah Berlin remembers him as loving to argue 'on and on . . .'. A. J. P. Taylor wrote, 'Hubert was wonderful intellectual company, away the best I have ever known. His mind never relaxed. It was the intellectual equivalent of being in a mid-west saloon. You had to keep your hand on the gun all the time; otherwise you would be shot and maybe in the back.' Henderson was not in JMK's class as a theorist; but he was a shrewd judge of JMK's character, and had a strong sense for what was practicable. Much of his economic credo is contained in the letter he wrote JMK on 10 July 1925: 'it is fearfully dangerous to advocate anything which depends for its success on conditions of clear-sighted resolution in execution, which are most unlikely to be forthcoming, and which otherwise will be a visible and dramatic failure. . . . The moral is that one should only advocate ideas, which would do more good than harm, if applied in a feeble and wavering way.'

HICKS, JOHN (b. 1904), economist and Nobel prizewinner. Lecturer, LSE, 1926–35; Fellow of Gonville and Caius College, Cambridge, 1935–8. His 'generalisation' of JMK's *General Theory* in 1937 was crucial in gaining it acceptance among economists. The most powerful synthesising, mathematical mind in twentieth-century British economics, Hicks was held in only moderate esteem by JMK.

HILL, ARCHIBALD VIVIAN (1886–1977), physiologist and Nobel prizewinner. He married JMK's sister MARGARET (1885–1970) in 1913. Their daughter Mary Eglantyne ('POLLY') (*b.* 1914) studied economics at Cambridge, but not under JMK, though she subsequently worked on the Index of the *Economic Journal*.

HINDLEY-SMITH, JAMES (1894–1974), connoisseur. Helped guarantee the London Artists' Association with JMK and Samuel Courtauld.

HOBSON, JOHN ATKINSON (1858–1940), economist and journalist. Best known for his doctrine of underconsumption, and as a critic of imperialism who influenced Lenin. He failed to get a university job, remarking, 'I hardly realized that in appearing to question the virtue of unlimited thrift I had committed the unpardonable sin.' JMK, who had savaged his views before the First World War, made handsome amends in the *General Theory*, and the two men developed a mutual sympathy in the 1930s. His nephew, OSCAR RUDOLF HOBSON (1886–1961), a City journalist, had been at KCC before the First World War. 'Like all the Hobsons,' JMK wrote, 'he will always put justice before expediency.'

HOOVER, CALVIN BRYCE (1897–1974), American agricultural economist, who, as Lydia Keynes remarked, 'always gets into an upheavaled country and scribbles its effects' – this in reference to his studies of Soviet Russia and Nazi Germany. JMK had dinner with him in Washington in 1934, giving him a lesson in the multiplier with bath towels.

HOOVER, HERBERT (1874–1964), American statesman. President of the United States, 1929–33.

HOPKINS, SIR RICHARD (1880–1955), civil servant. Cambridge-educated, with first-class honours in classics and history, he was chairman of the Board of Inland Revenue, 1922–7; controller of finance at the Treasury, 1927–32; second secretary, 1932–42. JMK's toughest Treasury adversary before the Macmillan Committee. Robbins wrote of him, 'Diminutive in stature, with a general appearance rather like that of an extremely intelligent monkey, on the general subject of government finance he was an intellectual match for anyone of his generation.'

HUTCHINSON, MARY ST JOHN (1889–1977), wife of the barrister St John Hutchinson, mistress of Clive Bell till 1927. Lydia wrote to her on 17 February 1937 soliciting support for the Cambridge Arts Theatre, 'You are an important element in all sets 1) the high brow, 2) the smart set, 3) the mezzo world where we all live. Can you entice all the people to come and see us.'

IBSEN, HENRIK (1828–1906), Norwegian playright. Lydia acted memorably in two of his plays, *A Doll's House* and *The Master-Builder*. Powerfully appealed to JMK's imagination.

IDZIKOVSKY, STANISLAS (1894–1972), Polish-born dancer, who often partnered Lydia.

JOHNSON, WILLIAM ERNEST (1858–1931), logician. JMK's theory of probability was influenced by his work. 'A merciful release', JMK wrote to Lydia Keynes on his death, 'as his mind had broken down completely . . .'.

JOHNSTON, THOMAS (1881–1965), Labour politician. JMK debated socialism with him at the Liberal Summer School, 1928.

KAHN, RICHARD (1905–88), economist. Took a first in Part II of the economics tripos, 1928; Fellow of KCC from 1930. JMK's 'favourite pupil', who often stayed with him at Tilton. His outstanding contribution to the Keynesian Revolution was his multiplier theory of 1931; but his own particular interest lay in linking the theory of imperfect competition associated with Sraffa to the macroeconomic revolution associated with JMK. Sheppard called him 'a very nice boy'. Preferred to remain behind the scenes, helping with the work of others rather than bringing his own work to fruition.

KALDOR, NICHOLAS (1908–86), Hungarian-born economist. Took a first in economics at the LSE in 1930, and taught there from 1932 to 1947. One of the most powerful 'intuitive' economists of this century, his article 'Professor Pigou on Money Wages in Relation to Unemployment' in the *Economic Journal* of December 1937 was crucial in winning acceptance for Keynes's ideas.

KALECKI, MICHAL (1899–1970), Polish economist. 'Acknowledged posthumously as an independent creator of many of the elements of the "Keynesian" system' (Blaug).

KAPITSA, PYOTR (1895–1984), Soviet physicist, who received the Nobel prize in 1978 for his contribution to low-temperature physics. JMK met him several times in the 1920s when he was working under Rutherford at the Cavendish Laboratory in Cambridge – work which contributed to the 'splitting of the atom'. The Kapitsa Club, based on Trinity College, mingled scientific and political discussion, and helped spread communism among young Cambridge scientists in the 1920s.

KARSAVINA, TAMARA (1885–1978), friend of Lydia and one of the greatest classical ballerinas, who settled in London in 1918.

KENNEDY, GEORGE (1882–1954), architect. A friend of JMK, who got him a number of commissions, including the rebuilding of KCC, the building of the Cambridge Arts Theatre, and the reconstruction of parts of Tilton. Against the modern functionalist movement, he specialised in alterations to private houses.

KEYNES family. JMK's parents JOHN NEVILLE KEYNES (1852–1949) and FLORENCE ADA KEYNES (1861–1958) both outlived him. Neville Keynes retired from the job of University Registrary in 1925, devoting himself to his hobbies. Florence Keynes remained active in Cambridge and women's affairs, becoming Mayor of Cambridge, 1932–3. JMK's brother, SIR GEOFFREY KEYNES (1887–1982), was a notable surgeon and bibliographer, competing with JMK in purchases of antiquarian books. His wife MARGARET, *née* Darwin (1890–1974) and their four sons, RICHARD (*b.* 1919), QUENTIN (*b.* 1921), MILO (*b.* 1924) and STEPHEN (*b.* 1927), were often at Tilton.

KIDDY, ARTHUR WILLIAM (1868–1950), financial journalist. Member of the Tuesday Club.

KNIGHT, FRANK (1885–1972), American economist. Professor of Economics, Chicago University, 1928–55. First to develop the crucial distinction between risk and uncertainty (1921), but bitterly opposed to JMK's *General Theory*. JMK referred to his 'passionate, expiring cries'.

KNOX, DILLWYN (1885–1943), classicist and cryptographer. An old schoolfriend of JMK. At the KCC Founder's Day Feast, 1926, JMK said, 'It is not fitting that the best Greek scholar in the world, a card player of genius, a dear and beloved card himself, should languish in some obscure government office.'

KREUGER, IVAR (1880–1932), Swedish match king, uncovered as a fraud and committed suicide. JMK saw him as more a victim than a criminal.

LABORDÈRE, MARCEL (1869–1946), French financial journalist. First got in touch with JMK in 1911, and they corresponded till JMK died. Hardly any of JMK's letters have survived, but sixty of Labordère's are to be found in the Keynes Papers. He wrote with a thick pen, and in elegant, precise English. They thought of each other as poets of economics. Any assessment of Labordère's influence on JMK's theories of stock-market behaviour and 'animal spirits' requires the tracing of JMK's letters.

LAMBERT, CONSTANT (1905–51), composer and conductor. Conductor of the Camargo Society, and wrote music for many of Fred Ashton's ballets. Friend of Lydia Keynes, and regular guest at her Sunday lunches. A great drinker, he found the hospitality at Tilton too frugal for his taste.

LAMONT, THOMAS WILLIAM (1870–1948), American banker, partner in J. P. Morgan & Co. JMK met him at the Paris Peace Conference. Conservative critic of JMK's theories.

LASKI, HAROLD (1893–1950), jurist and politician, Professor of Political Science, LSE, 1926–50. JMK defended his freedom to utter nonsense in 1934.

LAVINGTON, FREDERICK (1881–1927), economist. Lavington came to Cambridge in 1908, as a 'mature student', gaining a first in both parts of the economics tripos. Girdler's Lecturer in Economics, 1920, and Fellow of Emmanuel College, 1922. Lavington was the most orthodox of the Cambridge economists of the 1920s, his favourite dictum being 'It's all in Marshall.' On the other hand, his notion of the rate of interest as, in part, a 'payment for uncertainty' has a very Keynesian ring to it.

LAWRENCE, THOMAS EDWARD (1888–1935), 'Lawrence of Arabia'. JMK spent enough time with him at the Paris Peace Conference to count him as a friend and be consulted on his character by David Garnett when Garnett came to edit his letters.

LAYTON, SIR WALTER (1884–1966), Cambridge-educated economist, editor of *The Economist*, 1922–38; chairman of the Liberal Industrial Inquiry, 1926–8. One of the Liberal mandarins of the inter-war years.

LEAF, WALTER (1852–1927), banker. Chairman of the Westminster Bank. Prominent in debate surrounding the return to the gold standard.

LEITH-ROSS, SIR FREDERICK ('Leithers') (1888–1968), civil servant. Deputy controller of finance at the Treasury, 1925–32; chief economic adviser to the government, 1932–46. Partially converted to Keynes's ideas in the 1930s.

LENIN, VLADIMIR ILYICH (1870–1924), Soviet statesman. JMK worked out his remedies for capitalism under his gigantic shadow.

LERNER, ABBA (1903–82), Russian-born economist. Student and assistant lecturer at the LSE in the 1930s, he was one of a number of Hayek's students who deserted to the Keynesian camp. Chiefly known for his theory of 'functional finance', developed during the Second World War.

LIPPMANN, WALTER (1889–1974), American journalist. Columnist for the *New Republic*, 1913–19; *New York World*, 1922–31; *New York Herald Tribune*, 1931–63. The most intellectual and influential newspaper columnist of this century, who was educated by JMK in economics, and educated JMK in the realities of American public life. 'My friendship with Keynes was one of the happiest of my life', Lippmann recalled, but, according to his biographer Ronald Steel, he never knew 'how to connect the Bloomsbury Keynes with the government adviser and economic theorist'.

LLOYD GEORGE, DAVID (1863–1945), Liberal statesman. Prime Minister, 1916–22; Leader of the Liberal Party, 1926–31. JMK was reconciled to him in 1926, and provided the intellectual substance for Lloyd George's pledge to 'conquer unemployment' in 1929. JMK called him the 'Professor of Political Practice' in a speech to the Cambridge University Liberal Club in 1928.

LOPUKHOV family. Lydia Lopokova's parents were FYODOR (*d.* 1914?) and CONSTANZA ('Karlusha') (1860–1942). Her elder sister EUGENIA (1885–1943), her elder brother FYODOR (1886–1973) and her younger brother ANDREJ (1898–1947) were all ballet dancers, Fyodor a noted choreographer with the Maryinsky Theatre, and its director from 1922–30 and again after the war.

LUCAS, FRANK LAURENCE ('Peter') (1894–1967), classicist and anti-Leavisite literary critic. Apostle; Fellow of KCC, 1920; College and University lecturer in English from 1922. Married the novelist E. B. C. ('Topsy') Jones in 1921, and secondly, Prudence Wilkinson in 1932. JMK greatly admired his book, *Tragedy in Relation to Aristotle's Poetics* (1922). A would-be man of action with the 'sensitive face of a poet'.

MACAULAY, WILLIAM HERRICK (1853–1936), Apostle, mathematician, bursar of KCC. JMK got money out of his brother Reginald for the rebuilding of KCC in 1925.

MACCARTHY, DESMOND (1877–1952), literary critic. Bloomsbury waited for his masterpiece, which never came. His wife MARY ('Molly') (1882–1953) started the Memoir Club to get him to write it.

MACDONALD, JAMES RAMSAY (1866–1937), Labour statesman. Prime Minister, 1924, 1929–35. MacDonald used JMK as an adviser after 1929, but was too pessimistic to take his advice, preferring the more cautious Hubert Henderson. His brainchild, the Economic Advisory Council, faded away in the 1930s.

MCKENNA, REGINALD (1863–1943), Liberal politician and banker. Chancellor of the Exchequer, 1915–16, when JMK was his favourite official; chairman of the Midland Bank, 1922–43. JMK and McKenna were allies against Lloyd George's great gun programme in

1915, against the return to the gold standard in 1925, against deflation in the late 1920s, and on the Macmillan Committee; but JMK felt that 'McKenna always lets you down in the end' – notably by not resigning over conscription in 1916, and by backing down over the gold standard. However, McKenna was a very able advocate of monetary reform in the 1920s, and the influence of the two men on each other is worth exploring.

MACMILLAN, DANIEL (1886–1965), publisher. Macmillan was the publisher of all JMK's books, and from the 1930s of his pamphlets as well. JMK was also one of Macmillan's readers for books on economics. He dealt increasingly with Daniel's younger brother HAROLD (1891–1986) on publishing as well as political matters, supporting Harold's effects to 'socialise' Conservatism in the 1930s.

MAINE, BASIL (1894–1972), music critic. Lydia's 'platonic lover', who played her the piano. He later became a clergyman.

MAISKY, IVAN (1884–1975), Soviet diplomat, surprisingly long-lived. Ambassador to Britain, 1932–43. JMK first encountered him in 1922 in connection with the Reconstruction Supplements when he was chief of the Press Department at the Foreign Office, Moscow. JMK and Lydia Keynes cultivated him mainly for the protection of her family, but he was unable to arrange for her brothers to come to the West, especially after the defection of Balanchine.

MARSHALL, ALFRED (1842–1924), economist. Founder of the Cambridge school of economics. JMK's attitude to him as an economist and as a person was ambivalent; not so to his widow MARY PALEY MARSHALL (1850–1944), whom he and Lydia Keynes loved, and of whom he wrote a touching memorial which ended: 'Modest as Morn; as Mid-day bright; / Gentle as Ev'ning; cool as Night'.

MARTIN, KINGSLEY (1897–1969), journalist. Editor of the *New Statesman*, 1931–62, of which JMK was the proprietor.

MASSINE, LÉONIDE (1896–1979), Russian dancer and choreographer. He choreographed *The Good Humoured Ladies* and *La Boutique Fantasque*, in which Lydia Lopokova made her mark in London in 1918–19, and they danced together in the early 1920s. Lydia found him selfish as a dancer, and his witty choreography gave little scope for her dramatic talents.

MEADE, JAMES (*b.* 1907), economist. First in PPE at Oxford, 1930; Fellow and lecturer in economics at Hertford College, Oxford, 1930–7; he spent a postgraduate year in Cambridge, 1930–1, as a member of the Keynes 'Circus'. Meade's contribution to the Keynesian Revolution was, firstly, 'Mr. Meade's Relation', an extension of Kahn's original multiplier theory; second, his 'A Simplified Model of Mr. Keynes's System', *Review of Economic Studies*, 4, 1937. JMK 'considered [Meade] to be of excellent promise' in 1932.

MELCHIOR, CARL (1877–1933), German banker. Partner in the Hamburg merchant bank, M. M. Warburg & Co. A member of the Wilhelmine 'Kaiserjuden' establishment, Melchior had served the German government on special missions in Eastern Europe during the First World War. His meetings with JMK early in 1919 during the armistice negotiations are the subject of the latter's memoir 'Dr. Melchior: A Defeated Enemy' read to Bloomsbury's Memoir Club in 1920, in which JMK praised Melchior for his courage and dignity in defeat. JMK's estimate of Germany's 'capacity to pay' reparations in his *Economic Consequences of the Peace* was identical to that put forward by Melchior at Versailles in 1919. As *persona grata* to the Allies, particularly the British, Melchior played a key part in the reparation diplomacy of the early 1920s, he and Keynes working together to try to bring about an Anglo-German financial agreement in 1923. The only German to be elected to the League of Nations' Financial Committee, Melchior became its chairman in 1930.

MONTAGU, EDWIN (1879–1924), Liberal politician. Secretary of State for India, 1917–22. JMK withdrew in 1922 from the Fiscal Commission on Indian tariff policy, to which Montagu had appointed him, to be with Lydia.

MORRELL, LADY OTTOLINE (1873–1938), famous pre-war Bloomsbury hostess. Her house in Oxford, Garsington, provided a refuge for pacifists and conscientious objectors during the war. JMK went on seeing her during the inter-war years.

MORTIMER, RAYMOND (1895–1980), literary critic, member of post-war Bloomsbury. He stayed with JMK and Lydia Lopokova at Studlands, Dorset, in 1923, contributed reviews and articles to the *Nation*, and became literary editor of the *New Statesman* in 1935.

MOSLEY, SIR OSWALD (1896–1980), politician. Chancellor of the Duchy of Lancaster, 1929–30, in MacDonald's government; leader of the New Party, 1930–2, and the British Union of Fascists, 1932–40. The first (and only prominent) political advocate of Keynes's monetary and fiscal policies in the period 1924–31. In his *Revolution by Reason* (1925), Mosley anticipated JMK in identifying 'lack of effective demand' as the cause of unemployment, and stating the task of policy as removing the 'gap' between actual and full employment output. JMK was in sympathetic contact with him up to 1931; Lydia dreamt she was being seduced by him!

MUIR, RAMSAY (1872–1941), historian. One of the architects of post–1918 liberalism, he was, in effect, rejected by JMK as editor of the *Nation* in 1923. 'He dealt in fine generalities, but he was perhaps deficient in the saving ballast of particulars and details' (*DNB*).

NEWBOLD, JOHN TURNER WALTON (1888–1943), writer and politician. A Manchester man, with a Quaker, agricultural and trade background. Communist MP, 1922–3; resigned from the Party, 1924; a member of the Macmillan Committee, 1929–31. JMK found him interesting, but woolly.

NORMAN, MONTAGU (1871–1950), governor of the Bank of England, 1920–42. JMK clashed with Norman on the American debt settlement, 1923; the return to the gold standard, 1925; and the effects of monetary policy – notably before the Macmillan Committee; but they agreed on reparations. JMK supported Norman's initiative in setting up the Bank of International Settlements in 1931, and relations between the two men thawed in the 1930s. Norman was an obsessively shy, secretive man, who travelled abroad as Mr Skinner – the name of his secretary. Whereas he wrought his alchemy by his prolonged silences, JMK spun his magic with his flow of words.

PENROSE family. Three Quaker brothers were part of JMK's Cambridge circle in the early 1920s. ALEC (1896–1950), KCC, Apostle, designed the scenery for the *Oresteia*, 1921, and produced Lytton Strachey's play, *The Son of Heaven*, 1925, in which Dennis Robertson acted the part of the head eunuch; LIONEL (1898–1972), St John's, Apostle, was an eminent geneticist, who married the daughter of Pavlov; ROLAND (1900–83), Queens' College, was a painter, art critic and biographer of Picasso. A fourth brother, BERNARD ('Beakus'), came up a few years later, after a spell in the merchant navy. After visiting him in Falmouth in 1926, Lytton Strachey wrote, 'His existence is a sordid insignificance which . . . opens up vistas in human pointlessness hitherto undreamt of.'

PIGOU, ARTHUR CECIL (1877–1959), economist. Succeeded Marshall as Professor of Political Economy, Cambridge in 1907, holding the chair till 1943. Member of the Cunliffe and Chamberlain–Bradbury Committees on the Currency, and served with JMK on the Committee of Economists, 1930. Pioneer of welfare economics, in which 'he elaborated Marshall's invention of the concept of externalities into a general economic theory of government intervention' (Blaug). After his heart attack in 1927, he became a physical shadow of his former self, but went on working. In 1930, JMK remarked of him, 'Here comes a man who has ruined his health with manly exertion' – a reference to Pigou's love of mountain-climbing. Wrote one of the most hostile reviews of the *General Theory*, provoked by what he considered JMK's unfairness to Marshall and also to his own *Theory of Unemployment* (1933).

RAMSEY, FRANK PLUMPTON (1903–30), philosopher. Trinity College, Cambridge, 1920–3; Apostle; first in Parts I and II of the mathematical tripos; Fellow of KCC, 1924. JMK thought him a genius, and his criticism of JMK's *Treatise on Probability* edged JMK away from his theory of probability as an 'objective relation'. Captured the philosophic mood of the 1920s when he said the aim of philosophy was not to answer questions but to cure headaches. Summed up Wittgenstein's *Tractatus* as 'What you can't say, you can't say, and you can't whistle either.'

REDDAWAY, WILLIAM BRIAN (*b.* 1913), economist. Studied economics under JMK, obtaining a first in economics, Part II, 1934. JMK called him 'by far the best economist of his year'.

ROBBINS, LIONEL (1898–1984), economist. Professor of Economics, LSE, 1929–61. Defended free trade and the policy of diminishing public spending in a slump against JMK, their quarrel coming to a head on the Committee of Economists, 1930. On the first, he later believed he was right; on the second, he acknowledged he was wrong. In his autobiography he argued that economics as a study of 'remoter effects' was still a better guide to policy than the 'gay reminder' that 'in the long run we are all dead'. Admired JMK as an artist, but mistrusted his reasoning and panaceas. JMK thought him 'difficult and queer'.

ROBERTS, WILLIAM (1895–1980), English artist, influenced by Cubism and Futurism, who painted a much reproduced portrait of JMK and Lydia in 1931–2. JMK greatly admired his work, bought six of his paintings and continued to subsidise him after the end of the London Artists' Association in 1934.

ROBERTSON, DENNIS HOLME (1890–1963), economist. JMK's chief stimulus in the 1920s, Robertson rejected JMK's 'revolution' in the 1930s, and their intellectual relationship collapsed, with some effect on their personal one. Robertson thought industrial fluctuations were an inevitable, and necessary, accompaniment of economic progress; the use of money aggravated, but did not cause, them; monetary policy should be designed to limit them to what was 'appropriate' or 'warranted'. Robertson regarded JMK's *General Theory* as the theory of a one-off, deep slump, not a 'general' analysis of the working of the capitalist system, and rejected its stagnationist presuppositions. Robertson wrote in a witty, but on the whole private, language; his typical ideas were too subtle for most to grasp; and he had little impact outside Cambridge.

ROBINSON, AUSTIN (1897–1993), economist. One of the first generation of post-war Cambridge economists, graduating from Christ's College in 1921. University lecturer in economics, Cambridge, 1929–49; assistant editor, *Economic Journal*, 1934–44. Member of the Keynes 'Circus', 1930–1. An excellent chronicler of the Keynesian Revolution, he did not play much part in it.

ROBINSON, JOAN (*née* Maurice) (1903–83), economist. Studied economics at Girton College, Cambridge, failing to get a first in 1925. Appointed assistant lecturer, 1931. One of the most powerful minds, and outstanding personalities, in Cambridge economics for half a century, she made her reputation with her first book, *The Economics of Imperfect Competition* (1933), helped by Richard Kahn, with whom she had her most intense intellectual and emotional partnership. JMK thought increasingly highly of her, and she was one of the ablest expositors, and simplifiers, of his ideas. A favourite saying was: 'As I never learnt mathematics, I have had to think.' The only woman (so far) among the great economists.

ROOSEVELT, FRANKLIN DELANO (1882–1945), American statesman. President of the United States, 1933–45. JMK put his hope in Roosevelt for a democratic escape from the Depression. Roosevelt had a 'grand talk' with JMK in Washington in 1934; JMK noticed that his hands while 'firm and fairly strong' were 'not clever or with finesse'.

ROTHSCHILD, VICTOR (1910–1990), scientist and administrator. Apostle; prize Fellow of Trinity College, Cambridge, 1935–9. In the 1930s JMK used to dine frequently with Victor and his first wife Barbara, daughter of Mary and St John Hutchinson, at their house in Newmarket.

ROWSE, ALFRED LESLIE (*b.* 1903), historian. Fellow of All Souls College, Oxford, 1925–74. A strong advocate of Keynes's ideas in the Labour Party, his pamphlet *Mr Keynes and the Labour Movement* (1936), was dedicated to Herbert Morrison in 'High Hopes for the Future'.

RUNCIMAN family. JMK knew SIR WALTER RUNCIMAN (1870–1949), the Liberal politician, and his second son, STEVEN (*b.* 1903), the historian of the Crusades, an Eton scholar (with George Orwell), undergraduate and fellow of Trinity College, Cambridge. He much preferred the son to the father.

RYLANDS, GEORGE HUMPHREY WOLFERSTAN ('Dadie') (*b.* 1902). He arrived at KCC from Eton in 1921, became an Apostle, took a first in English in 1924, and became a fellow of KCC in 1927. In the mid-1920s he shared rooms with Douglas Davidson at 37 Gordon Square, while working on his dissertation. Cambridge's leading actor–director in the inter-war years, and closely involved with JMK's and Lydia's ballet and dramatic projects. Became a close friend of JMK only after his return to KCC in 1927, Sheppard having earlier – as he told JMK – 'made it entirely impossible for me to know you or be known by you, I suppose unconsciously'. Lytton Strachey was 'luckily (*almost* entirely) immune from his yellow hair', but 'those who are not . . . ah! I pity them'.

SALTER, SIR ARTHUR (1881–1975), civil servant and politician. General secretary, Reparation Commission, 1920–2; director, Economic Section of the League of Nations, 1922–31; member, Committee of Economic Information, 1931–7. A good example of the Middle Way in search of a theory.

SAMUEL, SIR HERBERT (1870–1963), Liberal politician. At the Founder's Feast at KCC, 6 December 1935, at which he was a guest, JMK remarked tactfully, 'For myself working with him in the production of the famous Liberal Yellow Book I knew well the powers of his criticism and at the same time the justice and fairness of his mind.' Lloyd George's comment was tarter: 'When they circumcised him, they threw the wrong piece away.'

SANGER, CHARLES PERCY (1872–1930), statistician and barrister. Pre-war friend of JMK. Reviewed JMK's *Treatise on Probability*. According to Lowes Dickinson, he was of the type of Cambridge man 'unworldly without being saintly, unambitious without being inactive, warm-hearted without being sentimental'.

SCHUMPETER, JOSEPH ALOIS (1883–1950), Austrian-born economist. Austrian Minister of Finance, 1920; Professor of Economics at the University of Bonn, 1925–32; at Harvard, 1932–50. The most wide-ranging, encyclopaedic economist of the twentieth century. 'In an astonishing book, *Theory of Economic Development* (1912), written at the early age of 28, he replaced Marx's greedy, blood-sucking capitalist by the dynamic, innovating entrepreneur as the linchpin of the capitalist system, responsible not just for technical progress but the very existence of a positive rate of profit on capital' (Blaug). Schumpeter was scathing about the Anglo-Saxon tradition for not properly distinguishing interest and profit, investment and enterprise; and for concentrating on the conditions of static equilibrium rather than the forces of innovation. He had little sympathy, therefore, for JMK's method. 'Most people who admire Keynes', he wrote in 1933, 'accept the stimulus, take from him what is congenial to them, and leave the rest.' JMK thought Schumpeter a bit of a charlatan; Schumpeter thought the same of JMK.

SCHUSTER, SIR FELIX (1854–1936), banker. Dominant in the City before the First World War, his old-fashioned banking principles made him anathema to JMK. He died at Ruthin Castle in Wales shortly before JMK's arrival there.

SCOTT, CHARLES PRESTWICH (1846–1932), editor of the *Manchester Guardian*. JMK worked with him, and his son EDWARD (1883–1932) on the *Manchester Guardian Commercial* Reconstruction Supplements, 1922–3. C. P. Scott thought JMK brilliant, but self-centred.

SCOTT, FRANCIS CLAYTON (1881–1979), chairman of the Provincial Insurance Company, on whose board JMK served.

SCOTT, WILLIAM ROBERT (1868–1940), economic historian. Sponsored JMK, unsuccessfully, for election to the British Academy, 1920.

SHAW, GEORGE BERNARD (1856–1950), Irish-born playwright, philosopher and self-proclaimed genius, who dazzled the first half of this century with his intellectual playfulness and verbal pyrotechnics, which he, nevertheless, used to promote his idea of socialism brought about by Nietzschean supermen. Despite the generation gap, and his obsolete economics, JMK loved GBS for his wit and inexhaustible fancy, and wrote him probably the most quoted of all his letters in 1935, explaining the purpose of the *General Theory*. GBS, in turn, thought JMK (aged fifty-one) 'a bright and promising youth, frightfully handicapped by the Cambridge nullification process, with some inextinguishable sparks of culture' in him.

SHEPPARD, JOHN TRESSIDER (1881–1968), classicist. Fellow of KCC, 1909; Provost, 1933–54. Pre-war friend of JMK, and frequent visitor to Tilton, he proved an eccentric but effective provost, giving an astonishing amount of attention to the undergraduates. 'I like him very much . . . but that's true of practically all of them,' Sheppard wrote about one of them to Nathaniel Wedd in 1929. Lytton Strachey described the new flames he acquired each year as 'exhalations whizzing in the air'.

SHOVE, GERALD (1887–1947), economist. Fellow of KCC, 1926. Cambridge's hardest-working teacher of economics between the wars, he relieved JMK of much of his teaching duties, but published almost nothing in consequence. JMK estimated that in the early 1920s he was doing five lectures, and supervising fifty or sixty pupils, a week. Shove's 1913 fellowship dissertation, 'Notes on the Application of G. E. Moore's System of Ethics to Some Problems of Political Theory', would repay study, as showing how the pre-war Apostles saw the connection between ethics and politics.

SICKERT, WALTER (1860–1942), English painter. Painted Lydia in 1924, told her her head was like a pigeon's.

SIMON, SIR ERNEST DARWIN (1879–1960), Liberal politician and social reformer. Leader of post-First World War Manchester liberalism which started the Liberal Summer Schools, he sat with JMK on the board of the *Nation*, served on the Liberal Industrial Inquiry, and so on.

SIMON, SIR JOHN (1873–1954), Liberal politician. Annoyed JMK by his legalistic attitude to the General Strike. Lloyd George made the best quip about him: 'He has sat so long on the fence, the iron has entered his soul.'

SMUTS, JAN CHRISTIAN (1870–1950), South African statesman. Prime Minister of South Africa, 1919–24, 1939–48. He and JMK were allies over reparations.

SNOWDEN, PHILIP LORD, (1864–1937), Labour politician. As Chancellor of the Exchequer, 1929–31, he was the main obstacle to a radical unemployment policy. Ethel Snowden (1881–1951) epitomised the social-climbing Labour wife.

SPICER, ROBERT HENRY SCANES (1897–1956), business economist and statistician. Apostle, 1919. One of JMK's favourites immediately after the war.

SPRAGUE, OLIVER (!873–1953), economist. Economic adviser to the Bank of England, 1930–3. The butt of one of JMK's typical sallies at the Keynes Club. Sprague had argued that deflation applied at the top of the boom would lessen the pain later. JMK: 'I suppose, my dear Sprague, that in that situation your pathological propensities would do less harm.'

SPROTT, WALTER JOHN HERBERT ('Sebastian') (1897–1971), psychologist. Clare College, Cambridge, 1919–22; Apostle, 1920; first in moral sciences; demonstrator at Psychological Laboratory, 1922–5; lecturer in psychology at Nottingham, 1925. JMK's affair with Sprott after the war overlapped his courtship of Lydia. At Nottingham he was known for his wit and brilliant oratory. Wives of colleagues entertained in his house were served with great courtesy by discharged prisoners carrying small trays of wine in their fists.

SRAFFA, PIERO (1898–1983), Italian economist. Fellow of Trinity College, Cambridge, lecturer in economics, 1927–31; assistant director of research in economics, 1935–63 – a job JMK invented to keep him in Cambridge, so great was his horror of teaching. A *curiosum* of twentieth-century economics. Arriving with a great reputation on the wings of his article, 'The Laws of Return under Competitive Conditions', in the *Economic Journal*, December 1926, he proceeded to spend thirty years editing an eleven-volume edition of Ricardo's works, pausing briefly to demolish Hayek's theory of business cycles in 1932, before resurrecting his reputation as a theorist with a largely incomprehensible ninety-nine-page book published in 1960, though mainly written in the 1920s. JMK used to 'potter with Piero' round the antiquarian bookshops on Saturday afternoons. Influenced both JMK and Wittgenstein, without accepting the ideas of either. Joan Robinson recalls having 'innumerable discussions with Piero Sraffa but they always consisted of his heading me off from errors; he would never say anything positive'. His strongest emotional attachment was to his mother.

STAMP, JOSIAH CHARLES (1880–1941), statistician, foremost expert on the taxation system. 'A great gun loaded with statistics' is how Oswald Falk described him. One of the few in Keynes's circle – or that of the inter-war great and good – who had worked himself up from the ranks. Entering the Inland Revenue service as a boy clerk in 1896, he had proceeded, via an external B.Sc. at London University in 1911 (in which he gained an outstanding first), to occupy a series of top positions in the 'semi-public' corporations of the day, as well as serving on important advisory committees, like the Colwyn Committee on National Debt and Taxation, the Economic Advisory Council and the Committee of Economists. As British representative on the Dawes and Young Committees he played a crucial part in settling the reparation problem. He was perhaps JMK's model for the businessman of the future – part technical expert, part public servant – required for managing business life in the 'age of stabilisation'.

STRACHEY family. GILES LYTTON STRACHEY (1880–1932), biographer and literary critic, remained a continued moral presence in JMK's life; his brother JAMES (1887–1967) kept him in touch with psychoanalytic theory. JOHN STRACHEY (1901–63), the Labour politician, who sought a 'revolution by reason' first with Mosley then with Marx, was the son of JOHN ST LOE STRACHEY (1860–1927), editor of the *Spectator* and Lytton Strachey's uncle. JMK's last few exchanges with Lytton are typical of the untroubled state their friendship had reached. 'My dearest Lytton,' JMK wrote (3 December 1928), on receipt of Strachey's *Elizabeth and Essex*, 'Thank you most affectionately for Elizabeth. . . . I don't believe it is essentially as good as Victoria. But the *natural pleasure* of reading it is enormous. You seem, on the whole, to imagine yourself as Elizabeth; but I see from the pictures that it is Essex whom you have got up as yourself. But I expect you have managed to get the best of both worlds.' 'Dearest Maynard,' wrote Lytton (31 October 1930), on receipt of JMK's *Treatise on Money*, 'What a delightful and imposing present! Thank you for something more than Commodity Money, Managed Money, Fiat Money, State Money, Bank Money, Reserve Money and Current Money can buy. You see I have read the first chapter.'

STRAKOSCH, SIR HENRY (1871–1943), banker. Montagu Norman described him as a 'visionary arbitrageur'. JMK was involved with him in a number of projects relating to South African gold mining and banking immediately after the First World War.

TARSHIS, LAURIE (b. 1911), Canadian economist. Attended JMK's lectures, 1932–5. Spread JMK's ideas at Tufts and Harvard in late 1930s. His article 'Changes in Real and Money Wages', *Economic Journal*, March 1939, showing that real and money wages moved pro-cyclically, was important in dispelling fears of the inflationary consequences of Keynesian policy.

TAUSSIG, FRANK WILLIAM (1859–1940), American economist. Professor of Economics, Harvard University, 1892–1935. His *Principles of Economics* (1st edn, 1911) is regarded as epitomising the classical school against which JMK wrote the *General Theory*. If discovered, JMK's letters to Taussig (1914–15) might throw interesting light on JMK's attitude to the First World War.

TINBERGEN, JAN (*b.* 1903), Dutch economist and Nobel prizewinner. Professor, Netherlands School of Economics, 1933–73. JMK had a famous controversy with him on the theory of econometrics, 1938–9.

TROUTON, RUPERT (1897–1965), economist and businessman. Served in the Treasury under JMK, 1916–19, then read economics at KCC, gaining a first in both parts of the tripos, 1920–1. Stockbroker with Laurence, Keen and Gardener, 1928–61; director of the Hector Whaling Company, in which JMK invested. Economic adviser to Mosley's New Party, 1931. He and his wife were frequent guests at Tilton.

VINER, JACOB (1892–1970), American economist. Professor of Economics, Chicago University, 1925–46. 'A leading interwar price and trade theorist and quite simply the greatest historian of economic thought that ever lived' (Blaug). Viner's review of the *General Theory* was one of the few critical notices which JMK took seriously. It contained the famous remark: 'In a world organized in accordance with Keynes' specifications there would be a constant race between the printing press and the business agents of the trade unions, with the problem of unemployment largely solved if the printing press could maintain a constant lead. . . .'

WALRAS, LÉON (1834–1910), French economist and failed engineering student. The founder of general equilibrium theory, in which equilibrium is a solution to a simultaneous-equation model of the economy. Became probably the most influential economist (in terms of method) of all time, especially following the translation of his *Elements of Pure Economics* (1844–77) into English in 1954. In Schumpeter's view it is 'the only work by an economist that will stand comparison with the achievements of theoretical physics'. Others (including JMK) believe it led to the graveyard of sterile formalism. It is interesting that what economists regard as essentially an Anglo-American science should have increasingly followed a style which is classically French.

WEBB. JMK and Lydia developed a warm relationship with SIDNEY (1859–1947) and BEATRICE (1858–1943) between the wars, JMK being won over by her *My Apprenticeship*, published in 1926. To JMK they embodied the spirit of disinterested public spirit, and he was moved by Beatrice's struggle to replace her lost Christianity by service to humanity. Beatrice admired his intellectual energy, but doubted his seriousness. Lydia reported on her visit to Passfield Corner in 1933, 'The old lady is magnificent, be it in a Dutch cap she wears in the afternoon, or lying on the sofa with black silks in the evening.'

WELLS, HERBERT GEORGE (1866–1946). Wells 'adored' JMK. JMK admired Wells's idea of a Samurai leading mankind to better things, but repeatedly pointed out to him that he gave them no idea of what to do.

WICKSELL, KNUT (1851–1926), Swedish economist, founder of the Stockholm school. JMK referred to him as his 'great grandparent' in errancy. His distinction between the 'money' and 'natural' rates of interest (and their possible divergence) was adopted by JMK in his *Treatise on Money* (1930). JMK underestimated Wicksell, thinking him too academic and formal, but did not know his work well. Like JMK, Wicksell combined free-thinking in private life (he was once imprisoned for blasphemy) with the attempt to stabilise economic systems, seeing the 'solution' of the economic problem as a necessary condition for an improved quality of life.

WILSON, WOODROW (1856–1924), American statesman. President of the United States, 1913–22. JMK's description of him as a 'blind and deaf Don Quixote' alienated many of his natural liberal allies in the United States, though its contribution to US 'isolationism' has been greatly exaggerated.

WITTGENSTEIN, LUDWIG (1889–1951), Austrian philosopher. JMK revered him as a genius, but found his company wearying. Wittgenstein's relations with JMK were 'marred by his hypersensitivity and his neurotic propensity to misinterpret minor incidents as symptomatic of alienation or disloyalty' (*Times Literary Supplement*, 18 October 1974). Frances Partridge writes that 'in mixed company [Wittgenstein's] conversation was often trivial in the extreme, and loaded with feeble jokes accompanied by a wintry smile'. Wayne Parsons argues that the epistemological position of JMK and Wittgenstein was very close. They had a joint belief 'in the necessity of shared languages and "forms of life" as a pre-requisite to the possibility of meaningful, if not rational, discussion and communication' – that is, one had to 'see' things in the same way first, before discussion could be fruitful.

WOOLF. LEONARD (1880–1963) was literary editor of the *Nation*, 1923–30. One of JMK's oldest friends, who did not really like him. His wife VIRGINIA (1882–1942), *née* Stephen, is constantly critical of JMK, and his relationship with Lydia, in her diary. Their joint view was that he had a brilliant, even great, mind, but bad character – selfish, domineering, unreflective.

WRIGHT, HAROLD (1883–1934), economist. Staff of the *Nation*, 1923–31; editor, 1930–1. Wrote *Population* (1923) for the Cambridge Economic Handbook series. JMK's (unpublished) letter to him of 18 April 1923 on the book is a good example of his neo-Malthusianism: 'I think you might rub in a little more the hopelessness of emigration as anything better than a temporary expedient on the ground that a country which is already feeling the strain of population is in no position to afford the breeding up of human beings to the productive age and then exporting them free of charge.'

YOUNG, SIR EDWARD HILTON, LORD KENNET (1879–1960), Liberal politician, and pre-war friend of JMK, the 'sphinx without a secret'. Minister of Health in the National Government, 1931–5. JMK tried to get him to enlarge the expenditure of his department in 1933.

Index

NOTES

Works by Keynes appear under titles; those by others under the author's name.

Titles and ranks are generally the highest mentioned in the text.

Aberconway, Christabel, Lady, 114, 504
Academic Assistance Council, 486
Ackerley, Joe Randolph, 36
Adcock, Frank, 400
Addis, Sir Charles, 22, 107, 147, 162, 191, 193–4, 196–8
Addison, Errol, 213
Adeney, Bernard, 243n
Allen, Clifford, 438
Allen, Thomas, 393
'Alternative Theories of the Rate of Interest', 598
Altschul, Frank, 435
'Am I a Liberal?' (talk), 229–31, 259
Anderson, Sir John, 22, 197
Anglo-Spanish Friendship Society, 379
Annan, Noël, Baron, 228, 406, 516
Anrep, Boris, 214
Apostles: JMK's membership, ix–x, 6–7, 56–7, 65, 138, 210, 293–4, 521; and Marxism, 516
Arts Theatre, Cambridge *see* Cambridge Arts Theatre
Arts Theatre Club, London, 381–2, 503
Arundell, Dennis, 294, 295
Ashton, (Sir) Frederick, 95, 381–2, 480, 531
Asquith, Cyril, 434n
Asquith, Herbert Henry, 1st Earl of Oxford and Asquith: JMK's relations with, 21, 114; and Miss Bentwich, 50; contributes to *Manchester Guardian* Supplements, 103;

and Liberal summer schools, 135; and control of business cycles, 222; retains Party leadership, 245; and 1926 Liberal split, 249, 293; and General Strike, 251–5; stroke and death, 256; resigns Party leadership, 258
Asquith, Margot, Countess of Oxford and Asquith, 21, 252, 254–6
Atkin, Gabriel, 35–6, 50, 93, 96
Atkins, Robert, 633
Auden, W. H., 36, 628
Austin Motor Company, 342
Australia, 441
Austrian School (of economics), 331, 455, 600

Bachelier, Louis, 73
Bagehot, Walter, 244, 461
Bagenal, Barbara (*née* Hiles), 36, 141, 182
Bakst, Leon, 99
Balanchine, George, 99, 338–9
Baldwin, Stanley: Victorianism, 17; as Chancellor, 121; and war debts, 123–4; succeeds Law as Prime Minister, 127; and German reparations, 128; favours cheap money, 147, 151; on protection and unemployment, 151; on JMK's Order of the Bath, 179; 1924 election victory, 195; on wage reduction and miners' strike, 203; JMK on, 204, 232;

decency, 231; conflict with unions, 240; Mosley on, 242; and General Strike, 250–1; in 1929 election, 301; and Treasury view, 359

Balfour, Arthur James, 1st Earl, 117; Committee on Trade and Industry, 201–2; on Committee on the Economic Outlook, 363

Ballets Russes, 93, 98, 175

Balogh, Thomas, 25

banana parable, 323–5, 331, 350, 457, 499

Bank of England: JMK's disagreement with, 20; and monetary policy, 40; and bank rate, 147–8; supports return to gold, 190, 192; JMK's view of, 192; and deflation, 204; semi-autonomy, 227, 244, 336; control of money supply, 281, 356; international influence, 327; and Macmillan Committee, 356–7, 362; arranges international loan, 394–5; and 1931 devaluation, 396–7; JMK supports nationalisation of, 437; and JMK's expansionism, 473, 475

bank rate, 147–8; *modus operandi* of, 325–8, 330, 346–8, 350–1, 358

banks and banking: and monetary theory, 39, 91, 156–7, 335–6; and business cycles, 281; and price stabilisation, 315–17; in *Treatise on Money*, 319–20; and cost inflation, 329; and credit cycle, 331–2; maintenance of stable economies, 410

Barbusse, Henri, 104

Baring Brothers: 1890 crisis, 334

Barlow, Sir Montague, 189n

Barnes, George, 513

Barocchi, Randolfo, 95–6, 98, 101, 142, 176

Barrie, James Matthew, 145

Barry, Norman, 408–9

Barthou, Louis, 118

Baruch, Bernard, 19–20

Bateman, Bradley, 83

Bates, Sir Percy, 527

Batum (Georgia), 95–6

Bauer, Peter (*later* Baron), 522

Baynes, Keith, 243n

Bean, Lewis, 506

Beaumont, Cyril, 94–5, 116

Beaumont, Comte Etienne de, 177–9

Beaverbrook, William Maxwell Aitken, 1st Baron, 27, 124, 189, 255, 375

Beckhart, Benjamin Haggot, 572n

Békássy, Ferenc, 7, 16

Belgium, 125

Bell, Clive: in Bloomsbury group, 10–13, 140, 407; and Mary Hutchinson, 35; on JMK and Lydia, 93, 111–13, 142; reviews in *Nation*, 138; and Lydia, 179, 211–12; on JMK's marriage, 208, 210; on London Artists exhibition, 243; investments, 343; aesthetics, 407; on Lydia's acting, 624; *Civilisation*, 16

Ball, Daniel, 234

Bell, Julian: attends ballet with JMK, 14; heroic stance, 16; friendship with JMK, 293; at Cambridge, 293–4, 296, 339, 496, 515; Marxism, 515–16; irreligion, 517–18; killed in Spain, 634

Bell, Quentin, 13n; as favourite of JMK, 14; on Bloomsbury values, 16; on Sprott, 36; on Lydia and JMK, 100; 15th birthday, 208; on JMK's assurance, 428; on Lydia's acting, 503

Bell, Vanessa: paintings damaged, 4; Cambridge murals, 5; in Bloomsbury group, 10, 12, 140, 213; at Charleston, 13–14, 91; relations with Duncan Grant, 14, 35–6; on decline of Bloomsbury, 17; advises JMK on art purchases, 28; finances JMK's currency speculations, 41; Italy holiday, 42; on Berenson, 42; and JMK's earnings, 92; and JMK's attachment to Lydia, 93, 96, 100–1, 111–13, 116, 178, 182; designs logo for *Manchester Guardian Commercials*, 103; relations with Lydia, 140–2, 146; portrait of Lydia, 141; loses money in 1924 election, 195; antipathy to Keyneses, 217; and London Artists Association, 243–4, 380, 527; visits Cambridge, 293; quarrel with JMK over hanging of pictures, 380; on JMK's appearance, 433; and Julian's death, 634

Bellerby, J. R., 287

Beltram, Luc, 442

Benjamin, D. K. & Kochin, L. A., 349

Benn, William Wedgwood (*later* 1st Viscount Stansgate), 245–6

Bennett, Arnold, 388

Bensusan-Butt, D. M., 521, 537, 573

Bentham, Jeremy, 225–6

Bentwich, Naomi (*later* Birnberg): in love with JMK, 36–8, 51–5; as JMK's secretary, 49–51, 54; marries Birnberg, 55; 'Lucifer in Starlight: a Human Document' (unpublished), 37

Berenson, Bernard, 42

Bergen, George, 380

Bergson, Henri, 418
Berkeley, George, Bishop of Cloyne, 75
Berlin: 1922 conference, 116, 118–20
Berlin, Sir Isaiah, 427
Bernal, J. D., 293
Bernoulli, Jacques, 78, 80
Beveridge, Sir William: in Liberal radical circle, 22; and business barometers, 106; and Carnegie Endowment, 114; dispute with JMK over unemployment, 150; urges Economic Advisory Council, 343; supports free trade, 386; Beatrice Webb meets, 400; dislikes JMK, 400; offers professorship to Hayek, 456
Beves, Donald, 49, 294
Bevin, Ernest, 345, 349, 356, 363, 393
Bewley, T. K., 505
Bibesco, Princess Elizabeth (née Asquith), 91
Birch, Frank, 294, 296, 529
Birkenhead, F. E. Smith, 1st Earl of, 250–1
Birnberg, Jonas, 55
Birrell, Francis, 11–12, 13n, 138, 296; death, 432
Blackett, Basil: and College rentals, 9; influenced by JMK, 19; in JMK circle, 22; loan to JMK, 43; writes for Manchester Guardian, 103; at Genoa Conference, 107; and Balfour Note, 117; on JMK's Tract, 161; and gold standard, 399; chairs PEP, 438; on Economic Advisory Council committee, 468; international recovery plan, 471
Blair-Cunynghame, (Sir) James, 521
Bloomsbury group: JMK's involvement in, 10–17, 34, 175, 407; nature and values, 16–18; and JMK's economics, 83; attitude to Lydia, 112, 141–3, 145, 182; London homes, 112–13, 116; and Nation, 137–8; aesthetic theory, 407
Blum, Léon, 104, 583
Blunt, Anthony, 293, 514, 516–17, 523
Blyumin, I. G., 582
Böhm-Bawerk, Eugen von, 455
Bonham-Carter, Maurice ('Bongie'), 253
Bonham-Carter, Lady Violet, 11, 253
Bonn, Moritz, 118
'Boom Control', 629
Boris, Georges, 583
Bosanquet, Bernard, 76
Bowen, Harold, 115, 142–4, 177–80, 214
Bowen, Vera: friendship with Lydia, 115–16, 142–6, 177–80, 214, 480; at

JMK–Lydia wedding, 207; relations with Lydia cool, 531
Bowley, A. L., 106
Boyle, Andrew, 516
Bradbury, Sir John (later 1st Baron): on Reparation Commission, 20, 49, 117–18, 121; and Treasury control of finances, 40; and Chamberlain Committee, 191–2; Committee report, 197, 203; and gold, 198, 200, 243, 348; on Macmillan Committee, 345, 348
Bradley, Francis Herbert: Appearance and Reality, 75–7, 86, 224
Brailsford, H. N., 246
Braithwaite, Richard, 4, 7, 9, 71, 292, 294
Brand, Phyllis, 119
Brand, Robert Henry, 1st Baron: in Liberal-radical circle, 22–3; hesitancy, 23; on bank largesse, 39; at Genoa Conference, 107; on currency reform commission, 118–19; respects JMK's mind, 144; favours gold standard, 161; and JMK's anti-laissez faire views, 186; in Tuesday Club, 197; criticises Mosley, 246; at Liberal summer school, 264n; on private and public business, 266–7; on Macmillan Committee, 345, 351, 361; advocates public expenditure economies, 385; opposes JMK's international expansionism, 475; 'Why I Am Not a Socialist', 266–7
Brandeis, Louis Dembitz, 505, 518n
Brenan, Gerald, 13n
Bretton Woods, 108, 472
Briand, Aristide, 47, 49, 107, 116
Briggs, Hedley, 633
Brinkman, Carl, 581
Britain's Industrial Future (Liberal Party publication), 264, 267–8, 343
British Academy, 19
'British Balance of Trade, The', 300
British Union of Fascists, 436, 495
Broad, C. D., 67, 71, 73
Broadberry, S.: The British Economy Between the Wars, 369n
Brooke, A. E., 248–9
Brooke, Rupert, 7, 16
Broun, Heywood, 97
Brown, Alice (cook), 389
Brown, Ada Haydon (JMK's grandmother), 8
Brown, Frances, 286
Brown, Harold, 8
Brown, Jessie (JMK's aunt), 286
Brown, John (JMK's grandfather), 8

Brown, Kenneth, 176, 286
Brown, Neville (JMK's cousin), 8, 261, 504
Brown, Sir Walter Langdon- ('Uncle Walrus'), 286, 343, 632–3
Brüning, Heinrich, 435
Bryce, Robert, 460, 461n, 464n, 510, 532, 560n, 580
Bullock, Charles, 106, 340–1
Bullock Report, 1976, 265
Bulmer, Bertram, 144
Burgess, Guy, 496, 516–17
Burke, Edmund, 57, 61–4, 224, 409
Burnham, James, 227
Burt, Cyril, 414
business cycles, 275–6, 281, 569
Butler, Richard Austen, 232
Buttress, S. J., 106

Cadbury, Laurence, 135, 260
Cadman, Sir John, 363
Caillaux, Joseph, 104
Cain, Neville, 449, 451; 'Hawtrey and Multiplier Theory', 445n
Cairncross, Alexander, 460, 465
Camargo Society, 296, 339, 381–3, 480, 527
Cambridge: Lydia's flat in, 626
Cambridge Arts Theatre: JMK plans and builds, 9, 502, 510, 513–14, 528–31; opening, 530, 536, 624; transferred to University trustee, 530n; management, 624, 632; catering, 624, 626; Lydia plays at, 624, 631
Cambridge Chamber of Commerce, 476
'Cambridge Circus' (group), 441, 447–52, 453, 455
Cambridge Platonism, 74, 76
Cambridge University: JMK teaches and lectures at, 5, 174–5, 496–500, 510–12, 521–2; economics at, 5–6, 286–90; communism at, 292–3, 496, 514–17; theatre and arts in, 294–6; anti-war demonstration at, 496
'Can Lloyd George Do It?' (JMK and Henderson), 303, 365, 371, 449
Canada, 183–4
Cannan, Edwin, 162–4, 169, 191, 245, 438
Cannes, 632–3
capitalism: historical origins, 332–5
Carabelli, Anna, 83–6, 88
Carrington, Dora, 14–15, 92, 432
Carroll, Sydney, 633
Case, Walter, 385, 390, 392, 395, 504–6, 513
Cassel, Sir Ernest, 43

Cassel, Gustav, 103, 107, 118–19, 123, 153, 169, 473
Cecchetti, Enrico, 94, 142
Cecil, Lord Robert (later 5th Marquess of Salisbury), 103, 127
Chalmers, Robert, 1st Baron, 15
Chamberlain, Austen, 19, 39–40; Committee on the Note Issue, 189, 191–3, 197, 203
Chamberlain, Joseph, 387
Chamberlain, Neville: as Chancellor, 127n, 433–6; on balancing budget, 474–5; and JMK's devaluation plan, 481; and ideas, 570; borrows for rearmament, 630
Champernowne, David, 460, 521–3, 574–5, 603–4
Chanak crisis, 1922, 118
Channel Tunnel, 363
Charleston (Sussex house), 13, 34–5, 91, 112, 217
Chicago Council on Foreign Relations, 391–2
Chicago school (of economists), 573, 578–80
Chicherin, Georgi V., 108–10
Chrysler, Walter, 504
Churchill, Winston S.: on gold standard as Chancellor, 197–200, 203, 243, 252, 399; and exchange rates, 202; Currency Bill criticised by JMK, 285; and 1929 election, 306; and Treasury view, 359; and convertibility, 397
Citrine, Sir Walter, 343, 363, 399, 467
Clapham, Sir John Harold, 248, 400
Clark, Colin, 363, 449
Clark, Kenneth, Baron, 427
Clark, R. & R. (printers), 282–3
Clarke, Peter, 222–3, 299, 439–41, 443
Clay, Henry, 103, 343, 357–8, 362, 384
Clemenceau, Georges, 28, 32, 90
coal mining and miners, 203–4, 223, 250, 260
'Coal: A Suggestion', 260
Coase, Ronald, 456
Cockerell, Douglas, 91
Coddington, Alan, 540
Cole, G. D. H., 343, 363, 467
Cole, Dr Leslie B., 633
Colefax, Sibyl, Lady, 214
Collard, David: 'A. C. Pigou', 597n
collectivism, 406–7
Columbia University, New York, 504, 506
Committee on Civil Research, 343, 363

Committee on Economic Information, 467–9
Committee on the Economic Outlook, 363
Committee on Unemployment, 468
commodity inflation, 331
Commons, John Rogers, 229–30, 236, 608
Communism: JMK on, 32, 235, 488, 517–19; and student politics, 496, 515
Connolly, Cyril, 626
Conservative Party, 231–2, 400
Cooke, Sidney Russell, 43, 103, 264n, 343
Coolidge, Calvin, 124
Corcoran, Tom, 505
Cornford, John, 523
Cornish, Francis Warre, 293–4
Cosgrave, William T., 479
cotton industry, 260–3, 378
Cotton Yard Association, 261–2
Coughlin, Father Charles Edward, 508
Courtauld, Elizabeth ('Lil'), 96, 143–4, 177, 217, 339, 383, 400; death, 480
Courtauld, Samuel: and Lydia, 96, 143–4, 177, 217, 480, 531; patronises artists, 243; friendship with JMK, 258, 339; relations with JMK cool, 343; meagre support for Camargo Society, 382–3; and 1931 election, 400; on JMK's conservatism, 437; on US economy, 504; and London Artists' Association, 527; appetite, 531
Cranium Club, London, 12–13
Cranston, Maurice, 223
Cravath, Paul, 103
credit cycle, 331–2, 525
Croce, Benedetto, 104
Croly, Herbert, 28
Crosfield, G. B. 521
Crosland, Charles Anthony Raven, 232
Cunard, Maud Alice (Emerald), Lady, 144
Cunliffe, Walter, 1st Baron, 47n, 190; Report, 1918, 40, 148, 187, 189
Cuno, Wilhelm, 103, 107, 115n, 118, 120–2, 126–8
Cuppi, Anna, 381
Currie, Lauchlin, 580
Curzon, Francis, 426, 525
Curzon of Kedleston, George Nathaniel, Marquess, 125–7
Cuthbertson, J. R. 521

D'Abernon, Edgar Vincent, Baron (later Viscount), 117–19, 120, 125, 338
Daily Mail, 469–70, 481
Dalton, Hugh, 163, 363, 376, 438

Dark Red Roses (film), 338–9
Darlington, W. A., 502
Dartington Hall, Devon, 522
Davenport, Nicholas, 25–6, 103, 139, 188, 438
David, Gustave, 528
Davidson, Angus, 13n, 91–2, 182, 295
Davidson, Douglas, 13n, 91–2, 182, 214
Davidson, J. C. C., 124, 289
Davies, Hugh Sykes, 516
Davies, J. Conway, 344n
Davies, Richard Llewellyn, 516
Davis, John, 83
Dawes, Charles Gates: plan and loan, 123, 129, 309
Dawson, Geoffrey, 27, 202, 469–70
Debenhams, 27
deficient aggregate demand, 484
de Morgan, Augustus, 411
Denikin, General Anton Ivanovich, 96
depressions (economic): 1920–22, 130–2; Great (1929–32), 130, 340–2, 378, 436; JMK's analysis of, 439–41; JMK on recovery from, 467; causes, 468
Derain, André, 633
de Valera, Eamon, 480
de Valois, Ninette, 94, 339, 381–2, 480
devaluation (sterling), 190–1, 394–5; (dollar), 480; (franc), 206, 583
Diaghilev, Serge, 93, 95–100, 143, 179–80, 244; death, 339
Dicey, Albert Venn, 406
Dickinson, Goldsworthy Lowes, 13n, 103, 427; death, 432
Dimsdale, Helen, 296
'Do We Want Prices to Fall?' (lecture), 45
Dobb, Maurice, 5, 46, 209, 287, 292
Dobson, Frank, 13n, 145, 214, 243n
Dobson, Lettice, 217
Doggart, James Hamilton, 6
Dolin, Anton, 175, 213, 338
Doone, Rupert, 178
Douglas, Major Clifford Hugh, 416, 511, 569
Douglas, Henry, 575
Doumer, Paul, 48
Dublin, 476–80
Dubois, Leopold, 118, 119n
Duffy, Bruce, 69
Dulles, John Foster, 114
Duncan, Sir Andrew, 343
Dunlop, John Thomas, 604
Dunoyer de Segonzac, André, 179
Durbin, Evan M. F., 438, 575, 602
Durnford, Hugh, 512, 526

Durnford, Walter, 248

Econometric Conference, Oxford, 1936, 613
econometrics, JMK's views on, 106, 413–14, 620
Economic Advisory Council: JMK serves on, 21, 343–5, 363–78; economic committee, 364; report, 376–8; and world depression, 378; advises Ramsay MacDonald, 468
'Economic Aspects of the Peace Treaty, The' (lectures), 3
'Economic Consequences of Mr Churchill, The', 188, 200, 202, 260
Economic Consequences of the Peace, The, reputation, 3, 6, 29; writing, 14, 26; Strachey praises, 14; official reaction to, 18–20; and JMK's writings, 27–8; serialised, 28; translations, 28; and German reparations, 31; on inflation, 40, 46; on food prices, 150; on 19th century achievements, 220; Freudianism in, 234; success, 422; on Europe's trade balance with USA, 429; and duty of non-consumption, 542, 554n
Economic Journal: JMK edits, 137, 175, 244–5
'Economic Possibilities for Our Grandchildren' (essay), 234, 236–9, 324, 554n, 565
'Economic Transition in England, The' (talk), 229
Economist (journal), 22
Edgeworth, Francis Ysidro, 244, 412–13
Edward VIII, King (*later* Duke of Windsor), 628
effective demand, theory of, 442–3, 461–2, 484, 545, 554
Egorova, Lubov, 99
Einaudi, Luigi, 103, 105
Einstein, Albert, 239, 486–7
Eliot, T. S., 17, 138, 517, 626
Eliot, Vivien, 625
Elmhirst, Leonard, 522
Elsham (estate), Lincolnshire, 526
empiricism, 74
'End of *Laissez-Faire*, The' (lecture), 180, 183, 225–9, 442
Engels, Friedrich, 520
Essays in Biography, 416, 460, 469
Essays in Persuasion, 387, 431, 439, 460
ethics, 57–9, 64–6, 71

'Ethics in Relation to Conduct' (paper), 57
Eugenics Society, 620
Europe: JMK's view of, 485
'Europe's Economic Outlook' (articles), 90
Evans, Edwin, 381
Everybody's (US magazine), 27
' "Ex Ante" Theory of the Rate of Interest, The', 598
exchange rates, 105, 107–8, 131–3; and monetary policy, 154, 158–9; and wages, 187; and gold standard, 188; and price stability, 316
exports (British): decline, 131, 133; and balance of payments, 298–300

Falk, Oswald Toynbee ('Foxy'): at Treasury, 18; and Tuesday Club, 22–3, 197; on JMK's dominance, 23; as JMK's business collaborator, 25–7, 29; and currency speculation, 41–3; writes for *Manchester Guardian*, 103; and JMK's business indexes, 106; JMK stays with, 113; attitude to JMK and Lydia, 144; on level of US investment, 299; and Wall Street crash, 339–40, 342–3;
JMK ends collaboration with, 342–3; and US banking weakness, 390; and Independent Trust liabilities, 394; and JMK's investment policy, 401; criticises JMK, 432; and PR Investment Trust, 524
Fallgatter, Martin, 460, 501
fascism, 484–5
Fay, C. R., 46, 184, 407
Federal Reserve Board (USA): role, 158, 193, 195, 198, 336, 489; and Great Depression, 340–1, 435; and domestic considerations, 355; and JMK's 1931 visit to USA, 390–1
Feis, Herbert, 505
Ferrer, Gaspar, 191–2
Ferrero, Guglielmo, 104
Finlay Lecture, Dublin, 1933, 476–9
Firbank, Ronald, 35
Fisher, Irving, 103, 105, 153, 168, 173, 277–8, 314, 409, 418, 601
Fiske, Minnie, 97
Fitzgibbons, Athol, 83–4, 87–9, 526
Fokine, Mikhail Mikhailovich, 99
Fonteyn, Margot, 531
'Footnotes to the General Theory' (unfinished), 611
Forbes-Robertson, Jean, 624

Forster, E. M., ix, 13n, 35, 138

Foxwell, Herbert Somerton, 412, 628

France: attitude to Germany, 31–3, 119–20, 123, 125–6; financial problems, 32; and German reparations, 47–9, 128, 299, 390; war debts, 47, 123; differences with Britain over Germany, 116–17; JMK–Melchior policy on, 122–3; occupies Ruhr, 123–5; JMK attacks, 126; gold hoarding, 355; remains on gold standard, 434, 583; reception of *General Theory* in, 582–4

France, Anatole, 104

Franck, Paul, 28, 104

Frankfurter, Felix, 38, 489, 491–2, 505–6, 518n

Frazer, Sir James: *The Golden Bough*, 85

free trade, 151–2, 353, 371–2, 386; as cause of war, 477; *see also* protection

Freeden, Michael, 222–3

Freud, Sigmund: and 'death instinct', 7; Bloomsbury and, 17; and anal-sadistic character, 88; on gold and money, 188; influence on JMK, 234, 237; JMK on theories of, 414

Friedman, Milton, 153, 435, 578–80, 588

Fry, Geoffrey, 115

Fry, Roger: paintings damaged, 4; in Cranium Club, 13n; and Vanessa Bell's view on Berenson, 42; and Lydia, 111, 116, 140–1; on JMK's marriage, 210; Lydia on, 213; and London Artists Association, 243–4, 380, 527; and JMK's views on financial history, 333; investments, 343; quarrel with JMK, 380; aesthetics, 407; death, 432; funeral, 510

Furness, Robert, 217

Furst, Gaston, 54

Gage, Harold Rainald, 6th Viscount, 214

Gaitskell, Hugh, 438

Galbraith, John Kenneth, 580

Galton, Francis, 410, 415, 429, 631

Galton Lecture, 1937, 608

Garnett, Angelica, 14, 293

Garnett, David ('Bunny'): marriage, 11; in Bloomsbury group, 12–13; at Charleston, 14, 35, 495; relations with JMK, 14; reviews in *Nation*, 138; Lydia on, 213; investments, 343; receives JMK's annuity, 528; and Cambridge Arts Theatre, 529; and literary editorship of *New Statesman*, 536

Garnett, Ray (*née* Marshall), 11

Garraty, John, 485

Garvin, J. L., 139, 388

Gathorne-Hardy, Edward, 13n

Gathorne-Hardy, Robert, 13n

Genée, Adeline, 115, 381

General Elections: 1923, 151–2; 1924, 195; 1929, 285, 297–303, 306; 1935, 536

'General Theory of Employment, The' (paper), 616–18

General Theory of Employment, Interest and Money, The: and new economics, 3, 29, 318; and probability, 82–4, 87–8; and irrational behaviour, 88–9, 539–40; and monetary reform, 169, 543; and wage behaviour, 223, 371, 463, 549; and psychology, 271; abstract nature of, 319; on investors, 336; and Macmillan Committee, 346, 362; on Robbins, 368; on disequilibrium, 373, 442, 540; and low-income equilibrium, 392; on economic heretics, 415–16; and output, 421; on nature of economic life, 425; on dissensions among economists, 438; argument and concepts, 439–45, 462–3, 466, 510–12, 533–5, 548–71; reception, 443; and 'Cambridge Circus', 447; and Sraffa's commodity rates of exchange, 458; Hayek and, 458–9; and effective demand, 461–2; and JMK's Cambridge lectures, 496–500; writing of, 510, 532; proofs circulated and criticised, 532–4; publication, 536; qualities and 'vision', 537–48; as social reflection, 541, 543; difficulty, 548; controversy and reaction to, 572–93; foreign translations, 581–3; differences with classical and continental economics, 593–5, 606–10; neglects long-period theory, 600, 605; historical content, 606–7; mathematical and generalised versions, 612–24

General Strike, 1926, 223, 249–56

Genoa Economic Conference, 1922, 27, 106–11, 116

George V, King, 17

'German Transfer Problem, The', 300

Germany: reparations (Great War), 19–20, 27, 31–4, 46–50, 54, 107, 117–21, 123, 127–9, 299, 309–11, 316, 390; ended, 433; JMK's view of, 31–2; relations with France, 32–3, 122–3; inflation in, 90, 107, 117, 120, 129, 156; and 1922 Berlin conference, 119–20; and French occupation of Ruhr, 123–4; transfer problem, 309–12, 316; and collapse of Vienna bank, 390; 1931 default, 393; JMK visits (1922), 118; (1923), 127; (1926), 239–49; (1932), 434–5; economic revival, 486; persecution in, 486–7; JMK's *General Theory* in, 581–2

Germany, Grace, 100, 146

Gesell, Silvio, 497, 511, 569

Giannini, A., 103

Giblin, Lyndhurst Faulkner, 441, 594n

Gielgud, John, 530

Gifford, Charles, 293

Gifford, P. J., 521

Gilpin, E. H., 258

Gladstone, Herbert, 249

Gogarty, Oliver St John, 480

gold prices (USA), 493n

gold standard: calls for resumption of, 20, 40, 130, 132; JMK opposes, 45, 129, 136, 147, 154, 158–62, 173, 188–90, 193–4, 200–2, 204–7, 336, 472; Norman and, 25, 397–8; and exchange rates, 107–8, 132, 188–9, 317; and price levels, 158; management of, 158, 169; and gold reserves, 159; Cannan defends, 163; British return to, 187–90, 195–200; and wage system, 330; abolished in Britain, 393–4, 397–400; France retains, 434, 481, 583; USA abandons, 480–1

Goldenweiser, Emmanuel, 360

Gompers, Samuel, 104

Goodenough, Charles, 198

Gordon Square, London, 10–12, 213

Gore, Muriel, 143, 145, 176

Gorki, Maxim, 104

Goschen, Sir Henry, 191

Gosse, Sir Edmund, 14, 15n

Gramsci, Antonio, 289

Grant, Duncan, xi; paintings damaged, 4; Cambridge murals, 5; on Gordon Square, 10–12; in Cranium Club, 13n; at Charleston, 14, 91; relations with JMK, 14, 92, 101, 432; relations with Vanessa Bell, 14, 35; on Barbara Bagenal and JMK, 36; advises JMK on art purchases, 28; finances JMK's currency speculation, 41, 43; Italy holiday, 42; mistaken for JMK at I Tatti, 42; and JMK's attachment to Lydia, 96, 100–1, 112; designs logo for *Manchester Guardian Commercials*, 103; and Tomlin, 141; devises ballet, 182; loses money in 1924 election, 195; at JMK's wedding, 207–8; attitude to

Keyneses, 217; and London Artists Association, 243–4, 380, 527; and JMK's theories, 332; quarrel with JMK, 380; affair with Bergen, 380; visits Versailles, 407; visits Cambridge, 513; Cunard reject *Queen Mary* panels, 527; annuity from JMK, 528; at Tilton, 536

Gray, C. J., 248

Green, T. H., 224

Gregory, Theodor Emmanuel, 345, 361, 469

Grenfell, Edward ('Teddy'), 143

Grenfell, Florence ('Florrie'), 143–4, 177, 208, 211

Grey, Sir Edward (Viscount Grey of Fallodon), 249, 252, 255

Grigg, P. J., 189, 200

Hacking, Ian, 77

Haberler, Gottfried: *Prosperity and Depression*, 618

Hahn, Frank, 426

Hall, Radclyffe: *The Well of Loneliness*, 18

Halley-Stewart Lecture, 1932, 439, 441, 464

Hamburg, 435

Hamilton, Alfred Douglas Douglas-Hamilton, 13th Duke of, 145

Hamilton, Earl J., 334

Hammond, J. L., 102, 134

Hannen, Peter, 294

Hanotaux, Gabriel, 113

Hansen, Alvin, 538, 576, 580, 605; *A Guide to Keynes*, 550n

Harcourt, Alfred, 284

Harding, Warren, 116

Hargreaves, F. A., 139

Hargreaves, Mary, 176

Harland, Mrs (cook), 216, 389

Harmer, Frederick, 6, 287

Harris, Frank, ix, 111

Harris, Seymour, 580

Harris Lecture, 1931, 461

Harris Memorial Foundation (USA), 389

Harrison, George Leslie, 393

Harrod, Roy: on effect of *Economic Consequences*, 18; meets JMK, 114; and JMK–Cuno initiative, 128; on JMK's *Tract*, 160; and JMK's foreign investment lecture, 186; and note issue, 190; and economic theory, 406; and JMK's view of economists, 413; and effective demand, 466; letter of support for JMK, 473; attacks JMK's interest rate theory, 500; comments on *General Theory*, 532–5, 557, 572, 583, 615; teaches at Oxford, 533; and IS–LM Keynesianism, 538, 613–14; and JMK's provocativeness, 547; on interest rate and adjusting saving and investment, 559–60; reviews *General Theory*, 575; as intermediary, 584; and Henderson's views on *General Theory*, 587; defends Tinbergen, 620; 'The Scope and Method of Economics' (address), 619

Harvard University, 580

Harvey, Sir Ernest Musgrave, 356

Harvey, Miss J. M., 528–9

Harwood, Professor, 494

Haskell, Arnold, 381–2

Haslam, W. H., 106

Havenstein, Rudolf, 117, 120

Hawtrey, Ralph: at Genoa Conference, 20, 107–8; and JMK's view of 'inflation tax', 159; and gold standard, 161, 399; economic theory, 174; and Churchill, 198; and US prices, 204; at Harvard, 282; and 1929 Liberal initiative, 298–9; relations with JMK, 424, 441; on *Treatise on Money*, 444–6, 448, 453; on cheap money, 468; on gold value of pound, 473; JMK sees as mad, 495; reads and comments on *General Theory*, 532–3, 559, 586, 593, 600; reviews *General Theory*, 584, 586; disagreements with JMK, 600–1; *The Art of Central Banking*, 445; *Capital and Employment*, 586; *Currency and Credit*, 169, 445n; *Good and Bad Trade*, 277

Hayek, Friedrich: proposes abolition of credit, 331; and nature's cure, 379; controversies with JMK, 424, 441, 452, 455–9, 499; influence, 438; at London School of Economics, 455–6; Sraffa and, 457–8, 566; personal relations with JMK, 459; supports balanced budget policy, 469; and Bryce's exposition of *General Theory*, 532; fears incontinence of money, 543; silence on *General Theory*, 573; on market system, 577; on depressions, 597; on wage bargaining, 603; 'Capital Consumption', 459; *Constitution of Liberty*, 229; *Prices and Production*, 457–8

Head, Sir Henry, 146n

Heard, Gerald, 13n

Heckscher, Eli Filip, 535

Hegel, Georg Wilhelm Friedrich, 75–6

Helburn, Suzanne, 83

Hemming, A. F., 364, 376

Henderson, Alexander, 522

Henderson, Faith, 137, 145, 208, 217, 339

Henderson, Hubert: leaves Cambridge, 5; in Liberal-radical group, 22; edits *Nation*, 134–8; friendship with JMK, 145, 208, 217, 339, 424; and political economy, 174; and Liberal economics, 222; on Liberal-Labour alliance, 245; on Lloyd George in General Strike, 253; and Liberal Party, 258, 264n, 306; JMK works with, 272; and 1929 Liberal initiative, 299, 303–5; relations with JMK cool during Great Depression, 343; work for Economic Advisory Council, 344, 363–5, 370, 373–8, 468; changes views, 365–6; opposes free trade, 376; on JMK's budget pronouncements, 385; leaves *Nation*, 388; and JMK's 1931 US visit, 390; foresees British economic crisis, 393; on JMK as *enfant terrible*, 423; controversies with JMK, 436, 495, 532; sides with Treasury on public works, 449; rejects multiplier theory, 452; on Committee on Economic Information, 467; devises international recovery plan, 471; and JMK's expansionist plan, 474; and US recovery, 491; at All Souls, 532, 587; and *General Theory*, 532, 584, 587–8, 593, 599; breach with JMK, 587–8; criticises Robertson's article on *General Theory*, 589; and Robertson's position at Cambridge, 593; on interest rate, 593; on political interference, 597; on wage increases, 603; and JMK's boom control, 628; *Can Lloyd George Do It?* (with JMK), 303, 365, 371, 449

Herriot, Edouard, 104, 129

Hession, Charles, 424

Hicks, John, 328, 412, 439, 455, 538, 546; on *General Theory*, 572–3, 575–6, 611–16, 618; 'Mr Keynes and the Classics', 575, 611, 622–4

Hicks, Sir William Joynson, 17, 299

Higgins, Norman Oppenshaw, 528–9

Hilferding, Rudolf, 103

Hill, A. V., 7, 41, 296, 343

Hill, David (JMK's nephew), 8

Hill, Janet (JMK's niece), 8

Hill, Margaret (*née* Keynes; JMK's sister), 7, 529

Hill, Maurice (JMK's nephew), 8

Hill, Polly (JMK's niece), 8, 95, 146, 536, 626
Hill, Vivian, 296
Hiller, Wendy, 530
Hindley-Smith, Frank, 243, 527
Hirsch, Fred, 237n
Hirst, F. W., 114
'Historical Retrospect' (lecture), 464
Hitchens, Ivon, 527
Hitler, Adolf, 31, 338, 440, 485, 495, 578
Hobhouse, Arthur, 15
Hobhouse, L. T., 134, 224
Hobson, J. A., 134, 224, 247, 301, 317, 343, 535, 545n, 569
Hodgskin, Thomas, 416
Hogarth Press, 17
Hollis, Martin, 71
Hoover, Calvin, 505
Hoover, Herbert, 390, 489
Hopkin, Bryan, 521-2
Hopkins, Sir Richard, 21, 298, 302, 354, 358-61, 384-5, 436, 473
Horne, Sir Robert, 107
Housman, A. E., 626
'How Far Are Bankers Responsible for the Alternation of Crisis and Depression' (talk), 277
'How to Avoid a Slump', 629
'How to Organise a Wave of Prosperity', 297
Howe, Bea (later Lubbock), 182
Howson, Susan, 40, 364
Hubback, David, 22
Hume, David, 58, 60, 61, 310
Hutchins, Robert, 491
Hutchinson, Mary, 12, 35, 111-13
Hutchison, Terence, 631
Hutton, Graham, 397
Huxley, Aldous, 495-6

Ibsen, Henrik: Lydia acts in plays of, 503, 530, 625; JMK on, 423
Idealism, 74-7
Idzikovsky, Stanislas, 93, 99, 176
Iford, Sussex: Oaklands (house), 208-10
Import Duties Act, 1931, 377
Independent Investment Trust, 394, 524
Independent Labour Party, 246n; summer school, 257
India, 91, 93, 102, 174
Indian Currency and Finance, 153
inflation: post-Great War, 39-41, 44-6; JMK on effects of, 155-6; debate with Robertson on, 277-80; and supply of

consumption goods, 331; and boom, 629-30
Inglis, Professor, 529
Institute of Bankers, 121, 132
interest rates, 500-2, 555-6, 559-66, 591, 593, 597-9
International Economic Society, 434
International Monetary Fund, 100, 472
intuitions, 407n, 414
Invergordon mutiny, 1931, 396
Ireland, 479-80
IS–LM diagram, 538, 575, 612, 616n
Isherwood, Christopher, 36, 627

Jacobsson, Per, 460
Japan, 488
Jay, Douglas, 575
Jeffreys, Harold, 452
Jenks, Jeremiah, 118
Jeune, Alick de, 511
Jevons, William Stanley, 411-12, 415, 423, 606, 624-5; The Coal Question, 415
Jews, 238-9; persecuted in Germany, 485, 487
Johannsen, Nicholas: Neglected Points in Connection with Crises, 545n, 594n
Johnson, Alvin, 161, 391
Johnson, Elizabeth, 18, 223
Johnson, W. E., 37-8, 51-2, 55, 80
Johnston, Thomas, 233, 394
Jones, Brent, 604
Jones, Eric, 606
Jones, Thomas, 111, 114; Whitehall Diary, 343
Jonson, Ben: Volpone, x, xii
Jooss, Kurt, 522, 531
Joseph, Horace, 224
Joshi, J. V., 6, 114
Joynson Hicks, Sir William see Hicks, Sir William Joynson
Judson, Stanley, 633
Jung, Carl Gustav, 20

Kahn, Richard ('Ferdinand'): studies at Cambridge, 6, 287-8, 290; King's Fellowship, 9; Jewishness, 239, 288; and 'employment multiplier', 304, 373-5, 377, 445n, 448-52, 471, 594n; on economists' committee of Economic Advisory Council, 364, 371, 377; on Marshall, 418; on 'short period', 421;

conversations with JMK, 424, 436, 495, 510; nurses JMK, 432; in 'Cambridge Circus', 447–8; creative influence, 448; relations with Joan Robinson, 448, 495, 536; challenges Hayek, 456; lectures in USA, 471; and US recovery, 491; reads *General Theory*, 495, 532; replaces Durnford, 512; and JMK's credit cycle investments, 525; visits Tilton, 536, 625; on public works, 563; translates Wicksell, 580; attracts research students, 593; and JMK's 'generalised system', 611; and revolutionary nature of *General Theory*, 613; manages King's accounts, 626; replies to Hutchison, 630; *The Making of the General Theory*, 452n; 'Public Works and Inflation' (paper), 451; 'The Relation of Home Investment to Unemployment', 449

Kaldor, Nicholas, 346, 412, 452, 456, 478n, 573, 597n, 607n

Kalecki, Michal, 451, 594n, 604

Kamenka, B., 118

Kant, Immanuel, 75

Kapitsa, Peter, 292–3

'Kappa' *see* Ratcliffe, S. K.

Karsavina, Tamara, 98, 382

Kennedy, George Lawrence, 13n, 176, 215, 285, 510, 513, 528–30

Kenworthy, Joseph Montague (10th Baron Strabolgi), 245; *Sailors*, 340

Kerr, Philip (*later* 11th Marquess of Lothian), 22, 265

Keynes, Florence Ada (JMK's mother): in Cambridge, 7; and JMK's financial losses, 43; meets Lydia, 176–7; at JMK's wedding, 207–8; as mayor of Cambridge, 339; visits Tilton, 535; and JMK's health, 627, 632–3

Keynes, Geoffrey (JMK's brother): family, 7, 296; destroys letters, 36; currency speculation, 42; rescues Virginia Woolf, 146n; and Lydia, 183; visits JMK and Lydia, 208, 339; career, 339; investments, 343; adapts Blake's *Job* for Camargo Society, 382; and JMK's illness, 634

Keynes, John Maynard
  career and activities: teaching and lecturing at Cambridge, 4–5, 174, 496–501, 510–12, 521–2; as bursar of King's College, 8–9, 285–6, 512–13; official influence, 18–24; writing, 24, 27–8; business interests, 25–7; and

Manchester Guardian Supplements, 92, 100, 102–6, 113, 117, 120–1, 153n, 289; at Genoa Conference, 106–11, 116; at 1922 Berlin conference, 116, 118–20; manages *Nation*, 134–9, 175; serves on Macmillan Committee, 343–58, 361–2; on Economic Advisory Council, 343–5, 363–78

  characteristics: playfulness, xi–xii; intelligence and verbal powers, 23, 422, 427; creativity, 210–11, 443; stinginess, 218; intuitions, 219, 414–15, 424; attitudes and values, 406–12, 422–3; excellence as teacher, 414; self-confidence, 422–3, 425; style, 423–4, 470; multiplicity of talents, 423–4; achievements, 424–5; ridicule, 425; manner, 426–7; artistic tastes, 427; fastidiousness, 427; working methods, 427–8; credulousness, 428; vision, 502, 537; concentration, 502; imaginative ardour, 509–10; gambling instinct, 524–5; commitment to countryside, 526; generosity, 527; forgetfulness, 626

  personal and private life: appearance and dress, ix, 9, 38, 208, 213, 422, 427, 433; love life, xi, 35–6, 51, 92–3, 101; family, 7–8; riding, 9; in Bloomsbury group, 10–17, 34, 175, 407; at Charleston, 14, 34–5; relations with Bunny Garnett and Duncan Grant, 14; earnings, 24–6, 92, 102; currency speculation, 26, 28–9, 38, 41–3, 90–1; art collection, 28–9, 141, 427, 527–8; and Naomi Bentwich, 38–9, 51–5; loses money, 43; and Wittgenstein, 72; entertaining, 92, 217–18; courts Lydia, 93, 100–1, 104, 111–16, 144, 146; correspondence with Lydia, 109–10, 180–1; need for praise, 110; sexual relations with Lydia, 110–11; lives with Lydia, 140; social life, 144; backs play, 144; campaigns in 1923 election, 151–2; engagement and marriage, 173–6, 179, 207–11; language, 173–4; and ancient coin and money, 175; visits USSR, 208–9, 235–6, 626; marriage relations, 210–13; occupies Tilton, 214–17; interest in theatre, 294–5; commodity losses in Great Depression, 342; backs Camargo Society, 382; health breakdown, 389, 432–3; 1931 visits and lectures in USA, 389–92; voice and speech, 422; lectures in Dublin,

476–80; weakness in foreign languages, 485; supports Lydia's acting, 502–3; 1934 visit to USA, 504–9; wisdom teeth removed, 509; wealth and investments, 524–5; benefactions, 526, 528; collects books and manuscripts, 527–8; plans and builds Cambridge Arts Theatre, 528–31; votes Labour in 1935, 536; ill health, 624, 628–9, 633–4; in Cannes, 633–4

views and opinions: party politics, 3–4, 21–2, 151–2, 231–2, 301–4, 436–7; on war, 7; on civilisation, 8, 18; anti-Americanism, 20; on economics, 29, 122, 618–19; on ethics, 56–61, 64–6, 71; on government, 61–4; on property, 63; on tragedy, 64–6; on exchange rate, 105, 107–8, 132; on Bolshevism, 108; on US war debts and intervention, 123–4; on German reconstruction and reparations, 125–7; on unemployment, 131–3; on wages, 133–4; on Liberal Party policies, 135–7, 222–4; on population, 149–51, 221, 429–30, 608–9, 631; on society, 221, 223, 233–4; utopianism, 234, 237; on 'love of money', 236–7; on Jews, 238–9, 421n; on businessmen, 258–60; on origins of capitalism, 332–4; favours tariffs, 371–2, 375–7, 386–8, 395; on 1931 financial crisis, 395–6; on investment policy, 401; on greatness, 410–11; on earlier economists, 410–20; on mathematics in economics, 412–14; on eccentricity and crankiness, 415–16; on self as great economist, 422; on socialism, 437–8; on historical studies, 464–6; on budget, 468–9; opposes Marxism, 517–21, 523; on religion, 517–18; on history, 606–8; advocates rearmament, 626–7, 630–1

see under title for individual publications by JMK

Keynes, Margaret (*née* Darwin; Geoffrey's wife), 7, 296, 625

Keynes, Margaret (JMK's sister) *see* Hill, Margaret

Keynes, Milo (JMK's nephew), 7, 625

Keynes, Neville (JMK's father); in Cambridge, 7; finances JMK's currency speculation, 41–2; writes off loan to JMK, 43; relations with Lydia, 176; on JMK's obituary of Marshall, 181; entertains JMK, 286; investments, 343; JMK's attachment to,

416–17; visits Tilton, 535; depressed over pre-war Europe, 626

Keynes, Quentin (JMK's nephew), 7

Keynes, Richard (JMK's nephew), 7

Keynes, Stephen (JMK's nephew), 7, 625

Keynes Club *see* Political Economy Club, Cambridge

Kiddy, A. W., 22

King's College, Cambridge: JMK's post-Great War return to, 4–6; life in, 8; JMK's service as bursar, 8–9, 285–6, 512–13; improvements and rebuilding, 175–6, 285, 503; 1926 provostship election, 248–9; and theatre, 294; Sheppard elected provost, 496, 503; investments, 524–5; and Arts Theatre, 528

Kipling, Rudyard, 626

Kisch Plan, 481

Kitson, A. W., 416

Klotz, Lucien, 239

Klugman, James, 523

Knight, Frank, 576–8, 599

Knox, Dillwyn ('Dilly'), 91

Kocherthaler, Ernst, 119n

Kreuger, Ivar, 435

Kries, J. von, 79

Kumar, Dharma, 419

Labordère, Marcel: on King's College, 8, 517; influence on JMK, 25, 275–6; friendship with JMK, 122, 426; on JMK's *Tract*, 158; influence on Robertson, 275–8; correspondence with JMK on money, 312–13, 558, 567n; and JMK's investments, 526; comments on *General Theory*, 583–4

Labour Party: 1923 government, 151, 161; JMK's attitude to, 174, 232–4, 437; and gold standard, 189; proposed alliance with Liberals, 245; economic policy, 246–7; 1929 government, 306; rejects Mosley's New Deal, 378; loses power (1931), 393, 395; in 1931 election, 400, 437; suspicion of JMK, 438; public works programme, 472–3; JMK votes for in 1935, 536; opposes borrowing for rearmament, 629

laissez-faire: JMK opposes, 160, 173, 180, 183, 185–7, 219–21, 225, 609; as policy, 219; and economic theory, 405, 484

Lambardi, Zampart, 522

Lambert, Constant, 13n, 381–2, 480, 633

Lamont, Thomas, 103, 397–8

Lancashire: cotton industry, 174, 260–3
Lancashire Cotton Corporation, 262
Lange, Oscar, 615
Laplace, Marquis Pierre Simon de, 78
Largentaye, Jean de, 582–3
Larranaga, P. J. M., 416, 519
Laski, Harold, 38, 103, 400, 432, 518
Lausanne Conference, 1932, 433
Lautenbach, Wilhelm, 582
Lavington, Frederick, 5, 287
Law, Andrew Bonar: and monetary policy, 40, 190; declines to contribute to *Manchester Guardian*, 104; premiership, 120–1; and German–French relations, 123, 125–6; and US war debts, 124; resignation, 126–7; and protection, 151
Lawrence, D. H.: *Lady Chatterley's Lover*, 18
Lawrence, Susan, 505
Lawson, Tony, 83, 88
Layton, Walter, 5, 22, 103, 135–6, 197, 258, 343, 468–9
Leaf, Walter, ix, 191, 194, 244
League of Nations, 338, 618–20
Lees-Smith, H. B., 380
Leffingwell, Russell, 18–19, 103, 105, 397–8, 509
Leibnitz, Gottfried Wilhelm, Freiherr von, 77
Leijohnhufvud, Axel, 444
Leith-Ross, Sir Frederick, 20, 298, 302, 317, 468
Lenin, V. I., 40, 104, 110
Leontief, Wassily, 616
Lerner, Abba P., 456, 573–5, 578–9
Letiche, J. M., 582
Lewis, Sir Alfred, 467
Lewis, Wyndham, 11
Liberal Party: decline, 21–2, 134–5, 137, 436; summer schools, 135–6, 144, 149, 186, 222, 233; and JMK's policies, 136–7, 174, 222–4; in 1924 election, 195; Industrial Inquiry, 222, 258, 263–4, 269; loses supporters, 245; proposed alliance with Labour, 245; 1926 split, 249; Lloyd George resumes leadership, 258; on private and public industry, 265–7; and increased investment, 298; programme in 1929 election, 298, 301–6; JMK parts from, 344; in 1931 election, 400
Lindahl, Erik, 488, 547, 580, 601
Lippmann, Walter: friendship with JMK, 3; and JMK's influence, 19; and *New Republic*, 28; writes for *Manchester Guardian*, 103; on *Nation*, 139; and gold

standard, 398; and New Deal, 491, 494; and JMK's 1934 visit to USA, 507–8; letter from Leffingwell, 509
liquidity preference ('propensity to hoard'), 561–5, 578, 592, 628
List, Friedrich, 476
Littleboy, Bruce, 83
Living Way, The (ILP pamphlet), 247
Lloyd, Muriel (JMK's cousin), 286
Lloyd George, David: takes over Liberal Party leadership (1926), 21, 258; and German reparations, 32, 47–9, 54; and inflation, 39–40; and politics of lying, 63; Clemenceau on, 90; JMK on, 90, 118; and Genoa Conference, 106–11, 116; political decline, 116, 118, 134–5; JMK supports, 174, 249, 293; advocates public works programme, 184; and JMK's economic theory, 222; as Party chairman, 245; fund, 245 and n, 258; and General Strike, 251–6; JMK's relations with, 251, 258; and Industrial Inquiry, 264, 269; pledge to reduce unemployment, 269, 301; in 1929 election, 297–8, 302–3, 306; proposes improved investment, 298–9, 354, 359, 361; JMK visits, 339, 400; attack on City, 385; and JMK's tariff proposals, 387–8; and decline of Liberal Party, 436; praises Roosevelt, 490
Locarno Treaty, 1925, 338
Locke, John, 60
Loeser, Charles, 42
logical positivism, 69
London and Cambridge Economic Service, 106
London Artists' Association, 92, 143, 175, 243, 380, 382; wound up, 527
London School of Economics, 438, 455–6, 532
Long, Huey, 508
Long, Leo, 516
Lopokova, Lydia (Mrs JMK): JMK courts, 93, 100–1, 104, 111–16, 146; character and appearance, 94, 142, 144, 211–13; dancing, 93, 95–6, 98–9, 109, 113–14, 116, 140, 176–8, 181–2, 244, 249, 338–9, 381–2; disappearance, 95–6; life and family background, 96–8; correspondence with JMK, 109–10, 180–1; sexual relations with JMK, 110–11; Bloomsbury hostility to, 112–13, 141–3, 145, 182, 210–11; London homes, 112–13, 116; on *Nation*,

140; JMK lives with, 140–1; on English
life-style, 140–1; Vanessa Bell's
portrait of, 141; divorce from Barocchi,
142, 176; acting, 142, 295–6, 380–2,
480, 502–3, 530, 625, 632; friends,
142–3; Virginia Woolf describes, 145;
on free trade, 152; engagement and
marriage to JMK, 173–6, 179, 207–8,
210–11; in Monte Carlo, 173; meets
JMK's mother, 175; in Paris, 177–81;
in USSR, 208–9, 488, 626; marriage
relations, 210–13; spoken English,
211–12, 295–6; writings on ballet,
212–13; home-making and
entertaining, 213–14, 218; at Tilton,
215–18; recreations, 218, 295; on Jews,
238; loses child, 294, 480; and
Cambridge theatre, 295, 529–30; and
1928 election, 306; dances in film,
338–9; founds Camargo Society, 339,
381; in Spain, 380; buys blankets, 384;
1931 visit to USA, 389–90, 392; on
Webbs, 399; favours Labour in 1931
election, 400; effect on JMK, 428;
refuses to visit Strachey and
Carrington, 432; and JMK's illness,
432; final ballet appearance, 480;
'Russian lunches', 480, 503; 1934 US
visit, 504–5; supports JMK's lecturing,
511; largesse at Tilton, 526, 536; ballet
comments, 531; broadcasts, 531; and
reaction to General Theory, 573; rests at
Tilton, 625; in Cannes, 632; nurses
JMK, 633
Lopukhov, Fyodor, 488–9
Lopukhova, Eugenia (Lydia's sister), 96–7,
488
Lopukhov, Fedor (Lydia's brother), 96–7
Lopukhov, Karlusha (Lydia's mother),
208, 488, 626
Loucheur, Louis, 49, 243
'love of money', 236–40, 424
Lubbock, Cecil, 196, 345, 361
Lucas, E. B. C. ('Topsy'; née Jones), 7, 217,
296
Lucas, Frank Laurence ('Peter'): revives
Apostles, 6; marriage, 7; King's
Fellowship, 9; at Charleston, 35, 91;
book on tragedy, 65; friendship with
JMK, 217, 294, 296, 339; separates, 296
Luce, Gordon, xi, 208, 217, 249
Ludwig Mond Lecture, 1929, 347, 352, 365,
369n

Macaulay, Reginald, 286
Macaulay, W. H., 285–6
MacCarthy, Desmond, 12, 115
MacCarthy, Molly, 12, 115
McCloskey, Donald, 424
MacDonald, James Ramsay: Victorianism,
17; writes for Manchester Guardian, 103;
1923 government, 151; rhetoric, 232;
and proposed alliance with Liberals,
245; sets up Economic Advisory
Council, 343–4, 363–4, 468; and
Mosley's resignation, 364; favours
Henderson, 365; blames capitalism for
slump, 378; and JMK's tariff proposals,
387; and May report, 393–5; and
devaluation, 394; heads National
Government, 395, 400, 436; JMK's
relations with, 436; and Committee on
Economic Information, 467, 469; at
World Economic Conference, 481; and
Roosevelt's programme, 491
McDougall, Walter, 32, 34
McEagar, W., 264n
McFadyean, Sir Andrew, 20
MacGregor, A. G., 416
Macgregor, David H., 245, 469
MacIntyre, Alastair: After Virtue, 407n
McKenna, Reginald: absent from JMK's
Liberal–radical circle, 22; JMK's view
of, 23; forms syndicate with JMK, 43;
JMK stays with, 115; and war debts
to USA, 124; and German reparations,
127–8; on bank rate, 147; and
Chamberlain Committee, 191–2; and
gold standard, 200; speeches on credit,
283–4; JMK admires, 286; obstructs
Kahn, 288, 301; and 1929 Liberal
initiative, 301–2; on Macmillan
Committee, 345, 347, 356, 361, 393;
supports tariffs, 393
Maclean, Sir Donald, 249
Macmillan, Hugh Pattison Maclean,
Baron, 345, 349, 361; Committee on
Finance and Industry, 1929–30, 321,
343–62, 371, 382, 393, 422, 608
Macmillan, Daniel, 43, 56, 210, 282, 285
Macmillan, Harold (later 1st Earl of
Stockton), 232, 436, 438
Macmillan (publishers), 470
McTaggart, John, 76–7, 85
Maine, Basil, 143
Maisky, Ivan, 104, 489
Malcolm, Neil, 49
Malthus, Daniel, 416
Malthus, Thomas: JMK's respect for,

410–11, 413, 416–17, 419, 426, 429, 464–5, 484, 545n, 569, 588; on population and unemployment, 632

Manchester Guardian (newspaper), 27, 48, 50, 54; Commercial Supplements, 92, 100, 102–6, 113, 117, 120–1, 153n, 289; JMK covers Genoa Conference for, 106–7

Manchester System, 570

Mandeville, Bernard: *Fable of the Bees*, 465, 541, 552, 569

Mann, A. H. ('Daddy'), 144

Marjolin, Robert, 583

Markova, Alicia, 531

Marks, Geoffrey, 25

Marshall, Alfred: JMK's obituary article on, 119, 181–2, 410–11; on money, 156, 409, 461; Cannan and, 163; and economic control, 170; and business vocation, 259; teaching, 272; criticisms of, 288, 290, 413; on long-run prices, 320, 420–1; influence, 405, 409, 412, 418–20; and Jevons, 411–12; on time and periods, 419–21; on partial equilibrium, 425; on purchasing, 550; mocked in *General Theory*, 585; *Principles of Economics*, 418–20

Marshall, Frances *see* Partridge, Frances

Marshall, Mary, 181–2, 217, 282, 510

Marshall, Tom, 13n, 294

Marshall Society, 456, 587

Martin, Kingsley, 3–4, 388–9, 436, 486, 488, 536

Martynov, General, 95–6

Marx, Karl: doctrines, 221, 226, 293, 379, 439, 484, 488, 497, 511; appeal, 514–16; JMK opposes, 517–21, 523, 538; and commodities, 542; and ideas, 570; and class war, 595; *Das Kapital*, 538–9

Mary, Queen, 17

Masquerade (ballet), 143–4

Massine, Léonide, 99, 109, 111, 176, 180; ballets: *Le Beau Danube*, 178; *La Boutique Fantasque*, 95–6; *The Good-Humoured Ladies*, 93

Massingham, Hugh, 134–5

Masterman, Charles, 22

Matthews, K. C. P., 206n

Maurice, Joan *see* Robinson, Joan

May, Sir George, 384; Report, 1931, 393–5

Meade, James, 447–9, 450–1, 533, 538, 572, 613–15

'Means to Prosperity, The', 435, 451–2, 454, 470, 472, 475, 493

Meehan, James, 478–9

Melchior, Carl: and German

reconstruction, 102, 107, 115n, 119–21, 125–8; relations with JMK, 122, 485; exile and death, 486

Meltzer, Allan, 605n

Memoir Club, 12, 16, 36, 238, 252, 525

Memoranda on Certain Proposals Relating to Unemployment (Treasury, 1929), 301

Mendès-France, Pierre, 583

Menken, J., 264n

Mercury Theatre Club, 381

Meyer, Eugene, 389

Micklin, John M., 124n

Midas, King, (legend of) 175, 193, 322, 425, 498n, 566, 608

Middlemas, Keith, 543

Middleton, Roger: *Towards the Managed Economy*, 630n

Middle Way, The, 22, 222, 229, 231–4, 239, 263, 265, 437, 569

Mill, John Stuart, 63

Milne, A. A., 139

Mini, P. V., 83, 88, 483

Mirsky, Prince Dimitri, 12, 139, 379; *The Intelligentsia of Great Britain*, 233

'Miscellanea Ethica' (notes), 57, 83

Mises, Ludwig von, 331

Mitchell, Wesley, 333

Mitrany, David, 102, 243

modernism, 406–7

Moggridge, Donald, 41n, 198–9, 206, 425

Mond, Sir Alfred, 245, 259, 344n, 345

'Monetary Theory of Production, The' (lectures), 4, 460, 546

'Monetary Theory of Production, A' (essay), 460

Montagu, Edwin, 91

Monte Carlo, 175

Moore, George Edward: influence on JMK, 50, 56–8, 60, 62, 68–9, 72, 75–6, 84, 224, 228, 407–9, 517, 541; attacks Idealism, 407n; Julian Bell rejects, 515; *Principia Ethica*, 58, 64, 66, 74, 86, 408, 517; 'The Refutation of Idealism', 77

Mordkin, Mikhail, 97

Morgan, E. V., 39, 45

Morgan, John Pierpont, 395

Morgenthau, Henry, Jr., 505

Morrell, Lady Ottoline, 11, 113, 236

Morrell, Philip, 11

Mortimer, Raymond, 13n, 138, 145, 536, 626, 631

Mosley, Sir Oswald: on Baldwin and wage reduction, 242; reputation, 246; economic proposals, 246; political career, 339, 344; resigns from

government, 364, 436; advocates public works programme, 367; favours protective tariffs, 376–7; starts New Party, 377; Labour Rejects New Deal, 378; denied help by Courtauld, 383; JMK praises Manifesto, 383; on state intervention, 384; hears JMK's address in House, 395–6; and 1931 financial crisis, 396; founds British Union of Fascists, 436, 495; JMK rebukes, 478; *Revolution by Reason*, 246
Moulton, J. F., x–xiii
Muir, Ramsay, 22, 135–6, 222, 258, 264
multiplier theory, 449–52, 454, 466, 470–1, 474, 498, 554–5, 590–1
Murray, Gilbert, 22
Mussolini, Benito, 103, 118, 191, 289, 338
'My Early Beliefs', 55, 88, 408, 525
Myers, Leopold Hamilton, 13n, 243
Myrdal, Gunnar, 488, 547, 559, 580–1

Namier, Lewis B., 102
Nash, Paul, 243
Nathan, H. L., 264n
Nation and Athenaeum (journal), 22; JMK manages, 134–9, 175; merges with *New Statesman*, 139, 386, 388; Lydia on, 140; Wight edits, 344; wound up, 388
National Government, 395, 400
National Liberal Club, London, 152
National Liberal Federation, 297
National Mutual Life Assurance Company, 25–6, 524
'National Self-Sufficiency' articles, 483
Neisser, Hans, 591
Nelson, Francis St George, 100
Nevinson, H. W., 134
Newbold, John Turner Walton, 345, 361
New Deal (USA), 467, 489–90, 493, 504, 506, 508–9, 558
New Fabian Research Bureau, 438, 447
New Leader (journal), 246 and n
New Nation company, 135–6
New Party (Mosley's), 377
New Republic (US magazine), 27
New Statesman (weekly), 22; absorbs *Nation*, 139, 386, 388–9; left-wing stance, 436, 488; JMK writes to, 626
Newton, Sir Isaac, 411, 414, 423, 626
New York, 389–91, 504, 506
Next Five Years Group, 438
Nicod, Jean, 73
Nicolson, Harold, 440
Nicolson, Nigel, 218

Niemeyer, Otto, 19, 22, 191, 197–200, 243, 298, 473
Nietzsche, Friedrich, 544
Nightingale, Frederick, 215
Nijinska, Bronislava, 99, 180
Nijinsky, Vaslav Fomich, 98–9, 143
1917 Club, London, 11
Nitti, Francesco, 104, 207
Noel-Baker, Philip, 22
Norman, Montagu: and repayment of US war debt, 20, 123–4; at Political Economy Club, 22; friendship with Strakosch, 23; Falk and, 25; and Lloyd George's monetary policy, 40–1; and JMK's 1922 visit to Berlin, 120; and German loan, 128; and bank rate increase, 147; limits foreign lending, 187; and return to gold standard, 189–90, 194–5, 197, 397–8; and unemployment, 286, 356; and JMK at Macmillan Committee, 351; testimony to Macmillan Committee, 356–7; Stamp on, 368; and 1931 drop in sterling exchange, 393; obstructs Ottawa Conference, 434; and JMK's devaluation plan, 481
North, Douglass, 606
Norton, Harry, 35

O'Brien, George, 478
O'Casey, Sean, 529
O'Donnell, Roderick, 57, 83–6, 88
Ogden, C. K., 4, 68
Ohlin, Bertil, 186, 300, 309–11, 327–8, 426, 488, 580, 592, 598, 600–1, 604, 628
Olson, Mancur, 230, 607
Omega Workshops, 17
'Open Letter to the President' (i.e. Roosevelt), 492, 494
Ord, Boris, 144
Orlando, Vittorio Emanuele, 104
Ottawa Conference, 1932, 434
Otter, William, Bishop of Chichester, 416
output, theory of, 461
Owen, Wilfred, 6
Oxford University, 224

Paget, Lady Muriel, 488
Painlevé, Paul, 103
Paish, F. W., 46
Paish, Sir George, 191
Paris Peace Conference, 1919, x, 18, 20, 26, 47–8

Partridge, Frances (*née* Marshall), 11, 13n, 182, 339
Partridge, Ralph, 92
Patinkin, Don, 443, 447–8, 461–2, 579n; *Anticipation of the General Theory*, 462n, 551n, 594n; 'On Different Interpretations of the *General Theory*', 616n; 'The Process of Writing the *General Theory*', 616n
Pavlova, Anna, 97, 216
Peacock, Sir Edward, 107
Pearson, Alfred Chilton, 91
Pearson, Karl, 61, 429, 618
Peddie, John Taylor, 416
Penrose, Alexander, 6, 13n, 92, 294
Penrose, Bernard, 92
Penrose, Lionel, 6–7, 92
Penrose, Roland, 92
Perkins, Frances, 505
Pethick-Lawrence, Frederick William, Baron, 630
Petrushka (ballet), 212
Peyser, Henry de, 49
Phillips, Sir Frederick, 21, 249, 468, 473
Phillips, William, 505
Pigou, Arthur Cecil: in Keynes Club, 5; excluded by British Academy, 19; on monetary policy, 45, 461; writes for *Manchester Guardian*, 103; Cambridge equation, 156; on JMK's *Tract*, 161; memorial lecture on Marshall, 182; on devaluation, 191; and Chamberlain Committee, 193; and return to gold standard, 197; at Cambridge, 272, 292, 375, 447; heart trouble, 282, 286–7, 367; aloofness, 287, 367, 586; and JMK's *Treatise on Money*, 320; on Economic Advisory Council committee, 364, 367, 370, 372–3, 375–7; JMK disagrees with methods, 367; JMK questions at Macmillan Committee, 371; on economic results, 405; theory of money, 409; relations with JMK, 424; letter on unemployment, 468–9; and *General Theory*, 532–3, 548, 549–50, 565, 578, 586, 597, 599, 614; Harrod on, 533; influence on Champernowne, 574; reviews *General Theory*, 584–6, 603; on JMK–Robertson controversy, 593; on political interference, 597; and interest rates, 597; defends classical view, 599; and wage levels, 604; historical sense, 607–8; *Industrial Fluctuations*, 282; *Theory of Unemployment*, 497
Planck, Max, 119

Plant, Arnold, 469
Plumptre, A. F. W., 237, 409
Poincaré, Raymond, 48, 104, 107, 116–17, 122–4, 126, 129
Political and Economic Planning (PEP), 438
'Political Doctrines of Edmund Burke, The' (essay), 57, 61–3
Political Economy Club, Cambridge ('Keynes Club'), 5, 287, 532–3, 627; (London), 22, 277, 281, 416
Pollock, Sir Frederick, ix
Popham, Brynhild (*née* Olivier), 432
population: in Europe, 46; policy, 220; JMK on, 429–30, 608–9, 631
'Population' (unpublished), 429
Porter, Frederick, 243n
Potts, F. A., 301
pound sterling: overvaluation, 206–7; 1931 devaluation, 394, 433; currency bloc, 434
Powell, Anthony: *Books Do Furnish a Room*, 11
PR Investment Trust, 524
Prentice, C. H. C., 13n
Preobrazhensky, E., 209
'Present Disorders of the World's Monetary System, The' (lecture), 44
prices: stabilisation of, 45–6, 148–50, 165, 315–16, 320–1, 329–30; 1920s fall in, 131–3, 149; indexes, 148, 320; and expectation of rise, 155; and monetary theory, 156–7; and deflation, 203–5; adjustments to, 444; in *General Theory*, 567
Pringle, W. M., 246, 249
'Private and the Public Concern, The' (talk), 264
probability: JMK on, 56–61, 67, 73–4, 77–87, 174, 224; Wittgenstein on, 69, 292; Ramsey on, 70–1, 73; history of, 77–82
'Problem of the Next Slump, The', 627
Procter, R. W., 46
'Proposals for a Revenue Tariff', 386
protection (trade), 151–2, 353, 360; JMK supports, 371–2, 375–7, 386–8, 434; Robbins opposes, 375–6
Provincial Insurance Company, 524
'Pure Theory of Money, The' (lectures), 460

quantity theory of money, 156–7, 162
Queen Mary, RMS, 527

Radin, Professor Max, 239
Raine, Sir Walter, 353
Rambert, Marie, 381
Ramsey, Frank: in Keynes Club, 5; in
    Apostles, 7, 68; King's Fellowship, 9;
    on JMK's *Treatise on Probability*, 67–8,
    70–1, 73, 85; qualities, 67–8, 71–2;
    translates Wittgenstein, 68, 70; death,
    72, 380; on saving theory, 284;
    relations with Wittgenstein, 292
Ramsey, Lettice, 292, 380, 389
Ransome, Arthur, 102, 104
Rapallo, Treaty of, 1922, 110
Ratcliffe, Samuel Kerkham ('Kappa'), 139
Rathenau, Walther, 54, 103, 110
rationality, 83–4, 88–9, 292
Raverat, Gwen, 382
Raverat, Jacques, 145, 183
Realism, 74
Reddaway, Brian, 521–2, 566, 574, 609, 615
Redgrave, Michael, 293–6, 389
Rees, Miss (JMK's secretary), 102, 114
Reparation Commission, 46, 54, 117, 119,
    123
reparations *see* Germany
Revelstoke, John Baring, 2nd Baron, 196
Revision of the Treaty, A, 14, 90, 96, 124
Rhineland, 47, 117, 578
Ricardo, David, 289–91, 293, 413, 417,
    419–20, 464–5, 588
Richardson, J. H., 103
Richardson, Philip, 381
Ries, Frank, 97
Rist, Charles, 582
Robbins, Lionel: on origins of US slump,
    341; on Economic Advisory Council,
    364, 367–9, 373, 375–6, 468; opposes
    tariffs, 372, 377, 386, 433; at London
    School of Economics, 438, 455; and
    Hayek, 455; supports balanced budget
    policy, 469; silence on *General Theory*,
    573; influenced by continental view of
    capitalism, 596; on depressions, 597;
    *Essay on the Nature and Significance of
    Economic Science*, 619
Roberts, John, 388, 527
Robertson, Dennis: in Keynes Club, 5; as
    Liberal–radical, 22; on JMK's
    economic ideas, 29; writes for *Manchester
    Guardian*, 103; collaborates with JMK,
    137, 272, 274–5, 418; plays Silenus, 144,
    274–5; economic theories vocabulary,
    174, 306–9; in Tuesday Club, 197;
    friendship with JMK, 207, 217, 272,
    296, 424, 510; on Jews, 238; on Lloyd

George, 252; and Liberal Party, 258,
    264n; background and character,
    272–4; debate with JMK on business
    cycles and inflation, 275–80, 307–8, 315,
    326; 1926–7 absence, 282; and JMK's
    Treatise on Money, 283, 453; on short-
    term problems, 314; on credit cycle,
    331–2; relations with JMK cool during
    Great Depression, 343; at Macmillan
    Committee, 358; criticisms of JMK,
    412, 499; correspondence with JMK,
    441, 452–4, 512; absent from
    'Cambridge Circle', 447; rejects
    multiplier theory, 452, 454, 590–1; on
    credit expansion, 455; comments on
    General Theory, 512, 532, 540, 547, 560;
    personal troubles, 532; on interest
    rates, 563–4, 598; and JMK's reaction
    to criticisms of *General Theory*, 573;
    influence on Champernowne, 574; on
    General Theory, 584, 589–93, 600, 603,
    611; and Henderson at Marshall
    Society meeting, 587; relations with
    JMK, 589–93, 598, 616; takes London
    professorship, 593; influenced by
    continental economics, 596; on wage
    demands, 603–4; *Banking Policy and the
    Price Level*, 6, 278–80, 284, 289, 306,
    308–9, 322, 591; *Money*, 272–3, 278,
    283; 'Some Notes on Mr Keynes'
    General Theory of Employment',
    590–1; *A Study of Industrial Fluctuation*,
    275, 276–8
Robertson, H. M., 286, 465
Robertson, Revd James, 272
Robinson, Sir Arthur, 474
Robinson, Austin: in Keynes Club, 5, 287;
    attends JMK lectures, 46; friendship
    with JMK, 207, 414, 424, 513; on Pigou,
    287; marriage, 287; in 'Cambridge
    Circus', 447–8; reviews *General Theory*,
    589
Robinson, Joan (*née* Maurice): excluded
    from Keynes Club, 5; at Cambridge,
    287, 290, 424, 513; in 'Cambridge
    Circus', 447–8; relations with Kahn,
    448, 495, 536; and Hayek's dispute with
    JMK, 458; reads *General Theory*, 532;
    on 'bastard Keynesianism', 538, 621;
    attacks Henderson, 587; attracts
    research students, 593; champions
    Kalecki, 594n; dismisses fears of
    inflation, 603; on population, 609; and
    JMK's 'generalised system', 611; and
    revolutionary nature of *General Theory*,

613; JMK reads proofs of book, 627;
Contributions to Modern Economics, 594n;
The Theory of Imperfect Competition, 448
Roosevelt, Franklin Delano, 470, 475;
    economic programme (New Deal),
    481–2, 485, 489–94, 504–5; JMK's open
    letter to, 492–4; unpredictability, 501;
    JMK meets, 506; JMK's advice to,
    507–8
Ropke, Wilhelm, 581
Rorty, M. C., 416, 491
Rosanvallon, Pierre, 582–3
Rose, Archie, xi, 208
Rosenberg, von, 127–8
Roseveare, Henry, 20
Rothermere, Harold Sidney Harmsworth,
    1st Viscount, 375, 386
Rothschild, Barbara (*née* Hutchinson), 495,
    513, 627
Rothschild, Victor, 495–6, 513, 516, 627
Rowland, Peter, 252
Rowntree family, 134–5
Rowntree, Arnold, 135–6
Rowntree, Seebohm, 22, 301
Rowse, A. L., 438, 575
Royal Commission on Employment
    Insurance, 384
Royal Commission on Finance and
    Industry, 21
Royal Commission on Indian Currency
    and Finance, 174
Royal Society, London, 625
Royal Statistical Society, 625
Rueff, Jacques, 300, 309–10, 349, 582–3
Ruhr, 123–5
Runciman, Steven, 273
Runciman, Walter, 1st Viscount, 246, 249,
    252, 254–5, 479–80
Russell, Bertrand: absent from Apostles
    dinner, ix; in Cranium Club, 13n; and
    Naomi Bentwich, 37–8; on JMK's
    Treatise on Probability, 67; approach to
    philosophy, 68–9, 75–7, 84, 224, 407n;
    Wittgenstein and, 69–70; influence on
    JMK, 73–4; on logic, 79; *The Principles
    of Mathematics*, 68, 74, 86
Russell, Dora, 519
Rustow, Alexander, 581
Ryan, John, 261–2, 378
Rylands, George ('Dadie'): in Apostles, 7;
    King's Fellowship, 9; in Cranium
    Club, 13n; Cambridge theatricals, 49,
    176, 294, 381n, 382; relations with
    JMK, 92, 145; reviews in *Nation*, 138;
    in Duncan Grant ballet, 182; and

Lydia, 214, 382; Robertson and, 273;
    entertains at Cambridge, 293, 389; and
    Lydia's acting, 502–3; on Cambridge
    Arts Theatre Board, 528–9, 624;
    productions at Arts Theatre, 530
Rymes, T. K.: *Keynes' Lectures, 1932–5*, 560n

Sackville-West, Edward, 13n
Sackville-West, Vita, 380
St George *see* Nelson, Francis St George
Salant, Walter, 460
Salter, Sir Arthur, 19, 22, 467–9, 473
Salter, F. R., 264n, 399
Samuel, Sir Herbert, 242, 250–1, 258
Samuelson, Paul, 441–2, 548, 573, 580
Sanger, Charles, 13n, 67
Sargant-Florence, Philip, 5
Sassoon, Siegfried, 6, 35
Savannah Conference, 100
Say's Law, 497, 499, 511, 547, 550, 552,
    559, 562–5, 577, 590
Schacht, Hjalmar, 103, 129, 476
Schaeffer, Robert and David: 'The Political
    Philosophy of J. M. Keynes', 238n
Schlesinger, Arthur, 490
Schuker, Stephen A., 43n
Schumpeter, Joseph, 182, 225, 234, 287,
    326, 334, 411, 493, 539–40; reviews
    General Theory, 576–7, 580
Schuster, Sir Felix, 190–1, 197
Schwartz, G. L., 478n
Scott, C. P., 48, 91, 102, 105, 135, 245
Scott, E. J. (Ted), 102, 108, 135
Scott, Francis C., 524, 528, 534
Scott, J. R., 102
Scott, W. R., 19
Seeckt, General Hans von, 48
Segonzac, André *see* Dunoyer de Segonzac,
    André
Seydoux Plan, 1920, 47 and n
Shackle, G. L. S., 5, 82, 88, 610
Shakespeare, William: *A Lover's Complaint*,
    295–6
Sharp, Clifford, 388
Shaw, E. S., 598
Shaw, George Bernard, 247–8, 259, 510,
    513, 518–20
Sheppard, John T.: and Apostles, 6; as
    King's vice-provost, 9; bids for Greek
    professorship, 91–2; gambling, 115, 175;
    theatricals, 144, 176, 294; friendship
    with JMK, 208, 217–18, 339; and
    JMK's marriage, 210; and 1931

election, 400; as Provost of King's, 496, 503
Shone, Richard, 42n
Short View of Russia, A, 210, 235, 238, 519
Shove, Gerald, 5, 9, 102, 287, 424, 512
Sickert, Walter, 11
Sidgwick, Arthur, x
Sidgwick, Henry, 68
Sidney Ball Lecture, 1924, 180, 183, 225, 229
Simon, Christopher, 522
Simon, Sir Ernest, 22, 468
Simon, E. D., 135–6, 258, 264, 386
Simon, Sir John, 249–52, 255
Simons, Henry, 579 and n
Simons, Walter, 49
Simpson, Mrs Wallis (*later* Duchess of Windsor), 628
Sitwell, Sacheverell, 99
Skidelsky, Arcadius, 46
Slaughter, F. W., 139
Sloan, Alfred, 504
Smith, Adam, 405, 411, 465, 476, 608
Smith, J. H., 113
Smith, Matthew, 243
Smith, W. H. (company), 627
Smithers, Waldron, 426
Smithies, Arthur, 425
Smythe, Ethel, 380
Snowden, Ethel, 388
Snowden, Philip: writes for *Manchester Guardian*, 103; supports gold, 189; socialist values, 246; and Macmillan Committee, 344–5, 363–5; dismisses JMK's economists report, 377; on unemployment, 384; and JMK's tariff proposals, 387, 395; suspends convertibility, 397; supports National Government in 1931 election, 400
socialism: JMK's attitude to, 232–4
Sokolova, Lydia, 98, 211
Solow, Robert, 580
Sombart, Werner, 239, 581
'Some Economic Consequences of a Declining Population' (talk), 631
Souter, Helen, 339
'Soviet Russia' (3 articles), 210
Spa, 122
Spain, 333–5, 379–80
Spencer-Smith, E. M. S., 197
Spender, Stephen, 440
Spengler, Oswald: *Decline of the West*, 485
Spesivtseva, Olga, 99
Spicer, Robert Henry Scanes, 6
Spiethoff, Arthur, 460, 486

Sprague, Oliver, 103, 340, 357, 391
Sprott, Jack ('Sebastian'): in Apostles, 6; riding, 9; in Cranium Club, 13n; relations with JMK, 15, 35–6, 51, 92–3, 100–1, 115, 142, 176, 339, 514; at Charleston, 91; in Nottingham, 207; and JMK's entertaining, 218; Carrington and, 432
Squire, Sir John Collings, 14, 15n
Sraffa, Piero: at Cambridge, 6, 289–92, 296, 380, 514; writes on Italian banking, 103; half-Jewish origins, 239; on Marshall, 288, 290; in 'Cambridge Circus', 447; reviews Hayek, 458–9, 566; and Malthus–Ricardo correspondence, 464; and JMK's attack on Marx, 523; JMK helps to stay in Cambridge, 536; criticises Robertson's article on *General Theory*, 589; visits Tilton, 626; *Production of Commodities by Commodities*, 291
Stalin, Josef V., 338, 488–9, 518–19, 570
Stamp, Sir Josiah: at Political Economy Club, 22; on price collapse, 41; and JMK's desertion of gold, 161; in Tuesday Club, 197; on Liberal Industrial Inquiry, 258; writes Dawes Report, 309; and MacDonald's lunches for Economic Advisory Council, 343; serves on EAC, 364–5, 368–9, 376–7, 468; chairs Committee on Economic Information, 467; letter on consumption and unemployment, 469; supports unbalanced budget, 473; and Irish negotiations, 479
standardisation (of consumer goods), 240
Stark, Werner, 416
Steel, Ronald, 28
Steel-Maitland, Sir Arthur Herbert Drummond Ramsay-, 299
Stein, Herbert, 490, 493
Stephen, Adrian, 10, 13n
Stephen, Karen (*née* Berenson), 10
Stephen, Leslie: *English Thought in the Eighteenth Century*, 225
Stephen, Thoby, 16
sterling *see* pound sterling
Stewart, Sir Kenneth, 343
Stewart, Michael, 551
Stewart, Walter W., 357–8, 361
Stockholm: school (of economics), 573, 580–1; JMK lectures in, 616, 626, 632
Stoll, Sir Oswald, 99–100, 176
Strabolgi, 10th Baron *see* Kenworthy, Joseph Montague

Strachey, Alix (*née* Sargant-Florence), 10–11, 113

Strachey, Giles Lytton: at Apostles dinner, ix; in Bloomsbury group, 10–11, 35; on self as civilisation, 13; in Cranium Club, 13n; relations with Carrington, 14; attitude to JMK, 14–15; irony, 17, 154; and JMK's metaphysical longings, 68; on JMK's Cambridge life, 92; on Tchaikovsky, 99; and JMK's attachment to Lydia, 101; writes for *Nation*, 138, 140; praises JMK's obituary of Marshall, 182; visits JMK and Lydia, 210, 218; visits Cambridge, 294; investments, 343; background, 406; and Moore, 408; letters from JMK, 427, 432; death, 432; *Books and Characters*, 92; *Eminent Victorians*, xii, 14, 17, 406; *Queen Victoria*, 14–15, 17, 35

Strachey, James, ix, 10, 12, 14, 113, 188, 234

Strachey, John, 246–7, 432, 516

Strachey, Marjorie, 178

Strachey, Oliver, 13n

Straight, Dorothy (*later* Elmhirst), 28, 522

Straight, Michael, 28, 510, 516, 522–3

Strakosch, Sir Henry, 19, 22–3, 107, 197, 205, 399, 525

Strauss, Lewis, 114

Stravinsky, Igor, 99; *The Soldier's Tale* (ballet), 295

Streseman, Gustav, 129

Strong, Benjamin, 195, 342, 398

Sumner, John Andrew Hamilton, 1st Viscount, 47n

Sunday Times, 27, 90

Sutherland, Ian: *The Monetary Puzzle*, 416

Sweden, 487–8, 580–1, 600; *see also* Stockholm

Swithinbank, Bernard, xi

Sydney-Turner, Saxon, 13n

Symes, J. E., x

Szeliski, Victor von, 508

Takahashi, Korekiyo, 488

Tappan, Marjorie (*later* Holland), 287

tariffs *see* protection

Tarshis, Laurie (Lorie), 460, 462, 574, 580, 604

Tattersall, Lincoln, 262

Tatti, I (house, Italy), 42

Taussig, Frank William, 580, 616

Taylor, Mrs (bedmaker), 432

Taylor, A. J. P., 378

Taylor, Alonzo, 48, 103

Taylor, Cecil ('Madame'), 115

Taylor, Frater, 393

Tchaikovsky, Peter Ilich: *The Sleeping Princess*, 98–100

Tennessee Valley Authority, 490

'Theory of Money, The' (lectures), 4

Thomas, J. H., 245, 344, 363–4, 480

Thomas, Robert Paul, 606

Thompson, Logan, 526

Thomson, George, 294, 296, 480

thrift, paradox of, 499, 541, 553

Tilton (Sussex house): JMK occupies, 214–17; life at, 338–9, 535–6; estate and farming, 526; rebuilt, 528, 626

Times, The: hostility to JMK, 27; JMK writes for, 431–2, 469–73, 605, 627–9

Tinbergen, Jan, 618–20

Tobin, James, 580

Tomlin, Garrow, 13n

Tomlin, Stephen ('Tommy'), 13n, 141

Townshend, Hugh, 621

Trachtenberg, Marc, 33–4

Tract on Monetary Reform, 20, 26, 45–6; on 'long-run', 62, 153–4; on property, 63; uses *Manchester Guardian* articles, 105, 153n; publication and contents, 153–60, 173, 314, 409–10; tone, 154, 159–61; reception, 160–5, 169; on exchange rate, 187, 191, 316–17; attacks gold standard, 188–90; and 'inflation tax', 278; Sraffa translates, 289; and price levels, 316; and Macmillan Report, 393; on forward exchanges, 558

trade unions: and inflation, 44; and labour costs, 130–1

tragedy, 64–6

Treasury: JMK's influence at, 19–20; and inflation, 40; and 1929 Liberal initiative, 297–9, 301–4; and Macmillan Committee, 356, 358–61; and budgetary policy, 435, 468, 473–4

Treatise on Money: influence, 6, 318–19; on price indexes, 148, 316; planning, 164, 175; cites Freud, 188; writing and rewriting, 281–5, 299, 338, 380, 446, 459; publication, 285, 297, 314; concepts and 'new theory', 301, 314, 318–32, 350–2, 410, 439, 442, 499; on disequilibrium, 315–16, 320–2, 546; style, 317–20; on historical capitalism, 332–5; policy proposals, 335–7; and Great Depression, 341; JMK uses model on US visit, 391–2; reception and criticism of, 438, 444–6, 452–9;

background to, 439–40; and *General Theory*, 441–4; 'widow's cruse' fallacy, 447–8; Hayek criticises, 458; on liquidity preference, 561; historical content, 608

Treatise on Probability: writing, 14, 35, 56; philosophical content, 56–63, 77, 80–9; reception, 67–73; on history of probability, 77–80; and *General Theory*, 83–4, 87

Trefilova, Vera, 99

Trevelyan, R. C., 50

Trotsky, Leon, 233

Trouton, Billie, 535

Trouton, Rupert, 6, 46, 296, 535, 633

Trustee Acts, 183

Tuesday Club, 22, 40, 196–7, 282, 436

Tugwell, Rexford, 505

Tulloch, A. A. G., 393

Turtle, Mrs (charwoman), 385

unemployment: inter-war, 38, 334, 369n, 468; and British economy, 130–3; rate, 147, 184–5; and monetary policy, 148, 151–2, 203; and population, 149–50; and investment, 184–6; Churchill on, 198, 203; and Bank of England, 286, 356; and prices, 298; and state action, 298; 'multiplier', 304, 373, 375, 377; Macmillan Committee on, 359–60; Economic Advisory Council views on, 365–6, 369–73; and purchasing process, 449–50; Committee on, 468; and underperformance, 498n; and government policy, 629–30

Union of Soviet Socialist Republics (USSR): at Genoa Conference, 108–11; JMK visits, 208–9, 234–6, 626; socialism in, 233; JMK's attitude to, 235–6, 488; terror in, 338, 489; rise to dominance, 485; appeal to western intellectuals, 488; *General Theory* neglected in, 582

United States of America: JMK's attitude to, 20, 489; and French financial problems, 32; Allied war debts to, 47, 107, 121, 123, 433; and JMK's exchange rates plan, 108, 198–9, 201–2; intervention in European reconstruction, 123, 128–9; gold management, 158, 336; cost of living index, 201; standardisation in, 240; savings and investment in, 299–300; and German transfer problem, 309–11;

speculation in, 338; and Great Depression, 339–42, 435; JMK and Lydia visit in 1931, 389–92; New Deal recovery programme, 467, 489–94, 508–9; abandons gold standard, 480–1; dominance, 485; maintains capitalist civilisation, 489; JMK and Lydia visit in 1934, 504–9; reaction to *General Theory* in, 576–80

Vaizey, John, 421

Valéry, Paul, 479

Valois, Ninette de *see* de Valois, Ninette

Vanderlip, Frank, 107

Venn, John: *Logic of Chance*, 78–9

Versailles: JMK on water works at, 407

Versailles, Treaty of, 1919, 3, 21; *see also* Germany: reparations

Viner, Jacob, 33, 492, 494, 576, 578–9, 602, 616

Vinson, Fred, 100

Vissering, G., 107, 118

Vogue (ballet), 178

Voigt, R. A., 102

Wadsworth, A. P., 102

wages (British): and labour costs, 131, 133–4; control of levels, 203–6, 242, 348–9, 369n, 372; in JMK's *Treatise on Money*, 328, 334; lag, 334; Macmillan Committee discusses, 348–9, 355; Economic Advisory Council on, 369–72; in *General Theory*, 462–3, 603–4

Waley, Arthur (*born* Schloss), 13n

Wall Street: 1929 crash, 339–40, 342–3, 378

Wallas, Graham, 22

Wallenberg, Markus, 107, 488

Walras, Léon, 615

Walter, William Grey, 516

Walton, William, 382

war debts (Allied), 47, 107, 121–3, 433

Ward, Dudley, 103

Warming, Jens, 449, 452

Warnock, G. J.: *English Philosophy since 1900*, 76n

Warren, George F., 493n

Watson, Alister, 293, 496, 516

Waugh, Evelyn, 17

Webb, Beatrice, 224, 247, 257, 399–400, 488

Webb, Sidney, 103, 161, 399, 488

Weber, Alfred, 582

Weber, Max, 236, 335, 542

Wedgwood, Josiah, 162
Weir, William Douglas Weir, 1st Baron, 343
Weller, Andrei, 216
Weller, Barry, 216
Weller, Edgar, 216, 380, 510, 526
Weller, Penny ('Auntie'), 217
Weller, Ruby, 216
Weller, Sonia, 216
Wells, H. G., 114, 139, 161, 248, 252, 258–9, 265, 510, 513, 518–19
West, Rebecca, 626
White, Harry Dexter, 472
Wicksell, Knut, 168, 169–70, 315, 326, 409, 580–1, 598, 601
widow's cruse fallacy, 447–8
Wigforss, Ernst, 488
Wiley, Louis, 398
Williams, John H., 103
Wilson, Mary, 11
Wilson, Woodrow, 20, 27, 32–3, 90, 270
Winch, Donald, 225, 364
Windsor, Edward, Duke of see Edward VIII, King
Windsor, Wallis, Duchess of see Simpson, Mrs Wallis
Winslow, Ted, 83, 88
Wirth, Joseph, 54, 118
Withers, Hartley, 22
Wittgenstein, Ludwig: on metaphysics, 56, 69; genius and qualities, 68–70; JMK and, 72–3, 210; visits JMK, 208; half-Jewish origins, 239; at Cambridge, 291–2, 294, 296, 380; Tractatus Logico-Philosophicus, 69, 72, 292
Woizikovsky, Leon, 99, 218
Wollaston, Sandy, 380
Woolf, Leonard: in Cranium Club, 13n; attitude to JMK, 15, 432; on violent pacifists, 134; as literary editor of Nation, 138, 145; relations with Keyneses, 217; Jewishness, 239; sees

Lydia dance, 249; in General Strike, 250; leaves Nation, 388; criticises JMK's style, 470; 'The Civilised Man', 16
Woolf, Virginia: praises JMK's Cambridge room, 5; on F. L. Lucas, 6; and Bloomsbury, 10–11; criticises JMK, 15; on Clive Bell's Civilisation, 16; visits Charleston, 35; and JMK's liking for praise, 110; writes for Nation, 140; on Lydia, 141, 143, 145, 182–3, 212, 625; suicide attempt, 146n; faintings, 208, 380–1; JMK visits at Rodmell, 209; on JMK's marriage, 210–11, 213; Lydia on, 213; relations with Keyneses, 217–18; marriage to Jew, 239; on JMK and King's provostship, 248–9; visits Cambridge, 293; on Lydia's acting, 502–3; on JMK's imaginative ardour, 509–10; on Eliot's Christianity, 517; and Shaw's letter to JMK, 520; and JMK's illness, 633; Jacob's Room, 15, 35; Night and Day, 15n; The Voyage Out, 15n; The Waves, 16
World Economic Conference, 1933, 470, 472, 476, 480–2, 486
Worthington-Evans, Sir Laming, 303
Woytinsky, Vladimir, 485
Wright, Harold, 344
Wright, Quincy, 389
Wright, Ralph, 13n

XYZ Club, 438

Young, Allyn, 341
Young, Hilton, 245, 469
Young, Owen D., 309
Young, Warren, 612–13
Yudenitch, General Nicholas N., 96

Zanfretta, Madame, 381